Making and Doing Deals: Contracts in Context

DAVID G. EPSTEIN
Charles E. Tweedy, Jr. Chairholder of Law
The University of Alabama School of Law

BRUCE A. MARKELL
Doris S. and Theodore B. Lee Professor of Law
William S. Boyd School of Law
The University of Nevada, Las Vegas

LAWRENCE PONOROFF
Dean and Mitchell Franklin Professor of Law of Private and Commercial Law
Tulane Law School

LexisNexis™

Library of Congress Cataloging-in-Publication Data

Epstein, David G., 1943-
Making and doing deals: contract and related law / David G. Epstein, Bruce A. Markell, Lawrence Ponoroff.
p. cm.
Includes index
ISBN 0-8205-5393-X
1. Contracts—United States—Cases. I. Markell, Bruce A. II. Ponoroff, Lawrence. III. Title.

KF801.A7 E65 2002
346.7302—dc21

2002016059

Editorial Offices
744 Broad Street, Newark, NJ 07102 (973) 820-2000
201 Mission St., San Francisco, CA 94105-1831 (415) 908-3200
701 East Water Street, Charlottesville, VA 22902-7587 (804) 972-7600
www.lexis.com

Dedications

To Diane Floca Epstein, the "other party " to the best deal that I ever made
DGE

To Ava, Amanda and Michelle, without whom nothing is worthwhile
BAM

To my wife, Monica, and in memory of her father and my friend, James E. Moses
LP

Preface

Our primary objectives[1] in writing this book were to give you a better understanding of:

(1) how to do contract law in law school—what legal issues arise when there is a dispute[2] over a deal and what legal concepts law students should use in addressing these issues; and

(2) how to do contract law in the "real world"—what a lawyer can do to minimize the possibility that her client will be involved in disputes and maximize the possibility that if disputes nonetheless arise, resolution will be favorable to her client.

The book, like most law school "case books," is mostly cases.[3] Some of the cases are "classics," part of a legal culture shared by lawyers regardless of the law school they attended or the case book their contracts professor selected. Other cases have been selected because they raise interesting questions or contain insightful analysis of important legal issues. We have also tried, whenever possible, to include recent cases that involve contemporary issues such as shrinkwrap contracts and arbitration clauses. We don't agree with the reasoning or result of all of the cases in the book; your teacher won't; you shouldn't.

---

[1]The objectives of making money, gaining academic prestige, convincing David Kelley to develop a new television series about contract law professors were, of course, secondary.

[2]People may disagree about (i) whether they ever made a deal or (ii) what the terms of the deal are or (iii) whether the other guy did what he agreed to do or (iv) if there is some legal excuse for not doing what you agreed to do or (v) how courts should enforce deals.

[3]Additionally, the book has both textual notes before the cases to give you some idea of what you are supposed to look for in the case and also questions after the cases to give you some idea of whether you found it. While we are of course proud of every word we have written, we want to single out the material in the Appendix on what is a contract, what is contract law, and what is a law school course on contracts. We urge you to read these pages at some point during the first few weeks of the semester.

We just want you to think about the cases. Not "think like a lawyer," just think.

Through law school and beyond, we have heard the phrase "think like a lawyer." We still don't know what it means. Each of us practiced law for more than eight years, and have been partners in large law firms; each of us approaches legal issues differently. While we disagree over the phrase "think like a lawyer," we agree with the phrase that "lawyers think."

A big part of that thinking is questioning constantly what you read. It is important that you read the cases and other materials in this book, asking yourself questions such as:

(1) What facts in this case are important?

(2) What were the questions that the court decided?

(3) What were the reasons for the decision? Do I agree with the result? Do I agree with the reasons for the result?

(4) Why is this case in the book? How is it similar to and different from other cases in the book?

(5) How can the decision in this case be helpful in avoiding other disputes or in resolving other disputes?

(6) How come Epstein, Markell and Ponoroff are funnier and more interesting than my contracts teacher?

One last point before you turn the page. When communicating in writing, people often use footnotes. In this book, the footnotes that are noted with asterisks contain material that we, the casebook editors, have written for explanatory or other purposes. Footnotes with actual numbers are the footnotes from the original material, be it actual cases, articles, or the like. In addition, we have retained the original numbers of these footnotes. You should keep this in mind because, due to our sometimes heavy editing, these numbered footnotes do not always appear in consecutive numerical order.

We have had fun writing this book, and we learned a lot. We hope that you have fun using the book and that you also learn a lot.

HAVE A GREAT FIRST YEAR.

David G. Epstein

Bruce A. Markell

Lawrence Ponoroff

Tuscaloosa, Las Vegas and New Orleans,

February 2002

Acknowledgments

Actress' Settlement Ends Long Legal Saga, LOS ANGELES TIMES, at page B2 (May 27, 1999), reprinted with permission of the Los Angeles Times Syndicate.

Atiyah, Patrick S., AN INTRODUCTION TO THE LAW OF CONTRACTS (5th ed. 1975), by permission of Oxford University Press.

Brennan, Justice William J., Jr., *In Memoriam: J. Skelly Wright*, 102 HARV. L. REV. 361 (1988).

Eisenberg, Melvin Aron, *The World of Contract and the World of Gift*, 85 CALIF. L. REV. 821 (1997).

Esptein, Richard A., *Unconscionability: A Critical Appraisal*, 18 J. LAW & ECON. 293 (1975).

Farber, Daniel A. & Matheson, John E., *Beyond Promissory Estoppel: Contract Law and the Invisible Handshake*, 52 U. CHI. L. REV. 903, 945 (1985), reprinted with permission.

Farnsworth, E. Allan, *Precontractual Liability and Preliminary Agreements: Fair Dealing and Failed Negotiations*, 87 COLUM. L. REV. 217, 257–58 (1987), reprinted with permission of the Columbia Law Review and Professor Farnsworth.

Farnsworth, E. Allan, *The Past of Promise: An Historical Introduction to Contract*, 69 COLUM. L. REV. 576, 592–98 (1969), reprinted with permission of the Columbia Law Review and Professor Farnsworth.

Fessler, Daniel Wm., TEACHING NOTES FOR FESSLER & LOISEAUX'S CONTRACTS: MORALITY, ECONOMICS AND THE MARKETPLACE 47–48 (1982), reprinted with permission.

Friedman, Lawrence M., CONTRACT LAW IN AMERICA 17–18, 20–22 (1965), reprinted by permission of The University of Wisconsin Press.

Farnsworth, E. Allan, CHANGING YOUR MIND 13–14, 16–18, 24, 26–27 (1998), reprinted with permission of The Yale University Press.

Fuller, Lon, *Consideration and Form*, 41 COLUM. L. REV. 799, 821–22 (1941), reprinted with permission.

Herman, Shael, *Detrimental Reliance in Louisiana Law—Past, Present, and Future: The Code Drafter's Perspective*, 58 TULANE L. REV. 707, 715 (1984), reprinted with permission of the Tulane Law Review Association.

Hillman, Robert A., *Contract Modifications Under the Restatement (Second) of Contracts*, 67 CORNELL L. REV. 680 (1982), reprinted with permission.

Kasterly, Amy H., *Cogs or Cyborgs, Blasphemy and Irony in Contract Theories*, 90 NW. L. REV. 132, 138 (1995), reprinted with permission.

Kidwell, John, *Ruminations on Teaching the Statute of Frauds*, 44 ST. LOUIS U. L.J. 1427 (2000).

Kozinski, Alex, *Who Gives a Hoot About Legal Scholarship?*, 37 HOUSTON L. REV. 295, 289–99 (2000), reprinted with permission from Judge Kozinski.

Leslie, Melanie B., *Enforcing Family Promises: Reliance, Reciprocity and Relational Contract*, 77 N.C. L. REV. 551 (1999).

Macneil, Ian R., *A Primer of Contract Planning*, 48 S. CAL. L. REV. (1975), reprinted with the permission of the Southern California Law review and Professor MacNeil.

Markell, Bruce A., *A View From the Field: Some Observations on the Effect of Interpretational Commercial Law Reform Efforts on the Rule of Law*, 6 IND. J. OF GLOBAL LEGAL STUDIES, 497, 498–99 (1999), reprinted with permission.

McConnaughey, Janet, *Court: Failed Fantasy Worth Only $57,500*, THE BATON ROUGE ADVOCATE, at page 7B (Aug. 14, 1998), reprinted with permission of the Associated Press.

Patterson, Edwin W., *The Interpretation and Construction of Contracts,* 64 COLUM. L. REV. 833, 852–54 (1964), reprinted with permission.

Peters, Ellen, *In Memory of Grant Gilmore: Grant Gilmore and the Illusion of Certainty*, 92 YALE L.J. 8, 11 (1982), reprinted with permission of the Yale Law Journal.

Posner, Richard, *In Memoriam: Henry J. Friendly*, 99 HARV. L. REV. 1724 (1986), reprinted with the permission of the Harvard Law Review.

Restatement (Second) of Contracts. Copyright 1981 by the American Law Institute. Reprinted with permission. All rights reserved.

Threedy, Debora L., *Feminists and Contract Doctrine,* 32 IND. L. REV. 1347 (1999), reprinted by permission.

Uniform Commercial Code. Copyright 2000 by the American Law Institute and the National Conference of Commissioners on Uniform State Laws. Reproduced with the permission of the Permanent Editorial Board for the Uniform Commercial Code. All rights reserved.

Wade, John, W., *Restitution for the Benefit Conferred Without Request,* 19 VAND. L. REV. 1183, 1183–84, 1211–12 (1966), reprinted with permission.

Waters, Antony Jon, *The Property in the Promise – A Study of the Third Party Beneficiary Rule,* 98 HARV. L. REV. 1109, 1117, 1148–51 (1985), reprinted with permission.

Yorio, Edward & Thel, Steve, *The Promissory Basis of § 90,* 101 YALE L.J. 111, 116–17 (1991), reprinted by permission of the Yale Law Journal Company and William S. Hein Company.

Epstein thanks Alabama law students, especially Kris Aungst, Thomas Casey, and Adam Plant, for their help with the book, especially with Markell and Ponoroff's parts of the book. And Erica Nicholson for turning the words that I put on disks and the words that I meant to be put on disks into a book.

Markell wishes to thank Natalie Cox, of the William S. Boyd School of Law's charter 2001 class, and Elizabeth Bradley and Carla Kok, of the Boyd School of Law's 2003 class, for their superb and tireless research assistance. A big tip o' the hat is due Dan McNutt, also of the Boyd School of Law's charter class for his comments (some of which were constructive) and help (all of which was needed) as a teaching assistant. Teresa Eckersall, Markell's secretary and assistant, was invaluable for her patient and competent handling of all the messes Markell makes. Finally, the biggest thanks go to Markell's students at the Boyd School of Law who, for the past three years, were cheerful (albeit involuntary) participants in the creation of this book; they were great, each and every one of them.

Ponoroff wishes to thank Michelle Emmert, Tulane Law School class of 2002, for her able assistance, including a harrowing trip to the courthouse archives in Shreveport, Louisiana to track down a copy of the contract in *Ever-Tite Roofing v. Green*. He would also like to thank the students in the classes of 2002 and 2003 in his Contracts I section who, without too much grousing, served as guinea pigs on earlier manuscripts of this book and, in the process, provided enormously useful feedback and, on occasion, painful (but constructive) criticism.

Table of Contents

Introduction

WHAT ARE WE GOING TO BE DOING IN THIS COURSE?*

SECTION 1: WHAT IS A CONTRACT?

People often use the word "contract" to refer to the writing that embodies an agreement or deal. For example, you turn on the television and see Alex ("A-Rod") Rodriguez jubilantly waiving a piece of paper after having agreed to play shortstop for the Texas Rangers for $252,000,000. People think of the A-Rod/Rangers contract as being that piece of paper.

That piece of paper is not a contract. At least, it is not a "contract" as we will be using the word "contract." At most, that piece of paper is a memorialization of the contract between A-Rod and the Rangers.

In law school (and usually in the practice of law), a contract is a promise or a set of promises that the law will enforce. A-Rod promises to play shortstop; the Rangers promise to pay. That is the A-Rod/Rangers contract.

To state the obvious (we hope), there are thus two key elements to the existence of a contract:

(1) a promise or promises AND
(2) enforcement.

Let's briefly consider "promise" first. A "promise" is a commitment as to the happening or non-happening of some future event: "I promise I will

*There is a more traditional (and more complete) introduction to the study of contracts in Appendix A. We (especially Ponoroff, who wrote it) urge you to read it.

paint your house" or "I promise I will not sell my 1973 Cadillac to anyone else for ten days."

"Enforcement" means legal enforcement—an award of damages or some other order by a court of law. Not all promises are legally enforceable. In some instances, the making of a promise creates a moral obligation but not a legal obligation.

SECTION 2: WHAT IS A FIRST YEAR COURSE IN CONTRACTS?

Contracts will be your easiest first year subject. Part of what makes contracts the easiest first year course is that you have already done contracts—apartment leases, automobile purchases, employment agreements, etc. And, part of what makes contracts the easiest first year course is that it only covers seven somewhat related, overlapping* questions:

1. Is there a deal?
2. If so, is it a deal that the law will enforce?
3. What are the terms of the deal?
4. When is someone who made an enforceable deal excused from doing what she agreed to do?
5. How does the law enforce a deal?
6. When can someone assert legal rights because of a deal made by others?
7. What are the alternatives to contracts and contract law?

Indeed, contract law is so easy that, when you get out of law school, you will re-learn (learn?) everything that you need to know about contracts for the bar exam in six to nine hours of lecture in a bar review course.

Why then do law schools spend four to nine months on contracts instead of just six to nine hours? The six to nine hours of bar review coverage of contracts helps prepare you for two days of fairly predictable contract law questions from bar examiners. The next four to nine months of law school coverage of contracts helps prepare you for a career of unpredictable contracts questions and assignments from clients, judges, and other lawyers in your law

*In the world of practicing law, most of your work assignments will involve more than one of these seven questions. In the world of learning law, we will, to the extent possible, consider these questions in this order, one question at a time.

firm—a career of writing contracts so as to minimize if not eliminate later problems—a career of resolving those problems that contract drafting did not eliminate.

As a part of that preparation, your teacher will regularly ask unpredictable questions—questions different from the questions in the book, and different from the questions that you anticipated. And, you will find that most of your professors' questions in law school (like most of the questions from clients, judges, and other lawyers in the "real world") do not have simple answers—or even answers at all.

In dealing with these questions, you will discover the importance of:

1. *Knowing vocabulary*

   Contract law has its own vocabulary—familiar words with new meanings. For example, a "contract" is more than just an agreement; an "offer" is similar but not identical to a proposal; "acceptance" is a special form of response to an offer; and "consideration" has a meaning that is even more "special." And, lots of new terms such as "executory contract," "parol evidence," and "promissory estoppel."

2. *Understanding history*

   Contract law has a long history. Ancient Rome had its own form of contract law. Roman contract law influenced the development of contract law in England in medieval times. And, English contract law, in turn, influenced the development of American contract law.

   Even today, lawyers and judges continue to use terms and concepts derived from Roman law and early English law: quantum meruit, assumpsit, etc. Obviously, the particular problems and more general policy concerns in 21st century America are different from those in ancient Rome, or medieval England or even 18th century America. Obviously, there are challenges in adapting long-accepted contract concepts to 21st century deals such as e-commerce or surrogate parenting agreements.

3. *Reading cases and statutes*

   Most contract law in law school comes from the written opinions of judges in decided cases. This is commonly called "common law."

American courts, with the partial exception of state courts in Louisiana, follow the English common law tradition. Louisiana and most of the rest of the world operate under a civil law system.

In a civil law system, the legislature makes the laws and courts basically interpret and apply these legislative enactments. Legislatures in a common law system also enact laws which are interpreted and applied by courts. For example, the legislatures in all 50 states have enacted Article 2 of the Uniform Commercial Code which governs contracts for the sale of "goods" (things that are movable).

The essential difference between a common law system and a civil law system is that in a common law system courts also make laws. A common law court's decision not only resolves the specific dispute between the parties but also becomes a part of the law in that court that is to be applied when similar disputes arise in the future.

In other, new, words, a common law system is based on "*stare decisis*," *i.e.*, judicial adherence to past decisions that are "precedents." A law dictionary defines "precedent" as "a decided case that furnishes a basis for determining an identical or similar case that might arise later, or a similar question of law."*

A big part of the practice of law is reading judicial opinions to determine which cases are "precedent" that will affect how the court will decide "your" case. And so, learning to read cases is a big part of law school.

4. *Considering competing policies*

While our common law system is based on judicial adherence to precedent, courts can and do avoid following earlier cases. Often, courts distinguish earlier decisions: different court, different facts, different legal arguments, etc. Less often, a court decides in a later case that the rule it established in an earlier decision should no longer be followed.

In such instances, courts turn to "policy". For example, contract law should be fair. **Equitable.** Contract law should apply even-handedly to all members of society. **Consistent.** Contract law should be certain so that businesses and individuals can act accordingly. **Predictable.**

*Bryan A. Garner, A Dictionary of Modern Legal Usage 680 (2nd ed. 1995).

Contract law should reflect our free market economy. **Freedom of contract.**

While most of us would have trouble challenging any of these policies in the abstract, all of us will have trouble this year in reconciling these policies in particular situations. Such as the situation in *Hill v. Gateway 2000*, below.

It's a simple story—the Hills bought a computer from Gateway, over the telephone, paying for the computer with a credit card. They were unhappy with the way that the computer performed and sued Gateway. While the Hills' complaint was not based on contract law, Gateway's answer was. Gateway argued that, under contract law, the "Standard Terms and Conditions Agreement" that was in the box that the computer was shipped in prevents the Hills from bringing the law suit. The parts of that Agreement relevant to the case were:

> "This document contains Gateway 2000's Standard Terms and Conditions. By keeping your Gateway 2000 computer system beyond thirty (30) days after the date of delivery, you accept these Terms and Conditions."
>
> "Any dispute or controversy arising out of or relating to this Agreement or its interpretation shall be settled exclusively and finally by arbitration. The arbitration shall be conducted in accordance with the Rules of Conciliation and Arbitration of the International Chamber of Commerce. The arbitration shall be conducted in Chicago, Illinois, U.S.A. before a sole arbitrator. Any award rendered in any such arbitration proceeding shall be final and binding on each of the parties, and judgment may be entered thereon in a court of competent jurisdiction."

Hill v. Gateway 2000, Inc.

105 F.3d 1147 (7th Cir. 1997)

Easterbrook, Circuit Judge

A customer picks up the phone, orders a computer, and gives a credit card number. Presently a box arrives, containing the computer and a list of terms, said to govern unless the customer returns the computer within 30 days. Are these terms effective as the parties' contract, or is the contract term-free because the order-taker did not read any terms over the phone and elicit the customer's assent?

One of the terms in the box containing a Gateway 2000 system was an arbitration clause. Rich and Enza Hill, the customers, kept the computer more than 30 days before complaining about its components and performance. They filed suit in federal court. * * * Gateway asked the district court to enforce the arbitration clause; the judge refused, writing that "[t]he present record is insufficient to support a finding of a valid arbitration agreement between the parties or that the plaintiffs were given adequate notice of the arbitration clause." Gateway took an immediate appeal, as is its right.

The Hills say that the arbitration clause did not stand out: they concede noticing the statement of terms but deny reading it closely enough to discover the agreement to arbitrate, and they ask us to conclude that they therefore may go to court. * * * A contract need not be read to be effective; people who accept take the risk that the unread terms may in retrospect prove unwelcome. Terms inside Gateway's box stand or fall together. If they constitute the parties' contract because the Hills had an opportunity to return the computer after reading them, then all must be enforced.

ProCD, Inc. v. Zeidenberg, 86 F.3d 1447 (7th Cir. 1996), holds that terms inside a box of software bind consumers who use the software after an opportunity to read the terms and to reject them by returning the product. * * * Gateway shipped computers with the same sort of accept or return offer ProCD made to users of its software. * * *

Plaintiffs ask us to limit ProCD to software, but where's the sense in that? ProCD is about the law of contract, not the law of software. Payment preceding the revelation of full terms is common for air transportation, insurance, and many other endeavors. Practical considerations support allowing vendors to enclose the full legal terms with their products. Cashiers cannot be expected to read legal documents to customers before ringing up sales. If the staff at the other end of the phone for direct-sales operations such as Gateway's had to read the four-page statement of terms before taking the buyer's credit card number, the droning voice would anesthetize rather than enlighten many potential buyers. Others would hang up in a rage over the waste of their time. And oral recitation would not avoid customers' assertions (whether true or feigned) that the clerk did not read term X to them, or that they did not remember or understand it. Writing provides benefits for both sides of commercial transactions. Customers as a group are better off when vendors skip costly and ineffectual steps such as telephonic recitation, and use instead a simple approve-or-return device. Competent adults are bound by such documents, read or unread. For what little it is worth, we add that the box from Gateway was crammed with software. The computer came with an operating system, without which it was useful only as a boat anchor. * * * So the Hills' effort to limit ProCD to software would not avail them factually, even if it were sound legally—which it is not.

For their second sally, the Hills contend that ProCD should be limited to executory contracts (to licenses in particular), and therefore does not apply because both parties' performance of this contract was complete when the box arrived at their home. This is legally and factually wrong: legally because the question at hand concerns the *formation* of the contract rather than its *performance*, and factually because both contracts were incompletely performed. ProCD did not depend on the fact that the seller characterized the transaction as a license rather than as a contract; we treated it as a contract for the sale of goods and reserved the question whether for other purposes a "license" characterization might be preferable. All debates about characterization to one side, the transaction in ProCD was no more executory than the one here: Zeidenberg paid for the software and walked out of the store with a box under his arm, so if arrival of the box with the product ends the time for revelation of contractual terms, then the time ended in ProCD before Zeidenberg opened the box. But of course ProCD had not completed performance with delivery of the box, and neither had Gateway. One element of the transaction was the warranty, which obliges sellers to fix defects in their products. The Hills have invoked Gateway's warranty and are not satisfied with its response, so they are not well positioned to say that Gateway's obligations were fulfilled when the motor carrier unloaded the box. What is more, both ProCD and Gateway promised to help customers to use their products. Long-term service and information obligations are common in the computer business, on both hardware and software sides. Gateway offers "lifetime service" and has a round-the-clock telephone hotline to fulfil this promise. Some vendors spend more money helping customers use their products than on developing and manufacturing them. The document in Gateway's box includes promises of future performance that some consumers value highly; these promises bind Gateway just as the arbitration clause binds the Hills.

* * *

At oral argument the Hills propounded still another distinction: the box containing ProCD's software displayed a notice that additional terms were within, while the box containing Gateway's computer did not. The difference is functional, not legal. Consumers browsing the aisles of a store can look at the box, and if they are unwilling to deal with the prospect of additional terms can leave the box alone, avoiding the transactions costs of returning the package after reviewing its contents. Gateway's box, by contrast, is just a shipping carton; it is not on display anywhere. Its function is to protect the product during transit, and the information on its sides is for the use of handlers rather than would-be purchasers.

Perhaps the Hills would have had a better argument if they were first alerted to the bundling of hardware and legal-ware after opening the box and wanted to return the computer in order to avoid disagreeable terms, but were dissuaded by the expense of shipping. What the remedy would be in such a case—could it exceed the shipping charges?—is an interesting question, but one that need not detain us because the Hills knew before they ordered the computer that the carton would include some important terms, and they did not seek to discover these in advance. Gateway's ads state that their products come with limited warranties and lifetime support. How limited was the warranty—30 days, with service contingent on shipping the computer back, or five years, with free onsite service? What sort of support was offered? Shoppers have three principal ways to discover these things. First, they can ask the vendor to send a copy before deciding whether to buy. * * * Concealment would be bad for business, scaring some customers away and leading to excess returns from others. Second, shoppers can consult public sources (computer magazines, the Web sites of vendors) that may contain this information. Third, they may inspect the documents after the product's delivery. Like Zeidenberg, the Hills took the third option. By keeping the computer beyond 30 days, the Hills accepted Gateway's offer, including the arbitration clause.

The Hills' remaining arguments, including a contention that the arbitration clause is unenforceable as part of a scheme to defraud, do not require more than a citation to *Prima Paint Corp. v. Flood & Conklin Mfg. Co.*, 388 U.S. 395, 87 S. Ct. 1801, 18 L. Ed.2d 1270 (1967). Whatever may be said pro and con about the cost and efficacy of arbitration (which the Hills disparage) is for Congress and the contracting parties to consider. * * * The decision of the district court is vacated, and this case is remanded with instructions to compel the Hills to submit their dispute to arbitration.

QUESTIONS AND NOTES

1. Questions about the facts of this case

   1.1. Who sued whom for what?

1.2. Who won at the trial court? On appeal?

1.3. Do we know why the Hills did not want to settle their dispute with Gateway by arbitration in Chicago under the International Chamber of Commerce Rules? Do you know what the International Chamber of Commerce Rules are? Did the Hills? Did Judge Easterbrook?

1.4. Did the Hills know before they ordered the computer that the carton would include some important terms?

1.5. Do we know why the Hills did not return the computer within 30 days? Did Judge Easterbrook care? Do you care?

1.6. Do we know when the Hills first read the Standard Terms and Conditions? Did Judge Easterbrook care? Do you care?

1.7. The decision of the trial court judge was "vacated." Did the trial court judge get the facts "wrong"?

2. Questions about the law

2.1. What is the question in this case? What does Judge Easterbrook mean by his statement "the question at hand concerns the formation of the contract"?

2.2. What is a "contract"? What resulted in the "formation of the contract" in this case? The Hills' ordering a computer and giving their credit card number? Gateway's shipping the computer? The Hills' reading the Standard Terms and Condition? Did Judge Easterbrook's opinion answer this question? What does Judge Easterbrook mean by his statement "by keeping the computer beyond 30 days, the Hills accepted Gateway's offer, including the arbitration clause"?

2.3. Would the Seventh Circuit have decided this case differently if Gateway sent the Hills the Standard Terms and Conditions in a separate envelope that arrived one day after the computer?

2.4. The Hills tried unsuccessfully to convince the court to limit the *ProCD* decision holding to "executory contracts." What is the *ProCD* holding? What is an "executory contract"? What is the argument for limiting the *ProCD* holding to executory contracts?

2.5. Your friend Bill calls. He wants your help with his New York landlord who won't let him keep his dog in the apartment. Bill rented the apartment by telephone outside a bar in Cancun. Bill paid for the first month's rent and the security deposit by credit card. The landlord told Bill that when he arrived, he would give Bill a copy of the apartment rules and regulations. The rules and regulations which Bill received (but did not read) clearly provides "no dogs." What do you tell Bill?

2.6. Is the holding in this case consistent with the policy objective that contract law should be "fair"? Do you think that "terms in a box" are fair? Assume that Microsoft becomes disenchanted with its present legal counsel and hires your firm. Would you encourage Microsoft to do business different from Gateway and ProCD? Is this what Bill Gates had in mind when he talked about "thinking outside the box"?

2.7. Is the holding in this case consistent with the policy objective of freedom of contract? Could the Hills have bought a Gateway computer without "agreeing" to arbitration of disputes?

3. Notes

3.1. Like virtually all of the cases in this book and the other "casebooks" that you will be using in law school, this is a decision of the appellate court. A lawsuit begins in a trial court. The trial court hears testimony from the witnesses and arguments from the attorneys as to what the relevant facts are, what the relevant law is, and how the law should be applied to the facts. The trial court then makes a decision.

After the trial court has made its decision as to who "wins" and who "loses," the losing party makes a decision as to whether to incur the additional costs of an appeal. In making that decision, the losing party's attorney knows that an appellate court will reverse the trial court's decision if, through her briefs and oral argument, she can convince a majority of the judges on the appellate court that the trial court got the law "wrong," or the facts wrong. An appellate court does *de novo* review of questions of law.

Appellate review of a factual basis for the trial court's decision is much more limited. Since an appellate court does not hear new testimony or consider new evidence, the trial court's resolution of factual disputes will be reversed on appeal only if clearly erroneous. Accordingly, most appeals and most appellate court opinions focus on questions of law.

Think about what this means about the cases that you will be studying in law school. *Gateway* and the other cases in this book and your other casebooks involve questions of law sufficiently close and unclear that someone was willing to incur the costs of litigating the questions in a trial court and then again on appeal.

3.2. This case, like most of the other cases in this book, is heavily edited. In writing opinions, judges focus on resolving all the factual and legal issues raised by the litigants.

We have a different focus. In editing these opinions, we have focused on teaching first year law students about contract law, one new concept at a time. For example, we have omitted Judge Easterbrook's citations to seven other cases, his reference to the Magnuson-Moss Warranty Act which will be covered in an advanced Consumer Law course, and his discussion of section 2-207 of the Uniform Commercial Code which will be covered later in this course.

3.3. Consider what this case illustrates about a court's and a lawyer's use of precedent.

3.4. Consider what this case illustrates about a lawyer's use of precedent. Do you think that the Hills' lawyers knew about the *ProCD* case? If so, why did they still appeal to the United States Court of Appeals for the Seventh Circuit?

3.5. *Gateway* is a very controversial case that has been criticized by many law professors. For example, Professor James J. White of the University of Michigan Law School describes the shrinkwrap contract in cases like *ProCD* and *Gateway* as an "autistic contract":

> Parties to modern form contracts sometimes interact with one another in the same way a parent of an autistic child interacts with that child. When a licensor offers a software license with the assertion that it will infer acceptance of all the license terms if the licensee removes the power cord from its plastic wrapper, the licensor is drawing an inference from the licensee's behavior just as doubtful as the inference a hopeful parent draws from an autistic child's apparently knowing response to the parent's statement.

James J. White, *Autistic Contracts*, 45 WAYNE L. REV. 1693 (2000). Why should you care what Jim White, a short, old, bald guy* who teaches at another law school, thinks about the *Gateway* decision? Why does your professor care about what you think about the *Gateway* decision?

3.6. *Hill v. Gateway* is not the only reported decision on shrinkwrap agreements, not the only reported decision on shrinkwrap agreements to arbitrate, and not the only reported decision on Gateway's shrinkwrap agreement to arbitrate. *See*** *Klocek v. Gateway, Inc.*, 104 F. Supp. 2d 1332 (U.S.D.C. Kan. 2000), *infra*, at 163; *Westendorf v. Gateway 2000, Inc.*, 2000 WL 307369 (Del. Ch. 2000); *Brower v. Gateway 2000, Inc.*, 676 N.Y.S.2d 569 (1998).

---

*White is even older than Epstein! We disagree as to whether White is shorter or balder than Ponoroff.

**"See" does not mean that you are really supposed to go see these cases. "See" is an "introductory signal" that indicates that "the cited authority directly states or clearly supports the proposition." *See* (sic) THE BLUEBOOK: A UNIFORM SYSTEM OF CITATIONS R. 1.2(a) at 22 (Columbia Law Review Ass'n et al. eds., 16th ed. 1996). All of you will actually see "the Bluebook" in your first year of law school (and your second and third years of law school if you "make law review.") A law professor with a Garrison Keillor-like sense of humor describes the Bluebook as the "Bible of citation form" or even the "KamaSutra of legal citation." It is at once "Divine Word" and Divine Comedy, holy writ and sexual manual rolled in one. (Yes, that is why they say "Make love, not law review"). Gil Grantmore, *The Death of Contra*, 52 STAN. L. REV. 889, 890 (2000) (The use of the phony name, Gil Grantmore, is what passes for humor in stuff written by law professors; it is a "spoof" of the name of a "famous," and dead, law professor, Grant Gilmore who wrote a book entitled The Death of Contract.)

Chapter One

HAS YOUR CLIENT MADE A DEAL?

The first of the seven general questions that we will be considering in this course is whether your client has made an agreement—whether there is a deal. In the *Gateway* case, it seems clear that there was some sort of an agreement by the Hills to buy a computer from Gateway and an agreement by Gateway to sell the Hills a computer. What is not yet clear is how and when the deal was made and what the terms of the deal were. Did the Hills make a deal with Gateway by ordering the computer over the telephone? By taking delivery of the box from Gateway? By failing to return the computer within 30 days? How do you know whether and when your client has made a deal? In other words, when do the parties cross the line from "mere negotiations"—from which either party may walk away without liability—to "agreement"—which may commit the parties to mutual performance obligation.

Remember, however, that just because we have an agreement does not mean we have a "contract"—an agreement that the law recognizes by way of enforcement. The question of which agreements are enforceable and which are not is one we take up in Chapter 2. On the other hand, if there is no agreement, there's not much point in talking about anything else. So let's begin by considering how you know whether your client has made a deal.

SECTION 1: DETERMINING THE MEETING OF THE MINDS

It is frequently said that an agreement is formed when there is a "meeting of the minds" between the parties on all of the essential terms of the proposed transaction. Often, however, one party will contend that there was such a meeting of the minds while the other will assert that there was never any intention to be bound. When faced with this disputed testimony, how is the court to decide whether a bargain in fact was indeed struck? As you read the next three cases, which illustrate the traditional approach for determining when negotiations have ripened into mutual assent to a bargain, ask yourself what the policy considerations are which explain or justify this approach?

Lucy v. Zehmer
Supreme Court of Virginia
196 Va. 493, 84 S.E.2d 516 (1954)

Buchanan, J.

This suit was instituted by W. O. Lucy and J. C. Lucy, complainants, against A. H. Zehmer and Ida S. Zehmer, his wife, defendants, to have specific performance of a contract by which it was alleged the Zehmers had sold to W. O. Lucy a tract of land owned by A. H. Zehmer in Dinwiddie county containing 471.6 acres, more or less, known as the Ferguson farm, for $50,000. J. C. Lucy, the other complainant, is a brother of W. O. Lucy, to whom W. O. Lucy transferred a half interest in his alleged purchase.

The instrument sought to be enforced was written by A. H. Zehmer on December 20, 1952, in these words: "We hereby agree to sell to W. O. Lucy the Ferguson Farm complete for $50,000.00, title satisfactory to buyer," and signed by the defendants, A. H. Zehmer and Ida S. Zehmer.

The answer of A. H. Zehmer admitted that at the time mentioned W. O. Lucy offered him $50,000 cash for the farm, but that he, Zehmer, considered that the offer was made in jest; that so thinking, and both he and Lucy having had several drinks, he wrote out "the memorandum" quoted above and induced his wife to sign it; that he did not deliver the memorandum to Lucy, but that Lucy picked it up, read it, put it in his pocket, attempted to offer Zehmer $5 to bind the bargain, which Zehmer refused to accept, and realizing for the first time that Lucy was serious, Zehmer assured him that he had no intention of selling the farm and that the whole matter was a joke. Lucy left the premises insisting that he had purchased the farm.

Depositions were taken and the decree appealed from was entered holding that the complainants had failed to establish their right to specific

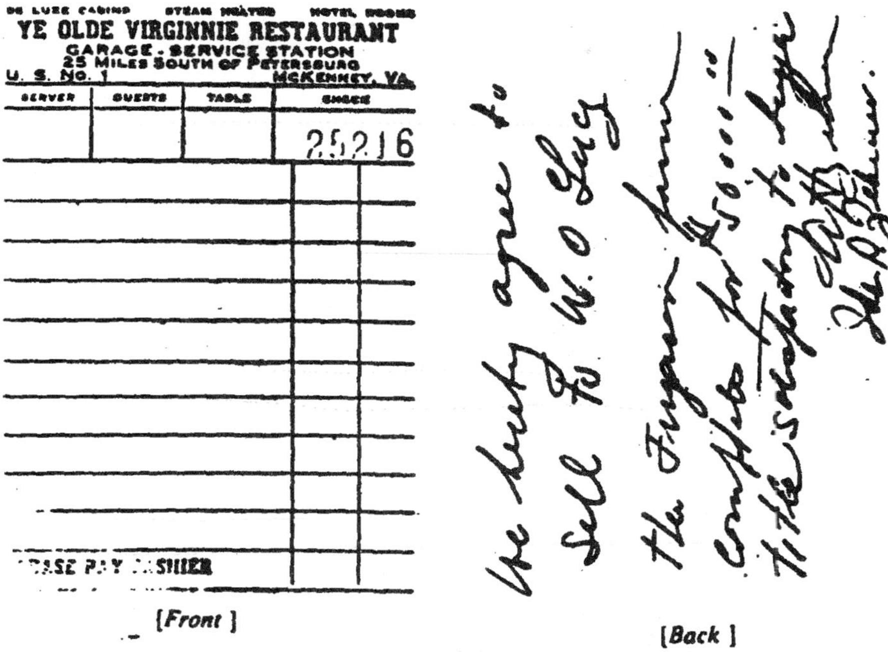

Lucy Contract

performance, and dismissing their bill. The assignment of error is to this action of the court.

W. O. Lucy, a lumberman and farmer, thus testified in substance: He had known Zehmer for fifteen or twenty years and had been familiar with the Ferguson farm for ten years. Seven or eight years ago he had offered Zehmer $20,000 for the farm which Zehmer had accepted, but the agreement was verbal and Zehmer backed out. On the night of December 20, 1952, around eight o'clock, he took an employee to McKenney, where Zehmer lived and operated a restaurant, filling station and motor court. While there he decided to see Zehmer and again try to buy the Ferguson farm. He entered the restaurant and talked to Mrs. Zehmer until Zehmer came in. He asked Zehmer if he had sold the Ferguson farm. Zehmer replied that he had not. Lucy said, "I bet you wouldn't take $50,000.00 for that place." Zehmer replied, "Yes, I would too; you wouldn't give fifty." Lucy said he would and told Zehmer to write up an agreement to that effect. Zehmer took a restaurant check and wrote on the back of it, "I do hereby agree to sell to W. O. Lucy the Ferguson Farm for $50,000 complete." Lucy told him he had better change it to "We" because Mrs. Zehmer would have to sign it too. Zehmer then tore up what he had written, wrote the agreement quoted above and asked Mrs. Zehmer, who was at the other end of the counter ten or twelve feet away, to sign it. Mrs. Zehmer said she would for $50,000 and signed it. Zehmer brought it back and gave it to Lucy, who offered him $5 which Zehmer refused, saying, "You don't need to give me any money, you got the agreement there signed by both of us."

The discussion leading to the signing of the agreement, said Lucy, lasted thirty or forty minutes, during which Zehmer seemed to doubt that Lucy could raise $50,000. Lucy suggested the provision for having the title examined and Zehmer made the suggestion that he would sell it "complete, everything there," and stated that all he had on the farm was three heifers.

Lucy took a partly filled bottle of whiskey into the restaurant with him for the purpose of giving Zehmer a drink if he wanted it. Zehmer did, and he and Lucy had one or two drinks together. Lucy said that while he felt the drinks he took he was not intoxicated, and from the way Zehmer handled the transaction he did not think he was either.

December 20 was on Saturday. Next day Lucy telephoned to J. C. Lucy and arranged with the latter to take a half interest in the purchase and pay half of the consideration. On Monday he engaged an attorney to examine the title. The attorney reported favorably on December 31 and on January 2 Lucy wrote Zehmer stating that the title was satisfactory, that he was ready to pay the purchase price in cash and asking when Zehmer would be ready to close the deal. Zehmer replied by letter, mailed on January 13, asserting that he had never agreed or intended to sell.

Mr. and Mrs. Zehmer were called by the complainants as adverse witnesses. Zehmer testified in substance as follows:

He bought this farm more than ten years ago for $11,000. He had had twenty-five offers, more or less, to buy it, including several from Lucy, who had never offered any specific sum of money. He had given them all the same answer, that he was not interested in selling it. On this Saturday night before Christmas it looked like everybody and his brother came by there to have a drink. He took a good many drinks during the afternoon and had a pint of his own. When he entered the restaurant around eight-thirty Lucy was there and he could see that he was "pretty high." He said to Lucy, "Boy, you got some good liquor, drinking, ain't you?" Lucy then offered him a drink. "I was already high as a Georgia pine, and didn't have any more better sense than to pour another great big slug out and gulp it down, and he took one too."

After they had talked a while Lucy asked whether he still had the Ferguson farm. He replied that he had not sold it and Lucy said, "I bet you wouldn't take $50,000.00 for it." Zehmer asked him if he would give $50,000 and Lucy said yes. Zehmer replied, "You haven't got $50,000 in cash." Lucy said he did and Zehmer replied that he did not believe it. They argued "pro and con for a long time," mainly about "whether he had $50,000 in cash that he could put up right then and buy that farm."

Finally, said Zehmer, Lucy told him if he didn't believe he had $50,000, "you sign that piece of paper here and say you will take $50,000.00 for the farm." He, Zehmer, "just grabbed the back off of a guest check there" and wrote on the back of it. * * *

After Zehmer had, as he described it, "scribbled this thing off," Lucy said, "Get your wife to sign it." Zehmer walked over to where she was and she at first refused to sign but did so after he told her that he "was just needling him [Lucy], and didn't mean a thing in the world, that I was not selling the farm." Zehmer then "took it back over there * * * and I was still looking at the dern thing. I had the drink right there by my hand, and I reached over to get a drink, and he said, 'Let me see it.' He reached and picked it up, and when I looked back again he had it in his pocket and he dropped a five dollar bill over there, and he said, 'Here is five dollars payment on it.' * * * I said, 'Hell no, that is beer and liquor talking. I am not going to sell you the farm. I have told you that too many times before.'"

Mrs. Zehmer testified that when Lucy came into the restaurant he looked as if he had had a drink. When Zehmer came in he took a drink out of a bottle that Lucy handed him. She went back to help the waitress who was getting things ready for next day. Lucy and Zehmer were talking but she did not pay too much attention to what they were saying. She heard Lucy ask Zehmer if he had sold the Ferguson farm, and Zehmer replied that he had not and did not want to sell it. Lucy said, "I bet you wouldn't take $50,000 cash for that farm," and Zehmer replied, "You haven't got $50,000 cash." Lucy said, "I can get it." Zehmer said he might form a company and get it, "but you haven't got $50,000.00 cash to pay me tonight." Lucy asked him if he would put it in writing that he would sell him this farm. Zehmer then wrote on the back of a pad, "I agree to sell the Ferguson Place to W. O. Lucy for $50,000.00 cash." Lucy said, "All right, get your wife to sign it." Zehmer came back to where she was standing and said, "You want to put your name to this?" She said "No," but he said in an undertone, "It is nothing but a joke," and she signed it.

She said that only one paper was written and it said: "I hereby agree to sell," but the "I" had been changed to "We". However, she said she read what she signed and was then asked, "When you read 'We hereby agree to sell to W. O. Lucy,' what did you interpret that to mean, that particular phrase?" She said she thought that was a cash sale that night; but she also said that when she read that part about "title satisfactory to buyer" she understood that if the title was good Lucy would pay $50,000 but if the title was bad he would have a right to reject it, and that that was her understanding at the time she signed her name.

On examination by her own counsel she said that her husband laid this piece of paper down after it was signed; that Lucy said to let him see it, took it, folded it and put it in his wallet, then said to Zehmer, "Let me give you $5.00," but Zehmer said, "No, this is liquor talking. I don't want to sell the farm, I have told you that I want my son to have it. This is all a joke." Lucy then said at least twice, "Zehmer, you have sold your farm," wheeled around and started for the door. He paused at the door and said, "I will bring you $50,000.00 tomorrow. * * * No, tomorrow is Sunday. I will bring it to you Monday." She said you could tell definitely that he was drinking and she said to her husband, "You should have taken him home," but he said, "Well, I am just about as bad off as he is."

The waitress referred to by Mrs. Zehmer testified that when Lucy first came in "he was mouthy." When Zehmer came in they were laughing and joking and she thought they took a drink or two. She was sweeping and cleaning up for next day. She said she heard Lucy tell Zehmer, "I will give you so much for the farm," and Zehmer said, "You haven't got that much." Lucy answered, "Oh, yes, I will give you that much." Then "they jotted down something on paper * * * and Mr. Lucy reached over and took it, said let me see it." He looked at it, put it in his pocket and in about a minute he left. She was asked whether she saw Lucy offer Zehmer any money and replied, "He had five dollars laying up there, they didn't take it." She said Zehmer told Lucy he didn't want his money "because he didn't have enough money to pay for his property, and wasn't going to sell his farm." Both of them appeared to be drinking right much, she said.

She repeated on cross-examination that she was busy and paying no attention to what was going on. She was some distance away and did not see either of them sign the paper. She was asked whether she saw Zehmer put the agreement down on the table in front of Lucy, and her answer was this: "Time he got through writing whatever it was on the paper, Mr. Lucy reached over and said, 'Let's see it.' He took it and put it in his pocket," before showing it to Mrs. Zehmer. Her version was that Lucy kept raising his offer until it got to $50,000.

The defendants insist that the evidence was ample to support their contention that the writing sought to be enforced was prepared as a bluff or dare to force Lucy to admit that he did not have $50,000; that the whole matter was a joke; that the writing was not delivered to Lucy and no binding contract was ever made between the parties.

It is an unusual, if not bizarre, defense. When made to the writing admittedly prepared by one of the defendants and signed by both, clear evidence is required to sustain it.

In his testimony Zehmer claimed that he "was high as a Georgia pine," and that the transaction "was just a bunch of two doggoned drunks bluffing to see who could talk the biggest and say the most." That claim is inconsistent with his attempt to testify in great detail as to what was said and what was done. It is contradicted by other evidence as to the condition of both parties, and rendered of no weight by the testimony of his wife that when Lucy left the restaurant she suggested that Zehmer drive him home. The record is convincing that Zehmer was not intoxicated to the extent of being unable to comprehend the nature and consequences of the instrument he executed, and hence that instrument is not to be invalidated on that ground. * * * It was in fact conceded by defendants' counsel in oral argument that under the evidence Zehmer was not too drunk to make a valid contract.

The evidence is convincing also that Zehmer wrote two agreements, the first one beginning "I hereby agree to sell." Zehmer first said he could not remember about that, then that "I don't think I wrote but one out." Mrs. Zehmer said that what he wrote was "I hereby agree," but that the "I" was changed to "We" after that night. The agreement that was written and signed is in the record and indicates no such change. * * *

The appearance of the contract, the fact that it was under discussion for forty minutes or more before it was signed; Lucy's objection to the first draft because it was written in the singular, and he wanted Mrs. Zehmer to sign it also; the rewriting to meet that objection and the signing by Mrs. Zehmer; the discussion of what was to be included in the sale, the provision for the examination of the title, the completeness of the instrument that was executed, the taking possession of it by Lucy with no request or suggestion by either of the defendants that he give it back, are facts which furnish persuasive evidence that the execution of the contract was a serious business transaction rather than a casual, jesting matter as defendants now contend.

* * *

If it be assumed, contrary to what we think the evidence shows, that Zehmer was jesting about selling his farm to Lucy and that the transaction was intended by him to be a joke, nevertheless the evidence shows that Lucy did not so understand it but considered it to be a serious business transaction and the contract to be binding on the Zehmers as well as on himself. The very next day he arranged with his brother to put up half the money and take a half interest in the land. The day after that he employed an attorney to examine the title. The next night, Tuesday, he was back at Zehmer's place and there Zehmer told him for the first time, Lucy said, that he wasn't going to sell and he told Zehmer, "You know you sold that place fair and square." After receiving the report from his attorney that the title was good he wrote to Zehmer that he was ready to close the deal.

Not only did Lucy actually believe, but the evidence shows he was warranted in believing, that the contract represented a serious business transaction and a good faith sale and purchase of the farm.

In the field of contracts, as generally elsewhere, "We must look to the outward expression of a person as manifesting his intention rather than to his secret and unexpressed intention. 'The law imputes to a person an intention corresponding to the reasonable meaning of his words and acts.'" *First Nat. Bank v. Roanoke Oil Co.*, 169 Va. 99, 114, 192 S.E. 764, 770.

At no time prior to the execution of the contract had Zehmer indicated to Lucy by word or act that he was not in earnest about selling the farm. They had argued about it and discussed its terms, as Zehmer admitted, for a long time. Lucy testified that if there was any jesting it was about paying $50,000 that night. The contract and the evidence show that he was not expected to pay the money that night. Zehmer said that after the writing was signed he laid it down on the counter in front of Lucy. Lucy said Zehmer handed it to him. In any event there had been what appeared to be a good faith offer and a good faith acceptance, followed by the execution and apparent delivery of a written contract. Both said that Lucy put the writing in his pocket and then offered Zehmer $5 to seal the bargain. Not until then, even under the defendants' evidence, was anything said or done to indicate that the matter was a joke. Both of the Zehmers testified that when Zehmer asked his wife to sign he whispered that it was a joke so Lucy wouldn't hear and that it was not intended that he should hear.

The mental assent of the parties is not requisite for the formation of a contract. If the words or other acts of one of the parties have but one reasonable meaning, his undisclosed intention is immaterial except when an unreasonable meaning which he attaches to his manifestations is known to the other party. Restatement of the Law of Contracts, Vol. I, § 71, p. 74.

"* * * The law, therefore, judges of an agreement between two persons exclusively from those expressions of their intentions which are communicated between them. * * *." Clark on Contracts, 4 ed., § 3, p. 4.

An agreement or mutual assent is of course essential to a valid contract but the law imputes to a person an intention corresponding to the reasonable meaning of his words and acts. If his words and acts, judged by a reasonable standard, manifest an intention to agree, it is immaterial what may be the real but unexpressed state of his mind. * * *

So a person cannot set up that he was merely jesting when his conduct and words would warrant a reasonable person in believing that he intended a real agreement * * *.

Whether the writing signed by the defendants and now sought to be enforced by the complainants was the result of a serious offer by Lucy and a serious acceptance by the defendants, or was a serious offer by Lucy and an acceptance in secret jest by the defendants, in either event it constituted a binding contract of sale between the parties.

Defendants contend further, however, that even though a contract was made, equity should decline to enforce it under the circumstances. These circumstances have been set forth in detail above. They disclose some drinking by the two parties but not to an extent that they were unable to understand fully what they were doing. There was no fraud, no misrepresentation, no sharp practice and no dealing between unequal parties. The farm had been bought for $11,000 and was assessed for taxation at $6,300. The purchase price was $50,000. Zehmer admitted that it was a good price. There is in fact present in this case none of the grounds usually urged against specific performance.

* * *

The complainants are entitled to have specific performance of the contracts sued on. The decree appealed from is therefore reversed and the cause is remanded for the entry of a proper decree requiring the defendants to perform the contract in accordance with the prayer of the bill.

Reversed and remanded.

QUESTIONS AND NOTES

1. Questions about the facts of this case

   1.1. Was there a "meeting of the minds" in *Lucy*? In considering the existence of a contract, the court is ostensibly attempting to ascertain the intention of the parties, but did Mr. Zehmer really intend to sell the farm to Lucy or was he jesting? How about Mrs. Zehmer?

   1.2. Did Lucy believe that his neighbor was jesting?

   1.3. What about Zehmer's contention that he was "high as a Georgia pine"? Did the court think that either Lucy or Zehmer were intoxicated? Should that matter? Can you enter into a legally binding contract when you're drunk? This is a question of "capacity" to contract, a topic we take up in Chapter 2.

   1.4. If you were representing Zehmer, what facts would you emphasize? If you represented Lucy, what facts would you emphasize?

   1.5. How reasonable was Lucy in going out the next day and hiring an attorney to examine title and arranging with his brother for financing?

2. Questions about the law

   2.1. Does the court in *Lucy* take an objective or subjective approach to contract formation? What is the difference between the two?

   2.2. How would the case have been decided if Lucy believed that Zehmer was jesting?

   2.3. Of what relevance was Zehmer's refusal to accept the $5 that Lucy offered after the "guest check" had been signed? Was acceptance of the payment necessary to seal the deal? If the rationale for the objective theory is to protect the reasonable expectation of parties, for how long was Lucy reasonable in his belief that Zehmer intended to be bound? Should it make a difference at what stage the offeror tells the offeree he's not serious?

2.4. Can you now articulate the legal standard for ascertaining mutual assent? If not, don't worry, just keep reading!

3. Notes

3.1. In fact, in ascertaining the existence of a binding contract, the courts examine and give legal effect to the outward manifestation of the parties, regardless of what either party may have privately or secretly intended. The question then is not what the offeror may have actually meant by what she said, but the reasonable impression created in the mind of the offeree by the words used and the conduct engaged in by the offeror. This is known as the *objective theory* of contract formation. Consider this statement from the United States Court of Appeals for the Seventh Circuit: "The premise—that a 'meeting of the minds' is required for a binding contract is strained. Most contract disputes arise because the parties did not foresee and provide for some contingency that has not materialized—so there was no meeting of the minds on the matter at issue—yet such disputes are treated as disputes over contractual meaning. * * * So a literal meeting of the minds is not required for an enforceable contract, which is fortunate, since courts are not renowned as mind readers." *Colfax Envelope Corp. v. Local No. 458-3M*, 20 F.3d 750, 752 (7th Cir. 1994). If a literal meeting of the minds is not required to establish mutual assent, what sort of meeting of the minds will suffice?

3.2. The notion that the law of contracts is not concerned with the parties' undisclosed intent and ideas is traditionally regarded as a relatively new concept. Throughout most of the nineteenth century, courts viewed contractual liability as arising from the conscious, *subjective* agreement on the same undertaking. Hence the origins of the term *meeting of the minds. See* LAWRENCE FRIEDMAN, CONTRACT LAW IN AMERICA 87 (1965) (suggesting that the shift from subjective to objective theory of contract formation was a response to the law's concern around the turn of the last century with reducing business risk and enhancing the predictability of market transactions); *but see*

Joseph M. Perillo, *The Origins of Objective Theory of Contract Formation and Interpretation,* 69 FORDHAM L. REV. 427, 428–430 (2000) (arguing that objective approaches predominated in the common law of contracts from "time immemorial"). Subjective theory would certainly be consistent with the nineteenth century's general emphasis on free will and individualism. The objective theory of mutual assent obviously places a higher priority on one party's right to rely on the reasonable expectations created by an apparent agreement of the other, a priority perceived as also assuring the need in the marketplace for certainty and predictability. Although not without its critics, objective theory ultimately triumphed, thanks, in large measure, to the support of its greatest advocate, Professor Samuel Williston, Reporter for the first *Restatement of Contracts.* Objective theory also found its way into the Second Restatement. *See Restatement (Second) of Contracts* § 24. However, it is important to recognize that the objective theory of assent has two components, only one of which is purely objective: (1) would a reasonable person in the position of the offeree understand from the offeror's words and conduct an intent to be bound? and (2) did the offeree in fact so believe?

3.3. Does objective theory mean that the offeror's subjective belief as to the existence of a contract is never relevant? *See Kabil Developments Corp. v. Mignot*, 566 P.2d 505 (Ore. 1977) (noting that a person's own view of his position in a negotiation may bear on his behavior as perceived by others). Surely, no court would find a contract if neither party thought the other intended to be bound.

3.4. In a frequently-quoted passage from his opinion in *Hotchkiss v. National City Bank of New York*, 200 F. 287, 293 (S.D.N.Y. 1911) the distinguished jurist Learned Hand wrote:

> A contract has, strictly speaking, nothing to do with the personal, or individual, intent of the parties. A contract is an obligation attached by the mere force of law to certain acts of the parties, which ordinarily accompany and represent a known intent. If, however, it were proved by twenty bishops that either party when he used the words intended something else than the usual meaning which the law imposes on them, he would still be held [liable]. . . .

Is this view consistent with *Lucy*? Thirty-five years after *Hotchkiss* was decided, Judge Jerome Frank, actually concurring in an opinion written by then Second Circuit Judge Hand, criticized the "objectivists" as having gone too far. He complained:

> The objectivists transferred from the field of torts that stubborn anti-subjectivist, the 'reasonable-man'; so that, in part at least, advocacy of the 'objective' standard in contracts appears to have represented a desire for legal symmetry, legal uniformity, a desire seemingly prompted by aesthetic impulses. * * * At any rate, the sponsors of complete 'objectivity' in contracts largely won out in the wider generalization of the Restatement of Contracts and in some judicial opinions.

Ricketts v. Pennsylvania R. Co., 153 F.2d 757, 761 (2d Cir. 1946).

3.5. If contract law is distinguished from tort law as being consent rather than fault-based, does Judge Frank make a fair point? What do you suppose were the "aesthetic impulses" that accounted for Professor Williston's wholesale adoption of objective theory in the first *Restatement of Contracts*?

3.6. Even accepting the court's explanation in *Lucy* for how the existence of contractual assent is to be ascertained by the courts when there is a dispute between the parties, is it all that clear that a person in Lucy's position would have inferred from Zehmer's outward manifestations an intent to sell the farm for $50,000? Is it appropriate to look only at the words used? If not, what other factors were relevant in *Lucy* that were arguably overlooked by the court of appeals? Even if the court of appeals concluded that the trial court had applied the wrong legal standard for determining intention to be bound, was it appropriate for the court of appeals to decide, as a matter of law, that Lucy was entitled to judgment for specific performance?

Leonard v. Pepsico, Inc.
United States District Court for the Southern District of New York
88 F. Supp. 2d 116 (1999)

WOOD, U.S.D.J.

Plaintiff brought this action seeking, among other things, specific performance of an alleged offer of a Harrier Jet, featured in a television advertisement for defendant's "Pepsi Stuff" promotion. Defendant has moved for summary judgment pursuant to Federal Rule of Civil Procedure 56. For the reasons stated below, defendant's motion is granted.

I. Background

This case arises out of a promotional campaign conducted by defendant, the producer and distributor of the soft drinks Pepsi and Diet Pepsi. The promotion, entitled "Pepsi Stuff," encouraged consumers to collect "Pepsi Points" from specially marked packages of Pepsi or Diet Pepsi and redeem these points for merchandise featuring the Pepsi logo. Before introducing the promotion nationally, defendant conducted a test of the promotion in the Pacific Northwest from October 1995 to March 1996. A Pepsi Stuff catalog was distributed to consumers in the test market, including Washington State. Plaintiff is a resident of Seattle, Washington. While living in Seattle, plaintiff saw the Pepsi Stuff commercial that he contends constituted an offer of a Harrier Jet.

A. The Alleged Offer

Because whether the television commercial constituted an offer is the central question in this case, the Court will describe the commercial in detail. The commercial opens upon an idyllic, suburban morning, where the chirping of birds in sun-dappled trees welcomes a paperboy on his morning route. As the newspaper hits the stoop of a conventional two-story house, the tattoo of a military drum introduces the subtitle, "MONDAY 7:58 AM." The stirring strains of a martial air mark the appearance of a well-coiffed teenager preparing to leave for school, dressed in a shirt emblazoned with the Pepsi logo, a red-white-and-blue ball. While the teenager confidently preens, the military drumroll again sounds as the subtitle "T-SHIRT 75 PEPSI POINTS" scrolls across the screen. Bursting from his room, the teenager strides down the hallway wearing a leather jacket. The drumroll sounds again, as the subtitle "LEATHER JACKET 1450 PEPSI POINTS" appears. The teenager opens the door of his house and, unfazed by the glare of the early morning sunshine, puts on a pair of sunglasses. The drumroll then accompanies the subtitle "SHADES 175 PEPSI POINTS." A voiceover then intones, "Introducing the new Pepsi Stuff catalog," as the camera focuses on the cover of the catalog.

The scene then shifts to three young boys sitting in front of a high school building. The boy in the middle is intent on his Pepsi Stuff Catalog, while the boys on either side are each drinking Pepsi. The three boys gaze in awe at an object rushing overhead, as the military march builds to a crescendo. The Harrier Jet is not yet visible, but the observer senses the presence of a mighty plane as the extreme winds generated by its flight create a paper maelstrom in a classroom devoted to an otherwise dull physics lesson. Finally, the Harrier Jet swings into view and lands by the side of the school building, next to a bicycle rack. Several students run for cover, and the velocity of the wind strips one hapless faculty member down to his underwear. While the faculty member is being deprived of his dignity, the voiceover announces: "Now the more Pepsi you drink, the more great stuff you're gonna get."

The teenager opens the cockpit of the fighter and can be seen, helmetless, holding a Pepsi. "Looking very pleased with himself," the teenager exclaims, "Sure beats the bus," and chortles. The military drumrol sounds a final time, as the following words appear: "HARRIER FIGHTER 7,000,000 PEPSI POINTS." A few seconds later, the following appears in mcre stylized script: "Drink Pepsi—Get Stuff." With that message, the music and the commercial end with a triumphant flourish.

Inspired by this commercial, plaintiff set out to obtain a Harrier Jet. Plaintiff explains that he is "typical of the 'Pepsi Generation' . . . he is young, has an adventurous spirit, and the notion of obtaining a Harrier Jet appealed to him enormously." Plaintiff consulted the Pepsi Stuff Catalog. The Catalog features youths dressed in Pepsi Stuff regalia or enjoying Pepsi Stuff accessories, such as "Blue Shades" ("As if you need another reason to look forward to sunny days), "Pepsi Tees" ("Live in 'em. Laugh in 'em. Get in 'em."), "Bag of Balls" ("Three balls. One bag. No rules."), and "Pepsi Phone Card" ("Call your mom!"). The Catalog specifies the number of Pepsi Points required to obtain promotional merchandise. The Catalog includes an Order Form which lists, on one side, fifty-three items of Pepsi Stuff merchandise redeemable for Pepsi Points Conspicuously absent from the Order Form is any entry or description of a Harrier Jet. The amount of Pepsi Points required to obtain the listed merchandise ranges from 15 (for a "Jacket Tattoo" ("Sew 'em on your jacket, not your arm.")) to 3300 (for a "Fila Mountain Bike" ("Rugged. All-terrain. Exclusively for Pepsi.")). It should be noted that plaintiff objects to the implication that because an item was not shown in the Catalog, it was unavailable.

The rear foldout pages of the Catalog contain directions for redeeming Pepsi Points for merchandise. These directions note that merchandise may be ordered "only" with the original Order Form. The Catalog notes that in the event that a consumer lacks enough Pepsi Points to obtain a desired item, additional Pepsi Points may be purchased for ten cents each; however, at least fifteen original Pepsi Points must accompany each order.

Although plaintiff initially set out to collect 7,000,000 Pepsi Points by consuming Pepsi products, it soon became clear to him that he "would not be able to buy (let alone drink) enough Pepsi to collect the necessary Pepsi Points fast enough." Reevaluating his strategy, plaintiff "focused for the first time on the packaging materials in the Pepsi Stuff promotion," and realized that buying Pepsi Points would be a more promising option. Through acquaintances, plaintiff ultimately raised about $700,000.

B. Plaintiff's Efforts to Redeem the Alleged Offer

On or about March 27, 1996, plaintiff submitted an Order Form, fifteen original Pepsi Points, and a check for $700,008.50. Plaintiff appears to have been represented by counsel at the time he mailed his check; the check is drawn on an account of plaintiff's first set of attorneys. At the bottom of the Order Form, plaintiff wrote in "1 Harrier Jet" in the "Item" column and "7,000,000" in the "Total Points" column. In a letter accompanying his submission, plaintiff stated that the check was to purchase additional Pepsi Points "expressly for obtaining a new Harrier jet as advertised in your Pepsi Stuff commercial."

On or about May 7, 1996, defendant's fulfillment house rejected plaintiff's submission and returned the check, explaining that:

> The item that you have requested is not part of the Pepsi Stuff collection. It is not included in the catalogue or on the order form, and only catalogue merchandise can be redeemed under this program.
>
> The Harrier jet in the Pepsi commercial is fanciful and is simply included to create a humorous and entertaining ad. We apologize for any misunderstanding or confusion that you may have experienced and are enclosing some free product coupons for your use.

Plaintiff's previous counsel responded on or about May 14, 1996, as follows:

> Your letter of May 7, 1996 is totally unacceptable. We have reviewed the video tape of the Pepsi Stuff commercial . . . and it clearly offers the new

> Harrier jet for 7,000,000 Pepsi Points. Our client followed your rules explicitly. . . .
>
> This is a formal demand that you honor your commitment and make immediate arrangements to transfer the new Harrier jet to our client. If we do not receive transfer instructions within ten (10) business days of the date of this letter you will leave us no choice but to file an appropriate action against Pepsi . . . .

This letter was apparently sent onward to the advertising company responsible for the actual commercial, BBDO New York ("BBDO"). In a letter dated May 30, 1996, BBDO Vice President Raymond E. McGovern, Jr., explained to plaintiff that:

> I find it hard to believe that you are of the opinion that the Pepsi Stuff commercial ("Commercial") really offers a new Harrier Jet. The use of the Jet was clearly a joke that was meant to make the Commercial more humorous and entertaining. In my opinion, no reasonable person would agree with your analysis of the Commercial.

* * *

II. Discussion

* * *

B. Defendant's Advertisement Was Not An Offer

1. Advertisements as Offers

The general rule is that an advertisement does not constitute an offer. The Restatement (Second) of Contracts explains that:

> Advertisements of goods by display, sign, handbill, newspaper, radio or television are not ordinarily intended or understood as offers to sell. The same is true of catalogues, price lists and circulars, even though the terms of suggested bargains may be stated in some detail. It is of course possible to make an offer by an advertisement directed to the general public (see § 29), but there must ordinarily be some language of commitment or some invitation to take action without further communication.

Restatement (Second) of Contracts § 26 cmt. b (1979). Similarly, a leading treatise notes that:

> It is quite possible to make a definite and operative offer to buy or sell goods by advertisement, in a newspaper, by a handbill, a catalog or circular or on a placard in a store window. It is not customary to do this, however; and the presumption is the other way. . . . Such advertisements are understood to be mere requests to consider and examine and negotiate; and no one can reasonably regard them as otherwise unless the circumstances are exceptional and the words used are very plain and clear.

1 Arthur Linton Corbin & Joseph M. Perillo, Corbin on Contracts § 2.4, at 116–17 (rev. ed. 1993) (emphasis added); see also 1 E. Allan Farnsworth, Farnsworth on Contracts § 3.10, at 239 (2d ed. 1998); 1 Samuel Williston & Richard A. Lord, A Treatise on the Law of Contracts § 4:7, at 286–87 (4th ed. 1990). New York courts adhere to this general principle. * * *

The Court finds, in sum, that the Harrier Jet commercial was merely an advertisement. * * *

C. An Objective, Reasonable Person Would Not Have Considered the Commercial an Offer

Plaintiff's understanding of the commercial as an offer must also be rejected because the Court finds that no objective person could reasonably have concluded that the commercial actually offered consumers a Harrier Jet.

1. Objective Reasonable Person Standard

In evaluating the commercial, the Court must not consider defendant's subjective intent in making the commercial, or plaintiff's subjective view of what the commercial offered, but what an objective, reasonable person would have understood the commercial to convey. *See Kay-R Elec. Corp. v. Stone & Weber Constr. Co.*, 23 F.3d 55, 57 (2d Cir. 1994) ("We are not concerned with what was going through the heads of the parties at the time [of the alleged contract]. Rather, we are talking about the objective principles of contract law."). * * *.

If it is clear that an offer was not serious, then no offer has been made:

> What kind of act creates a power of acceptance and is therefore an offer? It must be an expression of will or intention. It must be an act that leads the offeree reasonably to conclude that a power to create a contract is conferred. This applies to the content of the power as well as to the fact of its existence. It is on this ground that we must exclude invitations to deal or acts of mere preliminary negotiation, and acts evidently done in jest or without intent to create legal relations.

Corbin on Contracts, § 1.11 at 30. An obvious joke, of course, would not give rise to a contract. *See, e.g., Graves v. Northern N.Y. Pub. Co.*, 260 A.D. 900, 22 N.Y.S.2d 537 (App. Div. 4th Dept. 1940) (dismissing claim to offer of $1000, which appeared in the "joke column" of the newspaper, to any person who could provide a commonly available phone number). On the other hand, if there is no indication that the offer is "evidently in jest," and that an objective, reasonable person would find that the offer was serious, then there may be a valid offer. See [*Barnes v. Treece*, 549 P.2d 437, 549 P.2d 1152, 1155 (Wash. Ct. App. 1976)] ("If the jest is not apparent and a reasonable hearer would believe that an offer was being made, then the speaker risks the formation of a contract which was not intended."); *see also Lucy v. Zehmer*, 196 Va. 493, 84 S.E.2d 516, 518, 520 (Va. 1954) (ordering specific performance of a contract to purchase a farm despite defendant's protestation that the transaction was done in jest as "'just a bunch of two doggoned drunks bluffing'").

2. Necessity of a Jury Determination

Plaintiff also contends that summary judgment is improper because the question of whether the commercial conveyed a sincere offer can be answered only by a jury. Relying on dictum from *Gallagher v. Delaney*, 139 F.3d 338 (2d Cir. 1998), plaintiff argues that a federal judge comes from a "narrow segment of the enormously broad American socio-economic spectrum," and, thus, that the question whether the commercial constituted a serious offer must be decided by a jury composed of, inter alia, members of the "Pepsi Generation," who are, as plaintiff puts it, "young, open to adventure, willing to do the unconventional." Plaintiff essentially argues that a federal judge would view his claim differently than fellow members of the "Pepsi Generation."

Plaintiff's argument that his claim must be put to a jury is without merit. Gallagher involved a claim of sexual harassment in which the defendant allegedly invited plaintiff to sit on his lap, gave her inappropriate Valentine's

Day gifts, told her that "she brought out feelings that he had not had since he was sixteen," and "invited her to help him feed the ducks in the pond, since he was 'a bachelor for the evening.'" *Gallagher*, 139 F.3d at 344. The court concluded that a jury determination was particularly appropriate because a federal judge lacked "the current real-life experience required in interpreting subtle sexual dynamics of the workplace based on nuances, subtle perceptions, and implicit communications." This case, in contrast, presents a question of whether there was an offer to enter into a contract, requiring the Court to determine how a reasonable, objective person would have understood defendant's commercial. Such an inquiry is commonly performed by courts on a motion for summary judgment. * * *

3. Whether the Commercial Was "Evidently Done In Jest"

Plaintiff's insistence that the commercial appears to be a serious offer requires the Court to explain why the commercial is funny. Explaining why a joke is funny is a daunting task; as the essayist E.B. White has remarked, "Humor can be dissected, as a frog can, but the thing dies in the process . . . ."[11] The commercial is the embodiment of what defendant appropriately characterizes as "zany humor."

First, the commercial suggests, as commercials often do, that use of the advertised product will transform what, for most youth, can be a fairly routine and ordinary experience. The military tattoo and stirring martial music, as well as the use of subtitles in a Courier font that scroll terse messages across the screen, such as "MONDAY 7:58 AM," evoke military and espionage thrillers. The implication of the commercial is that Pepsi Stuff merchandise will inject drama and moment into hitherto unexceptional lives. The commercial in this case thus makes the exaggerated claims similar to those of many television advertisements: that by consuming the featured clothing, car, beer, or potato chips, one will become attractive, stylish, desirable, and admired by all. A reasonable viewer would understand such advertisements as mere puffery, not as statements of fact, * * * and refrain from interpreting the promises of the commercial as being literally true.

Second, the callow youth featured in the commercial is a highly improbable pilot, one who could barely be trusted with the keys to his parents' car, much less the prize aircraft of the United States Marine Corps. Rather than checking the fuel gauges on his aircraft, the teenager spends his precious

---

[11]Quoted in Gerald R. Ford, Humor and the Presidency 23 (1987).

preflight minutes preening. The youth's concern for his coiffure appears to extend to his flying without a helmet. Finally, the teenager's comment that flying a Harrier Jet to school "sure beats the bus" evinces an improbably insouciant attitude toward the relative difficulty and danger of piloting a fighter plane in a residential area, as opposed to taking public transportation.

Third, the notion of traveling to school in a Harrier Jet is an exaggerated adolescent fantasy. In this commercial, the fantasy is underscored by how the teenager's schoolmates gape in admiration, ignoring their physics lesson. The force of the wind generated by the Harrier Jet blows off one teacher's clothes, literally defrocking an authority figure. As if to emphasize the fantastic quality of having a Harrier Jet arrive at school, the Jet lands next to a plebeian bike rack. This fantasy is, of course, extremely unrealistic. No school would provide landing space for a student's fighter jet, or condone the disruption the jet's use would cause.

Fourth, the primary mission of a Harrier Jet, according to the United States Marine Corps, is to "attack and destroy surface targets under day and night visual conditions." United States Marine Corps, Factfile: AV-8B Harrier II (last modified Dec. 5, 1995) <http://www.hqmc.usmc.mil//factfile.nsf>. Manufactured by McDonnell Douglas, the Harrier Jet played a significant role in the air offensive of Operation Desert Storm in 1991. The jet is designed to carry a considerable armament load, including Sidewinder and Maverick missiles. As one news report has noted, "Fully loaded, the Harrier can float like a butterfly and sting like a bee—albeit a roaring 14-ton butterfly and a bee with 9,200 pounds of bombs and missiles." Jerry Allegood, Marines Rely on Harrier Jet, Despite Critics, News & Observer (Raleigh), Nov. 4, 1990, at C1. In light of the Harrier Jet's well-documented function in attacking and destroying surface and air targets, armed reconnaissance and air interdiction, and offensive and defensive anti-aircraft warfare, depiction of such a jet as a way to get to school in the morning is clearly not serious even if, as plaintiff contends, the jet is capable of being acquired "in a form that eliminates [its] potential for military use."

Fifth, the number of Pepsi Points the commercial mentions as required to "purchase" the jet is 7,000,000. To amass that number of points, one would have to drink 7,000,000 Pepsis (or roughly 190 Pepsis a day for the next hundred years—an unlikely possibility), or one would have to purchase approximately $700,000 worth of Pepsi Points. The cost of a Harrier Jet is roughly $23 million dollars, a fact of which plaintiff was aware when he set out to gather the amount he believed necessary to accept the alleged offer. Even if an objective, reasonable person were not aware of this fact, he would conclude that purchasing a fighter plane for $700,000 is a deal too good to be true.

Plaintiff argues that a reasonable, objective person would have understood the commercial to make a serious offer of a Harrier Jet because there was "absolutely no distinction in the manner" in which the items in the commercial were presented. Plaintiff also relies upon a press release highlighting the promotional campaign, issued by defendant, in which "no mention is made by [defendant] of humor, or anything of the sort." These arguments suggest merely that the humor of the promotional campaign was tongue in cheek. Humor is not limited to what Justice Cardozo called "the rough and boisterous joke . . . [that] evokes its own guffaws." *Murphy v. Steeplechase Amusement Co.*, 250 N.Y. 479, 483, 166 N.E. 173, 174 (1929). In light of the obvious absurdity of the commercial, the Court rejects plaintiff's argument that the commercial was not clearly in jest.

* * *

III. Conclusion

* * *

In sum, there are three reasons why plaintiff's demand cannot prevail as a matter of law. First, the commercial was merely an advertisement, not a unilateral offer. Second, the tongue-in-cheek attitude of the commercial would not cause a reasonable person to conclude that a soft drink company would be giving away fighter planes as part of a promotion. * * * [The third reason related to the absence of a "writing" as required under a contract law doctrine known as the "Statute of Frauds."]

For the reasons stated above, the Court grants defendant's motion for summary judgment. The Clerk of Court is instructed to close these cases. Any pending motions are moot.

SO ORDERED.

QUESTIONS

1. Questions about the facts of this case

   1.1. From Judge Wood's description of the television commercial, what do you think you would have understood had you seen the Pepsi promotion?

   1.2. Are there facts that tend to show that Justin Leonard regarded the commercial as serious? Does that matter?

   1.3. If a federal judge lacks "the current real-life experience required in interpreting subtle sexual dynamics of the workplace based on nuances, subtle perceptions, and implicit communications," how can that same judge, coming from a "narrow segment of the enormously broad American socioeconomic spectrum," relate to how a member of the "Pepsi Generation" might perceive the commercial? Just who is this reasonable, objective person?

2. Questions about the law

   2.1. Pepsi was only joking, and so it gets off the hook; Zehmer was only joking, but he gets stuck with liability. Are *Leonard* and *Lucy* inconsistent?

   2.2. What do you suppose is the basis for the general rule that ordinarily an advertisement does not constitute an offer? Can you couch your explanation in terms of objective theory?

   2.3. When is the question of whether a promise conveys an offer a question for the jury and when should it be decided by a judge? Should Judge Wood have at least let this question go to a jury of Mr. Leonard's peers?

Smith v. Boyd
Supreme Court of Rhode Island
553 A.2d 131 (1989)

Murray, Justice

This case is an appeal by the defendants James F. and Virginia Boyd, and the defendant-intervenors, Philip and Patricia Durigan. The case was tried in the Superior Court by a justice sitting without a jury. The trial court judgment permanently enjoined the Boyds from selling their Narragansett realty to the Durigans, and required them to convey instead to the plaintiffs. We reverse.

The record contains the following pertinent facts. The Boyds own a Cape Cod house on Boston Neck Road in the town of Narragansett. The Boyds decided to sell their house. On January 28, 1988, they listed the home for $325,000 with a real estate broker, Joan Carter. The Boyds discussed with Carter their willingness to include various appliances with the house. They received a written offer to purchase their home by prospective buyers, the Duxburys, but the sale was never completed.

On February 21, 1988, the Smiths viewed the Boyd's house accompanied by their realtor, Gerald Connors. Later that day, Joan Carter called the Boyds and told them that the Smiths were interested in purchasing the house and certain items of personalty for $325,000. The items of personalty were the refrigerator, stove, washer, dryer, dining room draperies, and bedroom curtains. The Smiths and Boyds negotiated over these items through their respective brokers. The parties agreed on a possible closing date of April 25, 1988. Joan Carter filled out a standard purchase-and-sales-agreement form. She filled in the blanks with the items of personalty and the closing date, and the Smiths signed the form.

Meanwhile, the Durigans had visited the Boyds' home with their realtor, Muriel Sullivan. The Durigans decided that they would like to purchase the house. They did not request to purchase any personalty. Sullivan made up a purchase-and-sales-agreement form. She filled out the blanks in the form and filled in April 25, 1988 as the date of closing. The Durigans signed the form.

Joan Carter delivered the two purchase-and-sales-agreement forms to the Boyds simultaneously. She told them that they could accept either or reject both. The Boyds decided to accept the Durigans' offer, and reject the Smiths'. The Boyds signed the Durigans' purchase-and-sales-agreement form. The Smiths then commenced an action seeking specific performance of their alleged oral contract to purchase the Boyds' home.

This case presents the issue of whether the trial justice erred in finding that the discussions between the Boyds and the Smiths progressed beyond negotiations to form a contract. We believe that a contract was never formed. * * *

A contract is a consensual endeavor. Farnsworth, § 3.1 at 106. To form a valid contract, each party to the contract must have the intent to promise or be bound. * * * Farnsworth, § 3.1 at 106. In general, assent to be bound is analyzed in two steps: offer and acceptance. Farnsworth, § 3.3 at 108. Under traditional contract theory, an offer and acceptance are indispensable to contract formation, and without such assent a contract is not formed. * * *

There are two types of intent to contract: objective and subjective. Farnsworth, Contracts § 3.6 at 113. In general, it is a party's objective intent that will be considered as creating either an offer or acceptance. * * * That is, this court shall look to an external interpretation of the party's or parties' intent as manifested by action. * * *

Hence, in order for an offer or acceptance to occur, the party must manifest an objective intent to promise or be bound. Sometimes, however, the individual or subjective intent of a party will be indicative of objective intent. Thus, although it is objective intent that controls in contract formation, subjective intent may be one of the factors which comprises objective intent.

There are instances in which a party intends that his agreement to terms of a contract will have no legal consequences. In this situation, there is no intent to be bound. Farnsworth, § 3.7 at 116–17. In general, courts will honor such intent not to contract if the other party has reason to know of it. *Id*. One instance in which parties may not wish their assent to particular terms to form a contract is when a written instrument is contemplated. The Supreme Court of Maine has held:

"If the party sought to be charged intended to close a contract prior to the formal signing of a written draft, or if he signified such an intention to the other party, he will be bound by the contract actually made, though the signing of the written draft be omitted. If on the other hand, such party neither had nor signified such an intention to close the contract until it was fully expressed in a written instrument and attested by signatures, then he will not be bound until the signatures are affixed." *Mississippi & Dominion Steamship Co. v. Swift*, 86 Me. 248, 258, 29 A. 1063, 1066–67 (1894) * * *.

Thus, where the parties understand that a written instrument is to be executed, whether an oral contract is formed may turn upon whether the party denying the contract manifested an objective intent to be bound before signing the written instrument. We hold that when the parties to an agreement understand that the agreement is to be reduced to writing, and extensive preparation or performance has not begun, the burden of proof to show an objective intent to be bound before execution of the written contract is on that party who wishes to enforce the alleged oral contract.

An important policy underlies today's holding. Business transactions require that parties to a contract be able to negotiate without fear that they will be bound by mere discussion. In circumstances where the parties understand that the agreement is to be reduced to writing, and extensive preparation or performance has not begun, the parties to a contract need autonomy to determine whether a bargain will be struck before or upon the execution of such written contract.

In determining whether a party's objective intent was to be bound before or upon execution of the written contract, one must examine the particular case. We shall consider, among other things, the practice of the trade or profession, the prior practice between the parties, whether the written contract was to be drawn up by persons other than the parties, and statements made during the negotiations. Most persuasive will be the fact that at the time of negotiation, a party states that he or she does not intend to be bound contractually until the written agreement is executed.

The findings of a trial justice sitting without a jury are accorded great deference and will not be disturbed unless the trial justice misconceived material evidence or was otherwise clearly wrong. * * * Moreover, this principle applies to inferences and conclusions drawn by the trial justice with respect to the ultimate issues of fact derived from the testimony and evidence. * * *. In the case at bar, we believe that the trial justice misconceived material evidence in determining that Dr. Boyd manifested an objective intent to enter into a binding contract before signing a purchase-and-sales agreement.

Applying the above-enunciated considerations to the case at bar, we note that it is a widespread real estate practice that an offer to purchase realty is made in writing by the purchaser's signature on a purchase-and-sales-agreement form, and a contract formed by the seller's countersignature on the same document. Indeed, Joan Carter did not believe the Smiths and Boyds had entered into a binding contract.

As far as the prior practice of at least the Boyds, Doctor Boyd testified that Carter was retained to solicit offers to buy the Boyds' house. This was also Joan Carter's understanding of her role. Prior to the Smiths' and the Durigans' offers, the Boyds received a written offer from other prospective buyers, the Duxburys. Thus it is logical for the Boyds to assume and intend that offers to buy would be made in writing, and that a deal would be consummated only upon their signing a purchase-and-sales agreement. In regard to the preparation of the purchase-and-sales agreement, Doctor Boyd testified:

"I have been involved in * * * several real estate transactions with Mrs. Carter, and I know that at some point in the transaction, when the prospective buyer is going to make an offer and put down a check, at that point an agreement is produced by somebody."

That is, Dr. Boyd believed that the offer would be made by the buyer executing the purchase-and-sales-agreement form. We believe Dr. Boyd's understanding of the transaction was a reasonable and objective view.

We note that as the written contract was to be drawn up by the realtors, the parties and their realtors had to discuss what was to be stated in the written agreement. The purchase-and-sales-agreement form is a standardized document, but nevertheless a real estate agent must fill in the blanks. To fill in the blanks, the appropriate information must be discussed by the parties and their agents. We are convinced that such discussion, considered alone, does not manifest an objective intent to contract before the written agreement is executed.

As far as the statements made during the negotiations, it is true that the Boyds and the Smiths did engage in some very specific discussion in regard to appliances, draperies, and the date of closing. In the complaint, the Smiths stated that:

> "5. Plaintiffs on said date agreed to all of the terms of the sale, each term having been defined, and agreed to by the Defendants, and accepted by the Defendants."

Paragraph 4 of the defendants' answer admitted to the allegations in paragraph 5 of the complaint. However, that the terms of the sale were agreed to does not necessarily mean that the Boyds intended tc be bound by such agreed-upon terms before they executed the written document. On the contrary, there is much evidence that the Boyds did not intend to contract before signing a written purchase-and-sales-agreement form.

We reverse the judgment below and its order of permanent injunction. The defendants' appeal is sustained, and the papers in this case are remanded to Superior Court.

QUESTIONS AND NOTE

1. Questions about the facts of this case

   1.1. Did the Smiths and Boyds agree to all of the terms of the sale on February 21, 1988?

   1.2. Did Dr. Boyd believe that he had agreed to sell the house to the Smiths on February 21, 1988? Is that relevant? What did the Smiths believe? Were the Smiths reasonable in their belief that the Boyds intended to be bound on February 21, 1988?

   1.3. What did the trial court believe about the parties intent on February 21, 1988?

2. Questions about the law

   2.1. What "material evidence" was "misconstrued" by the trial court judge?

   2.2. What does the court mean by the statement, "Sometimes, however, the individual or subjective intent of a party will be indicative of objective intent"?

   2.3. Based on *Lucy, Leonard,* and *Smith* do you want to try again to articulate the legal standard for determining whether the parties have mutually assented to a bargain?

   2.4. Why exactly were the Smiths not reasonable in their belief that the Boyds intended to be bound when the parties appeared to reach agreement on February 21, 1988? Was it because the Boyds were joking? Can you reconcile the result in *Smith* with the result in *Lucy*? How about with *Leonard*?

3. Note

Observe that in *Smith* the plaintiffs were seeking to enforce an *oral* contract. While some wags have insisted that an oral contract is not worth the paper it's written on, in fact, oral contracts, if proven, are perfectly enforceable. However, by virtue of a law (known as the "Statute of Frauds") first enacted by the English Parliament in the seventeenth century, some agreements, in order to be enforceable, must be evidenced by a written note or memoranda "signed by the party to be charged." Recall that the statute of frauds issue also came up in *Leonard.* We will examine the statute of frauds at some length in Chapter 2. For now, it's sufficient to point out that among these agreements required to be in writing are contracts involving the sale of any interest in real estate. However, an exception to this writing requirement is recognized where the defendant admits under oath all of the elements necessary to a contract. Thus, in *Smith,* the issue boiled down to whether the Boyds, who acknowledged that all of the terms of sale had been agreed upon, also admitted the elements necessary to the existence of a contract. Obviously, the Supreme Court of Rhode Island concluded not; can you identify what element(s) was missing? If you're still confused, take a look at *Restatement (Second) of* Contract § 27, cmt. c and see if that helps. *See also Continental Laboratories v. Scott Paper Co.*, 759 F. Supp. 538 (S.D. Ia. 1990), aff'd, 938 F.2d 184 (8th Cir. 1991) (applying the cited *Restatement* provision).

Note on the Intention to be Legally Bound

Did you notice that in none of the first three cases did the defendants make any reference in their alleged contracts to an *intention* to assume a legally binding obligation? And yet, the decisions seem unconcerned with this point in analyzing whether a contract may have been formed. This is because, ordinarily, such an express manifestation of intent to be bound is not required in order for a promise to bind the promisor; rather, it is inferred from the very act of making the promise. However, should an express manifestation of intention *not* to assume a legal obligation affect the enforceability of a promise? Can you justify a distinction under objective theory? Often, in sophisticated business transactions, such as corporate mergers and asset acquisitions, the deal will entail several individual points of agreement that cannot be arrived at simultaneously, but which, together, may be critical to the willingness of one or both of the parties to proceed with the transaction. Assume you represent one of these parties. Once agreement in principle has been reached on some but less than all of the deal points, how would you propose to protect your client's interests? *See, e.g., Phoenix Mutual Life Insurance Co. v. Shady Grove Plaza Limited Partnership*, 734 F. Supp. 1181 (1990). We will consider this question in greater detail in Section 7 of this chapter.

As we saw in *Lucy*, the law does not require, as a condition of enforceability, that a promise be accompanied by an express statement of the promisor acknowledging her intention to be legally bound by her promise. Just the opposite is generally true, however, in the context of promises made in a social or familial setting. Why is this the case? Suppose one of your new classmates invites you out to dinner, "Dutch treat," promising an evening of good food and good fellowship, but then reneges. Do you have a valid claim for breach of promise? If not, why not? If so, what are your damages? Does your answer (or perhaps your inability to fashion a satisfactory answer) to the last question begin to reveal some of the reasons for the presumption against the enforceability of social and familial contracts?

Notwithstanding the law's bias against treating promises among family members as enforceable obligations, in recent years, courts have begun to enforce promises between non-married cohabitants even in the absence of an express statement of the promisor's intent that the promise should be regarded as creating a legally enforceable obligation. For example, in famous case of *Marvin v. Marvin*, 557 P.2d 1106 (Cal. 1976), the court enforced an oral promise made by actor Lee Marvin (of *Cat Ballou* and *The Dirty Dozen* fame) to his cohabitant of seven years, Michelle Marvin, that they would share equally any property acquired during the course of their relationship. Can you distinguish these cases from other kinds of social and domestic promises where there is a general presumption of non-enforceability unless the parties manifest an express intention that legal consequences should attach to a breach of promise?

Professor Melanie Leslie has argued that the traditional distinction drawn in contract law between "self-interested" market-activity and "altruistic" family relations is misguided. *See* Leslie, *Enforcing Family Promises: Reliance, Reci-*

procity, and Relational Contract, 77 N.C. L. REV. 551 (1999). She maintains that while personal considerations frequently prevent parties in family and personal situations from casting their understandings in bargain terms, "the ability to make gratuitous transfers, and, more importantly, to promise to make such transfers, is a tool that the donor uses to obtain desired intangible 'goods' and 'services' for which there is no comparable market substitute." *Id.* at 568–69. If this is so, should the law's bias against enforcing family promises be reconsidered. Are there other considerations, beyond intention, that make enforcement problematic?

Problems on Mutual Assent

1. Ponoroff offers to sell his car to Epstein for $20,000. However, Ponoroff actually misspoke. He meant to say $22,000, but before Ponoroff could correct the error, Epstein promptly accepted. Who bears the risk of Ponoroff's mistake? What if Epstein was aware that Ponoroff had misspoken when he offered the car for $20,000? Would it make a difference if Ponoroff had said he would sell Epstein the car for $2,000? What additional facts would you like to know before giving an answer?

2. Markell had a written employment contract with Epstein's Construction Co. which expired on December 15, 2001. Before the agreement expired, Markell had tried without success to arrange a meeting with the president of the company, Epstein, to discuss renewal of his contract. Two days before Christmas, at the height of Epstein's busy season, Markell finally met with Epstein and advised him that unless satisfactory arrangements for a new one-year contract were worked out he would have no choice but to quit on the spot and seek another job. Epstein replied: "Go ahead, you're all right; get your men out and don't let that worry you." Markell assumed this meant that his contract was renewed for another year and, therefore, did not seek alternative employment. However, on March 1, 2002, Epstein advised Markell that Markell's position was being terminated and that, in two weeks, he would be let go by the company. Markell sued for breach of contract claiming that a contract for an additional year was created during the course of the conversation on December

23. At trial, Epstein testified that he had no recollection of ever making the "you're all right" statement and that, in any event, he was in a hurry during this conversation and had no intention at that point to renew the contract. Instead, his intent was to defer the issue until after the busy season. The trial judge instructed the jury that in order to return a verdict for Markell "you must find not only that the conversation occurred as Markell claimed, but that both parties intended by that conversation to contract with each other for Markell's employment for an additional year on the same terms as his prior agreement." The jury returned a verdict for Epstein. Markell has now appealed, claiming that the trial court erred by giving the jury this instruction. You are a law clerk to the court of appeals judge who has been assigned to write the opinion on appeal. The judge has asked you to advise her as to how she should rule in this case and why. What will you tell her?

SECTION 2: OFFER

We observed in Section 1 that the courts employ objective theory in deciding whether or not the parties assented to be bound. Now we shift focus from the overall method courts use to ascertain mutual assent to the mechanics of assent. An objective manifestation of assent can occur in numerous ways. As a practical matter, in many instances, assent occurs simply by mutual concurrence and understanding of the parties. For example, when you sign the rental agreement presented to you at the Hertz counter, there is a mutual understanding that the company is agreeing to let you use one of its cars for a specified period of time at a fixed price, and you are agreeing to pay that price for the use of the car. Conventionally, however, the method used to illustrate mutual assent is the more formalized, two-step process consisting of an *offer* and an *acceptance.*

As we have seen, an offer is a manifestation of assent that essentially says to the offeree "I've decided to deal on these terms. You now have the power to seal the deal with your assent to the terms of this offer." The *Restatement (Second) of Contracts* § 24 provides that:

> *An offer is the manifestation of willingness to enter into a bargain, so made as to justify another person in understanding that his assent to that bargain is invited and will conclude it.*

Consider this definition as you read the cases in this section.

Lonergan v. Scolnick

Court of Appeal of California

129 Cal. App. 2d 179, 276 P.2d 8 (1954)

Barnard, J.

This is an action for specific performance or for damages in the event specific performance was impossible.

The complaint alleged that on April 15, 1952, the parties entered into a contract whereby the defendant agreed to sell, and plaintiff agreed to buy a 40-acre tract of land for $2,500; that this was a fair, just and reasonable value of the property; that on April 28, 1952, the defendant repudiated the contract and refused to deliver a deed; that on April 28, 1952, the property was worth $6,081; and that plaintiff has been damaged in the amount of $3,581. The answer denied that any contract had been entered into, or that anything was due to the plaintiff.

By stipulation, the issue of whether or not a contract was entered into between the parties was first tried, reserving the other issues for a further trial if that became necessary. The issue as to the existence of a contract was submitted upon an agreed statement, including certain letters between the parties, without the introduction of other evidence.

The stipulated facts are as follows: During March, 1952, the defendant placed an ad in a Los Angeles paper reading, so far as material here, "Joshua Tree vic. 40 acres, . . . need cash, will sacrifice." In response to an inquiry resulting from this ad the defendant, who lived in New York, wrote a letter to the plaintiff dated March 26, briefly describing the property, giving directions as to how to get there, stating that his rock-bottom price was $2,500 cash, and further stating that "This is a form letter." On April 7, the plaintiff wrote a letter to the defendant saying that he was not sure he had found the property, asking for its legal description, asking whether the land was all level or whether it included certain jutting rock hills, and suggesting a certain bank as escrow agent "should I desire to purchase the land." On April 8, the defendant wrote to the plaintiff saying "From your description you have found the property"; that this bank "is O.K. for escrow agent"; that the land was fairly level; giving the legal description; and then saying, "If you are really interested, you will have to decide fast, as I expect to have a buyer in the next week or so." On April 12, the defendant sold the property to a third party for $2,500. The plaintiff received defendant's letter of April 8 on April 14. On April 15 he wrote to the defendant thanking him for his letter "confirming that I was on the right land," stating that he would immediately proceed to have the escrow opened and would deposit $2,500 therein "in conformity with your offer," and asking the defendant to forward a deed with his instructions to the escrow agent. On April 17, 1952, the plaintiff started an escrow and placed in the hands of the escrow agent $100, agreeing to furnish an additional $2,400 at an unspecified time, with the provision that if the escrow was not closed by May 15, 1952, it should be completed as soon thereafter as possible unless a written demand for a return of the money or instruments was made by either party after that date. It was further stipulated that the plaintiff was ready and willing at all times to deposit the $2,400.

The matter was submitted on June 11, 1953. On July 10, 1953, the judge filed a memorandum opinion stating that it was his opinion that the letter of April 8, 1952, when considered with the previous correspondence, constituted an offer of sale which offer was, however, qualified and conditioned upon prompt acceptance by the plaintiff; that in spite of the condition thus imposed, the plaintiff delayed more than a week before notifying the defendant of his acceptance; and that since the plaintiff was aware of the necessity of promptly communicating his acceptance to the defendant his delay was not the prompt action required by the terms of the offer. Findings of fact were filed on October 2, 1953, finding that each and all of the statements in the agreed statement are true, and that all allegations to the contrary in the complaint are untrue. As conclusions of law, it was found that the plaintiff and defendant did not enter into a contract as alleged in the complaint or otherwise, and that the defendant is entitled to judgment against the plaintiff. Judgment was entered accordingly, from which the plaintiff has appealed.

The appellant contends that the judgment is contrary to the evidence and to the law since the facts, as found, do not support the conclusions of law upon which the judgment is based. It is argued that there is no conflict in the evidence, and this court is not bound by the trial court's construction of the written instruments involved; that the evidence conclusively shows that an offer was made to the plaintiff by the defendant, which offer was accepted by the mailing of plaintiff's letter of April 15; that upon receipt of defendant's letter of April 8 the plaintiff had a reasonable time within which to accept the offer that had been made; that by his letter of April 15 and his starting of an escrow the plaintiff accepted said offer; and that the agreed statement of facts establishes that a valid contract was entered into between the parties. In his briefs the appellant assumes that an offer was made by the defendant, and confined his argument to contending that the evidence shows that he accepted that offer within a reasonable time.

There can be no contract unless the minds of the parties have met and mutually agreed upon some specific thing. This is usually evidenced by one party making an offer which is accepted by the other party. Section 25 of the Restatement of the Law on Contracts reads:

"If from a promise, or manifestation of intention, or from the circumstances existing at the time, the person to whom the promise or manifestation is addressed knows or has reason to know that the person making it does not intend it as an expression of his fixed purpose until he has given a further expression of assent, he has not made an offer."

The language used in *Niles v. Hancock*, 140 Cal. 157[,73 P. 840], "It is also clear from the correspondence that it was the intention of the defendant that the negotiations between him and the plaintiff were purely preliminary," is applicable here. The correspondence here indicates an intention on the part of the defendant to find out whether the plaintiff was interested, rather than an intention to make a definite offer to the plaintiff. The language used by the defendant in his letters of March 26 and April 8 rather clearly discloses that they were not intended as an expression of fixed purpose to make a definite offer, and was sufficient to advise the plaintiff that some further expression of assent on the part of the defendant was necessary.

The advertisement in the paper was a mere request for an offer. The letter of March 26 contains no definite offer, and clearly states that it is a form letter. It merely gives further particulars, in clarification of the advertisement, and tells the plaintiff how to locate the property if he was interested in looking into the matter. The letter of April 8 added nothing in the way of a definite offer. It merely answered some questions asked by the plaintiff, and stated that if the plaintiff was really interested he would have to act fast. The statement that he expected to have a buyer in the next week or so indicated that the defendant intended to sell to the first-comer, and was reserving the right to do so. From this statement, alone, the plaintiff knew or should have known that he was not being given time in which to accept an offer that was being made, but that some further assent on the part of the defendant was required. Under the language used the plaintiff was not being given a right to act within a reasonable time after receiving the letter; he was plainly told that the defendant intended to sell to another, if possible, and warned that he would have to act fast if he was interested in buying the land.

Regardless of any opinion previously expressed, the court found that no contract had been entered into between these parties, and we are in accord with the court's conclusion on that controlling issue. The court's construction of the letters involved was a reasonable one, and we think the most reasonable one, even if it be assumed that another construction was possible.

The judgment is affirmed.

QUESTIONS

1. Questions about the facts of this case

   1.1. What is the specific communication that Lonergan points to as constituting the offer to which he maintains his April 15 communication was an acceptance?

   1.2. Of what significance was the fact that on April 17, Lonergan started an escrow and placed $100 in the hands of the escrow agent? By the way, just what is an "escrow" anyway?

2. Questions about the law

   2.1. The court of appeal affirms the judgment of the trial court in *Lonergan*, but did the two courts take a different legal journey in reaching the same destination?

   2.2. If Lonergan's letter of April 15 was not an acceptance, what was it?

2.3. Section 25 of the first *Restatement of Contracts*, quoted in *Lonergan*, is carried forward in *Restatement (Second) of Contracts* § 26, which provides that

> *A manifestation of willingness to enter into a bargain is not an offer if the person to whom it is addressed knows or has reason to know that the person making it does not intend to conclude a bargain until he has made a further manifestation of assent.*

How did Lonergan know, or have reason to know, that Scolnick was not, by means of his April 8 letter, making an offer?

Fairmount Glass Works v. Grunden-Martin Woodenware Co.
Court of Appeals of Kentucky
106 Ky. 659, 51 S.W. 196 (1899)

Hobson, J.

On April 20, 1895, appellee wrote appellant the following letter:

> "St. Louis, Mo., April 20, 1895. Gentlemen: Please advise us the lowest price you can make us on our order for ten car loads of Mason green jars, complete, with caps, packed one dozen in a case, either delivered here, or f. o. b. cars your place, as you prefer. State terms and cash discount. Very truly, Grunden-Martin W. W. Co."

To this letter appellant answered as follows:

> "Fairmount, Ind., April 23, 1895. Grunden-Martin Wooden Ware Co., St. Louis, Mo—Gentlemen: Replying to your favor of April 20, we quote you Mason fruit jars, complete, in one-dozen boxes, delivered in East St. Louis, Ill.: Pints $4.50, quarts $5.00, half gallons $6.50, per gross, for immediate acceptance, and shipment not later than May 15, 1895; sixty days' acceptance, or 2 off, cash in ten days. Yours, truly, Fairmount Glass Works.
>
> "Please note that we make all quotations and contracts subject to the contingencies of agencies or transportation, delays or accidents beyond our control."

For reply thereto, appellee sent the following telegram on April 24, 1895:

> "Fairmount Glass Works, Fairmount, Ind.: Your letter twenty-third received. Enter order ten car loads as per your quotation. Specifications mailed. Grunden-Martin W. W. Co."

In response to this telegram, appellant sent the following:

> "Fairmount, Ind., April 24, 1895. Grunden-Martin W. W. Co., St. Louis, Mo.: Impossible to book your order. Output all sold. See letter. Fairmount Glass Works."

Appellee insists that, by its telegram sent in answer to the letter of April 23d, the contract was closed for the purchase of 10 car loads of Mason fruit jars. Appellant insists that the contract was not closed by this telegram, and that it had the right to decline to fill the order at the time it sent its telegram of April 24. This is the chief question in the case. The court below gave judgment in favor of appellee, and appellant has appealed, earnestly insisting that the judgment is erroneous.

We are referred to a number of authorities holding that a quotation of prices is not an offer to sell, in the sense that a completed contract will arise out of the giving of an order for merchandise in accordance with the proposed terms. There are a number of cases holding that the transaction is not completed until the order so made is accepted. 7 Am. & Eng. Enc. Law (2d Ed.) p. 138; Smith v. Gowdy, 8 Allen, 566; Beaupre v. Telegraph Co., 21 Minn. 155. But each case must turn largely upon the language there used. In this case we think there was more than a quotation of prices, although appellant's letter uses the word "quote" in stating the prices given. The true meaning of the correspondence must be determined by reading it as a whole. Appellee's letter of April 20th, which began the transaction, did not ask for a quotation of prices. It reads: "Please advise us the lowest price you can make us on our order for ten car loads of Mason green jars. * * * State terms and cash discount." From this appellant could not fail to understand that appellee wanted to know at what price it would sell it ten car loads of these jars; so when, in answer, it wrote: "We quote you Mason fruit jars * * * pints $4.50, quarts $5.00, half gallons $6.50, per gross, for immediate acceptance; * * * 2 off, cash in ten days,"—it must be deemed as intending to give appellee the information it had asked for. We can hardly understand what was meant by the words "for immediate acceptance," unless the latter was intended as a proposition to sell at these prices if accepted immediately. In construing every contract, the aim of the court is to arrive at the intention of the parties. In none of the cases to which we have been referred on behalf of appellant was there on the face of the correspondence any such expression of intention to make an offer to sell on the terms indicated. In Fitzhugh v. Jones, 6 Munf. 83, the use of the expression that the buyer should reply as soon as possible, in case he was disposed to accede to the terms offered, was held sufficient to show that there was a definite proposition, which was closed by the buyer's acceptance. The expression in appellant's letter, "for immediate acceptance," taken in connection with appellee's letter, in effect, at what price it would sell it the goods, is, it seems to us, much stronger evidence of a present offer, which, when accepted immediately, closed the contract. Appellee's letter was plainly an inquiry for the price and terms on which appellant would sell it the goods, and appellant's answer to it was not a quotation of prices, but a definite offer to sell on the terms indicated, and could not be withdrawn after the terms had been accepted. It will be observed that the telegram of acceptance refers to the specifications mailed. These specifications were contained in the following letter: "St. Louis, Mo., April 24, 1895. Fairmount Glass-Works Co., Fairmount, Ind.—Gentlemen: We received your letter of 23rd this morning, and telegraphed you in reply as follows: 'Your letter 23rd received. Enter order ten car loads as per your quotation. Specifications mailed,'—which we now confirm. We have accordingly entered this contract on our books for the ten cars Mason green jars, complete, with caps and rubbers, one dozen in case, delivered to us in East St. Louis at $4.50 per gross for pint, $5.00 for quart, $6.50 for one-half gallon. Terms, 60 days' acceptance, or 2 per cent, for cash in ten days, to be shipped not later than May 15, 1895. The jars and caps to be strictly first-quality goods. You may ship the first car to us here assorted: Five gross pint, fifty-five gross quart, forty gross one-half gallon. Specifications for the remaining 9 cars we will send later. Grunden-Martin W. W. Co." It is insisted for appellant that this was not an acceptance of the offer as made; that the stipulation, "The jars and caps to be strictly first-quality goods," was not in their offer; and that, it not having been accepted as made, appellant is not bound. But it will be observed that appellant declined to furnish the goods before it got this letter, and in the correspondence with appellee it nowhere complained of these words as an addition to the contract. Quite a number of other letters passed, in which the refusal to deliver the goods was placed on other grounds, none of which have been sustained by the evidence. Appellee offers proof tending to show that these words, in the trade in which parties were engaged, conveyed the same meaning as the words used in appellant's letter, and were only a different form of expressing the same idea. Appellant's conduct would seem to confirm this evidence.

Appellant also insists that the contract was indefinite, because the quantity of each size of the jars was not fixed, that 10 car loads is too indefinite a specification of the quantity sold, and that appellee had no right to accept the goods to be delivered on different days. The proof shows that "10 car loads" is an expression used in the trade as equivalent to 1,000 gross, 100 gross being regarded a car load. The offer to sell the different sizes at different prices gave the purchaser the right to name the quantity of each size, and, the offer being to ship not later than May 15th, the buyer had the right to fix the time of delivery at any time before that. * * * The petition, if defective, was cured by the judgment, which is fully sustained by the evidence. Judgment affirmed.

QUESTIONS AND NOTES

1. Question about the facts of this case

   The court states that "each case must turn largely on the language used." What language turned this case?

2. Question about the law

   What is the meaning (and the relevance) of the court's statement: "In construing every contract the aim of the court is to arrive at the intention of the parties"?

3. Notes

   3.1. In *Nebraska Seed Co. v. Harsh*, 98 Neb. 89, 152 N.W. 310 (1915), the defendant sent a letter to plaintiff in which he stated he had about 1,800 bushels of millet seed, of which he was mailing plaintiff a sample. He further stated: "I want $2.25 per cwt. for this seed f.o.b. Lowell." Upon receipt of the letter the plaintiff replied in part: "Sample and letter received. Accept your offer." The defendant refused to deliver and the plaintiff brought suit for such nondelivery.

The court ruled that the defendant's letter was not an offer but was an invitation for offers, quoting in part:

> If a proposal is nothing more than an invitation to the person to whom it is made to make an offer to the proposer, it is not such an offer as can be turned into an agreement by acceptance. Proposals of this kind, although made to definite persons and not to the public generally, are merely invitations to trade; they go no further than what occurs when one asks another what he will give or take for certain goods. Such inquiries may lead to bargains, but do not make them. They ask for offers which the proposer has a right to accept or reject as he pleases.

Id. at 91, 152 N.W. at 311. Some decisions suggest that the reason for the general rule that a price quote is not an offer is that the price quote lacks sufficient words of commitment, such as "agree" or "offer". *See Courteen Seed v. Abraham,* 587 P. 994 (Or. 1929). Is that a sufficient explanation? Does it explain the difference in the outcomes in *Fairmount* and *Nebraska Seed*? Identify the interests of the merchant who makes the quote and those of the prospective buyer who reads it, and see if that helps to sharpen the focus.

3.2. Should it make a difference whether the quote is in response to a particular inquiry? How important are the contextual circumstances in which the price quote is made? What other problems do you see with treating a price quotation as an offer? What if the quote is not made to the buyer but to the public at large? Does that help or hinder the argument for making the case that the price quote is an offer? Perhaps the next case will shed some light for you on this last question.

Note on U.C.C. Article 2

Because the transaction in *Fairmount* involved a transaction in goods, today Article 2 of the U.C.C. would supply the law governing the case. Section 2-204 is the Article 2 provision that addresses the formation of a contract. It is plain to see from that section that the U.C.C. takes a fairly liberal approach to contract formation, recognizing any manner of assent as sufficient to show agreement of the parties. In turn, U.C.C. § 1-201(3) defines the term *agree-*

ment broadly to mean the parties *bargain in fact,* derived not only from what was spoken between them but also "from other circumstances, including course of dealing or usage of trade or course of performance." The inclusion of all three of those concepts as part of the agreement of the parties in fact is consistent with the Code's general philosophy of bringing the law into line with prevailing commercial reality and expectation. Judge Posner put it this way: "The Uniform Commercial Code, its draftsmen mindful of the haste and sloppiness, and disregard for lawyerly niceties, that characterize commercial dealing, tolerates a good deal of incompleteness and even contradiction in offer and acceptance." *Architectural Metal Systems v. Consolidated Systems,* 58 F.3d 1227, 1230 (1995). The test for an offer, according to Judge Posner, is whether it induces a reasonable belief in the recipient that his acceptance is all that is necessary to seal the deal. Thus, the statement "I would like to buy your hamster" is not intended to empower the recipient of that solicitation to reply: "My price is $1 million. We have a contract." *Id.* at 1229.

Article 2's incorporation of course of dealing, usage of trade, and course of performance into the parties' bargain-in-fact means that if a party to a commercial transaction does *not* want a particular prior course of dealing or trade usage to become part of a new contract she must affirmatively say so in the new agreement. In a manner of speaking, this reverses the usual presumption that the terms of the contract consist only of those matters which the parties deliberately chose to *include.* Does this violate the principle of freedom of contract or *freedom from contract*? How might course of dealing or usage of trade evidence been used in *Fairmount*?

Despite the U.C.C.'s efforts to ensure that an agreement does not fail if the parties intended to make a contract, the Code does not define the term *offer.* Where then should a court, in considering whether a particular communication was an offer, look to determine the appropriate standard? The answer can be found in U.C.C. § 1-103 which states the general principle that the U.C.C. is intended to displace the common law to the least extent possible and that, therefore, if the U.C.C. does not directly speak to a particular issue, the answer is supplied by the common law. Hence, the definition of "offer" contained in *Restatement (Second) of Contracts* § 24 may also apply in the case of contracts for the sale of goods.

Donovan v. RRL Corporation

Supreme Court of California
26 Cal.4th 261, 27 P.3d 702 (2001)

Opinion by: George

* * *

I

While reading the April 26, 1997, edition of the Costa Mesa Daily Pilot, a local newspaper, plaintiff noticed a full-page advertisement placed by defendant. The advertisement promoted a "PRE-OWNED COUP-A-RAMA SALE!/2-DAY PRE-OWNED SALES EVENT" and listed, along with 15 other used automobiles, a 1995 Jaguar XJ6 Vanden Plas. The advertisement described the color of this automobile as sapphire blue, included a vehicle identification number, and stated a price of $ 25,995. The name Lexus of Westminster was displayed prominently in three separate locations in the advertisement, which included defendant's address along with a small map showing the location of the dealership. The following statements appeared in small print at the bottom of the advertisement: *"All cars plus tax, lic., doc., smog & bank fees. On approved credit. Ad expires 4/27/97[.]"*

Also on April 26, 1997, plaintiff visited a Jaguar dealership that offered other 1995 Jaguars for sale at $8,000 to $10,000 more than the price specified in defendant's advertisement. The following day, plaintiff and his spouse drove to Lexus of Westminster and observed a blue Jaguar displayed on an elevated ramp. After verifying that the identification number on the sticker was the same as that listed in defendant's April 26 Daily Pilot advertisement, they asked a salesperson whether they could test drive the Jaguar. Plaintiff mentioned that he had seen the advertisement and that the price "looked really good." The salesperson responded that, as a Lexus dealer, defendant might offer better prices for a Jaguar automobile than would a Jaguar dealer. At that point, however, neither plaintiff nor the salesperson mentioned the specific advertised price.

After the test drive, plaintiff and his spouse discussed several negative characteristics of the automobile, including high mileage, an apparent rust problem, and worn tires. In addition, it was not as clean as the other Jaguars they had inspected. Despite these problems, they believed that the advertised price was a very good price and decided to purchase the vehicle. Plaintiff told the salesperson, "Okay. We will take it at your price, $ 26,000."

When the salesperson did not respond, plaintiff showed him the advertisement. The salesperson immediately stated, "That's a mistake."

After plaintiff asked to speak with an individual in charge, defendant's sales manager also told plaintiff that the price listed in the advertisement was a mistake. The sales manager apologized and offered to pay for plaintiff's fuel, time, and effort expended in traveling to the dealership to examine the automobile. Plaintiff declined this offer and expressed his belief that there had been no mistake. Plaintiff stated that he could write a check for the full purchase price as advertised. The sales manager responded that he would not sell the vehicle at the advertised price. Plaintiff then requested the sales price. After performing some calculations, and based upon defendant's $35,000 investment in the automobile, the sales manager stated that he would sell it to plaintiff for $37,016. Plaintiff responded, "No, I want to buy it at your advertised price, and I will write you a check right now." The sales manager again stated that he would not sell the vehicle at the advertised price, and plaintiff and his spouse left the dealership.

Plaintiff subsequently filed this action against defendant for breach of contract, fraud, and negligence. In addition to testimony consistent with the facts set forth above, the following evidence was presented to the municipal court, which acted as the trier of fact.

Defendant's advertising manager compiles information for placement in advertisements in several local newspapers, including the Costa Mesa Daily Pilot. Defendant's advertisement published in the Saturday, April 19, 1997, edition of the Daily Pilot listed a 1995 Jaguar XJ6 Vanden Plas, but did not specify a price for that automobile; instead, the word "Save" appeared in the space where a price ordinarily would have appeared. The following Thursday afternoon, defendant's sales manager instructed the advertising manager to delete the 1995 Jaguar from all advertisements and to substitute a 1994 Jaguar XJ6 with a price of $ 25,995. The advertising manager conveyed the new information to a representative of the Daily Pilot that same afternoon.

Because of typographical and proofreading errors made by employees of the Daily Pilot, however, the newspaper did not replace the description of the 1995 Jaguar with the description of the 1994 Jaguar, but did replace the word "Save" with the price of $ 25,995. Thus, the Saturday, April 26, edition of the Daily Pilot erroneously advertised the 1995 Jaguar XJ6 Vanden Plas at a price of $ 25,995. The Daily Pilot acknowledged its error in a letter of retraction sent to defendant on April 28. No employee of defendant reviewed a proof sheet of the revised Daily Pilot advertisement before it was published, and defendant was unaware of the mistake until plaintiff attempted to purchase the automobile.

Except for the 1995 Jaguar XJ6 Vanden Plas, defendant intended to sell each vehicle appearing in the April 26, 1997, Daily Pilot advertisement at the advertised price. Defendant's advertisements in the April 26 editions of several other newspapers correctly listed the *1994* Jaguar XJ6 with a price of $ 25,995. In May 1997, defendant's advertisements in several newspapers listed the 1995 Jaguar XJ6 Vanden Plas for sale at $ 37,995. Defendant subsequently sold the automobile for $ 38,399.

The municipal court entered judgment for defendant. During the trial, the court ruled that plaintiff had not stated a cause of action for negligence, and it precluded plaintiff from presenting evidence in support of such a claim. After the close of evidence and presentation of argument, the municipal court concluded as a matter of law that a newspaper advertisement for an automobile generally constitutes a valid contractual offer that a customer may accept by tendering payment of the advertised price. The court also determined that such an advertisement satisfies the requirements of the statute of frauds when the dealer's name appears in the advertisement. Nevertheless, the municipal court held that in the present case there was no valid offer because defendant's unilateral mistake of fact vitiated or negated contractual intent. The court made factual findings that defendant's mistake regarding the advertisement was made in good faith and was not intended to deceive the public. The municipal court also found that plaintiff was unaware of the mistake before it was disclosed to him by defendant's representatives.

Plaintiff appealed from the judgment to the appellate department of the superior court, limiting his contentions to the breach of contract claim. The appellate department reversed the judgment for defendant and directed the municipal court to calculate plaintiff's damages. Relying upon the public policies underlying Vehicle Code section 11713.1, subdivision (e), the appellate department concluded that the advertisement constituted an offer capable of acceptance by tender of the advertised price. Section 11713.1, subdivision (e), provides that it is a violation of the Vehicle Code for a dealer to "fail to sell a vehicle to any person at the advertised total price . . . while the vehicle remains unsold, unless the advertisement states the advertised total price is good only for a specified time and the time has elapsed." The appellate department further concluded that defendant bore the risk of the mistaken transmission of its offer, because plaintiff was unaware of the mistake.

The appellate department of the superior court certified the appeal to the Court of Appeal, which ordered the case transferred to it for hearing and decision. Like the appellate department, the Court of Appeal reversed the judgment of the municipal court and held that defendant's advertisement constituted a contractual offer that invited acceptance by the act of tendering the advertised price, which plaintiff performed.* Acknowledging that the question was close, however, the Court of Appeal reasoned that Vehicle Code section 11713.1, subdivision (e), "tips the scale in favor of . . . construing the advertisement as an offer . . . ." The court disagreed with the municipal court's conclusion that defendant's unilateral mistake of fact, unknown to plaintiff at the time he tendered the purchase price, precluded the existence of a valid offer. With regard to the contention that defendant should not bear the risk of an error resulting solely from the negligence of the newspaper, the Court of Appeal made a factual finding based upon the appellate record (Code Civ. Proc., § 909) that defendant's failure to review a proof sheet for the Daily Pilot advertisement constituted negligence that contributed to the placement of the erroneous advertisement.

We granted defendant's petition for review and requested that the parties include in their briefing a discussion of the effect, if any, of California Uniform Commercial Code division 2, chapter 2, sections 2-201–2-210, upon the present case.

II

An essential element of any contract is the consent of the parties, or mutual assent. Mutual assent usually is manifested by an offer communicated to the offeree and an acceptance communicated to the offeror. (1 Witkin, Summary of Cal. Law (9th ed. 1987) Contracts, § 128, p. 153 (hereafter Witkin).) "'"An offer is the manifestation of willingness to enter into a

*In the opening paragraph of its opinion, the Court of Appeal offered this assessment of the case: "A first year law student would not be surprised to be called upon to answer the questions we address here. Does an advertisement for a specific used car at a designated price constitute an offer that may be accepted by tendering the purchase price? Does a statute prohibiting an automobile dealer from refusing to sell a vehicle at the advertised price affect the answer? Finally, does the answer change if the erroneous price inserted in the advertisement was the result of an error? We believe the answers are respectively 'possibly,' 'yes,' and 'no.' However, since such cryptic answers would not entitle our hypothetical law student to a passing grade, we must explain these answers below." Eds.

bargain, so made as to justify another person in understanding that his assent to that bargain is invited and will conclude it."' [Citations.]" * * * The determination of whether a particular communication constitutes an operative offer, rather than an inoperative step in the preliminary negotiation of a contract, depends upon all the surrounding circumstances. (1 Corbin, Contracts (rev. ed. 1993) § 2.2, p. 105.) The objective manifestation of the party's assent ordinarily controls, and the pertinent inquiry is whether the individual to whom the communication was made had reason to believe that it was intended as an offer. (1 Witkin, *supra*, Contracts, § 119, p. 144; 1 Farnsworth, Contracts (2d ed. 1998) § 3.10, p. 237.)

In the present case, the municipal court ruled that newspaper advertisements for automobiles generally constitute offers that can be accepted by a customer's tender of the purchase price. Its conclusion that defendant's advertisement for the 1995 Jaguar did not constitute an offer was based solely upon the court's factual determination that the erroneous price in the advertisement was the result of a good faith mistake.

Because the existence of an offer depends upon an objective interpretation of defendant's assent as reflected in the advertisement, however, the mistaken price (not reasonably known to plaintiff to be a mistake) is irrelevant in determining the threshold question whether the advertisement constituted an offer. In this situation, mistake instead properly would be considered in deciding whether a contract resulted from the acceptance of an offer containing mistaken terms, or whether any such contract could be voided or rescinded. * * * Thus, the municipal court did not make any factual findings relevant to the issue whether defendant's advertisement constituted an offer, and we shall review the question de novo. * * *

Some courts have stated that an advertisement or other notice disseminated to the public at large generally does not constitute an offer, but rather is presumed to be an invitation to consider, examine, and negotiate. (* * * see Rest.2d Contracts, § 26, com. b, p. 76; 1 Corbin, Contracts, *supra*, § 2.4, p. 116; 1 Farnsworth, Contracts, *supra*, § 3.10, p. 242; 1 Williston, Contracts (4th ed. 1990) § 4:7, pp. 285–287, 294.) Nevertheless, certain advertisements have been held to constitute offers where they invite the performance of a specific act without further communication and leave nothing for negotiation. Advertisements for rewards typically fall within this category, because performing the requested act (e.g., returning a lost article or supplying particular information) generally is all that is necessary to accept the offer and conclude the bargain. (1 Witkin, *supra*, Contracts, § 188,

p. 200; Rest.2d Contracts, § 29, com. b, illus. 1, p. 84; 1 Corbin, Contracts, *supra*, § 2.4, p. 119.)

Various advertisements involving transactions in goods also have been held to constitute offers where they invite particular action. For example, a merchant's advertisement that listed particular goods at a specific price and included the phrase "First Come First Served" was deemed to be an offer, because it constituted a promise to sell to a customer at that price in exchange for the customer's act of arriving at the store at a particular time. (*Lefkowitz v. Great Minneapolis Surplus Store* (1957) 251 Minn. 188 [86 N.W.2d 689, 691]; Rest.2d Contracts, § 26, com. b, illus. 1, p. 76.) * * * Similarly, external wording on the envelope of an item of bulk rate mail promising to give the recipient a watch "just for opening the envelope" before a certain date was held to constitute an operative offer accepted by performance of the act of opening the envelope. (*Harris v. Time, Inc., supra*, 191 Cal. App. 3d 449, 455–456.) In addition, an advertisement stating that anyone who purchased a 1954 automobile from a dealer could exchange it for a 1955 model at no additional cost constituted an offer that was accepted when the plaintiff purchased the 1954 vehicle. (*Johnson v. Capital City Ford Co.* (La.Ct.App. 1955) 85 So. 2d 75, 79–80; *see also Cobaugh v. Klick-Lewis* (Pa.Super.Ct. 1989) 385 Pa. Super. 587, 561 A.2d 1248, 1249–1250 [sign at golf course stated "hole-in-one wins" an automobile at a specified price].) In such cases, courts have considered whether the advertiser, in clear and positive terms, promised to render performance in exchange for something requested by the advertiser, and whether the recipient of the advertisement reasonably might have concluded that by acting in accordance with the request a contract would be formed. (1 Williston, Contracts, *supra*, § 4:7, pp. 296–297; 1 Corbin, Contracts, *supra*, § 2:4, pp. 116–117; see, e.g., *Chang v. First Colonial Sav. Bank* (1991) 242 Va. 388 [410 S.E.2d 928, 929–930] [bank's newspaper advertisement stating "Deposit $ 14,000 and receive . . . $ 20,136.12 upon maturity in 3 1/2 years" constituted an offer that was accepted by the plaintiffs' deposit of that sum for the specified period].)

Relying upon these decisions, defendant contends that its advertisement for the 1995 Jaguar XJ6 Vanden Plas did not constitute an offer, because the advertisement did not request the performance of a specific act that would conclude the bargain. According to defendant, plaintiff's assertion that the advertisement was an offer conflicts with the generally accepted "black-letter" rule that an advertisement that simply identifies goods and specifies a price is an invitation to negotiate.

This court has not previously applied the common law rules upon which defendant relies, including the rule that advertisements generally constitute invitations to negotiate rather than offers. Plaintiff observes that such rules governing the construction of advertisements have been criticized on the ground that they are inconsistent with the reasonable expectations of consumers and lead to haphazard results. (See Eisenberg, *Expression Rules in Contract Law and Problems of Offer and Acceptance* (1994) 82 Cal. L.Rev. 1127, 1166–1172.) Plaintiff urges this court to reject the black-letter advertising rule.

In the present case, however, we need not consider the viability of the black-letter rule regarding the interpretation of advertisements *in general*. Like the Court of Appeal, we conclude that a licensed automobile dealer's advertisement for the sale of a particular vehicle at a specific price—when construed in light of Vehicle Code section 11713.1, subdivision (e)—reasonably justifies a consumer's understanding that the dealer intends the advertisement to constitute an offer and that the consumer's assent to the bargain is invited and will conclude it. ROL

Vehicle Code section 11713.1 sets forth comprehensive requirements governing a licensed automobile dealer's advertisements for motor vehicles. This statute requires, among other things, that an advertisement for a specific automobile identify the vehicle by its identification number or license number (*id*., subd. (a)), disclose the type of charges that will be added to the advertised price at the time of sale (*id*., subd. (b)), and refrain from containing various types of misleading information (*id*., subds. (i), (l), (o), (p), (r)).

In addition, Vehicle Code section 11713.1, subdivision (e) (hereafter section 11713.1(e)), states that it is a violation of the Vehicle Code for the holder of any dealer's license to "fail to sell a vehicle to any person at the advertised total price, exclusive of [specified charges such as taxes and registration fees], while the vehicle remains unsold, unless the advertisement states the advertised total price is good only for a specified time and the time has elapsed."

The administrative regulation implementing section 11713.1(e) states in relevant part: "A specific vehicle advertised by a dealer . . . shall be willingly shown and sold at the advertised price and terms while such vehicle remains unsold . . ., unless the advertisement states that the advertised price and terms are good only for a specific time and such time has elapsed. Advertised vehicles must be sold at or below the advertised price irrespective of whether or not the advertised price has been communicated to the purchaser." (Cal. Code Regs., tit. 13, § 260.04, subd. (b).)[2]

Plaintiff asserts that because a dealer is prohibited by section 11713.1(e) from failing to sell a particular vehicle at the advertised price, an advertisement for such a vehicle cannot be a mere request for offers from consumers or an invitation to negotiate, but instead must be deemed an operative offer that is accepted when a consumer tenders the full advertised price. We agree that, in light of the foregoing regulatory scheme, a licensed automobile dealer's advertisement for a particular vehicle at a specific price constitutes an offer.

As one commentator has observed, legislation can affect consumer expectations and cause reasonable individuals to regard certain retail advertisements for the sale of goods as offers to complete a bargain. (1 Corbin, Contracts, *supra*, § 2.4, p. 118.) By authorizing disciplinary action against a licensed automobile dealer that fails to sell a vehicle at the advertised price, section 11713.1(e) creates a reasonable expectation on the part of consumers that the dealer intends to make an offer to sell at that price, and that the consumer can accept the offer by paying the price specified in the advertisement. Interpreted in light of the regulatory obligations imposed upon dealers, an advertisement for a particular automobile at a specific price constitutes an objective manifestation of the dealer's willingness to enter into a bargain on the stated terms, and justifies the consumer's understanding that his or her assent to the bargain is invited and will conclude it. Such an advertisement therefore constitutes an offer that is accepted when a consumer tenders the advertised price.

Defendant and its supporting *amici curiae* contend that section 11713.1(e) was not intended to modify the common law of contracts, and that therefore the statute should not be considered in determining whether a contract arose from defendant's advertisement and plaintiff's tender of the advertised price. * * * [W]e agree that section 11713.1(e) does not reflect a legislative intent to supplant the common law governing contracts for the sale of motor vehicles by licensed dealers. Nevertheless, the statute does govern the conduct of dealers and thus creates an objective expectation that dealers intend to sell vehicles at the advertised price. Therefore, even though section 11713.1(e) does not alter the applicable common law re-

[2]A dealer's violation of section 11713.1(e) constitutes a ground for suspension or revocation of the dealer's license by the Department of Motor Vehicles and is a misdemeanor. (Veh. Code, §§ 11705, subd. (a)(10), 40000.11, subd. (a).)

garding contractual offers, consumer expectations arising from the statute are relevant in determining whether defendant's advertisement constituted an offer pursuant to governing principles of contract law.

Amicus curiae California Motor Car Dealers Association further asserts that an advertisement for the sale of a vehicle does not constitute an offer because consumers have reason to believe that an automobile dealer does not intend to conclude the bargain until agreement is reached with regard to numerous terms other than price and until the contract is reduced to writing. (See Rest.2d Contracts, § § 26, 27; 1 Witkin, *supra*, Contracts, § 142, pp. 166–167.) For example, a written contract for the sale of an automobile by a dealer typically includes terms such as the form of payment, warranties, insurance, title, registration, delivery, taxes, documentation fees, and, if applicable, financing. * * * In addition, specific written disclosures, required by statute, must appear in the contract. (E.g., Veh. Code, § 11713.1, subd. (v) [retail automobile sales contract clearly and conspicuously must disclose whether the vehicle is being sold as used or new], subd. (x) [dealer must disclose on the face of the contract whether the transaction is or is not subject to a fee received by an "autobroker" as defined in the Vehicle Code].)

Plaintiff, on the other hand, contends that the existence of a contract is not defeated by the circumstance that he and defendant might have included additional terms in their ultimate written agreement, or that acceptance of defendant's offer might have been communicated by means other than tender of the purchase price, for example by signing a written contract. Plaintiff relies upon the following principle: "Manifestations of assent that are in themselves sufficient to conclude a contract will not be prevented from so operating by the fact that the parties also manifest an intention to prepare and adopt a written memorial thereof; but the circumstances may show that the agreements are preliminary negotiations." (Rest.2d Contracts, § 27.) Plaintiff also observes that "an offer to make a contract shall be construed as inviting acceptance in any manner and by any medium reasonable in the circumstances," unless otherwise indicated. (Cal. U. Com. Code, § 2-206, subd. (1)(a).)

Although dealers are required by statute to prepare a written contract when selling an automobile, and such a contract contains terms other than the price of the vehicle, we agree with plaintiff that a dealer's advertisement specifying a price for a particular vehicle constitutes a sufficient manifestation of the dealer's assent to give rise to a contract. As we have explained, in light of section 11713.1(e) such an advertisement objectively reflects the dealer's intention to sell the vehicle to a member of the public who tenders the full advertised price while the vehicle remains unsold and before the advertisement expires. The price almost always is the most important term of the bargain, and the dealer's intention to include other terms in a written contract does not preclude the existence of mutual assent sufficient to conclude a contract.

In sum, because section 11713.1(e) makes it unlawful for a dealer not to sell a particular vehicle at the advertised price while the vehicle remains unsold and before the advertisement expires, plaintiff reasonably could believe that defendant intended the advertisement to be an offer. Therefore, we conclude that defendant's advertisement constituted an offer that was accepted by plaintiff's tender of the advertised price.

III

Defendant contends that even if its advertisement constituted an offer that was accepted by plaintiff's tender of the purchase price, plaintiff is not authorized by law to enforce the resulting contract, because there was no signed writing that satisfied the requirements of the statute of frauds for the sale of goods. Plaintiff, on the other hand, maintains that defendant's name, as it appeared in the newspaper advertisement for the sale of the vehicle, constituted a signature within the meaning of the statute.

[The court concluded that the defendant's printed name in the advertisement was a sufficient signature satisfying the statute of frauds.]

IV

Having concluded that defendant's advertisement for the sale of the Jaguar automobile constituted an offer that was accepted by plaintiff's tender of the advertised price, and that the resulting contract satisfied the statute of frauds, we next consider whether defendant can avoid enforcement of the contract on the ground of mistake.

[The court decided that recession of the contract was warranted under the doctrine of unilateral mistake of fact because the mistake was made in good faith and enforcement of the contract with the erroneous price would be unconscionable. We examine the doctrine of "mistake" as a defense to contract liability in Chapter 2.]

Having determined that defendant satisfied the requirements for rescission of the contract on the ground of unilateral mistake of fact, we conclude that the municipal court correctly entered judgment in defendant's favor.

V

The judgment of the Court of Appeal is reversed.

QUESTIONS AND NOTES

1. Questions about the facts of this case

   1.1. Was the defendant aware of the mistake made by the newspaper? Is that fact important in determining whether the advertisement constituted an offer?

   1.2. Are there any facts that suggest that maybe the plaintiff was aware of the mistake concerning the advertisement. Why would that be important?

   1.3. What exactly was the role of the California Motor Car Dealers Association in this case? The court refers to this Association as "*Amicus curiae.*" Does that help? Why can't courts just speak English?

2. Questions about the law

   2.1. Why do some courts hold that "an advertisement or other notice disseminated to the public at large generally does not constitute an offer, but rather is presumed to be an invitation to consider, examine, and negotiate"? Is this why the ad in *Leonard v. Pepsi Co., supra,* was not regarded as an offer?

   2.2. Why might the language "First Come, First Served" convert an ad into an offer? What does the Supreme Court of California have to say about the "black-letter" rule that an advertisement that simply identifies goods and specifies a price is an invitation to negotiate"?

   2.3. What was the significance of § 11713.1 of the California Vehicle Code in this case? Is that statute about contract law? Is it a criminal statute? Given that the existence of the statute obviously played a pivotal role in the outcome, do you think this court would have decided the case differently if the ad had been for a lawn mower instead of a car?

2.4. If a merchant displays an item with a price is that an offer or invitation to offer? What does your common sense tell you?

2.5. Why is the existence of a "mistaken price (not reasonably known to plaintiff to be a mistake) irrelevant in determining the threshold question whether the advertisement constituted an offer"? When might this fact become relevant?

3. Notes

3.1. In the famous case of *Lefkowitz v. Great Minneapolis Supply Store, Inc.*, 251 Minn. 188, 86 N.W.2d 689 (1957) (which by the way is the basis for the *Restatement* illustration referred to by the court in *Donovan*), the defendant placed advertisements in a local newspaper on two consecutive weeks offering certain expensive items of apparel for one dollar each *"First Come, First Served."* On both occasions, the plaintiff was the first to show-up and indicated a readiness to pay the dollar, but the defendant refused to sell the merchandise to him, stating on the first occasion that by a "house rule" the offer was intended for women only and sales would not be made to men, and on the second visit that plaintiff knew defendant's house rules. The court ruled that "[w]hether in any individual instance a newspaper advertisement is an offer rather than an invitation to make an offer depends on the legal intention of the parties and the surrounding circumstances." In this case, because the ads in question were "clear, definite, and left nothing open for negotiation," the court concluded that an offer had been made which the plaintiff accepted when he successfully managed to be the first person to appear at the defendant's store and tendered the stated purchase price. The court quickly dispatched of the defendant's further argument that the offer had been modified by the "house rule" since the ad itself contained no such restriction. Was the court's holding in *Lefkowitz* concerning the undisclosed house rule consistent with objective theory? Even if so, could you draw a distinction between the first and second transactions based on the existence of this rule?

3.2. The defendant in *Donovan* urged that the advertisement did not constitute an offer because, unlike *Lefkowitz* and other cases finding an offer originating in an ad, it *did not request the performance of a specific act* that would conclude a bargain. The Court of Appeal in *Donovan* responded to that argument by concluding that the "characterization of the contract as either unilateral or bilateral [is not] essential to our decision." In fact, the distinction between offers for unilateral and bilateral contracts has been de-emphasized under modern contract law as tending to promote unnecessary formalism and rigidity in analyzing the question of whether a contract was formed. Under classical contract law, however, all offers were characterized as offers either for a unilateral or a bilateral contract. The distinction was based on an assessment of whether the offeror was bargaining for, respectively, a specific act by the offeree, or a return promise. A unilateral contract is one that, instantly upon its formation, is wholly performed on one side. *Lefkowitz* was an example of such a contract because there was no contract until Lefkowitz had accepted the offer by performing the requested act; *i.e.*, showing up at the store first, ready to pay the dollar. Thus, at the time the contract is formed, the offeror has already received what he was bargaining for in exchange for his promise. A bilateral contract, by contrast, involves an exchange of promises, so that on formation the contract is usually unperformed (executory) on both sides. These terms—unilateral and bilateral contract—are not found anywhere in either the *Restatement (Second) of Contracts* or Article 2 of the Uniform Commercial Code, but they do show up occasionally in the caselaw and, as we will see later in this chapter, may have significant implications in the contract formation analysis.

3.3. You'll recall that in *Leonard v. Pepsico, Inc.,* the court rejected the argument that Pepsi's advertisement should be construed as an offer. Is that ruling inconsistent with *Lefkowitz?* Here's what Judge Wood had to say about that:

> The present case is distinguishable from *Lefkowitz*. First, the commercial cannot be regarded in itself as sufficiently definite, because it specifically reserved the details of the offer to a separate writing, the Catalog. The commercial itself made no mention of the steps a potential offeree would be required to take to accept the alleged offer of a Harrier Jet. The advertisement in *Lefkowitz*, in contrast,

"identified the person who could accept." * * * FARNSWORTH [ON CONTRACTS], § 310, at 239 [(2nd ed. 1998)] ("The fact that a proposal is very detailed suggests that it is an offer, while omission of many terms suggests that it is not."). Second, even if the Catalog had included a Harrier Jet among the items that could be obtained by redemption of Pepsi Points, the advertisement of a Harrier Jet by both television commercial and catalog would still not constitute an offer. As the *Mesaros* court explained, the absence of any words of limitation such as "first come, first served," renders the alleged offer sufficiently indefinite that no contract could be formed. *See* Mesaros [v. United States], 845 F.2d 1576, 1581 (Fed. Cir. 1988). "A customer would not usually have reason to believe that the shopkeeper intended exposure to the risk of a multitude of acceptances resulting in a number of contracts exceeding the shopkeeper's inventory." FARNSWORTH, *supra*, at 242. There was no such danger in *Lefkowitz*, owing to the limitation "first come, first served."

3.4. We've noted that an offer involves some *manifestation* by the offeror of a willingness to be bound upon assent by the offeree. But does that assent have to be expressed in either spoken or written words? The answer is clearly not. What must be *expressed* is the manifestation of intent, but this expression can be *implied* from conduct. Thus, courts sometimes distinguish between express and implied-in-fact contracts, but there is no legal difference between the two, both are contracts in the strict sense of the word. Thus, if you are passing a hot dog vendor who holds out a sandwich that you take and consume, it should be fairly clear that there is an obligation to pay for it. While purely implied-in-fact contracts may be somewhat rare, many, if not most, contracts are partially express and partially implied-in-fact. For example, when a lawyer expressly agrees to handle a new client's case, there is an implied understanding that the client will pay for those services even if nothing is said about fees (although we hasten to add that we personally think that it is always advisable to have an express agreement concerning fees; the point being, however, that it often doesn't happen that way). However, in situations involving family members or parties who otherwise have an intimate relationship, courts have generally been reluctant to find the existence of a binding obligation to pay for the services. Should it matter, insofar as contractual liability is concerned, whether the client is a stranger or the lawyer's spouse? How about the lawyer's father-in-law? Try to couch your answer in terms of objective theory.

3.5. Because of the general rule that advertisements are not offers, contract law doctrine and remedies often proved of little help to consumers who were "taken in" by a false or misleading ad. Recognizing the need for additional protection, Section 5 of the Federal Trade Commission Act proscribes certain "deceptive" trade practices, including the notorious "bait and switch" advertising. 16 C.F.R. § 238. The bait and switch was used by unscrupulous merchants to lure customers into their stores with "promises" of deals too good to be true. When the consumer showed to take advantage of the deals, they would be told that the advertised merchandise (the bait) was no longer available, and then be steered into a higher priced product (the switch). However, because the Federal Trade Commission Act provides for only administrative remedies, such as cease and desist orders, many states have promulgated their own false or deceptive advertising laws that permit for a monetary recovery, including attorney's fees, by aggrieved consumers. For example, Georgia's Fair Business Practices Acts, OCGA § 10-1-390 *et seq.* provides a private right of action in favor of any person who suffers an injury or damages as a result of consumer practices in violation of the act. In *Agnew v. Great Atlantic & Pacific Tea Co.,* 502 S.E.2d 735 (Ga. App. 1998). Gary Agnew, a lawyer, saw a large sign in front of a grocery store which read: *"Nobody's Gonna Beat Us Now. Buy One Get One Free. 1=2 Sale. All This Week. Single Purchases Will be Charged Regular Retail Price, Second Item Free."* The sign contained no additional limitations. Agnew entered the store, selected two bags of sugar, two boxes of Rice-A-Roni, and two boxes of crackers. The cashier rang up his purchases but no discount appeared. When Agnew inquired about the promotional sale he was told it only applied to certain items, not including those he had selected. Agnew paid full price for his purchases, but then filed a complaint under the Georgia Fair Business Practice Act against the grocery store claiming that the sign caused him injury when he paid full price for the six items. The court concluded that because he purchased the items with knowledge that the sign did not mean what it said, his deliberate choice, and not the misleading sign, was the proximate cause of his injury. Therefore, the court sustained the trial court's dismissal of his claim. Would Agnew have been better off suing for breach of contract? How would you analyze such a claim?

SECTION 3: DESTROYING THE OFFER

An offer, once communicated to the offeree, creates in the offeree the power of acceptance. But how long does this power last? Two events that terminate an offer are a revocation by the offeror or a rejection by the offeree. Revocation simply requires notifying the offeree that the offeror no longer desires to be bound on the terms of the offer. At that point the offeree is no longer reasonable in the belief that all that is necessary to seal the deal is her assent. Similarly, if the offeree declines the offer by notifying the offeror that she is not interested in doing a deal on the terms of the offer, this also terminates the power of acceptance and the offer cannot be revived unless the offeror affirmatively elects to renew it. But suppose the offer is neither revoked nor rejected, does it continue into perpetuity? If not, when does it expire? Moreover, beyond an affirmative statement to the offeree that the offeror "hereby officially withdraws her offer" what kind of communication is sufficient to revoke an offer and when is it effective? These are some of the questions that we address in this section.

A. Indirect Revocation

Dickinson v. Dodds
Court of Appeal, Chancery Division
2 Ch. Div. 463 (1876)

On Wednesday, the 10th of June, 1874, the Defendant John Dodds signed and delivered to the Plaintiff, George Dickinson, a memorandum, of which the material part was as follows:

> I hereby agree to sell to Mr. George Dickinson the whole of the dwelling-houses, garden ground, stabling, and outbuildings thereto belonging,

situate at Croft, belonging to me, for the sum of £800. As witness my hand this tenth day of June, 1874.

£800 /signed/ John Dodds

P.S.—This offer to be left open until Friday, 9 o'clock, A.M. J.D. (the twelfth), 12th June 1874.

/signed/ J. Dodds

The bill alleged that Dodds understood and intended that the Plaintiff should have until Friday 9 a.m. within which to determine whether he would or would not purchase, and that he should absolutely have until that time the refusal of the property at the price of £800, and that the Plaintiff in fact determined to accept the offer on the morning of Thursday, the 11th of June, but did not at once signify his acceptance to Dodds, believing that he had the power to accept it until 9 a.m. on the Friday.

In the afternoon of the Thursday the Plaintiff was informed by a Mr. Berry that Dodds had been offering or agreeing to sell the property to Thomas Allan, the other Defendant. Thereupon the Plaintiff, at about half-past seven in the evening, went to the house of Mrs. Burgess, the mother-in-law of Dodds, where he was then staying, and left with her a formal acceptance in writing of the offer to sell the property. According to the evidence of Mrs. Burgess this document never in fact reached Dodds, she having forgotten to give it to him.

On the following (Friday) morning, at about seven o'clock, Berry, who was acting as agent for Dickinson, found Dodds at the Darlington railway station, and handed to him a duplicate of the acceptance by Dickinson, and explained to Dodds its purport. He replied that it was too late, as he had sold the property. A few minutes later Dickinson himself found Dodds entering a railway carriage, and handed him another duplicate of the notice of acceptance, but Dodds declined to receive it, saying, "You are too late. I have sold the property."

It appeared that on the day before, Thursday, the 11th of June, Dodds had signed a formal contract for the sale of the property to the Defendant Allan for £800, and had received from him a deposit of £40.

The bill in this suit prayed that the Defendant Dodds might be decreed specifically to perform the contract of the 10th of June, 1874; that he might be restrained from conveying the property to Allan; that Allan might be restrained from taking any such conveyance; that, if any such conveyance had been or should be made, Allan might be declared a trustee of the property for, and might be directed to convey the property to, the Plaintiff; and for damages.

The cause came on for hearing before Vice-Chancellor Bacon on the 25th of January, 1876.

[Vice Chancellor Bacon declared that Allan had no interest in the property and entered a decree of specific performance in favor of Dickinson, from which Dodds and Allan appealed]

JAMES, L.J., after referring to the document of the 10th of June, 1874, continued:—

The document, though beginning "I hereby agree to sell," was nothing but an offer, and was only intended to be an offer, for the Plaintiff himself tells us that he required time to consider whether he would enter into an agreement or not. Unless both parties had then agreed there was no concluded agreement then made; it was in effect and substance only an offer to sell. * * * There was no consideration given for the undertaking or promise, to whatever extent it may be considered binding, to keep the property unsold until 9 o'clock on Friday morning; but apparently Dickinson was of opinion, and probably Dodds was of the same opinion, that he (Dodds) was bound by that promise, and could not in any way withdraw from it, or retract it, until 9 o'clock on Friday morning, and this probably explains a good deal of what afterwards took place. But it is clear settled law, on one of the clearest principles of law, that this promise, being a mere *nudum pactum*, was not binding, and that at any moment before a complete acceptance by Dickinson of the offer, Dodds was as free as Dickinson himself. Well, that being the state of things, it is said that the only mode in which Dodds could assert that freedom was by actually and distinctly saying to Dickinson, "Now I withdraw my offer." It appears to me that there is neither principle nor authority for the proposition that there must be an express and actual withdrawal of the offer, or what is called a retraction. It must, to constitute a contract, appear that the two minds were at one, at the same moment of time, that is, that there was an offer continuing up to the time of the acceptance. If there was not such a continuing offer, then the acceptance comes to nothing. Of course it may well be that the one man is bound in some way or other to let the other man know that his mind with regard to the offer has been changed; but in this case, beyond all question, the Plaintiff knew that Dodds was no longer minded to sell the property to him as plainly and clearly as if Dodds had told him in so many words, "I withdraw the offer." This is evident from the Plaintiff's own statements in the bill.

* * *

It is to my mind quite clear that before there was any attempt at acceptance by the Plaintiff, he was perfectly well aware that Dodds had changed his mind, and that he had in fact agreed to sell the property to Allan. It is impossible, therefore, to say there was ever that existence of the same mind between the two parties which is essential in point of law to the making of an agreement. I am of opinion, therefore, that the Plaintiff has failed to prove that there was any binding contract between Dodds and himself.

MELLISH, L.J.:

I am of the same opinion. * * * He [Dodds] was not in point of law bound to hold the offer over until 9 o'clock on Friday morning. He was not so bound either in law or in equity. Well, that being so, when on the next day he made an agreement with Allan to sell the property to him, I am not aware of any ground on which it can be said that that contract with Allan was not as good and binding a contract as ever was made. Assuming Allan to have known (there is some dispute about it, and Allan does not admit that he knew of it, but I will assume that he did) that Dodds had made the offer to Dickinson, and had given him till Friday morning at 9 o'clock to accept it, still in point of law that could not prevent Allan from making a more favorable offer than Dickinson, and entering at once into a binding agreement with Dodds.

Then Dickinson is informed by Berry that the property has been sold by Dodds to Allan. Berry does not tell us from whom he heard it, but he says that he did hear it, that he knew it, and that he informed Dickinson of it. Now, stopping there, the question which arises is this—If an offer has been made for the sale of property, and before that offer is accepted, the person who has made the offer enters into a binding agreement to sell the property to somebody else, and the person to whom the offer was first made receives notice in some way that property has been sold to another person, can he after that make a binding contact by the acceptance of the offer? I am of opinion that he cannot. The law may be right or wrong in saying that a person who has given to another a certain time within which to accept an offer is not bound by his promise to give that time; but, if he is not bound by that promise, and may still sell the property to some one else, and if it be the law that, in order to make a contract, the two minds must be in agreement at some one time, that is, at the time of the acceptance, how is it possible that when the person to whom the offer has been made knows that the person who made the offer has sold the property to someone else, and that, in fact, he has not remained in the same mind to sell it to him, he can be at liberty to accept the offer and thereby make a binding contract? It seems to me that would be simply absurd. * * * If the rule of law is that a mere offer to sell property, which can be withdrawn at any time, and which is made dependent on the acceptance of the person to whom it is made, is a mere *nudum pactum*, how is it possible that the person to whom the offer has been made can by acceptance make a binding contract after he knows that the person who has made the offer has sold the property to some one else? * * * I am clearly of opinion that * * * once the person to whom the offer was made knows that the property has been sold to some one else, it is too late for him to accept the offer, and on that ground I am clearly of opinion that there is no binding contact for the sale of this property by Dodds to Dickinson, and even if there had been, it seems to me that the sale of the property to Allan was first in point of time. However, it is not necessary to consider, if there had been two binding contracts, which of them would be entitled to priority in equity, because there is no binding contact between Dodds and Dickinson.

QUESTIONS AND NOTE

1. Questions about the facts of this case

   1.1. If you'll excuse the expression, Dodds dodged the bullet in this case because of the court's holding that the offer was revoked once Dickinson learned through Berry that Dodds was no longer of a mind to sell the property to him. How much did Dickinson really know, however, about the dealings between Dodds and Allan?

   1.2. The court obviously considered Berry to be a reliable messenger. Why was that fact important to the court? Do you agree with the court's judgment?

2. Questions about the law

2.1. Is the holding in *Dickinson* consistent with objective theory of contract formation? Suppose Berry was mistaken in what he told Dickinson. Is the offer still revoked? What if Berry was not just mistaken, but deliberately lying to Dickinson? Does that change the analysis?

2.2. The court states that although Dodds promised that his offer would be held open until Friday morning, this promise was unenforceable *even though* both parties probably believed that Dodds was bound by that promise. Why was this so? How could this promise have been made binding? We will take up the subject of when offers will be regarded as irrevocable in the next section of this chapter. For the time being, accepting the court's statement of the law as true, how would you have advised Dodds to proceed once he decided that he might be interested in selling the property to Allan?

2.3. Suppose that even though Dodds entered into an agreement with Allan for the sale of the property, Dickinson did not learn of this fact, directly or indirectly, until after he had accepted the offer. This is the problem that Lord Judge Mellish says at the end of his concurring opinion that the court does not have to address. If, however, the court were faced with those circumstances, would a contract have been formed with Allan? Would a contract also be formed between Dickinson and Dodds? Is it possible to have *two* contracts for the same property? If so, and both purchasers sue for specific performance, who gets the property? What does the other party get? Is there any way in which a person in Dickinson's position can protect himself against an intervening contract buyer?

2.4. Suppose the facts in *Dickinson* had been different so that what happened is that Dodds learned from a reliable source on the afternoon of Thursday, June 11, that Dickinson was not interested in buying his property and, in fact, was actively negotiating with someone else for the purchase of another parcel of land. Would the offer then be terminated by indirect rejection? But suppose that information was inaccurate and, before 9 a.m. on Friday, Dickinson accepts. Would Dodds be obligated to sell?

3. Note

In a case where an offer is made by a public advertisement, does the offeror retain the power to revoke the offer? If so, how is it done? Does the offeror have to personally contact everyone that might have read the advertisement? *See Shuey v. United States*, 92 U.S. 73 (1875), involving an attempt to collect a reward that had been offered for the apprehension of John H. Surratt, an alleged accomplice of John Wilkes Booth in the murder of President Lincoln.

B. Lapse

Minnesota Linseed Oil Co. v. Collier White Lead Co.

Circuit Court, District of Minnesota
17 F. Cas. 447 (1876)

* * * The plaintiff seeks to recover the sum of $2,151.50, with interest from September 20, 1875—a balance claimed to be due for oil sold to the defendant. The defendant, in its answer, alleges that on August 3d, 1875, a contract was entered into between the parties, whereby the plaintiff agreed to sell and deliver to the defendant, at the city of St. Louis, during the said month of August, twelve thousand four hundred and fifty (12,450) gallons of linseed oil for the price of fifty-eight (58) cents per gallon, and that the plaintiff has neglected and refused to deliver the oil according to the contract; that the market value of oil after August 3d and during the month was not less than seventy (70) cents per gallon, and therefore claims a set-off or counter-claim to plaintiff's cause of action. The reply of the plaintiff denies that any contract was entered into between it and defendant.

* * * The contract is alleged to have been made by telegraph.

The plaintiff sent the following dispatch to the defendant: *"Minneapolis, July 29, 1875. To Alex. Easton, Secretary Collier White Lead Company, St. Louis, Missouri: Account of sales not enclosed in yours of 27th. Please wire us best offer for round lot named by you—one hundred barrels shipped. Minnesota Linseed Oil Company."*

The following answer was received: *"St. Louis, Mo., July 30, 1875. To the Minnesota Linseed Oil Company: Three hundred barrels fifty-five cents here, thirty days, no commission. August delivery. Answer. Collier Company."*

The following reply was returned: *"Minneapolis, July 31, 1875. Will accept fifty-eight cents (58c), on terms named in your telegram. Minnesota Linseed Oil Company."*

This dispatch was transmitted Saturday, July 31, 1875, at 9:15 p.m., and was not delivered to the defendant in St. Louis, until Monday morning, August 2, between eight and nine o'clock.

On Tuesday, August 3, at 8:53 a.m., the following dispatch was deposited for transmission in the telegraph office: *"St. Louis, Mo., August 3, 1875. To Minnesota Linseed Oil Company, Minneapolis: Offer accepted—ship three hundred barrels as soon as possible. Collier Company."*

The following telegrams passed between the parties after the last one was deposited in the office at St. Louis: *"Minneapolis, August 3, 1875. To Collier Company, St. Louis: We must withdraw our offer wired July 31st. Minnesota Linseed Oil Company."*

Answered: *"St. Louis, August 3, 1875. Minnesota Linseed Oil Company: Sale effected before your request to withdraw was received. When will you ship? Collier Company."*

It appeared that the market was very much unsettled, and that the price of oil was subject to sudden fluctuations during the month previous and at the time of this negotiation, varying from day to day, and ranging between fifty-five and seventy-five cents per gallon. It is urged by the defendant that the dispatch of Tuesday, August 3d, 1875, accepting the offer of the plaintiff transmitted July 31st, and delivered Monday morning, August 2d, concluded a contract for the sale of the twelve thousand four hundred and fifty gallons of oil. The plaintiff, on the contrary, claims, 1st, that the dispatch accepting the proposition made July 31st, was not received until after the offer had been withdrawn; 2d, that the acceptance of the offer was not in due time; that the delay was unreasonable, and therefore no contract was completed.

NELSON, District Judge.

It is well settled by the authorities in this country, and sustained by the later English decisions, that there is no difference in the rules governing the negotiation of contracts by correspondence through the post-office and by telegraph, and a contract is concluded when an acceptance of a proposition is deposited in the telegraph office for transmission. * * *

The reason for this rule is well stated in Adams v. Lindsell, 1 Barn. & Ald. 681. The negotiation in that case was by post. The court said: 'That if a bargain could not be closed by letter before the answer was received, no contract could be completed through the medium of the post-office; that if the one party was not bound by his offer when it was accepted (that is, at the time the letter of acceptance is deposited in the mail), then the other party ought not to be bound until after they had received a notification that the answer had been received and assented to, and that so it might go on ad infinitum.' * * * In the case at bar the delivery of the message at the telegraph office signified the acceptance of the offer. If any contract was entered into, the meeting of minds was at 8:53 of the clock, on Tuesday morning, August 3d, and the subsequent dispatches are out of the case. * * *.

This rule is not strenuously dissented from on the argument, and it is substantially admitted that the acceptance of an offer by letter or by telegraph completes the contract, when such acceptance is put in the proper and usual way of being communicated by the agency employed to carry it; and that when an offer is made by telegraph, an acceptance by telegraph takes effect when the dispatch containing the acceptance is deposited for transmission in the telegraph office, and not when it is received by the other party. Conceding this, there remains only one question to decide, which will determine the issues: Was the acceptance of defendant deposited in the telegraph office Tuesday, August 3d, within a reasonable time, so as to consummate a contract binding upon the plaintiff?

It is undoubtedly the rule that when a proposition is made under the circumstances in this case, an acceptance concludes the contract if the offer is still open, and the mutual consent necessary to convert the offer of one party into a binding contract by the acceptance of the other is established, if such acceptance is within a reasonable time after the offer was received.

The better opinion is, that what is, or is not, a reasonable time, must depend upon the circumstances attending the negotiation, and the character of the subject matter of the contract, and in no better way can the intention of the parties be determined. If the negotiation is in respect to an article stable in price, there is not so much reason for an immediate acceptance of the offer, and the same rule would not apply as in a case where the negotiation related to an article subject to sudden and great fluctuations in the market.

The rule in regard to the length of the time an offer shall continue, and when an acceptance completes the contract, is laid down in Parsons on Contracts (volume 1, p. 482). He says: "It may be said that whether the offer be made for a time certain or not, the intention or understanding of the parties is to govern. * * * If no definite time is stated, then the inquiry as to a reasonable time resolves itself into an inquiry as to what time it is rational to suppose the parties contemplated; and the law will decide this to be that time which as rational men they ought to have understood each other to have had in mind." Applying this rule, it seems clear that the intention of the plaintiff, in making the offer by telegraph, to sell an article which fluctuates so much in price, must have been upon the understanding that the acceptance, if at all, should be immediate, and as soon after the receipt of the offer as would give a fair opportunity for consideration. The delay here was too long, and manifestly unjust to the plaintiff, for it afforded the defendant an opportunity to take advantage of a change in the market, and accept or refuse the offer as would best subserve its interests.

Judgment will be entered in favor of the plaintiff for the amount claimed. The counter-claim is denied. Judgment accordingly.

QUESTIONS AND NOTES

1. Questions about the facts of this case

   1.1. Why is the party alleged to have breached the contract the *plaintiff* in this action?

   1.2. Can you identify the key fact that, in the court's estimation, made the August 3 transmission untimely as an acceptance?

2. Questions about the law

   2.1. If a prompt acceptance was critical to the plaintiff in this case, why didn't it say so? Was it proper for the court to read a time limitation into the offer that the plaintiff had neglected to include of its own accord?

   2.2. Can you justify the court's decision under objective theory?

2.3. The parties seemed to be in agreement in *Minnesota Linseed Oil* that if the offer were still open, a contract would have been completed when the defendant's August 3 telegraph was deposited for transmission. Is this rule consistent with objective theory? If you're confused, you ought to be, but keep the faith because we return to the issue of when an acceptance is effective in Section 5 of this chapter. For purposes of this case, however, it didn't matter when the acceptance would have been effective—transmission or receipt—because of the court's conclusion that the offer *lapsed* prior to either of those events.

3. Notes

3.1. *Minnesota Linseed Oil* suggests that an offer for an unstated period lapses after a *reasonable* time. If Epstein approaches Markell and offers him employment for a specific wage and Markell does not respond during that conversation but instead sends notice of acceptance the next day, is there a contract between Epstein and Markell? *See Akers v. J.B. Sedberry, Inc.*, 286 S.W.2d 617 (Tenn. App. 1955). If not, what is the proper legal characterization of Markell's notice of "acceptance"? *Compare Restatement (Second) of Contracts* § 70, *with* Art. 21(2), *United Nations Convention on Contracts for the International Sale of Goods* and Article 2.9(1), *UNIDROIT Principles of International Commercial Contracts* (both providing that a late acceptance may be effective as an acceptance if the offeror gives notice to that effect without undue delay).* Does it change your answer if, during the conversation, Markell replies, "Alright, I accept, but you really should pay me more"? See *Brangier v. Rosenthal,* 337 F.2d 952 (9th Cir. 1964), involving a so-called "grumbling acceptance."

3.2. As illustrated by *Dickinson v. Dodds, supra,* an offer for a stated period of time ("will give you eight days to accept") remains open, unless earlier revoked, for the time stated in the offer. But when does that time period begin to run when there is a delay between the date the offer is made and the date it is received? *See Caldwell v. Cline, 156 S.E. 55* (W. Va. 1930). Which party is in the best position to

*What are the *U.N. Convention of Contracts for the International Sales of Goods* and the *UNIDROIT Principles of International Commercial Contracts* you ask? What kind of contracts do they apply to? Take a look at Section 5 of the Appendix describing the sources of modern contract law.

avoid the ambiguity? Should that affect the determination? If so, and you are drafting an offer for a client intended to be good for eight days, how will you express this intention?

C. Death (or Incapacity) of the Offeror

New Headley Tobacco Warehouse Co. v. Gentry's Ex'r

Court of Appeals of Kentucky
307 Ky. 857, 212 S.W.2d 325 (1948)

STANLEY, Commissioner

The question at issue is whether a lessee lost its right to an extension of a lease.

On September 1, 1932, P. T. Gentry executed a lease to New Headley Tobacco Warehouse Company of property in Lexington for a term of 21 years and 6 months at an annual rental of $1,200 and payment of taxes. The contract contained no provision for extension or renewal. Nearly ten years later, on March 24, 1942, Gentry addressed the following letter to the Company:

> "In the event you build within the next five years (from March 1st, 1942) an addition to your warehouse at a cost of not less than $25.000.00 on the property you have under lease from me, I agree,
>
> "First, to extend your present lease so you will have a total term of twenty-two years (22 years) from March 1st of the year the addition is built.
>
> "Second, the extended term of lease shall carry a net rental to me of Sixteen Hundred Dollars ($1,600.00) per annum instead of the present net rental of Twelve Hundred Dollars per annum.
>
> "Third, in all other respects the terms and conditions of the extended lease shall be the same as the present lease."

The lessee had not made any response or started construction of the building before Gentry died on September 29, 1945. It was not until April 16, 1946, more than four years after the offer to extend the lease had been made, and nearly seven months after Gentry's death, that the lessee communicated any acceptance of the offer. On that day the Warehouse Company addressed a letter to Gentry's executor advising it that the company accepted the offer of March 24, 1942. A confirmatory letter was written the executor on May 21, 1946, reciting that the company had made due application to the federal war bureau, known as the Civilian Production Administration, for a permit to acquire material and erect the building contemplated by the offer, but it had been denied. The date of the application was not given, but it is later shown to have been April 17, 1946, the day after the first letter was written the executor. The company later offered to deposit $25,000 in escrow to guarantee construction of the building in accordance with the terms of the offer to extend the lease, and it later made a tender of the sum. This and other efforts to obtain recognition of a right were futile.

This suit seeks a judicial declaration of the lessee's right to the extension of the lease. The judgment was adverse to the lessee.

The arguments cover several interesting points, but it seems to us the question may be decided upon common principles of the law of contracts.

We have, first, a simple offer without consideration to make a bilateral contract. Ordinarily an option of extension or renewal of a lease given for a good consideration runs with the land and is not terminated by the death of the offeror or optioner but is binding on his successors. * * *. But an option for a lease, like that of a sale, for which there is no consideration, being unilateral and voluntary and imposing no legal duty on either party, is subject to withdrawal or revocation by the optioner before acceptance or, perhaps in some instances, before the other party has done something in reliance upon the offer which works to his detriment. * * * Restatement of the Law of Contracts, sec. 41. The form of the proposal in the instant case did not purport to be a grant upon consideration of an option to extend the lease. It was a mere voluntary offer, submitted without consideration, and under no contractual duty. It imposed no obligation on either party and could, therefore, be withdrawn at any time before acceptance. That could have been done by a definite word of assent or reciprocal promise, communicated to the offeror, or by performance of the condition precedent, thereby effecting a binding bilateral contract and holding the option open until it expired by its terms. * * * Silence certainly did not supply the part indispensable to the completed contract. * * * Nor did the fact of mere possession or right under the present lease give rise to any equity preventing the lapse of the offer, as the appellant submits. * * *

The offer having been subject to withdrawal or revocation by the lessor personally any time before he died, the question is as to the effect of his death upon the right of the optionee, the lessee, to accept it thereafter before the end of the five year period, as it undertook to do.

In the making of a contract there must be two minds, at least, concurring at the moment of its completion. But this can not occur if there be but one of the contracting parties in existence. Hence, the death of a party who had the right of revocation or withdrawal of an offer to contract renders the completion impossible and terminates the negotiations or proceedings at the very point where they were when he died. So, an acceptance by the optionee or the other party subsequent to that event is ineffectual to close the bargain. Therefore, the death of a party while a contract is being made, even though only a single act remains to be done, renders the completion of the contract impossible. * * * The question has been set at rest. Its pertinence excuses the relative length of the following quotation from *Chain v. Wilhelm*, 4 Cir., 84 F.2d 138, 140:

> "The effect of death upon a revocable offer is thus stated in Restatement of Contracts, sec. 48: 'A revocable offer is terminated by the offeror's death or such insanity as deprives him of legal capacity to enter into the proposed contract.' See, also, section 35. This rule has been criticized on the ground that under the modern view of the formation of contracts, it is not the actual meeting of the minds of the contracting parties that is the determining factor, but rather the apparent state of mind of the parties embodied in an expression of mutual consent; so that the acceptance by an offeree of an offer, which is apparently still open, should result in an enforceable contract notwithstanding the prior death of the offeror unknown to the offeree. On the other hand, it has been forcibly suggested that ordinarily the condition is implied in an offer that the offeror will survive to supervise the performance if his offer is accepted, and therefore an acceptance after death is ineffective even though the acceptor be ignorant of the offeror's death. * * * Williston on Contracts (Rev. Ed.) sec. 62. These conflicting views, however, were given consideration in the preparation of the Restatement, and the rule announced was adopted as representing the weight of authority and professional opinion. See Proceedings of the American Law Institute, vol. 3, sec. 35, pp. 196 to 202."

We are of opinion, therefore, the right of the appellant to accept the offer to extend its lease terminated with the death of the lessor. The circuit court so adjudged.

Judgment affirmed.

QUESTIONS AND NOTE

1. Questions about the facts of this case

   1.1. What did the offer say insofar as manner of acceptance was concerned? Was this an offer for a promise or a performance?

   1.2. What did the offer say insofar as the effect on the offer of Gentry's death? On April 16, 1946, was New Headley aware that Gentry had died?

2. Questions about the law

   2.1. Would the outcome in this case have been different if the substance of Gentry's March 24, 1942 letter had been included in the original lease? Why?

   2.2. What would the outcome in the case have been if New Headley had begun, but not completed, construction prior to Gentry's death?

   2.3. In justifying the rule that death terminates an offer regardless of notice to the offeree, it has been stated that "In a contract for sale there must be two minds, at least, concurring at the moment of its completion; but this cannot be if there be but one contracting party in existence." *American Chain Co. v. Arrow Grip Mfg.*, 235 N.Y.S. 228, 235 (1929). Was the court *American Chain* taking the "meeting of the minds" requirement for contract formation a little too literally? On the other hand, if it is not possible to form a contract *with* a dead person, how can a contract formed before death be enforced *against* a dead person?

   2.4. The court in *New Headley* states that the rule that a "revocable offer is terminated by the offeror's death" has been criticized as out-of-step with the modern view of formation of contracts. Do you agree with that criticism? Does the rule work any unfairness in this case? Here's what Professor Corbin had to say about the issue:

> It is very generally said that the death of the offeror terminates the offeree's power of acceptance even though the offeree has no knowledge of such death. Such general statements arose out of the earlier notion that a contract cannot be made without an actual meeting of minds at a single moment of time, a notion that has long been abandoned. The rule has also been supposed to follow by some logical necessity from the dictum that it takes two persons to make a contract. It is not contrary to that dictum to deny that death terminates power to accept; the offer was made by a living man and is accepted by another living man.

1 CORBIN, CONTRACTS § 54 at 229–30 (1963).

3. Note

Is the rule that death terminates an offer regardless of notice consistent with objective theory? Of course not. The *Restatement (Second) of Contracts* § 48 nevertheless continues to follow the rule, but suggests it is without much support. *Restatement (Second) of Contracts* § 48 cmt. a. To appreciate the illogic of the rule concerning automatic termination on death (or disability), consider the following problems.

Problems on Termination of Offer by Death

To induce Ponoroff to sell provisions to Markell, a younger individual with a shaky credit history, on November 11, 2000, Epstein, an older and more responsible person, entered into a written agreement of "continuing guaranty" with Ponoroff undertaking to pay at maturity all indebtedness of Markell for goods sold and delivered to Markell by Ponoroff. Among other provisions, the agreement signed by Epstein purported to cover all liabilities that Markell might incur until ten days after receipt of notice from Epstein or his legal representatives of withdrawal of the guaranty. No notice of withdrawal was ever given by Epstein or his representatives. However, Epstein died on January 16, 2001, and this fact did not become known to Ponoroff until March 1, 2001, at which point he ceased making sales to Markell on credit. Between January 16 and March 1, however, Markell incurred $8,509.60 of indebtedness for merchandise supplied by Ponoroff. Markell is now insolvent and has filed a petition under Chapter 7 of the Bankruptcy Code. Ponoroff made a claim against Epstein's estate for the $8,509.60, which was rejected by the executor, whereupon Ponoroff brought an action against the estate to recover the $8,509.60, plus interest. Epstein's estate has defended by asserting that the continuing guaranty constituted a series of offers for unilateral contracts which was terminated as to *future* transactions upon the death of the guarantor, citing *American Chain Co. v. Arrow Grip Mfg.*, 235 N.Y.S. 228 (1929). This is a case of first impression in the jurisdiction in which the action is pending.

(a) If you represent Ponoroff, what arguments will you make in support of recovery? *Cf. Swift & Company v. Smigel*, 115 N.J. Super. 391; 279 A.2d 895 (Sup. Ct. of N.J., App. Div. 1971)?

(b) If the court accepts the executor's position regarding the effect of Epstein's death on outstanding offers, is there any other way to analyze the continuing guaranty that would permit your client to prevail? *See In re Lorch's Estate*, 248 Pa. 500, 131 A. 381 (1925).

(c) How does it affect the analysis if, instead of dying, the event giving rise to the defense under the guaranty was that Epstein had been adjudged mentally incompetent on January 16? See the Note which follows.

Note on Termination by Supervening Incapacity

At common law, the offeror's supervening mental incapacity, as established by an adjudication of incompetence or appointment of a guardian, has the same effect on the offeree's power of acceptance as the offeror's death. Professor Arthur Corbin, never a fan to begin with of the rule that the death of the offeror automatically terminates the offeree's power of acceptance, opined that the case for terminating an offer on the subsequent insanity of the offeror without the knowledge of the offeree is "even more doubtful than the rule as to the offeror's death." 1 CORBIN, CONTRACTS § 54, at 231. Why do you suppose Corbin felt that way? Bear in mind that we are speaking of incapacity occurring *after* the offer has been made, and, of course, before it is accepted. Mental incompetence at the time the offer is made raises a different issue, namely *capacity* to contract, a subject we take up in the next chapter. As you will see, such a contract is voidable at the instance of the mentally incompetent party. That means that if Epstein offers to sell his Lexus to Ponoroff for $100 before he loses his mind, the issue of whether or not Ponoroff can enforce his deal will turn on whether Epstein's dementia occurs before or after Ponoroff accepts the offer, regardless of what Ponoroff knows about Epstein's condition at the time he accepts. On the other hand, if Epstein was already around the bend at the time the offer is made, he (or his guardian) can avoid the contract. Is that logical or is Professor Corbin beginning to make some sense to you?

SECTION 4: PRESERVING THE OFFER

Sometimes, even though an offer is attractive to the offeree, the offeree may not be ready to commit to the deal. For example, the offeree may need time to be sure he can arrange necessary financing or order his other affairs (locate customers, suppliers, etc.) in a manner that ensures that the proposed contract will be a beneficial one. If the offeree simply accepts the offer now, he assumes the risk if the contingencies creating the uncertainty do not occur. The logical course of action, therefore, is to request the offeror's agreement to hold the offer open—make it irrevocable—for a specified period of time. If the offeror agrees, in effect, a separate, ancillary promise has been made under the terms of which the offeror surrenders his right to revoke the offer for the principal contract for the agreed period of time. But what has the offeror received in return? If the offeror receives nothing in return, can this ancillary promise be enforced? You may recall that in *Dickinson v. Dodds, supra,* the court answered that question in the negative. Therefore, the cases and materials collected in this section address the issues of the circumstances under which a promise of irrevocability may become binding on the offeror and the consequences of irrevocability.

Beall v. Beall

Court of Special Appeals of Maryland

45 Md. App. 489, 413 A.2d 1365 (1980)

rev'd on other grounds, 291 Md. 224, 434 A.2d 1015 (Md. App. 1981)

Moore, J.

This appeal concerns an alleged option agreement and a suit by Carlton G. Beall for the specific performance thereof. The Circuit Court for Prince George's County (Melbourne, J.) found the agreement unsupported by consideration and dismissed plaintiff's bill of complaint pursuant to Maryland Rule 535. From that order, he appeals to this Court.

I

In 1968, the plaintiff, Carlton G. Beall, purchased a farm in Prince George's County from Pearl Beall. At that time, the property was farmed by Pearl's son, Calvin Beall. The record discloses that Carlton, the plaintiff, and Calvin were second cousins. Calvin was married to Cecelia M. Beall, the defendant herein. Carlton agreed that Calvin could continue to farm the property if he would pay the annual property taxes. Calvin and Cecelia owned and resided on a parcel of about one-half acre that was bordered on three sides by the farm bought by the plaintiff; and it is that parcel that is the subject of this dispute.

On the day that plaintiff contracted to buy Pearl's farm, he obtained a three-year option to purchase Calvin's and Cecelia's parcel for $28,000.00. The option recited a consideration of $100.00 which was paid by check. In 1971, the parties executed a new option, for five years, but on the same terms and reciting an additional $100.00 consideration.

This 1971 option was never exercised by the plaintiff, but prior to its expiration the following language was appended at the bottom of the page:

> "As of October 6, 1975, we, Calvin E. Beall and Cecelia M. Beall, agree to continue this option agreement three more years—Feb. 1, 1976 to Feb. 1, 1979.
>
> /s/ Calvin E. Beall
>
> /s/ Cecelia M. Beall."

It is this purported extension that forms the basis for plaintiff's bill of complaint seeking specific performance of the agreement. Calvin died in August 1977, and Cecelia now holds the fee simple title by right of survivorship. In letters dated May 24, 1978 and September 14, 1978, the plaintiff advised Cecelia that he was electing to exercise the option. He scheduled settlement for October 5, 1978. As the chancellor found:

> "It is undisputed in this case that Mr. Carlton Beall did eventually hire attorneys to search the title, set a settlement date, attend the settlement, and was ready, willing and able to perform the contract."

Cecelia refused to attend settlement, and this suit for specific performance ensued.

At trial, after plaintiff presented his evidence, Cecelia moved to dismiss the bill of complaint. The chancellor granted the motion because she felt that the option agreements were not supported by consideration in that "no benefit . . . flowed to Cecelia Beall." In addition, as to the 1975 alleged option, the chancellor ruled:

> "[T]here is no consideration recited in that extension or purported extension of the original option contract. And the one extension that had occurred in the interim, even then would also fail because there is no consideration stated in the extension. It is clear that consideration must pass for the extension each time, in some form of consideration. None is stated within the written four lines."

On appeal, the plaintiff contends that the chancellor erred in dismissing the bill of complaint and in excluding certain testimony relative to oral transactions with Calvin, the deceased husband of the defendant.

II

Under Maryland law it is clear that "an option is not a mere offer to sell, which can be withdrawn by the optionor at any time before acceptance, but a binding agreement if supported by consideration." *Blondell v. Turover*, 195 Md. 251, 256, 72 A.2d 697, 699 (1950). In other words, an option is an agreement to keep an offer open that requires consideration to give it its irrevocable character. * * * Once the option is exercised by the optionee a binding contract is created that may be enforced through a decree commanding specific performance. * * * It is apparent, then, that an option must be supported by consideration in order to be irrevocable for the period provided in the option.

When, however, the consideration allegedly supporting an option fails or is nonexistent, the option is no longer irrevocable but rather it becomes "a mere offer to sell, which can be withdrawn by the optionor at any time before acceptance. . . ." *Blondell v. Turover, supra*, 195 Md. at 256, 72 A.2d at 699. The failure of consideration destroys the irrevocability of the option; it nonetheless retains its essential characteristic as an offer to buy or sell for the period stated in the option or until revoked. It has been recognized that equity will enforce a resulting contract despite lack of consideration for the option:

> "While the rule that equity will enforce a contract consummated by the acceptance of an option within the time and upon the terms of the option is often stated in such a way as to suggest or imply the necessity of consideration for the option, all that is meant in most cases is that a consideration is necessary to prevent the defendant from asserting his withdrawal of the option before its acceptance by the plaintiff and before the expiration of the time fixed in the option within which acceptance could be made."

71 Am. Jur. 2d, Specific Performance § 143 (1973) (footnotes omitted). See 1A Corbin on Contracts § 263 (1963). See generally *Kahn v. General Development Corp.*, 40 Del. Ch. 83, 92, 174 A.2d 307, 312 (1961) (failure of consideration "destroyed the irrevocability of the option"). * * *

Assuming, arguendo, that the 1975 option was unsupported by consideration, it remained as an offer to sell the parcel for $28,000. The offer was open until February 1, 1979, but it was revocable at any time by action of Calvin and Cecelia Beall. As stated in the case of *Holifield v. Veterans' Farm & Home Board*, 218 Miss. 446, 450, 67 So. 2d 456, 457 (1953):

> "It is well settled that an option is not binding as a contract where there is no consideration, unless it is accepted within the time limit and before the offer is withdrawn. Since there was no consideration paid by the Veterans' Farm and Home Board and Mauldin for the option, it could have been revoked by the Holifields at any time before the Veterans' Farm and Home Board and Mauldin notified them that they intended to buy the land; *but since the offer was accepted within the time limit and before withdrawal, the contract became binding upon all parties as it was*

> *thereafter supported by the consideration of the mutual promises*." (Emphasis added.)

This statement is generally in accord with the Maryland cases, *supra*.

The chancellor should, therefore, have determined whether or not there was a valid, unrevoked offer to sell the property in dispute and whether or not there was a proper acceptance of that offer sufficient to create a contract specifically enforceable in equity.[1] These issues of offer and acceptance primarily involve factual determinations that initially must be evaluated by the chancellor. As an appellate court, we are limited to a review of the chancellor's findings under the "clearly erroneous" standard. Md. Rule 1086. But our review is dependent upon the existence of factual findings on the issues material to the case. Such findings were not made below.

It was error for the chancellor to dismiss plaintiff's bill of complaint at the close of his case. A new trial, in accordance with this opinion, s necessitated.

Order reversed; cause remanded for a new trial in accordance with this opinion; costs to abide the final result.

QUESTIONS AND NOTES

1. Questions about the facts of this case

   1.1. In 1975, when the option was extended for an additional three years, what was each side bargaining for?

   1.2. What was the mistake that Carlton made in 1975? According to the court, when did Carlton's option to purchase the Calvin/Ceceila property expire?

---

[1]We express no opinion concerning the validity of the chancellor's finding that there was no consideration for the option.

2. Questions about the law

   2.1. What is the specific issue that the chancellor will have to resolve on remand in *Beall*? If you represent Carlton, what evidence will you seek to put forward? How about if you represent Cecelia?

   2.2. Why does the law impose a requirement that the promise of irrevocability be supported by a separate consideration? Would the outcome in *Beall* have been different if, in 1971, the extension of the option had been for eight years instead of five even though the consideration remained $100? How about if, during that eight-year period, but before Carlton exercised the option, Cecelia joined Calvin in the great beyond? Does an option, if enforceable, survive the death of the optionor?

3. Notes

   3.1. Option contracts can take a variety of different forms, such as an offer with an ancillary contract not to revoke (*"I offer to sell you my land for $50,000 and, in consideration of $50, I agree not to revoke this offer for 30 days"*) or a contract with a condition (*"In consideration of $50, I agree to sell you my land if, within 30 days, you pay me $50,000"*). In either case, it comes down to pretty much the same thing. For some separate consideration, the offeror is bound for a period of time pending a decision by the offeree.

   3.2. As a general rule, in civil law systems, the mere statement of irrevocability will be enforced. Indeed, both the *U.N. Convention on Contracts for the International Sales of Goods*, § 16(2)(a), and the *UNIDROIT Principles of International Commercial Contracts, Principle* 2.4(2)(a), effectively provide that an offer cannot be revoked if it states that it is irrevocable, whether by providing a fixed time for acceptance or otherwise. You might wonder why the rule is different in common law jurisdictions. Your answer lies in the common law's general requirement of consideration as a condition for enforcement of promises, a topic that we examine in depth in the next chapter. The next case, however, considers what it takes to satisfy this requirement of consideration in the context of an option contract.

Board of Control of Eastern Michigan University v. Burgess
Court of Appeals of Michigan
45 Mich. App. 183, 206 N.W.2d 256 (1973)

Opinion by: Burns

On February 15, 1966, defendant signed a document which purported to grant to plaintiff a 60-day option to purchase defendant's home. That document, which was drafted by plaintiff's agent, acknowledged receipt by defendant of "One and no/100 ($1.00) Dollar and other valuable consideration". Plaintiff concedes that neither the one dollar nor any other consideration was ever paid or even tendered to defendant. On April 14, 1966, plaintiff delivered to defendant written notice of its intention to exercise the option. On the closing date defendant rejected plaintiff's tender of the purchase price. Thereupon, plaintiff commenced this action for specific performance.

At trial defendant claimed that the purported option was void for want of consideration [and] that any underlying offer by defendant had been revoked prior to acceptance by plaintiff. * * * The trial judge * * * held that defendant's acknowledgment of receipt of consideration bars any subsequent contention to the contrary. Accordingly, the trial judge entered judgment for plaintiff.

Defendant appeals. She claims that acknowledgment of receipt of consideration does not bar the defense of failure of consideration. * * *

Options for the purchase of land, if based on valid consideration, are contracts which may be specifically enforced. * * * Conversely, that which purports to be an option, but which is not based on valid consideration, is not a contract and will not be enforced. * * * One dollar is valid consideration for an option to purchase land, provided the dollar is paid or at least tendered. * * * In the instant case defendant received no consideration for the purported option of February 15, 1966.

A written acknowledgment of receipt of consideration merely creates a rebuttable presumption that consideration has, in fact, passed. [Nothing] * * * bars the presentation of evidence to contradict any such acknowledgment. * * *

It is our opinion that the document signed by defendant on February 15, 1966, is not an enforceable option, and that defendant is not barred from so asserting.

The trial court premised its holding to the contrary on *Lawrence v McCalmont*, 43 U.S. (2 How) 426, 452; 11 L Ed 326, 336 (1844). That case is significantly distinguishable from the instant case. Mr. Justice Story held that "[t]he guarantor acknowledged the receipt of one dollar, and is now estopped to deny it." However, in reliance upon the guaranty substantial credit had been extended to the guarantor's sons. The guarantor had received everything she bargained for, save one dollar. * * * In the instant case defendant claims that she never received any of the consideration promised her.

That which purports to be an option for the purchase of land, but which is not based on valid consideration, is a simple offer to sell the same land. * * * An option is a contract collateral to an offer to sell whereby the offer is made irrevocable for a specified period. * * * Ordinarily, an offer is revocable at the will of the offeror. Accordingly, a failure of consideration affects only the collateral contract to keep the offer open, not the underlying offer.

A simple offer may be revoked for any reason or for no reason by the offeror at any time prior to its acceptance by the offeree. * * * Thus, the question in this case becomes, "Did defendant effectively revoke her offer to sell before plaintiff accepted that offer?"

* * *

Defendant testified that within hours of signing the purported option she telephoned plaintiff's agent and informed him that she would not abide by the option unless the purchase price was increased. Defendant also testified that when plaintiff's agent delivered to her on April 14, 1966, plaintiff's notice of its intention to exercise the purported option, she told him that "the option was off".

Plaintiff's agent testified that defendant did not communicate to him any dissatisfaction until sometime in July, 1966.

If defendant is telling the truth, she effectively revoked her offer several weeks before plaintiff accepted that offer, and no contract of sale was created. If plaintiff's agent is telling the truth, defendant's offer was still open when plaintiff accepted that offer, and an enforceable contract was created. The trial judge thought it unnecessary to resolve this particular dispute. In light of our holding the dispute must be resolved.

An appellate court cannot assess the credibility of witnesses. We have neither seen nor heard them testify. * * * Accordingly, we remand this case to the trial court for additional findings of fact based on the record already before the court.

* * *

QUESTIONS AND NOTES

1. Questions about the facts of this case

    1.1. Why didn't the university just pay the silly dollar?

    1.2. What was the "other valuable consideration"?

    1.3. Who drafted the February 15, 1966 document? Was that a factor in the case? Should it have been?

    1.4. On February 15, 1966, do you think that the defendant believed that the university had a nonrevocable 60-day option to purchase her property? What do you think the university believed?

2. Questions about the law

    2.1. How did the reasoning of the trial court and the court of appeals differ?

    2.2. How is the Michigan Court of Appeals' decision in *Board of Control* distinguishable from the U.S. Supreme Court's holding *Lawrence v. McCalmont,* the case on which the trial court relied?

    2.3. Is the holding in *Board of Control* consistent with *Beall*?

    2.4. Just what is a "rebuttable presumption"?

3. Notes

    3.1. Not all courts agree with *Board of Control* insofar as the effect of a recital of consideration is concerned. Some courts, for example, treat the recital as a binding acknowledgement of payment. *See Real Estate Co. v. Rudolph*, 153 A. 438 (Pa. 1930). The *Restatement (Second) of Contracts* adopts a somewhat different approach in § 87(1)(a). Take a look at that provision now. How would *Board of Control* have been decided if the court of appeals had applied that rule? As a general proposition, most lay people like it when the law conforms to their own intuitive, common sense judgment of what the law ought to be. Which rule—*Board of Control* or *Restatement (Second)* § 87(1)(a)—more closely conforms to what the true intentions of the parties probably are in these cases where the contract recites a consideration?

3.2. The brief remaining materials in this section consider whether there are any other circumstances in our legal system where a promise of irrevocability will be enforced despite the absence of consideration. By now you have surely learned in law school that there are few rules without exception and so it will come as no surprise to you to learn that such circumstances do indeed exist.

Note on Option Contracts and Firm Offers

The classical view that a mere promise to hold an offer open for a stated period of time is not itself enforceable is carried forward in the *Restatement (Second) of Contracts* § 25, which provides that: *"An option contract is a promise which meets the requirements for the formation of a contract and limits the promisor's power to revoke an offer."* Of course, the central "requirement for the formation of a contract" is the existence of consideration given in exchange for the promise of irrevocability, separate and apart from the consideration supporting the underlying offer. At common law, a promise not to revoke an offer would be enforced if given under seal, but the seal has been abolished in most states by statute. *See, e.g., Hill v. Corbett*, 33 Wash.2d 219, 204 P.2d 845 (1949). Thus, today, a typical option contract might take the following form: "In return for payment of $100, A hereby grants B the right through January 5, 2002, to purchase his property for $100,000." The consideration for the promise of irrevocability in this example is the $100, while the consideration for the property, if B elects before the expiry of the option to accept, is $100,000.

Consistent with its philosophy of conforming the governing principles of commercial law with the norms and expectations of the marketplace, the U.C.C. creates an exception to the rule set forth in *Beall* that an offer, even though stated to be irrevocable, may be revoked unless supported by consideration. The exception is in § 2-205 for so-called "firm offers." Under this provision, if a "merchant" (defined in § 1-201(4)) makes an offer, in writing, signed, and which contains an assurance that it will be held open, then it will be regarded as irrevocable in spite of the absence of consideration for either the period stated or, if no period is stated, for a reasonable time, but in no event exceeding three months. The theory behind this provision, as stated in the Official Comments, is that when a merchant makes such a promise he understands and intends for it to be binding, and such offers are so understood in the marketplace. Thus, the provision gives effect to this deliberate intention and reasonable expectation. The requirements that the promise be signed and in writing ensures the seriousness of the merchant's promise to effectively create an option contract. A similar form of statutory option contract, applicable to merchants in the non-sale of goods context, can be found in § 5-1109 of the New York General Obligations Law. However, in either case, it is important to bear in mind that there cannot be an enforceable *firm offer* until there is an *offer*, ascertained in the usual way. *See Coastal Aviation, Inc. v. Commander Aircraft Co.*, 937 F. Supp. 1051 (S.D.N.Y. 1996) (holding that the defendant's statement concerning its intent to hold a particular area open for the plaintiff in connection with a proposed exclusive dealership arrangement did not evince an intent to be bound by a promise to do so and, hence, could not be enforced as a "firm offer" within the meaning of U.C.C. § 2-205).

Note on Option Contracts and Reliance

So far, our examination of irrevocability can be boiled down to the following set of rules: All offers are revocable, even when they're stated to be irrevocable (or open for a specified period of time), *unless* the promise of irrevocability is supported by independent consideration (including perhaps the mere recital of consideration) or made enforceable by statute. Are there any other circumstances where an offer will be deemed irrevocable?

Suppose Epstein offers Markell, a recent law school graduate with significant student loans, a job as an associate at Epstein's highly successful law firm in Atlanta. Epstein tells Markell, "this offer is good for one week." At the time, Markell is working for another firm, which although not as prestigious or lucrative as Epstein's, still pays a decent wage. Flush with excitement over the offer, the next day Markell calls his current boss and tells him, in no uncertain terms, to take this job and shove it. Thereupon he calls Epstein to accept the offer, but before Markell can say anything, Epstein says: "Sorry pal, but I must revoke my offer." Markell responds: "You can't do that, I just quit my other job as you had to know I would; this is unfair"! Epstein's rejoinder is short and sweet: "Look, Ace, maybe you should have paid a little more attention in Contracts. My offer could be revoked at any time before acceptance regardless of how long I said it would be good for; if you wanted an option you should have paid for one." Under the traditional rules of contract law does Markell have any recourse? How about under *Restatement (Second) of Contracts* § 87(2)? Does it change your answer at all if Epstein's offer had not been for a stated period of time; i.e., one week? We will return to § 87(2) in the next chapter when we examine "consideration substitutes." For now, however, we shift our attention from "offer" to "acceptance."

SECTION 5: MODES AND METHODS OF ACCEPTANCE

In Section 2 we saw that an offer, so long as it remains open, confers on the offeree the power of acceptance. The acceptance is the other piece of the mutual assent puzzle. But how does an offeree exercise this power of acceptance? What constitutes an acceptance and when is it effective? These are some of the questions we examine in this section. *Restatement (Second) of Contracts* § 50(1) provides that "Acceptance of an offer is a manifestation of assent to the terms thereof made by the offeree in a manner invited or required by the offer." Is that definition consistent with the objective theory of contract formation? Bear that definition in mind as you consider the next two cases dealing with who controls the permitted form of acceptance.

A. Control Over the Manner of Acceptance

The plaintiff in the next case is a bank acting in its capacity as a trustee of a trust. A trust is a common law invention whose original purpose was to avoid taxes—in 14th and 15th Century England! Whether from utility or sheer cussedness, trusts survive to this day. Most trusts involve large sums of money entrusted to banks and other moneyed interests to administer for others. In these cases, a trust consists of property (often called the "*res*" from the Latin for "thing") transferred to the trusted individual (the "trustee") who has legal title to the property but holds it for the use or benefit of another (the "beneficiary"). All things considered, it is good to be the beneficiary of a trust. In fact, if we were trust beneficiaries we might not have written this book.

In the next case, however, the common law origins of tax and regulatory avoidance play a role. In Illinois and some other states, land or other real property is often held in a "land trust" in which the legal title holder is the trustee. That trustee holds title for the benefit of the beneficiary. So far, so good; the format is just like regular trusts. But why would the beneficiary not just take title directly? The twist here is that Illinois common law considers beneficial interests in land trusts as *personal* property and not as *real* property, even if the trust *res* is dirt. Thus, in Illinois, those who hold property in a land trust are not listed in the public record as owners. Also, they can transfer their interests quickly without the inherited formality that usually attends a real estate transfer.

Such an arrangement, however, involves risk to the bank/trustee. They are on the title, and are in a position to make mistakes. As a consequence, they charge a fee for their services, and they also very carefully specify what they need to do and what they do not need to do in the contract creating the trust. This care usually permeates the formation process, because the bank/trustee certainly doesn't want to sign documents indicating it will buy property if the beneficiary suddenly has a change of heart and refuses to put up the funds to buy the land.* Keep this background in mind when reading the next case.

---

*For those curious about Illinois land trusts, see Eric T. Freyfogle, *Land Trusts and the Decline of Mortgage Law*, 1988 U. ILL. L. REV. 67.

La Salle National Bank v. Vega
Appellate Court of Illinois, Second District
167 Ill. App.3d 154, 520 N.E.2d 1129 (1988)

Lindberg, J.

* * *

Plaintiff's first amended complaint alleged the existence of a contract for the sale of real estate between it and Mel [Vega] and sought specific performance of the alleged contract and damages from defendants for willfully and intentionally breaching it. Borg was permitted to intervene and filed a counterclaim naming plaintiff and defendants as counterdefendants. As finally amended, the counterclaim sought specific performance of a different contract for sale of the same real estate to Borg; a judgment declaring the alleged contract between Mel and plaintiff void and holding it for naught; and, if the alleged contract with plaintiff was "held to be a valid and enforceable contract," damages from defendants for fraud for failure to disclose the contract with plaintiff to Borg.

Borg moved for partial summary judgment * * * requesting a determination by the court that the alleged contract between plaintiff and Mel was unenforceable because it was not "signed in accordance with its terms and provisions" and because plaintiff abandoned it. The trial court granted partial summary judgment on the basis of the first ground argued by Borg.

In its verified first amended complaint, plaintiff alleged, inter alia:

> "The Defendant, MEL VEGA, on March 12, 1985, in his own behalf and in behalf of all the owners of record, entered into a Real Estate Sale Contract (herein 'Contract') with the Plaintiff, a true and correct copy of said Contract is attached hereto and incorporated herein as Exhibit A."

Exhibit A is a document, drafted by counsel for plaintiff, entitled "Real Estate Sale Contract." On the first page of this document appears the date March 12, 1985, and the statement that "Attached Rider is part of this Contract." One of the Rider's provisions states:

> "This contract has been executed and presented by an authorized agent for the purchaser, the beneficiaries of the La Salle National Bank, under Trust No. 109529, as Trustee aforesaid for the benefit of the Trust only and not personally. Upon execution of this contract by the Seller, this contract shall be presented to the trust for full execution. Upon the trust's

> execution, this contract will then be in full force and a copy of a fully executed contract along with evidence of the earnest money deposit will be delivered back to Seller."

The document was signed by Bernard Ruekberg as the purchaser's purchasing agent and by Mel Vega (on March 19, 1985, according to the date by his signature on the Rider) as the seller but not by the trustee for the purchaser.

* * *

The trial court held that there was no genuine issue of material fact that no contract was formed because the offer was made by Mel, the offer could only be accepted by execution of the document at issue by the trust, and the document was not executed by the trust. Plaintiff argues that the trial court erred because there were genuine issues of material fact regarding whether the document was ever executed by the trust and whether execution of the document by the trust was necessary to the formation of a contract. Plaintiff is incorrect on both of these points.

[The court first rejected the argument that there was a genuine issue of material fact concerning whether the document was executed by the trust, noting that the exhibit attached to the plaintiff's complaint, which was alleged to be a "true and correct copy" of the written instrument on which the claim of plaintiff was founded, did not show execution by the trust. Therefore, the plaintiff had effectively admitted that the document was never executed by the trust]

* * *

Whether a contract was formed without execution of the document by the trust may now be considered. This requires first an analysis of the events which occurred with respect to the document in terms of offer and acceptance.

The pertinent provision of the document stated:

> "This contract has been executed and presented by an authorized agent for the purchaser, the beneficiaries of the La Salle National Bank, under Trust No. 109529, as Trustee aforesaid for the benefit of the Trust only and not personally. Upon execution of this contract by the Seller, this contract shall be presented to the trust for full execution. Upon the trust's execution, this contract will then be in full force and a copy of a fully exe-

cuted contract along with evidence of the earnest money deposit will be delivered back to Seller."

Thus, a specific order of events was contemplated, after which the contract would be in full force. Ruekberg (the purchasing agent) was to execute the document and present it to Mel (the seller). Then Mel was to execute it. After Mel executed it, the document was to be presented to the trust for execution. Finally, "upon the trust's execution," the contract would be in full force.

An offer is an act on the part of one person giving another person the legal power of creating the obligation called a contract. * * * Where "the so-called offer is not intended to give the so-called offeree the power to make a contract there is no offer." * * * From the provisions contained in the document at bar, particularly the language quoted, it is apparent that there was to be no contract (i.e., the "contract" was not to be in full force) until it was executed by the trust. Thus, Ruekberg's presentation of the document he had executed to Mel was not an offer because it did not give Mel the power to make a contract by accepting it. On the other hand, when Mel executed the document and gave it back to Ruekberg he made an offer which could be accepted by execution of the document by the trust.

An offeror has complete control over an offer and may condition acceptance to the terms of the offer. * * * The language of an offer may moreover govern the mode of acceptance required, and where an offer requires a written acceptance, no other modes may be used. * * * In the case at bar, the document at issue stated clearly that the contract would be in full force upon the trust's execution. This indicates that the only mode by which Mel's offer could be accepted was execution of the document by the trust. The trust not having executed the document, there was no acceptance of the offer, and so there was no contract. * * *

Affirmed.

Ever-Tite Roofing Corp. v. Green

Court of Appeal of Louisiana
83 So. 2d 449 (1955)

Ayers, J.

This is an action for damages allegedly sustained by plaintiff as the result of the breach by the defendants of a written contract for the re-roofing of defendants' residence. Defendants denied that their written proposal or offer was ever accepted by plaintiff in the manner stipulated therein for its acceptance, and hence contended no contract was ever entered into. The trial court sustained defendants' defense and rejected plaintiff's demands and dismissed its suit at its costs. From the judgment thus rendered and signed, plaintiff appealed.

Defendants executed and signed an instrument June 10, 1953, for the purpose of obtaining the services of plaintiff in re-roofing their residence situated in Webster Parish, Louisiana. The document set out in detail the work to be done and the price therefor to be paid in monthly installments. This instrument was likewise signed by plaintiff's sale representative, who, however, was without authority to accept the contract for and on behalf of the plaintiff. This alleged contract contained these provisions:

> "This agreement shall become binding only upon written acceptance hereof, by the principal or authorized officer of the Contractor, *or upon commencing performance of the work.* This contract is Not Subject to Cancellation. * * *" (Emphasis supplied.)

Inasmuch as this work was to be performed entirely on credit, it was necessary for plaintiff to obtain credit reports and approval from the lending institution which was to finance said contract. With this procedure defendants were more or less familiar and knew their credit rating would have to be checked and a report made. On receipt of the proposed contract in plaintiff's office on the day following its execution, plaintiff requested a credit report, which was made after investigation and which was received in due course and submitted by plaintiff to the lending agency. Additional information was requested by this institution, which was likewise in due course transmitted to the institution, which then gave its approval.

The day immediately following this approval, which was either June 18 or 19, 1953, plaintiff engaged its workmen and two trucks, loaded the trucks with the necessary roofing materials and proceeded from Shreveport to defendants' residence for the purpose of doing the work and performing the services allegedly contracted for the defendants. Upon their arrival at defendants' residence, the workmen found others in the performance of the work which plaintiff had contracted to do. Defendants notified plaintiff's workmen that the work had been contracted to other parties two days before and forbade them to do the work.

Formal acceptance of the contract was not made under the signature and approval of an agent of plaintiff. It was, however, the intention of plaintiff to accept the contract by commencing the work, which was one of the ways provided for in the instrument for its acceptance, as will be shown by reference to the extract from the contract quoted hereinabove. Prior to this time, however, defendants had determined on a course of abrogating the agreement and engaged other workmen without notice thereof to plaintiff.

The basis of the judgment appealed was that defendants had timely notified plaintiff before 'commencing performance of work'. The trial court held that notice to plaintiff's workmen upon their arrival with the materials that defendants did not desire them to commence the actual work was sufficient and timely to signify their intention to withdraw from the contract. With this conclusion we find ourselves unable to agree.

Defendants' attempt to justify their delay in thus notifying plaintiff for the reason they did not know where or how to contact plaintiff is without merit. The contract itself, a copy of which was left with them, conspicuously displayed plaintiff's name, address and telephone number. Be that as it may, defendants at no time, from June 10, 1953, until plaintiff's workmen arrived for the purpose of commencing the work, notified or attempted to notify plaintiff of their intention to abrogate, terminate or cancel the contract.

Defendants evidently knew this work was to be processed through plaintiff's Shreveport office. The record discloses no unreasonable delay on plaintiff's part in receiving, processing or accepting the contract or in commencing the work contracted to be done. No time limit was specified in the contract within which it was to be accepted or within which the work was to be begun. It was nevertheless understood between the parties that some delay would ensue before the acceptance of the contract and the commencement of the work, due to the necessity of compliance with the requirements relative to financing the job through a lending agency. The evidence as referred to hereinabove shows that plaintiff proceeded with due diligence.

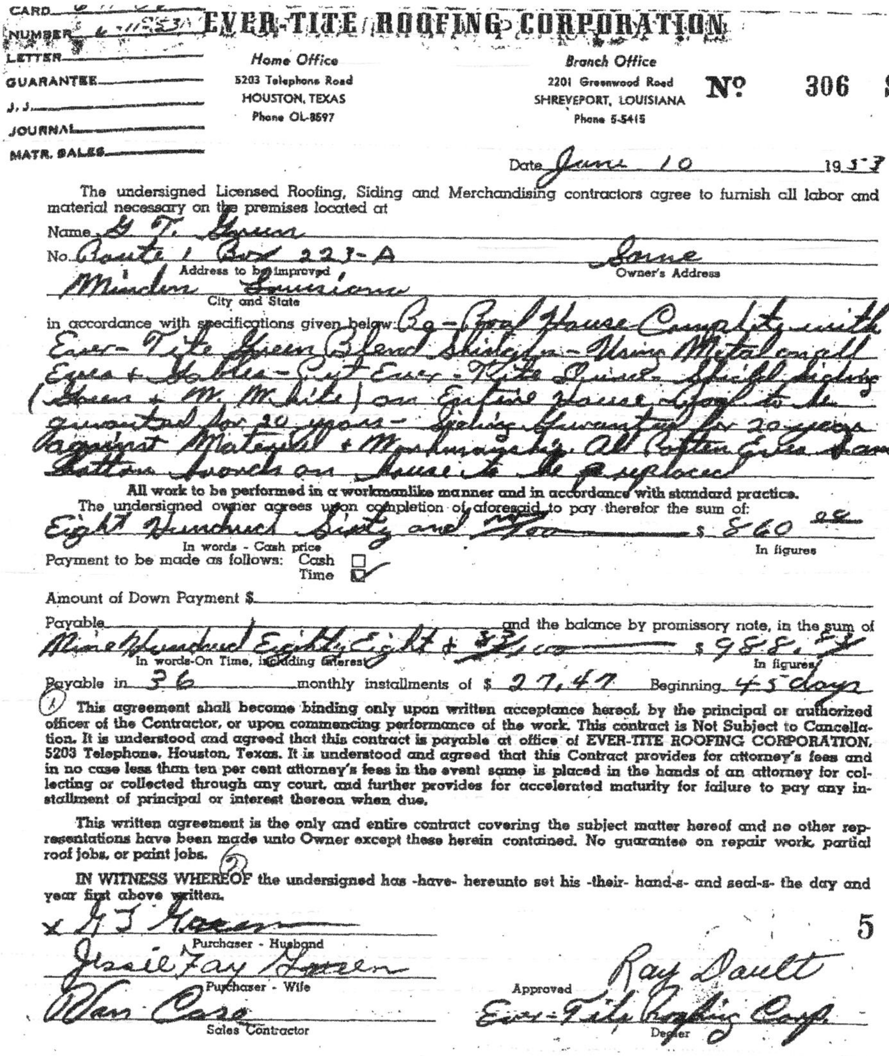

CARD
NUMBER
LETTER
GUARANTEE
J. J.
JOURNAL
MATR. SALES

EVER-TITE ROOFING CORPORATION

Home Office
5203 Telephone Road
HOUSTON, TEXAS
Phone OL-8597

Branch Office
2201 Greenwood Road
SHREVEPORT, LOUISIANA
Phone 5-5415

Nº 306 S

Date June 10 1957

The undersigned Licensed Roofing, Siding and Merchandising contractors agree to furnish all labor and material necessary on the premises located at

Name G. T. Green

No. Route 1 Box 223-A — Address to be improved — Same — Owner's Address

Minden Louisiana — City and State

in accordance with specifications given below: Re-Roof House Completely with Ever-Tite Green Blend Shingles - Using Metal on all Eves + Gables - Put Ever-Tite Insul. Shield Siding (Green + M. White) on Entire House. Roof to be guaranteed for 20 years - Siding Guaranteed for 20 years against Material + Workmanship. All Rotten Eves, Facia Boards on House to be replaced

All work to be performed in a workmanlike manner and in accordance with standard practice.

The undersigned owner agrees upon completion of aforesaid to pay therefor the sum of:

Eight Hundred Sixty and 00/100 — In words - Cash price — $ 860.00 — In figures

Payment to be made as follows: Cash ☐ Time ☑

Amount of Down Payment $

Payable ____ and the balance by promissory note, in the sum of

Nine Hundred Eighty Eight + [illegible]/100 — In words-On Time, including interest — $ 988.[illegible] — In figures

Payable in 36 monthly installments of $ 27.47 Beginning 45 days

(1) This agreement shall become binding only upon written acceptance hereof, by the principal or authorized officer of the Contractor, or upon commencing performance of the work. This contract is Not Subject to Cancellation. It is understood and agreed that this contract is payable at office of EVER-TITE ROOFING CORPORATION, 5203 Telephone, Houston, Texas. It is understood and agreed that this Contract provides for attorney's fees and in no case less than ten per cent attorney's fees in the event same is placed in the hands of an attorney for collecting or collected through any court, and further provides for accelerated maturity for failure to pay any installment of principal or interest thereon when due.

This written agreement is the only and entire contract covering the subject matter hereof and no other representations have been made unto Owner except these herein contained. No guarantee on repair work, partial roof jobs, or paint jobs. (2)

IN WITNESS WHEREOF the undersigned has -have- hereunto set his -their- hand-s- and seal-s- the day and year first above written.

x G T Green — Purchaser - Husband

Jessie Fay Green — Purchaser - Wife

Wm Case — Sales Contractor

5

Approved Ray Dault — Ever-Tite Roofing Corp. — Dealer

Ever-Tite Contract

The general rule of law is that an offer proposed may be withdrawn before its acceptance and that no obligation is incurred thereby. This is, however, not without exceptions. For instance, Restatement of the Law of Contracts stated:

"(1) The power to create a contract by acceptance of an offer terminates at the time specified in the offer, or, if no time is specified, at the end of a reasonable time.

'What is a reasonable time is a question of fact depending on the nature of the contract proposed, the usages of business and other circumstances of the case which the offeree at the time of his acceptance either knows or has reason to know."

* * *

Therefore, since the contract did not specify the time within which it was to be accepted or within which the work was to have been commenced, a reasonable time must be allowed therefor in accordance with the facts and circumstances and the evident intention of the parties. A reasonable time is contemplated where no time is expressed. What is a reasonable time depends more or less upon the circumstances surrounding each particular case. The delays to process defendants' application were not unusual. The contract was accepted by plaintiff by the commencement of the performance of the work contracted to be done. This commencement began with the loading of the trucks with the necessary materials in Shreveport and transporting such materials and the workmen to defendants' residence. Actual commencement or performance of the work therefore began before any notice of dissent by defendants was given plaintiff. The proposition and its acceptance thus became a completed contract.

By their aforesaid acts defendants breached the contract. They employed others to do the work contracted to be done by plaintiff and forbade plaintiff's workmen to engage upon that undertaking. By this breach defendants are legally bound to respond to plaintiff in damages. * * *

Plaintiff expended the sum of $85.37 in loading the trucks in Shreveport with materials and in transporting them to the site of defendants' residence in Webster Parish and in unloading them on their return, and for wages for the workmen for the time consumed. Plaintiff's Shreveport manager testified that the expected profit on this job was $226. None of this evidence is controverted or contradicted in any manner.

True, as plaintiff alleges, the contract provides for attorney's fees where an attorney is employed to collect under the contract, but this is not an action on the contract or to collect under the contract but is an action for damages for a breach of the contract. The contract in that respect is silent with reference to attorney's fees. In the absence of an agreement for the payment of attorney's fees or of some law authorizing the same, such fees are not allowed.

For the reasons assigned, the judgment appealed is annulled, avoided, reversed and set aside and there is now judgment in favor of plaintiff, Ever-Tite Roofing Corporation, against the defendants, G. T. Green and Mrs. Jessie Fay Green, for the full sum of $311.37, with 5 per cent per annum interest thereon from judicial demand until paid, and for all costs.

Reversed and rendered.

Note on Required Form of Acceptance

The following statements in *LaSalle National Bank*, "An offeror has complete control over an offer and may condition acceptance to the terms of the offer. * * * The language of an offer may moreover govern the mode of acceptance required, and, where an offer requires a written acceptance, no other mode may be used" reflect an important feature of the law relating to contract formation, namely, that the offeror is "sovereign," with complete control and mastery over the terms of her offer. Thus, if an offer prescribes the time, place, and/or manner of assent, the purported acceptance—the manifestation of intent to be bound—in order to be effective *must* comply without variation to the terms of the offer. This notion is, of course, consistent with the core policy of freedom of and *from* contract. The offeror has the unfettered right to determine the terms on which she is willing to deal, such that, if the offer requires as a condition to acceptance that the offeree place a paper bag over his head, dance in circles, and squawk like a chicken, then nothing less than what is bargained for will be sufficient to constitute a valid acceptance of the offer.

Sometimes, however, this rule, which is obviously intended to protect the offeror from liability other than on her terms, will end up frustrating the offeror. Consider again *LaSalle National Bank.* Obviously, Mel intended to sell the property to the bank and certainly the bank wanted the property (why else did it sue?). We are often reminded in the caselaw that contract law is about "effectuating the intention of the parties." And yet, Mel was able to escape liability because, by the bank's own requirement, the proposal could not ripen into a contract until the document had been fully executed by an authorized trust officer of the bank. We think this raises some interesting questions, the answers to which may have a bearing on your advice to clients engaged in contract negotiations.

Questions About *Lasalle* and *Ever-Tite*

1. In *LaSalle National Bank,* how important was "full execution" to the bank? Who was that provision intended to protect? Suppose it was just a formality? If so, under the guise of protecting the offeror (the sovereign), have we not assisted the offeree in walking on the deal?

2. Why didn't LaSalle National Bank simply have an officer in its trust department execute the Real Estate Sale Contract before the bank filed its complaint against Mel?

3. Returning to *Ever-Tite,* what does the following statement from the Ever-Tite form mean: "written acceptance, hereof, by the principal . . ."? What does the following statement from the *Ever-Tite* opinion mean: "Formal acceptance of the contract was not made under the signature and approval of an agent of the plaintiff"?

4. Suppose that the day before Ever-Tite planned to do the job the Greens had called and said they were no longer interested. Would there have been a contract? Would it have mattered if, at the time they called, the Greens were aware that their credit had checked out? How could Ever-Tite have protected itself?

5. According to the courts' decisions, who were the offerors in *LaSalle National Bank* and *Ever-Tite*? Who drafted the instruments on which the assertion of contractual liability was based? Did that have a bearing on the outcome in either case? Should it have? Is it the *offeror* who controls the terms of the offer or is it more accurate to say that it is the terms of the *offer* that control the deal?

6. In *Ever-Tite*, the trial court had concluded that the work did not "commence" until the Ever-Tite workers arrived at the site. Is this a less reasonable construction of the language in the instrument than the loading of the trucks? Even if so, was that a judgment that was appropriate to make on appeal? Accepting, *arguendo*, the trial court's construction of when the work commenced, did that justify the trial court's conclusion that there was no contract? There was still no communication from the Greens, so how did they *manifest* their intent to revoke the offer? Does this square with the objective theory of contract formation?

7. What happens when the offer does not stipulate the required manner or method of acceptance? Consider the next case and the material that follows.

Davis v. Jacoby

Supreme Court of California
1 Cal. 2d 370, 34 P.2d 1026 (1934)

Per Curiam

Plaintiffs appeal from a judgment refusing to grant specific performance of an alleged contract to make a will. The facts are not in dispute and are as follows:

The plaintiff Caro M. Davis was the niece of Blanche Whitehead who was married to Rupert Whitehead. Prior to her marriage in 1913 to her coplaintiff Frank M. Davis, Caro lived for a considerable time at the home of the Whiteheads, in Piedmont, California. The Whiteheads were childless and extremely fond of Caro. The record is replete with uncontradicted testimony of the close and loving relationship that existed between Caro and her aunt and uncle. During the period that Caro lived with the Whiteheads she was treated as and often referred to by the Whiteheads as their daughter. In 1913, when Caro was married to Frank Davis the marriage was arranged at the Whitehead home and a reception held there. After the marriage Mr. and Mrs. Davis went to Mr. Davis' home in Canada, where they have resided ever since. During the period 1913 to 1931 Caro made many visits to the Whiteheads, several of them being of long duration. The Whiteheads visited

Mr. and Mrs. Davis in Canada on several occasions. After the marriage and continuing down to 1931 the closest and most friendly relationship at all times existed between these two families. They corresponded frequently, the record being replete with letters showing the loving relationship.

By the year 1930 Mrs. Whitehead had become seriously ill. She had suffered several strokes and her mind was failing. Early in 1931 Mr. Whitehead had her removed to a private hospital. The doctors in attendance had informed him that she might die at any time or she might linger for many months. Mr. Whitehead had suffered severe financial reverses. He had had several sieges of sickness and was in poor health. The record shows that during the early part of 1931 he was desperately in need of assistance with his wife, and in his business affairs, and that he did not trust his friends in Piedmont. On March 18, 1931, he wrote to Mrs. Davis telling her of Mrs. Whitehead's condition and added that Mrs. Whitehead was very wistful. "Today I endeavored to find out what she wanted. I finally asked her if she wanted to see you. She burst out crying and we had great difficulty in getting her to stop. Evidently, that is what is on her mind. It is a very difficult matter to decide. If you come it will mean that you will have to leave again, and then things may be serious. I am going to see the doctor, and get his candid opinion and will then write you again. .... Since writing the above, I have seen the doctor, and he thinks it will help considerably if you come." * * * On March 24, 1931, Mr. Davis, at the request of his wife, telegraphed to Mr. Whitehead as follows: "Your letter received. Sorry to hear Blanche not so well. Hope you are feeling better yourself. If you wish Caro to go to you can arrange for her to leave in about two weeks. Please wire me if you think it advisable for her to go." On March 30, 1931, Mr. Whitehead wrote a long letter to Mr. Davis, in which he explained in detail the condition of Mrs. Whitehead's health and also referred to his own health. He pointed out that he had lost a considerable portion of his cash assets but still owned considerable realty, that he needed someone to help him with his wife and some friend he could trust to help him with his business affairs and suggested that perhaps Mr. Davis might come to California. He then pointed out that all his property was community property; that under his will all the property was to go to Mrs. Whitehead; that he believed that under Mrs. Whitehead's will practically everything was to go to Caro. Mr. Whitehead again wrote to Mr. Davis under date of April 9, 1931, pointing out how badly he needed someone he could trust to assist him, and giving it as his belief that if properly handled he could still save about $150,000. He then stated: "Having you [Mr. Davis] here to depend on and to help me regain my mind and courage would be a big thing." Three days later, on April 12, 1931, Mr. Whitehead again wrote, addressing his letter to "Dear Frank and Caro", and in this letter made the definite offer, which offer it is claimed was accepted and is the basis of this action. In this letter he first pointed out that Blanche, his wife, was in a private hospital and that "she cannot last much longer . . . my affairs are not as bad as I supposed at first. Cutting everything down I figure 150,000 can be saved from the wreck." He then enumerated the values placed upon his various properties and then continued "my trouble was caused by my friends taking advantage of my illness and my position to skin me

"Now if Frank could come out here and be with me, and look after my affairs, we could easily save the balance I mentioned, provided I dont get into another panic and do some more foolish things.

"The next attack will be my end, I am 65 and my health has been bad for years, so, the Drs. dont give me much longer to live. So if you can come, Caro will inherit everything and you will make our lives happier and see Blanche is provided for to the end

"My eyesight has gone back on me, I cant read only for a few lines at a time. I am at the house alone with Stanley [the chauffeur] who does everything for me and is a fine fellow. Now, what I want is some one who will take charge of my affairs and see I dont lose any more. Frank can do it, if he will and cut out the booze.

"Will you let me hear from you as soon as possible, I know it will be a sacrifice but times are still bad and likely to be, so by settling down you can help me and Blanche and gain in the end. If I had you here my mind would get better and my courage return, and we could work things out."

This letter was received by Mr. Davis at his office in Windsor, Canada, about 9:30 A. M. April 14, 1931. After reading the letter to Mrs. Davis over the telephone, and after getting her belief that they must go to California, Mr. Davis immediately wrote Mr. Whitehead a letter, which, after reading it to his wife, he sent by air mail. This letter was lost, but there is no doubt that it was sent by Davis and received by Whitehead, in fact the trial court expressly so found. Mr. Davis testified in substance as to the contents of this letter. After acknowledging receipt of the letter of April 12, 1931, Mr. Davis unequivocally stated that he and Mrs. Davis accepted the proposition of Mr. Whitehead and both would leave Windsor to go to him on April 25th. This letter of acceptance also contained the information that the reason they could not leave prior to April 25th was that Mr. Davis had to appear in court on April 22d as one of the executors of his mother's estate. The testimony is uncontradicted and ample to support the trial court's finding that this letter was sent by Davis and received by Whitehead. In fact under date of April 15, 1931, Mr. Whitehead again wrote to Mr. Davis and stated "Your letter by air mail received this a. m. Now, I am wondering if I have put you to unnecessary trouble and expense, if you are making any money dont leave it, as things are bad here. . . . You know your business and I dont and I am half crazy in the bargain, but I dont want to hurt you or Caro

"Then on the other hand if I could get some one to trust and keep me straight I can save a good deal, about what I told you in my former letter."

This letter was received by Mr. Davis on April 17, 1931, and the same day Mr. Davis telegraphed to Mr. Whitehead "Cheer up—we will soon be there, we will wire you from the train."

Between April 14, 1931, the date the letter of acceptance was sent by Mr. Davis, and April 22d, Mr. Davis was engaged in closing out his business affairs, and Mrs. Davis in closing up their home and in making other arrangements to leave. On April 22, 1931, Mr. Whitehead committed suicide. Mr. and Mrs. Davis were immediately notified and they at once came to California. From almost the moment of her arrival Mrs. Davis devoted herself to the care and comfort of her aunt, and gave her aunt constant attention and care until Mrs. Whitehead's death on May 30, 1931. * * *

After the death of Mrs. Whitehead, for the first time it was discovered that the information contained in Mr. Whitehead's letter of March 30, 1931, in reference to the contents of his and Mrs. Whitehead's wills was incorrect. By a duly witnessed will dated February 28, 1931, Mr. Whitehead, after making several specific bequests, had bequeathed all of the balance of his estate to his wife for life, and upon her death to respondents Geoff Doubble and Rupert Ross Whitehead, his nephews. Neither appellant was mentioned in his will. * * *

After the discovery of the manner in which the property had been devised was made, this action was commenced upon the theory that Rupert Whitehead had assumed a contractual obligation to make a will whereby "Caro Davis would inherit everything"; that he had failed to do so; that plaintiffs had fully performed their part of the contract; * * *

It should also be added that the evidence shows that as a result of Frank Davis leaving his business in Canada he forfeited not only all insurance business he might have written if he had remained, but also forfeited all renewal commissions earned on past business. According to his testimony this loss was over $8,000.

The trial court found that the relationship between Mr. and Mrs. Davis and the Whiteheads was substantially as above recounted and that the other facts above stated were true; * * *

The theory of the trial court and of respondents on this appeal is that the letter of April 12th was an offer to contract, but that such offer could only be accepted by performance and could not be accepted by a promise to perform, and that said offer was revoked by the death of Mr. Whitehead before performance. In other words, it is contended that the offer was an offer to enter into a unilateral contract, and that the purported acceptance of April 14th was of no legal effect.

The distinction between unilateral and bilateral contracts is well settled in the law. It is well stated in section 12 of the American Institute's Restatement of the Law of Contracts as follows:

> "A unilateral contract is one in which no promisor receives a promise as consideration for his promise. A bilateral contract is one in which there are mutual promises between two parties to the contract; each party being both a promisor and a promisee."

This definition is in accord with the law of California. (*Christman v. Southern Cal. Edison Co.*, 83 Cal. App. 249[, 256 Pac. 618].)

In the case of unilateral contracts no notice of acceptance by performance is required. Section 1584 of the Civil Code provides, "Performance of the conditions of a proposal, . . . is an acceptance of the proposal." * * *

Although the legal distinction between unilateral and bilateral contracts is thus well settled, the difficulty in any particular case is to determine whether the particular offer is one to enter into a bilateral or unilateral contract. Some cases are quite clear cut. Thus an offer to sell which is accepted is clearly a bilateral contract, while an offer of a reward is a clear-cut offer of a unilateral contract which cannot be accepted by a promise to perform, but only by performance. * * * Between these two extremes is a vague field where the particular contract may be unilateral or bilateral depending upon the intent of the offerer and the facts and circumstances of each case. The offer to contract involved in this case falls within this category. By the provisions of the Restatement of the Law of Contracts it is expressly provided that there is a presumption that the offer is to enter into a bilateral contract. Section 31 provides:

> "In case of doubt it is presumed that an offer invites the formation of a bilateral contract by an acceptance amounting in effect to a promise by the offeree to perform what the offer requests, rather than the formation of one or more unilateral contracts by actual performance on the part of the offeree."

Professor Williston in his Treatise on Contracts, volume 1, section 60, also takes the position that a presumption in favor of bilateral contracts exists.

In the comment following section 31 of the Restatement the reason for such presumption is stated as follows:

> "It is not always easy to determine whether an offerer requests an act or a promise to do the act. As a bilateral contract immediately and fully protects both parties, the interpretation is favored that a bilateral contract is proposed."

While the California cases have never expressly held that a presumption in favor of bilateral contracts exists, the cases clearly indicate a tendency to treat offers as offers of bilateral rather than of unilateral contracts. * * *

Keeping these principles in mind we are of the opinion that the offer of April 12th was an offer to enter into a bilateral as distinguished from a unilateral contract. Respondents argue that Mr. Whitehead had the right as offerer to designate his offer as either unilateral or bilateral. That is undoubtedly the law. It is then argued that from all the facts and circumstances it must be implied that what Whitehead wanted was performance and not a mere promise to perform. We think this is a non sequitur, in fact the surrounding circumstances lead to just the opposite conclusion. These parties were not dealing at arm's length. Not only were they related, but a very close and intimate friendship existed between them. The record indisputably demonstrates that Mr. Whitehead had confidence in Mr. and Mrs. Davis, in fact that he had lost all confidence in everyone else. The record amply shows that by an accumulation of occurrences Mr. Whitehead had become desperate, and that what he wanted was the promise of appellants that he could look to them for assistance. He knew from his past relationship with appellants that if they gave their promise to perform he could rely upon them. The correspondence between them indicates how desperately he desired this assurance. Under these circumstances he wrote his offer of April 12th, above quoted, in which he stated, after disclosing his desperate mental and physical condition, and after setting forth the terms of his offer:

"Will you let me hear from you as soon as possible–I know it will be a sacrifice but times are still bad and likely to be, so by settling down you can help me and Blanche and gain in the end." By thus specifically requesting an immediate reply Whitehead expressly indicated the nature of the acceptance desired by him–namely, appellants' promise that they would come to California and do the things requested by him. This promise was immediately sent by appellants upon receipt of the offer, and was received by Whitehead. It is elementary that when an offer has indicated the mode and means of acceptance, an acceptance in accordance with that mode or means is binding on the offerer.

* * *

For the foregoing reasons we are of the opinion that the offer of April 12, 1931, was an offer to enter into a bilateral contract which was accepted by the letter of April 14, 1931. * * *

For the foregoing reasons the judgment appealed from is reversed.

QUESTIONS AND NOTES

1. Questions about the facts of this case

   1.1. Did Rupert Whitehead make an offer to Frank and Caro Davis? If so, what was it?

   1.2. Did that offer invite or require acceptance in any particular manner?

   1.3. Did Rupert Whitehead ever revoke that offer? What is the importance of the April 14th letter? What about the February 28th will?

   1.4. Who was Jacoby?

2. Questions about the law

   2.1. How did Frank and Caro accept? Can every offer be accepted by a mere promise? How would *Restatement (Second)* § 32 answer that question? *See* Note 3.2 below.

2.2. What if the letter of March 30th had said, "Caro and you can accept this offer to inherit everything only by moving to California"? What is the difference between that hypothetical language and the language of the April 12th letter—"So if you can come, Caro will inherit everything"?

2.3. What do you think Mr. Whitehead was *really* bargaining for, the Davis' promise or their performance? Do you think he even thought about it in those terms? If not, should important legal consequences—such as when an acceptance is effective and whether notice of acceptance is required—turn on the distinction between offers for unilateral and bilateral contracts?

3. Notes

3.1. We will deal more directly with the question of what a party to an agreement was bargaining for when we deal with consideration in Chapter 2. Examination of "incapacity" is also deferred until Chapter 2. Professor Monroe Freedman of Hofstra Law School suggests that the lawyers for Davis and Jacoby also decided to defer consideration of incapacity:

> [T]he adversary system will occasionally fail to bring out facts or arguments that might be highly relevant to the court's decision. One illustration is *Davis v. Jacoby*, where the contest was between parties claiming under a will and parties claiming under a contract to make a different will. A material fact was that the testator/contractor was very likely incompetent during the period of time when both instruments were executed. Accordingly, neither party appears to have argued the legal relevance of the testator/contractor's mental condition, one side because they did not want to impeach the will, the other side because they did not want to impeach the contract."

Monroe H. Freedman, *Arguing the Law in the Adversary System*, 16 GA. L. REV. 833, 838 (1982).

3.2. *Davis* reflects the attitude of the common law and the first *Restatement of Contracts,* consistent with the view of offeror as sovereign, that every offer had to be regarded as an offer for a bilateral or a unilateral contract. In turn, of course, this affected the manner in which the offer could be accepted. For instance, in *Davis,* the respondents urged the court to characterize Mr. Whitehead's proposed arrangement as a unilateral contract, thereby rendering the Davis' promissory acceptance ineffective. The perspective of the *Restatement (Second) of Contracts*, and for that matter the U.C.C., was to make the law less formal and less rigid so that failure to comply with some legal nicety does not inadvertently frustrate actual contractual intent. It was for this reason that the drafters of the *Restatement (Second)* decided to refrain from referring to the bilateral/unilateral contract terminology anywhere in the document. The thinking was that in most instances the offeror is indifferent as to what manner of assent, promise or performance, is necessary to accept the offer. If that's so, by construing the offer as requiring one or the other, we run the risk that contractual intent might be defeated because of the failure of the acceptance to comport with the form of the offer. This is almost what happened in *Davis.*

The approach of the *Restatement (Second)*, when an offer specifies a manner of acceptance, is to tilt the presumption in the other direction. As a starting point, § 50(1) provides that "[a]cceptance of an offer is a manifestation of assent to the terms thereof made by the offeree in a manner invited or required by the offer." This provision recognizes the principle that the offeror can dictate the permissible manner of assent. However, § 30(2) creates a presumption that, "unless otherwise indicated by the language or circumstances," an offer will be treated as inviting acceptance in any manner that is reasonable under the circumstances. Section 32 then continues that, "[i]n the case of doubt an offer is interpreted as inviting the offeree to accept either by promising to perform what the offeror requests or by rendering the performance as the offeree chooses." How would the analysis in *Davis* have differed if the case were to be decided today under these rules?

The above provisions of the *Restatement (Second)* are consistent with the general approach taken by the U.C.C. concerning acceptance. Specifically, § 2-206(1)(a) provides that "[u]nless otherwise unambiguously indicated by the language or circumstances an offer to make a contract shall be construed as inviting acceptance in any manner and by any medium reasonable in the circumstances." This provision also reflects a belief that, in the vast majority of cases, the offeror is indifferent to the manner in which assent is expressed. Is that a fair assumption?

B. Effectiveness of Promissory Acceptance

Introduction to *Hendricks*

Davis v. Jacoby illustrates that a promise can be effective as an acceptance, at least under most circumstances. The next two cases raise two different questions relating to the *point in time* at which a promise as an acceptance is effective. In the first case, *Hendricks*, we see an attempt to accept and an attempt to revoke an offer. Accordingly, the time at which each becomes is effective is going to be critical in determining whether or not there is mutual assent.

Hendricks v. Behee

Court of Appeals of Missouri, Southern District
786 S.W.2d 610 (1990)

Flanigan, J.

Plaintiff Steve L. Hendricks, d/b/a Hendricks Abstract & Title Co., instituted this interpleader action,* against defendants Eugene Behee, Artice Smith, and Pearl Smith. Plaintiff was the escrowee of $5,000 which had been paid by defendant Behee as a deposit accompanying Behee's offer to purchase real estate owned by defendants Artice and Pearl Smith, husband

*This is a procedural device that is available in the following kind of circumstances: Epstein holds certain property which he acknowledges does not belong to him and as to which he asserts no claim. He simply wants to return the property to its rightful owner. The problem is that both Markell and Ponoroff claim that they are entitled to the property and they both demand that Epstein turn it over to them or they will sue! Epstein does not really care who is right, he just doesn't want to run the risk of turning it over to the wrong party and then incurring liability to the rightful owner. The solution for Epstein is to bring a lawsuit, naming both Markell and Ponoroff as defendants, in which Epstein *interpleads* the property with the court saying, in effect, "here it is, you decide who gets it, Judge, just leave me out of it, except I think I ought to be reimbursed my costs by the real parties in interest here." Eds.

and wife, in Stockton, Missouri. A dispute between Behee and the Smiths as to whether their dealings resulted in a binding contract prompted the interpleader action. Behee filed a crossclaim against the Smiths.

After a nonjury trial, the trial court awarded plaintiff $997.50 to be paid out of the $5,000 deposit. None of the parties challenges that award. The trial court awarded the balance of $4,002.50 to defendant Behee. Defendants appeal.

In essence the Smiths contend that the dealings between them and Behee ripened into a contract and entitled the Smiths to the balance of $4,002.50, and that the trial court erred in ruling otherwise.

After Behee, as prospective buyer, and the Smiths, as prospective sellers, had engaged in unproductive negotiations, Behee, on March 2, 1987, made a written offer of $42,500 for the real estate and $250 for a dinner bell and flower pots. On March 3 that offer was mailed to the Smiths, who lived in Mississippi, by their real estate agent. There were two real estate agents involved. The trial court found that both were the agents of the Smiths, and that finding has not been disputed by the Smiths in this appeal. For simplicity, the two agents will be considered in this opinion as one agent who acted on behalf of the Smiths.

On March 4 the Smiths signed the proposed agreement in Mississippi. Before Behee was notified that the Smiths had accepted the offer, Behee withdrew the offer by notifying the real estate agent of the withdrawal. That paramount fact is conceded by this statement in the Smiths' brief: "On either March 5, 6 or 7, 1987, Behee contacted [the Smiths' real estate agent] and advised her that he desired to withdraw his offer to purchase the real estate. Prior to this communication, Behee had received no notice that his offer had been accepted by the Smiths."

* * *

An uncommunicated intention to accept an offer is not an acceptance. * * * When an offer calls for a promise, as distinguished from an act, on the part of the offeree, notice of acceptance is always essential. * * * A mere private act of the offeree does not constitute an acceptance. * * * Communication of acceptance of a contract to an agent of the offeree is not sufficient and does not bind the offeror. * * *

Unless the offer is supported by consideration, * * * an offeror may withdraw his offer at any time "before acceptance and communication of that fact to him." * * * To be effective, revocation of an offer must be communicated to the offeree before he has accepted. * * *

Notice to the agent, within the scope of the agent's authority, is notice to the principal, and the agent's knowledge is binding on the principal. * * *

Before Behee was notified that the Smiths had accepted his offer, Behee notified the agent of the Smiths that Behee was withdrawing the offer. The notice to the agent, being within the scope of her authority, was binding upon the Smiths. Behee's offer was not supported by consideration and his withdrawal of it was proper. * * *

The judgment is affirmed.

QUESTIONS

1. Questions about the facts of this case

   1.1. What did Mr. Behee indicate to the Smiths concerning the permissible or required manner of acceptance?

   1.2. The court notes that the real estate agents involved in the deal were both agents of the Smiths. Why is that fact important? How would the analysis change if one or both of the agents were agent(s) for Behee?

2. Questions about the law

   2.1. Did the court construe Mr. Behee's offer as an offer for a unilateral or a bilateral contract? Was this proper?

   2.2. Does the holding in *Hendricks* suggest that in *Ever-Tite Roofing, supra,* had an authorized representative of the Ever-Tite corporation actually signed the Green's offer as soon as their credit checked out that there would still have been no contract until notice of the signature had been given to the Greens? Why not? By the same token how could the loading of the truck in *Ever-Tite* have constituted acceptance by commencement of performance if the Greens were not aware that the trucks were being loaded?

2.3. Is *Restatement (Second) of Contracts* § 50(3) consistent with the holding in *Hendricks*?

Introduction to *Adams v. Lindsell*

When, under the terms of the offer, acceptance by return promise is permitted or required an issue arises if the parties are not face-to-face. *Hendricks* suggests that an uncommunicated intention to accept an offer is not an acceptance; that notice of acceptance is always an essential aspect of a promissory acceptance. Is this consistent with objective theory? In *Hendricks*, there is no indication that the Smiths made any attempt to communicate their acceptance to Behee before Behee withdrew his offer. What about, however, if the offeree does send off an acceptance? Unless the parties are face-to-face, inevitably there will be some length of time between the moment the acceptance is actually sent and the moment it is received. If the mails are involved, this could be a matter of days, or, as we all know, even longer. The period of transmission will be much shorter of course if the offeree uses FedEx or another overnight courier, but, even then, there may be a gap. Thus, the question arises whether during this period of transmission a contract exists or whether the offeror is still sovereign until the acceptance is actually received. Based on objective theory of contract formation, what would you predict? Of course, you would say that the acceptance is not effective until received by the offeror. However, you may recall that in *Minnesota Linseed Oil Co. v. Collier Whitehead Co., supra,* at 76, the court suggested that a different rule pertains in these circumstances, citing the next case, *Adams v. Lindsell.* Now we get to see what that case was all about.

Adams v. Lindsell

Court of King's Bench
106 Eng. Rep. 250 (1818)

Action for non-delivery of wool according to agreement. At the trial at the last Lent Assizes for the county of Worcester, before Burrough J. it appeared that the defendants who were dealers in wool, at St. Ives, in the county of Huntingdon, had, on Tuesday the 2d of September 1817, written the following letter to the plaintiffs, who were woolen manufacturers residing in Bromsgrove, Worcestershire. "We now offer you eight hundred tods of wether fleeces, of a good fair quality of our country wool, at 35s. 6d. per tod, to be delivered at Leicester, and to be paid for by two months' bill in two months, and to be weighed up by your agent within fourteen days, receiving your answer in course of post."

This letter was misdirected by the defendants, to Bromsgrove, Leicestershire, in consequence of which it was not received by the plaintiffs in Worcestershire till 7 p.m. on Friday, September 5th. On that evening the plaintiffs wrote an answer, agreeing to accept the wool on the terms proposed. The course of the post between St. Ives and Bromsgrove is through London, and consequently this answer was not received by the defendants till Tuesday, September 9th. On Monday September 8th, the defendants not having, as they expected, received an answer on Sunday September 7th, (which in case their letter had not been misdirected, would have been in the usual course of the post,) sold the wool in question to another person. Under these circumstances, the learned Judge held, that the delay having been occasioned by the neglect of the defendants, the jury must take it, that the answer did come back in due course of post; and that then the defendants were liable for the loss that had been sustained; and the plaintiffs accordingly recovered the verdict.

Jervis having in Easter term obtained a rule nisi for a new trial, on the ground that there was no binding contract between the parties,

Dauncey, Puller, and Richardson, showed cause. They contended, that at the moment of the acceptance of the offer of the defendants by the plaintiffs, the former became bound. And that was on the Friday evening, when there had been no change of circumstances. They were then stopped by the Court, who called upon Jervis and Campbell in support of the rule. They relied on *Payne v Cave* [3 T.R. 148], and more particularly on *Cooke v. Oxley* [Ibid. 653]. In that case, Oxley, who had proposed to sell goods to Cooke, and given him a certain time at his request, to determine whether he would buy them or not, was held not liable to the performance of the contract, even though Cooke, within the specified time, had determined to buy them, and given Oxley notice to that effect. So here the defendants who have proposed by letter to sell this wool are not to be held liable, even though it be now admitted that the answer did come back in due course of post. Till the plaintiffs' answer was actually received, there could be no binding contract between the parties; and before then, the defendants had retracted their offer, by selling the wool to other persons. But—

The Court said, that if that were so, no contract could ever be completed by the post. For if the defendants were not bound by their offer when accepted by the plaintiffs till the answer was received, then the plaintiffs ought not to be bound till after they had received notification that the defendants had received their answer and assented to it. And so it might go on ad infinitum. The defendants must be considered in law as making, during every instant of the time their letter was travelling, the same identical offer to the plaintiffs; and then the contract is completed by the acceptance of it by the latter. Then as to the delay in notifying the acceptance, that arises entirely from the mistake of the defendants, and it therefore must be taken as against them, that the plaintiffs answer was received in course of post.

Rule discharged.

QUESTIONS AND NOTES

1. Questions about the facts of this case

   1.1. *Adams* is celebrated for establishing the so-called "mailbox rule," which holds that an acceptance is effective on *dispatch* rather than *receipt.* This rule continues to the present day. *See Restatement (Second) of Contracts* § 63. Along with automatic termination of an offer on death or disability of the offeror, the dispatch rule represents perhaps the most glaring exception to the objective theory of contract formation. However, the dispatch rule is only operative under certain circumstances. What was the critical fact in *Adams* that convinced the court to employ this rule?

   1.2. In *Adams*, the court invoked the mailbox rule to protect the plaintiffs since the misdirection of the offer letter was the fault of the defendants. However, review the facts closely. Did the court need to resort to the mailbox rule in order to find for the plaintiffs? Also, is it clear that plaintiffs were entitled to protection? Shouldn't the plaintiffs have been aware that by September 8 the defendants might no longer be interested in selling the fleeces to them? If so, did they still have the power of acceptance?

1.3. Just how much was at stake in this case? According to Markell, who frequently travels to Europe (Epstein only goes to Ethiopia and Ponoroff doesn't like to leave this country), a "tod" is equivalent to 28 pounds, so the contract involved 22,400 pounds of "wether fleeces" (fleeces from castrated male sheep). At 35S. 6d. per tod, or roughly $15.00, we're talking about $12,000 worth of wool, not an inconsiderable sum in 1818.

1.4. By the way, are you as impressed as we are with the speed of the early nineteenth century English post?

2. Questions about the law

2.1. What justification does the court offer for the "mailbox rule"? How satisfying do you find that rationale?

2.2. If the offeror is truly sovereign and, as such, entitled to dictate the terms on which she is willing to deal, is there some way in which the offeror can protect herself against the mailbox rule; against having legal consequences established based on uncommunicated intent?

2.3. Who is the superior bearer of the risk that a communication will be lost or delayed during transit? Does your answer to this question suggest a more principled justification for the rule than the one offered by the court in *Adams*? *See* A. CORBIN, CONTRACTS § 78 (1950).

2.4. Under the rationale of *Adams,* if an offer is made by FedEx, and the acceptance by return post, does the mailbox rule apply? How about the other way around?

2.5. As the pace of technology has made communications between parties almost instantaneous even when those parties are at a distance from one another, e.g., facsimile transmissions and e-mail, does the rationale for the mailbox rule breakdown? How so? *Cf. Restatement (Second) of Contracts* § 64, cmt. a ("*Where the parties are in each other's presence, the offeree can accept without being in doubt as to whether the offeror has attempted to revoke his offer or whether the offeror has received the acceptance.*")

3. Notes

3.1. There is an emerging body of statutory law being developed to deal with so-called "electronic contracts"; that is, contracts formed by means of computer transmissions or over the Internet and stored solely in the form of an electronic record. This includes the federal Electronic Signature in Global and National Commerce (E-Sign) Act and the Uniform Electronic Transactions Act, both designed to give legal effect to electronic signatures. What role would you anticipate that the "dispatch rule" will or should play in the legal rules governing these contracts? Current Article 2 is silent about the "mailbox" rule. Early drafts of Revised Article 2 had provided that: "If an offer evokes an electronic response, a contract is formed, if at all . . . when the record is received." The most current version, however, eliminates that provision and provides simply that: "A contract for the sale of goods may be made in any manner sufficient to show agreement, including . . . the interaction of electronic agents." Revised § 2-204(1). An "Electronic Agent" means a computer program or an electronic or other automated means used independently to initiate an action or respond to electronic records or performances in whole or in part, without review or action by an individual. For the most part, the law has treated electronic contracts as tending to raise issues of *form* (*e.g.*, when is an electronic signature effective) rather than involving new substantive rules. Therefore, we discuss electronic contracting again in Chapter 2 as part of our study of the Statute of Frauds.

3.2. In *Dick v. United States*, 82 F. Supp. 326, 113 Ct. Cl. 94 (1949), a contractor received, on March 8, 1945, a purchase order by mail from the Navy for two sets of new propeller equipment consisting of two propellers and a propeller bow each. Believing that the bid was for one set of propellers and a propeller bow (a single "shipset"), the plaintiff mailed its acceptance on March 15, 1945. The following day, plaintiff notified the Navy that he had made a mistake and that the price should be doubled. The plaintiff proceeded with the manufacture and delivery of two shipsets of propellers, but the Navy paid for only one. Thereafter the plaintiff brought an action to recover the value of the second shipset of propeller equipment. In response to the Navy's argument that a binding contract had been formed upon the mailing of plaintiff's acceptance on March 15, the court cited a change in postal regulation permitting anyone who had sent a letter to reclaim it by wiring the postmaster at the destination point. Thus, because the court concluded that the letter of acceptance was not out of the plaintiff's control until it had been delivered, the posting of the letter did not constitute an acceptance. Does this ruling make sense? *See also Rhode Island Tool Co. v. United States,* 128 F. Supp. 417, 130 Ct. Cl. 698 (1955). *But see Soldau v. Organon Inc.,* 860 F.2d 355 (9th Cir. 1988) (holding that, contrary to *Dick,* an acceptance made by mail was effective when dispatched even though the acceptance was later retrieved from the mailbox).

Problems Concerning Application of the "Mailbox Rule"

1. Assume that, on November 26, Ponoroff executes a contract for the purchase and sale of certain real property and mails it to Markell for acceptance. On receipt of the agreement, Markell executes it and sends it, by return mail, to Ponoroff's attorney. Subsequently, Markell changes his mind and calls Ponoroff's attorney to inform her that he is not interested in selling and that she should ignore the agreement when it shows up. The next day, the signed agreement arrives at Ponoroff's attorney's office. What should the attorney advise Ponoroff in terms of whether or not he has a binding contract to buy the property? *See Morrison v. Thoelke,* 155 So. 2d 889 (Fla. App. 1963). Would it affect your advice if Markell failed to inform the attorney during their telephone conversation that he had already signed and mailed back the agreement? In that case, suppose, after being informed of the telephone call by his attorney, Ponoroff goes out and enters into a contract to purchase another parcel of property. Thereafter, the signed agreement arrives in Ponoroff's attorney's office and Markell brings an action for specific performance. Is there a contract between Ponoroff and Markell? If so, does Ponoroff have a defense to liability?

2. Assume the same facts as stated at the beginning of Problem 1 above, except that, instead of mailing the agreement to Ponoroff's attorney, Markell mails it to his own lawyer with instructions to deliver to it Ponoroff. Can Markell still change his mind? If so, up to what point

in time? Why didn't the mailbox rule protect the sellers in *Hendricks v. Behee, supra*?

3. Suppose that, on Day 1, Epstein sends Markell an offer by mail. The offer does not contain any specification relating to manner of acceptance. On Day 2, Epstein changes his mind and mails a revocation of the offer. On Day 3, Markell receives the offer and immediately mails an acceptance. On Day 5 the revocation arrives and on Day 6 the acceptance arrives.

   (a) Has a contract been formed? If so, when?

   (b) Does it change your answer if, on Day 2, right after dropping his letter in the mail, Epstein clutches his chest and dies right there at the mailbox?

   (c) How about if Epstein dies on Day 3? Is there anything else you want to know?

   (d) How does it affect your answer if, before Epstein dies on Day 3, Markell mails a rejection and then changes his mind and mails an acceptance? *See Restatement (Second) of Contracts* § 40.

   (e) Assume the same facts as part (d), except that Epstein doesn't die at all. In analyzing whether a contract is formed, does it matter which communication arrives first?

4. Now assume that, on February 1, Epstein sends Markell an offer by mail agreeing that, in return for $100, he will grant Markell a 60-day option (to expire on April 2) to purchase Epstein's house for $150,000. Markell promptly pays the $100. There are no further communications between the parties until, on March 29, Markell sends a letter to Epstein notifying him that he is exercising the option. The letter reaches Epstein on April 3, whereupon Epstein calls Markell and tells him that it's "too late," and he has already arranged to sell the property to Ponoroff for $155,000. Does Markell have a claim against Epstein? *See Smith v. Hervo Realty Corp.*, 199 Conn. 330, 507 A.2d 980 (1986); *Restatement (Second)* § 63, cmt. f. How about against Ponoroff?

C. Effectiveness of Acceptance by Performance

Subject to the mailbox rule, we've seen that an acceptance in the form of a return promise is not effective until communicated to the offeror. However, recall that *"[U]nless otherwise indicated by the language or the circumstances, an offer [is treated as inviting] acceptance in any manner and by any medium reasonable in the circumstances." Restatement (Second) of Contracts* § 30(2). Thus, in most cases, acceptance may occur by performance as well as by promise. If the offeree accepts by performance, when is the acceptance effective? Is it when the act is begun; when it is completed; or when the offeror receives notice that the act has been completed? The next two cases and the material that follow address these questions and the answers may just surprise you.

Carlill v. Carbolic Smoke Ball Co.
Court of Appeal
1 Q.B. 256 (1893)

[The defendant, a London-based company, ran an advertisement promising to pay a 100£ "reward" to anyone who contracted the flu after inhaling the company's smoke ball three times daily for a two-week period in accordance with the printed directions. The ad noted that, in a gesture of its sincerity, the company had deposited 1,000£ pounds with a local bank. This action was brought by Lilli Carlill who, after seeing the ad, purchased a smoke ball and used it as directed for a period of two months whereupon she contracted influenza.]

LINDLEY, L.J. [The Lord Justice stated the facts, and proceeded:]

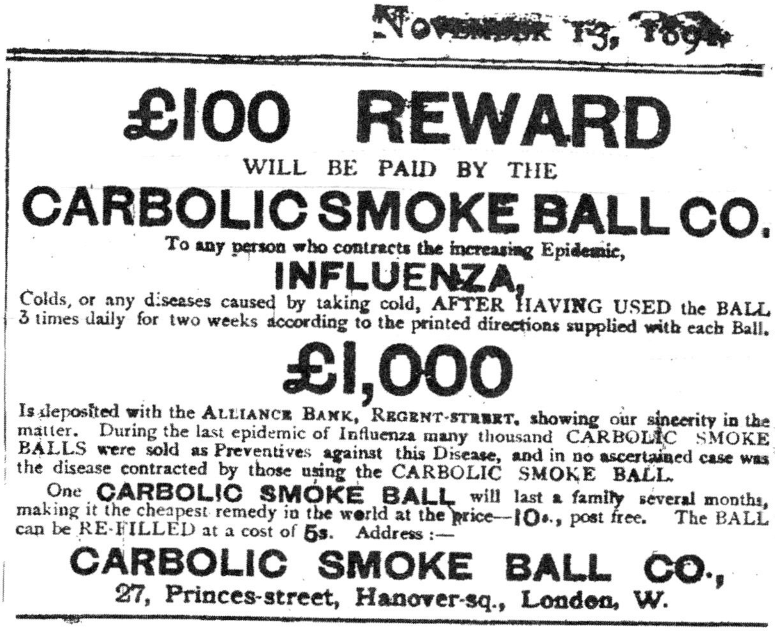

Smoke Ball Contract

I will begin by referring to two points which were raised in the Court below. I refer to them simply for the purpose of dismissing them. First, it is said no action will lie upon this contract because it is a policy. You have only to look at the advertisement to dismiss that suggestion. Then it was said that it is a bet. Hawkins, J., came to the conclusion that nobody ever dreamt of a bet, and that the transaction had nothing whatever in common w th a bet. I so entirely agree with him that I pass over this contention also as not worth serious attention.

Then, what is left? The first observation I will make is that we are not dealing with any inference of fact. We are dealing with an express promise to pay 100£ in certain events. Read the advertisement how you will, and twist it about as you will, here is a distinct promise expressed in language which is perfectly unmistakable—"100£ reward will be paid by the Carbolic Smoke Ball Company to any person who contracts the influenza after having used the ball three times daily for two weeks according to the printed directions supplied with each ball."

We must first consider whether this was intended to be a promise at all, or whether it was a mere puff which meant nothing. Was it a mere puff? My answer to that question is No, and I base my answer upon this passage: "1000£ is deposited with the Alliance Bank, showing our sincerity in the matter." Now, for what was that money deposited or that statement made except to negative the suggestion that this was a mere puff and meant nothing at all? The deposit is called in aid by the advertiser as proof of his sincerity in the matter—that is, the sincerity of his promise to pay this 100£ in the event which he has specified. I say this for the purpose of giving point to the observation that we are not inferring a promise; there is the promise, as plain as words can make it.

Then it is contended that it is not binding. In the first place, it is said that it is not made with anybody in particular. Now that point is common to the words of this advertisement and to the words of all other advertisements offering rewards. They are offers to anybody who performs the conditions named in the advertisement, and anybody who does perform the condition accepts the offer. In point of law this advertisement is an offer to pay 100£ to anybody who will perform these conditions, and the performance of the conditions if the acceptance of the offer. * * *

But then it is said, "Supposing that the performance of the conditions is an acceptance of the offer, that acceptance ought to have been notified." Unquestionably, as a general proposition, when an offer is made, it is necessary in order to make a binding contract, not only that it should be accepted, but that the acceptance should be notified. But is that so in cases of this kind? I apprehend that they are an exception to that rule, or, if not an exception, they are open to the observation that the notification of the acceptance need not precede the performance. This offer is a continuing offer. It was never revoked, and if notice of acceptance is required—which I doubt very much, for I rather think the true view is that which was expressed and explained by Lord Blackburn in the case of *Brogden v. Metropolitan By Co.*—if notice of acceptance is required, the person who makes the offer gets the notice of acceptance contemporaneously with his notice of the performance of the condition. If he gets notice of the acceptance before his offer is revoked, that in principle is all you want. I, however, think that the true view, in a case of this kind, is that the person who makes the offer shows by his language and from the nature of the transaction that he does not expect and does not require notice of the acceptance apart from notice of the performance.

We, therefore, find here all the elements which are necessary to form a binding contract enforceable in point of law, subject to two observations. First of all it is said that this advertisement is so vague that you cannot really construe it as a promise—that the vagueness of the languages shows that a legal promise was never intended or contemplated. The language is vague and uncertain in some respects, and particularly in this, that the 100£ is to be paid to any person who contracts the increasing epidemic after having used the balls three times daily for two weeks. It is said, When are they to be used? According to the language of the advertisement no time is fixed, and, construing the offer most strongly against the person who has made it, one might infer that any time was meant. I do not think that was meant, and to hold the contrary would be pushing too far the doctrine of taking language most strongly against the person using it. I do not think that business people or reasonable people would understand the words as meaning that if you took a smoke ball and used it three times daily for two weeks you were to be guaranteed against influenza for the rest of your life, and I think it would be pushing the language of the advertisement too far to construe it as meaning that. But if it does not mean that, what does it mean? It is for the defendants to show what it does mean; and it strikes me that there are two, and possibly three reasonable constructions to be put on this advertisement, any one of which will answer the purpose of the plaintiff. Possibly it may be limited to persons catching the "increasing epidemic" (that is, the then prevailing epidemic), or any colds or diseases caused by taking cold, during the prevalence of the increasing epidemic. That is one suggestion; but it does not commend itself to me. Another suggested meaning is that you are warranted free from catching this epidemic, or colds or other diseases caused by taking cold, whilst you are using this remedy after using it for two weeks. If that is the meaning, the plaintiff is right, for she used the remedy for two weeks and went on using it till she got the epidemic. Another meaning, and the one which I rather prefer, is that the reward is offered to any person who contracts the epidemic or other disease within a reasonable time after having used the smoke ball. Then it is asked, What is a reasonable time? It has been suggested that there is no standard of reasonableness; that it depends upon the reasonable time for a germ to develop! I do not feel pressed by that. It strikes me that a reasonable time may be ascertained in a business sense and in a sense satisfactory to a lawyer, in this way; find out from a chemist what the ingredients are; find out from a skilled physician how long the effect of such ingredients on the system could be reasonable expected to endure so as to protect a person from an epidemic or cold, and in that way you will get a standard to be laid before a jury, or a judge without a jury, by which they might exercise their judgement as to what a reasonable time would be. It strikes me, I confess, that the true construction of this advertisement is that 100£ will be paid to anybody who uses this smoke ball three times daily for two weeks according to the printed directions, and who gets the influenza or cold or other diseases caused by taking cold within a reasonable time after so using it; and if that is the true construction, it is enough for the plaintiff.

I come now to the last point which I think requires attention—that is, the consideration. It has been argued that this is nudum pactum—that there is no consideration. We must apply to that argument the usual legal tests. Let us see whether there is advantage to the defendants. It is said that the use of the ball is no advantage to them, and that what benefits them is the sale; and the case is put that a lot of these balls might be stolen, and that it would be no advantage to the defendants if the thief or other people used them. The answer to that, I think, is as follows. It is quite obvious that in the view of the advertisers a use by the public of their remedy, if they can only get the public to have confidence enough to use it, will react and produce a sale which is directly beneficial to them. Therefore, the advertisers get out of the use an advantage which is enough to constitute a consideration.

But there is another view. Does not the person who acts upon this advertisement and accepts the offer put himself to some inconvenience at the request of the defendants? Is it nothing to use the ball three times daily for two weeks according to the directions at the request of the advertiser? Is that to go for nothing? It appears to me that there is a distinct inconvenience, not to say a detriment, to any person who so uses the smoke ball. I am of opinion, therefore, that there is ample consideration for the promise.

It appears to me, therefore, that the defendants must perform their promise, and, if they have been so unwary as to expose themselves to a great many actions, so much the worse for them.

QUESTIONS AND NOTES

1. Questions about the facts of this case

    1.1. The court dismissed "as not worth serious consideration" the argument that the advertisement was a bet. Did the Carbolic Smoke Ball

Company really think inhalation of its smoke ball would prevent the flu or was it betting that most users would not contract the flu anyway?

1.2. What's the difference between a promise and a "puff"?

1.3. The court in *Carlill* describes the Carbolic's advertisement as offering a *reward*. Is this a fair analogy? How does the advertisement differ from an offer of "$50 for anyone who returns my lost dog"? More on this advertisement/reward distinction below.

1.4. The court rejected the Carbolic Smoke Ball Company's argument that the offer was too vague to enforce on the basis that the promise was to give the reward to anyone contracting influenza within a *reasonable* time after using the smoke ball for two weeks as directed. Some lay people might suggest that this is an equally vague standard but, as you probably already know from your Torts class, for whatever reasons, lawyers are perfectly content with the "reasonable" answer. So just how long is a reasonable time?

2. Questions about the law

2.1. According to the court, Ms. Carlill's acceptance was effective when she performed the acts requested by the offer even though the Carbolic Smoke Ball Company had not been notified of this fact. Why should the rule on notice to the offeror be different when acceptance is by performance rather than promise?

2.2. Can this rule be reconciled with objective theory? Is there anything the offeror can do to alter this rule?

2.3. *See Restatement (Second) of Contracts* § 54. Are the *Restatement* rules regarding notice of acceptance by performance consistent with the holding in *Carlill*? If not, how do they differ?

2.4. In distinguishing the situation in *Carlill* from the typical advertisement case, Lord Justice Lindley construed the advertisement as offering a *reward* and noted that "advertisements offering rewards . . . are offers to anybody who performs the conditions named in the advertisement, and anybody who performs the condition accepts the offer." Justin Leonard tried to make the same argument in *Leonard v. Pepsi Co., supra*, at 25, but, in a portion of the opinion we edited out, Judge Wood rejected the argument noting that: "Because the alleged offer in this case was, at most, an advertisement to receive offers rather than an offer of reward, plaintiff cannot show that there was an offer made in the circumstances of this case." Do you agree that *Carlill* and *Leonard* are distinguishable on this basis?

2.5. Suppose you were able to get your hands on a Carbolic smoke ball today and snort (er, we mean inhale) it three times daily for two weeks and then, within a reasonable time thereafter, develop the flu. Could you collect the reward?

3. Notes

3.1. Assume another customer, Mortimer Markell (great, great grandfather of guess who) purchased a Carbolic smoke ball with no knowledge of the company's advertisement. After using the ball as directed for two weeks, Mortimer also contracted the flu. While at the doctor's office, he ran into Lilli Carlill and, upon striking up a conversation, the two discovered the similarity of their circumstances. Carlill told Mortimer that she planned to sue the Carbolic Smoke Ball Co. and he decided he would as well. Should Mortimer also prevail in his suit? *See Hawkeye Land Co. v. Iowa Power & Light Co.*, 497 N.W.2d 480 (Iowa App. 1993). Would it change your answer if Mortimer learned of the advertisement *after* he purchased the smoke ball but *before* he finished the two-week regime? *See Restatement (Second) of Contracts* § 51.

3.3. Under traditional analysis, an offeree must know of the offer before there can be mutual assent. Is this rule consistent with objective theory? Should it apply in a reward case? If Ponoroff posts a $50 reward for the return of his lost dog and Epstein does not learn of the reward until after he's found the dog, should Ponoroff be able to refuse payment of the $50? Hasn't Ponoroff gotten what he bargained for, regardless of what Epstein knew or didn't know? *See Glover v. Jewish War Veterans*, 68 A.2d 233 (D.C. 1949). What is the situation if, upon reading of the reward, Epstein calls Ponoroff and says, "I accept, I am now off to look for your dog"? If Epstein doesn't find the dog, is he liable to Ponoroff? How about if he gets distracted by a show on TV and never even goes out to look?

In *Carlill,* the offeree had fully performed what was requested by the offer and so the court found that the offeror was bound, notice notwithstanding. Suppose, however, the offeree has only begun performance when the offeror changes his mind and revokes the offer. Is the revocation too late? Is there a contract? If not, are both parties free to walk away without any further liability? Assume that Markell offers Epstein $1,000 to paint Markell's house. Right after Epstein starts painting, Ponoroff tells Markell that he will paint the house for only $600. Can Markell still revoke his offer to Epstein? Or, if Sharon Stone offers Epstein a job as a co-star in her next movie, can Epstein stop painting Markell's house without liability? Does the next case, involving a revocation of an offer to pay commission to a real estate agent, help you answer any of these questions? (Or do you just wish we'd stop asking so many questions!)

Marchiondo v. Scheck
Supreme Court Of New Mexico
78 N.M. 440, 432 P.2d 405 (1967)

WOOD, Judge

The issue is whether the offeror had a right to revoke his offer to enter a unilateral contract.

Defendant, in writing, offered to sell real estate to a specified prospective buyer and agreed to pay a percentage of the sales price as a commission to the broker. The offer fixed a six-day time limit for acceptance. Defendant, in writing, revoked the offer. The revocation was received by the broker on the morning of the sixth day. Later that day, the broker obtained the offeree's acceptance.

Plaintiff, the broker, claiming breach of contract, sued defendant for the commission stated in the offer. On the above facts, the trial court dismissed the complaint.

We are not concerned with the revocation of the offer as between the offeror and the prospective purchaser. With certain exceptions, the right of a broker to the agreed compensation, or damages measured thereby, is not defeated by the refusal of the principal to complete or consummate a transaction. * * *

Plaintiff's appeal concerns the revocation of his agency. As to that revocation, the issue between the offeror and his agent is not whether defendant had the power to revoke; rather, it is whether he had the right to revoke. * * *

When defendant made his offer to pay a commission upon sale of the property, he offered to enter a unilateral contract; the offer was for an act to be performed, a sale. * * *

Many courts hold that the principal has the right to revoke the broker's agency at any time before the broker has actually procured a purchaser. * * * The reason given is that until there is performance, the offeror has not received that contemplated by his offer, and there is no contract. Further, the offeror may never receive the requested performance because the offeree is not obligated to perform. Until the offeror receives the requested performance, no consideration has passed from the offeree to the offeror. Thus, until the performance is received, the offeror may withdraw the offer. * * *

Defendant asserts that the trial court was correct in applying this rule. However, plaintiff contends that the rule is not applicable where there has been part performance of the offer.

Hutchinson v. Dobson-Bainbridge Realty Co., [31 Tenn. App. 490 (1946)], states:

> "A greater number of courts, however, hold that part performance of the consideration may make such an offer irrevocable and that where the offeree or broker manifests his assent to the offer by entering upon performance and spending time and money in his efforts to perform, then the offer becomes irrevocable during the time stated and binding upon the principal according to its terms. * * *"

Defendant contends that the decisions giving effect to a part performance are distinguishable. He asserts that in these cases the offer was of an exclusive right to sell or of an exclusive agency. Because neither factor is present here, he asserts that the "part performance" decisions are not applicable.

Many of the decisions do seem to emphasize the exclusive aspects of the offer. * * *.

Defendant's offer did not specifically state that it was exclusive. * * * [However,] [i]t is not the exclusiveness of the offer that deprives the offeror of the right to revoke. It is the action taken by the offeree which deprives the offeror of that right. Until there is action by the offeree—a partial performance pursuant to the offer—the offeror may revoke even if his offer is of an exclusive agency or an exclusive right to sell. * * *

Once partial performance is begun pursuant to the offer made, a contract results. This contract has been termed a contract with conditions or an option contract. This terminology is illustrated as follows:

> "If an offer for a unilateral contract is made, and part of the consideration requested in the offer is given or tendered by the offeree in response thereto, the offeror is bound by a contract, the duty of immediate performance of which is conditional on the full consideration being given or tendered within the time stated in the offer, or, if no time is stated therein, within a reasonable time." Restatement of Contracts, § 45 (1932).

Restatement (Second) of Contracts, § 45, Tent. Draft No. 1, (approved 1964, Tent. Draft No. 2, p. vii) states:

> "(1) Where an offer invites an offeree to accept by rendering a performance and does not invite a promissory acceptance, an option contract is created when the offeree begins the invited performance or tenders part of it.
>
> "(2) The offeror's duty of performance under any option contract so created is conditional on completion or tender of the invited performance in accordance with the terms of the offer."

Restatement (Second) of Contracts, § 45, Tent. Draft No. 1, comment (g), says:

> "This Section frequently applies to agency arrangements, particularly offers made to real estate brokers. * * *"

See Restatement (Second) of Agency § 446, comment (b).

The reason for finding such a contract is stated in *Hutchinson v. Dobson-Bainbridge Realty Co.*, *supra*, as follows:

> "This rule avoids hardship to the offeree, and yet does not hold the offeror beyond the terms of his promise. It is true by such terms he was to be bound only if the requested act was done; but this implies that he will let it be done, that he will keep his offer open till the offeree who has begun can finish doing it. At least this is so where the doing of it will neces-

sarily require time and expense. In such a case it is but just to hold that the offeree's part performance furnishes the 'acceptance' and the 'consideration' for a binding subsidiary promise not to revoke the offer, or turns the offer into a presently binding contract conditional upon the offeree's full performance."

We hold that part performance by the offeree of an offer of a unilateral contract results in a contract with a condition. The condition is full performance by the offeree. Here, if plaintiff-offeree partially performed prior to receipt of defendant's revocation, such a contract was formed. Thereafter, upon performance being completed by plaintiff, upon defendant's failure to recognize the contract, liability for breach of contract would arise. Thus, defendant's right to revoke his offer depends upon whether plaintiff had partially performed before he received defendant's revocation. * * *

What constitutes partial performance will vary from case to case since what can be done toward performance is limited by what is authorized to be done. Whether plaintiff partially performed is a question of fact to be determined by the trial court.

The trial court denied plaintiff's requested finding concerning his partial performance. It did so on the theory that partial performance was not material. In this the trial court erred.

Because of the failure to find on the issue of partial performance, the case must be remanded to the trial court. * * *.

The cause is remanded for findings on the issue of plaintiff's partial performance of the offer prior to its revocation, and for further proceedings consistent with this opinion and the findings so made.

It is so ordered.

QUESTIONS

1. Questions about the facts of this case

   1.1. How many offers did the defendant make in this case?

   1.2. How, if at all, did the plaintiff perform?

1.3. Did the specified prospective buyer agree to buy the real property? Was that important?

1.4. Did the specified prospective buyer agree to buy the real property before the plaintiff received the defendant's revocation? Was that important?

2. Questions about the law

2.1. What does the court mean by the statement that, "part performance by the offeree of a unilateral contract results in a condition. The condition is full performance by the offeree"?

2.2. Is there any language that the defendant could have added to its offer to the plaintiff that would have eliminated the possibility of this litigation?

2.3. The New Mexico Supreme Court looked to what eventually became *Restatement (Second) of Contracts* § 45. Take a look at that section yourself. How can a real estate agent prove that she "begins the invited performance"? How can the real estate agent deal with the "performance/preparation" distinction of *comment f* to § 45 which provides: "What is begun or tendered must be part of the actual performance invited in order to preclude revocation under this Section. Beginning preparations, though they may be essential in carrying out the contract or accepting the offer is not enough"?

2.4. Assuming, on remand, that the trial court does find that the plaintiff partially performed before the defendant's attempted revocation, is there consideration for holding the defendant's offer irrevocable? If not, what is the basis for finding an enforceable option contract?

Problems on Acceptance by Promise, Performance and Part Performance

Consider how the following hypotheticals would be resolved both under classical principles of contract law and under the *Restatement (Second) of Contracts*:

1. Markell says to Ponoroff, "I'll pay you $20 if you wash and wax my car." Ponoroff says, "I accept." Has a contract been formed? If Ponoroff fails to take care of Markell's car is he in breach? How about if Ponoroff says nothing but begins washing Markell's car? *See Restatement (Second)* §§ 50(2) & 62.

2. Suppose Markell's offer is phrased, "I'll pay you $20 if you wash and wax my car, and what I want is the job done, not your promise." Ponoroff replies, "I accept." Is either party bound at this point? How about if Ponoroff goes out and buys some rags and a can of wax to do the job? What about when he actually begins the job? Suppose he's nearly finished, having put in over two hours on the job, and Markell walks up to him and says, "I revoke my offer." Will Ponoroff prevail in a suit for breach of contract? *See Restatement (Second)* § 45. If Markell does not revoke, and instead Ponoroff abandons the job without finishing, can Markell sue for breach?

3. Now suppose Markell's offer is phrased, "I'll pay you $20 if you will agree to wash and wax my car this weekend, but I want your promise." Ponoroff replies, "I accept." Is either party bound at this point? Suppose Ponoroff says nothing, but that weekend he shows up and begins working on Markell's car. Has a contract been formed? Suppose just prior to completing the job, Markell shows up and says, "I revoke my offer." Will Ponoroff prevail if he sues Markell for breach? How about if Markell says nothing until after Ponoroff has completed the job and then Markell revokes? *See Restatement (Second)* § 50(3).

4. Finally, suppose Markell makes the offer, "I'll pay you $20 to wash and wax my car," and then promptly heads off to Monaco to try to win enough money so that he can take a year off from teaching contracts. Ponoroff locates Markell's car and gives it a first class wash and wax. Two weeks later, Markell, who has lost all his money, e-mails Ponoroff from Monaco to tell him that he is withdrawing his offer. Ponoroff fires back a reply, "Too late, dude, I did the job two weeks ago. Did you forget *Carlill*? You owe me the money." Markell responds with the following message: "Spare me the 19th century case law from merry old England, Bud, go read § 54(2) of the *Restatement (Second) of Contracts*." Was there a contract here? Can Ponoroff recover his $20?

D. Acceptance by Silence or Inaction

Laredo National Bank v. Gordon
United States Court of Appeals, Fifth Circuit
61 F.2d 906 (1932)

BRYAN, Circuit Judge.

This is an action at law by an attorney Bernard Gordon, against his client, Laredo National Bank, to recover $12,500 as a fee agreed upon in the settlement of a suit which the attorney had brought for the bank against Abraham Rosenblum, Aaron Rosenblum, and the Abe Rosenblum Corporation. The suit against the Rosenblums was to recover $144,000 which it was alleged they and one Joseph Rosenblum had fraudulently procured from the bank by means of drafts to which were attached fictitious delivery orders falsely purporting to cover actual carload shipments of produce. Gordon brought the suit upon an agreement that he was to receive a contingent fee of 25 per cent. of the amount recovered. While the suit was pending, the bank and its local attorney entered into negotiations with the Rosenblums for a compromise settlement. During the continuance of those negotiations, and on March 4, 1930, the bank wired Gordon that, acting upon his suggestion, it would refuse to accept a proposition of settlement which the Rosenblums had made, but added "in case there should be a counter proposition from them which we may consider acceptable advise what are your minimum fees." On the same day Gordon replied by wire that he felt confident his fee could be adjusted reasonably in the light of prior arrangements and subsequent developments, but that he would welcome the bank's suggestion in regard to his fee. On March 10 the bank wired Gordon, stating that its proposition had not been accepted, but that "we must know immediately what will be your fees in the event we accept settlement offered us. Answer quick"; and Gordon replied, "Answering today's telegram twelve thousand five hundred dollars." Nothing further was said about fees pending negotiations for settlement, which continued until June 16, 1930, when the bank received in settlement of its claim against the Rosenblums about $50,000 in cash, securities of the estimated value of $94,000, and a note of Joseph Rosenblum for $66,000. On June 29 the local attorney for the bank, who lived at Laredo, Tex., addressed a letter to Gordon who lived in New York, advising that a settlement had been effected, directing dismissal of the suit which Gordon had brought in New York and which was still pending, and stating that the bank's president "will write you direct and take up the matter of your fee and its payment." On July 3, 1930, the bank's president wrote Gordon that the bank would pay a reasonable fee, but that the amount mentioned in his telegram of March 10 was beyond reason. Gordon testified that before he received this last-mentioned letter he had already dismissed the suit against the Rosenblums, in compliance with the directions of the bank's local attorney. At the close of the evidence in this case, both sides moved for a directed verdict; whereupon the trial court charged the jury to render a verdict in favor of Gordon for $12,500 with interest. After this charge was given, the bank undertook to withdraw its motion, and requested the court to submit to the jury the question whether it had accepted Gordon's offer contained in his telegram of March 10 to take $12,500 in settlement of his fee.

It is argued that the bank never became bound to pay the $12,500 fee, because it never replied to or accepted Gordon's offer to take that amount in settlement for his services. It is true that, generally speaking, an offeree has a right to make no reply to offers, and hence that his silence is not to be construed as an acceptance. But, where the relation between the parties is such that the offeror is justified in expecting a reply, or the offeree is under a duty to reply, the latter's silence will be regarded as acceptance. Under such circumstances, "one who keeps silent, knowing that his silence will be misinterpreted, should not be allowed to deny the natural interpretation of his conduct," etc. It was upon the bank's insistence that Gordon agreed to accept the fee he named in his telegram, in order that the bank might go ahead with its compromise settlement. It was not until after a settlement had been made, the suit against the Rosenblums had been dismissed, and Gordon had lost all opportunity of earning a larger contingent fee, that the bank made any objection or expressed any dissatisfaction with the amount of the fee Gordon had agreed to accept in the event of a compromise settlement. Its silence amounted to conduct which misled its attorney to his detriment, for the bank could not have failed to know that Gordon was acting in the belief that the fee which he had agreed to accept would be paid without question. Under the circumstances, the bank's silence was equivalent to its acceptance of and assent to Gordon's offer to forego his contingent fee and receive instead the lump sum payment which he named.

* * *

It is true, of course, that an attorney ought not to take advantage of his client, or be permitted to drive a hard bargain. But the evidence shows that Gordon thought a better settlement could be made with the Rosenblums, did not suggest giving up the trial of the case, was reluctant to accept the bank's suggestion of a compromise and its taking the case out of his hands, and expressed himself as perfectly willing to let the question of his fee be postponed until the case in which he was employed was disposed of. It was only when the bank insisted upon making its own settlement that he agreed to accept a fee which was less than he would have been entitled to receive if he had been paid the contingent fee originally agreed upon. So far as this record shows, his conduct was above reproach. The duty of fair dealing applies to the client as well as to the attorney. The record before us leaves no room for reasonable doubt that Gordon was justly entitled to the verdict which the court directed the jury to render in his favor.

The judgment is affirmed.

QUESTIONS AND NOTES

1. Questions about the facts of this case

   1.1. Is it just us, or did the Laredo National Bank get a pretty good settlement on its $144,000 case against the Rosenblums?

   1.2. The court states that Gordon thought a better settlement could be obtained and that it was only after the settlement had been arranged and he lost the opportunity for a larger contingency fee that the bank made any objection. But could Gordon really hold up a settlement that his client wanted because of the prospect of earning a larger fee?

2. Questions about the law

   2.1. What is the basis for the general rule that silence or inaction does not constitute an exception?

   2.2. *Restatement (Second) of Contracts* § 69 codifies the general rule that silence or inaction will ordinarily not be construed to signify assent, but there are three exceptions. Which exception would have applied in *Gordan*?

   2.3. Who are the exceptions in § 69 intended to benefit, the offeror or the offeree? Are these exceptions consistent with objective theory?

2.4. What is the relationship between circumstances where silence is considered an acceptance and an implied-in-fact contract?

3. Notes

3.1. Assume Broker represents a party looking to purchase new warehouse space. Broker is aware of what may be suitable space and shows it to his client, who expresses some interest. Thereupon, Broker sends Owner, with whom Broker has never dealt before, a letter stating that "if you are successful in selling this property to my client, I shall be entitled to a 5% commission at closing." Owner acknowledged receipt of the letter and began negotiations with Broker's client that ultimately culminated in a sale. When Broker demanded his 5% commission, Owner responded that an agreement regarding payment of such a commission was never consummated and, therefore, there is no liability for the commission. Broker claims that if Owner disagreed with Broker's request for the commission, Owner had a duty to repudiate the terms of Broker's letter. Assess the validity of these arguments. *Cf. Feist & Feist Realty Corp. v. Dockside Urban Renewal Corp.*, 255 N.J. Super. 100, 604 A.2d 653 (1992).

3.2. In the leading case of *Austin v. Burge*, 156 Mo. App. 286, 137 S.W. 618 (1911), the defendant's subscription for a newspaper expired, but the publisher continued to have it sent to him, even though the defendant ordered the paper stopped. When the publisher sued for the subscription price, the defendant argued that there was no contract. The court disagreed, observing that because the defendant had continued accepting and reading the paper, even after his order to stop delivery, the defendant had accepted the publisher's offer for the price of the paper. In light of this case, what should you do when a merchant continues to send you unordered goods through the mails? Does this open the door to abusive marketing practices? Are the rules of contract law adequate to address the abuse? If not, what should be done? *See United States v. Random Stationers, Inc.*, 1984 U.S. Dist. LEXIS 24709 (S.D. Fla. 1984) (applying a federal statute, 39 U.S.C. § 3009, adopted as part of the Postal Reorganization Act of 1970, making it an unfair trade practice in violation of § 5 of the Federal Trade Commission Act to bill a recipient for unsolicited merchandise and permitting such merchandise to be retained by the recipient as a gift).

E. Imperfect Acceptances

If Ponoroff offers to buy Epstein's car for $100 and Epstein replies, "I want $110," nobody would seriously regard Epstein's reply as an acceptance. Indeed, that reply would be treated as a *counteroffer* which is simultaneously an implied rejection of the original offer and a new offer over which Ponoroff now has the power of acceptance. But suppose Ponoroff answers, "I won't pay $110," and Epstein replies, "Ok, I'll take $100." Is there a contract? Consider that question in the context of the next case.

Introduction to *Egger v. Nesbit*

It's a little hard in *Egger v. Nesbit* to keep the parties straight without a scorecard, so we though we'd give you one to help make reading this case just a little less painful. Playing first base (and also the plaintiff in this case) is Fredolin Egger (sometimes referred to as "F. Egger") of Appleton City, Missouri. Fredolin purchased a certain 80-acre tract of land at a tax sale and subsequently sold the property to Mr. Larkin (who is not a party in this case). Playing second base (and, coincidentally, the defendant in this action) is Scot Nesbit of Washington, D.C. Mr. Nesbit held the patent title to the 80 acres of land which had been purchased and re-sold by Fredolin. At third base is John B. Egger, who is Fredolin's son (a Ken Griffey/Ken Griffey Jr. kind of thing), and who has agreed to serve as an intermediary of sorts between his father and Scot Nesbit in consummating the transaction at issue. J.B. Egger is also not a party to this suit. Now, who's on first?

Egger v. Nesbit

Supreme Court of Missouri
27 S.W. 385, 122 Mo. 667 (1894)

Burgess, J.

This is an action for specific performance of a contract of sale by defendant to plaintiff of 80 acres of land, to wit, E. 1/2 of the N. E. 1/4 of section 36, in township 38, range 28, in St. Clair county, Mo. Plaintiff bought the land at a sale of it for taxes, and subsequently sold it to one Larkin, who took possession of and improved it. The petition avers that defendant owns the patent title to the land, which he, for and in consideration of the sum of $400, to be paid to him by plaintiff, agreed and promised in writing to convey to him, plaintiff, and that he is ready and willing to pay said purchase money, here offers to do so, and prays that defendant be required to comply with the terms of his contract, and for all proper relief. The answer is a general denial. Defendant had acquired the patent title to the land, and plaintiff began negotiating with him for its purchase, and wrote to him in regard to the matter. To this letter defendant replied from Washington City, where he then resided, as follows:

> "Washington, D. C., Feb. 26, 1890. F. Egger, Esq., Appleton City, Mo.—Dear Sir: Your letter of December 30th was addressed to me at Osceola, Missouri, and, although I was in Osceola about that time, I received all my mail at Lowry City, and the letter laid at Osceola for some time, and when forwarded to me here went wrong in some way, and I only received it a short time ago. Your letter was a very kind one, under the circumstances, and I will try to act in the same spirit; and, although we are somewhat apart in our views of this matter, I hope we can adjust it now, and in good feeling. When I first purchased these titles, I assure you that I did not know that it would in any way bring me in conflict with you or your interests, as I told you that Mr. Larkin owned the other claim, and I did not know who he got it from. I bought the title from all the heirs, and paid in cash to them $200.00, and to agents, attorneys, and for recording, etc., about $60.00 or $70.00 more. This, at ten per cent. interest, would amount to about $400.00 at this time. I am willing to make a Q. C. deed either to you or to Larkin, pay the costs of the suit, and dismiss it for $400.00. I feel that this is a liberal offer, from the standpoint from which I view this case, which is about this: You purchased a tax title against a man who had died in 1855, and I think also the records show

> that it was sold in the name of Alexander Corder, when the correct name was Alexander Cowden, as is shown in the original patent, which I have. I hold deeds from all his legal heirs, which I think clearly gives me the title. I think you sold the land, many years ago, to Larkin, for $800.00. You have had the use of this money all these years on a tax title which only cost you a few dollars. I have laid out of my money for five years, and the amount named will only let me out whole, while you still have a small profit, and will be able to keep good faith with your purchaser, Mr. Larkin, and close the entire matter with all parties satisfied. The suit was only filed to save the statute of limitation, and was in no way intended to annoy you; but, if we are to settle it, please let me hear from you soon, as I think your court comes in March or April, and, like you, I don't want any law whatever between us. We are well. Yours, with respect, Scott Nesbit."

To this letter plaintiff made reply, March 4, 1890. Leaving out the formal parts and immaterial matter, the reply is as follows:

> "I will accept your proposition, with the understanding that you will deliver to me all the papers you have in reference to the land,—U. S. patent and other deeds. You may make Q. C. deed in blank, and send it, with the other papers, to J. B. Egger, and authorize him to insert either my name of Mr. Larkin's, whichever may be proper, and he will return the four hundred dollars to you as you may direct."

Plaintiff received no reply from the defendant to the above letter, and on March 14th again wrote to the defendant, as follows:

> "Scott Nesbit, Esq., Washington, D. C.—Dear Sir: On the 4th inst. I sent you a letter in reply to your letter of February 26, stating that I accept your offer in regard to the Alexander Cowden land, e. h. f. n. e. 1/4, sec. 36, town. 38, range 28, St. Clair county, and requested you to send Q. C. deed, name of party blank, and authorize J. B. Egger to insert either my name or Mr. Larkin's, as may be found proper. As no answer or deed from you is received yet, I would request you, if deed is not yet sent, to please make it complete, and insert my name, Fredolin Egger. John B. Egger will remit the amount, four hundred dollars, to you as stated in my former letter. I will perhaps be compelled to be away for some time, and wish to have this business settled before."

Both of the above letters from plaintiff to the defendant were deposited upon the dates they were written, respectively, sealed in envelopes, directed to Scott Nesbit, 1333 F Street N. W., Washington, D. C., in the United States post office at Appleton City, Mo., with the postage thereon fully prepaid. The address to which the above-named letters were sent was "Scott Nesbit, 1333 F Street N. W., Washington, D. C." On March 31, 1890, plaintiff caused to be sent to defendant to the same address as above the following dispatch:

> "F. Egger has deposited four hundred dollars, to be paid to you on receipt of certain deeds. John B. Egger, Cashier."

Plaintiff had then deposited in the First National Bank at Appleton City, Mo., the $400 to be paid to defendant upon the delivery of the deed to said land. Defendant did not receive the letter of March 4th, but did receive that of March 14th, and also the dispatch, which was sent to the same address. On May 1, 1890, defendant addressed a letter to John B. Egger, which is as follows:

> "Washington, D. C., May 1, 1890. John B. Egger, Esq., Appleton City, Mo.—Dear Sir: Some weeks ago (March 31st) I received a telegram from you saying that F. Egger had deposited four hundred dollars, subject to a receipt of a 'certain deed,' and about the same date a letter from your father, saying that he had addressed two letters to me, and asking if they had been received. I at once wrote to you that such letters had not been received, and asking their purport, and to what deed he had referred. I took it that it meant the Larkin-Cowden land, as way along, I think, in February last, I had written to him again, trying to adjust that cause before I had to take depositions, etc.; but, as I did not hear from him, concluded that he did not wish to settle, and made other arrangements. This was about the substance of my letter. As I have not heard from you, thought you had overlooked in some way. Please let me hear from you. All well and busy. Yours, truly, Scott Nesbit."

At the close of plaintiff's evidence the court found for defendant, dismissed the petition, and rendered judgment against plaintiff for costs. Plaintiff, after taking the usual course, prosecutes his appeal to this court.

It may be conceded that a contract may be made by letter or telegram, and when the offer is made by letter and is accepted by letter, although the letter accepting the offer never reaches the hand of the person making the offer, providing the acceptance is mailed in due time, postage prepaid, and directed to the proper address of the person making the offer, or, if accepted by telegram, the charges being prepaid, and directed as before stated, in regard to the acceptance by letter; the acceptance must be made within a reasonable time, no time being fixed, or before the offer is withdrawn. * * * But the acceptance must be unconditional, and in strict accordance with the proposition; that is, the mind of the person making the offer and of the one accepting it must meet in regard to the same subject-matter and terms of sale. * * * In *Bruner v. Wheaton,* 46 Mo. 363, the court says:

> "In order that an acceptance may be operative, it must be unequivocal, unconditional, and without variance of any sort between it and the proposal, and it must be communicated to the other party without unreasonable delay. To constitute a valid contract, there must be a mutual assent of the parties thereto, and they must assent to the same thing in the same sense. Therefore an absolute acceptance of a proposal, coupled with any qualification or condition, will not be regarded as a complete contract, because there at no time exists the requisite mutual assent to the same thing in the same sense. Any words manifesting an *aggregatio mentium* are sufficient to constitute a contract, but the mutual consent—the *aggregatio mentium*—cannot be attained without the assent of both parties."

Measured by the rule thus announced, defendant's [*sic*. Should be *plaintiff's*. Eds.] letter to plaintiff [*sic.* Should be *defendant's*. Eds.] of March 4, 1890, was not an acceptance of the proposition contained in defendant's letter to him of date February 26, 1890, for the reason that the acceptance was not unconditional, but with the understanding that plaintiff [*sic*. Should be *defendant*. Eds.] would deliver to him all the papers in reference to the land,—United States patents and other deeds,—about which there was nothing said in defendant's letter or proposition, thereby making a new proposition of his own, and imposing new burdens upon defendant, though light they may have been. As the conditions upon which the proposition was accepted materially differed from the original proposition, it amounted to the rejection of the offer. * * *

It is contended by plaintiff that, even if his letter of March 4, 1890, was no more than a conditional acceptance, yet his letter of March 14, 1890, written prior to any withdrawal of defendant's offer, was an unconditional acceptance of defendant's offer, and that thereby the offer was accepted, and the contract closed. Upon the other hand, the contention is that the plaintiff, having rejected the offer of defendant by his conditional acceptance, the offer was at an end, and could not be renewed by a subsequent acceptance of it by plaintiff. *Judd v. Day,* 50 Iowa, 247, it relied upon by plaintiff as sustaining his position, but in that case there was no conditional acceptance of the offer to purchase, and it was rightly held that the offer was a continuing one, unless otherwise specified or withdrawn. Mr. Parsons, in his work on Contracts (page 477, 7th Ed.), says: "The party making the offer may renew it; but the party receiving it cannot reply accepting with modifications, and, when these are rejected, again reply, accepting generally, and upon his acceptance claim the right of holding the other party to his first offer." So in *Baker v. Johnson Co.,* 37 Iowa, 186, it is held that a proposal to accept, or an acceptance of an offer upon different terms from those contained in the offer amounts to a rejection of it. * * *

In the case in hand, plaintiff directed the deed to be made out in blank, to be sent to the bank, and, upon receipt thereof, the money to be paid over to defendant. This was not an acceptance of the offer to sell as made by defendant. The burden of proof rested upon the plaintiff to show by clear and satisfactory evidence the contract which he seeks to have specifically enforced—that is, that his acceptance of the offer of defendant was unequivocal, unconditional, and without any variance at any sort between it and the proposal—and, as he failed in this, he was not entitled to the relief which he sought. The judgment is affirmed. All of this division concur.

QUESTIONS AND NOTES

1. Questions about the facts of this case

   1.1. Why did Fredolin Egger want the patent title to this land in the first place? After all, he had already sold the property to Larkin. While we're at it, just what is a patent title? If you studied *Pennoyer v. Neff* in Civil Procedure you might recall that case involved a patent title, too. If not, you better haul out *Black's Law Dictionary.*

   1.2. How important do you suppose it was to F. Egger that Nesbit would deliver to him all papers related to the land? Should it matter?

2. Questions about the law

2.1. In Section 3, we noted that when an offeree *expressly* rejects an offer the offer is terminated and may not be revived unless the offeror elects to renew it. In this case, by responding on March 4 to the offer with a form of acceptance that altered the terms of the original offer, the court suggests that the offeree, F. Egger has *implicitly* rejected the offer. What is the legal effect of an implied rejection?

2.2. When was F. Egger's March 4 letter effective, on receipt or on dispatch? After that letter became effective, who had the power of acceptance?

2.3. If F. Egger's March 4 letter never reached Nesbit, why couldn't Egger's March 14 letter be construed as an acceptance?

2.4. What is the effect of a counteroffer when the original offer is an irrevocable offer? In other words, suppose on February 1, in exchange for $100, Markell granted Epstein a 60-day option to acquire certain real property owned by Markell for $150,000. Epstein pays the $100 at the time the option is granted. On March 1, Epstein calls Markell and offers to give him $145,000 for the property. Markell refuses. Ten days later Markell contacts Epstein to tell him that he has decided to exercise the option and buy the property for $150,000. Markell, however, citing *Egger,* contends that it is too late. Does Epstein have a claim for breach against Markell? *See Humble Oil & Refining Co. v. Westside Investment Corp.,* 428 S.W.2d 92 (Tex. 1968) and *Restatement (Second) of Contracts* § 37. How, if at all, does it affect your answer if, in the March 1 conversation, Epstein explicitly told Markell that he was simply not interested in the property at the $150,000 price?

3. Notes

3.1. *Egger* illustrates the common law "mirror image" rule, which derives from the first principle that the offeror is sovereign. Specifically, that the offeror is not to be required to deal other than on the terms she specified in her offer. Thus, the mirror image rule holds that an acceptance must be an unconditional assent on the terms of the offer. Any variation, request or condition in the acceptance, a so-called "imperfect acceptance," renders it ineffective to form a contract.

However, what if the reason that the purported acceptance varies or adds to the terms of the offer is that the offeree simply makes a mistake in fashioning her reply, which she is quick to rectify upon having it pointed out to her? In *Minneapolis & St. Louis Railway Co. v. Columbia Rolling-Mill Co.,* 119 U.S. 149 (1886), the defendant offered iron rails at $54 per gross ton for quantities of between 2,000 and 5,000 tons. The plaintiff responded by ordering 1,200 tons at the quoted price. When the defendant replied that it was impossible to book the order at that price because it was below the minimum quantity, the plaintiff entered an order for 2,000 tons, but the defendant refused to deliver, denying the existence of a contract. What result on plaintiff's claim for breach?

3.2. *Restatement (Second) of Contracts* §§ 59–61 attempt to draw a distinction between a truly conditional acceptance, which operates as a counteroffer, and an acceptance with suggestions or inquiries, which is still sufficient to form a contract. Is this a break with the common law mirror image rule? Read those sections and decide whether there is mutual assent in either of these situations. Epstein says to Markell, "I'll sell you my car for $3,000." Markell replies, "I accept; will you take a check?" How about if Markell replies, "I accept, but you fix the brakes?"

Just like the rule that the *manner* of acceptance must abide by the terms of the offer (recall *La Salle National Bank, supra,* at 100), the mirror image rule, which focuses on the *substance* of the acceptance, can work some harsh and unexpectedly restrictive results, both with respect to the aim of protecting the interests of the offeror and in enforcing an arrangement with respect to which the parties indeed intended to be bound. For example, suppose in *Egger,* after receiving F. Egger's March 14th letter, Scott Nesbit considered that the parties had a deal, regarding the duty to deliver the documentation pertaining to his title as a mere formality. However, before having any contact with Egger, Nesbit learned that the value of his patent title was about to increase significantly in value. Because of the operation of the mirror image rule, he could claim no contract existed and, effectively, walk on a deal even though there truly had been an agreement reached by the parties on all of the essential terms of the transaction.

The problem is compounded in an era when so much business is done on the basis of an exchange of standard printed forms between buyer and seller containing lots of detailed and technical language, typically prepared by the parties' lawyers, which neither party may be reading very carefully or capable of understanding. Under the mirror image rule, any divergence in the fine print of these forms prevents formation of a contract on the documents. Nevertheless, if the parties have commenced performance before a dispute occurs or a problem arises, clearly there is a contract of some type, but what are its terms if we can't rely on the documents? To address both this issue and the problem of the offeree being able to manipulatively use the mirror image rule to renege on a deal, the drafters of the U.C.C. came up with § 2-207 applicable in contracts involving the sale of goods. That provision has been subjected to considerable criticism as flawed in its design and unnecessarily cumbersome in it application. As you read the next two cases, see if you agree with those critics.

Dorton v. Collins & Aikman Corporation
United States Court of Appeals, Sixth Circuit
453 F.2d 1161 (1972)

CELEBREZZE, Circuit Judge.

This is an appeal from the District Court's denial of Defendant-Appellant's motion for a stay pending arbitration, pursuant to Section 3 of the United States Arbitration Act of 1925, 9 U.S.C. § 3. The suit arose after a series of over 55 transactions during 1968, 1969, and 1970 in which Plaintiffs-Appellees [hereinafter The Carpet Mart], carpet retailers in Kingsport, Tennessee, purchased carpets from Defendant-Appellant [hereinafter Collins & Aikman], incorporated under the laws of the State of Delaware, with its principal place of business in New York, New York, and owner of a carpet manufacturing plant [formerly the Painter Carpet Mills, Inc.] located in Dalton, Georgia. The Carpet Mart originally brought this action in a Tennessee state trial court, seeking compensatory and punitive damages in the amount of $450,000 from Collins & Aikman for the latter's alleged fraud, deceit, and misrepresentation in the sale of what were supposedly carpets manufactured from 100% Kodel polyester fiber. The Carpet Mart maintains that in May, 1970, in response to a customer complaint, it learned that not all of the carpets were manufactured from 100% Kodel polyester fiber but rather some were composed of a cheaper and inferior carpet fiber. After the cause was removed to the District Court on the basis of diversity of citizenship, Collins & Aikman moved for a stay pending arbitration, asserting that The Carpet Mart was bound to an arbitration agreement which appeared on the reverse side of Collins & Aikman's printed sales acknowledgment forms. Holding that there existed no binding arbitration agreement between the parties, the District Court denied the stay. For the reasons set forth below, we remand the case to the District Court for further findings.

* * *

The primary question before us on appeal is whether the District Court, in denying Collins & Aikman's motion for a stay pending arbitration, erred in holding that The Carpet Mart was not bound by the arbitration agreement appearing on the back of Collins & Aikman's acknowledgment forms. In reviewing the District Court's determination, we must look closely at the procedures which were followed in the sales transactions which gave rise to the present dispute over the arbitration agreement.

In each of the more than 55 transactions, one of the partners in The Carpet Mart, or, on some occasions, Collins & Aikman's visiting salesman, telephoned Collins & Aikman's order department in Dalton, Georgia, and ordered certain quantities of carpets listed in Collins & Aikman's catalogue. There is some dispute as to what, if any, agreements were reached through the telephone calls and through the visits by Collins & Aikman's salesman. After each oral order was placed, the price, if any, quoted by the buyer was checked against Collins & Aikman's price list, and the credit department was consulted to determine if The Carpet Mart had paid for all previous shipments. After it was found that everything was in order, Collins & Aikman's order department typed the information concerning the particular order on one of its printed acknowledgment forms. Each acknowledgment form bore one of three legends: "Acknowledgment," "Customer Acknowledgment," or "Sales Contract." The following provision was printed on the face of the forms bearing the "Acknowledgment" legend:

> "The acceptance of your order is subject to all of the terms and conditions on the face and reverse side hereof, including arbitration, all of which are accepted by buyer; it supersedes buyer's order form, if any. It shall become a contract either (a) when signed and delivered by buyer to seller and accepted in writing by seller, or (b) at Seller's option, when buyer shall have given to seller specification of assortments, delivery

> dates, shipping instructions, or instructions to bill and hold as to all or any part of the merchandise herein described, or when buyer has received delivery of the whole or any part thereof, or when buyer has otherwise assented to the terms and conditions hereof."

Similarly, on the face of the forms bearing the "Customer Acknowledgment" or "Sales Contract" legends the following provision appeared:

> "This order is given subject to all of the terms and conditions on the face and reverse side hereof, including the provisions for arbitration and the exclusion of warranties, all of which are accepted by Buyer, supersede Buyer's order form, if any, and constitute the entire contract between Buyer and Seller. This order shall become a contract as to the entire quantity specified either (a) when signed and delivered by Buyer to Seller and accepted in writing by Seller or (b) when Buyer has received and retained this order for ten days without objection, or (c) when Buyer has accepted delivery of any part of the merchandise specified herein or has furnished to Seller specifications or assortments, delivery dates, shipping instructions, or instructions to bill and hold, or when Buyer has otherwise indicated acceptance of the terms hereof."

The small print on the reverse side of the forms provided, among other things, that all claims arising out of the contract would be submitted to arbitration in New York City. Each acknowledgment form was signed by an employee of Collins & Aikman's order department and mailed to The Carpet Mart on the day the telephone order was received or, at the latest, on the following day. The carpets were thereafter shipped to The Carpet Mart, with the interval between the mailing of the acknowledgment form and shipment of the carpets varying from a brief interval to a period of several weeks or months. Absent a delay in the mails, however, The Carpet Mart always received the acknowledgment forms prior to receiving the carpets. In all cases The Carpet Mart took delivery of and paid for the carpets without objecting to any terms contained in the acknowledgment form.

In holding that no binding arbitration agreement was created between the parties through the transactions above, the District Court relied on * * * [UCC § 2-207], * * *

The District Court found that Subsection 2-207(3) controlled the instant case, quoting the following passage from 1 W. Hawkland, A Transactional Guide to the Uniform Commercial Code § 1.090303, at 19–20 (1964):

> "If the seller . . . ships the goods and the buyer accepts them, a contract is formed under subsection (3). The terms of this contract are those on which the purchase order and acknowledgment agree, and the additional terms needed for a contract are to be found throughout the U.C.C. . . . [T]he U.C.C. does not impose an arbitration term on the parties where their contract is silent on the matter. Hence, a conflict between an arbitration and an [sic] no-arbitration clause would result in the noarbitration clause becoming effective."

Under this authority alone the District Court concluded that the arbitration clause on the back of Collins & Aikman's sales acknowledgment had not become a binding term in the 50-odd transactions with The Carpet Mart.

In reviewing this determination by the District Court, we are aware of the problems which courts have had in interpreting Section 2-207. This section of the UCC has been described as a "murky bit of prose," Southwest Engineering Co. v. Martin Tractor Co., 205 Kan. 684, 694, 473 P.2d 18, 25 (1970), as "not too happily drafted," Roto-Lith Ltd. v. F. P. Bartlett & Co., 297 F.2d 497, 500 (1st Cir. 1962), and as "one of the most important, subtle, and difficult in the entire Code, and well it may be said that the product as it finally reads is not altogether satisfactory." Duesenberg & King, Sales and Bulk Transfers under the Uniform Commercial Code, (Vol. 3, Bender's Uniform Commercial Code Service) § 3.03, at 3-12 (1969). Despite the lack of clarity in its language, Section 2-207 manifests definite objectives which are significant in the present case.

As Official Comment No. 1 indicates, UCC § 2-207 was intended to apply to two situations:

> "The one is where an agreement has been reached either orally or by informal correspondence between the parties and is followed by one or both of the parties sending formal acknowledgments or memoranda embodying the terms so far as agreed upon and adding terms not discussed. The other situation is one in which a wire or letter expressed and intended as the closing or confirmation of an agreement adds further minor suggestions or proposals such as 'ship by Tuesday,' 'rush,' 'ship draft against bill of lading inspection allowed,' or the like." * * *

Although Comment No. 1 is itself somewhat ambiguous, it is clear that Section 2-207, and specifically Subsection 2-207(1), was intended to alter the "ribbon matching" or "mirror" rule of common law, under which the terms of an acceptance or confirmation were required to be identical to the terms of the offer or oral agreement, respectively. * * * Under the common law, an acceptance or a confirmation which contained terms additional to or different from those of the offer or oral agreement constituted a rejection of the offer or agreement and thus became a counter-offer. The terms of the counter-offer were said to have been accepted by the original offeror when he proceeded to perform under the contract without objecting to the counter-offer. Thus, a buyer was deemed to have accepted the seller's counter-offer if he took receipt of the goods and paid for them without objection.

Under Section 2-207 the result is different. This section of the Code recognizes that in current commercial transactions, the terms of the offer and those of the acceptance will seldom be identical. Rather, under the current "battle of the forms," each party typically has a printed form drafted by his attorney and containing as many terms as could be envisioned to favor that party in his sales transactions. Whereas under common law the disparity between the fineprint terms in the parties' forms would have prevented the consummation of a contract when these forms are exchanged, Section 2-207 recognizes that in many, but not all, cases the parties do not impart such significance to the terms on the printed forms. * * * Subsection 2-207(1) therefore provides that "[a] definite and seasonable expression of acceptance or a written confirmation . . . operates as an acceptance even though it states terms additional to or different from those offered or agreed upon, unless acceptance is expressly made conditional on assent to the additional or different terms." Thus, under Subsection (1), a contract is recognized notwithstanding the fact that an acceptance or confirmation contains terms additional to or different from those of the offer or prior agreement, provided that the offeree's intent to accept the offer is definitely expressed, see Sections 2-204 and 2-206, and provided that the offeree's acceptance is not expressly conditioned on the offeror's assent to the additional or different terms. When a contract is recognized under Subsection (1), the additional terms are treated as "proposals for addition to the contract" under Subsection (2), which contains special provisions under which such additional terms are deemed to have been accepted when the transaction is between merchants. Conversely, when no contract is recognized under Subsection 2-207(1)—either because no definite expression of acceptance exists or, more specifically, because the offeree's acceptance is expressly conditioned on the offeror's assent to the additional or different terms—the entire transaction aborts at this point. If, however, the subsequent conduct of the parties—particularly, performance by both parties under what they apparently believe to be a contract—recognizes the existence of a contract, under Subsection 2-207(3) such conduct by both parties is sufficient to establish a contract, notwithstanding the fact that no contract would have been recognized on the basis of their writings alone. Subsection 2-207(3) further provides how the terms of contracts recognized thereunder shall be determined.

With the above analysis and purposes of Section 2-207 in mind, we turn to their application in the present case. We initially observe that the affidavits and the acknowledgment forms themselves raise the question of whether Collins & Aikman's forms constituted acceptances or confirmations under Section 2-207. The language of some of the acknowledgment forms ("The acceptance of your order is subject to . . .") and the affidavit of Mr. William T. Hester, Collins & Aikman's marketing operations manager, suggest that the forms were the only acceptances issued in response to The Carpet Mart's oral offers. However, in his affidavit Mr. J. A. Castle, a partner in The Carpet Mart, asserted that when he personally called Collins & Aikman to order carpets, someone from the latter's order department would agree to sell the requested carpets, or, alternatively, when Collins & Aikman's visiting salesman took the order, he would agree to the sale, on some occasions after he had used The Carpet Mart's telephone to call Collins & Aikman's order department. Absent the District Court's determination of whether Collins & Aikman's acknowledgment forms were acceptances or, alternatively, confirmations of prior oral agreements, we will consider the application of section 2-207 to both situations for the guidance of the District Court on remand.

Viewing Collins & Aikman's acknowledgment forms as acceptances under Subsection 2-207(1), we are initially faced with the question of whether the arbitration provision in Collins & Aikman's acknowledgment forms were in fact "additional to or different from" the terms of The Carpet Mart's oral offers. In the typical case under Section 2-207, there exist both a written purchase order and a written acknowledgment, and this determination can be readily made by comparing the two forms. In the present case, where the only written forms were Collins & Aikman's sales acknowledgments, we believe that such a comparison must be made between the oral offers and the written acceptances. Although the District Court apparently assumed that The Carpet Mart's oral orders did not include in their terms the arbitration provision which appeared in Collins & Aikman's acknowledgment forms, we believe that a specific finding on this point will be required on remand.

Assuming, for purposes of analysis, that the arbitration provision was an addition to the terms of The Carpet Mart's oral offers, we must next determine whether or not Collins & Aikman's acceptances were "expressly made conditional on assent to the additional . . . terms" therein, within the proviso of Subsection 2-207(1). As set forth in full above, the provision appearing on the face of Collins & Aikman's acknowledgment forms stated that the acceptances (or orders) were "subject to all of the terms and conditions on the face and reverse side hereof, including arbitration, all of which are accepted by buyer." The provision on the "Acknowledgment" forms further stated that Collins & Aikman's terms would become the basis of the contract between the parties * * *.

Although Collins & Aikman's use of the words "subject to" suggests that the acceptances were conditional to some extent, we do not believe the acceptances were "expressly made conditional on [the buyer's] assent to the additional or different terms," as specifically required under the Subsection 2-207(1) proviso. In order to fall within this proviso, it is not enough that an acceptance is expressly conditional on additional or different terms; rather, an acceptance must be expressly conditional on the offeror's assent to those terms. Viewing the Subsection (1) proviso within the context of the rest of that Subsection and within the policies of Section 2-207 itself, we believe that it was intended to apply only to an acceptance which clearly reveals that the offeree is unwilling to proceed with the transaction unless he is assured of the offeror's assent to the additional or different terms therein. * * * That the acceptance is predicated on the offeror's assent must be "directly and distinctly stated or expressed rather than implied or left to inference." * * *

Although the UCC does not provide a definition of "assent," it is significant that Collins & Aikman's printed acknowledgment forms specified at least seven types of action or inaction on the part of the buyer which—sometimes at Collins & Aikman's option—would be deemed to bind the buyer to the terms therein. These ranged from the buyer's signing and delivering the acknowledgment to the seller—which indeed could have been recognized as the buyer's assent to Collins & Aikman's terms—to the buyer's retention of the acknowledgment for ten days without objection—which could never have been recognized as the buyer's assent to the additional or different terms where acceptance is expressly conditional on that assent.

To recognize Collins & Aikman's acceptances as "expressly conditional on [the buyer's] assent to the additional . . . terms" therein, within the proviso of Subsection 2-207(1), would thus require us to ignore the specific language of that provision. Such an interpretation is not justified in view of the fact that Subsection 2-207(1) is clearly designed to give legal recognition to many contracts where the variance between the offer and acceptance would have precluded such recognition at common law.

Because Collins & Aikman's acceptances were not expressly conditional on the buyer's assent to the additional terms within the proviso of Subsection 2-207(1), a contract is recognized under Subsection (1), and the additional terms are treated as "proposals" for addition to the contract under Subsection 2-207(2). Since both Collins & Aikman and The Carpet Mart are clearly "merchants" as that term is defined in Subsection 2-104(1), the arbitration provision will be deemed to have been accepted by The Carpet Mart under Subsection 2-207(2) unless it materially altered the terms of The Carpet Mart's oral offers. * * * [UCC § 2-207(2) (b)]. We believe that the question of whether the arbitration provision materially altered the oral offer under Subsection 2-207(2) (b) is one which can be resolved only by the District Court on further findings of fact in the present case. If the arbitration provision did in fact materially alter The Carpet Mart's offer, it could not become a part of the contract "unless expressly agreed to" by The Carpet Mart. * * * [UCC § 2-207], Official Comment No. 3.

We therefore conclude that if on remand the District Court finds that Collins & Aikman's acknowledgments were in fact acceptances and that the arbitration provision was additional to the terms of The Carpet Mart's oral orders, contracts will be recognized under Subsection 2-207(1). The arbitration clause will then be viewed as a "proposal" under Subsection 2-207(2) which will be deemed to have been accepted by The Carpet Mart unless it materially altered the oral offers.

If the District Court finds that Collins & Aikman's acknowledgment forms were not acceptances but rather were confirmations of prior oral agreements between the parties, an application of Section 2-207 similar to that above will be required. Subsection 2-207(1) will require an initial determination of whether the arbitration provision in the confirmations was "additional to or different from" the terms orally agreed upon. Assuming that the District Court finds that the arbitration provision was not a term of the oral agreements between the parties, the arbitration clause will be treated as a "proposal" for addition to the contract under Subsection 2-207(2), as was the case when Collins & Aikman's acknowledgments were viewed as acceptances above. The provision for arbitration will be deemed to have been accepted by The Carpet Mart unless the District Court finds that it materially altered the prior oral agreements, in which case The Carpet Mart could not become bound thereby absent an express agreement to that effect.

* * *

For the reasons set forth above, the case is remanded to the District Court for further findings consistent with this opinion.

QUESTIONS AND NOTE

1. Questions about the facts of this case

   1.1. U.C.C. § 2-207 is often called the "battle of the forms" provision. Did *Dorton* involve a battle of *forms*?

   1.2. In *Dorton,* when were the contracts for the purchase of carpeting formed? Were these contracts oral or written? When did the district court think the contracts were formed?

   1.3. Why did The Carpet Mart accept and pay for the carpet shipments if it objected to the arbitration provisions contained in the acknowledgements, which were admittedly received prior to delivery of each shipment?

2. Questions about the law

   2.1. How would the *Dorton* case have been decided under the common law mirror image rule? Does U.C.C. § 2-207 change the result?

   2.2. In the classic battle of the forms scenario, the buyer's purchase order and the seller's acknowledgement don't match, but the goods are nevertheless shipped by the seller and accepted by the buyer. Section 2-207 was designed to eliminate the unearned "last-shot" advantage that the offeree/seller would enjoy under the common law mirror image rule, *i.e.*, acknowledgment is a counteroffer which buyer accepts by paying for the goods. Did § 2-207 accomplish this objective in *Dorton*?

   2.3. If the some of the contracts were formed during the telephone conversations between The Carpet Mart and Collins & Aikman, does the court's opinion suggest that § 2-207 can be used to alter the terms of an existing agreement? If so, is this a proper interpretation of the statute? *See* U.C.C. § 2-207, Official Comment 1. As lawyer for the buyer, what steps could you take to prevent this possibility?

2.4. In *Dorton,* the court found that Collins & Aikman's acceptances were *not* expressly conditional on The Carpet Mart's assent to the additional terms. Thus, a contract was deemed to exist under § 2-207(1) and the only issue is, what were its terms? If the acceptances had been made expressly conditional on the offeror's assent to such additional terms, could The Carpet Mart's acceptance of and payment for the goods be recognized as assent?

2.5. Ultimately, what difference would it make under § 2-207 if, on remand, the district court determined that the Collins & Aikman acknowledgements were confirmations of prior oral agreements rather than acceptances?

2.6. How did the district court and the Sixth Circuit's § 2-207 analyses in *Dorton* differ? Did it affect the result?

3. Note

Section 2-207(1) makes an "imperfect acceptance" effective as an acceptance rather than as a counteroffer, provided that it constitutes a "definite and seasonable expression of acceptance" but one which is not the mirror image of the offer because it contains terms additional to or different from those specified in the offer. There are, however, a couple of points about the scope of § 2-207 that you need to be aware of. First, § 2-207(1) does not create a contract in every instance where there are additional or different terms. Remember the hypothetical we started this section with? Ponoroff offered to buy Epstein's car for $100 and Epstein replied that he wanted $110. Would that reply operate as an acceptance under § 2-207(1)? Certainly not, because the parties are still negotiating; they have not reached agreement on all of the bargained-for points of the transaction. Therefore, § 2-207 does not apply. Secondly, even when the reply would otherwise operate as an acceptance under § 2-207(1), the offeree can prevent its application by expressly making his assent conditional on the offeror's assent to the additional or different terms contained in the reply. This is because of the proviso in the last part of § 2-207(1). In *Dorton,* however, the court stated, "In order to fall within this proviso, it is not enough that an acceptance is expressly conditional on additional or different terms; rather, an acceptance must be expressly conditional on the offeror's assent to those terms." What does that mean? Do you agree with that interpretation of the language of the statute? How would you draft a conditional acceptance that would satisfy the court in *Dorton*? Assuming you are able to do so, what is the effect of the conditional acceptance?

Introduction to *Klocek v. Gateway, Inc.*

Let's go back to the first case we read in the Introduction, *Hill v. Gateway 2000, Inc.* Another argument made by the Hills in that case, the discussion of which we omitted from the reprinted version, was that the arbitration clause contained inside the box was a proposal for an additional term under § 2-207(2). The Hills continued that since they were not merchants and had not assented to the additional term, it could not have become part of their contract with Gateway. Here's what Judge Easterbrook had to say about that: "[W]hen there is only one form, § 2-207 is irrelevant." 105 F.3d at 1150. Is that a fair reading of the statute or did the court give inadequate consideration to the Hills' argument? Here's what another court had to say on the matter.

Klocek v. Gateway, Inc.
United States District Court for the District of Kansas
104 F. Supp. 2d 1332 (2000)

MEMORANDUM AND ORDER

William S. Klocek brings suit against Gateway, Inc. * * * on claims arising from purchases of a Gateway computer . * * * This matter comes before the Court on the Motion to Dismiss which Gateway filed November 22, 1999 . * * * For reasons stated below, the Court overrules Gateway's motion to dismiss * * * .

A. Gateway's Motion to Dismiss

Plaintiff brings. . . claims against Gateway, alleging that it induced him . . . to purchase [a] computer[] and special support package[] by making false promises of technical support. Individually, plaintiff also claims breach of contract and breach of warranty, in that Gateway breached certain warranties that its computer would be compatible with standard peripherals and standard internet services.

Gateway asserts that plaintiff must arbitrate his claims under Gateway's Standard Terms and Conditions Agreement ("Standard Terms"). Whenever it sells a computer, Gateway includes a copy of the Standard Terms in the box which contains the computer battery power cables and instruction manuals. At the top of the first page, the Standard Terms include the following notice:

> NOTE TO THE CUSTOMER:
>
> This document contains Gateway 2000's Standard Terms and Conditions. By keeping your Gateway 2000 computer system beyond five (5) days after the date of delivery, you accept these Terms and Conditions.

The notice is in emphasized type and is located inside a printed box which sets it apart from other provisions of the document. The Standard Terms are four pages long and contain 16 numbered paragraphs. Paragraph 10 provides the following arbitration clause:

> DISPUTE RESOLUTION. Any dispute or controversy arising out of or relating to this Agreement or its interpretation shall be settled exclusively and finally by arbitration. The arbitration shall be conducted in accordance with the Rules of Conciliation and Arbitration of the International Chamber of Commerce. The arbitration shall be conducted in Chicago, Illinois, U.S.A. before a sole arbitrator. Any award rendered in any such arbitration proceeding shall be final and binding on each of the parties, and judgment may be entered thereon in a court of competent jurisdiction.[1]

---

[1]Gateway states that after it sold plaintiff's computer, it mailed all existing customers in the United States a copy of its quarterly magazine, which contained notice of a change in the arbitration policy set forth in the Standard Terms. The new arbitration policy afforded customers the option of arbitrating before the International Chamber of Commerce ("ICC"), the American Arbitration Association ("AAA"), or the National Arbitration Forum ("NAF") in Chicago, Illinois, or any other location agreed upon by the parties. Plaintiff denies receiv-

* * *

Gateway bears an initial summary-judgment-like burden of establishing that it is entitled to arbitration. * * * Thus, Gateway must present evidence sufficient to demonstrate the existence of an enforceable agreement to arbitrate. * * * If Gateway makes such a showing, the burden shifts to plaintiff to submit evidence demonstrating a genuine issue for trial. * * * In this case, Gateway fails to present evidence establishing the most basic facts regarding the transaction. The gaping holes in the evidentiary record preclude the Court from determining what state law controls the formation of the contract in this case and, consequently, prevent the Court from agreeing that Gateway's motion is well taken.

Before granting a stay or dismissing a case pending arbitration, the Court must determine that the parties have a written agreement to arbitrate. See 9 U.S.C. §§ 3 and 4; * * *. When deciding whether the parties have agreed to arbitrate, the Court applies ordinary state law principles that govern the formation of contracts. * * * The existence of an arbitration agreement "is simply a matter of contract between the parties; [arbitration] is a way to resolve those disputes–but only those disputes–that the parties have agreed to submit to arbitration." * * * If the parties dispute making an arbitration agreement, a jury trial on the existence of an agreement is warranted if the record reveals genuine issues of material fact regarding the parties' agreement.

* * *

[The court at this point engaged in a discussion of which state law to apply: Missouri, where the plaintiff lived, or Kansas, where plaintiff claimed he purchased the computer at a Gateway store. Ultimately, the court concluded that it did not matter because the issue was one of first impression in both jurisdictions.]

Regardless whether plaintiff purchased the computer in person or placed an order and received shipment of the computer, the parties agree that plaintiff paid for and received a computer from Gateway. This conduct clearly demonstrates a contract for the sale of a computer. * * * Thus the issue is whether the contract of sale includes the Standard Terms as part of the agreement.

---

ing notice of the amended arbitration policy. Neither party explains why–if the arbitration agreement was an enforceable contract–Gateway was entitled to unilaterally amend it by sending a magazine to computer customers.

State courts in Kansas and Missouri apparently have not decided whether terms received with a product become part of the parties' agreement. Authority from other courts is split. *Compare Step-Saver* [*Data Sys., Inc. v. Wyse Tech.*], 939 F.2d 91 (printed terms on computer software package not part of agreement); *Arizona Retail Sys., Inc. v. Software Link, Inc.*, 831 F. Supp. 759 (D. Ariz. 1993) (license agreement shipped with computer software not part of agreement); and *U.S. Surgical Corp. v. Orris, Inc.*, 5 F. Supp. 2d 1201 (D. Kan. 1998) (single use restriction on product package not binding agreement); *with Hill v. Gateway 2000, Inc.*, 105 F.3d 1147 (7th Cir.), cert. denied, 522 U.S. 808 (1997) (arbitration provision shipped with computer binding on buyer); *ProCD, Inc. v. Zeidenberg*, 86 F.3d 1447 (7th Cir. 1996) (shrinkwrap license binding on buyer);[6] and *M.A. Mortenson Co., Inc. v. Timberline Software Corp.*, 140 Wn.2d 568, 998 P.2d 305 (Wash. 2000) (following *Hill* and *ProCD* on license agreement supplied with software).[7] It appears that at least in part, the cases turn on whether the court finds that the parties formed their contract *before* or *after* the vendor communicated its terms to the purchaser. *Compare Step-Saver*, 939 F.2d at 98 (parties' conduct in shipping, receiving and paying for product demonstrates existence of contract; box top license constitutes proposal for additional terms under § 2-207 which requires express agreement by purchaser); *Arizona Retail*, 831 F. Supp. at 765 (vendor entered into contract by agreeing to ship goods, or at latest by shipping goods to buyer; license agreement constitutes proposal to modify agreement under § 2-209 which requires express assent by buyer); and *Orris*, 5 F. Supp. 2d at 1206 (sales contract concluded when vendor received consumer orders; single-use language on product's label was proposed modification under § 2-209 which requires

[6]The term "shrinkwrap license" gets its name from retail software packages that are covered in plastic or cellophane "shrinkwrap" and contain licenses that purport to become effective as soon as the customer tears the wrapping from the package. *See ProCD*, 86 F.3d at 1449.

[7]The *Mortenson* court also found support for its holding in the proposed Uniform Computer Information Transactions Act ("UCITA") (formerly known as proposed UCC Article 2B) (text located at www.law.upenn.edu/library/ulc/ucita/UCITA99.htm), which the National Conference of Commissioners on Uniform State Laws approved and recommended for enactment by the states in July 1999. *See Mortenson*, 998 P.2d at 310 n.6, 313 n.10. The proposed UCITA, however, would not apply to the Court's analysis in this case. The UCITA applies to computer information transactions, which are defined as agreements "to create, modify, transfer, or license computer information or informational rights in computer information." UCITA, §§ 102(11) and 103. In transactions involving the sale of computers, such as our case, the UCITA applies only to the computer programs and copies, not to the sale of the computer itself. *See* UCITA § 103(c)(2).

express assent by purchaser); *with ProCD*, 86 F.3d at 1452 (under § 2-204 vendor, as master of offer, may propose limitations on kind of conduct that constitutes acceptance; § 2-207 does not apply in case with only one form); *Hill*, 105 F.3d at 1148–49 (same); and *Mortenson*, 998 P.2d at 311–314 (where vendor and purchaser utilized license agreement in prior course of dealing, shrinkwrap license agreement constituted issue of contract formation under § 2-204, not contract alteration under § 2-207).

Gateway urges the Court to follow the Seventh Circuit decision in *Hill*. That case involved the shipment of a Gateway computer with terms similar to the Standard Terms in this case, except that Gateway gave the customer 30 days–instead of 5 days–to return the computer. In enforcing the arbitration clause, the Seventh Circuit relied on its decision in *ProCD*, where it enforced a software license which was contained inside a product box. *See Hill*, 105 F.3d at 1148–50. In *ProCD*, the Seventh Circuit noted that the exchange of money frequently precedes the communication of detailed terms in a commercial transaction. *See ProCD*, 86 F.3d at 1451. Citing UCC § 2-204, the court reasoned that by including the license with the software, the vendor proposed a contract that the buyer could accept by using the software after having an opportunity to read the license.[8] *ProCD*, 86 F.3d at 1452. Specifically, the court stated:

> A vendor, as master of the offer, may invite acceptance by conduct, and may propose limitations on the kind of conduct that constitutes acceptance. A buyer may accept by performing the acts the vendor proposes to treat as acceptance.

ProCD, 86 F.3d at 1452. The *Hill* court followed the *ProCD* analysis, noting that "practical considerations support allowing vendors to enclose the full legal terms with their products." *Hill*, 105 F.3d at 1149.[9]

---

[8]Section 2-204 provides: "A contract for sale of goods may be made in any manner sufficient to show agreement, including conduct by both parties which recognizes the existence of such contract." [U.C.C. § 2-204].

[9]Legal commentators have criticized the reasoning of the Seventh Circuit in this regard. *See, e.g.,* Jean R. Sternlight, Gateway Widens Doorway to Imposing Unfair Binding Arbitration on Consumers, Fla. Bar J., Nov. 1997, at 8, 10-12 (outcome in Gateway is questionable on federal statutory, common law and constitutional grounds and as a matter of contract law and is unwise as a matter of policy because it unreasonably shifts to consumers search cost of ascertaining existence of arbitration clause and return cost to avoid such clause); Thomas J. McCarthy et al., Survey: Uniform Commercial Code, 53 Bus. Law. 1461, 1465-66 (Seventh Circuit finding that UCC § 2-207 did not apply is inconsistent with official comment);

The Court is not persuaded that Kansas or Missouri courts would follow the Seventh Circuit reasoning in *Hill* and *ProCD*. In each case the Seventh Circuit concluded without support that UCC § 2-207 was irrelevant because the cases involved only one written form. *See ProCD,* 86 F.3d at 1452 (citing no authority); *Hill*, 105 F.3d at 1150 (citing *ProCD*). This conclusion is not supported by the statute or by Kansas or Missouri law. Disputes under § 2-207 often arise in the context of a "battle of forms," * * * but nothing in its language precludes application in a case which involves only one form. The statute provides:

> Additional terms in acceptance or confirmation.
>
> (1) A definite and seasonable expression of acceptance or a written confirmation which is sent within a reasonable time operates as an acceptance even though it states terms additional to or different from those offered or agreed upon, unless acceptance is expressly made conditional on assent to the additional or different terms.
>
> (2) The additional terms are to be construed as proposals for addition to the contract [if the contract is not between merchants]. . . .

[U.C.C. § 2-207.] By its terms, § 2-207 applies to an acceptance or written confirmation. It states nothing which requires another form before the provision becomes effective. In fact, the official comment to the section specifically provides that §§ 2-207(1) and (2) apply "where an agreement has been reached orally ... and is followed by one or both of the parties sending formal memoranda embodying the terms so far agreed and adding terms not discussed." Official Comment 1 of UCC § 2-207. Kansas and Missouri

---

Batya Goodman, Honey, I Shrink-Wrapped the Consumer: the Shrinkwrap Agreement as an Adhesion Contract, 21 Cardozo L. Rev. 319, 344-352 (Seventh Circuit failed to consider principles of adhesion contracts); Jeremy Senderowicz, Consumer Arbitration and Freedom of Contract: A Proposal to Facilitate Consumers' Informed Consent to Arbitration Clauses in Form Contracts, 32 Colum. J.L. & Soc. Probs. 275, 296-299 (judiciary (in multiple decisions, including Hill) has ignored issue of consumer consent to an arbitration clause). Nonetheless, several courts have followed the Seventh Circuit decisions in *Hill* and *ProCD*. *See, e.g., Mortenson*, 2000 WL 550845 (license agreement supplied with software); Rinaldi v. Iomega Corp., 1999 Del. Super. LEXIS 563, 1999 WL 1442014, Case No. 98C-09-064-RRC (Del. Sept. 3, 1999) (warranty disclaimer included inside computer Zip drive packaging); Westendorf v. Gateway 2000, Inc., 2000 Del. Ch. LEXIS 54, 2000 WL 307369, Case No. 16913 (Del. Ch. March 16, 2000) (arbitration provision shipped with computer); Brower v. Gateway 2000, Inc., 246 A.D.2d 246, 676 N.Y.S.2d 569 (N.Y. App. Div. 1998) (same); Levy v. Gateway 2000, Inc., 1997 WL 823611, 33 U.C.C. Rep. Serv. 2d (Callaghan) 1060 (N.Y. Sup. Ct. August 12, 1997) (same).

courts have followed this analysis. *See Southwest Engineering Co. v. Martin Tractor Co.*, 205 Kan. 684, 695, 473 P.2d 18, 26 (1970) (stating in dicta that § 2-207 applies where open offer is accepted by expression of acceptance in writing or where oral agreement is later confirmed in writing); *Central Bag Co. v. W. Scott and Co.*, 647 S.W.2d 828, 830 (Mo. App. 1983) (§§ 2-207(1) and (2) govern cases where one or both parties send written confirmation after oral contract). Thus, the Court concludes that Kansas and Missouri courts would apply § 2-207 to the facts in this case. * * *

In addition, the Seventh Circuit provided no explanation for its conclusion that "the vendor is the master of the offer." *See ProCD*, 86 F.3d at 1452 (citing nothing in support of proposition); *Hill*, 105 F.3d at 1149 (citing *ProCD*). In typical consumer transactions, the purchaser is the offeror, and the vendor is the offeree. *See Brown Mach., Div. of John Brown, Inc. v. Hercules, Inc.*, 770 S.W.2d 416, 419 (Mo. App. 1989) (as general rule orders are considered offers to purchase); *Rich Prods. Corp. v. Kemutec Inc.*, 66 F. Supp. 2d 937, 956 (E.D. Wis. 1999) (generally price quotation is invitation to make offer and purchase order is offer). While it is possible for the vendor to be the offeror, see *Brown Machine*, 770 S.W.2d at 419 (price quote can amount to offer if it reasonably appears from quote that assent to quote is all that is needed to ripen offer into contract), Gateway provides no factual evidence which would support such a finding in this case. The Court therefore assumes for purposes of the motion to dismiss that plaintiff offered to purchase the computer (either in person or through catalog order) and that Gateway accepted plaintiff's offer (either by completing the sales transaction in person or by agreeing to ship and/or shipping the computer to plaintiff).[11] *Accord Arizona Retail*, 831 F. Supp. at 765 (vendor entered into contract by agreeing to ship goods, or at latest, by shipping goods).

Under § 2-207, the Standard Terms constitute either an expression of acceptance or written confirmation. As an expression of acceptance, the Standard Terms would constitute a counter-offer only if Gateway expressly made its acceptance conditional on plaintiff's assent to the additional or different terms. [U.C.C. § 2-207(1).] "The conditional nature of the acceptance must be clearly expressed in a manner sufficient to notify the offeror that the offeree is unwilling to proceed with the transaction unless the additional or

[11]UCC § 2-206(b) provides that "an order or other offer to buy goods for prompt or current shipment shall be construed as inviting acceptance either by a prompt promise to ship or by the prompt or current shipment ..." The official comment states that "either shipment or a prompt promise to ship is made a proper means of acceptance of an offer looking to current shipment." UCC § 2-206, Official Comment 2.

different terms are included in the contract." *Brown Machine*, 770 S.W.2d at 420.[12] Gateway provides no evidence that at the time of the sales transaction, it informed plaintiff that the transaction was conditioned on plaintiff's acceptance of the Standard Terms. Moreover, the mere fact that Gateway shipped the goods with the terms attached did not communicate to plaintiff any unwillingness to proceed without plaintiff's agreement to the Standard Terms. *See, e.g., Arizona Retail,* 831 F. Supp. at 765 (conditional acceptance analysis rarely appropriate where contract formed by performance but goods arrive with conditions attached); *Lighton Indus., Inc. v. Callier Steel Pipe & Tube, Inc.*, 1991 WL 18413, *6, Case No. 89-C-8235 (N.D.Ill. Feb. 6, 1991) (applying Missouri law) (preprinted forms insufficient to notify offeror of conditional nature of acceptance, particularly where form arrives after delivery of goods).

Because plaintiff is not a merchant, additional or different terms contained in the Standard Terms did not become part of the parties' agreement unless plaintiff expressly agreed to them. *See* [U.C.C. §-2-207] Comment 2 (if either party is not a merchant, additional terms are proposals for addition to the contract that do not become part of the contract unless the original offeror expressly agrees). Gateway argues that plaintiff demonstrated ac-

---

[12]Courts are split on the standard for a conditional acceptance under § 2-207. *See Daitom* [*v. Pennwalt Corp.*], 741 F.2d 1569, 1576 (finding that Pennsylvania would most likely adopt "better" view that offeree must explicitly communicate unwillingness to proceed with transaction unless additional terms in response are accepted by offeror). On one extreme of the spectrum, courts hold that the offeree's response stating a materially different term solely to the disadvantage of the offeror constitutes a conditional acceptance. *See Daitom*, 741 F.2d at 1569 (citing *Roto-Lith. Ltd v. F.P. Bartlett & Co.*, 297 F.2d 497 (1st Cir. 1962)). At the other end of the spectrum courts hold that the conditional nature of the acceptance should be so clearly expressed in a manner sufficient to notify the offeror that the offeree is unwilling to proceed without the additional or different terms. *See Daitom*, 741 F.2d at 1569 (citing *Dorton v. Collins & Aikman Corp.*, 453 F.2d 1161 (6th Cir. 1972)). The middle approach requires that the response predicate acceptance on clarification, addition or modification. *See Daitom*, 741 F.2d at 1569 (citing *Construction Aggregates Corp. v. Hewitt-Robins, Inc.*, 404 F.2d 505 (7th Cir. 1968)). The First Circuit has since overruled its decision in *Roto-Lith, see Ionics, Inc. v. Elmwood Sensors, Inc.*, 110 F.3d 184, and the Court finds that neither Kansas nor Missouri would apply the standard set forth therein. *See Boese-Hilburn Co. v. Dean Machinery Co.*, 616 S.W.2d 520, (Mo. App. 1981) (rejecting *Roto-Lith* standard); *Owens-Corning Fiberglas Corp. v. Sonic Dev. Corp.*, 546 F. Supp. 533, 538 (D. Kan. 1982) (acceptance is not counteroffer under Kansas law unless it is made conditional on assent to additional or different terms (citing *Roto-Lith* as comparison)); *Daitom*, 741 F.2d at 1569 (finding that *Dorton* is "better" view). Because Gateway does not satisfy the standard for conditional acceptance under either of the remaining standards (*Dorton* or *Construction Aggregates*), the Court does not decide which of the remaining two standards would apply in Kansas and/or Missouri.

ceptance of the arbitration provision by keeping the computer more than five days after the date of delivery. Although the Standard Terms purport to work that result, Gateway has not presented evidence that plaintiff expressly agreed to those Standard Terms. Gateway states only that it enclosed the Standard Terms inside the computer box for plaintiff to read afterwards. It provides no evidence that it informed plaintiff of the five-day review-and-return period as a condition of the sales transaction, or that the parties contemplated additional terms to the agreement.[14] * * * The Court finds that the act of keeping the computer past five days was not sufficient to demonstrate that plaintiff expressly agreed to the Standard Terms. *Accord Brown Machine*, 770 S.W.2d at 421 (express assent cannot be presumed by silence or mere failure to object). Thus, because Gateway has not provided evidence sufficient to support a finding under Kansas or Missouri law that plaintiff agreed to the arbitration provision contained in Gateway's Standard Terms, the Court overrules Gateway's motion to dismiss.

* * *

IT IS THEREFORE ORDERED that the Motion to Dismiss . . . which defendant Gateway filed November 22, 1999 be and hereby is **OVERRULED**. * * * .

QUESTIONS AND NOTES

1. Questions about the facts of this case

   1.1. How did Klocek buy his computer? Was it by mail order, as in *Hill*, or at a physical "Gateway Country" store? Does it matter?

   1.2. What are the differences between the arbitration clause in *Klocek* and the arbitration clause in *Hill*, *supra*, at 5? Do they matter?

   1.3. Below is Gateway's current arbitration language. Is it different? Does it matter?

---

[14]The Court is mindful of the practical considerations which are involved in commercial transactions, but it is not unreasonable for a vendor to clearly communicate to a buyer–at the time of sale–either the complete terms of the sale or the fact that the vendor will propose additional terms as a condition of sale, if that be the case.

> 9. DISPUTE RESOLUTION. You agree that any Dispute between You and Gateway will be resolved exclusively and finally by arbitration administered by the National Arbitration Forum (NAF) and conducted under its rules, except as otherwise provided below. The arbitration will be conducted before a single arbitrator, and will be limited solely to the Dispute between You and Gateway. The arbitration shall be held at any reasonable location near your residence by submission of documents, by telephone, online or in person. Any decision rendered in such arbitration proceedings will be final and binding on each of the parties, and judgment may be entered thereon in any court of competent jurisdiction. Should either party bring a Dispute in a forum other than NAF, the arbitrator may award the other party its reasonable costs and expenses, including attorneys' fees, incurred in staying or dismissing such other proceedings or in otherwise enforcing compliance with this dispute resolution provision. You understand that You would have had a right to litigate disputes through a court, and that You have expressly and knowingly waived that right and agreed to resolve any Disputes through binding arbitration. This arbitration agreement is made pursuant to a transaction involving interstate commerce, and shall be governed by the Federal Arbitration Act, 9 U.S.C. Section 1, et seq. For the purposes of this section, the term "Dispute" means any dispute, controversy, or claim arising out of or relating to (i) this Agreement, its interpretation, or the breach, termination, applicability or validity thereof, or (ii) the purchase or use of any product, accessory, service or otherwise from Gateway; the term "Gateway" means Gateway, Inc, its subsidiaries, affiliates, directors, officers, employees, beneficiaries, agents or assigns; the term "You" means you the original purchaser, your agents, beneficiaries, or heirs.
>
> Information may be obtained from the NAF on line at www.arbforum.com, by calling 800-474-2371 or writing to P.O. Box 50191, Minneapolis, MN, 55405.
>
> http://www.gateway.com/help/support/8505295.shtml (visited September 15, 2000).

2. Questions about the law

2.1. If Gateway had told Klocek that before he could have the computer, he would "have to agree to our terms," would that have changed the result? How about if Gateway had made Klocek separately sign the additional terms or recorded his assent to them over the telephone?

2.2. Under § 2-207(1), does it matter who is the offeror and who is the offeree?

2.3. In footnote 12 of the case, the court describes the split in the caselaw on what constitutes a "conditional acceptance" for purposes of § 2-207(1). *Dorton*, of course, is cited for the strict view while other courts take a much more expansive view of when an acceptance should be regarded as conditional. Given the purposes of and policies behind § 2-207, which view do you think has the better of it?

2.4. If you were Gateway's counsel, what would you tell Gateway's sales division that they should do to ensure that in the future purchasers of Gateway computers would be bound to arbitrate their disputes against the company?

3. Notes

3.1. One might have expected that Gateway would take the district court's decision refusing to dismiss Klocek's complaint and compel arbitration up to the Sixth Circuit. As it happened, Gateway had a better idea. Shortly after this opinion was rendered, Gateway filed a motion to dismiss for lack of subject matter jurisdiction alleging that plaintiff had not satisfied his burden of establishing the requisite amount in controversy to invoke the court's diversity jurisdiction. Klocek conceded the point and the case was dismissed. *See* 2000 WL 1372886 (D. Kan., Sept. 6, 2000). Left lingering is the precedential value of this decision in light of the subsequent dismissal. Because the court in the order of dismissal did not vacate its earlier opinion, we think *Klocek* continues to have some persuasive force as a source of law and, of course, the subsequent dismissal does not in any way lessen its instructional value, which is important because in our view this court got it right—even if it ended up not really counting.

3.2. The drafters of Revised Article 2 have made several proposals to rework and clarify § 2-207. The most recent proposal is aimed at providing a mechanism that (1) assures a party that it will not unexpectedly find itself subject to terms to which that party did not expressly agree, and (2) confers greater discretion on the court to include or exclude certain terms. Revised U.C.C. § 2-207 provides:

> If (i) conduct by both parties recognizes the existence of a contract although their records do not otherwise establish a contract, (ii) a contract is formed by offer and acceptance, or (iii) a contract formed in any manner is confirmed by a record which contains terms additional to or different from those in the contract being confirmed, the terms of the contract . . . are: (1) terms that appear in the records of both parties, (2) terms, whether in a record or not, to which both parties agree, and (3) terms supplied or incorporated under any provision of this Act.

Is this an improvement over the present version of § 2-207? What specific problems does it solve?

3.3. The approach of the *U.N. Convention on Contracts for the International Sales of Goods* to the "battle of the forms" problem is contained in Article 19, which provides:

> (1) A reply to an offer which purports to be an acceptance but contains additions, limitations or other modifications is a rejection of the offer and constitutes a counter-offer
>
> (2) However, a reply to an offer which purports to be an acceptance but contains additional or different terms which do not materially alter the terms of the offer constitutes an acceptance unless the offeror, without undue delay, objects orally to the discrepancy or dispatches a notice to that effect. If he does not so object, the terms of the contract are the terms of the offer with the modifications contained in the acceptance.
>
> (3) Additional or different terms relating, among other things, to the price, payment, quality, or quantity of the goods, place and time of delivery, extent of one party's liability to the other or the settlement of disputes are considered to alter the terms of the offer materially.

How would *Dorton* and *Klocek* have been decided under this provision?

Problems on U.C.C. § 2-207

1. Assume in *Dorton* that The Carpet Mart's offers to purchase the carpet had been in the form of written purchase orders containing an explicit provision to the effect that any disputes arising between the parties would be resolved by arbitration. Assume further that the acknowledgment forms from Collins & Aikman contained an express provision to the effect that disputes will *not* be resolved by arbitration. When a disagreement concerning the quality of the carpet breaks out, how should the court go about determining whether there is an obligation to submit the matter to binding arbitration? Based on the caselaw thus far, there are at least three possibilities for dealing with "different" terms. Can you figure out what they are? *See* J. WHITE & R. SUMMERS, UNIFORM COMMERCIAL CODE § 1-3 (4th ed. 1995). *See also Northrop Corp. v. Litronic Industries*, 29 F.3d 1173 (7th Cir. 1994).

2. Many § 2-207 cases involve disputes over warranties. In order to understand these issues it's important for you first to understand a few things about the U.C.C. Article 2 warranty scheme, a topic we take up in much greater depth in Chapter 3. In particular, § 2-314 provides that in every contract for the sale of goods in which the seller is a merchant (i.e., someone in the business of selling goods of that kind) there is an implied warranty of *merchantability*. The implied warranty of merchantability is an assurance that the goods are fit for the ordinary purposes for which such goods are used. Thus, if Epstein were to buy a lawnmower from Sears that didn't cut grass very well, there would probably be a breach of this warranty. However, if Epstein, having grown up in the South where it doesn't snow much, naively purchased a lawn mower to blow snow off of his driveway, there would be no breach of the implied warranty of merchantability even though the lawnmower didn't do a very good job on clearing the driveway. Finally, you need to be aware that § 2-316 allows the seller to exclude any and all warranties from the contract of sale by making an effective *disclaimer* of warranties. Ok, now on to the problem.

   Assume Ponoroff sends a purchase order for widgets that says nothing about warranties. Markell responds with an acknowledgment that matches all of the terms of the purchase order with respect to price, quantity, shipment terms, etc., but also contains a provision that says: *"Markell hereby disclaims all warranties with respect to these widgets, including the warranty of merchantability. This acknowledgment, if issued in response to an offer, shall only constitute an acceptance of such offer subject to the express condition that Ponoroff assent to any terms herein which vary, add to, or conflict with such offer."* Ponoroff never assents to the disclaimer, but when the goods are shipped Ponoroff accepts and pays for them. Later, it turns out that the widgets are defective. Ponoroff sues for breach of the implied warranty of merchantability. Markell moves to dismiss, pointing to the disclaimer in the acknowledgment form. How would this case be decided under the mirror image rule? Does § 2-207 change the result?

SECTION 6: COMPLETING THE AGREEMENT

Introduction

Sometimes the parties will have manifested an assent to be bound but, because of haste, lack of sophistication, or carelessness, they will have failed to express the terms of their understanding clearly or in sufficient detail to provide an adequate basis for a remedy should one party fail to perform. In these circumstances enforcement may not be possible. *Restatement (Second) of Contracts* § 33 provides that:

> *Even though a manifestation of intention is intended to be understood as an offer, it cannot be accepted so as to form a contract unless the terms of the contract are reasonably certain.*

Analytically, *indefiniteness* can be viewed as a *defense* to liability rather than as an aspect of contract formation. However, it is equally appropriate to conceptualize the requirement of definiteness as an aspect of the bargaining process that must be satisfied, no less than mutual assent, in order for a contract to arise. The purpose of contract enforcement is, as we shall to see in Chapter 5, to protect the promisee's *expectation* in the event of breach; that is, to put the non-breaching party in as good a position as performance would have. If the parties have not expressed their agreement with sufficient clarity or completeness to permit the court to fashion an appropriate remedy, than an essential component of contract formation is missing.

As a practical matter, it is impossible for the parties' agreement to speak to every aspect of their relationship. Unquestionably, the requirement of definiteness means something less than specific agreement down to the finest minutiae. The real question we address in this section then is as follows: when the parties have intended to make a contract but have failed to express their mutual obligations with perfect clarity, how far will and should the court go in resolving ambiguities and supplying missing terms in order to provide a remedy for nonperformance? Moreover, because the failure to complete the agreement is sometimes inadvertent and sometimes intentional, our examination of this area is broken into two parts: the first dealing with circumstances where the parties have failed in their agreement to express their intention clearly or completely and the second where the parties have deliberately left a term open intending to reach later agreement.

A. Indefiniteness and Open Terms

Varney v. Ditmars

Court of Appeals of New York

217 N.Y. 223, 111 N.E. 822 (1916)

Chase, J.

This is an action brought for an alleged wrongful discharge of an employee. The defendant is an architect employing engineers, draftsmen and other assistants. The plaintiff is an architect and draftsman. In October, 1910, he applied to the defendant for employment and when asked what wages he wanted, replied that he would start for $40 per week. He was employed at $35 per week. A short time thereafter he informed the defendant that he had another position offered to him and the defendant said that if he would remain with him and help him through the work in his office he thought he could offer him a better future than anybody else. He continued in the employ of the defendant and became acquainted with a designer in the office and said designer and the plaintiff from time to time prior to the 1st of February, 1911, talked with the defendant about the work in his office.

On that day by arrangement the two remained with the defendant after the regular office hours and the defendant said: "I am going to give you $5 more a week; if you boys will go on and continue the way you have been and get me out of this trouble and get these jobs started that were in the office three years, on the first of next January I will close my books and give you a fair share of my profits. That was the result of the conversation. That was all of that conversation." The plaintiff was given charge of the drafting. Thereafter suggestions were made by the plaintiff and said designer about discharging many of the defendant's employees and employing new men and such suggestions were carried out and the two worked in the defendant's office over time and many Sundays and holidays. At least one piece of work that the defendant said had been in his office for three years was completed. The plaintiff on his cross-examination told the story of the employment of himself and said designer as follows: 'And he says at that time 'I am going to give you $5 more a week starting this week.' This was about Thursday. He says 'You boys go on and continue the work you are doing and the first of January next year I will close my books and give you a fair share of my profits.' Those were his exact words."

Thereafter the plaintiff was paid $40 a week. On November 6, 1911, the night before the general election in this state, the defendant requested that all of his employees that could do so, should work on election day. The plaintiff told the defendant that he wanted to remain at home to attend an election in the village where he lived. About four o'clock in the afternoon of election day he was taken ill and remained at his house ill until a time that as nearly as can be stated from the evidence was subsequent to December 1, 1911. On Saturday, November 11, the defendant caused to be delivered to the plaintiff a letter in which he said:

> "I am sending you herewith your pay for one day's work of seven hours, performed on Monday, the 6th inst. On Monday night, I made it my special duty to inform you that the office would be open all day Election Day and that I expected you and all the men to report for work. Much to my surprise and indignation, on Tuesday you made no appearance and all the men remained away, in obedience of your instructions to them of the previous evening. An act of this kind I consider one of extreme disloyalty and insubordination and I therefore am obliged to dispense with your services."

After the plaintiff had recovered from his illness and was able to do so he went to the defendant's office (the date does not appear) and told him that he was ready, willing and able to continue his services under the agreement. The defendant denied that he had any agreement with him and refused to permit him to continue in his service. Thereafter and prior to January 1, 1912, the plaintiff received for special work about $50.

The plaintiff seeks to recover in this action for services from November 7, 1911, to December 31, 1911, inclusive, at $40 per week and for a fair and reasonable percentage of the net profits of the defendant's business from February 1, 1911, to January 1, 1912, and demands judgment for $1,680.

At the trial he was the only witness sworn as to the alleged contract and at the close of his case the complaint was dismissed.

The statement alleged to have been made by the defendant about giving the plaintiff and said designer a fair share of his profits is vague, indefinite and uncertain and the amount cannot be computed from anything that was said by the parties or by reference to any document, paper or other transaction. The minds of the parties never met upon any particular share of the defendant's profits to be given the employees or upon any plan by which such share could be computed or determined. The contract so far as it related to the special promise or inducement was never consummated. It was left subject to the will of the defendant or for further negotiation. It is urged that the defendant by the use of the word "fair" in referring to a share of his profits, was as certain and definite as people are in the purchase and sale of a chattel when the price is not expressly agreed upon, and that if the agreement in question is declared to be too indefinite and uncertain to be enforced a similar conclusion must be reached in every case where a chattel is sold without expressly fixing the price therefor.

The question whether the words "fair" and "reasonable" have a definite and enforceable meaning when used in business transactions is dependent upon the intention of the parties in the use of such words and upon the subject-matter to which they refer. In cases of merchandising and in the purchase and sale of chattels the parties may use the words "fair and reasonable value" as synonymous with "market value." A promise to pay the fair market value of goods may be inferred from what is expressly agreed by the parties. The fair, reasonable or market value of goods can be shown by direct testimony of those competent to give such testimony. The competency to speak grows out of experience and knowledge. The testimony of such witnesses does not rest upon conjecture. The opinion of this court in *United Press v. N. Y. Press Co.*, (164 N. Y. 406) was not intended to assert that a contract of sale is unenforceable unless the price is expressly mentioned and determined.

In the case of a contract for the sale of goods or for hire without a fixed price or consideration being named it will be presumed that a reasonable price or consideration is intended and the person who enters into such a contract for goods or service is liable therefor as on an implied contract. Such contracts are common, and when there is nothing therein to limit or prevent an implication as to the price, they are, so far as the terms of the contract are concerned, binding obligations.

The contract in question, so far as it relates to a share of the defendant's profits, is not only uncertain but it is necessarily affected by so many other facts that are in themselves indefinite and uncertain that the intention of the parties is pure conjecture. A fair share of the defendant's profits may be any amount from a nominal sum to a material part according to the particular views of the person whose guess is considered. Such an executory contract must rest for performance upon the honor and good faith of the parties making it. The courts cannot aid parties in such a case when they are unable or unwilling to agree upon the terms of their own proposed contract.

It is elementary in the law that, for the validity of a contract, the promise, or the agreement, of the parties to it must be certain and explicit and that their full intention may be ascertained to a reasonable degree of certainty. Their agreement must be neither vague nor indefinite, and, if thus defective, parol proof cannot be resorted to. * * *

The courts in this state, in reliance upon and approval of the rule as stated in the *United Press* case, have decided many cases involving the same rule. Thus, in *Mackintosh v. Thompson,* (58 App. Div. 25), and again in *Mackintosh v. Kimball,* (101 App. Div. 494), the plaintiff sought to recover compensation in addition to a stated salary which he had received and which additional amount rested upon a claim by him that while he was employed by the defendants he informed them that he intended to leave their employ unless he was given an increase in salary, and that one of the defendants said to him that they would make it worth his while if he would stay on, and would increase his salary, and that his idea was to give him an interest in the profits on certain buildings that they were then erecting. The plaintiff further alleges that he asked what would be the amount of the increase and was told, "You can depend upon me; I will see that you get a satisfactory amount." The court held that the arrangement was too indefinite to form the basis of any obligation on the part of the defendants.

In *Bluemner v. Garvin,* (120 App. Div. 29), the plaintiff and defendant were architects, and the plaintiff alleged that he drew plans for a public building in accordance with a contract held by the defendant and pursuant to a special agreement that if the plans were accepted the defendant would give him a fair share of the commissions to be received by him. The court held that a good cause of action was stated on quantum meruit, but that the contract was too vague and indefinite to be enforced.

* * *

The rule stated from the *United Press* case does not prevent a recovery upon quantum meruit in case one party to an alleged contract has performed in reliance upon the terms thereof, vague, indefinite and uncertain though they are. In such case the law will presume a promise to pay the reasonable value of the services. Judge Gray, who wrote the opinion in the *United Press* case, said therein: "I entertain no doubt that, where work has been done, or articles have been furnished, a recovery may be based upon quantum meruit, or quantum valebat; but, where a contract is of an executory character and requires performance over a future period of time, as here, and it is silent as to the price which is to be paid to the plaintiff during its term, I do not think that it possesses binding force. As the parties had omitted to make the price a subject of covenant, in the nature of things, it would have to be the subject of future agreement, or stipulation." (p. 412.)

* * *

So, in this case, while I do not think that the plaintiff can recover anything as extra work, yet if the work actually performed as stated was worth more than $40 per week, he having performed until November 7, 1910, could, on a proper complaint, recover its value less the amount received. * * *

The plaintiff claims that he at least should have been allowed to go to the jury on the question as to whether he was entitled to recover at the rate of $40 per week from November 7, 1911, to December 31, 1911, inclusive. He did not perform any services for the defendant from November 6 until some time after December 1st, by reason of his illness. He has not shown just when he offered to return. It appears that between the time when he offered to return and January 1st he received $50 for other services.

The amount that the plaintiff could recover, therefore, if any, based upon the agreement to pay $40 per week would be very small, and he did not present to the court facts from which it could be computed. His employment by the defendant was conditional upon his continuing the way he had been working, getting the defendant out of his trouble and getting certain unenumerated jobs that were in the office three years, started. There was nothing in the contract specifying the length of service except as stated. It was not an unqualified agreement to continue the plaintiff in his service until the first of January, and it does not appear whether or not the special conditions upon which the contract was made had been performed. Even apart from the question whether the plaintiff's absence from the defendant's office by reason of his illness would permit the defendant to refuse to take him back into his employ, I do not think that on the testimony as it appears before us it was error to refuse to leave to the jury the question whether the plaintiff was entitled to recover anything at the rate of $40 per week.

The judgment should be affirmed, with costs.

CARDOZO, J. (dissenting).

I do not think it is true that a promise to pay an employee a fair share of the profits in addition to his salary is always and of necessity too vague to be enforced * * * The promise must, of course, appear to have been made with contractual intent * * * But if that intent is present, it cannot be said from the mere form of the promise that the estimate of the reward is inherently impossible. The data essential to measurement may be lacking in the particular instance, and yet they may conceivably be supplied. It is possible, for example, that in some occupations an employee would be able to prove a percentage regulated by custom. The difficulty in this case is not so much in the contract as in the evidence. Even if the data required for computation might conceivably have been supplied, the plaintiff did not supply them. He would not have supplied them if all the evidence which he offered, and which the court excluded, had been received. He has not failed because the nature of the contract is such that damages are of necessity incapable of proof. He has failed because he did not prove them.

There is nothing inconsistent with this view in *United Press v. N. Y. Press Co.,* (164 N. Y. 406). The case is often cited as authority for the proposition that an agreement to buy merchandise at a fair and reasonable price is so indefinite that an action may not be maintained for its breach in so far as it is still executory. Nothing of the kind was decided, or with reason could have been. What the court did was to construe a particular agreement, and to hold that the parties intended to reserve the price for future adjustment. If instead of reserving the price for future adjustment, they had manifested an intent on the one hand to pay and on the other to accept a fair price, the case is far from holding that a jury could not determine what such a price would be and assess the damages accordingly. Such an intent, moreover, might be manifested not only through express words, but also through reasonable implication. It was because there was neither an express statement nor a reasonable implication of such an intent that the court held the agreement void to the extent that it had not been executed.

On the ground that the plaintiff failed to supply the data essential to computation, I concur in the conclusion that profits were not to be included as an element of damage. I do not concur, however, in the conclusion that he failed to make out a case of damage to the extent of his loss of salary. The amount may be small, but none the less it belongs to him. The hiring was not at will * * * . The plain implication was that it should continue until the end of the year when the books were to be closed. The evidence would permit the jury to find that the plaintiff was discharged without cause, and he is entitled to damages measured by his salary for the unexpired term.

The judgment should be reversed and a new trial granted, with costs to abide the event.

QUESTIONS

1. Questions about the facts of this case

   1.1. What did the defendant intend when he told plaintiff and the designer that if they would continue the work they had been doing he would give them "a fair share of my profits"?

   1.2. What was the term of the plaintiff's employment contract according to Justice Chase? How about in Justice Cardozo's view?

2. Questions about the law

   2.1. The majority opinion in *Varney* represents the traditional common law attitude toward issues of definiteness. What is the concern that accounts for this attitude? What is Justice Cardozo's take and how does it differ from the approach adopted by the majority?

   2.2. The majority opinion seems concerned that the determination of a "fair share of profits" is inherently more speculative than the determination of a "fair" or "reasonable" price for goods. Do you agree? Does Justice Cardozo agree? What kind of evidence would you seek to adduce to prove a fair share of the profits if given the opportunity?

Nora Beverages, Inc. v. Perrier Group of America, Inc.
United States Court of Appeals, Second Circuit
164 F.3d 736 (1988)

POOLER, Circuit Judge:

Plaintiff Nora Beverages, Inc., ("Nora") appeals from a grant of summary judgment entered on December 10, 1997, in the United States District Court for the District of Connecticut (Ellen Bree Burns, Judge). The judgment dismissed Nora's statutory and common law claims against defendants Perrier Group of America, Inc. ("PGA"), Poland Spring Corporation ("Poland Spring"), Zephyrhills Corporation ("Zephyrhills"), Arrowhead Water Corporation ("Arrowhead"), and Calistoga Mineral Water Company, Inc. ("Calistoga") (collectively, "Perrier"). * * * [W]e reverse the district court's entry of judgment on one of Nora's two contractual claims. * * *

BACKGROUND

Nora, a Canadian company with its principal place of business in Quebec, Canada, bottles at the source and markets a natural spring water brand known as NAYA. Since beginning its spring water operation in May 1986, Nora has bottled and sold NAYA water in 1.5-liter clear plastic bottles, made from a resin called polyethylene terephthalate ("PET"). Prior to introducing NAYA in 1986, Nora reviewed approximately fifty to sixty potential designs, ultimately adopting a 1.5-liter PET ribbed bottle with a "waist" that created a "bottle upon bottle" effect. The NAYA bottle bears a dark blue label with a lighter blue insert containing the word "NAYA" in dark blue letters outlined in white.

PGA, a Delaware corporation with its headquarters in Connecticut, distributes and markets various brands of domestically produced bottled water throughout the United States. PGA's former subsidiary corporations—Poland Spring, Zephyrhills, Arrowhead, and Calistoga—are all American companies principally engaged in the distribution and marketing of spring water under various brand names in diverse regions of the United States. Although

Poland Spring, Zephyrhills, Arrowhead, and Calistoga all sold spring water in the United States prior to Nora's entry into the market, defendants did not sell spring water in "convenience-size" 1.5-liter bottles.

Wishing to enter the market for convenience-size spring water, PGA—in 1986 and 1987—negotiated with both Johnson Controls, Inc. ("Johnson") and Sewell Plastics, Inc. ("Sewell") to produce PET bottles for its waters. In dealing with both bottlers, PGA indicated a preference for all or part of the NAYA bottle design. PGA selected Sewell as its bottler, but Sewell proved technically unable to perform the work.

Thus, in early 1988, PGA began to discuss with Nora the possibility of Nora supplying bottles to PGA and its subsidiaries. On March 1, 1988, Nora sent Perrier a letter offering two prices for its bottles: (1) to the extent that defendants furnished their own water, Nora would bottle it in 1.5-liter bottles for $3.25 per case and (2) Nora would provide both NAYA water and bottling services for $3.75 per case. Nora proposed that it would provide approximately three million bottles during 1988 and indicated that its quote would be valid for one month. Nora also promised PGA a quote on twelve-ounce bottles within three weeks.

On March 23, 1988, Frank Szczesniak, PGA's purchasing manager, wrote to Dr. Malek Basbous, a former president of Nora who acted on Nora's behalf in the contract negotiations with PGA:

> This letter will serve as our agreement and understanding between Nora Beverages and the Perrier Group regarding contract packaging a 1.5-liter container.
>
> —The contract price will be $3.25 per case without water or $3.75 using your water.
>
> —The contract price will include a bottle, label, case, and cap.
>
> —Our projections are 1/2 to 1 million cases for the 1.5 liter container.
>
> —We expect to make the initial finished product shipments the first week in May.
>
> —We will provide Poland Springs water in 6300 tankers to your Mirabel facility.
>
> The Zephyrhills product will use your water.

Over the next several months, the parties circulated draft contracts for some of the PGA subsidiaries. In a communication received by Basbous on April 6, 1988, Nora's president, Ahmad Hbouss, confirmed that Basbous would receive a five percent commission "in the event of conclusion of a contract between our company and Perrier." On May 17, 1998, Naji Barsoum, Nora's export manager, sent Jean-Guy Lord, Nora's executive vice-president, an office memorandum indicating that negotiations with PGA had stopped.

PGA selected Johnson to supply its bottles in May 1988. In early 1989, defendants introduced convenience-size bottles of Poland Spring, Arrowhead, and Zephyrhills water, packaged in 1.5-liter ribbed PET bottles. PGA's bottles—with the exception of distinctive labels—are virtually identical to NAYA's. Both the NAYA bottles and the various PGA brand bottles are made of clear PET. The top half of each bottle has an indentation for the product's label. Below the label is a rib and below the rib is an indented rib or "waist." Below the waist is a series of ribs.

Nora filed a complaint in the district court for the District of Connecticut on December 3, 1991. Nora sued * * * PGA for breach of contract (with respect to both the 1.5-liter and twelve-ounce bottles) and in quantum meruit. On October 13, 1994, defendants moved for summary judgment dismissal of Nora's complaint. Nora cross-moved for partial summary judgment on its 1.5-liter contractual claim and its twelve-ounce contractual claim with respect to the Poland Spring and Zephyrhills brands only * * *.

In a December 3, 1997, ruling, the district court granted defendants' motion for summary judgment and denied plaintiff's motion for partial summary judgment. The court found that (1) Nora failed to establish the formation of a contract for sale of either the 1.5-liter or the twelve-ounce bottles because the March 23, 1988, letter was "merely a predicate to further negotiations among the parties," * * * and the March 23 letter could not be construed as a requirements contract; * * * and (2) the facts did not support a claim for quantum meruit or unjust enrichment. * * * Nora appealed from the December 10, 1997, judgment incorporating the district court's holding.

* * *

III. The Contractual Claims

* * *

The UCC governs contracts for the sale of goods. [§ 2-102]. However, the alleged contract between Nora and PGA required Nora to provide both goods (the bottles) and bottling services. To determine whether a contract including both goods and services is governed by the U.C.C., the court must determine "whether the dominant factor or 'essence' of the transaction is the sale of the materials or the services." * * * The record does not indicate whether the alleged contracts predominantly involved goods or services. Therefore, we will consider whether issues of fact exist on contract formation under either the U.C.C. or Connecticut common law.

C. The Alleged 1.5-Liter Contract

We first consider whether there are issues of fact concerning formation of the 1.5-liter contract under the U.C.C. Pursuant to the Code, "[a] contract for sale of goods may be made in any manner sufficient to show agreement, including conduct by both parties which recognizes the existence of such a contract." [§ 2-204(1)]. The contract will not fail for indefiniteness because "one or more terms are left open . . . if the parties have intended to make a contract and there is a reasonably certain basis for giving an appropriate remedy." [§ 2-204(3)]. However, "the more terms the parties leave open, the less likely it is that they have intended to conclude a binding agreement." Id., cmt.

* * *

PGA argues * * * that there was no contract because the parties had not agreed on the critical terms of duration of the contract or quantity. We believe that a reasonable fact finder could determine that PGA and Nora reached at least a limited agreement on both quantity and duration. Arguably, the March 23 letter obligated PGA to purchase at least 500,000 cases of the 1.5-liter bottles. The record also contains information from which a finder of fact could infer that the parties had arrived at a duration term. The March 1 letter from Nora to PGA offers a price and projects a quantity of 3,000,000 bottles for 1988. The March 23 letter from PGA to Nora confirms the price per case and increases the projected quantity to a minimum of 500,000 cases of twelve bottles each. From this sequence, the fact-finder could infer that PGA and Nora contracted for the sale of at least 500,000 cases during the balance of 1988. Moreover, the record contains some evidence that PGA understood that it would have to commit to a term of between two and three years to obtain PET bottles. Sandy Albert, PGA's purchasing manager, testified that most companies required a two-to-three year commitment prior to undertaking a new PET project. In addition, a Sewell Plastics representative testified that "as was fairly common in the plastics industry," Sewell wanted a multi-year arrangement prior to entering into a bottling agreement. Because the UCC does not treat open terms as defeating a contract if there is a reasonable commercial basis for supplying the term, see §2-204, cmt, and the fact finder reasonably could infer duration either from PGA's concession on industry practice or from the March 1 letter read together with the March 23 letter, we find that under the U.C.C. there are issues of fact as to whether PGA and Nora arrived at a contract for the 1.5-liter bottles.

* * *

We also conclude that Nora demonstrated issues of fact on contract formation using a common law analysis. Under the Connecticut common law, we must first examine the March 23 letter to see if it expressly requires the execution of a formal contract. *See Atlantic Terra Cotta Co. v. Chesapeake Terra Cotta Co.,* 96 Conn. 88, 113 A. 156, 158 (Conn. 1921). If it does not, "it becomes a question of fact whether the parties intended the agreement in a certain memorandum to constitute a contract or intended that there should be no contract until the execution of a formal written contract." *See* 113 A. at 158–59.

Because the March 23 letter contained no express condition of a formal contract, we must determine whether there are issues of fact concerning the parties' intent. The same evidence that persuaded us to find issues of fact under the U.C.C. convince us that there are issues of fact as to the parties' intent under the common law. We also believe that there are issues of fact as to whether the parties sufficiently defined the terms of their agreement to create a contract. Connecticut common law requires that a contract "be definite and certain as to its terms and requirements." *Dunham v. Dunham,* 204 Conn. 303, 528 A.2d 1123, 1129 (Conn. 1987) (citations omitted). However, the trier of fact determines whether an agreement has been made and what the terms of the agreement are. * * * Moreover, if the trier of fact can find a reasonable basis for implying a missing term—such as price—the absence of the term is not fatal to the contract. * * *

Applying these standards, we do not believe that the omissions the district court identified in the PGA-Nora contract–indemnification, insurance, price increases, quality control, choice of law, length of contract and confidentiality–are necessarily fatal to the contract's existence. As previously discussed, we disagree with the district court's conclusion that the contract necessarily lacked a quantity term. Therefore, we must reverse the district court's grant of summary judgment on the 1.5-liter bottle contract claim.

D. The Alleged Twelve-Ounce Contract

We agree with the district court that there are no facts in the record from which the finder of fact reasonably could infer that PGA and Nora entered into a contract with regard to the supply of twelve-ounce bottles to PGA. The March 23 letter serves as an "agreement and understanding between Nora Beverages and the Perrier Group regarding contract packaging a 1.5 liter container." The letter's only reference to the twelve-ounce size is Szczesniak's expressed hope to receive a timetable within the next few days. It does not contain either a price or a quantity term and contains no basis from which price or quantity readily could be inferred. Moreover, Barsoum's March 1, 1988, letter to Lisa Hatem of PGA refers to the twelve-ounce bottle only in passing. We have reviewed all of the evidence that Nora claims creates issues of fact on the formation of a contract for provision of the twelve-ounce bottle and find nothing from which a reasonable fact finder could infer that Nora and PGA reached an agreement.

* * *

QUESTIONS AND NOTES

1. Questions about the facts of this case

   1.1. What was the relationship between the Perrier Group of America and the other defendants in this action?

   1.2. Who won the first time in the trial court? Who will win the second time or will there be a second time at all? If you represented Perrier, what would you recommend after this decision came down?

2. Questions about the law

2.1. On remand should the trial court apply the Uniform Commercial Code or common law? Are the contract prices helpful in answering this question?

2.2. If, on remand, the trial court does apply the Uniform Commercial Code, should it apply § 2-207?

2.3. The trial court found that the March letter from PGA could not be "construed as a requirements contract." What is a "requirements contract"? If Epstein agrees to buy all of the Viagra he needs from Jim Meyers Pharmacy, is that a requirements contract? *See* U.C.C. § 2-306. Why wasn't the March 23rd letter a requirements contract?

2.4. Can there be an enforceable agreement to buy bottles even though the number of bottles that the buyer is buying is "left open"? Did the court in *Nora Beverages* conclude that the quantity term was left open in this case?

2.5. How would the *Varney* court have decided *Nora Beverages*? Do the facts of the two cases raise the same legal issues? Are the statements as to the number of bottles in *Nora Beverages* any less "vague, indefinite, and uncertain" than the statement as to the amount of profits in *Varney?*

2.6. *Nora Beverages* suggests that the court may imply a missing term when there is a "reasonable basis" for doing so. Does this refer to a reasonable basis for assuming that the parties *intended* that the court would fill in the omitted or ambiguous item, or just an objectively reasonable basis for supplying or construing that missing or vague term?

3. Notes

3.1. While *Nora Beverages* reflects the contemporary attitude of increasing tolerance of indefiniteness, even today some courts still take the definiteness requirement quite seriously. In *Goldstick v. ICM Reality,* 788 F.2d 456, 461 (7th Cir. 1986), for example, Judge Posner, in insisting that the parties must express their agreement with sufficient definiteness to guide the court in determining what they intended, observed: "The parties have a competitive advantage over the court in deciding on what terms a voluntary transaction is value-maximizing; that is the premise of a free enterprise system." Do you agree? Is the concern over inadvertent, judicially-created market inefficiencies sufficient to justify depriving a party of his "fair share of the profits"?

3.2. Should the reason why the parties failed to address some aspect of their relationship with definiteness affect the court's willingness to supply the missing or ambiguous term? For instance, would it make a difference to you if the parties left an item open because they were unable to reach agreement? How about if they left the item open because of the inability to accurately forecast at the time of contracting what the needs of the parties were likely to be over the life of a contract?

Note on U.C.C. Gap Fillers

The Uniform Commercial Code takes a very liberal attitude toward the definiteness requirement once it is established that the parties intended to be bound. Section 2-204(3), applied by the court in *Nora Beverages*, makes clear that the fact that one or more terms of a contract are left open does not render the contract too indefinite as long as there is a reasonable basis for affording an appropriate remedy. This break with the traditional disinclination of common law judges to "make" a contract for the parties is consistent with the general philosophy of the drafters of the U.C.C. to bring the law into line with prevailing commercial practices and expectation. In many business contexts it is desirable, and sometimes even necessary, for the parties to be less than entirely clear in specifying one of the essential terms of the transaction. This can occur for a variety of reasons, ranging from uncertainty about future events to, in the case of agreements involving a series of performances over a lengthy period of time, an inability at the time of contracting to foresee every eventuality. For instance, in connection with the purchase and sale of a particular commodity subject to rapid price fluctuations, neither party may wish today to take the risk of an adverse move in the market. Nevertheless, if it is clear that they intend to be bound to one another at prevailing market prices at the time or times for performance, the thinking of the drafters was that this intention should not be frustrated merely because the parties left the price term open or tied it to an external standard. Similarly, if the parties clearly manifested an intention to be bound and expressed all of the other critical terms of their agreement but for, due to oversight, the place where delivery should occur, a contract for the sale of goods will not fail for indefiniteness.

The Code deals with these "open terms" in two ways. First, § 1-201(3) defines "Agreement" as the parties' bargain-in-fact as ascertained not only from the language used but implied from "other circumstances including course of dealing or usage of trade or course of performance as provided in this Act." We will take up each of these concepts in Chapter 3 when we consider what are the terms of the deal. Second, as also discussed in more detail when we get to Chapter 3, the U.C.C. contains numerous "gap filling" provisions in Article 2. These provisions operate as default rules that supply the governing rule as to various aspects of the agreement if the parties, though intending to be bound, have failed to address the particular term.

In theory, default rules are designed to emulate what the parties *would have* agreed to had they spoken to the issue. In reality, they will sometimes hit their mark and sometimes miss. Moreover, we do not necessarily mean what *these* parties would have agreed to, since they failed to tell us what they wanted, but rather what reasonable persons in the position of these parties would have agreed to assuming that they were bargaining from relatively equal positions of strength. Some commentators have urged that perhaps it would be better in some instances if the default rule was not one that the parties would likely have agreed to had they spoken to the issue. Instead, it has been suggested that if the default rule is an unattractive one—one that neither party would presumably want—then there is more incentive for the parties to express their preference by negotiating more complete agreements. *See* Ian Ayres & Robert Gertner, *Filling Gaps in Incomplete Contracts: An Economics Theory of Default Rules,* 99 YALE L.J. 87 (1989) (distinguishing between "tailored" and "penalty" default rules and urging that in the interests of minimizing the costs of contracting "efficiency-minded courts and legislatures" should move "beyond the received wisdom that default rules should simply be what the majority of contracting parties would have wanted").

B. Agreements to Agree

Recall that the trial court in *Nora Beverages* found that the March 23rd letter on which Nora relied to establish a contract was "merely a predicate to further negotiations between the parties." Such "predicates" are commonly known as non-binding "letters of intent," a topic we take up in Section 7 of this Chapter. On some occasions, however, the parties leave a key term of their agreement open not because they have failed yet to reach agreement, but because, although they consider themselves bound, they have decided to defer agreement until a later time. We call such arrangements "agreements to agree," and if the parties later reach agreement on the open term everything is copasetic. However, when the parties fail to come to agreement, the issue for the courts is whether the agreement as struck is too indefinite to enforce or whether the court should supply the missing term in order to save the deal.

Walker v. Keith

Court of Appeals of Kentucky
382 S.W.2d 198 (1964)

CLAY, Commissioner.

In this declaratory judgment proceeding the plaintiff appellee sought an adjudication that he had effectively exercised an option to extend a lease, and a further determination of the amount of rent to be paid. The relief prayed was granted by the Chancellor. The principal issue is whether the option provision in the lease fixed the rent with sufficient certainty to constitute an enforceable contract between the parties.

In July 1951 appellants, the lessors, leased a small lot to appellee, the lessee, for a 10-year term at a rent of $100 per month. The lessee was given an option to extend the lease for an additional 10-year term, under the same terms and conditions except as to rental. The renewal option provided:

> "rental will be fixed in such amount as shall actually be agreed upon by the lessors and the lessee with the monthly rental fixed on the comparative basis of rental values as of the date of the renewal with rental values

at this time reflected by the comparative business conditions of the two periods."

The lessee gave the proper notice to renew but the parties were unable to agree upon the rent. Preliminary court proceedings finally culminated in this lawsuit. Based upon the verdict of an advisory jury, the Chancellor fixed the new rent at $125 per month.

The question before us is whether the quoted provision is so indefinite and uncertain that the parties cannot be held to have agreed upon this essential rental term of the lease. There have been many cases from other jurisdictions passing on somewhat similar lease provisions and the decisions are in hopeless conflict. We have no authoritative Kentucky decision.

At the outset two observations may be made. One is that rental in the ordinary lease is a very uncomplicated item. It involves the number of dollars the lessee will pay. It, or a method of ascertaining it, can be so easily fixed with certainty. From the standpoint of stability in business transactions, it should be so fixed.

Secondly, as an original proposition, uncomplicated by subtle rules of law, the provision we have quoted, on its face, is ambiguous and indefinite. The language used is equivocal. It neither fixes the rent nor furnishes a positive key to its establishment. The terminology is not only confusing but inherently unworkable as a formula.

The above observations should resolve the issue. Unfortunately it is not that simple. Many courts have become intrigued with the possible import of similar language and have interpolated into it a binding obligation. The lease renewal option has been treated as something different from an ordinary contract. The law has become woefully complicated. For this reason we consider it necessary and proper to examine this question in depth.

The following basic principles of law are generally accepted:

"It is a necessary requirement in the nature of things that an agreement in order to be binding must be sufficiently definite to enable a court to give it an exact meaning." Williston on Contracts (3rd Ed.) Vol. 1, section 37 (page 107).

"Like other contracts or agreements for a lease, the provision for a renewal must be certain in order to render it binding and enforceable. Indefiniteness, vagueness, and uncertainty in the terms of such a provision will render it void unless the parties, by their subsequent conduct or acts

> supplement the covenant and thus remove an alleged uncertainty. The certainty that is required is such as will enable a court to determine what has been agreed upon." 32 Am.Jur., Landlord and Tenant, section 958 (page 806).
>
> "The terms of an extension or renewal, under an option therefor in a lease, may be left for future determination by a prescribed method, as by future arbitration or appraisal; but merely leaving the terms for future ascertainment, without providing a method for their determination, renders the agreement unenforceable for uncertainty." 51 C.J.S. Landlord and Tenant 56b (2), page 597. * * *

The degree of certainty is the controlling consideration. An example of an appropriate method by which a non-fixed rental could be determined appears in *Jackson v. Pepper Gasoline Co.,* 280 Ky. 226, 133 S.W.2d 91, 126 A.L.R. 1370. The lessee, who operated an automobile service station, agreed to pay "an amount equal to one cent per gallon of gasoline delivered to said station". Observing that the parties had created a definite objective standard by which the rent could with certainty be computed, the court upheld the lease as against the contention that it was lacking in mutuality. * * *

On the face of the rent provision, the parties had not agreed upon a rent figure. They left the amount to future determination. If they had agreed upon a specific method of making the determination, such as by computation, the application of a formula, or the decision of an arbitrator, they could be said to have agreed upon whatever rent figure emerged from utilization of the method. This was not done.

It will be observed the rent provision expresses two ideas. The first is that the parties agree to agree. The second is that the future agreement will be based on a comparative adjustment in the light of "business conditions". We will examine separately these two concepts and then consider them as a whole.

The lease purports to fix the rent at such an amount as shall "actually be agreed upon." It should be obvious that an agreement to agree cannot constitute a binding contract. Williston on Contracts (3rd Ed.) Vol. 1, section 45 (page 149) * * * .

As said in Williston on Contracts (3rd Ed.) Vol. 1, section 45 (page 149):

> "Although a promise may be sufficiently definite when it contains an option given to the promisor, yet if an essential element is reserved for the

> future agreement of both parties, the promise gives rise to no legal obligation until such future agreement. Since either party, by the very terms of the agreement, may refuse to agree to anything the other party will agree to, it is impossible for the law to fix any obligation to such a promise."

We accept this because it is both sensible and basic to the enforcement of a written contract. We applied it in *Johnson v. Lowery, Ky.,* 270 S.W.2d 943, page 946, wherein we said:

> "To be enforceable and valid, a contract to enter into a future covenant must specify all material and essential terms and leave nothing to be agreed upon as a result of future negotiations."

This proposition is not universally accepted as it pertains to renewal options in a lease. *Hall v. Weatherford,* 32 Ariz. 370, 259 P. 282, 56 A.L.R. 903; *Rainwater v. Hobeika,* 208 S.C. 433, 38 S.E.2d 495, 166 A.L.R. 1228. We have examined the reasons set forth in those opinions and do not find them convincing. The view is taken that the renewal option is for the benefit of the lessee; that the parties intended something; and that the lessee should not be deprived of his right to enforce his contract. This reasoning seems to overlook the fact that a party must have an enforceable contract before he has a right to enforce it. We wonder if these courts would enforce an original lease in which the rent was not fixed, but agreed to be agreed upon.

Surely there are some limits to what equity can or should undertake to compel parties in their private affairs to do what the court thinks they should have done. * * * In any event, we are not persuaded that renewal options in leases are of such an exceptional character as to justify emasculation of one of the basic rules of contract law. An agreement to agree simply does not fix an enforceable obligation.

As noted, however, the language of the renewal option incorporated a secondary stipulation. Reference was made to "comparative business conditions" which were to play some part in adjusting the new rental. It is contended this provides the necessary certainty, and we will examine a leading case which lends support to the argument.

In *Edwards v. Tobin,* 132 Or. 38, 284 P. 562, 68 A.L.R. 152, the court upheld and enforced a lease agreement which provided that the rent should be "determined" at the time of renewal, "said rental to be a *reasonable rental* under the then existing conditions". (Our emphasis) Significance was attached to the last quoted language, the court reasoning that since the parties had agreed upon a reasonable rent, the court would hold the parties to the agreement by fixing it.

All rents tend to be reasonable. When parties are trying to reach an agreement, however, their ideas or claims of reasonableness may widely differ. In addition, they have a right to bargain. They cannot be said to be in agreement about what is a reasonable rent until they specify a figure or an exact method of determining it. The term "reasonable rent" is itself indefinite and uncertain. Would an original lease for a "reasonable rent" be enforceable by either party? The very purpose of a rental stipulation is to remove this item from an abstract area.

It is true courts often must imply such terms in a contract as "reasonable time" or "reasonable price". This is done when the parties fail to deal with such matters in an otherwise enforceable contract. Here the parties were undertaking to fix the terms rather than leave them to implication. Our problem is not what the law would imply if the contract did not purport to cover the subject matter, but whether the parties, in removing this material term from the field of implication, have fixed their mutual obligations.

We are seeking what the agreement actually was. When dealing with such a specific item as rent, to be payable in dollars, the area of possible agreement is quite limited. If the parties did not agree upon such an unequivocal item or upon a definite method of ascertaining it, then there is a clear case of nonagreement. The court, in fixing an obligation under a nonagreement, is not enforcing the contract but is binding the parties to something they were patently unable to agree to when writing the contract.

The opinion in the *Tobin* case, which purportedly was justifying the enforcement of a contractual obligation between the lessor and lessee, shows on its face the court was doing something entirely different. This question was posed in the opinion: "What logical reason is there for equity to refuse to act when the parties themselves *fail to agree* on the rental?" (Our emphasis) The obvious logical answer is that even equity cannot enforce as a contract a nonagreement. No distortion of words can hide the fact that when the court admits the parties "fail to agree," then the contract it enforces is one it makes for the parties.

* * *

We have examined the *Tobin* case at length because it exemplifies lines of reasoning adopted by some courts to dredge certainty from uncertainty. Other courts balk at the process. The majority of cases, passing upon the question of whether a renewal option providing that the future rent shall be dependent upon or proportionate to the valuation of the property at the time of renewal, hold that such provision is not sufficiently certain to constitute an enforceable agreement. * * * The valuation of property and the ascertainment of "comparative business conditions," which we have under consideration, involve similar uncertainties.

* * *

We do not think our problem can be solved by determining which is the "majority" rule and which is the "minority" rule. We are inclined, however, to adhere to a sound basic principle of contract law unless there are impelling reasons to depart from it, particularly so when the practical problems involved in such departure are so manifest. Let us briefly examine those practical problems.

What the law requires is an adequate key to a mutual agreement. If "comparative business conditions" afforded sufficient certainty, we might possibly surmount the obstacle of the unenforceable agreement to agree. This term, however is very broad indeed. Did the parties have in mind local conditions, national conditions, or conditions affecting the lessee's particular business?

* * *

We realize that litigation is oft times inevitable and courts should not shrink from the solution of difficult problems. On the other hand, courts should not expend their powers to establish contract rights which the parties, with an opportunity to do so, have failed to define. As said in *Morrison v. Rossignol,* 5 Cal. 64, quoted in 30 A.L.R. at page 579:

> "A court of equity is always chary of its power to decree specific performance, and will withhold the exercise of its jurisdiction in that respect, unless there is such a degree of certainty in the terms of the contract as will enable it at one view to do complete equity."

That cannot be done in this case.

Stipulations such as the one before us have been the source of interminable litigation. Courts are called upon not to enforce an agreement or to determine what the agreement was, but to write their own concept of what would constitute a proper one. Why this paternalistic task should be undertaken is difficult to understand when the parties could so easily provide any number of workable methods by which rents could be adjusted. As a practical matter, courts sometimes must assert their right not to be imposed upon. This thought was thus summed up in *Slayter v. Pasley, Or.*, 264 P.2d 444, page 449:

> "We should be hesitant about completing an apparently legally incomplete agreement made between persons sui juris enjoying freedom of contract and dealing at arms' length by arbitrarily interpolating into it our concept of the parties' intent merely to validate what would otherwise be an invalid instrument, lest we inadvertently commit them to an ostensible agreement which, in fact, is contrary to the deliberate design of all of them. It is a dangerous doctrine when examined in the light of reason. Judicial paternalism of this character should be as obnoxious to courts as is legislation by judicial fiat. Both import a quality of jural ego and superiority not consonant with long-accepted ideas of legistic propriety under a democratic form of government. If, however, we follow the urgings of the lessee in the instant matter, we will thereby establish a precedent which will open the door to repeated opportunities to do that which, in principle, courts should not do and, in any event, are not adequately equipped to do."

We think the basic principle of contract law that requires substantial certainty as to the material terms upon which the minds of the parties have met is a sound one and should be adhered to. A renewal option stands on the same footing as any other contract right. Rent is a material term of a lease. If the parties do not fix it with reasonable certainty, it is not the business of courts to do so.

The renewal provision before us was fatally defective in failing to specify either an agreed rental or an agreed method by which it could be fixed with certainty. Because of the lack of agreement, the lessee's option right was illusory. The Chancellor erred in undertaking to enforce it.

The judgment is reversed.

QUESTIONS

1. Questions about the facts of this case

   1.1. Why didn't the parties simply fix the rent for the option period in their original lease agreement?

   1.2. The reported decision in *Walker* does not indicate why the parties were unable to reach agreement upon the rent for the option period. Suppose it was because the lessor insisted on an outrageously high figure relative to market value or the lessee demanded an equally outrageous number on the low side. Would those facts have been relevant to the court? Do you think the reason why the parties were unable to reach agreement should matter to a court in deciding whether to imply a "reasonable rate" of rent?

2. Questions about the law

   2.1. If, as the court suggests, the determination of rental value is such an uncomplicated affair, why did the court of appeals set aside the Chancellor's determination of $125 per month?

   2.2. The court in *Walker* indicates that the parties did not in their original agreement specify an objective method or standard for determining rent in the option period. Do you agree with this conclusion? How would you redraft the renewal option provision so as to satisfy the court of appeals?

   2.3. As the court seems to recognize, the effect of its decision in *Walker* is to leave the lessee without the right to enforce the option. Do you think that's what the parties contemplated when the renewal option was negotiated, that the lessee would have an option enforceable only at the pleasure of the lessor?

Moolenaar v. Co-Build Companies, Inc.
United States District Court, District of the Virgin Islands
354 F. Supp. 980 (1973)

WARREN H. YOUNG, District Judge.

This case involves the proper construction of the renewal clause in a lease. Briefly stated, two issues are presented. First, is a valid and specifically enforceable renewal option created by a clause which leaves the rent for this period to be determined by subsequent agreement between the parties? And secondly, if the clause is valid but the parties are unable to agree on the rent, how is this rental figure to be determined? Here I must decide whether the court must look to fair market value at the time when the option is exercised, or whether the court may take a lower figure if it is shown that the parties contemplated that the land would be put to less than its most remunerative use. For the reasons given below, I hold that such a renewal clause contains an implicit term that the new rent shall be fixed at its "reasonable" or "fair market" value. The clause is thus specific enough to be valid and enforceable. I further hold that parol evidence is admissible to explain this implicit term, and to show that the parties intended the rent to be set at the fair market value of the land as if it were subject to certain use restrictions.

The facts of this case are not in dispute. In October of 1967, plaintiff Moolenaar, a sheep and goat farmer, leased 150 acres of land from one Aurea Correa. His leasehold was to run for a period of five years with an option to renew for an additional five. Moolenaar was to pay $375 per month during the initial term, but the rent for the renewal period "shall be renegotiated."[1] Moolenaar took possession under this lease and expanded his sheep and goat farm onto the demised premises. Before the time came to exercise the renewal option, however, Mrs. Correa sold the land to real estate speculators who in turn sold it to West Indies Enterprises, the predecessor corporation to the defendant Co-Build Companies, Inc. ("Co-Build"). The new owners nonetheless took subject to Moolenaar's rights under the pre-existing and duly recorded lease. At this point I should mention that the testimony disclosed, and I so find, that the representatives of Co-Build ne-

---

[1]The renewal clause provides in full as follows:

> 4. OPTION OF RENEWAL: Provided that Tenant shall not be declared in default at any time during the term hereof, the Tenant shall be entitled to an option to extend the term of this lease for an additional period of FIVE (5) YEARS upon the same terms and conditions except that the rental shall be renegotiated.

gotiating the purchase of the land had actual knowledge of the lease and its renewal clause. They discussed its validity or purported lack of validity with their counsel and accepted title insurance with an exception taken by the title insurer to the rights of the tenant in possession, including the lease renewal clause.

In April of 1972, some six months before the first five year term expired, Moolenaar informed Co-Build of his intention to exercise the renewal option. Co-Build expressed its willingness to extend the lease at a "renegotiated" rent of $17,000 per month. Co-Build justified this figure by the high price it had paid for the land, and by its unquestionably great value if put to industrial use. Such a rent, however, is obviously beyond the resources of the less profitable goat husbandry business. Moolenaar therefore proposed a considerably lower figure and indicated his desire to meet for direct negotiations. All such offers were declined. Upon Co-Build's refusal to recede from its initial position, Moolenaar filed the present action for a declaratory judgment setting out the rights of the parties under the lease.

I

The threshold question is, of course, whether Moolenaar possesses a renewal option at all. A number of jurisdictions would hold that he does not, reasoning that a clause which neglects to stipulate the rent is void for uncertainty and indefiniteness. * * * The better view, however, would hold that such a clause intends renewal at a "reasonable" rent, and would find that market conditions are ascertainable with sufficient certainty to make the clause specifically enforceable. A number of policy considerations support this result. First, it will probably effectuate the intent of the parties better than would striking out the clause altogether. A document should be construed where possible to give effect to every term, on the theory that the signatories inserted each for a reason and if one party had agreed to the clause only in the secret belief that it would prove unenforceable, he should be discouraged from such paths. Secondly, a renewal option has a more sympathetic claim to enforcement than do most vague contractual terms, since valuable consideration will often have already been paid for it. The option of renewal is one factor inducing the tenant to enter into the lease, or to pay as high a rent as he did during the initial period. To this extent the landlord benefited from the tenant's reliance on the clause, and so the tenant has a stronger claim to receive the reciprocal benefit of the option. * * *

It then remains to be determined only whether this resolution is within the powers of the Court. In the absence of an applicable statute, the Restatement of Contracts has been designated as positive law in this jurisdiction. Section 32 of the Restatement provides that a contract is valid if it is "so definite in its terms" that the "performances to be rendered by each party are reasonably certain." Under this standard the renewal clause would appear sufficiently definite to be binding. * * *

Even if it were thought that the Restatement is ambiguous or silent on the precise issue *sub judice*, Moolenaar would still recover. In that case we must make our determination under the common law "as generally understood" in courts of other jurisdictions. The rule which I have followed here is admittedly the minority view. * * * But for the reasons which I gave in an earlier opinion, I think it is appropriate to give greater weight to recent decisions rather than weighing the authorities on a strictly numerical basis. * * * Briefly, the common law is in a state of perpetual evolution and recent decisions will more accurately reflect the current understanding on an issue. For the issue at hand the minority view is nonetheless a widely followed one * * * and has been gaining adherents at a rate which indicates that the common law is moving in that direction. * * * And while, of course, not controlling here, the U.C.C. provisions on the Sale of Goods also illustrate the approach of the modern law, with its emphasis on reasonable commercial dealings and its rejection of technical requirements. [U.C.C. § 2-305] provides as follows:

> (1) The parties if they so intend can conclude a contract for sale even though the price is not settled. In such a case the price is a reasonable price at the time for delivery if
>
> (a) nothing is said as to price; or
>
> (b) the price is left to be agreed by the parties and they fail to agree . . . ."

The comments to this section are also informative, and state in part as follows:

> This article rejects in these instances the formula that "an agreement to agree is unenforceable" . . . and rejects also defeating such agreements on the grounds of "indefiniteness." Instead this Article recognizes the dominant intention of the parties to have the deal continue to be binding upon both.

For all the above reasons, I hold that the renewal clause is valid and enforceable.

II

Given that the clause is enforceable, there remains the question of what rent Moolenaar should pay during the additional five years. As a general rule the "reasonable rent" will be established at its "fair market value," which is to say, at the highest rent which a responsible bidder is apt to offer. This in turn suggests that the leasehold should be valued at its "highest and best use," for a lessee using the land in the most intensive and remunerative way possible will be able to outbid a person who would use it less efficiently. From this Co-Build asks us to conclude that the rent should be many times higher than it had been, since the 150 acres are now zoned 1-2 and may be subdivided for light industry.

Nonetheless, I believe that Moolenaar is entitled to have the rent established at its fair value for the land as used for agricultural or animal husbandry purposes only. I conclude that this will most accurately reflect the intent of the original signatories to the lease. From the testimony presented at trial, I find that Mrs. Correa intended that Moolenaar be able to use the land for the purpose of raising sheep and goats during the renewal period, and that the rent be set at a fair value for this purpose. It is true that under this arrangement she will lose the possibility of a higher rent if circumstances changed to make a more profitable use practicable. But one purpose of a long-term lease, or of a renewal clause, is precisely to insulate the parties from such changes in circumstances. In any event, I further find that Mrs. Correa was aware of such possibilities but determined that she was willing to see the land remain in an agricultural state for ten years, and so accepted a rent low enough to make this possible.

Co-Build then took title to the land subject to the provisions of the lease as outlined above. In other circumstances, a new owner who has purchased land subject to a lease might defeat the lower agricultural-use rental by arguing lack of notice. The lease states that the land may be used for any legal purpose, and from that a purchaser might reasonably conclude that the rent is to be set according to the "highest and best" such purpose. Nothing in the document indicates the contrary, and a bona fide purchaser charged with constructive notice of the recorded lease ordinarily should not be bound by additional parol understandings which would depart from the basic presumption of fair market valuation.

I believe, however, that Co-Build is fairly chargeable with actual notice of the circumstances here. At the time the company acquired the property in 1970, it was zoned R-10. This classification permitted agricultural use or residential in quarter-acre lots. The latter use is obviously impractical where, as here, the land can be held only for an additional five year term. Thus, it was evident that the landlord and tenant had contemplated continuous agricultural or animal husbandry use. When Co-Build bought the land, it could well have deduced the nature of the underlying understanding in the lease agreement which encumbered the land. It was to this agreement that the company succeeded when it acquired the land. A subsequent change in the zoning laws should not be permitted to defeat that understanding. I find that the "renegotiation" clause was intended to deal only with fluctuations in real estate values and was not intended to permit a response to the major contingency of rezoning. In any event, the clause had a built-in "red flag" to put Co-Build on a duty of inquiry, since execution of the lease under the old zoning law would at least have left the intentions of the parties unclear. This duty would not have been burdensome; those who participated in the drafting of the original lease were available on St. Croix and in San Juan.

Since the parties have been unable to agree on a fair rental value for agricultural purposes, that figure will now be determined by the Court. The testimony at trial indicated that the present rental of $375 per month is, if anything, somewhat high for grazing use. Nonetheless I must take this figure as a freely bargained one, and hence fair. I also feel that I should make a rough adjustment for intervening inflation. A round figure of $400 per month would seem appropriate in the circumstances. Therefore, from the expert testimony given by Mr. Roebuck who has been engaged for many years in St. Croix in the sheep and goat husbandry business, and from the expert testimony of Mr. Hamilton who made an appraisal of the land on a rather novel but nonetheless convincing basis, I find that a reasonable rental would be $400 per month. With all due respect to Mr. Gaztambide, a most learned, respected and highly professional real property appraiser in Puerto Rico and the Virgin Islands, I must reject his appraisal but only for the reason that it was determined on the basis of the land's highest and most productive use—which, for the reasons explained herein—cannot be used in arriving at the reasonable rental for the use contemplated by the original parties to the lease agreement.

* * *

A declaratory judgment will be entered in accordance with this Opinion.

DECLARATORY JUDGMENT

For the reasons set forth in the Memorandum Opinion above, it is hereby adjudged and declared as follows:

1. The renewal clause is valid and enforceable.
2. The clause contemplates a rent for the additional term at a reasonable rate, as calculated by the value of the land for agricultural and animal husbandry purposes.
3. The fair rental in this case is $400 per month, retroactive to the end of the original five-year term.

QUESTIONS AND NOTES

1. Questions about the facts of this case

   1.1. Review the renewal option provisions in both *Walker* and *Moolenaar.* Which provision provided a greater insight into the intention of the parties concerning rent for the option term?

   1.2. Of what significance was the fact in *Moolenaar* that Co-Build refused to meet for direct negotiations?

   1.3. Other than its "roundness," on what factual basis does the court conclude that $400 per month constituted a reasonable rent?

2. Questions about the law

   2.1. In *Walker,* the court dismissed the lessee's equities in the renewal option stating that the lessee is not deprived of the right to enforce the option provision if there is no enforceable contract to begin with. How does the *Moolenaar* court's analysis of the issue differ?

   2.2. Does Co-Build have any claim against the prior owners of the property based on the fact that it will be precluded for five years from putting the land to its highest and best use? Does the answer to that question have any bearing on *Moolenaar's* right to have rent determined based on the value of the land used for agricultural and animal husbandry, rather than industrial, purposes?

2.3. Would the case have been decided differently if, after further negotiations, Co-Build had agreed to $1,000 per month in rent during the option term? How about $500 per month? In other words, does the lessee have a claim any time there's a failure to agree?

3. Notes

3.1. The basis for the traditional reluctance to enforce agreements to agree, even when the parties have manifested an intent to be immediately bound, has been that since there is no assurance that the parties themselves would have reached agreement on the postponed term, the court has no basis for supplying the omitted term in order to enforce the contract. Thus, the courts tended to distinguish cases where the parties simply *neglected* to include a material term—implying a reasonable term—from cases where the parties acknowledged a conscious awareness of the term and deliberately chose to defer agreement. Nevertheless, doubtless influenced by the liberal attitude taken in the Uniform Commercial Code toward enforcing incomplete agreements, decisions like *Moolenaar* represent the trend of modern authority. *Restatement (Second) of Contracts* § 33, illus. 11 offers the following example.

A promises B to construct a building according to stated plans and specification, and B promises to pay A $30,000 therefor. It is also provided that the character of the window fastners shall be subject to further agreement of the parties. Unless a contrary intention is manifested, the indefiniteness of the agreement with reference to this matter will not prevent the formation of a contract.

3.2. If a particular agreement is too indefinite at its inception to enforce, may that initial indefiniteness as to material terms subsequently be cured by construing those indefinite terms with reference to the parties' performance up to the point that the dispute arises? *See Blackhawk Heating & Plumbing Co. v. Data Lease Financial Corp.*, 302 So. 2d 404 (Fla. 1974).

3.3. Obviously, careful drafting of the agreement at the onset can eliminate most of the issues relating to indefiniteness. This is true even when the parties deliberately decide to leave a term open because neither wants to take the risk of adverse market fluctuations or the parties otherwise desire to defer agreement on a particular term until a later time. In either case, the keys are to clearly manifest somewhere in the writing the parties' intention to be bound and then to point the court toward a mechanism for supplying the missing term. For instance, if the price term is deliberately left open, it behooves the drafter to set forth in the agreement the parties' intention that the price should be set by "fair market value" or some other measurable external standard as of a date certain. Sometimes, however, particular terms of an agreement will not be addressed because the parties have not really reached agreement on an important issue and perhaps don't want to address it for fear of having the whole deal fall apart over it. If the lawyer who is commissioned to document the deal makes a point of pressing the matter she is likely to receive a chilly reception from her client. On the other hand, if she drafts the agreement without addressing this important term there is a risk that it will not be enforceable, a result also likely to make for an unhappy client. How would you handle this dilemma if you were that lawyer?

3.4. Particular problems arise when the omitted term relates to quantity. Nevertheless, sometimes a buyer will want to be assured of a specific source of supply and will even be willing to commit to a fixed price, but does not yet know what its needs are and does not wish to be obligated to purchase more than it needs or have a commitment for less than is required. Because, unlike the price term, it is virtually impossible for a court to determine what is a *reasonable* quantity, how would you address this problem as a drafting matter from your buyer/client's perspective? Can similar issues arise from the seller's side?

Problem: "*Love in the Time of Faxes*"

Richard Roth is a movie producer who lives in California and carries out his projects through Richard Roth Productions. Gabriel Garcia Marquez, an internationally renowned author who won the Nobel Prize for Literature in 1982, has written numerous bestselling novels. Garcia Marquez has resided in

Mexico City for the last sixteen years. Carmen Balcells is the president of a literary agency headquartered in Barcelona, Spain. A resident of Barcelona, Balcells has been Garcia Marquez' literary agent for more than 25 years.

In late 1986, Roth contacted Garcia Marquez in Mexico City to express his interest in making a film based on *Love in the Time of Cholera*. Roth flew to Havana, Cuba for a meeting with Garcia Marquez on this matter. Garcia Marquez told Roth that he would consider selling film rights under the following three conditions:

1) Roth would agree to pay him a large sum of money (later Balcells specified the sum of five million dollars);
2) Roth would agree to use a Latin American director; and
3) Roth would shoot the film in Colombia.

Garcia Marquez later authorized Balcells to pursue negotiations with Roth.

Negotiations dragged on with disputes both about the price for the option and the identity of the possible director. Roth traveled a number of times to Barcelona and Mexico City to meet with Balcells and Garcia Marquez, and repeated calls, letters, and faxes passed between the parties. Marquez agreed that Roth could shoot the film in Brazil, not Colombia, but he remained firm on the other two terms.

On November 17, 1988, Roth and Garcia Marquez met in Los Angeles. Later that day, Alan Schwartz, Roth's representative, faxed a letter to Balcells in Barcelona. The letter offered Garcia Marquez $200,000 for the grant of an option of two years on the film rights, the right to extend the option for another year for an additional $100,000, these monies to be applied against $1,250,000 to be paid when the option was exercised, $400,000 more on the release of the video, $350,000 more on the release of television showing, and 5% of the net profits of the film. On January 19, 1989, Schwartz faxed another letter, which changed the first sum of $200,000 for the option to $400,000. The letter stated that the first paragraph of the November 17, 1988, letter was changed to the following:

> (a) A payment of $400,000 for an option of two years to acquire the motion picture and allied rights to this novel. The option shall commence upon signature by Gabriel Garcia Marquez to the formal agreement and the return of said signed agreement to me or Richard Roth, at which time

> the option payment shall be made to you as agent for Gabriel Garcia Marquez.

The letter also stated: "On behalf of Richard Roth and myself I am very happy to confirm the final agreement between Richard and Gabriel Garcia Marquez . . ." and "Please convey to Garcia Marquez the excitement Richard and I feel in being able finally to get this project moving."

Balcells countersigned the letter and faxed back the following the next day:

> Thank you for today's fax and I am happy that this deal is finally concluded. I had no time to tell Gabo [Marquez] about this conclusion. In any case, I am returning your letter duly signed. I shall await the formal agreement at your earliest convenience.

That same day, Roth wrote independently to Balcells thanking her "so much for concluding the deal" and telling her he was "putting the best champagne on ice so we can celebrate and drink it together."

In late February, Schwartz transmitted the twenty-five page formal agreement to Balcells. Balcells objected to a number of points, particularly the omission of clauses about a Latin American director and the site of the shooting. Balcells communicated these objections, and weeks of renewed negotiations failed to produce an agreement. Garcia Marquez never signed the formal agreement, and the money was never paid him.

Roth sues to enforce the option contract. What result? *See Roth v. Marquez*, 942 F.2d 617 (9th Cir. 1991)

Note on Long-Term Agreements and Relational Contracts

The basic principles of contract law, including the requirement of definiteness, evolved in simpler economic times. Most contractual relations tended to involve discrete, "one-shot" transactions of short duration and limited interpersonal dealings between the parties. Understandably, many of the basic rules of contract law were developed to accommodate this type of transaction. However, increasingly contractual dealings are characterized by long-term, on-going relations between the contracting parties involving a complex series of performances over time. Of necessity, circumstances will change over the course of this relationship and, because it is impossible to anticipate all of these changes at the inception of the relationship, adjustments inevitably will have to be made by the parties during the course of performance. In a series of articles and an important book, Professor Ian R. Macneil has challenged many of the assumptions upon which both classical and contemporary principles of contract law are based as still misguidedly wedded to the traditional conception of contracts involving discrete transactions rather a long-term *relational* dealings between the parties. *See* MACNEIL, THE NEW SOCIAL CONTRACT (1980). Professor Macneil's work has important implications for the contract formation process, including the traditional demand of classical contract law that all material terms be agreed to at the moment of contracting. He suggests that while this may be possible in the typical one-shot deal, it is unrealistic in the long-term relational contract and is at odds with the needs of the parties to work collaboratively, rather than purely out of self-interest, during the course of their relationship. Ideally, the relational contract will serve more as a private constitution for the parties—setting forth the general standards that will govern their relationship—than an ordinary contract—setting forth in specific detail the terms of performance. In Professor Macneil's view, this should not make the contract any less enforceable in the eyes of the law.

While this is not the place to discuss the full impact of Professor Macneil's work, recognition of the relational character of many modern contracts does help provide perspective on the definiteness requirement and the impracticability of requiring complete projection of the transaction into the future through promises as a condition of meeting the law's demand for certainty. Indeed, while not necessarily reflected in the black-letter rules of contract law, the reality of contract litigation is that the character of the contract and the needs of the parties ultimately affect the degree of indefiniteness that the courts may be willing to allow. This tolerance suggests that the drafter of the long-term contract may be able to preserve some measure of flexibility for the parties in fashioning the agreement without running a serious risk that the agreement will later be declared to be too indefinite to enforce.

SECTION 7: PRE-CONTRACT FORMATION LIABILITY

We have seen that until such time as there is mutual assent between the parties in the form of an offer and acceptance, either party is free to break off negotiations without fear of being in breach of contract. In the business world, no less than in the flea market, fervent negotiations sometimes lead nowhere and the parties go off in search of other opportunities. Inevitably, time and money are spent during the course of these negotiations in the hope that they will lead to the consummation of a mutually advantageous bargain. If these hopes are not ultimately realized, ordinarily each party absorbs its own out-of-pocket expenses, recognizing them simply as the costs of doing business.

In certain circumstances, however, these costs can be substantial and one party may feel that the other *ought* to be held accountable for them. But on what basis? Common law courts, steeped in the traditional approach to contractual liability, were reluctant to establish an intermediate point after the commencement of negotiations but before the conclusion of the final agreement at which liability might attach. But the traditional "contract/no contract" distinction was a product of a simpler time and simpler transactions. Sophisticated modern business transactions, such as corporate mergers and acquisitions, require multiple points of agreement that must be reached before the deal is final, and because of the number and complexity of issues to be resolved, the agreement tends to come together in stages or pieces over time. These transactions are "heavily lawyered," and at some stage in the process the lawyers will memorialize the points of agreement reached so far, and the matters still subject to negotiation, in a document typically called an "agreement in principle" or "letter of intent." Professor Farnsworth described additional purposes for the letter of intent as follows:

> Usually the parties expect that a record of the understandings that they have reached at a particular stage will facilitate further negotiations. Such a record may prevent misunderstandings, suggest formulas for reaching further agreements, and provide a basis for drafting a definitive text. The parties may also anticipate that it will inform others of the progress of the negotiations. It may be of interest to employees or shareholders of the negotiating parties and to third parties such as prospective lenders and investors. At least one party may hope that it will enhance its position in future negotiations. Thus it may make it harder for the other party to

withdraw concessions, especially if they have been made known to prospective lenders and investors, and more disadvantageous for the other party to allow the negotiations to fail, especially if the prospect of success has been made public.

E. Alan Farnsworth, *Precontractual Liability and Preliminary Agreements: Fair Dealing and Failed Negotiations*, 87 COLUM. L. REV. 217, 257–58 (1987).

Because neither of the parties is ready at the letter of intent stage to commit to the transaction *in toto*, the letter of intent will also almost always contain a standard "not legally binding" clause indicating that the writing is not intended as a legal agreement or that the understandings expressed in the letter shall not be binding pending, among other things, regulatory approvals, execution of definitive documentation, or further agreement on matters as yet unresolved. Under the *Restatement (Second) of Contracts* § 21, express manifestations of the parties that their legal relations are not to be affected are generally accorded deference by the courts. In some cases, however, a court may be persuaded that the letter, though denominated "non-binding," nevertheless evidenced the parties' intention to make a binding agreement. *See Borg-Warner Corp. v. Anchor Coupling,* 156 N.E.2d 513 (Ill. 1958). A less extreme view is to regard the letter of intent as imposing a duty to negotiate in good faith independent of the underlying transaction. Under this view, while neither party is yet bound to the principal transaction, neither may walk away from negotiations without having made every reasonable effort to conclude the deal. If one party breaches such "contract to bargain," how should the other party's damages be measured? If the parties do not express an undertaking to engage in further good faith negotiations, how far should the court go in implying one? Are there alternative legal theories that a disappointed suitor might pursue when the other party breaks off negotiations before a final agreement can be concluded? One court's answer to some of these questions can be found in the next case.

Budget Marketing, Inc. v. Centronics Corporation

United States Court of Appeals, Eighth Circuit
927 F.2d 421 (1991)

GIBSON, Circuit Judge.

Budget Marketing, Inc. (BMI) and Charles A. Eagle appeal from an order of summary judgment denying their claims against Centronics Corporation for: (1) breach of implied duty to negotiate in good faith; (2) promissory estoppel; and (3) negligent misrepresentation. This suit arises out of the breakdown in negotiations for the purchase of BMI by Centronics. The district court also entered summary judgment against Centronics on its counterclaim of negligent misrepresentation. Both parties appeal. We affirm in part, but reverse on BMI's and Eagle's claim of promissory estoppel and remand for further consideration of this issue.

BMI is a Des Moines-based firm that markets and services magazine subscription agreements. Eagle is the president and principal shareholder of BMI. Centronics is a Delaware corporation based in New Hampshire.

In April 1987, BMI and Centronics executed a letter of intent outlining the basic terms of a proposed acquisition of BMI by Centronics. The letter stated that: (1) initial consideration would be $10 million; (2) additional consideration of up to $7 million would be contingent upon BMI meeting certain cash flow objectives over a 36-month period; (3) Centronics would provide additional capital during the 36-month "earn out" period, but BMI was responsible for cash needs until closing; and (4) BMI was responsible for dealing with any outstanding Federal Trade Commission or Federal Reserve complaints. The letter of intent also stated that completion of the merger depended on four express conditions: (1) satisfactory completion of an accounting, legal, and business review of BMI by Centronics; (2) purchase by BMI of "key man" life insurance coverage for Eagle; (3) avoidance by Centronics of a "significant cash outlay" for taxes because of BMI's planned change in accounting methods; and (4) execution of a definitive and legally binding agreement between BMI and Centronics.

The letter of intent provided that the transaction was subject to approval by the boards of directors of both corporations and by the BMI shareholders. It also contained a specific disclaimer: "This letter shall not be construed as a binding agreement on the part of BMI or Centronics." The letter set a target date for a definitive agreement of May 31, 1987.

Between January and May 1987, Centronics' officials carefully evaluated BMI. On May 21, the parties executed an addendum to the letter of intent that included changes favorable to Centronics. The Centronics' board approved the addendum on May 26, 1987. The addendum changed the target date for the definitive documents to June 30, 1987.

Other steps leading to the proposed merger followed: Centronics' public relations firm issued a press release about the letter of intent, the directors of BMI's parent company and the BMI shareholders approved the proposed merger, and Centronics received all documents necessary to complete the legal, business, and accounting review of BMI.

At the same time, Centronics began considering the acquisition of companies larger than BMI, and, in June 1987, made a formal proposal to acquire the assets of Ecko Group, Inc., for $127 million. In August, Centronics sent its draft of the final agreement to BMI.

Meanwhile, BMI and Eagle began taking the steps necessary to meet the conditions imposed by the letter of intent. Eagle borrowed $750,000 for BMI's use that he personally secured. BMI opened additional branch offices and expanded existing branch operations. BMI also purchased "key man" life insurance coverage for Eagle. Throughout the summer and fall of 1987, Eagle kept Centronics informed of BMI's expansion efforts and the other developments.

During this time, Centronics did not disclose that it might not complete the deal. In August, a Centronics representative confirmed a planned closing date no later than September 30 during a conversation with an official of Norwest Bank, BMI's lender. In mid-September, a Centronics executive participated in a meeting with BMI representatives, an investment banker from R.G. Dickinson, and representatives of Norwest Bank regarding post-closing financing for BMI. All of those present at the meeting proceeded on the assumption that the deal would close, and the Centronics representative said nothing to the contrary. In October, a Centronics representative discussed with a BMI official a necessary SEC filing that would have to be completed after closing. Also in October, Centronics' president and chief executive officer, Robert Stein, told Philip Boesel, an investment banker with R.G. Dickinson who had been involved with the planned merger, that Centronics was ready to move toward closing the deal with BMI.

In November 1987, Centronics abruptly halted preparations for the merger. After evaluating proposed federal tax legislation, Stein sent a letter to Eagle stating that in spite of Centronics' "good faith efforts," conditions beyond its control made the deal "no longer feasible." The letter stated that the merger would lead to a cash outlay for taxes because of BMI's change in accounting methods, thereby triggering one of the negative conditions of the letter of intent.

On appeal, BMI challenges Centronics' stated reason for terminating negotiations as mere "pretext"[3] because the proposed tax legislation did not apply to the proposed merger and the change of accounting methods would not in fact have resulted in Centronics having to make a cash outlay for taxes.

Eagle and BMI brought this action against Centronics, alleging that together they had invested "hundreds of thousands of dollars" to meet the cash flow requirements of the letter of intent. Eagle and BMI originally filed suit in an Iowa district court, but Centronics removed the case to federal court. Centronics filed a counterclaim alleging negligent misrepresentation concerning an FTC investigation of BMI and BMI's financial prospects.

The district court granted Centronics' motion for summary judgment, concluding that: (1) Centronics breached no agreement to acquire BMI: (2) the letter of intent disclaimed a duty to negotiate in good faith; (3) Centronics made no agreement or promise that was sufficiently definite to support recovery under promissory estoppel; and (4) Centronics owed BMI and Eagle no duty to supply the information upon which the negligent misrepresentation claim was based. * * * The court also granted BMI's motion for summary judgment on Centronics' counterclaim. Both parties appeal.

* * *

I.

BMI concedes that the letter of intent did not constitute a binding agreement to merge, but it contends that the letter did establish a duty on the part of both parties to negotiate in good faith. Breach of that duty, it argues, entitles BMI to reliance damages. Specifically, BMI points to language in the letter setting a target date for executing a definitive agreement and stating that the definitive agreement "will contain mutually agreed terms." BMI further points to the extensive efforts devoted by both parties to bring the merger to fruition during the months preceding and following the execution of the letter as confirming the existence of a good faith duty.

---

[3]BMI alleges that the October 1987 stock market "crash" caused Centronics to be interested in other, more lucrative acquisition opportunities.

Centronics counters by arguing that the specific language in the letter stating that it "shall not be construed as a binding agreement on the part of BMI or Centronics" means that no binding agreement to negotiate in good faith existed between the parties.

The district court found that the language of the letter of intent "plainly disclaimed any such [implied] duty." * * *

BMI relies primarily on three cases, Teachers Insurance & Annuity Association v. Tribune Company, 670 F. Supp. 491 (S.D.N.Y. 1987); Channel Home Centers v. Grossman, 795 F.2d 291 (3d Cir. 1986); Itek Corp. v. Chicago Aerial Industries, Inc., 248 A.2d 625 (Del. 1968), arguing that the overall language of the letter, coupled with the parties' conduct, gave rise to an implied duty to negotiate in good faith. The facts of these three cases are plainly distinguishable from the facts before us now.

In *Teachers Insurance & Annuity Association*, the parties had signed a financing commitment letter that, far from disclaiming an intent to be bound, stated that the parties had entered a " 'binding agreement.' " 670 F. Supp. at 491. The court concluded that " 'the intention to create mutually binding contractual obligations is stated with unmistakable clarity. . . .'" *Id.* at 499.

Such an intent is not present here. The letter of intent between BMI and Centronics clearly stated that it should not be construed as a binding agreement "except for the confidentiality obligations set forth in paragraphs 11 and 12." The fact that the parties expressly designated the confidentiality obligations as the sole exception to the general disclaimer lends further support to our conclusion that no binding agreement to negotiate in good faith can be implied from the overall language of the letter. In *Teachers Insurance & Annuity Association*, the court observed that it must determine the intent of the parties "at the time of their entry into the understanding," 670 F. Supp. at 499, and that a party not wanting to be bound by a preliminary letter can "very easily protect itself by not accepting language that indicates a 'firm commitment' or 'binding agreement.'" *Id*. With these observations in mind, we conclude that the parties here evinced no intent to be bound at the time they signed the letter; the letter clearly disclaims that it is a binding agreement.

Similarly, in *Channel Home Centers*, the Third Circuit found that a detailed letter of intent, signed by a property owner and a prospective tenant, gave rise to a duty to negotiate in good faith because the parties intended their promise to be binding. 795 F.2d at 299–300. The court concluded that the agreement contained "an unequivocal promise by [the landlord] to withdraw the store from the rental market and to negotiate the proposed leasing transaction with [the prospective tenant] to completion." *Id.* at 299. No such binding promises are contained in the letter signed by BMI and Centronics. Moreover, *Channel Home Centers* does not suggest that such promises can be implied in the presence of express language disclaiming an intent to be bound.

Finally, *Itek* is equally unpersuasive. The *Itek* court, applying Illinois law, concluded that a jury could find that the parties entered a binding agreement to negotiate in good faith. 248 A.2d at 629. The court relied in part on language in the letter of intent stating that although the parties would have "'no further obligation'" to each other if they failed to reach ultimate agreement, they would "'make every reasonable effort'" to agree upon and execute a final contract. *Id.* at 627. The letter signed by BMI and Centronics did not contain similar language. To the contrary, the letter expressly stated that the parties were not bound.

The language of the letter of intent signed by BMI and Centronics is clear, and its interpretation is therefore a matter of law for the court. * * * *Chariton Feed and Grain, Inc. v. Harder,* 369 N.W.2d 777, 785 (Iowa 1985).

Our conclusion that the letter of intent is not binding and did not give rise to an implied agreement to negotiate in good faith is consistent with Iowa authorities. See *Chariton,* 369 N.W.2d at 785 ("in construction of written contracts, the cardinal principle is that the intent of the parties must control; and except in cases of ambiguity, this is determined by what the contract itself says") * * *.

Courts are reluctant to find implied covenants. * * * They "must arise from the language used or be indispensable to effecting the intention of the parties." [*Pathology Consultants v. Gratton,* 343 N.W.2d 428, 434 (Iowa 1984).] While the court may find an implied term on a point not covered by the express terms of the agreement, "there can be no implied contract on a point fully covered by an express contract and in direct conflict therewith." *Snater v. Walters,* 250 Iowa 1189, 98 N.W.2d 302, 307 (1959). Because the facts here fail to meet the Iowa test for an implied contract and because finding an implied duty would contradict the express disclaimer of the letter of intent, we conclude that the parties did not bind themselves to an obligation to negotiate in good faith, and that the district court did not err in so holding.

II.

BMI next argues that oral promises made by Centronics after the execution of the letter of intent establish a triable claim based on promissory estoppel. BMI contends that Centronics, on numerous occasions, gave oral assurances that the deal would be consummated.[5] Relying on those promises, BMI spent substantial sums of money to comply with the conditions stated in the letter of intent. The record shows that BMI regularly apprised Centronics of its efforts and achievements.

Centronics argues that a promissory estoppel claim is foreclosed by the letter of intent, again relying on the disclaimer language. The district court did not rely on the disclaimer, but rejected BMI's promissory estoppel claim because the statements by Centronics were "vague" rather than "clear and definite." * * *

Under Iowa law, a party claiming recovery under promissory estoppel must establish: (1) a clear and definite agreement; (2) that it acted to its detriment in reasonable reliance on the agreement; and (3) that the equities support enforcement of the agreement. *National Bank of Waterloo v. Moeller,* 434 N.W.2d 887, 889 (Iowa 1989). Moeller further states that while no Iowa case has "squarely defined" the first element of "agreement," that earlier cases of the Iowa Supreme Court demonstrate that agreement can include a "promise" in which the promisor clearly understands that "the promisee was seeking an assurance upon which he could rely and without which he would not act." *Id.* at 889. This approach, Moeller states, adheres to the definition of promissory estoppel found in the Restatement (Second) of Contracts, which states:

> A promise which the promisor should reasonably expect to induce action or forbearance on the part of the promisee or a third person and which does induce such action or forbearance is binding if injustice can be

---

[5]BMI specifically points to: (1) an October 1987 telephone conversation between Stein and Boesel, the investment banker from R.G. Dickinson, in which Stein stated that Centronics was ready to move ahead toward closing; (2) an oral confirmation in August of a September 30 closing date during a conversation between a Centronics representative and a Norwest Bank official; (3) a mid-September meeting at Norwest Bank in which all of those present, including the Centronics representative, proceeded on the assumption the deal would close; (4) a statement by Stein in June 1987 that he wanted to defer closing until BMI met July sales projections, which BMI subsequently did; and (5) a statement in October by a Centronics' official to a BMI representative that a certain SEC filing would have to be made after closing, implicitly indicating that the deal would close.

> avoided only by enforcement of the promise. The remedy granted for breach may be limited as justice requires.

Restatement (Second) of Contracts § 90(1) (1979). * * *

Our study of the record convinces us that BMI's promissory estoppel claim should be submitted to a jury. Reasonable jurors could find that Centronics provided oral assurances to BMI and others that it would close on the deal. In October 1987, for instance, Stein told the investment banker, Boesel, that Centronics was ready to "move ahead toward a closing" of the deal. Eagle stated in his deposition and in a November 1987 letter to Stein that he and Boesel relied on Stein's "positive assurance" during that conversation to go ahead with the loan that R. G. Dickinson subsequently made to Eagle.[7]

In alleged reliance on Centronics' oral assurances, Eagle and BMI endeavored to meet all of the conditions imposed by the letter of intent. BMI opened new offices, expanded existing operations, hired more dealers and "independents," arranged for necessary credit, and purchased "key man" life insurance coverage for Eagle. BMI contends that it expended considerable effort and incurred substantial expense in doing so. Centronics was promptly apprised of the developments at BMI. We conclude that the evidence of Centronics' oral assurances, coupled with BMI's alleged reliance and Centronics' awareness of BMI's reliance, is substantial enough to establish a triable claim under Iowa's promissory estoppel doctrine. * * *

We also observe that the facts of this case closely resemble those in the Second Circuit case, *Arcadian Phosphates, Inc. v. Arcadian Corp.,* 884 F.2d 69 (2d Cir. 1989). In *Arcadian*, the parties had negotiated under the terms of a letter of intent which stated that a "'binding sales agreement'" would be completed at a later date. *Id.* at 70. After both sides took numerous steps to consummate the deal, the seller changed its position on what percentage of ownership it wanted to retain, thereby triggering suit by the buyer. The Second Circuit reversed summary judgment for the defendant on the plaintiffs' promissory estoppel claim, stating that "Appellants' . . . claim is based on evidence that [the defendant] knew and approved of [the plaintiffs'] expen-

---

[7]The conversation between Stein and Boesel and the subsequent loan to Eagle illustrate a necessary element of promissory estoppel, that of detrimental reliance. Logically, the promise must precede the promisee's alleged reliance. See *Moeller, 434 N.W.2d at 889.* In the case before us, BMI alleges a series of assurances, or promises, and a series of actions taken in reliance on those promises. To ultimately prevail on its promissory estoppel claim, BMI will have to establish that it took specific actions in reliance on specific promises.

ditures and collateral contracts, but . . . suddenly demanded a majority interest in [the plaintiff corporation] when the phosphate fertilizer business became 'dramatically' profitable." *Id.* at 74. The court concluded that triable issues existed as to whether the seller had made a clear and unambiguous promise to bargain in good faith, whether the buyer had reasonably and foreseeably relied on that promise, and whether the buyer had sustained an injury. *Id.* The court observed that prevailing on a promissory estoppel claim might not entitle the buyer to benefit-of-the-bargain damages. *Id.* at 73. Damages under promissory estoppel are often limited by the extent of the promisee's reliance rather than by the terms of the promise. *Id. See also* Restatement (Second) of Contracts, § 90 comment d; § 349 comment b (1979) (discussion of reliance damages).

* * *

Looking at the facts in the light most favorable to BMI, as we are required to do in determining a motion for summary judgment, we conclude that BMI has established a triable claim of promissory estoppel that would support an award of reliance damages. We therefore reverse the district court's grant of summary judgment on this issue.

III.

BMI finally argues that it also established a triable claim of negligent misrepresentation based on Centronics' oral assurances that the deal would close. We reject this claim under the rule of *Meier v. Alfa-Laval, Inc.*, 454 N.W.2d 576, 580–82 (Iowa 1990), a case recently decided by the Iowa Supreme Court.

Meier states that the tort of negligent misrepresentation applies to "a person in the profession or business of supplying information or opinions" and that such a person "owes a duty of reasonable care to clients or others." *Id.* at 581. The tort does not properly apply to a "vendor of merchandise," *Meier* concludes, citing with approval a Columbia Law Review article that differentiates between those "engaged in the business or profession of supplying guidance to others" and parties dealing at "arm's length" in commercial transactions. *Id.* (citing Hill, *Damages for Innocent Misrepresentation*, 73 Colum. L. Rev. 679, 688 (1973)).

The parties here were not in the business of supplying guidance to others; they were negotiating a commercial transaction at arm's length. The rule of *Meier* bars not only BMI's negligent misrepresentation claim, but also

Centronics' counterclaim based on negligent misrepresentation. We therefore affirm the district court's grant of summary judgment on these claims.

For the reasons stated above, we affirm in part the district court's order and remand for further consideration of BMI's promissory estoppel claim.

QUESTIONS AND NOTES

1. Questions about the facts of this case

   1.1. What was the purpose for the letter of intent between BMI and Centronics?

   1.2. What expressly did BMI and Centronics agree to in the letter of intent?

   1.3. The court distinguished all three cases on which BMI relied in support of its contention that the letter of intent established a duty on each party to negotiate in good faith. What were the critical factual distinctions between those cases and the case at hand? Were those differences enough to justify the difference in outcome?

   1.4. What facts will BMI have to establish on remand in order to prevail on its promissory estoppel claim? If BMI is successful, what will it recover from Centronics?

   1.5. Did we make a mistake by including this case in the book? Is this really a "contracts" case at all?

2. Questions about the law

   2.1. Assuming that a court concludes that a binding duty to negotiate in good faith does arise out of a letter of intent, what exactly does that mean? Is it bad faith if one party terminates negotiation for no apparent reason? How about if that party receives a better offer from a third party, or if the reason is that the first party won't yield to that party's demands?

2.2. Does the duty to negotiate in good faith include a duty to accept all reasonable terms? In stressing that a precontractual duty to negotiate in good faith does not encompass an automatic duty to approve the final deal, consider the following observation from the Seventh Circuit:

> In a business transaction both sides presumably try to get the best of the deal. This is the essence of bargaining and the free market. And in the context of this case, no legal rule bounds the run of business interest. No particular demand in negotiations could be termed dishonest, even if it seemed outrageous to the other party. The proper recourse is to walk away from the bargaining table, not to sue for "bad faith" in negotiations.

Apothekernes Laboratorium v. I.M.C. Chemical, 873 F.2d 155, 159 (7th Cir. 1989), *quoting Feldman v. Allegheny International, Inc.*, 850 F.2d 1217, 1223 (7th Cir. 1988).

2.3. In its summary of the facts giving rise to this lawsuit, the court discusses several events occurring *after* the letter of intent was signed. Should the parties' post-signing conduct be relevant to the determination of whether a duty to negotiate in good faith arose out of the letter? In its analysis of the legal issue, did the court give sufficient weight to that conduct?

2.4. How do the pre-contract formation liability cases like *Budget Marketing* differ from the "agreement to agree" cases that we examined in Section 6 of this chapter? Ponoroff argues that in the later cases the parties have manifested an intention to be bound at the time of the initial agreement and the only issue is whether the court may imply a reasonable term if the parties fail to subsequently agree or whether the agreement is fatally indefinite from the inception. In cases like *Budget Marketing*, there is clearly no intention to be bound to the terms of the deal in principle, but the question remains whether the parties' negotiations have proceeded to the point where liability may be imposed if one party breaks off negotiations in bad faith. Epstein believes that Ponoroff is splitting hairs and the analytic distinction between the two types of cases is just not all that sharp. Markell thinks Ponoroff and Epstein need to get a life. What do you think?

3. Notes

3.1. The clearer the letter of intent is with respect to whether or not it is intending to impose any precontractual obligations on the parties to negotiate in good faith, the more likely it is that this expressed intent will be enforced, although, as *Budget Marketing* suggests, other theories may be available where one party "misbehaves." If a letter of intent is ambiguous, however, the issue of whether a cause of action may lie for breach of the duty to negotiate in good faith must be ascertained from the specificity of the language used by the parties as well as all of the surrounding circumstances. For example, in *Schwanbeck v. Federal Mogul Corp.,* 578 N.E.2d 789 (Mass Ct. App. 1991), one corporation was negotiating to acquire the assets of another corporation. The parties reached the stage where they had their lawyers draft a letter of intent. The letter contained one provision stating that, "this letter is not intended to create, nor do you or we presently have any binding legal obligation whatever in any way relating to such sale and purchase . . ." and a later provision stating that, "it is our intention, and, we understand, your intention immediately to proceed in good faith in the negotiation of . . . a binding definitive agreement." In determining whether the selling corporation had breached its duty of good faith when it arranged a sale of the assets to a third party before attempting to conclude a deal with the first buyer, the court of appeals commented: "To the degree this cordial language [speaking of the second provision] smoothed the hard edge of the 'this is not yet a binding deal' language that had preceded it, the letter soon (on the second page) reverts to a 'keep-your-hands-on-your-wallet' tone." Thus, the court concluded that, "even if given legal effect to some extent, we are of opinion that, in the context of a proposed business acquisition, as to which the parties have agreed not to be bound by their preliminary agreement, and the seller has reserved the right to deal with other buyers, the obligation to proceed in good faith means something less than unremitting efforts to get to 'yes,' with the players at all times playing their cards face up." *Id.* at 795. On further appeal, the Supreme Judicial Court of Massachusetts concurred with the result in the court of appeal, but decided "that it is not necessary to determine what constitutes an obligation to negotiate in good faith or whether [the selling corporation] breached any such obligation, because we conclude that the parties did not bind themselves contractually to any such obligation." 592 N.E.2d 1289, 1291 (Mass. 1992).

3.2. Perhaps the most famous case involving precontractual liability was not a contracts case at all, but a tort action. In 1983, Pennzoil, seeking to acquire control of its substantial oil reserves, negotiated with Getty Oil and its major shareholder for the purchase of 57% of that company's stock at $110 per share. Although awaiting documentation of the transaction, the parties entered into a letter of intent. Subsequently, Texaco offered $128 per share for all of the stock of Getty Oil, which was promptly accepted by Getty Oil's major shareholder. Pennzoil then sued Texaco for the common law tort of inducement of breach of contract. Obviously, central to recovery under this theory was the requirement that the court find a binding obligation under the letter of intent. It did. *Texaco, Inc. v. Pennzoil Co.*, 729 S.W.2d 768 (Tex.App. 1987), *cert. denied* 485 U.S. 994 (1998). The result was entry of a judgment against Texaco and in favor of Pennzoil for $7.53 *billion* with an additional $1 billion in punitive damages thrown in for good measure. As a result of this judgment, Texaco eventually had to file for reorganization under the federal Bankruptcy Code. Clearly this case serves as a warning to the corporate lawyers negotiating and drafting these sorts of "gentlemen's agreements," and boards of directors properly seeking the best price for the company's shareholders, that the mere fact that *final* documents have not yet been prepared and signed may not prevent the assignment of liability if the circumstances point to the manifestation of assent by the parties.

SECTION 8: DEFEATING AGREEMENTS BASED ON MISUNDERSTANDING OF THE TERMS

Introduction

So far in this chapter we have been focused on various dimensions of the issue of when an agreement is formed, *i.e.*, up to what point in time is either party free to walk from the deal without liability? We have also considered how complete the expression of that agreement must be in order for it to be enforced by the court.

In this final section of the chapter we consider a related problem, namely, what happens when the parties both believe they have assented to a deal, but each of them has attached a materially different meaning or understanding to their outward manifestations of assent?

In these situations, the party challenging the agreement will claim not that she has a *defense* to liability, but rather that the differences in the parties' understanding of their respective intentions is so fundamental that there never was a deal to begin with, notwithstanding what the parties may have initially thought. In other words, that there can be no mutual assent if the parties have assented to different things. The questions you should be asking yourself as you review this material are: 1) under what conditions should such a misunderstanding preclude a finding that a contract was formed; 2) are those conditions satisfied in each of the next two cases; and 3) which of the parties ends up in these cases bearing the risk of the misunderstanding?

Raffles v. Wichelhaus
Court of Exchequer
1 H.& C. 906, 159 Eng. Rep. 375 (1864)

Declaration. For that it was agreed between the plaintiff and the defendants, to wit, at Liverpool, that the plaintiff should sell to the defendants, and the defendants buy of the plaintiff, certain goods, to wit, 125 bales of Surat cotton, guaranteed middling fair merchant's Dhollarah, to arrive ex "Peerless" from Bombay; and that the cotton should be taken from the quay, and that the defendants would pay the plaintiff for the same at a certain rate, to wit, at the rate of 17¼ d. per pound, within a certain time then agreed upon after the arrival of said goods in England. Averments: that the said goods did arrive by the said ship from Bombay in England, to wit, at Liverpool, and the plaintiff was then and there ready and willing and offered to deliver the said goods to the defendants, &c. Breach: that the defendants refused to accept the said goods or pay the plaintiff for them.

Plea. That the said ship mentioned in the said agreement was meant and intended by the defendants to be the ship called the "Peerless," which sailed from Bombay, to wit, in October; and that the plaintiff was not ready and willing, and did not offer to deliver to the defendants any bales of cotton which arrived by the last-mentioned ship, but instead thereof was only ready and willing, and offered to deliver to the defendants 125 bales of Surat cotton which arrived by another and different ship, which was also called the "Peerless," and which sailed from Bombay, to wit, in December.

Demurrer, and joinder therein.

Milward, in support of the demurrer. The contract was for the sale of a number of bales of cotton of a particular description, which the plaintiff was ready to deliver. It is immaterial by what ship the cotton was to arrive, so that it was a ship called the "Peerless." The words "to arrive ex 'Peerless,'" only mean that if the vessel is lost on the voyage, the contract is to be at an end. [Pollock, C.B. It would be a question for the jury whether both parties meant the same ship called the "Peerless."] That would be so if the contract was for the sale of a ship called the "Peerless"; but it is for the sale of cotton on board a ship of that name. [Pollack, C.B. The defendant only bought that cotton which was to arrive by a particular ship. It may as well be said, that if there is a contract for the purchase of certain goods in warehouse A., that is satisfied by the delivery of goods of the same description in warehouse B.] In that case there would be goods in both warehouses; here it does not appear that the plaintiff had any goods on board the other "Peerless." [Martin, B. It is imposing on the defendant a contract different from that which he entered into. Pollack, C.B. It is like a contract for the purchase of wine coming from a particular estate in France or Spain, where there are two estates of that name.] The defendant has no right to contradict by parol evidence a written contract good upon the face of it. He does not impute misrepresentation or fraud, but only says that he fancied the ship was a different one. Intention is of no avail, unless stated at the time of the contract. [Pollock, C.B. One vessel sailed in October and the other in December.] The time of sailing is no part of the contract.

Mellish (Cohen with him), in support of the plea. There is nothing on the face of the contract to shew that any particular ship called the "Peerless" was meant; but the moment it appears that two ships called the "Peerless" were about to sail from Bombay there is a latent ambiguity, and parol evidence may be given for the purpose of shewing that the defendant meant one "Peerless," and the plaintiff another. That being so, there was no consensus ad idem, and therefore no binding contract. He was then stopped by the Court.

PER CURIAM. There must be judgment for the defendants.

Judgment for the defendants.

QUESTIONS

1. Questions about the facts of this case

   1.1. Who sets out the facts of the case? Who were Milward and Mellish?

   1.2. Why did it matter what the parties privately may have intended when they made reference to the ship *Peerless*? And while we're at it, why did it even matter what vessel the cotton was being shipped by? Wasn't the important thing that the plaintiff delivered the proper quantity of the agreed-upon commodity to the defendant? Why then did the parties even specify the ship on which the cotton would be carried? Was it to establish the time of delivery or to protect the seller if the ship went down? Does that make a difference?

   1.3. Why do you suppose that the defendant refused to accept the cotton that arrived on the December *Peerless*? Did the court understand that? Did it care? Presumably, the October *Peerless* arrived in London some weeks or even months before the December *Peerless* and yet there is no indication that defendant raised any inquiry as to why his cotton was not on the October ship.

   1.4. As a result of the court's decision that no contract was formed, were the parties simply left in the same position they were before the purported agreement was entered into or did the decision actually benefit one party over the other?

2. Questions about the law

   2.1. Is *Raffles* consistent with objective theory? In discussing *Raffles,* Justice Holmes said, "The true ground of the decision was not that each party meant a different thing from the other, as has been implied in the explanation that has been mentioned, but that each said a different thing." O.W. HOLMES, THE COMMON LAW 242 [1881] (Howe ed. 1963). Do you agree with that analysis? Here's what Professor Gilmore had to say about it: "The magician who could 'objectify' *Raffles v. Wichelhaus* . . . could, the need arising, objectify anything. But why bother?" GRANT GILMORE, THE DEATH OF CONTRACT 41 (1974).

2.2. Did the *Raffles* court go pretty "light" on Mellish compared to Milward? What else might you have asked if you sat on the bench in this case before you were convinced that there was no contract?

Hill-Shafer Partnership v. Chilson Family Trust
Supreme Court of Arizona
165 Ariz. 469, 799 P.2d 810 (1990)

MOELLER, Justice.

JURISDICTION

A buyer sued for specific performance of a contract for the sale of land. The seller counterclaimed, seeking rescission of the contract. The trial court held there was a lack of mutual assent and granted summary judgment to the seller. The court of appeals reversed, holding that the facts did not present an issue of lack of mutual assent, but remanded for further proceedings on a theory of unilateral mistake. We granted seller's petition for review and have jurisdiction pursuant to A.R.S. § 12-120.24 and Ariz. Const. art. 6, § 5(3).

ISSUES

1. Whether, under the facts of this case, rescission of a real estate purchase contract on grounds of lack of mutual assent is precluded because the misunderstanding relates to a legal description of land.

2. Whether the trial court, on the particular facts before it, correctly granted summary judgment rescinding the real estate purchase contract on the grounds of lack of mutual assent.

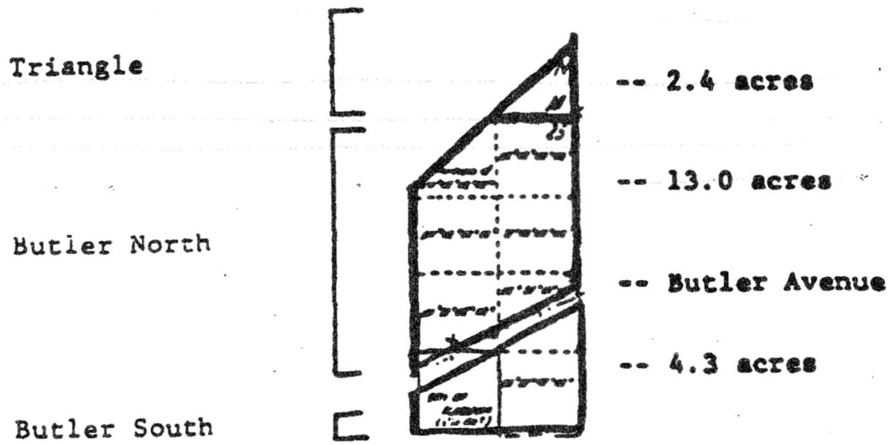

Chilson Family Trust Tract

FACTS

Ernest Chilson and Evelyn Chilson, trustees of the Chilson Family Trust, own approximately twenty acres of land south of Flagstaff on Butler Avenue. The tract, although contiguous, can be divided into three distinct units, as shown in the diagram below. The large parcel, containing about 17.3 acres, is bisected by Butler Avenue into "Butler North" and "Butler South." The smaller parcel, called the "Triangle," is a 2.4 acre triangular piece of land north of the larger parcel.

The Chilsons originally acquired the property in two separate transactions. Later, they directed a title agency to prepare one deed to include the property north of Butler and another deed to include the property south of Butler. The Chilsons used these two deeds to convey the property to themselves as trustees of a family trust.

In December 1984, the Chilsons listed the Triangle and Butler North with a broker, seeking a tenant for a long-term lease. Daniel Hill and Craig Shafer, general partners in the Hill-Shafer Partnership (buyer), saw a sign posted on the north side of Butler Avenue and became interested. Buyer contacted seller's broker and obtained a copy of the appraisal which listed the property as "15 acres of vacant land on the north side of Butler Avenue, one-quarter mile west of the Butler Interstate 40 interchange." The appraisal valued the property at $620,500.

Buyer inspected the land, and submitted a letter of intent proposing terms to purchase the listed property for the appraised value of $620,500. Buyer's letter of intent described the Triangle and Butler North plots of land, as had the listing and the appraisal. Buyer proposed that the final price of $620,500 be subject to an adjustment, depending on the actual acreage to be determined by a survey. The offer also contained certain proposed representations and warranties by seller as to location and size.

Seller rejected the proposal and, instead, directed its attorney to prepare a "take it or leave it" counter-offer at the same purchase price. Seller refused throughout negotiations to include a map as a part of the contract, and also refused to indicate the size of the parcel of land or to describe its location in lay terms or by reference to nearby landmarks. Seller also refused to agree to a price-per-acre adjustment mechanism or to make price in any way contingent upon an acreage figure to be determined by survey. Instead, seller insisted that the price be fixed at $620,500, and that the land be identified by legal description alone. Seller also proposed to make close of escrow contingent upon buyer's satisfaction with an economic and feasibility study that buyer would perform at its expense after receipt of a survey from seller.

The legal description contained in seller's counter-offer did not, in fact, describe the Triangle and Butler North. Rather, it described Butler North and Butler South. Buyer "accepted" seller's counter-offer and the parties entered into a contract. Escrow instructions were signed on July 5, 1985. When seller reviewed the escrow instructions in mid-July, he discovered the error in the legal description. Seller has consistently contended it always intended to sell Butler North and the Triangle, and that the use of the legal description which instead described Butler North and Butler South was due to an error. Seller contends the error originated in one of the two earlier deeds prepared by the title company by which the Chilsons transferred the property to the trust. Seller borrowed the description from one of the earlier deeds on the mistaken assumption that it described the Triangle and Butler North.

Upon discovery of the error, seller prepared an amendment to correct the legal description. Buyer refused to accept the amendment and contended it was entitled to a conveyance of the property included in the legal description. As a result of the dispute, seller cancelled the escrow, and buyer sued for specific performance. Seller counterclaimed, alleging fraudulent concealment and racketeering, and also sought rescission and a decree quieting title in it. The trial court granted summary judgment against seller on the fraud and racketeering claims, which are not involved in this appeal. The trial court also granted summary judgment against buyer on the specific performance claim and for seller on the quiet title claim, rescinding the contract for lack of mutual assent.

Buyer appealed from the summary judgment, and seller cross-appealed from what it considered to be an inadequate award of attorney's fees. The court of appeals reversed the summary judgment, holding that because the legal description in the contract was not ambiguous or vague, no misunderstanding concerning it could be the basis for relief on a theory of lack of mutual assent. The court of appeals remanded for further proceedings on a theory of unilateral mistake. * * * We granted seller's petition for review. We conclude the trial court properly granted summary judgment on a theory of lack of mutual assent.

DISCUSSION

* * *

In the case before us, assuming all inferences in favor of buyer, we are convinced, as was the trial judge, that reasonable minds could only conclude that there was no mutual assent by the parties. All parties agree that initially all negotiations were directed towards Butler North and the Triangle. Both the appraisal and the letter of intent described and set a price only for the property north of Butler. Buyer's essential contention is that once seller made a counter-offer, the entire posture of the deal changed. Buyer argues that, although it offered to buy only the property north of Butler, once the seller insisted the property be identified by legal description alone, buyer's intent shifted (although uncommunicated to seller) and it thereafter intended to purchase whatever was contained in the legal description, regardless of what it was or where it was.

* * *

A careful examination of the deposition testimony demonstrates that no testimony or reasonable inference rebuts seller's testimony that seller only intended to convey the property north of Butler. Absent any such testimony or inference, buyer relies solely on the fact that seller insisted that a legal description govern. Our review of the evidence leads us to hold that, under these particular facts, the only reasonable conclusion to be drawn from the evidence is that seller insisted on use of a legal description to avoid a price adjustment based on the actual acreage of the property north of Butler. There is no evidence that the parties ever discussed any property south of Butler. The first and only time Butler South crept into the deal was in the legal description contained in seller's counter-offer. Buyer's agents testified that, although they knew they were purchasing property in the Butler area, they had no specific knowledge of how many acres were involved. Buyer was not even sure seller owned the parcel south of Butler. Seller, on the other hand, was interested only in selling Butler North and the Triangle.

Generally, if a seller intends to sell and a buyer intends to buy land other than that described in a deed, a case of mutual mistake is presented. * * * A mutual mistake exists where there has been a meeting of the minds of the parties, and an agreement is actually entered into, but the agreement in its written form does not express what was really intended by the parties. * * * Justice Holmes wrote:

> When both parties to a conveyance have intended to describe a certain parcel of land identified by their senses, and by the words of their previous agreement, and have used words supposed by them to be apt for their purpose, but in fact describing that parcel, and something more, the full purport of all their acts, taken together, is only to convey the parcel intended . . . .

Goode v. Riley, 153 Mass. 585, 586, 28 N.E. 228, 228 (1891).

Because we view the evidence in the light most favorable to buyer, we accept its contention that it intended to purchase whatever the legal description identified, regardless of size or location. Because seller did not have a similar intent and did not intend to convey whatever was included within the legal description, this case does not present a problem of mutual mistake but, rather, a problem of lack of mutual assent.

It is well-established that before a binding contract is formed, the parties must mutually consent to all material terms. A distinct intent common to both parties must exist without doubt or difference, and until all understand alike there can be no assent. * * * If one party thinks he is buying one thing and the other party thinks he is selling another thing, no meeting of the minds occurs, and no contract is formed. * * *

The most famous statement of this point of law arose in the case of *Raffles v. Wichelhaus*, 2 Hurl. 906, 159 Eng.Rep. 375 (1864). In *Raffles*, the parties agreed on a sale of goods which was to be delivered from Bombay by the ship "Peerless." In fact, two ships named "Peerless" were sailing from Bombay at different times, and each party had a different ship in mind. The arrival time of the merchandise was of the essence to the contract. Because the understandings of the parties were different as to a material term, no binding contract was formed.

Importantly, however, mutual assent is based on objective evidence, not on the hidden intent of the parties. * * * In other words, what is operative is the objective manifestations of assent by the parties. * * * As the Restatement describes it, a contract is formed if there is "manifestation of mutual assent to the exchange and a consideration." Restatement (Second) of Contracts § 17 (1979). Additionally, the Restatement explains the effect of misunderstandings on contracts:

> 20. Effect of Misunderstanding
>
> (1) There is no manifestation of mutual assent to an exchange if the parties attach materially different meanings to their manifestations and
>
> (a) neither party knows or has reason to know the meaning attached by the other; or
>
> (b) each party knows or each party has reason to know the meaning attached by the other.
>
> (2) The manifestations of the parties are operative in accordance with the meaning attached to them by one of the parties if
>
> (a) that party does not know of any different meaning attached by the other, and the other knows the meaning attached by the first party; or
>
> (b) that party has no reason to know of any different meaning attached by the other, and the other has reason to know the meaning attached by the first party.

Restatement (Second) of Contracts § 20 (1979).

The first subsection describes the circumstances under which the parties' misunderstanding of the meaning of their manifestations prevents formation of an enforceable bargain. The second subsection describes the circumstances under which a bargain may be enforceable in accordance with the meaning that one party has attached. Under Section 20(1), "Even though the parties manifest mutual assent to the same words of agreement, there may be no contract because of material difference of understanding as to the terms of the exchange." Restatement (Second) of Contracts § 20 comment c, see also comment d. Insofar as the land in this litigation is concerned, we believe the case is governed by Section 20(1)(a) and, therefore, do not reach the alternative provisions of Section 20.

The court of appeals held that no lack of mutual assent can be found due to a misunderstanding where no ambiguity or vagueness exists in the words of a contract. The court of appeals relied on the reporter's note to Section 20, which states:

> A contract should be held nonexistent under this section only when the misunderstanding goes to conflicting and irreconcilable meanings of a material term that could have either but not both meanings.

Relief is proper if the writing evidencing the purported agreement is uncertain or ambiguous. * * * 1 S. Williston, Contracts § 95 (3d ed. 1957). The legal description contained in the contract, the court of appeals reasoned, contained no ambiguity or ambivalence. In fact, a legal description is the most precise description that can be devised. Therefore, the court of appeals held that the seller cannot claim a misunderstanding occurred or that no meeting of the minds existed as to an essential term. Although the court of appeals' logic has a certain force to it, we cannot agree with it.

A dual meaning is only one situation in which a court can find a lack of mutual assent. As stated by the court in *Buckmaster v. Dent*, some extrinsic facts could create "a latent ambiguity in otherwise clear and intelligible language." 146 Ariz. 521, 523, 707 P.2d 319, 321 (App. 1985). * * *

In *Buckmaster*, buyer and seller signed a contract for the purchase of property. The purchase contract reserved an "easement" to the sellers. The sellers claimed that the word "easement" did not refer to a single easement but actually referred to two easements. Despite the rather clear language of the contract, the court of appeals looked to the extrinsic facts surrounding the contract and the conduct of the parties and held the parties reasonably had different understandings. Consequently, no contract was formed and summary judgment rescinding the contract was appropriate.

As long as the misunderstandings of the parties are reasonable under the specific circumstances of the case, a court may properly find a lack of mutual assent. We do not believe that the fact that a legal description is the source of the misunderstanding precludes relief.

The legal description in this case reads as follows:

> The following described real property situated in Coconino County, Arizona:
>
> The East half of the Northeast quarter of the Northeast quarter of Section 23, Township 21 North, Range 7 East;
>
> EXCEPT the Southwest quarter of the Southeast quarter of the Northeast quarter of the Northeast quarter; and
>
> EXCEPT a strip of land 88.00 feet in width, the centerline of which is described as follows:
>
> BEGINNING at a point from which the Northeast corner of Section 23, Township 21 North, Range 7 East, Gila and Salt River Base and Meridian is North 0 degrees 44 minutes 59 seconds west a distance of 753.26 feet; Thence South 70 degrees 09 minutes 11 seconds West a distance of 32.67 feet to the point of curvature of the curve to the left having a radius of 600.000 feet and a central angle of 12 degrees 48 minutes 25 seconds; Thence along a side curve a distance of 134.11 feet to a point of tangency; Thence South 57 degrees 20 minutes 46 seconds West a distance of 340.23 feet to the North line of the Southwest quarter of the Southeast quarter of the Northeast quarter of said Section 23.

The seller believed the description covered only the property north of Butler. It did not. To an untrained person, the language of a legal description is susceptible of different interpretations. In fact, the parties in this case testified they could not understand the technical terminology of the legal description. Shafer, the buyer, testified the description looked "like Greek" to him. Chilson, the seller, testified that: "I just had to assume that it was correct of what we intended to do, and found out later it wasn't, however." As stated earlier, the price of $620,500 was determined after an appraisal of the Triangle and Butler North. Buyer submitted a letter of intent only on the property north of Butler. The property south of Butler was never discussed. Seller believed the description contained in the offer described the property that had been listed and discussed. Had buyer accepted the offer on that basis and with the same intent, a binding contract (subject to reformation) might well have been formed for the sale of the land north of Butler. However, buyer's intent varied from seller's. Buyer's understanding was that it would acquire whatever was included in the legal description, regardless of size or location. We disagree with the court of appeals' conclusion that the preciseness of a legal description, as a matter of law, prevented a rescission based on a misunderstanding. Any reasonable view of the evidence inevitably leads to the conclusion that there was no meeting of the minds and no enforceable contract was formed. We conclude that the trial court properly granted summary judgment in favor of the seller.

DISPOSITION

The evidence supports the trial court's conclusion that, as a matter of law, there was no mutual assent. Therefore, the trial court's grant of summary judgment in favor of the seller is affirmed. The court of appeals' decision is vacated.

QUESTIONS

1. Questions about the facts of this case

   1.1. According to the Supreme Court of Arizona, what did the seller intend to sell and what did the buyer intend to buy?

   1.2. Was there an actual meeting of the minds in this case? Was there an apparent meeting of the minds?

   1.3. Do you believe the buyer's assertion that "it intended to purchase whatever was contained in the legal description"? Was that fact important?

2. Questions about the law

   2.1. The court of appeals remanded on the theory of unilateral mistake. If this was a case of unilateral mistake, under objective theory, who would ordinarily bear the risk of that mistake?

   2.2. The Arizona Supreme Court obviously did not believe this to be a case of unilateral mistake; it also stated, "this case does not present a problem of mutual mistake but, rather, a problem of lack of mutual assent." What's the difference between the two? Hint: look at the second to last paragraph of the court's decision.

   2.3. We will consider the doctrine of mutual mistake in the next chapter. After you read those cases—*Sherwood v. Walker* and *Cummings v.*

Dusenberg—consider whether the *Hill-Shafer* case is more like those decisions than it is like *Raffles.*

2.4. Since the buyer in *Chilson* has lost his claim for specific performance of the contract concerning the Butler North and South plots of land, can it now go back and sue the seller for what the seller apparently was willing to sell on these terms, namely, the Butler South and Triangle plots?

2.5. Is *Restatement (Second) of Contracts* § 20, cited and applied in *Chilson,* a codification of the Court of Exchequer's decision in *Raffles*?

Problem on Mutual Misunderstanding

Epstein has two prized hunting dogs: Gober and Goober. For several days Ponoroff had been negotiating with Epstein to purchase Gober. After much haggling, Epstein finally says, "Ok, I'll sell you Goober for $1,000." Ponoroff knew that Epstein was uncommonly attached to Goober and that Epstein would never part with Goober for any price, but he nonetheless promptly replied, "I accept your offer." Goober and Gober are roughly of the same age and pedigree. Consult § 20 of *Restatement (Second) of Contracts* and answer the following questions:

- Is there a contract here, and, if so, is it for the sale of Goober or Gober?
- How, if at all, does it change your answer if Ponoroff had no reason to know of Epstein's unusual "attachment" to Goober?
- How, if at all, does it change your answer if the facts were different in that Epstein knowingly offered Goober, a less valuable retriever, hoping, as it turns out correctly, that Ponoroff would assume he meant Gober and accept? Suppose Ponoroff is aware what Epstein is up to but still accepts intending to assert a claim for Gober?

Well, now that you know whether your client has made a deal, assuming she has, it's time to find out whether it's a deal that the law will enforce. Ready for Chapter 2?

Chapter Two

IS IT A DEAL THAT THE LAW WILL ENFORCE?

SECTION 1: PREVIEW OF HOW THE LAW ENFORCES AN AGREEMENT AND AN OVERVIEW OF WHY THE LAW DOES NOT ENFORCE SOME AGREEMENTS

In the first chapter, we considered whether there was an agreement. In this chapter, we consider the different, but closely related, question of which agreements are legally enforceable.

If you read the previous sentence carefully you should have three other questions of your own:

(1) What do courts do to enforce agreements?
(2) How come all agreements are not legally enforceable?
(3) Which agreements are not legally enforceable?

Chapter Five deals with the first question of how a court enforces an agreement. We will see that a court generally requires a person who has not done what he agreed to do to pay money damages.

Consider the following example/multiple choice question: Epstein agreed to mow Ponoroff's yard every Monday for $10 a week for the forty weeks that is summer in New Orleans. Epstein now refuses to do what he agreed to do. No one else is willing to mow Ponoroff's yard for less than $15 a week. Ponoroff sues Epstein for breach of contract. How will a court enforce the agreement? By:

A. Putting Epstein in jail?

B. Making Epstein pay a fine?
C. Going each week out to Ponoroff's house in the Garden District and making sure that Epstein mows Ponoroff's lawn and does it right?
D. Requiring Epstein to pay Ponoroff damages of $600 (40 × 15)?
E. Requiring Epstein to pay Ponoroff damages of $400 (40 × 10)?
F. Requiring Epstein to pay Ponoroff damages of $200 (40 × [15–10])?

Most courts would pick F.

As you will learn in the later chapter on how courts enforce agreements, the usual remedy for breach of a contract is a damages award measured by the dollars that it takes to put the plaintiff in the same position that he would have been in if the contract had been performed. If Epstein had performed, Ponoroff would have his lawn mowed at a cost to him of $10 a week. Now, if Epstein pays Ponoroff damages which amount to $5 a week, Ponoroff will have his lawn mowed at a cost to him of $10 a week.

This chapter surveys possible legal grounds for NOT enforcing such an agreement. What are possible reasons that Epstein should be able to "rescind" his agreement to mow Ponoroff's yard or otherwise get out of doing what he agreed to do?

We will see that arguments against enforcing an agreement can be based on legal issues related to (1) the deal-making process, (2) the parties to the deal, or (3) the terms of the deal itself. More specifically,

What if Epstein made a mistake? *E.g.*, Epstein thought Ponoroff's yard, like other yards in the Garden District, was two-tenths of an acre instead of the 2 acres it actually is.

What about Ponoroff's fraud or misrepresentation? *E.g.*, Ponoroff told Epstein that the yard was two-tenths of an acre instead of the 2 acres that it actually is.

What about Epstein's lack of capacity? *E.g.*, Epstein was obviously drunk as a skunk when he made the agreement with Ponoroff.

What about Ponoroff's duress or undue influence? *E.g.*, Ponoroff was pointing a gun at Epstein's dog and threatening to shoot when Epstein finally agreed.

What about the illegality of the subject matter of the contract? *E.g.*, the agreement was in violation of Louisiana minimum wage laws.

What about the "unconscionability," the "statute of frauds," or the absence of "consideration" or "promissory estoppel"?

The "point" of this series of questions is to show you (i) what the most common legal grounds for not enforcing an agreement are and (ii) that the point and purpose (*i.e.*, the "how come") of most but not all of these legal grounds for not enforcing an agreement is obvious.

SECTION 2: MISTAKEN, UNSTATED FACTUAL ASSUMPTIONS

All agreements are based on various factual assumptions. Sometimes, these assumptions can be found in the terms of the agreement, and the terms of the agreement sometimes spell out whether a party can cancel the agreement if such an express factual assumption turns out to be erroneous.

It is unlikely, however, that even the most comprehensive commercial agreement sets out all of the factual assumptions of the parties. And, agreements prepared by the parties themselves are likely to omit many if not most factual assumptions. This part of the book focuses on such mistaken, unstated factual assumptions.

Assume, for example, that Epstein, Markell, and Ponoroff enter into an agreement with LEXIS to write a 1000 page contracts book. Subsequently, LEXIS tries to recover the substantial advance it paid to your three authors, alleging that all parties erroneously believed that most law schools required students to take a six-hour contracts class. Or assume that Epstein, Markell, and Ponoroff agree that they will spend two summers in Tuscaloosa working on the contracts book. Subsequently, Markell and Ponoroff try to get out of the agreement, alleging that they erroneously believed that there was a five-star French restaurant in Tuscaloosa.

What factual issues and legal questions are presented by these hypotheticals? The two hypotheticals and subsequent cases raise three core problems for courts and lawyers.

First, there is the problem of proof. How can a lawyer prove what her client was thinking about but did not say when he entered into the agreement?

Second, there is problem of policy. Why should courts excuse a person from doing what she agreed to do because of a mistaken, unstated factual assumption? Is the concern conceptual—mistake somehow prevents mutual assent, *i.e.*, no meeting of the minds? Is the concern ethical—it is somehow unfair for one party to benefit from mistaken, factual assumptions? Is the concern economic—the law should reward efficient bargaining behavior, whatever that is?

Third, there is the related problem of "rules." Once the courts have decided what the relevant policy consideration(s) is (are), what rule with respect to relief for unstated factual assumptions advances that policy? Should it matter whether the mistake relates to "quality" or "nature"? Whether the mistake is a mistake of judgment or a clerical error? Whether the mistake relates to facts of law? Whether both parties have made the same mistake?

Sherwood v. Walker
Supreme Court of Michigan
66 Mich. 568, 33 N.W. 919 (1887)

Morse, J.

Replevin for a cow. Suit commenced in justice's court; Judgment for plaintiff; Appealed to circuit court of Wayne county, and verdict and judgment for plaintiff in that court. The defendants bring error, and set out 25 assignments of the same.

* * *

The Walkers are importers and breeders of polled Angus cattle.

The plaintiff is a banker living at Plymouth, in Wayne county. He called upon the defendants at Walkerville for the purchase of some of their stock, but found none there that suited him. Meeting one of the defendants afterwards, he was informed that they had a few head upon this Greenfield farm. He was asked to go out and look at them, with the statement at the time that they were probably barren, and would not breed.

May 5, 1886, plaintiff went out to Greenfield and saw the cattle. A few days thereafter, he called upon one of the defendants with the view of purchasing a cow, known as "Rose 2d of Aberlone." After considerable talk, it was agreed that defendants would telephone Sherwood at his home in Plymouth in reference to the price. The second morning after this talk he was called up by telephone, and the terms of the sale were finally agreed upon. He was to pay five and one-half cents per pound, live weight, fifty pounds shrinkage. He was asked how he intended to take the cow home, and replied that he might ship her from King's cattle-yard. He requested defendants to confirm the sale in writing, which they did by sending him the following letter:

Walkerville, May 15, 1886.

T. C. Sherwood,

President, etc.,—

Dear Sir: We confirm sale to you of the cow Rose 2d of Aberlone, lot 56 of our catalogue, at five and a half cents per pound, less fifty pounds shrink. We inclose herewith order on Mr. Graham for the cow. You might leave check with him, or mail to us here, as you prefer.

Yours truly,

Hiram Walker & Sons.

The order upon Graham inclosed in the letter read as follows:

Walkerville, May 15, 1886.

George Graham: You will please deliver at King's cattle-yard to Mr. T. C. Sherwood, Plymouth, the cow Rose 2d of Aberlone, lot 56 of our catalogue. Send halter with cow, and have her weighed.

Yours truly,

Hiram Walker & Sons.

On the twenty-first of the same month the plaintiff went to defendants' farm at Greenfield, and presented the order and letter to Graham, who informed him that the defendants had instructed him not to deliver the cow. Soon after, the plaintiff tendered to Hiram Walker, one of the defendants, $80, and demanded the cow. Walker refused to take the money or deliver the cow. The plaintiff then instituted this suit.

* * *

It appears from the record that both parties supposed this cow was barren and would not breed, and she was sold by the pound for an insignificant sum as compared with her real value if a breeder. She was evidently sold and purchased on the relation of her value for beef, unless the plaintiff had learned of her true condition, and concealed such knowledge from the defendants. Before the plaintiff secured possession of the animal, the defendants learned that she was with calf, and therefore of great value, and undertook to rescind the sale by refusing to deliver her. The question arises whether they had a right to do so.

The circuit judge ruled that this fact did not avoid the sale, and it made no difference whether she was barren or not. I am of the opinion that the court erred in this holding. I know that this is a close question, and the dividing line between the adjudicated cases is not easily discerned. But it must be considered as well settled that a party who has given an apparent consent to a contract of sale may refuse to execute it, or he may avoid it after it has been completed, if the assent was founded, or the contract made, upon the mistake of a material fact,—such as the subject-matter of the sale, the price, or some collateral fact materially inducing the agreement; and this can be done when the mistake is mutual.

If there is a difference or misapprehension as to the substance of the thing bargained for; if the thing actually delivered or received is different in substance from the thing bargained for and intended to be sold,—then there is no contract; but if it be only a difference in some quality or accident, even though the mistake may have been the actuating motive to the purchaser or seller, or both of them, yet the contract remains binding.

The difficulty in every case is to determine whether the mistake or misapprehension is as to the substance of the whole contract, going, as it were, to the root of the matter, or only to some point, even though a material point, an error as to which does not affect the substance of the whole consideration.

It has been held, in accordance with the principles above stated, that where a horse is bought under the belief that he is sound, and both vendor and vendee honestly believe him to be sound, the purchaser must stand by his bargain, and pay the full price, unless there was a warranty.

It seems to me, however, in the case made by this record, that the mistake or misapprehension of the parties went to the whole substance of the agreement. If the cow was a breeder, she was worth at least $750; if barren, she was worth not over $80. The parties would not have made the contract of sale except upon the understanding and belief that she was incapable of breeding, and of no use as a cow. It is true she is now the identical animal that they thought her to be when the contract was made; there is no mistake as to the identity of the creature. Yet the mistake was not of the mere quality of the animal, but went to the very nature of the thing. A barren cow is substantially a different creature than a breeding one. There is as much difference between them for all purposes of use as there is between an ox and a cow that is capable of breeding and giving milk. If the mutual mistake had simply related to the fact whether she was with calf or not for one season, then it might have been a good sale; but the mistake affected the character of the animal for all time, and for her present and ultimate use. She was not in fact the animal, or the kind of animal, the defendants intended to sell or the plaintiff to buy. She was not a barren cow, and, if this fact had been known, there would have been no contract. The mistake affected the substance of the whole consideration, and it must be considered that there was no contract to sell or sale of the cow as she actually was. The thing sold and bought had in fact no existence. She was sold as a beef creature would be sold; she is in fact a breeding cow, and a valuable one.

The court should have instructed the jury that if they found that the cow was sold, or contracted to be sold, upon the understanding of both parties that she was barren, and useless for the purpose of breeding, and that in fact she was not barren, but capable of breeding, then the defendants had a right to rescind, and to refuse to deliver, and the verdict should be in their favor.

The judgment of the court below must be reversed, and a new trial granted, with costs of this Court to defendants.

SHERWOOD, J., (dissenting.)

I do not concur in the opinion given by my brethren in this case. I think the judgments before the justice and at the circuit were right. * * *

As has already been stated by my brethren, the record shows that the plaintiff is a banker and farmer as well, carrying on a farm, and raising the best breeds of stock, and lived in Plymouth, in the county of Wayne, 23 miles from Detroit; that the defendants lived in Detroit, and were also dealers in stock of the higher grades; that they had a farm at Walkerville, in Canada, and also one in Greenfield in said county of Wayne, and upon these farms the defendants kept their stock. The Greenfield farm was about 15 miles from the plaintiff's. In the spring of 1886 the plaintiff, learning that the defendants had some "polled Angus cattle" for sale, was desirous of purchasing some of that breed, and meeting the defendants, or some of them, at Walkerville, inquired about them, and was informed that they had none at Walkerville, "but had a few head left on their farm in Greenfield, and asked the plaintiff to go and see them, stating that in all probability they were sterile and would not breed." In accordance with said request, the plaintiff, on the fifth day of May, went out and looked at the defendants' cattle at Greenfield, and found one called "Rose, Second," which he wished to purchase, and the terms were finally agreed upon at five and a half cents per pound, live weight, 50 pounds to be deducted for shrinkage. The sale was in writing, and the defendants gave an order to the plaintiff directing the man in charge of the Greenfield farm to deliver the cow to plaintiff. This was done on the fifteenth of May. On the twenty-first of May plaintiff went to get his cow, and the defendants refused to let him have her; claiming at the time that the man in charge at the farm thought the cow was with calf, and, if such was the case, they would not sell her for the price agreed upon. The record further shows that the defendants, when they sold the cow, believed the cow was not with calf, and barren; that from what the plaintiff had been told by defendants (for it does not appear he had any other knowledge or facts from which he could form an opinion) he believed the cow was farrow, but still thought she could be made to breed. The foregoing shows the entire interview and treaty between the parties as to the sterility and qualities of the cow sold to the plaintiff. The cow had a calf in the month of October.

There is no question but that the defendants sold the cow representing her of the breed and quality they believed the cow to be, and that the purchaser so understood it. And the buyer purchased her believing her to be of the breed represented by the sellers, and possessing all the qualities stated, and even more. He believed she would breed. There is no pretense that the plaintiff bought the cow for beef, and there is nothing in the record indicating that he would have bought her at all only that he thought she might be made to breed. Under the foregoing facts,—and these are all that are contained in the record material to the contract,—it is held that because it turned out that the plaintiff was more correct in his judgment as to one quality of the cow than the defendants, and a quality, too, which could not by any possibility be positively known at the time by either party to exist, the contract may be annulled by the defendants at their pleasure. I know of no law, and have not been referred to any, which will justify any such holding, and I think the circuit judge was right in his construction of the contract between the parties.

It is claimed that a mutual mistake of a material fact was made by the parties when the contract of sale was made. There was no warranty in the case of the quality of the animal. When a mistaken fact is relied upon as ground for rescinding, such fact must not only exist at the time the contract is made, but must have been known to one or both of the parties. Where there is no warranty, there can be no mistake of fact when no such fact exists, or, if in existence, neither party knew of it, or could know of it; and that is precisely this case. If the owner of a Hambletonian horse had speeded him, and was only able to make him go a mile in three minutes, and should sell him to another, believing that was his greatest speed, for $300, when the purchaser believed he could go much faster, and made the purchase for that sum, and a few days thereafter, under more favorable circumstances, the horse was driven a mile in 2 min. 16 sec., and was found to be worth $20,000, I hardly think it would be held, either at law or in equity, by any one, that the seller in such case could rescind the contract. The same legal principles apply in each case.

In this case neither party knew the actual quality and condition of this cow at the time of the sale. The defendants say, or rather said, to the plaintiff, "they had a few head left on their farm in Greenfield, and asked plaintiff to go and see them, stating to plaintiff that in all probability they were sterile and would not breed." Plaintiff did go as requested, and found there these cows, including the one purchased, with a bull. The cow had been exposed, but neither knew she was with calf or whether she would breed. The defendants thought she would not, but the plaintiff says that he thought she could be made to breed, but believed she was not with calf. The defendants sold the cow for what they believed her to be, and the plaintiff bought her as he believed she was, after the statements made by the defendants. No conditions whatever were attached to the terms of sale by either party. It was in fact as absolute as it could well be made, and I know of no precedent as authority by which this court can alter the contract thus made by these parties in writing,—interpolate in it a condition by which, if the defendants should be mistaken in their belief that the cow was barren, she could be returned to them and their contract should be annulled. It is not the duty of courts to destroy contracts when called upon to enforce them, after they have been legally made. There was no mistake of any material fact by either of the parties in the case as would license the vendors to rescind. There was no difference between the parties, nor misapprehension, as to the substance of the thing bargained for, which was a cow supposed to be barren by one party, and believed not to be by the other. As to the quality of the animal, subsequently developed, both parties were equally ignorant, and as to this each party took his chances. If this were not the law, there would be no safety in purchasing this kind of stock.

I entirely agree with my brethren that the right to rescind occurs whenever "the thing actually delivered or received is different in substance from the thing bargained for, and intended to be sold; but if it be only a difference in some quality or accident, even though the misapprehension may have been the actuating motive" of the parties in making the contract, yet it will remain binding. In this case the cow sold was the one delivered. What might or might not happen to her after the sale formed no element in the contract. * * * The judgment should be affirmed.

QUESTIONS AND NOTES

1. Questions about the facts of this case

1.1. Who sued whom for what?

1.2. What is "replevin"?

1.3. Was Sherwood in the cattle business? Was Walker? Did that matter to the court? Should it have?

1.4. Could the parties have determined whether Rose 2d was "with calf"? (At last, a question that students who did their undergraduate work at Auburn can answer.)

1.5. Did either party sustain a loss because the court refused to enforce the sale agreement? Would either party have sustained a loss if the court had enforced the agreement?

1.6. The Michigan Supreme Court ordered a new trial with the following direction to the trial court: "the court should have instructed the jury that if they found that the cow was sold, or contracted to be sold, upon the understanding of both parties that she was barren . . . then the defendant has the right to rescind." If you were the attorney for the plaintiff/buyer, would you give up and dismiss? If not, what known facts would you emphasize at this new trial?

2. Questions about the law

2.1. How is this case different from *Raffles*? How is the use of the term "Rose 2d" in this case different from the use of the term "Peerless" in *Raffles*?

2.2. What is the *Sherwood v. Walker* test for determining whether a mistake is a defense to enforcement of an agreement?

2.3. Apply that test to the following problem: Markell buys a painting from Ponoroff for $23,000. Both believe that it is a major work by Warhol. Markell later learns that while the painting is by Warhol, it is one of his minor works and is worth no more than $1000. Markell wants out of the agreement and he wants his money back.

2.4. Is it possible to distinguish mistakes "running to the value," from mistakes "touching the substance of the consideration" in agreements with a subject matter other than the sale of goods? For example,

(a) A and B agree that A will pay $240 to support C, B's child. At the time of the agreement, both A and B mistakenly assume that A is the father of C. When A later learns that D is C's father, A asserts mutual mistake of fact as a defense to enforcement of the child support agreement.

(b) P is injured in an automobile accident caused by D. P agrees to release D from any liability for injuries from the accident for $24. At the time of the agreement, both P and D mistakenly assume that P is not seriously injured. When P later learns that she has suffered serious internal injuries, P asserts mutual mistake of fact as a defense to enforcement of the release agreement.

2.5. Ninety-five years after *Sherwood v. Walker*, the Michigan Supreme Court, in *Lenawee County Board of Health v. Messerly*, 417 Mich. 17, 331 N.W.2d 203 (1982), described the test in *Sherwood* as "inexact and confusing," stated that *Sherwood* should be "limited to [its] facts," and adopted the rule stated in the *Restatement (Second) of Contracts*:

We think that the better-reasoned approach is a case-by-case analysis whereby rescission is indicated when the mistaken belief relates to a basic assumption of the parties upon which the con-

> tract is made, and which materially affects the agreed performance of the parties. [Restatement (Second) of Contracts § 152.] . . . Rescission is not available, however, to relieve a party who has assumed the risk of loss, in connection with a mistake. [Restatement (Second) of Contracts §§ 152, 154.]

Is the *Restatement (Second)* test less "inexact and confusing" than the *Sherwood* test?

3. Notes

3.1. A substantial body of case law supports an important but unacknowledged rule of contract doctrine: the proper legal response to certain problems resulting from contracts that are "incomplete" or "not fully specified" is to leave the parties alone. . . .

. . . The party who balked at performing will not be forced to proceed, but the completed exchange will not be recalled. . . .

. . . [I]f the parties have not allocated the risk of a particular windfall or casualty to one of them, neither have they allocated it to the other.

Andrew Kull, *Mistake, Frustration and the Windfall Principle of Contracts Remedies*, 43 HASTINGS L. J. 1, 5–6 (1991).

3.2. "[I]t is plain that contract law needs a rule or principle that affords relief in cases involving clerical mistakes, arithmetical blunders, misidentification of persons or property and the like. The rule, however, needs to be confined to cases of just that sort . . . —one roughly speaking that separates inadvertent errors from misjudgments." MARVIN A. CHIRELSTEIN, CONCEPTS AND CASE ANALYSIS IN THE LAW OF CONTRACTS 147 (4th ed. 2001).

Burggraff v. Baum
Supreme Judicial Court of Maine
1998 ME 262; 720 A.2d 1167 (1998)

Rudman, J.

1. Verna and Joseph Baum appeal from the judgment entered after a bench trial in the Superior Court (Knox County, Marsano, J.) rescinding a

contract for the purchase of land. They argue the trial court erred by applying the doctrine of mutual mistake of fact to rescind their contract. We agree and vacate the judgment.

2. This case arises from an installment contract to purchase roughly eight-and-a-half acres of undeveloped shorefront property at Mill Cove in St. George. Verna Baum and her husband, Joseph Baum, agreed to sell the lot to David Burggraff and his wife, Roberta Rubly-Burggraff, in July 1994. Roberta drafted the contract, which did not include a contingency clause, and the parties signed it without the advice of counsel.

3. The parties originally became acquainted in April 1993 when the Burggraffs began renting the Baums' house on nearby Patten Point. The couples became close friends, "almost like family." During the summer or fall of 1993, the Burggraffs offered to buy a portion of the Baums' land at Mill Cove after Verna joked that she would gladly sell the property if she could get the amount of the town's latest tax assessment. The Burggraffs wanted the lot because it had an ocean view and a potential building site near the water. Negotiations proceeded slowly because the land had been in Verna Baum's family for generations and had sentimental value to her. During this time, the parties discussed in detail their plans for the land, both emphasizing potential building sites and the importance of limiting development that could detract from its natural beauty.

4. The Burggraffs planned to build both a primary residence and a cabin on the lot. They desired (and the Burggraffs [sic?] understood) that the cabin be located within seventy-five feet of the water, with the residence up the hill from the water in the woods. * * * Verna Baum testified that she understood the cabin was to be a building near the water for meditation and to store kayaks. * * *

5. Roberta Rubly-Burggraff researched some of the zoning statutes that applied to the land. She determined that the general state setback was 100 feet, while the St. George setback was only seventy-five feet. Both parties believed, based on her efforts and what they called "common knowledge," that those were the only relevant zoning ordinances that applied to the lot. In April 1995, after the contract was signed, the Burggraffs hired a civil engineer to discuss improving an access road that led to the building site of the primary residence. He informed the Burggraffs that the land was in the town's Resource Protection District (RPD), which generally extends 250 feet from the water's edge. While the site chosen for the main residence would

not be affected, neither the access road nor the cabin could be built in the RPD without permits from various local authorities.

6. When the Burggraffs informed the Baums that the lot was in the RPD, they asked for a price reduction. The Baums responded by saying they would consider it, but first wanted to see if the town would reduce the property tax assessment. In light of the zoning restrictions, the Baums were able to convince the town to reduce the assessment. When the parties returned to negotiate a reduction in price, they were unable to come to an agreement, and in October 1995, the Burggraffs stopped making payments and demanded a refund.

7. In June 1996, the Burggraffs filed a complaint seeking rescission of the contract. After a bench trial, the court found that neither party knew the land was in the RPD, and granted rescission based on the doctrine of mutual mistake of fact. It is well-settled that a contract is not legally binding if both parties have entered into it laboring under a good-faith mistake of fact. A mistake of fact, however, differs from a mistake of law. When, as here, both parties know the facts, yet have an erroneous conclusion as to their legal effect, the misconception is a mistake of law.

8. Both the Burggraffs and the Baums were aware that the property was subject to at least some land use restrictions. As evidenced by Rubly-Burggraff's attempt to research the zoning ordinances that applied to the property, the parties could have informed themselves accurately of what could be built at Mill Cove. Her research, however, failed to uncover the existence of the RPD, and therefore the parties interpreted the local land use regulations to permit their proposed building plans. They were not mistaken about the fact that restrictions applied to the lot, but rather about what those restrictions were and what legal effect they had. That is a mistake of law, and not a basis to rescind a contract. The rationale behind this rule is that the parties are presumed to know the law, or at least capable of verifying it, whereas they cannot be expected to be acquainted with all factual matters, regardless of their diligence. *See also* Letter from Thomas Jefferson to Andre Limozin (Dec. 22, 1787), in Papers of Thomas Jefferson, at 451 (Julian P. Boyd ed., 1955) ("Ignorance of the law is no excuse in any country. If it were, the laws would lose their effect, because it can always be pretended."). We therefore conclude that the parties labored under a mistake of law, and that rescission of the contract is inappropriate.

The entry is:

Judgment vacated. Remanded for entry of judgment in favor of defendant.

QUESTIONS AND NOTE

1. Questions about the facts of this case

   1.1. Was there any language in the land sale agreement about land use restrictions?

   1.2. Did either party sustain a loss because the court refused to enforce the agreement? Would either party have sustained a loss if the court had enforced the agreement?

   1.3. What facts, if any, were essential to the court's decision?

2. Questions about the law

   2.1. How would Thomas Jefferson have decided this case? Professor Kull? Professor Chirelstein?

   2.2. The *Restatement (Second) of Contracts* does not distinguish between mistakes of fact and mistakes of law—the law governing the agreement is a part of the facts. How would a court such as the Michigan Supreme Court that has adopted the *Restatement (Second) of Contracts* § 152 have decided this case?

   2.3. P and D enter into an agreement settling P's tort claim against D. At the time of the agreement, they both assume P's recovery would be limited by the case of *Markell v. Ponoroff*. That was a mistaken assumption, as two days before the P-D agreement, the State Supreme Court overruled *Markell v. Ponoroff* in another case. Should a court refuse to enforce the settlement agreement because of the mutual mistake?

3. Note

In *Sherwood* and *Bruggraff*, the courts considered the argument that a mutual mistake should be a defense to enforcement of an agreement. Unilateral mistake occurs when only one party to the agreement has an erroneous assumption concerning an important aspect of the deal that makes the deal far less favorable to him than he had assumed. Because, in these cases, only one party is mistaken and the other is "innocent," courts have traditionally been more reluctant to grant relief based on unilateral mistake unless there is a showing that perhaps that other party took advantage of a deal that was literally too good to believe. Nevertheless, as illustrated by the next case, courts and commentators are not in complete agreement over whether and when a unilateral mistake should be a defense to enforcement of an agreement.

Donovan v. RRL Corp.
Supreme Court of California
26 Cal. 4th 261, 27 P.3d 702 (2001)

[Defendant is a car dealer. Plaintiff noticed defendant's newspaper advertisement listing a 1995 Jaguar XJ6 Vanden Plas for sale for $25,959. The advertisement described the car and included the vehicle advertisement number. When plaintiff attempted to buy the car at the advertised price, defendant refused to sell it. Plaintiff filed this action against defendant alleging breach of contract. The trial court found that the newspaper that published the advertisement made a mistake—that the advertisement was supposed to list the price of the 1995 Jaguar XJ6 Vanden Plas at $37,995 and ruled for the defendant on the ground that the mistake precluded the existence of a contract. The intermediate court of appeals reversed, relying in part upon a California statute, Vehicle Code 1713.1, which makes it unlawful for an automobile dealer to refuse to sell a motor vehicle at the advertised price while the vehicle remains unsold. The California Supreme Court then ruled for the defendant, reversing the intermediate court of appeals and affirming the trial court.

The portion of the California Supreme Court decision dealing with whether an advertisement is an offer is set out *supra* at 55. The part of the opinion discussing rescission of the contract on the ground of unilateral mistake is set out below. We will later consider the portions of the *Donovan* opinion dealing with unconscionability and the statute of frauds.]

George, J:

* * *

Having concluded that defendant's advertisement for the sale of the Jaguar automobile constituted an offer that was accepted by plaintiff's tender of the advertised price, [*see* page 55 *supra*] and that the resulting contract satisfied the statute of frauds [*see* page 484 *supra*] we next consider whether defendant can avoid enforcement of the contract on the ground of mistake.

A party may rescind a contract if his or her consent was given by mistake. (Civ. Code, § 1689, subd. (b)(1).) A factual mistake by one party to a contract, or unilateral mistake, affords a ground for recission in some circumstances. Civil Code section 1577 states in relevant part: "Mistake of fact is a mistake, not caused by the neglect of a legal duty on the part of the person making the mistake, and consisting in: 1. An unconscious ignorance or forgetfulness of a fact past or present, material to the contract . . ." * * *

Under the first Restatement of Contracts, unilateral mistake did not render a contract voidable unless the other party knew of or caused the mistake. * * *

* * * [T]he Restatement Second of Contracts authorizes recission for a unilateral mistake of fact where "the effect of the mistake is such that enforcement of the contract would be unconscionable." (Rest. 2d Contracts, § 153, subd. (a).) The comment following this section recognizes "a growing willingness to allow avoidance where the consequences of the mistake are so grave that enforcement of the contract would be unconscionable. * * *

Because the rule in section 153, subdivision (a), of the Restatement Second of Contracts, authorizing recission for unilateral mistake of fact where enforcement would be unconscionable, is consistent with our previous decisions, we adopt the rule as California law. * * *

Having concluded that a contract properly may be rescinded on the ground of unilateral mistake of fact as set forth in section 153, subdivision (a), of the Restatement Second of Contracts, we next consider whether the requirements of that provision, construed in light of our previous decision, are satisfied in the present case. Where the plaintiff has no reason to know of and does not cause the defendant's unilateral mistake of fact, the defendant must establish the following facts to obtain recission of the contract: (1) the defendant made a mistake regarding a basic assumption upon which the defendant made the contract; (2) the mistake has a material effect upon the agreed exchange of performances that is adverse to the defendant; (3) the defendant does not bear the risk of the mistake; and (4) the effect of the mistake is such that enforcement of the contract would be unconscionable. We shall consider each of these requirements below.

A significant error in the price term of a contract constitutes mistake regarding a basic assumption upon which the contract is made, and such a mistake ordinarily has a material effect adverse to the mistaken party. * * * In establishing a material mistake regarding a basic assumption of the contract, the defendant must show that the resulting imbalance in the agreed exchange is so severe that it would be unfair to require the defendant to perform. (Rest. 2d Contracts, § 152, com. c.) * * *

* * * Plaintiff implicitly concedes that defendant's mistake was material.

The parties and amici curiae vigorously dispute, however, whether defendant should bear the risk of its mistake. Section 154 of the Restatement Second of Contracts states: "A party bears the risk of a mistake when (a) the risk is allocated to him by agreement of the parties, or (b) he is aware, at the time the contract is made, that he has only limited knowledge with respect to the facts to which the mistake relates but treats his limited knowledge as sufficient, or (c) the risk is allocated to him by the court on the ground that it is reasonable in the circumstances to do so." Neither of the first two factors applies here. Thus, we must determine whether it is reasonable under the circumstances to allocate to defendant the risk of the mistake in the advertisement. * * *

Plaintiff contends that section 11713.1(e) imposes a legal duty upon licensed automobile dealers to ensure that their advertisements containing sale prices are accurate. Section 11713.1(e) provides that it is a violation of the Vehicle Code for a dealer to "fail to sell a vehicle to any person at the advertised total price . . . while the vehicle remains unsold, unless the advertisement states the advertised total price is good only for a specified time and the time has elapsed." Plaintiff also relies upon Vehicle Code section 11713, subdivision (a), which provides that a licensed dealer shall not "make or disseminate . . . in any newspaper . . . any statement which is untrue or misleading . . . ." * * *

* * * Allowing automobile dealers to avoid contracts because of carelessness in proofreading advertisements, plaintiff asserts, would undermine the

legislative intent and public policy favoring the protection of consumers and ensuring accuracy in advertisements. * * *

Section 11713(e) does not eliminate mistake as a ground for recission of the contract, as plaintiff contends. The statute is part of a regulatory scheme that subjects licensed dealers to potential discipline for a violation of the duties set forth therein. Nothing in section 11713.1(e) or the regulatory scheme reflects a legislative intent completely to remove the contract-making process from the purview of the common law. At most, section 11713.1(e) reflects an intent to *supplement* contract law by establishing a ceiling for the price term of a contract for the sale of an advertised vehicle. Therefore, the common law, including the law governing mistake, remains applicable. * * *

The final factor defendant must establish before obtaining recission based upon mistake is that enforcement of the contract for the sale of the 1995 Jaguar XJ6 Vanden Plas at $25,995 wold be unconscionable. * * * [T]he standards of unconscionability warranting recission for mistake are similar to those for unconscionability justifying a court's refusal to enforce a contract or term. * * * [We will consider the standards for unconscionability justifying a refusal to enforce a contract or term *infra*, at 329–341.]

Having determined that defendant satisfied the requirements for recission of the contract on the ground of unilateral mistake of fact, we conclude that the municipal court correctly entered judgment in defendant's favor.

QUESTIONS AND NOTE

1. Questions about the facts of the case

   1.1. What was the mistake in this case?

   1.2. Who made the mistake?

   1.3. Why does the court describe the mistake as a unilateral mistake?

2. Questions about the law

   2.1. Would the California Supreme Court have ruled differently if an employee of the defendant instead of an employee of the newspaper had made the mistake? Assume for example that Epstein, one of the defendant's employees, had transposed the price of the 1995 Jaguar XJ6 Vanden Plas with the price of a 1995 Volvo in the copy that he had delivered to the newspaper. Should defendant still be excused from performing because of its unilateral mistake?

2.2. The California Supreme Court mentions the first *Restatement of Contracts'* provision on excuse of performance because of unilateral mistake. Section 503 of the 1932 *Restatement of Contracts* provided "A mistake of only one party that forms the basis on which he enters into a transaction does not of itself render the transaction voidable." The comment to the section adds, "There is a contract formed by the acceptance of an offer even though the offer is under a mistake or fails to express what the offeror intends. * * * Additional facts may render a transaction voidable where only one party is mistaken, namely, (1) where the mistake of one party is due to the fault of the other, or (2) a party knows or has reason to know that there is a mistake when the transaction is entered into." How would *Donovan* have been decided under the first *Restatement of Contracts*?

2.3. Is the holding in *Donovan* consistent with objective theory of contract formation? Could you defend the result on that basis?

2.4. Recall that Professor Chirlestein would distinguish between "clerical mistakes, mathematical blunders" on the one hand and "errors from misjudgments on the other." What is the policy basis for such a distinction? How would Professor Chirelstein have decided the *Donovan* case?

3. Note

When a contractor submits a bid in which the owner has reason to know that a mistake has been made, courts consistently hold that such a unilateral mistake prevents contract formation. Professor Kull explains such cases on the basis that "the owner cannot form a contract on terms he knows the contractor does not intend." Andrew Kull, *Unilateral Mistake: The Baseball Card Case,* 70 WASH. U. L.Q. 57, 70 (1992). Professor Corbin offered a different explanation for the same result:

> Suppose . . . a bidding contractor makes an offer to supply specified goods or to do specified work for a definitely named price, and that he was caused to name this price by an antecedent error of

> computation. If, before acceptance, the offeree knows, or has reason to know, that a material error has been made, he is seldom mean enough to accept; and if he does accept, the courts have no difficulty in throwing him out. He is not permitted 'to snap up' such an offer and profit thereby. If, without knowledge of the mistake and before any revocation, he has accepted the offer, it is natural for him to feel a sense of disappointment at not getting a good bargain, when the offeror insists on withdrawal; but a just and reasonable man will not insist upon profiting by the other's mistake. There are now many decisions to the effect that if the error was a substantial one and notice is given before the other party has made such a change of position that he cannot be put substantially in status quo, the bargain is voidable and rescission will be decreed.

3 Arthur Linton Corbin, Corbin on Contracts § 609 at pages 680–82 (1960).

SECTION 3: FRAUD, FRAUDULENT OR MATERIAL MISREPRESENTATION, AND NONDISCLOSURE

The contract law of misrepresentation is similar to the tort law of fraud and misrepresentation. Both are based in part on common law as it evolved in England and in part on common sense.

First, the old common law part—procedure. Recall that in old England, a writ of assumpsit was the prescribed procedure for enforcement of an agreement. In such assumpsit actions, misrepresentation was not a defense to the enforcement of an agreement. Instead the person who had been a victim of the misrepresentation had to bring a separate tort action in deceit for damages.

While misrepresentation was not a defense in actions at law under assumpsit, courts of equity did allow a person who entered into an agreement because of a misrepresentation to avoid the agreement by means of the equitable remedy of rescission. In rescission, each party returns what she received.

Today, as at early common law, misrepresentation can be the basis for either a tort action or a contract action. The tort action is generally a suit for actual (and possibly punitive damages) for deceit or fraud or misrepresentation. And, the contract action is generally a suit for rescission to make an agreement unenforceable.

Second, the common sense part—the requirements for an action to rescind an agreement because of misrepresentation. In determining whether an agreement should not be enforced or should be rescinded because of one party's misrepresentation, courts generally look to how important (*i.e.*, material) the representation was, whether the other party relied on that misrepresentation, and whether that reliance was reasonable. *Cf. Restatement (Second) of Contracts* § 164. Common sense stuff.

Assume, for example, that Markell and Ponoroff agree to do a contract book with Epstein. Should Markell and Ponroff be able to get out of their agreement with Epstein because he told them that he had a masters degree in law from the Harvard Law School, when in reality his LL.M. degree was from the Havahd Law School, Tanning and Nail Boutique, if (i) Epstein honestly believes that he went to Harvard (at his age, he gets confused a lot), or (ii) Markell and Ponoroff could have easily checked on LEXIS whether Epstein graduated from Harvard?

The next case, *Halpert v. Rosenthal*, involves equally easy facts—a defendant buyer who is arguing that a court should not enforce an agreement to buy the plaintiff's house because of the plaintiff's misrepresentation as to termites. As you read the case, please notice the court's fairly obvious distinctions between tort actions based on misrepresentations and contract actions based on misrepresentations and the court's (the Restatement's?) more "subtle" distinction between contract actions based on fraudulent misrepresentations and contract actions based on material misrepresentations.

Halpert v. Rosenthal

Supreme Court of Rhode Island
107 R.I. 406, 267 A.2d 730 (1970)

Kelleher, J.

This is a civil action wherein the plaintiff vendor seeks damages for the breach by the defendant vendee of a contract for the sale of real estate. The defendant filed a counter-claim in which he sought the return of his deposit.

A jury trial was held in the Superior Court. The jury found for the defendant and judgment followed. The case is before us on the plaintiff's appeal.

On February 21, 1967, the parties hereto entered into a real estate agreement whereby plaintiff agreed to convey a one-family house located in Providence on the southeasterly corner of Wayland and Upton Avenues to defendant for the sum of $54,000. The defendant paid a deposit of $2,000 to plaintiff. The agreement provided for the delivery of the deed and the payment of the balance of the purchase price by June 30, 1967.

On May 17, 1967, a termite inspection was made of the premises, and it was discovered that the house was inhabited by termites. The defendant then notified plaintiff that, because of the termite infestation, he was not going to purchase the property. The defendant did not appear for the title closing which plaintiff had scheduled for June 30, 1967.

The plaintiff immediately commenced this suit. Her complaint prayed for specific performance or monetary damages. When the case came on for trial, the property had been sold to another buyer for the sum of $35,000. The plaintiff then sought to recover from defendant the $19,000 difference between the selling price called for in the sales agreement and the actual selling price. The defendant in his answer alleged that plaintiff and her agent had, during the preagreement negotiation, intentionally misrepresented the house as being free of termites. The defendant's counterclaim sought the return of the $2,000 deposit.

At the conclusion of the presentation of all the evidence, plaintiff made a motion for a directed verdict on the issue of the alleged fraudulent misrepresentations. The trial justice reserved decision on the motion and submitted the case to the jury. After the jury's verdict, he denied the motion.

This case is unique in that plaintiff made no motion for a new trial. Her appeal is based for the most part on the trial court's refusal to direct a verdict in her favor on the counterclaim. She has also alleged that the trial justice erred in certain portions of his charge to the jury and in failing to adopt some 15 requests to charge submitted by plaintiff.

The absence of a motion for a new trial narrows the scope of an inquiry on appeal. Instead of being concerned with the credibility of witnesses or the weight of the evidence as we would be were we reviewing the usual motion for a new trial, we apply the standards applicable to a motion for a directed verdict. In doing so, it is our duty to consider all of the evidence and reasonable inferences deducible therefrom in the light most favorable to defendant.

Since we consider only the evidence favorable to defendant, we shall set forth defendant's version of three different occasions in 1967 when the alleged misrepresentations relative to absence of any termites were made.

1. In early February, defendant and his wife inspected the Halpert home. They asked the agent about termites and he told them that there was no termite problem and that he had never experienced any termite problem with any of the houses he sold in the East Side section of Providence.

2. Later on in February, defendant, his wife, his sister-in-law and his brother-in-law met plaintiff. The brother-in-law inquired about the presence of termites; plaintiff said that there were no termites in the house.

3. When defendant was about to sign the purchase and sales agreement, he asked plaintiff's real estate agent whether it might not be advisable if the home be inspected for termites before the agreement was signed. The agent told defendant that such a step was unnecessary because there were no termite problems in the house.

* * *

In contending that she was entitled to a directed verdict, plaintiff contends that to sustain the charge of fraudulent misrepresentation, some evidence had to be produced showing that either she or her agent knew at the time they said there were no termites in the house, that such a statement was untrue. Since the representations made to defendant were made in good faith, she argues that, as a matter of law, defendant could not prevail on his counterclaim.

The defendant concedes that there was no evidence which shows that plaintiff or her agent knowingly made false statements as to the existence of the termites but he maintains that an innocent misrepresentation of a material fact is grounds for rescission of a contract where, as here, a party relies to his detriment on the misrepresentation.

We affirm the denial of the motion for a directed verdict.

The plaintiff, when she made her motion for a directed verdict, stated that her motion was restricted to the issue of "fraud." The word "fraud" is a generic term which embraces a great variety of actionable wrongs. It is a word of many meanings and defies any one all-inclusive definition. Fraud may become important either for the purpose of giving the defrauded person the right to sue for damages in an action for deceit or to enable him to rescind the contract. In this jurisdiction a party who has been induced by fraud to enter into a contract may pursue either one of two remedies. He may elect to rescind the contract to recover what he has paid under it, or he may affirm the contract and sue for damages in an action for deceit.

The distinction between a claim for damages for intentional deceit and a claim for rescission is well defined. Deceit is a tort action, and it requires some degree of culpability on the misrepresenter's part. An individual who sues in an action of deceit based on fraud has the burden of proving that the defendant in making the statements knew they were false and intended to deceive him. On the other hand, a suit to rescind an agreement induced by fraud sounds in contract. It is this latter aspect of fraud that we are concerned with in this case, and the pivotal issue before us is whether an innocent misrepresentation of a material fact warrants the granting of a claim for rescission. We believe that it does.

When he denied plaintiff's motion, the trial justice indicated that a false, though innocent, misrepresentation of a fact made as though of one's knowledge may be the basis for the rescission of a contract. While this issue is one of first impression in this state, it is clear that the trial judge's action finds support in the overwhelming weight of decisional and textual authority which has established the rule that where one induces another to enter into a contract by means of a material misrepresentation, the latter may rescind the contract. It does not matter if the representation was "innocent" or fraudulent.

In 12 Williston, *supra,* § 1500 at 400–01, Professor Jaeger states:

> It is not necessary, in order that a contract may be rescinded for fraud or misrepresentation, that the party making the misrepresentation should have known that it was false. Innocent misrepresentation is sufficient, for though the representation may have been made innocently, it would be unjust and inequitable to permit a person who has made false representations, even innocently, to retain the fruits of a bargain induced by such representations.

This statement of law is in accord with Restatement of Contracts, § 476 at 908 which states: "Where a party is induced to enter into a transaction with another party that he was under no duty to enter into by means of the latter's fraud or material misrepresentation, the transaction is voidable as against the latter * * *." Misrepresentation is defined as " * * * any manifestation by words or other conduct by one person to another that, under the circumstances, amounts to an assertion not in accordance with the facts." Restatement of Contracts, § 470 at 890–91.

The comment following this section explains that a misrepresentation may be innocent, negligent or known to be false. A misrepresentation becomes material when it becomes likely to affect the conduct of a reasonable man with reference to a transaction with another person. Restatement of Contracts, § 470 (2) at 891. * * *

A misrepresentation, even though innocently made, may be actionable, if made and relied on as a positive statement of fact. The question to be resolved in determining whether a wrong committed as the result of an innocent misrepresentation may be rectified is succinctly stated in 12 Williston, *supra*, § 1510 at 462 as follows:

> "When a defendant has induced another to act by representations false in fact although not dishonestly made, and damage has directly resulted from the action taken, who should bear the loss?"

The question we submit is rhetorical. The answer is obvious. Simple justice demands that the speaker be held responsible. Accordingly, we hold that here defendant vendee could maintain his counterclaim.

* * *

Before leaving this phase of plaintiff's appeal, we think it appropriate that we allude to the tendency of many courts to equate an innocent misrepresentation with some species of fraud. Usually the word "fraud" connotes a conscious dishonest conduct on the part of the misrepresenter. Fraud, however, is not present if the speaker actually believes that what he states as the truth is the truth. We believe that it would be better if an innocent misrepresentation was not described as some specie of fraud. Unqualified statements imply certainty. Reliance is more likely to be placed on a positive statement of fact than a mere expression of opinion or a qualified statement. The speaker who uses the unqualified statement does so at his peril. The risk of falsity is his. If he is to be liable for what he states, the liability is imposed because he is to be held strictly accountable for his words. Responsibility for an innocent misrepresentation should be recognized for what it is—an example of absolute liability rather than as many courts have said, an example of constructive fraud.

* * *

The appeal of the plaintiff is denied and dismissed, and the case is remanded to the Superior Court for entry of judgment thereon.

Motion for reargument denied.

QUESTIONS AND NOTES

1. Questions about the facts of this case

   1.1. Who is suing whom for what?

   1.2. Which of the various statements by the seller or the seller's agent was most favorable to the defendant buyer's position?

   1.3. Did the seller or the seller's agent know that there were termites in the house? Was that important to the court? Should it be important?

2. Questions about the law

   2.1. Earlier we considered cases involving mistakes of fact. How do the facts of *Halpert* differ from the facts of these cases? How does the law of misrepresentation differ from the law of mutual mistake?

   2.2. Would the case have been decided differently if the court had applied *Restatement (Second) of Contracts* § 164, which provides:

   If a party's manifestation of assent is induced by either a fraudulent or a material misrepresentation by the other party upon which the recipient is justified in relying, the contract is voidable by the recipient.

   How is this different from *Restatement of Contracts* § 476 which the court relied on? More importantly, how is a "fraudulent" misrepresentation different from a "material" misrepresentation? *See also Restatement (Second) of Contracts* §§ 159, 160, 162.

   2.3. Would the case have been decided differently if the seller and the seller's agent had simply and truthfully said "we have not seen any termites" or "I do not believe that there are any termites in the house"?

2.4. Would the case have been decided differently if the contract had provided that "this house has not been inspected for termites and so seller makes no representation as to whether there are termites"?

2.5. Would the case have been decided differently if the buyer was not a consumer, but instead an experienced investor, who regularly bought and sold houses?

2.6. This case uses the terms "deceit," "fraud," and "misrepresentation." How do these terms differ? Which is involved in this case?

2.7. In negotiating to buy Epstein's 1973 Cadillac, Ponoroff tells Epstein that "$400 is my best offer—it is as much as I am willing to pay for the car." Being an extremely trusting sort of person, Epstein believes Ponoroff and agrees to sell him the car for $400. Shortly thereafter, Epstein learns from Markell that Ponoroff had said that he was willing to pay as much as $1600 for the car. Can Epstein argue a fraud, deceit, or misrepresentation defense to the enforcement of his agreement to sell the car to Ponoroff based on Ponoroff's statement to him?

3. Notes

3.1. The facts in *Halpert* (and the facts in the various examples in *Restatement (Second) of Contracts* § 164) involve a statement or representation that is not a part of the contract language.

It is of course possible to include representations in the contract language. For example, in a typical business acquisition agreement, the seller will make representations about the conditions of the business and the agreement will provide that the buyer can walk away from the deal if any of the "representations" are instead "misrepresentations." *See generally* JAMES C. FREUND, ANATOMY OF A MERGER: STRATEGIES AND TECHNIQUES FOR NEGOTIATING CORPORATE ACQUISITIONS Chapter 7 (1975):

There are no known statistics on the subject, but I'm willing to bet my briefcase that lawyers spend more time negotiating 'Representations and Warranties of the Seller' than any other single article in

> the typical acquisition agreement. It is a nit-picker's delight, a forum for expending prodigious amounts of energy in debating the merits of what sometimes seem to be relatively insignificant items.

Id. at 229.

3.2. *Halpert* shows the legal consequences of a misstatement that was aguably innocent. In the next two cases, we consider the legal consequences of a "non-statement" that was arguably not so innocent.

Swinton v. Whitinsville Savings Bank

Supreme Judicial Court of Massachusetts
311 Mass. 677, 42 N.E.2d 808 (1942)

[Plaintiff-appellant Swinton sued defendant-appellee Whitinsville Savings Bank to recover damages for defendant's alleged fraudulent concealment in the sale of a house to plaintiff. Plaintiff appeals an order by the court below which sustained the defendant's demurrer to plaintiff's declaration.]

Qua, J.

The declaration alleges that on or about September 12, 1938, the defendant sold the plaintiff a house in Newton to be occupied by the plaintiff and his family as a dwelling; that at the time of the sale the house "was infested with termites, an insect that is most dangerous and destructive to buildings"; that the defendant knew the house was so infested; that the plaintiff could not readily observe this condition upon inspection; that, "knowing the internal destruction that these insects were creating in said house," the defendant falsely and fraudulently concealed from the plaintiff its true condition; that the plaintiff at the time of his purchase had no knowledge of the termites, exercised due care thereafter, and learned of them about August 30, 1940; and that, because of the destruction that was being done and the dangerous condition that was being created by the termites, the plaintiff was put to great expense for repairs and for the installation of termite control in order to prevent the loss and destruction of said house.

There is no allegation of any false statement or representation, or of the uttering of a half truth which may be tantamount to a falsehood. There is no intimation that the defendant by any means prevented the plaintiff from acquiring information as to the condition of the house. There is nothing to show any fiduciary relation between the parties, or that the plaintiff stood in a position of confidence toward or dependence upon the defendant. So far as appears the parties made a business deal at arm's length. The charge is concealment and nothing more; and it is concealment in the simple sense of mere failure to reveal, with nothing to show any peculiar duty to speak. The characterization of the concealment as false and fraudulent of course adds nothing in the absence of further allegations of fact.

If this defendant is liable on this declaration every seller is liable who fails to disclose any nonapparent defect known to him in the subject of the sale which materially reduces its value and which the buyer fails to discover. Similarly it would seem that every buyer would be liable who fails to disclose any nonapparent virtue known to him in the subject of the purchase which materially enhances its value and of which the seller is ignorant. The law has not yet, we believe, reached the point of imposing upon the frailties of human nature a standard so idealistic as this. That the particular case here stated by the plaintiff possesses a certain appeal to the moral sense is scarcely to be denied. Probably the reason is to be found in the facts that the infestation of buildings by termites has not been common in Massachusetts and constitutes a concealed risk against which buyers are off their guard. But the law cannot provide special rules for termites and can hardly attempt to determine liability according to the varying probabilities of the existence and discovery of different possible defects in the subjects of trade. * * *

The order sustaining the demurrer is affirmed, and judgment is to be entered for the defendant.

So ordered.

QUESTIONS AND NOTES

1. Questions about the facts of this case

   1.1. Did the defendant know that the house was infested with termites?

   1.2. Did the defendant make any representation to the plaintiff about termites?

   1.3. Did the plaintiff ask the defendant about termites?

2. Notes

2.1. "Of the forms of animal life known to modern science, few, if any, classifications other than Homo sapiens have been the subject of as much legal controversy as the members of the order Isoptera. The species involved in this particular lawsuit does not appear in the record, but it is likely it was from the genus Reticulitermes of the family of Rhinotermitidae, known to the nonbiologically oriented as 'termites.' The wooden edifices of man represent nothing more to these despicable insects than an abundant source of cellulose, which is their principal food." *Hughes v. Stusser*, 68 Wash.2d 707, 708, 415 P.2d 89 (1966).

2.2. *Swinton* is an old case. Even older than Epstein. *Swinton* remains "good law" in Massachusetts. The rule of *Swinton*—no defense to enforcement of an agreement based on nondisclosure (silence)—was reaffirmed most recently in *Parisi v. Poole Construction Co.*, 2001 WL 792783 (Mass. Superior Ct. 2001).

2.3. There are, however, much older cases on nondisclosure. Perhaps the best known such case, the United States Supreme Court decision in *Laidlaw v. Organ*, 15 U.S. 178 (1817),* goes back to the end of the War of 1812. During that war, the British blockade of New Orleans depressed the price of tobacco and other exportable commodities. Organ, a tobacco merchant, obtained advance information that a peace treaty had been signed and bought a large quantity of tobacco from Peter Laidlaw & Co., a New Orleans tobacco broker, without revealing the news of the war's end. When peace was announced, the price of tobacco shot up by almost 50%. The tobacco seller sued to avoid the contract because of Organ's nondisclosure. Chief Justice Marshall wrote: "The question in this case is, whether the intelligence of extrinsic circumstances, which might influence the price of

*Even earlier, Cicero addressed the question of nondisclosure in a hypothetical case of a grain merchant who was the first to visit a town suffering from famine. Cicero's question was whether the merchant should inform the townspeople that other merchants were coming even though this disclosure would lower the price people would pay for his grain. "Holding things back does not always amount to concealment; but it does when you want people, for your own profit, to be kept in the dark about something which you know and would be useful for them to know." *Cicero on Duties III*, in SELECTED WORKS 157, 177 (Michael Grant trans. 1971) Cicero then describes a person who would engage in such concealment as "shifty" and "underhanded." *Id.*

> the commodity, and which was exclusively within the knowledge of the vendee, ought to have been communicated by him to the vendor? The court is of the opinion that he was not bound to communicate it. It would be difficult to circumscribe the contrary doctrine within proper limits, where the means of intelligence are equally accessible to both parties.

Weintraub v. Krobatsch

Supreme Court of New Jersey
64 N.J. 445, 317 A.2d 68 (1974)

Jacobs, J.

* * *

Mrs. Weintraub owned and occupied a six-year-old English-town home which she placed in the hands of a real estate broker (The Serafin Agency, Inc.) for sale. The Krobatsches were interested in purchasing the home, examined it while it was illuminated and found it suitable. On June 30, 1971 Mrs. Weintraub, as seller, and the Krobatsches, as purchasers, entered into a contract for the sale of the property for $42,500. The contract provided that the purchasers had inspected the property and were fully satisfied with its physical condition, that no representations had been made and that no responsibility was assumed by the seller as to the present or future condition of the premises. A deposit of $4,250 was sent by the purchasers to the broker to be held in escrow pending the closing of the transaction. The purchasers requested that the seller have the house fumigated and that was done. A fire after the signing of the contract caused damage but the purchasers indicated readiness that there be adjustment at closing.

During the evening of August 25, 1971, prior to closing, the purchasers entered the house, then unoccupied, and as they turned the lights on they were, as described in their petition for certification, "astonished to see roaches literally running in all directions, up the walls, drapes, etc." On the following day their attorney wrote a letter to Mrs. Weintraub, care of her New York law firm, advising that on the previous day "it was discovered that the house is infested with vermin despite the fact that an exterminator has only recently serviced the house" and asserting that "the presence of vermin in such great quantities, particularly after the exterminator was done, rendered the house as unfit for human habitation at this time and therefore, the contract is rescinded." On September 2, 1971 an exterminator wrote to Mr. Krobatsch advising that he had examined the premises and that "cockroaches were found to have infested the entire house." He said he could eliminate them for a relatively modest charge by two treatments with a twenty-one day interval but that it would be necessary to remove the carpeting "to properly treat all the infested areas."

Mrs. Weintraub rejected the rescission by the purchasers and filed an action in the Law Division joining them and the broker as defendants. Though she originally sought specific performance she later confined her claim to damages in the sum of $4,250, representing the deposit held in escrow by the broker. * * * There were opposing motions for summary judgment by the purchasers and Mrs. Weintraub * * *. At the argument on the motions it was evident that the purchasers were claiming fraudulent concealment or nondisclosure by the seller as the basis for their rescission. Thus at one point their attorney said: "Your honor, I would point out, and it is in my clients' affidavit, every time that they inspected this house prior to this time every light in the place was illuminated. Now, these insects are nocturnal by nature and that is not a point I think I have to prove through someone. I think Webster's dictionary is sufficient. By keeping the lights on, it keeps them out of sight. These sellers had to know they had this problem. You could not live in a house this infested without knowing about it."

The Law Division denied the motion by the purchasers for summary judgment but granted Mrs. Weintraub's motion and directed that the purchasers pay her the sum of $ 4,250. * * * On appeal, the Appellate Division sustained the summary judgment in Mrs. Weintraub's favor * * *.

Before us the purchasers contend that they were entitled to a trial on the issue of whether there was fraudulent concealment or nondisclosure entitling them to rescind; if there was then clearly they were under no liability to either the seller or the broker and would be entitled to the return of their deposit held by the broker in escrow.

Mrs. Weintraub asserts that she was unaware of the infestation and the Krobatsches acknowledge that, if that was so, then there was no fraudulent concealment or nondisclosure on her part and their claim must fall. But the purchasers allege that she was in fact aware of the infestation and at this stage of the proceedings we must assume that to be true. She contends, however, that even if she were fully aware she would have been under no duty to speak and that consequently no complaint by the purchasers may legally be grounded on her silence. She relies primarily on cases such as *Swinton v. Whitinsville Sav. Bank*, 311 Mass. 677, 42 N.E. 2d 808, 141 A.L.R. 965 (1942) * * *. *Swinton* is pertinent but, as Dean Prosser has noted, it is one of a line of "singularly unappetizing cases" which are surely out of tune with our times.

In *Swinton* the plaintiff purchased a house from the defendant and after he occupied it he found it to be infested with termites. The defendant had made no verbal or written representations but the plaintiff, asserting that the defendant knew of the termites and was under a duty to speak, filed a complaint for damages grounded on fraudulent concealment. The Supreme Judicial Court of Massachusetts sustained a demurrer to the complaint and entered judgment for the defendant. In the course of its opinion the court acknowledged that "the plaintiff possesses a certain appeal to the moral sense" but concluded that the law has not "reached the point of imposing upon the frailties of human nature a standard so idealistic as this." 42 N.E. 2d at 808–809. That was written several decades ago and we are far from certain that it represents views held by the current members of the Massachusetts court. *See Kannavos v. Annino*, 356 Mass. 42, 247 N.E. 2d 708, 711 (1969). In any event we are certain that it does not represent our sense of justice or fair dealing and it has understandably been rejected in persuasive opinions elsewhere. *See Obde v. Schlemeyer,* 56 Wash. 2d 449, 353 P. 2d 672 (1960).

In *Obde v. Schlemeyer,* 353 P. 2d 672, the defendants sold an apartment house to the plaintiffs. The house was termite infested but that fact was not disclosed by the sellers to the purchasers who later sued for damages alleging fraudulent concealment. The sellers contended that they were under no obligation whatever to speak out and they relied heavily on the decision of the Massachusetts court in *Swinton* (311 Mass. 677, 42 N.E. 2d 808, 141 A.L.R. 965). The Supreme Court of Washington flatly rejected their contention, holding that though the parties had dealt at arms length the sellers were under "a duty to inform the plaintiffs of the termite condition" of which they were fully aware. In the course of its opinion the court quoted approvingly from Dean Keeton's article in 15 Tex. L. Rev. 1. There the author first expressed his thought that when Lord Cairns suggested in *Peek v. Gurney*, L.R. 6 H.L. 377 (1873), that there was no duty to disclose facts, no matter how "morally censurable" (at 403), he was expressing nineteenth century law as shaped by an individualistic philosophy based on freedom of contracts and unconcerned with morals. He then made the following comments which fairly embody a currently acceptable principle on which the holding in *Obde* may be said to be grounded:

> In the present stage of the law, the decisions show a drawing away from this idea, and there can be seen an attempt by many courts to reach a just result in so far as possible, but yet maintaining the degree of certainty which the law must have. The statement may often be found that if either party to a contract of sale conceals or suppresses a material fact which he is in good faith bound to disclose then his silence is fraudulent.
>
> The attitude of the courts toward nondisclosure is undergoing a change and contrary to Lord Cairns' famous remark it would seem that the object of the law in these cases should be to impose on parties to the transaction a duty to speak whenever justice, equity, and fair dealing demand it. This statement is made only with reference to instances where the party to be charged is an actor in the transaction. This duty to speak does not result from an implied representation by silence, but exists because a refusal to speak constitutes unfair conduct.

15 Tex. L. Rev. at 31.

* * *

The purchasers here were entitled to withstand the seller's motion for summary judgment. They should have been permitted to proceed with their efforts to establish by testimony that they were equitably entitled to rescind because the house was extensively infested in the manner described by them, the seller was well aware of the infestation, and the seller deliberately concealed or failed to disclose the condition because of the likelihood that it would defeat the transaction. The seller may of course defend factually as well as legally and since the matter is primarily equitable in nature the factual as well as legal disputes will be for the trial judge alone.

If the trial judge finds such deliberate concealment or nondisclosure of the latent infestation not observable by the purchasers on their inspection, he will still be called upon to determine whether, in the light of the full presentation before him, the concealment or nondisclosure was of such significant nature as to justify rescission. Minor conditions which ordinary sellers and purchasers would reasonably disregard as of little or no materiality in the transaction would clearly not call for judicial intervention. While the described condition may not have been quite as major as in the termite cases which were concerned with structural impairments, to the purchasers here it apparently was of such magnitude and was so repulsive as to cause them to rescind immediately though they had earlier indicated readiness that there be adjustment at closing for damage resulting from a fire which occurred after the contract was signed. We are not prepared at his time to say that on their showing they acted either unreasonably or without equitable justification.

Our courts have come a long way since the days when the judicial emphasis was on formal rules and ancient precedents rather than on modern concepts of justice and fair dealing. While admittedly our law has progressed more slowly in the real property field than in other fields, there have been notable stirrings even there. * * * [W]e are satisfied that current principles grounded on justice and fair dealing, embraced throughout this opinion, clearly call for a full trial below; to that end the judgment entered in the Appellate Division is:

Reversed and remanded.

QUESTIONS

1. Questions about the facts of this case

   1.1. Did the contract mention cockroaches?

   1.2. Did either the seller or the buyer mention cockroaches before the contract was signed?

   1.3. Did the buyer allege that the seller concealed the cockroaches?

2. Questions about the law

   2.1. What is the new New Jersey test for determining when an agreement will not be enforced because of a non-disclosure?

   2.2. The New Jersey court quotes a Washington court's quote from a law review article by Dean Keeton which (to quote yet again) advocates:

   > The attitude of the courts toward non-disclosure is undergoing a change and contrary to Lord Cairns' famous remark it would seem that the object of the law in these cases should be to impose on

parties to the transaction a duty to speak whenever justice, equity, and fair dealing demand it." (emphasis added)

What does the underscored language mean?

2.3. "Legislation mandating disclosure of residential real property conditions has been enacted by the majority of the states . . . The legislation requires sellers to disclose salient property defects on a mandated form." Gary S. Moore and Gerald Smolen, *Real Estate Disclosure Forms and Information Transfer*, 28 Real Estate Law Journal 319 (2000).

S contracts to sell her house to B. S fails to disclose that cockroaches had infested the entire house. Should the court permit B to rescind the contract if the relevant disclosure law did not expressly require disclosure of cockroach infestation?

2.4. *Weintraub* involved a consumer transaction. Should nondisclosure be a basis for rescission of commercial transactions? B Corp. contracts to buy S Food Processing, Inc. After entering into the contract but before closing on the contract, B Corp. learns that S Food Processing, Inc. had health department licensing problems that it failed to disclose. Should B Corp. be able to rescind the contract? *Cf. Restatement Second of Contracts* § 161.

SECTION 4: CAPACITY

Some agreements are not enforceable because of who made the agreement. Assume for example that Bruce, a six year old child who is big fan of Tinky Winky, signs a "contract" to purchase a purple 4-door slant back Hummer for $95,000. Should that agreement be legally enforceable against Bruce? What if Bruce, the buyer of the $95,000 purple Hummer, is a forty-six year old intoxicated law professor who is a big fan of The Artist once and once again known as Prince? Should that agreement to pay $95,000 for a purple Hummer be legally enforceable against Bruce? Was there a "meeting of the minds"? Did the Bruces have the capacity to contract?

Common law and then statutes have long recognized categories of individuals who do not have the capacity to contract. At one time, the law of capacity to contract considered a person's sex, color, and even occupation. The present law of capacity in most states resembles *Restatement (Second) of Contracts* § 12:

> *(2) A natural person who manifests assent to a transaction has full legal capacity to incur contractual duties thereby unless he is*
>
> *(a) under guardianship, or*
> *(b) an infant, or*
> *(c) mentally ill or defective, or*
> *(d) intoxicated.*

Historically, an infant or minor was anyone under the age of 21. Today, in most states, the "age of majority" is 18. The following case involves a car dealer's efforts to enforce an agreement by a 20 year old married infant, who was the father of a real infant, to pay for a used station wagon.

Kiefer v. Fred Howe Motors, Inc.
Supreme Court of Wisconsin
39 Wis. 2d 20, 158 N.W.2d 288 (1968)

SYLLABUS: On August 9, 1965, the plaintiff, Steven Kiefer, entered into a contract with the defendant, Fred Howe Motors, Inc. ("dealer" hereinafter) for the purchase of a 1960 Willys station wagon. Kiefer paid the contract price of $412 and took possession of the car. At the time of the sale Kiefer was twenty years old, married, and the father of one child.

Kiefer had difficulty with the car which he claimed was caused by a cracked block. Kiefer contacted the dealer and asked it to take the car back. Several other attempts to secure some adjustment with the dealer failed and Kiefer contacted Attorney Paul C. Konnor. The attorney wrote a letter to the dealer advising it that Kiefer was under twenty-one at the time of the sale. The letter declared the contract void, tendered return of the automobile and demanded repayment of the purchase price. There was no response so this action was commenced to recover the $412 purchase price. After a trial to the court, a judgment for the plaintiff was entered and the defendant appeals.

Wilkie, J.

Three issues are presented on this appeal. They are:

1. Should an emancipated minor over the age of eighteen be legally responsible for his contracts?
2. Was the contract effectively disaffirmed?
3. Is the plaintiff liable in tort for misrepresentation?

Legal Responsibility of Emancipated Minor.

The law governing agreements made during infancy reaches back over many centuries. The general rule is that ". . . the contract of a minor, other than for necessaries, is either void or voidable at his option." The only other exceptions to the rule permitting disaffirmance are statutory or involve contracts which deal with duties imposed by law such as a contract of marriage or an agreement to support an illegitimate child. The general rule is not affected by the minor's status as emancipated or unemancipated.

Appellant does not advance any argument that would put this case within one of the exceptions to the general rule, but rather urges that this court, as a matter of public policy, adopt a rule that an emancipated minor over eighteen years of age be made legally responsible for his contracts.

The underpinnings of the general rule allowing the minor to disaffirm his contracts were undoubtedly the protection of the minor. It was thought that the minor was immature in both mind and experience and that, therefore, he should be protected from his own bad judgments as well as from adults who would take advantage of him. The doctrine of the voidability of minors' contracts often seems commendable and just. If the beans that the young naive Jack purchased from the crafty old man in the fairy tale "Jack and the Bean Stalk" had been worthless rather than magical, it would have been only fair to allow Jack to disaffirm the bargain and reclaim his cow. However, in today's modern and sophisticated society the "infancy doctrine" seems to lose some of its gloss.

Paradoxically, we declare the infant mature enough to shoulder arms in the military, but not mature enough to vote; mature enough to marry and be responsible for his torts and crimes, but not mature enough to assume the burden of his own contractual indiscretions. In Wisconsin, the infant is deemed mature enough to use a dangerous instrumentality—a motor vehicle—at sixteen, but not mature enough to purchase it without protection until he is twenty-one.

No one really questions that a line as to age must be drawn somewhere below which a legally defined minor must be able to disaffirm his contracts for nonnecessities. The law over the centuries has considered this age to be twenty-one. Legislatures in other states have lowered the age. We suggest that the appellant might better seek the change it proposes in the legislative halls rather than this court. * * *

Undoubtedly, the infancy doctrine is an obstacle when a major purchase is involved. However, we believe that the reasons for allowing that obstacle to remain viable at this point outweigh those for casting it aside. Minors require some protection from the pitfalls of the marketplace. Reasonable minds will always differ on the extent of the protection that should be afforded. For this court to adopt a rule that the appellant suggests and remove the contractual disabilities from a minor simply because he becomes emancipated, which in most cases would be the result of marriage, would be to suggest that the married minor is somehow vested with more wisdom and maturity than his single counterpart. However, logic would not seem to dictate this result especially when today a youthful marriage is oftentimes indicative of a lack of wisdom and maturity.

Disaffirmance.

The appellant questions whether there has been an effective disaffirmance of the contract in this case.

Williston, while discussing how a minor may disaffirm a contract, states:

> "Any act which clearly shows an intent to disaffirm a contract or sale is sufficient for the purpose. Thus a notice by the infant of his purpose to disaffirm . . . a tender or even an offer to return the consideration or its proceeds to the vendor, . . . is sufficient."

2 Williston, *Contracts* (3d ed.), p. 26, sec. 234.

The testimony of Steven Kiefer and the letter from his attorney to the dealer clearly establish that there was an effective disaffirmance of the contract.

Misrepresentation

Appellant's last argument is that the respondent should be held liable in tort for damages because he misrepresented his age. Appellant would use these damages as a set-off against the contract price sought to be reclaimed by respondent.

The 19th-century view was that a minor's lying about his age was inconsequential because a fraudulent representation of capacity was not the equivalent of actual capacity. This rule has been altered by time. There appear to be two possible methods that now can be employed to bind the defrauding minor: He may be estopped from denying his alleged majority, in which case the contract will be enforced or contract damages will be allowed; or he may be allowed to disaffirm his contract but be liable in tort for damages. Wisconsin follows the latter approach.

* * *

The "motor vehicle purchase contract" signed by Steven Kiefer contained the following language just above the purchaser's signature:

> I represent that I am 21 years of age or over and recognize that the dealer sells the above vehicle upon this representation.

Whether the inclusion of this sentence constitutes a misrepresentation depends on whether elements of the tort have been satisfied. They were not. In [*First Nat. Bank in Oshkosh v. Scieszinski*, 25 Wis. 2d 569, 131 N.W.2d 308 (1964)], it is said:

> A party alleging fraud has the burden of proving it by clear and convincing evidence. The elements of fraud are well established:
>
> To be actionable the false representation must consist, first of a statement of fact which is untrue; second, that it was made with intent to defraud and for the purpose of inducing the other party to act upon it; third, that he did in fact rely on it and was induced thereby to act, to his injury or damage.

No evidence was adduced to show that the plaintiff had an intent to defraud the dealer. To the contrary, it is at least arguable that the majority of minors are, as the plaintiff here might well have been, unaware of the legal consequences of their acts.

Without the element of scienter being satisfied, the plaintiff is not susceptible to an action in misrepresentation. Furthermore, the reliance mentioned in *Scieszinski* must be, as Prosser points out, "justifiable reliance." We fail to see how the dealer could be justified in the mere reliance on the fact that the plaintiff signed a contract containing a sentence that said he was twenty-one or over. The trial court observed that the plaintiff was sufficiently immature looking to arouse suspicion. The appellant never took any affirmative steps to determine whether the plaintiff was in fact over twenty-one. It never asked to see a draft card, identification card, or the most logical indicium of age under the circumstances, a driver's license. Therefore, because there was no intent to deceive, and no justifiable reliance, the appellant's action for misrepresentation must fail.

By the Court: Judgment affirmed.

Hallows, C. J. (dissenting).

The majority opinion on the issue of whether an emancipated minor legally should be responsible for his contracts "doth protest too much." After giving very cogent reasons why the common-law rule should be abandoned, the opinion refrains from reshaping the rule to meet reality. Minors are emancipated by a valid marriage and also by entering military service. If they are mature enough to become parents and assume the responsibility of raising other minors and if they are mature enough to be drafted or volunteer to bear arms and sacrifice their life for their country, then they are mature enough to make binding contracts in the marketplace. The magical age limit of twenty-one years as an indication of contractual maturity no longer has a basis in fact or in public policy.

My second ground of the dissent is that an automobile to this respondent was a necessity and therefore the contract could not be disaffirmed. Here, we have a minor, aged twenty years and seven months, the father of a child, and working. While the record shows there is some public transportation to his present place of work, it also shows he borrowed his mother's car to go to and from work. Automobiles for parents under twenty-one years of age to go to and from work in our current society may well be a necessity and I think in this case the record shows it is. An automobile as a means of transportation to earn a living should not be considered a non-necessity because the owner is five months too young. I would reverse.

QUESTIONS AND NOTES

1. Questions about the facts of this case

 1.1. Is 20 year old Steven Kiefer "distinguishable" (*i.e.*, different) from 6 year old Bruce?

 1.2. Did the plaintiff deny that he agreed to pay and did pay $412 for the five year old station wagon?

 1.3. Did the plaintiff deny that he represented to the seller that he was twenty-one?

 1.4. Did the plaintiff contend that he did not understand the contract he signed?

 1.5. Did the plaintiff contend that the agreement was unfair?

 1.6. Did the plaintiff need the car?

 1.7. Was the plaintiff "emancipated"?

 1.8. How much did the car cost? How much did it cost to litigate and appeal this case?

2. Questions about the law

 2.1. In September 1965, Epstein (the only one of your authors who was over 21 in 1965) offers Fred Howe Motors, Inc., $3,000 for a 1960 Willys station wagon. Can Fred Howe Motors, Inc. get the car back from Steve Kiefer on the ground that the sale contract was not effective since Kiefer was a minor?

 2.2. How can you contract with a minor? Your firm represents Jive Records, Inc. which wants to sign Gooberhead, an 11 year old bluegrass rapper, to a recording contract. What do you advise?

 2.3. Is the discussion of misrepresentation in the *Kiefer* case consistent with the earlier discussion of misrepresentation in *Halpert v. Rosenthal, supra*?

 2.4. Epstein's thirteen year old niece, Bubbette Epstein, uses the $3000 she has received in bat mitzvah presents to buy a new computer from M&P Computers, Inc. Months later, when there is a new, improved model of the computer on the market, can Bubbette disaffirm her contract with M&P, return the computer, and get her money back?

3. Questions about the law generally—Statutes in a common law system

3.1. What was the basis for the *Kiefer* court's decision that the contract of a minor is voidable?

3.2. Why did Fred Howe Motors, Inc.'s attorney appeal?

4. Notes

4.1. "The right of disaffirmance as taught in our law schools has increasingly had little practical import in the billion dollar juvenile marketplace. . . . It [infant incapacity] has been preserved in the cloistered domain of black letter law. In reality, it has been dismantled piece by piece by twin adversaries: the courthouse and the statehouse. The right of disaffirmance has been judicially limited by the creation of an assortment of subdoctrines intended to mollify the harsh effects of the per se rule."

LARRY L. DIMATTEO, CONTRACT THEORY—THE EVOLUTION OF CONTRACTUAL INTENT 103 (1998).

4.2. The *Kiefer* case illustrates a couple of these limiting judicial "subdoctrines": (i) infants' liability for "necessaries" and (ii) infants' liability for misrepresentation of age.

4.3. Another such mollifying subdoctrine is ratification. By her actions or inactions after reaching the age of majority (or otherwise gaining capacity) a person can lose the right of disaffirmance through ratification. For example, ratification prevented Bob Dylan from saying "I'll just say fare thee well, gal" to Columbia Records.

When [CBS/Columbia Records] signed him, Dylan was twenty and a minor under New York state contract law. The folksinger said he had no parent to countersign for him, which was untrue. After his first album bombed, Dylan sent Columbia a letter declaring his contract void. [The letter was] handed over to [Clive] Davis. Clive asked whether Dylan had used the CBS studio since turning twenty-one. Six or seven times [was the response]. In that case, Clive said Dylan had affirmed his contract. Dylan was forced to rescind the letter.

FREDRIC DANNEN, HIT MEN: POWER BROKERS AND FAST MONEY INSIDER THE MUSIC BUSINESS 67–68 (1991).

4.4. One of Epstein's young research assistants understandably asks: why is there a "bright line" statutory rule to decide who is too young to contract but no similar rule to decide who is too old to contract?

SECTION 5: PRESSURE—DURESS AND UNDUE INFLUENCE

In the previous subchapter on capacity, the defense to enforceability of an agreement was based on who happened to make the agreement. In these materials on duress and undue influence, the defense to enforceabilty of an agreement is based primarily on how the agreement happened.

Obviously, if Epstein agrees to write a book with Markell and Ponoroff only because they have guns pointed at his head, that agreement should not be legally enforceable. Physical duress! Restatement (Second) of Contracts § 174. As Professor Atiyah of Oxford explained, duress is not limited to physical duress:

P.S. ATIYAH, AN INTRODUCTION TO THE LAW OF CONTRACT
265–67 (5th ed. 1995)

All persons over the age of 18 and of sound mind are generally treated as of equal capacity for the purpose of contracting, and the law is reluctant to admit the direct plea that the contract is unfair, and that one party was in a position to dictate the terms to the other. But while maintaining the sanctity of contracts as a general principle, the law has, from time to time, stepped in to redress the balance between the strong and the weak.

* * *

A person who does something under the most severe constraints (such as throwing his cargo overboard to save his ship during a storm), is, said Aristotle, still acting voluntarily, of his own free will. He is choosing between two very unpalatable courses, but he is still making a free choice. Similarly, a person who signs a contract at the point of a gun may be said to be simply choosing between being shot and signing the document. He signs, not because he has no will—indeed, the more strongly he believes in the gunman's threats, the more willing he is likely to be to sign—but because it is the lesser of the two evils open to him.

But this analysis leads to a new difficulty. If even the gunman's victim is acting of his free will, then we must say that all (or anyhow nearly all) contracts are made voluntarily, but we must also admit that all contracts are made under pressure of some sort. Not only is there no such thing as a totally involuntary contract, there is equally no such thing as a totally unconstrained choice. Every contract we make is made under some form of pressure, every contractual offer is made backed by some sort of threat. The pressure and the threats are implicit in the whole concept of exchange, because the offeror is always demanding something in return for his offer, which is only another way of saying that he is threatening not to supply what you want, unless you can give him what he wants in return. This means that some way must be found of distinguishing between the kinds of pressure and the kinds of threats which will be permissible, which will not invalidate a contract, and those pressures and threats which will be ruled out, and which will invalidate a contract. The distinction which the law seeks to draw, therefore, must be that between legitimate and illegitimate pressure, or threats, and has nothing to do with 'overborne wills.'

This excursion into theory is not without practical import, because the questions raised by these two possible approaches are quite different. If the law were truly concerned with the degree to which a choice was an exercise of free will, the question before the court would presumably be a psychological (or even philosophical) question of no little difficulty, and it would also be a question of fact in each case: has the will been overborne? On the other hand, if the true question concerns the legitimacy of the pressure or threats used, the question must be one of law which has nothing to do with the psychological state of mind of the party in question.

As Professor Atiyah points out, the law of duress is not limited to physical duress. As the next two cases point out, the law of duress is not limited to individuals: businesses can avoid the legal enforcement of an agreement by establishing "illegitimate pressure or threats."

Austin Instrument, Inc. v. Loral Corporation

Court of Appeals of New York
29 N.Y.2d 124, 272 N.E.2d 533 (1971)

Fuld, C.J.

The defendant, Loral Corporation, seeks to recover payment for goods delivered under a contract which it had with plaintiff Austin Instrument, Inc., on the ground that the evidence establishes, as a matter of law, that it was forced to agree to an increase in price on the items in question under circumstances amounting to economic duress.

In July of 1965, Loral was awarded a $6,000,000 contract by the Navy for the production of radar sets. The contract contained a schedule of deliveries, a liquidated damages clause applying to late deliveries and a cancellation clause in case of default by Loral. The latter thereupon solicited bids for some 40 precision gear components needed to produce the radar sets, and awarded Austin a subcontract to supply 23 such parts. That party commenced delivery in early 1966.

In May, 1966, Loral was awarded a second Navy contract for the production of more radar sets and again went about soliciting bids. Austin bid on all 40 gear components but, on July 15, a representative from Loral informed Austin's president, Mr. Krauss, that his company would be awarded the subcontract only for those items on which it was low bidder. The Austin officer refused to accept an order for less than all 40 of the gear parts and on the next day he told Loral that Austin would cease deliveries of the parts due under the existing subcontract unless Loral consented to substantial increases in the prices provided for by that agreement—both retroactively for parts already delivered and prospectively on those not yet shipped—and placed with Austin the order for all 40 parts needed under Loral's second Navy contract. Shortly thereafter, Austin did, indeed, stop delivery. After contacting 10 manufacturers of precision gears and finding none who could produce the parts in time to meet its commitments to the Navy, Loral acceded to Austin's demands; in a letter dated July 22, Loral wrote to Austin that:

> We have feverishly surveyed other sources of supply and find that because of the prevailing military exigencies, were they to start from scratch as would have to be the case, they could not even remotely begin to deliver on time to meet the delivery requirements established by the Gov-

> ernment. * * * Accordingly, we are left with no choice or alternative but to meet your conditions.

Loral thereupon consented to the price increases insisted upon by Austin under the first subcontract and the latter was awarded a second subcontract making it the supplier of all 40 gear parts for Loral's second contract with the Navy. Although Austin was granted until September to resume deliveries, Loral did, in fact, receive parts in August and was able to produce the radar sets in time to meet its commitments to the Navy on both contracts. After Austin's last delivery under the second subcontract in July, 1967, Loral notified it of its intention to seek recovery of the price increases.

On September 15, 1967, Austin instituted this action against Loral to recover an amount in excess of $17,750 which was still due on the second subcontract. On the same day, Loral commenced an action against Austin claiming damages of some $22,250—the aggregate of the price increases under the first subcontract—on the ground of economic duress. The two actions were consolidated and, following a trial, Austin was awarded the sum it requested and Loral's complaint against Austin was dismissed on the ground that it was not shown that "it could not have obtained the items in question from other sources in time to meet its commitment to the Navy under the first contract." A closely divided Appellate Division affirmed. * * *

The applicable law is clear and, indeed, is not disputed by the parties. A contract is voidable on the ground of duress when it is established that the party making the claim was forced to agree to it by means of a wrongful threat precluding the exercise of his free will. The existence of economic duress or business compulsion is demonstrated by proof that "immediate possession of needful goods is threatened" or, more particularly, in cases such as the one before us, by proof that one party to a contract has threatened to breach the agreement by withholding goods unless the other party agrees to some further demand. However, a mere threat by one party to breach the contract by not delivering the required items, though wrongful, does not in itself constitute economic duress. It must also appear that the threatened party could not obtain the goods from another source of supply and that the ordinary remedy of an action for breach of contract would not be adequate.

We find without any support in the record the conclusion reached by the courts below that Loral failed to establish that it was the victim of economic duress. On the contrary, the evidence makes out a classic case, as a matter of law, of such duress.

It is manifest that Austin's threat—to stop deliveries unless the prices were increased—deprived Loral of its free will. As bearing on this, Loral's relationship with the Government is most significant. As mentioned above, its contract called for staggered monthly deliveries of the radar sets, with clauses calling for liquidated damages and possible cancellation on default. Because of its production schedule, Loral was, in July, 1966, concerned with meeting its delivery requirements in September, October and November, and it was for the sets to be delivered in those months that the withheld gears were needed. Loral had to plan ahead, and the substantial liquidated damages for which it would be liable, plus the threat of default, were genuine possibilities. Moreover, Loral did a substantial portion of its business with the Government, and it feared that a failure to deliver as agreed upon would jeopardize its chances for future contracts. * * * It was perfectly reasonable for Loral, or any other party similarly placed, to consider itself in an emergency, duress situation.

* * *

Loral, as indicated above, also had the burden of demonstrating that it could not obtain the parts elsewhere within a reasonable time, and there can be no doubt that it met this burden. The 10 manufacturers whom Loral contacted comprised its entire list of "approved vendors" for precision gears, and none was able to commence delivery soon enough. As Loral was producing a highly sophisticated item of military machinery requiring parts made to the strictest engineering standards, it would be unreasonable to hold that Loral should have gone to other vendors, with whom it was either unfamiliar or dissatisfied, to procure the needed parts. * * *

It is hardly necessary to add that Loral's normal legal remedy of accepting Austin's breach of the contract and then suing for damages would have been inadequate under the circumstances, as Loral would still have had to obtain the gears elsewhere with all the concomitant consequences mentioned above. In other words, Loral actually had no choice, when the prices were raised by Austin, except to take the gears at the "coerced" prices and then sue to get the excess back. * * *

In sum, the record before us demonstrates that Loral agreed to the price increases in consequence of the economic duress employed by Austin. Accordingly, the matter should be remanded to the trial court for a computation of its damages.

The order appealed from should be modified, with costs, by reversing so much thereof as affirms the dismissal of defendant Loral Corporation's claim and, except as so modified, affirmed.

* * *

QUESTIONS

1. Questions about the facts of this case

   1.1. Which company is larger, Austin or Loral? Does size matter? Is Austin's powers relevant?

   1.2. Did Loral agree to Austin's demand for price increases?

   1.3. Do you think that Loral's July 22d letter was written, or at least reviewed, by a lawyer? By a lawyer familiar with the concept of excuse by reason of economic duress?

   1.4. Why did Austin ask for price increases? According to the statement of facts in the Appellate Division opinion,

   > Austin claimed that it was losing a substantial sum on the existing job; that it could not afford to do this; and that the prices being paid to it were only a fraction of what it was entitled to. Parenthetically, we note that it is well known that in this time of continual rising of material and manufacturing costs, renegotiation of contract prices does sometimes occur in business and commercial dealings.

   316 N.Y.S. 2d 530. Is that relevant?

2. Questions about the law

   2.1. Is this case covered by Article 2 of the Uniform Commercial Code?

   2.2. Professor Atiyah suggested that the law needs to distinguish between "legitimate and illegitimate pressure." How did the court in *Austin* distinguish between the two? What did Austin do that was "illegitimate"?

Totem Marine Tug & Barge, Inc. v. Alyeska Pipeline Service Company
Supreme Court of Alaska
584 P.2d 15 (1978)

Burke, J.

This appeal arises from the superior court's granting of summary judgment in favor of defendants-appellees Alyeska Pipeline Services, et al., in a contract action brought by plaintiffs-appellants Totem Marine Tug & Barge, Inc., Pacific, Inc., and Richard Stair.

The following summary of events is derived from the materials submitted in the summary judgment proceedings below.

Totem is a closely held Alaska corporation which began operations in March of 1975. Richard Stair, at all times relevant to this case, was vice-resident of Totem. In June of 1975, Totem entered into a contract with Alyeska under which Totem was to transport pipeline construction materials from Houston, Texas, to a designated port in southern Alaska, with the possibility of one or two cargo stops along the way. In order to carry out this contract, which was Totem's first, Totem chartered a barge (The "Marine Flasher") and an ocean-going tug (the "Kirt Chouest"). * * *

By the terms of the contract, Totem was to have completed performance by approximately August 15, 1975. From the start, however, there were numerous problems which impeded Totem's performance of the contract. For example, according to Totem, Alyeska represented that approximately 1,800 to 2,100 tons of regular uncoated pipe were to be loaded in Houston, and that perhaps another 6,000 to 7,000 tons of materials would be put on the barge at later stops along the west coast. Upon the arrival of the tug and barge in Houston, however, Totem found that about 6,700 to 7,200 tons of coated pipe, steel beams and valves, haphazardly and improperly piled, were in the yard to be loaded. This situation called for remodeling of the barge and extra cranes and stevedores, and resulted in the loading taking thirty days rather than the three days which Totem had anticipated it would take to load 2,000 tons. The lengthy loading period was also caused in part by Alyeska's delay in assuring Totem that it would pay for the additional expenses, bad weather and other administrative problems.

The difficulties continued after the tug and barge left Houston. It soon became apparent that the vessels were travelling more slowly than anticipated because of the extra load. In response to Alyeska's complaints and with its verbal consent, on August 13, 1975, Totem chartered a second tug, the "N. Joseph Guidry." When the "Guidry" reached the Panama Canal, however, Alyeska had not yet furnished the written amendment to the parties' contract. Afraid that Alyeska would not agree to cover the cost of the second tug, Stair notified the "Guidry" not to go through the Canal. After some discussions in which Alyeska complained of the delays and accused Totem of lying about the horsepower of the first tug, Alyeska executed the amendment on August 21, 1975.

By this time the "Guidry" had lost its preferred passage through the Canal and had to wait two or three additional days before it could go through. Upon finally meeting, the three vessels encountered the tail of a hurricane which lasted for about eight or nine days and which substantially impeded their progress.

The three vessels finally arrived in the vicinity of San Pedro, California, where Totem planned to change crews and refuel. On Alyeska's orders, however, the vessels instead pulled into port at Long Beach, California. At this point, Alyeska's agents commenced off-loading the barge, without Totem's consent, without the necessary load survey, and without a marine survey, the absence of which voided Totem's insurance. After much wrangling and some concessions by Alyeska, the freight was off-loaded. Thereafter, on or about September 14, 1975, Alyeska terminated the contract. The termination was affirmed a few days later at a meeting at which Alyeska officials refused to give a reason for the termination.

Following termination of the contract, Totem submitted termination invoices to Alyeska and began pressing the latter for payment. The invoices came to something between $260,000 and $300,000. An official from Alyeska told Totem that they would look over the invoices but that they were not sure when payment would be made—perhaps in a day or perhaps in six to eight months. Totem was in urgent need of cash as the invoices represented debts which the company had incurred on 10-30 day payment schedules. Totem's creditors were demanding payment and according to Stair, without immediate cash, Totem would go bankrupt. Totem then turned over the collection to its attorney, Roy Bell, directing him to advise Alyeska of Totem's financial straits. Thereafter, Bell met with Alyeska officials in Seattle, and after some negotiations, Totem received a settlement offer from Alyeska for $97,500. On November 6, 1975, Totem, through its president Stair, signed an agreement releasing Alyeska from all claims by Totem in exchange for $97,500.

On March 26, 1976, Totem, Richard Stair, and Pacific filed a complaint against Alyeska, which was subsequently amended. In the amended complaint, the plaintiffs sought to rescind the settlement and release on the ground of economic duress and to recover the balance allegedly due on the original contract. In addition, they alleged that Alyeska had wrongfully terminated the contract and sought miscellaneous other compensatory and punitive damages.

Before filing an answer, Alyeska moved for summary judgment against the plaintiffs on the ground that Totem had executed a binding release of all claims against Alyeska and that as a matter of law, Totem could not prevail on its claim of economic duress. In opposition, plaintiffs contended that the purported release was executed under duress in that Alyeska wrongfully terminated the contract; that Alyeska knew that Totem was faced with large debts and impending bankruptcy; that Alyeska withheld funds admittedly owed knowing the effect this would have on plaintiffs and that plaintiffs had no alternative but to involuntarily accept the $97,500 in order to avoid bankruptcy. Plaintiffs maintained that they had thus raised genuine issues of material fact such that trial was necessary, and that Alyeska was not entitled to judgment as a matter of law. Alyeska disputed the plaintiffs' assertions.

On November 30, 1976, the superior court granted the defendant's motion for summary judgment. This appeal followed.

* * *

As was noted above, a court's initial task in deciding motions for summary judgment is to determine whether there exist genuine issues of material fact. In order to decide whether such issues exist in this case, we must examine the doctrine allowing avoidance of a release on grounds of economic duress.

This court has not yet decided a case involving a claim of economic duress or what is also called business compulsion. At early common law, a contract could be avoided on the ground of duress only if a party could show that the agreement was entered into for fear of loss of life or limb, mayhem or imprisonment. The threat had to be such as to overcome the will of a person of ordinary firmness and courage. Subsequently, however, the concept has been broadened to include myriad forms of economic coercion which force a person to involuntarily enter into a particular transaction. The test has come to be whether the will of the person induced by the threat was overcome rather than that of a reasonably firm person.

At the outset it is helpful to acknowledge the various policy considerations which are involved in cases involving economic duress. Typically, those claiming such coercion are attempting to avoid the consequences of a modification of an original contract or of a settlement and release agreement. On the one hand, courts are reluctant to set aside agreements because of the notion of freedom of contract and because of the desirability of having private dispute resolutions be final. On the other hand, there is an increasing recognition of the law's role in correcting inequitable or unequal exchanges between parties of disproportionate bargaining power and a greater willingness to not enforce agreements which were entered into under coercive circumstances.

There are various statements of what constitutes economic duress. * * * Section 492(b) of the Restatement of Contracts defines duress as:

> any wrongful threat of one person by words or other conduct that induces another to enter into a transaction under the influence of such fear as precludes him from exercising free will and judgment, if the threat was intended or should reasonably have been expected to operate as an inducement.

Professor Williston states the basic elements of economic duress in the following manner:

1. The party alleging economic duress must show that he has been the victim of a wrongful or unlawful act or threat, and
2. Such act or threat must be one which deprives the victim of his unfettered will.

Many courts state the test somewhat differently, eliminating use of the vague term "free will," but retaining the same basic idea. Under this standard, duress exists where: (1) one party involuntarily accepted the terms of another, (2) circumstances permitted no other alternative, and (3) such circumstances were the result of coercive acts of the other party. The third element is further explained as follows:

> In order to substantiate the allegation of economic duress or business compulsion, the plaintiff must go beyond the mere showing of reluctance to accept and of financial embarrassment. There must be a showing of acts on the part of the defendant which produced these two factors. The assertion of duress must be proven by evidence that the duress resulted

from defendant's wrongful and oppressive conduct and not by the plaintiff's necessities.

[*W. R. Grimshaw Co. v. Nevil C. Withrow Co.*, 248 F.2d 896, 904 (1957)].

As the above indicates, one essential element of economic duress is that the plaintiff show that the other party by wrongful acts or threats, intentionally caused him to involuntarily enter into a particular transaction. Courts have not attempted to define exactly what constitutes a wrongful or coercive act, as wrongfulness depends on the particular facts in each case. This requirement may be satisfied where the alleged wrongdoer's conduct is criminal or tortious but an act or threat may also be considered wrongful if it is wrongful in the moral sense.

In many cases, a threat to breach a contract or to withhold payment of an admitted debt has constituted a wrongful act. Implicit in such cases is the additional requirement that the threat to breach the contract or withhold payment be done in bad faith.

Economic duress does not exist, however, merely because a person has been the victim of a wrongful act; in addition, the victim must have no choice but to agree to the other party's terms or face serious financial hardship. Thus, in order to avoid a contract, a party must also show that he had no reasonable alternative to agreeing to the other party's terms, or, as it is often stated, that he had no adequate remedy if the threat were to be carried out. What constitutes a reasonable alternative is a question of fact, depending on the circumstances of each case. An available legal remedy, such as an action for breach of contract, may provide such an alternative. Where one party wrongfully threatens to withhold goods, services or money from another unless certain demands are met, the availability on the market of similar goods and services or of other sources of funds may also provide an alternative to succumbing to the coercing party's demands. * * *

* * * For example, in [*Austin Instrument, Inc. v. Loral Corp.*, 29 N.Y.2d 124 (1971)], duress was found in the following circumstances: A subcontractor threatened to refuse further delivery under a contract unless the contractor agreed to modify the existing contract between the parties. The contractor was unable to obtain the necessary materials elsewhere without delay, and if it did not have the materials promptly, it would have been in default on its main contract with the government. In each case such default would have had grave economic consequences for the contractor and hence it agreed to the modifications. In both, the courts found that the al-

ternatives to agreeing to the modification were inadequate (i.e., suing for breach of contract or obtaining the materials elsewhere) and that modifications therefore were signed under duress and voidable.

* * *

Turning to the instant case, we believe that Totem's allegations, if proved, would support a finding that it executed a release of its contract claims against Alyeska under economic duress. Totem has alleged that Alyeska deliberately withheld payment of an acknowledged debt, knowing that Totem had no choice but to accept an inadequate sum in settlement of that debt; that Totem was faced with impending bankruptcy; that Totem was unable to meet its pressing debts other than by accepting the immediate cash payment offered by Alyeska; and that through necessity, Totem thus involuntarily accepted an inadequate settlement offer from Alyeska and executed a release of all claims under the contract. If the release was in fact executed under these circumstances,[5] we think that under the legal principles discussed above that this would constitute the type of wrongful conduct and lack of alternatives that would render the release voidable by Totem on the ground of economic duress. We would add that although Totem need not necessarily prove its allegation that Alyeska's termination of the contract was wrongful in order to sustain a claim of economic duress, the events leading to the termination would be probative as to whether Alyeska exerted any wrongful pressure on Totem and whether Alyeska wrongfully withheld payment from Totem.[6]

* * *

Our examination of the materials presented by Totem in opposition to Alyeska's motion for summary judgment leads us to conclude that Totem has made a sufficient factual showing as to each of the elements of economic duress to withstand that motion. There is no doubt that Alyeska disputes many of the factual allegations made by Totem[7] and drawing all infer-

---

[5]By way of clarification, we would note that Totem would not have to prove that Alyeska admitted to owing the precise sum Totem claimed it was owed upon termination of the contract but only that Alyeska acknowledged that it owed Totem approximately that amount which Totem sought.

[6]We make no comment as to whether Alyeska's termination of the contract was wrongful nor as to the truth of Totem's other allegations.

[7]For example, Alyeska has denied that it ever admitted to owing any particular sum to Totem and has disputed the truthfulness of Totem's assertions of impending bankruptcy. Other factual issues which remain unresolved include whether or not Alyeska knew of Totem's fi-

ences in favor of Totem, we believe that genuine issues of material fact exist in this case such that trial is necessary. Admittedly, Totem's showing was somewhat weak in that, for example, it did not produce the testimony of Roy Bell, the attorney who represented Totem in the negotiations leading to the settlement and release. At trial, it will probably be necessary for Totem to produce this evidence if it is to prevail on its claim of duress. However, a party opposing a motion for summary judgment need not produce all of the evidence it may have at its disposal but need only show that issues of material fact exist. Therefore, we hold that the superior court erred in granting summary judgment for appellees and remand the case to the superior court for trial in accordance with the legal principles set forth above.

* * *

QUESTIONS AND NOTES

1. Questions about the facts of this case

   1.1. The opinion mentions two different agreements: (i) the June transport agreement and (ii) the November settlement agreement. Which agreement is involved in this litigation?

   1.2. Does the plaintiff Totem Marine Tug & Barge, Inc. allege a breach of the June transport agreement? Does it allege a breach of the November settlement agreement?

2. Questions about the law

   2.1. According to the first *Restatement* definition of duress quoted by the Alaska Supreme Court, duress requires a "wrongful" threat or conduct. What "wrongful" threat or conduct does the plaintiff allege?

   2.2. The *Totem* decision discusses the *Austin* case. As the attorney for Alyeska, how would you distinguish the *Austin* case?

---

nancial situation after termination of the contract and whether Alyeska did in fact threaten by words or conduct to withhold payment unless Totem agreed to settle.

2.3. On remand, what does the trial court have to find in order to rescind the November settlement agreement on the ground of economic duress? Will the plaintiff establish economic duress by establishing that the value of its claim was more than $97,500? Significantly more than $97,500? *Cf. Restatement (Second) of Contracts* § 74.

3. Notes

3.1. Recently, the Alaska Supreme Court discussed the *Totem* decision in *Northern Fabrication Co., Inc. v. Unocal and Star North Services, Inc.*, 980 P.2d 958 (Alaska 1999), a case with markedly similar facts to *Totem*. There, Northern Fabrication, a company on the brink of bankruptcy, settled its $170,000+ contract cost overruns claim against Unocal and then later sued to rescind the settlement on the ground of economic duress. Unocal moved for summary judgment. In *Northern Fabrication*, unlike *Totem*, the Alaska Supreme Court granted the summary judgment motion distinguishing *Totem*:

> Herein lies the difference between *Totem* and the case at bar. In *Totem*, it was alleged that the other party deliberately withheld payment of an acknowledged debt. Deliberately withholding payment of an acknowledged debt constitutes an action "wrongful in the moral sense" that satisfies the third prong of the test for economic duress. Here NFC has not produced evidence that UNOCAL ever acknowledged its debt to NFC for the full amount of the cost overruns.

3.2. While the first Restatement of Contracts used the term "wrongful" in defining "duress," the *Restatement (Second) of Contracts* §§ 175 and 176 use the term "improper." The examples of an "improper threat" for this purpose include a threat that is "a breach of the duty of good faith and fair dealing under a contract with the recipient." *Restatement (Second) of Contracts* § 176(d).

3.3. In *Rich & Whillock, Inc. v. Ashon Development, Inc.*, 157 Cal. App. 3d 1154, 1158 (1984), another case with facts similar to *Totem*, the court discussed two conflicting policy concerns: (i) "the reluctance to set aside agreements because of the notion of freedom of contract and . . . the desirability of having private dispute resolution be final" and (ii) "the recognition of the law's role in correcting inequitable . . . exchanges between parties of disproportionate bargaining power and

. . . not to enforce agreements which were entered into under coercive circumstances."

3.4. The next case considers "undue influence." According to the note in the Restatement (Second) of Contracts, introducing the sections on duress and undue influence: "Undue influence involves unfair persuasion, a milder form of pressure than duress."

Odorizzi v. Bloomfield School District

Court of Appeal of California, Second Appellate District
246 Cal. App. 2d 123, 54 Cal.Rptr. 533 (1966)

Fleming, J.

Appeal from a judgment dismissing plaintiff's amended complaint on demurrer.

Plaintiff Donald Odorizzi was employed during 1964 as an elementary school teacher by defendant Bloomfield School District and was under contract with the district to continue to teach school the following year as a permanent employee. On June 10 he was arrested on criminal charges of homosexual activity, and on June 11 he signed and delivered to his superiors his written resignation as a teacher, a resignation which the district accepted on June 13. In July the criminal charges against Odorizzi were dismissed under Penal Code, section 995, and in September he sought to resume his employment with the district. On the district's refusal to reinstate him he filed suit for declaratory and other relief.

Odorizzi's amended complaint asserts his resignation was invalid because obtained through duress, fraud, mistake, and undue influence and given at a time when he lacked capacity to make a valid contract. Specifically, Odorizzi declares he was under such severe mental and emotional strain at the time he signed his resignation, having just completed the process of arrest, questioning by the police, booking, and release on bail, and having gone for 40 hours without sleep, that he was incapable of rational thought or action. While he was in this condition and unable to think clearly, the superintendent of the district and the principal of his school came to his apartment. They said they were trying to help him and had his best interests at heart, that he should take their advice and immediately resign his position with the district, that there was no time to consult an attorney, that if he did not resign immediately the district would suspend and dismiss him from his position and publicize the proceedings, his "aforedescribed arrest" and cause him "to suffer extreme embarrassment and humiliation"; but that if he resigned at once the incident would not be publicized and would not jeopardize his chances of securing employment as a teacher elsewhere. Odorizzi pleads that because of his faith and confidence in their representations they were able to substitute their will and judgment in place of his own and thus obtain his signature to his purported resignation. A demurrer to his amended complaint was sustained without leave to amend.

By his complaint plaintiff in effect seeks to rescind his resignation pursuant to Civil Code, section 1689,* on the ground that his consent had not been real or free * * *, but had been obtained through duress, menace, fraud, undue influence, or mistake. * * * In our view the facts in the amended complaint are insufficient to state a cause of action for duress, menace, fraud, or mistake, but they do set out sufficient elements to justify rescission of a consent because of undue influence. We summarize our conclusions on each of these points.

1. No duress or menace has been pleaded. Duress consists in unlawful confinement of another's person, or relatives, or property, which causes him to consent to a transaction through fear. Duress is often used interchangeably with menace, but in California menace is technically a threat of duress or a threat of injury to the person, property, or character of another. We agree with respondent's contention that neither duress nor menace was involved in this case, because the action or threat in duress or menace must be unlawful, and a threat to take legal action is not unlawful unless the party making the threat knows the falsity of his claim. The amended complaint shows in substance that the school representative announced their intention to initiate suspension and dismissal proceedings under Education Code, section 13403,** 13408,*** et seq. at a time when the filing of such pro-

*§ 1689. "(b) A party to a contract may rescind the contract in the following cases: (1) If the consent of the party rescinding, or of any party jointly contracting with him, was given by mistake, or obtained through duress, menace, fraud, or undue influence, exercised by or with the connivance of the party as to whom he rescinds, or of any other party to the contract jointly interested with such party." Eds.

**§ 134.03. "Grounds for dismissal of permanent employee. No permanent employee shall be dismissed except for one or more of the following causes: (a) Immoral or unprofessional conduct. * * * (k) Knowing membership by the employee in the Communist Party." Eds.

***§ 13408. "Immediate suspension of permanent employee; hearing upon certain charges. Upon the filing of written charges, duly signed and verified by the person filing them with the governing board of a school district, or upon a written statement of charges formulated

3. Notes

3.1. Professor Peter Birks of Oxford University and Professor Chin Nyuk Yin of University of West Australia have suggested that duress and undue influence be combined: "It is time in this field that we overcame the old jurisdictional duality. It would be better that pressure should be litigated as pressure." Peter Birks & Chin Nyuk Yin, *On the Nature of Undue Influence* in JACK BEASON & DANIEL FRIEDMANN, GOOD FAITH AND FAULT IN CONTRACT LAW 57, 63 (1995).

3.2. Profesor Curtis Nyquist of New England School of Law and two students active in the Les-Bi-Gay-Trans Caucus at New England School of Law suggest that the study of the *Odorizzi* case be combined with the study of LBGT issues: "we think it is impossible to understand the pressures felt by Odorizzi without considering LBGT issues in depth. Domination undue influence is fundamentally a claim that a particular person, at the time of the agreement, suffered from diminished mental capacity. Ruiz (a "heteroqueer evolved-male") and Smith's (a "gay-white biologically male law student") participation in the class provided context for students' understanding of the impact on Odorizzi of the arrest and threat of public proceedings." Curtis Nyquist, Patrick Ruiz, and Frank Smith, *Using Students as Discussion Leaders on Sexual Orientation and Gender Identity Issues in First-Year Courses*, 49 J. LEGAL EDUC. 535 (1999).

SECTION 6: ILLEGALITY AND PUBLIC POLICY

It is easy to think of agreements that are illegal and understand why an agreement's illegal subject matter makes the agreement unenforceable by either party. For example, Chiam, one of Epstein's contracts students, hires Bubba, another of Epstein's contracts students, to injure Epstein. That agreement would be unenforceable by either Chiam or Bubba. It is against the law to injure someone—even a contracts professor.

ceedings was not only their legal right but their positive duty as school officials. (Ed.Code, § 13409*). * * *

2. Nor do we find a cause of action for fraud, either actual or constructive.

* * *

3. As to mistake, the amended complaint fails to disclose any facts which would suggest that consent had been obtained through a mistake of fact or of law. * * *

4. However, the pleading does set out a claim that plaintiff's consent to the transaction had been obtained through the use of undue influence.

Undue influence, in the sense we are concerned with here, is a shorthand legal phrase used to describe persuasion which tends to be coercive in nature, persuasion which overcomes the will without convincing the judgment. The hallmark of such persuasion is high pressure, a pressure which works on mental, moral, or emotional weakness to such an extent that it approaches the boundaries of coercion. In this sense, undue influence has been called overpersuasion. Misrepresentations of law or fact are not essential to the charge, for a person's will may be overborne without misrepresentation. By statutory definition undue influence includes "taking an unfair advantage of another's weakness of mind, or . . . taking a grossly

---

by the governing board, charging a permanent employee of the district with immoral conduct, conviction of a felony or of any crime involving moral turpitude, with incompetency due to mental disability, with violation of Section 8455 of this code, with knowing membership by the employee in the Communist Party or with violation of any provision in Sections 12952 to 12958, inclusive, of this code, the governing board may, if it deems such action necessary, immediately suspend the employee from his duties and give notice to him of his suspension, and that 30 days after service of the notice, he will be dismissed, unless he demands a hearing." Eds.

*§ 13409. "Compulsory leave of absence on charge of sex offenses and narcotics offenses; effect on salary of acquittal. Whenever any certificated employee of a school district is charged with the commission of any sex offense as defined in Section 12912 by complaint, information or indictment filed in a court of competent jurisdiction, the governing board of the school district shall immediately place the employee upon compulsory leave of absence for a period of time extending for not more than 10 days after the date of the entry of the judgement in the proceedings. The governing board of the school district may extend the compulsory leave of absence of the employee beyond such period by giving notice to the employee within 10 days after the entry of judgment in the proceedings that the employee will be dismissed at the expiration of 30 days from the date of service of the notice, unless the employee demands a hearing as provided in Sections 13313, 13327 and 13338, and Sections 13403 to 13441, inclusive." Eds.

oppressive and unfair advantage of another's necessities or distress." While most reported cases of undue influence involve persons who bear a confidential relationship to one another, a confidential or authoritative relationship between the parties need not be present when the undue influence involves unfair advantage taken of another's weakness or distress.

We paraphrase the summary of undue influence given the jury by Sir James P. Wilde in *Hall v. Hall*, L.R. 1, P. & D. 481, 482 (1868): To make a good contract a man must be a free agent. Pressure of whatever sort which overpowers the will without convincing the judgment is a species of restraint under which no valid contract can be made. Importunity or threats, if carried to the degree in which the free play of a man's will is overborne, constitute undue influence, although no force is used or threatened. A party may be led but not driven, and his acts must be the offspring of his own volition and not the record of someone else's.

In essence undue influence involves the use of excessive pressure to persuade one vulnerable to such pressure, pressure applied by a dominant subject to a servient object. In combination, the elements of undue susceptibility in the servient person and excessive pressure by the dominating person make the latter's influence undue, for it results in the apparent will of the servient person being in fact the will of the dominant person.

Undue susceptibility may consist of total weakness of mind which leaves a person entirely without understanding; or, a lesser weakness which destroys the capacity of a person to make a contract even though he is not totally incapacitated; or, the first element in our equation, a still lesser weakness which provides sufficient grounds to rescind a contract for undue influence. Such lesser weakness need not be longlasting nor wholly incapacitating, but may be merely a lack of full vigor due to age, physical condition, emotional anguish, or a combination of such factors. The reported cases have usually involved elderly, sick, senile persons alleged to have executed wills or deeds under pressure. In some of its aspects this lesser weakness could perhaps be called weakness of spirit. But whatever name we give it, this first element of undue influence resolves itself into a lessened capacity of the object to make a free contract.

In the present case plaintiff has pleaded that such weakness at the time he signed his resignation prevented him from freely and competently applying his judgment to the problem before him. Plaintiff declares he was under severe mental and emotional strain at the time because he had just completed the process of arrest, questioning, booking, and release on bail and had been without sleep for forty hours. It is possible that exhaustion and emotional turmoil may wholly incapacitate a person from exercising his judgment. As an abstract question of pleading, plaintiff has pleaded that possibility and sufficient allegations to state a case for rescission.

Undue influence in its second aspect involves an application of excessive strength by a dominant subject against a servient object. Judicial consideration of this second element in undue influence has been relatively rare, for there are few cases denying persons who persuade but do not misrepresent the benefit of their bargain. Yet logically, the same legal consequences should apply to the results of excessive strength as to the results of undue weakness. Whether from weakness on one side, or strength on the other, or a combination of the two, undue influence occurs whenever there results "that kind of influence or supremacy of one mind over another by which that other is prevented from acting according to his own wish or judgment, and whereby the will of the person is overborne and he is induced to do or forbear to do an act which he would not do, or would do, if left to act freely." *Webb v. Saunders*, 79 Cal. App. 2d 863,871. Undue influence involves a type of mismatch which our statute calls unfair advantage. Whether a person of subnormal capacities has been subjected to ordinary force or a person of normal capacities subjected to extraordinary force, the match is equally out of balance. If will has been overcome against judgment, consent may be rescinded.

The difficulty, of course, lies in determining when the forces of persuasion have overflowed their normal banks and become oppressive flood waters. There are second thoughts to every bargain, and hindsight is still better than foresight. Undue influence cannot be used as a pretext to avoid bad bargains or escape from bargains which refuse to come up to expectations. A woman who buys a dress on impulse, which on critical inspection by her best friend turns out to be less fashionable than she had thought, is not legally entitled to set aside the sale on the ground that the saleswoman used all her wiles to close the sale. A man who buys a tract of desert land in the expectation that it is in the immediate path of the city's growth and will become another Palm Springs, an expectation cultivated in glowing terms by the seller, cannot rescind his bargain when things turn out differently. If we are temporarily persuaded against our better judgment to do something about which we later have second thoughts, we must abide the consequences of the risks inherent in managing our own affairs.

However, overpersuasion is generally accompanied by certain characteristics which tend to create a pattern. The pattern usually involves several of the following elements: (1) discussion of the transaction at an unusual or inappropriate time, (2) consummation of the transaction in an unusual place, (3) insistent demand that the business be finished at once, (4) extreme emphasis on untoward consequences of delay, (5) the use of multiple persuaders by the dominant side against a single servient party, (6) absence of third-party advisers to the servient party, (7) statements that there is no time to consult financial advisers or attorneys. If a number of these elements are simultaneously present, the persuasion may be characterized as excessive. * * *

The difference between legitimate persuasion and excessive pressure * * * rests to a considerable extent in the manner in which the parties go about their business. For example, if a day or two after Odorizzi's release on bail the superintendent of the school district had called him into his office during business hours and directed his attention to those provisions of the Education Code compelling his leave of absence and authorizing his suspension on the filing of written charges, had told him that the district contemplated filing written charges against him, had pointed out the alternative of resignation available to him, had informed him he was free to consult counsel or any adviser he wished and to consider the matter overnight and return with his decision the next day, it is extremely unlikely that any complaint about the use of excessive pressure could ever have been made against the school district.

But, according to the allegations of the complaint, this is not the way it happened, and if it had happened that way, plaintiff would never have resigned. Rather, the representatives of the school board undertook to achieve their objective by overpersuasion and imposition to secure plaintiff's signature but not his consent to his resignation through a high-pressure carrot-and-stick technique—under which they assured plaintiff they were trying to assist him, he should rely on their advice, there wasn't time to consult an attorney, if he didn't resign at once the school district would suspend and dismiss him from his position and publicize the proceedings, but if he did resign the incident wouldn't jeopardize his chances of securing a teaching post elsewhere.

Plaintiff has thus pleaded both subjective and objective elements entering the undue influence equation and stated sufficient facts to put in issue the question whether his free will had been overborne by defendant's agents at a time when he was unable to function in a normal manner. It was sufficient to pose " . . . the ultimate question . . . whether a free and competent judgment was merely influenced, or whether a mind was so dominated as to prevent the exercise of an independent judgment." (*Williston on Contracts*, § 1625 [rev. ed.]; Rest., Contracts, § 497, com. c.) The question cannot be resolved by an analysis of pleading but requires a finding of fact.

We express no opinion on the merits of plaintiff's case, or the propriety of his continuing to teach school, or the timeliness of his rescission. We do hold that his pleading, liberally construed, states a cause of action for rescission of a transaction to which his apparent consent had been obtained through the use of undue influence.

The judgment is reversed.

QUESTIONS AND NOTES

1. Questions about the facts of this case

   1.1. There are two Odorizzi/Bloomfield School District agreements: (i) an employment contract for the 1964–65 school year and (ii) Odorizzi's June resignation. Which is involved in this litigation?

   1.2. Do we know the grounds for dismissal in the employment contract? Is that relevant? Do we know the grounds for dismissal in the California Education Code? Is that relevant?

2. Questions about the law

   2.1. The *Odorizzi* case identifies two elements of undue influence and lists seven elements of overpersuasion. The two elements of undue influence are (i) the susceptibility of the weaker party and (ii) the overpersuasion of the stronger party. Which of these two elements is more important?

   2.2. The *Odorizzi* opinion then lists seven elements of "overpersuasion." Which of the seven elements were alleged by the plaintiff?

   2.3. *Odorizzi* holds that the facts are insufficient for duress but sufficient for undue influence. How is duress different from undue influence?

   2.4. Why didn't Loral in the *Austin* case allege undue influence?

The law in question does not have to be a criminal law. We all know and understand that a court will not enforce an agreement to pay interest in excess of the rate set in the usury laws or an agreement to combine businesses that violates the antitrust laws.

A more common illegality problem is the enforceability of an agreement by someone who has failed to comply with a licensing statute. Consider the following illustrative problem.

Problem

Louisiana Revised Statute 37:1367 provides in part that: "No natural person shall engage in doing the work of a plumber unless he possesses a license or renewal thereof issued by the board [Louisiana State Plumbing Board]." Louisiana Revised Statute 37:1374 then provides: "Whoever violates the provisions of this Chapter shall be fined not less than five hundred dollars nor more than five thousand dollars, or imprisoned for not more than ninety days or both."

Ponoroff enters into an agreement with Epstein, who is not a licensed plumber, to pay Epstein $200 to install a urinal in his office. Epstein does the agreed work. Ponoroff refuses to pay. Should Epstein be able to enforce the agreement even though Epstein acted in violation of the state licensing statute? (Board regulations describe the work of a plumber as including the installation of plumbing fixtures.) How would you answer the problem? How would the *Restatement (Second)* answer the problem?

> *§ 181 Effect of Failure to Comply With Licensing or Similar Requirement*
>
> *If a party is prohibited from doing an act because of his failure to comply with a licensing, registration or similar requirement, a promise in consideration of his doing that act or of his promise to do it is unenforceable on grounds of public policy if*
>
> *(a) the requirement has a regulatory purpose, and*
> *(b) the interest in the enforcement of the promise is clearly outweighed by the public policy* <u>*behind the requirement*</u>*.*

(Emphasis added).

The defense of public policy is not limited to agreements that directly or even indirectly violate a legislative enactment. *Restatement (Second) of Contracts* § 178 provides:

> *A promise or other term of an agreement is unenforceable on grounds of public policy if legislation provides that it is unenforceable or the interest in its enforcement is clearly outweighed in the circumstances by a public policy against the enforcement of such terms.*

Some of the policies considered in the examples following § 178 and in the following cases are the product of judicial development.

Who decides whether there is a "public policy against the enforcement"? In the next case, how did the intermediate appellate court in Florida decide that there was a public policy against exculpatory clauses?

Covert v. South Florida Stadium Corporation

Court of Appeal of Florida, Third District
762 So. 2d 938 (2000)

Appellant/plaintiff Michael James Covert, M.D. appeals a judgment on the pleadings in favor of the appellee/defendant South Florida Stadium Corp [Stadium]. We reverse.

Covert sued the Stadium for personal injuries he sustained while attending a Miami Dolphin football game at Pro Player Stadium as a club-level season-ticket holder when allegedly intoxicated fans beat him up. The trial court found that the affirmative defense raised by the Stadium based on an exculpatory clause contained in the contract signed by Covert when he purchased his season tickets entitled the Stadium to judgment on the pleadings. Under the terms of the clause, the Stadium is relieved of liability for negligence and is also indemnified for any payments it is required to make in the event of injury caused by the ticket holder or any one else.[1] Covert de-

---

[1] Paragraph 3.4 of the ticket contract provides:

> Owner shall not be liable or responsible for any loss, damage, or injury to any person or to any property of Licensee or Licensee's guests in or upon the Stadium, resulting from any cause whatsoever, including but not limited to theft and vandalism, and including the sole or joint negligence of Owner, unless due to the intentional misconduct of Owner or Owner's employees, agents or other representatives. In addition, Licensee agrees to indemnify and hold Owner harmless from and against any liability, losses, claims, demands, costs and expenses including attorney's fees and litigation expenses arising out

nied the affirmative defense and responded that the exculpatory clause was illegal as against the public interest and lacked mutuality. He also argued that an ambiguity was created in the contract because, in another clause, the contract states that it does not confer any greater or lesser rights and privileges to Covert than to any other ticket holder.[2]

* * *

We have also held that "[e]xculpatory provisions which attempt to relieve a party of his or her own negligence are generally looked upon with disfavor, and Florida law requires that such clauses be strictly construed against the party claiming to be relieved of liability." Sunny Isles Marina, Inc. v. Adulami, 706 So. 2d 920, 922 (Fla. 3d DCA 1998). For such provisions to be found valid and enforceable by Florida courts, the intention of the parties must be made clear and unequivocal. * * *

As in Sunny Isles, the contract here contains two ambiguous provisions and this ambiguity precludes judgment on the pleadings. Paragraph 3.4 absolves the Stadium of liability except for "intentional misconduct" while paragraph 1.1 states that the agreement does not confer any greater or lesser rights and privileges on Covert than those held by other ticket holders. Covert offered evidence that regular season ticket-holders were not required to execute any licensing agreement and thus the Stadium was not exonerated from liability to those ticket holders. Obviously, under the Stadium's interpretation, Covert was indeed conferred a lesser right when he signed the contract for his club-level seats.

The clause also suffers from the same internal ambiguity as the clause in Sunny Isles. Under the terms of paragraph 3.4 of the contract, the Stadium is not liable for any loss, except that "due to the intentional misconduct of [the Stadium] or [the Stadium's] employees, agents or other representa-

---

> of any personal injury or property damage occurring in or upon the Stadium due to or resulting from the breach by Licensee or Licensee's guests of any of the terms and conditions of this Agreement or of any applicable laws, rules, regulations or orders of any governmental agency having appropriate jurisdiction over the Stadium, the Seat or over any actions or negligence of Licensee, or from any other cause whatsoever, including but not limited to the sole or joint negligence by the Owner.

[2]Paragraph 1.1 provides, in pertinent part:

> This Agreement provides Licensee only with the right and privilege to possess and use the Seat in the manner set forth herein, and except as pertains to the special right and privilege to so possess and use the Seat, this Agreement does not confer upon Licensee or Licensee's guests any greater or lesser rights and privileges with respect to admission to the Stadium than afforded to other holders of tickets for admission thereto.

tives." In case of theft, an intentional act, liability would be excluded under the first part of the sentence but ostensibly included under the second, assuming the "unless" clause modifies the "theft and vandalism" clause earlier in the sentence or the sentence immediately preceding which addresses the "sole or joint negligence of" the Stadium. The terms of the indemnity clause further complicate the issue because, under a literal reading, Covert would arguably have to indemnify the Stadium for a loss by theft suffered by Covert's guest due to the sole negligence of the Stadium. Furthermore, these clauses must be read in pari materia with the clause that purports not to confer any greater or lesser rights on Covert than those afforded to other ticket-holders. In this case, we find that the various clauses are so ambiguous that an ordinary and knowledgeable party would not know what he or she was contracting away. Since construction of the ambiguous exculpatory and indemnity clauses is required in this case, the judgment on the pleadings in favor of the Stadium must be reversed.

Reversed and remanded.

QUESTIONS AND NOTES

1. Questions about the facts of this case

   1.1. Did Dr. Covert sign the ticket contract?

   1.2. Did Dr. Covert read the ticket contract before he signed it? Is that relevant?

   1.3. Did you read the portions of the agreement in footnotes 1 and 2? If so, was the "wording clear and understandable"? If not, how would you change the contract to make the "wording clear and understandable"?

   1.4. If Dr. Covert had read the ticket contract before he signed it and objected to paragraph 3.4, would South Florida Stadium Corp. have agreed to eliminate the exculpatory clause?

2. Questions about the law

   2.1. What is an exculpatory clause?

2.2. Has Florida enacted legislation making exculpatory clauses illegal?

2.3. Are exculpatory clauses against public policy?

3. Notes

3.1. The Restatement offers this "rationale" for a public policy against exculpatory agreements:

a. Rationale. The law of torts imposes standards of conduct for the protection of others against unreasonable risk of harm. One cannot exempt himself from such liability for harm that is caused either intentionally or recklessly. However, a party to a contract can ordinarily exempt himself from liability for harm caused by his failure to observe the standard of reasonable care imposed by the law of negligence.

b. Relation to other rules. Language inserted by a party in an agreement for the purpose of exempting him from liability for negligent conduct is scrutinized with particular care and a court may require specific and conspicuous reference to negligence under the general principle that language is interpreted against the draftsman. Furthermore, a party's attempt to exempt himself from liability for negligent conduct may fail as unconscionable.

Restatement (Second) of Contracts § 195, comments a and b. Is that a rationale for the *Restatement* position on exculpatory contracts or merely a restatement of the *Restatement*?

3.2. A week before the *Covert* opinion, the same Florida intermediate appellate issued an opinion in *Goeden v. CM III, Inc.*, 756 So. 2d 1105 (Dist Ct. App. Fl. 3d Dist. 2000), holding that an agreement signed by a motorcyclist releasing a motorcycle rider school from liability for its negligence was enforceable without mentioning the language of the agreement.

The reported cases on whether an agreement in the form of a "covenant not to compete" is against public policy are equally divided. Covenants not to compete are fairly common in the business world. For example, a buyer of a tavern might want some assurances that her seller is not going to open a competing tavern in the same neighborhood. Or a business employer might want assurances that a key employee will not later work for a competitor.

And law suits challenging the enforceability of covenants not to compete are fairly common in the "legal" world. The holding of a particular case depends in the main on facts relating to the business need for a protective agreement and the reasonableness of the protective agreement; the opinions regularly discuss the public policies of (i) freedom of contract, (ii) freedom to compete, and (iii) employee mobility.

The next case, involving a covenant not to compete agreement among various doctors, discusses an additional "public policy" as the basis for not enforcing the agreement.

Valley Medical Specialists v. Farber
Supreme Court of Arizona
982 P.2d 1277 (1999)

Feldman, J.

We granted review to determine whether the restrictive covenant between Dr. Steven Farber and Valley Medical Specialists is enforceable. We hold that it is not. Public policy concerns in this case outweigh Valley Medical's protectable interests in enforcing the agreement. We thus vacate the court of appeals' opinion, affirm the trial court's judgment, and remand to the court of appeals to resolve any remaining issues. * * *

FACTS AND PROCEDURAL HISTORY

In 1985, Valley Medical Specialists ("VMS"), a professional corporation, hired Steven S. Farber, D.O., an internist and pulmonologist who, among other things, treated AIDS and HIV-positive patients and performed brachytherapy—a procedure that radiates the inside of the lung in lung cancer patients. Brachytherapy can only be performed at certain hospitals that have the necessary equipment. A few years after joining VMS, Dr. Farber became a shareholder and subsequently a minority officer and director. In 1991, the three directors, including Dr. Farber, entered into new stock and employment agreements. The employment agreement contained a restrictive covenant, the scope of which was amended over time.

In 1994, Dr. Farber left VMS and began practicing within the area defined by the restrictive covenant, which at that time read as follows:

> The parties recognize that the duties to be rendered under the terms of this Agreement by the Employee are special, unique and of an extraordinary character. The Employee, in consideration of the compensation to be paid to him pursuant to the terms of this Agreement, expressly agrees to the following restrictive covenants:
>
> (a) The Employee shall not, directly or indirectly:
>
> (i) Request any present or future patients of the Employer to curtail or cancel their professional affiliation with the Employer;
>
> (ii) Either separately, jointly, or in association with others, establish, engage in, or become interested in, as an employee, owner, partner, shareholder or otherwise, or furnish any information to, work for, or assist in any manner, anyone competing with, or who may compete with the Employer in the practice of medicine.
>
> * * *
>
> (iv) Either separately, jointly or in association with others provide medical care or medical assistance for any person or persons who were patients or [sic] Employer during the period that Employee was in the hire of Employer.
>
> * * *
>
> (d) The restrictive covenants set forth herein shall continue during the term of this Agreement and for a period of three (3) years after the date of termination, for any reason, of this Agreement. The restrictive covenants set forth herein shall be binding upon the Employee in that geographical area encompassed within the boundaries measured by a five (5) mile radius of any office maintained or utilized by Employer at the time of execution of the Agreement or at any time thereafter.
>
> (e) The Employee agrees that a violation on his part of any covenant set forth in this Paragraph 17 will cause such damage to the Employer as will be irreparable and for that reason, that Employee fur-

> ther agrees that the Employer shall be entitled, as a matter of right, and upon notice as provided in Paragraph 20 hereof, to an injunction from any court of competent jurisdiction, restraining any further violation of said covenants by Employee, his corporation, employees, partners or agents. Such right to injunctive remedies shall be in addition to and cumulative with any other rights and remedies the Employer may have pursuant to this Agreement or law, including, specifically with regard to the covenants set forth in subparagraph 17(a) above, the recovery of liquidated damages equal to forty percent (40%) of the gross receipts received for medical services provided by the Employee, or any employee, associate, partner, or corporation of the Employee during the term of this Agreement and for a period of three (3) years after the date of termination, for any reason, of this Agreement. The Employee expressly acknowledges and agrees that the covenants and agreement contained in this Paragraph 17 are minimum and reasonable in scope and are necessary to protect the legitimate interest of the Employer and its goodwill.

VMS filed a complaint against Dr. Farber seeking (1) preliminary and permanent injunctions enjoining Dr. Farber from violating the restrictive covenant, (2) liquidated damages for breach of the employment agreement, and (3) damages for breach of fiduciary duty, conversion of patient files and confidential information, and intentional interference with contractual and/or business relations.

Following six days of testimony and argument, the trial court denied VMS's request for a preliminary injunction, finding that the restrictive covenant violated public policy or, alternatively, was unenforceable because it was too broad. Specifically, the court found that: any covenant over six months would be unreasonable; the five-mile radius from each of the three VMS offices was unreasonable because it covered a total of 235 square miles; and the restriction was unreasonable because it did not provide an exception for emergency medical aid and was not limited to pulmonology.

The court of appeals reversed, concluding that a modified covenant was reasonable. The court noted that there were eight hospitals outside the restricted area where Dr. Farber could practice. Although the covenant made no exceptions for emergency medicine, the court held that the severability clause permitted the trial court to modify the covenant so Dr. Farber could provide emergency services within the restricted area. Moreover, VMS was allowed to stipulate that Dr. Farber could perform brachytherapy and treat AIDS and HIV patients within the restricted area, again even though the covenant contained no such exceptions.

The court of appeals found the restriction, when so modified, reasonable as to time and place. Although non-emergency patients might be required to travel further to see Dr. Farber, they could continue to see him if they were willing to drive that far. Three years was reasonable because the record contained testimony that it might take Dr. Farber's replacement three to five years to develop his pulmonary practice referral sources to the level they were when Dr. Farber resigned.

The court found that the restrictive covenant did not violate public policy, believing that courts must not unnecessarily restrict the freedom of contract. Moreover, the record was void of any evidence that the availability of pulmonologists in the restricted area would be inadequate without Dr. Farber.

History of restrictive covenants

A brief reference to basic principles is appropriate. Historically, covenants not to compete were viewed as restraints of trade and were invalid at common law. Eventually, ancillary restraints, such as those incident to employment or partnership agreements, were enforced under the rule of reason. To be enforced, the restriction must do more than simply prohibit fair competition by the employee. In other words, a covenant not to compete is invalid unless it protects some legitimate interest beyond the employer's desire to protect itself from competition.

It is true that in this case, unlike typical employer-employee agreements, Dr. Farber may not have been at a bargaining disadvantage, which is one of the reasons such restrictive covenants are strictly construed. Unequal bargaining power may be a factor to consider when examining the hardship on the departing employee. But in cases involving the professions, public policy concerns may outweigh any protectable interest the remaining firm members may have. Thus, this case does not turn on the hardship to Dr. Farber.

The doctor-patient relationship is special and entitled to unique protection. It cannot be easily or accurately compared to relationships in the commercial context. In light of the great public policy interest involved in covenants not to compete between physicians, each agreement will be strictly construed for reasonableness.

Reasonableness of covenant

Reasonableness is a fact-intensive inquiry that depends on the totality of the circumstances. A restriction is unreasonable and thus will not be enforced: (1) if the restraint is greater than necessary to protect the employer's legitimate interest; or (2) if that interest is outweighed by the hardship to the employee and the likely injury to the public. Thus, in the present case, the reasonableness inquiry requires us to examine the interests of the employer, employee, patients, and public in general. Balancing these competing interests is no easy task and no exact formula can be used.

VMS's protectable interest

VMS contends, and the court of appeals agreed, that it has a protectable interest in its patients and referral sources. In the commercial context, it is clear that employers have a legitimate interest in retaining their customer base. In the medical context, however, the personal relationship between doctor and patient as well as the patient's freedom to see a particular doctor, affects the extent of the employer's interest.

Even in the commercial context, the employer's interest in its customer base is balanced with the employee's right to the customers. Where the employee took an active role and brought customers with him or her to the job, courts are more reluctant to enforce restrictive covenants. Dr. Farber was a pulmonologist. He did not learn his skills from VMS.

Scope of the restrictive covenant

The restriction cannot be greater than necessary to protect VMS's legitimate interests. A restraint's scope is defined by its duration and geographic area. The frequency of contact between doctors and their patients affects the permissible length of the restraint. The idea is to give the employer a reasonable amount of time to overcome the former employee's loss, usually by hiring a replacement and giving that replacement time to establish a working relationship.

In this case, the trial judge found that the three-year period was an unreasonable duration because all of the experts agree that the practice of pulmonology entails treating patients with chronic conditions which require more hospital care than office care and which requires regular contact with the treating physician at least once within each six-month period so that any provision over six months is onerous and unnecessary to protect VMS's economic interests where virtually all of Dr. Farber's VMS patients had an opportunity by late 1994 or early 1995 (Farber left September 12, 1994) to decide which pulmonologist . . . they would consult for their ongoing treatment[.]

On this record, we cannot say this factual finding was clearly erroneous. The three-year duration is unreasonable.

The activity prohibited by the restraint also defines the covenant's scope. The restraint must be limited to the particular specialty of the present employment. On its face, the restriction here is not limited to internal medicine or even pulmonology. It precludes any type of practice, even in fields that do not compete with VMS. Thus, we agree with the trial judge that this restriction is too broad. * * *

Public policy

The court of appeals held that the restrictive covenant does not violate public policy, pointing out that the record contains nothing to suggest there will be a lack of pulmonologists in the restricted area if Dr. Farber is precluded from practicing there. Even if we assume other pulmonologists will be available to cover Dr. Farber's patients, we disagree with this view. It ignores the significant interests of individual patients within the restricted area. * * * A court must evaluate the extent to which enforcing the covenant would foreclose patients from seeing the departing physician if they desire to do so.

Concluding that patients' right to see the doctor of their choice is entitled to substantial protection, VMS's protectable interests here are comparatively minimal. The geographic scope of this covenant encompasses approximately 235 square miles, making it very difficult for Dr. Farber's existing patients to continue treatment with him if they so desire. After six days of testimony, the trial judge concluded that this restrictive covenant was unreasonably broad and against public policy. Specifically, the judge found:

(1) the three year duration was unreasonable because pulmonology patients typically require contact with the treating physician once every six months. Thus, a restriction over six months is unnecessary to protect VMS's economic interests. Patients would have had opportunity within approximately six months to decide which doctor to see for continuing treatment;

(2) the five mile radius was unreasonable because with the three offices, the restriction covered more than 235 square miles;

(3) the restriction was unreasonable because it did not expressly provide for an exception for emergency medical treatment;

(4) the restriction was overly broad because it is not limited to pulmonology;

(5) the covenant violates public policy because of the sensitive and personal nature of the doctor-patient relationship.

Given the facts and the principles discussed, that finding is well supported factually and legally.

Severance—the blue pencil rule

This contract contains a severance clause. The court of appeals accepted a stipulation by VMS that the restriction would not prohibit Dr. Farber from treating HIV-positive and AIDS patients or from performing brachytherapy. On its face, however, the restriction is broader than that, restricting him from providing "medical care or medical assistance for any person or persons who were patients or [sic] Employer during the period that Employee was in the hire of Employer." Arizona courts will "blue pencil" restrictive covenants, eliminating grammatically severable, unreasonable provisions. Here, however, the modifications go further than cutting grammatically severable portions. The court of appeals, in essence, rewrote the agreement in an attempt to make it enforceable. This goes too far. "Where the severability of the agreement is not evident from the contract itself, the court cannot create a new agreement for the parties to uphold the contract."

Even the blue pencil rule has its critics. For every agreement that makes its way to court, many more do not. Thus, the words of the covenant have an in terrorem effect on departing employees. Employers may therefore create ominous covenants, knowing that if the words are challenged, courts will modify the agreement to make it enforceable. *Id.* Although we will tolerate ignoring severable portions of a covenant to make it more reasonable, we will not permit courts to add terms or rewrite provisions.

* * *

CONCLUSION

We hold that the restrictive covenant between Dr. Farber and VMS cannot be enforced. Valley Medical Specialists' interest in enforcing the restriction is outweighed by the likely injury to patients and the public in general. In so holding, we need not reach the question of the hardship imposed on Dr. Farber. The public policy implications here are enough to invalidate this particular agreement. We stop short of holding that restrictive covenants between physicians will never be enforced, but caution that such restrictions will be strictly construed. The burden is on the party wishing to enforce the covenant to demonstrate that the restraint is no greater than necessary to protect the employer's legitimate interest, and that such interest is not outweighed by the hardship to the employee and the likely injury to the public. Here VMS has not met that burden. The restriction fails because its public policy' implications outweigh the legitimate interests of VMS.

* * *

QUESTIONS AND NOTES

1. Questions about the facts of this case

   1.1. Was the defendant an experienced physician when he joined Valley Medical Specialists? How many of his patients were originally patients of other Valley Medical Specialists doctors? Are any of these questions relevant?

   1.2. Was there any evidence that there is a shortage of pulmonologists in the Valley of the Sun?

2. Questions about the law

   2.1. Reconsider the first three sentences of the opinion: "We granted review to determine whether the restrictive covenant between Dr. Steven Farber and Valley Medical Specialists is enforceable. We hold that it is not. Public policy concerns in this case outweigh Valley Medical's protectable interests in enforcing this agreement." What are the public policy concerns? What are Valley Medical's protectable interests?

   2.2. Dr. S, a pulmonologist, decides to retire. She sells her medical practice to Dr. B. The sale agreements include a covenant not to compete similar in scope to the covenant not to compete in *Valley Medical*

Specialists. Later, Dr. S decides that she would like to resume her practice. Would this court find her covenant not to compete agreement unenforceable because of public policy?

2.3. A is an accountant. His employment agreement with Valley Accountancy Specialists, Inc., includes a covenant not to compete similar in scope to the covenant not to compete in *Valley Medical Specialists*. A has now decided that he would like to leave Valley Accountancy Specialists, Inc. and start his own accounting practice. Would this court find his covenant not to compete unenforceable because of public policy?

2.4. Would the court have had the same public policy concerns and issued the same ruling if the covenant not to compete had been limited (i) in time to one year and (ii) in place to five miles from Valley Medical's principal office?

2.5. In discussing the contrary ruling of the court of appeals, the opinion mentions a "severability clause"—"the severability clause permitted the trial court to modify the covenant so Dr. Farber could provide emergency service within the restricted area." What is a severability clause? How is a severability clause connected to the blue pencil rule discussed later in the opinion?

3. Notes

3.1. There are courts that "reform" covenants not to compete that are excessive in time or space. For example, *Ferrofluidics Corp. v. Advanced Vacuum Components, Inc.*, 968 F.2d 1463 (1st Cir. 1992) found that a five year covenant not to compete in an employment agreement was excessive and so enforced it for a three year term. *See generally* Samuel C. Darren, *The Theory of Involuntary Contracts: The Judicial Rewriting of Unreasonable Covenants Not to Compete*, 6 TEX. WESLEYAN L. REV. 71 (1999).

3.2. Although most states rely on courts and precedent to shape public policy on covenants not to compete, a significant number of states have enacted legislation prohibiting or regulating covenants not to compete.

3.3. Professor Ronald Gilson, a prominent law professor at Stanford, recently studied the effect of covenants not to compete on the high tech industries in California's Silicon Valley and Massachusetts' Route 128. California has enacted legislation prohibiting covenants not to compete in employment contracts; Massachusetts still permits such covenants. Professor Gilson concludes that (i) because California does not enforce covenants not to compete, high tech firms in the Silicon Valley gain from knowledge spillovers between firms and (ii) these knowledge spillovers have allowed Silicon Valley firms to thrive while Route 128 firms have deteriorated. Ronald J. Gilson, *The Legal Infrastructure of High Technology Industrial Districts: Silicon Valley, Route 128 and Covenants Not to Compete*, 74 N.Y.U. L. REV. 575 (1999). Can you think of any other reasons for the greater growth of the California high tech industry? Have you been to Massachusetts in January? Is *Baywatch* set in Massachusetts Bay?

The most complicated and controversial cases considering a public policy defense to enforceability of an agreement are cases affecting family relationships such as palimony agreements or surrogacy contracts in which a woman agrees to relinquish any parental rights to the child to whom she gives birth. Attorneys, judges, and professors continue to discuss the gender, moral, political, and religious issues raised by these contracts. The following case is illustrative.

R.R. v. M.H.

Supreme Judicial Court of Massachusetts
426 Mass. 501, 689 N.E.2d 790 (1998)

Wilkins, C.J.

On a report by a judge in the Probate and Family Court, we are concerned with the validity of a surrogacy parenting agreement between the plaintiff (father) and the defendant (mother). Both the mother and the father are married but not to each other. A child was conceived through artificial insemination of the mother with the father's sperm, after the mother and father had executed the surrogate parenting agreement. The agreement provided that the father would have custody of the child. During the sixth month of her pregnancy and after she had received funds from the father pursuant to the surrogacy agreement, the mother changed her mind and decided that she wanted to keep the child.

The father thereupon brought this action and obtained a preliminary order awarding him temporary custody of the child. * * * The judge's order granting the preliminary injunction is before us on her report of the propriety of that order which was based in part on her conclusion that the father was likely to prevail on his assertion that the surrogacy agreement is enforceable. On our own motion, we transferred here the appeal and the report, which a single justice of the Appeals Court had consolidated. The question of the enforceability of the surrogacy agreement is before us and, although we could defer any ruling until there is a final judgment entered, the issue is one on which we elect to comment because it is fully briefed and is of importance to more than the parties. This court has not previously dealt with the enforceability of a surrogacy agreement.

The Facts

The baby girl who is the subject of this action was born on August 15, 1997, in Leominster. The defendant mother and the plaintiff father are her biological parents. The father and his wife, who live in Rhode Island, were married in June, 1989. The wife is infertile. * * * In April, 1996, responding to a newspaper advertisement for surrogacy services, they consulted a Rhode Island attorney who had drafted surrogacy contracts for both surrogates and couples seeking surrogacy services. On the attorney's advice, the father and his wife consulted the New England Surrogate Parenting Advisors (NESPA), a for-profit corporation that helps infertile couples find women willing to act as surrogate mothers. They entered into a contract with NESPA in September, 1996, and paid a fee of $6,000.

Meanwhile, in the spring of 1996, the mother, who was married and had two children, responded to a NESPA advertisement. She reported to NESPA that her family was complete and that she desired to allow others less fortunate than herself to have children. The mother submitted a surrogacy application to NESPA. The judge found that the mother was motivated to apply to NESPA by a desire to be pregnant, in order to earn money, and to help an infertile couple.

In October, Dr. Angela Figueroa of NESPA brought the mother together with the father and his wife. They had a seemingly informative exchange of information and views. The mother was advised to seek an attorney's advice concerning the surrogacy agreement. Shortly thereafter, the mother, the father, and his wife met again to discuss the surrogacy and other matters. The mother also met with a clinical psychologist as part of NESPA's evaluation of her suitability to act as a surrogate. The psychologist, who also evaluated the father and his wife, advised the mother to consult legal counsel, to give her husband a chance to air his concerns, to discuss arrangements for contact with the child, to consider and discuss her expectations concerning termination of the pregnancy, and to arrange a meeting between her husband and the father and his wife.[2] The psychologist concluded that the mother was solid, thoughtful, and well grounded, that she would have no problem giving the child to the father, and that she was happy to act as a surrogate. The mother told the psychologist that she was not motivated by money, although she did plan to use the funds received for her children's education. The mother's husband told the psychologist by telephone that he supported his wife's decision.

The mother signed the surrogate parenting agreement and her signature was notarized on November 1. The father signed on November 18. The agreement stated that the parties intended that the "Surrogate shall be inseminated with the semen of Natural Father" and "that, on the birth of the child or children so conceived, Natural Father, as the Natural Father, will have the full legal parental rights of a father, and surrogate will permit Natural Father to take the child or children home from the hospital to live with he [sic] and his wife." The agreement acknowledged that the mother's parental rights would not terminate if she permitted the father to take the child home and have custody, that the mother could at any time seek to enforce her parental rights by court order, but that, if she attempted to obtain custody or visitation rights, she would forfeit her rights under the agreement and would be obligated to reimburse the father for all fees and expenses paid to her under it. The agreement provided that its interpretation would be governed by Rhode Island law.

The agreement provided for compensation to the mother in the amount of $10,000 "for services rendered in conceiving, carrying and giving birth to the Child." Payment of the $10,000 was to be made as follows: $500 on verification of the pregnancy; $2,500 at the end of the third month; $3,500 at the end of the sixth month; and $3,500 at the time of birth "and when delivery of child occurs." The agreement stated that no payment was made in connection with adoption of the child, the termination of parental rights, or

[2]Her husband had had a vasectomy in 1994 and did not have sexual relations with the mother after October, 1996.

consent to surrender the child for adoption. The father acknowledged the mother's right to determine whether to carry the pregnancy to term, but the mother agreed to refund all payments if, without the father's consent, she had an abortion that was not necessary for her physical health. The father assumed various expenses of the pregnancy, including tests, and had the right to name the child. The mother would be obliged, however, to repay all expenses and fees for services if tests showed that the father was not the biological father of the child, or if the mother refused to permit the father to take the child home from the hospital. The agreement also provided that the mother would maintain some contact with the child after the birth.

The judge found that the mother entered into the agreement on her own volition after consulting legal counsel. There was no evidence of undue influence, coercion, or duress. The mother fully understood that she was contracting to give custody of the baby to the father. She sought to inseminate herself on November 30 and December 1, 1996. The attempt at conception was successful.

The lawyer for the father sent the mother a check for $500 in December, 1996, and another for $2,500 in February. In May, the father's lawyer sent the mother a check for $3,500. She told the lawyer that she had changed her mind and wanted to keep the child. She returned the check uncashed in the middle of June. The mother has made no attempt to refund the amounts that the father paid her, including $550 that he paid for pregnancy-related expenses.

Procedure

Approximately two weeks after the mother changed her mind and returned the check for $3,500, and before the child was born, the father commenced this action against the mother seeking to establish his paternity, alleging breach of contract, and requesting a declaration of his rights under the surrogacy agreement. Subsequently, the wife's [*sic*. Should be "the mother's." Eds.] husband was added as a defendant. The judge appointed a guardian ad litem to represent the interests of the unborn child. Proceedings were held on aspects of the preliminary injunction request (now resolved) and on the mother's motion to determine whether surrogacy contracts are enforceable in Massachusetts.

On August 4, 1997, the judge entered an order directing the mother to give the child to the father when it was discharged from the hospital and granting the father temporary physical custody of the child. She did so based on her determination that the father's custody claim was likely to prevail on the merits of the contract claim, and, if not on that claim, then on the basis of the best interests of the child. The mother was granted the right to frequent visits.

On August 13, 1997, the judge reported the propriety of her August 1 order which, as we have said, was based in part on her conclusion that the surrogacy contract was enforceable. * * *

Other Jurisdictions

A significant minority of States have legislation addressing surrogacy agreements. Some simply deny enforcement of all such agreements. [Arizona, Indiana, Michigan, New York, North Dakota, Utah.] Others expressly deny enforcement only if the surrogate is to be compensated. [Kentucky, Louisiana, Nebraska, Washington.] Some States have simply exempted surrogacy agreements from provisions making it a crime to sell babies. [Alabama, Iowa, West Virginia.] A few States have explicitly made unpaid surrogacy agreements lawful. [Florida, Nevada, New Hampshire, Virginia.] Florida, New Hampshire, and Virginia require that the intended mother be infertile. New Hampshire and Virginia place restrictions on who may act as a surrogate and require advance judicial approval of the agreement.[6] Last, Arkansas raises a presumption that a child born to a surrogate mother is the child of the intended parents and not the surrogate.

There are few appellate court opinions on the enforceability of traditional surrogacy agreements. * * *

The best known opinion is that of the Supreme Court of New Jersey in *Matter of Baby M.*, 109 N.J. 396, 537 A.2d 1227 (1988), where the court invalidated a compensated surrogacy contract because it conflicted with the law and public policy of the State. The *Baby M* surrogacy agreement involved broader concessions from the mother than the agreement before us because it provided that the mother would surrender her parental rights and would allow the father's wife to adopt the child. The agreement, therefore, directly conflicted with a statute prohibiting the payment of money to obtain an adoption and a statute barring enforcement of an agreement to adoption made prior to the birth of the child. The court acknowledged that an award

---

[6]New Hampshire permits the surrogate to opt out of the agreement to surrender custody at any time up to seventy-two hours after birth. Virginia allows a surrogate who is the child's genetic mother to terminate the agreement within 180 days of the last assisted conception.

of custody to the father was in the best interests of the child, but struck down orders terminating the mother's parental rights and authorizing the adoption of the child by the husband's wife. The court added that it found no "legal prohibition against surrogacy when the surrogate mother volunteers, without any payment, to act as a surrogate and is given the right to change her mind and to assert her parental rights."

Discussion

1. The governing law. The agreement before us provided that "Rhode Island Law shall govern the interpretation of this agreement." * * * The child was conceived and born in Massachusetts, and the mother is a Massachusetts resident, all as contemplated in the surrogacy arrangement. The significance, if any, of the surrogacy agreement on the relationship of the parties and on the child is appropriately determined by Massachusetts law.

2. General Laws c. 46, § 4B. The case before us concerns traditional surrogacy, in which the fertile member of an infertile couple is one of the child's biological parents. Surrogate fatherhood, the insemination of the fertile wife with sperm of a donor, often an anonymous donor, is a recognized and accepted procedure. If the mother's husband consents to the procedure, the resulting child is considered the legitimate child of the mother and her husband.[9] In the case before us, the infertile spouse is the wife. No statute decrees the consequences of the artificial insemination of a surrogate with the sperm of a fertile husband. This situation presents different considerations from surrogate fatherhood because surrogate motherhood is never anonymous and her commitment and contribution is unavoidably much greater than that of a sperm donor.

We must face the possible application of G. L. c. 46, § 4B, to this case. Section 4B tells us that a husband who consents to the artificial insemination of his wife with the sperm of another is considered to be the father of any resulting child. In the case before us, the birth mother was married at the time of her artificial insemination. Despite what he told the psychologist, her husband was not supportive of her desire to become a surrogate parent but acknowledged that it was her decision and her body. The husband, who filed a complaint for divorce on August 8, 1997, may have simply been indifferent because he knew that the marriage was falling apart. The judge

[9]General Laws c. 46, § 4B, states: "Any child born to a married woman as a result of artificial insemination with the consent of her husband, shall be considered the legitimate child of the mother and such husband."

found that he was not the biological father of the child. His interest might have been vastly greater if he had been informed that § 4B literally says that any child produced by the artificial insemination of his wife with his consent would be his legitimate child whom he would have a duty to support. It is doubtful, however, that the Legislature intended § 4B to apply to the child of a married surrogate mother. Section 4B seems to concern the status of a child born to a fertile mother whose husband, presumably infertile, consented to her artificial insemination with the sperm of another man so that the couple could have a child biologically related to the mother.

3. Adoption statutes. Policies underlying our adoption legislation suggest that a surrogate parenting agreement should be given no effect if the mother's agreement was obtained prior to a reasonable time after the child's birth or if her agreement was induced by the payment of money. Adoption legislation is, of course, not applicable to child custody, but it does provide us with some guidance. Although the agreement makes no reference to adoption and does not concern the termination of parental rights or the adoption of the child by the father's wife, the normal expectation in the case of a surrogacy agreement seems to be that the father's wife will adopt the child with the consent of the mother (and the father). Under G. L. c. 210, § 2, adoption requires the written consent of the father and the mother but, in these circumstances, not the mother's husband. Any such consent, written, witnessed, and notarized, is not to be executed "sooner than the fourth calendar day after the date of birth of the child to be adopted." *Id.* That statutory standard should be interpreted as providing that no mother may effectively agree to surrender her child for adoption earlier than the fourth day after its birth, by which time she better knows the strength of her bond with her child. Although a consent to surrender custody has less permanency than a consent to adoption, the legislative judgment that a mother should have time after a child's birth to reflect on her wishes concerning the child weighs heavily in our consideration whether to give effect to a prenatal custody agreement. No private agreement concerning adoption or custody can be conclusive in any event because a judge, passing on custody of a child, must decide what is in the best interests of the child.

Adoptive parents may pay expenses of a birth parent but may make no direct payment to her. *See* G. L. c. 210, § 11A; 102 Code Mass. Regs. § 5.09 (1997). Even though the agreement seeks to attribute that payment of $10,000, not to custody or adoption, but solely to the mother's services in carrying the child, the father ostensibly was promised more than those services because, as a practical matter, the mother agreed to surrender custody of the child. She could assert custody rights, according to the agreement, only if she repaid the father all amounts that she had received and also reimbursed him for all expenses he had incurred. The statutory prohibition of payment for receiving a child through adoption suggests that, as a matter of policy, a mother's agreement to surrender custody in exchange for money (beyond pregnancy-related expenses) should be given no effect in deciding the custody of the child.

4. Conclusion. The mother's purported consent to custody in the agreement is ineffective because no such consent should be recognized unless given on or after the fourth day following the child's birth. In reaching this conclusion, we apply to consent to custody the same principle which underlies the statutory restriction on when a mother's consent to adoption may be effectively given. Moreover, the payment of money to influence the mother's custody decision makes the agreement as to custody void. Eliminating any financial reward to a surrogate mother is the only way to assure that no economic pressure will cause a woman, who may well be a member of an economically vulnerable class, to act as a surrogate. It is true that a surrogate enters into the agreement before she becomes pregnant and thus is not presented with the desperation that a poor unwed pregnant woman may confront. However, compensated surrogacy arrangements raise the concern that, under financial pressure, a woman will permit her body to be used and her child to be given away.

There is no doubt that compensation was a factor in inducing the mother to enter into the surrogacy agreement and to cede custody to the father. If the payment of $10,000 was really only compensation for the mother's services in carrying the child and giving birth and was unrelated to custody of the child, the agreement would not have provided that the mother must refund all compensation paid (and expenses paid) if she should challenge the father's right to custody. Nor would the agreement have provided that final payment be made only when the child is delivered to the father. We simply decline, on public policy grounds, to apply to a surrogacy agreement of the type involved here the general principle that an agreement between informed, mature adults should be enforced absent proof of duress, fraud, or undue influence.

We recognize that there is nothing inherently unlawful in an arrangement by which an informed woman agrees to attempt to conceive artificially and give birth to a child whose father would be the husband of an infertile wife. We suspect that many such arrangements are made and carried out without disagreement.

If no compensation is paid beyond pregnancy-related expenses and if the mother is not bound by her consent to the father's custody of the child unless she consents after a suitable period has passed following the child's birth, the objections we have identified in this opinion to the enforceability of a surrogate's consent to custody would be overcome. Other conditions might be important in deciding the enforceability of a surrogacy agreement, such as a requirement that (a) the mother's husband give his informed consent to the agreement in advance; (b) the mother be an adult and have had at least one successful pregnancy; (c) the mother, her husband, and the intended parents have been evaluated for the soundness of their judgment and for their capacity to carry out the agreement; (d) the father's wife be incapable of bearing a child without endangering her health; (e) the intended parents be suitable persons to assume custody of the child; and (f) all parties have the advice of counsel. The mother and father may not, however, make a binding best-interests-of-the-child determination by private agreement. Any custody agreement is subject to a judicial determination of custody based on the best interests of the child.

The conditions that we describe are not likely to be satisfactory to an intended father because, following the birth of the child, the mother can refuse to consent to the father's custody even though the father has incurred substantial pregnancy-related expenses. A surrogacy agreement judicially approved before conception may be a better procedure, as is permitted by statutes in Virginia and New Hampshire. A Massachusetts statute concerning surrogacy agreements, pro or con, would provide guidance to judges, lawyers, infertile couples interested in surrogate parenthood, and prospective surrogate mothers.

We do not reach but comment briefly on the mother's argument that the agreement was unconscionable. She actively sought to become a surrogate and entered into the surrogacy agreement voluntarily, advised by counsel, not under duress, and fully informed. Unconscionability is not apparent on this record.

A declaration shall be entered that the surrogacy agreement is not enforceable. Such further orders as may be appropriate, consistent with this opinion, may be entered in the Probate and Family Court.

So ordered.

QUESTIONS AND NOTE

1. Questions about the facts of this case

   1.1. Was the surrogate mother married? Was that relevant to the court's decision? Should it be?

   1.2. Was it in the best interests of the child to remain with her birth mother? Was that relevant to the court's decision? Should it be?

   1.3. Did the agreement require the father to make payments to the mother? Was that relevant to the court's decision? Should it be?

   1.4. Did the court order that the mother return payments from the father to him?

2. Questions about the law

   2.1. The court noted that "surrogate fatherhood, the insemination of the fertile wife with the sperm of a donor, often an anonymous donor, is a recognized and accepted procedure." Assume that Epstein enters into an artificial insemination agreement whereby (i) he provides sperm, (ii) Mrs. X pays Epstein $10,000, and (iii) Mr. and Mrs. X will have custody of any child that results from Mrs. X's artificial insemination. Epstein later changes his mind about relinquishing custody rights. Would this court find such a surrogacy agreement unenforceable?

   2.2. Another medically-accepted surrogacy procedure involves implanting the embryo created by the egg and sperm of a man and woman in another woman. If the agreement for such a surrogacy arrangement was similar to the agreement in *R.R. v. M.H.*, would this court find the agreement unenforceable?

   2.3. Still another medically-accepted surrogacy procedure involves implanting the egg of one woman into another, infertile woman. Mr. and Mrs. X contract with Ms. Y for $2000 for Ms. Y to provide a fertile egg for implanting into Mrs. X. Ms. Y agrees to forfeit any claim to custody of any child born of that egg. The egg is artificially inseminated with Mr. X's sperm and implanted in Mrs. X. Just before the baby's birth, Ms. Y decides she wants custody of the baby. Would the court in *R.R. v. M.H.* enforce the agreement?

3. Note

According to Professor Gillian Hatfield of University of Toronto Law School, "contract pregnancy" raises two difficult questions.

> The first is a public-law question and is concerned with whether, as a society, we should permit individuals to contract for the conception of a child and the allocation of parental status. This question raises the specter of commodification, and feminists grapple with the implications for children, women and sexuality of the use of market mechanisms to structure childbirth and parenting. The second question is a private-law contract puzzle. It is concerned with whether in a given case in which the birth mother refuses to relinquish her parental status and in the absence of public-law prohibition, contract law should find that the birth mother has a contractual obligation to release the child. Further, the second question asks whether any breach of this obligation should be remedied with an order of specific performance as opposed to an order for compensation.

Gillian K. Hatfield, *An Expressive Theory of Contract: From Feminist Dilemmas to a Reconceptualization of Rational Choice in Contract Law*, 146 U. PA. L. REV. 1235, 1240 (1998). Professor Richard Epstein of University of Chicago Law School has answers for Professor Hatfield's questions: unless there is fraud or duress, there should be "full contract enforcement" for surrogacy contracts. Richard A. Epstein, *Surrogacy: The Case For Full Contractual Enforcement*, 81 VA. L. REV. 2305 (1995). Reconsider Professor Hatfield's questions and (and Professor Epstein's answers) when we examine specific performance and other remedies in Chapter Five.

SECTION 7: UNCONSCIONABILITY

In studying duress and undue influence, misrepresentation, and nondisclosure, we have seen courts refuse to enforce agreements because of problems in the bargaining process. And, in studying illegality and public policy, we have seen courts refuse to enforce agreements because of problems with the substance of the bargain.

Unconscionability, in a sense, is a combination of all that. Unconscionability looks to both the bargaining process and the terms of the bargain.

Scholars trace the concept of unconscionability back to Roman law and find traces of an unconscionability doctrine in basic equity maxims such as "clean hands." The modern American law of unconscionability has its roots in section 2-302 of the Uniform Commercial Code and in the next case, *Williams v. Walker-Thomas Furniture Co.*, a case in which the United States of Court of Appeals for the District of Columbia overruled the District of Columbia Court of Appeals in holding that, under common law, a court could refuse to enforce a contract for the sale of consumer goods on credit that provided "[T]he amount of each periodical installment payment * * * shall be credited pro rata on all outstanding leases, bills and accounts due the Company by (purchaser) at the time each such payment is made."

Williams v. Walker-Thomas Furniture Company

Court of Appeals, District of Columbia
198 A.2d 914 (1964)

QUINN, Associate Judge.

Appellant, a person of limited education separated from her husband, is maintaining herself and her seven children by means of public assistance. During the period 1957–1962 she had a continuous course of dealings with appellee from which she purchased many household articles on the installment plan. These included sheets, curtains, rugs, chairs, a chest of drawers, beds, mattresses, a washing machine, and a stereo set. In 1963 appellee filed a complaint in replevin for possession of all the items purchased by appellant, alleging that her payments were in default and that it retained title to the goods according to the sales contracts. By the writ of replevin appellee obtained a bed, chest of drawers, washing machine, and the stereo set. After hearing testimony and examining the contracts, the trial court entered judgment for appellee.

Appellant's principal contentions on appeal are (1) there was a lack of meeting of the minds, and (2) the contracts were against public policy.

Appellant signed fourteen contracts in all. They were approximately six inches in length and each contained a long paragraph in extremely fine print. One of the sentences in this paragraph provided that payments, after the first purchase, were to be prorated on all purchases then outstanding. Mathematically, this had the effect of keeping a balance due on all items until the time balance was completely eliminated. It meant that title to the first purchase, remained in appellee until the fourteenth purchase, made some five years later, was fully paid.

At trial appellant testified that she understood the agreements to mean that when payments on the running account were sufficient to balance the amount due on an individual item, the item became hers. She testified that most of the purchases were made at her home; that the contracts were signed in blank; that she did not read the instruments; and that she was not provided with a copy. She admitted, however, that she did not ask anyone to read or explain the contracts to her.

We have stated that "one who refrains from reading a contract and in conscious ignorance of its terms voluntarily assents thereto will not be relieved from his bad bargain." "One who signs a contract has a duty to read it and is obligated according to its terms." "It is as much the duty of a person who cannot read the language in which a contract is written to have someone read it to him before he signs it, as it is the duty of one who can read to peruse it himself before signing it."

A careful review of the record shows that appellant's assent was not obtained "by fraud or even misrepresentation falling short of fraud." This is not a case of mutual misunderstanding but a unilateral mistake. Under these circumstances, appellant's first contention is without merit.

Appellant's second argument presents a more serious question. The record reveals that prior to the last purchase appellant had reduced the balance in her account to $164. The last purchase, a stereo set, raised the balance due to $678. Significantly, at the time of this and the preceding purchases, appellee was aware of appellant's financial position. The reverse side of the stereo contract listed the name of appellant's social worker and her $218 monthly stipend from the government. Nevertheless, with full knowledge that appellant had to feed, clothe and support both herself and seven children on this amount, appellee sold her a $514 stereo set.

We cannot condemn too strongly appellee's conduct. It raises serious questions of sharp practice and irresponsible business dealings. A review of the legislation in the District of Columbia affecting retail sales and the pertinent decisions of the highest court in this jurisdiction disclose, however, no ground upon which this court can declare the contracts in question contrary to public policy. We think Congress should consider corrective legislation to protect the public from such exploitive contracts as were utilized in the case at bar.

Affirmed.

Williams v. Walker-Thomas Furniture Company
U.S. Court of Appeals, District of Columbia Circuit
350 F.2d 445 (1965)

J. Skelly Wright, Circuit Judge.

* * *

We do not agree that the court lacked the power to refuse enforcement to contracts found to be unconscionable. In other jurisdictions, it has been held as a matter of common law that unconscionable contracts are not enforceable. While no decision of this court so holding has been found, the notion that an unconscionable bargain should not be given full enforcement is by no means novel. In *Scott v. United States*, 79 U.S. (12 Wall.) 443, 445, 20 L.Ed. 438 (1870), the Supreme Court stated:

> "* * * If a contract be unreasonable and unconscionable, but not void for fraud, a court of law will give to the party who sues for its breach damages, not according to its letter, but only such as he is equitably entitled to. * * *"

Since we have never adopted or rejected such a rule, the question here presented is actually one of first impression.

Congress has recently enacted the Uniform Commercial Code, which specifically provides that the court may refuse to enforce a contract which it finds to be unconscionable at the time it was made. The enactment of this section, which occurred subsequent to the contracts here in suit, does not mean that the common law of the District of Columbia was otherwise at the time of enactment, nor does it preclude the court from adopting a similar rule in the exercise of its powers to develop the common law for the District of Columbia. In fact, in view of the absence of prior authority on the point, we consider the congressional adoption of § 2-302 persuasive authority for following the rationale of the cases from which the section is explicitly derived. Accordingly, we hold that where the element of unconscionability is present at the time a contract is made, the contract should not be enforced.

Unconscionability has generally been recognized to include an absence of meaningful choice on the part of one of the parties together with contract terms which are unreasonably favorable to the other party. Whether a meaningful choice is present in a particular case can only be determined by consideration of all the circumstances surrounding the transaction. In many cases the meaningfulness of the choice is negated by a gross inequality of bargaining power. The manner in which the contract was entered is also relevant to this consideration. Did each party to the contract, considering his obvious education or lack of it, have a reasonable opportunity to understand the terms of the contract, or were the important terms hidden in a maze of fine print and minimized by deceptive sales practices? Ordinarily one who signs an agreement without full knowledge of its terms might be held to assume the risk that he has entered a one-sided bargain. But when a party of little bargaining power, and hence little real choice, signs a commercially unreasonable contract with little or no knowledge of its terms, it is hardly likely that his consent, or even an objective manifestation of his consent, was ever given to all the terms. In such a case the usual rule that the terms of the agreement are not to be questioned should be abandoned and the court should consider whether the terms of the contract are so unfair that enforcement should be withheld.

In determining reasonableness or fairness, the primary concern must be with the terms of the contract considered in light of the circumstances existing when the contract was made. The test is not simple, nor can it be mechanically applied. The terms are to be considered "in the light of the general commercial background and the commercial needs of the particular trade or case." Corbin suggests the test as being whether the terms are "so extreme as to appear unconscionable according to the mores and business practices of the time and place." We think this formulation correctly states the test to be applied in those cases where no meaningful choice was exercised upon entering the contract.

Because the trial court and the appellate court did not feel that enforcement could be refused, no findings were made on the possible unconscionability of the contracts in these cases. Since the record is not sufficient for our deciding the issue as a matter of law, the cases must be remanded to the trial court for further proceedings.

So ordered.

DANAHER, Circuit Judge (dissenting):

The District of Columbia Court of Appeals obviously was as unhappy about the situation here presented as any of us can possibly be. Its opinion in the *Williams* case, quoted in the majority text, concludes: "We think Congress should consider corrective legislation to protect the public from such exploitive contracts as were utilized in the case at bar."

My view is thus summed up by an able court which made no finding that there had actually been sharp practice. Rather the appellant seems to have known precisely where she stood.

There are many aspects of public policy here involved. What is a luxury to some may seem an outright necessity to others. Is public oversight to be required of the expenditures of relief funds? A washing machine, e.g., in the hands of a relief client might become a fruitful source of income. Many relief clients may well need credit, and certain business establishments will take long chances on the sale of items, expecting their pricing policies will afford a degree of protection commensurate with the risk. * * *

I mention such matters only to emphasize the desirability of a cautious approach to any such problem, particularly since the law for so long has allowed parties such great latitude in making their own contracts. I dare say there must annually be thousands upon thousands of installment credit transactions in this jurisdiction, and one can only speculate as to the effect the decision in these cases will have.

I join the District of Columbia Court of Appeals in its disposition of the issues.

QUESTIONS AND NOTES

1. Questions about the facts of the case

   1.1. Who is suing whom for what?

1.2. Was there a written agreement?

1.3. Was there any dispute over the terms of the agreement?

1.4. Did the Walker-Thomas Furniture Company do anything that it was not permitted to do under the agreement?

1.5. What did the Walker-Thomas Furniture Company do "wrong"?

2. Questions about the law

2.1. What was unconscionable about the agreement between Ms. Williams and the Walker-Thomas store? What did Judge Wright decide?

2.2. How would Judge Wright have decided this case if all agreements contained the following warning in bold print: CAUTION. IF YOU DO NOT PAY ON TIME FOR WHAT YOU JUST BOUGHT, WE MAY BE ABLE TO TAKE BACK EVERYTHING WE EVER SOLD YOU? *See generally* Arthur A. Leff, *Contract As Thing*, 19 AM. U. L. REV. 131, 155 (1970).

2.3. On remand, what evidence would you try to introduce if you represented Ms. Williams? Would it be helpful to show her education and economic situation? Would it be helpful to show why she purchased a $514 stereo? Would it be helpful to show that repossessed "sheets, curtains, rugs" have almost no resale value to Walker-Thomas? Would it be helpful to show that other merchants in the area used similar contracts?

2.4. On remand, what evidence would you try to find and introduce if you represented Walker-Thomas? Would it be helpful to show that other merchants in the area used similar contracts? Would it be helpful to show that consumer goods lose value more rapidly than paying off the purchase price? Would it be helpful to show that D.C. law restricted Walker-Thomas to the recovery of the debt owed by Ms. Williams and its collection costs?

3. Notes

3.1. According to Professor David Slawson of University of Southern California Law School, "The theoretical underpinnings of unconscionablity . . . are not simple, and to some extent they are self-contradictory. They require one to accept the legitimacy of contracts to which one party did not give meaningful consent but to deny their legitimacy to the extent that they operate unfairly." W. DAVID SLAWSON, BINDING PROMISES 144 (1996)

3.2. Richard Epstein* favors a limited use of unconscionability, to police the bargaining process, but not the bargain:

> One of the major conceptual tools used by courts in their assault upon private agreements has been the doctrine of unconscionability. That doctrine has a place in contract law, but it is not the one usually assigned it by its advocates. The doctrine should not, in my view, allow courts to act as roving commissions to set aside those agreements whose substantive terms they find objectionable. Instead, it should be used only to allow courts to police the process whereby private agreements are formed, and in that connection, only to facilitate the setting aside of agreements that are as a matter of probabilities likely to be vitiated by the classical defenses of duress, fraud, or incompetence.
>
> When the doctrine of unconscionability is used in its substantive dimension, be it in a commercial or consumer context, it serves only to undercut the private right of contract in a manner that is apt to do more social harm than good. The result of the analysis is the same even if we view the question of unconscionability from the lofty perspective of public policy. "[I]f there is one thing which more than another public policy requires, it is that men of full age and competent understanding shall have the utmost liberty of contracting, and that their contracts when entered into freely and voluntarily shall be held sacred and shall be enforced by Courts of justice."

Richard Epstein, *Unconscionability: A Critical Reappraisal*, 18 J. L. & ECON. 293, 294–5, 314 (1975)

3.3. Judge Wright was from New Orleans; he served on the D.C. Circuit rather than the Fifth Circuit for "political reasons." Justice William Brennan, Jr. described Judge Wright as "one of the outstanding ju-

*Richard consented to our reproducing this excerpt from his article on the conditions that (i) we make clear that he is not in any way related to David Epstein and (ii) David Epstein acknowledge that Richard Epstein was a much better basketball player than David Epstein was during the two terms that the University of Chicago let David Epstein teach there.

rists of the nation's history" and acknowledged Judge Wright's judicial activism:

> It is of course true that some of his most notable decisions were greeted with harsh and bitter invective. The charge was that he was an "activist judge," exceeding his proper role. This, of course, is not an unfamiliar charge. But since our beginnings, lively, even acrimonious, debate about the proper role of judges in a democratic society has been with us. The judge who believes that the judicial power should be made creative and vigorously effective is labeled "activist." The judge inclined to question the propriety of judicial intervention to redress even the most egregious failures of democracy is labeled "neutralist" or "passivist." The labels are not synonymous with "conservative" or "liberal"; where yesterday "activist" was pinned on liberals, today it's on conservatives. As often as not, however, such labels are used merely to express disapproval of a particular judge's decisions. If useful at all, the labels may be more serviceable to distinguish the judge who sees his role as guided by the principle that "justice or righteousness is the source, the substance and the ultimate end of the law," from the judge for whom the guiding principle is that "courts do not sit to administer justice, but to administer the law." Such legendary names as Justice Holmes and Judge Learned Hand have been associated with the latter view. Holmes' imaginary society of Jobbists is limited to judges who hold a tight rein on humanitarian impulse and compassionate action, stoically doing their best to discover and apply already existing rules. But judges acting on the former view, and Skelly Wright was one, believe that the judicial process demands a good deal more than that. Because constitutions, statutes, and precedents rarely speak unambiguously, a just choice between competing alternatives has to be made to decide concrete cases. Skelly Wright would argue that in such cases "the judge's role necessarily is a creative one—he must legislate; there is no help for it; when the critical moment comes and he must say yea or nay, he is on his own; he has nothing to rely on but his own intellect, experience and conscience.

Justice William J. Brennan, Jr., *In Memoriam: J. Skelly Wright*, 102 HARV. L. REV. 361 (1988).

In the 35 years since the *Walker-Thomas* decision, there have been numerous reported cases that have considered the argument that an agreement or part of an agreement should not be enforced because it is unconscionable. As the next case illustrates, (1) the argument is not always successful, and (2) success depends on the facts.

Morrison v. Circuit City Stores, Inc.
U.S. District Court, Southern District of Ohio
70 F. Supp. 2d 815 (1999)

ORDER

SPIEGEL, Senior District Judge.

This matter is before the Court on a Motion by Defendant Circuit City Stores, Inc. to Compel Arbitration and Stay or Dismiss Proceedings.

This is an employment discrimination action brought by Plaintiff Lillian Pebbles Morrison pursuant to Title VII of the Civil Rights Act of 1964.

Prior to her discharge on December 12, 1997, Plaintiff worked as a store manager for one of Defendant's Cincinnati area stores. According to Defendant, Plaintiff was 30 years old with an undergraduate degree from the U.S. Air Force Academy and a master's degree from Central Michigan University when she applied for a position with Defendant on July 10, 1995. Defendant hired Plaintiff on December 1, 1995.

As part of the application and hiring process, Plaintiff signed two identical application forms, the first on July 10, 1995, and the second on December 27, 1995. Each application sets forth identical language about the "Circuit City Dispute Resolution Agreement" (hereinafter, the "Agreement"). In addition, each application states that the company will not consider any applicant for employment unless he or she also signs the Agreement.

The Agreement provides, in pertinent part, that an applicant will resolve:

> any and all previously unasserted claims, disputes or controversies arising out of or relating to [his or her] application or candidacy for employment, employment and/or cessation of employment with Circuit City, **exclusively** by final and binding **arbitration** before a neutral Arbitrator. By way of example only, such claims include claims under federal, state and local statutory or common law, such as the Age Discrimination in Employment Act, Title VII of the Civil Rights Act of 1964, as amended, in-

cluding the amendments of the Civil Rights Act of 1991, the Americans with Disabilities Act, the law of contract and law of tort.

Above the text of the Agreement, the application states in boldface type that:

> With this application you should have received the *Rules and Procedures of the Agreement*. You should familiarize yourself with these rules and procedures prior to signing the Agreement. If you did not receive the Rules and Procedures you must request a copy from a Circuit City representative prior to signing the Agreement.

Once an applicant signs the Agreement, the Agreement allows the applicant three days in which to withdraw his or her consent to the Agreement. The applicant may also take the application package home and return it later with his or her signature affixed.

Furthermore, the Agreement states that: "The Dispute Resolution Agreement and the Dispute Resolution Rules and Procedures affect your legal rights. You may wish to seek legal advice before signing this Dispute Resolution Agreement". The following clauses offer some detail as to how legal rights will be affected by the Agreement:

> I understand that if I do file a lawsuit regarding a dispute arising out of or relating to my application or candidacy for employment, employment or cessation or employment, Circuit City may use this Agreement in support of its request to the court to dismiss the lawsuit and require me instead to use arbitration.
>
> * * *
>
> This Agreement will be enforceable throughout the application process, my employment, and thereafter with respect to any claims arising from or relating to my application or candidacy for employment, employment or cessation of employment with Circuit City. I then must arbitrate all employment-related claims, and I may not file a lawsuit in court.

Defendant now moves this Court to compel arbitration and stay these proceedings pursuant to the Federal Arbitration Act ("FAA"), or, in the alternative, to dismiss this case entirely pursuant to Rule 12(b)(1) or Rule 12(b)(6) of the Federal Rules of Civil Procedure, because Plaintiff and Defendant are parties to this Agreement requiring them to resolve this type of dispute through final and binding arbitration.

Plaintiff responds that the Agreement is invalid and unenforceable because it fails to comply with common law principles of contract law. * * *

Plaintiff urges the Court to find the Agreement unenforceable, arguing that the Agreement is an unconscionable adhesion contract that limits Plaintiff's substantive rights and remedies under Title VII and Ohio Rev.Code § 4112. * * *

Plaintiff first claims that the Agreement is an unconscionable contract of adhesion. The Ohio Supreme Court referred to Black's Law Dictionary in describing a contract of adhesion as a "'[s]tandardized contract form offered . . . on essentially [a] 'take it or leave it' basis.'" Meanwhile, unconscionability is defined as "'an absence of meaningful choice on the part of one of the parties to a contract, combined with contract terms that are unreasonably favorable to the other party.'"

Ohio courts conduct a two-prong inquiry into whether a contract is unconscionable. The first prong looks at whether the contract terms are so unfair and unreasonable as to constitute substantive unconscionability while the second prong focuses on the relative bargaining power of the contracting parties to determine whether procedural unconscionability exists.

In support of her argument that the Agreement is a contract of adhesion, Plaintiff alleges that she was "forced" to sign the Agreement as part of the application in order to be considered for employment by Defendant. Plaintiff also contends that Defendant, a large company with retail facilities across the country, is more sophisticated and maintains more bargaining power than Plaintiff. She states that she was extremely surprised to learn that the Agreement amounted to a waiver of her right to a judicial forum and a jury trial. Plaintiff further argues that the Agreement is unconscionable because it threatens to deny her the substantive rights and remedies provided by Title VII and Ohio Rev. Code § 4112.

In contrast, Defendant asserts that the Agreement is not a contract of adhesion simply because Plaintiff had to sign it before she could be considered for employment. Defendant states that several other electronics retailers exist in the Cincinnati area, and it argues that Plaintiff could have applied for positions with these retailers. Defendant cites *Beauchamp v. Great West Life Assurance Co.*, 918 F. Supp. 1091, 1098 (E.D. Mich.1996), and *EEOC v. Frank's Nursery & Crafts*, 966 F. Supp. 500, 504 (E.D. Mich.1997) (*rev'd on other grounds*, 177 F.3d 448, 454–55 (6th Cir.1999)), in support of the proposition that adhesion contracts do not exist where applicants have a choice of where to apply for a job. In Beauchamp, the court indicated its reluctance in finding a contract of adhesion in a context where a plaintiff could choose to work for other employers without signing arbitration agreements. Likewise, the court in Frank's Nursery & Crafts stated that "[i]f [the applicant] disagreed with anything contained in the application she was free to simply look elsewhere for employment. . . . (When a party. . . voluntarily agrees to something in an attempt to obtain employment, they are not being 'forced' to do anything").

Defendant also contends that the application and its arbitration provisions are not unconscionable just because Plaintiff was only one of many employees working for a large, nationwide retailer. Defendant notes that the court in *Beauchamp* responded to a similar balance-of-power argument, stating: "Under plaintiff's theory, practically every condition of employment would be an 'adhesion contract' which could not be enforced because it would have been presented to the employee by the employer in a situation of unequal bargaining power on a 'take it or leave it' basis." Moreover, in *Gilmer,* the Supreme Court stated that the "[m]ere inequality in bargaining power . . . is not a sufficient reason to hold that arbitration agreements are never enforceable in the employment context."

Defendant further alleges that Plaintiff is "a well-educated, mature and experienced manager, who certainly understood the effect of the arbitration agreement and fully appreciated her choices". In addition, Defendant argues that the Agreement signed by both Plaintiff and Defendant pursuant to the application was "clear and unambiguous" and could not lead to the type of surprise Plaintiff now asserts. *See Frank's Nursery & Crafts*, 966 F. Supp. at 504 (agreeing with the *Beauchamp* court and stating that "[t]he simple fact of the matter is that if [the applicant] did not understand or intend to agree to arbitration she should not have signed her name until she did understand or consulted with someone.").

The Court finds Defendant's arguments persuasive, and we conclude that Plaintiff fails to show the unfairness or undue oppression necessary to support a finding that the Agreement amounted to an unconscionable contract of adhesion on a substantive or procedural basis. Furthermore, we find that the terms of the Agreement are fair and reasonable. We also find here that the balance of power between Plaintiff as an applicant and Defendant as a potential employer was not so disproportionate as to prevent a voluntary meeting of the minds on the issue of arbitration. * * *

Accordingly, since the Court holds (1) that this case falls within the coverage of the Federal Arbitration Act; (2) that the Agreement is broad enough to cover the disputes asserted in this case; and (3) that the Agreement is valid and enforceable, we hereby COMPEL arbitration of Plaintiff's claims.

QUESTIONS AND NOTES

1. Questions about the facts of this case

 1.1. Was there an arbitration agreement between the plaintiff and the defendant? Was it a negotiated agreement?

 1.2. Was it a clear agreement? How would you change the agreement so that people who sign the agreement are not later "surprised to learn that the Agreement amounted to a waiver of her right to a judicial forum and trial"?

2. Questions about the law

 2.1. Both the plaintiff and the court use the term "contract of adhesion." What is a contract of adhesion?

 2.2. While neither the U.C.C. nor the *Restatement (Second) of Contracts* uses the term "adhesion contracts," the term "adhesion contracts" is widely used in cases and adhesion contracts are widely used in the "real world." Have any of the cases previously considered in this book involved adhesion contracts? Have you ever been party to an adhesion contract?

 2.3. Would this court have found the arbitration agreement in *Hill v. Gateway* unconscionable? How would Judge Wright have ruled?

3. Notes

 3.1. In the real world, a litigant does not limit herself to a single, contract law concept. In this case, for example, Ms. Morrison also argued lack of consideration, her rights under federal laws on employment discrimination, etc. Because we are now learning about unconscionability, we edited out the court's discussion of all other legal and factual issues.*

3.2. Later, in *Hooters v. Phillips, infra,* we will consider a successful challenge to an arbitration agreement based on the concept of consideration. That case is also edited; you will read only the portion of the opinion on consideration. In the real case, Ms. Phillips also argued, and the court found, that the arbitration agreement was an unconscionable contract of adhesion.**

3.3. Earlier in *Donovan v. RRL Corp., supra,* at 55, 254 (the case involving the newspaper's mistake on the price of the Vamden Plas Jaguar), the California Supreme Court considered whether a buyer's efforts to compel a car dealer to sell a car at the advertised price was unconscionable:

> [T]he standards of unconscionability warranting rescission for mistake are similar to those for unconscionability justifying a court's refusal to enforce a contract or term. * * * An unconscionable contract ordinarily involves both a procedural and a substantive element: (1) oppression or surprise due to unequal bargaining power, and (2) overly harsh or one-sided results. * * * In ascertaining whether rescission is warranted for a unilateral mistake of fact, substantive unconscionability often will constitute the determinative factor, because the oppression and surprise ordinarily results from the mistake—not from inequality in bargaining power. Accordingly, even though defendant is not the weaker party to the contract and its mistake did not result from unequal bargaining power, defendant was surprised by the mistake, and in these circumstances overly harsh or one-sided results are sufficient to establish unconscion-

---

*In a labor law class you might consider the Circuit City Dispute Resolution Agreement again in connection with *Circuit City Stores, Inc. v. Adams,* 532 U.S. 105, 121 S.Ct. 1302 (2001), which involved a challenge to the arbitration agreement based on The Federal Arbitration Act.

**The *Morrison* case considers and distinguishes the *Hooters* case, primarily on differences between the Circuit City's arbitration procedures and Hooters' arbitration procedures. 70 F. Supp. 2d at 824. A recent law review article advocates teaching unconscionability through agreements to arbitrate employment claims: "Testing the social utility of these arbitration agreements in the employer-employee context should provoke lively inquiry along with serious analysis, and ultimately provide a most interesting and challenging vehicle for teaching unconscionability." Susan A. Fitzgibbon, *Teaching Unconscionability Through Agreements to Arbitrate Employment Claims,* 44 ST. LOUIS. U. L.J. 1401 (2000).

> ability entitling defendant to rescission. * * * In the present case, enforcing the contract with the mistaken price of $25,995 would require defendant to sell the vehicle to plaintiff for $12,000 less than the intended advertised price of $37,995—an error amounting to 32 percent of the price defendant intended.

A buyer acting unconscionably in his dealing with a used car dealer?

SECTION 8: CONSIDERATION

The great English contracts scholar Patrick Atiyah provides the following introduction to consideration:

> The 'doctrine' of consideration is generally seen by lawyers as a set of rules which limits the freedom of individuals to make binding legal promises. Only those promises which are supported by a legal consideration are legally binding; other promises are not binding, even if the promisor *intends* to bind himself by his promise. Thus to many lawyers the central function of the doctrine of consideration is to prevent people from making gratuitous promises, because the typical gratuitous promise is made without any consideration as lawyers understand that term. On this view, the purpose of the law of consideration is to distinguish between gratuitous and non-gratuitous promises. This may, indeed, be one of the chief purposes of the doctrine of consideration, but it is doubtful if it is the only purpose, and certainly this has not traditionally been the only purpose of this doctrine in its very long history. Moreover, to over-emphasize this particular function of the doctrine of consideration is to risk ignoring the relationship between that doctrine and other parts of the law of obligations. Indeed, this has very largely happened in the history of this subject, and for that reason it may be worth stressing at the outset the way in which the doctrine of consideration has roots linking contract law with other parts of the law of obligations. * * *
>
> The doctrine of consideration has traditionally rested on two main legs. The first of these is the idea that a promise is legally binding if it is given in return for some benefit which is rendered, or to be rendered, to the promisor. The second is the notion that a promise becomes binding if the

promisee incurs a detriment by reliance upon it, that is, if he changes his position in reliance on the promise in such a way that he would be worse off if the promise were broken than he would have been if the promise had never been made at all. * * *

The doctrine is in a sense a *limitation* on the free power of individuals to bind themselves as they wish. It is, therefore, a paternalistic device. If a promise or a contract is declared not binding even where there has been a clear promise, on the ground of absence of consideration, the law is in effect saying that it is better that individuals should not bind themselves unless they receive some benefit in return, or unless the other party has suffered some detrimental reliance. * * *

In the nineteenth century the doctrine of consideration came to be widely regarded as technical and anomalous, precisely because of its inherent paternalistic tendency. What is much more curious is that in the twentieth century lawyers have continued to regard the doctrine in this critical fashion despite the very paternalistic tendencies of so much modern law. The oddity is even stronger when it is noted that two of the chief trends of modern law have been on the one side, the whittling down of the binding nature of bare promises and on the other side, the great expansion in benefit-based and reliance-based liabilities. These developments were not accompanied by recognition that their obvious corollary ought to have been a renewed faith in the value of the doctrine of consideration. But today, when there is such a resurgence in classical principles, the outlook on many of these matters looks blurred. It seems unlikely that there will be much turning back from the great increase in benefit-based and reliance-based liabilities; but perhaps criticism of the doctrine of consideration will become stronger again, as lawyers once again take their stand on the ability of individuals to make their own judgements.

P.S. ATIYAH, AN INTRODUCTION TO THE LAW OF CONTRACT, 118, 120–121 (5th ed. 1995).

The history of consideration goes back to 13th century England, to a time when the enforceability of an agreement was limited by the common law system of pleading. A case had to fit within a specific form of pleading or writ.

One such early common law writ, covenant, was largely limited to writings with a seal. Today, in England and most states, the absence or existence of a seal does not affect the enforceability of an agreement. Professor Arthur Allen Leff explained seals as follows:

> Seals thus exemplify one of the strongest impulses of legal ordering, to signal formally to people at critical moments that they are about to leave the world of social interaction for the world of compulsion, bureaucracy and impersonality. It is a way of saying "this counts," "this is for keeps," "we're not kidding around any more" and similar things. Seals are not the only mechanism of that kind: the archaic language and ceremony of marriage, the creamy paper and multiple witnesses of a will, even the formal "One dollar in hand paid" recited in a real-estate man's option form has something of the same intent . . . With seals, of course, the modern problem has been that as the form of the seal has been attenuated (down to a preprinted "seal"), its cautionary effect has been vitiated apace. Hence there is a modern trend to render seals powerless to confer legal rights which would not otherwise be conferred.

Arthur Allen Leff, *A Letter from Professor Leff to a Prospective Publisher*, 94 YALE L.J. 1852 (1985).

Assumpsit developed as the primary common law writ for the enforcement of agreements without seals. Assumpsit had a series of requirements that came to be described as "consideration."

Courts and lawyers no longer use the writ of assumpsit, but they continue to use the term "consideration." While courts consistently use the term "consideration," the term is not used consistently and it is not a real issue in many real world problems or cases. In other words,

1. courts, lawyers and law professors (especially law professors) regularly mention "consideration" BUT
2. there is not a single, universally accepted definition of consideration AND
3. it is unusual for an agreement to be unenforceable because of a lack of consideration.

The following three definitions of consideration are representative. First, the California Civil Code defines consideration as follows:

§ 1605. Good consideration, what

Any benefit conferred, or agreed to be conferred, upon the promisor, by any other person, to which the promisor is not lawfully entitled, or any prejudice suffered, or agreed to be suffered, by such person, other than such as he is at the time of consent lawfully bound to suffer, as an inducement to the promisor, is a good consideration for a promise.

Cal. Civ. Code § 1605.

Second, *Restatement (Second) of Contracts* § 71 defines consideration as follows:

§ 71 Requirement of exchange; types of exchange

(1) To constitute consideration, a performance or a return promise must be bargained for.
(2) A performance or return promise is bargained for if it is sought by the promisor in exchange for his promise and is given by the promisee in exchange for that promise.
(3) The performance may consist of
  (a) an act other than a promise, or
  (b) a forbearance, or
  (c) the creation, modification, or destruction of a legal relation.
(4) The performance or return promise may be given to the promisor or to some other person. It may be given by the promisee or by some other person.

Third, the Alabama Supreme Court has approved the following pattern jury instruction* regarding consideration:

APJI 10.03 Consideration–Definition

A sufficient consideration to support a valid contract is anything of value promised or received, or the doing or promising to do something which one has a legal right to do, or a promise not to do something which one has a legal right to do, as the inducement to enter into the contract.

*In Alabama, as in most states, a committee of judges and lawyers have prepared model jury instructions which are reviewed and "recommended" by the state supreme court–"their use by the trial judges of this state are recommended but without prejudice to the rights of any litigant to make and reserve for review any objection thereto as to form, substance or application."

1 ALABAMA PATTERN JURY INSTRUCTION CIVIL, p. 165 (2nd ed. 1993).

Keep in mind these three definitions of consideration as you read the following cases which are representative of cases in which consideration was an issue.*

A. Changing Your Mind About Agreeing to Give—Looking for Bargained for Benefit to Promisor or Detriment to Promisee

Recall that Professor Atiyah suggested that one purpose of consideration is to distinguish between gratuitous and non-gratuitous promises. The next two cases, *Kirksey v. Kirksey*, and *Hamer v. Sidway*, use the concept of consideration to determine whether an intrafamily promise to make a gift is legally enforceable.

Kirksey v. Kirksey
Supreme Court of Alabama
8 Ala. 131 (1845)

ASSUMPSIT by the defendant, against the plaintiff in error. The question is presented in this Court, upon a case agreed, which shows the following facts:

The plaintiff was the wife of defendant's brother, but had for some time been a widow, and had several children. In 1840, the plaintiff resided on public land, under a contract of lease, she had held over, and was comfortably settled, and would have attempted to secure the land she lived on. The defendant resided in Talladega county, some sixty, or seventy miles off. On the 10th October, 1840, he wrote to her the following letter:

> "Dear sister Antillico—Much to my mortification, I heard, that brother Henry was dead, and one of his children. I know that your situation is one of grief, and difficulty. You had a bad chance before, but a great deal worse now. I should like to come and see you, but cannot with convenience at present. * * * I do not know whether you have a preference on

---

*The cases are not representative in that consideration is not an issue in most contract cases.

> the place you live on, or not. If you had, I would advise you to obtain your preference, and sell the land and quit the country, as I understand it is very unhealthy, and I know society is very bad. If you will come down and see me, I will let you have a place to raise your family, and I have more open land than I can tend; and on the account of your situation, and that of your family, I feel like I want you and the children to do well."

Within a month or two after the receipt of this letter, the plaintiff abandoned her possession, without disposing of it, and removed with her family, to the residence of the defendant, who put her in comfortable houses, and gave her land to cultivate for two years, at the end of which time he notified her to remove, and put her in a house, not comfortable, in the woods, which he afterwards required her to leave.

A verdict being found for the plaintiff, for two hundred dollars, the above facts were agreed, and if they will sustain the action, the judgment is to be affirmed, otherwise it is to be reversed.

ORMOND, J.

The inclination of my mind, is, that the loss and inconvenience, which the plaintiff sustained in breaking up, and moving to the defendant's, a distance of sixty miles, is a sufficient consideration to support the promise, to furnish her with a house, and land to cultivate, until she could raise her family. My brothers, however think, that the promise on the part of the defendant, was a mere gratuity, and that an action will not lie for its breach. The judgment of the Court below must therefore be reversed, pursuant to the agreement of the parties.

QUESTIONS AND NOTES

1. Questions about the facts of this case

   1.1. Did the defendant deny that he made a promise to plaintiff? Did the defendant deny that he did not do what he promised to do?

   1.2. Why did the plaintiff move to Talladega County?

2. Questions about the law

   2.1. Did Judge Ormond believe that there was "sufficient consideration" to make the defendant's promise legally enforceable? Why/why not?

2.2. What is "sufficient" consideration? How does "sufficient consideration" differ from "consideration"?

2.3. How would this case have been decided under the Alabama jury instruction on consideration? Under the *Restatement (Second) of Contracts* definition of consideration?

3. Notes

3.1. Promises, agreements and contracts

Up to this point, most of the cases in this chapter have discussed whether an "agreement" is legally enforceable. *Kirksey,* like most cases in which consideration is the issue, asks whether a "promise" is legally enforceable.

Thinking about the relationship between an "agreement" and a "promise" can be real confusing. If you are going to think about it, keep in mind that

(a) Most agreements or deals involve two promises. *E.g.* (i) P promises to paint H's house and H promises to pay P for her work; and (ii) S promises to sell Crimsonacre to B and B promises to pay S for Blackacre.

(b) Such an agreement with two promises is often labeled "bilateral." And, so long as neither party has fully performed his promise, the agreement is described as "executory."

(c) If the agreement (as in *Kirksey*) is unilateral in form (a promise requesting some act) or is fully "executed" by either party, then there is only one promise to be enforced.

(d) Regardless of whether an agreement is bilateral or unilateral or executory or executed, courts generally are asked to determine the enforceability of a particular promise. P sues D for not doing what she promised to do. D contends that her promise is not enforceable because there is no consideration for her promise. The court is thus asked to determine whether that particular promise is enforceable.

In review, an agreement may have one or two unperformed promises. If one party to an agreement sues because the other party to the agreement is not performing as promised, a possible legal argument by the defendant is that her promise is not legally enforceable because there was no bargained for benefit to her or detriment to the promisee. *Cf. Restatement (Second) of Contracts* § 1.

3.2. Judge Ormond's cryptic opinion does not answer the questions (i) why is a promise not enforceable because it is a "mere gratuity"? and (ii) how can a court (and, more importantly, a law student) determine whether a promise is supported by consideration or a "mere gratuity"? Does the following excerpt from *Maughs v. Porter*, 157 Va. 415, 418, 161 S.E. 242, 243 (Va. Ct. App. 1931), answer these questions?

A gift is a contract without a consideration, and, to be valid, must be executed. A valid gift is, therefore, a contract executed. It is to be executed by the actual delivery by the donor to the donee, or some one for him, of the thing given, or by delivery of the means of obtaining the subject of the gift, without further act of the donor to enable the donee to reduce it to his own possession. "The intention to give must be accompanied by a delivery, and the delivery must be made with an intention to give." Otherwise there is only an intention or promise to give, which, being gratuitous, would be a mere nullity. Delivery of possession of the thing given or of the means of obtaining it so as to make the disposal of it irrevocable, is indispensable to a valid gift.

Clearly then, the plaintiff, under the facts shown here, cannot recover unless defendant is bound by a promise which is supported by a consideration sufficient to support the action. It is often quite difficult to determine in such cases whether or not there is such a consideration. 1 Williston on Contracts, section 112, page 232, thus illustrates the difficulty: "If a benevolent man says to a tramp: 'If you go around the corner to the clothing shop there, you may purchase an overcoat on my credit,' no reasonable person would understand that the short walk was requested as the consideration for the promise, but that in the event of the tramp going to the shop the promisor would make him a gift. Yet the walk to the shop is in its nature capable of being consideration. It is a legal detriment to the tramp to make the walk, and the only reason why the walk is not consideration is because on a reasonable construction it must be held that the walk was not requested as the price of the promise, but was merely a condition of a gratuitous promise. It is often difficult to determine whether words of condition in a promise indicate a request for consideration or state a mere condition in a gratuitous promise. An aid, though not a conclusive test, in determining which construction of the promise is more reasonable is an inquiry whether the happening of the condition will be a benefit to the promisor. If so, it is a fair inference that the happening was requested as a consideration. On the other hand, if, as in the case of the tramp stated above, the happening of the condition will be not only of no benefit to the promisor but is obviously merely for the purpose of enabling the promisee to receive a gift, the happening of the event on which the promise is conditional, though brought about by the promisee in reliance on the promise, will not properly be construed as consideration. In case of doubt where the promisee has incurred a detriment on the faith of the promise, courts will naturally be loath to regard the promise as a mere gratuity and the detriment incurred as merely a condition. But in some cases it is so clear that a conditional gift was intended that even though the promisee has incurred detriment, the promise has been held unenforceable."

3.3. Professor Williston included *Kirksey* in his casebook on contracts and concluded that the result in the case was unjust. *See* Carol Weisbrod, *An Uncertain Trumpet: A Gloss on* Kirksey v. Kirksey, 32 CONN. L. REV. 1699, 1701 (2000). Do you believe that the facts of *Kirksey* are different from the facts of Williston's tramp hypothetical?

3.4. Professor Debora Threedy of University of Utah Law School suggests that the outcome of *Kirksey* might have been different if both the Kirkseys had been male:

Not all bargains between family members are excluded from contract law, however. A pair of first year contract law cases illustrates the tensions between "family" and "market." When an uncle promised his nephew $5000 if the nephew would refrain from smoking, drinking and gambling until he turned twenty-one, the court concluded they were bargaining; thus, the nephew's refraining constituted consideration and the parties had contracted. When, however, a brother-in-law promised to give his widowed sister-in-law a place to raise her family if she would give up homesteading and mover closer to him, the court did not perceive them as bargaining; moving was not consideration and the parties had not contracted.

> One explanation for these divergent outcomes is that in the first case the intra-familial agreement occurs between two males, while in the latter it occurs between a male and female relation. Bargaining, like beauty, is in the eye of the beholder and judges may be less likely to perceive contract bargaining between the sexes in a family context.
>
> Debora L.Threedy, *Feminists & Contract Doctrine*, 32 IND. L. REV. 1247, 1251(1999). The case of the uncle's promise to the nephew, a guy thing, is set out below.

Hamer v. Sidway

Court of Appeals of New York
124 N.Y. 538, 27 N.E. 256 (1891)

[The facts of this case are somewhat confusing in that none of the parties to the agreement was named either "Hamer" or "Sidway." Both were named "William Story." The older William was the uncle and the promisor to the younger William who was (obviously) the nephew and the promisee. The trial court found that the promise was legally enforceable; the intermediate appellate court reversed, and then this court reversed the intermediate appellate court and reinstated the decision of the trial court. The intermediate appellate court* provided the following information about the promise:

The testimony introduced by the plaintiff was to the effect that in March, 1869, when the testator and William E. Story were attending the golden wedding of the father of the testator, he said to William: "Willie, I am going to make you a proposition." William told him he would like to hear it. That the testator then said: "If you will not drink any liquor, will not smoke, will not play cards or billiards until you are 21, I will give you $5,000 that day. Of course, if you want to play for fun, that I don't consider playing cards." William said he would endeavor to carry it out; that he would do it. When William became 21 years of age he wrote the testator the following letter: "Dear Uncle: I am twenty-one years old to-day, and I am now my own boss, and I believe, according to agreement, that there is due me five thousand dollars. I have lived up to the contract to the letter in every sense of the word." The testator's reply to this letter, so far as material to the questions involved in this case, was as follows: "Buffalo, February 26, 1875. W. E. Story, Jr.—Dear Nephew: Your letter of the 31st ult. came to hand all right, saying you had lived up to the promise made me several years ago. I have no doubt

*11 N.Y. Supp 182 (N.Y. Supreme Court, 4th Dept. 1890). Eds.

lived up to the promise made me several years ago. I have no doubt but what you have, for which you shall have $5,000, as I promised you. I had the money in the bank the day you were twenty-one years old that I intended for you, and you shall have the money certain. Now, Willie, I do not intend to interfere with this money in any way until I think you are capable of taking care of it, and the sooner that time comes the better it will please me. I would hate very much to have you start out in some adventure that you thought all right, and lose this money in one year. The first five thousand dollars I got together cost me a heap of hard work. * * * Willie, you are twenty-one, and you have many a thing to learn yet. This money you have earned much easier than I did, besides acquiring good habits at the same time, and you are quite welcome to the money. Hope you will make good use of it. I was ten long years getting this together after I was your age. Now, hoping this will be satisfactory, I stop. *** P.S. You can consider this money on interest."

Uncle William then died before paying nephew William; the executor of Uncle William's estate refused to pay the promised $5,000 to nephew William and this law suit was filed.]

* * *

Parker, J.

The question which provoked the most discussion by counsel on this appeal, and which lies at the foundation of plaintiff's asserted right of recovery, is whether by virtue of a contract defendant's testator, William E. Story, became indebted to his nephew, William E. Story, 2d, on his twenty-first birthday in the sum of $5,000. The trial court found as a fact that "on the 20th day of March, 1869, * * * William E. Story agreed to and with William E. Story, 2d, that if he would refrain from drinking liquor using tobacco, swearing, and playing cards or billiards for money until should become twenty-one years of age, then he, the said William E. Story, would at that time pay him, the said William E. Story, 2d, the sum of $5,000 for such refraining, to which the said William E. Story, 2d, agreed," and that he "in all things fully performed his part of said agreement." The defendant contends that the contract was without consideration to support it, and therefore invalid. He asserts that the promisee, by refraining from the use of liquor and tobacco, was not harmed, but benefitted; that which he did was best for him to do, independently of his uncle's promise,—and insists that it follows that, unless the promisor was benefitted, the contract was without consideration,—a contention which, if well founded, would seem to leave open for controversy in many cases whether that which the promisee did or omitted to do was in fact of such benefit to him as to leave no consideration to support the enforcement of the promisor's agreement. Such a rule could not be tolerated, and is without foundation in the law. The exchequer chamber in 1875 defined "consideration" as follows: "A valuable consideration, in the sense of the law, may consist either in some right, interest, profit, or benefit accruing to the one party, or some forbearance, detriment, loss, or responsibility given, suffered, or undertaken by the other." Courts "will not ask whether the thing which forms the consideration does in fact benefit the promisee or a third party, or is of any substantial value to any one. It is enough that something is promised, done, forborne, or suffered by the party to whom the promise is made as consideration for the promise made to him." Anson, Cont. 63. "In general a waiver of any legal right at the request of another party is a sufficient consideration for a promise." Pars. Cont. "Any damage, or suspension, or forbearance of a right will be sufficient to sustain a promise." 2 Kent, Comm. (12th Ed.) Pollock in his work on Contracts, (page 166,) after citing the definition given by the exchequer chamber, already quoted, says: "The second branch of this judicial description is really the most important one. 'Consideration' means not so much that one party is profiting as that the other abandons some legal right in the present, or limits his legal freedom of action in the future, as an inducement for the promise of the first." Now, applying this rule to the facts before us, the promisee used tobacco, occasionally drank liquor, and he had a legal right to do so. That right he abandoned for a period of years upon the strength of the promise of the testator that for such forbearance he would give him $5,000. We need not speculate on the effort which may have been required to give up the use of those stimulants. It is sufficient that he restricted his lawful freedom of action within certain prescribed limits upon the faith of his uncle's agreement, and now, having fully performed the conditions imposed, it is of no moment whether such performance actually proved a benefit to the promisor, and the court will not inquire into it; but, were it a proper subject of inquiry, we see nothing in this record that would permit a determination that the uncle was not benefitted in a legal sense.

The order appealed from should be reversed, and the judgment of the special term affirmed, with costs payable out of the estate. All concur.

QUESTIONS AND NOTES

1. Questions about the facts of this case

   1.1. Did Sidway, the executor for the estate of William E. Story, contend that Mr. Story did not promise to pay his nephew $5000 if he refrained from drinking, using tobacco, swearing, and playing cards or billiards for money?

   1.2. Did Sidway contend that the nephew did not so refrain?

2. Questions about the law

   2.1. Recall that nephew William was a minor when Uncle William made the promise. And, recall the law of capacity. Why didn't Sidway assert William's lack of capacity as a defense?

   2.2. What was the consideration in *Hamer*?

   2.3. The *Hamer* opinion quotes from an 1875 Exchequer Chamber definition of consideration. Apply the definition to the facts of the *Hamer* case. Was there a "benefit accruing to the one party"? Was there a "forbearance, detriment, loss or responsibility given, suffered or undertaken by the other"?

   2.4. Would *Hamer* have been decided differently under the California statutory definition of consideration? Under *Restatement (Second) of Contracts* § 71? Under the Alabama jury instruction?

   2.5. Would *Hamer* have been decided differently if the promise had been made just after Nephew William turned 21 and was "Since you did not drink any liquor or smoke or play cards or billiards for money until you reached the age of 21, I will give you $5000 at your birthday party next week"?

   2.6. Would *Hamer* have been decided differently if (i) the original conversation between Uncle William and Nephew William had simply been "Willie, you are a fine lad. I will give you $5000 when you are 21" and (ii) Willie then decided on his own to show his uncle what a fine lad he really was by not drinking liquor, playing cards or billiards, or smoking until he was 21?

2.7. Would *Hamer* have been decided differently if Uncle William had promised $5,000,000 instead of $5000? $5 instead of $5000?

3. Notes

3.1. Professor Melvin Eisenberg of University of California at Berkeley Law School argues that the world of contracts and the world of donative promises are two different worlds:

> To begin with, the world of contract is a market world, largely driven by relatively impersonal considerations and focused on commodities and prices. The impersonal organs of the state are an appropriate means to enforce promises made in such a world. In contrast, much of the world of gift is driven by affective considerations like love, affection, friendship, gratitude, and comradeship. That world would be impoverished if it were to be collapsed into the world of contract. * * *
>
> Similarly, making simple, affective donative promises enforceable would have the effect of commodifying the gift relationship. Under an enforceability regime, it could never be clear to the promisee, or even to the promisor, whether a donative promise that was made in a spirit of love, friendship, affection, or the like, was also performed for those reasons, or instead was performed to discharge a legal obligation or avoid a lawsuit. Accordingly, gifts made pursuant to simple, affective donative promises would be seriously impoverished, because at the point of the transfer, the promisor's motives would invariably be mixed.
>
> It can now be seen that the principle that simple donative promises are unenforceable does not show that the law fails to value donative promises. Just the opposite is true. The principle that simple donative promises are unenforceable is justified not because simple donative promises are less important than bargain promises, but because they are more important.

Melvin Aron Eisenberg, *The World of Contract and the World of Gift*, 85 CAL. L. REV. 821, 846 (1997).

3.2. Professor Melanie Leslie of Yeshiva Law School recently studied the cases in which someone attempted to bring a family promise into the world of contracts and concluded:

The scarcity of cases involving breach of promise within intimate relationships reflects two factors: the often indefinite nature of personal agreements and the unwillingness of parties to sue until the relationship is beyond repair.

Even if one family member wanted to sue another for breach of promise, it would be hard to isolate particular promises and acts of reliance within the relationship. Very few cases would display the easy clarity of the rare, but often cited, war horses like *Hamer v. Sidway*, in which a nephew sued his uncle for breaching an express promise to pay the nephew if he forswore drinking and swearing. Agreements within long-term, intimate relationships are most often implicit and multifaceted. The relationships themselves are premised on reciprocity, constructed of a multitude of mutual and simultaneous promises and actions generated, at least in part, by reliance on those promises. The closer and more interdependent the parties, the less likely promises and agreements will be isolated and clearly spelled out, because the parties operate in accordance with implied understandings, and because the value generated by those implied understandings is greatly enhanced if the reciprocal nature of the duties within the relationship is left unspoken. The relationship simply cannot be diagrammed as a series of discrete transactions that fit neatly into the classical contract paradigm of bargained-for exchange, nor should it be.

Of course, indefiniteness alone is not an adequate explanation for family members' reluctance to resort to legal process. After all, courts have become increasingly willing to enforce indefinite agreements in the commercial context. More importantly, family members do not look to the law because doing so would destroy the familial relationship. Personal interdependent relationships are most often characterized by a high degree of trust. When trust disintegrates, it does so slowly, and disappointed parties generally harbor hopes that a disintegrating relationship will improve. In family relationships especially, strong psychological ties often inspire the promisee to hope for reconciliation. Moreover, the promisee would prefer that the promisor's performance be voluntary rather than coerced; the performance is valuable, in large measure, because it is motivated, or appears to be motivated, by love rather than self-interest. The disappointed promisee will abandon hope only when the relationship clearly is beyond repair, and the promisee is sufficiently angered by the promisor's betrayal that she is willing to sever the relationship entirely. Short of that, there will be no lawsuit because the promisee knows that a suit would quickly and finally destroy whatever trust is left. Often, family relationships end only at divorce or death.

Melanie B. Leslie, *Enforcing Family Promises: Reliance, Reciprocity, and Relational Contract,* 77 N.C. L. REV. 551, 555 (1999).

3.3. A later New York Court of Appeals decision, *Weiner v. McGraw-Hill, Inc.*, 443 N.E.2d 441 (N.Y. Ct. App. 1982) describes *Hamer* as the "seminal" case on consideration. *Hamer* appears as a principal case in virtually every contracts casebook. *Hamer,* with variations, can be used to illustrate such basic consideration concepts as:

- legal detriment different from actual detriment
- no inquiry into adequacy of amount of consideration
- promise as consideration
- bargained for requirement
- past consideration

B. Changing Your Mind About Agreeing to Settle Past Claims or Release Future Claims

In the last case, *Hamer v. Sidway*, the promise looked like a gift, and the court held that it was a contract. In the next case, *Schnell v. Nell,* the agreement looks like a contract, and the court holds that it is a gift. What gives?

Schnell v. Nell

Supreme Court of Indiana
17 Ind. 29 (1861)

Perkins, J.

Action by J.B. Nell against Zacharias Schnell, upon the following instrument:

> This agreement, entered into this 13th day of February, 1856, between Zach. Schnell, of Indianapolis, Marion county, State of Indiana, as party of the first part, and J.B. Nell, of the same place, Wendelin Lorenz, of

> Stilesville, Hendricks county, State of Indiana, and Donata Lorenz, of Frickinger, Grand Duchy of Baden, Germany, as parties of the second part, witnesseth: The said Zacharias Schnell agrees as follows: whereas his wife, Theresa Schnell, now deceased, has made a last will and testament, in which, among other provisions, it was ordained that every one of the above named second parties, should receive the sum of $200; and whereas the said provisions of the will must remain a nullity, for the reason that no property, real or personal, was in the possession of the said Theresa Schnell, deceased, in her own name, at the time of her death, and all property held by Zacharias and Theresa Schnell jointly, therefore reverts to her husband; and whereas the said Theresa Schnell has also been a dutiful and loving wife to the said Zach. Schnell, and has materially aided him in the acquisition of all property, real and personal, now possessed by him; for, and in consideration of all this, and the love and respect he bears to his wife; and, furthermore, in consideration of one cent, received by him of the second parties, he, the said Zach. Schnell, agrees to pay the above named sums of money to the parties of the second part, to wit: $200 to the said J.B. Nell; $200 to the said Wendelin Lorenz; and $200 to the said Donata Lorenz, in the following installments, viz., $200 in one year from the date of these presents; $200 in two years, and $200 in three years; to be divided between the parties in equal portions of $66 2/3 each year, or as they may agree, till each one has received his full sum of $200.
>
> And the said parties of the second part, for, and in consideration of this, agree to pay the above named sum of money [one cent], and to deliver up to said Schnell, and abstain from collecting any real or supposed claims upon him or his estate, arising from the said last will and testament of the said Theresa Schnell, deceased.
>
> In witness whereof, the said parties have, on this 13th day of February, 1856, set hereunto their hands and seals.
>
> Zacharias Schnell, [seal.]
>
> J. B. Nell, [seal.]
>
> Wen. Lorenz. [seal.]

The complaint contained no averment of a consideration for the instrument, outside of those expressed in it; and did not aver that the one cent agreed to be paid, had been paid or tendered.

A demurrer to the complaint was overruled.

The defendant answered, that the instrument sued on was given for no consideration whatever.

He further answered, that it was given for no consideration, because his said wife, Theresa, at the time she made the will mentioned, and at the time of her death, owned, neither separately, nor jointly with her husband, or any one else (except so far as the law gave her an interest in her husband's property), any property, real or personal, &c.

The will is copied into the record, but need not be into this opinion.

The Court sustained a demurrer to these answers, evidently on the ground that they were regarded as contradicting the instrument sued on, which particularly set out the considerations upon which it was executed. But the instrument is latently ambiguous on this point.

The case turned below, and must turn here, upon the question whether the instrument sued on does express a consideration sufficient to give it legal obligation, as against Zacharias Schnell. It specifies three distinct considerations for his promise to pay $600:

1. A promise, on the part of the plaintiffs, to pay him one cent.
2. The love and affection he bore his deceased wife, and the fact that she had done her part, as his wife, in the acquisition of property.
3. The fact that she had expressed her desire, in the form of an inoperative will, that the persons named therein should have the sums of money specified.

The consideration of one cent will not support the promise of Schnell. It is true, that as a general proposition, inadequacy of consideration will not vitiate an agreement. But this doctrine does not apply to a mere exchange of sums of money, of coin, whose value is exactly fixed, but to the exchange of something of, in itself, indeterminate value, for money, or, perhaps, for some other thing of indeterminate value. In this case, had the one cent mentioned, been some particular one cent, a family piece, or ancient, remarkable coin, possessing an indeterminate value, extrinsic from its simple money value, a different view might be taken. As it is, the mere promise to pay six hundred dollars for one cent, even had the portion of that cent due from the plaintiff been tendered, is an unconscionable contract, void, at first blush, upon its face, if it be regarded as an earnest one. The consideration of one cent is, plainly, in this case, merely nominal, and intended to be so. As the will and testament of Schnell's wife imposed no legal obligation upon him to discharge her bequests out of his property, and as she had none of her own, his promise to discharge them was not legally binding upon him, on that ground. A moral consideration, only, will not support a promise. And for the same reason, a valid consideration for his promise can not be found in the fact of a compromise of a disputed claim; for where such claim is legally groundless, a promise upon a compromise of it, or of a suit upon it, is not legally binding. There was no mistake of law or fact in this case, as the agreement admits the will inoperative and void. The promise was simply one to make a gift. The past services of his wife, and the love and affection he had borne her, are objectionable as legal considerations for Schnell's promise, on two grounds: 1. They are past considerations. * * * 2. The fact that Schnell loved his wife, and that she had been industrious, constituted no consideration for his promise to pay J. B. Nell, and the Lorenzes, a sum of money. Whether, if his wife, in her lifetime, had made a bargain with Schnell, that, in consideration of his promising to pay, after her death, to the persons named, a sum of money, she would be industrious, and worthy of his affection, such a promise would have been valid and consistent with public policy, we need not decide. Nor is the fact that Schnell now venerates the memory of his deceased wife, a legal consideration for a promise to pay any third person money.

The instrument sued on, interpreted in the light of the facts alleged in the second paragraph of the answer, will not support an action. The demurrer to the answer should have been overruled.

Per Curiam.—The judgment is reversed, with costs. Cause remanded &c.

QUESTIONS

1. Questions about the facts of this case

   1.1. Did the defendant Mr. Schnell contend that he did not agree to pay the plaintiff J.B. Nell $200?

   1.2. Do you think that Mr. Schnell wrote the agreement himself?

1.3. Why did the defendant Schnell enter into such an agreement, complete with seals? Was Schnell's reason for making the agreement relevant to the court's reasoning?

1.4. Was it ethical for Schnell to take the position that his promise to pay was not enforceable? Was it ethical for Schnell's lawyer to take that position? Would it have been ethical for Schnell's lawyer to refuse to take that position?

2. Questions about the law

2.1. Modern concepts of consideration. How would this case be decided under *Restatement (Second) of Contracts* § 71? Under the Alabama jury instruction?

2.2. An even more modern concept. If you were representing the plaintiffs, and the judge deciding your suit against Schnell was Judge Judy, what arguments would you make?

2.3. A real old concept—seals. Did the court mention that Schnell not only signed the agreement but affixed a seal thereto? Why not?

2.4. Adequacy of consideration. The court describes the "consideration of one cent" as "nominal." What does nominal mean? Will one penny always be "nominal"? What if the consideration recited and actually paid was $1.70? $18? $190?

2.5. Adequacy of consideration. What if the document had recited consideration of "an autographed picture of David Epstein" and the plaintiffs had provided such a picture? Would that be "nominal"? What if the document had recited consideration of a "mere peppercorn" and the plaintiffs had given Schnell a peppercorn? According to Professor Atiyah, "At one time it was traditional to stipulate a peppercorn as nominal consideration in certain transactions, and this has always been sufficient to satisfy the law's requirements." P.S. ATIYAH, AN INTRODUCTION TO THE LAW OF CONTRACT 127 (5th ed. 1995).

2.6. Past consideration. If the plaintiffs had rescued Schnell's pet hog on January 15, 1856, and that was the consideration recited in the February 13, 1856, agreement, would a court applying *Restatement (Second)* § 71 have enforced Schnell's agreement to pay?

2.7. Settlement of a claim. Why wasn't the plaintiffs' agreement to "abstain from collecting any real or supposed claims upon him or his estate, arising from the said last will and testament" consideration? Reconsider the court's answer in *Schnell* after considering the next case, *Dyer v. National By-Products*, which more completely discusses promises to release claims as consideration.

Dyer v. National By-Products, Inc.

Supreme Court of Iowa
380 N.W.2d 732 (1986)

SCHULTZ, Justice.

The determinative issue in this appeal is whether good faith forbearance to litigate a claim, which proves to be invalid and unfounded, is sufficient consideration to uphold a contract of settlement. The district court determined, as a matter of law, that consideration for the alleged settlement was lacking because the forborne claim was not a viable cause of action. We reverse and remand.

On October 29, 1981, Dale Dyer, an employee of National By-Products, lost his right foot in a job-related accident. Thereafter, the employer placed Dyer on a leave of absence at full pay from the date of his injury until August 16, 1982. At that time he returned to work as a foreman, the job he held prior to his injury. On March 11, 1983, the employer indefinitely laid off Dyer.

Dyer then filed the present lawsuit against his employer claiming that his discharge was a breach of an oral contract. He alleged that he in good faith believed that he had a valid claim against his employer for his personal injury. Further, Dyer claimed that his forbearance from litigating his claim was made in exchange for a promise from his employer that he would have lifetime employment. The employer specifically denied that it had offered a lifetime job to Dyer after his injury.

Following extensive discovery procedures, the employer filed a motion for summary judgment claiming there was no genuine factual issue and that it was entitled to judgment as a matter of law. The motion was resisted by Dyer. The district court sustained the employer's motion on the basis that: (1) no reciprocal promise to work for the employer for life was present, and

(2) there was no forbearance of any viable cause of action, apparently on the ground that workers' compensation provided Dyer's sole remedy.

On appeal, Dyer claims that consideration for the alleged contract of lifetime employment was his forbearance from pursuing an action against his employer. Accordingly, he restricts his claim of error to the second reason advanced by the district court for granting summary judgment. Dyer generally contends that an unresolved issue of material fact remains as to whether he reasonably and in good faith forbore from asserting a claim against his employer and his coemployees in exchange for the employer's alleged promise to employ him for life. Specifically, he asserts that the trial court erred because: (1) the court did not consider the reasonab eness and good faith of his belief in the validity of the claim he forbore from asserting, and (2) the court considered the legal merits of the claim itself which Dyer forbore from asserting.

The employer, on the other hand, maintains that workers' compensation[1] benefits are Dyer's sole remedy for his injury and that his claim for damages is unfounded. It then urges that forbearance from asserting an unfounded claim cannot serve as consideration for a contract. For the purpose of this discussion, we shall assume that Dyer's tort action is clearly invalid and he had no basis for a tort suit against either his employer or his fellow employees. We recognize that the fact issue, as to whether Dyer in good faith believed that he had a cause of action based in tort against the employer, remains unresolved. The determinative issue before the district court and now on appeal is whether the lack of consideration for the alleged promise of lifetime employment has been established as a matter of law.

Preliminarily, we observe that the law favors the adjustment and settlement of controversies without resorting to court action. Compromise is favored by law. Compromise of a doubtful right asserted in good faith is sufficient consideration for a promise.

---

[1] It is undisputed that the employee was covered under workers' compensation. The Iowa workers' compensation act states in pertinent part that:

> The rights and remedies provided in this chapter. . . . for an employee on account of injury . . . for which benefits under this chapter . . . are recoverable, shall be the exclusive and only rights and remedies of such employee . . . at common law or otherwise, on account of such injury . . . against:
>
> (1) his or her employer. . .

Iowa Code S 85.20 (1983).

The more difficult problem is whether the settlement of an unfounded claim asserted in good faith is consideration for a contract of settlement. Professor Corbin presents a view favorable to Dyer's argument when he states:

> [F]orbearance to press a claim, or a promise of such forbearance, may be a sufficient consideration even though the claim is wholly ill-founded. It may be ill-founded because the facts are not what he supposes them to be, or because the existing facts do not have the legal operation that he supposes them to have. In either case, his forbearance may be a sufficient consideration, although under certain circumstances it is not. The fact that the claim is ill-founded is not in itself enough to prevent forbearance from being a sufficient consideration for a promise.

Further, in the same section, it is noted that:

> The most generally prevailing, and probably the most satisfactory view is that forbearance is sufficient if there is any reasonable ground for the claimant's belief that it is just to try to enforce his claim. He must be asserting his claim "in good faith"; but this does not mean he must believe that his suit can be won. It means that he must not be making his claim or threatening suit for purposes of vexation, or in order to realize on its "nuisance value."

The Restatement (Second) of Contracts section 74 (1979), supports the Corbin view and states:

> Settlement of Claims
>
> (1) Forbearance to assert or the surrender of a claim or defense which proves to be invalid is not consideration unless
>
> (a) the claim or defense is in fact doubtful because of uncertainty as to the facts or the law, or
>
> (b) the forbearing or surrendering party believes that the claim or defense may be fairly determined to be valid. * * *
>
> Comment:
>
> * * *
>
> b. Requirement of good faith. The policy favoring compromise of disputed claims is clearest, perhaps, where a claim is surrendered at a time

when it is uncertain whether it is valid or not. Even though the invalidity later becomes clear, the bargain is to be judged as it appeared to the parties at the time; if the claim was then doubtful, no inquiry is necessary as to their good faith. Even though the invalidity should have been clear at the time, the settlement of an honest dispute is upheld. But a mere assertion or denial of liability does not make a claim doubtful, and the fact that invalidity is obvious may indicate that it was known. In such cases Subsection (1)(b) requires a showing of good faith.

However, not all jurisdictions adhere to this view. Some courts require that the claim forborne must have some merit in fact or at law before it can provide consideration and these jurisdictions reject those claims that are obviously invalid.

Additionally, Professor Williston notes that:

> While there is a great divergence of opinion respecting the kind of forbearance which will constitute consideration, the weight of authority holds that although forbearance from suit on a clearly invalid claim is insufficient consideration for a promise, forbearance from suit on a claim of doubtful validity is sufficient consideration for a promise if there is a sincere belief in the validity of the claim.

We believe, however, that the better reasoned approach is that expressed in the Restatement (Second) of Contracts section 74. Even the above statement from Williston, although it may have been the state of the law in 1957, is a questionable assessment of the current law. As noted before, as a matter of policy the law favors compromise and such policy would be defeated if a party could second guess his settlement and litigate the validity of the compromise. The requirement that the forbearing party assert the claim in good faith sufficiently protects the policy of law that favors the settlement of controversies. Our holdings which are to the contrary to this view are overruled.

In the present case, the invalidity of Dyer's claim against the employer does not foreclose him, as a matter of law, from asserting that his forbearance was consideration for the alleged contract of settlement. However, the issue of Dyer's good faith must still be examined. In so doing, the issue of the validity of Dyer's claim should not be entirely overlooked:

> Although the courts will not inquire into the validity of a claim which was compromised in good faith, there must generally be reasonable grounds

> for a belief in order for the court to be convinced that the belief was honestly entertained by the person who asserted it. Sufficient consideration requires more than the bald ascertion by a claimant who has a claim, and to the extent that the validity or invalidity of a claim has a bearing upon whether there were reasonable grounds for believing in its possible validity, evidence of the validity or invalidity of a claim may be relevant to the issue of good faith.

15A Am.Jur.2d Compromise and Settlement § 17, at 790. We conclude that the evidence of the invalidity of the claim is relevant to show a lack of honest belief in the validity of the claim asserted or forborne.

Under the present state of the record, there remains a material fact as to whether Dyer's forbearance to assert his claim was in good faith. Summary judgment should not have been rendered against him. Accordingly, the case is reversed and remanded for further proceedings consistent with this opinion.

REVERSED AND REMANDED.

QUESTIONS

1. Questions about the facts of this case

   1.1 Was there a written agreement in this case?

   1.2. Does National By-Products, Inc. (the employer) deny that it promised the plaintiff lifetime employment? Did the trial court find that the employer made such a promise?

   1.3. According to the plaintiff, what was the consideration for that promise?

   1.4. What evidence should the plaintiff's attorneys introduce on remand?

2. Questions about the law

   2.1. Dyer apparently made a mistake as to the workers compensation law. We previously considered the effect of a mistake of law in *Burggraff v. Baum*. Is this case consistent with the *Burggraff* case?

2.2. Would the court that decided *Schnell* affirm the district court's ruling that forbearance to assert a claim which is invalid and unfounded cannot be consideration?

2.3. Note that Corbin and Williston disagree over whether settlement of an invalid claim can be consideration. What policy reasons support the Williston position? The Corbin position?

2.4. Why didn't the plaintiff's attorney argue that plaintiff's loss of his right foot was consideration for the employer's promise of life-time employment? Isn't losing a foot even more detriment than refraining from "drinking liquor, using tobacco, swearing, and playing cards and billiards for money"?

2.5. Would you have represented the plaintiff in this case on a contingency fee basis?

Schnell and *Dyer* illustrate some of the consideration issues that can be raised when a person who promised to settle past claims changes his mind. The next short case, *Reed*, considers the argument that an agreement to release possible future claims should not be enforced because of consideration issues.

Reed v. University Of North Dakota* and The North Dakota Association For The Disabled, Inc.

Supreme Court of North Dakota

589 N.W.2d 880 (1999)

[The plaintiff, Jace Reed, was a student at the University of North Dakota (UND) on a hockey scholarship. As part of UND's preseason conditioning program, Reed ran in a ten kilometer race sponsored by the North Dakota Association for the Disabled (NDAD). As a result of the race, Reed himself became "disabled," suffering extensive damage to his kidneys and liver as a result of dehydration. More specifically, Reed required one kidney and two liver transplants.

*Reed's suit against the University of North Dakota was dismissed on the ground of "sovereign immunity," a concept that you have discussed, will discuss or should discuss in torts. Eds.

Reed sued NDAD on a tort theory, alleging that NDAD negligently failed to provide adequate medical services and water at the race site. NDAD defended on a contract theory, alleging that the race registration form that Reed signed was a contract releasing NDAD from any liability. The trial court granted NDAD's motion for summary judgment. Reed appealed.]

Maring, Justice.

Jace Reed appealed a summary judgment dismissing his * * * claims against the North Dakota Association for the Disabled (NDAD). We hold * * * a valid release exonerates NDAD from liability for its alleged negligence * * *. We affirm.

* * *

A

Reed contends a release in a race registration form signed by him does not bar his negligence claim against NDAD. Before the race, Reed signed a registration form which provided, in part:

> I am entering this event at my own risk and assume all responsibility for injuries I may incur as a direct or indirect result of my participation. For myself and my heirs, I agree not to hold the participating sponsors and their directors, employees, and/or agents responsible for any claims. I also give permission for the free use of my name and/or picture in a broadcast, telecast, or other account of this event.

According to Reed, UND coaches presented the registration form to him before the race, and he had to sign it to run the race, which was a mandatory part of the UND hockey team's preseason conditioning program.

Reed asserts the release is not enforceable, because it was not supported by consideration. Consideration may be any benefit conferred or detriment suffered. See N.D.C.C. § 9-05-01. The forbearance of a legal right is a legal detriment which constitutes good consideration. The existence of consideration is a question of law.

As part of their preseason conditioning program, the UND hockey players were allowed to run on the same course during NDAD's road race. When the hockey players, including Reed, signed the registration form, they agreed not to hold the participating sponsors responsible for any claims arising from their participation in the event and NDAD agreed to let them run on the course during NDAD's road race. Reed's surrender of a legal right in exchange for NDAD allowing him to run the course during the race constitutes consideration for the release. *See Malecha v. St. Croix Valley Skydiving Club,* 392 N.W.2d 727, 731 (Minn. App. 1986) (holding payment of fee and surrender of right to sue for negligence in exchange for skydiving training course constitutes valid consideration for release).

* * *

V

We affirm the summary judgment dismissing Reed's complaint against NDAD. * * *

QUESTIONS

1. Questions about the facts of this case

   1.1. Did either party contend that there was no agreement in this case?

   1.2. What did the plaintiff, Mr. Reed, agree to do or forbear from doing?

   1.3. What did the defendant, North Dakota Association for the Disabled, Inc., agree to do or forbear from doing?

2. Questions about the law

   2.1. The *Reed* decision cites a North Dakota statute for its definition of consideration. That statute provides:

   9-05-01 Good consideration defined.

   Any benefit conferred or agreed to be conferred upon the promisor by any other person to which the promisor is not entitled lawfully, or any prejudice suffered or agreed to be suffered by such person, other than such as he, at the time of consent, is lawfully bound to suffer as an inducement to the promisor, is a good consideration for a promise.

N.D. Cent. Code § 9-05-01 (1997). Is the definition of consideration in the North Dakota statute different from the definition of consideration in *Hamer*?

2.2. Apply the North Dakota statute to the facts of *Reed*. Who is the "promisor"? Was there any "benefit conferred or agreed to be conferred upon the promisor"?

2.3. The *Reed* decision restates the holding of *Hamer*: "The forbearance of a legal right is a legal detriment which constitutes good consideration." What is the relevance of that statement to the issue before the court?

2.4. How would you restate the holding in this case? As "Reed's surrender of a legal right in exchange for NDAD allowing him to run the course during the race constitutes consideration for the release"?

2.5. Markell purchases (but does not read) the Burning Man ticket set out below. While attending Burning Man, Markell is beaten up by drunken law students. Markell sues the Burning Man promoters. The promoters move for summary judgment based on the exculpatory language in the ticket. How would the *Reed* court rule? How would the *Covert* court rule?

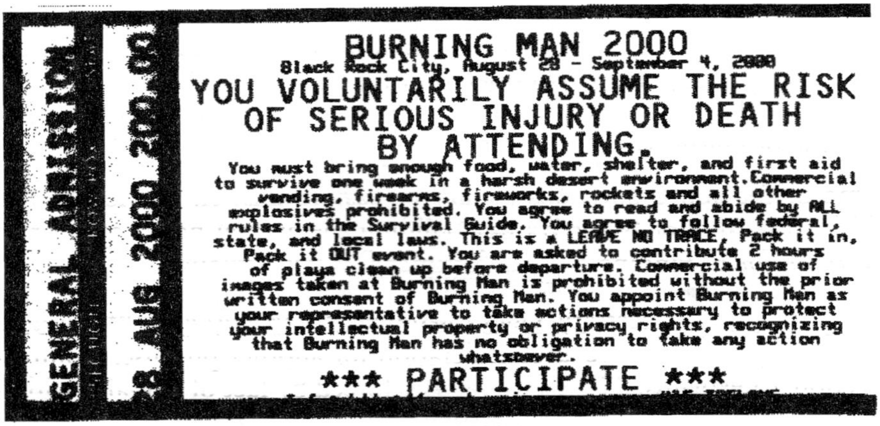

Burning Man Ticket

In *Reed*, the consideration took the form of performance by the promisee: NDAD allowed the promisor Reed to run in its race in exchange for his promise not to sue. Earlier, in *Hamer*, the consideration took the form of forbearance by the promisee: the nephew Willie refrained from drinking, etc., until he reached the age of 21.

Most business transactions involve an exchange of promises to do something (or not do something) in the future. Consider the following problems.

Problems

1. Faber Veterinary Clinic (F) contracts with Blutarsky Building Contractors (B) for the construction of a new animal hospital. B promises to complete the building by April 5. F promises to pay $400,000 within 30 days after completion of the building. B never even starts on the building. F hires Stratton Construction Company (S) which builds the building at a cost of $500,000. Can F sue B for breach of contract? What was the consideration for B's promise? Since F did not yet pay B, what is the detriment to the promisee F or the benefit to promisor B?
2. In October, Mitch McDeere (M), a law student, accepts a job with the law firm of Bandini, Lambert & Locke (B) for $150,000 per year starting in August. M later changes his mind and goes out on his own instead of starting work at B. Can B sue M for breach of contract? What was the consideration for M's promise? Since B did not yet pay M, what is the detriment to the promisee B or the benefit to the promisor M?

Some of the above questions should be easy to answer. Obviously, there should be a legal remedy for B's not building the animal house and for M's not working for B. Finding a "legal detriment" is less obvious.

And perhaps, less necessary. Under *Restatement (Second) of Contracts* §§ 71 and 75, a promise can serve as consideration for another promise. Comment a to section 75 explains: "The promise is enforced by fact of bargain, without more."

The *Restatement* comment (and our first hypothetical) is taken from the following article on consideration by Professor Lon Fuller who taught contracts at Harvard Law School:

B promises to build a house for A, and A, in return, promises to pay B $5000 on the completion of the house. B defaults in his promise, and A, without having had occasion to pay anything on the contract, sues B for damages. Judicial intervention in this kind of case apparently began in England toward the end of the sixteenth century. It is now generally assumed that so far as consideration is concerned the executory bilateral contract is on a complete parity with the situation where the plaintiff has already paid the price of the defendant's promised performance. Yet if we examine the executory bilateral contract in terms of the policies underlying consideration, it will become apparent that this assumption is unjustified.

Where a bilateral contract remains wholly executory the arguments for judicial intervention have been considerably diminished in comparison with the situation of the half-completed exchange. There is here no unjust enrichment. Reliance may or may not exist, but in any event will not be so tangible and direct as where it consists in the rendition of the price of the defendant's performance. On the side of form, we have lost the natural formality involved in the turning over of property or the rendition and acceptance of services. There remains simply the fact that the transaction is an exchange and not a gift.

In the situation of the half-completed exchange, the element of exchange is only one factor tending toward enforcement. Since that element is there reinforced by reliance, unjust enrichment, and the natural formality involved in the surrender and acceptance of a tangible benefit, it is unnecessary to analyze the concept of exchange closely, and it may properly be left vague. In the executory bilateral contract, on the other hand, the element of exchange stands largely alone as a basis of liability and its definition becomes crucial. Various definition are possible. We may define exchange vaguely as a transaction from which each participant derives a benefit, or, more restrictively, as a transaction in which the motives of the parties are primarily economic rather than sentimental. The problem of choosing among these varying conceptions may seem remote and unimportant, yet it underlies some of the most familiar problems of contract law. For example, suppose a nephew promises his uncle that he will not smoke until he is twenty-one, and the uncle promises him $5000 as a reward if he will keep his promise. Where the nephew sues after having earned the reward by following the prescribed line of conduct recovery has been permitted. But would such an agreement be enforced as an

> executory bilateral contract? Could the uncle, for example, sue the nephew for smoking a cigarette? In answering this question it is at once apparent that we are faced with the necessity of defining the particular kind of exchange which is essential to the enforcement of a bilateral contract. A similar problem underlies many of the cases involving "illusory promises."
>
> Like consideration, exchange is a complex concept. To the problem of the executory exchange we may, within a narrower compass, apply the same general approach that we have applied to the problem of consideration as a whole. Here our "archetype" is the business trade of economic values in the form of goods, services, or money. To the degree that a particular case deviates from this archetype, the incentives to judicial intervention decrease, until a point is reached where relief will be denied altogether unless the attenuated element of exchange is reinforced, either on the formal side by some formal or informal satisfaction of the desiderata underlying the use of legal formalities, or on the substantive side by a showing of reliance or unjust enrichment, or of some special need for a regulation of the relations involved by private autonomy.

Lon Fuller, *Consideration and Form*, 41 COLUM. L. REV. 799, 816–18 (1941). Professor Fuller refers to an "illusory promise." The next case involves such a promise.

C. Changing Your Mind About Employment Agreements

We have seen various legal challenges to agreements to arbitrate. In the next case, *Hooters v. Phillips*, a case of overreaching by Hooters, an employee argues that an arbitration agreement with her employer is unenforceable because of the lack of consideration.

Hooters of America, Inc. v. Phillips

United States District Court, District of South Carolina
39 F. Supp. 2d 582 (1998)

Currie, J.

* * *

I. BACKGROUND

[From 1989 to 1996, Annette Phillips was employed by Hooters of Myrtle Beach (HOMB), a franchisee of Hooters of America, Inc. (HOA). She alleges that in June of 1996, she was sexually harassed by the brother of HOMB's principal owner. After complaining to her manager and being told to "let it go," she instead let her job go and retained an attorney. The attorney contacted HOA, alleging that the sexual harassment and HOMB's failure to address it violated Title VII of the Civil Rights Act of 1964. HOA responded that Ms. Phillips had executed a binding agreement to arbitrate and so was required to submit any claim to arbitration. HOA then initiated this legal proceeding.]

This is a declaratory judgment and Title VII case involving a former "Hooters Girl," who complains of sexual harassment by Hooter's managers and the brother of the company's CEO. * * * Unlike the party alignment in the typical employment discrimination case, the plaintiff here is the former employer, Hooters of America, Inc. ("hereinafter HOA") and the employee, Ms. Phillips, is the defendant (hereinafter "Phillips"). * * *[1]

The matter is before the court on HOA's "Motion for Preliminary Injunction," filed November 8, 1996, treated as a motion to compel arbitration under *9 U.S.C. § 3.* * * * For the reasons given below, the court finds that HOA's motion to compel arbitration * * * should be DENIED.

II. PROCEDURAL HISTORY

This case has a long and convoluted procedural history. * * *

The case commenced when HOA filed a complaint * * *, seeking a declaratory judgment, 28 U.S.C. § 2201, that the November 25, 1994, and April 23, 1995, arbitration agreements signed by Phillips were valid and enforceable. * * *

---

[1] Collectively the two defendants, HOA and HOMB, will be referred to as "Hooters."

* * * The answer denied that Phillips had entered into an enforceable arbitration agreement covering her dispute with HOA. Phillips asserted that the agreements were neither knowingly nor voluntarily entered into, and were unconscionable adhesion contracts violative of public policy. Moreover, the answer asserted that the alleged arbitration agreements were not supported by adequate consideration and were illusory. * * *

III. HOA'S § 4 MOTION TO COMPEL ARBITRATION

* * *

Hooters points to the broad language of the arbitration clause executed by Phillips on two occasions:

> In consideration of the Company offering you employment and employing you, you and the company each agrees [sic] that, provided, when appropriate, the employee, complies with the company's open door policy and/or compliance resolution procedure, the employee and the company agree to resolve any claims pursuant to the company's rules and procedures for alternative resolution of employment-related disputes, as promulgated by company from time to time (the "Rules"). Company will make available or provide a copy of the rules upon written request of the employee.

* * *

Fulcher [a Hooters manager] testified (1) that each of his employees was required to hold the arbitration agreement at least five days before signing it in his presence and the presence of another witness; (2) that he told employees, including Phillips, that they should have the arbitration agreement reviewed by a lawyer, if they wished; (3) that he also informed employees they could decline to sign the arbitration agreement, but that they would not be eligible for further promotion; and (4) that he informed employees that the procedural rules to be used in arbitration, while not available at HOMB, were available by request in writing to a Divisional Vice-President. Unquestionably Phillips executed an arbitration agreement, dated November 25, 1994, that expressly covered sexual harassment claims. * * *

Phillips also challenges the arbitration agreement's validity on the separate ground that the agreement and Rules are illusory. Because in the present case no new consideration in tangible benefit (cash, a promotion, etc. . .) was advanced at the time of execution of the arbitration agreement, the question becomes whether the parties exchanged mutually binding promises that could serve as adequate consideration. It is hornbook contract law that in order for a promise to be enforceable against a promisor, the promisee must have given some consideration for the promise. An illusory contract is also regarded as "an apparent promise which makes performance optional with the promisor . . . is in fact no promise . . . ." Consideration is defined as a bargained for exchange whereby the promisor (here Hooters) receives some benefit or the promisee (here Phillips) suffers a detriment. *Gibson v. Neighborhood Health Clinics, Inc.,* 121 F.3d 1126 (7th Cir. 1997). In order for Phillips' agreement to be enforceable, there must be a detriment to Hooters or benefit to Phillips that was bargained for in exchange for Phillips' promise to arbitrate her statutory claims.

"Often, consideration for one party's promise to arbitrate is the other party's promise to do the same." Thus, in *Gibson* the Seventh Circuit found an arbitration agreement illusory and unenforceable where it was one-sided, and only the employee was bound to submit claims to arbitration. In contrast, in the present case Hooters executed an arbitration agreement that bound it to arbitrate disputes ("you and the company each agrees [sic] that . . . the employee and the company agree to resolve any claims pursuant to the company's rules and procedures for alternative resolution of employment-related disputes, as promulgated by the company from time to time. . ."). However, under the Rules, incorporated into the arbitration agreement, "These Rules and Procedures may be modified, in whole or in part, by the Company from time to time, without notice." Rule 24-1. Moreover, "the Company may cancel the Agreement and Procedure on 30 days written notice," but no termination authority is given to the employee. Rule 23-1.

The question is whether the imperfect mutuality of obligation expressed in the Rules vitiates Hooters' promise to arbitrate set forth in the agreement. The Fourth Circuit has recognized that a promise whereby the promisor "retained an unlimited right to decide later the nature or extent of her performance" is, "in law no promise." The court finds this principle applicable to the present situation. Here, it is clear that the obligations encompassed in the Rules dwarfed whatever promises were contained in the agreement. And even a casual inspection of the Rules yields that the obligations of the two parties are not in equilibrium. For example, under the Rules, an employee's claim would be considered "waived" if arbitration were not commenced within specified time limits, but no similar waiver provision applies to Hooters. Rule 2-3. Similarly, when the employee initiates a claim he must file a detailed "content of notice" settling forth the particulars of his claim, Rule 6-2, but Hooters is under no similar obligation. The employee's witnesses must be sequestered, Rule 13-5, but not Hooters' witnesses. Under the Rules, Hooters retains exclusive authority to compile the record of the proceeding. Rule 18-1. Moreover, although Hooters may vacate under 9 U.S.C. § 10 any award if it proves merely "by the preponderance of the evidence" that the arbitrator exceeded his powers, Rule 21-4, it is not clear under the Rules that employees have any authority to seek a review of any arbitration award. Several additional disparities in obligation are contained in the Rules, but the preceding examples should suffice to illustrate the point.

Upon review of the differing obligations set forth in the Rules, the court concludes that Hooters retained to itself an unfettered "right to decide later the nature or extent of [its] performance" by reserving the authority to modify the Rules, or terminate the agreement, at its choice, while denying the same to Phillips. The court finds the agreement and Rules illusory, and unenforceable under South Carolina law on that basis.

* * *

VII. CONCLUSION

IT IS THEREFORE ORDERED that Plaintiff's November 8, 1996, Motion for a Preliminary Injunction, treated by the court as a motion to compel arbitration pursuant to the Federal Arbitration Act, 9 U.S.C. § 4, is DENIED.

* * *

QUESTIONS AND NOTES

1. Questions about the facts of this case

    1.1. Was there a written arbitration agreement?

    1.2. Was Ms. Phillips employed by Hooters before she signed the arbitration agreement?

    1.3. Why did Ms. Phillips sign the arbitration agreement? Did she have to sign the agreement in order to keep her job? In order to be considered for promotion? Do you think that it was important to Ms. Phillips that Hooters was also agreeing to submit any claims that it might have against her to arbitration? Is determining what is important to Ms Phillips important to determining whether there was consideration for her promise to arbitrate?

1.4. Do you agree with the court's identification of the parties, *i.e.* Hooters as the "promisor"? Should we have added a "sic" after this statement?

1.5. Why did Hooters sign the arbitration agreement? What was the benefit to Hooters? Is that relevant? What was the detriment to Hooters? Is that relevant? Was there at least a peppercorn of detriment to Hooters in promising to arbitrate? If so, was it bargained for?

2. Questions about the law

2.1. Can a promise be consideration? If so, can a promise to arbitrate be consideration?

2.2. What is an illusory promise?

2.3. It is clear from the authorities cited in *Hooters* that an illusory promise is not consideration. *See also Restatement (Second) of Contracts* § 77. It is less clear what made Hooters' promise to arbitrate illusory. Why is Hooters' promise to arbitrate illusory?

2.4. Assume that Hooters had sued Ms. Phillips in the United States District Court for keeping her tips in violation of company rules. Could Ms. Phillips have compelled Hooters to submit the claim to arbitration?

2.5. The Hooters opinion states that "even a casual inspection of the Rules yields that the obligations of the two parties are not in equilibrium." What does this statement mean? Is it relevant in determining whether Hooters' promise to arbitrate was an illusory promise? Is it relevant to determining whether there was any consideration for the defendant's promise to arbitrate?

2.6. Markell hires Epstein to perform at UNLV's Annual Purim Party. Markell promises to pay $2400 and Epstein promises "I will show up and play at the Purim party unless I change my mind." Was Epstein's promise an illusory promise? Will that be relevant if Epstein does not show up and Markell sues him for breach of contract? Will that be relevant if Markell sends Epstein a certified letter stating that the deal is off and Epstein sues Markell for breach of contract?

2.7. Would your answer to question 2.6 change if Epstein's promise is changed to "I will play at the Purim Party unless I give you written notice at least two days before the Purim Party that I have changed my mind."?

3. Notes

3.1. The agreements recited consideration: "In consideration of the Company offering you employment . . . " This recital was of course false—Ms. Phillips was already employed. The district court opinion did not discuss the question whether a mere recital of consideration should be sufficient on the basis that the recital is a kind of legal formality, like a seal, that evidences an intent to contract. The *Restatement (Second) of Contracts* does discuss this question and concludes "a mere pretense of bargain does not suffice, as where there is a false recital of consideration." *Restatement (Second) of Contracts*, § 71, comment b.

3.2. In affirming this decision by the district court, the Fourth Circuit made no mention of illusory promises or lack of consideration. Its statement of holding was: "Because Hooters set up a dispute resolution process utterly lacking in the rudiments of even-handedness, we hold that Hooters breached its agreement [contract?] to arbitrate. Thus, we affirm the district court's refusal to compel arbitration." 173 F.3d 933, 935 (4th Cir. 1999). By focusing on the district court's discussion of consideration and illusory promises, the editors of this casebook omitted the extensive discussion of contracts of adhesion and public policy, which was covered earlier.

3.3. More recently, the Sixth Circuit in *Floss v. Ryan's Family Steak Houses, Inc.*, 211 F.3d 306 (6th Cir. 2000) held that an agreement to arbitrate between a third-party arbitration services provider (EDSI) and employee lacked consideration, stating:

> Where a promisor retains an unlimited right to decide later the nature or extent of his performance, the promise is too indefinite for

> legal enforcement. The unlimited choice in effect destroys the promise and makes it merely illusory.
>
> EDSI's illusory promise does not create a binding obligation. The purported arbitration agreement therefore lacks a mutuality of obligation. Without a mutuality of obligation, the agreement lacks consideration and, accordingly, does not constitute an enforceable arbitration agreement.
>
> Ryan's has pursued an acceptable objective in an unacceptable manner. An employer may enter an agreement with employees requiring the arbitration of all employment disputes, including those involving federal statutory claims. Yet an employer cannot seek to do so in such a way that leaves employees with no consideration for their promise to submit their disputes to arbitration. Here, we find that Floss and Daniels did not receive any consideration for their promise to arbitrate their disputes. We thus refuse to enforce their promise in favor of Ryan's.

211 F.3d at 315.

3.4. What is "mutuality of obligation"? Is it different from consideration? According to the Maine Supreme Court in *Zamore v. Whitten*, 395 A.2d 435, 443 n.3 (Me. 1978):

> The phrase "mutuality of obligation" has caused much confusion to courts and commentators over the years. Professor Corbin criticizes the expression for its tendency to connote a need for obligations equivalent in terms of detriment and value.
>
> In fact, mutuality embodies a particularized application of the consideration doctrine in the context of formation of a bilateral contract. In a bilateral contract, one promise is good consideration for another. If the promisee fails to give the required return promise, mutual obligations are not, in fact, created. It is less confusing, and equally accurate, however, to conclude that no contract exists due to the promisee's failure to give legally sufficient consideration.

3.5. While the Hooters case uses the phrase "mutuality of obligation," it does not use "bilateral/unilateral" terminology. Was Hooters' agreement with its employees a bilateral agreement? Is that important? Reconsider your answer after considering the next case, *Asmus v. Pacific Bell*, 999 P.2d 71 (Cal. 2000) (involving an employer's unilateral modification of a unilateral contract).

Asmus v. Pacific Bell (skip this case)
Supreme Court of California
999 P.2d 71 (2000)

CHIN, J.

We granted the request of the United States Court of Appeals for the Ninth Circuit for an answer to the following certified question of law, "Once an employer's unilaterally adopted policy—which requires employees to be retained so long as a specified condition does not occur—has become a part of the employment contract, may the employer thereafter unilaterally [terminate] the policy, even though the specified condition has not occurred?" We conclude the answer to the certified question is yes. An employer may unilaterally terminate a policy that contains a specified condition, if the condition is one of indefinite duration, and the employer effects the change after a reasonable time, on reasonable notice, and without interfering with the employees' vested benefits. * * *

In 1986, Pacific Bell issued the following "Management Employment Security Policy" (MESP): "It will be Pacific Bell's policy to offer all management employees who continue to meet our changing business expectations employment security through reassignment to and retraining for other management positions, even if their present jobs are eliminated. This policy will be maintained so long as there is no change that will materially affect Pacific Bell's business plan achievement."

In January 1990, Pacific Bell notified its managers that industry conditions could force it to discontinue its MESP. * * *

Nearly two years later, in October 1991, Pacific Bell announced it would terminate its MESP on April 1, 1992, so that it could achieve more flexibility in conducting its business and compete more successfully in the marketplace. That same day, Pacific Bell announced it was adopting a new layoff policy (the Management Force Adjustment Program) that replaced the MESP but provided a generous severance program designed to decrease management through job reassignments and voluntary and involuntary terminations. Employees who chose to continue working for Pacific Bell would receive enhanced pension benefits. Those employees who opted to retire in December 1991 would receive additional enhanced pension benefits, including increases in monthly pension and annuity options. Employees who chose to resign in November 1991 would receive these additional enhanced pension benefits as well as outplacement services, medical and life insurance for one year, and severance pay equaling the employee's salary and bonus multiplied by a percentage of the employee's years of service.

Plaintiffs are 60 former Pacific Bell management employees who were affected by the MESP cancellation. They chose to remain with the company for several years after the policy termination and received increased pension benefits for their continued employment while working under the new Management Force Adjustment Program. All but eight of them signed releases waiving their right to assert claims arising from their employment under the MESP or its termination.

Plaintiffs filed an action in federal district court against Pacific Bell and its parent company, Pacific Telesis Group, seeking declaratory and injunctive relief, as well as damages for breach of contract, breach of fiduciary duty, fraud, and violations of the Employee Retirement Income Security Act (ERISA). The parties filed countermotions for partial summary judgment before conducting discovery. The district court granted summary judgment in Pacific Bell's favor against the 52 plaintiffs who signed releases. In an unpublished opinion, the Ninth Circuit affirmed the district court's judgment in this respect.

The district court granted summary judgment on the breach of contract claim in favor of the eight plaintiffs who did not sign releases. It held that even if an employer had the right unilaterally to terminate a personnel policy creating a contractual obligation, that right would not apply in cases where the original employment policy incorporated a term for duration or conditions for rescission, absent stronger evidence of the employees' assent to the policy modification than their continued employment. The court concluded that Pacific Bell could not terminate its MESP unless it first demonstrated (paraphrasing the words of the MESP) "a change that will materially alter Pacific Bell's business plan achievement."

Thereafter, the parties entered into a stipulation providing in part that Pacific Bell "elected not to present any further evidence in this action with respect to the question of whether there has been 'a change that will materially alter Pacific Bell's business plan achievement' . . . and agreed that summary judgment may be entered in favor of the eight remaining Plaintiffs on the issue of liability for their claims of breach of contract by breach of the MES policy. . . ." On May 5, 1997, the district court entered an order approving the stipulation and entered judgment in plaintiffs' favor on the issue.

Pursuant to the parties' agreement, the court certified for interlocutory appeal the issue whether Pacific Bell breached the MESP, and the Ninth

Circuit accepted the interlocutory appeal. In a published opinion the Ninth Circuit stated its certification request and noted that our answer to the certified question would determine the remaining portion of the case pending before it. The court agreed to abide by our answer. * * *

In some cases, an employer adopts a no-layoff policy or provides employees with an employment security policy in order to earn the employees' loyalty in exchange for granting them job security. This exchange is fair and it may, depending on the facts, provide the basis for an enforceable unilateral contract, i.e., one in which the promisor does not receive a promise in return as consideration.

In a unilateral contract, there is only one promisor, who is under an enforceable legal duty. The promise is given in consideration of the promisee's act or forbearance. As to the promisee, in general, any act or forbearance, including continuing to work in response to the unilateral promise, may constitute consideration for the promise.[4]

As a Court of Appeal observed, "Of late years the attitude of the courts (as well as of employers in general) is to consider [employment security agreements] which offer additional advantages to employees as being in effect offers of a unilateral contract which offer is accepted if the employee continues in the employment, and not as being mere offers of gifts. They

---

[4]An employment contract in which the employer promises to pay an employee a wage in return for the employee's work is typically described as a unilateral contract. Scholars observe, however, that it is not always easy to determine whether an offer creates a unilateral or bilateral contract. . . . Indeed, the distinction between the contract types often exaggerates the importance of the particular bargain compelling performance without commitment. "In response to these concerns, the Restatement (Second) of Contracts has abandoned the terms 'unilateral' and 'bilateral,' without, however, abandoning the concepts behind them." . . . In the Restatement Second of Contracts, the unilateral contract is preserved in the phrase, "Where an offer invites an offeree to accept by rendering a performance and does not invite a promissory acceptance. . . ." (Rest.2d Contracts, § 45(1).)

Most legal scholars, however, prefer to rely on the traditional terminology to distinguish between the two types of offers and promises because the use of unilateral contract analysis has been growing in recent years, particularly in employment cases. (1 Corbin on Contracts, *supra*, § 1.23, p. 95.) As one scholar observed, "Sometimes innovation does not take the form of a new substantive rule but rather of a new perspective on the problem reflected in the substitution of a new terminology or analysis for a traditional one. For example, the Restatement (Second) abandons the terms 'unilateral' and 'bilateral' as descriptive of contracts. . . . There is no way to assess the extent to which such innovations in terminology and analysis portend innovations of substance." (Farnsworth, *Ingredients in the Redaction of the Restatement (Second) of Contracts* (1981) 81 Colum. L. Rev. 1, 5-6, fns. omitted.) In this case, we retain the distinction between unilateral and bilateral contracts.

make the employees more content and happier in their jobs, cause the employees to forego their rights to seek other employment, assist in avoiding labor turnover, and are considered of advantage to both the employer and the employees." (Chinn v. China Nat. Aviation Corp. (1955) 138 Cal. App. 2d 98, 99–100, 291 P.2d 91.) * * *

The parties agree that California law permits employers to implement policies that may become unilateral implied-in-fact contracts when employees accept them by continuing their employment. We do not further explore the issue in the context here, although we note that whether employment policies create unilateral contracts will be a factual question in each case. The parties here disagree on how employers may terminate or modify a unilateral contract that has been accepted by the employees' performance. Plaintiffs assert that Pacific Bell was not entitled to terminate its MESP until it could demonstrate a change materially affecting its business plan, i.e., until the time referred to in a clause in the contract. Pacific Bell asserts that because it formed the contract unilaterally, it could terminate or modify that contract as long as it did so after a reasonable time, gave affected employees reasonable notice, and did not interfere with the employees' vested benefits (e.g., pension and other retirement benefits). Even if we were to require additional consideration, Pacific Bell contends it gave that consideration by offering enhanced pension benefits to those employees who chose to remain with the company after the modification took effect. Both parties rely on cases from other jurisdictions to support their respective positions.

Plaintiffs contend that Pacific Bell gave no valid consideration to bind the proposed MESP termination and subsequent modification. According to plaintiffs, when Pacific Bell unilaterally terminated the contract to create a new contract with different terms, it left its employees with no opportunity to bargain for additional benefits or other consideration. The parties' obligations were unequal, and hence, there was no mutuality of obligation for the change.

We disagree. The general rule governing the proper termination of unilateral contracts is that once the promisor determines after a reasonable time that it will terminate or modify the contract, and provides employees with reasonable notice of the change, additional consideration is not required. The mutuality of obligation principle requiring new consideration for contract termination applies to bilateral contracts only. In the unilateral contract context, there is no mutuality of obligation. For an effective modification, there is consideration in the form of continued employee services. Here, Pacific Bell replaced its MESP with a subsequent layoff policy. Plaintiffs' continued employment constituted acceptance of the offer of the modified unilateral contract. As we have observed, a rule requiring separate consideration in addition to continued employment as a limitation on the ability to terminate or modify an employee security agreement would contradict the general principle that the law will not concern itself with the adequacy of consideration.

The corollary is also true. Just as employers must accept the employees' continued employment as consideration for the original contract terms, employees must be bound by amendments to those terms, with the availability of continuing employment serving as adequate consideration from the employer. When Pacific Bell terminated its original MESP and then offered continuing employment to employees who received notice and signed an acknowledgment to that effect, the employees accepted the new terms, and the subsequent modified contract, by continuing to work. Continuing to work after the policy termination and subsequent modification constituted acceptance of the new employment terms.

Plaintiffs alternatively claim that Pacific Bell's MESP would be an illusory contract if Pacific Bell could unilaterally modify it. Plaintiffs rely on the rule that when a party to a contract retains the unfettered right to terminate or modify the agreement, the contract is deemed to be illusory.

Plaintiffs are only partly correct. Scholars define illusory contracts by what they are not. As Corbin observes, "if a promise is expressly made conditional on something that the parties know cannot occur, no real promise has been made. Similarly, one who states 'I promise to render a future performance, if I want to when the time arrives,' has made no promise at all. It has been thought, also, that promissory words are illusory if they are conditional on some fact or event that is wholly under the promisor's control and bringing it about is left wholly to the promisor's own will and discretion. This is not true, however, if the words used do not leave an unlimited option to the one using them. It is true only if the words used do not in fact purport to limit future action in any way." Thus, an unqualified right to modify or terminate the contract is not enforceable. But the fact that one party reserves the implied power to terminate or modify a unilateral contract is not fatal to its enforcement, if the exercise of the power is subject to limitations, such as fairness and reasonable notice.

As Pacific Bell observes, the MESP was not illusory because plaintiffs obtained the benefits of the policy while it was operable. In other words, Pacific Bell was obligated to follow it as long as the MESP remained in effect. Although a permanent no-layoff policy would be highly prized in the modern workforce, it does not follow that anything less is without significant value to the employee or is an illusory promise. As long as the MESP remained in force, Pacific Bell could not treat the contract as illusory by refusing to adhere to its terms; the promise was not optional with the employer and was fully enforceable until terminated or modified.

Under contract theory, an employer may terminate a unilateral contract of indefinite duration, as long as its action occurs after a reasonable time, and is subject to prescribed or implied limitations, including reasonable notice and preservation of vested benefits. The facts clearly show that employees enjoyed the benefits of the MESP for a reasonable time period, and that Pacific Bell gave its employees reasonable and ample notice of its intent to terminate the MESP. The company also did not at any time interfere with employees' vested benefits in effecting the MESP termination. In addition, the employees accepted the company's modified policy by continuing to work in light of the modification. Therefore, in response to the Ninth Circuit's certification request, we conclude that we should answer as follows: An employer may terminate a written employment security policy that contains a specified condition, if the condition is one of indefinite duration and the employer makes the change after a reasonable time, on reasonable notice, and without interfering with the employees' vested benefits.

QUESTIONS

1. Questions about the facts of this case

   1.1. What is the contract in this case? Is the contract limited to MESP?

   1.2. Why did Pacific Bell terminate its MESP?

   1.3. Why did the plaintiffs continue to work for Pacific Bell "for several years after the policy termination"?

   1.4. Are our first three questions relevant to the question certified by the United States Court of Appeals for the Ninth Circuit?

2. Questions about the law

   2.1. If you represented Hooters in California, would the *Asmus* case be helpful to you in determining how the California Supreme Court would rule in a case with facts similar to *Phillips v. Hooters*?

2.2. The California Supreme Court uses the phrase "terminate or modify." Did Pacific Bell "terminate" its contract with the plaintiffs or "modify" its contract with the plaintiffs? Does that matter?

2.3. Reconsider the California Supreme Court's consideration of unilateral contracts. Do you agree with the court's determination that the contract between Pacific Bell and the plaintiffs was a unilateral contract?

2.4. Was the determination that the employment contract between Pacific Bell and the plaintiffs was a unilateral contract important to the California Supreme Court's answer to the Ninth Circuit's certified question? Should the requirement for consideration for termination or modification of unilateral contracts be treated differently from termination or modification of bilateral contracts? The next two cases more directly consider the question of whether agreements to modify contracts require new consideration in order to be enforceable.

D. Changing Your Mind About Agreeing to Change the Deal

Alaska Packers' Ass'n v. Domenico
Circuit Court of Appeals, Ninth Circuit
117 F. 99 (1902)

Ross, Circuit Judge:

[This is a case involving the enforceability of an employer's written agreement to modify an employment agreement by increasing employees' minimum salary. The employer contends that this modification agreement is not enforceable because of lack of consideration. More specifically, the employer, Alaska Packers ("appellant"), owned a salmon packing factor in Alaska. The employees ("libelants"*) were California sailors and fishermen who contracted to work for appellant in Alaska during the salmon season for $50 per sailor or fisherman plus two cents for each red salmon he caught. The libelants arrived in Alaska in April; in late May, the libelants stopped worked and demanded an increase in salary. It was impossible for the appellant to find any replacement workers in Alaska or bring replacement workers from California in time to take full advantage of the short

*A libelant is the admiralty counterpart to a plaintiff.

salmon season. The appellant agreed in writing to increased the libelants' fixed salary from $50 to $100. The libelants returned to work. After the catch was in and the libelants returned to California, appellant refused to pay more than the amount originally promised. Libelants sued to enforce the agreement modifying the employment contract.]

* * *

On the trial in the court below, the libelants undertook to show that the fishing nets provided by the respondent were defective, and that it was on that account that they demanded increased wages. On that point, the evidence was substantially conflicting, and the finding of the court was against the libelants the court saying:

> The contention of libelants that the nets provided them were rotten and unserviceable is not sustained by the evidence. The defendants' interest required that libelants should be provided with every facility necessary to their success as fishermen, for on such success depended the profits defendant would be able to realize that season from its packing plant, and the large capital invested therein. In view of this self-evident fact, it is highly improbable that the defendant gave libelants rotten and unserviceable nets with which to fish. It follows from this finding that libelants were not justified in refusing performance of their original contract.'

The evidence being sharply conflicting in respect to these facts, the conclusions of the court, who heard and saw the witnesses, will not be disturbed.

* * * From the foregoing statement of the case, it will have been seen that the libelants agreed in writing, for certain stated compensation, to render their services to the appellant in remote waters where the season for conducting fishing operations is extremely short, and in which enterprise the appellant had a large amount of money invested; and, after having entered upon the discharge of their contract, and at a time when it was impossible for the appellant to secure other men in their places, the libelants, without any valid cause, absolutely refused to continue the services they were under contract to perform unless the appellant would consent to pay them more money. Consent to such a demand, under such circumstances, if given, was, in our opinion, without consideration, for the reason that it was based solely upon the libelants' agreement to render the exact services, and none other, that they were already under contract to render.

* * * The circumstances of the present case bring it, we think, directly within the sound and just observations of the supreme court of Minnesota in the case of King v. Railway Co., 61 Minn. 482, 63 N.W. 1105:

> No astute reasoning can change the plain fact that the party who refuses to perform, and thereby coerces a promise from the other party to the contract to pay him an increased compensation for doing that which he is legally bound to do, takes an unjustifiable advantage of the necessities of the other party. Surely it would be a travesty on justice to hold that the party so making the promise for extra pay was estopped from asserting that the promise was without consideration. A party cannot lay the foundation of an estoppel by his own wrong, where the promise is simply a repetition of a subsisting legal promise. There can be no consideration for the promise of the other party, and there is no warrant for inferring that the parties have voluntarily rescinded or modified their contract. The promise cannot be legally enforced, although the other party has completed his contract in reliance upon it.

In Lingenfelder v. Brewing Co., 103 Mo. 578, 15 S.W. 844, the court, in holding void a contract by which the owner of a building agreed to pay its architect an additional sum because of his refusal to otherwise proceed with the contract, said:

> It is urged upon us by respondents that this was a new contract. New in what? Jungenfeld was bound by his contract to design and supervise this building. Under the new promise, he was not to do anything more or anything different. What benefit was to accrue to Wainwright? He was to receive the same service from Jungenfeld under the new, that Jungenfeld was bound to tender under the original, contract. What loss, trouble, or inconvenience could result to Jungenfeld that he had not already assumed? No amount of metaphysical reasoning can change the plain fact that Jungenfeld took advantage of Wainwright's necessities, and extorted the promise of five per cent. on the refrigerator plant as the condition of his complying with his contract already entered into. Nor had he even the flimsy pretext that Wainwright had violated any of the conditions of the contract on his part. Jungenfeld himself put it upon the simple proposition that 'if he, as an architect, put up the brewery, and another company put up the refrigerating machinery, it would be a detriment to the Empire Refrigerating Company,' of which Jungenfeld was president. To permit plaintiff to recover under such circumstances would be to offer a premium upon bad faith, and invite men to violate their most sacred

contracts that they may profit by their own wrong. That a promise to pay a man for doing that which he is already under contract to do is without consideration is conceded by respondents. The rule has been so long imbedded in the common law and decisions of the highest courts of the various states that nothing but the most cogent reasons ought to shake it. (Citing a long list of authorities.) But it is 'carrying coals to Newcastle' to add authorities on a proposition so universally accepted, and so inherently just and right in itself. The learned counsel for respondents do not controvert the general proposition. Their contention is, and the circuit court agreed with them, that, when Jungenfeld declined to go further on his contract, the defendant then had the right to sue for damages, and not having elected to sue Jungenfeld, but having acceded to his demand for the additional compensation defendant cannot now be heard to say his promise is without consideration. While it is true Jungenfeld became liable in damages for the obvious breach of his contract, we do not think it follows that defendant is estopped from showing its promise was made without consideration. * * * What we hold is that, when a party merely does what he has already obligated himself to do, he cannot demand an additional compensation therefor; and although, by taking advantage of the necessities of his adversary, he obtains a promise for more, the law will regard it as nudum pactum, and will not lend its process to aid in the wrong.

* * *

It results from the views above expressed that the judgment must be reversed, and the cause remanded, with directions to the court below to enter judgment for the respondent, with costs. It is so ordered.

QUESTIONS AND NOTE

1. Question about the facts of this case

    1.1. Did the libelants argue that there was consideration for appellant's promise to pay more? If so, what?

    1.2. Why it is "highly improbable" that appellant gave libelants "rotten and unserviceable nets"? Should the condition of the nets be relevant to the enforceability of appellant's promise?

2. Questions about the law

2.1. If the court deciding *Alaska Packers* followed the *Restatement (Second)* § 71 definition of consideration—"a performance or return promise must be bargained for," what is appellant's strongest legal argument?

2.2. Consider the following hypothetical based on *Alaska Packers* posed by Professor David Snyder in a recent article critical of the case: "Say the seamen in Alaska stopped work and said to the boss 'We want our wages doubled. In return, we'll spread the word back in San Fran that you are a great employer.' The boss, with no other labor for thousands of miles, is just as stuck as in the actual Alaska Packers case, and he agrees to the sailors' proposal." David V. Snyder, *The Law of Contract and the Concept of Change: Public and Private Attempts to Regulate Modification, Waiver and Estoppel,* 1999 WISC. L. REV. 607, 614. How would Professor Snyder's hypothetical be decided under our definitions of consideration?

3. Note

Professor Debora L. Threedy of University of Utah Law School has explored the historical and social background of the *Alaska Packers* case and concludes: "I confess from my first reading of the case I was skeptical about the reality of the traditional reading, doubting that Alaska Packers was ever at the mercy of the fishermen. Everything that I have since learned about the case has only deepened my skepticism." Debora L. Threedy, *A Fish Story:* Alaska Packers' Association v. Domenico, 2000 UTAH L. REV. 185, 197, n. 78.

Angel v. Murray

Supreme Court of Rhode Island
113 R.I. 482, 322 A.2d 630 (1974)

Roberts, C.J.

This is a civil action brought by Alfred L. Angel and others against John E. Murray, Jr., Director of Finance of the City of Newport, the city of Newport, and James L. Maher, alleging that Maher had illegally been paid the sum of $20,000 by the Director of Finance and praying that the defendant Maher be ordered to repay the city such sum. The case was heard by a justice of the Superior Court, sitting without a jury, who entered a judgment ordering Maher to repay the sum of $20,000 to the city of Newport. Maher is now before this court prosecuting an appeal.

The record discloses that Maher has provided the city of Newport with a refuse-collection service under a series of five-year contracts beginning in 1946. On March 12, 1964, Maher and the city entered into another such contract for a period of five years commencing on July 1, 1964, and terminating on June 30, 1969. The contract provided, among other things, that Maher would receive $137,000 per year in return for collecting and removing all combustible and noncombustible waste materials generated within the city.

In June of 1967 Maher requested an additional $10,000 per year from the city council because there had been a substantial increase in the cost of collection due to an unexpected and unanticipated increase of 400 new dwelling units. Maher's testimony, which is uncontradicted, indicates the 1964 contract had been predicated on the fact that since 1946 there had been an average increase of 20 to 25 new dwelling units per year. After a public meeting of the city council where Maher explained in detail the reasons for his request and was questioned by members of the city council, the city council agreed to pay him an additional $10,000 for the year ending on June 30, 1968. Maher made a similar request again in June of 1968 for the same reasons, and the city council again agreed to pay an additional $10,000 for the year ending on June 30, 1969.

The trial justice found * * * that Maher was not entitled to extra compensation because the original contract already required him to collect all refuse generated within the city and, therefore, included the 400 additional units. The trial justice further found that these 400 additional units were within the contemplation of the parties when they entered into the contract. It appears that he based this portion of the decision upon the rule that Maher had a preexisting duty to collect the refuse generated by the 400 additional units, and thus there was no consideration for the two additional payments.

* * *

As previously stated, the city council made two $10,000 payments. The first was made in June of 1967 for the year beginning on July 1, 1967, and ending on June 30, 1968. Thus, by the time this action was commenced in October of 1968, the modification was completely executed. That is, the money had been paid by the city council, and Maher had collected all of the refuse. * * *

It is generally held that a modification of a contract is itself a contract, which is unenforceable unless supported by consideration. In *Rose v. Daniels,* 8 R. I. 381 (1866), this court held that an agreement by a debtor with a creditor to discharge a debt for a sum of money less than the amount due is unenforceable because it was not supported by consideration.

Rose is a perfect example of the preexisting duty rule. Under this rule an agreement modifying a contract is not supported by consideration if one of the parties to the agreement does or promises to do something that he is legally obligated to do or refrains or promises to refrain from doing something he is not legally privileged to do. In *Rose* there was no consideration for the new agreement because the debtor was already legally obligated to repay the full amount of the debt.

* * *

The primary purpose of the preexisting duty rule is to prevent what has been referred to as the "hold-up game." A classic example of the "hold-up game" is found in *Alaska Packers' Ass'n v. Domenico,* 117 F. 99 (9th Cir. 1902). There 21 seamen entered into a written contract with Domenico to sail from San Francisco to Pyramid Harbor, Alaska. They were to work as sailors and fishermen out of Pyramid Harbor during the fishing season of 1900. The contract specified that each man would be paid $50 plus two cents for each red salmon he caught. Subsequent to their arrival at Pyramid Harbor, the men stopped work and demanded an additional $50. They threatened to return to San Francisco if Domenico did not agree to their demand. Since it was impossible for Domenico to find other men, he agreed to pay the men an additional $50. After they returned to San Francisco, Domenico refused to pay the men an additional $50. The court found that the subsequent agreement to pay the men an additional $50 was not supported by consideration because the men had a preexisting duty to work on the ship under the original contract, and thus the subsequent agreement was unenforceable.

Another example of the "hold-up game" is found in the area of construction contracts. Frequently, a contractor will refuse to complete work under an unprofitable contract unless he is awarded additional compensation. The courts have generally held that a subsequent agreement to award additional compensation is unenforceable if the contractor is only performing work which would have been required of him under the original contract.

These examples clearly illustrate that the courts will not enforce an agreement that has been procured by coercion or duress and will hold the parties to their original contract regardless of whether it is profitable or unprofitable. However, the courts have been reluctant to apply the pre-existing duty rule when a party to a contract encounters unanticipated difficulties and the other party, not influenced by coercion or duress, voluntarily agrees to pay additional compensation for work already required to be performed under the contract.

* * *

Although the preexisting duty rule has served a useful purpose insofar as it deters parties from using coercion and duress to obtain additional compensation, it has been widely criticized as a general rule of law. With regard to the preexisting duty rule, one legal scholar has stated: "There has been a growing doubt as to the soundness of this doctrine as a matter of social policy. * * * In certain classes of cases, this doubt has influenced courts to refuse to apply the rule, or to ignore it, in their actual decisions. Like other legal rules, this rule is in process of growth and change, the process being more active here than in most instances. The result of this is that a court should no longer accept this rule as fully established. It should never use it as the major premise of a decision, at least without giving careful thought to the circumstances of the particular case, to the moral deserts of the parties, and to the social feelings and interests that are involved. It is certain that the rule, stated in general and all-inclusive terms, is no longer so well-settled that a court must apply it though the heavens fall." 1A Corbin, [Contracts] § 171 [(1963)] * * *.

The modern trend appears to recognize the necessity that courts should enforce agreements modifying contracts when unexpected or unanticipated difficulties arise during the course of the performance of a contract, even though there is no consideration for the modification, as long as the parties agree voluntarily.

Under the Uniform Commercial Code, § 2-209(1), which has been adopted by 49 states, "[an] agreement modifying a contract [for the sale of goods] needs no consideration to be binding." Although at first blush this section appears to validate modifications obtained by coercion and duress, the comments to this section indicate that a modification under this section must meet the test of good faith imposed by the Code, and a modification obtained by extortion without a legitimate commercial reason is unenforceable.

The modern trend away from a rigid application of the preexisting duty rule is reflected by § 89D(a) of the American Law Institute's Restatement Second of the Law of Contracts, which provides: "A promise modifying a duty under a contract not fully performed on either side is binding (a) if the modification is fair and equitable in view of circumstances not anticipated by the parties when the contract was made * * *."

We believe that § 89D(a) is the proper rule of law and find it applicable to the facts of this case. It not only prohibits modifications obtained by coercion, duress, or extortion but also fulfills society's expectation that agreements entered into voluntarily will be enforced by the courts. Section 89D(a), of course, does not compel a modification of an unprofitable or unfair contract; it only enforces a modification if the parties voluntarily agree and if (1) the promise modifying the original contract was made before the contract was fully performed on either side, (2) the underlying circumstances which prompted the modification were unanticipated by the parties, and (3) the modification is fair and equitable.

* * *

The evidence, which is uncontradicted, reveals that in June of 1968 Maher requested the city council to pay him an additional $10,000 for the year beginning on July 1, 1968, and ending on June 30, 1969. This request was made at a public meeting of the city council, where Maher explained in detail his reasons for making the request. Thereafter, the city council voted to authorize the Mayor to sign an amendment to the 1954 contract which provided that Maher would receive an additional $10,000 per year for the duration of the contract. Under such circumstances we have no doubt that the city voluntarily agreed to modify the 1964 contract.

Having determined the voluntariness of this agreement, we turn our attention to the three criteria delineated above. First, the modification was made in June of 1968 at a time when the five-year contract which was made in 1964 had not been fully performed by either party. Second, although the 1964 contract provided that Maher collect all refuse generated within the city, it appears this contract was premised on Maher's past experience that the number of refuse-generating units would increase at a rate of 20 to 25 per year. Furthermore, the evidence is uncontradicted that the 1967–1968 increase of 400 units "went beyond any previous expectation." Clearly, the circumstances which prompted the city council to modify the

1964 contract were unanticipated.[4] Third, although the evidence does not indicate what proportion of the total this increase comprised, the evidence does indicate that it was a "substantial" increase. In light of this, we cannot say that the council's agreement to pay Maher the $10,000 increase was not fair and equitable in the circumstances.

It is clearly a contractual provision requiring the contractor to hold the city harmless and to defend it in any litigation arising out of the performance of his obligations under the contract, whether a result of affirmative action or some omission or neglect on the part of Maher or his agents or employees. We are persuaded that the portion of sec. 2(a) specifically referred to by the court refers to losses resulting to Maher from some action or omission on the part of his own agents or employees. It cannot be disputed, however, that any losses that resulted from an increase in the cost of collecting from the increased number of units generating refuse in no way resulted from any action on the part of either Maher or his employees. Rather, whatever losses he did entail by reason of the requirement of such extra collection resulted from actions completely beyond his control and thus unanticipated.

The judgment appealed from is reversed, and the cause is remanded to the Superior Court for entry of judgment for the defendants.

QUESTIONS AND NOTE

1. Questions about the facts of this case

   1.1. Who agreed to make the additional payments to Maher?

---

[4]The trial justice found that sec. 2(a) of the 1964 contract precluded Maher from recovering extra compensation for the 400 additional units. Section 2(a) provided: "*The Contractor, having made his proposal after his own examinations and estimates, shall take all responsibility for, and bear, any losses resulting to him in carrying out the contract;* and shall assume the defence of, and hold the City, its agents and employees harmless from all suits and claims arising from the use of any invention, patent, or patent rights, material, labor or implement, by or from any act, omission or neglect of, the Contractor, his agents or employees, in carrying out the contract." (Emphasis added). The trial justice, quoting the italicized portion of sec. 2(a), found that this section required that any losses incurred in the performance of the contract were Maher's responsibility. In our opinion, however, the trial justice overlooked the thrust of sec. 2(a) when read in its entirety.

1.2. Why did the city agree to make the additional payments to Maher? Is that relevant to the court's decision?

1.3. Under the 1964 contract, was Maher legally obligated to collect refuse from the 400 additional units? Should that be relevant to the court's decision?

2. Questions about the law

2.1. The *Murray* decision discusses the *Alaska Packers* case and the pre-existing duty rule. What was the holding in *Alaska Packers*? What is the pre-existing duty rule? Is the holding in *Murray* consistent with the holding in *Alaska Packers*? Consistent with the pre-existing duty rule?

2.2. The *Murray* case involves a question about the enforceability of a modification to a contract. (Didn't the *Hooters* case and the *Asmus* case also involve a contract modification?) Should courts treat the question of whether a contract modification is legally enforceable differently from the question of whether an agreement is legally enforceable?

2.3. *Murray* holding: A later decision of the Rhode Island Supreme Court, *Fondedile, S.A. v. C.E. Maguire, Inc.*, 610 A.2d 87, 92 (1992), cites the *Murray* decision for the following proposition: "parties to a contract can mutually assent to modify the contract if the modification does not violate the law or public policy and the modification is supported by adequate consideration." Is that an accurate summary of the *Murray* decision?

2.4. *Murray* reasoning: The court in *Murray* cites to and relies on the provisions in § 89 of the *Restatement (Second) of Contracts. Restatement (Second)* § 89(a) now states "A promise modifying a duty under a contract not fully performed on either side is binding (a) if the modification is fair and equitable in view of the circumstances not anticipated by the parties when the contract was made." Is the Rhode Island Supreme Court obligated to follow the statements in the *Restatement*?

2.5. Was the contract in *Murray* a bilateral or a unilateral contract? Was that important to the Rhode Island Supreme Court? Would it be important to the California Supreme Court that decided *Asmus*?

2.6. More *Murray* reasoning: Note that the court in *Murray* discusses § 2-209 of the Uniform Commercial Code. Is the Rhode Island Supreme Court obligated to follow the sections of the Uniform Commercial Code? Does the *Murray* case involve a sale of goods? If not, why does the court consider § 2-209 of the Uniform Commercial Code?

2.7. Modification of contracts for sale of goods: How does § 2-209 of the Uniform Commercial Code differ from *Restatement (Second)* § 89(a)? Apply § 2-209 to the following sale of goods problem: Ponoroff contracts to deliver thirty-three pounds of crayfish meat to Markell for $400. Ponoroff then discovers that catching crayfish and extracting crayfish meat is much harder than he expected. He asks Markell to modify the contract by reducing the quantity from thirty-three pounds to twenty-two pounds without reducing the price. Markell agrees. Markell later changes his mind. Is the modification agreement legally enforceable?

2.8. D owes C $3,200. The debt is due right now and undisputed. D and C agree that if D pays C $2,000 then C will release the rest of the debt. D pays C $2,000. Is the release agreement legally enforceable? Should it be?

2.9. Ponoroff (P) contracts with Markell (M) to perform at M's Las Vegas night club, The Bottoms Up Review, as the featured "dancer." Under the contract, P is to be paid $3,300. Just before the time advertised for P to perform, as the inebriated and impatient crowd is shouting for P, P tells M that he will not perform unless he is paid $4,000. M agrees to pay $4,000. P performs. M only pays P the original $3,300 contract price. Is M's promise to pay the additional $700 legally enforceable? Is this hypothetical distinguishable from *Alaska Packers*? From *Murphy*? From *Austin Instrument, Inc. v. Loral Corp., supra*, in which the court found the agreement to modify a contract unenforceable because of duress?

3. Note

Professor Robert Hillman of Cornell Law School is critical of the pre-existing duty rule and *Restatement (Second) of Contracts* § 89(a):

> The approach of the Restatement (Second) of Contracts to modification enforceability suffers from a lack of clarity and fails to reflect the goals of

contract-modification law. The weaknesses of the approach stem both from adherence to the preexisting-duty doctrine–a doctrine which, most commentators agree, has outlived its usefulness–and from failure to apply the doctrine of economic duress directly to the modification problem.

The Restatement (Second) approach suffers from lack of clarity because of the difficulties of defining "unanticipated circumstances" and the broadness of the "fair and equitable," "honesty" and "justice requires" terminology. In addition, in light of the goals of contract modification law, the approach wrongly bars the enforcement of voluntary mocification in the absence of consideration, "unanticipated circumstances," or material reliance (unless the promisee reasonably or honestly believes in a defense to performance). The approach is also potentially harmful because the occurrence of "unanticipated circumstances" does not ensure the voluntariness of a modification and because the "fair and equitable" and "pretense of a bargain" language may be insufficient to direct courts to the issue of economic duress.

Proper application of each of the sections of the Restatement Second examined here (sections 73, 74, 89(a), and 89(c)) ultimately requires reference to the issues of duress. Accordingly, to cut through the morass of technical and unclear rules of the past, the duress doctrine should be applied to the problem of contract modification directly. Duress is a superior vehicle for analyzing the voluntariness of a modification because it requires inquiry into all of the factual elements that are probative of the issue. Undoubtedly, courts will face difficult decisions in weighing the various factors involved in the duress inquiry. Nevertheless, even if terms such as "unanticipated circumstances" were capable of clear definition and increased predictability of results, use of such tests would come at the expense of the appropriate broader inquiry–the voluntariness of modifications.

Robert A. Hillman, *Contract Modification Under the Restatement (Second) of Contracts*, 67 CORNELL L. REV. 680, 702–703 (1982).

The pre-existing duty rule is the end of our consideration of the contract law doctrine of consideration. What are the ends served by the contract law doctrine of consideration? Should courts and legislatures consider ending use of the doctrine of consideration? *See generally* James D. Gordon, III, *A Dialogue About the Doctrine of Consideration*, 75 CORNELL L. REV. 987 (1990), which begins by comparing consideration to Elvis* and concludes by quoting Cardozo.**

SECTION 9: CONSIDERATION SUBSTITUTES—ENFORCING AGREEMENTS AND PROMISES WITHOUT A BARGAINED-FOR LEGAL DETRIMENT

Even though courts and the legislatures have not yet heeded the call of Professor Gordon and others to abolish consideration as a legal requirement for the enforcement of agreements and promises, courts and legislatures have developed concepts that are alternatives to or substitutes for consideration.

A. Promises to "Pay" for Something that Happened Before the Promise

Recall that consideration is bargained for: "To constitute consideration, a performance or a return promise must be bargained for." *Restatement of Contracts (Second)* § 71(1). You can't bargain for someone to do something that she has already done—stuff that happened before a promise can't be "bargained for"; can't be consideration. Or, as the *Restatement* more elegantly puts it, " 'Past consideration' is inconsistent with the meaning of consideration stated in section 71." *Restatement (Second) of Contracts* § 86, cmt. a.

Assume, for example, that Oprah Winfrey recommends our contracts book during the Oprah Book Club feature on her show. That week, the book makes the *New York Times* best seller list. Markell and Ponoroff are so grate-

---

*The comparison of consideration to Elvis is in a footnote: "Consideration is to contract law as Elvis is to rock and roll—the King. Revisionists have questioned Elvis's greatness. They have wrestled with one disturbing issue: if Elvis is so great, how come he is buried in his own back yard—like a hamster." *Id.* at 987, fn 3.

**Professor Gordon's Cardozo quote is not exactly about either Elvis or consideration: "Benjamin Cardozo observed that the time has come 'when the old forms seem ready to decay and the old rules of action lose their binding force.' Perhaps someday contract law will more closely reflect common sense and modern commercial practice and business people will not have to seek legal advice reflecting irrational rules from centuries long past." *Id.* at 1006.

ful* that they promise to take Ms. Winfrey to Commander's Palace on all-you-can-eat night. Markell and Ponoroff later change their minds. Ms. Winfrey's sues, and Markell and Ponoroff contend that their promise should not be enforced because Ms. Winfrey's plugging the book, which occurred before their promise, cannot be consideration for their promise. Should the court enforce their promise nevertheless? Would the courts that decided the next two cases have enforced their promise?

Harrington v. Taylor
Supreme Court of North Carolina
225 N.C. 690, 36 S.E.2d 227 (1945)

Per Curium

The plaintiff in this case sought to recover of the defendant upon a promise made by him under the following peculiar circumstances:

The defendant had assaulted his wife, who took refuge in plaintiff's house. The next day the defendant gained access to the house and began another assault upon his wife. The defendant's wife knocked him down with an axe, and was on the point of cutting his head open or decapitating him while he was laying on the floor, and the plaintiff intervened, caught the axe as it was descending, and the blow intended for defendant fel upon her hand, mutilating it badly, but saving defendant's life.

Subsequently, defendant orally promised to pay the plaintiff her damages; but, after paying a small sum, failed to pay anything more. So, substantially, states the complaint.

The defendant demurred to the complaint as not stating a cause of action, and the demurrer was sustained. Plaintiff appealed.

The question presented is whether there was a consideration recognized by our law as sufficient to support the promise. The Court is of the opinion that however much the defendant should be impelled by common gratitude to alleviate the plaintiff's misfortune, a humanitarian act of this kind, voluntar-

*As the secretary who is typing this, I can tell you, Epstein is by nature an ungrateful sort—and he does not proof my work carefully, Erica.

ily performed, is not such consideration as would entitle her to recover at law.

The judgment sustaining the demurrer is

Affirmed.

Mills v. Wyman
Supreme Judicial Court of Massachusetts
20 Mass. (3 Pick.) 207 (1825)

This was an action of assumpsit brought to recover a compensation for the board, nursing, etc. of Levi Wyman, son of the defendant, from the 5th to the 20th of February 1821. The plaintiff then lived in Hartford, in Connecticut; the defendant, as Shrewsbury, in this county. Levi Wyman, at the time when the services were rendered, was about 25 years of age, and had long ceased to be a member of his father's family. He was on his return from a voyage at sea, and being suddenly taken sick at Hartford, and being poor and in distress, was relieved by the plaintiff in the manner and to the extent above stated. On the 24th of February, after all the expenses had been incurred, the defendant wrote a letter to the plaintiff, promising to pay him such expenses. There was no consideration for this promise, except what grew out of the relation which subsisted between Levi Wyman and the defendant, and Howe J., before whom the cause was tried in the Court of Common Pleas, thinking this not sufficient to support the action, directed a nonsuit. To this direction the plaintiff filed exceptions.

PARKER, Chief Justice.

General rules of law established for the protection and security of honest and fair-minded men, who may inconsiderably make promises without any equivalent, will sometimes screen men of a different character from engagements which they are bound in *foro conscientiae* to perform. This is a defect inherent in all human systems of legislation. The rule that a mere verbal promise, without any consideration, cannot be enforced by action, is universal in its application, and cannot be departed from to suit particular cases in which a refusal to perform such a promise may be disgraceful.

The promise declared on in this case appears to have been made without any legal consideration. The kindness and services toward the sick son of the defendant were not bestowed at his request. The son was in no respect under the care of the defendant. He was twenty-five years old, and had long left his father's family. On his return from a foreign country he fell sick among strangers, and the plaintiff acted the part of the good Samaritan, giving him shelter and comfort until he died. The defendant, his father, on being informed of this event, influenced by transient feeling of gratitude, promises in writing to pay the plaintiff for the expenses he had incurred.* But he has determined to break this promise, and is willing to have his case appear on record as a strong example of particular injustice sometimes necessarily resulting from the operation of general rules.

It is said a moral obligation is sufficient consideration to support an express promise; and some authorities lay down the rule thus broadly; but upon examination of the case we are satisfied that the universality of the rule cannot be supported, and that there must have been some pre-existing obligation, which has become inoperative by positive law, to form a basis for an effective promise. The cases of debts barred by the statute of limitations, of debts incurred by infants, of debts of bankrupts, are generally put for illustration of the rule. Express promises founded on such pre-existing equitable obligations may be enforced; there is a good consideration for them; they merely remove an impediment created by law to the recovery of debts honestly due, but which public policy protects the debtors from being compelled to pay. In all these cases there was originally a quid pro quo; and according to the principle of natural justice the party receiving ought to pay; but the legislature has said he shall not be coerced; then comes the promise to pay the debt that is barred, the promise of the man to pay the debt of the infant, of the discharged bankrupt to restore to his creditor what by the law he has lost. In all these cases there is a moral obligation founded upon

*The letter is not reproduced in the opinion. Through some nice detective work, Dr. Watson found the letter and reproduced it in his article on *Mills v. Wyman*:

> Dear Sir:
>
> I received a line from you relating to my Son Levi's sickness and requesting me to come up and see him, but as the going is very bad I cannot come up at the present, but I wish you to take all possible care of him and if you cannot have him at your house I wish you to remove him to some convenient place and if her cannot satisfy you for it I will.
>
> I want that you should write me again immediately how he does and greatly oblige your most obedient servant
>
> Seth Wyman Feb 24th 1821.

Geoffrey R. Watson, *In the Tribunal of Conscience: Mills v. Wyman Reconsidered*, 71 TUL. L. REV. 1749, 1758 (1997). Eds.

an antecedent valuable consideration. These promises therefore have a sound legal basis. They are not promises to pay something for nothing; not naked pacts; but the voluntary revival or creation of obligation which before existed in natural law, but which had been dispensed with, not for the benefit of the party obliged solely, but principally for the public convenience. If moral obligation, in its fullest sense, is a good substratum for an express promise, it is not easy to perceive why it is not equally good to support an implied promise. What a man ought to do, generally he ought to be made to do, whether he promise or refuse. But the law of society has left most of such obligations to the *interior* forum, as the tribunal of conscience has been aptly called. Is there not a moral obligation upon every son who has become affluent by means of the education and advantages bestowed upon him by his father, to relieve that father from pecuniary embarrassment, to promote his comfort, and happiness, and even to share with him his riches, if thereby he will be made happy? And yet such a son may, with impunity, leave such a father in any degree of penury above that which will expose the community in which he dwells, to the danger of being obliged to preserve him from absolute want. Is not a wealthy father under strong moral obligation to advance the interest of an obedient, well disposed son, to furnish him with the means of acquiring and maintaining a becoming rank in life, to rescue him from the horrors of debt incurred by misfortune? Yet the law will uphold him in any degree of parsimony, short of that which would reduce his son to the necessity of seeking public charity.

Without doubt there are great interests of society which justify withholding the coercive arm of the law from these duties of imperfect obligation, as they are called; imperfect, not because they are less binding upon the conscience than those which are called perfect, but because the wisdom of the social law does not impose sanctions upon them.

A deliberate promise in writing, made freely and without any mistake, one which may lead the party to whom it is made into contracts and expenses, cannot be broken without a violation of moral duty. But if there was nothing paid or promised for it, the law, perhaps wisely, leaves the execution of it to the conscience of him who makes it. It is only when the party making the promise gains something, or he to whom it is made loses something, that the law gives the promise validity. And in the case of a promise of an adult to pay the debt of the infant, of the debtor discharged by the statute of limitations or bankruptcy, the principle is preserved by looking back to the origin of the transaction, where an equivalent is to be found. An exact equivalent is not required by the law; for there being a consideration, the parties are left to estimate its value; though here the courts of equity will step in to relieve from gross inadequacy between the consideration and the promise.

These principles are deduced from the general current of decided cases upon the subject, as well as from the known maxims of the common law. The general position, that moral obligation is a sufficient consideration for an express promise, is to be limited in its application to cases where at some time or other a good or valuable consideration has existed.

* * *

For the foregoing reasons, we are all of the opinion that the nonsuit directed by the Court of Common Pleas was right, and that judgment be entered thereon for the costs of the defendant.

QUESTIONS AND NOTES

1. Questions about the facts of this case

   1.1. Who is suing whom for what?

   1.2. Why did the plaintiff Mills take care of Levi Wyman? Was he a doctor? Was he expecting to be paid?

   1.3. Why didn't Mills sue Levi Wyman's estate? Why did Mills sue Seth Wyman, Levi's father?

   1.4. Did Mills continue to take care of Levi Wyman after receiving the letter from the defendant? Is that important to the court's decision?

2. Questions about the law

   2.1. Did Chief Justice Parker conclude that Seth Wyman was morally obligated to pay the plaintiff for taking care of his son? What is the basis for any such moral obligation?

   2.2. Should Parker, C.J. have ruled that Seth Wyman's promise to pay Mills for the costs that Mills incurred in taking care of Seth's son was legally enforceable? Could Parker, C.J. have so ruled? Would Judge Judy, TV. J, have so ruled?

   2.3. Is there a pre-existing duty issue in this case? Why not?

3. Notes

3.1. Here's one writer's view of *Mills*:

> Many lawyers remember great common-law cases more for their facts than their reasoning. Ask a lawyer about the holding of *Mills v. Wyman* and you probably get a blank look. Ask if the lawyer remembers the case about father promising to pay the Good Samaritan for caring for the sick son, and you may get a smile of recognition. * * * Everyone remembers the facts; no one remembers the holding.
>
> For *Mills*, perhaps that is the way it should be. The rule in the case is eminently forgettable: it is as incoherent as it is inefficient. It will be a dead letter in another hundred years. But the facts of the case are memorable. Indeed, the story told by Justice Parker—Seth's hasty promise in a fleeting moment of gratitude, the death of Levi Wyman, Seth's willingness to stand up in court and be counted as a scoundrel—is more compelling than the story told by the surviving documents, in which Seth makes no promise, Levi does not die, and Seth deserves to win. For the law teacher, the reported facts stand as a morality play for lawyers and as a reminder of the limits of the profession. The mythical facts of Mills are an important part of our legal culture.

Geoffrey R. Watson, *In the Tribunal of Conscience:* Mills v. Wyman *Reconsidered,* 71 TUL. L. REV. 1749, 1806 (1997).

3.2. Lord Mansfield, Lord Chief Justice from 1756 to 1788 of the King's Bench, and a giant figure in the development of the commercial law in England, authored several opinions advancing the view that the moral obligation associated with any *written* agreement ought to serve as a sufficient basis to make that agreement enforceable. *See, e.g., Hawkes v. Saunders,* 1 Cowper 289, 98 Eng. Rep. 1091 (K.B. 1782). He regarded the existence of the writing as a suitable substitute for the evidentiary and cautionary functions purportedly served by the doctrine of consideration or, in early time, the seal. However, by Mansfield's time, the requirement of consideration was too deeply embedded in the common law to be uprooted, although it was not until 1840 that moral obligation alone was eliminated in England as satisfying the requirement of a good consideration for a promise. *See Eastwood v. Kenyon, 11 Ad. & E. 438, 113 Eng. Rep. 482.* As the decisions in *Harrington* and *Mills* illustrate, courts in this country were also skeptical of accepting moral obligation as a sufficient basis for enforcement of a promise. In *Manwill v. Oyler*, 361 P.2d 177, 178 (1961), the Utah Supreme Court expressed the generally-held sentiment that "if a mere moral, as distinguished from a legal, obligation were recognized as a valid consideration for a contract, that would practically erode to the vanishing point the necessity for finding a consideration" in the first place. Clearly, Chief Justice Parker in *Mills* was bothered by the defendant's abnegation of his promise, indicating his apparent disbelief that Wyman was "willing to have his case appear on record." How much of a deterrent do you suppose this form of shaming is likely to be in the case of persons already inclined to avoid their promises because of the technical absence of consideration?

3.3. The court in *Mills* makes reference to three circumstances in which the law has long recognized exceptions to the rule that past consideration is not good consideration: (1) a promise reviving a previously legally enforceable obligation now barred by an applicable limitations period, (2) a promise to pay an obligation rendered discharged by insolvency, and (3) a promise to pay an obligation incurred by an infant. The enforceability of the first type of promise—reviving an earlier enforceable obligation—is now recognized in *Restatement (Second) of Contracts* § 82, although many states also require a writing as a condition to the enforceability of such promises. *See, e.g., Manwill v. Oyler, supra.* As for the second type of promise, Section 83 of *Restatement (Second) of Contracts* provides that an express promise to pay all or part of a debt discharged in bankruptcy is binding. Since 1978, however, the matter has been preempted by the federal Bankruptcy Code, which expressly makes promises to repay a discharged debt unenforceable. On the other hand, agreements (called "reaffirmations") by a bankruptcy debtor to reinstate personal liability for debts that would otherwise be subject to the discharge may, subject to certain stringent conditions, be binding provided that they are entered into and approved by the court *prior* to the entry of the discharge in bankruptcy. *See Bankruptcy Code* §§ 524(c) & (d). In addition, purely *voluntary* repayment of discharged debts is permitted under the bankruptcy law. *See Bankruptcy Code* § 524(f). Finally, as to the third type of promise, modern courts continue to recognize that a minor with the power to avoid by disaffirmance his contractual obligations may, upon reaching the age of majority and without the requirement of new consideration, make a new enforceable undertaking to perform his duties under the contract. *See generally Restatement (Second) of Contracts* § 85.

3.4. The civil law has a little easier time with these cases, as illustrated by the following decision, bearing remarkable factual similarity to *Mills v. Wyman*, but decided under the Louisiana Civil Code rather than the common law.

Thomas v. Bryant
Court of Appeal of Louisiana, Second Circuit
639 So. 2d 378 (1994)

Brown, J.

Plaintiff, Jerald Thomas, instituted this action to collect a promissory note. Defendant, Myles Bryant, admitted his signature as co-maker of the note but claimed lack of consideration, fraud and nonperformance. Bryant appeals the trial court's judgment for plaintiff. We affirm.

FACTS

Myles and Theresa Bryant, husband and wife, jointly executed a promissory note for $5750 payable to Jerald Thomas on February 22, 1989. At that time, David Thomas, the 21-year-old son of Jerald Thomas and Theresa Bryant, was in Charter Forest Hospital because of alcohol and drug abuse problems. The amount of the note represented one-half of the medical bill owed to Charter Forest Hospital.

On November 28, 1989, Thomas filed suit against Myles and Theresa Bryant, seeking payment of the note, together with interest and attorney fees. Though married when the note was executed, defendant, Myles Bryant, and David's mother, Theresa Bryant, separated and at the time of trial were divorced. Myles Bryant answered plaintiff's petition asserting lack of consideration * * *

A default judgment was rendered against Theresa Bryant on April 2, 1990. Thomas successfully moved for summary judgment against Myles

Bryant. This court granted a writ to review the summary judgment decision. The trial court's judgment was reversed and the case remanded for trial because material issues of fact remained unresolved. *Thomas v. Bryant,* 597 So.2d 1065 (La. App. 2d Cir. 1992). Trial was held on January 15, 1993.

DISCUSSION

CAUSE

Plaintiff initially carried his burden of proof when Bryant admitted his signature as co-maker of the promissory note. As between the parties to the instrument, however, Bryant could assert all defenses available in a contract action. *See Thomas v. Bryant, supra.* A civil obligation grants to the creditor the right to enforce its performance. Consideration for the civil obligation, in the context of a negotiable note, is what is received in return for the obligation. LSA-R.S. 10:3-408. An obligation cannot exist without a lawful cause. LSA-C.C. art. 1966. Cause is the reason a party enters into an obligation. LSA-C.C. art. 1967.

In this case, Bryant had no civil or legal duty to pay any part of the medical charges incurred by his adult stepson. Although he had no legal duty to pay, when Bryant executed the promissory note, he entered into a promise to pay half of these expenses. For this promise to be enforceable, consideration or a lawful cause must be shown. While a natural obligation is not judicially enforceable, it can serve as the cause or consideration for a civil obligation. LSA-C.C. art. 1761.

The Louisiana Civil Code does not define natural obligations, but states that they arise from circumstances in which the law implies a particular moral duty to render a performance. LSA-C.C. art. 1760; Litvinoff, The Law of Obligations § 2.2, 5 *Louisiana Civil Law Treatise* (1992). A moral duty is traditionally defined as a duty of conscience; a legal duty, on the other hand, is correlative of a right to demand a performance. Litvinoff, *supra*, § 2.2.

Not every moral duty will serve as the basis of a natural obligation. In order for a duty to rise to the level of a natural obligation, the following requirements must be present:

(1) The moral duty must be felt towards a particular person, not all persons in general.

(2) The person involved feels so strongly about the moral duty that he truly feels he owes a debt.

(3) The duty can be fulfilled through rendering a performance whose object is of pecuniary value.

(4) A recognition of the obligation by the obligor must occur, either by performing the obligation or by promising to perform. This recognition brings the natural obligation into existence and makes it a civil obligation.

(5) Fulfillment of the moral duty must not impair the public order.

Litvinoff, The Law of Obligations § 2.4, 5 *Louisiana Civil Law Treatise* (1992).

The issue of whether a natural obligation arises from a particular situation is raised only after a person has voluntarily rendered a performance or has promised to perform. Litvinoff, *supra*, § 2.6. If in performing or promising to perform, the person was obeying dictates of his conscience that prompted him to fulfill a strongly felt moral duty, the performance is valid and cannot be reclaimed or the promise is valid and is enforceable by the creditor. The person's belief in the existence of the moral duty is as important as its reality. *Id.*

Great discretion must be exercised by the courts in determining whether, in a given situation, a moral duty rises to the level of a natural obligation. *Id.*

When asked why he signed the note, Bryant testified that he did so because his friend and stepson, David Thomas, needed help. According to Bryant, when David was approximately three weeks into the treatment program, Thomas told Bryant that he could no longer afford to keep David in Charter Forest and that he would have to take his son out of treatment. Bryant stated that he executed the note in order to keep David in the treatment center. Bryant testified that he and Thomas agreed that Thomas would pay Charter Forest and that Bryant would reimburse him one-half of the cost of David's treatment. According to Bryant, he executed the note voluntarily, not out of any sense of obligation, financial or otherwise.

The trial court found that Bryant, David Thomas's friend and stepfather, specifically intended to fulfill a duty of natural justice and that this natural obligation was the legal cause for the note's execution.

* * *

Bryant testified that he executed the promissory note voluntarily and that he was willing to bear one-half the cost of David's treatment because David was his friend in addition to being his stepson. The trial court's conclusion that Bryant felt a moral duty to pay for David's treatment and that this moral duty met the requirements of a natural obligation (i.e. Bryant felt this duty was owed to David specifically; Bryant felt so strongly that he truly believed he owed a debt; the object of Bryant's performance, one-half of the cost of David's treatment for alcohol and drug addiction, has a pecuniary value; Bryant recognized his obligation by promising to perform (executing the promissory note); and fulfillment of Bryant's duty is not such that it would impair the public order) is reasonable, therefore not manifestly erroneous or clearly wrong.

* * *

CONCLUSION

For the reasons set forth above, the judgment of the trial court is affirmed. Costs are assessed to defendant-appellant, Myles Bryant.

VICTORY, J., concurring.

I am not persuaded that Mr. Bryant was shown to have a natural obligation to help pay medical expenses for his stepson, David Thomas. However, he promised Mr. Thomas he would pay for half of the anticipated medical expenses by signing the note. Mr. Thomas reasonably relied on Bryant's written promise to his detriment by continuing David Thomas's treatment at Charter Forest Hospital. Thus, Bryant is liable on the note under La. Civ. Code article 1967 which reads in relevant part:

> A party may be obligated by a promise when he knew or should have known that the promise would induce the other party to rely on it to his detriment and the other party was reasonable in so relying.

Except as stated herein, I agree with the majority opinion.

Webb v. McGowin
Court of Civil Appeals of Alabama
27 Ala. App. 82, 168 So. 196 (1935)

BRICKEN, Presiding Judge.

This action is in assumpsit. The complaint as originally filed was amended. The demurrers to the complaint as amended were sustained, and because of this adverse ruling by the court the plaintiff took a non-suit, and the assignment of errors on this appeal are predicated upon said action or ruling of the court.

A fair statement of the case presenting the questions for decision is set out in appellant's brief, which we adopt.

> "On the 3d day of August, 1925, appellant while in the employ of the W. T. Smith Lumber Company, a corporation, and acting within the scope of his employment, was engaged in clearing the upper floor of mill No. 2 of the company. While so engaged he was in the act of dropping a pine block from the upper floor of the mill to the ground below; this being the usual and ordinary way of clearing the floor, and it being the duty of the plaintiff in the course of his employment to so drop it. The block weighed about 75 pounds.
>
> "As appellant was in the act of dropping the block to the ground below, he was on the edge of the upper floor of the mill. As he started to turn the block loose so that it would drop to the ground, he saw J. Greeley McGowin, testator of the defendants, on the ground below and directly under where the block would have fallen had appellant turned it loose. Had he turned it loose it would have struck McGowin with such force as to have caused him serious bodily harm or death. Appellant could have remained safely on the upper floor of the mill by turning the block loose and allowing it to drop, but had he done this the block would have fallen on McGowin and cause him serious injuries or death. The only safe and reasonable way to prevent this was for appellant to hold to the block and divert its direction in falling from the place where McGowin was standing and the only safe way to divert it so as to prevent its coming into contact with McGowin was for appellant to fall with it to the ground below. Appellant did this, and by holding to the block and falling with it to the ground below, he diverted the course of its fall in such way that McGowin was not injured. In thus preventing the injuries to McGowin appellant himself received serious bodily injuries, resulting in his right leg

being broken, the heel of his right foot torn off and his right arm broken. He was badly crippled for life and rendered unable to do physical or mental labor.

"On September 1, 1925, in consideration of appellant having prevented him from sustaining death or serious bodily harm and in consideration of the injuries appellant had received, McGowin agreed with him to care for and maintain him for the remainder of appellant's life at the rate of $15 every two weeks from the time he sustained his injuries to and during the remainder of appellant's life; it being agreed that McGowin would pay this sum to appellant for his maintenance. Under the agreement McGowin paid or caused to be paid to appellant the sum so agreed on up until McGowin's death on January 1, 1934. After his death the payments were continued to and including January 27, 1934, at which time they were discontinued. Thereupon plaintiff brought suit to recover the unpaid installments accruing up to the time of the bringing of the suit.

"The material averments of the different counts of the original complaint and the amended complaint are predicated upon the foregoing statement of facts."

In other words, the complaint as amended averred in substance: (1) That on August 3, 1925, appellant saved J. Greeley McGowin, appellee's testator, from death or grievous bodily harm; (2) that in doing so appellant sustained bodily injury crippling him for life; (3) that in consideration of the services rendered and the injuries received by appellant, McGowin agreed to care for him the remainder of appellant's life, the amount to be paid being $15 every two weeks; (4) that McGowin complied with this agreement until he died on January 1, 1934, and the payments were kept up to January 27, 1934, after which they were discontinued.

The action was for the unpaid installments accruing after January 27, 1934, to the time of the suit.

The principal grounds of demurrer to the original and amended complaint are: (1) It states no cause of action; (2) its averments show the contract was without consideration; (3) it fails to allege that McGowin had, at or before the services were rendered, agreed to pay appellant for them; (4) the contract declared on is void under the statute of frauds.

1. The averments of the complaint show that appellant saved McGowin from death or grievous bodily harm. This was a material benefit to him of infinitely more value than any financial aid he could have received. Receiving

this benefit, McGowin became morally bound to compensate appellant for the services rendered. Recognizing his moral obligation, he expressly agreed to pay appellant as alleged in the complaint and complied with this agreement up to the time of his death; a period of more than 8 years.

Had McGowin been accidentally poisoned and a physician, without his knowledge or request, had administered an antidote, thus saving his life, a subsequent promise by McGowin to pay the physician would have been valid. Likewise, McGowin's agreement as disclosed by the complaint to compensate appellant for saving him from death or grievous bodily injury is valid and enforceable.

Where the promisee cares for, improves, and preserves the property of the promisor, though done without his request, it is sufficient consideration for the promisor's subsequent agreement to pay for the service, because of the material benefit received. * * *

In *Boothe v. Fitzpatrick,* 36 Vt. 681, the court held that a promise by defendant to pay for the past keeping of a bull which had escaped from defendant's premises and been cared for by plaintiff was valid, although there was no previous request, because the subsequent promise obviated that objection; it being equivalent to a previous request. On the same principle, had the promisee saved the promisor's life or his body from grievous harm, his subsequent promise to pay for the services rendered would have been valid. Such service would have been far more material than caring for his bull. Any holding that saving a man from death or grievous bodily harm is not a material benefit sufficient to uphold a subsequent promise to pay for the service, necessarily rests on the assumption that saving life and preservation of the body from harm have only a sentimental value. The converse of this is true. Life and preservation of the body have material, pecuniary values, measurable in dollars and cents. Because of this, physicians practice their profession charging for services rendered in saving life and curing the body of its ills, and surgeons perform operations. The same is true as to the law of negligence, authorizing the assessment of damages in personal injury cases based upon the extent of the injuries, earnings, and life expectancies of those injured.

In the business of life insurance, the value of a man's life is measured in dollars and cents according to his expectancy, the soundness of his body, and his ability to pay premiums. The same is true as to health and accident insurance.

It follows that if, as alleged in the complaint, appellant saved J. Greeley McGowin from death or grievous bodily harm, and McGowin subsequently agreed to pay him for the service rendered, it became a valid and enforceable contract.

2. It is well settled that a moral obligation is a sufficient consideration to support a subsequent promise to pay where the promisor has received a material benefit, although there was no original duty or liability resting on the promisor. * * * In the case of *State ex rel. Bayer v. Funk, supra,* [105 Or. 134, 199 P. 592] the court held that a moral obligation is a sufficient consideration to support an executory promise where the promisor has received an actual pecuniary or material benefit for which he subsequently expressly promised to pay.

The case at bar is clearly distinguishable from that class of cases where the consideration is a mere moral obligation or conscientious duty unconnected with receipt by promisor of benefits of a material or pecuniary nature. * * * Here the promisor received a material benefit constituting a valid consideration for his promise.

3. Some authorities hold that, for a moral obligation to support a subsequent promise to pay, there must have existed a prior legal or equitable obligation, which for some reason had become unenforceable, but for which the promisor was still morally bound. This rule, however, is subject to qualification in those cases where the promisor, having received a material benefit from the promisee, is morally bound to compensate him for the services rendered and in consideration of this obligation promises to pay. In such cases the subsequent promise to pay is an affirmance or ratification of the services rendered carrying with it the presumption that a previous request for the service was made. * * *

Under the decisions above cited, McGowin's express promise to pay appellant for the services rendered was an affirmance or ratification of what appellant had done raising the presumption that the services had been rendered at McGowin's request.

4. The averments of the complaint show that in saving McGowin from death or grievous bodily harm, appellant was crippled for life. This was part of the consideration of the contract declared on. McGowin was benefited. Appellant was injured. Benefit to the promisor or injury to the promisee is a sufficient legal consideration for the promisor's agreement to pay. * * *

5. Under the averments of the complaint the services rendered by appellant were not gratuitous. The agreement of McGowin to pay and the acceptance of payment by appellant conclusively shows the contrary.

6. The contract declared on was not void under the statute of frauds.

* * *

From what has been said, we are of the opinion that the court below erred in the ruling complained of; that is to say, in sustaining the demurrer, and for this error the case is reversed and remanded.

SAMFORD, Judge (Concurring)

The questions involved in this case are not free from doubt, and perhaps the strict letter of the rule, as stated by judges, though not always in accord, would bar a recovery by plaintiff, but following the principle announced by Chief Justice Marshall in *Hoffman v. Porter, Fed.Cas. No. 6,577,* 2 Brock. 156, 159, where he says, "I do not think that law ought to be separated from justice, where it is at most doubtful," I concur in the conclusions reached by the court.

Webb v. McGowin
Supreme Court of Alabama
168 So. 199 (1936)

Foster, J

We do not in all cases in which we deny a petition for certiorari to the Court of Appeals approve the reasoning and principles declared in the opinion, even though no opinion is rendered by us. But when the opinion of the Court of Appeals asserts important principles or their application to new situations, and it may be uncertain whether this court agrees with it in all respects, we think it advisable to be specific in that respect when the certiorari is denied. We think such a situation here exists.

Neither this court nor the Court of Appeals has had before it questions similar to those here presented.

The opinion of the Court of Appeals here under consideration recognized and applies the distinction between a supposed moral obligation of the promisor, based upon some refined sense of ethical duty, without material benefit to him, and one in which such a benefit did in fact occur. We agree with that court that if the benefit be material and substantial, and was to the person of the promisor rather than to his estate, it is within the class of material benefits which he has the privilege of recognizing and compensating either by an executed payment or an executory promise to pay. The cases are cited in that opinion. The reason is emphasized when the compensation is not only for the benefits which the promisor received, but also for the injuries either to the property or person of the promisee by reason of the service rendered.

Writ denied.

QUESTIONS AND NOTES

1. Questions about the facts of this case

   1.1. Was there a written promise in *Webb*?

   1.2. Why was plaintiff paid $15 every two weeks until January 27, 1934? Why did the payments stop on January 27, 1934?

   1.3. Can the facts of *Webb* be distinguished from the facts of *Mills*? Which, if any, of the factual differences explain the different legal result?

   1.4. Recall that in *Webb* the Alabama Court of Appeals reproduced the statement of facts from the appellant/plaintiff's brief. What were the grounds for the defendant's demurrers that were sustained by the trial court?

2. Questions about the law

   2.1. Did the Court of Appeals in *Webb* hold that there was an agreement to pay plaintiff $15 every two weeks? That there was consideration for such a promise?

   2.2. Would a court applying any of our definitions of consideration hold that such a promise was enforceable because of consideration?

   2.3. Both the Alabama Court of Appeals decision and the Alabama Supreme Court decision mention "material benefit." The Reporter to

Restatement (Second) of Contracts described section 86, set out below, as a "material benefit rule":*

§ 86 Promise for Benefit Received

(1) A promise made in recognition of a benefit previously received by the promisor from the promisee is binding to the extent necessary to prevent injustice.

(2) A promise is not binding under Subsection (1)

(a) if the promisee conferred the benefit as a gift or for other reasons the promisor has not unjustly enriched; or

(b) to the extent that its value is disproportionate to the benefit.

How would *Webb* be decided by a court applying this *Restatement* provision? How would *Mills* be decided by a court applying this *Restatement* provision? Is there a difference between *Webb* and *Mills* in terms of the circumstances under which the services were rendered? If so, does this help you reconcile the decisions? Can you reconcile *Webb* and *Harrington* on the same basis?

3. Notes

3.1 Professor Charles Fried, a Harvard law professor, describes the Alabama Court of Appeals decision in *Webb* as "a process of reasoning too strained to repeat." CHARLES FRIED, CONTRACT AS PROMISE 33 (1981). Do you agree?

3.2 In his widely-celebrated book, THE DEATH OF CONTRACT, written in 1974, Professor Grant Gilmore, pointing to the general direction being taken in the *Restatement (Second) of Contracts,* concluded that, "we might say that what is happening is that 'contract' is being reabsorbed into the mainstream of 'tort'." *Id.* at 95. As one of the primary illustrations of this trend, Professor Gilmore pointed to allowing enforcement of a promise made in recognition of a past benefit. He noted: "The principal thing is that *Restatement (Second)* gives overt recognition to an important principle whose existence *Restatement (First)* ignored and, by implication denied. By the time we get

---

*Robert Braucher, *Freedom of Contract and the Second Restatement*, 78 YALE L. J. 598, 615 (1969).

to Restatement (Third) it may well be that § 89A* will have flowered like Jack's bean-stalk in the same way that § 90 did between *Restatement (First)* and *Restatement (Second)*." *Id.* at 76.

3.3 Twenty-one years later, Professor Kastely offered the following evaluation of this prediction.:

This prediction has not proved true. Very few reported decisions since 1974 have even mentioned Section 86, and most of those references have been made only in passing, often in reference to contract actions barred by the statute of limitations. I have found only four reported decisions involving Section 86; in two, the courts found that Section 86 would not support enforcement of the promise. Moreover, the two cases holding that Section 86 might support enforcement of the promise involve situations that fit a traditional quasi-contract model**—one involved service rendered by a broker and another care provided by a sister. These cases do not represent movement toward the idea that "to prevent unjust enrichment, any benefit received by a defendant must be paid for unless it was clearly meant as a gift" as Gilmore suggested.

Following some initial expansion, many courts have domesticated the doctrines of promissory estoppel and promise for benefit received, making them compatible with classical contract theory, or at least much less of a threat to it. Most current versions of these doctrines offer little threat to the idea that no one should be liable for anything, at least not anything that she or he has not explicitly agreed to do. It seems that the pressures of contract ideology are so strong that, over time, they have reshaped the rebellious versions of these doctrines, fitting them into line with contract ideology.

Amy H. Kastely, *Cogs or Cyborgs, Blasphemy and Irony in Contract Theories*, 90 NW. U. L. REV. 132, 138–39 (1995).

---

*Section 89A, to which Professor Gilmore refers, became § 86 in the final draft of the *Restatement (Second)*. Eds.

**We take up the subject of "quasi contract" in Chapter 7. Eds.

B. Promissory Estoppel

1. Overview

Classical contract law was primarily concerned with protecting the promisee's expectation interest in an exchange transaction. The requirement of consideration, as we have seen, ensures that promises that are part of a bargained-for exchange will be enforceable. By the same token, mere reliance on a promise that was not part of an economic exchange was not cognizable in the eyes of the law; hence, the adage that gift promises are not enforceable. Nonetheless, there are circumstances where leaving a party who detrimentally changed her position in reliance on a promise without a remedy of any sort was perceived as unduly harsh. Accordingly, one of the most important developments in contract law over the course of the twentieth century was the evolution of the principle that, in an appropriate case, unbargained-for reliance may provide a suitable basis for enforcing a promise, even in a non-exchange transaction. This evolution culminated in the *Restatement (Second) of Contracts'* revision of § 90, which now provides:

> (1) *A promise which the promisor should reasonably expect to induce action or forbearance on the part of the promisee or a third person and which does induce such action or forbearance is binding if injustice can be avoided only by enforcement of the promise. The remedy granted for breach may be limited as justice requires.*

Compare this formulation with § 90 of the first *Restatement of Contracts*

> *A promise which the promisor should reasonably expect to induce action or forbearance of a definite and substantial character on the part of the promisee and which does induce such action or forbearance is binding if injustice can be avoided only by enforcement of the promise.*

Section 90 has been described as "perhaps the most radical and expansive development of this century in the law of promissory liability." *See* Charles L. Knapp, *Reliance in the Revised* Restatement: *The Proliferation of Promissory Estoppel*, 81 COLUM. L. REV. 52, 52 (1981). Reliance, or more properly, compensation for harm suffered as a consequence of reliance on a promise, plays a central role in the *Restatement (Second)*. Section 90 offers a mechanism whereby a purely gratuitous promise might be enforced. In fact, one might not unfairly regard reliance as a substitute for consideration in cases to which § 90 applies. Thus, § 90 has vastly expanded the potential scope of contractual responsibility to the point, at least according to one commentator, that it has "swallowed up the bargain principle" embodied in the doctrine of consideration. GRANT GILMORE, THE DEATH OF CONTRACT 77 (1974).

From where did this seemingly revolutionary doctrine arise? Professor Williston is generally given credit for coining the term "promissory estoppel" in the first edition of his famous Contracts treatise originally published in 1920. 1 WILLISTON ON CONTRACT § 139 (1st ed. 1920). Not surprisingly, Williston was instrumental in the incorporation of the doctrine of promissory estoppel into the first *Restatement of Contracts* in the form of § 90, quoted above. In Anglo/American jurisprudence, however, the roots of the doctrine go back to at least the nineteenth century, although, as we see in our first case, the courts were not always sure into what category of the law the doctrine belonged.

---

2. Historical Development

Ricketts v. Scothorn
Supreme Court of Nebraska
57 Neb. 51, 77 N.W. 365 (1898)

Sullivan, J.

In the district court of Lancaster county the plaintiff, Katie Scothorn, recovered judgment against the defendant, Andrew D. Ricketts, as executor of the last will and testament of John C. Ricketts, deceased. The action was based upon a promissory note, of which the following is a copy:

"May the first, 1891. I promise to pay to Katie Scothorn on demand, $2,000, to be at 6 per cent. per annum. J. C. Ricketts."

In the petition the plaintiff alleges that the consideration for the execution of the note was that she should surrender her employment as bookkeeper for Mayer Bros., and cease to work for a living. She also alleges that the note was given to induce her to abandon her occupation, and that, relying on it, and on the annual interest, as a means of support, she gave up the employment in which she was then engaged. These allegations of the petition are denied by the administrator. The material facts are undisputed. They are as follows: John C. Ricketts, the maker of the note, was the grandfather of the plaintiff. Early in May—presumably on the day the note bears date—he called on her at the store where she was working. What transpired between them is thus described by Mr. Flodene, one of the plaintiff's witnesses:

> "A. Well, the old gentleman came in there one morning about nine o'clock, probably a little before or a little after, but early in the morning, and he unbuttoned his vest, and took out a piece of paper in the shape of a note; that is the way it looked to me; and he says to Miss Scothorn, 'I have fixed out something that you have not got to work any more.' He says, none of my grandchildren work, and you don't have to.
>
> Q. Where was she?
>
> A. She took the piece of paper and kissed him, and kissed the old gentleman, and commenced to cry."

It seems Miss Scothorn immediately notified her employer of her intention to quit work, and that she did soon after abandon her occupation. The mother of the plaintiff was a witness, and testified that she had a conversation with her father, Mr. Ricketts, shortly after the note was executed, in which he informed her that he had given the note to the plaintiff to enable her to quit work; that none of his grandchildren worked, and he did not think she ought to. For something more than a year the plaintiff was without an occupation, but in September, 1892, with the consent of her grandfather, and by his assistance, she secured a position as bookkeeper with Messrs. Funke & Ogden. On June 8, 1894, Mr. Ricketts died. He had paid one year's interest on the note, and a short time before his death expressed regret that he had not been able to pay the balance. In the summer or fall of 1892 he stated to his daughter, Mrs. Scothorn, that if he could sell his farm in Ohio he would pay the note out of the proceeds. He at no time repudiated the obligation. We quite agree with counsel for the defendant that upon this evidence there was nothing to submit to the jury, and that a verdict should have been directed peremptorily for one of the parties. The testimony of Flodene and Mrs. Scothorn, taken together, conclusively establishes the fact that the note was not given in consideration of the plaintiff pursuing, or agreeing to pursue, any particular line of conduct. There was no promise on the part of the plaintiff to do, or refrain from doing, anything. Her right to the money promised in the note was not made to depend upon an abandonment of her employment with Mayer Bros., and future abstention from like service. Mr. Ricketts made no condition, requirement, or request. He exacted no quid pro quo. He gave the note as a gratuity, and looked for nothing in return. So far as the evidence discloses, it was his purpose to place the plaintiff in a position of independence, where she could work or remain idle, as she might choose. The abandonment of Miss Scothorn of her position as bookkeeper was altogether voluntary. It was not an act done in fulfillment of any contract obligation assumed when she accepted the note. The instrument in suit, being given without any valuable consideration, was nothing more than a promise to make a gift in the future of the sum of money therein named. Ordinarily, such promises are not enforceable, even when put in the form of a promissory note. * * * But it has often been held that an action on a note given to a church, college, or other like institution, upon the faith of which money has been expended or obligations incurred, could not be successfully defended on the ground of a want of consideration. * * * In this class of cases the note in suit is nearly always spoken of as a gift or donation, but the decision is generally put on the ground that the expenditure of money or assumption of liability by the donee on the faith of the promise constitutes a valuable and sufficient consideration. It seems to us that the true reason is the preclusion of the defendant, under the doctrine of estoppel, to deny the consideration. Such seems to be the view of the matter taken by the supreme court of Iowa in the case of *Simpson Centenary College v. Tuttle,* 71 Iowa, 596, 33 N. W. 74, where Rothrock, J., speaking for the court, said:

> Where a note, however, is based on a promise to give for the support of the objects referred to, it may still be open to this defense [want of consideration], unless it shall appear that the donee has, prior to any revocation, entered into engagements, or made expenditures based on such promise, so that he must suffer loss or injury if the note is not paid. This is based on the equitable principle that, after allowing the donee to incur obligations on the faith that the note would be paid, the donor would be estopped from pleading want of consideration.

And in the case of *Reimensnyder v. Gans,* 110 Pa. St. 17, 2 Atl. 425, which was an action on a note given as a donation to a charitable object, the court said: "The fact is that, as we may see from the case of *Ryerss v. Trustees,* 33 Pa. St. 114, a contract of the kind here involved is enforceable rather by way of estoppel than on the ground of consideration in the original undertaking." It has been held that a note given in expectation of the payee performing certain services, but without any contract binding him to serve, will not support an action. *Hulse v. Hulse,* 84 E. C. L. 709. But when the payee changes his position to his disadvantage in reliance on the promise, a right of action does arise. * * *

Under the circumstances of this case, is there an equitable estoppel which ought to preclude the defendant from alleging that the note in controversy is lacking in one of the essential elements of a valid contract? We think there is. An estoppel in pais is defined to be "a right arising from acts, admissions, or conduct which have induced a change of position in accordance with the real or apparent intention of the party against whom they are alleged." Mr. Pomeroy has formulated the following definition: "Equitable estoppel is the effect of the voluntary conduct of a party whereby he is absolutely precluded, both at law and in equity, from asserting rights which might, perhaps, have otherwise existed, either of property, of contract, or of remedy, as against another person who in good faith relied upon such conduct, and has been led thereby to change his position for the worse, and who on his part acquires some corresponding right, either of property, of contract, or of remedy." 2 Pom. Eq. Jur. 804. According to the undisputed proof, as shown by the record before us, the plaintiff was a working girl, holding a position in which she earned a salary of $10 per week. Her grandfather, desiring to put her in a position of independence, gave her the note, accompanying it with the remark that his other grandchildren did not work, and that she would not be obliged to work any longer. In effect, he suggested that she might abandon her employment, and rely in the future upon the bounty which he promised. He doubtless desired that she should give up her occupation, but, whether he did or not, it is entirely certain that he contemplated such action on her part as a reasonable and probable consequence of his gift. Having intentionally influenced the plaintiff to alter her position for the worse on the faith of the note being paid when due, it would be grossly inequitable to permit the maker, or his executor, to resist payment on the ground that the promise was given without consideration. The petition charges the elements of an equitable estoppel, and the evidence conclusively establishes them. If errors intervened at the trial, they could not have been prejudicial. A verdict for the defendant would be unwarranted. The judgment is right, and is affirmed.

QUESTIONS AND NOTES

1. Questions about the facts of this case

   1.1. Why did Katie's grandfather offer to pay her the $2000? Did he want her to quit her job? Did she?

   1.2. We've seen enough of these kinds of cases now to know that executors never seem to want to pay! Why do you suppose this is?

2. Questions about the law

   2.1. Equitable estoppel (estoppel *in pais*) is a doctrine that prohibits one party from asserting the truth of a matter previously misrepresented by that party. The elements of equitable estoppel are "conduct by one party which leads another party, in reliance thereon, to adopt a course of action resulting in detriment or damage if the first party is permitted to repudiate his conduct." *United American Life Insurance Co. v. Zions First National Bank,* 641 P.2d 158 (Utah 1982). In this case, Katie's grandfather's estate was estopped to deny the existence of consideration for the promise to pay her $2000. But did John Ricketts ever misrepresent that there was consideration for his promise? What's going on here? Is this a proper application of the doctrine of equitable estoppel? If not, why do you suppose the court invoked the doctrine?

   2.2. Why wasn't Katie's quitting her job consideration for the promise? Is there any less of a bargain here in terms of benefit to the promisor or detriment to the promisee than in *Hamer v. Sidway, supra.*?

   2.3. Would Katie have been better off if the court accepted the argument made in the original petition that John Ricketts' execution of the note met the traditional requirements for enforcement, *i.e.,* that it was supported by consideration?

   2.4. Suppose Katie had taken her old job back a week after her grandfather's promise. Would she have been in breach? Even if not, would she have been entitled to recover the whole $2000? How would the case come out under *Restatement (Second) of Contracts* § 90? What are the similarities between the first and second *Restatements*' versions of § 90? What are the differences?

3. Notes

3.1. Until fairly recently, enforcement of non-bargain promises based on reliance was limited to certain categories of cases that existed outside of or on the periphery of the marketplace and where the equities favoring enforcement were unusually compelling. Most notable among these was the willingness of courts to enforce gratuitous promises made to charitable organizations. Sometimes courts would do this by stretching the doctrine of consideration. For example, in *Allegheny College v. National Chautauqua County Bank,* 159 N.E. 173 (N.Y. 1927), Justice Cardozo concluded that the donor's desire for posthumous remembrance, coupled with the college's agreement to set up a memorial fund in her name, constituted good consideration to support the donor's pledge to have her estate pay the college $5000 30 days after her death. Other courts took a more direct approach to enforcing donative promises by invoking an estoppel in situations where the donee could demonstrate detrimental reliance on the promise. *See, e,g, Gittings v. Matthews,* 6 Md. 113 (1854). For more than you ever wanted to know about Justice Cardozo's *Allegheny College* opinion, see Markell's summary and analysis on the Internet at http://www2.law.cornell.edu/cgi-bin/foliocgi.exe/Allegheny. Today, in spite of its halting and at times uncertain origins, promissory estoppel is regularly applied in a wide variety of commercial contexts as demonstrated by the cases that follow in this section.

3.2. Students (and sometimes courts) are often confused by the distinction between a promissory and an equitable estoppel. While doctrinally distinct, the two can sometimes overlap. Consider the following scenario: Suppose Ponoroff signs a promissory note promising to pay Epstein $24,000 in 48 equal monthly installments of $500 each together with interest. The note expressly provides that payments are due on the first of each month and that, in the event of nonpayment, Epstein shall have the right to declare the entire debt due and owing in full (*i.e.*, an "acceleration" clause). For the first 18 months, Ponoroff makes all the required payments, but always pays between the 5th and the 10th of the month. Epstein says nothing about this. However, when Epstein fails to receive the 19th monthly payment on the first of the month Epstein immediately declares a default. Even though Ponoroff promptly tenders the past due monthly installment, Epstein brings suit for breach of contract seeking recovery of the entire outstanding balance of the note. In Ponoroff's defense (usually something nobody is much interested in, but then this is a hypothetical), can you successfully raise a defense based on estoppel? Is that an equitable or a promissory estoppel? Are there any other defenses you can think of? What if the contract rate of interest was 6% and the market rate of interest had risen over 18 months to 11%?

3.3. Although widely regarded as a creature of the common law developed as a necessary tool to blunt the occasional harshness of the bargain theory of consideration, in fact, as demonstrated in the excerpt which follows, the doctrine of promissory estoppel has roots going back at least as far as Roman Law.

Shael Herman, *Detrimental Reliance In Louisiana Law—Past, Present, and Future: The Code Drafter's Perspective*
58 TUL. L. REV. 707, 715 (1984)

Anglo-American jurisprudence did not invent detrimental reliance as a substitute for consideration or a basis for enforcement. On the continent, it already had long and venerable antecedents before the Norman Conquest. It appeared in Roman texts, and so venerable was the idea of detrimental reliance that it even acquired its own Latin maxim: venire contra proprium factum (no one can contradict his own act). In its usual applications, the maxim performed the function of estoppel: after an assertion that a certain fact presently existed, reliance on the assertion barred proof that the assertion was false.

In classical sources, there were even traces of reliance as a ground for the limited enforcement of gift promises. The Digest, for example, narrates a case in which a promisor promised another a sum of money if he took a trip. After the promisee had taken the trip, the promisor sued for recovery of the money he had meanwhile paid him. Although the promisee received a deduction for his expenditures from the payor's recovery of the money, he was denied damages in excess of that sum.

The concept of detrimental reliance is also present in many modern civil law systems. A study of French and German cases has led Dawson to conclude that French courts, at least sub rosa, must factor detrimental reliance into their decisions, even though reliance rarely constitutes an express ground for enforcement because French courts prefer to search for "onerosity" in the donor's motive. By contrast, in the more recent German decisions that use the good faith clause of the German Civil Code to dispense with requirements of form, the promisee's reliance can at times appear as the predominant reason for enforcement and may now be almost a requirement for the promisee's recovery. In the twentieth century, detrimental reliance as a fundamental principle has gained ground among some European authors. Some twentieth-century German and Italian writers have urged the express adoption of detrimental reliance as a basis for enforcing promises that "fall in the borderland between exchange and gift."

---

3. Contemporary Applications of the Doctrine

Katz v. Danny Dare, Inc.
Court of Appeals of Missouri
610 S.W.2d 121 (1980)

Turnage, J.

I. G. Katz filed three suits in the Associate Division of the Circuit Court seeking pension payments for three separate time periods alleged to be due from Danny Dare, Inc. Two suits resulted in judgment in favor of Katz, but a request for a trial de novo was filed and those causes were assigned to a circuit judge for trial. The other suit pending in the Associate Division was transferred to the same circuit judge and all the cases were consolidated for trial without a jury. Judgment was entered in favor of Dare in all cases. On this appeal Katz contends the promise of pension payments made to him by Dare is binding under the Doctrine of Promissory Estoppel. Reversed and remanded.

There is little or no dispute as to the facts in this case. Katz began work for Dare in 1950 and continued in that employ until his retirement on June 1, 1975. The president of Dare was Harry Shopmaker, who was also the brother of Katz's wife. Katz worked in a variety of positions including executive vice president, sales manager, and a member of the board of directors, although he was not a member of the board at the time of his retirement. In

February 1973, Katz was opening a store, operated by Dare, for business and placed a bag of money on the counter next to the cash register. A man walked in, picked up the bag of money and left. When Katz followed him and attempted to retrieve the money, Katz was struck in the head. He was hospitalized and even though he returned to work he conceded he had some difficulties. His walk was impaired and he suffered some memory loss and was not able to function as he had before. Shopmaker and others testified to many mistakes which Katz made after his return at considerable cost to Dare. Shopmaker reached the decision that he would have to work out some agreeable pension to induce Katz to retire because he did not feel he could carry Katz as an employee. At that time Katz's earnings were about $23,000 per year.

Shopmaker began discussions with Katz concerning retirement but Katz insisted that he did not want to retire but wanted to continue working. Katz was 65 at the time of his injury and felt he could continue performing useful work for Dare to justify his remaining as an employee. However, Shopmaker persisted in his assessment that Katz was more of a liability than an asset as an employee and continued negotiating with Katz over a period of about 13 months in an effort to reach an agreement by which Katz would retire with a pension from Dare. Shopmaker first offered Katz $10,500 per year as a pension but Katz refused. Thereafter, while Katz was on vacation, Shopmaker sent Katz a letter to demonstrate how Katz could actually wind up with more take-home pay by retiring than he could by continuing as an employee. In the letter Shopmaker proposed an annual pension payable by Dare of $13,000, added the Social Security benefit which Katz and his wife would receive after retirement, and added $2,520 per year which Katz could earn for part-time employment, but not necessarily from Dare, to demonstrate that Katz would actually realize about $1,000 per year more in income by retiring with the Dare pension over what he would realize if he continued his employment. Shopmaker testified that he sent this letter in an effort to persuade Katz to retire.

Katz acceded to the offer of a pension of $13,000 per year for life, and on May 22, 1975, the board of directors of Dare unanimously approved the following resolution:

> WHEREAS, I. G. Katz has been a loyal employee of Danny Dare, Inc. and its predecessor companies for more than 25 years; and,
>
> WHEREAS, the said I. G. Katz has requested retirement because of failing health; and,

> WHEREAS, it has been the custom in the past for the company to retire all executives having loyally served the company for many years with a remuneration in keeping with the sum received during their last five years of employment;
>
> NOW THEN BE IT RESOLVED, That Danny Dare, Inc. pay to I. G. Katz the sum of $500.00 bi-weekly, or a total of $13,000.00 per year, so long as he shall live.

Katz retired on June 1, 1975, at age 67, and Dare began payment of the pension at the rate of $500 every other week. Katz testified that he would not have retired without the pension and relied on the promise of Dare to pay the pension when he made his decision to retire. Shopmaker testified that at the time the board resolution was passed, the board intended for Katz to rely on the resolution and to retire, but he said Katz would have been fired had he not elected to retire.

In the Fall of 1975, Katz began working for another company on 3 to 4 half-days per week. At the end of that year Shopmaker asked Katz if he could do part-time work for Dare and Katz told him he could work one-half day on Wednesdays. For the next two and one-half years Katz continued to work for Dare one-half day per week.

In July, 1978, Dare sent a semi-monthly check for $250 instead of $500. Katz sent the check back and stated he was entitled to the full $500. Thereafter Dare stopped sending any checks. Shopmaker testified that he cut off the checks to Katz because he felt Katz's health had improved to the point that he could work, as demonstrated by the part-time job he held. Katz testified the decrease was made after Shopmaker told him he would have to work one-half day for five days a week for Dare or his pension would be cut in half. Katz testified, without challenge, that he was not able to work 40 hours per week in 1978 at age 70.

The trial court entered a judgment in which some findings of fact were made. The court found that Katz based his claim on the Doctrine of Promissory Estoppel as applied in *Feinberg v. Pfeiffer Company,* 322 S.W.2d 163 (Mo. App. 1959). The court found that Katz was not in the same situation as *Feinberg* had been because Katz faced the prospect of being fired if he did not accept the pension offer whereas there was no such evidence in the *Feinberg* case. The court found the pension from Dare did not require Katz to do anything and he was in fact free to work for another company. The court found Katz did not give up anything to which he was legally entitled when he elected to retire. The court found that since Katz had the choice of accepting retirement and a pension or being fired, that it could not be said that he suffered any detriment or significant change of position when he elected to retire. The court further found that it could not find any injustice resulting to Katz because by the time payments had been terminated, he had received about $40,000 plus a paid vacation for his wife and himself to Hawaii. The court found these were benefits he would not have received had he been fired.

Katz contends he falls within the holding in *Feinberg* and Dare contends that because Katz faced the alternative of accepting the pension or being fired that he falls without the holding in *Feinberg*.

At the outset it is interesting to note in view of the argument made by Dare that the court in *Feinberg* stated at p. 165:

> It is clear from the evidence that there was no contract, oral or written, as to plaintiff's length of employment, and that she was free to quit, and the defendant to discharge her, at any time.

In *Feinberg* the board of directors passed a resolution offering Feinberg the opportunity to retire at any time she would elect with retirement pay of $200 per month for life. Feinberg retired about two and one-half years after the resolution was passed and began to receive the retirement pay. The pay continued for about seven years when the company sent a check for $100 per month, which Feinberg refused and thereafter payments were discontinued.

The court observed that Section 90 of the Restatement of the Law of Contracts had been adopted by the Supreme Court in *In Re Jamison's Estate,* 202 S.W.2d 879 (Mo. 1947). The court noted that one of the illustrations under § 90 was strikingly similar to the facts in *Feinberg*. The court applied the Doctrine of Promissory Estoppel, as articulated in § 90, and held that Feinberg had relied upon the promise of the pension when she resigned a paying position and elected to accept a lesser amount in pension. The court held it was immaterial as to whether Feinberg became unable to obtain other employment before or after the company discontinued the pension payment. The court held the reliance by Feinberg was in giving up her job in reliance on the promise of a pension. Her subsequent disability went to the prevention of injustice which is part of the Doctrine of Promissory Estoppel.

There are three elements to be satisfied to invoke the Doctrine of Promissory Estoppel. These are: (1) a promise; (2) a detrimental reliance on such promise; and (3) injustice can be avoided only by enforcement of the promise.

This court is not convinced that the alternative Shopmaker gave to Katz of either accepting the pension and retiring or be fired takes this case out of the operation of Promissory Estoppel. The fact remains that Katz was not fired, but instead did voluntarily retire, but only after the board of directors had adopted the resolution promising to pay Katz a pension of $13,000 per year for life. Thus, the same facts are present in this case as were present in Feinberg. When Katz elected to retire and give up earnings of about $23,000 per year to accept a pension of $13,000 per year, he did so as a result of a promise made by Dare and to his detriment by the loss of $10,000 per year in earnings. It is conceded Dare intended that Katz rely on its promise of a pension and Dare does not contend Katz did not in fact rely on such promise. The fact that the payments continued for about three years and that Katz at age 70 could not work full-time was unquestioned. Thus, the element that injustice can be avoided only by enforcement of the promise is present, because Katz cannot now engage in a full-time job to return to the earnings which he gave up in reliance on the pension.

Dare's argument that the threat of being fired removes this case from the operation of Promissory Estoppel is similar to an argument advanced in *Trexler's Estate,* 27 Pa.Dist. & Co. Rep. 4 (1936), cited with approval in *Fried v. Fisher,* 328 Pa. 497, 196 A. 39 (1938). In *Trexler* the depression had forced General Trexler to decide whether to fire several employees who had been with him for many years or place them on a pension. The General decided to promise them a pension of $50 per month and at his death, the employees filed a claim against his estate for the continuation of the payments. The court observed that the General could have summarily discharged the employees, but was loath to do this without making some provision for their old age. This was shown by the numerous conferences which the General had with his executives in considering each employee's financial situation, age and general status. The court said it was clear that the General wanted to reduce overhead and at the same time wanted to give these faithful employees some protection. The court stated it as an open question of what the General would have done if the men had not accepted his offer of a lifetime pension. The court said it would not speculate on that point but it was sufficient to observe that the men accepted the offer and received the pension. The court applied § 90 of the Restatement and held that under the

Doctrine of Promissory Estoppel the estate was bound to continue the payments.

The facts in this case are strikingly similar to *Trexler*. Shopmaker undoubtedly wanted to reduce his overhead by reducing the amount being paid to Katz and it is true that Katz could have been summarily discharged. However, it is also true that Shopmaker refused to fire Katz, but instead patiently negotiated for about 13 months to work out a pension which Katz did agree to accept and voluntarily retired.

While Dare strenuously urges that the threat of firing effectively removed any legitimate choice on the part of Katz, the facts do not bear this out. The fact is that Katz continued in his employment with Dare until he retired and such retirement was voluntary on the part of Katz. Had Shopmaker desired to terminate Katz without any promise of a pension he could have done so and Katz would have had no recourse. However, the fact is that Shopmaker did not discharge Katz but actually made every effort to induce Katz to retire voluntarily on the promise of a pension of $13,000 per year.

Dare appears to have led the trial court into error by relying on *Pitts v. McGraw-Edison Co.,* 329 F.2d 412 (6th Cir. 1964). Pitts was informed that the company had retired him and would pay him a certain percentage of sales thereafter. Thus, the main distinction between this case and *Pitts* is that Pitts did not elect to retire on the promise of any payment, but was simply informed that he had been retired by the company and the company would make payment to him. There was no promise made to Pitts on which he acted to his detriment. In addition, the court was applying the law of Tennessee and the court stated that Tennessee had not adopted § 90 of the Restatement. The court in *Pitts* found that Pitts had not given up anything to which he was legally entitled and was not restricted in any way in his activities after being placed in retirement by his company.

The facts in *Pitts* would not enable Pitts to recover under Promissory Estoppel in Missouri because there was no action taken by Pitts in reliance on a promise. The test to be applied in this case is not whether Katz gave up something to which he was legally entitled, but rather whether Dare made a promise to him on which he acted to his detriment. The legally entitled test could never be met by an employee such as Katz or Feinberg because neither could show any legal obligation on the company to promise a pension. The Doctrine of Promissory Estoppel is designed to protect those to whom a promise is made which is not legally enforcible until the requirements of the doctrine are met. *Pitts* is not applicable either on the facts or the law.

The trial court misapplied the law when it held that Katz was required to show that he gave up something to which he was legally entitled before he could enforce the promise of a pension made by Dare. The elements of Promissory Estoppel are present: a promise of a pension to Katz, his detrimental reliance thereon, and injustice can only be avoided by enforcing that promise. The judgment is reversed and the case is remanded with directions to enter judgment in both suits in favor of Katz for the amount of unpaid pension.

All concur.

QUESTIONS AND NOTES

1. Questions about the facts of this case

   1.1. How did Katz change his position in reliance on the promise of a pension from Danny Dare? What would have happened if he didn't take this action?

   1.2. How might the fact that Shopmaker was Katz's brother-in-law have influenced the outcome?

2. Questions about the law

   2.1. Why did the trial court in *Danny Dare* think the fact that Katz faced being fired if he did not accept retirement (with the promise of the pension) made the case distinguishable from *Feinberg v. Pfeiffer*, the case on which the court of appeals placed considerable reliance? Are the cases distinguishable? Here's what one law professor had to say about *Danny Dare*, see if you agree:

   The *Danny Dare* decision is one that I teach in my class, and it causes no small level of consternation because of the court's distinction between a legal entitlement to employment (which the plaintiff did not have) and an interest in relying on a promise that the promisor may not have been obligated to make (the defendant

> really could have fired the plaintiff anytime he wanted to). Students catch on to this kind of reasoning and conclude, * * * that what we really have is judicial acrobatics to achieve a desired result.

Craig L. Jackson, *Traditional Contract Theory: Old and New Attacks and Old and New Defenses*, 33 NEW ENG. L. REV. 365, 422 (1998).

2.2. The court in *Danny Dare* entered judgment for Katz for the amount of the unpaid pension obligations that had accrued from the date of discontinuance of those payments to the date of judgment. If the basis for the recovery was Katz's detrimental reliance, why should he have been entitled to any payments after he learned that the company no longer intended to continue the pension?

2.3. Would the outcome in *Danny Dare* be different if the promise was made by one of Katz's friends rather than an official of the company? How about if Katz overheard Shopmaker telling another employee that the company was going to pay this pension after Katz retired? *See Restatement (Second) of Contracts* § 90, cmt. c.

2.4. According to the court in *Danny Dare*, what are the elements of a recovery under promissory estoppel? Keep them in mind as you read the next case.

3. Notes:

3.1. Mr. Katz's victory over Danny Dare may have been even more impressive than he realized. Recently, Professor Robert Hillman published the results of an empirical study he conducted of promissory estoppel cases in the employment context decided during the period from 1994 through 1996. Surprisingly, he found that the employees succeeded *less than five percent* of the time. *See* Robert A. Hillman, *The Unfulfilled Promise of Promissory Estoppel in the Employment Setting*, 31 RUTGERS L. J. 1 (1999). In part, Professor Hillman attributed this low rate of success to an increasing judicial preference for written contracts supported by traditional bargained-for consideration. Indeed, like the rumors of Mark Twain's death, it is possible that Grant Gilmore's fear that promissory estoppel might "swallow up" the bargain principle in contract enforcement was vastly exaggerated!

3.2. In *Langer v. Superior Steel,* 161 A. 571 (Penn. Supr. Ct. 1932), the president of the defendant/employer sent a letter to the plaintiff, Langer, upon his retirement promising "a pension of $100 per month as long as you live and preserve your present attitude of loyalty to the company and its officers and are not employed in any competitive occupation." After four years, the company ceased the payments and Langer sued. The company defended on the basis that the letter was a gratuitous promise and, as such, unenforceable. The court, however, concluded that there was a sufficient consideration because the company had received a benefit in Langer's not seeking employment with a competitor. Do you think the promise in *Langer* was any less gratuitous than the one in *Danny Dare*? Could you make an argument, based on *Langer*, that Danny Dare's promise was enforceable under traditional bargain theory?

3.3. Until the enactment in 1974 of the Employee Retirement Income Security Act (ERISA), enforcement of private employer-sponsored pension plans was handled under state common law theories of breach of contract and promissory estoppel. ERISA, which was adopted to strengthen and improve pension and welfare security payments for plan participants, establishes a statutory enforcement mechanism that preempts state law. However, the common law contract theories remain viable as to plans that are unfunded or otherwise exempt from ERISA. *See also Schonholz v. Long Island Jewish Medical Center, 87 F.3d 72 (2d Cir. 1996)* (holding that promissory estoppel theory might be applied even in an ERISA case under extraordinary circumstances). The resolution granting Katz's pension likely was not covered by ERISA because it was not a company "plan," but rather a one-time obligation incurred to a single employee.

Midwest Energy, Inc. v. Orion Food Systems, Inc.
Court of Appeals of Missouri
14 S.W.3d 154, 2000 Mo. App. LEXIS 112 (2000)

Charles B. Blackmar, Senior Judge

The trial court granted summary judgment on all three counts of the plaintiff's petition and entered final judgment for both defendants. * * *

The plaintiff Midwest, a Missouri corporation, operates a chain of service station convenience stores in Southeast Missouri. The defendant Orion, a South Dakota corporation, has developed recipes and equipment for several fast food systems for which it issues franchises to local outlets. Defendant Ted Ries at material times was the district sales manager for Orion in the area in which Midwest has facilities.

In early 1996 Midwest undertook the construction of a substantial building in Fruitland, Missouri, designed for the operation of a service station and convenience store and estimated to cost $800,000. Its president and sole stockholder, Laura Younghouse, inquired into the possibility of a franchise for some of Orion's product lines. On March 27, 1996, Ries visited Younghouse and delivered to her an offering circular required by the Federal Trade Commission accompanied by a specimen franchise agreement in which the blank spaces were not filled in. The circular contained a caution about taking any further action until Midwest had been notified in writing that its application had been approved. Younghouse receipted for these documents and read them.

Ries advised Younghouse he had to check with other Orion franchisees in the area to determine whether they had any contractual protection from nearby competition. He checked particularly with Rhodes Oil, which had Orion franchises at several nearby locations. On April 13, 1996 Ries again visited with Younghouse, advising her that Rhodes and other franchisees interposed no obstacle and that "we can go forward with the franchise." Younghouse had already filled out and delivered a franchise application on behalf of Midwest for the new location. Midwest's building contractor was present at this conference and discussed the proposed construction with Ries and Younghouse.

During the next several months Orion provided drawings and specifications setting forth its requirements for the area in which its franchised products would be prepared and dispensed. Ries was in touch with both the general contractor and the electrician. He pointed out the need to enlarge the convenience store area to 800 square feet to meet Orion's special requirements. This was a larger area than Younghouse had originally planned. The final store layout and design was provided by Orion to Midwest on July 2, 1996.

Ries reported his contacts with Midwest to his immediate supervisor, Keith Watts, who told him to "go ahead" at the Midwest location. Orion prepared orders for the equipment necessary to prepare and serve the franchised products.

Under date of September 4, 1996 Midwest received from Orion an unsigned franchise agreement specifying an opening date of November 8, 1996. On September 13, Ries called to advise Younghouse he would call on September 18, 1996 to "pick up the franchise agreement." He did not appear on that date and did not respond to Younghouse's persistent attempts to get in touch with him. There is evidence that his superiors instructed him to "make himself scarce" while they reevaluated the franchise situation.

On September 30, 1996 Younghouse executed the franchise agreement on behalf of Midwest and mailed it to Orion. In the meantime a representative of Rhodes, Midwest's potential competitor, had called Orion to report that he had seen a notice of Midwest's opening date of November 8 for the new facility and was not pleased at the thought of competition. Orion's executives decided not to issue the franchise to Midwest, and one Schendel, an analyst, was instructed to write a letter to Midwest conveying this decision. For some reason the letter was not mailed until October 11, 1996. On October 1, however, Watts called Younghouse to advise her Orion was "withdrawing the franchise offer."[2]

The foregoing is an abbreviated summary of the bare facts that might be found. The record provided on summary judgment is voluminous, and other facts will be stated in the discussion of each of the several counts.

Midwest's petition declares in three counts as follows: (I) Breach of contract by Orion in failing to grant a franchise to Midwest; (II) Promissory estoppel against Orion in accordance with the provisions of Section 90 of the Restatement (2d) of Contracts; and (III) Fraud and deceit against Ries for willfully misstating the extent of his authority. We affirm the judgment on

[2]The record does not show whether Watts had received the franchise agreement signed by Younghouse and returned by mail to Orion when he made this call, but, for want of Orion's signature, the time of receipt is not legally significant.

Count I, but find error in the entry of summary judgment on Counts II and III, and so remand this portion of the case for further proceedings.

Count I—Breach of Contract

Count I declares on the five-year franchise agreement submitted to Midwest on September 4, 1996 as a contract between Midwest and Orion. The contract, however, is not signed by Orion. It cannot be performed within one year of its stated effective date of November 8, 1996. This contract is clearly unenforceable under section 432.010 RSMo 1994, known as the "Statute of Frauds," and nothing short of Orion's signature can make it into an enforceable contract. * * *

Our cases clearly hold that a contract otherwise unenforceable because of the Statute of Frauds cannot be made into a fully enforceable contract through any doctrine of promissory estoppel. * * *

There was no error in granting summary judgment on Count I.

Count II—Promissory Estoppel

Count II seeks to state a claim under Section 90, Restatement (2d) of Contracts which reads in pertinent part as follows:

> Section 90. Promise Reasonably Inducing Action or Forbearance
>
> (1) A promise which the promisor should reasonably expect to induce action or forbearance on the part of the promisee or a third person and which does induce such action or forbearance is binding if injustice can be avoided only by enforcement of the promise. The remedy granted for breach may be limited as justice requires.

Promissory estoppel has been part of the law of Missouri for many years, and our courts have cited Section 90 of both the First and Second Restatements of Contracts. * * * The doctrine is closely related to equitable estoppel, and there are statements in the cases that it is an equitable remedy. * * * We have found no case, however, which rules the issue of availability of trial by jury in an action at law. There is language suggesting the doctrine should only be applied "in extreme cases to avoid unjust results." * * * This is a standard somewhat difficult of application, and may influence the decision as to whether trial by jury is available. Inasmuch as the issue of trial by jury has not been briefed to us, we forego ruling the point pending further proceedings. We do observe that the question of whether the remedy is necessary seems inappropriate for decision on summary judgment, if the elements of promissory estoppel are arguably present.

Numerous cases, involving widely different fact situations, have considered the requirements for recovery under Section 90. In some the opinions seem overexpansive, seeking to lay down rules which are broader than required for the resolution of the immediate problem. We seek to apply the governing principle of the Restatement. * * *

We have found no case discussing the method of jury instruction in Section 90 cases, and there are no MAI patterns. Nor do we find discussion of the appropriate form for findings of fact. There is some variation in the manner of stating essential elements, but, as Judge Shrum observed in *Delmo*, all pertinent opinions list the elements as: (1) A promise; (2) foreseeability of reliance; (3) reliance; and (4) injustice absent enforcement. [*Delmo, Inc. v. Maxima Elec. Sales, Inc.,* 878 S.W.2d 499at 504 (Mo. App. 1994)]. * * *

The sense of the cases, and especially the recent cases, is that a plaintiff who can point to evidence which, if believed, would permit a judge or jury to find each of these elements, is entitled to go to trial without prior judicial determination as to whether the case is "extreme." All cases agree the essence of the plaintiff's case is justifiable reliance causing damage. Under Section 90 recoveries have been permitted which might not have been allowed under traditional contract doctrine.[4] We proceed therefore to determine whether Midwest has demonstrated that there is a genuine issue of fact as to each one of the essential elements as defined in the cases. If there is, then the motion for summary judgment on Count II was improvidently granted. If there is no genuine issue as to the existence of any one of these elements, then summary judgment is appropriate. We conclude that Midwest's proffer is sufficient to establish fact questions as to all four essential elements.

* * *

---

[4]*Prenger v. Baumhoer,* 939 S.W.2d 23, 27 (Mo. App. 1997), discerns a "Missouri rule" in Section 90 cases to the effect that a promise must be contractually enforceable in order to meet the requirements of Section 90. That case involved a situation in which the parties each contemplated further bargaining, and is for that reason distinguishable from the cases cited in subsection (1) of this Section [dealing with the breach of contract claim], in which the only problem relates to the Statute of Frauds.

(1) Promise

The record shows several promissory statements made by Ries. On April 13, 1996, Ries called on Younghouse and told her he had received clearance from other franchisees and that "[we can] go forward with the franchise." He repeated his assurances that all was in order, providing floor plans, lists of required equipment, and, on July 2, 1996, a definitive layout. On September 4, 1996 Orion mailed to Younghouse a franchise agreement providing for an opening date of November 8, 1996. This document was not signed by anyone purporting to act on behalf of Orion, but Ries advised Younghouse he would appear on September 18 to pick up the franchise agreement. Younghouse understood that Ries proposed to sign on behalf of Orion. From the facts just stated the trier of fact could find Ries promised Midwest that a franchise conforming to the specimen provided to Midwest in March would be issued as soon as Midwest was ready to operate, and that Midwest could make preparations based on those assurances.

* * *

(2) Foreseeable Reliance

The trier of fact could certainly find that, between April 13 and September 4, Orion and Midwest wanted to do business with each other. Ries was Orion's authorized liaison with Midwest in order to further preparation for undertaking the franchise. He had every reason to believe Midwest would hasten to comply with his directions, for fear that the tender of the franchise would be withdrawn. To the extent that his requests, on behalf of Orion, required expenditure or forbearance, he could confidently expect these would be forthcoming. Whatever authority Ries had with regard to executing franchise documents, he could surely forestall the granting of a franchise by expressing his disapproval.

(3) Reliance in Fact

The record shows, at the very least, that Midwest relied on Ries's promises by making changes in its plans for the fast food area and by forbearing attempts to interest other possible franchisors in its new facility. These, in and of themselves, are sufficient to demonstrate reliance and, when the reliance proved to be unjustified, damages. There may be other provable damages. There is no briefing of the issue, and argument did not focus on the quantitative scope of recovery. This trier of fact may be totally unimpressed with Midwest's evidence of damages, but enough has been shown to raise a factual issue.

Orion asserts emphatically that Midwest had no right to rely on anything Ries said as being binding on Orion. It is not necessary to show, however, that Ries had authority to determine that a franchise should be granted. As has been said earlier, it could be found that he had the authority to transmit Orion's instructions and requirements so as to assist Midwest in putting itself in a position to commence operations under an Orion franchise. He could also confirm Orion's continued interest in Midwest as a franchisee and advise Midwest as to further necessary steps.

Orion also points to the cautionary language in the offering circular required by the Federal Trade Commission and in the specimen franchise agreement delivered with the circular on the occasion of Ries's first visit. These documents confirm the franchise agreement as the sole agreement between the parties, strongly suggest that Midwest avail itself of legal counsel in examining the documents, and expressly warn Midwest that it should not take any other action in anticipation of receiving the franchise unless and until it should have an executed franchise agreement in hand. The promises on which Midwest relies to invoke Section 90, however, came after these documents were delivered, at a time when Orion was encouraging Midwest to make active preparation to undertake the franchise. Under Section 90 Orion is not necessarily free to encourage reliance by promises made in the expectation of reliance, simply by reason of a prior written warning that its promises mean nothing until both parties have signed a franchise agreement. The situation is analogous to one in which a contract provides it may be modified only by an instrument in writing, but the parties later agree to an oral modification. * * * The examples to Section 90 show, moreover, that the plaintiff is not necessarily required to exercise perfect diligence.

Orion also argues that Younghouse, shown to be experienced in business, did not act reasonably in relying on oral promises. Whether her reliance was reasonable or not is a question of fact.

(4) Injustice Absent Enforcement

This element is not cast with precision. Numerous writings on Section 90 make it clear it is designed to protect the reliance interest. Damages are measured by the degree of reliance. When the other elements of a Section 90 claim are present, the "injustice" element is not appropriate for determination in a summary judgment proceeding. The parties will have to work with the trial court in determining the appropriate manner of submission.

We again caution that our somewhat detailed expostulation of the fact governing Count II represents only our conception of the permissible findings the trier of fact might make. We do not suggest in any respect that the fact-finder should make any particular finding, or that any particular conclusion is preferable. The record is voluminous, and we simply say we perceive genuine issues of material fact on each of the essential elements of an action under Section 90 sufficient to withstand a motion for summary judgment.

Count III—Fraud and Deceit against Ries

Count III seeks actual and punitive damages on account of Ries's alleged misrepresentation of his authority to act for Orion regarding the grant of a franchise to Midwest. Since Count II is predicated on Ries's authority to do as he did, Count III is necessarily alternative to Count II. Our rules, however, permit alternative pleadings. Rule 55.10.

* * *

All parties should understand that, if Midwest should recover on Count II, it would not be proper to enter an additional judgment on Count III.

The judgment for Orion on Count I is affirmed. The judgments on Counts II and III are reversed, and the case is remanded for appropriate proceedings consistent with this opinion.

QUESTIONS

1. Questions about the facts of this case

   1.1. The court in *Midwest Energy* suggests that whether or not Younghouse's reliance was reasonable is a question of fact. On remand, what facts would you point to if you represented Midwest Energy? How about if you represent Orion?

1.2. The court also says that the injustice element is not appropriate for summary judgment. Why not? Is "injustice absent enforcement" a fact question or a question of law?

2. Questions about the law

2.1. What are the elements of a claim under promissory estoppel according to the court in *Midwest Energy*? How do they differ from the elements delineated by the court in *Danny Dare*?

2.2. If Midwest Energy is able to make out a case under promissory estoppel at trial, how should its damages be determined?

2.3. Did the court in *Midwest Energy* agree with Orion that entitlement to relief under the doctrine of promissory estoppel was an equitable issue for the court to decide? If you were the trial judge on remand how would you go about deciding whether or not this claim should be tried to a jury?

2.4. Why did Midwest Energy's breach of contract claim fail? Suppose the reason that the agreement was not reduced to writing had been that Orion informed Midwest Energy, "Don't worry about that; we don't need a formal written agreement, our handshake is our bond." If Orion later tries to use the absence of a writing as a defense to a breach of contract claim should it be estopped from doing so? *Cf. Restatement (Second) of Contracts* § 139. Is that an equitable or a promissory estoppel?

Introduction to *Pavel Enterprises*

We saw in Chapter 1 that all offers, even offers stated to be irrevocable, are in fact revocable at the will of the offeror *unless*: 1) the promise of irreovcability is supported by some consideration, or 2) the promise of irrevocability is made enforceable by statute—thereby, in either case, creating an *option contract*. However, you may recall that we also saw certain situations where the *Restatement (Second) of Contracts* fashions a sort of option contract to protect the offeree's reliance interest. For example, where the offer *requires* acceptance by full performance, and the offeree commences performance, under *Restatement (Second) of Contracts* § 45 the offeree has a reasonable time to complete the performance and, during that time, the offer may not be revoked. *See, e.g., Marchiondo v. Scheck, supra*, at 135. In *Marchiondo*, of course, the court concluded that "[w]hat constitutes partial performance will vary from case to case since what can be done toward performance is limited by what is authorized to be done."

Another recurring circumstance where the courts have shown some willingness to create an option contract in order to protect the offeree arises in the construction contract situation. In terms of context, in the conventional scenario (and particularly in government projects), the property owner will seek bids from general contractors for the construction of a building on, or other improvement to, the owner's property. Inevitably, the contractor will plan to perform some portion of its obligations under the prime contract by contracting for services with, and acquiring materials from, an array of subcontractors and suppliers. In order to formulate its bid on the prime contract, therefore, the general contractor often will solicit bids in advance from these subcontractors. These bids, of course, are only *offers*, but the general contractor typically *relies* on these bids in determining what it can bid on the prime contract and still make a profit. Obviously, the general contractor does not want to accept the sub-bids unless and until it knows that its primary bid has been accepted. As you can see, the issue of "fairness" arises when the general contractor, who has been awarded the prime contract having relied on particular subcontractor bids, is faced suddenly with a revocation of a sub-bid before it can accept.

The next case describes the approaches that have been developed over the past seventy years or so to deal with this particular problem. As you read the case, think about what might be done to protect the general contractor's interest *ex ante*, eliminating the need to rely, after the fact and with apologies to Tennessee Williams, on the kindness of judges.

Pavel Enterprises, Inc. v. A. S. Johnson Company, Inc.

Court of Appeals of Maryland
342 Md. 143, 674 A.2d 521 (1996)

Karwacki, J.

In this case we are invited to adapt the "modern" contractual theory of detrimental reliance, or promissory estoppel, to the relationship between general contractors and their subcontractors. Although the theory of detrimental reliance is available to general contractors, it is not applicable to the facts of this case. For that reason, and because there was no traditional bilateral contract formed, we shall affirm the trial court.

I

The National Institutes of Health [hereinafter, "NIH"], solicited bids for a renovation project on Building 30 of its Bethesda, Maryland campus. The proposed work entailed some demolition work, but the major component of the job was mechanical, including heating, ventilation and air conditioning ["HVAC"]. Pavel Enterprises Incorporated [hereinafter, "PEI"], a general contractor from Vienna, Virginia and appellant in this action, prepared a bid for the NIH work. In preparing its bid, PEI solicited sub-bids from various mechanical subcontractors. The A. S. Johnson Company [hereinafter, "Johnson"], a mechanical subcontractor located in Clinton, Maryland and the appellee here, responded with a written scope of work proposal on July 27, 1993.[2] On the morning of August 5, 1993, the day NIH opened the general contractors' bids, Johnson verbally submitted a quote of $898,000 for the HVAC component. Neither party disputes that PEI used Johnson's sub-bid in computing its own bid. PEI submitted a bid of $1,585,000 for the entire project.

General contractors' bids were opened on the afternoon of August 5, 1993. PEI's bid was the second lowest bid. The government subsequently disqualified the apparent low bidder, however, and in mid-August, NIH notified PEI that its bid would be accepted.

---

[2]The scope of work proposal listed all work that Johnson proposed to perform, but omitted the price term. This is a standard practice in the construction industry. The subcontractor's bid price is then filled in immediately before the general contractor submits the general bid to the letting party.

With the knowledge that PEI was the lowest responsive bidder, Thomas F. Pavel, president of PEI, visited the offices of A. S. Johnson on August 26, 1993, and met with James Kick, Johnson's chief estimator, to discuss Johnson's proposed role in the work. Pavel testified at trial to the purpose of the meeting:

> "I met with Mr. Kick. And the reason for me going to their office was to look at their offices, to see their facility, to basically sit down and talk with them, as I had not done, and my company had not performed business with them on a direct relationship, but we had heard of their reputation. I wanted to go out and see where their facility was, see where they were located, and basically just sit down and talk to them. Because if we were going to use them on a project, I wanted to know who I was dealing with."

* * *

Following that meeting, PEI sent a fax to all of the mechanical subcontractors from whom it had received sub-bids on the NIH job. The text of that fax is reproduced:

> Pavel Enterprises, Inc.
>
> TO: PROSPECTIVE MECHANICAL SUBCONTRACTORS FROM: ESTIMATING DEPARTMENT REFERENCE: NIH, BLDG 30 RENOVATION
>
> We herewith respectfully request that you review your bid on the above referenced project that was bid on 8/05/93. PEI has been notified that we will be awarded the project as J.J. Kirlin, Inc. [the original low bidder] has been found to be nonresponsive on the solicitation. We anticipate award on or around the first of September and therefor request that you supply the following information.

* * *

On August 30, 1993, PEI informed NIH that Johnson was to be the mechanical subcontractor on the job. On September 1, 1993, PEI mailed and faxed a letter to Johnson formally accepting Johnson's bid. That letter read:

Pavel Enterprises, Inc.

September 1, 1993

Mr. James H. Kick, Estimating Mngr. A.S. Johnson Company 8042 Old Alexandria Ferry Road Clinton, Maryland 20735

Re: NIH Bldg 30 HVAC Modifications IFB # 263-93-B (CM) - 0422

Subject: Letter of Intent to award Subcontract

Dear Mr. Kick;

We herewith respectfully inform your office of our intent to award a subcontract for the above referenced project per your quote received on 8/05/93 in the amount of $898,000.00. This subcontract will be forwarded upon receipt of our contract from the NIH, which we expect any day. A preconstruction meeting is currently scheduled at the NIH on 9/08/93 at 10 AM which we have been requested that your firm attend.

As discussed with you, a meeting was held between NIH and PEI wherein PEI confirmed our bid to the government, and designated your firm as our HVAC Mechanical subcontractor. This action was taken after several telephonic and face to face discussions with you regarding the above referenced bid submitted by your firm. We look forward to working with your firm on this contract and hope that this will lead to a long and mutually beneficial relationship.

Sincerely,

/s/ Thomas F. Pavel, President

Upon receipt of PEI's fax of September 1, James Kick called and informed PEI that Johnson's bid contained an error, and as a result the price was too low. According to Kick, Johnson had discovered the mistake earlier, but because Johnson believed that PEI had not been awarded the contract, they did not feel compelled to correct the error. Kick sought to withdraw Johnson's bid, both over the telephone and by a letter dated September 2, 1993:

A. S. Johnson Co.

September 2, 1993

PEI Construction 780 West Maples Avenue, Suite 101 Vienna, Virginia 22180

Attention: Thomas Pavel, President

Reference: NIH Building 30 HVAC Modifications

Dear Mr. Pavel,

We respectfully inform you of our intention to withdraw our proposal for the above referenced project due to an error in our bid.

As discussed in our telephone conversation and face to face meeting, the management of A. S. Johnson Company was reviewing this proposal, upon which we were to confirm our pricing to you.

Please contact Mr. Harry Kick, General Manager at [telephone number deleted] for any questions you may have.

Very truly yours,

/s/ James H. Kick Estimating Manager

PEI responded to both the September 1 phone call, and the September 2 letter, expressing its refusal to permit Johnson to withdraw.

On September 28, 1993, NIH formally awarded the construction contract to PEI. PEI found a substitute subcontractor to do the mechanical work, but at a cost of $930,000. PEI brought suit against Johnson in the Circuit Court for Prince George's County to recover the $32,000 difference between Johnson's bid and the cost of the substitute mechanical subcontractor.

The case was heard by the trial court without the aid of a jury. The trial court made several findings of fact, which we summarize:

1. PEI relied upon Johnson's sub-bid in making its bid for the entire project;
2. The fact that PEI was not the low bidder, but was awarded the project only after the apparent low bidder was disqualified, takes this case out of the ordinary;
3. Prior to NIH awarding PEI the contract on September 28, Johnson, on September 2, withdrew its bid; and
4. PEI's letter to all potential mechanical subcontractors, dated August 26, 1993, indicates that there was no definite agreement between PEI and Johnson, and that PEI was not relying upon Johnson's bid.

The trial court analyzed the case under both a traditional contract theory and under a detrimental reliance theory. PEI was unable to satisfy the trial judge that under either theory that [sic] a contractual relationship had been formed.

PEI appealed to the Court of Special Appeals, raising both traditional offer and acceptance theory, and "promissory estoppel." Before our intermediate appellate court considered the case, we issued a writ of certiorari on our own motion.

II

The relationships involved in construction contracts have long posed a unique problem in the law of contracts. A brief overview of the mechanics of the construction bid process, as well as our legal system's attempts to regulate the process, is in order.

A. CONSTRUCTION BIDDING.

Our description of the bid process in *Maryland Supreme Corp. v. Blake Co.,* 279 Md. 531, 369 A.2d 1017 (1977) is still accurate:

> "In such a building project there are basically three parties involved: the letting party, who calls for bids on its job; the general contractor, who makes a bid on the whole project; and the subcontractors, who bid only on that portion of the whole job which involves the field of its specialty. The usual procedure is that when a project is announced, a subcontractor, on his own initiative or at the general contractor's request, prepares an estimate and submits a bid to one or more of the general contractors interested in the project. The general contractor evaluates the bids made by the subcontractors in each field and uses them to compute its total bid to the letting party. After receiving bids from general contractors, the letting party ordinarily awards the contract to the lowest reputable bidder."

Id. at 533–34, 369 A.2d at 1020–21 (citing The Firm Offer problem).

B. THE CONSTRUCTION BIDDING CASES—AN HISTORICAL OVERVIEW.

The problem the construction bidding process poses is the determination of the precise points on the timeline that the various parties become bound to each other. The early landmark case was *James Baird Co. v. Gimbel Bros., Inc.,* 64 F.2d 344 (2d Cir. 1933). The plaintiff, James Baird Co., ["Baird"] was a general contractor from Washington, D.C., bidding to construct a government building in Harrisburg, Pennsylvania. Gimbel Bros., Inc., ["Gimbel"], the famous New York department store, sent its bid to supply linoleum to a number of bidding general contractors on December 24, and Baird received Gimbel's bid on December 28. Gimbel realized its bid was based on an incorrect computation and notified Baird of its withdrawal on December 28. The letting authority awarded Baird the job on December 30. Baird formally accepted the Gimbel bid on January 2. When Gimbel refused to perform, Baird sued for the additional cost of a substitute linoleum supplier. The Second Circuit Court of Appeals held that Gimbel's initial bid was an offer to contract and, under traditional contract law, remained open only until accepted or withdrawn. Because the offer was withdrawn before it was accepted there was no contract. Judge Learned Hand, speaking for the court, also rejected two alternative theories of the case: unilateral contract and promissory estoppel. He held that Gimbel's bid was not an offer of a unilateral contract that Baird could accept by performing, i.e., submitting the bid as part of the general bid; and second, he held that the theory of promissory estoppel was limited to cases involving charitable pledges.

Judge Hand's opinion was widely criticized, *see* Note, *Contracts-Promissory Estoppel*, 20 VA. L. REV. 214 (1933) [hereinafter, "Promissory Estoppel"]; Note, *Contracts-Revocation of Offer Before Acceptance-Promissory Estoppel*, 28 ILL. L. REV. 419 (1934), but also widely influential. The effect of the *James Baird* line of cases, however, is an "obvious injustice without relief of any description." *Promissory Estoppel*, at 215. The general contractor is bound to the price submitted to the letting party, but the subcontractors are not bound, and are free to withdraw.

As one commentator described it, "If the subcontractor revokes his bid before it is accepted by the general, any loss which results is a deduction from the general's profit and conceivably may transform overnight a profitable contract into a losing deal." Franklin M. Schultz, *The Firm Offer Puzzle: A Study of Business Practice in the Construction Industry*, 19 U. CHI. L. REV. 237, 239 (1952).

The unfairness of this regime to the general contractor was addressed in *Drennan v. Star Paving,* 333 P.2d 757, 51 Cal. 2d 409 (1958). Like James Baird, the *Drennan* case arose in the context of a bid mistake. Justice Traynor, writing for the Supreme Court of California, relied upon § 90 of the *Restatement (First) of Contracts*:

> "A promise which the promisor should reasonably expect to induce action or forbearance of a definite and substantial character on the part of the promisee and which does induce such action or forbearance is binding if injustice can be avoided only by enforcement of the promise."

Restatement (First) of Contracts § 90 (1932).

Justice Traynor reasoned that the subcontractor's bid contained an implied subsidiary promise not to revoke the bid. As the court stated:

> "When plaintiff [, a General Contractor,] used defendant's offer in computing his own bid, he bound himself to perform in reliance on defendant's terms. Though defendant did not bargain for the use of its bid neither did defendant make it idly, indifferent to whether it would be used or not. On the contrary it is reasonable to suppose that defendant submitted its bid to obtain the subcontract. It was bound to realize the substantial possibility that its bid would be the lowest, and that it would be included by plaintiff in his bid. It was to its own interest that the contractor be awarded the general contract; the lower the subcontract bid, the lower the general contractor's bid was likely to be and the greater its chance of acceptance and hence the greater defendant's chance of getting the paving subcontract. Defendant had reason not only to expect plaintiff to rely on its bid but to want him to. Clearly defendant had a stake in plaintiff's reliance on its bid. Given this interest and the fact that plaintiff is bound by his own bid, it is only fair that plaintiff should have at least an opportunity to accept defendant's bid after the general contract has been awarded to him."

Drennan, 51 Cal. 2d at 415, 333 P.2d at 760. The *Drennan* court however did not use "promissory estoppel" as a substitute for the entire contract, as is the doctrine's usual function. Instead, the *Drennan* court, applying the principle of § 90, interpreted the subcontractor's bid to be irrevocable. Justice Traynor's analysis used promissory estoppel as consideration for an implied promise to keep the bid open for a reasonable time. Recovery was then predicated on traditional bilateral contract, with the sub-bid as the offer and promissory estoppel serving to replace acceptance.

The *Drennan* decision has been very influential. Many states have adopted the reasoning used by Justice Traynor. * * *

Despite the popularity of the *Drennan* reasoning, the case has subsequently come under some criticism. The criticism centers on the lack of symmetry of detrimental reliance in the bid process, in that subcontractors are bound to the general, but the general is not bound to the subcontractors. The result is that the general is free to bid shop,[13] bid chop[14], and to encourage bid peddling,[15] to the detriment of the subcontractors. One commentator described the problems that these practices create:

> "Bid shopping and peddling have long been recognized as unethical by construction trade organizations. These 'unethical,' but common practices have several detrimental results. First, as bid shopping becomes common within a particular trade, the subcontractors will pad their initial bids in order to make further reductions during post-award negotiations. This artificial inflation of subcontractor's offers makes the bid process less effective. Second, subcontractors who are forced into post-award negotiations with the general often must reduce their sub-bids in order to avoid losing the award. Thus, they will be faced with a Hobson's choice between doing the job at a loss or doing a less than adequate job. Third, bid shopping and peddling tend to increase the risk of loss of the time and money used in preparing a bid. This occurs because generals and subcontractors who engage in these practices use, without expense, the bid estimates prepared by others. Fourth, it is often impossible for a general to obtain bids far enough in advance to have sufficient time to properly prepare his own bid because of the practice, common among many subcontractors, of holding sub-bids until the last possible moment in order to avoid pre-award bid shopping by the general. Fifth, many subcontractors refuse to submit bids for jobs on which they expect bid shopping. As a result, competition is reduced, and, consequently, construction prices are increased. Sixth, any price reductions gained through the use of post-award bid shopping by the general will be of no benefit to the awarding authority, to whom these price reductions would normally accrue as a result of open competition before the award of the

[13]Bid shopping is the use of the lowest subcontractor's bid as a tool in negotiating lower bids from other subcontractors post-award.

[14]"The general contractor, having been awarded the prime contract, may pressure the subcontractor whose bid was used for a particular portion of the work in computing the overall bid on the prime contract to reduce the amount of the bid." Closen & Weiland, at 566 n.6 [13 J. Marshall L. Rev. 565 (1980)].

[15]An unscrupulous subcontractor can save estimating costs, and still get the job by not entering a bid or by entering an uncompetitive bid. After bid opening, this unscrupulous subcontractor, knowing the price of the low sub-bid, can then offer to perform the work for less money, precisely because the honest subcontractor has already paid for the estimate and included that cost in the original bid. This practice is called bid peddling.

> prime contract. Free competition in an open market is therefore perverted because of the use of post-award bid shopping."

Bid Shopping, at 394–96 [18 UCLA L. Rev. 389 (1970] (citations omitted).
* * *

The doctrine of detrimental reliance has evolved in the time since *Drennan* was decided in 1958. The American Law Institute, responding to *Drennan*, sought to make detrimental reliance more readily applicable to the construction bidding scenario by adding § 87. This new section was intended to make subcontractors' bids binding:

> § 87. Option Contract
>
> . . .
>
> (2) An offer which the offeror should reasonably expect to induce action or forbearance of a substantial character on the part of the offeree before acceptance and which does induce such action or forbearance is binding as an option contract to the extent necessary to avoid injustice.

Restatement (Second) of Contracts § 87 (1979).

Despite the drafter's intention that § 87 of the *Restatement (Second) of Contracts* (1979) should replace *Restatement (First) of Contracts* § 90 (1932) in the construction bidding cases, few courts have availed themselves of the opportunity. * * *

Courts and commentators have also suggested other solutions intended to bind the parties without the use of detrimental reliance theory. The most prevalent suggestion is the use of the firm offer provision of the Uniform Commercial Code. Maryland Code (1992 Repl. Vol.), § 2-205 of the Commercial Law Article. That statute provides:

> "An offer by a merchant to buy or sell goods in a signed writing which by its terms gives assurance that it will be held open is not revocable, for lack of consideration, during the time stated or if no time is stated for a reasonable time, but in no event may such period of irrevocability exceed three months; but any such term of assurance on a form supplied by the offeree must be separately signed by the offeror."

In this manner, subcontractor's bids, made in writing and giving some assurance of an intent that the offer be held open, can be found to be irrevocable.

The Supreme Judicial Court of Massachusetts has suggested three other traditional theories that might prove the existence of a contractual relationship between a general contractor and a sub: conditional bilateral contract analysis; unilateral contract analysis; and unrevoked offer analysis. *Loranger Constr. Corp. v. E. F. Hauserman Co.,* 384 N.E.2d 176, 376 Mass. 757 (1978). If the general contractor could prove that there was an exchange of promises binding the parties to each other, and that exchange of promises was made before bid opening, that would constitute a valid bilateral promise conditional upon the general being awarded the job. *Loranger,* 384 N.E.2d at 180, 376 Mass. at 762. This directly contrasts with Judge Hand's analysis in *James Baird*, that a general's use of a sub-bid constitutes acceptance conditional upon the award of the contract to the general. *James Baird,* 64 F.2d at 345–46.

Alternatively, if the subcontractor intended its sub-bid as an offer to a unilateral contract, use of the sub-bid in the general's bid constitutes part performance, which renders the initial offer irrevocable under the *Restatement (Second) of Contracts* § 45 (1979). *Loranger,* 384 N.E.2d at 180, 376 Mass. at 762. This resurrects a second theory dismissed by Judge Learned Hand in James Baird.

Finally, the *Loranger* court pointed out that a jury might choose to disbelieve that a subcontractor had withdrawn the winning bid, meaning that acceptance came before withdrawal, and a traditional bilateral contract was formed. *Loranger,* 384 N.E.2d at 180, 376 Mass. at 762–63.

Another alternative solution to the construction bidding problem is no longer seriously considered-revitalizing the common law seal. William Noel Keyes, *Consideration Reconsidered-The Problem of the Withdrawn Bid,* 10 STAN. L. REV. 441, 470 (1958). Because a sealed option contract remains firm without consideration this alternative was proposed as a solution to the construction bidding problem.

It is here that the state of the law rests.

III

If PEI is able to prove by any of the theories described that a contractual relationship existed, but Johnson failed to perform its end of the bargain, then PEI will recover the $32,000 in damages caused by Johnson's breach of contract. Alternatively, if PEI is unable to prove the existence of a contractual relationship, then Johnson has no obligation to PEI. We will test the facts of the case against the theories described to determine if such a relationship existed.

The trial court held, and we agree, that Johnson's sub-bid was an offer to contract and that it was sufficiently clear and definite. We must then determine if PEI made a timely and valid acceptance of that offer and thus created a traditional bilateral contract, or in the absence of a valid acceptance, if PEI's detrimental reliance served to bind Johnson to its sub-bid. We examine each of these alternatives, beginning with traditional contract theory.[22]

A. TRADITIONAL BILATERAL CONTRACT.

The trial judge found that there was not a traditional contract binding Johnson to PEI. A review of the record and the trial judge's findings make it clear that this was a close question. On appeal however, our job is to assure that the trial judge's findings were not clearly erroneous. * * * This is an easier task.

The trial judge rejected PEI's claim of bilateral contract for two separate reasons: 1) that there was no meeting of the minds; and 2) that the offer was withdrawn prior to acceptance. Both need not be proper bases for decision; if either of these two theories is not clearly erroneous, we must affirm.

There is substantial evidence in the record to support the judge's conclusion that there was no meeting of the minds. PEI's letter of August 26, to all potential mechanical subcontractors, reproduced *supra*, indicates, as the trial judge found, that PEI and Johnson "did not have a definite, certain

[22]Because they were not raised, either below or in this Court, we need not address the several methods in which a court might interpret a subcontractor's bid as a firm, and thus irrevocable, offer. Nevertheless, for the benefit of bench and bar, we review those theories as applied to this case. First, PEI could have purchased an option, thus supplying consideration for making the offer irrevocable. This did not happen. Second, Johnson could have submitted its bid as a sealed offer. [U.C.C. § 5-102]. An offer under seal supplants the need for consideration to make an offer firm. This did not occur in the instant case. The third method of Johnson's offer becoming irrevocable is by operation of [U.C.C. § 2-205]. We note that Johnson's sub-bid was made in the form of a signed writing, but without further evidence we are unable to determine if the offer "by its terms gives assurance that it will be held open" and if the sub-bid is for "goods" as that term is defined by [U.C.C. § § 2-105(1)] and by decisions of this Court * * *.

meeting of the minds on a certain price for a certain quantity of goods . . . ." Because this reason is itself sufficient to sustain the trial judge's finding that no contract was formed, we affirm.

Alternatively, we hold, that the evidence permitted the trial judge to find that Johnson revoked its offer prior to PEI's final acceptance. We review the relevant chronology. Johnson made its offer, in the form of a sub-bid, on August 5. On September 1, PEI accepted. Johnson withdrew its offer by letter dated September 2. On September 28, NIH awarded the contract to PEI. Thus, PEI's apparent acceptance came one day prior to Johnson's withdrawal.

The trial court found, however, "that before there was ever a final agreement reached with the contract awarding authorities, that Johnson made it clear to [PEI] that they were not going to continue to rely on their earlier submitted bid." Implicit in this finding is the judge's understanding of the contract. Johnson's sub-bid constituted an offer of a contingent contract. PEI accepted that offer subject to the condition precedent of PEI's receipt of the award of the contract from NIH. Prior to the occurrence of the condition precedent, Johnson was free to withdraw. See 2 *Williston on Contracts* § 6:14 (4th ed.). On September 2, Johnson exercised that right to revoke.[23] The trial judge's finding that withdrawal proceeded valid final acceptance is therefore logical and supported by substantial evidence in the record. It was not clearly erroneous, so we shall affirm.

B. DETRIMENTAL RELIANCE

PEI's alternative theory of the case is that PEI's detrimental reliance binds Johnson to its bid. We are asked, as a threshold question, if detrimental reliance applies to the setting of construction bidding. Nothing in our previous cases suggests that the doctrine was intended to be limited to a specific

[23] We have also considered the possibility that Johnson's offer was not to enter into a contingent contract. This is unlikely because there is no incentive for a general contractor to accept a non-contingent contract prior to contract award but it would bind the general to purchase the subcontractor's services even if the general did not receive the award. Moreover, PEI's September 1 letter clearly "accepted" Johnson's offer subject to the award from NIH. If Johnson's bid was for a non-contingent contract, PEI's response substantially varied the offer and was therefore a counter-offer, not an acceptance. * * *

factual setting. The benefits of binding subcontractors outweigh the possible detriments of the doctrine.[24]

This Court has decided cases based on detrimental reliance as early as 1854, and the general contours of the doctrine are well understood by Maryland courts. The historical development of promissory estoppel, or detrimental reliance, in Maryland has mirrored the development nationwide. It was originally a small exception to the general consideration requirement, and found in "cases dealing with such narrow problems as gratuitous agencies and bailments, waivers, and promises of marriage settlement." Jay M. Feinman, Promissory Estoppel and Judicial Method, *97 HARV. L. REV. 678, 680 (1984).* The early Maryland cases applying "promissory estoppel" or detrimental reliance primarily involve charitable pledges.

* * *

Detrimental reliance doctrine has had a slow evolution from its origins in disputes over charitable pledges, and there remains some uncertainty about its exact dimensions. * * *

To resolve these confusions we now clarify that Maryland courts are to apply the test of the *Restatement (Second) of Contracts* § 90(1) (1979), which we have recast as a four-part test:

1. a clear and definite promise;
2. where the promisor has a reasonable expectation that the offer will induce action or forbearance on the part of the promisee;
3. which does induce actual and reasonable action or forbearance by the promisee; and
4. causes a detriment which can only be avoided by the enforcement of the promise.

In a construction bidding case, where the general contractor seeks to bind the subcontractor to the sub-bid offered, the general must first prove that the subcontractor's sub-bid constituted an offer to perform a job at a given price. We do not express a judgment about how precise a bid must be to constitute an offer, or to what degree a general contractor may re-

[24]General contractors, however, should not assume that we will also adopt the holdings of our sister courts who have refused to find general contractors bound to their subcontractors. *See, e.g., N. Litterio & Co. v. Glassman Constr. Co.,* 115 U.S. App. D.C. 335, 319 F.2d 736 (D.C. Cir. 1963).

quest to change the offered scope before an acceptance becomes a counter-offer. That fact-specific judgment is best reached on a case-by-case basis. In the instant case, the trial judge found that the sub-bid was sufficiently clear and definite to constitute an offer, and his finding was not clearly erroneous.

* * *

Second, the general must prove that the subcontractor reasonably expected that the general contractor would rely upon the offer. The subcontractor's expectation that the general contractor will rely upon the sub-bid may dissipate through time.[30]

In this case, the trial court correctly inquired into Johnson's belief that the bid remained open, and that consequently PEI was not relying on the Johnson bid. The judge found that due to the time lapse between bid opening and award, "it would be unreasonable for offers to continue." This is supported by the substantial evidence. James Kick testified that although he knew of his bid mistake, he did not bother to notify PEI because J J. Kirlin, Inc., and not PEI, was the apparent low bidder. The trial court's finding that Johnson's reasonable expectation had dissipated in the span of a month is not clearly erroneous.

As to the third element, a general contractor must prove that he actually and reasonably relied on the subcontractor's sub-bid. We decline to provide a checklist of potential methods of proving this reliance, but we will make several observations. First, a showing by the subcontractor, that the general contractor engaged in "bid shopping," or actively encouraged "bid chopping," or "bid peddling" is strong evidence that the general did not rely on the sub-bid. Second, prompt notice by the general contractor to the subcontractor that the general intends to use the sub on the job, is weighty evidence that the general did rely on the bid.[31] Third, if a sub-bid is so low that a reasonably prudent general contractor would not rely upon it, the trier of fact may infer that the general contractor did not in fact rely upon the erroneous bid.

---

[30] We expect that evidence of "course of dealing" and "usage of the trade," *see Restatement (Second) of Contracts* § 219-223 (1979), will provide strong indices of the reasonableness of a subcontractor's expectations.

[31] Prompt notice and acceptance also significantly dispels the possibility of b d shopping, bid chopping, and bid peddling.

In this case, the trial judge did not make a specific finding that PEI failed to prove its reasonable reliance upon Johnson's sub-bid. We must assume, however, that it was his conclusion based on his statement that "the parties did not have a definite, certain meeting of the minds on a certain price for a certain quantity of goods and wanted to renegotiate . . . ." The August 26, 1993, fax from PEI to all prospective mechanical subcontractors, is evidence supporting this conclusion. Although the finding that PEI did not rely on Johnson's bid was indisputably a close call, it was not clearly erroneous.

Finally, as to the fourth prima facie element, the trial court, and not a jury, must determine that binding the subcontractor is necessary to prevent injustice. This element is to be enforced as required by common law equity courts—the general contractor must have "clean hands." This requirement includes, as did the previous element, that the general did not engage in bid shopping, chopping or peddling, but also requires the further determination that justice compels the result. The fourth factor was not specifically mentioned by the trial judge, but we may infer that he did not find this case to merit an equitable remedy.

Because there was sufficient evidence in the record to support the trial judge's conclusion that PEI had not proven its case for detrimental reliance, we must, and hereby do, affirm the trial court's ruling.

V

In conclusion, we emphasize that there are different ways to prove that a contractual relationship exists between a general contractor and its subcontractors. Traditional bilateral contract theory is one. Detrimental reliance can be another. However, under the evidence in this case, the trial judge was not clearly erroneous in deciding that recovery by the general contractor was not justified under either theory.

JUDGMENT AFFIRMED, WITH COSTS.

QUESTIONS AND NOTES

1. Questions about the facts of this case

   1.1. Try to put together a chronology of events. On what date did Johnson make its offer for the sub-bid? On what date did PEI accept? On what date did Johnson attempt to withdraw its offer? Now look at your chronology of the facts. Does it support the holding in the case?

   1.2. With respect to PEI's promissory estoppel claim, in its summary of the findings of fact made by the trial court, the court of appeals notes that "PEI relied upon Johnson's sub-bid in making the bid for the entire project." Later in the decision, the court states: "In this case, the trial judge did not make a specific finding that PEI failed to prove its reasonable reliance upon Johnson's sub-bid. . . . Although the finding that PEI did not rely on Johnson's bid was indisputably a close call, it was not clearly erroneous." What's going on here?

   1.3. See if you can identify the critical factual distinctions between Justice Traynor's holding in *Drennan v. Star Paving*, discussed at length in the *Pavel Enterprises* opinion, and the *Pavel* case itself.

2. Questions about the law

   2.1. One of the limitations in *Restatement (Second) of Contracts* § 87(2), which expressly adopts the *Drennan* approach, is that the promise is only enforceable "to the extent necessary to prevent injustice." Of course, the same language appears in § 90. What does that language mean in this context? Is it an injustice if, as result of the revocation of the subcontractor's bid, the general contractor will make *less* profit, or is it only an injustice if, because of the price of the next lowest bid, the general contractor will now actually lose money on the job? Who makes that determination?

   2.2. Despite the different theories under which a general contractor may bind the subcontractor to hold its bid open, as *Pavel Enterprises* illustrates, there is no guarantee that the general contractor will prevail on any of these theories. Therefore, in representing a general contractor who is figuring its costs in reliance on specific subcontractor bids, what advice would you give to ensure protection of your client's interests? Correspondingly, if you represent a subcontractor preparing to make its bid and concerned about application of the rule in *Drennan*, what steps would you advise your client to take?

2.3. The court in *Pavel Enterprises* concluded that a traditional bilateral contract had not been formed and that PEI's detrimental reliance would not serve to bind Johnson. Nevertheless, it was undisputed that Pavel used Johnson's sub-bid in computing its own bid. Given this fact, could you construct an argument either for acceptance by performance or, invoking *Restatement (Second) of Contracts* § 45, for irrevocability of the sub-bid based on part performance?

3. Notes

3.1. In the *Drennan* case, Justice Traynor employed the doctrine of promissory estoppel to find that the subcontractor could not revoke its bid once it had been relied upon by the general contractor. However, as the court in *Pavel Enterprises* noted, this was really an expansion of the doctrine of promissory estoppel since the bid involved an offer for an *exchange* transaction and not a gift promise. Thus, in *Drennan*, the court used promissory estoppel (or detrimental reliance) to *imply* a promise of irrevocability where none actually existed, as well as to *enforce* that promise despite the absence of consideration.

3.2. Recognizing the one-sided nature of the option contract created by *Drennan*, and the potential for bid-shopping by the general contractor that it creates, in 1963 the California legislature adopted a statute that 1) requires the general contractor in any public project to list the identities of its subcontractors in its bid, and then, 2) proscribes the substitution by the general contractor of any subcontractor listed in the original bid, except upon a showing of exceptional circumstances such as the subcontractor's insolvency or refusal to do the work. Cal. Gov't Code §§ 4100–4108 (Subletting and Subcontractors Fair Practices Act). Does such an approach, which has been followed in other states, level the playing field for general and subcontractors?

Note on Promissory Estoppel and Pre-Contract Negotiations

Drennan and *Restatement (Second) of Contracts* § 87(2), discussed in the *Pavel Enterprises* case, demonstrate that courts will sometimes use a promissory estoppel theory as a basis for barring an offeror from revoking an offer on which the offeree has relied. This raises the broader question of to what extent will the courts invoke promissory estoppel to police conduct occurring in the stage of pre-contract negotiations? How do you suppose the court in *Midwest Energy* would answer that question in light of the "Missouri rule" referred to in footnote 4 of the case?

In perhaps the most far-reaching application of the doctrine of promissory estoppel, the Wisconsin Supreme Court, in *Hoffman v. Red Owl Stores, Inc,* 133 N.W.2d 267 (Wis. 1967), held that assurances made by a grocery store franchisor to a prospective franchisee concerning the award of a store at a new location could form the basis for recovery of out-of-pocket expenses incurred by the promisee in anticipation of the contract, even though the negotiations of the parties never ripened into a contractually enforceable promise.

The *Restatement (Second) of Contracts* appears to approve of the holding in *Red Owl. See* § 90 cmt. d, illus 10. Nevertheless, the decision represents a significant expansion of the doctrine of promissory estoppel as a basis for enforcing gift promises inducing reliance since there was no actual offer or "promise" in *Red Owl.* In other words, negotiations had not advanced to the point where there was a sufficiently clear and definite agreement that might have supported an action for breach of contract. Instead, recovery of reliance expenditures was based solely on positive assurances made by the franchisor during the course of negotiations that ultimately failed to reach fruition. Failed negotiations are, of course, a fact of life in business. Thus, something else was going on in *Red Owl.* What do you suppose it was? Go back and review *Budget Marketing, Inc. v. Centronics Corp., supra,* at 213. Does that offer any hints? Sometimes we begin to wonder whether this class is about contracts or torts. Maybe you're wondering the same thing.

Problem on Promissory Estoppel

Let's assume that, in his third year of law school, Epstein accepts a job offer upon graduation from Cornbath, Swine & Moorg, a highly prestigious Wall Street firm with a reputation for paying the highest new associate salaries in the country. Secure in his decision, Epstein turns down other interviews with firms paying well, but not as well as old CS&M. After graduation, Epstein packs up his belongings and moves to New York to begin studying for the bar and working for CS&M. The day before he is to begin work, he receives a call at home from the hiring partner who informs Epstein that CS&M has a policy of only employing new associates who graduated in the top 5% of their law school class. Because, in his last semester of law school, Epstein dropped just below the top 5%, the partner tells him that the firm has filled his slot by hiring someone else. Enraged, Epstein responds by reminding the partner that he had a contract with the firm. The partner replies by telling him, "Ah, but that's where you're wrong. Because this was an employment at will, either party could terminate at any time. This bilateral power of termination means neither of us was committed to performance to the other. Therefore, these mutual so-called promises were illusory and could not give rise to a contract in fact. Perhaps if you studied a little harder, Dave, you would have known that, as well as graduated in the top 5%." Feeling betrayed, lamenting the money he spent to move to New York, and thinking about the other attractive interviews he passed up, Epstein decides to sue. Assuming the partner is right that, under applicable law, no contract arose between Epstein and CS&M, can Epstein successfully bring an action under the theory of promissory estoppel? If so, what damages should he seek?

---

4. Remedial Considerations

Edward Yorio & Steve Thel, The Promissory Basis of § 90

101 YALE L.J. 111, 116–17 (1991).

During the 1926 proceedings of the American Law Institute, a member of the audience asked Professor Samuel Williston, the reporter for the First Restatement of Contracts, about the following hypothetical. Uncle, aware that Nephew is thinking about buying a car, promises to give Nephew

$1000. Nephew buys a car for $600. If Uncle reneges on his promise and Nephew sues, what does the Nephew recover, $1000 or $600? Williston responded that Uncle would be liable for $1000, the amount of his promise. Although Williston's response satisfied the immediate questioner, Frederic Coudert, the famous New York lawyer, challenged Williston's answer in an exchange that has since become one of the most quoted passages in American contract law:

> MR. COUDERT: Allow me to trespass once more, Mr. Reporter, by asking this question. Please let me see if I understand it rightly. Would you say, Mr. Reporter, in your case of Johnny and the uncle, the uncle promising the $1000 and Johnny buying the car—say, he goes out and buys the car for $500—that uncle would be liable for $1000 or would he be liable for $500?
>
> MR. WILLISTON: If Johnny had done what he was expected to do, or is acting within the limits of his uncle's expectation, I think the uncle would be liable for $1000; but not otherwise.
>
> MR. COUDERT: In other words, substantial justice would require that uncle should be penalized in the sum of $500.
>
> MR. WILLISTON: Why do you say "penalized"?. . . .
>
> MR. COUDERT: Because substantial justice there would require, it seems to me, that Johnny get his money for his car, but should he get his car and $500 more? I don't see.

Coudert's bewilderment was shared by other members of the audience, who returned repeatedly to the car hypothetical:

> HOMER ALBERS (Massachusetts): I am still not satisfied that Johnny could have the car and $500 both, if he bought a second-hand Buick for $500 . . .
>
> JUDGE PAGE: To get back to Johnny, how is injustice going to be done Johnny if he is not going to get the other $500; how is he going to be done an injustice, if he only paid $500 for the car?

In the face of this assault, Williston stood his ground:

> MR. WILLISTON: Either the promise is binding or it is not. If the promise is binding it has to be enforced as it is made.

Many commentators have urged that the remedy in promissory estoppel cases should be limited to *reliance* damages—the amount necessary to put the promisee back in the position she would have been had the promise not been made. In fact, however, most cases support Professor Williston's view and award *expectation* damages or even specific performance. Expectation damages are measured by the amount necessary to put the promisee in as good of a position as performance would have. Which measure of damages did the court recommend as appropriate on remand in *Midwest Energy*? How about in *Ricketts*? Can you explain the reasons for the difference?

When we enforce a promise because the promisee detrimentally relied, arguably what we're saying is that we'll hold the promisor liable because it would be wrong to allow him to walk away after foreseeably causing harm or loss to the promisee. In other words, the promisee has been damaged and it is the promisor's fault. Doesn't this suggest that the promisee's recovery should be determined based on the amount necessary to compensate her for her loss, to restore her to the position she would have been in had the promise never been made? How does this rationale differ from the rationale for enforcing exchange promises—those supported by a bargained-for consideration? Should this make a difference in how damages are calculated? What about the language in § 90 that allows courts to limit the remedy "as justice requires"? Consider these questions in light of the discussion which follows about the continued role of reliance in promissory estoppel cases.

---

5. The Diminishing Importance of Reliance

Oddly, even though the doctrine of promissory estoppel developed in the context of charitable subscription cases, proving reliance in the form of action or forbearance is often most difficult for the promisee in those cases. If you pledge $100 to your alma mater and then stiff the school, how can the institution show that it was *induced* by your pledge to take a particular course of action that it would not otherwise have taken? Chances are, it can't. Thus, courts typically engage in various fictions to find detrimental reliance when none exist in fact. In the next case the court deals with the issue of reliance more honestly. See if you agree with the public policy that the court cites in support of its holding.

Salsbury v. Northwestern Bell Telephone Company
Supreme Court of Iowa
221 N.W.2d 609 (1974)

Harris, J.

This is the third appeal in which we have considered a claim of charitable subscription following the collapse of an attempt to establish a college in Charles City. In *Pappas v. Hauser,* 197 N.W.2d 607 (Iowa 1972) and *Pappas v. Bever,* 219 N.W.2d 720 (Iowa 1974) we held pledges not legally binding. In this case a letter was sent by the subscriber in lieu of executing the pledge form. The trial court held the letter bound its sender. We affirm.

* * *

John Salsbury (plaintiff) participated in the efforts to establish Charles City College (the college). He was the first and only chairman of the college's board of trustees. The funding project for the college was described in *Pappas v. Hauser, supra.* As part of the funding drive Peter Bruno, a professional fund raiser, solicited a subscription from Northwestern Bell Telephone Company (defendant). Defendant's office manager in Charles City was Daryl V. Winder who was also active in the campaign to raise money for the college. Bruno negotiated a number of times with Winder for the subscription from defendant.

As a fund solicitor Winder had been given a kit which included pledge forms of the type described in *Pappas v. Hauser, supra,* and *Pappas v. Bever, supra.* [These pledge forms or cards were generally given and received with the understanding that they were not binding. Eds.] Winder lacked authority to bind defendant for a pledge but conveyed the request to superiors in defendant corporation. Winder apparently did not have a pledge form available when he received defendant's consent for the subscription. Accordingly he wrote a letter to Bruno as follows:

> "This is to advise you that the contribution from Northwestern Bell Telephone Co. to the Charles City College has been approved by Mr. E. A. McDaniel, District Manager, Mason City.
>
> "The $15,000 contribution will be made over a three year period, in three equal payments. Our first $5000 payment will be made in 1968.
>
> "We are very pleased to add our name to the list of contributors to this fine community undertaking.

"If I can be of further assistance, please feel free to contact me."

The college and all others treated the letter exactly as another pledge card. In common with executed pledge cards it was assigned to a material supplier of the college. The letter itself was not transmitted to the supplier. A pledge card form was typed-in to reflect the $15,000 pledge though it was not signed by defendant. If any document reflecting defendant's intended contribution was forwarded in connection with the assignment to the supplier it was a copy of the typed-in pledge card.

Plaintiff executed a personal guaranty in order to gain credit from the supplier. Subscription pledges secured the obligation. The supplier then assigned the pledges to American Acceptance Corporation of Philadelphia, Pennsylvania, and finally, after settling with plaintiff, American Acceptance Corporation assigned them to him. In all assignments no copy of the letter was shown or given. Plaintiff conceded he had no knowledge of the letter. He acted in the belief defendant was obligated in the same manner as those who executed pledge cards.

As we have seen in the earlier cases cited the college failed after a short operation. In this appeal we are faced with the question of whether defendant is bound to pay his subscription by reason of the letter. *Pappas v. Bever, supra,* stands as authority defendant would not be bound had it executed only the pledge card.

I.

The trial court held the letter was a promissory undertaking which constituted a basis for contractual liability. This holding is challenged as being at variance with the understanding of the parties when the letter was given and received.

* * *

Plaintiff conceded letters, such as defendant's, were sometimes taken "in lieu of" pledge cards and were accepted on the "same basis." Plaintiff also admitted he had not seen defendant's letter until trial and had been unaware of its contents until two months before trial. * * *

The trial court refused to proceed from plaintiff's concession that letters were taken "in lieu of" and on the "same basis" as pledge cards. Defendant assumes it must follow the parties agreed any liabilities and rights under any letter, no matter how it was worded, were fixed by the wording of the pledge cards. The trial court did not agree. It ruled: "* * * A pledge card * * * was never presented to or signed by the defendant, and is irrelevant to any undertaking of the defendant. Any obligation of the defendant must be based on its letter."

We find nothing in plaintiff's concession which rises to an admission all letters were understood to bind the signer in exact accordance with the wording of an unsigned pledge card. The record supports the trial court's determination that defendant's letter set its own terms and was impervious to defenses which might avail against the pledge cards. It follows the trial court was right in excluding as irrelevant the evidence of circumstances surrounding execution of pledge cards.

II.

Defendant separately assigns the claim the trial court failed to apply fundamental contract principles. It is argued there was a failure of consideration because the college failed before any sums were scheduled for payment under the terms of the letter. It is also claimed the trial court should have given the letter the practical construction adopted by the college when it treated it the same as a pledge card. These assignments presuppose a charitable subscription should be viewed by routine contract standards. Many cases, including our own, have considered charitable subscriptions as desirable but enforceable only upon a showing of consideration sufficient for contractual liability.

Cases throughout the country clearly reflect a conflict between the desired goal of enforcing charitable subscriptions and the realities of contract law. The result has been strained reasoning which has been the subject of considerable criticism. This criticism is directed toward efforts by the courts to secure a substitute for consideration in charitable subscriptions. These efforts were thought necessary to bind the subscriber on a contract theory. Yet, in the nature of charitable subscriptions, it is presupposed the promise is made as a gift and not in return for consideration. 1 Williston on Contracts, Third Ed., § 116, page 473.

Consideration sufficient for a binding contract has been found under various criticized theories. *Id.* at 476–479. We have found consideration in the promises of other subscribers. *Brokaw v. McElroy,* 162 Iowa 288, 143 N.W. 1087; *Trustees v. Noyes,* 165 Iowa 601, 146 N.W. 848; *In re Estate of Leigh,* 186 Iowa 931, 173 N.W. 143; *Young Men's Christian Assn. v. Caward,* 213 Iowa 408, 239 N.W. 41. This theory is also criticized:

"* * * The difficulty with this view is its lack of conformity to the facts. It is doubtless possible for two or more persons to make mutual promises that each will give a specified amount to a charity or other object, but in the case of ordinary charitable subscriptions, the promise of each subscriber is made directly to the charity or its trustees, and it is frequently made without any reference to the subscription of others. If induced at all by previous or expected subscriptions, this inducement only affects the motive of the subscriber; it cannot be said that the previous subscriptions were given in exchange for the later one. Indeed the earlier subscriptions would be open to the objection of being past consideration so far as a later subscription was concerned. * * *." 1 Williston on Contracts, *supra*, pages 476–477.

In reaction to this widespread criticism a number of courts have turned to promissory estoppel as an alternative for the consideration requirement. 1 Williston on Contracts, Third Ed., § 140 * * * .

If promissory estoppel were to be the standard or criterion for enforcement this defendant probably could not be bound on the pledge. * * * Plaintiff relied on defendant's letter but not the form of it. Plaintiff conceded he had not even seen the letter until shortly before trial. And it is the form of the letter that distinguishes it from the pledge cards we have held not to be binding. *Pappas v. Bever, supra.*

We acknowledge as valid the criticism of cases which enforce charitable subscriptions only on a fictional finding of consideration. But we are reluctant to adopt promissory estoppel as the sole alternative basis for such enforcement.

"* * * Wide variation in reasoning indicates the difficulty of enforcing a charitable subscription on grounds of consideration. Yet, the courts have generally striven to find grounds for enforcement, indicating the depth of feeling in this country that private philanthropy serves a highly important function in our society.

"Of late, courts have tended to abandon the attempt to utilize traditional contract doctrines to sustain subscriptions and have placed their decision on grounds of promissory estoppel. Surprisingly, however, if promissory estoppel, in its traditional form, is widely adopted as the grounds upon which such subscriptions are to be tested, fewer subscriptions are likely to be enforced than previously. Under previous holdings, despite the conceptual inadequacy of the reasoning, promises were frequently enforced without regard to detrimental reliance on the promise. It was enough that the promisor had subscribed. If enforcement of charitable subscriptions is a desirable goal, it would seem sounder to view the preponderance of the cases as supporting the proposition that a charitable subscription is enforceable without consideration and without detrimental reliance. This seems to be the position taken in Restatement Second. Recognition of such a rule would also put an end to the flood of needless litigation created by the caution of executors and administrators who, for self-protection against surcharging, will not pay out on a subscription without a court decree." Calamari & Perillo, Law of Contracts, § 103, pages 177–178.

The tentative draft of Restatement of Contracts, Second, includes a new subparagraph 2. Section 90 now reads as follows: * * *

> "(2) A charitable subscription or a marriage settlement is binding under Subsection (1) without proof that the promise induced action or forbearance."

We believe public policy supports this view. It is more logical to bind charitable subscriptions without requiring a showing of consideration or detrimental reliance.

Charitable subscriptions often serve the public interest by making possible projects which otherwise could never come about. It is true some fund raising campaigns are not conducted on a plan which calls for subscriptions to be binding. In such cases we do not hesitate to hold them not binding. *Pappas v. Bever, supra.* However where a subscription is unequivocal the pledgor should be made to keep his word.

AFFIRMED.

QUESTIONS

1. Obviously, the approach to charitable subscriptions adopted in *Salsbury* has found its way into the final version of the *Restatement (Second) of Contracts.* Does this mean if you call and make a $10 pledge to Jerry's Kids on Labor Day but fail to follow-up with the money that the Muscular Dystrophy Association can sue you and recover? What if your donation was made in an uncontrollable surge of emotion after watching a particu-

larly poignant segment of the telethon, but you cannot really afford to pay the amount you pledged? Speaking of pledges, what exactly was the difference from a legal standpoint between the pledge cards and the letter in *Salsbury*?

2. Reliance remains a necessary element of promissory estoppel under § 90 in the commercial context. But what kind of showing is required? Must the reliance result in some form of measurable economic loss? In *Vastoler v. American Can Co.*, 700 F.2d 916 (3d Cir. 1983), the plaintiff brought suit against his former employer to enforce a promise to the effect that his years of service on behalf of the company occurring prior to his promotion would count for purposes of calculating his pension benefits at retirement. The plaintiff's acceptance of the promotion was conditioned on receiving this credit, so when, at retirement, the employer did not count the years of past service, the plaintiff sued on a promissory estoppel theory alleging the promise induced him to accept the promotion. The trial court granted the employer's summary judgment motion on the basis that the plaintiff had not been disadvantaged by accepting a promotion. The court of appeals reversed and remanded the case for trial, noting that the district court's reasoning contained the following flaw:

> The second error in the district court's reasoning involves an even more fundamental deficiency. It failed to consider the human dynamics and anxieties inherent in supervisory positions. All jobs are not the same, and work involves more than one's "daily bread" and the weekly paycheck. Certain jobs have higher levels of stress and anxiety. Often, increased responsibilities torture the mind as well as the body. The different levels of stress associated with different jobs explains why some qualified people do not want to be President of Fortune 500 corporations, nominee for the Presidency of the United States, or foreman of their plants. Some privates do not want the decision-making burdens of majors and generals. Following Justice Frankfurter's admonition that "this Court should not be ignorant as judges of what we know as men [or women]," *Watts v. Indiana,* 338 U.S. 49, 52, 69 S.Ct. 1347, 1349, 93 L.Ed. 1801 (1949), we find that the trial judge erred in failing to recognize that absorption of the stress and anxiety inherent in supervisory positions could be one of the factors that constitutes detrimental reliance.

700 F.2d at 919.

Do you think this is the kind of detrimental reliance the drafters of the *Restatement (Second)* had in mind? Reliance, of course, is very much a tort-based concept. If proof of reliance is becoming less central to recovery under promissory estoppel, does that help explain the trend we discussed in the Subsection 4, *supra,* concerning the tendency of the courts to award expectation damages rather than reliance damages in promissory estoppel cases? By way of conclusion, consider the following thoughts from Professors Farber and Matheson.

Daniel A. Farber & John E. Matheson, *Beyond Promissory Estoppel: Contract Law and the Invisible Handshake*
52 U. CHI. L REV. 903, 945 (1985)

Based on our survey of recent promissory estoppel cases, we believe that promissory estoppel is losing its link with reliance. In key cases promises have been enforced with only the weakest showing of any detriment to the promisee. Reliance-based damages are the exception, not the rule. With the decline of reliance, promissory estoppel is moving away from tort law. It has become a means of enforcing promises differing in doctrinal detail from traditional contract law but sharing a common goal. That goal, we have argued, is to foster trust between economic actors. Trust is a moral good, but it is also an economic asset. It allows coordination and planning between economic actors and fosters the formation of valuable economic institutions.

Perhaps in an earlier age traditional contract law was adequate to foster the degree of trust society needed in economic activities. Today, an increasingly interdependent society needs to foster trust in a variety of relationships not readily organized through the device of the formal contract. Promissory estoppel is one of several mechanisms courts have used to try to close what we have called the "relational gap"' in contract law.

In our view, recent cases expansively applying promissory estoppel are steps on the road to a broader rule of promissory obligation. We have proposed as a new standard for enforcement that all promises made in furtherance of economic activities be enforced without regard to the presence of consideration or reliance. Although we recognize that courts have not yet articulated this standard, we believe they are moving in this direction.

SECTION 10: STATUTE OF FRAUDS

Because of the statute of frauds, *some* agreements are not enforceable unless there is *special* proof that the agreement was made. This relatively simple sentence raises five not always simple questions that lawyers and law students need to be able to answer.

1) What is a statute of frauds?
2) What are the reasons for a statute of frauds?
3) Which agreements are covered by a statute of frauds, *i.e.* "within" the statute of frauds?
4) How are the requirements of a statute of frauds met, *i.e.*, satisfied?
5) What are the legal consequences of failure to satisfy the statute of frauds?

First, what is a statute of frauds? The first statute of frauds was enacted in England in 1677: "An Act for Prevention of Frauds and Perjuries." It required that certain kinds of agreements must be in writing to be legally enforceable. It remained the law in England until 1954 when most of its provisions were repealed.

While the statute of frauds has been virtually eliminated from the law of contracts in England, it remains an important (albeit unpopular) part of the law of contracts in the United States. Virtually every state has enacted one or more statutes of frauds providing that certain kinds of agreements are not legally enforceable unless set out in a signed writing.

Second, what are the reasons for a statute of frauds? The title of the first statute of fraud sets out the purpose of a statute of frauds: "Prevention of Frauds or Perjuries." As the note preceding § 110 of the *Restatement (Second) of Contracts* explains: "In general, the primary purpose of the Statute of Frauds is assumed to be evidentiary, to provide reliable evidence of the existence and terms of the contract, and the classes of contracts covered seem for the most part to have been selected because of importance or complexity."

Third, what kinds of agreements are covered by the statute of frauds? Again, statutes of frauds vary from state to state. Section 110 of the *Restatement (Second) of Contracts* sets out the kinds of agreements generally covered by a state's statutes of frauds.

§ 110 Classes of Contracts Covered

(1) The following classes of contracts are subject to a statute, commonly called the Statute of Frauds, forbidding enforcement unless there is a written memorandum or an applicable exception;
   (a) a contract of an executor or administrator to answer for a duty of his decedent (the executor-administrator provision);
   (b) a contract to answer for the duty of another (the suretyship provision);
   (c) a contract made upon consideration of marriage (the marriage provision);
   (d) a contract for the sale of an interest in land (the land contract provision);
   (e) a contract that is not to be performed within one year from the making thereof (the one-year provision).

(2) The following classes of contracts, which were traditionally subject to the Statute of Frauds, are now governed by Statute of Frauds provisions of the Uniform Commercial Code:
   (a) a contract for the sale of goods for the price of $500 or more (Uniform Commercial Code § 2-201).

* * *

The following three cases illustrate three kinds of contracts that are commonly within a state's statute of frauds* (1) land transfer agreements, (2) agreements to buy or sell goods for $500 or more and (3) agreements that cannot be performed within one year from the date the agreement was made. Additionally, the cases show the answers to questions 4—how are the requirements of a statute of frauds satisfied? and 5—what are the consequences of failure to satisfy the statute of frauds? In the first of the cases, *Radke v. Brenon*, the court considers whether a typed letter offering to sell land was sufficient to comply with the statute of frauds so that the person who received the letter and accepted the offer could get the court to enforce the agreement.

---

*While the *Restatement* capitalizes the Statute of Frauds, Bryan Garner doesn't—at least we think he doesn't. *See* BRYAN A. GARNER, A DICTIONARY OF MODERN LEGAL USAGE 831 (2nd ed. 1995).

Radke v. Brenon
Supreme Court of Minnesota
271 Minn. 35, 134 N.W.2d 887 (1965)

ROGOSHESKE, Justice.

Defendants appeal from a judgment of the district court decreeing specific performance of a contract for the sale of real estate.

The judgment was entered upon findings made after trial that "subsequent to the Defendant acquiring" the property in question they "did offer to sell the property to the Plaintiff for the sum of Two Hundred Sixty-two ($262.00) Dollars, which offer the Plaintiff did accept"; and that "at all times relevant, the Plaintiff has been ready, willing and able to complete the agreement for the sale of Defendants' property but the Defendants have refused to do so." The court concluded that defendants "have wrongfully and improperly failed and refused" to deliver a deed of the property to plaintiff.

Resolving the conflicts in the evidence in plaintiff's favor, as we must, these appear to be the facts. Plaintiff and defendants are neighbors owning adjoining lots in Wakefield Park addition in Ramsey County. At the times each acquired ownership, their lots and eight neighboring lots did not extend to the west shoreline of Wakefield Lake, located nearby. The strip of land between the shoreline of the lake and the east boundary of the platted lots was owned by Dr. Gulden * * * until December 1, 1959, when defendants acquired ownership of the entire strip. Preston Brenon, hereinafter referred to as defendant, was a licensed real estate agent. Following his purchase, he had the property surveyed, and on June 28, 1960, he sent an identical letter to plaintiff and the eight other neighbors offering to sell them the irregular parcels that separated their lots from the lake. In the letter he explained that since he was interested only in that part of the strip adjoining his property, he had no desire to retain the remainder. He stated he had "no desire to make any profit on this transaction if everyone owning adjoining property is willing to buy their portion" and divide the cost "equally among all 10 including (him)self." He itemized the total cost at $2,120 and offered to sell each lot for $212 on any terms agreeable. This letter was not signed by defendant but his name was typewritten thereon, he having authorized this and considered such to be tantamount to his signature. Previous to the receipt of this letter, plaintiff and defendant had discussed the latter's intent of acquiring the property for the neighborhood on at least two occasions. About [two] weeks after plaintiff received this offer, he orally accepted it.

Sometime later, plaintiff learned from a neighbor that two neighbors declined to purchase, and thus the divided cost of each lot was increased to $262 * * *. It is clear that plaintiff accepted defendant's offer on May 7, at which time plaintiff knew of the price increase. Defendant testified:

> 'Q. * * * And did he agree to buy that time?
>
> 'A. At that time he did.'

On August 14, plaintiff delivered to his attorney a check for $262 payable to defendants for the purpose of completing the sale. On August 16, plaintiff's attorney wrote defendant informing him that he held the check for payment of the sale price to be delivered on receipt of a deed. Sometime after August 16, plaintiff received a letter from defendant dated August 16 informing him that the offer to sell was revoked.

The question is whether these facts establish a valid and enforceable contract for the sale of land. Defendants contend they do not.

As admitted by defendant, an oral contract to sell the land was made, and the trial court was clearly justified in so finding. There being no formal, integrated, written contract, however, the problem is whether the oral contract is unenforceable because it comes within Minn. St. 513.05[1] of the statute of frauds. Briefly, that provision decrees void any contract for the sale of lands unless the contract or some memorandum of the contract is in writing. The precise issue in this case is whether, under the circumstances, the letter written by defendant offering the land to plaintiff is a memorandum sufficient to satisfy the requirements of the statute.

The statute expresses a public policy of preventing the enforcement by means of fraud and perjury of contracts that were never in fact made. To inhibit perversion of this policy by those who would deny an oral contract actually made, the statute itself permits enforcement of an oral contract if there exists a note or memorandum as evidence of the contract. To the courts, then, is left promotion of the policy of the statute, either by denying enforcement urged by defrauders or by granting enforcement against wrongful

[1]Minn. St. 513.05 provides: "Every contract for the leasing for a longer period of than one year or for the sale of any lands, or any interest in lands, shall be void unless the contract, or some note or memorandum thereof, expressing the consideration, is in writing and subscribed by the party by whom the lease or sale is to be made, or by his lawful agent thereunto authorized in writing; and no such contract, when made by an agent, shall be entitled to record unless the authority of such agent be also recorded."

repudiators. As an aid in this objective, the statute itself lists some requisites of a memorandum and this court has added others, so that we have some indication of what content a memorandum normally must have in order to be sufficient evidence of the contract.

The statute requires that the writing express the consideration and that it be subscribed by the party by whom the sale is to be made or by his lawful agent authorized in writing. This court has stated that the memorandum is sufficient when, in addition to the above requirements, it states expressly or by necessary implication the parties to the contract, the lands involved, and the general terms and conditions upon which the sale will be made.

These latter elements are clearly present in the letter written by defendant. Plaintiff's name is included in the inside address heading the letter, and Brenon's name is typewritten at the bottom. The land to be sold is positively delineated. The letter offers "their portion" to "everyone owning adjoining property," and the survey map accompanying the letter depicts each tract. Considering the conversation both before the after the letter was sent, it is inconceivable that the parties could be uncertain concerning the land to be sold. As to other terms of the contract, such as manner of payment, Brenon merely held himself ready "to work out any kind of terms" with the purchasers.

The elements expressly required by statute are not so obvious. First, the consideration of $212 stated in the letter is not the same as the $262 tendered in accord with the oral understanding. Despite this discrepancy, we think that the letter sufficiently expresses the consideration because the $212 represented an equal share of the cost divided by all ten interested parties. As Brenon said in the letter, "I feel the only fair way to share the cost is to divide equally among all 10 including myself." There is no dispute that the price was changed from that stated in the letter when two property owners declined to buy. The consideration then was simply a mathematical computation according to the formula specified in the letter. We do not believe this variation in the dollar amount renders the letter's expression of the consideration insufficient, especially since plaintiff paid more under the admitted agreement than he would have paid according to the letter.

The necessity of a subscription presents the final problem. A "subscription" is the same as a "signing," and it is clear that Brenon's typewritten name, which according to his testimony was typed with the intent that it be tantamount to a written signature, is a sufficient subscription. A problem here is that his wife, who owned the property with him in joint tenancy, apparently neither signed the letter nor authorized him in writing to sell her share. But this deficiency was at no time claimed or asserted before the trial court or in defendants' brief to this court. It was suggested for the first time upon oral argument. If it is a fact, it was not a part of the theory upon which the case was tried and submitted. We must therefore adhere to our well-settled rule that an unlitigated issue may not be asserted for the first time on appeal.

We by no means intend to hold that Brenon's letter would be a sufficient memorandum in every case. We will overlook technical requirements only if proof of the oral contract is clear and uncontradicted as in this case where defendant admitted that a contract had been made. But those technical requirements are only aids to discern where the truth lies in a given case, and we will not blindly apply those technicalities if they lead to a conclusion repugnant to common sense. As Professor Williston has said:

> "In brief, the Statute 'was intended to guard against the perils of perjury and error in the spoken word.' Therefore, if after a consideration of the surrounding circumstances, the pertinent facts and all the evidence in a particular case, the court concludes that enforcement of the agreement will not subject the defendant to fraudulent claims, the purpose of the Statute will best be served by holding the note or memorandum sufficient even though it be ambiguous or incomplete."

Most persuasive is defendant's admission during trial that a contract was in fact made between plaintiff and himself. Although we have followed the majority rule that admission of the contract does not preclude assertion of the statute of frauds, an admission that a contract was made certainly cannot be ignored when all other evidence submitted supports the same conclusion. Even though it may be argued that the formal requirements contemplated by the statute are lacking, when all the evidence is taken into account we are of the opinion that the letter should be held a sufficient memorandum in this case. The policy of the statute of frauds would be perverted if the admitted contract were not enforced. The judgment of the trial court is therefore affirmed.

QUESTIONS AND NOTES

1. Questions about the facts of this case

   1.1. Was the letter from the defendant to the plaintiff a contract or an offer?

   1.2. Did the defendant sign the letter?

   1.3. Was there a writing signed by the plaintiff in which he agreed to buy the land?

   1.4. Did the defendant contend that he did not offer to sell the land? Did the defendant argue that the plaintiff did not accept his offer?

2. Questions about the law

   2.1. What was the reason for the court's statement: "We by no means hold that Brenon's letter would be a sufficient memorandum in every case"?

   2.2. Why was the defendant's admission of an agreement "most persuasive"? Would the court have reached the same result if defendant's June 28 offer to sell was in an e-mail message? In a voice mail message left on plaintiff's answering machine? In some states, statutes of fraud have been revised to answer these questions. California's answers are set out in the footnote.*

   2.3. Assume that the buyer Radke, not the seller Brenon, changed his mind about the deal and Brenon was suing Radke for $262 for

*Cal. Civ. Code section 1624:

(3) There is sufficient evidence that a contract has been made in any of the following circumstances:

(A) There is evidence of an electronic communication (including, without limitation, the recording of a telephone call or the tangible written text produced by computer retrieval), admissible in evidence under the laws of this state, sufficient to indicate that in the communication a contract was made between the parties. * * *

(4) For purposes of this subdivision, the tangible written text produced by telex, telefacsimile, computer retrieval, or other process by which electronic signals are transmitted by telephone or otherwise shall constitute a writing, and any symbol executed or adopted by a party with the present intention to authenticate a writing shall constitute a signing.

breach of contract. Would the agreement be enforceable against Radke?

2.4. How would the Minnesota Supreme Court have decided *Smith v. Boyd, supra*, at 36?

3. Notes

3.1. The Minnesota statute of frauds seems to be contemplate a single writing: "the contract, some note or memorandum thereof." Such language is typical of statutes of fraud. Nonetheless, courts generally conclude that several writings can be pieced together to satisfy the statute of frauds, even though anyone of the writings taken alone would not have been sufficient. *See Restatement (Second) of Contracts* § 132.

3.2. The Minnesota statute of frauds also requires a writing "expressing the consideration." The requirements for satisfying a statute of frauds vary from state to state, and from statute to statute within a state. Compare the requirements of the Minnesota statute of frauds set out in the *Radke* case with the requirements of the Uniform Commercial Code's statute of frauds for sales of goods for $500 or more set out below. Note the differences in (i) what the writing must provide (2-201(1)), (ii) who must sign the writing (2-201(2)) and (iii) the significance of an admission that there was an agreement (2-201(3)(b)).

§ 2-201 Formal Requirements; Statute of Frauds

(1) Except as otherwise provided in this section a contract for the sale of goods for the price of $500 or more is not enforceable by way of action or defense unless there is some writing sufficient to indicate that a contract for sale has been made between the parties and signed by the party against whom enforcement is sought or by his authorized agent or broker. A writing is not insufficient because it omits or incorrectly states a term agreed upon but the contract is not enforceable under this paragraph beyond the quantity of goods shown in such writing.

(2) Between merchants if within a reasonable time a writing in confirmation of the contract and sufficient against the sender is received and the party receiving it has reason to know its contents, it satisfies the requirements of subsection (1) against such party un-

less written notice of objection to its contents is given within 10 days after it is received.

(3) A contract which does not satisfy the requirements of subsection (1) but which is valid in other respects is enforceable

(a) if the goods are to be specially manufactured for the buyer and are not suitable for sale to others in the ordinary course of the seller's business and the seller, before notice of repudiation is received and under circumstances which reasonably indicate that the goods are for the buyer, has made either a substantial beginning of their manufacture or commitments for their procurement; or

(b) if the party against whom enforcement is sought admits in his pleading, testimony or otherwise in court that a contract for sale was made, but the contract is not enforceable under this provision beyond the quantity of goods admitted; or

(c) with respect to goods for which payment has been made and accepted or which have been received and accepted (Sec. 2-606).

3.3. Reconsider the phrase in section 2-201(1): "signed by the party against whom enforcement is sought." Who is the "party against whom enforcement is sought"? What is "signed"?

Section 1-201 defines "signed" as including "any symbol executed or adopted by a party with present intent to authenticate a writing." In *Donovan v. RRL Corp.*, 27 P.3d 702 (Cal. 2001), *supra*, at 55 and 254 (the Jaguar newspaper advertisement case), the court concluded that "defendant's printed name in the advertisement similarly evidenced an intention to authenticate the advertisement as an offer and therefore constituted a signature satisfying the statute of frauds."

While a writing, or writings, is the most common method of satisfying the statute of frauds, note the alternatives in section 2-201(3). The next case deals with the "judicial admission" alternative set out in 2-201(3)(b).

DF Activities Corporation v. Brown

United States Court of Appeals, Seventh Circuit
851 F.2d 920 (1988)

Posner, Circuit Judge.

This appeal in a diversity breach of contract case raises an interesting question concerning the statute of frauds, in the context of a dispute over a chair of more than ordinary value. The plaintiff, DF Activities Corporation (owner of the Domino's pizza chain), is controlled by a passionate enthusiast for the work of Frank Lloyd Wright. The defendant, Dorothy [sic] Brown, a resident of Lake Forest (a suburb of Chicago) lived for many years in a house designed by Frank Lloyd Wright—the Willits House—and became the owner of a chair that Wright had designed, the Willits Chair. This is a stark, high-backed, uncomfortable-looking chair of distinguished design that DF wanted to add to its art collection. In September and October 1986, Sarah-Ann Briggs, DF's art director, negotiated with Dorothy Brown to buy the Willits Chair. DF contends—and Mrs. Brown denies—that she agreed in a phone conversation with Briggs on November 26 to sell the chair to DF for $60,000, payable in two equal installments, the first due on December 31 and the second on March 26. On December 3 Briggs wrote Brown a letter confirming the agreement, followed shortly by a check for $30,000.* Two weeks later Brown returned the letter and the check with the following handwritten note at the bottom of the letter: "Since I did not hear from you until December and I spoke with you the middle of November, I have made other arrangements for the chair. It is no longer available for sale to you." Sometime later Brown sold the chair for $198,000, precipitating this suit for

---

*The letter stated:

Dear Mrs. Brown:

This letter is to confirm our agreement to purchase from you the high back dining chair from the Ward W. Willits Residence (Highland Park, Illinois, 1901) for $60,000. As agreed to down payment of $30,000 is to be paid in December 1986 and the remaining $30,000 within 90 days. On completion of payment I will contact you to make transportation arrangements for the chair to Domino's Farms.

Domino's Pizza will carry insurance on the chair. Also, we would like to illustrate the chair in future publications. Do you have a transparency we could use?

Sincerely,

Sara-Ann B. Briggs

Director, Archives & Galleries

Eds.

the difference between the price at which the chair was sold and the contract price of $60,000. Brown moved under Fed. R. Civ. P. 12(b)(6) to dismiss the suit as barred by the statute of frauds in the Uniform Commercial Code. See UCC § 2-201. * * * Attached to the motion was Brown's affidavit that she had never agreed to sell the chair to DF or its representative, Briggs.* The affidavit also denied any recollection of a conversation with Briggs on November 26, and was accompanied by both a letter from Brown to Briggs dated September 20 withdrawing an offer to sell the chair and a letter from Briggs to Brown dated October 29 withdrawing DF's offer to buy the chair.

---

* AFFIDAVIT OF DOROTHEA F. BROWN

I, Dorothea F. Brown, having been first duly deposed and sworn to all states as follows:

i. My name is Dorothea F. Brown and I reside at 671 Beverly Place, Lake Forest, Illinois.

ii. I am the defendant in the above-captioned case.

iii. On August 19, 1986, I drafted a letter to Domino's Pizza Incorporated regarding my Frank Lloyd Wright chair, which is the subject matter of this suit.

iv. In response to my letter, Helen M. McNulty drafted her August 26, 1986 correspondence. (exhibit A)

v. For a short while thereafter, I negotiated with Sarah Briggs of Domino's Pizza relative to a possible sale of my chair to Domino Farms.

vi. I terminated my negotiation with the Plaintiff, herein with my correspondence dated September 20, 1986. (exhibit B)

vii. On October 29, 1986, the agent working on behalf of Domino's Farms drafted her letter to terminate further negotiation with respect to the chair, (exhibit C)

viii. Thereafter, I was contacted by a person who represented that she was Sarah Briggs and in a November 6, 1986 phone conversation, she further discussed the matter with me, but I did not agree to sell my chair to them.

ix. To the best of my recollection, I had no conversation with Sarah Ann Briggs on November 26, 1986.

x. I did not accept any offer from Domino's Farms or Sarah Briggs for their purchase of my chair.

xi. I did not sign any agreement to sell my chair to DF Activities, Sarah Briggs, or Domino's Farms nor was any person or entity authorized to enter into any alleged agreement in my behalf.

xii. I have not accepted any payment whatsoever from Domino's Farms or Sarah Briggs with respect to this matter.

Further deponent saith not.

Eds.

The district judge granted the motion to dismiss and dismissed the suit. DF appeals, contending that although a contract for a sale of goods at a price of $500 or more is subject to the statute of frauds, the (alleged) oral contract made on November 26 may be within the statutory exception for cases where "the party against whom enforcement is sought admits in his pleading, testimony or otherwise in court that a contract for sale was made." UCC § 2-201(3)(b). DF does not argue that Brown's handwritten note at the bottom of Briggs' letter is sufficient acknowledgment of a contract to bring the case within the exemption in section 2-201(1).

At first glance DF's case may seem quite hopeless. Far from admitting in her pleading, testimony, or otherwise in court that a contract for sale was made, Mrs. Brown denied under oath that a contract had been made. DF argues, however, that if it could depose her, maybe she would admit in her deposition that the affidavit was in error, that she had talked to Briggs on November 26, and that they had agreed to the sale of the chair on the terms contained in Briggs' letter of confirmation to her.

There is remarkably little authority on the precise question raised by this appeal—whether a sworn denial ends the case or the plaintiff may press on, and insist on discovery. In fact we have found no authority at the appellate level, state or federal. Many cases hold, it is true, that the defendant in a suit on an oral contract apparently made unenforceable by the statute of frauds cannot block discovery aimed at extracting an admission that the contract was made, simply by moving to dismiss the suit on the basis of the statute of frauds or by denying in the answer to the complaint that a contract had been made. There is also contrary authority * * *. We need not take sides on the conflict. When there is a bare motion to dismiss, or an answer, with no evidentiary materials, the possibility remains a live one that, if asked under oath whether a contract had been made, the defendant would admit it had been. The only way to test the proposition is for the plaintiff to take the defendant's deposition, or, if there is no discovery, to call the defendant as an adverse witness at trial. But where as in this case the defendant swears in an affidavit that there was no contract, we see no point in keeping the lawsuit alive. Of course the defendant may blurt out an admission in a deposition, but this is hardly likely, especially since by doing so he may be admitting to having perjured himself in his affidavit. Stranger things have happened, but remote possibilities do not warrant subjecting the parties and the judiciary to proceedings almost certain to be futile.

A plaintiff cannot withstand summary judgment by arguing that although in pretrial discovery he has gathered no evidence of the defendant's liability, his luck may improve at trial. The statement in a leading commercial law text that a defense based on the statute of fraud must always be determined at trial because the defendant might in cross-examination admit the making of the contract, see White & Summers, Handbook of the Law Under the Uniform Commercial Code 67 (1980), reflects a misunderstanding of the role of summary judgment; for the statement implies, contrary to modern practice, that a party unable to generate a genuine issue of fact at the summary judgment stage, because he has no evidence with which to contest an affidavit of his adversary may nevertheless obtain a trial of the issue. He may not. By the same token, a plaintiff in a suit on a contract within the statute of frauds should not be allowed to resist a motion to dismiss, backed by an affidavit that the defendant denies the contract was made, by arguing that his luck may improve in discovery. Just as summary judgment proceedings differ from trials, so the conditions of a deposition differ from the conditions in which an affidavit is prepared; affidavits in litigation are prepared by lawyers, and merely signed by affiants. Yet to allow an affiant to be deposed by opposing counsel would be to invite the unedifying form of discovery in which the examining lawyer tries to put words in the witness's mouth and construe them as admissions.

The history of the judicial-admission exception to the statute of frauds reinforces our conclusion. The exception began with common-sense recognition that if the defendant admitted in a pleading that he had made a contract with the plaintiff, the purpose of the statute of frauds—protection against fraudulent or otherwise false contractual claims—was fullfilled. (The situation would be quite otherwise, of course, with an oral admission, for a plaintiff willing to testify falsely to the existence of a contract would be equally willing to testify falsely to the defendant's having admitted the existence of the contract.) Toward the end of the eighteenth century the courts began to reject the exception, fearing that it was an invitation to the defendant to perjure himself. Later the pendulum swung again, and the exception is now firmly established. The concern with perjury that caused the courts in the middle period to reject the exception supports the position taken by Mrs. Brown in this case. She has sworn under oath that she did not agree to sell the Willits Chair to DF. DF wants an opportunity to depose her in the hope that she can be induced to change her testimony. But if she changes her testimony this will be virtually an admission that she perjured herself in her affidavit (for it is hardly likely that her denial was based simply on a faulty recollection). She is not likely to do this. What is possible is that her testimony will be sufficiently ambiguous to enable DF to argue that there should be still further factual investigation—perhaps a full-fledged trial at which Mrs. Brown will be questioned again about the existence of the contract.

With such possibilities for protraction, the statute of frauds becomes a defense of meager value. And yet it seems to us as it did to the framers of the Uniform Commercial Code that the statute of frauds serves an important purpose in a system such as ours that does not require that all contracts be in writing in order to be enforceable and that allows juries of lay persons to decide commercial cases. The methods of judicial factfinding do not distinguish unerringly between true and false testimony, and are in any event very expansive. People deserve some protection against the risks and costs of being hauled into court and accused of owing money on the basis of an unacknowledged promise. And being deposed is scarcely less unpleasant than being cross-examined—indeed, often it is more unpleasant, because the examining lawyer is not inhibited by the presence of a judge or jury who might resent hectoring tactics. The transcripts of depositions are often very ugly documents.

Some courts still allow the judicial-admission exception to be defeated by the defendant's simple denial, in a pleading, that there was a contract * * *. To make the defendant repeat the denial under oath is already to erode the exception (as well as to create the invitation to perjury that so concerned the courts that rejected the judicial-admission exception altogether), for there is always the possibility, though a very small one, that the defendant might be charged with perjury. But, in any event, once the defendant has denied the contract under oath, the safety valve of section 2-201(3)(b) is closed. The chance that at a deposition the defendant might be badgered into withdrawing his denial is too remote to justify prolonging an effort to enforce an oral contract in the teeth of the statute of frauds. If Dorothy [sic] Brown did agree on November 27 to sell the chair to DF at a bargain price, it behooved Briggs to get Brown's signature on the dotted line, posthaste.

Affirmed.

Flaum, Circuit Judge, dissenting.

Because I disagree with the majority's holding that additional discovery is prohibited whenever a defendant raises a statute of frauds defense and submits a sworn denial that he or she formed an oral contract with the plaintiff, I respectfully dissent. Neither would I hold, however, that a plaintiff is automatically entitled to additional discovery in the face of a defendant's sworn denial that an agreement was reached. Rather, in my view district courts should have the authority to exercise their discretion to determine the limits of permissible discovery in these cases. This flexibility is particularly important where, as here, the defendant's affidavit does not contain a conclusive denial of contract formation. * * *

QUESTIONS AND NOTES

1. Questions about the facts of this case

   1.1. Why didn't the defendant, Dorothea Brown, want to sell the chair to the plaintiff, D.F. Activities Corporation, for $60,000?

   1.2. Did the defendant admit that she orally agreed to sell the chair to the plaintiff for $60,000?

   1.3. Whom do you believe? Whom did the trial court believe?

2. Questions about the law

   2.1. Writing: Why didn't the December 3rd letter satisfy the statute of frauds? Would the writing have satisfied the statute of frauds if the defendant was a merchant?

   2.2. Ethics: Would it be ethical for the defendant's attorney to advise her client to file an affidavit denying that she made an oral agreement if she did indeed make an oral agreement? Would it be ethical for defendant's attorney to file a motion to dismiss the suit as barred by the statute of frauds if she knew that Mrs. Brown had made such an oral agreement?

   2.3. Part performance: Why didn't the $30,000 payment satisfy the statute of frauds? *See* U.C.C. § 2-201(3)(c).

   2.4. Review: Does section 2-201 apply to the computer purchase agreement in *Hill v. Gateway, supra,* at 5? If so, how and when was the statute of frauds satisfied?

3. Notes

3.1. Common law judicial admission exception: Notwithstanding the dictum in *DF Activities* that the "judicial admissions exception is firmly established," cases not governed by U.C.C. § 2-201(3) are divided as to whether an oral judicial admission satisfies the Statute of Frauds. Remember the dictum in the *Radke* case.

3.2. Uniform Commercial Code § 2-201(3) judicial admission exception: In addition, the co-authors of the most widely used U.C.C. text are now divided as to whether a defendant in a case under § 2-201(3) can prevail on a motion to dismiss by demurring to a complaint that alleges an oral contract for the sale of goods for $500 or more and denying in a sworn affidavit that the oral contract was made. JAMES J. WHITE & ROBERT S. SUMMERS, UNIFORM COMMERCIAL CODE 79 (5th ed. 2000)

3.3. Recall that England abolished the Statute of Frauds in 1954. More recently, the United Nations Convention on Contracts for the International Sale of Goods, eliminated any statute of frauds. Article 11 of UNCISG provides: "A contract of sale need not be concluded in or evidenced by writing . . . It may be proved by any means, including witnesses."

The final statute of frauds case involves an employment agreement. Many employment agreements are oral (including many employment agreements between law firms and their young lawyers). Does the statute of frauds require that an employment agreement has to be in writing in order to be legally enforceable?

McIntosh v. Murphy
Supreme Court of Hawaii
469 P.2d 177 (1970)

LEVINSON, Justice.

This case involves an oral employment contract which allegedly violates the provision of the Statute of Frauds requiring "any agreement that is not to be performed within one year from the making thereof" to be in writing in order to be enforceable. HRS § 656-1(5). In this action the plaintiff-employee Dick McIntosh seeks to recover damages from his employer, George Murphy and Murphy Motors, Ltd., for the breach of an alleged one-year oral employment contract.

While the facts are in sharp conflict, it appears that defendant George Murphy was in southern California during March, 1964 interviewing prospective management personnel for his Chevrolet-Oldsmobile dealerships in Hawaii. He interviewed the plaintiff twice during that time. The position of sales manager for one of the dealerships was fully discussed but no contract was entered into. In April, 1964 the plaintiff received a call from the general manager of Murphy Motors informing him of possible employment within thirty days if he was still available. The plaintiff indicated his continued interest and informed the manager that he would be available. Later in April, the plaintiff sent Murphy a telegram to the effect that he would arrive in Honolulu on Sunday, April 26, 1964. Murphy then telephoned McIntosh on Saturday, April 25, 1964, to notify him that the job of assistant sales manager was open and work would begin on the following Monday, April 27, 1964. At that time McIntosh expressed surprise at the change in job title from sales manager to assistant sales manager but reconfirmed the fact that he was arriving in Honolulu the next day, Sunday. McIntosh arrived on Sunday, April 26, 1964, and began work on the following day, Monday, April 27, 1964.

As a consequence of his decision to work for Murphy, McIntosh moved some of his belongings from the mainland to Hawaii, sold other possessions, leased an apartment in Honolulu and obviously forwent any other employment opportunities. In short, the plaintiff did all those things which were incidental to changing one's residence permanently from Los Angeles to Honolulu, a distance of approximately 2,200 miles. McIntosh continued working for Murphy until July 16, 1964, approximately two and one-half months, at which time he was discharged on the grounds that he was unable to close deals with prospective customers and could not train the salesmen.

At the conclusion of the trial, the defense moved for a directed verdict arguing that the oral employment agreement was in violation of the Statute of Frauds, there being no written memorandum or note thereof. The trial court ruled that as a matter of law the contract did not come within the Statute, reasoning that Murphy bargained for acceptance by the actual commencement of performance by McIntosh, so that McIntosh was not bound by a contract until he came to work on Monday, April 27, 1964.

Therefore, assuming that the contract was for a year's employment, it was performable within a year exactly to the day and no writing was required for it to be enforceable. Alternatively, the court ruled that if the agreement was made final by the telephone call between the parties on Saturday, April 25, 1964, then that part of the weekend which remained would not be counted in calculating the year, thus taking the contract out of the Statute of Frauds. With commendable candor the trial judge gave as the motivating force for the decision his desire to avoid a mechanical and unjust application of the Statute.[1]

The case went to the jury on the following questions: (1) whether the contract was for a year's duration or was performable on a trial basis, thus making it terminable at the will of either party; (2) whether the plaintiff was discharged for just cause; and (3) if he was not discharged for just cause, what damages were due the plaintiff. The jury returned a verdict for the plaintiff in the sum of $12,103.40. The defendants appeal to this court on four principal grounds, three of which we find to be without merit. The remaining ground of appeal is whether the plaintiff can maintain an action on the alleged oral employment contract in light of the prohibition of the Statute of Frauds making unenforceable an oral contract that is not to be performed within one year.

I. TIME OF ACCEPTANCE OF THE EMPLOYMENT AGREEMENT

The defendants contend that the trial court erred in refusing to give an instruction to the jury that if the employment agreement was made more than one day before the plaintiff began performance, there could be no recovery by the plaintiff. The reason given was that a contract not to be performed within one year from its making is unenforceable if not in writing.

The defendants are correct in their argument that the time of acceptance of an offer is a question of fact for the jury to decide. But the trial court alternatively decided that even if the offer was accepted on the Saturday prior to the commencement of performance, the intervening Sunday and part of Saturday would not be counted in computing the year for the purposes of

[1]THE COURT: You make the law look ridiculous, because one day is Sunday and the man does not work on Sunday; the other day is Saturday; he is up in Fresno. He can't work down there. And he is down here Sunday night and shows up for work on Monday. To me that is a contract within a year. I don't want to make the law look ridiculous, Mr. Clause, because it is one day after, one day too much, and that one day is a Sunday, and a non-working day.

the Statute of Frauds. The judge stated that Sunday was a non-working day and only a fraction of Saturday was left which he would not count. In any event, there is no need to discuss the relative merits of either ruling since we base our decision in this case on the doctrine of equitable estoppel which was properly briefed and argued by both parties before this court, although not presented to the trial court.

II. ENFORCEMENT BY VIRTUE OF ACTION IN RELIANCE ON THE ORAL CONTRACT

In determining whether a rule of law can be fashioned and applied to a situation where an oral contract admittedly violates a strict interpretation of the Statute of Frauds, it is necessary to review the Statute itself together with its historical and modern functions. The Statute of Frauds, which requires that certain contracts be in writing in order to be legally enforceable, had its inception in the days of Charles II of England. Hawaii's version of the Statute is found in HRS § 656-1 and is substantially the same as the original English Statute of Frauds.

The first English Statute was enacted almost 300 years ago to prevent "many fraudulent practices, which are commonly endeavored to be upheld by perjury and subornation of perjury." Certainly, there were compelling reasons in those days for such a law. At the time of enactment in England, the jury system was quite unreliable, rules of evidence were few, and the complaining party was disqualified as a witness so he could neither testify on direct-examination nor, more importantly, be cross-examined. The aforementioned structural and evidentiary limitations on our system of justice no longer exist.

Retention of the Statute today has nevertheless been justified on at least three grounds: (1) the Statute still serves an evidentiary function thereby lessening the danger of perjured testimony (the original rationale); (2) the requirement of a writing has a cautionary effect which causes reflection by the parties on the importance of the agreement; and (3) the writing is an easy way to distinguish enforceable contracts from those which are not, thus channeling certain transactions into written form.

In spite of whatever utility the Statute of Frauds may still have, its applicability has been drastically limited by judicial construction over the years in order to mitigate the harshness of a mechanical application. Furthermore, learned writers continue to disparage the Statute regarding it as "a statute for promoting fraud" and a "legal anachronism."

Another method of judicial circumvention of the Statute of Frauds has grown out of the exercise of the equity powers of the courts. Such judicially imposed limitations or exceptions involved the traditional dispensing power of the equity courts to mitigate the "harsh" rule of law. When courts have enforced an oral contract in spite of the Statute, they have utilized the legal labels of "part performance" or "equitable estoppel" in granting relief. Both doctrines are said to be based on the concept of estoppel, which operates to avoid unconscionable injury.

Part performance has long been recognized in Hawaii as an equitable doctrine justifying the enforcement of an oral agreement for the conveyance of an interest in land where there has been substantial reliance by the party seeking to enforce the contract. Other courts have enforced oral contracts (including employment contracts) which failed to satisfy the section of the Statute making unenforceable an agreement not to be performed within a year of its making. This has occurred where the conduct of the parties gave rise to an estoppel to assert the Statute.

It is appropriate for modern courts to cast aside the raiments of conceptualism which cloak the true policies underlying the reasoning behind the many decisions enforcing contracts that violate the Statute of Frauds. There is certainly no need to resort to legal rubrics or meticulous legal formulas when better explanations are available.

In seeking to frame a workable test which is flexible enough to cover diverse factual situations and also provide some reviewable standards, we find very persuasive section [139] of the Second Restatement of Contracts. That section specifically covers those situations where there has been reliance on an oral contract which falls within the Statute of Frauds. Section [139] states:

> (1) A promise which the promisor should reasonably expect to induce action or forbearance on the part of the promisee or a third person and which does induce the action or forbearance is enforceable notwithstanding the Statute of Frauds if injustice can be avoided only by enforcement of the promise. The remedy granted for breach is to be limited as justice requires.
>
> (2) In determining whether injustice can be avoided only by enforcement of the promise, the following circumstances are significant: (a) the availability and adequacy of other remedies, particularly cancellation and restitution; (b) the definite and substantial character of the action or forbear-

> ance in relation to the remedy sought; (c) the extent to which the action or forbearance corroborates evidence of the making and terms of the promise, or the making and terms are otherwise established by clear and convincing evidence; (d) the reasonableness of the action or forbearance; (e) the extent to which the action or forbearance was forseeable by the promisor.

We think that the approach taken in the Restatement is the proper method of giving the trial court the necessary latitude to relieve a party of the hardships of the Statute of Frauds. This is to be preferred over having the trial court bend over backwards to take the contract out of the Statute of Frauds. In the present case the trial court admitted just this inclination and forthrightly followed it.

There is no dispute that the action of the plaintiff in moving 2200 miles from Los Angeles to Hawaii was foreseeable by the defendant. In fact, it was required to perform his duties. Injustice can only be avoided by the enforcement of the contract and the granting of money damages. No other remedy is adequate. The plaintiff found himself residing in Hawaii without a job.

It is also clear that a contract of some kind did exist. The plaintiff performed the contract for two and one-half months receiving $3,484.60 for his services. The exact length of the contract, whether terminable at will as urged by the defendant, or for a year from the time when the plaintiff started working, was up to the jury to decide.

In sum, the trial court might have found that enforcement of the contract was warranted by virtue of the plaintiff's reliance on the defendant's promise. Naturally, each case turns on its own facts. Certainly there is considerable discretion for a court to implement the true policy behind the Statute of Frauds, which is to prevent fraud or any other type of unconscionable injury. We therefore affirm the judgment of the trial court on the ground that the plaintiff's reliance was such that injustice could only be avoided by enforcement of the contract.

Affirmed.

ABE, Justice (dissenting).

The majority of the court has affirmed the judgment of the trial court; however, I respectfully dissent.

I.

Whether alleged contract of employment came within the Statute of Frauds:

As acknowledged by this court, the trial judge erred when as a matter of law he ruled that the alleged employment contract did not come within the Statute of Frauds; however, I cannot agree that this error was not prejudicial as this court intimates.

On this issue, the date that the alleged contract was entered into was all important and the date of acceptance of an offer by the plaintiff was a question of fact for the jury to decide. In other words, it was for the jury to determine when the alleged one-year employment contract was entered into and if the jury had found that the plaintiff had accepted the offer[1] more than one day before plaintiff was to report to work, the contract would have come within the Statute of Frauds and would have been unenforceable.

II.

This court holds that though the alleged one-year employment contract came within the Statute of Frauds, nevertheless the judgment of the trial court is affirmed "on the ground that the plaintiff's reliance was such that injustice could only be avoided by enforcement of the contract."

I believe this court is begging the issue by its holding because to reach that conclusion, this court is ruling that the defendant agreed to hire the plaintiff under a one-year employment contract. The defendant has denied that the plaintiff was hired for a period of one year and has introduced into evidence testimony of witnesses that all hiring by the defendant in the past has been on a trial basis. The defendant also testified that he had hired the plaintiff on a trial basis.

Here on one hand the plaintiff claimed that he had a one-year employment contract; on the other hand, the defendant claimed that the plaintiff had not been hired for one year but on a trial basis for so long as his services were satisfactory. I believe the Statute of Frauds was enacted to avoid the consequences this court is forcing upon the defendant. In my opinion, the legislature enacted the Statute of Frauds to negate claims such as has been made by the plaintiff in this case. But this court holds that because the plaintiff in reliance of the one-year employment contract (alleged to have

[1]Plaintiff testified that he accepted the offer in California over the telephone.

been entered into by the plaintiff, but denied by the defendant) has changed his position, "injustice could only be avoided by enforcement of the contract." Where is the sense of justice?

Now assuming that the defendant had agreed to hire the plaintiff under a one-year employment contract and the contract came within the Statute of Frauds, I cannot agree, as intimated by this court, that we should circumvent the Statute of Frauds by the exercise of the equity powers of courts. As to statutory law, the sole function of the judiciary is to interpret the statute and the judiciary should not usurp legislative power and enter into the legislative field. Thus, if the Statute of Frauds is too harsh as intimated by this court, and it brings about undue hardship, it is for the legislature to amend or repeal the statute and not for this court to legislate.

QUESTIONS AND NOTES

1. Questions about the facts of this case

   1.1. The Hawaii statute of frauds requires that "the promise, contract, or agreement, upon which the action is brought, or some memorandum or note thereof, is in writing, and is signed by the party to be charged therewith." Is there such a writing in this case?

   1.2. Did the defendant admit that it agreed to employ the plaintiff for one year?

   1.3. What was the defendant's explanation for the plaintiff's moving from California to Hawaii and working for the defendant for two and half months? The plaintiff's explanation? Who did the jury believe? Who do you believe?

2. Questions about the law

   2.1. Not to be performed within one year from the making thereof

      (a) The plaintiff alleged that there was a one year oral employment contract. Can a one year employment contract "be performed within one year"? Is that relevant in this case?

      (b) Epstein hires you to work as his research assistant on the Corpus Juris Thirdundum project—an update and complete rewriting of Corpus Juris Secondum, and orally agrees that you will be paid $60,000 a year until the treatise is complete. Is the contract "not to be performed within one year from the making"?

2.2. Equitable estoppel/promissory estoppel

In *McIntosh*, the court states that we "base our decision in this case on equitable estoppel." Later in the opinion, the court refers to two cases decided under the theory of equitable estoppel and a case decided under the theory of promissory estoppel. And then, the court in *McIntosh* finds *Restatement (Second)* § 139 persuasive. Is *Restatement (Second)* § 139 equitable estoppel or promissory estoppel? How does equitable estoppel differ from promissory estoppel?

2.3. Part performance

The plaintiff worked for the defendant for two and half months. Was that important to the court's decision? "Part performance not amounting to full performance on one side does not in general take a contract out of the one-year provision." *Restatement Second of Contracts* §130, comment e. Why?

3. Notes

3.1. Judge Richard Posner is critical of the use of promissory estoppel "to get around" the statute of frauds, particularly in employment cases:

> Employment at will (i.e., without a contract of employment) remains the dominant type of employment relationship in this country, and would be seriously undermined if employees could use the doctrine of promissory estoppel to make alleged oral contracts of employment enforceable. Reliance is easily, perhaps too easily, shown in the employment setting. Agreeing to work for a particular employer, thereby giving up alternative opportunities for employment, can easily be described as reliance on the employer's alleged oral promises concerning the terms of employment. Maybe the cases that erode it in the area of promissory estoppel exaggerate the ability of courts to distinguish true oral promises from fabricated promises and language misunderstood as promissory. Maybe they overlook the simple logical point that the promisee should know the promise is unenforceable because of the statute of frauds and therefore shouldn't rely on it. But for what it is worth the logic of

such cases is that the element of reliance that is required to make a promise enforceable on grounds of estoppel takes the place of a writing in giving adequate assurance that the promise has not been fabricated, or misunderstood without fault on the part of the promisor. The "promisee" takes a great risk if he gives up something in purported reliance on a nonexistent promise, merely to bolster his claim that there was a promise.

Goldstick v. ICM Realty, 788 F.2d 456, 465 (7th Cir. 1986). Do you agree with Judge Posner? Would Justice Abe of the Hawaii Supreme Court agree?

3.2. Consider some of the ruminations Professor John Kidwell of University of Wisconsin Law School on teaching the statute of frauds:

[A] requirement that a contract be in writing is functionally very like the requirement of a seal. Such a requirement is attractive for the same reasons that the seal requirement is attractive. If everyone knew and followed the forms there would be less conflict, and justice would be speedy and certain. Social order would be enhanced. But we don't care just about social order. We care also about individual justice. And we know that not all people know the rules, and even when they do they might find reasons not to follow them. If we enforce the formal requirement in these cases, we sacrifice individual justice in favor of social order, which always at least makes us pause. And sometimes we yield to the urge to make an exception and soften the formal rule. I then suggest that it can be argued that every formal rule is under relentless pressure from our desire for individual justice. * * * We always are tempted to make exceptions to rules that depend on form because we always care, to some extent, about the injustice, which results when we enforce the formal requirement. Thus, formal requirements tend to decay. Not always, and not perhaps as dramatically as in the case of the seal, but often. Writing requirements, notice requirements, filing requirements, statutes of limitations—all invite exceptions.

John Kidwell, *Ruminations on Teaching the Statute of Frauds*, 44 ST. LOUIS U. L.J. 1427, 1432 (2000).

Chapter Three

WHAT ARE THE TERMS OF THE DEAL?

Up to this point, this book has focused on whether an enforceable contract exists; that is, whether the prerequisites for formation are present, whether consideration exists and whether the deal is subject to defenses. We now shift emphasis. From here on we assume, for the most part, that an enforceable contract exists, at least initially. What we are now concerned with are the duties and obligations that the contract creates. Put another way, we are concerned with the content of the contract.

Keep in mind that it is possible to agree that a contract exists but disagree on what it says or requires. Indeed, that is the heart of most contractual disputes: each side has a different view of what an acknowledged contract requires. This part of the casebook focuses on how courts determine what obligations the parties have created or assumed when they made a contract. In short, we examine how courts interpret contracts to find out what the parties agreed to.

Along the way, it's helpful to begin to formulate your own strategy for dealing with the interpretive rules courts use. We are convinced that most lawyers' work is not concerned with formation issues. Rather, for the deal lawyer, the daily focus is the task of drafting language so that a court or jury will construe the contract in the way the client intended. For a litigator, the parallel focus is the devising of strategies that will lead to a court or jury accepting your client's interpretation of language drafted long ago by another lawyer. To accomplish either of these goals, the deft lawyer will know and understand how courts will approach enforcement of a contract; that is, he or she must understand how courts will interpret the contractual language.

SECTION 1: THE AGREEMENT: BEYOND THE WRITTEN WORD

As stated on the first page of this casebook, there is a tendency to confuse the written paper signed by the parties with the contract that binds them. It is an easy mistake to make; everyone calls the signed paper "the contract." But that paper is, at best, only *evidence* of the contract. That is, the contract is represented by that paper; it is not that paper. Otherwise, if you tore the paper up (or spilled coffee on it) you would also tear up or water down the parties' obligations. While that may be the case with some types of obligations (such as checks or other negotiable instruments), that is not the case with regular, every day contracts.

So what is a contract? To go back to the introduction of this book, according to the *Restatement (Second) of Contracts*, it is "a promise or set of promises for the breach of which the law gives a remedy, or the performance of which the law in some way recognizes as a duty." *Restatement (Second) of Contracts* § 1.

Where do we find the promises recognized as the contract? We have many sources. Our first, but not exclusive source, is the utterances of the parties, be they written or oral. We'll have lots more to say about those terms later on. In particular, Section 2 looks at the parol evidence rule, which governs the relationship between written promises and other words or acts that lay claim to the status of an enforceable promise. Section 3, in turn, looks at interpretation; that is, how courts construe the agreed terms of a contract. Finally, in Section 4, we look at the world of implied terms, or terms that courts and legislatures feel ought to be added to what the parties have already agreed.

But for an introduction, our focus will be on what seems to be an oxymoron: promises contained in the contract (and thus enforceable) which the parties may not have spoken or put down in writing. The next case involves such promises in the context of an oral contract. The term at issue, however, was one which the parties never actually uttered. Try and focus on why the court wants to construe this provision as a term contained in the parties' contract, rather than some rule of law applicable to all contracts.

Threadgill v. Peabody Coal Co.
Court of Appeals of Colorado
34 Colo.App. 203, 526 P.2d 676 (1974)

Pierce, Judge.

Defendant, Peabody Coal Company (Peabody), appeals from a judgment holding it liable for damages for the loss of certain equipment owned by the plaintiff which was lost in the process of probing test holes drilled by Peabody. Plaintiff was an independent contractor hired by Peabody to probe the test holes for the purpose of locating coal deposits. After the test holes were sunk to the appropriate depth by Peabody, plaintiff's employees lowered a probing device to the bottom of each hole and proceeded to "log" the hole as the probe was retrieved. "Logging" consists of gathering soil samples and other data. During the probing of one of the test holes by the employees of the plaintiff, the probing device became stuck in the hole. Employees of Peabody then commenced recovery operations which were unsuccessful.

Plaintiff's complaint alleged two claims for relief: (1) that the loss of the probe was due to defendant's negligence in attempting to recover the probe, and (2) that the defendant was obligated under a contract between the parties to pay the value of any equipment owned by the plaintiff lost in the course of the probing operation. Defendant filed an answer containing several defenses and pleaded a counterclaim for expenses incurred in the recovery attempt based on the alleged negligence of plaintiff's employees.

Upon trial to the court, the court found that an oral contract for the services of the plaintiff did exist, but that there had been no express agreement, oral or otherwise, upon the placement of the risk of loss of the probing device. The court then found that the plaintiff had satisfactorily established "a certain practice or custom in the drilling industry which places the risk of probe loss on the driller (here the defendant) where, as here, there is no agreement otherwise." Furthermore, the court found that Peabody's employees had not been negligent in conducting the recovery operation but made no finding as to any negligence on the part of the plaintiff, or his employees. However, the court ruled that the negligence was immaterial under the trade practice, and thus, in effect, placed a duty of strict liability upon Peabody. The court then entered judgment in favor of the plaintiff and dismissed Peabody's counterclaim.

I

Peabody's first allegation of error is that the evidence is not sufficient to support the trial court's finding that a custom or trade usage existed that was binding on defendant.

In order to bind a party by a usage in the trade, it must be shown either that the party had actual knowledge of the existence of the trade usage or that the usage is so well established as to justify a finding of constructive knowledge. * * * The issue of knowledge of the trade usage, whether actual or constructive, is generally a question to be decided by the trier of fact. * * * Peabody's representatives testified that they had no knowledge of the alleged custom, and Peabody argues that, to show constructive knowledge, the custom or usage must be demonstrated to be "universal" and "notorious." Such terms have been used where the evidence was insufficient to support a finding that the alleged custom even existed. . . . However, these requirements are only applicable to the English law of custom by which accepted practices have developed into substantive rules of law. They do not apply to a trade usage which is offered only as evidence as to the intent of the parties. * * *

The proper test applicable to this issue is stated in the more recent case of *Ryan v. Fitzpatrick Drilling Co.*, 139 Colo. 471, 342 P.2d 1040. That is, to be binding upon a party, a trade usage must be "sufficiently general so that the parties could be said to have contracted with reference to it." *See Lorraine Mfg. Co. v. Allen Mfg. Co., supra.*[1]

Although contradicted on some points by Peabody's evidence, each of the plaintiff's witnesses testified as to his experience in the trade within the geographical locale of the instant operation and to the existence, within that locale, of the alleged trade usage. These witnesses further explained the usage by pointing out that the driller has primary control over the drilling of the hole and that since the prober has no connection with the operation until he begins the "logging" process, he must rely on the driller's judgment as to the readiness of the hole to receive the probe. Furthermore, once a probe becomes lodged in the hole, the prober must rely on the driller's equipment for recovery operations. The testimony of these witnesses also indicated

[1]While the Uniform Commercial Code does not govern this case, we think it significant to note that the drafters of the Code in defining a trade usage have adopted a similar standard focusing on the likelihood that the parties contracted with reference to the usage. *See* Uniform Commercial Code § 1-205(2) (C.R.S.1963, 155-1-205(2)). They have also rejected the "universal" and "notorious" language. Uniform Commercial Code § 1-205(2) (Comment 5).

that the loss of equipment was generally considered to be a cost to the owner of the land being probed; in this case, Peabody.

Finally, as pointed out by the trial court, the actions of the parties with regard to the recovery operation were consistent with the alleged usage. Such actions tending to demonstrate the intent of the parties are proper considerations for the fact finder. . . .

We hold that the evidence produced at trial was sufficient to support a finding of a general trade usage which permitted the inference that the parties must have contracted with reference to it.

Peabody also argues, however, that the evidence failed to establish that the alleged trade usage was sufficiently certain to permit its application to the facts before the court. It cites testimony to the effect that in some cases, the driller is obligated only to provide a certain number of "rig hours" for the purpose of recovering lost tools and that the obligation of the driller does not extend to liability for the value of unrecoverable tools. However, this testimony referred to cases in which the parties expressly agreed with respect to the obligations of the parties regarding the loss of the contractor's tools. Other witnesses testified that in the majority of logging jobs, as was the case here, no written agreement is actually entered into by the parties. Furthermore, the alleged trade usage which plaintiff sought to establish, and which the trial court found, provided a rule in cases in which no express agreement was reached by the parties.

The evidence in the record was sufficient to support the finding of the trial court that, in the absence of other factors, the trade usage would place on the driller the responsibility for the loss of the probing device in addition to the cost of the recovery attempt. That finding will not be disturbed upon review.

II

Peabody, however, also asserts that even though the trial court found the trade usage, the issue of plaintiff's negligence is not removed from the case. We agree with this contention.

In order for a trade custom or usage to be binding upon a person who has not expressly agreed to be bound by it, it must be reasonable. * * * This requirement in the law of trade usage generally specifies only that the usage not be illegal or in violation of public policy. * * *

The public policy of our state dictates that, generally, parties cannot contract away their potential liability for their own negligence. * * * If, under most circumstances, one cannot by express contract, immunize himself from the consequences of his own negligence, then an implied agreement to that effect arising out of a general custom or trade usage will not be given effect. . . . Only where such agreement is entered into by parties of equal bargaining power and where the agreement is express and unequivocal, have such clauses been held enforceable. * * * Here, there is no evidence in the record of such circumstances and the trial court erred in ruling that the trade usage applied regardless of the negligence of the parties. To the extent that the trade usage before us purports to relieve the contractor of the consequences of his own negligence, it is in conflict with the express public policy of this state.

Therefore, we hold that the findings of the trial court regarding the existence and generality of a trade usage placing the risk of loss upon the driller or owner in the absence of an express agreement are affirmed. The finding that negligence was made irrelevant by such usage is rejected, as a matter of law, and the case is remanded for further proceedings not inconsistent with this opinion.

Coyte and Smith, JJ., concur.

Judgment affirmed in part, reversed in part, and cause remanded with directions.

QUESTIONS AND NOTE

1. Questions about the facts of this case

    1.1. Did the court find that the parties had reached an express agreement on the risk of loss of Threadgill's gear?

    1.2. Did the court find that Peabody had no knowledge of the alleged custom?

2. Questions about the law

    2.1. The court makes a distinction between "accepted practices [that] have developed into substantive rules of law" and "trade usage which is offered only as evidence as to the intent of the parties." What is the difference?

2.2. If on remand the court finds that the trade practice did contemplate indemnity against Threadgill's negligence, what result? Does your answer change if the trial court also finds that Threadgill, although protected by the trade usage, was not negligent with respect to the probe stuck in Peabody's hole?

2.3. If you were Threadgill's lawyer, what type of defense would you prepare on remand?

3. Note

The *UNIDROIT Principles of International Commercial Contracts*, finalized in 1994, state that the "contractual obligations of the parties may be express or implied" (Article 5.1), and that implied obligations "stem from: (a) the nature and purpose of the contract; (b) practices established between the parties and usages; (c) good faith and fair dealing; (d) reasonableness." (Article 5.2). Given that such principles are meant to cover international contracts involving large sums of money, don't these principles seem to undercut certainty in commercial matters? Or do you suppose that are they just a reflection of actual practice?

Once you become accustomed to the baseline assumption that contracts need not be in writing (unless there are statute of frauds considerations), and that courts hold that customs, practices and past dealings form the basis of contract terms, even if they are not discussed, it is a short hop to thinking that contract interpretation is not much different than nailing jelly to a wall.

Resist that thought. There *is* order. It starts with fidelity to, and the completeness of, the written word. It is generally thought that those who order their lives with planning and care start by writing things down. With respect to contracts, they not only specify what exact terms bind the parties, but also what terms (or customs or practices) don't. But how does a judge distinguish between careful drafters and sloppy folk? In other words, how do we know that the writing is itself the final arbiter of completeness? Those questions lie within the domain of the parol evidence rule, and it is to that rule that these materials now turn.

SECTION 2: EXPRESS TERMS, PAROL EVIDENCE AND THE ARGUMENT OVER THE COMPLETENESS OF THE WRITTEN CONTRACT

A good lawyer not only wants to ensure that his or her clients understand the deal, but that a future court or jury will understand it too. This raises early on (at least as soon as drafting begins) the question of how a court will read the contract, or interpret the actions of the parties. One might draft differently if a court would adopt a strategy that would knowingly exclude relevant evidence. As a fanciful example, a court could make a general rule that the parties could only introduce one document and one witness in any contract case. This would cause the careful lawyer to line up in advance that one document and that one witness.

This system might also, over time, produce various exceptions. While the "one document, one witness" rule might work fine for small cases, what about the billion-dollar mega-merger? Or the complicated marital settlement? One can see that the long-term effect of such a rule would be to create shadings and variations of the rule to accommodate the wide array of contracts people enter into.

With some variations, this is the current state of the law. We have a rule—called the "parol evidence rule"*—that is applicable to written expressions of a contract. It is a rule of venerable heritage, as illustrated by the following explanation of its purpose, written by Chief Justice Popham almost four hundred years ago, but still relevant today:

> It would be inconvenient that matters in writing made by advice and on consideration, and which finally import the certain truth of the agreement of the parties should be controlled by averment of the parties to be

---

*"Parol" does not refer to the criminal justice system; properly, *that* word is "parol*e*." The word *parol* (without the "*e*") technically means an oral statement or utterance, and has its roots in the same Latin word that gives us the word parable.

In this course, however, "parol" means anything other than the written contract at issue, and thus can include writings, such as early drafts of the contract at issue.

proved by the uncertain testimony of slippery memory. And it would be dangerous to purchasers and farmers, and all others in such cases, if such averments against matter in writing should be admitted.

Countess of Rutland Case, 5 Co. 26a, 77 Eng. Rep. 89 (K.B. 1604).

Regardless of this salutary purpose, the effect of the parol evidence rule is to exclude evidence that you or I might think relevant to the interpretation of a contract. It is also full of (some might say riddled with) exceptions and shadings. Before stating the rule, however, it is wise to keep in mind the following statement about the rule by Professor James Thayer, as true now as it was when it was written over one hundred years ago: "Few things are darker than this, or fuller of subtle difficulties." JAMES B. THAYER , A PRELIMINARY TREATISE ON EVIDENCE AT THE COMMON LAW 390 (1898).

A. Common Law

The name parol evidence rule is a misnomer. As we will see, there is more than one rule, and it is not limited to parol statements. Moreover, it is more than just a rule of evidence. As Comment a to Section 213 of the *Restatement (Second) of Contracts* states:

> *[T]he parol evidence rule . . . is not a rule of evidence but a rule of substantive law. Nor is it a rule of interpretation; it defines the subject matter of interpretation. It renders inoperative prior written agreements as well as prior oral agreements. Where writings relating to the same subject matter are assented to as parts of one transaction, both form part of the integrated agreement. Where an agreement is partly oral and partly written, the writing is at most a partially integrated agreement.*

So what is this substantive rule of law? As with most rules in this course, there is no definitive statement of the parol evidence rule—it is a rule of common law origin, which means that it must be derived from cases applying it. For purposes of our study, however, we can start with the *Restatement (Second)*, as it provides a workable statement of the general rule:

> *§ 213 Effect of Integrated Agreement on Prior Agreements (Parol Evidence Rule)*
>
> *(1) A binding integrated agreement discharges prior agreements to the extent that it is inconsistent with them.*

(2) *A binding completely integrated agreement discharges prior agreements to the extent that they are within its scope.*

This text seems fine, but mentions an "integrated agreement." Indeed, the statement of the rule in Section 213 makes the presence of a "completely" or "partially" integrated agreement critical to the application of the parol evidence rule.

So what's an integrated agreement? This next case explores that concept in the context of an agreement signed by a Super Bowl quarterback—someone who obviously can afford good legal talent.

When reading this case, keep in mind some practices often followed in large acquisitions. First, the parties will often sign a binding contract to acquire a business well ahead of the time that they anticipate the actual change of ownership will occur. You may have seen this in buying a house—first you sign the contract, and then later on you "close" by actually transferring title. The interim period allows the parties to finalize their financing, take care of obtaining permissions that may be necessary to effectuate the transfer and other tasks.

Second, many businesses borrow money. When ownership changes, the borrowers may be a better or worse credit risk, and thus it is an event that lenders care deeply about. Accordingly, lenders customarily draft their loan documents to require payment in full whenever ownership changes. In actual practice, however, the lender may be persuaded by the buyer to "rollover" the loan, or agree to let the new owners assume the debt outstanding. The lender may agree if it is comfortable in the expertise of the new owners, or if it is comfortable that it, as a lender, will be paid in full before or at the same time the exiting owners are paid anything.

In this case, both of these assumptions come into play. As in most matters financial, it is a good idea to "follow the money" when reading this case; keep in mind not just who is making contracts, but who is benefitting, and when, from the contracts made.

Nelson v. Elway
Supreme Court of Colorado
908 P.2d 102 (1995)

Chief Justice VOLLACK delivered the Opinion of the Court.

We granted certiorari to review the decision by the court of appeals in *Nelson v. Elway*, No. 93CA0629 (Colo. App. May 26, 1994), affirming in part and reversing in part the trial court's grant of summary judgment in favor of the respondents. The court of appeals affirmed the trial court's entry of summary judgment in the respondents' favor as to the petitioners' allegations of breach of contract . . . . We . . . affirm . . . .

I.

Mel T. Nelson (Nelson) was the president and sole shareholder of two car dealerships, Metro Auto and Metro Toyota, Inc. General Motors Acceptance Corporation (GMAC) provided all the financing for both dealerships. In the first half of 1990, both dealerships were experiencing financial difficulties. In July of 1990, Nelson retained John J. Pico and the Aspen Brokerage Company (Pico) to represent him in the selling or refinancing of one or both of the dealerships.

In early 1991, Pico, acting on behalf of Nelson and Metro Toyota, began negotiations with John A. Elway, Jr. (Elway) and Rodney L. Buscher (Buscher) regarding the sale of Metro Toyota and the property upon which it was situated. On March 14, 1991, pursuant to those negotiations, Elway and Buscher signed a "Buy-Sell Agreement" and a separate real estate contract to purchase Metro Toyota. The closing was scheduled for April 15, 1991.

Soon after the signing of these documents, Pico asked Nelson if he would be willing to sell both Metro Auto and Metro Toyota to Elway. Nelson stated that he would be willing to sell both dealerships along with the land upon which they were located if he received sufficient personal remuneration. Pico then began negotiating with Elway and Buscher regarding the sale of both dealerships. Through these negotiations it became apparent that Elway and Buscher were unwilling or unable to pay the full purchase price for the dealerships and the land upon which they were located.

In order to consummate the transaction, Pico suggested to Nelson that Elway and Buscher reimburse Nelson for his interest in Metro Toyota by paying Nelson $50 per vehicle sold by both dealerships for a period of seven years commencing on May 1, 1991. In exchange for this compensation arrangement, Elway and Buscher would purchase Metro Auto from Nelson at a greatly reduced purchase price. These terms, referred to by the parties as the "Service Agreement," were reduced to writing but never signed by the parties. Subsequently, on March 16, 1991, the parties signed a "Buy-Sell Agreement" and a separate real estate contract for the purchase of Metro Auto. This written, signed agreement did not incorporate the terms of the Service Agreement.

By early 1991, the dealerships owed GMAC over $3 million. In order to protect its security interests, on April 3, 1991, GMAC required Nelson to execute agreements referred to as "keeper letters," allowing GMAC significant control over the dealerships. GMAC imposed this requirement as consideration for its agreement to pay [*sic.* Instead of "pay," this probably should read "finance for Elway" or "rollover and charge to Elway." Eds.] in excess of $890,000 in debt owed by Metro Auto and Metro Toyota at the closing of the sale of the dealerships to Elway and Buscher. Nelson knew that execution of these letters would preclude his ability to file for bankruptcy protection and proceed through re-organization. He alleges that he thus sought and received assurances from Elway and Buscher that the orally agreed upon, but as yet unsigned, Service Agreement would be honored.

On April 8, 1991, after the execution of the keeper letters, Pico, Elway, and Buscher met at Pico's office. During this meeting, GMAC telephoned Pico's office and informed Pico, Elway, and Buscher that as a condition to its agreement to finance the acquisition of the land and assets of the dealerships by Elway and Buscher, Nelson was not to receive any proceeds from the sale of the dealerships. The respondents then informed Nelson they would not be able to enter into the Service Agreement with him, and the Service Agreement was therefore not executed at the closing on April 12, 1991. After closing, Nelson demanded that the respondents honor the Service Agreement. When the respondents refused, Nelson filed the instant action.

In his complaint, Nelson sought damages from Elway and Buscher for breach of contract . . . .[Elway and Buscher] moved the trial court for summary judgment, which the court granted as to all counts.

* * *

IV.

The . . . issue is whether the court of appeals erred in upholding the trial court's entry of summary judgment on the petitioners' claim of breach of contract. The petitioners' claim for breach of contract is based on the alleged March 15, 1991, Service Agreement orally agreed upon by Nelson, Elway and Buscher.

A.

The first issue with regard to the breach of contract claim is whether the merger clauses in the Buy-Sell Agreements precluded the consideration of evidence that the parties intended the Service Agreement to be part of the overall agreement to sell the dealerships.[1] The petitioners argue that the court of appeals erred by ruling that the merger clauses precluded the consideration of the intent of the contracting parties. The respondents assert that the merger clauses wholly manifest the intention of the parties that only those terms of the transaction reduced to writing and signed at the closing would be enforceable terms of the agreement.

We agree with the court of appeals that the merger clauses preclude consideration of extrinsic evidence to ascertain the intent of the parties. Integration clauses generally allow contracting parties to limit future contractual disputes to issues relating to the express provisions of the contract. * * * Therefore, the terms of a contract intended to represent a final and complete integration of the agreement between the parties are enforceable, and extrinsic evidence offered to prove the existence of prior agreements is inadmissible. * * * Even when extrinsic evidence is admissible to ascertain the intent of the parties, such evidence may not be used to demonstrate an intent that contradicts or adds to the intent expressed in the writing. * * *

In this case, the merger clauses plainly and unambiguously manifest the intent of the parties that the Buy-Sell Agreements executed on March 16, 1991 constitute the entire agreement between the parties pertaining to the subject matter contained therein. Where, as here, sophisticated parties who

[1] Paragraph 14 of both of the Buy-Sell Agreements (the "Merger Clauses") for Metro Toyota and Metro Auto, both signed on March 16, 1991, by Nelson, Elway, and Buscher, states:

> This Agreement constitutes the entire Agreement between the parties pertaining to the subject matter contained herein, and supersedes all prior agreements, representations and understandings of the parties. No modification or amendment of this Agreement shall be binding unless in writing and signed by the parties. . . .

are represented by counsel have consummated a complex transaction and embodied the terms of that transaction in a detailed written document, it would be improper for this court to rewrite that transaction by looking to evidence outside the four corners of the contract to determine the intent of the parties.

The petitioners and respondents signed the March 16, 1991 Buy-Sell Agreements after extensive negotiation and numerous drafts of documents. By doing so, all parties expressly agreed, pursuant to the merger clauses, that the terms of those Buy-Sell Agreements would control the transaction and that all other agreements, oral or written, would be void. We will not step into a commercial transaction after the fact and attempt to ascertain the intent of the parties when that intent is clearly manifested by an express term in a written document. We thus conclude that the merger clauses in the March 16, 1991, Buy-Sell Agreements are dispositive as to the intent of the parties in this case. As there is no dispute as to any material fact with regard to this issue, the court of appeals correctly affirmed the trial court's order of summary judgment in favor of the respondents on this issue.

* * *

VI.

[The Court affirmed the summary judgment]

LOHR, J., dissents, and KIRSHBAUM and SCOTT, JJ., join in the dissent.

Justice LOHR dissenting:

Petitioners Mel T. Nelson and Metro Auto, Inc. (collectively "Nelson") appealed a trial court ruling dismissing their claims on summary judgment grounds. . . . On certiorari review in this court, the majority holds that Nelson's . . . . breach of contract . . . claims were all properly dismissed by the trial court on summary judgment.

I respectfully dissent. Summary judgment is a severe remedy. As the majority notes, in summary judgment proceedings courts must resolve all doubts as to the existence of genuine issues of material fact against the moving party. Maj. op. at 105. In view of the record and the procedural posture of this case, I would hold that Nelson's . . . breach of contract . . . claims were improperly dismissed. I would therefore reverse the judgment of the court of appeals upholding [the] breach of contract claims . . . .

I.

The following facts are derived from the record in this case, resolving all doubts against the party moving for summary judgment, as we must. . . . Mel T. Nelson was the president and sole shareholder of both Metro Toyota, Inc. ("Metro Toyota") and Metro Auto, Inc. ("Metro Auto"). Nelson also owned the land upon which the dealerships were located. Although Metro Auto was historically profitable, Metro Toyota was less successful. After hiring John J. Pico and Aspen Brokerage Co. (collectively "Pico") to serve as his agent and negotiator, Nelson agreed to sell Metro Toyota to John A. Elway, Jr., Rodney L. Buscher, J.R. Motors Company, and J.R. Motors Company South (collectively "Elway"). . . . The parties signed buy-sell and real estate contracts for the Metro Toyota concern on March 14, 1991, and set a closing date in April of 1991.

Soon after the Metro Toyota contracts were executed, Pico approached Nelson with the idea of selling Metro Auto to Elway as well. The parties agreed that any successful deal would have to meet two conditions: John A. Elway's total cash contribution would have to be limited to approximately $1.2 million dollars, and Nelson would have to receive enough personal compensation to make a sale of the historically profitable Metro Auto worthwhile. On March 15, 1991, Elway and Nelson agreed that if Nelson made the up-front concessions envisioned by Elway regarding the sale price for the real estate and dealership assets, Nelson would receive deferred personal compensation through a side agreement ("service agreement") providing that Nelson was to receive $50.00 for every new or used vehicle sold by the dealerships for the next seven years. Both buy-sell agreements noted that sale of the dealerships was contingent on GMAC approval. The parties subsequently signed buy-sell and real estate contracts for Metro Auto on March 16, 1991.

Anticipating the pending sale of the dealerships, GMAC insisted that Nelson relinquish control over the dealerships on April 3, 1991. Since Nelson and Elway had yet to sign the service agreement, Nelson contacted Rodney L. Buscher and received assurances that the service agreement would be honored before relinquishing control to GMAC.

On April 8 or 9, 1991, Pico and Elway met at the Landmark Hotel to discuss the sale of Nelson's dealerships. During the meeting, GMAC called Pico and told Elway that they would not finance the deal if Elway signed a side agreement with Nelson. Despite Nelson's understanding that Elway would honor the service agreement, Elway informed Nelson on April 8 or 9, 1991, that the service agreement would not be signed.

The parties disagree as to why Elway did not sign the service agreement. Elway contends that GMAC refused to approve the sale if the service agreement was executed. Nelson, on the other hand, alleges that Pico and Elway prompted GMAC to impose such conditions. Nelson suggests that Pico was interested in sabotaging the service agreement because of a fee dispute between Pico and Nelson. Nelson further contends that Elway realized that even if a portion of the money earmarked for the service agreement was diverted to pay Pico a commission, the total payout under any side agreements would be less if Nelson's compensation under the service agreement was eliminated. Nevertheless, Nelson proceeded with the sale of the dealerships because he already had turned control over to GMAC and thereby eliminated a bankruptcy reorganization alternative that was previously under consideration.

The parties' present dispute revolves around the enforceability of the service agreement. The district court dismissed Nelson's claims in a summary judgment proceeding . . . . Nelson then petitioned this court for certiorari review of the court of appeals' affirmance of the trial court's summary judgment ruling regarding his . . . breach of contract claims . . . .

* * *

IV.

Nelson . . . contends that Elway is liable for breach of contract in failing to honor the service agreement. The majority affirms the dismissal of Nelson's breach of contract claim on summary judgment, holding . . . that the merger clauses in the buy-sell agreements preclude consideration of the alleged service agreement . . . . I disagree with the majority . . .

First, merger clauses preclude consideration of extrinsic evidence only where the parties intend that the document containing the merger is exclusive. * * * The very essence of this case is a dispute regarding whether the parties intended the service agreement to be part and parcel of the overall deal. Because Nelson's position is adequately supported in the record, the intention of the parties regarding the exclusivity of the document containing the merger agreement is a disputed issue of material fact. As a result, this case is inappropriate for summary judgment disposition. . . .

* * *

A.

Nelson and Elway disagree regarding their intent to honor the alleged service agreement. The majority contends that the merger clauses in the buy-sell agreements affirmatively preclude consideration of extrinsic evidence such as the alleged oral service agreement, and refuses to look at "evidence outside the four corners of the contract to determine the intent of the parties." . . . Maj. op. at 107. However, the "four corners" approach to contract interpretation is in decline. * * * The "modern trend" . . . is that merger and integration clauses are to be afforded varying weight depending on the circumstances of the case. *Franklin v. White*, 493 N.E.2d 161, 166 (Ind.1986); *see also ARB*, 663 F.2d at 199 (court must consider "the circumstances surrounding the making of the contract" to ascertain whether an integration clause serves to "express the genuine intention of the parties to make the written contract the complete and exclusive statement of their agreement"); *Darner*, 140 Ariz. at 393, 682 P.2d at 398 ("Evidence on surrounding circumstances, including negotiation, prior understandings, subsequent conduct and the like, is taken to determine the parties' intent with regard to integration of the agreement. . . . This method obtains even though the parties have bargained for and written the actual words found in the instrument."); *Anderson*, 100 Idaho at 180, 595 P.2d at 714 (courts "should consider not only the language of the agreement but all extrinsic evidence relevant to the issue of whether the parties intended the written agreement to be a complete integration"); *Restatement (Second) of Contracts* § 209(2) (1979) ("Whether there is an integrated agreement is to be determined by the court as a question preliminary to determination of a question of interpretation or to application of the parol evidence rule."); *Restatement (Second) of Contracts* § 210 cmt. b (1979) (for purposes of proving a complete integration, "a writing cannot of itself prove its own completeness, and wide latitude must be allowed for inquiry into circumstances bearing on the intention of the parties") * * *.

Although I believe that merger and integration clauses are presumptively valid, in keeping with the honored tenets of contract law there is an exception such that "[w]here giving effect to the merger clause would frustrate and distort the parties' true intentions and understanding regarding the contract, the clause will not be enforced." * * * In particular, where the parties intend that both a written contract and an alleged oral agreement constitute components of an overall agreement, a merger clause does not preclude consideration of extrinsic evidence. * * *

The parties' intention that the buy-sell agreements constituted entire contracts, allegedly evidenced by the merger clauses within, was by no means clearly manifested. * * * In this case, despite the disclaimer in both merger clauses that each buy-sell agreement constituted the entire agreement, the overall deal involved two buy-sell agreements and two real estate contracts. Furthermore, each buy-sell agreement made reference to the real estate contracts despite the exclusivity disclaimer. Regardless of the standard merger and integration language in the buy-sell agreements, it is clear that the parties intended their ultimate bargain to encompass other agreements, although the substantive weight of the alleged service agreement remains unclear. * * *

When the parties disagree as to whether a document expresses the complete agreement of the parties, and a court subsequently finds that the evidence is conflicting or admits of more than one inference, the resolution of the parties' dispute requires a factual determination. * * *

VI.

In short, this case is singularly inappropriate for resolution in a summary judgment proceeding. . . . [T]he merger clauses in the parties' buy-sell agreements [do not] preclude[] Nelson's breach of contract claim for summary judgment purposes. At base, the parties are embroiled in a dispute regarding whether they intended the buy-sell agreements to be fully integrated and whether they intended the service agreement to be enforced. Nelson again supported his factual construction in the record, and as a result the parties' disagreement over the factual issues of integration . . . cannot properly be resolved by summary judgment.

* * *

For the aforementioned reasons, I respectfully dissent. I would reverse the judgment of the court of appeals upholding dismissal of Nelson's . . .breach of contract claim[ ] . . . .

Kirshbaum and Scott, JJ., join in this dissent.

QUESTIONS AND NOTE

1. Questions about the facts of this case

   1.1. What was the parol evidence that the majority thought ought not to be considered by the trier of fact?

   1.2. Did the parties contest that there was a side agreement negotiated and agreed to?

2. Questions about the law

   2.1. Did the court find as a matter of law that both Nelson and Elway intended the Buy-Sell Agreements to be the "final and complete integration of the agreement"? If so, what was the basis for such a finding?

   2.2. If the dissent is correct about the trend of the law (and it is), did the majority reach the correct result? In hindsight, what should have Nelson's litigation attorneys done differently to at least get the case to trial? What should have Nelson's lawyers done at the time of the 1991 closing?

   2.3. Again, assuming that the dissent is correct on the law, under the modern trend, what good is a merger clause?

3. Note

   Elway later sold these two dealerships, along with four others that he owned in the Denver area, for $82.5 million. *Huizenga Has Big Ideas about Selling Automobiles,* THE DENVER POST, June 11, 1998, p. C-01. What would have been the harm in honoring the agreement with Nelson in light of this development?

Parol evidence does not just apply to large mergers and intensely-lawyered deals. It applies to all contracts, including the one drafted by non-lawyers in the following case. Note, however, that this case was essentially decided before trial by the court's ruling on a "motion in limine;" that is, a motion to exclude evidence made before trial. Lawyers make this type of motion when they know the opposing side wants to introduce evidence that is potentially inadmissable. If the issue is resolved before trial, it reduces confusion during the trial, and also precludes the jury from hearing any reference to the evidence desired to be excluded.

Esbensen v. Userware International, Inc.

Court of Appeal of California, Fourth Appellate District
11 Cal. App.4th 631, 14 Cal. Rptr.2d 93 (1992)

Wiener, Acting Presiding Justice.

Plaintiff Daniel Esbensen sued his former employer, defendant Userware International, Inc. and several of its officers, alleging his employment as a computer programmer was wrongfully terminated without good cause. Because his written one-year employment contract did not specify a "good cause" requirement, Esbensen unsuccessfully sought to introduce evidence of oral assurances he was allegedly given by Userware management that the contract would be perpetually renewed as long as he performed his job competently.

Userware argues the written contract must be interpreted to allow for Esbensen's termination "at will" and that in any event, the contract was fully integrated precluding the admission of evidence to show an unwritten but consistent oral understanding. We reject both arguments. The more difficult question, we believe, is Userware's additional contention that the alleged oral assurances are inconsistent with the contract's one-year term. While it might be presumed that a one-year contract term, without more, means the parties have no obligations at the expiration of the one year, here Esbensen sought to overcome that presumption by introducing evidence of an express contrary oral understanding. While Esbensen may have difficulty proving such an understanding to the satisfaction of a jury, we conclude he is entitled to make the attempt. Accordingly, we reverse.

FACTUAL AND PROCEDURAL BACKGROUND

Userware is a company which provides computer-related services for small businesses and individuals. In 1977 Userware hired Esbensen as a computer programmer pursuant to an oral contract between Esbensen and Richard Rhodes, an officer and one of the founders of Userware. At Esbensen's insistence, the contract was later reduced to writing and beginning in May 1979, a series of three virtually identical one-year contracts was signed. In addition to a monthly salary, Esbensen was entitled to a ten percent "commission" on sales of software products he developed.

Several provisions of the final three-page contract executed in 1981 bear on the issues presented by this case. In the first paragraph, the contract specifies that Esbensen "will receive a regular weekly salary of $675.00 which amount will be reviewed on an annual basis." Paragraph IV is titled "Term of Agreement" and provides: "This agreement is effective June 1, 1981, for a period of one year; however, this agreement may be terminated earlier as hereinafter provided." Paragraph V, titled "Termination," goes on to state: "This agreement may be terminated by either party by giving two weeks written notice of termination to the other party. Upon termination for any reason, all salary shall cease on the effective date of termination. [Userware] will continue to pay commission as outlined in section II for a period of 180 days after the effective date of termination."

In January 1982, Esbensen was terminated by Userware allegedly, among other reasons, because he failed to timely report for work following a vacation. Esbensen responded by filing suit for breach of contract, asserting he had been told by Rhodes that the series of one-year contracts would be renewed perpetually as long as he was doing his job. In effect, according to Esbensen, his contract included an implied term that he could not be terminated except for good cause.

Userware filed a motion *in limine* to exclude evidence of any oral understanding between Esbensen and Rhodes concerning an implied "good cause" requirement for termination. The trial court agreed largely with Userware. It concluded Esbensen's employment contract was an integrated one-year agreement and Esbensen was precluded from "introduc[ing] parole [*sic*] evidence that his employment was to continue and that his contract was to be renewed so long as he performed his job capably. . . ." Esbensen was allowed to seek contract damages for breach of contract but those damages were limited to what would have been earned for six months following the expiration of the contract's one-year term. Because of the limitation of damages, Userware stipulated to judgment in the amount of $15,000, the maximum amount recoverable under the court's *in limine* rulings, and Esbensen proceeded with this appeal to challenge the correctness of those determinations. * * *

DISCUSSION

Userware makes a three-pronged argument in support of the trial court's ruling excluding Esbensen's proffered evidence of an oral agreement that he would not be terminated except for good cause. According to Userware, paragraph V of the contract, which provides for termination before the expiration of the one-year term, allows for termination at any time for any reason. Thus, Esbensen's testimony is assertedly inadmissible as inconsistent with this portion of the written contract. In any event, even if the employment agreement was not terminable at will, Userware asserts the parties intended the written agreement to be final, complete and exclusive, precluding the admission of parol evidence. Finally, even if the agreement is not integrated, Userware argues the oral understanding Esbensen seeks to prove is inconsistent with the one-year term specified in paragraph IV of the written contract and the parol evidence is therefore inadmissible on this additional ground as well.

Esbensen responds that paragraph V does not make the contract terminable "at will"; indeed, such an interpretation would make the one-year term of the contract meaningless. He goes on to argue why the contract is not integrated and concludes the parol evidence suggesting an oral understanding that the contract would be renewed perpetually is not inconsistent with paragraph IV and is admissible.

1. Is the employment relationship terminable at will?

We agree with Esbensen that paragraph V does not make the contract terminable at will. Userware relies on several cases in which the employment contracts specified that the employee could be terminated "at any time" and "for any reason." * * * Here, in contrast, the "for any reason" language relied on by Userware . . . does not refer to the grounds for termination but rather explains that Userware is not obliged to pay salary but is obliged to continue paying Esbensen's commission regardless of the reason for the termination. The written contract, as we read it, is silent on the acceptable grounds for termination.

2. Was the written contract fully integrated?

Even if the employment contract is not terminable at will, Userware argues the written agreement is fully integrated, precluding the admission of extrinsic evidence to add additional terms. In contract law, "integration" means the extent to which a writing constitutes the parties' final expression of their agreement. To the extent a contract is integrated, the parol evidence rule precludes the admission of evidence of the parties' prior or contemporaneous oral statements to contradict the terms of the writing, although parol evidence is always admissible to interpret the written agreement. * * *

Obviously where following negotiations the parties execute a written agreement, that agreement is at least "partially" integrated and parol evidence cannot be admitted to contradict the terms agreed to in the writing. * * * Evidence of related oral understandings, however, is admissible to prove additional terms of the contract not inconsistent with the express language of the writing. * * *

If a writing is intended by the parties as a "complete and exclusive statement of the terms of the agreement" * * *, the contract is "fully" or "completely" integrated and parol evidence is inadmissible even to add terms not inconsistent with the writing. Obviously such a determination must be based on proof of the parties' intent * * * and a critical element in that proof is the nature of the alleged oral understanding. * * * The Supreme Court has held that in order to bar evidence of a consistent oral understanding, the court must convince itself at a minimum that such an understanding would not "naturally" have been excluded from the writing. * * *

Here the court found that the agreement was "integrated" without specifying whether the integration was partial or complete.[4] Whatever the trial court's intent, we independently conclude the written employment contract represents only a partial integration. Here as in *Masterson*, the written contract "does not explicitly provide that it contains the complete agreement. . . ." * * * Moreover, as we explained earlier, the contract is silent as to the grounds for termination. It is hardly unnatural to think that small business entrepreneurs and a computer programmer, unsophisticated in legal matters and unadvised by lawyers, might have discussed those uncertainties and

---

[4]Although agreeing it is a question for the trial court rather than the jury. . . , cases have disagreed on whether the issue of "complete" integration is a question of law or a question of fact. Several cases have suggested that a substantial evidence standard of review applies to limit the ability of appellate courts to overturn trial court determinations. * * * Others have termed the issue a question of law and resolved it without deference to the trial court's factual findings, at least where the foundational extrinsic evidence is not in conflict. * * *

We read *Masterson v. Sine, supra*, 68 Cal.2d 222, 65 Cal. Rptr. 545, the seminal California Supreme Court case on the issue, to treat it as a question of law subject to plenary appellate review where the foundational extrinsic evidence is not in conflict. (*Id.* at pp. 228–231, 65 Cal. Rptr. 545) * * *

resolved them orally.[5] * * * Because it is only by implication that we can determine what the parties intended with regard to the proper bases for termination, that reasoning process ought to be informed by whatever relevant extrinsic evidence exists which casts light on the parties' intent.

3. Was the parol evidence offered to prove a consistent oral understanding?

Despite the parties' focus on the question of integration, our conclusion that the agreement was only partially integrated does not fully resolve the case. Assuming partial integration, parol evidence is admissible only to prove an oral term of the contract not inconsistent with the written memorialization. Parol evidence may not be offered to contradict the terms of even a partially integrated writing.

Esbensen sought to introduce evidence of his conversations with Rhodes to the effect that Userware had promised to renew the annual contracts so long as Esbensen performed competently. Userware argues that such an agreement would be flatly inconsistent with the written contract which provides, on one hand, for a term of one year and then creates a separate termination procedure which under some unspecified set of circumstances allows for dismissal before the expiration of the contract term. Even if it could not fire Esbensen for any reason at any time, at a minimum, Userware asserts, the fact that the contract was for a term of one year gives it the right to terminate Esbensen at the end of the year for any reason.

We agree with Userware that the one-year term provision of the contract must have some meaning. We disagree, however, that the only possible reason for including this provision was to allow for Esbensen's termination at the end of the year for any reason. As Esbensen points out, the contract specifically provided that his salary would be reviewed on an annual basis. If the written contract was supplemented by an oral understanding that the one-year agreements would be renewed absent good cause not to do so, it might be that the one-year contract term merely reflected the interval between salary reviews. Under such circumstances, "good cause" for nonrenewal would necessarily include the parties' failure to agree on the terms for renewal. In effect, the parties would be obligated to negotiate in good faith at the end of each year toward the goal of renewal on mutually acceptable terms.

---

[5] The evidence indicated that oral agreements were standard at Userware. Esbensen testified that he was the only Userware employee to have a written contract.

* * *

It could be argued that the failure to specify grounds necessarily implies that any reason was acceptable. As we have explained, however, the fact that something is presumed or implied in the absence of an express statement to the contrary does not preclude a party to an incomplete written contract from attempting to demonstrate an express oral agreement contrary to the term which would otherwise be presumed or implied.

We wish to emphasize that our conclusion parol evidence should have been admitted is but a small step on Esbensen's path to ultimate success. A jury must yet determine that the oral representations alleged by Esbensen were in fact made. Assuming they were, the jury must further determine the exact nature of the oral agreement between Rhodes and Esbensen. Assuming this is found to be an understanding that the contract would be perpetually renewed unless there was good cause not to do so, the jury must finally decide whether Userware had "good cause" to terminate Esbensen.

DISPOSITION

Judgment reversed. Appellant shall recover costs for this appeal.

Todd, and Huffman, JJ., concur.

QUESTIONS

1. Questions about the facts of this case

   1.1. What was the term that Esbensen thought was part of his contract?

   1.2. On remand, what issue is left for the jury to determine? What evidence will be given to them to consider?

2. Questions about the law

   2.1. Did the court determine that the contract was fully integrated?

   2.2. If your answer to question 2.1 was "no," then did the court determine that the contract was partially integrated? If so, on what terms was there integration?

2.3. What is this court's test for full or partial integration of written contracts?

2.4. If a writing is only partially integrated, is all parol evidence admissible? If not, then why was the parol evidence admissible in this case?

B. Uniform Commercial Code

According to *Elway* and *Esbensen*, the key to the applicability of the parol evidence rule is whether the document is "integrated." The Uniform Commercial Code has its own version of the parol evidence rule, which is reprinted below. Note that nowhere in the following section is the term "integrated" used. Nevertheless, does it appear that the U.C.C. also has an "integration" concept?

§ 2-202 Final Written Expression: Parol or Extrinsic Evidence

Terms with respect to which the confirmatory memoranda of the parties agree or which are otherwise set forth in a writing intended by the parties as a final expression of their agreement with respect to such terms as are included therein may not be contradicted by evidence of any prior agreement or of a contemporaneous oral agreement but may be explained or supplemented

(a) by course of dealing or usage of trade (Section 1-205) or by course of performance (Section 2-208); and

(b) by evidence of consistent additional terms unless the court finds the writing to have been intended also as a complete and exclusive statement of the terms of the agreement.

Does this language change the common law parol evidence rule? In reading the next case, focus on how the Supreme Court of South Dakota views or tries to determine the "final expression of their agreement" language in Section 2-202.

Herman Oil, Inc. v. Peterman
Supreme Court of North Dakota
518 N.W.2d 184 (1994)

LEVINE, Justice.

Herman Oil, Inc. appeals from a judgment dismissing its action to collect on a personal guaranty by Harvey and Shirley Peterman for the debts of Peterman Oil, Inc., a corporation owned by the Petermans and their son. We hold that the trial court's implicit determination that Herman Oil and Peterman Oil did not intend written invoices to be a final expression of their agreement was not clearly erroneous and permitted the court to rely on extrinsic evidence to determine the terms of that agreement. We further hold that the court's findings on the terms of that agreement were not clearly erroneous. We therefore affirm the judgment.

I

Herman Oil, a Williston-based North Dakota corporation engaged in the retail sale of fuel, purchased most of its petroleum products from Canadian refineries for resale in the United States. During 1990, Herman Oil sold fuel directly to a Canadian purchaser, Charles Mass, who transported the fuel back to Canada for resale. Herman Oil discontinued direct sales to Mass in November 1990, because it was concerned that those sales would jeopardize its supply of petroleum products from the Canadian refineries.

This lawsuit involves a dispute over the terms of an agreement between Herman Oil and Peterman Oil in the purchase of fuel by Mass. Herman Oil said it sold fuel directly to Peterman Oil, a North Dakota corporation engaged in trucking and selling fuel, and Peterman Oil independently sold that fuel to Mass. Herman Oil claimed that no special arrangement existed between it and Peterman Oil in the sale of fuel to Mass.

The Petermans told a different story. According to them, Herman Oil contacted Peterman Oil to "handle the paperwork" for the sales to Mass. The transactions with Mass were part of a "special arrangement" with Peterman Oil to act as a conduit for the sale of fuel by Herman Oil to Mass. Petermans explained that Mass initially issued checks to Peterman Oil for the fuel and Peterman Oil issued checks to Herman Oil, but that Peterman Oil and Herman Oil later agreed that Herman Oil would "hold" Peterman Oil's checks until Mass's checks to Peterman Oil were paid by his Canadian bank.

In April 1991, Peterman Oil issued a check to Herman Oil to pay for fuel for Mass. However, Mass ultimately failed to pay Peterman Oil for that fuel, and Peterman Oil's check to Herman Oil was returned for insufficient funds. Herman Oil sued Petermans individually to collect on their personal guaranty of Peterman Oil's obligations. The trial court determined that a "special arrangement" existed between Herman Oil and Peterman Oil for Mass's account, and, because of that arrangement and their agreement to hold Peterman Oil's checks until Mass's checks cleared his bank, Peterman Oil was not obligated to pay Herman Oil until Mass paid Peterman Oil. The court concluded that Petermans were not liable to Herman Oil on their personal guaranty of Peterman Oil's debts and dismissed Herman Oil's action against them. Herman Oil appealed.

II

Herman Oil argues that Article 2 of the Uniform Commercial Code makes the written invoices it issued to Peterman Oil separate contracts, each setting the price and payment terms for the fuel purchased under that invoice. It argues that because all prior and subsequent oral agreements between it and Peterman Oil contradicted payment terms in the written invoices, the parol evidence rule barred the trial court's consideration of those agreements. Petermans respond that Article 2 is not applicable because Peterman Oil's agreement with Herman Oil did not involve the "sale" of goods. They assert that Peterman Oil and Herman Oil orally agreed for Peterman Oil to act as a conduit for the sale of fuel to Mass . . . . They argue that the trial court did not err in considering extrinsic evidence relating to the parties' oral agreement and that the court's findings on the terms of that oral agreement are not clearly erroneous.

A

We initially consider whether the invoices issued by Herman Oil to Peterman Oil created enforceable contracts for the sale of goods.[1] [After finding that the U.C.C. applied to this case, and that there was no question un-

[1] "Goods" mean "all things (including specially manufactured goods) which are movable at the time of identification to the contract for sale other than the money in which the price is to be paid, investment securities (chapter 41-08), and things in action." N.D.C.C. § 41-02-05(2) [U.C.C. § 2-105(1)]. Here, the parties do not dispute that the subject of the invoices, fuel, is a "thing[ ] which [is] movable at the time of identification to the contract," thus satisfying the U.C.C.'s definition of goods. * * *

der the U.C.C.'s statute of frauds, the Court stated that] [u]nder N.D.C.C. § 41-02-08 [U.C.C. §2-201], the written invoices from Herman Oil to Peterman Oil evidenced enforceable contracts for the sale of fuel. * * * So the question becomes whether the parol evidence rule in the U.C.C. bars the court from considering extrinsic evidence about those invoices. * * *

B

Section 41-02-09, N.D.C.C. [U.C.C. § 2-202], outlines the scope of the parol evidence rule under the U.C.C.:

> "Final written expression—Parol or extrinsic evidence. Terms with respect to which the confirmatory memoranda of the parties agree or which are otherwise set forth in a writing intended by the parties as a final expression of their agreement with respect to such terms as are included therein may not be contradicted by evidence of any prior agreement or of a contemporaneous oral agreement but may be explained or supplemented:
>
> "1. By course of dealing or usage of trade (section 41-01-15) or by course of performance (section 41-02-15); and
>
> "2. By evidence of consistent additional terms unless the court finds the writing to have been intended also as a complete and exclusive statement of the terms of the agreement."

Section 41-02-09, N.D.C.C. [U.C.C. § 2-202], changes the common law of contracts and liberalizes the application of the parol evidence rule to writings evidencing a contract for the sale of goods. * * *

Under N.D.C.C. § 41-02-09 [U.C.C. § 2-202], the court must initially determine whether the parties intended a writing to be a final expression of their agreement on the written terms, or to be a complete and exclusive statement of their agreement. * * *

Section 41-02-09, N.D.C.C. [U.C.C. § 2-202], "definitely rejects ... [a]ny assumption that because a writing has been worked out which is final on some matters, it is to be taken as including all the matters agreed upon," and the requirement that, before extrinsic evidence may be considered, the written terms must be ambiguous. Official Comment 1 to U.C.C. § 2-202. * * *. There is no assumption that the parties intended a writing to be final or exclusive and, in fact, the assumption is to the contrary, unless the court expressly finds that the parties intended the contract to be completely integrated. * * *

In determining whether a writing is a final expression of the parties' agreement on the written terms, the most important factor is the intent of the parties. Sierra Diesel Injection Service, supra. The court may consider the nature and scope of the commercial setting surrounding the writing and the character of the alleged extrinsic terms not in writing. * * * The intent of the parties is a preliminary question of fact for the court, and the court's determination on that issue is reviewed under the clearly erroneous standard. * * * If the court determines that the parties did not intend a writing to be a final expression of the terms of their agreement, the court may rely on extrinsic evidence to determine the parties' agreement. * * *

Even if the court finds the parties intended a writing to be a final expression of written terms, N.D.C.C. § 41-02-09 [U.C.C. § 2-202] authorizes the court to consider extrinsic evidence of course of dealing and course of performance to supplement or explain the written terms. * * * As the official comment explains, a written contract need not be ambiguous for the admission of extrinsic evidence of course of performance, course of dealing, or usage of trade, because the proper construction of the writing requires familiarity with the commercial context of the agreement.* * *

In this case, the written invoices from Herman Oil to Peterman Oil evidenced an enforceable agreement and specified that Peterman Oil acknowledged the following pre-printed terms: "1.5% per month or 18% annual rate on all amounts 25 days or more past due from last statement." However, the invoices did not otherwise identify payments terms. The written invoices did not contain a merger clause[5] and there is no assumption that the parties intended the invoices to be a final expression of their agreement. Under N.D.C.C. § 41-02-09 [U.C.C. § 2-202], the trial court could consider extrinsic evidence of the commercial context of the parties' agreement, including evidence of their "special arrangement," to determine that the written invoices were not a final expression of their agreement about terms of payment. The court could also consider extrinsic evidence of the

[5]One commentator suggests that uncertainty about whether the parties intended a writing to be a final and complete and exclusive expression of the parties' agreement can be eliminated by a conspicuous written merger clause to the effect that the parties consider the signed agreement to be "a final written expression of all the terms of this agreement and is a complete and exclusive statement of those terms." 1 White and Summers, [Uniform Commercial Code], § 2-12 at p. 122. Although merger clauses are strong evidence of integration, they are not conclusive. * * *

parties' course of dealing and course of performance for Herman Oil to "hold" Peterman Oil's checks until Mass's bank paid his checks. * * * The trial court did not expressly find that the parties did not intend the written invoices to be the final expression of their agreement. However, in view of the court's finding that a special arrangement existed between Herman Oil and Peterman Oil and that they in fact agreed to make Peterman Oil's obligation subject to the condition that Mass's checks clear his bank, a condition not in the written invoices, we can infer no other finding but that the court determined the parties did not intend the invoices to be a final expression of their agreement. Hoff Companies, Inc., supra. The trial court's implicit determination is not clearly erroneous and permitted the court to rely on extrinsic evidence to determine the terms of the parties' agreement. . .

C

Herman Oil argues that the extrinsic evidence does not support the trial court's finding that the parties agreed that Herman Oil would hold Peterman Oil's checks until Mass's checks cleared his bank. In addition to Harvey Peterman's testimony of the parties' oral agreement to hold Peterman Oil's checks, there was also documentary evidence from which the court could infer a course of dealing and course of performance by Herman Oil to hold Peterman Oil's checks until Mass's checks cleared his bank. The evidence on the parties' agreement was conflicting. In that situation, N.D.R.Civ.P. 52(a) instructs that "due regard shall be given to the opportunity of the trial court to judge the credibility of the witnesses" and weigh conflicting evidence. We are not left with a definite and firm conviction that the trial court's finding about the parties' agreement to hold the checks was mistaken. Accordingly, we conclude the finding was not clearly erroneous.

The judgment is affirmed.

Vande Walle, C.J., and Sandstrom, Neumann and Meschke, JJ., concur.

QUESTIONS AND NOTES

1. Questions about the facts of this case

1.1. Did the court properly apply the facts with respect to the printed payment terms? Think of the following case: If Mass was 60 days late in paying Peterman, what argument could Peterman propose that would absolve him from paying 18% annual interest on days 26 to 60?

1.2. Does it strike you that if the relationship was as suggested by Peterman, that the method chosen by Herman Oil to document it (use of pre-printed invoices) was stunningly inappropriate? Did the court do anything with this observation?

1.3. If you represented Herman Oil, would you go back and change your standard form invoice after this case? If so, what would you change?

2. Questions about the law

2.1. What was Herman Oil's argument under U.C.C. section 2-202? What part of that argument did the Supreme Court of North Dakota reject?

2.2. The court states that section 2-202 "changes the common law of contracts and liberalizes the application of the parol evidence rule to writings evidencing a contract for the sale of goods." Do you agree?

2.3. Further on differences from the common law. Is there any real difference between an "integrated agreement" under the *Restatement's* definition and a writing which serves as "a final expression of [an] agreement with respect to such terms as are included therein" under the Uniform Commercial Code?

First, read comment 3 to Section 2-202. It states that:

> If the additional terms are such that, if agreed upon, they would certainly have been included in the document in the view of the court, then evidence of their alleged making must be kept from the trier of fact.

Then read Section 209(3) of the *Restatement (Second) of Contracts* which states that a writing is an integrated agreement if "in view of its completeness and specificity [it] reasonably appears to be a complete agreement."

Which is the tougher standard; that is, under which standard is it more difficult to introduce parol evidence?

2.4. Is Section 2-202(b) a parol evidence rule? Note that the title to the section in the U.C.C. is "parol or extrinsic evidence." What is the difference between "parol" and "extrinsic" evidence?

3. Notes

3.1. Note the structure of Section 2-202. It permits the introduction of parol evidence to "explain[] or supplement[] . . . by course of dealing or usage of trade (Section 1-205) or by course of performance (Section 2-208)" the terms of the contract. Under the Uniform Commercial Code, however, the "contract" is the enforceable agreement of the parties, § 1-201(11), and the agreement is the "bargain of the parties in fact as found in their language or by implication from other circumstances including course of dealing or usage of trade or course of performance." Thus, harkening back to *Threadgill*, the U.C.C. incorporates trade usage, course of dealing and usage of trade into each agreement within its scope. We'll see more of this later in Section 3, Subsection B.

3.2. Consider the difference between the statute of frauds and the parol evidence rule. The sales receipts in *Herman Oil* were held (i) to satisfy the statute of frauds but (ii) not to trigger the parol evidence rule. How can a writing satisfy the statute of frauds without even triggering the parol evidence rule?

C. Exceptions

As we have seen above, the finding that there is an integrated agreement carries with it significant consequences. It deprives the parties from introducing other terms that are inconsistent with the level of integration found: that is, if the agreement is *partially* integrated, the parol evidence rule bars evidence of terms inconsistent with the integrated terms (usually the ones written down); if *fully* integrated, the parol evidence rule bars introduction of any evidence of terms that may supplement or contradict the agreement.

There are, of course, cases to which these blanket statements don't apply. Although not an exception, note that the rule does not apply to evidence relating to terms discussed or agreed to *after* the execution of the agreement.

Technically, under the *Restatement*, the rule applies only to acts to "discharge[] *prior* agreements." *Restatement (Second) of Contracts* § 213(1) (emphasis added). This is a sensible result; if the rule acted prospectively, it would effectively eliminate any possibility of amendment or individual waiver of provisions of an integrated agreement. Contracts are typically not that static or rigid.

It would also be the height (or nadir) of formalism to deny a party the ability to introduce parol evidence to demonstrate that the contract was procured by fraud, or through mistake or some other affirmative defense. A species of such fraud, stemming from the common practice of signing documents in advance of their effectiveness would be to take an otherwise complete document and assert its validity before such validity was intended. This is often done when purchasing a home to facilitate the closing (the seller will sign the deed ahead of time, and give it to her attorney or escrow company), and in large corporate transactions given the sheer complexity and number of documents that attend such transactions). Thus, there is another exception that allows parties to show that there was an oral condition to the effectiveness of documents. *See Restatement (Second) of Contracts* § 217.

Problems on Parol Evidence

Try to synthesize your understanding thus far with the following problems based on the facts set out below:

> Ponoroff and Epstein are negotiating for the purchase of a cow. They reach agreement on a purchase price of $600, after several back and forth negotiations over the price involving other terms such as delivery date, veterinarian inspections and the like. At the end of negotiations, Ponoroff and Epstein sign the following document:
>
> Ponoroff agrees to sell to Epstein, and Epstein agrees to buy, for $600, Ponoroff's cow known as Bossie without any veterinarian's certificate. Payment to be by cashier's check.

1. One week after the signing, Epstein shows up at Ponoroff's barn and tries to give Ponoroff a cashier's check for $600. Ponoroff tells Epstein to leave. When Epstein sues Ponoroff for breach, can Epstein introduce evidence of discussions between them that tends to indi-

cate that Ponoroff and Epstein had a side agreement to deliver the cow on the date Epstein showed up?

2. If Epstein shows up with a personal check instead of a cashier's check, and Ponoroff refuses to accept it, may Epstein defend Ponoroff's lawsuit by offering evidence that, prior to signing the document, Ponoroff had indicated that a personal check from Epstein would be acceptable?

3. Does the result in Problem 2 above change if Epstein's evidence is that instead of before the signing, Ponoroff's assent to a personal check occurred *after* the signing?

4. Same facts as in Problem 1, except now the written agreement has an additional clause that states:

   This agreement, though short, contains all of the agreements of the parties on this subject, and is intended as a complete and final expression of all of the terms the parties deem relevant to this transaction.

5. Same facts as in Problem 4, except assume that, after signing, Epstein asked Ponoroff to hold the document "in escrow" until Epstein checked the cost of obtaining a cashier's check. When he found that the bank would charge him $25 for the check, Epstein asked Ponoroff to reduce the price to $575. Ponoroff said no. Later, Ponoroff sues Epstein for nonpayment of the $600. When Epstein tries to introduce evidence of their understanding about holding the agreement, Ponoroff asserts that, in light of the integration clause, Epstein is barred from doing so by the parol evidence rule. Who's right?

6. Same facts as in Problem 4, except that when Epstein appears, he demands a veterinarian's certificate attesting to the health of Bossie. Ponoroff points to the contractual term negating such a duty, but Epstein claims that such a certificate is customary in the cattle industry. In litigation over the point, it turns out that neither Epstein or Ponoroff (both experienced cattle merchants) have ever heard of a cattle transaction in which a veterinarian's certificate was not a precondition to payment.

D. A World Without Parol Evidence—*The Convention on the International Sale of Goods*

Before we leave direct consideration of the parol evidence rule, it is helpful to step back and wonder about its value. Would Western civilization as we know it collapse if the parol evidence rule were not part of our jurisprudence? The next case presents that issue. When reading it, check your statutory supplement for the *Convention on the International Sale of Goods*. It is the law of the United States, and potentially applicable to transactions in which you may be involved in the future.

MCC-Marble Ceramic Center, Inc. v. Ceramica Nuova D'Agostino, S.p.A.

U.S. Court of Appeals, Eleventh Circuit
144 F.3d 1384 (1998)

Appeal from the United States District Court for the Southern District of Florida.

Before EDMONDSON and BIRCH, Circuit Judges, and FAY, Senior Circuit Judge.

BIRCH, Circuit Judge:

This case requires us to determine whether a court must consider parol evidence in a contract dispute governed by the United Nations Convention on Contracts for the International Sale of Goods ("CISG").[1] The district court granted summary judgment on behalf of the defendant-appellee, relying on certain terms and provisions that appeared on the reverse of a pre-printed form contract for the sale of ceramic tiles. The plaintiff-appellant sought to rely on a number of affidavits that tended to show both that the parties had arrived at an oral contract before memorializing their agreement in writing and that they subjectively intended not to apply the terms on the reverse of the contract to their agreements. The magistrate judge held that the affidavits did not raise an issue of material fact and recommended that the district court grant summary judgment based on the terms of the contract. The

[1] United Nations Convention on Contracts for the International Sale of Goods, opened for signature April 11, 1980, S. Treaty Doc. No. 9, 98th Cong., 1st Sess. 22 (1983), 19 I.L.M. 671, reprinted at, 15 U.S.C. app. 52 (1997).

district court agreed with the magistrate judge's reasoning and entered summary judgment in the defendant-appellee's favor. We REVERSE.

BACKGROUND

The plaintiff-appellant, MCC-Marble Ceramic, Inc. ("MCC"), is a Florida corporation engaged in the retail sale of tiles, and the defendant-appellee, Ceramica Nuova d'Agostino S.p.A. ("D'Agostino") is an Italian corporation engaged in the manufacture of ceramic tiles. In October 1990, MCC's president, Juan Carlos Mozon, met representatives of D'Agostino at a trade fair in Bologna, Italy and negotiated an agreement to purchase ceramic tiles from D'Agostino based on samples he examined at the trade fair. Monzon, who spoke no Italian, communicated with Gianni Silingardi, then D'Agostino's commercial director, through a translator, Gianfranco Copelli, who was himself an agent of D'Agostino. The parties apparently arrived at an oral agreement on the crucial terms of price, quality, quantity, delivery and payment. The parties then recorded these terms on one of D'Agostino's standard, pre-printed order forms and Monzon signed the contract on MCC's behalf. According to MCC, the parties also entered into a requirements contract in February 1991, subject to which D'Agostino agreed to supply MCC with high grade ceramic tile at specific discounts as long as MCC purchased sufficient quantities of tile. MCC completed a number of additional order forms requesting tile deliveries pursuant to that agreement.

MCC brought suit against D'Agostino claiming a breach of the February 1991 requirements contract when D'Agostino failed to satisfy orders in April, May, and August of 1991. In addition to other defenses, D'Agostino responded that it was under no obligation to fill MCC's orders because MCC had defaulted on payment for previous shipments. In support of its position, D'Agostino relied on the pre-printed terms of the contracts that MCC had executed. The executed forms were printed in Italian and contained terms and conditions on both the front and reverse. According to an English translation of the October 1990 contract, the front of the order form contained the following language directly beneath Monzon's signature:

> [T]he buyer hereby states that he is aware of the sales conditions stated on the reverse and that he expressly approves of them with special reference to those numbered 1-2-3-4-5-6-7-8.

R2-126, Exh. 3 ¶ 5 ("Maselli Aff."). Clause 6(b), printed on the back of the form states:

> [D]efault or delay in payment within the time agreed upon gives D'Agostino the right to . . . suspend or cancel the contract itself and to cancel possible other pending contracts and the buyer does not have the right to indemnification or damages.

Id. ¶ 6.

D'Agostino also brought a number of counterclaims against MCC, seeking damages for MCC's alleged nonpayment for deliveries of tile that D'Agostino had made between February 28, 1991 and July 4, 1991. MCC responded that the tile it had received was of a lower quality than contracted for, and that, pursuant to the CISG, MCC was entitled to reduce payment in proportion to the defects.[4] D'Agostino, however, noted that clause 4 on the reverse of the contract states, in pertinent part:

> Possible complaints for defects of the merchandise must be made in writing by means of a certified letter within and not later than 10 days after receipt of the merchandise. . . .

Maselli Aff. ¶ 6. Although there is evidence to support MCC's claims that it complained about the quality of the deliveries it received, MCC never submitted any written complaints.

MCC did not dispute these underlying facts before the district court, but argued that the parties never intended the terms and conditions printed on the reverse of the order form to apply to their agreements. As evidence for this assertion, MCC submitted Monzon's affidavit, which claims that MCC had no subjective intent to be bound by those terms and that D'Agostino was aware of this intent. MCC also filed affidavits from Silingardi and Copelli, D'Agostino's representatives at the trade fair, which support Monzon's claim that the parties subjectively intended not to be bound by the terms on the reverse of the order form. The magistrate judge held that the affidavits, even if true, did not raise an issue of material fact regarding the interpretation or applicability of the terms of the written contracts and the district court accepted his recommendation to award summary judgment in D'Agostino's favor. MCC then filed this timely appeal.

---

[4]Article 50 of the CISG permits a buyer to reduce payment for nonconforming goods in proportion to the nonconformity under certain conditions. See CISG, art. 50.

DISCUSSION

* * *

The parties to this case agree that the CISG governs their dispute because the United States, where MCC has its place of business, and Italy, where D'Agostino has its place of business, are both States party to the Convention.[5] See CISG, art. 1.[6] Article 8 of the CISG governs the interpretation of international contracts for the sale of goods and forms the basis of MCC's appeal from the district court's grant of summary judgment in D'Agostino's favor.[7] MCC argues that the magistrate judge and the district court improperly ignored evidence that MCC submitted regarding the parties' subjective intent when they memorialized the terms of their agreement on D'Agostino's pre-printed form contract, and that the magistrate judge erred by applying the parol evidence rule in derogation of the CISG.

---

[5]The United States Senate ratified the CISG in 1986, and the United States deposited its instrument of ratification at the United Nations Headquarters in New York on December 11, 1986. *See* Preface to Convention, reprinted at 15 U.S.C. App. 52 (1997). The Convention entered into force between the United States and the other States Parties, including Italy, on January 1, 1988. *See id.; Filanto S.p.A. v. Chilewich Int'l Corp.*, 789 F. Supp. 1229, 1237 (S.D. N.Y.1992).

[6]Article 1 of the CISG states in relevant part:

> (1) This Convention applies to contracts of sale of goods between parties whose places of business are in different States:
>
> (a) When the States are Contracting States. . . .

CISG, art. 1.

[7]Article 8 provides:

> (1) For the purposes of this Convention statements made by and other conduct of a party are to be interpreted according to his intent where the other party knew or could not have been unaware what that intent was.
>
> (2) If the preceding paragraph is not applicable, statements made by and conduct of a party are to be interpreted according to the understanding a reasonable person of the same kind as the other party would have had in the same circumstances.
>
> (3) In determining the intent of a party or the understanding a reasonable person would have had, due consideration is to be given to all relevant circumstances of the case including the negotiations, any practices which the parties have established between themselves, usages and any subsequent conduct of the parties.

CISG, art. 8.

I. Subjective Intent Under the CISG

Contrary to what is familiar practice in United States courts, the CISG appears to permit a substantial inquiry into the parties' subjective intent, even if the parties did not engage in any objectively ascertainable means of registering this intent.[8] Article 8(1) of the CISG instructs courts to interpret the "statements . . . and other conduct of a party . . . according to his intent" as long as the other party "knew or could not have been unaware" of that intent. The plain language of the Convention, therefore, requires an inquiry into a party's subjective intent as long as the other party to the contract was aware of that intent.

In this case, MCC has submitted three affidavits that discuss the purported subjective intent of the parties to the initial agreement concluded between MCC and D'Agostino in October 1990. All three affidavits discuss the preliminary negotiations and report that the parties arrived at an oral agreement for D'Agostino to supply quantities of a specific grade of ceramic tile to MCC at an agreed upon price. The affidavits state that the "oral agreement established the essential terms of quality, quantity, description of goods, delivery, price and payment." * * * The affidavits also note that the parties memorialized the terms of their oral agreement on a standard D'Agostino order form, but all three affiants contend that the parties subjectively intended not to be bound by the terms on the reverse of that form despite a provision directly below the signature line that expressly and specifically incorporated those terms.[9]

---

[8]In the United States, the legislatures, courts, and the legal academy have voiced a preference for relying on objective manifestations of the parties' intentions. For example, Article Two of the Uniform Commercial Code, which most states have enacted in some form or another to govern contracts for the sale of goods, is replete with references to standards of commercial reasonableness. *See e.g.*, U.C.C. § 2-206 (referring to reasonable means of accepting an offer); *see also Lucy v. Zehmer*, 196 Va. 493, 503, 84 S.E.2d 516, 522 (1954) ("Whether the writing signed . . . was the result of a serious offer . . . and a serious acceptance . . . , or was a serious offer . . . and an acceptance in secret jest . . . , in either event it constituted a binding contract of sale between the parties."). Justice Holmes expressed the philosophy behind this focus on the objective in forceful terms: "The law has nothing to do with the actual state of the parties' minds. In contract, as elsewhere, it must go by externals, and judge parties by their conduct." Oliver W. Holmes, *The Common Law* 242 (Howe ed. 1963) quoted in JOHN O. HONNOLD, UNIFORM LAW FOR INTERNATIONAL SALES UNDER THE 1980 UNITED NATIONS CONVENTION § 107 at 164 (2nd ed. 1991) (hereinafter Honnold, Uniform Law).

[9]MCC makes much of the fact that the written order form is entirely in Italian and that Monzon, who signed the contract on MCC's behalf directly below this provision incorporating the terms on the reverse of the form, neither spoke nor read Italian. This fact is of no assis-

The terms on the reverse of the contract give D'Agostino the right to suspend or cancel all contracts in the event of a buyer's non-payment and require a buyer to make a written report of all defects within ten days. As the magistrate judge's report and recommendation makes clear, if these terms applied to the agreements between MCC and D'Agostino, summary judgment would be appropriate because MCC failed to make any written complaints about the quality of tile it received and D'Agostino has established MCC's non-payment of a number of invoices amounting to $108,389.40 and 102,053,846.00 Italian lira.

Article 8(1) of the CISG requires a court to consider this evidence of the parties' subjective intent. Contrary to the magistrate judge's report, which the district court endorsed and adopted, article 8(1) does not focus on interpreting the parties' statements alone. Although we agree with the magistrate judge's conclusion that no "interpretation" of the contract's terms could support MCC's position, article 8(1) also requires a court to consider subjective intent while interpreting the conduct of the parties. The CISG's language, therefore, requires courts to consider evidence of a party's subjective intent when signing a contract if the other party to the contract was aware of that intent at the time. This is precisely the type of evidence that MCC has provided through the Silingardi, Copelli, and Monzon affidavits, which discuss not only Monzon's intent as MCC's representative but also discuss the intent of D'Agostino's representatives and their knowledge that Monzon did not intend to agree to the terms on the reverse of the form contract. This acknowledgment that D'Agostino's representatives were aware of Monzon's subjective intent puts this case squarely within article 8(1) of the CISG, and therefore requires the court to consider MCC's evidence as it interprets the parties' conduct.

---

tance to MCC's position. We find it nothing short of astounding that an individual, purportedly experienced in commercial matters, would sign a contract in a foreign language and expect not to be bound simply because he could not comprehend its terms. We find nothing in the CISG that might counsel this type of reckless behavior and nothing that signals any retreat from the proposition that parties who sign contracts will be bound by them regardless of whether they have read them or understood them. *See e.g., Samson Plastic Conduit and Pipe Corp. v. Battenfeld Extrusionstechnik GMBH*, 718 F. Supp. 886, 890 (M.D. Ala.1989) ("A good and recurring illustration of the problem . . . involves a person who is ... unfamiliar with the language in which a contract is written and who has signed a document which was not read to him. There is all but unanimous agreement that he is bound. . . .")

II. Parol Evidence and the CISG

Given our determination that the magistrate judge and the district court should have considered MCC's affidavits regarding the parties' subjective intentions, we must address a question of first impression in this circuit: whether the parol evidence rule, which bars evidence of an earlier oral contract that contradicts or varies the terms of a subsequent or contemporaneous written contract, plays any role in cases involving the CISG. We begin by observing that the parol evidence rule, contrary to its title, is a substantive rule of law, not a rule of evidence. See II E. Allen Farnsworth, Farnsworth on Contracts, § 7.2 at 194 (1990). The rule does not purport to exclude a particular type of evidence as an "untrustworthy or undesirable" way of proving a fact, but prevents a litigant from attempting to show "the fact itself—he fact that the terms of the agreement are other than those in the writing." Id. As such, a federal district court cannot simply apply the parol evidence rule as a procedural matter—as it might if excluding a particular type of evidence under the Federal Rules of Evidence, which apply in federal court regardless of the source of the substantive rule of decision. *Cf. id.* § 7.2 at 196.[13]

The CISG itself contains no express statement on the role of parol evidence. See Honnold, Uniform Law § 110 at 170. It is clear, however, that the drafters of the CISG were comfortable with the concept of permitting parties to rely on oral contracts because they eschewed any statutes of fraud provision and expressly provided for the enforcement of oral contracts. Compare CISG, art. 11 (a contract of sale need not be concluded or evidenced in writing) with U.C.C. § 2-201 (precluding the enforcement of oral contracts for the sale of goods involving more than $500). Moreover, article 8(3) of the CISG expressly directs courts to give "due consideration . . . to all relevant circumstances of the case including the negotiations . . ." to determine the intent of the parties. Given article 8(1)'s directive to use the intent of the parties to interpret their statements and conduct, article 8(3) is

---

[13]An example demonstrates this point. The CISG provides that a contract for the sale of goods need not be in writing and that the parties may prove the contract "by any means, including witnesses." CISG, art. 11. Nevertheless, a party seeking to prove a contract in such a manner in federal court could not do so in a way that violated in the rule against hearsay. See Fed.R.Evid. 802 (barring hearsay evidence). A federal district court applies the Federal Rules of Evidence because these rules are considered procedural, regardless of the source of the law that governs the substantive decision. Cf. Farnsworth on Contracts § 7.2 at 196 & n. 16 (citing cases).

a clear instruction to admit and consider parol evidence regarding the negotiations to the extent they reveal the parties' subjective intent.

* * *

Our reading of article 8(3) as a rejection of the parol evidence rule, however, is in accordance with the great weight of academic commentary on the issue. As one scholar has explained:

> [T]he language of Article 8(3) that "due consideration is to be given to all relevant circumstances of the case" seems adequate to override any domestic rule that would bar a tribunal from considering the relevance of other agreements . . . . Article 8(3) relieves tribunals from domestic rules that might bar them from "considering" any evidence between the parties that is relevant. This added flexibility for interpretation is consistent with a growing body of opinion that the "parol evidence rule" has been an embarrassment for the administration of modern transactions.

Honnold, Uniform Law § 110 at 170–71.[17] * * * One of the primary factors motivating the negotiation and adoption of the CISG was to provide parties to international contracts for the sale of goods with some degree of certainty as to the principles of law that would govern potential disputes and remove the previous doubt regarding which party's legal system might otherwise apply. See Letter of Transmittal from Ronald Reagan, President of the United States, to the United States Senate, reprinted at 15 U.S.C. app. 70, 71 (1997). Courts applying the CISG cannot, therefore, upset the parties'

---

[17]*See also* LOUIS F. DEL DUCA, ET AL., SALES UNDER THE UNIFORM COMMERCIAL CODE AND THE CONVENTION ON INTERNATIONAL SALE OF GOODS, 173–74 (1993); Henry D. Gabriel, *A Primer on the United Nations Convention on the International Sale of Goods: From the Perspective of the Uniform Commercial Code*, 7 Ind. Int'l & Comp. L.Rev. 279, 281 (1997) ("Subjective intent is given primary consideration. . . . [Article 8] allows open-ended reliance on parol evidence...."); HERBERT BERSTEIN & JOSEPH LOOKOFSKY, UNDERSTANDING THE CISG IN EUROPE 29 (1997) ("[T]he CISG has dispensed with the parol evidence rule which might otherwise operate to exclude extrinsic evidence under the law of certain Common Law countries."); Harry M. Fletchner, *Recent Developments: CISG*, 14 J.L. & Com. 153, 157 (1995) (criticizing the Beijing Metals opinion and noting that "[c]ommentators generally agree that article 8(3) rejects the approach to the parol evidence questions taken by U.S. domestic law.") (collecting authority); John E. Murray, Jr., *An Essay on the Formation of Contracts and Related Matters Under the United Nations Convention on Contracts for the International Sale of Goods*, 8 J.L. & Com. 11, 12 (1988) ("We are struck by a new world where there is ... no parol evidence rule, among other differences."); Peter Winship, *Domesticating International Commercial Law: Revising U.C.C. Article 2 in Light of the United Nations Sales Convention*, 37 Loy L.Rev. 43, 57 (1991).

reliance on the Convention by substituting familiar principles of domestic law when the Convention requires a different result. We may only achieve the directives of good faith and uniformity in contracts under the CISG by interpreting and applying the plain language of article 8(3) as written and obeying its directive to consider this type of parol evidence.

This is not to say that parties to an international contract for the sale of goods cannot depend on written contracts or that parol evidence regarding subjective contractual intent need always prevent a party relying on a written agreement from securing summary judgment. To the contrary, most cases will not present a situation (as exists in this case) in which both parties to the contract acknowledge a subjective intent not to be bound by the terms of a pre-printed writing. In most cases, therefore, article 8(2) of the CISG will apply, and objective evidence will provide the basis for the court's decision. See Honnold, Uniform Law § 107 at 164–65. Consequently, a party to a contract governed by the CISG will not be able to avoid the terms of a contract and force a jury trial simply by submitting an affidavit which states that he or she did not have the subjective intent to be bound by the contract's terms. * * * Moreover, to the extent parties wish to avoid parol evidence problems they can do so by including a merger clause in their agreement that extinguishes any and all prior agreements and understandings not expressed in the writing.[19]

Considering MCC's affidavits in this case, however, we conclude that the magistrate judge and the district court improperly granted summary judgment in favor of D'Agostino. Although the affidavits are, as D'Agostino observes, relatively conclusory and unsupported by facts that would objectively establish MCC's intent not to be bound by the conditions on the reverse of the form, article 8(1) requires a court to consider evidence of a party's subjective intent when the other party was aware of it, and the Silingardi and Copelli affidavits provide that evidence. This is not to say that the affidavits are conclusive proof of what the parties intended. A reasonable finder of fact, for example, could disregard testimony that purportedly sophisticated international merchants signed a contract without intending to

---

[19]*See* Ronald A. Brand & Harry M. Fletchner, *Arbitration and Contract Formation in International Trade: First Interpretations of the U.N. Sales Convention*, 12 J.L. & Com. 239, 252 (1993) (arguing that article 8(3) of the CISG will not permit the consideration of parol evidence when the parties have expressly excluded oral modifications of the contract pursuant to article 29); *see also* I ALBERT KRITZER, GUIDE TO PRACTICAL APPLICATIONS OF THE UNITED NATIONS CONVENTION ON CONTRACTS FOR THE INTERNATIONAL SALE OF GOODS 125 (1989) (counseling the use of a merger clause to compensate for the absence of a parol evidence rule in the CISG).

be bound as simply too incredible to believe and hold MCC to the conditions printed on the reverse of the contract. Nevertheless, the affidavits raise an issue of material fact regarding the parties' intent to incorporate the provisions on the reverse of the form contract. If the finder of fact determines that the parties did not intend to rely on those provisions, then the more general provisions of the CISG will govern the outcome of the dispute.

MCC's affidavits, however, do not discuss all of the transactions and orders that MCC placed with D'Agostino. Each of the affidavits discusses the parties' subjective intent surrounding the initial order MCC placed with D'Agostino in October 1990. The Copelli affidavit also discusses a February 1991 requirements contract between the parties and reports that the parties subjectively did not intend the terms on the reverse of the D'Agostino order form to apply to that contract either. * * * D'Agostino, however, submitted the affidavit of its chairman, Vincenzo Maselli, which describes at least three other orders from MCC on form contracts dated January 15, 1991, April 27, 1991, and May 4, 1991, in addition to the October 1990 contract. * * *. MCC's affidavits do not discuss the subjective intent of the parties to be bound by language in those contracts, and D'Agostino, therefore, argues that we should affirm summary judgment to the extent damages can be traced to those order forms. It is unclear from the record, however, whether all of these contracts contained the terms that appeared in the October 1990 contract. Moreover, because article 8 requires a court to consider any "practices which the parties have established between themselves, usages and any subsequent conduct of the parties" in interpreting contracts, CISG, art. 8(3), whether the parties intended to adhere to the ten day limit for complaints, as stated on the reverse of the initial contract, will have an impact on whether MCC was bound to adhere to the limit on subsequent deliveries. Since material issues of fact remain regarding the interpretation of the remaining contracts between MCC and D'Agostino, we cannot affirm any portion of the district court's summary judgment in D'Agostino's favor.

CONCLUSION

MCC asks us to reverse the district court's grant of summary judgment in favor of D'Agostino. The district court's decision rests on pre-printed contractual terms and conditions incorporated on the reverse of a standard order form that MCC's president signed on the company's behalf. Nevertheless, we conclude that the CISG, which governs international contracts for the sale of goods, precludes summary judgment in this case because MCC has raised an issue of material fact concerning the parties' subjective intent to be bound by the terms on the reverse of the pre-printed contract. The CISG also precludes the application of the parol evidence rule, which would otherwise bar the consideration of evidence concerning a prior or contemporaneously negotiated oral agreement. Accordingly, we REVERSE the district court's grant of summary judgment and REMAND this case for further proceedings consistent with this opinion.

QUESTIONS

1. Questions about the facts of this case

   1.1. Let's get this straight. Monzon goes to Italy speaking no Italian, attends an Italian trade show, signs a document completely in Italian and then gets to say he really didn't mean to be bound by the acknowledged terms of that agreement? If that is the case, why didn't the court just say that he was not bound by the terms because he couldn't read them (see note 9 to the court's opinion)?

   1.2. If D'Agostino had insisted on a merger clause, would the result have been different? Would it have mattered if D'Agostino wrote the merger clause in English on the front of the order form?

2. Questions about the law

   2.1. As the Court indicates, the *CISG* is yet another source of law that must be consulted in this era of increasing globalization. Lazy lawyers, however, are assisted by Article 6 of the Convention, which states:

   The parties may exclude the application of this Convention or, subject to Article 12 [related to writing requirements], derogate from or vary the effect of any of its provisions.

   If Monzon had gone to Italy with a stamp (provided by his lawyers) that said (in English): "The provisions of the *Convention on the International Sales of Goods* do not apply to this contract," and had stamped it on D'Agostino's form, would the result have changed? What more would you need to know to answer this question?

How about if the stamp had said: "This contract is to be governed by the Uniform Commercial Code as in force in Florida, USA, on the date of this contract"?

2.2. It is clear that the *CISG* adopts a different view than Chief Judge Popham in the *Countess of Rutland* case, quoted above at 509. Does this mean that international transactions will be more litigation-prone in the future?

SECTION 3: AMBIGUOUS EXPRESS TERMS: USING PAROL EVIDENCE AND OTHER EXTRINSIC EVIDENCE TO DISCOVER THE MEANING OF THE TERMS USED

Another exception to the parol evidence rule is that extrinsic evidence may be admitted to interpret the agreement to establish "the meaning of the writing, whether or not it is integrated." *Restatement (Second) of Contracts* § 214(c).

If unchecked, this could be the loophole that swallows the parol evidence rule. As Oliver Wendell Holmes stated:

> [Y]ou cannot prove a mere private convention between the two parties to give language a different meaning from its common one. It would open too great risks if evidence were admissible to show that when they said five hundred feet they agreed it should mean one hundred inches, or that Bunker Hill Monument should signify the Old South Church.

Goode v. Riley, 153 Mass. 585, 586, 28 N.E. 228 (1891).

Just how courts approach the meaning of the words and language used by contracting parties is a diverse subject. This section tries to approach the study of this phenomena by looking at the types of extrinsic evidence parties try to use to convince courts that their "meaning" is the one that should control.

The next case, a classic, shows the tangles that can come from failing to appreciate that a word as common as "chicken" might cause disagreement.

Frigaliment Importing Co., Ltd., v. B.N.S. International Sales Corp.
U.S. District Court, Southern District of New York
190 F. Supp. 116 (1960)

FRIENDLY, J.:

OPINION:

The issue is, what is chicken? Plaintiff says 'chicken' means a young chicken, suitable for broiling and frying. Defendant says 'chicken' means any bird of that genus that meets contract specifications on weight and quality, including what it calls 'stewing chicken' and plaintiff pejoratively terms 'fowl'. Dictionaries give both meanings, as well as some others not relevant here. To support its [sic. The word "meaning" should probably be inserted here. Eds.], plaintiff sends a number of volleys over the net; defendant essays to return them and adds a few serves of its own. Assuming that both parties were acting in good faith, the case nicely illustrates Holmes' remark 'that the making of a contract depends not on the agreement of two minds in one intention, but on the agreement of two sets of external signs—not on the parties' having meant the same thing but on their having said the same thing.' The Path of the Law, in Collected Legal Papers, p. 178. I have concluded that plaintiff has not sustained its burden of persuasion that the contract used 'chicken' in the narrower sense.

The action is for breach of the warranty that goods sold shall correspond to the description, New York Personal Property Law, McKinney's Consol. Laws, c. 41, § 95. Two contracts are in suit. In the first, dated May 2, 1957, defendant, a New York sales corporation, confirmed the sale to plaintiff, a Swiss corporation, of

> 'US Fresh Frozen Chicken, Grade A, Government Inspected, Eviscerated 2 ½–3 lbs. and 1 ½–2 lbs. each all chicken individually wrapped in cryovac, packed in secured fiber cartons or wooden boxes, suitable for export
>
> 75,000 lbs. 2 ½–3 lbs....@ $ 33.00
>
> 25,000 lbs. 1 ½–2 lbs....@ $ 36.50
>
> per 100 lbs. FAS New York
>
> scheduled May 10, 1957 pursuant to instructions from Penson & Co., New York.'

The second contract, also dated May 2, 1957, was identical save that only 50,000 lbs. of the heavier 'chicken' were called for, the price of the smaller birds was $ 37 per 100 lbs., and shipment was scheduled for May 30. The initial shipment under the first contract was short but the balance was shipped on May 17. When the initial shipment arrived in Switzerland, plaintiff found, on May 28, that the 2 ½–3 lbs. birds were not young chicken suitable for broiling and frying but stewing chicken or 'fowl'; indeed, many of the cartons and bags plainly so indicated. Protests ensued. Nevertheless, shipment under the second contract was made on May 29, the 2 ½–3 lbs. birds again being stewing chicken. Defendant stopped the transportation of these at Rotterdam.

This action followed. Plaintiff says that, notwithstanding that its acceptance was in Switzerland, New York law controls under the principle of Rubin v. Irving Trust Co., 1953, 305 N.Y. 288, 305, 113 N.E.2d 424, 431; defendant does not dispute this, and relies on New York decisions. I shall follow the apparent agreement of the parties as to the applicable law.

Since the word 'chicken' standing alone is ambiguous, I turn first to see whether the contract itself offers any aid to its interpretation. Plaintiff says the 1 ½–2 lbs. birds necessarily had to be young chicken since the older birds do not come in that size, hence the 2 ½–3 lbs. birds must likewise be young. This is unpersuasive—a contract for 'apples' of two different sizes could be filled with different kinds of apples even though only one species came in both sizes. Defendant notes that the contract called not simply for chicken but for 'US Fresh Frozen Chicken, Grade A, Government Inspected.' It says the contract thereby incorporated by reference the Department of Agriculture's regulations, which favor its interpretation; I shall return to this after reviewing plaintiff's other contentions.

The first hinges on an exchange of cablegrams which preceded execution of the formal contracts. The negotiations leading up to the contracts were conducted in New York between defendant's secretary, Ernest R. Bauer, and a Mr. Stovicek, who was in New York for the Czechoslovak government at the World Trade Fair. A few days after meeting Bauer at the fair, Stovicek telephoned and inquired whether defendant would be interested in exporting poultry to Switzerland. Bauer then met with Stovicek, who showed him a cable from plaintiff dated April 26, 1957, announcing that they 'are buyer' of 25,000 lbs. of chicken 2 ½–3 lbs. weight, Cryovac packed, grade A Government inspected, at a price up to 33 cents per pound, for shipment on May 10, to be confirmed by the following morning, and were interested in further offerings. After testing the market for price,

Bauer accepted, and Stovicek sent a confirmation that evening. Plaintiff stresses that, although these and subsequent cables between plaintiff and defendant, which laid the basis for the additional quantities under the first and for all of the second contract, were predominantly in German, they used the English word 'chicken'; it claims this was done because it understood 'chicken' meant young chicken whereas the German word, 'Huhn,' included both 'Brathuhn' (broilers) and 'Suppenhuhn' (stewing chicken), and that defendant, whose officers were thoroughly conversant with German, should have realized this. Whatever force this argument might otherwise have is largely drained away by Bauer's testimony that he asked Stovicek what kind of chickens were wanted, received the answer 'any kind of chickens,' and then, in German, asked whether the cable meant 'Huhn' and received an affirmative response. Plaintiff attacks this as contrary to what Bauer testified on his deposition in March, 1959, and also on the ground that Stovicek had no authority to interpret the meaning of the cable. The first contention would be persuasive if sustained by the record, since Bauer was free at the trial from the threat of contradiction by Stovicek as he was not at the time of the deposition; however, review of the deposition does not convince me of the claimed inconsistency. As to the second contention, it may well be that Stovicek lacked authority to commit plaintiff for prices or delivery dates other than those specified in the cable; but plaintiff cannot at the same time rely on its cable to Stovicek as its dictionary to the meaning of the contract and repudiate the interpretation given the dictionary by the man in whose hands it was put. * * * Plaintiff's reliance on the fact that the contract forms contain the words 'through the intermediary of: __________', with the blank not filled, as negating agency, is wholly unpersuasive; the purpose of this clause was to permit filling in the name of an intermediary to whom a commission would be payable, not to blot out what had been the fact.

Plaintiff's next contention is that there was a definite trade usage that 'chicken' meant 'young chicken.' Defendant showed that it was only beginning in the poultry trade in 1957, thereby bringing itself within the principle that 'when one of the parties is not a member of the trade or other circle, his acceptance of the standard must be made to appear' by proving either that he had actual knowledge of the usage or that the usage is 'so generally known in the community that his actual individual knowledge of it may be inferred.' * * *. Here there was no proof of actual knowledge of the alleged usage; indeed, it is quite plain that defendant's belief was to the contrary. In order to meet the alternative requirement, the law of New York demands a showing that 'the usage is of so long continuance, so well established, so notorious, so universal and so reasonable in itself, as that the presumption is violent that the parties contracted with reference to it, and made it a part of their agreement.' * * *

Plaintiff endeavored to establish such a usage by the testimony of three witnesses and certain other evidence. Strasser, resident buyer in New York for a large chain of Swiss cooperatives, testified that 'on chicken I would definitely understand a broiler.' However, the force of this testimony was considerably weakened by the fact that in his own transactions the witness, a careful businessman, protected himself by using 'broiler' when that was what he wanted and 'fowl' when he wished older birds. Indeed, there are some indications, dating back to a remark of Lord Mansfield, Edie v. East India Co., 2 Burr. 1216, 1222 (1761), that no credit should be given 'witnesses to usage, who could not adduce instances in verification.' * * * While Wigmore thinks this goes too far, a witness' consistent failure to rely on the alleged usage deprives his opinion testimony of much of its effect. Niesielowski, an officer of one of the companies that had furnished the stewing chicken to defendant, testified that 'chicken' meant 'the male species of the poultry industry. That could be a broiler, a fryer or a roaster', but not a stewing chicken; however, he also testified that upon receiving defendant's inquiry for 'chickens', he asked whether the desire was for 'fowl or frying chickens' and, in fact, supplied fowl, although taking the precaution of asking defendant, a day or two after plaintiff's acceptance of the contracts in suit, to change its confirmation of its order from 'chickens,' as defendant had originally prepared it, to 'stewing chickens.' Dates, an employee of Urner-Barry Company, which publishes a daily market report on the poultry trade, gave it as his view that the trade meaning of 'chicken' was 'broilers and fryers.' In addition to this opinion testimony, plaintiff relied on the fact that the Urner-Barry service, the Journal of Commerce, and Weinberg Bros. & Co. of Chicago, a large supplier of poultry, published quotations in a manner which, in one way or another, distinguish between 'chicken,' comprising broilers, fryers and certain other categories, and 'fowl,' which, Bauer acknowledged, included stewing chickens. This material would be impressive if there were nothing to the contrary. However, there was, as will now be seen.

Defendant's witness Weininger, who operates a chicken eviscerating plant in New Jersey, testified 'Chicken is everything except a goose, a duck, and a turkey. Everything is a chicken, but then you have to say, you have to specify which category you want or that you are talking about.' Its witness Fox said that in the trade 'chicken' would encompass all the various classifications. Sadina, who conducts a food inspection service, testified that he would consider any bird coming within the classes of 'chicken' in the Department of Agriculture's regulations to be a chicken. The specifications approved by the General Services Administration include fowl as well as broilers and fryers under the classification 'chickens.' Statistics of the Institute of American Poultry Industries use the phrases 'Young chickens' and 'Mature chickens,' under the general heading 'Total chickens' and the Department of Agriculture's daily and weekly price reports avoid use of the word 'chicken' without specification.

Defendant advances several other points which it claims affirmatively support its construction. Primary among these is the regulation of the Department of Agriculture, 7 C.F.R. § 70.300–70.370, entitled, 'Grading and Inspection of Poultry and Edible Products Thereof.' and in particular 70.301 which recited:

> *Chickens.* The following are the various classes of chickens:
>
> (a) Broiler or fryer . . .
>
> (b) Roaster . . .
>
> (c) Capon . . .
>
> (d) Stag . . .
>
> (e) Hen or stewing chicken or fowl . . .
>
> (f) Cock or old rooster . . .

Defendant argues, as previously noted, that the contract incorporated these regulations by reference. Plaintiff answers that the contract provision related simply to grade and Government inspection and did not incorporate the Government definition of 'chicken,' and also that the definition in the Regulations is ignored in the trade. However, the latter contention was contradicted by Weininger and Sadina; and there is force in defendant's argument that the contract made the regulations a dictionary, particularly since the reference to Government grading was already in plaintiff's initial cable to Stovicek.

Defendant makes a further argument based on the impossibility of its obtaining broilers and fryers at the 33 cents price offered by plaintiff for the 2 ½–3 lbs. birds. There is no substantial dispute that, in late April, 1957, the price for 2 ½–3 lbs. broilers was between 35 and 37 cents per pound, and that when defendant entered into the contracts, it was well aware of this and intended to fill them by supplying fowl in these weights. It claims that plaintiff must likewise have known the market since plaintiff had reserved shipping space on April 23, three days before plaintiff's cable to Stovicek, or, at least, that Stovicek was chargeable with such knowledge. It is scarcely an answer to say, as plaintiff does in its brief, that the 33 cents price offered by the 2 ½–3 lbs. 'chickens' was closer to the prevailing 35 cents price for broilers than to the 30 cents at which defendant procured fowl. Plaintiff must have expected defendant to make some profit—certainly it could not have expected defendant deliberately to incur a loss.

Finally, defendant relies on conduct by the plaintiff after the first shipment had been received. On May 28 plaintiff sent two cables complaining that the larger birds in the first shipment constituted 'fowl.' Defendant answered with a cable refusing to recognize plaintiff's objection and announcing 'We have today ready for shipment 50,000 lbs. chicken 2 ½–3 lbs. 25,000 lbs. broilers 1 ½–2 lbs.,' these being the goods procured for shipment under the second contract, and asked immediate answer 'whether we are to ship this merchandise to you and whether you will accept the merchandise.' After several other cable exchanges, plaintiff replied on May 29 'Confirm again that merchandise is to be shipped since resold by us if not enough pursuant to contract chickens are shipped the missing quantity is to be shipped within ten days stop we resold to our customers pursuant to your contract chickens grade A you have to deliver us said merchandise we again state that we shall make you fully responsible for all resulting costs.'[2] Defendant argues that if plaintiff was sincere in thinking it was entitled to young chickens, plaintiff would not have allowed the shipment under the second contract to go forward, since the distinction between broilers and chickens drawn in defendant's cablegram must have made it clear that the larger birds would not be broilers. However, plaintiff answers that the cables show plaintiff was insisting on delivery of young chickens and that defendant shipped old ones at its peril. Defendant's point would be highly relevant on another disputed issue—whether if liability were established, the measure of damages should be the difference in market value of broilers and stewing chicken in New York or the larger difference in Europe, but I cannot give it weight on the issue of interpretation. Defendant points out also that plaintiff proceeded to deliver some of the larger birds in Europe, describing them as 'poulets'; defendant argues that it was only when plaintiff's customers complained about this that plaintiff developed the idea that 'chicken' meant

[2]These cables were in German; 'chicken', 'broilers' and, on some occasions, 'fowl,' were in English.

'young chicken.' There is little force in this in view of plaintiff's immediate and consistent protests.

When all the evidence is reviewed, it is clear that defendant believed it could comply with the contracts by delivering stewing chicken in the 2 ½–3 lbs. size. Defendant's subjective intent would not be significant if this did not coincide with an objective meaning of 'chicken.' Here it did coincide with one of the dictionary meanings, with the definition in the Department of Agriculture Regulations to which the contract made at least oblique reference, with at least some usage in the trade, with the realities of the market, and with what plaintiff's spokesman had said. Plaintiff asserts it to be equally plain that plaintiff's own subjective intent was to obtain broilers and fryers; the only evidence against this is the material as to market prices and this may not have been sufficiently brought home. In any event it is unnecessary to determine that issue. For plaintiff has the burden of showing that 'chicken' was used in the narrower rather than in the broader sense, and this it has not sustained.

This opinion constitutes the Court's findings of fact and conclusions of law. Judgment shall be entered dismissing the complaint with costs.

QUESTIONS AND NOTE

1. Questions about the facts of this case

   1.1. What was Frigaliment suing for? Put another way, why does Frigaliment think that BNS breached the contract?

   1.2. This is a trick question: Does the court hold that BNS did not breach the contract?

   1.3. Given the result and the Court's reason for its ruling, and the likely cost of procuring all the various experts and testimony about the meaning of chicken, what more could Frigaliment's lawyers done to persuade the Court that its definition of chicken was the intended one?

2. Questions about the law

   2.1. Did Judge Friendly consider parol evidence in interpreting the word "chicken"? Did Judge Friendly even consider the parol evidence rule?

2.2. According to this case, is the word "chicken" *always* ambiguous? Why or why not?

2.3. Change the facts somewhat. Instead of stopping the shipment at Rotterdam, and suing BNS for breach, assume that Frigaliment had accepted the second shipment of chickens, but paid BNS an amount equal to the contract price less its damages. If BNS was thereby forced to sue Frigaliment for the difference, does BNS win on the facts as alleged and proved at trial?

2.4. Think back to *Raffles v. Wichelhaus* and the cases regarding mistake in formation. Why doesn't the court rule that since neither party had the same conception of chicken, then no contract was formed? *See Restatement (Second) of Contracts* § 20.

3. Note

Judge Henry Friendly was one of the best federal judges in our nation's history. He not only wrote well-crafted opinions, but also contributed to the legal literature with numerous law review articles on many subjects. As noted by Judge Richard Posner:

> He was the greatest federal appellate judge of his time—in analytic power, memory, and application perhaps of any time. His opinions have exhibited greater staying power than that of any of his contemporaries on the federal courts of appeals. In addition, his extrajudicial scholarship has been extraordinarily influential, more so, perhaps, than any judge's since Cardozo.

Richard Posner, *In Memoriam: Henry J. Friendly*, 99 HARV. L. REV. 1724, 1724 (1986).

Before appointment to the federal Second Circuit Court of Appeals, Judge Friendly had been a successful business practitioner in New York City. As recalled by one of the attorneys involved in *Frigaliment*, "Judge Friendly [who had been appointed from practice directly to the Second Circuit without any trial experience] felt that he needed trial court experience in order to be able to perform his function as a appellate court judge and requested a case to be assigned to him as a trial judge. The *Frigaliment* case was assigned." One wonders if the parties knew then what lay in store for the reported opinion, which is a staple in all major contracts casebooks.

A. Course of Performance, Course of Dealing and Trade Usage (Again)

Frigaliment was decided before the Uniform Commercial Code, or the *Convention on the International Sale of Goods*, was in effect. The types of evidence adduced in *Frigaliment* would today come under the heading of trade usage—background assumptions regarding what the parties knew, or ought to have known, when contracting. As shown in *Threadgill* above, such concepts continue as part of the common law when the U.C.C. or the *CISG* do not apply, but when these codes apply, there are ready definitions of these practices.

In particular, the U.C.C. had codified these terms in Sections 1-205 (trade usage and course of dealing), and in 2-208 (on course of performance). They are set forth below.

§ 1-205. Course of Dealing and Usage of Trade.

(1) A course of dealing is a sequence of previous conduct between the parties to a particular transaction which is fairly to be regarded as establishing a common basis of understanding for interpreting their expressions and other conduct.

(2) A usage of trade is any practice or method of dealing having such regularity of observance in a place, vocation or trade as to justify an expectation that it will be observed with respect to the transaction in question. The existence and scope of such a usage are to be proved as facts. If it is established that such a usage is embodied in a written trade code or similar writing the interpretation of the writing is for the court.

(3) A course of dealing between parties and any usage of trade in the vocation or trade in which they are engaged or of which they are or should be aware give particular meaning to and supplement or qualify terms of an agreement.

(4) The express terms of an agreement and an applicable course of dealing or usage of trade shall be construed wherever reasonable as

consistent with each other; but when such construction is unreasonable express terms control both course of dealing and usage of trade and course of dealing controls usage of trade.

(5) An applicable usage of trade in the place where any part of performance is to occur shall be used in interpreting the agreement as to that part of the performance.

(6) Evidence of a relevant usage of trade offered by one party is not admissible unless and until he has given the other party such notice as the court finds sufficient to prevent unfair surprise to the latter.

§ 2-208. Course of Performance or Practical Construction.

(1) Where the contract for sale involves repeated occasions for performance by either party with knowledge of the nature of the performance and opportunity for objection to it by the other, any course of performance accepted or acquiesced in without objection shall be relevant to determine the meaning of the agreement.

(2) The express terms of the agreement and any such course of performance, as well as any course of dealing and usage of trade, shall be construed whenever reasonable as consistent with each other; but when such construction is unreasonable, express terms shall control course of performance and course of performance shall control both course of dealing and usage of trade (Section 1-205).

(3) Subject to the provisions of the next section on modification and waiver, such course of performance shall be relevant to show a waiver or modification of any term inconsistent with such course of performance.

The *CISG* also makes references to such practices, as shown below:

Article 9, *Convention on the International Sale of Goods*

(1) The parties are bound by any usages to which they have agreed and by any practices which they have established between themselves.

(2) The parties are considered, unless otherwise agreed, to have impliedly made applicable to their contract or its formation a usage of which the parties knew or ought to have known and which in international trade is widely known to, and regularly observed by, parties to contracts of the type involved in the particular trade concerned

Problems on Trade Usage and Course of Dealing

1. Under the U.C.C., what is the difference between a course of dealing and a course of performance? Can you ever have a course of performance in a contract to sell just one item (such as a car)?
2. Under either the U.C.C. or the *CISG*,* do you have to be a merchant to be bound by a usage of trade? If not, how do you protect yourself as a novice when buying something for which there is a recognized market and recognized practices of trade?
3. Note that under the U.C.C., a usage of trade may arise with respect to a "place, vocation or trade." What is the difference among these three items? Does the *CISG* have a similar broad application?

Note that Section 1-205(4) of the U.C.C. tries to prioritize conflicting claims to legitimacy between course of performance, course of dealing, trade usage and express terms. Is this a satisfactory ordering?

B. Ambiguity in Contract Terms—When Does It Exist, and How Do Courts Clarify the Deal?

Ambiguity seems ever present. It is difficult to pin down in writing exactly what is required or requested, especially if that writing is going to be read by someone not present at the negotiations, and probably isn't even very savvy regarding the subject matter of the contract.

But words are the stock in trade of the lawyer. She has to make them work for the client. Often, lack of clarity is not important; the parties do what each thought they should do without reference to any writing memorializing the terms.

Sometimes, however, words betray. When time comes for performance, the dispute isn't over what words are to be used (the province of the parol evidence rule), but over what the words that both sides agree are part of the contract mean. The particularly phrasing, for example, could be vague or ambiguous.

---

*The *CISG* does not apply to sales of goods bought for personal, family or household use, Article 2(a), but the U.C.C. does not have a similar limitation. So for this problem, assume that you are a entrepreneur seeking to buy goods for your business.

Of course, courts do not take claims of ambiguity at face value. A very difficult decision must be made as to when a party is to be allowed to pursue a claim of ambiguity; after all, both sides have already had an opportunity to clarify any ambiguities in the formation stage of the contract. In this quest for certainty, courts have developed rules or maxims of construction which aid the courts in reaching their decisions.

In the next case, the question involves whether words used at one time can encompass actions or developments that occur later on. Is such a situation one in which ambiguity is created?

Random House, Inc. v. Rosetta Books LLC
U.S. District Court, Southern District of New York
150 F. Supp. 2d 613 (2001)

Sidney H. Stein, U.S. District Judge.

In this copyright infringement action, Random House, Inc. seeks to enjoin Rosetta Books LLC and its Chief Executive Officer from selling in digital format eight specific works on the grounds that the authors of the works had previously granted Random House—not Rosetta Books—the right to "print, publish and sell the work[s] in book form." Rosetta Books, on the other hand, claims it is not infringing upon the rights those authors gave Random House because the licensing agreements between the publisher and the author do not include a grant of digital or electronic rights. Relying on the language of the contracts and basic principles of contract interpretation, this Court finds that the right to "print, publish and sell the work[s] in book form" in the contracts at issue does not include the right to publish the works in the format that has come to be known as the "ebook." Accordingly, Random House's motion for a preliminary injunction is denied.

BACKGROUND

In the year 2000 and the beginning of 2001, Rosetta Books contracted with several authors to publish certain of their works—including The Confessions of Nat Turner and Sophie's Choice by William Styron; Slaughterhouse-Five, Breakfast of Champions, The Sirens of Titan, Cat's Cradle, and Player Piano by Kurt Vonnegut; and Promised Land by Robert B. Parker—in digital format over the Internet. * * * On February 26, 2001 Rosetta Books launched its ebook business, offering those titles and others for sale in digital format. * * * The next day, Random House filed this complaint accusing Rosetta Books of committing copyright infringement and tortiously interfering with the contracts Random House had with Messrs. Parker, Styron and Vonnegut by selling its ebooks. It simultaneously moved for a preliminary injunction prohibiting Rosetta from infringing plaintiff's copyrights.

A. Ebooks

Ebooks are "digital book[s] that you can read on a computer screen or an electronic device." (Hrg. at 13; http://www.rosettabooks.com/pages/about_ebooks.html) Ebooks are created by converting digitized text into a format readable by computer software. The text can be viewed on a desktop or laptop computer, personal digital assistant or handheld dedicated ebook reading device. * * * Rosetta's ebooks can only be read after they are downloaded into a computer that contains either Microsoft Reader, Adobe Acrobat Reader, or Adobe Acrobat eBook Reader software.

Included in a Rosetta ebook is a book cover, title page, copyright page and "eforward" all created by Rosetta Books. Although the text of the ebook is exactly the same as the text of the original work, the ebook contains various features that take advantage of its digital format. For example, ebook users can search the work electronically to find specific words and phrases. They can electronically "highlight" and "bookmark" certain text, which can then be automatically indexed and accessed through hyperlinks. They can use hyperlinks in the table of contents to jump to specific chapters.

Users can also type electronic notes which are stored with the related text. These notes can be automatically indexed, sorted and filed. Users can also change the font size and style of the text to accommodate personal preferences; thus, an electronic screen of text may contain more words, fewer words, or the same number of words as a page of the original published book. In addition, users can have displayed the definition of any word in the text. * * * In one version of the software, the word can also be pronounced aloud.

Rosetta's ebooks contain certain security features to prevent users from printing, emailing or otherwise distributing the text. Although it is technologically possible to foil these security features, anyone who does so would be violating the licensing agreement accompanying the software. * * *

B. Random House's licensing agreements

While each agreement between the author and Random House differs in some respects, each uses the phrase "print, publish and sell the work in book form" to convey rights from the author to the publisher. * * *

1. Styron Agreements

Forty years ago, in 1961, William Styron granted Random House the right to publish The Confessions of Nat Turner. Besides granting Random House an exclusive license to "print, publish and sell the work in book form," Styron also gave it the right to "license publication of the work by book clubs," "license publication of a reprint edition," "license after book publication the publication of the work, in whole or in part, in anthologies, school books," and other shortened forms, "license without charge publication of the work in Braille, or photographing, recording, and microfilming the work for the physically handicapped," and "publish or permit others to publish or broadcast by radio or television . . . selections from the work, for publicity purposes. . . ." * * * Styron demonstrated that he was not granting Random House the rights to license publication in the British Commonwealth or in foreign languages by crossing out these clauses on the form contract supplied by Random House. * * *

The publisher agreed in the contract to "publish the work at its own expense and in such style and manner and at such a price as it deems suitable." * * * The contract also contains a non-compete clause that provides, in relevant part, that "the Author agrees that during the term of this agreement he will not, without the written permission of the Publisher, publish or permit to be published any material in book or pamphlet form, based on the material in the work, or which is reasonably likely to injure its sale." * * * Styron's contract with Random House for the right to publish Sophie's Choice, executed in 1977, is virtually identical to his 1961 contract to publish The Confessions of Nat Turner. * * *

2. Vonnegut Agreements

Kurt Vonnegut's 1967 contract granting Random House's predecessor-in-interest Dell Publishing Co., Inc. the license to publish Slaughterhouse-Five and Breakfast of Champions follows a similar structure to the Styron agreements. Paragraph # 1 is captioned "grant of rights" and contains those rights the author is granting to the book publisher. Certain rights on the publisher's form contract are crossed out, indicating that the author reserved them for himself. * * *One of the rights granted by the author includes the "exclusive right to publish and to license the Work for publication, after book publication . . . in anthologies, selections, digests, abridgements, magazine condensations, serialization, newspaper syndication, picture book versions, microfilming, Xerox and other forms of copying, either now in use or hereafter developed." * * *

Vonnegut specifically reserved for himself the "dramatic ... motion picture (silent and sound) . . . radio broadcasting (including mechanical renditions and /or recordings of the text) . . . [and] television" rights. * * * Unlike the Styron agreements, this contract does not contain a non-compete clause.

Vonnegut's 1970 contract granting Dell the license to publish The Sirens of Titan, Cat's Cradle, and Player Piano contains virtually identical grants and reservations of rights as his 1967 contract. However, it does contain a non-compete clause, which provides that "the Author . . . will not publish or permit to be published any edition, adaptation or abridgment of the Work by any party other than Dell without Dell's prior written consent." * * *

3. Parker Agreement

Robert B. Parker's 1982 contract granting Dell the license to publish Promised Land is similar to the 1970 Vonnegut contract. * * * Paragraph # 1 contains the "grant of rights," certain of which have been crossed out by the author. The contract does grant Random House the right to "Xerox and other forms of copying of the printed page, either now in use or hereafter developed." * * * Parker also reserved the rights to the "dramatic ... motion picture (silent and sound) . . . radio broadcasting . . . television . . . mechanical or electronic recordings of the text ...." * * * There is also a non-compete clause that provides, in relevant part, that "the Author . . . will not, without the written permission of Dell, publish or permit to be published any material based on the material in the Work, or which is reasonably likely to injure its sale." * * *

DISCUSSION

* * *

B. Ownership of a Valid Copyright

* * * It is well settled that although the authors own the copyrights to their works, "the legal or beneficial owner of an exclusive right under a copyright is entitled ... to institute an action for any infringement of that particular right committed while he or she is the owner of it." * * *The question for resolution, therefore, is whether Random House is the beneficial owner of the right to publish these works as ebooks.

1. Contract Interpretation of Licensing Agreements—Legal Standards

Random House claims to own the rights in question through its licensing agreements with the authors. Interpretation of an agreement purporting to grant a copyright license is a matter of state contract law. * * *

In New York, a written contract is to be interpreted so as to give effect to the intention of the parties as expressed in the contract's language. * * * The court must consider the entire contract and reconcile all parts, if possible, to avoid an inconsistency. * * *

Determining whether a contract provision is ambiguous is a question of law to be decided by the court. * * * Pursuant to New York law, "contract language is ambiguous if it is capable of more than one meaning when viewed objectively by a reasonably intelligent person who has examined the context of the entire integrated agreement and who is cognizant of the customs, practices, usages and terminology as generally understood in the particular trade or business." * * * "No ambiguity exists when contract language has a 'definite and precise meaning, unattended by danger of misconception in the purport of the [contract] itself, and concerning which there is no reasonable basis for a difference of opinion.'"

If the language of a contract is ambiguous, interpretation of the contract becomes a question of fact for the finder of fact and extrinsic evidence is admissible. * * *

These principles are in accord with the approach the U.S. Court of Appeals for the Second Circuit uses in analyzing contractual language in disputes, such as this one, "about whether licensees may exploit licensed works through new marketing channels made possible by technologies developed after the licensing contract—often called 'new use' problems." * * * The two leading cases in this Circuit on how to determine whether "new uses" come within prior grants of rights are Boosey [& Hawkes Music Publishers, Ltd v. Walt Disney Co., 145 F.3d 481 (2d Cir. 1998)] and Bartsch v. Metro-Goldwyn-Mayer, Inc., 391 F.2d 150 (2d Cir. 1968), decided three decades apart.

In *Bartsch*, the author of the play "Maytime" granted Harry Bartsch in 1930 "the motion picture rights [to 'Maytime'] throughout the world," including the right to "copyright, vend, license and exhibit such motion picture photoplays throughout the world; together with the further sole and exclusive rights by mechanical and/or electrical means to record, reproduce and transmit sound, including spoken words. . . ." 391 F.2d at 150. He in turn assigned those rights to Warner Bros. Pictures, which transferred them to MGM. In 1958 MGM licensed its motion picture "Maytime" for viewing on television. Bartsch sued, claiming the right to transmit the play over television had not been given to MGM.

Judge Henry Friendly, for the Second Circuit, wrote in 1968 that "any effort to reconstruct what the parties actually intended nearly forty years ago is doomed to failure."* * * He added that the words of the grant by Bartsch "were well designed to give the assignee [*i.e.*, MGM] the broadest rights with respect to its copyrighted property." * * * The words of the grant were broad enough to cover the new use—i.e. viewing on television—and Judge Friendly interpreted them to do so. This interpretation, he wrote, permitted the licensee to "properly pursue any uses which may reasonably be said to fall within the medium as described in the license." * * * That interpretation also avoided the risk "that a deadlock between the grantor and the grantee might prevent the work's being shown over the new medium at all." * * *

In *Boosey*, the plaintiff was the assignee of Igor Stravinsky's copyrights in the musical composition, "The Rite of Spring." In 1939, Stravinsky had licensed Disney's use of "The Rite of Spring" in the motion picture "Fantasia." Fifty-two years later, in 1991, Disney released "Fantasia" in video format and Boosey brought an action seeking, among other relief, a declaration that the grant of rights did not include the right to use the Stravinsky work in video format. In *Boosey*, just as in *Bartsch*, the language of the grant was broad, enabling the licensee "to record in any manner, medium or form, and to license the performance of, the musical composition [for use] in a motion picture." * * *.

At the Second Circuit, a unanimous panel focused on "neutral principles of contract interpretation rather than solicitude for either party." * * * "What governs," Judge Pierre Leval wrote, "is the language of the contract. If the contract is more reasonably read to convey one meaning, the party benefitted by that reading should be able to rely on it; the party seeking exception or deviation from the meaning reasonably conveyed by the words of the contract should bear the burden of negotiating for language that would express the limitation or deviation. This principle favors neither licensors nor licensees. It follows simply from the words of the contract." * * *

The Second Circuit's neutral approach was specifically influenced by policy considerations on both sides. On the one hand, the approach seeks to encourage licensees—here, the publishers—to develop new technologies that will enable all to enjoy the creative work in a new way. On the other hand, it seeks to fulfill the purpose underlying federal copyright law—to encourage authors to create literary works. * * *

2. Application of Legal Standards

Relying on "the language of the license contract and basic principles of interpretation," * * * as instructed to do so by *Boosey* and *Bartsch*, this Court finds that the most reasonable interpretation of the grant in the contracts at issue to "print, publish and sell the work in book form" does not include the right to publish the work as an ebook. At the outset, the phrase itself distinguishes between the pure content—i.e. "the work"—and the format of display—"in book form." The Random House Webster's Unabridged Dictionary defines a "book" as "a written or printed work of fiction or nonfiction, usually on sheets of paper fastened or bound together within covers" and defines "form" as "external appearance of a clearly defined area, as distinguished from color or material; the shape of a thing or person." Random House Webster's Unabridged Dictionary (2001), available in searchable form at http://www.allwords.com.

Manifestly, paragraph # 1 of each contract—entitled either "grant of rights" or "exclusive publication right"—conveys certain rights from the author to the publisher. * * * In that paragraph, separate grant language is used to convey the rights to publish book club editions, reprint editions, abridged forms, and editions in Braille. This language would not be necessary if the phrase "in book form" encompassed all types of books. That paragraph specifies exactly which rights were being granted by the author to the publisher. Indeed, many of the rights set forth in the publisher's form contracts were in fact not granted to the publisher, but rather were reserved by the authors to themselves. For example, each of the authors specifically reserved certain rights for themselves by striking out phrases, sentences, and paragraphs of the publisher's form contract. This evidences an intent by these authors not to grant the publisher the broadest rights in their works.

Random House contends that the phrase "in book form" means to faithfully reproduce the author's text in its complete form as a reading experience and that, since ebooks concededly contain the complete text of the work, Rosetta cannot also possess those rights. * * * While Random House's definition distinguishes "book form" from other formats that require separate contractual language—such as audio books and serialization rights—it does not distinguish other formats specifically mentioned in paragraph # 1 of the contracts, such as book club editions and reprint editions. Because the Court must, if possible, give effect to all contractual language in order to "safeguard against adopting an interpretation that would render any individual provision superfluous," * * * Random House's definition cannot be adopted.

Random House points specifically to the clause requiring it to "publish the work at its own expense and in such a style and manner and at such a price as [Random House] deems suitable" as support for its position. * * * However, plaintiff takes this clause out of context. It appears in paragraph # 2, captioned "Style, Price and Date of Publication," not paragraph # 1, which includes all the grants of rights. In context, the phrase simply means that Random House has control over the appearance of the formats granted to Random House in the first paragraph; i.e., control over the style of the book.

Random House also cites the non-compete clauses as evidence that the authors granted it broad, exclusive rights in their work. Random House reasons that because the authors could not permit any material that would injure the sale of the work to be published without Random House's consent, the authors must have granted the right to publish ebooks to Random House. This reasoning turns the analysis on its head. First, the grant of rights follows from the grant language alone. * * * Second, non-compete clauses must be limited in scope in order to be enforceable in New York. * * * Third, even if the authors did violate this provision of their Random House agreements by contracting with Rosetta Books—a point on which this Court does not opine—the remedy is a breach of contract action against the authors, not a copyright infringement action against Rosetta Books.* * *

The photocopy clause—giving Random House the right to "Xerox and other forms of copying, either now in use or hereafter developed"—similarly does not bolster Random House's position. Although the clause does appear in the grant language paragraph, taken in context, it clearly refers only to new developments in xerography and other forms of photocopying. Stretching it to include new forms of publishing, such as ebooks, would make the rest of the contract superfluous because there would be no reason for authors to reserve rights to forms of publishing "now in use." This interpretation also comports with the publishing industry's trade usage of the phrase. * * *

Not only does the language of the contract itself lead almost ineluctably to the conclusion that Random House does not own the right to publish the works as ebooks, but also a reasonable person "cognizant of the customs, practices, usages and terminology as generally understood in the particular trade or business," * * *, would conclude that the grant language does not include ebooks.[7] "To print, publish and sell the work in book form" is understood in the publishing industry to be a "limited" grant. * * *

In *Field v. True Comics*, the court held that "the sole and exclusive right to publish, print and market in book form"—especially when the author had specifically reserved rights for himself—was "much more limited" than "the sole and exclusive right to publish, print and market the book." * * * In fact, the publishing industry generally interprets the phrase "in book form" as granting the publisher "the exclusive right to publish a hardcover trade book in English for distribution in North America." * * *

III. CONCLUSION

Employing the most important tool in the armamentarium of contract interpretation—the language of the contract itself—this Court has concluded that Random House is not the beneficial owner of the right to publish the eight works at issue as ebooks. This is neither a victory for technophiles nor a defeat for Luddites. It is merely a determination, relying on neutral princi-

[7]Although *Boosey* recognizes that extrinsic evidence of industry custom is not likely to be helpful in analyzing the intent of the parties, it does not prohibit considering trade usage in understanding specific terms of the contract. * * *

Even were this Court to find the contracts ambiguous, thus allowing consideration of extrinsic evidence other than trade usage to determine whether Random House has a likelihood of success on the merits, a review of that evidence leads to the conclusion that it is unhelpful to either party.

ples of contract interpretation, that because Random House is not likely to succeed on the merits of its copyright infringement claim and cannot demonstrate irreparable harm, its motion for a preliminary injunction should be denied.

QUESTIONS AND NOTES

1. Questions about the facts of this case

   1.1. In the first paragraph of the opinion, Judge Stein states that his holding is based on "the language of the contracts and basic principles of contract interpretation." What contract language does he focus on? Who are the parties to the contracts? Do they include Rosetta Books, the defendant in the lawsuit? Why not?

   1.2. Why does Judge Stein treat all five contracts the same? Do any of the contracts contain language that would have warranted different treatment?

   1.3. Did the authors breach their contracts with Random House?

2. Questions about the law

   2.1. What's a preliminary injunction? What does it have to do with contract law?

   2.2. Were any of the contracts ambiguous? Did the court think so? Does it matter?

   2.3. What if Random House had released the authors' works in ebook format and the authors sued, claiming that Random House did not have the right to release their books in ebook format? Would the court have interpreted the contracts the same way?

   2.4. Is there any way Random House's attorneys could have drafted the contracts differently to avoid this problem?

3. Notes

   3.1. Strangely enough, in the brief of one of the parties that appeared as *amicus curiae* (a so-called "friend of the court") it was stated that two of Rosetta Books' exclusive distributors, Microsoft and Adobe, market the ebook format as being nearly identical to a hardcover book. *See* Brief of Amici Curiae Penguin Putnam, Inc., et al. at 8.

3.2. Still confused over the difference between a book and an ebook? You are not alone. The following is an excerpt from the deposition of Rosetta Books' CEO and co-founder, Arthur Klebanoff:

Q: Is an electronic book a book?

A: Is an electronic book a book. I guess—if I—my answer, to me, that would be I don't know.

Q: You never thought about that?

A: Well, in—an electronic book is not a book in the sense in which a physical book is a book.

Q: I think you testified to that earlier. My question was meant to be slightly broader . . . is the conception of a book broad enough in your estimation to include for the purpose of books other than physical books?

A: Electronic book incorporates the contents—can incorporate the contents of a physical book.

Q: But you're unprepared sitting here to state, in your view, that an e-book or . . . electronic book is a book.

A: Well, I would answer it this way. They call, it an ebook because it's an e-book.

Q: Who is they?

A: I mean people. The name e-book has come about I mean I would argue because it is actually a different form of a book.

Q: In what sense is it a different form of a book?

A: In the sense that it moves in a digital environment, that it's received in a digital environment, that it's read on a screen, that it's not on paper.

Klebanoff Dep. at 9, lines 4–25, to 10, lines 2–17. Note: we omitted the numerous objections of Mr. Klebanoff's attorney. He was not too happy with this line of questioning.

3.3. Two of the three co-founders of Rosetta Books, including Mr. Klebanoff, received law degrees from Harvard Law School and were editors of the Harvard Law Review. Do you think they knew what they were getting into when they founded Rosetta Books? Should Harvard be looking for a new Contracts Professor?

Rosetta Books takes a sensible—but expansive—view of what courts will consider when construing what a contract requires the parties to do. Maybe that's appropriate given its factual setting. When all is said and done, however, certainty of obligation and reduction of litigation may not be served by such an expansive rule.

In the next case, a federal judge applies similar state law, but in a widely different factual setting. The judge, Alex Kozinski of the Ninth Circuit Court of Appeals, is applying California law. And he doesn't like it.* When reading this opinion, keep in mind that Judge Kozinski and Judge Ideman (the trial court judge) both had the same texts relating to California law at their disposal, but came to diametrically opposite views. Has Judge Kozinski overplayed his hand? Or was Judge Ideman just trying to clear his docket?

Trident Center v. Connecticut General Life Ins. Co.

U.S. Court of Appeals, Ninth Circuit
847 F.2d 564 (1988)

Kozinski, Circuit Judge:

The parties to this transaction are, by any standard, highly sophisticated business people: Plaintiff is a partnership consisting of an insurance company and two of Los Angeles' largest and most prestigious law firms; defendant is another insurance company. Dealing at arm's length and from positions of roughly equal bargaining strength, they negotiated a commercial loan amounting to more than $ 56 million. The contract documents are lengthy and detailed; they squarely address the precise issue that is the

*He may not like it, but he has to apply California law. Federal law requires application of state law when the parties have invoked the federal court's diversity jurisdiction; that is, when both parties are citizens of different states. Thus, federal judges, who have no ability to extend or limit California law, must determine it and apply it (or some estimate of what it is in case of a lacuna) as it stands.

subject of this dispute; to all who read English, they appear to resolve the issue fully and conclusively.

Plaintiff nevertheless argues here, as it did below, that it is entitled to introduce extrinsic evidence that the contract means something other than what it says. This case therefore presents the question whether parties in California can ever draft a contract that is proof to parol evidence. Somewhat surprisingly, the answer is no.

Facts

The facts are rather simple. Sometime in 1983 Security First Life Insurance Company and the law firms of Mitchell, Silberberg & Knupp and Manatt, Phelps, Rothenberg & Tunney formed a limited partnership for the purpose of constructing an office building complex on Olympic Boulevard in West Los Angeles. The partnership, Trident Center, the plaintiff herein, sought and obtained financing for the project from defendant, Connecticut General Life Insurance Company. The loan documents provide for a loan of $ 56,500,000 at 12 1/4 percent interest for a term of 15 years, secured by a deed of trust on the project. The promissory note provides that "maker shall not have the right to prepay the principal amount hereof in whole or in part" for the first 12 years. Note at 6. In years 13–15, the loan may be prepaid, subject to a sliding prepayment fee. The note also provides that in case of a default during years 1–12, Connecticut General has the option of accelerating the note and adding a 10 percent prepayment fee.

Everything was copacetic for a few years until interest rates began to drop. The 12 1/4 percent rate that had seemed reasonable in 1983 compared unfavorably with 1987 market rates and Trident started looking for ways of refinancing the loan to take advantage of the lower rates. Connecticut General was unwilling to oblige, insisting that the loan could not be prepaid for the first 12 years of its life, that is, until January 1996.

Trident then brought suit in state court seeking a declaration that it was entitled to prepay the loan now, subject only to a 10 percent prepayment fee. Connecticut General promptly removed to federal court and brought a motion to dismiss, claiming that the loan documents clearly and unambiguously precluded prepayment during the first 12 years. The district court agreed and dismissed Trident's complaint. The court also "*sua sponte*, sanction[ed] the plaintiff for the filing of a frivolous lawsuit." * * *. Trident appeals both aspects of the district court's ruling.

Discussion

I

Trident makes two arguments as to why the district court's ruling is wrong. First, it contends that the language of the contract is ambiguous and proffers a construction that it believes supports its position. Second, Trident argues that, under California law, even seemingly unambiguous contracts are subject to modification by parol or extrinsic evidence. Trident faults the district court for denying it the opportunity to present evidence that the contract language did not accurately reflect the parties' intentions.

A. The Contract

As noted earlier, the promissory note provides that Trident "shall not have the right to prepay the principal amount hereof in whole or in part before January 1996." Note at 6. It is difficult to imagine language that more clearly or unambiguously expresses the idea that Trident may not unilaterally prepay the loan during its first 12 years. Trident, however, argues that there is an ambiguity because another clause of the note provides that "in the event of a prepayment resulting from a default hereunder or the Deed of Trust prior to January 10, 1996 the prepayment fee will be ten percent (10%)." Note at 6–7. Trident interprets this clause as giving it the option of prepaying the loan if only it is willing to incur the prepayment fee.

We reject Trident's argument out of hand. In the first place, its proffered interpretation would result in a contradiction between two clauses of the contract; the default clause would swallow up the clause prohibiting Trident from prepaying during the first 12 years of the contract. The normal rule of construction, of course, is that courts must interpret contracts, if possible, so as to avoid internal conflict. * * *

In any event, the clause on which Trident relies is not on its face reasonably susceptible to Trident's proffered interpretation. Whether to accelerate repayment of the loan in the event of default is entirely Connecticut General's decision. The contract makes this clear at several points. *See* Note at 4 ("in each such event [of default], the entire principal indebtedness, or so much thereof as may remain unpaid at the time, shall, *at the option of Holder*, become due and payable immediately" (emphasis added)); *id.* at 7 ("in the event Holder exercises its *option to accelerate* the maturity hereof . . ." (emphasis added)); Deed of Trust para. 2.01, at 25 ("in each such event [of default], Beneficiary *may* declare all sums secured hereby immediately due and payable . . ." (emphasis added)). Even if Connecticut General decides to declare a default and accelerate, it "may rescind any notice of breach or default." *Id.* para. 2.02, at 26. Finally, Connecticut General has the option of doing nothing at all: "Beneficiary reserves the right at its sole option to waive noncompliance by Trustor with any of the conditions or covenants to be performed by Trustor hereunder." *Id.* para. 3.02, at 29.

Once again, it is difficult to imagine language that could more clearly assign to Connecticut General the exclusive right to decide whether to declare a default, whether and when to accelerate, and whether, having chosen to take advantage of any of its remedies, to rescind the process before its completion.

Trident nevertheless argues that it is entitled to precipitate a default and insist on acceleration by tendering the balance due on the note plus the 10 percent prepayment fee.[1] The contract language, cited above, leaves no room for this construction. It is true, of course, that Trident is free to stop making payments, which may then cause Connecticut General to declare a default and accelerate. But that is not to say that Connecticut General would be required to so respond. The contract quite clearly gives Connecticut General other options: It may choose to waive the default, or to take advantage of some other remedy such as the right to collect "all the income, rents, royalties, revenue, issues, profits, and proceeds of the Property." Deed of Trust para. 1.18, at 22. By interpreting the contract as Trident suggests, we would ignore those provisions giving Connecticut General, not

[1]Trident's position is that the prepayment fee must either be a fee imposed as part of an "alternative method of performance" or "a liquidated damages provision specifying the amount of damages payable by Trident in the event that it defaults by prepaying the . . . loan." Appellant's Reply Brief at 12–13. Trident contends that if the prepayment fee is instead read as a provision for liquidated damages triggered by any default whatsoever, it would be invalid as a penalty because it would not be a reasonable estimate of the likely injury to Connecticut General resulting from most types of default: "If, for example, Trident were to default on the payment of a single installment, a fee of 10% of the outstanding balance of the loan would not qualify as a valid liquidated damages payment." *Id.* at 8.

California law is unsettled on this point and it may be that Connecticut General could not enforce the 10 percent fee in the event of certain defaults by Trident. *See generally* 1 H. Miller & M. Starr, *Current Law of California Real Estate* § 3:71 n.12 (Supp. 1987). But the contract assigns to Connecticut General alone the right to decide whether and under what circumstances to seek the prepayment fee. Connecticut General may well attempt to enforce the fee only in circumstances where it is valid. What the contract clearly does not provide is what Trident suggests. If the parties had wanted to give Trident the option of prepaying with a 10 percent fee, they certainly could have done so expressly.

Trident, the exclusive right to decide how, when and whether the contract will be terminated upon default during the first 12 years.

In effect, Trident is attempting to obtain judicial sterilization of its intended default. But defaults are messy things; they are supposed to be. Once the maker of a note secured by a deed of trust defaults, its credit rating may deteriorate; attempts at favorable refinancing may be thwarted by the need to meet the trustee's sale schedule; its cash flow may be impaired if the beneficiary takes advantage of the assignment of rents remedy; default provisions in its loan agreements with other lenders may be triggered. Fear of these repercussions is strong medicine that keeps debtors from shirking their obligations when interest rates go down and they become disenchanted with their loans.[4] That Trident is willing to suffer the cost and delay of a lawsuit, rather than simply defaulting, shows far better than anything we might say that these provisions are having their intended effect. We decline Trident's invitation to truncate the lender's remedies and deprive Connecticut General of its bargained-for protection.

B. Extrinsic Evidence

Trident argues in the alternative that, even if the language of the contract appears to be unambiguous, the deal the parties actually struck is in fact quite different. It wishes to offer extrinsic evidence that the parties had agreed Trident could prepay at any time within the first 12 years by tendering the full amount plus a 10 percent prepayment fee. As discussed above, this is an interpretation to which the contract, as written, is not reasonably susceptible. Under traditional contract principles, extrinsic evidence is inadmissible to interpret, vary or add to the terms of an unambiguous integrated written instrument. * * *

Trident points out, however, that California does not follow the traditional rule. Two decades ago the California Supreme Court in *Pacific Gas & Electric Co. v. G. W. Thomas Drayage & Rigging Co.*, 69 Cal. 2d 33, 442 P.2d 641, 69 Cal. Rptr. 561 (1968), turned its back on the notion that a contract can ever have a plain meaning discernible by a court without resort to extrinsic evidence. The court reasoned that contractual obligations flow not

[4]This provides a symmetry with the situation where interest rates go up and it is the lender who is stuck with a loan it would prefer to turn over at market rates. In an economy where interest rates fluctuate, it is all but certain that one side or the other will be dissatisfied with a long-term loan at some time. Mutuality calls for enforcing the contract as written no matter whose ox is being gored.

from the words of the contract, but from the intention of the parties. "Accordingly," the court stated, "the exclusion of relevant, extrinsic, evidence to explain the meaning of a written instrument could be justified only if it were feasible to determine the meaning the parties gave to the words from the instrument alone." 69 Cal. 2d at 38, 442 P.2d 641. This, the California Supreme Court concluded, is impossible: "If words had absolute and constant referents, it might be possible to discover contractual intention in the words themselves and in the manner in which they were arranged. Words, however, do not have absolute and constant referents." *Id.* In the same vein, the court noted that "the exclusion of testimony that might contradict the linguistic background of the judge reflects a judicial belief in the possibility of perfect verbal expression. This belief is a remnant of a primitive faith in the inherent potency and inherent meaning of words." *Id.* at 37 (citation and footnotes omitted).[5]

Under *Pacific Gas*, it matters not how clearly a contract is written, nor how completely it is integrated, nor how carefully it is negotiated, nor how squarely it addresses the issue before the court: the contract cannot be rendered impervious to attack by parol evidence. If one side is willing to claim that the parties intended one thing but the agreement provides for another, the court must consider extrinsic evidence of possible ambiguity. If that evidence raises the specter of ambiguity where there was none before, the contract language is displaced and the intention of the parties must be divined from self-serving testimony offered by partisan witnesses whose recollection is hazy from passage of time and colored by their conflicting interests. * * * We question whether this approach is more likely to divulge the original intention of the parties than reliance on the seemingly clear words they agreed upon at the time. * * *

Pacific Gas casts a long shadow of uncertainty over all transactions negotiated and executed under the law of California. As this case illustrates, even when the transaction is very sizeable, even if it involves only sophisticated parties, even if it was negotiated with the aid of counsel, even if it results in contract language that is devoid of ambiguity, costly and protracted litigation cannot be avoided if one party has a strong enough motive for

---

[5]In an unusual footnote, the court compared the belief in the immutable meaning of words with " 'the elaborate system of taboo and verbal prohibitions in primitive groups . . . [such as] the Swedish peasant custom of curing sick cattle smitten by witchcraft, by making them swallow a page torn out of the psalter and put in dough. . . .' " *Id.* n.2 (quoting Ullman, *The Principles of Semantics* 43 (1963)).

challenging the contract. While this rule creates much business for lawyers and an occasional windfall to some clients, it leads only to frustration and delay for most litigants and clogs already overburdened courts.

It also chips away at the foundation of our legal system. By giving credence to the idea that words are inadequate to express concepts, *Pacific Gas* undermines the basic principle that language provides a meaningful constraint on public and private conduct. If we are unwilling to say that parties, dealing face to face, can come up with language that binds them, how can we send anyone to jail for violating statutes consisting of mere words lacking "absolute and constant referents"? How can courts ever enforce decrees, not written in language understandable to all, but encoded in a dialect reflecting only the "linguistic background of the judge"? Can lower courts ever be faulted for failing to carry out the mandate of higher courts when "perfect verbal expression" is impossible? Are all attempts to develop the law in a reasoned and principled fashion doomed to failure as "remnant[s] of a primitive faith in the inherent potency and inherent meaning of words"?

Be that as it may. While we have our doubts about the wisdom of *Pacific Gas*, we have no difficulty understanding its meaning, even without extrinsic evidence to guide us. As we read the rule in California, we must reverse and remand to the district court in order to give plaintiff an opportunity to present extrinsic evidence as to the intention of the parties in drafting the contract.[6] It may not be a wise rule we are applying, but it is a rule that binds us. *Erie R.R. Co. v. Tompkins*, 304 U.S. 64, 78, 82 L. Ed. 1188, 58 S. Ct. 817 (1938).

II

In imposing sanctions on plaintiff, the district court stated:

> Pursuant to Fed. R. Civ. P. 11, the Court, *sua sponte*, sanctions the plaintiff for the filing of a frivolous lawsuit. The Court concludes that the language in the note and deed of trust is plain and clear. No reasonable person, much less firms of able attorneys, could possibly misunderstand

[6]Nothing we say should be construed as foreclosing Connecticut General from moving for summary judgment after completion of discovery; given the unambiguous language of the contract itself, such a motion would succeed unless Trident were to come forward with extrinsic evidence sufficient to render the contract reasonably susceptible to Trident's alternate interpretation, thereby creating a genuine issue of fact resolvable only at trial.

> this crystal-clear language. Therefore, this action was brought in bad faith.

Order of Dismissal at 3. Having reversed the district court on its substantive ruling, we must, of course, also reverse it as to the award of sanctions. While we share the district judge's impatience with this litigation, we would suggest that his irritation may have been misdirected. It is difficult to blame plaintiff and its lawyers for bringing this lawsuit. With this much money at stake, they would have been foolish not to pursue all remedies available to them under the applicable law. At fault, it seems to us, are not the parties and their lawyers but the legal system that encourages this kind of lawsuit. By holding that language has no objective meaning, and that contracts mean only what courts ultimately say they do, *Pacific Gas* invites precisely this type of lawsuit.[9] With the benefit of 20 years of hindsight, the California Supreme Court may wish to revisit the issue. If it does so, we commend to it the facts of this case as a paradigmatic example of why the traditional rule, based on centuries of experience, reflects the far wiser approach.

Conclusion

The judgment of the district court is REVERSED. The case is REMANDED for reinstatement of the complaint and further proceedings in accordance with this opinion. The parties shall bear their own costs on appeal.

QUESTIONS AND NOTE

1. Questions about the facts of this case

    1.1. Why do the law firms wish to prepay the loan? Where are they likely to get the money to make the payment?

    1.2. How do the law firms interpret the provisions regarding the inability to prepay the loan for the first twelve years of the loan?

    1.3. What possible extrinsic evidence could the law firms offer to support their position? And if the evidence does what the law firms want—

[9]This is not to say, of course, that all lawsuits seeking to challenge the interpretation of facially unambiguous contracts are necessarily immune from imposition of sanctions. Even under *Pacific Gas*, a party urging an interpretation lacking any objectively reasonable basis in fact might well be subject to sanctions for bringing a frivolous lawsuit.

establish a unilateral prepayment right—what answer do the law firms have as to why that wasn't spelled out more clearly in the contract?

2. Questions about the law

2.1. Do you agree with the following statement by Judge Kozinski? Why or why not?

> Under *Pacific Gas*, it matters not how clearly a contract is written, nor how completely it is integrated, nor how carefully it is negotiated, nor how squarely it addresses the issue before the court: the contract cannot be rendered impervious to attack by parol evidence.

2.2. Trident's second argument was that "under California law, even seemingly unambiguous contracts are subject to modification by parol or extrinsic evidence." Does either this case (or what you can discern from this case) or *Pacific Gas* so hold?

2.2. Is California law consistent with the statement of New York law set forth in *Rosetta Books*? How would Judge Kozinski, if freed from the restraining influence of state law, decide *Rosetta Books*?

3. Note

Judge Alex Kozinski is a judge on the federal Ninth Circuit Court of Appeals. Widely considered to be bright, engaging and conservative (or libertarian, depending on how the label is defined), he is a Romanian emigre, who arrived in this country at the age of twelve barely able to speak English. His moving account of his journey to the west can be read at *Freedom's Scents: A Romanian Remembers*, WALL ST. J., Nov. 28, 1989.

He learned quickly, however, and ultimately graduated first in his class at UCLA. He was one of the first clerks to Justice Anthony Kennedy (when the Justice sat on the Ninth Circuit), and then went on to clerk for Chief Justice Warren Burger. Appointed to the Ninth Circuit at the young age of 35 (after serving as Chief Judge for the Court of Claims), he is the author of many solid appellate opinions and a frequent speaker at Federalist Society events.

He also has an adventurous side. You can see him trying to bungee jump at http://juripole.u-nancy.fr/Magistrature/Laliberte/kozinskijump.avi. He also has written reviews of Nintendo Games. *See Guide to Nintendo Shopping*, WALL ST. J., Jan. 31, 1990, at A16. He was on the television show, *The Dating Game*—twice.

He also tweaks casebook authors from time to time. He recently said:

> How important do I think casebooks are? So important that, once in a while, I write an opinion precisely for the purpose of getting into one. Mind you, it doesn't change the outcome of the case, but it does change the way I write the opinion. The classic example happened about ten years ago. I had grown tired of law clerks who thought California Chief Justice Traynor was the cat's pajamas because he didn't believe that any contract could be interpreted without the use of extrinsic evidence. Whenever I would get a case where I thought the contract language was clear, they would quote me back some idiot line from Traynor about how this merely reflected the effete linguistic prejudices of judges. t turns out this came from Traynor's opinion in *Pacific Gas and Electric Co. v. G.W. Thomas Drayage & Rigging Co.*, which had found its way into every contracts casebook in the country. What the casebooks seemed to lack were cases responding to Traynor's argument.
>
> So I decided to write one. The case [was] Trident Center v. Connecticut General Life Insurance . . . .

Alex Kozinski, *Who Gives a Hoot About Legal Scholarship*, 37 HOUSTON L. REV. 295, 298–99 (2000).

C. The Use of Rules, Maxims and Extrinsic Evidence to Construe Contract Language

Once ambiguity exists, counsel for the parties can introduce extrinsic evidence to show what the parties meant by the words they used. Sometimes, as in the cases above, the extrinsic evidence can take the form of testimony of the parties who negotiated the contract.

Other times, however, the extrinsic evidence may be guides or manuals on style, or guides prepared by experts. In *In re Envirodyne Industries, Inc.*, 29

F.3d 301 (7th Cir. 1994), Chief Judge Posner had this to say about such extrinsic aids to interpretation:

> If the written contract is clear without extrinsic evidence, then such evidence could have no office other than to contradict the writing, and is therefore excluded. The object in excluding such evidence is to prevent parties from trying to slip out of their clearly stated, explicitly assumed contractual obligations through self-serving testimony or documents—which, though self-serving, might impress a jury— purporting to show that the parties didn't mean what they said in the written contract. Contractual obligations would be too uncertain if such evidence were allowed. But dictionaries, treatises, articles, and other published materials created by strangers to the dispute, like evidence of trade usage, which is also admissible because it is also evidence created by strangers rather than by a party trying to slip out of a contractual bind, do not present a similar danger of manufactured doubts and are therefore entirely appropriate for use in contract cases as interpretive aids. Appropriate, and sometimes indispensable. It would be passing odd to forbid people to look up words in dictionaries, or to consult explanatory commentaries that, like trade usage, are in the nature of specialized dictionaries.

Contract law has also developed common law rules for interpretation in doubtful cases. The *Restatement (Second) of Contracts* lists the following:

> *§ 203 Standards of Preference in Interpretation*
>
> *In the interpretation of a promise or agreement or a term thereof, the following standards of preference are generally applicable:*
>
> (a) *an interpretation which gives a reasonable, lawful, and effective meaning to all the terms is preferred to an interpretation which leaves a part unreasonable, unlawful, or of no effect;*
> (b) *express terms are given greater weight than course of performance, course of dealing, and usage of trade, course of performance is given greater weight than course of dealing or usage of trade, and course of dealing is given greater weight than usage of trade;*
> (c) *specific terms and exact terms are given greater weight than general language;*
> (d) *separately negotiated or added terms are given greater weight than standardized terms or other terms not separately negotiated.*

In addition, the *Restatement* adopts a rebuttable presumption that may trouble those who think that they should draft everything on behalf of their clients:

§ 206 Interpretation Against the Draftsman

In choosing among the reasonable meanings of a promise or agreement or a term thereof, that meaning is generally preferred which operates against the party who supplies the words or from whom a writing otherwise proceeds.

Finally, over 35 years ago, Professor Edwin Patterson set forth ten general maxims of interpretation, some of which are in Latin. An edited version of those ten maxims appears below.

Edwin W. Patterson, *The Interpretation and Construction of Contracts*
64 COLUM. L. REV. 833, 852–54 (1964)

In this brief treatment we can only quote a list of standard maxims, which may not be complete. The ones most often phrased in Latin are given first.

1. *Noscitur a sociis*. The meaning of a word in a series is affected by others in the same series; or, a word may be affected by its immediate context. The example for the next maxim may be taken to illustrate this one.

2. *Ejusdem generis*. A general term joined with a specific one will be deemed to include only things that are like (of the same genus as) the specific one. This one if applied usually leads to a restrictive interpretation. *E.g.*, S contracts to sell R his farm together with the "cattle, hogs, and other animals." This would probably not include S's favorite house-dog, but might include a few sheep that S was raising for the market.

3. *Expressio unius exclusio alterius*. If one or more specific items are listed, without any more general or inclusive terms, other items although similar in kind are excluded. *E.g.*, S contracts to sell R his farm together with "the cattle and hogs on the farm." This language would be interpreted to exclude the sheep and S's favorite house-dog.

4. *Ut magis valeat quam pereat*. By this maxim, an interpretation that makes the contract valid is preferred to one that makes it invalid.

5. *Omnia praesumuntur contra proferentem.* This maxim states that if a written contract contains a word or phrase which is capable of two reasonable meanings, one of which favors one party and the other of which favors the other, that interpretation will be preferred which is less favorable to the one by whom the contract was drafted. This maxim favors the party of lesser bargaining power, who has little or no opportunity to choose the terms of the contract, and perforce accepts one drawn by the stronger party. . . . [T]he maxim is commonly invoked in cases that do not reveal any disparity of bargaining power between the parties.

6. *Interpret contract as a whole.* A writing or writings that form part of the same transaction should be interpreted together as a whole, that is, every term should be interpreted as a part of the whole and not as if isolated from it. This maxim expresses the contextual theory of meaning, which is, perhaps, a truism.

7. *"Purpose of the parties."* "The principal apparent purpose of the parties is given great weight in determining the meaning to be given to manifestations of intention or to any part thereof." This maxim must be used with caution. In fact, the two parties to a (bargain) contract necessarily have different purposes, and if these are apparent, then the court can construe a principal or common purpose from the two as a guide to the interpretation of language or the filling of gaps. Thus a contract to sell, buy, and export scrap copper was construed to make the buyer's obtaining of an export license a condition of the seller's promise to deliver. However, if the purposes of the parties are obscure the court may well fall back upon "plain meaning."

8. *Specific provision is exception to a general one.* If two provisions of a contract are inconsistent with each other and if one is "general" enough to include the specific situation to which the other is confined, the specific provision will be deemed to qualify the more general one, that is, to state an exception to it. A lease of a truck-trailer provided that the lessee should be absolutely liable for loss or damage to the vehicle, yet another clause stated that no party's liability should be increased by this contract. It was held that the former was more specific and therefore controlled the general provision, hence the lessee was liable. A careful draftsman would have stated the former as an exception to the latter, and the court in effect does it for him.

9. *Handwritten or typed provisions control printed provisions*. Where a written contract contains both printed provisions and handwritten or typed provisions, and the two are inconsistent, the handwritten or typed provisions are preferred. This maxim is based on the inference that the language inserted by handwriting or by typewriter for this particular contract is a more recent and more reliable expression of their intentions than is the language of a printed form. While this maxim is used in interpreting insurance contracts and other contracts of adhesion, it is also applicable to all contracts drawn up on a printed form.

10. *Public interest preferred*. If a public interest is affected by a contract, that interpretation or construction is preferred which favors the public interest. The proper scope of application of this rule seems doubtful. It may have some appropriate uses in construing contracts between private parties. However, as applied to government contracts it would, if applied, be used to save the taxpayers' money as against those contracting with the government. But this is not, it is believed, a standard of interpretation or construction uniformly applied to government contracts.

Problems on Construction of Contracts

1. James wants to buy a sailboat at Sears. He seeks to use his Sears credit card to complete the purchase. On the credit card slip to be signed, right above where his signature is to be placed, are the words "By signing this, the Cardholder agrees to grant to Sears a security interest in the goods purchased hereby, as set forth in more detail in the most recent Cardholder agreement between Sears and the undersigned."

    a. James has no idea what a "security interest" is, but he signs anyway. He finds out what a security interest is when he doesn't pay his credit card bill, and Sears sends some of its workers over to "repossess" the sailboat, which they accomplish by sailing the boat away without any fuss. Assume for now (and you'll confirm this later in your Article 9 course) that Sears could do this only if they had been contractually granted a "security interest."

Based on your reading so far, have they been? What maxims or rules would help you here?

b. Now assume that James sees the language above his signature, and then crosses it out before signing. The clerk at the register makes no complaint, and lets James drive off with his new boat. If James doesn't pay, can Sears repossess the boat? What maxims or rules would help you here?

2. A contract to sell land states that the buyer is reserving all rights to "all coal and other minerals." Who gets the subsurface oil and gas? *See McCormick v. Union Pac. R.R. Co.*, 983 P.2d 84 (Colo. Ct. App. 1998).

3. Fred is a book collector. He advertises the following on eBay:

   For sale: One first edition Trollope, *circa* 1860. Signed by author. Excellent condition.

   Lucinda enters the auction, ultimately entering the highest bid of $500. When she receives the book, she notices that it is written and signed by Thomas Adolphus Trollope, the brother of Anthony Trollope. Thomas wrote travel books; Anthony was more in the literary vein. Both she and Fred believe they have a contract. Questions of mistake aside, what are the best arguments you can muster using the maxims that Lucinda should have received an Anthony Trollope book?

D. Special Interpretive Rules for Contracts of Adhesion?

How often have you wanted to rent a car or obtain some other good or service, and were then presented with a pre-printed form to sign (and no opportunity to negotiate anything)? Are these types of contracts just as valid as fully-negotiated, specially-prepared custom contracts? Are they subject to the same interpretive rules? The next two cases examine this issue.

Meyer v. State Farm Fire & Cas. Co.
Court of Special Appeals of Maryland
85 Md. App. 83, 582 A.2d 275 (1990)

OPINION:

For over 100 years, it has been common—indeed standard—for fire insurance policies to contain a clause requiring disputes concerning the amount of a covered loss suffered by the insured to be resolved through an appraisal process. Such a clause is at issue here. It provides, in relevant part, that, if the company and the insured are unable to agree on the amount of loss, either one can demand that the amount be determined by appraisal. Upon such a demand, each party is obliged to select an appraiser; the two appraisers so selected then "select a competent, impartial umpire." If the two appointed appraisers agree on an amount, that amount "shall be the amount of loss." If they are unable to agree, they submit their differences to the umpire. Written agreement signed by any two of the three then will constitute the amount of loss. The policy further provides that "[n]o action shall be brought unless there has been compliance with the policy provisions."

Appellants purchased a policy of fire insurance containing that clause from appellee. A fire occurred at their home, but, unfortunately, they and the company were unable to agree on the amount of loss. Although it is not entirely clear from the Agreed Statement of the Case that constitutes the record in this appeal, it appears that the company, at some point, sought to invoke the appraisal process. Appellants instead filed suit for damages in the Circuit Court for Wicomico County, contending that the appraisal provisions were invalid. The basis of their claim was that [among other things,] because the policy was a contract of adhesion and because they were actually unaware that it contained the appraisal provision, there was no effective waiver of their Constitutional right.

The company moved to dismiss the action. Though conceding the factual averments of appellants' complaint for purpose of the motion, it contended that the dispute resolution clause was not invalid and that, by omitting to allege compliance with it, appellants had failed to state a claim upon which relief could be granted. The court found merit in that defense and dismissed the action. Hence, this expedited appeal . . . .

* * *

[W]e are not dealing here with a statute mandating this form of dispute resolution. It is a contractual provision. The issue is whether appellants can escape its effect because the policy was a contract of adhesion and, as they were allegedly (and for purposes of this case concededly) unaware that such a provision was in the policy, they did not knowingly, voluntarily, and intelligently waive their right to try the issue of the amount of their loss before a jury. In urging their position, we think that the appellants give too expansive a meaning to both the requirements for waiving their right to a judicial resolution of the controversy and the effect of a contract of adhesion.

A contract of adhesion has been defined as one "that is drafted unilaterally by the dominant party and then presented on a 'take-it-or-leave-it' basis to the weaker party who has no real opportunity to bargain about its terms." *Restatement (Second) of Conflict of Laws* § 187, Comment b. The comment goes on to note that such contracts "are usually prepared in printed form, and frequently at least some of their provisions are in extremely small print." It is generally recognized that insurance policies qualify as contracts of adhesion, and so we shall assume that the policy at issue here is such a contract.

The fact that a contract is one of adhesion does not mean that either it or any of its terms are invalid or unenforceable. A court will, to be sure, look at the contract and its terms with some special care. As in most cases, it will refuse to enforce terms that it finds unconscionable and will construe ambiguities against the draftsman; but it will not simply excise or ignore terms merely because, in the given case, they may operate to the perceived detriment of the weaker party. *See*, in general, *Restatement (Second) of Contracts* § 211, Comment c; also *Corbin on Contracts* §§ 559, 1376.

There is no asserted ambiguity in the appraisal provision; indeed, in *Aetna Cas. & Sur., supra*, 293 Md. at 420, 445 A.2d 14, the Court declared such a provision "plain and unambiguous." Nor do we see anything unconscionable about it. The appraisal process has generally been regarded by the courts as a fair method of resolving disputes over the amount of loss. As Appleman notes, rather than being stricken down as unconscionable, appraisal provisions are usually *upheld* on grounds of public policy "since they tend to fair dealing and the prevention of litigation." J. Appleman, *Insurance Law and Practice* § 3921. Moreover, although certainly standard language in the policy, the appraisal provision at issue here is by no means "buried" or enunciated in the proverbial "fine print." It is worded in plain, colloquial English as part of the stated Conditions of the policy and, except for headings, is in the same size and type print as the other provisions of the policy.

It is true, of course, that a waiver of basic Constitutional rights is not ordinarily valid unless it is knowing and voluntary. * * * It is also true that where such a waiver is founded upon a provision in a contract of adhesion, the court will, as noted above, be especially careful to protect against an unconscionable result. * * *

These precepts, however, must be weighed against the equally well-established view that favors and enforces agreements to arbitrate disputes, including disputes over insured losses. An agreement to arbitrate either future or existing disputes involves more than just the waiver of a right to jury trial, although that is certainly implicit in such an agreement. It constitutes an election to use an alternative dispute resolution mechanism that the law not only recognizes but encourages. If appellants' position were correct, the whole foundation of the Federal and uniform arbitration acts could be placed in jeopardy. Arbitration clauses are standard not only in insurance contracts but in construction contracts, employment agreements, and a variety of other contracts that may, in some instances, be regarded as being of adhesion. If the "weaker" party to such contracts were able tc escape the duty to arbitrate on the premise that he was unaware of the arbitration clause and therefore had not validly waived his Federal or State Constitutional right to a jury trial, the viability of this favored method of dispute resolution would be significantly circumscribed.

We recognize that if the insertion of an arbitration clause in a contract is induced by *fraud*, the clause will not be enforced. * * * But that is not the case here. On the record before us, we hold that the appraisal clause is not invalid and that the procedure required by it must be used in good faith.

Judgment Affirmed; Appellants to Pay the Costs.

QUESTIONS

1. Questions about the facts of this case

   1.1. Did the insurance company refuse to pay anything on the policy?

   1.2. Why did Meyer pay money to State Farm if she had never read the contract under which State Farm provided her fire insurance?

2. Questions about the law

2.1. In Maryland, are parties always bound to contract language in adhesion contracts they don't read or understand? What exceptions would this court recognize?

2.2. Would it have made any difference to this court if the practice contained in the adhesion contract had not been "standard", that is, if the insurance company defendant had language different from all other insurance companies?

Lauvetz v. Alaska Sales and Service d/b/a National Car Rental

Supreme Court of Alaska

828 P.2d 162 (1991)

Opinion

Burke, Justice.

This matter is before the court on petition for review. By previous order, we agreed to examine the superior court's grant of partial summary judgment against the operator of a rental vehicle in an action against the operator for collision damage to the vehicle. The issue that we address is whether the operator is entitled to the coverage afforded by a collision damage waiver found in the vehicle rental agreement if the operator is intoxicated while operating the vehicle.

I

Vacationers John Osborne and Thomas Lauvetz arrived in Alaska on August 26, 1988. Before leaving Anchorage International Airport, they rented a previously reserved van from Alaska Sales and Service, doing business as National Car Rental (National). Although Osborne rented the vehicle, he listed Lauvetz as an authorized driver. While at the rental desk, Osborne was offered an optional collision damage waiver (CDW), which he accepted, and optional personal accident insurance, which he declined. The CDW added $ 8.95 per day to the basic daily rate of $ 70.00.

On the face of the Rental Agreement there is no indication of the scope of the CDW. Directly above the CDW box, in bold face and in the same size type as "Collision Damage Waiver Option," are the words "See Terms and Conditions." The National agent did not inform Osborne and Lauvetz where the terms and conditions could be found. The agent apparently made no representations about the scope of the CDW, nor did the agent indicate that the terms and conditions contained specific exclusions to the CDW.

The terms and conditions of the Rental Agreement were, in fact, on the inside of the travel folder in which the agent placed the Rental Agreement. The right flap of the travel folder opened into three panels containing the terms and conditions. The terms and conditions were printed in black on a white background and were legible. Lauvetz and Osborne did not read the terms and conditions.

Paragraph seven of the terms and conditions concerns the CDW option:

> If I [the renter] am involved in an accident or the car sustains collision damage, even from unknown causes, I am responsible for the resulting damages including loss of use, claims processing fees, and administrative charges regardless of fault. This financial responsibility is eliminated if I accept the CDW Option, pay for it, and comply with the Agreement, including all Terms and Conditions.
>
> I UNDERSTAND THAT CDW IS NOT INSURANCE. I understand that some automobile insurance policies cover loss and damages to the rental vehicle; that National cannot interpret the terms of my insurance policies; and that it is my responsibility to check with my insurance company and my insurance agent.
>
> If I accept the CDW Option, I agree to pay the charge per day shown on the Rental document for each full or partial day. I understand that CDW does not apply to interior or exterior damage to the Vehicle caused by negligent loading or unloading of baggage or equipment.

The Terms and Conditions also included a paragraph on prohibited uses:

> I agree that the Vehicle shall NOT be used by or for any of the following PROHIBITED USES:
>
> a. by an unauthorized driver;
>
> b. by any driver under the influence of intoxicants, drugs, or any other substance known to impair driving ability;

c. for any illegal purpose;

d. by anyone who gives the Company a false name, address, age or other false or misleading information;

e. in any abusive or reckless manner;

f. to carry persons or property for hire;

g. to tow or push anything;

h. in any race, test, contest, or training activity;

i. for any use in Mexico without the prior written permission of the renting location. All protection is void in Mexico. Your written permission must be obtained and special insurance must be purchased before entering Mexico.

I UNDERSTAND THAT IF THE VEHICLE IS OBTAINED OR USED FOR ANY PROHIBITED USE OR IN VIOLATION OF THIS AGREEMENT, THEN THE CDW OPTION SHALL BE VOID AND, WHERE PERMITTED BY THE LAW, THE LIABILITY AND COMPREHENSIVE PROTECTION, PAI, PEC, AND SLI INSURANCE SHALL BE VOID.

On August 29, 1988, the van was damaged while Lauvetz was driving. As a result of the accident, Lauvetz was charged with and pled no contest to reckless driving. AS 28.35.040.

National subsequently filed suit against Lauvetz and Osborne, seeking compensatory and punitive damages for the wreck of the van. The complaint alleged that Lauvetz was intoxicated at the time of the accident and that this intoxication was a causal factor of the accident. The complaint further claimed that the CDW did not apply, because Osborne and Lauvetz remained liable for any damage resulting from a prohibited use of the vehicle, specifically, use by an intoxicated driver or use in a reckless manner.

During preliminary proceedings, National sought and obtained partial summary judgment on the validity and enforceability of the exclusions to the CDW option. The superior court ruled that the "terms and provisions of the collision damage waiver in the car rental agreement governing drunk and reckless driving are valid, binding, and enforceable, and the Court rejects Defendants' position that the CDW is insurance." This court accepted Lauvetz's petition to review the grant of partial summary judgment.

II

Lauvetz argues that the exclusions were beyond the reasonable expectations of lessees accepting National's standardized contract. Before considering the parties' specific arguments, it is necessary to discuss the applicable law.

A

Section 211 of the Restatement Second of Contracts addresses the question of interpreting standardized form agreements:

> (1) Except as stated in Subsection (3), where a party to an agreement signs or otherwise manifests assent to a writing and has reason to believe that like writings are regularly used to embody terms of agreements of the same type, he adopts the writing as an integrated agreement with respect to the terms included in the writing.
>
> . . .
>
> (3) Where the other party has reason to believe that the party manifesting such assent would not do so if he knew that the writing contained a particular term, the term is not part of the agreement.

Restatement (Second) of Contracts § 211 (1981). Thus, this section establishes the general enforceability of the terms of standardized forms, without regard for whether the customer reads or understands those terms. Id. at comment b. This general enforceability, however, is subject to limitations of reasonableness: Customers "are not bound to unknown terms which are beyond the range of reasonable expectation." Id. at comment f.

Although we have never explicitly endorsed Section 211 as the appropriate analysis for standardized agreements, we have invoked a doctrine of reasonable expectations in analogous situations. * * *[T]hose cases involved insurance contracts. The operative fact * * *, however, was that the policy was a contract of adhesion, rather than a negotiated agreement. * * *As a consequence, the agreements were "construed according to the principle of reasonable expectations." * * *

These cases suggest that "reasonable expectations" are those expectations a consumer would have after reading the form. For example, we noted that an "insurance policy may be considered a contract of adhesion, and as such, should be construed to provide the coverage which a layperson would have reasonably expected, given a lay interpretation of the policy language." * * * Thus, this principle of reasonable expectations is somewhat different from the principle embodied in Section 211, which actually presumes that the customer does not read the contract. Restatement (Second) of Contracts § 211 comment b (1981) ("Customers do not in fact ordinarily understand or even read the standard terms.").

The distinction is significant in this case. Given the clarity of the terms and conditions, there is little room for argument that a Stordahl-type "lay interpretation" of the terms would differ from a legal interpretation. The Stordahl approach is inadequate, however, in cases where consumers probably will not read adhesive contracts and will not have any choice in the terms even if they do read them. * * * Section 211, on the other hand, emphasizes the reasonableness of the term or condition, no matter how clear its meaning might be to the layman if he happened to read it. The Arizona Supreme Court justified its endorsement of Section 211 by noting that

> to acknowledge standardized contracts for what they are—rules written by commercial enterprises—and to enforce them as written, subject to those reasonable limitations provided by law, is to recognize the reality of the marketplace as it now exists, while imposing just limits on business practice.

Darner Motor Sales v. Universal Underwriters Insurance Co., 140 Ariz. 383, 682 P.2d 388, 399 (Ariz. 1984). We agree and adopt the analysis of Section 211 with regard to standardized form agreements outside the insurance context.

B

National emphasizes that reasonableness is an objective concept, and adds that "no person who drives a car that does not belong to him can have any reasonable expectation that he can drive that car recklessly or while intoxicated." It argues that Lauvetz's claimed reasonable expectations are nothing more than "subjective and self-serving statements of [his] intent concerning the meaning of the CDW." Such subjective intent, National asserts, has no probative value, citing Peterson v. Wirum, 625 P.2d 866, 870 (Alaska 1981).

National notes that the doctrine of reasonable expectations is nothing more than a judicial construct for imposing community standards of reasonable behavior on the private law of contracts. National argues that under modern community standards, drunk driving is viewed as a serious threat to public safety. * * * Thus, National contends that Lauvetz's position that a prohibition against drunk and reckless driving is an unconscionable or unreasonable limit on the CDW is absurd.

National mischaracterizes the relevant question. It is not whether a prohibition against drunk driving is unreasonable; any renter would certainly know that the law prohibits drunk driving on pain of severe penalties. See AS 28.35.030(c) (mandating incarceration, a fine, and revocation of driver's license even for first conviction). Rather, the relevant question here is whether the purchaser of the damage waiver reasonably expected the waiver to be subject to any exclusions. We conclude that a consumer would not reasonably expect the damage waiver to be less than complete.

The common law rule is that bailees are not responsible "for damages unattributable to their fault." * * * This rule may be altered by contract. Id. The standardized form used by National did in fact purport to alter that common law rule by making the bailee responsible for any damage, however caused. The CDW then offered the bailee protection from National's unilateral alteration of the common law rule, ostensibly subject to the exclusions.

We think that the common law rule aptly expresses a bailee's reasonable expectation: He will be responsible for any damage caused by his fault. The average car renter would not parse that "fault" into the fine legal categories of "negligence," "recklessness" or "volitional conduct." When offered the CDW, the bailee would reasonably expect this option, at the not inconsiderable rate of $8.95 per day, to relieve him of responsibility even if the damage were caused by his fault. Again, the average car renter would not parse that fault into fine legal categories.

As the Colorado Supreme Court commented in a case similar to the present one, "lessors should know that the simple, highly readable summary of the collision responsibility alternatives will lead an average customer to reasonably conclude that he is protected against most, if not all, risks." * * * In this case, there was not even a summary of the responsibility alternatives. Lauvetz merely had the choice between a damage waiver and no waiver, protection against damaging the car or no protection. In deciding today that a consumer would reasonably expect that the rental company's waiver is complete, we join the large number of courts who have refused to enforce damage waiver exclusions under a variety of circumstances. * * *

The superior court's grant of partial summary judgment in favor of National on the enforceability of the CDW exclusions is REVERSED and this case REMANDED for further proceedings consistent with this opinion.

QUESTIONS AND NOTE

1. Questions about the facts of this case

    1.1. What did Lauvetz contend the CDW provision meant? In other words, what did it appear that he believed his $8.95 per day bought?

    1.2. Is the court saying that Lauvetz in any way relied on his reasonable expectation of the CDW provision in making the decision to purchase it?

2. Questions about the law

    2.1. In Alaska, can people now rent cars, get drunk, and not worry about what happens to the car when they wreck it? If you don't think so, what in the opinion would you point to that would exclude such an interpretation?

    2.2. Can you apply *Lauvetz* to an individually-negotiated contract to buy land? Even if it was documented by use of a standardized form?

    2.3. After *Lauvetz*, what evidence would a consumer introduce to establish reasonable expectations? What evidence would the purveyor of form contracts use?

    2.4. Which court has the better view of how to handle standard form contracts, *Lauvetz* or *Meyers*? Before answering that question, think about how companies offering goods or services through standard form contracts are going to react to decisions such as *Lauvetz*.

3. Note

The Alaska Supreme Court recently had another opportunity to review standard language in insurance contracts. In *Kim v. National Indemnity Co.*, 6 P.3d 264 (Alaska 2000), a taxicab driver, Kim, had sexually abused a minor passenger. After Kim's criminal conviction, the minor's parents sued Kim and his insurance company for the injuries suffered. The insurance contract Kim had purchased for his taxi operations provided up to $300,000 in coverage for injuries "caused by an accident and resulting from the ownership, maintenance or use of a covered auto." The insurance contract also had an exclusion from personal injury "expected or intended from the standpoint of the insured."

Without even mentioning *Lauvetz*, the Alaska Supreme Court found for Kim, and dismissed the lawsuit. They said that the contractual language required coverage only for accidents, and not for intentional injuries. Should the parties have cited *Lauvetz*? Should the court have distinguished it?*

SECTION 4: IMPLIED TERMS

It is a fact that parties often do not enter into contracts that spell everything out. Sometimes, courts will construe the parties' contract as incorporating background practices and understandings into the agreement, as shown by *Threadgill, supra*, at 503. Sometimes, legislatures will do the same, as shown by the U.C.C. and the *CISG*.

What happens, however, when the parties' actions after formation are consistent only with the fact that they jointly believe in the existence of a contract, but their words, written or otherwise, seem to be incomplete? The judicial response has been varied, and the following is a now-classic response.

---

*The Alaska Supreme Court partially overruled *Kim* in *Shaw v. State Farm Mut. Auto. Ins. Cos.*, 19 P.3d 588 (Alaska 2001) on the grounds that the minor was the "insured" under the uninsured motorist coverage, and the minor's acts were certainly not "intentional". The court let stand, however, the holding that the primary coverage's exclusion of non-accidental actions covered Kim's case. *Shaw* also did not cite or mention *Lauvetz*.

A. Terms Implied by Courts to Effectuate Assumed Intent

Wood v. Lucy, Lady Duff-Gordon

Court of Appeals of New York

222 N.Y. 88, 118 N.E. 214 (1917)

Cardozo, J:

The defendant styles herself "a creator of fashions." Her favor helps a sale. Manufacturers of dresses, millinery and like articles are glad to pay for a certificate of her approval. The things which she designs, fabrics, parasols and what not, have a new value in the public mind when issued in her name. She employed the plaintiff to help her to turn this vogue into money. He was to have the exclusive right, subject always to her approval, to place her indorsements on the designs of others. He was also to have the exclusive right to place her own designs on sale, or to license others to market them. In return, she was to have one-half of "all profits and revenues" derived from any contracts he might make. The exclusive right was to last at least one year from April 1, 1915, and thereafter from year to year unless terminated by notice of ninety days. The plaintiff says that he kept the contract on his part, and that the defendant broke it. She placed her indorsement on fabrics, dresses and millinery without his knowledge, and withheld the profits. He sues her for the damages, and the case comes here on demurrer.

The agreement of employment is signed by both parties. It has a wealth of recitals. The defendant insists, however, that it lacks the elements of a contract. She says that the plaintiff does not bind himself to anything. It is true that he does not promise in so many words that he will use reasonable efforts to place the defendant's indorsements and market her designs. We think, however, that such a promise is fairly to be implied. The law has outgrown its primitive stage of formalism when the precise word was the sovereign talisman, and every slip was fatal. It takes a broader view to-day. A promise may be lacking, and yet the whole writing may be "instinct with an obligation," imperfectly expressed. * * * If that is so, there is a contract.

The implication of a promise here finds support in many circumstances. The defendant gave an *exclusive* privilege. She was to have no right for at least a year to place her own indorsements or market her own designs except through the agency of the plaintiff. The acceptance of the exclusive agency was an assumption of its duties* * *. We are not to suppose that one party was to be placed at the mercy of the other* * *. Many other terms of the agreement point the same way. We are told at the outset by way of recital that "the said Otis F. Wood possesses a business organization adapted to the placing of such indorsements as the said Lucy, Lady Duff-Gordon has approved." The implication is that the plaintiff's business organization will be used for the purpose for which it is adapted. But the terms of the defendant's compensation are even more significant. Her sole compensation for the grant of an exclusive agency is to be one-half of all the profits resulting from the plaintiff's efforts. Unless he gave his efforts, she could never get anything. Without an implied promise, the transaction cannot have such business "efficacy as both parties must have intended that at all events it should have" (Bowen, L. J., in *The Moorcock*, 14 P. D. 64, 68). But the contract does not stop there. The plaintiff goes on to promise that he will account monthly for all moneys received by him, and that he will take out all such patents and copyrights and trademarks as may in his judgment be necessary to protect the rights and articles affected by the agreement. It is true, of course, as the Appellate Division has said, that if he was under no duty to try to market designs or to place certificates of indorsement, his promise to account for profits or take out copyrights would be valueless. But in determining the intention of the parties, the promise *has* a value. It helps to enforce the conclusion that the plaintiff *had* some duties. His promise to pay the defendant one-half of the profits and revenues resulting from the exclusive agency and to render accounts monthly, was a promise to use reasonable efforts to bring profits and revenues into existence. For this conclusion, the authorities are ample * * *.

The judgment of the Appellate Division should be reversed, and the order of the Special Term affirmed, with costs in the Appellate Division and in this court.

QUESTIONS AND NOTE

1. Questions about the facts of this case

   1.1. Why do you think the contract lacked any express obligation on the part of Wood to market the designs?

   1.2. Note that Wood brought this lawsuit. Why do you think Lady Duff-Gordon gave her indorsement to others without Wood's knowledge? Didn't she know that Wood would find out?

2. Questions about the law

   2.1. Assume that Lucy had not made another deal, and the case is instead Lucy suing Wood for breach of contract because Wood hadn't done a darn thing to market Lucy's fashions. What result?

   2.2. How is *Wood v. Lucy* similar to *Threadgill, supra*, at 503? How is it different?

   2.3. Would Cardozo have reached a different result if the agreement between Lucy and Wood had a merger clause?

3. Note

   In *Wood v. Lucy*, Cardozo states that "The law has outgrown its primitive stage of formalism when the precise word was the sovereign talisman, and every slip was fatal. It takes a broader view to-day." This is a hallmark of Cardozo; catchy language describing a common situation. But think about what it says. Is it true? Think back to our earlier materials about the required level of definiteness for a communication to be an offer. Have your views changed since then?

Lady Duff-Gordon had a curious career, as indicated by the following excerpt:*

DANIEL WM. FESSLER, TEACHING NOTES FOR FESSLER & LOISEAUX'S CONTRACTS: MORALITY, ECONOMICS AND THE MARKETPLACE 47–48 (1982)

For some reason I have become fascinated by Lady Duff-Gordon and over the years have collected a good deal of trivia concerning her exploits. The most famous affair involving Lady Duff grew out of her status as a passenger on the Titanic.** It seems that she was traveling with her husband,

---

*For those who can't get enough of Lady Duff-Gordon, or who just want to see a picture of her, you can go to *Encyclopedia Titanica: First Class Passenger: Lady Duff-Gordon (Lucy Christiana Sutherland)* (http://www.encyclopedia-titanica.org/bio/p/1st/duff-gordon_ce2.shtml).

**For the sharp-eyed, Lady Duff-Gordon is introduced to Leonardo DeCaprio's character in the movie, *Titanic*, in the scene in which Leonardo bluffs his way into the first class dining room. Eds.

Sir Cosmo Duff-Gordon, and her maid. In the midst of history's greatest marine disaster, Lady Duff, Sir Cosmo, the maid and two other passengers managed to appropriate a life boat with a capacity of 34. They were accompanied by seven members of the crew! As they were rowed to safety amidst the heroism and the death of the men who volunteered to remain on board Lady Duff is said to have declared to her maid: "Oh look, there goes my beautiful dressing gown." Later an Admiralty Court was to examine formal charges that Sir Cosmo had bribed members of the crew. It was established that Sir Cosmo had given £5 checks to the members of the crew on the life boat and had objected when one of the crew suggested that they go back in the attempt to pick up people who were in the sea and crying for help. Notwithstanding, the court acquitted Sir Cosmo of the charge of bribery. This acquittal shocked the press, perhaps because—or in spite of—Lady Duff appearance in the court as a witness. In a special dispatch to the New York Times on May 21, 1912, we find the following description of a dramatic figure: "[She was] dressed entirely in black except for a white lace collar." Harold Spencer reported that her second day on the stand gave quite a different impression from that of the first:

> . . . she is a fair creation, daintily chiseled, graceful in movement, arresting in speech. Her voice is tuned to the siren's note, her little face is pale and plaintive, and her whole being is braced to the edge of victory over her accusers. The white aigrette of Friday last, erect and challenging, had given place to the sweep of a large black picture hat, shading her eyes to the left and drooping with hint of tears over the right shoulder. A collar of exquisite lace ripples down from the shapely neck to the waist, very white and vivid against the black dress.

My colleague, Jack Ayer, supplied some further information respecting her business activities:

> It was big. When she died in 1935 at the age of 72, the New York Times described her as a 'pioneer in bringing freedom and grace back to women's dress after the Victorian era'. She was a Canadian, daughter of one Douglas Sutherland, sister of Elinor Glyn, the sexy novelist, widow of one James S. Wallace. She married Sir Cosmo in 1900; but before that she had undertaken the dressmaking business which later spanned the hemispheres. At her peak, she operated in London, Paris, Chicago and New York. Her name became synonymous with glamour and high style. Among her injunctions:

> A girl should never dress so that the dress subject her personality.
>
> One should never make 'sex appeal' on the street. Wear black by all means.
>
> One should never wear skirts so short as to allow a bit of leg above the top of the boots.

Her eye for fashion apparently did not translate into business sense. She went bankrupt in New York in 1922, and in London in 1924. At a bankruptcy inquiry in London, an examiner asked: "Can you give me some particulars on your shareholders?" To which she replied: "It is all Greek to me. I don't know what a share is."

Her success as a glamour girl seems to have been coupled with something of a sullen contempt for society at large. Her New York troubles began with an accusation that she engaged in conspiracy to defraud customs laws. In 1919, she gained notoriety of a small sort by answering a creditor's inquiry for non-payment of a $1,500 breach of contract judgment (not Woods!) in person. She wore a pearl necklace with an estimated worth of $5,000, and testified that she drew $365 per week from her firm, Lucille, Inc., and another $100 per week from International Features Services. What did she do for the $100? "Nothing" she replied. Her examiner asked if she ever bought Liberty Bonds. She replied: "Why should I buy any? This country means nothing to me. I have nothing but trouble over here. It is an awful country." She did add: "I believe I have one that my maid bought for me."

Courts are not the only ones who imply terms that are so basic that the parties' might be excused for not spelling them out.

Uniform Commercial Code

§ 2-312. Warranty of Title and Against Infringement.

(1) Subject to subsection (2) there is in a contract for sale a warranty by the seller that

(a) the title conveyed shall be good, and its transfer rightful; and

(b) the goods shall be delivered free from any security interest or other lien or encumbrance of which the buyer at the time of contracting has no knowledge.

> (2) A warranty under subsection (1) will be excluded or modified only by specific language or by circumstances which give the buyer reason to know that the person selling does not claim title in himself or that he is purporting to sell only such right or title as he or a third person may have.

As Comment 1 to this Section states,

> [s]ubsection (1) makes provision for a buyer's basic needs in respect to a title which he in good faith expects to acquire by his purchase, namely, that he receive a good, clean title transferred to him also in a rightful manner so that he will not be exposed to a lawsuit in order to protect it.

Note that this section does not make such a provision a part of every contract whether or not the parties want it. It can be excluded by specific language or by particular circumstances (such as in a foreclosure sale by a sheriff, or by selling goods or realty pursuant to a quitclaim deed).

B. Terms Implied by Courts to Effectuate Public Policy— The Implied Duty of Good Faith and Fair Dealing

In the introduction to this Section, the statement was made that perspective is necessary to appreciate the law of contract interpretation. We now need to add to that statement. A certain amount of cynicism is also necessary.

We are certain that not all lawsuits regarding contract interpretation are bona fide disputes. That is, if courts and juries could examine the hearts and minds of the litigants, we think in many cases they would find that the interpretations proffered were manufactured, or at least refined, only after some problem with the economics of the transaction surfaced. But courts and juries don't have that power. They must start from the interpretation offered, and work backwards to reach the best interpretation of the parties' original intent.

In this regard, courts have also implied terms into the parties' contract much in the same way that Justice Cardozo did in *Lucy*. The difference here is that the justification offered in *Lucy*—that of supplying what the parties surely forgot—is less obvious. Instead, we find courts (and with the case of the U.C.C., legislatures) implying terms and conditions in contracts to achieve substantial justice, whatever that may ultimately mean, or supplying terms that the parties would have agreed to had they thought about the matter at all. When assessing either of these types of terms, ask yourself whether the implication of such terms is based on pure public policy—that is, whether they represent society's collective judgment as to what ought to be in every contract. Also ask yourself to what extent such implication is based on rough empiricism—that is, do they represent society's collective judgment as to what parties in similar transactions would usually insert if they thought about it?*

Early on in our studies we encountered assertions that contract law, or at least the enforcement of contracts, is infused and imbued with notions of good faith. The next few cases examine that concept in several different contexts.

Locke v. Warner Bros., Inc.
Court of Appeal of California
57 Cal. App. 4th 354, 66 Cal. Rptr. 2d 921 (1997)

Klein, P. J.

Plaintiffs and appellants Sondra Locke (Locke) and Caritas Films, a California corporation (Caritas) (sometimes collectively referred to as Locke) appeal a judgment following a grant of summary judgment in favor of defendant and respondent Warner Bros., Inc. (Warner). * * *

We conclude triable issues are present with respect to whether Warner breached its development deal with Locke by categorically refusing to work with her * * * . The judgment therefore is reversed * * * .

FACTUAL AND PROCEDURAL BACKGROUND

1. Locke's dispute with Eastwood.

In 1975, Locke came to Warner to appear with Clint Eastwood in *The Outlaw Josey Wales* (Warner Bros. 1976). During the filming of the movie, Locke and Eastwood began a personal and romantic relationship. For the next dozen years, they lived in Eastwood's Los Angeles and Northern California homes. Locke also appeared in a number of Eastwood's films. In 1986, Locke made her directorial debut in *Ratboy* (Warner Bros. 1986).

*You also might ask yourself if you (or the judges deciding these cases) are in the best position to make that empirical call.

In 1988, the relationship deteriorated, and in 1989 Eastwood terminated it. Locke then brought suit against Eastwood, alleging numerous causes of action. That action was resolved by a November 21, 1990, settlement agreement and mutual general release. Under said agreement, Eastwood agreed to pay Locke additional compensation in the sum of $450,000 "on account of past employment and Locke's contentions" and to convey certain real property to her.

2. Locke's development deal with Warner.

According to Locke, Eastwood secured a development deal for Locke with Warner in exchange for Locke's dropping her case against him. Contemporaneously with the Locke/Eastwood settlement agreement, Locke entered into a written agreement with Warner, dated November 27, 1990. It is the Locke/Warner agreement which is the subject of the instant controversy.

The Locke/Warner agreement had two basic components. The first element states Locke would receive $250,000 per year for three years for a "non-exclusive first look deal." It required Locke to submit to Warner any picture she was interested in developing before submitting it to any other studio. Warner then had 30 days either to approve or reject a submission.

The second element of the contract was a $750,000 "pay or play" directing deal. The provision is called "pay or play" because it gives the studio a choice: It can either "play" the director by using the director's services, or pay the director his or her fee.

Unbeknownst to Locke at the time, Eastwood had agreed to reimburse Warner for the cost of her contract if she did not succeed in getting projects produced and developed. Early in the second year of the three-year contract, Warner charged $975,000 to an Eastwood film, *Unforgiven* (Warner Bros. 1992).

Warner paid Locke the guaranteed compensation of $1.5 million under the agreement. In accordance with the agreement, Warner also provided Locke with an office on the studio lot and an administrative assistant. However, Warner did not develop any of Locke's proposed projects or hire her to direct any films. Locke contends the development deal was a sham, that Warner never intended to make any films with her, and that Warner's sole motivation in entering into the agreement was to assist Eastwood in settling his litigation with Locke.

3. Locke's action against Warner.

On March 10, 1994, Locke filed suit against Warner, alleging four causes of action.

* * *

The second cause of action alleged that Warner breached the contract by refusing to consider Locke's proposed projects and thereby deprived her of the benefit of the bargain of the Warner/Locke agreement.

* * *

Warner answered, denied each and every allegation and asserted various affirmative defenses.

4. Warner's motion for summary judgment and opposition thereto.

On January 6, 1995, Warner filed a motion for summary judgment. Warner contended it did not breach its contract with Locke because it did consider all the projects she presented, and the studio's decision not to put any of those projects into active development or "hand" Locke a script which it already owned was not a breach of any express or implied contractual duty. Warner asserted the odds are slim a producer can get a project into development and even slimmer a director will be hired to direct a film. During the term of Locke's deal, Warner had similar deals with numerous other producers and directors, who fared no better than Locke.

* * *

In opposing summary judgment, Locke contended Warner breached the agreement in that it had no intention of accepting any project regardless of its merits. Locke also asserted Warner committed fraud by entering into the agreement without any intention of approving any project with Locke or allowing Locke to direct another film.

Locke's opposition papers cited the deposition testimony of Joseph Terry, who recounted a conversation he had with Bob Brassel, a Warner executive, regarding Locke's projects. Terry had stated to Brassel: " 'Well, Bob, this woman has a deal on the lot. She's a director that you want to work with. You have a deal with her. . . . I've got five here that she's interested in.' [¶] And then I would get nothing. [¶] . . . [¶] I was told [by Brassel], 'Joe, we're not going to work with her,' and then, 'That's Clint's deal.' And that's something I just completely did not understand."

Similarly, the declaration of Mary Wellnitz stated: She worked with Locke to set up projects at Warner, without success. Shortly after she began her association with Locke, Wellnitz submitted a script to Lance Young, who at the time was a senior vice-president of production at Warner. After discussing the script, Young told Wellnitz, "Mary, I want you to know that I think Sondra is a wonderful woman and very talented, but, if you think I can go down the hall and tell Bob Daly that I have a movie I want to make with her he would tell me to forget it. They are not going to make a movie with her here."

5. Trial court's ruling.

On February 17, 1995, the trial court granted summary judgment in favor of Warner. Thereafter, the trial court signed an extensive order granting summary judgment. The order stated:

> Under the contract, Warner had no obligation either to put into development any of the projects submitted to the studio for its consideration, or to 'hand off ' to Locke any scripts for her to direct that it previously had acquired from someone else. The implied covenant of good faith and fair dealing cannot be imposed to create a contract different from the one the parties negotiated for themselves. Warner had the option to pass on each project Locke submitted. Warner was not required to have a 'good faith' or 'fair' basis for declining to exercise its right to develop her material. Such a requirement would be improper and unworkable. A judge or jury cannot and should not substitute its judgment for a film studio's when the studio is making the creative decision of whether to develop or produce a proposed motion picture. Such highly subjective artistic and business decisions are not proper subjects for judicial review. Moreover, Warner had legitimate commercial and artistic reasons for declining to develop the projects Locke submitted.

* * *

Locke filed a timely notice of appeal from the judgment.

CONTENTIONS

Locke contends: The trial court erred by granting Warner's motion for summary judgment based on its conclusion there were no disputed issues of material fact; the trial court erred in weighing the evidence, resolving doubts against Locke, the nonmoving party, and adopting only those inferences favorable to Warner where the evidence supported contrary inferences; and the trial court committed reversible error first by failing to make any findings or evidentiary rulings and then by adopting Warner's defective ruling.

DISCUSSION

* * *

2. A triable issue exists as to whether Warner breached its contract with Locke by failing to evaluate Locke's proposals on their merits.

As indicated, the second cause of action alleged Warner breached the contract by "refusing to consider the projects prepared by [Locke] and depriving [Locke] of the benefit of the bargain of the Warner-Locke agreement."[3]

In granting summary judgment on this claim, the trial court ruled "[a] judge or jury cannot and should not substitute its own judgment for a film studio's when the studio is making the creative decision of whether to develop or produce a proposed motion picture. Such highly-subjective artistic and business decisions are not proper subjects for judicial review."

The trial court's ruling missed the mark by failing to distinguish between Warner's right to make a subjective creative decision, which is not reviewable for reasonableness, and the requirement the dissatisfaction be bona fide or genuine.

a. General principles.

"'[W]here a contract confers on one party a discretionary power affecting the rights of the other, a duty is imposed to exercise that discretion in good

[3]Contrary to Warner's contention Locke is raising an unpled claim for breach of the implied covenant of good faith and fair dealing, the second cause of action for breach of contract adequately alleges Warner deprived Locke of the benefit of the bargain of the development deal by refusing to consider her projects. Such conduct by Warner, if proven, would amount to a breach of the covenant, implied "in every contract that neither party will do anything which will injure the right of the other to receive the benefits of the agreement. {Citation.]" (*Comunale v. Traders & General Ins. Co.* (1958) 50 Cal. 2d 654, 658[, 328 P.2d 198, 68 A.L.R.2d 883]; accord, *Waller v. Truck Ins. Exchange, Inc.* (1995) 11 Cal. 4th 1, 36[, 44 Cal. Rptr. 2d 370, 900 P.2d 619].)

faith and in accordance with fair dealing.' [Citations.]"* * * It is settled that in " 'every contract there is an implied covenant that neither party shall do anything which will have the effect of destroying or injuring the right of the other party to receive the fruits of the contract. . . .'" * * *

Therefore, when it is a condition of an obligor's duty that he or she be subjectively satisfied with respect to the obligee's performance, the subjective standard of *honest satisfaction* is applicable.* * * "Where the contract involves matters of fancy, taste or judgment, the promisor is the sole judge of his satisfaction. If he asserts *in good faith* that he is not satisfied, there can be no inquiry into the reasonableness of his attitude. [Citations.] [¶] Traditional examples are employment contracts . . . and agreements to paint a portrait, write a literary or scientific article, or produce a play or vaudeville act. [Citations.]"* * * In such cases, "the promisor's determination that he is not satisfied, *when made in good faith*, has been held to be a defense to an action on the contract. [Citations.]" * * *

Therefore, the trial court erred in deferring entirely to what it characterized as Warner's "creative decision" in the handling of the development deal. If Warner acted in bad faith by categorically rejecting Locke's work and refusing to work with her, irrespective of the merits of her proposals, such conduct is not beyond the reach of the law.

b. Locke presented evidence from which a trier of fact reasonably could infer Warner breached the agreement by refusing to consider her proposals in good faith.

Merely because Warner paid Locke the guaranteed compensation under the agreement does not establish Warner fulfilled its contractual obligation. As pointed out by Locke, the value in the subject development deal was not merely the guaranteed payments under the agreement, but also the opportunity to direct and produce films and earn additional sums, and most importantly, the opportunity to promote and enhance a career.

Unquestionably, Warner was entitled to reject Locke's work based on its subjective judgment, and its creative decision in that regard is not subject to being second-guessed by a court. However, bearing in mind the requirement that subjective dissatisfaction must be an honestly held dissatisfaction, the evidence raises a triable issue as to whether Warner breached its agreement with Locke by not considering her proposals on their merits.

As indicated, the deposition testimony of Joseph Terry recounted a conversation he had with Bob Brassel, a Warner executive, regarding Locke's projects. In that conversation, Brassel stated " 'Joe, we're not going to work with her,' and then, 'That's Clint's deal.' "

Similarly, the declaration of Mary Wellnitz recalled a conversation she had with Lance Young, a senior vice-president of production at Warner. After discussing the script with Wellnitz, Young told her: "Mary, I want you to know that I think Sondra is a wonderful woman and very talented, but, if you think I can go down the hall and tell Bob Daly that I have a movie I want to make with her he would tell me to forget it. They are not going to make a movie with her here."

The above evidence raises a triable issue of material fact as to whether Warner breached its contract with Locke by categorically refusing to work with her, irrespective of the merits of her proposals. While Warner was entitled to reject Locke's proposals based on its subjective dissatisfaction, the evidence calls into question whether Warner had an honest or good faith dissatisfaction with Locke's proposals, or whether it merely went through the motions of purporting to "consider" her projects.

c. No merit to Warner's contention Locke seeks to rewrite the instant agreement to limit Warner's discretionary power.

Warner argues that while the implied covenant of good faith and fair dealing is implied in all contracts, it is limited to assuring compliance with the express terms of the contract and cannot be extended to create obligations not contemplated in the contract.* * *

This principle is illustrated in *Carma Developers (Cal.), Inc. v. Marathon Development California, Inc.* (1992) 2 Cal. 4th 342, 351–352 [6 Cal. Rptr. 2d 467, 826 P.2d 710], wherein the parties entered into a lease agreement which stated that if the tenant procured a potential sublessee and asked the landlord for consent to sublease, the landlord had the right to terminate the lease, enter into negotiations with the prospective sublessee, and appropriate for itself all profits from the new arrangement. *Carma* recognized "[t]he covenant of good faith finds particular application in situations where one party is invested with a discretionary power affecting the rights of another." (*Id.*, at p. 372.) The court expressed the view that "[s]uch power must be exercised in good faith." (*Ibid.*) At the same time, *Carma* upheld the right of the landlord under the express terms of the lease to freely exercise its discretion to terminate the lease in order to claim for itself—and deprive the tenant of—the appreciated rental value of the premises. (*Id.*, at p. 376.)

In this regard, *Carma* stated: "We are aware of no reported case in which a court has held the covenant of good faith may be read to prohibit a party from doing that which is expressly permitted by an agreement. On the contrary, as a general matter, implied terms should never be read to vary express terms. [Citations.] 'The general rule [regarding the covenant of good faith] is plainly subject to the exception that the parties may, by express provisions of the contract, grant the right to engage in the very acts and conduct which would otherwise have been forbidden by an implied covenant of good faith and fair dealing. . . . [¶] This is in accord with the general principle that, in interpreting a contract "an implication . . . should not be made when the contrary is indicated in clear and express words." 3 Corbin, Contracts, § 564, p. 298 (1960). . . . [¶] *As to acts and conduct authorized by the express provisions of the contract*, no covenant of good faith and fair dealing can be implied which forbids such acts and conduct. And if defendants were given the right to do what they did by the express provisions of the contract there can be no breach.' [Citation.]" * * *

In *Third Story Music, Inc. v. Waits* (1995) 41 Cal. App. 4th 798, 801 [48 Cal. Rptr. 2d 747], the issue presented was "whether a promise to market music, or to refrain from doing so, at the election of the promisor is subject to the implied covenant of good faith and fair dealing where substantial consideration has been paid by the promisor."

In that case, Warner Communications obtained from Third Story Music (TSM) the worldwide right to manufacture, sell, distribute and advertise the musical output of singer/songwriter Tom Waits. * * * The agreement also specifically stated that Warner Communications "'may at our election refrain from any or all of the foregoing.'" * * * TSM sued Warner Communications for contract damages based on breach of the implied covenant of good faith and fair dealing, claiming Warner Communications had impeded TSM's receiving the benefit of the agreement. * * * Warner Communications demurred to the complaint, alleging the clause in the agreement permitting it to "'at [its] election refrain' from doing anything to profitably exploit the music is controlling and precludes application of any implied covenant." * * * The demurrer was sustained on those grounds. * * *

The reviewing court affirmed, holding the implied covenant was unavailing to the plaintiff.* * * Because the agreement *expressly* provided Warner Communications had the right to *refrain* from marketing the Waits recordings, the implied covenant of good faith and fair dealing did not limit the discretion given to Warner Communications in that regard. * * *

Warner's reliance herein on *Third Story Music, Inc.*, is misplaced. The Locke/Warner agreement did not give Warner the express right to refrain from working with Locke. Rather, the agreement gave Warner *discretion* with respect to developing Locke's projects. The implied covenant of good faith and fair dealing obligated Warner to exercise that discretion honestly and in good faith.

In sum, the Warner/Locke agreement contained an implied covenant of good faith and fair dealing, that neither party would frustrate the other party's right to receive the benefits of the contract.* * * Whether Warner violated the implied covenant and breached the contract by categorically refusing to work with Locke is a question for the trier of fact.

* * *

DISPOSITION

The judgment is reversed . . . . Locke to recover costs on appeal.

Kitching, J., and Aldrich, J., concurred.

QUESTIONS AND NOTES

1. Questions about the facts of this case

    1.1. Was the contract term Ms. Locke claimed Warner Bros violated an express term of the contract? If not, how do the parties know what the term requires of them in their efforts to perform as promised?

    1.2. Did Ms. Locke not receive the compensation she was promised under the contract with Warner? If she did, what remedy does she want?

    1.3. Of what relevance is Clint Eastwood's relationship with Ms. Locke and his business dealings with Warner?

2. Questions about the law

2.1. Can you succinctly state the implied term of good faith that California (and indeed almost every other state) inserts into every contract?

2.2. Section 205 of the *Restatement (Second) of Contracts* states:

Every contract imposes upon each party a duty of good faith and fair dealing in its performance and its enforcement.

Comment d adds:

Subterfuges and evasions violate the obligation of good faith in performance even though the actor believes his conduct to be justified. But the obligation goes further: bad faith may be overt or may consist of inaction, and fair dealing may require more than honesty. A complete catalogue of types of bad faith is impossible, but the following types are among those which have been recognized in judicial decisions: evasion of the spirit of the bargain, lack of diligence and slacking off, willful rendering of imperfect performance, abuse of a power to specify terms, and interference with or failure to cooperate in the other party's performance.

Is California law, as set forth in *Locke*, consistent with these statements, or is it aberrational?

2.3. Would it be a valid defense on remand if Warner Bros. asserted that each idea that Ms. Locke pitched was silly or non-commercial?

2.4. What if Warner Bros. had given serious consideration to Ms. Locke's first 10 projects, but had found them all wanting and then just internally decided not to consider any more projects? What if its refusal came after only one project?

3. Notes

3.1. *Hey, That's Hollywood . . .* According to the *Los Angeles Times*, here's how the suit was resolved on remand:

Actress' Settlement Ends Long Legal Saga
LOS ANGELES TIMES, Part B, May 27, 1999, at 2

They said she'd never work in this town again, but all is forgiven between Sondra Locke and Warner Bros.

The actress is going back to work for the studio under terms of a legal settlement. The agreement came at the start of a trial on her lawsuit accusing Warner Bros. of harming her career by going along with a sham movie directing deal allegedly engineered by Locke's former lover and co-star, Clint Eastwood.

The last-minute settlement gives Locke a new lease on her career behind the camera, said her attorney, Neil Papiano.

The lawyer acknowledged that at times the three hours of settlement talks Monday more closely resembled a Hollywood pitch session as Locke discussed projects that caught her interest.

Asked how it felt to be back in business with a studio that a few years ago had rejected all her ideas, a beaming Locke quipped, "Hey, that's Hollywood."

The settlement came as jury selection was about to begin in a case that had been dismissed by a Los Angeles judge, then reinstated by a state appeals court.

The lawyers would not discuss the financial terms. But as he left the Burbank courthouse, Papiano said the agreement reaches beyond money considerations to create writing and directing opportunities for Locke, who had been all but blacklisted by the major studios for a decade.

"It involves a business arrangement beneficial to Ms. Locke," Papiano said. "She's going to be paid for her services—we believe handsomely."

Locke said, "This is my best day in a long, long time." She said she felt vindicated as a professional.

"We're happy too," said Warner Bros. attorney Robert Schwartz, who declined to discuss the matter further.

The case was the second installment in Locke's legal fight to regain her professional viability after the acrimonious split with Eastwood, a popular box office draw and Academy Award-winning director.

The lanky, laconic star settled with Locke for an undisclosed sum of money 2 ½ years ago, just as a jury was about to return a verdict in her favor. Testimony during that trial showed that he had paid $1.5 million under the table to subsidize her development deal with Warner Bros.

Eastwood acknowledged on the witness stand that he never told Locke about his role in subsidizing her development deal, struck as partial settlement of her palimony case against him.

Locke testified at the previous trial that she would never accept such a deal because it gave Eastwood too much control and sent a signal that she wasn't to be taken seriously.

Indeed, she pitched more than 30 ideas to the studio over three years, and none was accepted.

Monday's settlement finally lays to rest a long legal saga that began when Eastwood packed up Locke's belongings and changed the locks to their Brentwood home after the New Year's holiday in 1989.

Discovered in Nashville, Tenn., during a national talent search, Locke won a Golden Globe and an Academy Award nomination for her first film, "The Heart Is a Lonely Hunter."

She was in her 20s when she became romantically involved with Eastwood, and soon was his constant companion and co-star, even sharing billing with Clyde the orangutan in his "Every Which Way" films. The couple split after spending 14 years together.

3.2. All readers of this note will no doubt recall the joys of the SAT and LSAT exams. Did you ever wonder what would happen if, after getting 170 on the LSAT, you then got a letter from the Educational Testing Service questioning your performance, and refusing to forward your score to the schools of your choice? If you did wonder, you might well ask what contract law has to do with any answer.

That's where *Dalton v. Educational Testing Service*, 87 N.Y.2d 384, 663 N.E.2d 289, 639 N.Y.S.2d 977 (1995) would come in. In that case, Brian Dalton took the SAT test twice, improving his score by 410 points on the second try. After finding what it thought was different handwriting on each test, the test administrator, Educational Testing Service (ETS) canceled Dalton's second score. It believed it could do this because Dalton had signed a form agreement upon registering for the test allowing ETS to take such an action if it found any unexplained discrepancies.

But the form, held to be a contract by the New York Court of Appeals, also obligated ETS to "notif[y] the test taker of the reasons for questioning the score" and offer the test-taker the . . . five options:

(1) the opportunity to provide additional information, (2) confirmation of the score by taking a free retest, (3) authorization for ETS to cancel the score and refund all fees, (4) third-party review by any institution receiving the test score or (5) arbitration.

Dalton took the first option and supplied ETS with additional information (he had been ill during the first exam, and other tests indicated that his second score was a better indicator of his abilities). ETS promptly ignored this information, since they did not deem it relevant to whether Dalton had used a "ringer" in the second test.

This refusal, the court said, was a breach of the duty of good faith inherent in all contracts. "Where . . . ETS refuses to exercise its discretion . . . by declining even to consider relevant material submitted by the test-taker, the legal question is whether this refusal breached an express or implied term of the contract, ... Here, the courts below agreed that ETS did not consider the relevant information furnished by Dalton. By doing so, ETS failed to comply in good faith with its own test security procedures, thereby breaching its contract with Dalton."

So Dalton won the battle. Did he win the war and obtain an order forcing ETS to release his scores? No. "Dalton is entitled to relief that comports with ETS' contractual promise—good-faith consideration of the material he submitted to ETS. We cannot agree with Dalton's assumption that ETS will merely rubber-stamp its prior determination without good-faith attention to his documentation and that reconsideration by ETS will be an empty exercise. Our conclusion that the contract affords Dalton a meaningful remedy rests also on the provision in the Procedures for Questioned Scores [contained in the contract] allowing Dalton to utilize one or more of the remaining four options in combination with renewed consideration by the Board of Review. Those options—including third-party review by any institution receiving the test score as well as arbitration—remain available should ETS determine that the information submitted fails to resolve its concerns about the validity of the [second test] score."

Based on *Dalton*, how satisfying is it to prevail on a claim that someone did not consider information in good faith before making a decision related to a contract?

Hobin v. Coldwell Banker Residential Affiliates, Inc.
Supreme Court of New Hampshire
144 N.H. 626, 744 A.2d 1134 (2000)

Horton, J.

The plaintiff, Ross T. Hobin, the owner of a Coldwell Banker franchise, appeals from an order of the Superior Court (Gray, J.) dismissing his claims against the defendant, Coldwell Banker Residential Affiliates, Inc. (Coldwell Banker), relating to Coldwell Banker's alleged placement of addit onal franchises in Hobin's territory. The trial court dismissed the claims of breach of the implied covenant of good faith and fair dealing [and] breach of contract * * * for failure to state a claim. We affirm.

Upon review of the rulings on this motion to dismiss, we assume the following facts alleged by Hobin to be true for purposes of this appeal.* * * In 1994, Hobin, who operated a real estate office in Rye, contacted Coldwell Banker about becoming one of its franchisees. At the time, the nearest Coldwell Banker office was Marple Associates (Marple), located 5.5 miles away in Portsmouth. Marple maintained a Rye telephone number, but no office in Rye.

Although the real estate market was depressed and Coldwell Banker was having difficulty selling new franchises in the area, Hobin thought he could make a franchise successful if Marple did not expand into Rye. Hobin raised the issue of Marple's potential expansion in his discussions with a Coldwell Banker recruiter, who told him that Coldwell Banker treated Rye as a "small market" area for which it charged a reduced franchise fee, implying that it could not support a second franchise and that the probability of a second franchise in Rye would be unthinkable. Throughout discussions of other Coldwell Banker franchisees, including its largest, Hunneman Real Estate Corporation (Hunneman), the recruiter did not mention the possibility of any franchisee opening an office in Rye. The recruiter did, however, suggest that Coldwell Banker's internal policies and procedures for awarding franchises would not permit the placement of a second franchise in such proximity to an existing franchise as to jeopardize that franchisee's business. As a result of these representations, Hobin executed a franchise agreement effective July 25, 1994, and entered Coldwell Banker's Small Market Program.

Throughout the next two years, Hobin competed with the Joycelyn Caulfield Agency (Caulfield), which maintained two locations—the first in Rye, within 300 feet of Hobin's office, and the second in North Hampton, 3.2 miles away. Sometime around January 1997, Hunneman, which had purchased Marple in late 1995, also purchased Caulfield, resulting in its ownership of three offices within 5.5 miles of Hobin.

As represented to Hobin by the recruiter, Coldwell Banker maintains procedures for approving the placement of one franchise near or in another franchisee's territory. During Hobin's discussions with Coldwell Banker executives regarding his dissatisfaction with the additional Coldwell Banker offices in his territory, he discovered that those procedures include review of the proposed placement by a committee of ten to fifteen individuals and an opportunity for the existing franchisee to comment upon the placement. He also learned that, as Coldwell Banker's largest franchisee, Hunneman is given special preference and does not have to follow normal franchise-placement procedures. Coldwell Banker did not follow its procedures in permitting Hunneman to locate in Rye and North Hampton, but rather granted approval on a single telephone call from Hunneman's owner to Coldwell Banker's Franchise Development department.

Hobin brought a petition for injunctive relief against Coldwell Banker [seeking to enjoin the continued grant of a franchise to Hunneman] . . . . He appeals the dismissal of his claims against Coldwell Banker for breach of implied covenant of good faith and fair dealing [and] breach of contract * * *.

* * *

As a preliminary matter, we note that in the franchise agreement, which was appended to the petition, the parties chose the law of California, the State of Coldwell Banker's incorporation, to govern the agreement and their "legal relationships." . . . . We will . . . honor the parties' selection of California law.

Hobin's first issue is whether the trial court erred in dismissing his claim of breach of the implied covenant of good faith and fair dealing. The court dismissed the claim because the action of which Hobin complains, the grant of another franchise in Hobin's marketing area, is expressly permitted in the franchise agreement.

Hobin argues that although the agreement expressly reserved Coldwell Banker's right to place additional franchisees in Hobin's territory, Coldwell Banker had the duty to exercise its discretion in accordance with the covenant of good faith and fair dealing implied in all contracts. According to Hobin, allowing Coldwell Banker's largest franchisee to open two locations in his small-market territory, one within 300 feet of his office, was a breach of that duty.

Coldwell Banker counters that, under California law, the express terms of a contract always limit any implied covenants, and a party may not pursue a cause of action for breach of an implied covenant where the supposed covenant contradicts the express term.

The franchise agreement provided, in pertinent part:

> 1.02 Grant of Franchise
>
> (a) Franchisor hereby grants to Franchisee, and Franchisee hereby accepts, a non-exclusive franchise . . . . Nothing contained herein shall be deemed to grant Franchisee an exclusive territory and Franchisor . . . may . . . franchise or license others to locate and operate additional residential real estate brokerage businesses within the market area within which Franchisee conducts and operates the Franchised Business.

Although the parties agree that the agreement expressly provided that Coldwell Banker may place additional franchises in Hobin's market area, they disagree as to whether the implied covenant of good faith and fair dealing implied in every contract . . . operated to limit the extent of its discretion to do so.

In determining that a tenant had not breached the implied covenant of good faith and fair dealing against its landlord when the actions complained of were expressly allowed in the lease, . . . *Carma* [*Developers v. Marathon Dev. Cal.*, 2 Cal. 4th 342, 826 P.2d 710, 726 (Cal. 1992)] discussed two apparently inconsistent principles: that the covenant of good faith and fair dealing should be implied to limit the exercise of a discretionary power, and that express terms of a contract cannot be varied by an implied covenant. *Carma*, 826 P.2d at 726–28.

On one hand, as argued by Hobin, "the covenant of good faith finds particular application in situations where one party is invested with a discretionary power affecting the rights of another. Such power must be exercised in good faith." * * *

On the other hand, supporting Coldwell Banker's contentions, the court stated that it was

> aware of no reported case in which a court has held the covenant of good faith may be read to prohibit a party from doing that which is expressly permitted by an agreement. On the contrary, as a general matter, implied terms should never be read to vary express terms. The general rule regarding the covenant of good faith is plainly subject to the exception that the parties may, by express provisions of the contract, grant the right to engage in the very acts and conduct which would otherwise have been forbidden by an implied covenant of good faith and fair dealing . . . . As to acts and conduct authorized by the express provisions of the contract, no covenant of good faith and fair dealing can be implied which forbids such acts and conduct. And if defendants were given the right to do what they did by the express provisions of the contract there can be no breach.

Carma, 826 P.2d at 728 (quotation, citations, and brackets omitted).

A subsequent California Court of Appeal opinion reconciled these seemingly inconsistent principles. *Third Story Music, Inc. v. Waits*, 41 Cal. App. 4th 798, 48 Cal. Rptr. 2d 747 (Ct. App. 1995) (holding that the plaintiff music company had not stated a claim for breach of implied covenant of good faith and fair dealing when its contract with the defendant, to which it had sold certain music rights, expressly allowed the defendant to refrain from marketing the music). The *Third Story Music* court distinguished between the proper implication of a covenant of good faith and fair dealing "to contradict an express contractual grant of discretion when necessary to protect an agreement which otherwise would be rendered illusory and unenforceable," and situations in which a court may not imply such a covenant because "regardless of how such [discretionary] power [is] exercised, the agreement [is] supported by adequate consideration." * * *

The case before us is of the latter type. In consideration of Hobin's agreement to purchase and operate a Coldwell Banker franchise, his business accrued numerous benefits stemming from its association with a nationally recognized real estate marketing organization, including those resulting from chain identification, participation in a uniform system to promote and assist the business, training, and centralized programs for its use. Specifically, it received rights to the Coldwell Banker trademarks and trade names and the goodwill associated therewith, benefits accruing from Coldwell Banker's national and regional advertising, public relations and promotional campaigns, orientation and on-going training, operating advice and assistance, operational techniques and service concepts, on-site visits by Coldwell Banker field representatives, business-planning tools, sales and informational material, and available staff-recruitment, training, and advertising materials. Hobin was also eligible for cash awards based on his franchise's performance. Regardless of the extent of Coldwell Banker's exercise of its discretion—whether it chose to place competing franchises next door to Hobin or to leave the territory free of competitors—Hobin retained the right to the contractual benefits set forth above. Importantly, Coldwell Banker also incurred costs in providing its programs and assistance to Hobin. Even were we to adjudge the benefits accruing to Hobin to be worthless, the detriment Coldwell Banker incurred in providing its programs and assistance to Hobin was "sufficient to constitute consideration." * * * In sum, the consideration provided was "more than the peppercorn of consideration the law requires" to save the contract from unenforceability. * * *

The next issue presented is whether Hobin has stated a claim for breach of contract. Hobin concedes that Coldwell Banker did not breach an express term of the agreement. Given our holding that Hobin has not alleged a breach of the implied covenant of good faith and fair dealing, we conclude that Hobin has not alleged a breach of an implied term of the agreement. Therefore, we hold that he has failed to state a claim for breach of contract. * * *

Affirmed.

QUESTIONS

1. Questions about the facts of this case

   1.1. Why can't Hobin rely on the representations and discussions with Coldwell Banker's recruiter to make out a case for breach of contract?

   1.2. Did Coldwell Banker exercise its discretion with respect to Hunneman in good faith? Why would Coldwell Banker favor one broker over another?

1.3. Does Coldwell Banker's profit motive come into play here? Would you want to know the termination provisions in Hobin's contract before taking his case? Why?

2. Questions about the law

2.1. The court here applies California law. Based on *Locke, supra,* does the court apply it correctly? Is this case consistent with *Locke*?

2.2. Does this decision mean that Coldwell Banker could intentionally drive Hobin out of business by packing his market area indiscriminately with other, newer, brokers? Why, or why not?

2.3. If a client wished to have "total" discretion in making decisions under a contract, can you, after the last two cases, give her assurances that such a term will be honored? If you believe that you can, how would you go about drafting such a clause?

C. Terms Imposed by Legislatures

Courts are not alone in implying terms into contracts when the parties do not. Legislatures often write provisions that are to be adopted into every contract made with their jurisdiction. We have seen this in the Uniform Commercial Code with good faith (§ 1-203) and with adequate assurance of future performance (§ 2-609). But the U.C.C. implies many substantive terms in contracts as well. Some of the major ones are reprinted below:

§ 2-305. Open Price Term.

(1) The parties if they so intend can conclude a contract for sale even though the price is not settled. In such a case the price is a reasonable price at the time for delivery if

(a) nothing is said as to price; or

(b) the price is left to be agreed by the parties and they fail to agree; or

(c) the price is to be fixed in terms of some agreed market or other standard as set or recorded by a third person or agency and it is not so set or recorded. . . .

§ 2-308. Absence of Specified Place for Delivery.

Unless otherwise agreed

(a) the place for delivery of goods is the seller's place of business or if he has none his residence; but

(b) in a contract for sale of identified goods which to the knowledge of the parties at the time of contracting are in some other place, that place is the place for their delivery . . . .

§ 2-309. Absence of Specific Time Provisions . . . .

(1) The time for shipment or delivery or any other action under a contract if not provided in this Article or agreed upon shall be a reasonable time. . . .

Problems on Terms Implied by the U.C.C.

1. Epstein and Markell meet and agree that Markell will sell, and Epstein will buy, Markell's 1965 Cadillac convertible, painted fire engine red.

   Two months later, after calling Markell several times and getting no response, Epstein sues Markell for breach of contract. Issues of damages aside, who will prevail?

2. Markell and Ponoroff see each other at a Star Trek convention in Wawautosa, Wisconsin, and Markell agrees that he will purchase, and Ponoroff agrees he will sell, Ponoroff's prize pair of plastic Vulcan ears.

   Two weeks later, Markell shows up on Ponoroff's doorstep, flashes a crisp $100 bill at Ponoroff, and demands the ears. Ponoroff yawns and slams the door on Markell's face.

   Markell sues for breach. Issues of damages aside, who will prevail?

3. Ponoroff places an order for a Galaxy 950 computer over the telephone with Galaxy Computers, Inc. The price agreed upon is $999, but no delivery date is discussed. The next day, Galaxy sends a confirming invoice stating the computer will arrive in three weeks, and indicating a price of $1099. There is no explanation for the increase.

When the computer arrives in three weeks as indicated, Ponoroff refuses delivery, stating that it is late. Issues of damages aside, what result if Galaxy sues Ponoroff for breach?

4. Epstein sells asphalt; Ponoroff uses it to pave roads. Ponoroff and Epstein have a contract under which Epstein agrees to sell Ponoroff all of Ponoroff's requirements of asphalt for a period of five years, with the price to be the "posted price" at Tuscaloosa for Grade A asphalt. Epstein gets a bigger contract to supply asphalt, and doesn't want to supply Ponoroff's puny needs anymore. When Ponoroff orders some asphalt he needs for a job, Epstein tells him that they have no contract, because there is no agreement on price. What result?

D. Special Legislative Provisions—Warranties and the U.C.C.

1. Introduction

As we have seen, contract liability is promise-based. An alternative theory of obligation that may or may not be based on agreement of the parties is "warranty" liability. At its most basic level, a warranty is, in essence, an allocation of risk. That is to say, a party who makes a warranty accepts the risk of the untruth of the subject matter of that warranty. For instance, a seller of a business might warrant to the buyer that the assets of the company are free and clear of liens and encumbrances. If it should later turn out that some third party, perhaps a creditor or even the IRS, does have a claim against the assets of the business, then the seller must make it good to the buyer by satisfying the amount of the third party's claim. It makes no difference whether the seller-warrantor was aware of the claim, whether he intended to mislead the buyer, or even whether the buyer relied on the warranty in agreeing to buy the business. Unlike an action for fraud, which requires proof of bad intent, breach of warranty is a "strict liability" kind of offense.

The law recognizes several kinds of warranties concerning the nature or quality of one party's performance to the other. For instance, you may have learned in your property law class that many states recognize an implied "warrant of habitability" with respect to residential leases. If the premises are not habitable, the tenant has a defense to liability under the lease. Our focus in this section is on the statutory warranty scheme contained in Article 2 of the U.C.C. relating to contracts for the sale of goods. While you will probably receive more in-depth instruction on warranty theory in your upper-level commercial law courses, we think it is useful to briefly introduce warranty liability here for two reasons. First, it will allow you to contrast warranty liability with traditional contract liability. Second, it will give you an opportunity to engage in close statutory analysis which, as you will see, is very different from caselaw analysis.

The U.C.C. warranties come in two flavors: (1) "express warranties," which are statements made or assurances given by the seller concerning the quality or characteristics of the goods subject to the contract, and (2) "implied warranties," which are assurances concerning the seller's title to the goods and their basic quality. While express warranties arise from overt manifestations from the seller to the buyer, implied warranties are supplied by operation of law. That is to say, implied warranties are deemed to automatically become part of the contract *unless* they are excluded from the contract by affirmative agreement of the parties. Thus, warranties are "in" unless they are consciously taken "out." This is just the opposite from ordinary contract terms which are "out" unless they're deliberately put "in." Confused? Well, the U.C.C.'s warranty scheme is contained in § 2-312 through § 2-316. Review those provisions now before reading on to the next case, but bear in mind that we are only introducing warranty liability in this section. In most law schools, as we mentioned, the subject is treated in much more detail in one of the upper-level commercial law curriculum.

---

2. Express Warranties

We begin our examination of warranty liability by considering express wartanties. Unlike the other terms considered in this section, these are not implied terms. However, we think it will help you to understand the U.C.C. implied warranties if you first understand how the U.C.C. handles express warranties.

Section 2-313 of the U.C.C. provides that an express warranty may be created by (a) any affirmation of fact or promise that relates to the goods, (b) any description of the goods, or (c) any sample or model. In each case, however, the affirmation, description, or sample must be made part of the *basis of the bargain*. What does that language mean?

Daughtrey v. Ashe
Supreme Court of Virginia
243 Va. 73, 413 S.E.2d 336 (1992)

WHITING, Justice.

In this dispute between the buyers and the sellers of a diamond bracelet, the principal issues arise under the Uniform Commercial Code—Sales. [Article 2]. Specifically, they are: (1) whether the sellers' appraisal statement of the grade of diamonds on the bracelet is a description of the goods under Code § 8.2-313(1)(b), and therefore an express warranty; and (2) whether such a statement made the description "a part of the bargain" under Code § 8.2-313(1)(b), and therefore an express warranty, when the buyers did not know of the warranty until some time after the purchase price was paid and the bracelet was delivered. * * *

In October 1985, W. Hayes Daughtrey consulted Sidney Ashe (Ashe), a jeweler, about the purchase of a diamond bracelet as a Christmas gift for his wife, Fenton C. Daughtrey. Ashe exhibited, and offered to sell, a diamond bracelet to Daughtrey for $15,000. Although Ashe "knew" and "classified" the bracelet diamonds as v.v.s. grade (v.v.s. is one of the highest ratings in a quality classification system employed by gemologists and jewelers), he merely described the diamonds as "nice" in his conversation with Daughtrey. Ashe told Daughtrey that if he was later dissatisfied with the bracelet, he would refund the purchase price upon its return.

When Daughtrey later telephoned Ashe and told him he would buy the bracelet, Ashe had Adele Ashe, his business associate, complete an appraisal form which he signed. The form contained the following pertinent language:

> The following represents our estimate *for insurance purposes only, of the present retail replacement cost of identical items*, and not necessarily the amounts that might be obtained if the articles were offered for sale . . . .

DESCRIPTION	APPRAISED VALUE
platinum diamond bracelet, set with 28 brilliant full ct diamonds weighing a total of 10 carats. H color and v.v.s. quality.	$ 25,000.00

(emphasis added).

When Daughtrey came with his daughter to close the sale, he showed the bracelet to his daughter and then paid Ashe for it. As Ashe was counting the money, Daughtrey handed the bracelet to Adele Ashe, who put it in a box together with the appraisal and delivered the box to Daughtrey. Daughtrey later gave the bracelet to his wife as a Christmas present.

In February 1989, Daughtrey discovered that the diamonds were not of v.v.s. quality when another jeweler looked at the bracelet. Shortly thereafter, Daughtrey complained to Ashe, who refused to replace the bracelet with one mounted with diamonds of v.v.s. quality but offered to refund the purchase price upon return of the bracelet. Because the value of diamonds generally had increased in the meantime, Daughtrey declined Ashe's offer.

On May 8, 1989, Daughtrey and his wife filed this specific performance suit against Sidney Ashe and Adele Ashe t/a Ashe Jewelers (the Ashes) to compel them to replace the bracelet with one mounted with v.v.s. diamonds or pay appropriate damages. After hearing the evidence, the trial court found that the diamonds "were of substantially lesser grade" than v.v.s. Nevertheless, because it concluded that the Daughtreys had not proven that "the appraisal was a term or condition of the sale nor a warranty upon which [they] relied in the purchase of the bracelet," the court denied relief for breach of warranty.* The Daughtreys appeal.

First, we consider whether Ashe's statement of the grade of the diamonds was an express warranty. Code § 2-313 provides in pertinent part:

(1) Express warranties by the seller are created as follows:

. . .

*In conformity with the court's order, the Ashes refunded the purchase price without interest to the Daughtreys upon their return of the bracelet. However, the refund of the purchase price did not satisfy the Daughtreys' claim for the cost of replacing the bracelet with one with diamonds of v.v.s. quality.

> (b) any description of the goods which is made part of the basis of the bargain creates an express warranty that the goods shall conform to the description.

The Ashes argue that the statement in the appraisal form is not an express warranty for two reasons.

First, they say the "appraisal on its face stated that it was 'for insurance purposes only.' " However, we think that the balance of the emphasized language in the appraisal form demonstrates that the limiting language relates *only* to the statement of the *appraised value*. Therefore, Ashe's description of the grade of the diamonds should be treated as any other statement he may have made about them.

Second, the Ashes contend that Ashe's statement of the grade of the diamonds is a mere opinion and, thus, cannot qualify as an express warranty under Code § 2-313(2). Code § 2-313(2) provides:

> It is not necessary to the creation of an express warranty that the seller use formal words such as "warrant" or "guarantee" or that he have a specific intention to make a warranty, but an affirmation merely of the value of the goods or a statement purporting to be merely the seller's opinion or commendation of the goods does not create a warranty.

The Ashes rely principally upon a North Carolina case construing the identical code section from the North Carolina Uniform Commercial Code. *Hall v. T.L. Kemp Jewelry, Inc.,* 71 N.C. App. 101, 104, 322 S.E.2d 7, 10 (1984) (jeweler's assurance of value of jewels mere opinion under N.C. Gen. Stat. § 25-2-313, not warranty). However, here, Ashe did more than give a mere opinion of the value of the goods; he specifically described them as diamonds of "H color and v.v.s. quality."

Ashe did not qualify his statement as a mere opinion. And, if one who has superior knowledge makes a statement about the goods sold and does not qualify the statement as his opinion, the statement will be treated as a statement of fact. * * *

Nor does it matter that the opinions of other jewelers varied in minor respects. All of them said, and the trial judge found, that the diamonds were of a grade substantially less than v.v.s.

Clearly, Ashe intended to sell Daughtrey v.v.s. diamonds. He testified that he used only the term "nice" diamonds but "[n]ever mentioned vvs because

[Daughtrey] didn't know anything about vvs." Later, Ashe testified that "I know when I sold the bracelet and I classified it as vvs, I knew it was vvs."

Given these considerations, we conclude that Ashe's description of the goods was more than his opinion; rather, he intended it to be a statement of a fact. Therefore, the court erred in holding that the description was not an express warranty under Code § 2-313(2).

Next, the Ashes maintain that because the description of the diamonds as v.v.s. quality was not discussed, Daughtrey could not have relied upon Ashe's warranty and, thus, it cannot be treated as "a part of the basis of the bargain."

In our opinion, the "part of the basis of the bargain" language of Code § 2-313(1)(b) does not establish a buyer's reliance requirement. Instead, this language makes a seller's description of the goods that is not his mere opinion a representation that defines his obligation. * * *

Our construction of [Virginia's version of] § 2-313, containing language identical to § 2-313 of the Uniform Commercial Code, is supported by a consideration of the following pertinent portions of the Official Comment to the Uniform Commercial Code section:

> The present section deals with affirmations of fact by the seller, descriptions of the goods . . . exactly as any other part of a negotiation which ends in a contract is dealt with. No specific intention to make a warranty is necessary if any of these factors is made part of the basis of the bargain. In actual practice affirmations of fact made by the seller about the goods during a bargain are regarded as a part of the description of those goods; hence *no particular reliance* on such statements need be shown in order to weave them into the fabric of the agreement. Rather, any fact which is to take such affirmations, once made, out of the agreement requires clear affirmative proof. The issue normally is one of fact. Official Comment 3 (emphasis added).
>
> In view of the principle that *the whole purpose of the law of warranty is to determine what it is that the seller has in essence agreed to sell*, the policy is adopted of those cases which refuse except in unusual circumstances to recognize a material deletion of the seller's obligation. Thus, a contract is normally a contract for a sale of something describable and described. Official Comment 4 (emphasis added).

Paragraph (1)(b) makes specific some of the principles set forth above when a description of the goods is given by the seller. . . . Official Comment 5.

> The precise time when words of description or affirmation are made . . . is not material. The sole question is whether the language [is] fairly to be regarded as part of the contract. If language is used after the closing of the deal (as when the buyer when taking delivery asks and receives an additional assurance), the warranty becomes a modification, and need not be supported by consideration, if it is otherwise reasonable and in order (Section 2-209). Official Comment 7.
>
> Concerning affirmations of value or a seller's opinion or commendation under subsection (2), the basic question remains the same: What statements of the seller have in the circumstances and in objective judgment become part of the basis of the bargain? As indicated above, all of the statements of the seller do so unless good reason is shown to the contrary. The provisions of subsection (2) are included, however, since common experience discloses that some statements or predictions cannot fairly be viewed as entering into the bargain. Official Comment 8 (emphasis added).

We conclude from the language used in Code § 2-313 and the Official Comment thereto that the drafters of the Uniform Commercial Code intended to modify the traditional requirement of buyer reliance on express warranties. Such a requirement was contained in the following pertinent language of the earlier Uniform Sales Act § 12: "[a]ny affirmation of fact or any promise by the seller relating to the goods is an express warranty if the natural tendency of such affirmation or promise is to *induce* the buyer to purchase the goods, and if the buyer purchases the goods *relying thereon*." (Emphasis added.) We note that "induce" and "reliance" appear nowhere in Code § 2-313, as contrasted with the reference to buyer reliance in the subsequent section, Code § 2-315, dealing with an implied warranty of fitness for a particular purpose.

Hence, the seller's representation need only be "a part of the basis of the bargain," as set forth in Code § 2-313(1)(b). The term "bargain" is not defined in the Code, but it is used in the following definition of "agreement" as

> the bargain of the parties in fact as found in their language or by implication from other circumstances. . . . Whether an agreement has legal consequences is determined by the provisions of this act, if applicable; oth-

erwise by the law of contracts as provided in Code § 1-103. (Compare 'Contract'). Code § 1-201(3). The word " 'Contract' means the total legal obligation which results from the parties' agreement as affected by this act and any other applicable rules of law. (Compare 'Agreement')." Code § 1-201(11).

Ashe introduced no evidence of any factor that would take his affirmation of the quality of the diamonds out of the agreement. Therefore, his affirmation was "a part of the basis of the bargain." Accordingly, we hold that the Daughtreys are entitled to recover for their loss of bargain, and that the court erred in ruling to the contrary.

Therefore, we will reverse the judgment of the trial court and remand the case for further proceedings to ascertain the Daughtreys' damages.

Reversed and remanded.

QUESTIONS AND NOTES

1. Questions about the facts of this case

   1.1. How important to Mr. Daughtrey's purchase of the bracelet was the fact that the diamonds were of v.v.s. quality? Does that matter?

   1.2. Was the representation concerning the grade of the diamonds a contractual term of the sale?

   1.3. Should the fact that the appraisal was for "insurance purposes only" make a difference in determining whether the seller's statement was part of the "basis of the bargain"? Why wasn't it an important factor for the court in this case?

   1.4. Another issue raised by *Daughtrey* is whether the representation concerning the grade of the diamonds was a statement of fact or a "mere opinion." What is the distinction between the two? Would the outcome in the case have been different if the appraisal had not referred to "v.v.s. quality" but it turned out that, unrelated to changes in the market price for diamonds, the bracelet was worth considerably less than $25,000?

2. Questions about the law

2.1. The view in *Daughtrey* that the buyer need not prove that she *relied* on the seller's representation is widely followed. Thus, unlike proof of specific contract terms, the buyer does not have to establish that the statement or description was consciously *bargained for.* Does it affect the analysis, however, if the buyer *knows* prior to consummation of the sale that the goods are *not* as represented by the seller?

2.2. The court in *Daughtrey* specifically refers to the seller's *superior knowledge* about the goods. Does this suggest a different outcome if the Daughtreys knew only that the grade of the diamonds was less than v.v.s.? Or does it mean they must have known the actual grade of the diamonds? Whatever level of knowledge is required, should access to that knowledge be sufficient or must the buyer have actual knowledge? What are the practical consequences from a litigation standpoint of having the "basis of the bargain" requirement depend on the buyer's knowledge or access to knowledge? In *Rogath v. Sieberman,* 129 F.3d 261 (2d Cir. 1997), the court observed that the issue was not whether the buyer believed the truth of the seller's statement, but rather whether he was purchasing the seller's promise. Does that make sense?

2.3. In addition to determining (by virtue of factors such as superior knowledge) which party is best placed to bear the risk if the goods fail to conform to a specific statement or description, are there economic considerations that bear on the issue as well? Are you willing to pay more for goods with a warranty than without? If so, what does that tell you about how broadly the "basis of the bargain" language in § 2-313(a) should be construed?

2.4. Should the Ashes have argued that the alleged representation concerning the quality of the diamonds was barred by the parol evidence rule? By the same token, why didn't the Daughtreys argue misrepresentation in addition to breach of warranty?

2.5. What was Ashe prepared to give the Daughtreys when they found out the diamonds were not v.v.s. grade? What will they likely receive after remand as a result of the court's holding in this case?

3. Notes

3.1. Official Comment 7 to U.C.C. § 2-313, cited by the court in *Daughtrey,* makes clear that a statement or description made after the deal closes does not preclude that statement or description from constituting an express warranty as long as it is part of the basis for the bargain. The post-closing statement is simply considered a *modification* of the original agreement and, of course, under the U.C.C. modifications require no separate consideration. *See* U.C.C. § 2-209. However, if the buyer is completely unaware of the seller's affirmation of fact, arguably that statement did not become part of the basis of the bargain. This possible limitation played a key role in the well-known case of *Cipollone v. Liggett Group,* 893 F.2d 541 (3d Cir. 1990), *aff'd in part, rev'd in part,* 505 U.S. 504 (1992). In that case, the plaintiff brought suit against a cigarette manufacturer for breach of express warranty based on the company's general advertisements relating to its product. The court of appeals rejected the lower court's holding that an express warranty may be created by statements to the public at large *regardless* of whether the buyer heard or could remember hearing or seeing those advertisements. Instead, the court ruled that the "basis of the bargain" limitation requires the buyer to establish that she saw, heard, or was otherwise aware of the statements. Upon making this showing, there is a presumption that the statements did become part of the basis of the bargain. According to the court, however, the seller can rebut this presumption by "clear and affirmative" proof that the buyer *knew* the statements to be untrue, at which point, the plaintiff may still make out a claim by proving *reliance* despite the non-belief. You got all that? Is it any surprise that plaintiffs' lawyers in subsequent tobacco litigation turned their attention from warranty to tort theories of liability? Suppose you purchase an appliance which is accompanied by manual containing certain affirmations of fact about the product, but you're one of those people who never reads the manual. If the appliance doesn't comply with one of those affirmations are you just out of luck? How the heck is anyone going to know whether you read it or not? Also, can merchant-sellers have it both ways? Remember the first case we read, *Hill v. Gateway 2000, Inc.*? If sellers can add contract the terms they want by materials included inside of the box, should they also be able to claim that warranties contained in the box were not part of the basis of the bargain?

3.2. All courts recognize that there is some room for seller's to "talk up" their products without subsequently being held accountable under warranty theory. The terminology generally used to refer to these communications is "sales puffery." The next problem provides an opportunity to consider the fact/opinion (puffery) distinction further.

Problem on Express Warranty

Markell is in the market for a new car. As it happens, Epstein happens to have the make and model car that Markell is looking for and Epstein is interested in selling. Although Markell never specifically asked, during the course of their discussions over price and other terms, Epstein volunteered that the car was "a sweet runner" and that "you won't have any problems with her; I even had the carburetor rebuilt just last month." Eventually, the two agree on price and close the deal. Markell drives off with the car of his dreams, only to have things turn into a nightmare. Over the course of the next month, the car breaks down several times and it is anything but a "sweet runner." During one of his visits to the repair shop, Markell's mechanic informs him the carburetor is in bad shape and was never rebuilt. Does Markell have any claims against Epstein based on breach of express warranty. *Compare Crothers v. Cohen,* 384 N.W.2d 562 (Minn. App. 1986) *with Performance Motors, Inc. v. Allen,* 186 S.E.2d 161 (N.C. 1972). Are there any other facts you'd like to know before reaching a final conclusion? How, if at all, would it change your analysis if Epstein were a used car dealer and this was one of the cars on Epstein's lot?

---

3. Implied Warranties Generally

Article 2 contains two *implied* warranties relating to the quality of the goods forming the subject matter of the contract: an implied warranty of merchantability, provided that the seller is a merchant with respect to goods of that kind (§ 2-314), and, under certain circumstances, an implied warranty that the goods are fit for the particular purpose to which the buyer intends to put them (§ 2-315). We will briefly examine both of those warranties here. In addition, you will recall from our discussion in Section A, *supra*, of this section that the U.C.C. also provides implied warranties relating to the seller's *title* to the goods. Specifically, that the goods are free and clear of any third party claims, including liens, encumbrances, and claims arising by way of infringement or the like (§ 2-312). Bear in mind that implied warranties do not depend on anything the seller says or does. Recall as well that, unlike normal contract terms, an implied warranty becomes part of the contract without any affirmative undertaking by the seller. As we will see in Subsection 5, *infra*, however, a seller can, by taking affirmative steps under the Code, eliminate the warranty from the contract by way of an express disclaimer. First, however, let's look at each of these implied warranties.

4. Implied Warranty of Merchantability

Webster v. Blue Ship Tea Room, Inc.
Supreme Judicial Court of Massachusetts
347 Mass. 421, 198 N.E.2d 309 (1964)

Reardon, JJ.

This is a case which by its nature evokes earnest study not only of the law but also of the culinary traditions of the Commonwealth which bear so heavily upon its outcome. It is an action to recover damages for personal injuries sustained by reason of a breach of implied warranty of food served by the defendant in its restaurant. An auditor, whose findings of fact were not to be final, found for the plaintiff. On a retrial in the Superior Court before a judge and jury, in which the plaintiff testified, the jury returned a verdict for her. The defendant is here on exceptions to the refusal of the judge (1) to strike certain portions of the auditor's report, (2) to direct a verdict for the defendant, and (3) to allow the defendant's motion for the entry of a verdict in its favor under leave reserved.

The jury could have found the following facts: On Saturday, April 25, 1959, about 1 p.m., the plaintiff, accompanied by her sister and her aunt, entered the Blue Ship Tea Room operated by the defendant. The group was seated at a table and supplied with menus.

This restaurant, which the plaintiff characterized as "quaint," was located in Boston "on the third floor of an old building on T Wharf which overlooks the ocean."

The plaintiff, who had been born and brought up in New England (a fact of some consequence), ordered clam chowder and crabmeat salad. Within a few minutes she received tidings to the effect that "there was no more clam chowder," whereupon she ordered a cup of fish chowder. Presently, there was set before her "a small bowl of fish chowder." She had previously enjoyed a breakfast about 9 a.m. which had given her no difficulty. "The fish chowder contained haddock, potatoes, milk, water and seasoning. The chowder was milky in color and not clear. The haddock and potatoes were in chunks" (also a fact of consequence). "She agitated it a little with the spoon and observed that it was a fairly full bowl . . . . It was hot when she got it, but she did not tip it with her spoon because it was hot . . . but stirred it in an up and under motion. She denied that she did this because she was looking for something, but it was rather because she wanted an even distribution of fish and potatoes." "She started to eat it, alternating between the chowder and crackers which were on the table with . . . [some] rolls. She ate about 3 or 4 spoonfuls then stopped. She looked at the spoonfuls as she was eating. She saw equal parts of liquid, potato and fish as she spooned it into her mouth. She did not see anything unusual about it. After 3 or 4 spoonfuls she was aware that something had lodged in her throat because she couldn't swallow and couldn't clear her throat by gulping and she could feel it." This misadventure led to two esophagoscopies at the Massachusetts General Hospital, in the second of which, on April 27, 1959, a fish bone was found and removed. The sequence of events produced injury to the plaintiff which was not insubstantial.

We must decide whether a fish bone lurking in a fish chowder, about the ingredients of which there is no other complaint, constitutes a breach of implied warranty under applicable provisions of the Uniform Commercial Code,[1] the annotations to which are not helpful on this point. As the judge

---

[1]"(1) Unless excluded or modified by section 2-316, a warranty that the goods shall be merchantable is implied in a contract for their sale if the seller is a merchant with respect to goods of that kind. Under this section the serving for value of food or drink to be consumed either on the premises or elsewhere is a sale. (2) Goods to be merchantable must at least be such as . . . (c) are fit for the ordinary purposes for which such goods are used . . . ." G. L. c. 106, § 2-314.

". . . (3) (b) [W]hen the buyer before entering into the contract has examined the goods or the sample or model as fully as he desired or has refused to examine the goods there is no

put it in his charge, "Was the fish chowder fit to be eaten and wholesome? . . . [N]obody is claiming that the fish itself wasn't wholesome. . . . But the bone of contention here—I don't mean that for a pun—but was this fish bone a foreign substance that made the fish chowder unwholesome or not fit to be eaten?"

The plaintiff has vigorously reminded us of the high standards imposed by this court where the sale of food is involved (see *Flynn v. First Natl. Stores Inc.,* 296 Mass. 521, 523) and has made reference to cases involving stones in beans (*Friend v. Childs Dining Hall Co.,* 231 Mass. 65), trichinae in pork (*Holt v. Mann,* 294 Mass. 21, 22), and to certain other cases, here and elsewhere, serving to bolster her contention of breach of warranty.

The defendant asserts that here was a native New Englander eating fish chowder in a "quaint" Boston dining place where she had been before; that "[f]ish chowder, as it is served and enjoyed by New Englanders, is a hearty dish, originally designed to satisfy the appetites of our seamen and fishermen"; that "[t]his court knows well that we are not talking of some insipid broth as is customarily served to convalescents." We are asked to rule in such fashion that no chef is forced "to reduce the pieces of fish in the chowder to minuscule size in an effort to ascertain if they contained any pieces of bone." "In so ruling," we are told (in the defendant's brief), "the court will not only uphold its reputation for legal knowledge and acumen, but will, as loyal sons of Massachusetts, save our world-renowned fish chowder from degenerating into an insipid broth containing the mere essence of its former stature as a culinary masterpiece." Notwithstanding these passionate entreaties we are bound to examine with detachment the nature of fish chowder and what might happen to it under varying interpretations of the Uniform Commercial Code.

Chowder is an ancient dish preexisting even "the appetites of our seamen and fishermen." It was perhaps the common ancestor of the "more refined cream soups, purees, and bisques." *Berolzheimer, The American Woman's Cook Book* (Publisher's Guild Inc., New York, 1941) p. 176. The word "chowder" comes from the French "chaudiere," meaning a "cauldron" or "pot." "In the fishing villages of Brittany . . . 'faire la chaudiere' means to supply a cauldron in which is cooked a mess of fish and biscuit with some savoury condiments, a hodgepodge contributed by the fishermen themselves, each of whom in return receives his share of the prepared dish. The

implied warranty with regard to defects which an examination ought in the circumstances to have revealed to him . . . ." G. L. c. 106, § 2-316.

Breton fishermen probably carried the custom to Newfoundland, long famous for its chowder, whence it has spread to Nova Scotia, New Brunswick, and New England." *A New English Dictionary* (MacMillan and Co., 1893) p. 386. Our literature over the years abounds in references not only to the delights of chowder but also to its manufacture. A namesake of the plaintiff, Daniel Webster, had a recipe for fish chowder which has survived into a number of modern cookbooks[2] and in which the removal of fish bones is not mentioned at all. One old time recipe recited in the New English Dictionary study defines chowder as "A dish made of fresh fish (esp. cod) or clams, stewed with slices of pork or bacon, onions, and biscuit. 'Cider and champagne are sometimes added.' " Hawthorne, in *The House of the Seven Gables* (Allyn and Bacon, Boston, 1957) p. 8, speaks of "[a] codfish of sixty pounds, caught in the bay, [which] had been dissolved into the rich liquid of a chowder." A chowder variant, cod "Muddle," was made in Plymouth in the 1890s by taking "a three or four pound codfish, head added. Season with salt and pepper and boil in just enough water to keep from burning. When cooked, add milk and piece of butter."[3] The recitation of these ancient formulae suffices to indicate that in the construction of chowders in these parts in other years, worries about fish bones played no role whatsoever. This broad outlook on chowders has persisted in more modern cookbooks. "The chowder of today is much the same as the old chowder . . . ." *The American Woman's Cook Book*, supra, p. 176. The all embracing Fannie Farmer states in a portion of her recipe, fish chowder is made with a "fish skinned, but head and tail left on. Cut off head and tail and remove fish from backbone. Cut fish in 2-inch pieces and set aside. Put head, tail, and backbone broken in pieces, in stewpan; add 2 cups cold water and bring slowly to boiling point . . . ." The liquor thus produced from the bones is

---

[2] "Take a cod of ten pounds, well cleaned, leaving on the skin. Cut into pieces one and a half pounds thick, preserving the head whole. Take one and a half pounds of clear, fat salt pork, cut in thin slices. Do the same with twelve potatoes. Take the largest pot you have. Try out the pork first, then take out the pieces of pork, leaving in the drippings. Add to that three parts of water, a layer of fish, so as to cover the bottom of the pot; next a layer of potatoes, then two tablespoons of salt, 1 teaspoon of pepper, then the pork, another layer of fish, and the remainder of the potatoes. Fill the pot with water to cover the ingredients. Put over a good fire. Let the chowder boil twenty-five minutes. When this is done have a quart of boiling milk ready, and ten hard crackers split and dipped in cold water. Add milk and crackers. Let the whole boil five minutes. The chowder is then ready to be first-rate if you have followed the directions. An onion may be added if you like the flavor." "This chowder," he adds, "is suitable for a large fishing party." Wolcott, *The Yankee Cook Book* (Coward-McCann, Inc., New York City, 1939) p. 9.

[3] Atwood, Receipts for Cooking Fish (Avery & Doten, Plymouth, 1896) p. 8.

added to the balance of the chowder. Farmer, *The Boston Cooking School Cook Book* (Little Brown Co., 1937) p. 166.

Thus, we consider a dish which for many long years, if well made, has been made generally as outlined above. It is not too much to say that a person sitting down in New England to consume a good New England fish chowder embarks on a gustatory adventure which may entail the removal of some fish bones from his bowl as he proceeds. We are not inclined to tamper with age old recipes by any amendment reflecting the plaintiff's view of the effect of the Uniform Commercial Code upon them. We are aware of the heavy body of case law involving foreign substances in food, but we sense a strong distinction between them and those relative to unwholesomeness of the food itself, e.g., tainted mackerel (*Smith v. Gerrish,* 256 Mass. 183), and a fish bone in a fish chowder. Certain Massachusetts cooks might cavil at the ingredients contained in the chowder in this case in that it lacked the heartening lift of salt pork. In any event, we consider that the joys of life in New England include the ready availability of fresh fish chowder. We should be prepared to cope with the hazards of fish bones, the occasional presence of which in chowders is, it seems to us, to be anticipated, and which, in the light of a hallowed tradition, do not impair their fitness or merchantability. While we are buoyed up in this conclusion by *Shapiro v. Hotel Statler Corp.,* 132 F. Supp. 891 (S. D. Cal.), in which the bone which afflicted the plaintiff appeared in "Hot Barquette of Seafood Mornay," we know that the United States District Court of Southern California, situated as are we upon a coast, might be expected to share our views. We are most impressed, however, by *Allen v. Grafton,* 170 Ohio St. 249, where in Ohio, the Midwest, in a case where the plaintiff was injured by a piece of oyster shell in an order of friend [sic] oysters, Mr. Justice Taft (now Chief Justice) in a majority opinion held that "the possible presence of a piece of oyster shell in or attached to an oyster is so well known to anyone who eats oysters that we can say as a matter of law that one who eats oysters can reasonably anticipate and guard against eating such a piece of shell . . . ." (P. 259.)

Thus, while we sympathize with the plaintiff who has suffered a peculiarly New England injury, the order must be

Exceptions sustained. Judgment for the defendant.

QUESTIONS AND NOTES

1. Questions about the facts of this case

    1.1. Just how important was it to the court's decision in *Webster* that the plaintiff had been born and brought up in New England? Would the result have been different if the plaintiff was from Wyoming visiting Boston on vacation? And while we're at it, did the court conclude the chowder was merchantable because it contained no foreign substances or no *unexpected* foreign substances? If you find yourself intrigued by this question, you might want to take a look at *Green v. American Tobacco Co.*, 304 F.2d 70 (5th Cir. 1963), one of the early cigarette cases, where the court, in denying the claim, noted, "We are not dealing with an obvious, harmful foreign body in a product. . . . They (the cigarettes) are exactly like all others of the particular brand and virtually the same as all other brands on the market."

    1.2. Goods are "merchantable" if they *would pass in the trade* without objection or they are *fit for the ordinary purposes* for which such goods are used. But what does this mean? Obviously, the presence of a large fish bone did not render the chowder in *Webster* unmerchantable, but what if the facts had been that the bone was in a cup of cream of broccoli soup?

2. Questions about the law

    2.1. Should it make a difference in terms of warranty liability if the defect was latent and, therefore, not readily ascertainable to the buyer *or* the seller? In *Willis Mining. Inc. v. Noggle*, 509 S.E.2d 731 (Ga. 1998), the seller made just that argument with respect to granite blocks to be used by the buyer as gravestone monuments. About 18 months after sale of the blocks, they became discolored and had to be replaced. How would you expect the court to respond? Suppose the defect had been patent, rather than latent, and discoverable to the buyer upon exercise of reasonable diligence; how would that alter your analysis under § 2-314?

    2.2. Note that, unlike the provisions of § 2-313 relating to express warranties, the implied warranty of merchantability applies only if *the seller is a merchant with respect to goods of that kind*. What do you suppose is the reason for this limitation? How do you tell whether a seller is or is not a merchant? *See* U.C.C. § 2-104(1).

2.3. In *Bayliner Marine Corp. v. Crow*, 509 S.E.2d 499 (Va. 1999), the court suggested that the first phrase—would pass without objection in the trade—concerns whether a significant segment of the buying public would object to buying the goods, while the second phrase—fit for the ordinary purpose—concerns whether the goods are capable of performing their ordinary functions. The claim in *Crow* was that a certain fishing boat was unmerchantable because of its inability to reach a maximum speed of 30 miles per hour. How would you resolve that question under each of these tests of merchantability? What kind of evidence would be relevant to your determination? Would a significant segment of the public object to a creamy chowder that might mask the existence of a nasty fish bone? What is the ordinary function of a bowl of chowder?

3. Notes

3.1. Although most of the merchantability cases are litigated under the "fitness for the ordinary purpose" or the "would pass without objection in the trade" standard, to be merchantable for purposes of § 2-314(1) good must also, among other things, conform with any promises or representations made on the container or label. U.C.C. § 3-214(2)(f). Wouldn't such a promise or representation ordinarily constitute an express warranty? If so, what, if anything, does § 2-314(2)(f) add from the buyer's perspective?

3.2. Article 35(2)(a) of the *U.N. Convention on Contracts for the International Sale of Goods* has its own implied warranty of merchantability that requires that the goods be "fit for the purposes for which goods of the same description would ordinarily be used." How does this language compare with U.C.C. § 2-314(2)(c)?

3.3. Obviously, Justice Reardon, the author of the opinion in *Webster*, had a lot of fun with this case. Some people, however, think the term "judicial humor" is an oxymoron. Here's what Professor William Prosser (of tort law fame) had to say on the subject:

> Judicial humor is a dreadful thing. In the first place, the jokes are usually bad;. . .There seems to be something about the judicial er-

> mine which puts its wearer in the same general class with the radio comedian. He is just not funny. In the second place, the bench is not an appropriate place for levity. The litigant has vital interests at stake. His entire future, or even his life, may be trembling in the balance, and the robed buffoon who makes merry at his expense should be chocked with his own wig.

THE JUDICIAL HUMORIST: A COLLECTION OF JUDICIAL OPINIONS AND OTHER FRIVOLITIES (1952) vii–viii. We suspect Ms. Webster might be inclined to agree with Professor Prosser.

Note on Causation

Official Comment 13 to § 2-314 states that "it is of course necessary to show not only the existence of the warranty but the fact that the warranty was broken and that the breach was the *proximate cause* of the loss sustained" (emphasis added). In many cases, the trickiest element for the buyer in a claim for breach of the implied warranty of merchantability is establishing a causal link between the breach and the loss for which recovery is sought. And you thought causation issues only came up in torts? Sorry.

In *Reybold Group, Inc. v. Chemprobe Technologies, Inc.*, 721 A.2d 1267 (Del. 1998), the court suggested that proof of causation must "tend to negate other reasonable causes of the injury sustained." Thus, a buyer could presumably show that the defect in the seller's product was the cause in fact of her injury and still not prevail if she was unable to eliminate other intervening or supervening events. How can that be? Consider a buyer who purchases a chain saw from a hardware store. On assembling the product, buyer notices that the blade is not seated firmly in the housing. Nevertheless, buyer fires up the chain saw and proceeds to mangle his arm when the blade comes loose. Was the chain saw unmerchantable? Presumably so; this product would hardly pass muster in the trade. Was the defect in the chainsaw the cause in fact for buyer's injury? Sure, but for the defect the injury would never have occurred. But was the defect the proximate cause of buyer's injuries? Maybe not. Does it matter whether the instructions contained a warning not to use the chainsaw unless the blade is seated firmly in the housing?

The court in *Reybold* also stated that typically expert testimony is required to prove causation in a claim for breach of the implied warranty of merchantability. Why should this be so? Are there circumstances when the connection between the defect and the injury are so obvious that expert proof would be superfluous? Suppose the housing in which the chainsaw blade was seated was enclosed in a casing and not visible to the naked eye? If the buyer is injured when the blade comes loose is expert testimony really necessary to prove causation between the defect and the loss? And by the way, who are these experts? Do they work for free? Of course not, they're retained and paid for by the parties. Doesn't that tend to color their judgment? How can their testimony be taken seriously? Put another way, what safeguards exist to ensure that the expert will not just give the opinion that the party paying him or her wants? Are these safeguards adequate?

Problems on Merchantability

1. You all remember the "Clapper" don't you? That was the little device, marketed through television ads, which allowed you to turn an appliance on and off by clapping twice. Well it seems Edna Hubbs, an 80-year old woman suffering from arthritis and osteoporosis, purchased a Clapper. Alas, upon installing the Clapper, she found that her claps were not activating the device. Determined to make it work, Edna thereupon attempted one last, extra hard clap. Lamentably, however, the effort was too much and Edna sustained injuries to her hand and wrist. Edna proceeded to file suit against the manufacturer and the retailer of the device for breach of the warranty of merchantability. How should Edna's case be resolved? Lest you think we're making this up, see *Hubbs v. Joseph Enterprises,* 604 N.Y.S.2d 292 (N.Y. Sup. Ct. 1993).

2. Bruce Markell, Jr., a first year law student with a rare blood type, received a call from the local Red Cross office telling him that there was a critical shortage of his blood type and asking him to consider donating. The Red Cross official explained that a bloodmobile would be on campus the next week. Being a compassionate soul, Bruce showed up at the bloodmobile and donated a pint of his

blood. Afterwards, a nurse insisted that he have a glass of orange juice and some cookies supplied by the Red Cross to help him regain his strength and prevent light-headedness or even fainting. Bruce, never one to pass on freebies, had about six cookies along with his juice. As a good will gesture, Briesckes Bakery had donated the cookies to the Red Cross. Later that afternoon, Bruce became violently ill and had to be hospitalized. Tests revealed a form of food poisoning typically associated with bacteria that germinate in processed flour. Bruce is convinced that the cookies were the source of his woes. As a result of his illness, which came toward the end of the semester, Bruce was unable to take his final exams. Therefore, he will now have to spend an extra semester in law school in order to graduate. Bruce has brought a suit against both the Red Cross and Briesckes seeking to recover the additional education costs he will now incur and the wages he has lost by having to delay accepting full-time employment. What result in Bruce's case and why? *See, inter alia,* § 2-318.

---

5. Implied Warranty of Fitness for Particular Purpose

In many instances a buyer will have purchased goods for a particular purpose or with a particular objective in mind. In some of these cases the goods will not be fit for the particular purpose the buyer had in mind. If the seller affirmed that the goods would serve that purpose, the buyer will have a claim for breach of express warranty. In other situations, the goods will not accomplish the purpose because they are unmerchantable, *i.e.* not fit for the purposes for which such goods are ordinarily used. In still other cases, however, there will be no express warranty concerning the suitability of the goods to the purpose for which they were acquired *and* the failure to satisfy the buyer's purpose will not be attributable to a defect that renders the goods unmerchantable. What recourse does the buyer have in these situations? Sometimes, for example when the buyer was relying on her own judgment about the adequacy of the goods, there will be no recourse. In these cases, the hard lesson learned would be that the buyer should have done a more careful investigation into the suitability of the goods to the purpose for which they were acquired before purchasing. In other circumstances, however, the buyer may have recourse against the seller for breach of the implied warranty of fitness for a particular purpose under U.C.C. § 2-315. Nevertheless, establishing a breach of the fitness warranty when the goods fail to do what the buyer wanted them to do is a little trickier than establishing breach of the merchantability warranty when the goods are simply defective. The next case and the material that follow, are intended to help you to flesh out what the buyer must prove to make out a case under § 2-315.

Leal v. Holtvogt
Court of Appeals of Ohio
123 Ohio App.3d 51, 702 N.E.2d 1246 (1988)

FAIN, J.

* * *

Joseph and Claudia Holtvogt owned and operated Shady Glen Arabians, a horse barn in Miami County, Ohio. They were experienced in Arabian horse training, breeding, boarding, selling, and showing. In 1992, the Leals, novices in the equine industry, decided to begin raising horses. In April, 1993, Ferdinand Leal began visiting Shady Glen Arabians regularly to learn how to ride and handle horses. Before long, a friendship developed between the Holtvogts and Leals, and Ferdinand Leal began spending three to four days each week at the Holtvogts' barn helping Joseph Holtvogt with the horses.

In late 1993, the Leals decided they wanted to start a breeding program by purchasing a stallion to breed with a mare they owned. At first, they were interested in purchasing Procale, a stallion owned by John Bowman. After talking to Mr. Holtvogt about Procale, the Leals decided not to buy him. The Holtvogts then offered the Leals a one-half interest in Mc Que Jabask, an Arabian stallion that the Holtvogts owned. At trial, the Leals testified that before they agreed to invest in Mc Que Jabask, Mr. Holtvogt made a number of statements regarding the stallion, such as: Mc Que Jabask was a national top ten champion in three categories; he was an all-around winning stallion; he earns $20,000.00 per year in stud fees; he is capable of attaining national show titles again; and his foals were selling for $6,000 to $10,000 each [these statements will be referred to hereinafter as "the five contested statements"].

In January, 1994, the Leals and Holtvogts entered into a contract of sale for a one-half interest in Mc Que Jabask for $16,000. The contract also established a partnership agreement, which called for the parties to share equally in the expenses and profits arising from their joint ownership of Mc Que Jabask.

There was expert testimony that prior to January, 1994, Mc Que Jabask had been treated for lameness and was suffering a chronic lameness condition in his right rear and fore fetlocks. Mr. Holtvogt testified that he had taken the stallion for lameness treatments numerous times. He also stated that he did not disclose this information to the Leals.

By July, 1994, the Leals were dissatisfied with the partnership and indicated to the Holtvogts that they wanted either a refund of their money or a remedy for their concerns. In March, 1995, the mortality insurance on Mc Que Jabask lapsed when neither the Leals nor the Holtvogts paid the insurance premium.

* * *

On January 17, 1996, Mc Que Jabask died from stomach ulcer complications. Since neither party had renewed the stallion's mortality insurance, Mc Que Jabask was uninsured.

In February, 1995, the Leals filed suit against the Holtvogts, who then brought counterclaims against the Leals. The Miami Country Common Pleas Court found that the Holtvogts had negligently misrepresented the stallion's condition and that they had breached an "express warranty on the condition of the horse for the purposes intended" and awarded the Leals $16,000 in compensatory damages. * * *

II

The Holtvogts' Second Assignment of Error is as follows:

> THE TRIAL COURT COMMITTED REVERSIBLE ERROR WHEN IT HELD THAT DEFENDANTS' ACTIONS CONSTITUTED NEGLIGENT MISREPRESENTATION BECAUSE PLAINTIFFS FAILED TO PRESENT ANY FACTUAL EVIDENCE WHATSOEVER WHICH WOULD LEAD A REASONABLE PERSON TO BELIEVE THAT MC QUE JABASK WAS LAME AT THE TIME THE PARTIES ENTERED INTO THE PARTNERSHIP AGREEMENT OR THAT MC QUE JABASK WAS NOT FIT TO BE SHOWN.

* * *

Negligent misrepresentation is defined as follows:

> [One] who, in the course of his business, profession or employment, or in any other transaction in which he has a pecuniary interest, *supplies false information* for the guidance of others in their business transactions, is subject to liability for pecuniary loss caused to them by their justifiable reliance upon the information, if he fails to exercise reasonable care or competence in communicating the information. *Textron Financial Corp. v. Nationwide Mut. Ins. Co. (1996),* 115 Ohio App. 3d 137, 149, 684 N.E.2d 1261*, cert. denied*, 78 Ohio St. 3d 1425, 1425, 676 N.E.2d 531. (Emphasis in original.)

[The court ruled that the concealment of Mc Que Jabask's lameness did not support a claim of negligent misrepresentation since it was not an *affirmative* false statement. However, the court concluded that the record did support the trial court's finding that the Holtvogts negligently misrepresented to the Leals that Mc Que Jabask was fit to be shown, and thus overruled the Holtvogts' second assignment of error.]

III

The Holtvogts' First Assignment of Error is as follows:

> THE TRIAL COURT COMMITTED REVERSIBLE ERROR WHEN IT FOUND THAT DEFENDANTS' ACTIONS CONSTITUTED A BREACH OF AN EXPRESSED WARRANTY BECAUSE THE TRANSACTION BETWEEN THE PARTIES DOES NOT MEET THE DEFINITIONAL REQUIREMENTS UNDER OHIO EXPRESSED WARRANTY LAW; DEFENDANTS' CONDUCT DOES NOT RISE TO THE LEVEL OF AN EXPRESSED WARRANTY; AND THE INTEGRATION CLAUSE IN THE PARTNERSHIP AGREEMENT PRECLUDES THE COURT'S CONSIDERATION OF ANY AND ALL PRIOR ORAL REPRESENTATIONS.

The Holtvogts' argument that there was no breach of an express warranty is three-fold. First, they argue that Ohio's express warranty law is not applicable to their transaction. Second, they argue that their conduct was not sufficient to constitute an express warranty. Third, they argue that there was a clause in the parties' agreement precluding consideration of any oral representations.

We begin with the Holtvogts' argument that Ohio's express warranty law does not apply to the transaction that occurred between the parties. The Holtvogts contend that an express warranty can arise only if there has been a "sale" between the parties and that their transaction with the Leals created a "partnership agreement," not a "sale."

We first address this argument by noting that Ohio warranty law is governed by the Uniform Commercial Code, Sales, R.C. [Article 2]. The scope of [Article 2] is set forth in [§ 2-102], which provides in part that "sections [§§ 2-101 to 2-725], inclusive, of the Revised Code, apply to transactions in goods." Goods are defined as "all things * * * which are moveable at the time of identification to the contract for sale * * * [and] must be both existing and identified before any interest in them can pass." [§ 2-105(1), (2)]. The Arabian stallion, Mc Que Jabask, was moveable, existing, and could be identified at the time of the contract. Thus, he would qualify as a "good" under [§ 2-102].

As for the Holtvogts' contention that the transaction was not a "sale," they correctly argue that a "sale" is defined as "the passing of title from the seller to the buyer for a price." [§ 2-106(1)]. There is no statutory requirement, however, that full title to the good must pass from the buyer to the seller. In fact, [Article 2] explicitly states, in its definition of "goods," "there may be a sale of a part interest in existing identified goods." [§ 2-103(3)]. Thus, although the transaction involved the sale of only a half-interest in Mc Que Jabask, the transaction was within the definitional requirements of [Article 2] and thus is governed by Ohio warranty law. Therefore, the first part of the Holtvogts' argument is not well-taken.

We next address the Holtvogts' argument that their conduct did not amount to an express warranty. The trial court found that "* * * the [Holtvogts] engaged in 'puffing' at the time of the sale of the one-half interest in the horse but did not fraudulently misrepresent a material fact." Although the trial court did not enlighten us as to what part of the Holtvogts' conduct it believed to be "puffing," our review of the record leads us to believe that the trial court was talking about the five contested statements that the Leals claim the Holtvogts made. The Holtvogts contend that the trial court's finding that they engaged in "puffing" is inconsistent with the trial court's conclusion that they gave the Leals an express warranty.

* * *

"Puffing," or merely stating the seller's opinion, cannot amount to an express warranty. * * * The five contested statements were the subject of extensive testimony during the trial. Mr. Holtvogt denied making any of these statements and the Leals repeatedly testified that Mr. Holtvogt did make these statements. The trial court seems to have found the five contested statements to be "puffing." Our review of the record shows that there is credible and competent evidence that these five contested statements were no more than "puffing." The Holtvogts correctly argue that when statements are mere "puffing," they cannot constitute an express warranty.

We cannot sustain this Assignment of Error, however, because we find that the Holtvogts breached an implied warranty of fitness for a particular purpose.

In its entry, the trial court found the following:

> "* * * the information the [Holtvogts] failed to apprise the [Leals] was the lameness of the horse at the time the contract was executed in January 1994.
>
> The [Leals] suffered damages in the amount of $16,000.00 as a result of this negligent misrepresentation.
>
> The *same set of facts* establish a cause of action for breach of express warranty *on the condition of the horse for the purposes intended* * * * ." (emphasis added).

In its entry, the trial court did not just say an express warranty was breached, but rather said that an "express warranty on the condition of the horse for the purposes intended" was breached. We conclude that the trial court intended to say that an implied warranty of fitness for a particular purpose was breached. Our conclusion is supported by the trial court's statement that the same set of facts establishes claims for both a breach of express warranty on the condition of the horse for the purposes intended and negligent misrepresentation. We note that the elements of a claim for negligent misrepresentation and breach of an implied warranty of fitness for a particular purpose are quite similar, while the elements of negligent misrepresentation and breach of an express warranty are not similar. Thus, we conclude that the trial court, in its conclusions of law, intended to say that an implied warranty of fitness for a particular purpose was given and breached by the Holtvogts when they failed to disclose Mc Que Jabask's lameness to the Leals.

An implied warranty of fitness for a particular purpose is covered by the Uniform Commercial Code, Sales, [§ 2-315], which provides:

> "Where the seller at the time of contracting has reason to know any particular purpose for which the goods are required and that the buyer is relying on the seller's skill or judgment to select or furnish suitable goods, there is unless excluded or modified under section [2-316] of the Revised Code an implied warranty that the goods shall be fit for such purpose."

Ohio courts have set forth the following test to determine whether an implied warranty of fitness for a particular purpose has been created: (1) the seller must have reason to know of the buyer's particular purpose; (2) the seller must have reason to know that the buyer is relying on the seller's skill or judgment to furnish or select appropriate goods; and (3) the buyer must, in fact, rely upon the seller's skill or judgment. * * *

The first element requires that Mr. Holtvogt knew why the Leals decided to buy an interest in Mc Que Jabask. From our review of the record, we see that Mr. Holtvogt clearly knew that the Leals wanted to buy an interest in the stallion to start a breeding program. Mr. Holtvogt testified:

> " * * * [The Leals] had explained what type of horse they were looking for [and] it seemed to me that [Mc Que] Jabask fit the bill [of] what they were looking for and that's why I mentioned to them, uh, to Ferdinand that there might be a possibility that we would be interested in selling part interest in him.
>
> * * * The things that they were saying, * * * those things were, were present in, in [Mc Que] Jabask * * * .
>
> * * * It just, it made sense that, you know, in the fact that the Leals could breed to [Mc Que] Jabask * * * . * * * Um, we could, uh, with the experience and the reputation that we had we could help market their foals, um, it was, I really felt that it was something that could work."

Thus, evidence of the first element of an implied warranty of fitness for a particular purpose was presented at trial.

The second element requires that Mr. Holtvogt had reason to know that the Leals were relying on his skill and judgment to select or furnish the appropriate goods. Evidence presented at trial shows that Mr. Holtvogt knew, or at least should have known, that the Leals were relying on his judgment when they purchased an interest in the stallion. The relationship between Mr. Holtvogt and Mr. Leal was like that of a teacher and student. Mr. Leal spent a great deal of time at the Holtvogts' barn, helping Mr. Holtvogt with the horses and learning from Mr. Holtvogt. Mr. Holtvogt testified that he was an expert trainer and breeder with Arabian horses, and the evidence shows that he knew Mr. Leal knew very little about horses. Furthermore, the Leals testified that they were interested in purchasing another horse, Procale, but that Mr. Holtvogt steered them away from that horse, saying that horse was not the type of horse that the Leals wanted to buy. Mr. Holtvogt even testified that he mentioned Mc Que Jabask to the Leals because the stallion was the type of horse that they were looking for. Thus, evidence of the second element of an implied warranty of fitness for a particular purpose was presented at trial.

The third element requires that the Leals actually did rely upon Mr. Holtvogt's skill and judgment when they purchased an interest in the stallion. The trial court found that the Leals justifiably relied upon the Holtvogts' representations regarding the stallion. This finding is not against the manifest weight of the evidence. As stated earlier, there was competent and credible evidence presented at trial to support this finding as both Leals were novices in the horse industry and they testified that they trusted Mr. Holtvogt and considered him to be the expert. Thus, evidence of the third element was presented at trial.

Because all three elements were proven at trial, we conclude that an implied warranty of fitness for a particular purpose was given by the Holtvogts to the Leals at the time of the sale. There must be evidence that the warranty was breached if the Leals are to recover. *Delorise Brown, M.D., Inc.*, 86 Ohio App. 3d at 363. "Whether a warranty has failed to fulfill its essential purpose is ordinarily a determination for the factfinder." *Id.*

The trial court found that a warranty was breached by the Holtvogts because the horse was lame. As stated above, competent and credible evidence was presented to support the trial court's finding that Mc Que Jabask suffered from chronic lameness at the time of the sale. At trial, Dixie Gansmiller testified that even though a lame stallion could stand for stud, its lameness would affect her decision whether to breed her mares with it. Thus, we conclude that competent and credible evidence in the record does demonstrate that Mc Que Jabask was not fit for the particular purpose intended by the Leals when they invested in him.

* * *

Judgment accordingly.

QUESTIONS

1. Questions about the facts of this case

   1.1. Presumably, the court came up with the $16,000 in "compensatory damages" based upon the amount the Leals had paid for a one-half interest in Mc Que Jabask. Did that award really give the Leals the "benefit of their bargain"?

   1.2. What was the "purpose" for which the Leals acquired an interest in Mc Que Jabask? Did the horse's lameness make him no longer fit for that purpose?

   1.3. The court describes the relationship between Mr. Holtvogt and Mr. Leal as "like that of teacher and student." Why was that fact important?

2. Questions about the law

   2.1. The court of appeals in *Leal* agreed with the trial court that the "five contested statements" were no more than mere puffing. Do you agree? How do you think the court in *Daughtrey, supra,* at 624, would have characterized those statements? Should evidence relating to those statements have been excluded under the parol evidence rule?

   2.2. The court of appeals also concluded that the failure to disclose Mc Que Jabask's lameness could not support a negligent misrepresentation claim because it was not an *affirmative* false statement. Isn't deliberate concealment of a material fact tantamount to an affirmative misstatement of fact? Why didn't the Leals make a non-disclosure argument along the lines of *Weintraub v. Krobatsch, supra,* at 270?

   2.3. The court of appeals concludes that when the trial court in its entry of judgment stated not just that an express warranty was breached, but that an "express warranty on the condition of the horse for the purposes intended" was breached, it really meant to say that the sellers breached the implied warranty of fitness for a particular purpose. Do you think the trial court really just misspoke? If not, how should the court of appeals have disposed of the case?

2.4. Obviously, the Leals did not bring a claim for breach of the warranty of merchantability. Why do you suppose their lawyer made that judgment? What would you have done? Is there an upside to including alternative causes of action in a complaint even though you know they may be weak? Is there a downside? How does a court deal with multiple warranties? As for the last question, we offer you the next case.

The Singer Company v. E.I. du Pont de Nemours and Company
United States Court of Appeals, Eighth Circuit
579 F.2d 433 (1978)

HANSON, Senior District Judge.

In this diversity contract action, the Singer Company sued to recover losses incurred when the E.I. du Pont de Nemours and Company allegedly breached both an express warranty and an implied warranty of fitness in failing to provide plaintiff with suitable industrial paint for its plant operations at Red Bud, Illinois. The case was submitted to a jury only on the implied warranty theory, and judgment was returned for Singer in the amount of $108,367.00. Defendant was awarded no recovery on either of its two attendant counterclaims. Du Pont unsuccessfully moved for judgments notwithstanding the verdict and for new trial, contending that the trial court improperly instructed the jury and that there was insufficient evidence to support the jury verdicts. Du Pont appeals from those rulings. We affirm.

Singer became interested during late 1972 in obtaining an electrodeposition paint system for its Red Bud, Illinois plant, where until this time the metal, or ware, used in the manufacture of air-conditioners and furnaces had been painted in a spray system. Electrodeposition is a method of painting by which pretreated ware is conveyed through an electrically charged paint tank and the ware, serving as an anode, is coated with paint in an electroplating type of process. After a period of negotiation between representatives from the two parties, Du Pont, in September and October of 1972, was contracted to provide Singer with paint for its approximately 22,000 gallon tank. Three additional companies were contracted to provide other interrelated steps in the overall finishing process, steps such as pretreatment of the ware and conveyance of the ware through the entire system.

From the beginning, in October of 1973, Singer experienced problems with the electrodeposition system. Ware frequently emerged from the paint tank with "blotches" and "streaks." Repainting was necessary. Du Pont, which supervised the installation and starting up of this electrodeposition system, tried unsuccessfully for six months to correct this problem. Finally, in April of 1974, the Du Pont paint was removed from the tank and replaced with paint supplied by the Sherwin-Williams Company. This lawsuit was filed the following year.

The nub of the factual controversy in the trial court was the cause for the blotches and streaks on the painted ware. Du Pont maintained that the problem was with the substrate, pretreated ware; Singer, however, insisted that the paint was at fault. In countering Singer's claim, Du Pont argued that the paint provided to plaintiff met contract specifications until the substrate was altered in February of 1974, at which time Du Pont could no longer be held to have expressly warranted its product. Singer contends that even if the specifications of this express warranty were met, Du Pont had given an implied warranty of fitness for a particular purpose by representing throughout the period in question that its paint would satisfy plaintiff's needs. Over Du Pont's objection, the trial court instructed the jury on implied warranty for a particular purpose. The issue of express warranty was not submitted.

I. The Uniform Commercial Code

While disagreeing on whether the trial court should have instructed as to an implied warranty of fitness for a particular purpose, the parties are properly in accord that the Illinois adoption of the Uniform Commercial Code governs the disposition of this case. * * * . There is also no dispute that the "all tests" provision of the contract, which specified such set standards as color and texture that the paint was to satisfy upon pretreated laboratory test panels, was an express warranty pursuant to Section 2-313(1)(b) of the U.C.C. But Singer claims that the contract further preserved an implied warranty of fitness, a warranty that pursuant to Section 2-315 assured plaintiff the paint supplied would satisfactorily cover its substrate. A paragraph in the contract provided:

> None of the provisions or remedies herein are in lieu of any claims for damages Buyer may have at law or equity under the Uniform Commer-

cial Code or otherwise, for the breach of any contracts or warranties with Buyer, which rights are specifically reserved by Buyer.

Du Pont contends that parties who have an express warranty regarding a contracted for item cannot also have an implied warranty of fitness for that same item. The warranty of fitness for a specific purpose is alleged to have been limited by expressly defining it in a set of specifications, and Du Pont claims that to find otherwise would permit Singer to escape the parties' true contractual bargain.

* * *

Pertinent sections of the U.C.C., and the comments pursuant thereto, lend inferential support to Singer's position that the implied warranty of fitness was cumulative to and not excluded by the express warranty. Section 2-316(2), with regard to the exclusion or modification of such warranties, states:

> . . . To exclude or modify any implied warranty of fitness the exclusion must be a writing and *conspicuous*. (Emphasis added.)

Comment 9 to that section provides in part:

> The situation in which the buyer gives precise and complete *specifications to the seller* is not explicitly covered in this section, but this is a frequent circumstance by which the implied warranties may be excluded. The warranty of fitness for a particular purpose would not normally arise since in such a situation there is usually *no reliance on the seller by the buyer*. (Emphasis added.)

See also U.C.C. § 2-315, comment 2. Because the evidence in this case fully indicates that it was not the buyer but the seller who in fact recommended and supplied the paint specifications, and remained in control of the paint tank, it would appear that the trial court did not err in its determination that an implied warranty of fitness was at issue. This is especially so in view of the purported exclusion of this warranty, which could be scarcely termed "conspicuous."

A reading of the U.C.C. to suggest that an express warranty and an implied warranty of fitness are not necessarily mutually exclusive, as Singer has argued, receives support from Code authority.

> The fact that a warranty of fitness for a particular purpose does or does not exist has no bearing on any other warranty or theory of product liability. Conversely, the fact that there may be some other basis for liability of the defendant does not preclude the existence of a warranty for a particular purpose. *Thus the fact that there is a warranty of conformity to sample [an express warranty] does not preclude the existence of a warranty for a particular purpose.* (Emphasis added.) Anderson, Uniform Commercial Code § 2-315:5 (1970).

* * * Relevant case law, in the balance, further indicates that an express warranty would not control under the circumstances of this case.

Cases can be found prior to the adoption of the U.C.C. to support Du Pont's argument of mutual exclusiveness. This Court, without specific adoption of the position, recognized in *Hercules Powder Co. v. Rich,* 3 F.2d 12 (8th Cir. 1924) that there was law to the effect that an implied warranty of fitness could not prevail in the presence of an express warranty on the same item or subject.

An express warranty excludes an implied warranty relating to the same subject or of the same general nature, on the theory that no warranty should be implied where the parties with relation to the very same subject have expressed by words the warranty by which they will be bound. *Id.* at 18.

There was also case law to the contrary. * * * But while there may have once been a split of authority, we fail to find since the general adoption of the above-quoted sections of the U.C.C. any case holding directly in favor of Du Pont's mutual exclusivity agreement. In fact unless the exclusion of the implied warranty of fitness is specifically and conspicuously excluded, courts, often relying upon Section 2-317,[4] have found that such implied and express warranties can be cumulative and co-exist within the same agreement. * * * .

Du Pont, in arguing the law upon appeal, relies principally upon two types of cases that have arisen under the U.C.C.: those in which there has been a showing that the buyer, in possession or control of the item, failed to follow the express warranty specifications; and those where an enforceable disclaimer of an implied warranty has been established. With respect to the first type of case, it is clear that the trial court did not confront a situation

[4]Section 2-317 of the U.C.C. provides in part:

> Warranties whether express or implied shall be construed as consistent with each other and as cumulative. . . .

where a buyer in possession or control of an item failed to follow seller's specifications, used the item in a manner for which it was not intended, lost that for which he had contracted, and then erroneously claimed a breach of an implied warranty for fitness. * * * Here, Du Pont, as the seller, was in control of the disputed item. No one denies that Du Pont was throughout this time in control of Singer's paint tank, directing its operation and determining its contents.

The disclaimer cases are likewise inapplicable. Even without a paragraph in the contract reserving all further warranties under the U.C.C., Du Pont would have difficulty in arguing that an express warranty of the paint effected a disclaimer of any further warranty. It is clear from these cases that disclaimers under the Code are not favored and are limited whenever possible. * * *

Du Pont also argues in general that to permit Singer to assert an implied warranty of fitness would be to allow utilization of the U.C.C. in avoidance of the parties' true bargain. The true bargain, though, is less than apparent from the face of the contract. This was not a situation where a buyer ordered according to specifications and then claimed an implied warranty of fitness when the product failed to measure up to expectations. In this instance, the buyer approached the seller describing the results desired and the seller professed to be able to supply it, thereby inducing a reliance that created the possibility of an implied warranty of fitness. Notwithstanding the express warranty contained within the specifications particularly defining and describing the item to be supplied, there may have been a further warranty that an item with those specifications would accomplish certain results or be adequate for the specified purpose. That is, the accomplishment of the purpose might be viewed as the essence of the contractual undertaking, and not the mere furnishing of the specified item. Nothing within this contract, or in writings or statements subsequent to it, indicate whether the end of the agreement was the specified item or the use for which the item was intended. * * *

Du Pont simply failed to negotiate a contract that clearly delineated and limited allocation of risk. This case would never have arisen had defendant, as a party to and a scrivener of the contract, either inserted a specific disclaimer or demanded that the warranty savings clause be deleted.

Having left the contract ambiguous, the question as to whether use rather than supply of the product was intended to be of the essence, as well as questions regarding buyer's reliance and seller's knowledge of that reliance, are for jury determination. Such were submitted to the jury in this case under the trial court's following instruction.

> Your verdict on the plaintiff's claim must be for the plaintiff if you believe:
>
> First: The defendant sold paint to the plaintiff.
>
> Second: The defendant knew the use for which plaintiff purchased the paint, and
>
> Third: Plaintiff reasonably relied upon defendant's judgment for the suitability of the paint for such use, and,
>
> Fourth: The paint was not suitable for such use, and
>
> Fifth: As a direct result plaintiff was damaged.

Du Pont contends on appeal, as it did below, that the trial court was in error giving an instruction which allowed the jury to determine the construction of the contract. The question regarding the presence of an implied warranty, defendant maintains, constituted a question of law that should have been determined by the trial judge. Moreover, it is claimed that the jury should have been instructed with respect to the express warranty.

The better rule, when there remains an issue of contractual intent, is to submit the issue to the jury unless the evidence is so clear that no reasonable person would determine the issue but one way. * * * Du Pont fails to offer any sustaining reason as to why the construction of an ambiguous contract, which involves the existence or nonexistence of an implied warranty of fitness under the U.C.C., should also not be left to a jury determination. * * * The question of buyer's reliance and seller's knowledge of that reliance is a factual inquiry particularly well-suited for jury deliberation. U.C.C. §§ 2-316, 2-317 * * *

There was no prejudicial error in refusing to instruct the jury with respect to the express warranty. As concluded above, the law is that an implied warranty of fitness is not necessarily excluded by the presence of an express warranty. Thus, satisfaction of the express warranty, a factual issue that could be and was argued to the jury, would not preclude the jury from further consideration of the alleged implied warranty. We note that defendant, in presenting its appeal, did indicate that its primary purpose in requesting the express warranty instruction was to implement this mistaken contention that no implied warranty could be present by the fact that it had been specified and those specifications met. Plaintiff, while not conceding that the express warranty had been satisfied, agreed to go to the jury on the issue of implied warranty alone.

II. Substantial Evidence

Once having determined that the issue of implied warranty was properly submitted to the jury, sufficiency of the evidence becomes the controlling inquiry. We review the evidence to determine whether there was sufficient evidence for the jury to find that Singer reasonably relied upon Du Pont's judgment regarding the suitability of the paint, that Du Pont knew the use for which Singer purchased the paint, and that the paint was not suitable for such use. On appeal, Du Pont does not appear to contest the interrelated issues of buyer's "reliance" and seller's "knowledge." In view of the extensive negotiations prior to the contract, Du Pont's supervision of the installation of the paint tank, and the continuing presence of Du Pont in a supervisory capacity throughout the period in question, defendant's reason for not pursuing these lines of argument is apparent. Du Pont does contend, however, that there is insufficient proof to show that the paint was not suitable for Singer's use and was the cause of the blotches and streaks on the painted ware. It insists that an uneven pretreatment, with resulting un-uniform substrate, was the source of the problem.

[The court proceeded to review the evidence put on by Singer at trial concerning the cause for the blotches and streaks on painted ware. This consisted of expert scientific testimony to the effect that impurities and nonuniformity of elements within the paint tank were the source of the problem as well as evidence that after the Du Pont paint was removed and replaced with a different manufacturer's paint the problem was resolved.]

III. Conclusion

In reviewing the evidence pursuant to the judgment n.o.v. standards, we cannot conclude that Singer failed to offer the necessary evidence to sustain a jury verdict against Du Pont for a breach of an implied warranty of fitness. Clearly, Du Pont, which reviewed the entire finishing system, knew at the time of contracting the particularized use for which plaintiff purchased the paint, and Singer reasonably relied upon Du Pont's judgment that its paint was suitable for the electrodeposition system. Du Pont makes some argument that the change in substrate affected the suitability, but it was an argument not pressed upon appeal. In any event, if defendant did not consider itself bound by warranty to do anything more than furnish a paint of particular specifications, we find it difficult to explain not only why Du Pont supervised the installation of the system, but worked to alleviate the problems during the entire period its paint was in the tank.

Finally, in satisfaction of the last element necessary to an implied warranty of fitness, the evidence was sufficient to show that Du Pont's paint was not suitable for Singer's use. The evidence here presents a close question. Yet giving the "jury verdict the benefit of all reasonable inferences to be drawn from the evidence," this Court, though we might have cast our verdict otherwise, cannot say there was no more than a scintilla of evidence to support the jury verdict. The testimony of Singer employees and [plaintiff's expert] De Vittorio, and such evidence as the unexplained blotches and streaks upon the laboratory test panels, sufficiently takes this case from the undeterminative equipoise for which defendant argues. * * *

With respect to damages, which were reasonably assessed, we find the trial court did not err in denying a judgment n.o.v. on Du Pont's counterclaim for paint sold and delivered or further counterclaim for value of services rendered. Nor did the trial court abuse its discretion in denying defendant's motions for new trial.

The judgment appealed from is affirmed.

QUESTIONS AND NOTES

1. Questions about the facts of this case

    1.1. What specific facts were most favorable to Singer? What facts tended to support Du Pont's argument?

    1.2. What did Du Pont *expressly* warrant? Why do you suppose the issue of express warranty was not submitted to the jury? Why did Du Pont think it was prejudicial error not to submit the issue of express warranty to the jury?

    1.3. Of what significance was the fact that the Sherman-Williams paint apparently performed without any of the problems experienced with the Du Pont paint? Why does the court refer to the evidence regarding breach of the fitness warranty as presenting a close call?

What other facts would you like to know about the Sherwin-Williams paint?

2. Questions about the law

2.1. The decision in *Singer* is a good example of how a court goes about analyzing issues arising under a statute, but why did the court relegate its discussion of § 2-317 to a footnote? That curiosity aside, note how the court used the specific provisions of Article 2 and the Official Comments to dismantle each of Du Pont's contentions. Sometimes, however, the statute does not address every issue that arises in a case. For example, in *Singer,* Du Pont contended that the issue regarding the presence of a warranty is a question of law for the court and not one of fact for the jury. Article 2 simply does not offer any guidance as to whether the question should be regarded as one of law or fact. What should a court do in that situation? What did the *Singer* court do? *See* U.C.C. § 1-103.

2.2. In deciding that the issue of contractual intent was properly submitted to the jury, was the court saying that the issue of the presence of a fitness warranty was not a question of law?

2.3. According to the court in *Singer,* for there to be a breach of the fitness warranty the buyer must show that the seller *knew* both the buyer's purpose in acquiring the goods and that the buyer was relying on the seller's expertise in selecting suitable goods. Is that consistent with the *Leal* court's view of the elements of an action under § 2-315?

2.4. If you represent Du Pont, after the case is decided, what changes would you recommend that the company make in supply contracts of this type?

3. Notes

3.1. Article 35(2)(b) of the *U.N. Convention on Contracts for the International Sale of Goods* provides that goods will not be deemed as conforming to the contract unless they "are fit for any particular purpose expressly or impliedly made known to the seller at the time of the conclusion of the contract, except where the circumstances show that the buyer did not rely, or that it was unreasonable for him to rely, on the seller's skill and judgment." How does this provision differ from the comparable U.C.C. warranty? Can you construct a situation where there would be a breach of warranty under domestic law but not under *CISG*?

3.2. As the facts in *Singer* illustrate, sometimes warranties can conflict. Du Pont's argument that its express warranty negated the implied warranty of fitness was directly contradicted by § 2-317(c). However, the exception in that provision for the fitness warranty does not apply to other implied warranties, including an implied warranty of merchantability. Thus, if the two warranties cannot be construed consistently with one another, under the terms of § 2-317(c), the express warranty displaces the merchantability warranty. Is this an invitation to crafty sellers to deprive their buyers of a merchantability warranty with an express warranty that is not as broad? Suppose a seller warrants that her product is free from defects in workmanship and materials for three months. In the middle of the fourth month, the product breaks down because of a serious, latent manufacturing defect. Does the buyer have a valid breach of implied warranty claim? *See Koellmer v. Chrysler Motors Corp.*, 276 A.2d 807 (Conn. Cir. Ct. 1970). If so, what does the language in § 2-317(c) mean? If not, hasn't the seller effectively disclaimed the merchantability warranty without going thorough the required statutory procedure? To answer these questions, perhaps we better also take a look at the Code's provisions relating to warranty disclaimers.

---

6. Disclaimers of Warranties

The court in *Singer* obviously considered it relevant that Du Pont had not followed the regular statutory procedure for excluding an implied warranty of fitness for particular purpose. This implies, of course, that, had Du Pont been more conscientious, it could have disclaimed the warranty. But why should this ever be permitted? As we have discussed, the purpose for warranty theory is to allocate to the seller the risk that the goods do not conform to general or specific expectations. After all, usually the seller, and particularly a professional seller, is in the best position to know whether there is a problem with the goods and, in any event, the seller can pass the risk along via insurance, higher prices, etc. But this is not always the case. Sometimes the seller is in no better position than the buyer to avoid the loss. Moreover, sometimes the buyer is willing to accept the risk, typically because it means a better price. If warranties were absolute, the parties would lose the flexibility to negotiate over this term and the buyer would always pay the higher price. Have you purchased a computer, a television, or perhaps a stereo system lately? Did the cashier offer you an extended warranty? Did you take it? We bet you didn't. Why not?

The U.C.C.'s rules governing effective warranty disclaimers are set forth in U.C.C. § 2-316. Take a look at that statute right now. You'll see that the procedures differ depending on which warranty is at issue and that some warranties are harder to get rid of then others. It should also be apparent that the subject is a technical one. Therefore, an extended discussion of warranty disclaimers, and the related topic of seller efforts to limit liability for breach of warranty, must await the upper-level commercial law courses. However, we think it might be instructional, and perhaps even helpful in your personal life, to examine the basic framework right now.

Office Supply Co., Inc. v. Basic/Four Corporation

United States District Court, Eastern District of Wisconsin
538 F. Supp. 776 (1982)

REYNOLDS, Chief Judge.

This is an action for damages brought pursuant to 28 U.S.C. § 1332. The plaintiff Office Supply Co., Inc. ("Office Supply") is a corporation located in Racine, Wisconsin, which sells office supplies. The defendant Basic/Four Corporation ("Basic/Four") is a California corporation which manufactures and sells computer hardware and software. In 1975, Office Supply purchased computer hardware and leased computer software from Basic/Four. Office Supply claims that the system was defective and caused it to suffer substantial losses. It seeks compensation for "lost customers, income, good will and executive time and incurred additional hardware and software expense, office form expense, personnel expense and maintenance expense, all to its damage in the sum of $186,000 plus reasonable interest since April, 1975."

* * *

On January 31, 1975, the plaintiff's president, James F. Bruno, signed a contract for the purchase of computer hardware from the defendant and of computer software which was intended to control order processing, inventory control, sales analysis, and accounts receivable. Mr. Bruno mailed the contract to the defendant, and it was accepted by the defendant's assistant treasurer, R. C. Trost, on February 7, 1975. On April 1, 1975, the hardware was installed. In a letter dated May 22, 1975, the defendant advised the plaintiff that the warranty on the hardware would expire on July 1, 1975. The input of data on the software programs took longer to complete, and for a period of time the plaintiff ran parallel operations on the computer and manually as a check on the accuracy of the software applications. In a letter dated October 6, 1975, Mr. Bruno advised Basic/Four:

> "All of the applications anticipated by our company in agreeing to acquire our BASIC/FOUR System are complete and the system appears to be satisfactory. This fulfills your contractual obligation.
>
> "Although the applications programs appear to be operating satisfactorily, some 'defects' might become apparent [sic] later. (Defects might comprise misinterpretation of data, mishandling of a keyboarding error, or a confusing operator instruction—but would not include anything beyond the scope of the system design specification.) It is my understanding that you warrant your programs, when used in accordance with Basic/Four operating instructions, to be free from 'defects' for a period of ninety days, and that you will correct such 'defects' promptly when they are brought to your attention." (Exhibit E to defendant's memorandum in support of motion for summary judgment, filed December 15, 1981.)

Basic/Four took the position that its warranty on the software expired on January 6, 1976. As to complaints received after that date from Office Supply, it did continue to work with Office Supply in an effort to correct any claimed defects in the computer system. Office Supply also hired Ted Templeton, an independent programmer with a company called Computer Methods, Inc., who was recommended by Basic/Four, to work on its Basic/Four system starting some time after Basic/Four advised that the warranty period was over. The record established that Mr. Templeton made some modifications in the Basic/Four software. He also added at least one new program, the ABC program which involved inventory control, to the system. Starting in January 1978, Office Supply also hired a programmer, Marc Jerome, as a fulltime employee. He found what he claims were three major defects in the software system. The record establishes that two of those defects were in programs which Basic/Four did not supply to the plaintiff. The third defect was in the UJ portion of the Basic/Four accounts receivable program, but there is no evidence that the defect arose in the UJ program until after July 1976, which was after the end of the ninety-day period during which Basic/Four continued to warrant its software applications to be free from defects.

The plaintiff's vice president, David Carlson, testified during his deposition that starting at the end of October 1975 and continuing through early 1978, approximately 20% of the customer accounts were out of balance and the Basic/Four system performed up to 78% of expectation for Office Supply. Since February 1978, when Marc Jerome finished correcting the defects in the system, Carlson testified that it has performed up to 100% of expectation. The plaintiff's president, James Bruno, testified that the system only performed up to 50% of expectation prior to 1978, that the accounts receivable first went out of balance on the October 1975 monthly statement printed during the first week of November 1975, that it printed through for the first time in February 1976, but that thereafter the accounts receivable problem continued on an intermittent basis until it was corrected by Marc Jerome in early 1978. Both men testified that there were also problems with the hardware but that those problems were always corrected by Sorbus, a service corporation related to Basic/Four with which Office Supply had a hardware maintenance contract, with only a very few minimal extra charges not covered by the monthly maintenance charges.

On June 17, 1980, Office Supply commenced its action against Basic/Four.

The portion of the Office Supply-Basic/Four contract dealing with the purchase of the hardware is a straightforward document. It describes on the front of the document the computer model and features and the purchase price. Additional terms and conditions of sale are set forth on the reverse. In relevant part it provides on the reverse that it constitutes the entire agreement and understanding between the parties, that it shall be governed by the law of California, and as to warranties and remedies for breach of warranty:

> "3. For ninety (90) days after the Equipment is installed * * * the Seller warrants the Equipment to be free from defects in material, workmanship, and operating failure from ordinary use, and the Seller's liability is

> limited solely to correcting any such defect or failure without charge. * * *"

In italic print paragraph 3 also states:

> "The warranties contained in this Agreement are in lieu of all other warranties, express or implied, including any regarding merchantability or fitness for a particular purpose, arising out of or in connection with any Equipment (or the delivery, use or performance thereof). The Seller will not be liable * * * (b) for loss of profits or other incidental or consequential damages * * *."

The portion of the contract dealing with the lease of the software is not as clearly drafted. On its first page, which is page 3 of the contract, it states:

> "This Addendum to the Agreement for the Purchase of BASIC/FOUR Equipment, dated as of the 31 day of January 1975, between Basic/Four Corporation and Office Supply Inc. is hereby incorporated therein and made a part thereof."

Page 3 describes the program applications and their price. Additional terms and conditions are set forth on the reverse side. As to warranties and limitation of remedies, paragraph 3 provides:

> "The Seller believes that the programming being furnished hereunder is accurate and reliable and when programming accomplishes the results set forth in the 'Design Specifications,' to be agreed to by the Seller and the Purchaser, such programming will be considered completed."

Paragraph 3 continues in italics:

> "However, the amounts to be paid to the Seller under this Agreement and this Addendum do not include any assumption of risk, and the Seller disclaims any and all liability for incidental or consequential damages arising out of the delivery, use or operation of the programs provided herein.
>
> "If the purchaser, without the written consent of the Seller, makes any modification to the programming or any deviations from the operating instructions or violates the provisions of paragraph 2, all warranties set forth herein cease immediately.

> "All warranties set forth herein are in lieu of all other warranties, express or implied, including any regarding merchantability or fitness for a particular purpose, arising out of or in connection with any program (or the delivery, use or performance thereof)."

The contract also contains a fourteen-page description of the program applications.

The parties agree that the contract is a sales contract, that the choice of law provision which it contains is valid, and consequently that the parties' rights and liabilities are governed by the Uniform Commercial Code ("UCC") as adopted in California. They agree about very little else.

The defendant contends in its motion for summary judgment that * * * the warranty disclaimer and damage limitation provisions in the contact are valid and binding and therefore the plaintiff is entitled to no relief, * * * The plaintiff's summary judgment motion consists of a denial of each of those contentions and arguments favoring the application of contrary rules of law at the ultimate trial of this action.

Each of the defendant's contentions, along with the arguments as to the applicable legal principles raised by the plaintiff in opposing defendant's summary judgment motion, is discussed separately below.

* * *

(2) Disclaimer of Warranties

The Office Supply-Basic/Four contract specifically provides that it constitutes the entire agreement and understanding between the parties. That being so, parol evidence is not admissible under California law to vary the terms of the agreement. * * * The language of the contract must be interpreted in an effort to determine the intent of the contracting parties. * * *

If there are no exclusions or modifications in the contract, every sales contract governed by the UCC contains an implied warranty of merchantability and, if the seller has reason to know of a particular purpose for which the goods are required, an implied warranty of fitness for a particular purpose. Section 2315, Cal. Comm. Code [UCC § 2-315]. Express warranties are created if the seller makes an affirmation of fact or promise to the buyer and the affirmation becomes part of the bargain between the parties. Section 2313, Cal. Comm. Code [UCC § 2-313]. Thus, any express warranties must be found in the language of the contract. Implied warranties, in contrast, will be held to exist unless they are specifically excluded.

With regard to the computer hardware, the contract expressly warrants the hardware to be free from defects in material, workmanship, and operating failure from ordinary use for ninety days after installation.

With regard to the computer software, the most reasonable interpretation of the contract is that the same ninety-day warranty of material, workmanship, and operating failure applies, dating from the time when the "programming accomplishes the results set forth in the 'Design Specifications,' " which in this case was on October 6, 1975, when plaintiff's president so advised the defendant.

The plaintiff contends that the language just quoted is a warranty of future performance, and that in fact the programming did not accomplish the desired results until 1978. Courts have been parsimonious in finding warranties of future performance where there is no explicit language in the contract creating such a warranty. *Standard Alliance Industries, Inc. v. Black Clawson Company,* 587 F.2d 813, 820 (6th Cir. 1978). For example, a representation as to the performance ability of an existing product will not be construed as an explicit warranty of future performance ability of the product. *Jones & Laughlin Steel Corporation v. Johns-Manville Sales Corporation,* 626 F.2d 280, 291 (3d Cir. 1980) (interpreting California law). Section 2316(1), Cal. Comm. Code [UCC § 2-316(1)], provides in part:

> "(1) Words or conduct relevant to the creation of an express warranty and words or conduct tending to negate or limit warranty shall be construed wherever reasonable as consistent with each other, * * *."

The first page of the software addendum (page 3 of the contract) provides that it is incorporated within and made a part of the hardware purchase agreement. That agreement contains the ninety-day express warranty provision which, as a result of the incorporation, also applies to the software purchase. In light of the ninety-day express warranty, the most reasonable construction of the software addendum language regarding the results to be accomplished by the programming is that the completion of the programming and installation of all of the bargained-for applications starts the running of the ninety-day warranty period, and not that the applications are warranted to run perfectly once their installation is apparently successfully completed.

The UCC allows contracting parties to exclude or modify all implied warranties. There is no correlative requirement that if implied warranties are excluded, express warranties must be given. Thus it is permissible, for example, to exclude all implied warranties and to provide for a ninety-day express warranty limited to repair or replacement of defective goods. * * *

In order to make an effective waiver of implied warranties, the provisions of § 2316(2), Cal. Comm. Code [UCC § 2-316(2)], must be followed:

> "* * * to exclude or modify the implied warranty of merchantability or any part of it the language must mention merchantability and in case of a writing must be conspicuous, and to exclude or modify any implied warranty of fitness the exclusion must be by a writing and conspicuous.* * *"

There is no dispute that the language contained in the contract was in this case sufficient to waive all implied warranties. The issue is whether the disclaimer was "conspicuous." Section 1201(1), Cal. Comm. Code, [UCC § 1-201(1)] provides:

> "(10) 'Conspicuous.' A term or clause is conspicuous when it is so written that a reasonable person against whom it is to operate ought to have noticed it. A printed heading in capitals (as: NONNEGOTIABLE BILL OF LADING) is conspicuous. Language in the body of a form is 'conspicuous' if it is in larger or other contrasting type or color. But in a telegram any stated term is 'conspicuous.' Whether a term or clause is 'conspicuous' or not is for decision by the court."

Basic/Four points out that it disclaimed the implied warranties not once but twice, and that the disclaimers were written in italicized print, in contrast to the regular print used on the rest of the contract. Nevertheless, the disclaimers are not conspicuous. In *Dorman v. International Harvester Company,* 46 Cal. App. 3d 11, 120 Cal. Rptr. 516 (Cal. App. 1975), the California court of appeals noted that under pre-Code California law, disclaimers of warranty are strictly construed, and, applying the code, it found that an attempted disclaimer written in only slightly contrasting print and without a heading adequate to call the buyer's attention to the disclaimer clause was not effective. That decision controls in this case. The two disclaimers in the Office Supply-Basic/Four contract are on the reverse sides of the first two pages of the contract. They are not positioned close to the buyer's signature line. The contracts are printed on pale green paper and the disclaimers are set forth in print which, although italicized, is only slightly contrasting with the remainder of the contract. There are no headings noting the disclaimers of warranty. Since there is only " 'some slight contrasting set-off' " and there is " 'only a slight contrast with the balance of the instrument,' " *Dorman, supra,* 120 Cal. Rptr. at 522, *quoting Woodruff v. Clark County Farm Bureau Coop. Ass'n.,* (Ind. App. 1972), 153 Ind. App. 31, 286 N.E.2d 188, 198, *quoting* in turn *Greenspun v. American Adhesives, Inc.,* 320 F. Supp. 442 (E.D. Pa. 1970), therefore, the disclaimers are not conspicuous.

Discussion of the effectiveness of the disclaimer provisions in the contract does not end with the finding of lack of conspicuousness. In their treatise Uniform Commercial Code § 12-5 at 444 (2d ed. 1980), Messrs. White and Summers note "with apprehension" the growing number of cases which hold that if a buyer is actually aware of a warranty disclaimer, then the disclaimer is effective even if not conspicuous. * * * The Official Comment to UCC § 2-316 states that the section is designed "to protect a buyer from unexpected and unbargained language of disclaimer." Pointing to that language, the Court in *Dorman, supra, at 521–522,* indicated that California will follow the trend:

> "* * * [W]e must rely predominantly on the official comments to sections 2-316 and 1-201, subdivision (1), and to foreign law. The official comment to subdivision (10) of section 1201 states that the 'test [of conspicuousness] is whether attention can reasonably be expected to be called to [the disclaimer provision].' * * * We must examine this comment in the light of the official comment to section 2-316, which states: 'This section is designed principally to deal with those frequent clauses in sales contracts which seek to exclude "all warranties, express or implied." It seeks to protect a buyer from unexpected and unbargained language of disclaimer by denying effect to such language when inconsistent with language of express warranty and permitting the exclusion of implied warranties only by conspicuous language or other circumstances which protect the buyer from surprise.' In other words, section 2-316 seeks to protect the buyer from the situation where the salesman's 'pitch,' advertising brochures, or large print in the contract, giveth, and the disclaimer clause—in fine print—taketh away."

The *Dorman* Court also noted that under pre-Code California law as well, a provision disclaiming implied warranties "was ineffectual unless the buyer assented to the provision or was charged with notice of the disclaimer before the bargain was completed." *Id.* at 521.

James Bruno testified during his deposition taken on November 3, 1980, that before he purchased the Basic/Four system, he spent approximately two months comparing it with other systems, and that he drew up a written comparison of the Basic/Four and Qantel systems, including their guarantees. Basic/Four, 90 days; and Qantel had one year." He read the back of the contract before he signed it, when he received the contract from Basic/Four he made out a list of questions to ask Basic/Four before signing and one subject on his list was the ninety-day guarantee, and before he signed he showed the warranty provision in the contract to someone he knew in the data processing filed. He discussed the warranties with Basic/Four before signing and tried to have them modified:

"Q Did you read the provisions of the warranty?

"A Yes.

"Q And did you discuss those provisions with Basic/Four, or with someone from Basic/Four?

"A Yes.

"Q And what was said to you about those provisions?

"A That that was the condition that I had to accept.

"Q All right. And was that discussion before or after the contract as signed?

"A I would say before.

"Q * * * did you call up Darryl Bannister, for example, and say I want to buy this system but I refuse to agree to the warranty provisions in the contract?

"A Well, I argued with him, but it was to no avail. Nothing."

He also was aware of the warranty limitations before he signed the contract:

"Q Well, were you aware of the provisions of that warranty before you signed the contract?

"A That there were limitations?

"Q That there are limitations to the warranty? Were you aware of that?

"A Certainly.

"Q You were?

"A Yes."

That testimony establishes that the warranty disclaimers were neither unexpected nor unbargained for, and that, consequently, under *Dorman*, they should be enforced.

* * *

ORDER

For the foregoing reasons.

IT IS ORDERED that the plaintiff's motions to compel discovery and for partial summary judgment are denied.

IT IS FURTHER ORDERED that the defendant's motion for summary judgment is granted, and that judgment be entered dismissing this action with prejudice and awarding costs to the defendant.

QUESTIONS AND NOTES

1. Questions about the facts of this case

   1.1. What exactly did Basic/Four warrant with respect to the performance of its software programs and for how long?

   1.2. What facts did the court consider most important in making its finding that the Basic/Four warranty began to run on October 6, 1975?

   1.3. Were the Basic/Four software applications merchantable? Did that matter to the court?

   1.4. The court states at one point in its opinion that "the plaintiff is also an established commercial operation of significant size, and the plaintiff's president testified during his deposition that he is accustomed to engaging in contract negotiation on behalf of Office Supply." To what issue were those factual findings relevant?

2. Questions about the law

2.1. Most courts that have spoken to the issue agree with *Office Supply* that a non-conspicuous warranty disclaimer may be effective where it can be shown that the buyer had actual knowledge of the disclaimer. *See, e.g., Cate v. Dover Corp.,* 790 S.W.2d 559 (Tex. 1990). However, in a separate opinion in *Cate,* Justice Ray offered the following rationale against permitting this exception to the conspicuousness requirement:

> The statute, on its face, provides for no actual knowledge exception. There is no room for judicial crafting of those omitted by the legislature. I would hold that the extent of a buyer's knowledge of a disclaimer is irrelevant to a determination of enforceability under § 2-316(b) of the UCC.
>
> The effect of actual knowledge is subject to debate among leading commentators on commercial law. The purpose of the objective standard of conspicuousness adopted by the court today reflects the view that "The drafters intended rigid adherence to the conspicuousness requirement in order to avoid arguments concerning what the parties said about the warranties at the time of sale." J. White and R. Summers, Uniform Commercial Code § 12-5 (2d ed. 1980). An absolute rule that an inconspicuous disclaimer is invalid, despite the buyer's actual knowledge, encourages sellers to make their disclaimers conspicuous, thereby reducing the need for courts to evaluate swearing matches as to actual awareness in particular cases. * * * Today's decision condemns our court to a parade of such cases.

Do you agree with this argument? Does it make a difference if the transaction involves a consumer rather than a commercial sale? If actual knowledge is irrelevant, does that also mean that a conspicuous disclaimer is effective regardless of whether the buyer had actual knowledge of it? *See* U.C.C. § 1-201(10). How many buyer's seeking to establish a claim for breach of warranty do you think admit that they had knowledge of the disclaimer? No, we're not suggesting anyone would perjure themselves, we just think maybe it's not as big of a problem as some courts seem to have made it out to be.

2.2. We understand why the court applied Article 2 to the sales of the computer hardware, but should Article 2 have been applied to the *lease* of the software? Also, Article 2 applies to "transactions in goods." U.C.C. § 2-102. Is software a "good"?

2.3. In the course of its opinion, the court in *Office Supply* states that, "If there are no exclusions or modifications in the contract, *every* sale contract governed by the U.C.C. contains an implied warranty of merchantability . . . " (emphasis ours). What statute was Judge Reynolds reading? Not one we're acquainted with!

2.4. While the enforceability of disclaimers of implied warranties focuses on the conspicuousness of the language of disclaimer, § 2-316(1) adopts a different standard for attempts to disclaim express warranties. As noted in *Office Supply*, contractual language attempting to negate or limit an express warranty is required to be construed consistently with the language creating the warranty and, if that cannot be done, the negation or limitation is inoperative. In short, it's more difficult for a seller to get rid of an express warranty than an implied warranty. Is this as it should be? Why? Even if you agree with the judgment of the drafters on this point, there is one fly in the ointment. Look closely at the language in § 2-316(1). The negation of words of limitation that are inconsistent with an express warranty is made *subject* to § 2-202, the parol evidence rule for Article 2 contracts. Does this mean that a seller can effectively eliminate an express warranty made during the course of contract negotiations by including an expansive merger or integration clause into the final writing, thereby excluding introduction of the contradictory oral warranty? Technically it would seem so, but courts, not surprisingly, tend to have limited tolerance for that sort of elevation of form over substance. Thus, Professors White and Summers suggest that to be effective the merger clause needs to be 1) conspicuous, and 2) explicit that it is intended to exclude prior oral assurances made by the seller or its sales staff. *See* J. WHITE & R. SUMMERS, UNIFORM COMMERCIAL CODE, § 12-5, at p. 421 (4th ed. 1995). Is this a satisfactory resolution of the problem?

3. Notes

3.1. Note that in *Office Supply* the court was dealing not only with the effectiveness of Basic/Four's disclaimer under § 2-316, but also the enforceability of Basic/Four's attempt to: (1) limit the remedy (to repair and replacement) for breach of the express warranty that was given, and (2) exclude liability for consequential damages. In Article 2, the enforceability of remedy limitations and exclusions is governed by § 2-719. We omitted the portion of the opinion dealing with that provision because we cover limitations on damage remedies in Chapter 5. Suffice it to say for now that the relationship between § 2-719 and § 2-716 is subtle, but important. An effective disclaimer eliminates any cause of action for breach of warranty. A remedy limitation, by contrast, restricts the buyer's access to the remedy provisions of Article 2, or substitutes an entirely different remedy in their place, in the event of a breach. As we said, more on that to come.

3.2. The approach used by Basic/Four in *Office Supply* to include a limited express warranty that at the same time disclaims the broader Code warranties is not uncommon. In effect, the warranty "takes much and gives little." Recognizing that these provisions can be a trap for the unwary or the unsophisticated consumer, in 1975 Congress enacted the Magnuson-Moss Warranty Act (15 U.S.C. § 2301 *et seq.*). The Act, which only applies to the sale of goods used primarily for personal, family, and household purposes, is primarily a disclosure statute. This is consistent with the general approach taken in federal consumer protection legislation. Specifically, Magnuson-Moss requires manufacturers that elect to make written warranties do so in a manner that is least likely to mislead or confuse consumers. For example, § 103 of Magnuson-Moss requires sellers to designate their warranties as "full," meeting specified federal minimum standards in § 104, or "limited," not meeting those federal minimum standards. In addition, § 108 of the Act precludes a seller that makes any written warranty to a consumer from simultaneously attempting to disclaim or modify any implied warranty, except as to duration. Congress' hope was that many, if not most, manufacturers would feel competitive pressures to offer consumers full warranties. Alas, this hope has not been realized as will become obvious to you if you start reading the warranties that accompany the products you buy. Nevertheless, Magnuson-Moss, with its restrictions on disclaimers, has enlarged the scope of warranty protection for consumer buyers and, perhaps just as importantly, has provided an effective mechanism for enforcement of warranty obligations by allowing recovery of attorneys' fees by a consumer who is damaged by a seller's failure to comply with any obligation under the Act or under any written or implied warranty. *See* Magnuson-Moss § 110(d)(2).

Chapter Four

WHEN IS SOMEONE WHO MADE AN ENFORCEABLE DEAL EXCUSED FROM DOING WHAT SHE AGREED TO DO?

Once a contract is formed, and we know what it requires, then enforcement should be a snap, right? Unfortunately, it is not quite that simple. Because the law of contracts covers not only the simple sale of goods at the hardware store, but also the complex, long-term supply contract, we need to ask, in each case, why the party who is claimed to be in breach did not perform as agreed.

The reason may show that the putative breacher is innocent of the charge. The reason for non-performance could be as simple as the fact that the time for performance has not yet passed. Or that she is waiting for something else to happen first—as in cases in which people buy houses contingent on obtaining financing.

Even if these justifications are not present, and the duty is now due, there may be other reasons that the non-performance is not a breach of the contract. The reasons that justify non-performance are handled in contract law under the label of "excuse."

This chapter looks at the types of reasons that parties can assert to relieve them from performing as agreed. But first we look at the basic notion of what happens when someone does perform as agreed, a concept the law labels as "discharge."

SECTION 1: SATISFACTION OF MATURE OBLIGATIONS TO PERFORM: THE CONCEPT OF DISCHARGE

Discharge is a basic concept. As noted in Section 235 of the *Restatement (Second) of Contracts*:

> *§ 235 The Effect of Performance as Discharge and of Non-Performance as Breach*
>
> *(1) Full performance of a duty under a contract discharges the duty.*
> *(2) When performance of a duty under a contract is due any non-performance is a breach.*

Note the stark simplicity of these statements. Full performance, and only full performance, discharges a party from its contractual duties. Less than full performance, even if not the "fault" of the party from whom performance is due, is a breach. Comment *a* to this Section confirms this reading:

> *When performance is due, however, anything short of full performance is a breach, even if the party who does not fully perform was not at fault and even if the defect in his performance was not substantial. Nonperformance of a duty when performance is due is a breach whether the duty is imposed by a promise stated in the agreement or by a term supplied by the court (§ 204), as in the case of the duty of good faith and fair dealing (§ 205). Non-performance includes defective performance as well as an absence of performance.*

In *Metropolitan Transfer Station, Inc. v. Len Construction Co.*, 328 N.W.2d 532 (Iowa Ct. App. 1982), for example, Len had contracted with Metropolitan to build a retaining wall at a garbage transfer station for Metropolitan's use. The contract contained the following clause:

> That in the event the Metropolitan Transfer Station, Inc.'s facilities at 4198 Delaware are closed so that its normal course of business cannot be conducted thereon because of the fact that the retaining wall is under repair due to faulty construction thereof by Len Construction Company and Leonard C. DePhillips, then and in that event, Leonard C. DePhillips and Len Construction Company shall be responsible for all loss of revenue occasioned by said faulty construction.

The wall was defective, but Metropolitan did not immediately request repair. Sometime shortly thereafter, the premises were partially destroyed by fire. Metropolitan hired another firm to repair the fire damage, and requested that Len repair the defects at the same time. Len refused. The testimony was that during the additional time necessary to fix the wall, Metropolitan lost $60,000 in revenues and asked Len to pay that as damages.

Len defended on the basis that the stoppage in business was due to the fire, not the defect, and that in any event the plans under which it constructed the original wall were defective. The trial court agreed with Len, finding the stoppage due to the fire, and also finding that Len was excused at least as to half of the extra lost revenues because the plan Len used (and which Metropolitan had furnished to Len) was itself defective.

The appellate court reversed. It summarized the trial court's ruling as follows:

> The trial court, in fact, found defendants negligent in construction and prorated liability on a 50-50 basis. Yet the trial court excused performance of the contract on the basis that correction of construction defects "did not materially extend the time period that the transfer station was closed."

This ruling, the appellate court said, was in error. Why?

> Full performance of a duty under a contract discharges that duty. Conversely, nonperformance of a duty under the contract is a breach, unless performance is excused. See Restatement (Second) of Contracts § 235 (1979). . . .
>
> In the present case, the trial court found that in the contract of January 19, 1977, defendants "agreed to reimburse the plaintiff . . . for any loss of revenue occasioned by any [constructural defect]." The trial court further found that defendants "refused to make repairs . . . to the walls and floors." . . . Yet the trial court refused to impose the contractual obligation of defendants to reimburse plaintiff for lost revenues on the basis that corrections were "performed substantially at the same time as those design corrections and did not materially extend the time period that the transfer station was closed." We find that the trial court erred in excusing

defendants' performance under the contract for "not materially extend[ing] the time."

So are there any cases in which less than full performance will not result in breach? Of course. By now, as a first year law student, you may be cynical that any rule is absolute. But the exceptions here, although numerous, do make sense. For our purposes, there are roughly five categories of exceptions to the rule summarized in Section 235 (and which correspond, not surprisingly, to the next five sections). The buzz word usually associated with each category of exceptions is set out at the end of each of the next five paragraphs:

- Exceptions which exist because the duties, although known and agreed, are not yet due. There is something that has to happen first, or the time for performing has not yet occurred. An example of this might be the obligation to buy a house, which is usually conditioned upon the buyer being able to find acceptable financing, and which even then does not arise until a date certain. Category of exception: ***Conditions.***

- Exceptions which related to the fact that the performance agreed to at formation has been altered, either by amendment or modification of the contract, or by some action of the parties. An order for two dozen eggs, for example, might be changed to an order for three dozen eggs at the same price. Or a contract might call for an advance deposit, and the party receiving the deposit may decide not to require it. Categories of exception: ***Amendment, Modification, Waiver and Estoppel.***

- Exceptions which exist because some unanticipated event has occurred which significantly alters the nature of performance, such as when war breaks out unexpectedly in the area in which one party is to perform. Categories of exception: ***Impossibility, Impracticability and Frustration of Purpose.***

- Exceptions which relate to the actions of one of the parties before the time for performance is due—such as when one party tells the other flatly and without exception that she will not perform as agreed. Categories of exception: ***Repudiation, Actual and Anticipatory, and Failure of Adequate Assurance of Future Performance.***

- Exceptions which relate to the fact that the other party has materially breached its obligations, such as when one side fails to pay an amount agreed to be due in advance of delivery of goods. Category of exception: *Material Breach.*

SECTION 2: IS PERFORMANCE DUE?: CONDITIONS

A wag once said that time was God's way of making sure everything doesn't happen at once. In a similar sense, conditions serve to ensure that parties to a contract get what they bargained for, when they bargained to receive it. In this section we look at conditions, and how they differ from other parts of the contract. As we will see, often very important practical consequences attend the characterization of a contractual term as a condition, or as something else.

A. Conditions as Devices to Allocate Risk (of Express Conditions)

Conditions are terms of a contract. As we will see, they come in all sorts of flavors and shapes, from explicitly-dickered conditions to conditions implied by courts after the fact. Before we get into the effect of conditions, let us start with a definition:

Restatement (Second) of Contracts

§ 224 Condition Defined

A condition is an event, not certain to occur, which must occur, unless its non-occurrence is excused, before performance under a contract becomes due.

Thus, to have a condition, you must first have a contract or some other agreement. Conditions are about when, if ever, each party is to perform contractual duties. An example may serve: Markell proposes to buy Epstein's house on July 1 for $1000 (some Alabama shotgun shack), subject to the condition that Markell can obtain financing. If Epstein agrees in writing, there is a bilateral executory contract—both sides have exchanged promises to act in the future.

Markell's contractual obligations, however, are conditional; he need only cough up the $1000 if he can get financing, which (at least for now) we'll assume that he diligently pursues obtaining. Once he gets the financing, even if before July 1, he is bound to pay the $1000.

From this simple scenario, a thousand questions can be spun. What if Markell already has $1000 in the bank, and doesn't need to get financing? What if he has $100,000 in the bank (Hah!)? What if the only financing he can get is for 55% from Epstein & Vicious Lenders?

We'll try to work through some of these questions, but first let us look at the consequences of making obligations conditional. We will start with a contract that allows the government, in the form of the United States Postal Service, to make repairs to a post office in Louisiana.

West v. United States Postal Service

U.S. District Court, Eastern District of Virginia
907 F. Supp. 154 (1995)

Richard B. Kellam, J:

OPINION AND ORDER*

[Lincoln/West (sometimes just referred to as "West") lent money to RPP. The loan was secured by collateral in the form of a parcel of improved real property, and by any rents paid by tenants on that real property.

[RPP leased the property to the United States Postal Service ("USPS"), who apparently then sub-leased parts of it to others. Under the terms of the lease, as discussed in the opinion, RPP, as lessor, had certain duties to keep the heating and air conditioning in good repair. It failed in those duties, and the USPS made the necessary repairs itself.

[This action is about whether the USPS may reimburse itself for repairs made out of rents it has collected from sub-leasees, or whether it must turn over all such rents to the lender, Lincoln/West, who has a collateral security interest in them. All parties agree that their duties are governed by the

*We've condensed the facts, and our summary of them (and clarifications) appear in brackets. Eds.

master lease between USPS and RPP, which West knew about and acknowledged.]

II.

[Under] the applicable provisions of the lease [between RPP and USPS] . . . the Lessor [RPP] was required to maintain the building, equipment and fixtures in good repair. If repairs were needed, Lessor was required to make them to the satisfaction of the government. Failure so to do gave the government the right to cancel the lease, or itself make the repairs. However, before attempting to cancel the lease or make the repairs with the right to reimburse itself out of the accruing rents [from the USPS' subleasees], the government was first required to give Lessor written notice of the need of the repairs, with copy to Mortgagee [Lincoln/West], and allow Lessor 30 days to commence the repairs. If Lessor failed to take action within said time, before government could cancel the lease or itself undertake to make the repairs with the idea of deducting the costs from the rents, it was required to give Mortgagee a written notice of its intention to cancel the lease or itself make the repairs and deduct the costs thereof from the rents and allow Mortgagee an additional 30 days opportunity to commence the repairs.

The lease further provided that if the government

> becomes dissatisfied with Lessor's progress in making repairs, or any condition occurs which would give the government the right to cancel the lease or to incur a cost for which it could obtain reimbursement pursuant thereto, the government will not have said right or rights *unless and until* written notice thereof is first given to the assignee of money due or to become due hereunder and the mortgagee of any mortgage on the premises—and the government shall have afforded such assignee and mortgagee not less than 30 days opportunity, in addition to the aforesaid mentioned time allotted to lessor, to commence . . . necessary repairs . . . .

(Provisions of Lease, par. 10(a)). . . .

* * *

The evidence is clear that Postal Service did not give Lincoln/West any separate 30 day notice of Lessor's failure to make the requested repairs as required by the lease, and then allow Lincoln/West a period of 30 days to deal with the issue or make the repairs. The only notice to Lincoln/West was a copy of the 30 day notice given by Postal Service to Lessor requesting the repairs. Postal Service attempts to escape this requirement asserting that it sent Lincoln/West a copy of its notice to Lessor which substantially meets the requirements of the lease. The issue is whether Postal service has complied with the terms of the lease to permit it to deduct the costs of the repairs from the rents.

Lincoln/West assert that the language of the lease is clear and controlling; that under its terms Postal Service was required to give a 30 day written notice to Lessor with copy to Lincoln/West; that if Lessor failed or refused to perform, to thereafter give a 30 day written notice to Lincoln/West to enable it to deal with the issue as it might desire . . . . On the other hand, Postal Service asserts that Lincoln/West had constructive notice of the need and requirement for repairs and is therefore bound by the notice.

* * *

"Unless and Until" is a condition precedent. Postal service could not cancel the lease, or make the repairs and charge the costs against rents unless and until it gave the required notice. It could make the repairs and have a cause of action against the Lessor for the costs and subject Lessor's equity in the property to payment therefor "Unless" means "except." * * * "Unless" means except on the condition that; under any other circumstances than that; except on the condition that. *Webster's Third International Dictionary*. The same dictionary defines "unless" except "on the condition that; under any other circumstances than that; except on the condition that."

* * *

It was an express condition of the lease that "unless" and "until" the notice was first given to Lessor and upon its failure to act, a written notice was specifically given to mortgagee with an additional 30 day period to act, Postal Service was not authorized to cancel the lease or charge any repairs against the rents which had been assigned to Lincoln/West.

III.

* * *

Numerous cases have come before the courts where a contractor has been denied recovery for additional work under a contract because of failure to give the required notice of the costs before the work was done. In such cases the courts have generally held that giving the notice requires strict compliance and giving of the notice is a condition precedent. * * *

Postal Service breached the contract by failing to give plaintiff the required notice and is therefore not entitled to offset the costs of repairing the heating and air conditioning against any rent due to the Mortgagee, but only against any rents due the landlord.

[Judgment for West issued]

QUESTIONS

1. Questions about the facts of this case

   1.1. Do you think that West had anything to do with the lease provisions? If so, why did they, as a lender, insist on the notice with respect to the repairs?

   1.2. Is the result of this case that the USPS has to pay the full cost of all repairs, without deduction, if it can't obtain reimbursement from the lessor RPP? All for the want of sending what was probably an unnecessary notice?

2. Questions about the law

   2.1. This opinion speaks of "conditions." What are they? Are they express conditions or constructive conditions? Does it matter?

   2.2. Why does the court feel compelled to strictly apply the condition here? Doesn't strict application readjust the expectations of the parties in ways not anticipated at formation?

There are some other consequences of conditions. First, if a condition does not come to pass, there generally is no liability for its non-occurrence. If, to use the example that opened up this section, Markell legitimately cannot obtain financing by July 1, that is the end of the matter. Epstein cannot sue Markell, since Markell did not breach any provision of the contract; he was obligated to buy *only* if he obtained financing. After July 1, the condition can no longer occur, and thus the whole contract is discharged. *Restatement (Second) of Contracts* § 225(2).

B. Regulating Exchanges, or, Who is to Do What When (of Implied Conditions)

Conditions can be very powerful in regulating contractual relations. But for express conditions to assume that power, they must be just that—express (that is, agreed to and acknowledged terms of the contract). What if the parties haven't supplied the words for the conditions? To answer that requires a small detour into the history of conditions.

1. A Short History of Constructive Conditions

As we have seen, in every contract there are usually at least two obligations. In the typical bilateral contract, each party makes a promise to the other; if Epstein and Ponoroff agree that Epstein will sell Ponoroff his prized collection of road-kill recipes, Epstein has an obligation to transfer the recipes and Ponoroff has the duty to pay for them.

What's the timing of each party's performance? Does Epstein hold his recipes in one hand high in the air over Ponoroff's head (Epstein's taller, at least in physical stature) while extending the palm of his other hand towards Ponoroff to accept the payment? Does Ponoroff adopt a like stature? In short, who has to perform first and take the risk that the other will not honor his promise?

As indicated at the start of this chapter, conditions are a nice way to order things. They would seem to be tailor-made for regulating this type of exchange. A short detour into the common law, however, shows that it took some time for the common law to embrace this concept. Let's start with the state of the law in the early seventeenth century.

Nichols v. Raynbred

Hobart 88, 80 Eng. Rep. 238 (K.B. 1615)

Nichols brought an assumpsit against Raynbred, declaring that in consideration that Nichols promised to deliver the defendant to his own use a cow, the defendant promised to deliver him 50 shillings: adjudged for the plaintiff in both Courts, that the plaintiff need not to aver the delivery of the cow, because it is promise for promise. Note here the promises must be at one instant, for else they will be both nuda pacta.

That's all there is. What's going on here? What was the contract in this case? If you were Nichols, and could do it all over again, what would you put in the contract? In the complaint? As things stand, is Nichols out one cow?

The law evolved after *Nichols*. By 1772 (158 years later), the following case proved to be a turning point in the law of conditions.

Kingston v. Preston

2 Douglas 689, 99 Eng. Rep. 437 (K.B. 1773)

"It was an action of debt, for non-performance of covenants contained in certain articles of agreement between the plaintiff and the defendant. The declaration stated:—That, by articles made the 24th of March, 1770, the plaintiff, for the considerations thereinafter mentioned, covenanted, with the defendant, to serve him for one year and a quarter next ensuing, as a covenant-servant, in his trade of a silk-mercer, at £200 a year, and in consideration of the premises, the defendant covenanted, that at the end of the year and a quarter, he would give up his business of a mercer to the plaintiff, and a nephew of the defendant, or some other person to be nominated by the defendant, and give up to them his stock in trade, at a fair valuation; and that, between the young traders, deeds of partnership should be executed for 14 years, and from and immediately after the execution of the said deeds, the defendant would permit the said young traders to carry on the said business in the defendant's house. Then the declaration stated a covenant by the plaintiff, that he would accept the business and stock in trade, at a fair valuation, with the defendant's nephew, or such other person, &c., and execute such deeds of partnership, and, further, that the plaintiff should, and would, at, and before the sealing and delivery of the deeds, cause and procure good and sufficient security to be given to the defendant, to be approved of by the defendant, for the payment of £250 monthly, to the defendant, in lieu of a moiety of the monthly produce of the stock in trade, until the value of the stock should be reduced to £4,000.—Then the plaintiff averred, that he had performed, and been ready to perform, his covenants, and assigned for breach on the part of the defendant, that he had refused to surrender and give up his business, at the end of the said year and quarter.—The defendant pleaded, 1. That the plaintiff did not offer sufficient security; and, 2. That he did not give sufficient security for the payment of the £250, &c.—And the plaintiff demurred generally to both pleas.—On the part of the plaintiff, the case was argued by Mr. Buller, who contended, that the covenants were mutual and independent, and, therefore, a plea of the breach of one of the covenants to be performed by the plaintiff was no bar to an action for a breach by the defendant of one of which he had bound himself to perform, but that the defendant might have his remedy for the breach by the plaintiff, in a separate action. On the other side, Mr. Grose insisted, that the covenants were dependent in their nature, and, therefore, performance must be alleged: the security to be given for the money, was manifestly the chief object of the transaction, and it would be highly unreasonable to construe the agreement, so as to oblige the defendant to give up a beneficial business, and valuable stock in trade, and trust to the plaintiff's personal security, (who might, and, indeed, was admitted to be worth nothing,) for the performance of his part.—In delivering the judgment of the Court, Lord Mansfield expressed himself to the following effect: There are three kinds of covenants: 1. Such as are called mutual and independent, where either party may recover damages from the other, for the injury he may have received by a breach of the covenants in his favour, and where it is no excuse for the defendant, to allege a breach of the covenants on the part of the plaintiff. 2. There are covenants, which are conditions and dependent, in which the performance of one depends on the prior performance of another, and therefore, till this prior condition is performed, the other party is not liable to an action on his covenant. 3. There is also a third sort of covenants, which are mutual conditions to be performed at the same time; and, in these, if one party was ready, and offered, to perform his part, and the other neglected, or refused, to perform his, he who was ready, and offered, has fulfilled his engagement, and may maintain an action for the default of the other; though it is not certain that either is obliged to do the first act.—His Lordship then proceeded to say, that the dependence, or independence, of covenants, was to be collected from the evident sense and meaning of the parties, and, that, however transposed they might be in the deed, their precedency must depend on the order of time in which the intent of the transaction requires their performance. That, in the case before the Court, it would be the greatest injustice if the plaintiff should prevail: the essence of the agreement was, that the defendant should not trust to the personal security of the plaintiff, but before he delivered up his stock and business, should have good security for the payment of the money. The giving such security, therefore, must necessarily be a condition precedent.—Judgment was accordingly given for the defendant because the part to be performed by the plaintiff was clearly a condition precedent."*

Is Lord Mansfield finding something that isn't there? Did the parties insert a condition of concurrent exchange in their contract? Could they have? Is the rationale for implying a condition (in essence, writing it in when it isn't there) the same rationale Judge Cardozo would use 143 years later in *Wood v. Lucy, Lady Duff-Gordon* (*see infra*, at 596)?

Thus, promises of payment by the buyer and of delivery by the seller came to be dependent upon each other through the use of court-supplied assumptions called conditions. These assumptions are played out in the next case.

---

*The reason this case is reported within quotation marks is that it is not reported under its title, but is reported as part of the oral argument in another case, that being Jones v. Barkley, 2 Douglas 684, 99 Eng. Rep. 434 (1781). In 17th Century England there were no official reports of court decisions, and often the same case received several differing treatments. Indeed, in another report of this case, at 98 Eng. Rep. 606, Lord Mansfield is reported to have said:

> It would be the most monstrous case in the world, if the argument on the side of Mr. Buller's client was to prevail. It's of the very essence of the agreement, that the defendant will not trust the personal security of the plaintiff. A Court of Justice is to say, that by operation of law he shall, against his teeth. He is to let him into his house to squander every thing there, without any thing to rely on but what he has absolutely refused to trust. This payment, therefore, was a precedent condition before the covenant of putting into possession was to be performed on the part of the defendant.

Eds.

2. Constructive Conditions of Exchange in Current Practice

Pullman, Comley, Bradley and Reeves v. Tuck-it-away, Bridgeport, Inc.

Appellate Court of Connecticut
28 Conn. App. 460; 611 A.2d 435 (1992)

Freedman, J:

In this interpleader action,* the defendant, Vestpro Corporation, appeals from the judgment of the trial court awarding the other defendant, Tuck-it-away, Bridgeport, Inc., $100,000 as liquidated damages for Vestpro's default under the terms of a contract for the sale of real property.[2] Vestpro claims that the trial court improperly found that Tuck-it-away was entitled to the $100,000 as liquidated damages for Vestpro's default in performance of the contract of sale. We affirm the judgment of the trial court.

The parties stipulated to the following facts. On or about April 13, 1988, Tuck-it-away, as seller, and Vestpro, as buyer, signed a contract for the sale of real property located in Bridgeport. Pursuant to the contract, Vestpro deposited $100,000 in escrow with Tuck-it-away's attorneys, Pullman, Comley, Bradley and Reeves. This is the money presently in dispute between the parties. By correspondence dated October 14, 1988, Tuck-it-away and Vestpro agreed in writing to extend the closing date until December 10, 1988.

On December 10, 1988, a Saturday, no closing took place. On or about December 14, 1988, Tuck-it-away received from Vestpro a letter purporting to cancel the contract on the basis of three alleged title defects: (1) a lis pendens dated August 9, 1983, (2) a certificate of attachment dated June 27, 1988, and (3) a three foot nonconformity in one of the lengths in the legal description of the property as referenced in the contract.

---

*This action was commenced by the plaintiff, Pullman, Comley, Bradley and Reeves, as the holder of a $100,000 escrow deposit made by Vestpro in connection with the underlying real estate transaction here in dispute. The plaintiff sought and was granted an interlocutory judgment requiring the defendants to interplead concerning their claims to the funds so that the court could order the plaintiff to give the funds to the proper party and be released of any further obligations or liabilities to Vestpro.

[2]Paragraph 15 of the contract provided in pertinent part: "If the buyer fails to perform the terms of this contract, seller shall be entitled to retain all sums theretofore paid as provided in Sections 2 and 8 hereof which sums, to the extent held in escrow hereunder, shall be released from escrow and thereupon paid to the seller together with any accrued and unpaid interest thereon, as liquidated damages for loss of a bargain and not as a penalty. . . . "

Before December 10, 1988, Tuck-it-away's attorneys had in their possession a release of the August 9, 1983 lis pendens and a release of the June 27, 1988 attachment. At the time of execution of the contract, neither Tuck-it-away nor Vestpro was aware that the legal description contained an incorrect length. On or about September 16, 1988, attorneys for both Tuck-it-away and Vestpro received a survey from Preferred Land Title Services, Inc., showing a correct legal description of the property. At no time prior to the December 12, 1988 letter did Vestpro ever advise Tuck-it-away or complain to Tuck-it-away about the error in the legal description of the property contained in the contract.

In addition to these stipulated facts, other facts necessary to a resolution of this matter can be summarized as follows. The total purchase price due under the contract was $1,900,000. The contract provided that the closing date would be 120 days from the date of execution of the contract, but that Vestpro could obtain four extensions of time upon payment to Tuck-it-away of $15,000 for each extension. Because Vestpro exercised all four rights of adjournment, the actual closing date was December 10, 1988. The contract provided that time was of the essence.

As December 10 approached, Vestpro was short of the total funds necessary to complete the deal. On December 7, 1988, Alan Goldman, one of Vestpro's principals, met with Gerald Sprayragen, Tuck-it-away's president, to discuss the situation. At that meeting, Goldman indicated that Vestpro did not yet have the total funds necessary, but that it was close to attaining its goal, and optimistic that it would reach its goal, but that a further extension of time was needed. Although the express contractual language did not permit another extension, Sprayragen indicated that he would permit another extension if Vestpro would pay a fee for the extension. Vestpro refused to pay for a further extension, and as a result no agreement for an extension came from this meeting. Sprayragen also spoke with Stephen Hochman, a partner in Vestpro whose job was to solicit investors. He too indicated to Sprayragen that Vestpro was unable to close on December 10 and needed an extension of the closing date.

During that week, Michael Proctor, an attorney who represented Tuck-it-away in this deal, spoke with Gary Kleinman, an attorney who represented Vestpro in its negotiations and dealings with Tuck-it-away. Kleinman told Proctor that Vestpro would not be able to close on December 10 and needed another two weeks to secure the remaining funds. It thus was clear to Tuck-it-away that Vestpro would not be able to close the deal on December 10, 1988.

On December 9, 1988, Vestpro representatives met with their prospective investors to discuss the situation. During the meeting, the group received a call from Kleinman, who told the group "You got lucky" because he had discovered a discrepancy in one of the courses in the property description. As a result of this information, Vestpro decided to send a letter to Tuck-it-away electing to cancel the contract under its provisions because of Tuck-it-away's inability to convey title to the premises in accordance with the terms of the contract.[5] The letter represented to Tuck-it-away that Vestpro elected to cancel the contract because of the three alleged defects in title previously discussed. The letter was not mailed to Tuck-it-away until the end of the day on December 12, 1988, and Tuck-it-away did not receive the letter until December 14, 1988. * * *

Vestpro * * * argues that the trial court improperly found Vestpro in default for failing to appear for the closing on December 10, 1988. Vestpro claims that this finding was improper because Tuck-it-away also failed to appear for the closing and tender title to the property.

* * *

The trial court . . . found that Vestpro breached its duty to perform by not showing up at the closing on December 10 and tendering full payment of the purchase price, and that such a breach excused Tuck-it-away from its obligation to perform.

With respect to the time for performance of obligations contained in a contract, the general rule is: "Where all or part of the performances to be exchanged under an exchange of promises can be rendered simultaneously, they are to that extent due simultaneously, unless the language of [*sic.* Should be "or." Eds.] the circumstances indicate the contrary." 2 Restatement (Second), Contracts § 234 (1). Here, paragraph 4 of the contract provided: "At the closing, *on payment of the purchase price as provided above,* the seller shall deliver and the buyer shall accept, a full covenant Warranty deed . . . ." This language indicates that the parties agreed that the performances would not be rendered simultaneously, but rather that Vestpro's duty to perform would be a condition precedent to Tuck-it-away's obligation to tender and convey title.

---

[5]Paragraph 11 of the contract provided in pertinent part: "If the seller shall be unable to convey title to the buyer at the closing, or adjourned closing, in accordance with the terms of this contract, the buyer shall have the option of . . . (b) canceling this contract. . . ."

"A condition precedent is a fact or event which the parties intend must exist or take place before there is a right to performance." * * * ' 'Whether the performance of a certain act by a party to a contract is a condition precedent to the duty of the other party to act depends on the intent of the parties as expressed in the contract and read in light of the circumstances surrounding the execution of the instrument.' . . ." * * *

The express language of paragraph 4 of the contract evidences the parties' intent that Vestpro's duty to tender full payment of the purchase price is a condition precedent of Tuck-it-away's obligation to convey title to Vestpro. Because Vestpro failed on December 10, 1988, to tender the $1,800,000 balance due on the purchase price, Tuck-it-away was excused of its obligation to perform under the contract.

Vestpro argues, however, that Tuck-it-away's failure to go through the act of tendering a deed to the nonappearing buyer placed it in default and thus precluded it from recovering the $100,000 as liquidated damages. The law, however, does not require a party to undertake a futile act.* * * Because Vestpro failed to appear at the closing and perform its obligation, which was a condition precedent to Tuck-it-away's obligation to perform, it would have been an act in futility for Tuck-it-away to tender a deed to Vestpro. We will not require the seller in this situation to perform such a futile act.

We conclude that the trial court's factual findings were adequately supported by the record. The trial court, therefore, correctly awarded the $100,000 deposit to Tuck-it-away.

The judgment is affirmed.

QUESTIONS AND NOTE

1. Questions about the facts of this case

    1.1. What is the seller's law firm doing holding the $100,000? Would you do this for your client?

    1.2. Why did the buyer keep extending (or as the argot goes, "adjourning") the closing?

    1.3. Under the court's reasoning, who was obligated to perform first? Is that the same answer the old common law gave in *Nichols*? That Judge Mansfield gave in *Kingston*?

2. Questions about the law

   2.1. Why wasn't the contract terminated as of the December 7th meeting?

   2.2. Knowing what you know now, what would you have told the investors at the December 9th meeting when the call from Kleinman came in?

   2.3. Would it have made a difference if the December 12th letter had been hand delivered to the seller on December 9th?

   2.4. If you represented the seller, and received the December 12th letter on December 9th, what do you advise your client to do?

   2.5. Is this case an example of the rule set forth in Section 234 of the *Restatement (Second) of Contracts*? Or was that rule varied by the parties' agreement?

3. Note

   3.1. *Tuck-it-away* involved real estate and thus common law rules are appropriate to answer the issue presented. What of personal property? To go back to the road-kill recipe exchange mentioned above, does Epstein, the seller, have to hand over the recipes first, and then take the cash, or does Ponoroff, the buyer, first fork over the cash and then take delivery? Or do the parties need to deposit all items into escrow with a third person and then tell that person when she can deliver the items deposited to the respective parties?

   The U.C.C. follows the common law, and adopts neither. Section 2-507(1) of the U.C.C. states:

   (1) Tender of delivery is a condition to the buyer's duty to accept the goods and, unless otherwise agreed, to his duty to pay for them.

   So the seller must go first? Well, now read section 2-511(1):

   (1) Unless otherwise agreed tender of payment is a condition to the seller's duty to tender and complete any delivery.

   Seems that we have circular obligations. Buyer doesn't have to pay unless seller tenders delivery, but seller doesn't have to tender delivery until buyer tenders payment.

Comment 2 to Section 2-511 helps. It states that "Unless there is agreement otherwise the concurrence of the conditions as to tender of payment and tender of delivery requires their performance at a single place or time." Thus the delivery and payment are concurrent conditions; neither Epstein or Ponoroff have to go first.

This may sound clunky, but in practice it works. If the other side does not appear (as was the case in *Tuck-it-away*), then the party who did appear can say its obligation (to pay or to deliver) never arose. If both parties are present at the time and date for performance, then all that is required is "tender" of the performance. "Tender" in turn "contemplates an offer coupled with a present ability to fulfill all the conditions resting on the tendering party and must be followed by actual performance if the other party shows himself ready to proceed. . . . '[T]ender' connotes such performance by the tendering party as puts the other party in default if he fails to proceed in some manner." Comment 1 to U.C.C. § 2-503.

---

3. The Interplay Between Constructive and Express Conditions

The interplay between implied conditions which regulate the order of performance and express conditions which attempt to do the same was analyzed in *MXL Indust., Inc. v. Mulder*, 252 Ill. App. 3d 18, 623 N.E.2d 369, 191 Ill. Dec. 124 (1993). There, a lease had an early termination clause; the tenant could leave early upon the condition that it pay "all sums then due" plus four months' rent. This is the clause:

> (a) The term of this Lease shall be for a period of five (5) years commencing on the 1st day of March, 1987 and ending on the 29th day of February, 1992 (hereinafter referred to as 'the term of this Lease'). Notwithstanding the foregoing provisions of this Subsection 1 (a), at any time after the 29th day of February, 1988, Lessee may terminate this Lease by paying to Lessor all sums then due pursuant to the provisions of this Lease and an additional sum equal to four (4) months' rent specified in Section 2 hereof. If Lessee exercises such right, the term of this Lease shall end on the date on which Lessor receives such payment from Lessor [*sic*].

The tenant tried to exercise this option on February 28, 1988 by tendering $11,400, the amount of four months' rent (less a credit for a security deposit), and by vacating the premises. The landlord, however, correctly pointed out that one of the obligations of the lease was that, upon vacating the premises, the tenant was to repair certain damage. The exact amount of this obligation was debated for two months, and finally agreed to be $2000. When the tenant sent a check for that amount along with a check for four months' rent, the landlord rejected it, contending that the tenant owed rent for the two months during which the parties negotiated the settlement. The tenant disagreed, and contended that it had met the condition, or at least substantially met the condition, allowing it to terminate early by its February 28 tender. In response, the court said:

> Illinois courts define a condition precedent as one which must be performed either before a contract becomes effective or which is to be performed by one party to an existing contract before the other party is obligated to perform. * * * The satisfaction of a condition is generally subject to the rule of strict compliance. * * * Professor Williston explains, " 'since an express condition * * * depends for its validity on the manifested intention of the parties, it has the same sanctity as the promise itself. Though the court may regret the harshness of such a condition, as it may regret the harshness of a promise, it must, nevertheless, generally enforce the will of the parties.' "* * *A party seeking the benefit of a condition precedent, however, may waive strict compliance by conduct indicating that strict compliance with the provision will not be required. * * *
>
> Distinctly different, although analogous to the concept of a condition, are constructive conditions of exchange. The concept of constructive conditions of exchange was developed by the courts in order to allow the court to supply terms under which a party's duties to perform are conditioned on the performance to be given in return. * * * The purpose of constructive conditions of exchange is to play an integral role in assuring the parties to a bilateral contract that they will actually receive the performance that they have been promised.* * * A common application of the concept occurs when one party seeks to justify its own refusal to perform on the ground that the other party has committed a breach of the contract. In sum, the doctrine serves the salutary purpose of assuring each party to a bilateral contract that it will receive the promised return performance, and it expresses a judicial preference for dependent promises. * * *

> Because constructive conditions of exchange invoked the concept that one party's duty to perform was conditioned on the other party's performance, the need arose to ameliorate the rule of strict compliance ordinarily applied to express conditions. As explained by Professor Farnsworth, "the doctrine evolved that if one party's performance is a constructive condition of the other party's duty, only 'substantial performance' is required of the first party before that party can recover under the contract."(E. Farnsworth, Farnsworth on Contracts § 12, at 415 (1990).) Farnsworth further notes, however, that "the flexible requirement of substantial performance stands in sharp contrast to the requirement of strict compliance that protects a party that has taken the precaution of making its duty expressly conditional."(E. Farnsworth, Farnsworth on Contracts § 12, at 415 (1990).) Stated differently, the doctrine does not address substantial performance of a condition; rather, it focuses on substantial performance by one party of its obligations arising out of an agreed exchange of performances.* * * Accordingly, an express condition precedent, unless otherwise excused, operates by agreement of the parties to define the satisfaction of a necessary antecedent to a party's performance under the contract and is subject to the rule of strict compliance, unless such compliance is waived. In contrast, constructive or implied conditions of exchange operate to regulate the parties' course of performance and are subject to the rule of substantial performance.

The court found that the clause, being drafted by the parties, required strict compliance, and held that the tenant's $11,400 tender did not effectively terminate the lease. It was thus not only liable for the extra two months' rent, but also for the total amount of contract damages for the rest of the term (since it vacated and treated the lease as terminated, when it in fact was not); an amount claimed to be in excess of $230,000. And that was not all—because the tenant litigated the case and lost, it also wound up paying the landlord's attorneys' fees under the lease's attorneys' fees clause, and those fees were alleged to be in excess of $65,000.

C. Conditions vs. Covenants (of Interpreting Close Cases)

In the above examples and cases, it was fairly clear that a condition was meant. What if the wording and the conduct do not lead to so clear a result?

Peacock Const. Co., Inc. v. Modern Air Conditioning, Inc.
Supreme Court of Florida
353 So. 2d 840 (1977)

Boyd, Acting C.J.:

* * *

Peacock Construction was the builder of a condominium project. Modern Air Conditioning subcontracted with Peacock to do the heating and air conditioning work and Overly Manufacturing subcontracted with Peacock to do the "rooftop swimming pool" work. Both written subcontracts provided that Peacock would make final payment to the subcontractors,

> "within 30 days after the completion of the work included in this subcontract, written acceptance by the Architect and full payment therefor by the Owner."

Modern Air Conditioning and Overly Manufacturing completed the work specified in their contracts and requested final payment. When Peacock refused to make the final payments the two subcontractors separately brought actions in the Lee County Circuit Court for breach of contract. In both actions it was established that no deficiencies had been found in the completed work.[3] But Peacock established that it had not received from the owner[4] full payment for the subcontractors' work. And it defended on the basis that such payment was a condition which, by express term of the final payment provision, had to be fulfilled before it was obligated to perform under the contract. On motions by the plaintiffs, the trial judges granted summary judgments in their favor. The orders of judgment implicitly interpreted the contract not to require payment by the owner as a condition precedent to Peacock's duty to perform.

The Second District Court of Appeal affirmed the lower court's judgment in the appeal brought by Modern Air Conditioning. In so doing it adopted the view of the majority of jurisdictions in this country that provisions of the kind disputed here do not set conditions precedent but rather constitute absolute promises to pay, fixing payment by the owner as a reasonable time

---

[3]In fact, in the Modern Air Conditioning case the Architect stated in a sworn deposition that he felt the heating and air conditioning equipment, although not yet operated, was complete per the plans and specifications. Original Record, p. 37. Sup. Ct. Case No. 50,758.

[4]The owner, a corporation, had entered proceedings in bankruptcy.

for when payment to the subcontractor is to be made. When the judgment in the *Overly Manufacturing* case reached the Second District Court, *Modern Air Conditioning* had been decided and the judgment, therefore, was affirmed on the authority of the latter decision. These two decisions plainly conflict with [*Edward J. Gerrits, Inc. v. Astor Electric Service, Inc.*, 328 So. 2d 522 (Fla. 3d DCA 1976).]

In *Gerrits*, the Court had summarily ordered judgment for the plaintiff/subcontractor against the defendant/general contractor on a contractual provision for payment to the subcontractor which read,

> "The money to be paid in current funds and at such times as the General Contractor receives it from the Owner." * * *

In its review of the judgment, the Third District Court of Appeal referred to the fundamental rule of interpretation of contracts that it be done in accordance with the intention of the parties. Since the defendant had introduced below the issue of intention, a material issue, and since the issue was one that could be resolved through a factual determination by the jury, the Third District reversed the summary judgment and remanded for trial.

Peacock urges us to adopt *Gerrits* as the controlling law in this State. It concedes that the Second District's decisions are backed by the weight of authority. But it argues that they are incorrect because the issue of intention is a factual one which should be resolved after the parties have had an opportunity to present evidence on it. *Peacock* urges, therefore, that the causes be remanded for trial. If there is produced no evidence that the parties intended there be condition precedents, only then, says *Peacock*, should the judge, by way of a directed verdict for the subcontractors, be allowed to take the issue of intention from the jury.

The contractual provisions in dispute here are susceptible to two interpretations. They may be interpreted as setting a condition precedent or as fixing a reasonable time for payment. The provision disputed in *Gerrits* is susceptible to the same two interpretations. The questions presented by the conflict between these decisions, then, are whether ambiguous contractual provisions of the kind disputed here may be interpreted only by the fact-finder, usually the jury, or if they should be interpreted as a matter of law by the court, and if so what interpretation they should be given.

Although it must be admitted that the meaning of language is a factual question, the general rule is that interpretation of a document is a question of law rather than of fact. * * * If an issue of contract interpretation concerns the intention of parties, that intention may be determined from the written contract, as a matter of law, when the nature of the transaction lends itself to judicial interpretation. A number of courts, with whom we agree, have recognized that contracts between small subcontractors and general contractors on large construction projects are such transactions. * * * The reason is that the relationship between the parties is a common one and usually their intent will not differ from transaction to transaction, although it may be differently expressed.

That intent in most cases is that payment by the owner to the general contractor is not a condition precedent to the general contractor's duty to pay the subcontractors. This is because small subcontractors, who must have payment for their work in order to remain in business, will not ordinarily assume the risk of the owner's failure to pay the general contractor. And this is the reason for the majority view in this country, which we now join.

Our decision to require judicial interpretation of ambiguous provisions for final payment in subcontracts in favor of subcontractors should not be regarded as anti-general contractor. It is simply a recognition that this is the fairest way to deal with the problem. There is nothing in this opinion, however, to prevent parties to these contracts from shifting the risk of payment failure by the owner to the subcontractor. But in order to make such a shift the contract must unambiguously express that intention. And the burden of clear expression is on the general contractor.

The decisions of the Second District Court of Appeal to affirm the summary judgments were correct. We adopt, therefore, these two decisions as the controlling law in Florida and we overrule *Gerrits*, to the extent it is inconsistent with this opinion.

The orders allowing certiorari in these two causes are discharged. It is so ordered.

QUESTIONS

1. Questions on the facts of this case

   1.1. Do you understand the court's statement: "The contractual provisions in dispute here are susceptible to two interpretations. They may be interpreted as setting a condition precedent or as fixing a reasonable time for payment."? Do you agree with these statements? If so, state simply how the provisions could have been worded to avoid confusion.

1.2. Does the result of this case effectively mean that evidence of Peacock's intent is irrelevant? Modern Air's?

1.3. After this case, what can general contractors do, if anything, to reverse its effect on subsequent contracts?

2. Questions about the law

2.1. Do you get a different result if the sub-contractor is bigger and more well-established than the general contractor?

2.2. Do any of the "interpretive maxims" set forth above at 580–583 help in resolving this question? Or does this case (and the *Restatement* section quoted below) simply create another maxim?

2.3. Is this properly analyzed as a form of judicial adhesion contract, albeit one that is tilted in favor of the smaller party?

2.4. Is this a parol evidence case? What evidence did the parties offer to persuade the court to adopt their interpretation?

2.5. How should Peacock have "unambiguously expressed" its intent? What if the contract provided that payment will be made to subcontractors with thirty days after completion of the work "provided like payment shall be made by owner to general contractor"? *See Main Elec., Ltd. v. Printz Servs. Corp.*, 980 P.2d 522 (Colo. 1999).

Here's what the *Restatement* has to say about conditions versus promises. In reading the illustrations at the end, which one looks the most like *Peacock*?

§ 227 Standards of Preference with Regard to Conditions

(1) In resolving doubts as to whether an event is made a condition of an obligor's duty, and as to the nature of such an event, an interpretation is preferred that will reduce the obligee's risk of forfeiture, unless the event is within the obligee's control or the circumstances indicate that he has assumed the risk.

(2) Unless the contract is of a type under which only one party generally undertakes duties, when it is doubtful whether

(a) a duty is imposed on an obligee that an event occur, or

(b) the event is made a condition of the obligor's duty, or

(c) the event is made a condition of the obligor's duty and a duty is imposed on the obligee that the event occur, the first interpretation is preferred if the event is within the obligee's control. . . .

Comments

. . .

b. Condition or not. The non-occurrence of a condition of an obligor's duty may cause the obligee to lose his right to the agreed exchange after he has relied substantially on the expectation of that exchange, as by preparation or performance. The word "forfeiture" is used in this Restatement to refer to the denial of compensation that results in such a case. The policy favoring freedom of contract requires that, within broad limits . . . the agreement of the parties should be honored even though forfeiture results. When, however, it is doubtful whether or not the agreement makes an event a condition of an obligor's duty, an interpretation is preferred that will reduce the risk of forfeiture. . . . When the nature of the condition is such that the uncertainty as to the event will be resolved before either party has relied on its anticipated occurrence, both parties can be entirely relieved of their duties, and the obligee risks only the loss of his expectations. When, however, the nature of the condition is such that the uncertainty is not likely to be resolved until after the obligee has relied by preparing to perform or by performing at least in part, he risks forfeiture. If the event is within his control, he will often assume this risk. If it is not within his control, it is sufficiently unusual for him to assume the risk that, in case of doubt, an interpretation is preferred under which the event is not a condition. The rule is, of course, subject to a showing of a contrary intention, and even without clear language, circumstances may show that he assumed the risk of its non-occurrence.

Although the rule is consistent with a policy of avoiding forfeiture and unjust enrichment, it is not directed at the avoidance of actual forfeiture and unjust enrichment. Since the intentions of the parties must be taken as of the time the contract was made, the test is whether a particular interpretation would have avoided the risk of forfeiture viewed as of that time, not whether it will avoid actual forfeiture in the resolution of a dispute that has arisen later.

Illustrations:

1. A, a general contractor, contracts with B, a sub-contractor, for the plumbing work on a construction project. B is to receive $100,000, "no part of which shall be due until five days after Owner shall have paid Contractor therefor." B does the plumbing work, but the owner becomes insolvent and fails to pay A. A is under a duty to pay B after a reasonable time.

2. A, a mining company, hires B, an engineer, to help reopen one of its mines for "$10,000 to be payable as soon as the mine is in successful operation." $10,000 is a reasonable compensation for B's service. B performs the required services, but the attempt to reopen the mine is unsuccessful and A abandons it. A is under a duty to pay B $10,000 after the passage of a reasonable time.

3. A, a mining company, contracts with B, the owner of an untested experimental patented process, to help reopen one of its mines for $5,000 paid in advance and an additional "$15,000 to be payable as soon as the mine is in successful operation." $10,000 is a reasonable compensation for B's services. B performs the required services, but because the process proves to be unsuccessful, A abandons the attempt to reopen the mine. A is under no duty to pay B any additional amount.

D. Imposing Liability by Excusing Condition When One Party Prevents Condition from Occurring

The discussion of conditions up to now has been somewhat cut and dried. If an obligation is subject to an express condition, and the condition does not occur, the duty never matures. The person subject to the conditional duty incurs no liability for non-performance of the specified obligation for the simple reason that the obligation never matured.

But such a view of the world is brittle. What if the condition is within the control of the party subject to the duty? To be more concrete, assume that Markell has agreed to buy Epstein's house, subject to Markell obtaining financing. In this simple example, Markell's obligation to buy Epstein's house is conditioned up Markell getting financing. But Markell controls that issue. What if he sees a better deal with Ponoroff? Can he just do nothing until the date specified in the contract and avoid liability? See the following case.

Moore Brothers Co. v. Brown & Root, Inc.
U.S. Court of Appeals, Fourth Circuit
207 F.3d 717 (2000)

Murnaghan, Circuit Judge:

This case arises out of the construction of the Dulles Toll Road Extension, a privately owned and operated toll road connecting Dulles Airport and Leesburg, Virginia. [The issue on appeal is] whether a general contractor may rely on the non-occurrence of a valid "pay when paid" condition precedent in the subcontract as a defense to liability where the general contractor was partly responsible for the failure of the condition precedent. [W]e answer [the] question[] in the negative. . . .

I.

The Dulles Toll Road Extension ("DTRE") is a fourteen mile long private toll road between Dulles Airport and Leesburg, Virginia. It was built and is operated by the Toll Road Investors Partnership II ("TRIP"). In 1993, TRIP (the "Owners") awarded the general construction contract to Brown & Root, Inc. In addition to its role as general contractor, Brown & Root was also an equity partner in TRIP.

Brown & Root in turn entered into subcontracts with Moore Brothers Co., Inc. and The Lane Construction Corp., the plaintiffs, to build parts of the road. . . .

The subcontracts between Brown & Root and plaintiffs contain a general "pay when paid" clause:

> Notwithstanding any other provision hereof, payment by Owner to General Contractor is a condition precedent to any obligation of General Contractor to make payment hereunder; General Contractor shall have no obligation to make payment to Subcontractor for any portion of the Sublet Work for which General Contractor has not received payment from the Owner.
>
> * * *

The prime construction contract contains provisions for additional payment if the Owners order substantial design changes that constitute a "change in scope" of the project, including a provision for binding arbitration. The early drafts of the contract also contained several specific design change illustrations to clarify the type of situation in which Brown & Root would be entitled to additional payment from the Owners.

Changing the thickness of the pavement sub-base material was included in the examples of design changes that would warrant additional payment. Changing the thickness of the pavement sub-base is a common and costly design change in highway construction, and throughout the development of the DTRE project there was some uncertainty about the adequacy of the initial pavement design and the thickness of the sub-base material that would be required by the Virginia Department of Transportation. As early as 1991 the Brown & Root project manager knew that the initial pavement design for the DTRE was on the "marginal end."

The lenders who were financing the highway project, however, wanted to contain the costs of the project and insisted on a "high degree of certainty" in assessing the total project costs. They were hesitant to agree to a contract that contained specific illustrations of design changes that would warrant additional payment. The Owners and Brown & Root, therefore, agreed in July of 1993 to delete the specific illustrations of design changes from the prime contract to placate the lenders. At the same time, the Owners and Brown & Root assured the lenders that no substantial changes in the work, as defined in the base contract, were anticipated.

After deleting the design change illustrations from the prime contract, the Owners and Brown & Root incorporated the illustrations into a "Policy and Procedures" letter, the existence of which was not revealed to the lenders. In essence, the Owners and Brown & Root reached a side agreement concerning additional "change in scope" illustrations and then concealed that agreement from the lenders by placing it in a side letter, while leaving it out of the prime contract. Brown & Root did not tell the subcontractors that the design change illustrations and the potential need for additional "change in scope" work were hidden from, and therefore not adequately funded by, the lenders.

When the need for a thicker pavement sub-base became apparent, Brown & Root ordered the subcontractors to proceed with the additional work. Under the terms of the "pay when paid" condition precedent in the subcontract, Brown & Root knew that if payment for the additional work were not forthcoming from TRIP, it was the subcontractors who would assume the bulk of the loss.

After the additional work was completed, both Brown & Root and the subcontractors sought arbitration of their claim for additional payment from the Owners. The arbitrator concluded that the additional work did constitute a "change in scope" and therefore ordered the Owners to make payments beyond the base contract price. The arbitrator ordered TRIP to pay Brown & Root, who was subsequently required to pay the subcontractors.

Because the lenders were not made aware of the significant likelihood that additional work would be necessary, financing was never arranged to cover payment for additional "change in scope" work. TRIP, therefore, did not have the funds to pay Brown & Root the amount of the arbitration award. Brown & Root, as a result, claims that it is not obligated to pay the subcontractors for the additional work because of the "pay when paid" clause contained in the subcontracts.

* * *

Plaintiffs filed separate complaints against Brown & Root and its payment bond surety, Highlands, in the U.S. District Court for the Eastern District of Virginia in December of 1996. . . . On December 30, 1998, the district court issued extensive findings of fact and conclusions of law after a bench trial on the plaintiffs' claims against Brown & Root. The court held that Brown & Root is liable (1) to Lane for $ 1.4 million plus prejudgment interest for the additional "change in scope" work, (2) to Lane for $ 2.4 million for the early completion bonus, (3) to Moore for $ 2.1 million for the additional "change in scope" work, and (4) to Moore for $ 2.4 million for the early completion bonus.

Defendants appeal the . . . judgment against Brown & Root. . . .

* * *

III.

We next consider whether the district court properly found that Brown & Root is liable to the plaintiffs for payment for the additional "change in scope" work. . . .

A. Findings of fact

The district court found that Brown & Root's own actions in connection with the prime contract and the arrangements for financing additional "change in scope" work contributed to the non-occurrence of the condition precedent. The court found that Brown & Root knew that additional "change in scope" work on the DTRE project would likely be necessary to accommodate design changes regarding the thickness of the pavement sub-base material. Brown & Root nonetheless assured the lenders that no additional work would be necessary. Brown & Root then acquiesced in the decision to remove the "change in scope" illustrations from the contract to accommodate the lenders' interest in capping costs, while at the same time protecting themselves with the Policy and Procedures Letter which memorialized the change illustrations as a "side agreement."

In short, the district court found that Brown & Root agreed to remove the design change illustrations from the prime construction contract to placate the lenders, placed those illustrations in a side agreement (the existence of which was not revealed to the lenders), and assured the lenders that no additional work or design changes would be necessary. In finding these facts, the district court weighed the credibility of witnesses, the testimony offered during the prior arbitration, and various documents entered into evidence during the trial. Because the district court's findings of fact are consistent with the evidence contained in the record before this court, those findings are not clearly erroneous.

B. Conclusions of law

The subcontracts between Brown & Root and the plaintiffs contain a valid "pay when paid" condition precedent.* * * Because the Owners have not paid Brown & Root for the arbitration judgment regarding the additional "change in scope" work, Brown & Root can, as an initial matter, assert the nonoccurrence of the condition precedent as a valid defense to plaintiffs' claims.

Having found that by its own actions Brown & Root contributed to the non-occurrence of the condition precedent, however, the district court applied the "prevention doctrine" to waive the condition precedent and held that Brown & Root is liable to the plaintiffs for payment for the additional "change in scope" work notwithstanding the "pay when paid" clause in the subcontract.

The prevention doctrine is a generally recognized principle of contract law according to which if a promisor prevents or hinders fulfillment of a condition to his performance, the condition may be waived or excused. * * *

The prevention doctrine does not require proof that the condition would have occurred "but for" the wrongful conduct of the promisor; instead it only requires that the conduct have "contributed materially" to the non-occurrence of the condition. * * * The Supreme Court of Virginia does not require the plaintiff to prove "but for" causation. Rather, as that court specifically noted, "it is as effective an excuse of performance of a condition that the promisor has hindered performance as that he has actually prevented it." * * *

The district court found that Brown & Root misled the lenders regarding its expectations that potentially costly design changes would occur. By misleading the lenders in this way, Brown & Root made it less likely that the lenders would arrange additional financing to cover the cost of anticipated design changes. We therefore agree with the district court's conclusion that Brown & Root's conduct "hindered" the fulfillment of the condition precedent.

Brown & Root offers an alternative explanation for the failure of the condition precedent. The failure, they contend, was caused by the financial insolvency of the DTRE project, which was a result of lower than projected traffic flow on the DTRE. According to TRIP's Chief Financial Officer, because of the project's financial distress, sometime in December of 1995 the lenders halted all payments to Brown & Root since it was a partner in the DTRE project. Brown & Root concludes, therefore, that the May 1996 arbitration award would not have been paid regardless of whether additional contingency funding had been arranged by the lenders.

We are not persuaded by Brown & Root's argument. The fact that the lenders halted payments to Brown & Root under the circumstances as they existed in December of 1995 is not proof that the lenders would have forbidden TRIP to draw on some other source of funds to pay Brown & Root for the additional work after the arbitration award in May of 1996 under different circumstances. Had the lenders been apprised early on of the strong possibility that the pavement design would change, it is reasonable to infer that appropriate funding would have been arranged and made available for payment to Brown & Root.

The question is essentially a factual inquiry: why did TRIP fail to pay Brown & Root for the additional "change in scope" work? The district court found that TRIP failed to pay, at least in part, because of Brown & Root's misconduct. Because the district court's findings of fact are not clearly erroneous, and given the speculative nature of Brown & Root's alternative explanation, we do not find reversible error in the conclusions reached below as to the additional work claims. We agree that Brown & Root's misrepresentations "contributed materially" to TRIP's failure to pay for the additional "change in scope" work.

Having so concluded, we hold that the prevention doctrine was properly invoked and the performance of the condition precedent was correctly waived as to the additional "change in scope" work. Without the condition precedent as a defense, Brown & Root is liable to the plaintiffs for payment for the additional work.

* * *

VI.

For the reasons discussed above, we affirm the orders of the district court in part, reverse in part, and remand for further proceedings consistent with this opinion.

Affirmed in Part, Reversed in Part, and Remanded

Wilkins, Circuit Judge, concurring in part and dissenting in part:

. . . I would also conclude that the district court erred in holding that the prevention doctrine excused the nonfulfillment of the pay-when-paid condition with respect to the change in scope claims.

* * *

II.

I next address Brown & Root's contention that the district court erred in ruling that Brown & Root could not assert the nonfulfillment of the pay-when-paid condition as a defense to the change in scope claims because Brown & Root prevented or hindered the fulfillment of the condition.

Under the prevention doctrine, when a promisor hinders or prevents fulfillment of a condition and that hindrance or prevention "contributes materially" to the nonoccurrence of the condition, the condition is excused. * * * Because the prevention doctrine "is purely one of waiver," only "active conduct of the conditional promisor, preventing or hindering the fulfillment of the condition" excuses nonfulfillment of the condition. * * * Moreover, "the action of the party whose conduct is alleged to have prevented performance must be wrongful, and, accordingly, in excess of his legal rights." * * *

The district court found that four acts by Brown & Root excused the nonfulfillment of the pay-when-paid condition, none of which, in my view, supports excusing nonfulfillment. The primary act on which the district court relied—and the one on which the majority relies in affirming—was that Brown & Root "concealed from the lenders its expectation that changes in scope would occur." * * * The district court reasoned that absent the concealment, the lenders would have provided adequate contingency funding and "money would have been available to pay Brown & Root for the change in scope claims." * * * These findings were clearly erroneous because the district court had no reasonable basis for concluding that Brown & Root's concealment of its concern that scope changes would be necessary contributed materially to TRIP's failure to pay Brown & Root for the change in scope work.

In reviewing this issue, it is important to view the information concealed in light of the information that the lenders did have. The lenders must have been aware that there was a possibility that changes—particularly changes in the asphalt thickness—would occur: As the district court found, the consulting engineering firm retained by the lenders recommended the additional pavement thickness.* * * The lenders also must have been aware that a change in asphalt thickness and similar changes might entitle Brown & Root to additional payment under the contract: Although the parties had deleted language in the contract stating that a change in asphalt thickness would constitute a substantial change in project scope, the parties had not included language in the contract stating that such a change would not constitute a substantial change in project scope. Accordingly, the lenders were well aware that there was a possibility that TRIP would have to pay for increased asphalt thickness.

With this background, it is important to recognize that the only information that Brown & Root "concealed" from the lenders relating to whether extra work would be required was Brown & Root's concern that the lenders' own consultant's view that the asphalt needed to be thicker might prevail with the VDOT over the contrary view advanced by Brown & Root's engineering firm. The question then becomes what effect, if any, the lenders' knowledge of Brown & Root's concern would have had on the lenders' evaluation of the views of the lenders' own engineer. Importantly, there is no testimony from the lenders stating that had they known of Brown & Root's concern, they would have required further funding. Without such evidence, the district court could only speculate concerning whether the concealment had any effect at all on the lenders' evaluation of the probability that TRIP would have to pay for thicker asphalt.

It is possible that disclosure of Brown & Root's concern to the lenders would have had some effect on the lenders' assessment of the probability that TRIP ultimately would have to pay for thicker asphalt. Nevertheless, there simply was no reasonable, nonspeculative basis from which a fact-finder could conclude that this disclosure, had it been made, would have caused the lenders to decide that funding for the project was inadequate. And, even if such a basis existed, a factfinder still would have been left to speculate as to whether knowledge of Brown & Root's concern would have prompted the lenders to provide more funding or would have prompted the lenders to decide not to fund the project at all.[5] In short, the Subcontractors failed miserably in their attempt to prove that Brown & Root contributed materially to TRIP's failure to pay for the change in scope claims Accordingly, I believe the district court erred in excusing the nonfulfillment of the pay-when-paid condition by virtue of the prevention doctrine, and the majority errs in holding otherwise.

* * *

III.

In sum, I would reverse . . . the judgments against Brown & Root on the Subcontractors' change in scope claims. . . .

---

[5]The district court also found that had the Subcontractors known that the lenders had been misled concerning the scope of the project, the Subcontractors "could have refused to agree to the pay-when-paid condition." Lane Constr., 29 F. Supp. 2d at 724. However, the prevention doctrine would apply only if Brown & Root's conduct contributed materially to the nonfulfillment of the condition. The extent to which Brown & Root's conduct may have caused the pay-when-paid clause to come into existence is irrelevant. . . .

QUESTIONS

1. Questions about the facts of this case

   1.1. Did the court find prevention because Brown & Root had a conflict of interest due to the fact that it was both an owner and a contractor on the project?

   1.2. Was the lenders' concern for more "certainty" allayed or made worse by the actions taken in response to the request to remove the examples of items that would increase the cost?

   1.3. The court acts as though TRIP's only source of funds would be loan funds. Why do you suppose it makes that assumption?

2. Questions about the law

   2.1. In contrast to *Peacock Construction, supra*, at 695, how does the contract here allocate the risk of not getting paid by the owner in a large construction contract?

   2.2. On what points does the dissent depart from the majority? They both agree that the doctrine of prevention is an issue, but disagree on its application. Why?

   2.3. What is being "excused" here? Is it the obligation to perform? Or is it the satisfaction of a condition precedent to some other duty?

   2.4. If this case allows conditions to be excused (essentially, written out of the contract), how does that work? Does this case effectively say that Brown & Root has to pay the subcontractors even though they bargained for the right not to have to pay them until they themselves were paid?

E. Excusing Conditions When Strict Interpretation Would Amount to Forfeiture

What if no party plays games with conditions, but the agreed language doesn't work as one party thought it would (and mistake is not available as a defense)? This is particularly troublesome if the language is in a condition, thus acting as a block against the maturation of a duty. A party may render all it is to do under the contract, only to find that it may not be paid because the other side's duty to pay has not yet matured because all conditions to payment have not been satisfied. Under conditions, it is all or nothing; you don't receive part payment after part satisfaction of a condition.

Courts acknowledge that there may be circumstances in which all or nothing outcomes are not fair, or not in accordance with the original intention of the parties. For the most part, these courts focus on whether the operation of the clause at issue as a condition will work a forfeiture on one of the parties. The next case explores this concept.

Acme Markets, Inc. v. Federal Armored Express, Inc.
Superior Court of Pennsylvania
437 Pa. Super. 41, 648 A.2d 1218 (1994)

Opinion by Hester, J:

Acme Markets, Inc., appeals from the order entered in the Court of Common Pleas of Montgomery County on December 21, 1993, which granted Federal Armored Express, Inc. ("Federal") summary judgment. For the reasons set forth below, we reverse that order and remand the matter for further proceedings.

The procedural history of this case may be summarized as follows. On November 20, 1990, appellant filed a breach of contract complaint against Federal. In that complaint, appellant alleged that the parties had entered into a contract for armored car service and that the agreement later was amended to provide for the timely reimbursement of service-related losses. In addition, appellant averred that a Federal employee was robbed on May 19, 1990, after accepting possession of one of appellant's cashbags. Finally, appellant asserted that even though it had notified Federal promptly of the $62,544.32 loss, Federal had not made the reimbursement required by the agreement. Consequently, appellant requested, among other things, an award of damages equivalent to the amount of the loss.

On September 26, 1991, following the effectuation of service, appellant filed an answer and new matter. In connection with one of the defenses asserted in that document, Federal relied upon the fifth paragraph of the agreement which provides, "Responsibility of Federal under this contract shall begin when said [cash]bags or packages have been accepted and receipted for by Federal or its authorized employees, and shall terminate upon delivery to consignee or upon return to shipper." See Complaint at exhibit A. Specifically, Federal claimed that it bore no responsibility for the loss since neither it nor any of its employees had accepted the bag or provided the necessary receipt prior to the robbery.

On June 30, 1993, claiming that discovery was complete and that an examination of the record revealed no genuine issue of material fact, appellant moved for summary judgment. Federal responded by filing a cross-motion for summary judgment in which it acknowledged that one of its employees possessed appellant's cashbag at the time of the robbery. In addition, Federal noted that neither party disputed the fact that the employee in question had not provided a receipt for the bag prior to its loss. Consequently, relying upon both the fifth paragraph of the agreement and an affidavit demonstrating that the receipt requirement conformed with the custom of the armored car industry, Federal requested the entrance of judgment in its favor. On December 21, 1993, the trial court concluded that the fifth paragraph constituted a condition precedent to Federal's liability under the agreement. Thus, the court denied appellant's summary judgment motion and granted Federal relief. This timely appeal followed.

* * *

Appellant asserts that the trial court erroneously concluded that the fifth paragraph of the agreement constituted a condition precedent to Federal's liability for the lost bag. Specifically, appellant argues that since the paragraph was not labelled a condition precedent and does not contain other language normally associated with such a condition, "there is no means by which to state with the certainty required by Pennsylvania law that it creates a condition precedent." Appellant's brief at 13. We find appellant's claim devoid of merit.

Initially, we note that a condition precedent may be defined as a condition which must occur before a duty to perform under a contract arises. * * * While the parties to a contract need not utilize any particular words to create a condition precedent, an act or event designated in a contract will not be construed as constituting one unless that clearly appears to have been the parties' intention. * * * In addition, we note that the purpose of any condition set forth in a contract must be determined in accordance with the general rules of contractual interpretation. * * * Those rules may be summarized as follows.

> When construing agreements involving clear and unambiguous terms, this Court need only examine the writing itself to give effect to the parties['] understanding. * * * The court must construe the contract only as written and may not modify the plain meaning of the words under the guise of interpretation. * * *When the terms of a written contract are clear, this Court will not re-write it to give it a construction in conflict with the accepted and plain meaning of the language used. * * * Conversely, when the language is ambiguous and the intention of the parties cannot be reasonably ascertained from the language of the writing alone, the parol evidence rule does not apply to the admission of oral testimony to show both the intent of the parties and the circumstances attending the execution of the contract. * * *

Creeks v. Creeks, 422 Pa.Super. 432, 435, 619 A.2d 754, 756 (1993).

In the present case, the contested paragraph indicates that Federal's responsibility under the contract "shall begin when bags or packages have been accepted and receipted for by Federal or its employees. . . ." Complaint at exhibit A. Our reading of this plain language demonstrates that it clearly and unambiguously conditions Federal's performance under the contract upon both the acceptance of bags or packages and the granting of a receipt for them. Thus, it unquestionably delineates a condition precedent involving those requirements.

Since we have found that Federal's liability under the contract was subject to a condition precedent and neither party disputes that the receipt portion of the condition remained unfulfilled at the time of the robbery, we must determine whether satisfaction of that requirement may be excused. Apparently arguing that strict application of the condition would be unfair, appellant asserts that the receipt requirement was immaterial and could only be seen as incidental to the far more significant satisfied requirement of possession and acceptance by Federal's employee of appellant's property. See Appellant's brief at 15.

Restatement (Second) of Contracts § 229 discusses the excuse of a condition to avoid unfairness in connection with its strict enforcement. More specifically, that section relates to the excuse of a condition leading to a forfeiture, a term referring to "the denial of compensation that results when the obligee loses his right to the agreed exchange after he has relied substantially, as by preparation or performance on the expectation of that exchange." Restatement (Second) of Contracts § 229, comment b. Section 229 provides, "To the extent that the non-occurrence of a condition would cause disproportionate forfeiture, a court may excuse the non-occurrence of that condition unless its occurrence was a material part of the agreed exchange." Restatement (Second) of Contracts § 229. Since Pennsylvania law "abhors forfeitures and penalties and enforces them with the greatest reluctance when a proper case is presented[,]" * * * section 229 is consistent with the law of this Commonwealth. * * * Consequently, we will apply it in the present case.

There can be little doubt that the operation of the condition in question will lead to a forfeiture since the condition's nonoccurrence results in the denial of compensation for the loss of a cashbag possessed by Federal for transportation in accordance with the contract. Thus, the question becomes whether the forfeiture would be disproportionate.

> In determining whether the forfeiture is "disproportionate," [the] court must weigh the extent of the forfeiture by the obligee against the importance to the obligor of the risk from which he sought to be protected and the degree to which that protection will be lost if the nonoccurrence of the condition is excused to the extent required to prevent forfeiture.

Restatement (Second) of Contracts § 229, comment b.

In the present case, appellant obviously entered into the armored car service contract so that it would have a secure method of transporting cash and checks to the bank. Strict application of the condition precedent would result in the loss of appellant's ability to recover from Federal for the theft of the bag entrusted to Federal's care. Moreover, we believe that the receipting requirement was intended to provide Federal with proof that it accepted, at a specific time, a certain number of cashbags for shipment. Thus, in our opinion, the requirement probably was little more than an accounting device designed to track bags picked up in accordance with the agreement. Under such circumstances, the receipt primarily would serve to protect Federal rather than Acme from, among other things, theft by its own employees and disputes regarding the number of bags accepted. Those are two risks not at issue herein.

While we believe that the receipt requirement probably was an accounting device which had little impact upon the situation presently at issue, our examination of the certified record reveals that it is devoid of any evidence demonstrating the requirement's actual purpose. Thus, even though we have speculated on the matter, the record is inadequate to determine whether our speculation is accurate. In view of the inadequate record, we may not conduct the critical weighing analysis required by the Restatement or determine whether fulfillment of the condition may be excused. Indeed, we note that the trial court erroneously believed that its analysis ended upon concluding that a receipt was required to fulfill the condition precedent. Thus, the court did not consider whether the forfeiture would be disproportionate, decide if the receipt requirement constituted a material part of the exchange, or require the parties to provide an adequate record either for resolving those issues or deciding whether summary judgment in favor of Federal would be appropriate. Accordingly, we must reverse the trial court's grant of summary judgment and remand the matter for further proceedings.

On remand, the trial court should conduct an evidentiary hearing to determine the purpose of the receipt requirement and engage in the necessary weighing analysis. In addition, the court should determine whether the contested requirement constituted a material part of the agreement.[6] While this determination rests to a large extent on the analysis of the requirement's purpose, it also involves a consideration of the negotiations of the parties along with all other circumstances relevant to the formation of the contract or to the requirement itself, including the circumstances surrounding the theft.[7]

Order reversed. Case remanded for further proceedings. Jurisdiction relinquished.

QUESTIONS

1. Questions about the facts of this case

    1.1. When did the robbery occur relative to the handing over of the cashbags? Was it as the cashbags were being loaded? Is this clear, or even relevant?

    1.2. Do you think Acme thought about the order of performance when it signed the agreement? Should it have?

[6] We note that the form on which the requirement appears is pre-printed and does not contain any alterations. Thus, while not dispositive, our examination of that document suggests that the requirement was not specifically bargained-for.

[7] In light of our determination, we do not address appellant's two remaining claims which relate to whether Federal assumed liability for the bag immediately upon obtaining possession of it and whether satisfaction of the condition precedent may be excused since the failure of the condition resulted from the conduct of Federal's own employee.

1.3. Does anything other than a strict construction of the condition give Acme incentive to be sloppy at the handover (Along the lines of: "As long as you touch it, it is your responsibility")?

2. Questions about the law

2.1. You represent Acme on remand. What evidence do you introduce? Whom do you interview to get this evidence?

2.2. If the court is correct about the nature of the contract in note 6, would this case be better decided as a contract of adhesion?

SECTION 3: IS PERFORMANCE *STILL* DUE?: POST-FORMATION CONDUCT THAT CHANGES THE DEAL (AND HENCE THE NATURE OF THE REQUIRED PERFORMANCE)

One of the enduring facts about contracts and their performance is that it is the rare case in which contracts of any duration are not in some way modified before the scheduled performance. This may be done formally, as with a written amendment, or informally as when one side declines or neglects to complain about minor non-compliance by the other side.

There is a legal question raised by this divergence between the written word and practice. How or when can the party who is no longer getting exactly what it bargained for bring the other party back into compliance? Immediately? After a warning? Never? For lawyers advising clients in the middle of these contracts, advice on "what to do next"is the bread and butter of daily life. This section explores when an excuse or justification to perform can arise from the actions of the parties.

A. Amendment

People may modify their contractual obligations at any time. Under the U.C.C., such modifications do not even require consideration. §2-209(1). But a hallmark of modification or amendment is that both parties consent, or at least manifest assent, to the proposed modification. When that assent is express, as with a written amendment, few problems are presented. But what happens when consent for a permanent change could fairly be implied from conduct, not speech?

To take a common example, what happens if you just happen to be a week late in your rent payments every month? If six months into the lease, the landlord cries "Enough"and tries to evict you because you did not pay on time, do you have any legal arguments to aid your cause (after all, the text of the lease does say when the rent is due)? The next case has something to say about this fact pattern.

May Centers, Inc. v. Paris Croissant of Enfield Square, Inc., et al.
Superior Court of Connecticut
42 Conn. Supp. 77, 599 A.2d 407 (1991)

Satter, Judge.

The plaintiff is suing the corporate defendant, Paris Croissant of Enfield Square, Inc., (Paris) to recover unpaid rent, common assessments and attorney's fees pursuant to a lease, and is also suing the individual defendants* as guarantors of Paris' liability under the lease.

The facts are as follows. On February 4, 1986, the plaintiff as landlord and Paris as tenant entered into a ten year lease (prepared by the plaintiff) of commercial space at the Enfield Mall, commencing April 15, 1986. The lease provided for a minimum rent, to be paid in advance on the first day of each calendar month, the first month's minimum rent to be paid at the time of execution of the lease, a percentage rent and various assessments. If Paris failed "to remedy any default in the payment of any sum due under this lease for ten (10) days after notice" the plaintiff could reenter the premises and sublet them, or declare the lease at an end, evict Paris and collect the rent due over the balance of the term of the lease. Paris' failure to pay rent also entitled the plaintiff to charge interest at twelve percent on the unpaid balance, plus attorney's fees incurred to collect back rent. The lease also provided that "[n]o waiver of any default hereunder shall be implied from any omission by either party to take any action on account of such default if such default persists or is repeated. . . . The acceptance by landlord of rent

*Those individuals are represented by the "et al." in the case caption. Eds.

with knowledge of the breach of any of the covenants of this lease by tenant shall not be a waiver or any such breach."

The individual defendants executed a guaranty (prepared by the plaintiff) of the obligations of Paris under the lease. The guaranty provided that the guarantors "absolutely, unconditionally and irrevocably" guarantee to the plaintiff to be liable for full payment of all rent and other charges payable by Paris under the lease, and if Paris defaults, forthwith to pay such rent and charges to the plaintiff, without the necessity of any notice to the guarantors, which they expressly waive. The guaranty was to remain in effect during the first two years of the term of the lease. It further provided: "In the event [Paris] is in default or has failed to perform any of the terms and conditions of the lease as of the expiration of the second (2nd) year of the term of the lease, this [guaranty] shall remain in full force and effect during the entire term of the lease."

Paris, having paid the first month's minimum rent at the time the lease was executed on February 4, 1986, continued to pay the rent around the middle of each month. Thus, in 1986, the June rent was posted by the plaintiff as having been paid on June 13, the July rent on July 21, the August rent on August 14, the September rent on September 16, the October rent on October 13, the November rent on November 17, and, the December rent on December 11, 1986. Similar patterns persisted through 1987, although in some instances the rent was paid later. In 1988, the January rent was posted as having been paid on January 29, the February rent on February 22, the March rent on March 24, and the April rent on April 25. The two year period of the guaranty expired on April 14, 1988.

The procedure established by the plaintiff was that the tenants of Enfield Mall mailed their rent checks to a lock box in a St. Louis, Missouri bank. Bank employees deposited checks to the plaintiff's account and the next day posted the payment to the plaintiff. The evidence is that Paris' April, 1988 rent was posted to the plaintiff's account on April 25, 1988. That day was a Monday. The court infers the check was received in St. Louis on the previous Friday, or April 22, 1988. The defendant William Summers testified that he could not recall when he mailed the April rent check in Connecticut. It could possibly have been prior to April 15, although he regularly mailed such checks after the fifteenth of the month. This court, taking judicial notice of the mails between Enfield and St. Louis; *Lloyd & Elliott, Inc. v. Parke*, 114 Conn. 12, 14, 157 A. 272 (1931); concludes, from all the evidence, that Paris' April rent check was more probably than not mailed on April 20, 1988.

In June, 1987, the defendant Anthony Scussel sold his interest in Paris to Summers; Scussel thereafter ceased to be involved in Paris' business.

In July, 1988, Paris became erratic in its rent payments and the plaintiff started sending notices of default. Notices were sent in July, 1988, September, 1988, February, 1989, and April, 1989.

In May, 1989, Paris ceased paying rent and gave up its key to the plaintiff. The plaintiff boarded up the premises and eventually relet them in May, 1990. The unpaid rent, charges and assessments under the lease as of May, 1990, amount to $43,945. Interest on the arrearage to the date of trial amounts to $5799.35. Attorney's fees and costs of collection through the trial amount to $6223.70, totaling $55,968.05, which the plaintiff claims as damages.

On the first count against Paris, the plaintiff has proven its claim and is entitled to recover $55,968.05.

On the second count against the individual defendants as guarantors, the question is whether the plaintiff proved the existence of the condition precedent that triggered the extension of the guaranty beyond the initial two years. * * * More specifically, did the plaintiff prove Paris was in default in its rent (the only default the plaintiff claims) as of April 14, 1988? This court concludes that the plaintiff did not.

The lease term commenced on April 15, 1986. Paris paid the first month's minimum rent in February, 1986. The plaintiff's records are unclear whether this payment covered the period from April 15 to May 15, 1986, and the plaintiff produced no evidence to clarify this point. What is clear is that starting in June, 1986, Paris paid the rent each month around the fifteenth and the plaintiff accepted it without complaint. Although the lease provided for rent payments on the first of the month, it is a form lease and does not specifically take into account that the lease term started in the middle of the month.

A course of conduct may not only indicate the intent of the parties for the purpose of interpreting ambiguous language in a contract; * * * but also evince a subsequent modification of a contract or an abrogation of specific contract terms. * * * Proof that a contract has been modified is established by a showing of mutual consent; * * * which, in turn, " 'may be inferred from the attendant circumstances and conduct of the parties.' " * * *

In the present case, the court concludes from the starting date of the lease on April 15, 1986, and from the rent being regularly sent by Paris and accepted by the plaintiff without protest around the fifteenth of each month, that the parties indicated by their conduct their mutual consent to substitute the fifteenth as the due date for the rent. 2 Restatement (Second), Contracts § 279, comment (a).

The lease provides the tenant has ten days to remedy a default in rent payment before the plaintiff can take action. This is consistent with General Statutes § 47a-15a. The court interprets the lease as giving Paris a ten day grace period.

In the present case, Paris mailed the April, 1988 rent on April 20, 1988, and since the plaintiff directed that the rent be sent that way, that is the date the April rent was paid. * * * Since the court finds the April, 1988 rent was due on April 15, 1988, Paris was not in default in payment of that month's rent.

Even assuming the due date of the rent was April 1, 1988, and the April rent check was sent on April 20, 1988, while Paris technically may have been in default on April 14, 1988, it was not in default "as of" April 14, 1988, as required by the guaranty for the guaranty to be extended. When the plaintiff received the April rent check, it had several alternatives: (1) refuse the check because it was late and hold Paris in default; (2) return the check and declare it was holding it not as rent but as use and occupancy; (3) accept the check as payment of the April rent. The third is the alternative the plaintiff selected. The plaintiff could not both accept the check and claim a default. The law is clearly stated in the Restatement (Second) of Contracts § 278(1): "If an obligee accepts in satisfaction of the obligator's duty a performance by the obligor that differs from what is due, the duty is discharged." See also comment (a). Section 47a-19 of the General Statutes provides that "[a]cceptance of rent with the knowledge that such rent is overdue constitutes a waiver of the landlord's right to terminate the rental agreement for the tenant's failure to pay such rent when it was due." While the statute is not directly applicable, it reveals the general rule that a landlord cannot simultaneously accept a month's rent and claim a default because of late payment.

Particularly, the plaintiff cannot accept the April, 1988 rent, claim no default, (although in subsequent months in 1988 and 1989 the plaintiff sent out notices of default), then initiate this case in November, 1989, a year and a half later, and demand that this court find Paris in default in April, 1988, so that the guaranty was extended and the individual defendants are obligated for $55,968.05. Rather, this court finds that by the plaintiff's acceptance of the April, 1988 rent on April 20, 1988, any consequence of the late payment for April was cured. Paris was not in default as of April 14, 1988, and the guaranty was not extended.

The plaintiff argues that the nonwaiver provisions of the lease allow a claim of default despite payment. This court disagrees. The court interprets the language that no waiver of any default shall be implied from omission to take action "if such default persists or is repeated," to mean that a prior default, such as late payment, did not require the plaintiff to excuse and to accept a subsequent late payment, but when the plaintiff accepted the late payment, the default as to that payment was cured. The court interprets the language that acceptance by the landlord of rent with knowledge of the breach of any of the covenants of the lease "shall not be a waiver of any such breach" to mean breaches of covenants other than relating to rent.

In essence, the plaintiff wants this court to construe the lease so that the failure by Paris to pay the April rent exactly on April 1, 1988, constitutes a default, which the plaintiff did not waive by accepting the rent, and which extended the guaranty. The established standards of preference in interpreting contracts favor interpretations that are reasonable rather than unreasonable; * * * practical; * * * and consistent with common sense. The plaintiff's desired construction is unconscionable because it creates a lease and guaranty " 'no man in his right senses . . . would make . . . and . . . no honest and fair man would accept.' " 2 Restatement (Second), Contracts § 208, comment (b). This court exercises its prerogative to "limit the application of any unconscionable term [of a contract so] as to avoid any unconscionable result." 2 Restatement (Second), Contracts § 208.

Judgment may enter on the first count for the plaintiff against Paris for $55,968.05. Judgment may enter on the second count for the individual defendants.

QUESTIONS

1. Questions about the facts of the case

   1.1. Did the court find that the tenant Paris was liable for all of the rent? In making that determination, did the date the rent was due matter?

   1.2. If the court found that Paris was fully liable, why do you suppose May Centers is pursuing the individual guarantors?

1.3. How many contracts are involved in this case? Upon which of those contracts are the individual defendants liable? If the guarantors are not directly liable on the lease (they did not sign that document), then why is the question of whether the parties amended their obligations to change the due date for the rent payment relevant?

2. Questions about the law

2.1. Where does this court find the necessary consent for the amendment to the lease? Where does the court find the consideration necessary for the amendment to the lease?

2.2. If you represented May Centers, and wanted to hold the guarantors to their obligations, what would you advise May Centers to do with the rent check that showed up in late April?

2.3. The court finds a "discharge" of the obligation to pay rent from "acceptance" of the check. Is there anything that you might want to put in leases drafted in Connecticut after this case that could help you out under similar circumstances?

2.4. How does the court deal with the anti-waiver provision in the lease?

2.5. Is there a difference between modification and amendment?

B. Waiver and Estoppel

Amendment is permanent; that is, it changes the obligations now and for the rest of the contract. But what if you just want to excuse one instance of non-performance—for example, what if it is okay for the tenant to not pay rent on time this month, but no others? Can you do this? Of course; the next two cases explore the legal devices in your contracts toolbox that might help.

Clark v. West

Court of Appeals of New York
193 N.Y. 349, 86 N.E. 1 (1908)

Werner, J:

The contract before us, stripped of all superfluous verbiage, binds the plaintiff to total abstention from the use of intoxicating liquors during the continuance of the work which he was employed to do. The stipulations relating to the plaintiff's compensation provide that if he does not observe this condition he is to be paid at the rate of $ 2 per page, and if he does comply therewith he is to receive $ 6 per page.* The plaintiff has written one book under the contract known as "Clark & Marshall on Corporations," which has been accepted, published and copies sold in large numbers by the defendant. The plaintiff admits that while he was at work on this book he did not entirely abstain from the use of intoxicating liquors. He has been paid only $2 per page for the work he has done. He claims that, despite his breach of this condition, he is entitled to the full compensation of $6 per page because the defendant, with full knowledge of plaintiff's non-observance of this stipulation as to total abstinence, has waived the breach thereof and cannot now insist upon strict performance in this regard. This plea of waiver presents the underlying question which determines the answers to the questions certified.

Briefly stated, the defendant's position is that the stipulation as to plaintiff's total abstinence is the consideration for the payment of the difference between $2 and $6 per page and therefore could not be waived except by a new agreement to that effect based upon a good consideration; that the so-called waiver alleged by the plaintiff is not a waiver but a modification of the contract in respect of its consideration. The plaintiff on the other hand argues that the stipulation for his total abstinence was merely a condition precedent intended to work a forfeiture of the additional compensation in case of a breach and that it could be waived without any formal agreement to that effect based upon a new consideration. * * *

---

*The actual language was:

"In consideration of the above promises," the defendant agrees to pay the plaintiff $2 per page on each book prepared by him, and if he "abstains from the use of intoxicating liquor and otherwise fulfills his agreements as hereinbefore set forth, he shall be paid an additional $4 per page in manner hereinbefore stated." Eds.

The subject-matter of the contract was the writing of books by the plaintiff for the defendant. The duration of the contract was the time necessary to complete them all. The work was to be done to the satisfaction of the defendant, and the plaintiff was not to write any other books except those covered by the contract unless requested so to do by the defendant, in which latter event he was to be paid for that particular work by the year. The compensation for the work specified in the contract was to be $6 per page, unless the plaintiff failed to totally abstain from the use of intoxicating liquors during the continuance of the contract, in which event he was to receive only $2 per page. That is the obvious import of the contract construed in the light of the purpose for which it was made, and in accordance with the ordinary meaning of plain language. It is not a contract to write books in order that the plaintiff shall keep sober, but a contract containing a stipulation that he shall keep sober so that he may write satisfactory books. When we view the contract from this standpoint it will readily be perceived that the particular stipulation is not the consideration for the contract, but simply one of its conditions which fits in with those relating to time and method of delivery of manuscript, revision of proof, citation of cases, assignment of copyrights, keeping track of new cases and citations for new editions, and other details which might be waived by the defendant, if he saw fit to do so. * * *

It is obvious that the parties thought that the plaintiff's normal work was worth $6 per page. That was the sum to be paid for the work done by the plaintiff and not for total abstinence. If the plaintiff did not keep to the condition as to total abstinence, he was to lose part of that sum. Precisely the same situation would have risen if the plaintiff had disregarded any of the other essential conditions of the contract. The fact that the particular stipulation was emphasized did not change its character. It was still a condition which the defendant could have insisted upon, as he has apparently done in regard to some others, and one which he could waive just as he might have waived those relating to the amount of the advance payments, or the number of pages to be written each month. A breach of any of the substantial conditions of the contract would have entailed a loss or forfeiture similar to that consequent upon a breach of the one relating to total abstinence, in case of the defendant's insistence upon his right to take advantage of them. This, we think, is the fair interpretation of the contract, and it follows that the stipulation as to the plaintiff's total abstinence was nothing more nor less than a condition precedent. If that conclusion is well founded there can be no escape from the corollary that this condition could be waived; and if it was waived the defendant is clearly not in a position to insist upon the forfeiture which his waiver was intended to annihilate. The forfeiture must stand or fall with the condition. If the latter was waived, the former is no longer a part of the contract. Defendant still has the right to counterclaim for any damages which he may have sustained in consequence of the plaintiff's breach, but he cannot insist upon strict performance. * * *

This whole discussion is predicated of course upon the theory of an express waiver. We assume that no waiver could be implied from the defendant's mere acceptance of the books and his payment of the sum of $2 per page without objection. It was the defendant's duty to pay that amount in any event after acceptance of the work. The plaintiff must stand upon his allegation of an express waiver and if he fails to establish that he cannot maintain his action.

The theory upon which the defendant's attitude seems to be based is that even if he has represented to the plaintiff that he would not insist upon the condition that the latter should observe total abstinence from intoxicants, he can still refuse to pay the full contract price for his work. The inequity of this position becomes apparent when we consider that this contract was to run for a period of years, during a large portion of which the plaintiff was to be entitled only to the advance payment of $2 per page, the balance being contingent, among other things, upon publication of the books and returns from sales. Upon this theory the defendant might have waived the condition while the first book was in process of production, and yet when the whole work was completed, he would still be in a position to insist upon the forfeiture because there had not been strict performance. Such a situation is possible in a case where the subject of the waiver is the very consideration of a contract * * *, but not where the waiver relates to something that can be waived. In the case at bar, as we have seen, the waiver is not of the consideration or subject-matter, but of an incident to the method of performance. The consideration remains the same. The defendant has had the work he bargained for, and it is alleged that he has waived one of the conditions as to the manner in which it was to have been done. He might have insisted upon literal performance and then he could have stood upon the letter of his contract. If, however, he has waived that incidental condition, he has created a situation to which the doctrine of waiver very precisely applies.

The cases which present the most familiar phases of the doctrine of waiver are those which have arisen out of litigation over insurance policies where the defendants have claimed a forfeiture because of the breach of some condition in the contract* * *, but it is a doctrine of general application which is confined to no particular class of cases. A waiver has been defined to be the intentional relinquishment of a known right. It is voluntary and implies an election to dispense with something of value, or forego some advantage which the party waiving it might at its option have demanded or insisted upon * * * and this definition is supported by many cases in this and other states. In the recent case of *Draper v. Oswego Co. Fire R. Assn.* (190 N. Y. 12, 16) Chief Judge Cullen, in speaking for the court upon this subject, said: "While that doctrine and the doctrine of equitable estoppel are often confused in insurance litigation, there is a clear distinction between the two. A waiver is the voluntary abandonment or relinquishment by a party of some right or advantage. As said by my brother Vann in the Kiernan Case (150 N. Y. 190): 'The law of waiver seems to be a technical doctrine, introduced and applied by the court for the purpose of defeating forfeitures. * * * While the principle may not be easily classified, it is well established that if the words and acts of the insurer reasonably justify the conclusion that with full knowledge of all the facts it intended to abandon or not to insist upon the particular defense afterwards relied upon, a verdict or finding to that effect establishes a waiver, which, if it once exists, can never be revoked.' The doctrine of equitable estoppel, or estoppel in pais, is that a party may be precluded by his acts and conduct from asserting a right to the detriment of another party who, entitled to rely on such conduct, has acted upon it. * * * As already said, the doctrine of waiver is to relieve against forfeiture; it requires no consideration for a waiver, nor any prejudice or injury to the other party." * * *

It remains to be determined whether the plaintiff has alleged facts which, if proven, will be sufficient to establish his claim of an express waiver by the defendant of the plaintiff's breach of the condition to observe total abstinence. In the 12th paragraph of the complaint, the plaintiff alleges facts and circumstances which we think, if established, would prove defendant's waiver of plaintiff's performance of that contract stipulation. These facts and circumstances are that long before the plaintiff had completed the manuscript of the first book undertaken under the contract, the defendant had full knowledge of the plaintiff's non-observance of that stipulation, and that with such knowledge he not only accepted the completed manuscript without objection, but "repeatedly avowed and represented to the plaintiff that he was entitled to and would receive said royalty payments (i.e., the additional $4 per page), and plaintiff believed and relied upon such representations * * * and at all times during the writing of said treatise on corporations, and after as well as before publication thereof as aforesaid, it was mutually understood, agreed and intended by the parties hereto that notwithstanding plaintiff's said use of intoxicating liquors, he was nevertheless entitled to receive and would receive said royalty as the same accrued under said contract."

* * *

The three questions certified should be answered in the affirmative, the order of the Appellate Division reversed, the interlocutory judgment of the Special Term affirmed, with costs in both courts, and the defendant be permitted to answer the complaint within twenty days upon payment of costs.

QUESTIONS AND NOTE

1. Questions about the facts of this case

   1.1. Why did Clark want to find a waiver instead of an amendment?

   1.2. What facts on remand does Clark need to prove to show a waiver? Would one instance of West saying that it was all right for Clark to drink and write be enough? What if a West representative, upon receiving the first draft and being told that West drank while writing it, said "If you do stuff this good while blitzed, where can we buy you more beer?"

2. Questions about the law

   2.1. What is the difference between waiver and amendment?

   2.2. What is the difference between waiver and estoppel for this court?

   2.3. Recall that West had contracted with Clark to produce a series of books. If Clark later writes another of the books in the series while intoxicated, is West legally obligated to pay him $6 a page?

   2.4. If you were West's lawyer, and wanted to protect West from the effect of statements made after the conclusion of the contract that would waive various provisions of the contract, how would you do that? What types of clauses would you draft?

3. Note

Waiver differs from modification or amendment in that it can be unilateral; that is, the consent of both parties is not necessary to effectuate the waiver. But who gets to say when a provision is waived? That was the issue in *Wyler Summit Partnership v. Turner Broadcasting System, Inc.,* 135 F.3d 658 (9th Cir. 1998). There, successors to the estate of the director William Wyler sued to get more royalties for the movie "Ben-Hur," which Wyler directed and which is one of the most successful movies of all time.

To do this, Wyler's heirs had to find some way around the contract Wyler and MGM (the predecessor to Turner) had signed in 1958. That contract gave Wyler 3% of the revenues from the film, but capped the annual payments at $50,000 per year. (Accounting for inflation, the equivalent dollar amount in 2001 would be around $300,000). The reason for this cap was that when the deal was negotiated, in 1958, the marginal tax rates in this country were much higher than today—ranging between 89% and 91% on every dollar earned over $100,000. To minimize taxes over time, Wyler requested that his percentage interest not be changed, but that MGM/Turner would only be obligated to pay him $50,000 per year, with any amounts due over $50,000 to be paid in later years when the current income did not match $50,000.

By the time the lawsuit was filed, Turner had accumulated over $1.5 million in overages (the amounts in excess of $50,000 per year) after paying Wyler and his heirs over $1.8 million. So high was this amount—the $1.5 million—that Turner could just invest *part* of the money and ensure a perpetual flow of $50,000 to Wyler's heirs. Under the contract, Turner could use what it didn't pay to Wyler.

Wyler's heirs sued to "waive" this $50,000 cap, and have the $1.5 million paid directly to them. Not so fast, replied Turner. The law says that a contracting party may waive only those conditions placed in a contract solely for that party's benefit. The provision did not solely benefit Wyler; Turner got a benefit too, in the form of interest-free capital. Moreover, waiving the provision now, and forcing Turner to pay $1.5 million to Wyler's heirs, would change the basic nature of the deal, and one can't do that by a unilateral waiver. After answering the complaint, Turner moved for summary judgment and succeeded.

The court agreed with Turner's statement of the law, but not its application. It found that Wyler's heirs could go to trial on the factual issues of who was to benefit from the provision, and whether waiver of that provision would unilaterally unsettle the basic structure of the contract.

On remand, Turner again moved for summary judgment, and each side submitted written testimony showing the presence of a material issue of fact as to whether Wyler was the only intended beneficiary of the clause. In an interesting application of parol evidence, Wyler's heirs submitted an affidavit from a member of the 1958 negotiating team, 41 years after the fact, to show that Wyler was intended to be the sole beneficiary. *Wyler Summit Partnership v. Turner Broadcasting System*, 235 F.3d 1184 (9th Cir. 2000). The court agreed that there were material issues of fact, and again remanded the case for a trial on the merits. The final result is unknown at press time.

SECTION 4: UNANTICIPATED POST-FORMATION EVENTS THAT MAY EXCUSE PERFORMANCE

Often, the post-formation event is not a change of heart; it is a change of circumstance. It may not be the same deal if circumstances change too much.

But how much change is too much? While there might be cases in which we are willing to provide an excuse when something completely unanticipated occurs—such as war or a governmental regulation that forbids one side from rendering its performance—isn't one of the functions of contract to allocate risks of the unknown? Shouldn't we just let the chips fall where they may, and force parties to a contract to plan out every contingency? These questions form the focus of this section, and we start with the simple case of what happens when two parties contract to sell something that turns out to be impossible to convey.

A. Impossibility, Impracticability and Frustration of Purpose

Assume Markell is badly in need of tutoring in contracts. He hires Epstein to teach him because of Epstein's stellar reputation in the field of contracts. Markell pays the fee of $10,000 up front, and Epstein agrees in writing to a course of tutoring.

Alas, Epstein passes on before the lessons can begin. Markell's first words to the widow are not whispers of condolence; they are "Give me my money back."

Can he get it? Look at the following.

Restatement (Second) of Contracts

§ 262 Death or Incapacity of Person Necessary for Performance

If the existence of a particular person is necessary for the performance of a duty, his death or such incapacity as makes performance impracticable is an event the non-occurrence of which was a basic assumption on which the contract was made.

§ 261 Discharge by Supervening Impracticability

Where, after a contract is made, a party's performance is made impracticable without his fault by the occurrence of an event the non-occurrence of which was a basic assumption on which the contract was made, his duty to render that performance is discharged, unless the language or the circumstances indicate the contrary.

So does Markell get his money back? What if Markell had employed not Epstein, but a company of which Epstein (before his untimely demise) was the sole shareholder, but which employed others from time to time to tutor contracts (assume that the contract with this company does not specify that Epstein, and only Epstein, must perform the services)?

What if the contract was not for services from Epstein, but an unconditional loan from Epstein (and Epstein's estate is loaded)? Assess this in light of the next case.

Taylor v. Caldwell

122 Eng.Rep. 309 (K.B. 1863)

BLACKBURN, J. In this case the plaintiffs and defendants had, on the 27th May, 1861, entered into a contract by which the defendants agreed to let the plaintiffs have the use of The Surrey Gardens and Music Hall on four days then to come, viz., the 17th June, 15th July, 5th August and 19th August, for the purpose of giving a series of four grand concerts, and day and night fetes at the Gardens and Hall on those days respectively; and the plaintiffs agreed to take the Gardens and Hall on those days, and pay £100 for each day.

The parties inaccurately call this a "letting," and the money to be paid a "rent"; but the whole agreement is such as to shew that the defendants were to retain the possession of the Hall and Gardens so that there was to be no demise of them, and that the contract was merely to give the plaintiffs the use of them on those days. Nothing however, in our opinion, depends on this. The agreement then proceeds to set out various stipulations between the parties as to what each was to supply for these concerts and entertainments, and as to the manner in which they should be carried on. The effect of the whole is to shew that the existence of the Music Hall in the Surrey Gardens in a state fit for a concert was essential for the fulfilment of the contract,-such entertainment as the parties contemplated in their agreement could not be given without it.

After the making of the agreement, and before the first day on which a concert was to be given, the Hall was destroyed by fire. This destruction, we must take it on the evidence, was without the fault of either party, and was so complete that in consequence the concerts could not be given as intended. And the question we have to decide is whether, under these circumstances, the loss which the plaintiffs have sustained is to fall upon the defendants. The parties when framing their agreement evidently had not present to their minds the possibility of such a disaster, and have made no express stipulation with reference to it, so that the answer to the question must depend upon the general rules of law applicable to such a contract.

There seems no doubt that where there is a positive contract to do a thing, not in itself unlawful, the contractor must perform it or pay damages for not doing it, although in consequence of unforeseen accidents, the performance of his contract has become unexpectedly burdensome or even impossible. . . . But this rule is only applicable when the contract is positive and absolute, and not subject to any condition either express or implied; and there are authorities which, as we think, establish the principle that where, from the nature of the contract, it appears that the parties must from the beginning have known that it could not be fulfilled unless when the time for the fulfilment of the contract arrived some particular specified thing continued to exist, so that, when entering into the contract, they must have contemplated such continuing existence as the foundation of what was to be done; there, in the absence of any express or implied warranty that the thing shall exist, the contract is not to be construed as a positive contract, but as subject to an implied condition that the parties shall be excused in case, before breach, performance becomes impossible from the perishing of the thing without default of the contractor.

There seems little doubt that this implication tends to further the great object of making the legal construction such as to fulfill the intention of those who entered into the contract. For in the course of affairs men in making such contracts in general would, if it were brought to their minds, say that there should be such a condition.

* * *

There is a class of contracts in which a person binds himself to do something which requires to be performed by him in person; and such promises, e.g. promises to marry, or promises to serve for a certain time, are never in practice qualified by an express exception of the death of the party; and therefore in such cases the contract is in terms broken if the promisor dies before fulfilment. Yet it was very early determined that, if the performance is personal, the executors are not liable; Hyde v. The Dean of Windsor (Cro.Eliz. 552, 553). See 2 Wms.Exors. 1560, 5th ed., where a very apt illustration is given. "Thus," says the learned author, "if an author undertakes to compose a work, and dies before completing it, his executors are discharged from this contract: for the undertaking is merely personal in its nature, and, by the intervention of the contractor's death, has become impossible to be performed." For this he cites a dictum of Lord Lyndhurst in Marshall v. Broadhurst (1 Tyr. 348, 349), and a case mentioned by Patteson J. in Wentworth v. Cock (10 A. & E. 42, 45–46). In Hall v. Wright (E.B. & E. 746, 749), Crompton J., in his judgment, puts another case. "Where a contract depends upon personal skill, and the act of God renders it impossible, as, for instance, in the case of a painter employed to paint a picture who is struck blind, it may be that the performance might be excused."

It seems that in those cases the only ground on which the parties or their executors, can be excused from the consequences of the breach of the contract is, that from the nature of the contract there is an implied condition of the continued existence of the life of the contractor, and, perhaps in the case of the painter of his eyesight. In the instances just given, the person, the continued existence of whose life is necessary to the fulfilment of the contract, is himself the contractor, but that does not seem in itself to be necessary to the application of the principle; as is illustrated by the following example. In the ordinary form of an apprentice deed the apprentice binds himself in unqualified terms to "serve until the full end and term of seven years to be fully complete and ended," during which term it is covenanted that the apprentice his master "faithfully shall serve," and the father of the apprentice in equally unqualified terms binds himself for the performance by the apprentice of all and every covenant on his part. (See the form, 2 Chitty on Pleading, 370, 7th ed. by Greening.) It is undeniable that if the apprentice dies within the seven years, the covenant of the father that he shall perform his covenant to serve for seven years is not fulfilled, yet surely it cannot be that an action lie against the father? Yet the only reason why it would not is that he is excused because of the apprentice's death.

These are instances where the implied condition is of the life of a human being, but there are others in which the same implication is made as to the continued existence of a thing. For example, where a contract of sale is made amounting to a bargain and sale, transferring presently the property in specific chattels, which are to be delivered by the vendor at a future day; there, if the chattels, without fault of the vendor, perish in the interval, the purchaser must pay the price and the vendor is excused from performing his contract to deliver, which has thus become impossible.

It may, we think, be safely asserted to be now English law, that in all contracts of loan of chattels or bailments if the performance of the promise of the borrower or bailee to return the things lent or bailed, becomes impossible because it has perished, this impossibility (if not arising upon the fault of the borrower or bailee from some risk which he has taken upon himself) excuses the borrower or bailee from the performance of his promise to redeliver the chattel.

* * *

In none of these cases is the promise in words other than positive, nor is there any express stipulation that the destruction of the person or thing shall excuse the performance; but that excuse is by law implied, because from the nature of the contract it is apparent that the parties contracted on the basis of the continued existence of the particular person or chattel. In the present case, looking at the whole contract, we find that the parties contracted on the basis of the continued existence of the Music Hall at the time when the concerts were to be given; that being essential to their performance.

We think, therefore, that the Music Hall having ceased to exist, without fault of either party, both parties are excused, the plaintiffs from taking the gardens and paying the money, the defendants from performing their promise to give the use of the Hall and Gardens and other things. Consequently the rule must be absolute to enter the verdict for the defendants.

Rule absolute.

QUESTIONS AND NOTE

1. Questions about the facts of this case

   1.1. Was there any provision in the contract regarding the destruction of the hall?

   1.2. Would it have mattered if Caldwell had bought fire insurance on the building?

2. Questions about the law

   2.1. What is the legal device (fiction?) that the judge uses to find that both parties are excused?

   2.2. There are leases which expressly obligate the lessee to pay even if the premises are destroyed. They are sometimes referred to as "hell or high water" leases in the real estate industry. Would *Taylor* help the lessee in such a lease?

3. Note

In a modern day version of *Taylor*, the court in *The Opera Co. of Boston, Inc. v. The Wolf Trap Foundation for the Performing Arts*, 817 F.2d 1094 (4th Cir. 1987), faced the following situation. The Wolf Trap Foundation had hired The Opera Co. to give four operatic performances at the Filene Center in Wolf Trap Park in Boston. The agreed consideration was $272,000, and Wolf agreed to provide lighting and lighting equipment to The Opera Co.'s specifications (the performance was to be in the evening). The first three performances went off fine, but at 6:00 p.m. on the day of the fourth performance, a severe thunderstorm blew in, and its lightning struck a power source, depriving the park of all electricity. The performance was to begin at 8:00 p.m., and the estimates were that the electricity would not be restored until at least 11:00 p.m. After consultations with the Park Service which was responsible for the venue, the Wolf Trap Foundation canceled the show.

Five years after the cancellation, The Opera Co. sued to recover the payment due for the fourth performance. It claimed that it was ready to perform, and that Wolf breached by canceling the performance. Wolf claimed excuse due to impracticability.

After a review of *Taylor*, *Krell* (the next case) and about one hundred years' worth of impracticability jurisprudence, the Fourth Circuit reversed the judgment in favor of The Opera Co. As stated by the court:

Applying the law as above stated to the facts of this case, we conclude, as did the district judge, that the existence of electric power was necessary for the satisfactory performance by the Opera Company on the night of June 15. While he seems to conclude that public safety was the main consideration on which the cancellation was based, he found that the power outage was the reason assigned for cancellation, and in that connection he found it to be questionable that "a generator could [have been] set up to provide additional light for the theater itself (when power from the utility company became unavailable) and still provide adequate light for the people who had to move backstage." Such findings meet the requirement of Restatement (Second) on Contracts § 263 for an event, the "non-occurrence of which was a basic assumption on which the contract was made" and accordingly satisfies the definition of an impracticability which will relieve the obligor of his duty to perform as declared in section 265 of such Restatement (which we have accepted as the proper present statement of the doctrine of impossibility of performance as a defense to a breach of contract suit). . . . The district judge, however, refused to sustain the defense because he held that if the contingency that occurred was one that could have been foreseen reliance on the doctrine of impossibility as a defense to a breach of contract suit is absolutely barred. As we have said, this is not the modern rule and he found that the power outage was foreseeable. In this the district judge erred. Foreseeability, as we have said, is at best but one fact to be considered in resolving first how likely the occurrence of the event in question was and, second whether its occurrence, based on past experience, was of such reasonable likelihood that the obligor should not merely foresee the risk but, because of the degree of its likelihood, the obligor should have guarded against it or provided for non-liability against the risk. This is a question to be resolved by the trial judge after a careful scrutiny of all the facts in the case. The trial judge in this case made no

> such findings. The cause must be remanded for such findings. In connection with that remand, the parties may be permitted to offer additional evidence on the matters in issue.

817 F.2d at 1102–1103.

The dissent was not swayed by this logic. As he saw it, the evidence showed, and the trial court found

> that power failures were not only foreseeable in an abstract sense, but were, in fact, inevitable; that a theater without emergency capacity to carry on in case of a power outage is "incomplete"; that Hankenson [an agent of Wolf Trap] had advised "Claire," chairman of the theater board, of this opinion during the previous summer; that power outages had occurred on several previous occasions; that "Wolf Trap has been very lucky they did not occur during the evening when the performance would have been affected"; and that the "cost to the Foundation, the Park Service and the Opera Company of Boston for the evening's cancellation would go along [sic] way if not all the way toward providing emergency backup equipment to prevent such a recurrence."
>
> It would have taken only a few seconds to write into the contract a sentence which said, in effect, "If the electric power fails, Wolf Trap will not be responsible for any losses caused by the power failure."
>
> If the parties had agreed to such a provision I would not raise my voice.
>
> They did not so agree.
>
> I do not think we should write for the defendant a defense it did not write for itself.
>
> I would affirm the decision of the trial court.

Id. at 1104–1105.

Who gets the better of this argument?

Now, assume that Ponoroff had agreed to pay a premium for an apartment with a waterfront view of the Charles River next to Wolf Trap Park in order to hear the performance that was subsequently canceled. Does Ponoroff have to pay? What if he fronts the money—does he get it back? Read on.

Krell v. Henry
Court of Appeal
[1903] 2 K.B. 740

Appeal from a decision of DARLING, J. The plaintiff, Paul Krell, sued the defendant, C.S. Henry for £50, being the balance of a sum of £75, for which the defendant had agreed to hire a flat at 56A, Pall Mall on the days of June 26 and 27, for the purpose of viewing the processions to be held in connection with the coronation of His Majesty [Edward VII]. The defendant denied his liability, and counterclaimed for the return of the sum of £25, which had been paid as a deposit, on the ground that, the processions not having taken place owing to the serious illness of the King, there had been a total failure of consideration for the contract entered into by him.

The facts [were undisputed]. The plaintiff on leaving the country in March, 1902, left instructions with his solicitor to let his suite of chambers at 56A, Pall Mall on such terms and for such period (not exceeding six months) as he thought proper. On June 17, 1902, the defendant noticed an announcement in the windows of the plaintiff's flat to the effect that windows to view the coronation processions were to be let. The defendant interviewed the housekeeper on the subject, when it was pointed out to him what a good view of the processions could be obtained from the premises, and he eventually agreed with the housekeeper to take the suite for the two days in question for a sum of £75.

On June 20, the defendant wrote the following letter to the plaintiff's solicitor:

> "I am in receipt of yours of the 18th instant, inclosing form of agreement for the suite of chambers on the third floor at 56A, Pall Mall, which I have agreed to take for the two days the 26th and 27th instant, for the sum of £75. For reasons given you I cannot enter into the agreement, but as arranged over the telephone I inclose herewith cheque for £25, as deposit, and will thank you to confirm to me that I shall have the entire use of these rooms during the days (not the nights) of the 26th and 27th instant. You may rely that every care will be taken of the premises and their contents. On the 24th inst. I will pay the balance, viz., £50, to complete the £75 agreed upon."

On the same day the defendant received the following reply from the plaintiff's solicitor:

"I am in receipt of your letter of to-day's date inclosing cheque for £25 deposit on your agreeing to take Mr. Krell's chambers on the third floor at 56A, Pall Mall for the two days, the 26th and 27th June, and I confirm the agreement that you are to have the entire use of these rooms during the days (but not the nights), the balance, £50, to be paid to me on Tuesday next the 24th instant."

The processions not having taken place [on] June 26 and 27, the defendant declined to pay the balance of £50 alleged to be due from him under the contract in writing of June 20 constituted by the above two letters. Hence the present action. Darling J., on August 11, 1902, held, upon the authority of Taylor v. Caldwell, 3 B. & S. 826, and The Moorcock, (1889) 14 P.D. 64, that there was an implied condition in the contract that the procession should take place, and gave judgment for the defendant on the claim and counter-claim. The plaintiff appealed.

VAUGHAN Williams, L.J. The real question in this case is the extent of the application in English law of the principle of the Roman law which has been adopted and acted on in many English decisions, and notably in the case of Taylor v. Caldwell, 3 B. & S. 826. That case at least makes it clear that "where, from the nature of the contract, it appears that the parties must from the beginning have known that it could not be fulfilled unless, when the time for the fulfillment of the contract arrived, some particular specified thing continued to exist, so that when entering into the contract they must have contemplated such continued existence as the foundation of what was to be done; there, in the absence of any express or implied warranty that the thing shall exist, the contract is not to be considered a positive contract, but as subject to an implied condition that the parties shall be excused in case, before breach, performance becomes impossible from the perishing of the thing without default of the contractor."

* * *

I do not think that [the principle] is limited to cases in which the event causing the impossibility of performance is the destruction or nonexistence of some thing which is the subject-matter of the contract or of some condition or state of things expressly specified as a condition of it. I think that you first have to ascertain, not necessarily from the terms of the contract, but, if required, from necessary inferences, drawn from surrounding circumstances recognized by both contracting parties, what is the substance of the contract, and then to ask the question whether that substantial contract needs for its foundation the assumption of the existence of a particular state of things. If it does, this will limit the operation of the general words, and in such case, if the contract becomes impossible of performance by reason of the nonexistence of the state of things assumed by both contracting parties as the foundation of the contract, there will be no breach of the contract thus limited.

Now what are the facts of the present case? The contract is contained in [the] two letters of June 20. . . . These letters do not mention the coronation, but speak merely of the taking of Mr. Krell's chambers, or, rather, of the use of them. . . . [T]he plaintiff [had] exhibited on his premises, third floor, 56A, Pall Mall, an announcement to the effect that windows to view the Royal coronation procession were to be let, and [defendant] was induced by that announcement to apply to the housekeeper on the premises, who said that the owner was willing to let the suite of rooms for the purpose of seeing the Royal procession for both days, but not nights, of June 26 and 27. In my judgment the use of the rooms was let and taken for the purpose of seeing the Royal procession. It was not a demise of the rooms, or even an agreement to let and take the rooms. It is a license to use rooms for a particular purpose and none other. And in my judgment the taking place of those processions on the days proclaimed along the proclaimed route, which passed 56A, Pall Mall, was regarded by both contracting parties as the foundation of the contract; and I think that it cannot reasonably be supposed to have been in the contemplation of the contracting parties, when the contract was made, that the coronation would not be held on the proclaimed days, or the processions not take place on those days along the proclaimed route. . . .

It was suggested in the course of the argument that if the occurrence, on the proclaimed days, of the coronation and the procession in this case were the foundation of the contract, and if the general words are thereby limited or qualified, so that in the event of the nonoccurrence of the coronation and procession along the proclaimed route they would discharge both parties from further performance of the contract, it would follow that if a cabman was engaged to take some one to Epsom on Derby Day at a suitable enhanced price for such a journey, say £10, both parties to the contract would be discharged in the contingency of the race at Epsom for some reason becoming impossible; but I do not think this follows, for I do not think that in the cab case the happening of the race would be the foundation of the contract. No doubt the purpose of the engager would be to go to see the Derby, and the price would be proportionately high; but the cab had no special qualifications for the purpose which led to the selection of the cab for this particular occasion. Any other cab would have done as well. Moreover, I think that, under the cab contract, the hirer, even if the race went off, could have said, "Drive me to Epsom; I will pay you the agreed sum; you have nothing to do with the purpose for which I hired the cab," and that if the cabman refused he would have been guilty of a breach of contract, there being nothing to qualify his promise to drive the hirer to Epsom on a particular day. Whereas in the case of the coronation, there is not merely the purpose of the hirer to see the coronation procession, but it is the coronation procession and the relative position of the rooms which is the basis of the contract as much for the lessor as the hirer; and I think that if the King, before the coronation day and after the contract, had died, the hirer could not have insisted on having the rooms on the days named. It could not in the cab case be reasonably said that seeing the Derby race was the foundation of the contract. . . . Whereas in the present case, where the rooms were offered and taken, by reason of their peculiar suitability from the position of the rooms for a view of the coronation procession, surely the view of the coronation procession was the foundation of the contract, which is a very different thing from the purpose of the man who engaged the cab—namely, to see the race—being held to be the foundation of the contract. Each case must be judged by its own circumstances. In each case one must ask oneself first, what, having regard to all the circumstances, was the foundation of the contract? Secondly, was the performance of the contract prevented? Thirdly, was the event which prevented the performance of the contract of such a character that it cannot reasonably be said to have been in the contemplation of the parties at the date of the contract? If all these questions are answered in the affirmative (as I think they should be in this case), I think both parties are discharged from further performance of the contract. I think that the coronation procession was the foundation of this contract, and that the non-happening of it prevented the performance of the contract. . . . The test seems to be whether the event which causes the impossibility was or might have been anticipated and guarded against. It seems difficult to say, in a case where both parties anticipate the happening of an event, which anticipation is the foundation of the contract, that either party must be taken to have anticipated, and ought to have guarded against, the event which prevented the performance of the contract. . . .

I myself am clearly of opinion that in this case, where we have to ask ourselves whether the object of the contract was frustrated by the nonhappening of the coronation and its procession on the days proclaimed, parol evidence is admissible to shew that the subject of the contract was rooms to view the coronation procession, and was so to the knowledge of both parties. When once this is established, I see no difficulty whatever in the case. It is not essential to the application of the principle of Taylor v. Caldwell that the direct subject of the contract should perish or fail to be in existence at the date of performance of the contract. It is sufficient if a state of things or condition expressed in the contract and essential to its performance perishes or fails to be in existence at that time. In the present case the condition which fails and prevents the achievement of that which was, in the contemplation of both parties, the foundation of the contract, is not expressly mentioned either as a condition of the contract or the purpose of it; but I think for the reasons which I have given that the principle of Taylor v. Caldwell ought to be applied. This disposes of the plaintiff's claim for £50 unpaid balance of the price agreed to be paid for the use of the rooms. The defendant at one time set up a cross-claim for the return of the £25 he paid at the date of the contract. As that claim is now withdrawn it is unnecessary to say anything about it. I have only to add that the facts of this case do not bring it within the principle laid down in Stubbs v. Holywell Ry. Co., L.R., 2 Ex. 311, that in the case of contracts falling directly within the rule of Taylor v. Caldwell the subsequent impossibility does not affect rights already acquired, because the defendant had the whole of June 24 to pay the balance, and the public announcement that the coronation and processions would not take place on the proclaimed days was made early on the morning of the 24th, and no cause of action could accrue till the end of that day. . . .

Appeal dismissed.

QUESTIONS

1. Questions about the facts of this case

   1.1. Why did Henry want the use of the flat (to use the English terminology for an apartment)?

   1.2. Why did he not want to use it after all?

   1.3. Who gets the £25 that Henry paid? What if Henry had paid the full £75 up front?

2. Questions about the law

   2.1. Does this court read *Taylor* correctly?

2.2. What makes the Epsom Derby hypothetical in the *Krell* opinion different from the facts in *Krell*?

2.3. Professor Mark Gergen has stated "The doctrines on impracticability [and] mistake share a feature that is unusual in contract law. They give courts the power to excuse or modify terms in contracts between sophisticated parties who bargained over the terms of the contract with equal power and information." Mark Gergen, *A Defense of Judicial Reconstruction of Contracts*, 71 IND. L.J. 45, 45 (1995).

Is this true? Do sophisticated parties have better abilities to predict and account for the future than unsophisticated people? Or is that the wrong question to ask?

Problems on *Taylor* and *Krell*

1. The boy band B-Link has commenced the "Bad Boy World Tour," which consists of concerts in 54 cities in 75 days. One such city is Tuscaloosa, Alabama where the Redneck Bowl will serve as the outdoor venue for the band's performance. Arlene is an impressionable 10-year old who adores B-Link. Arlene's mother, Bertha, has bought tickets to the B-Link concert at the Redneck Bowl from Larry Link, a tour promoter. Larry has rented the Redneck Bowl for the performance for $30,000 for the one night of the concert, and has signed a deal with B-Link for the whole world tour, including the Tuscaloosa date.

What do *Taylor, WolfTrap* and *Krell* have to say about the following:

a. Thirty days into the tour, and just before the scheduled date of the Tuscaloosa concert, Ring-J, a member of the band, checks into a detox facility, and the band cancels the rest of the tour. Does Bertha get her money back? Must Larry pay the owners of the Redneck Bowl their $30,000?

b. Thirty days into the tour, and just before the scheduled date of the Tuscaloosa concert, the plane carrying B-Link crashes and all aboard are instantly killed. Does Bertha get her money back? Must Larry pay the owners of the Redneck Bowl their $30,000?

c. Thirty days into the tour, and just before the scheduled date of the Tuscaloosa concert, Larry dies unexpectedly. Does the Redneck Bowl have to make the stadium available to the band? If Larry prepaid the $30,000, will his estate get it back? If the Redneck Bowl doesn't allow the band to play, may Bertha get her money back?

2. In Epstein's town, all the hotels jack up their room rates around graduation time, and require a minimum two-day, non-refundable deposit. Six months before graduation, Ponoroff reserves a room in Epstein's town around graduation since his nephew is graduating from Epstein's school. He pays the two-day minimum. The day before graduation, a tornado sweeps through the town, leaving a trail of desolation and some disconsolate students—the school cancels graduation.

   Can Ponoroff get his money back? What if he was traveling to Epstein's town not to attend graduation, but rather to talk with Epstein about a new basketweaving textbook?

The line between assumed and unassumed risk is a blurred one, and one which is often difficult to draw. But in many cases, judges see things the way the dissent did in *The Opera Co., supra*, at 734, as shown by the following case.

Mel Frank Tool & Supply, Inc. v. Di-Chem Co.
Supreme Court of Iowa
580 N.W.2d 802 (1998)

Lavorato, Justice.

City authorities informed a lessee, a chemical distributor, that it could no longer use its leased premises to store its hazardous chemicals because of a recently enacted ordinance. The lessee vacated the premises, and the lessor sued for breach of the lease and for damages to the premises. The district court awarded the lessor judgment for unpaid rent and for damages to the premises. The lessee appeals, contending that the district court should have found that the city's actions constituted extraordinary circumstances rendering the performance of the lease impossible. . . . We affirm.

I. Facts.

Di-Chem Company is a chemical distributor. In May 1994, Di-Chem began negotiating with Mel Frank Tool & Supply, Inc. to lease a storage and distribution facility in Council Bluffs, Iowa. Mel Frank's real estate agent handled the negotiations so there were no actual face-to-face negotiations between the parties. However, a day before the lease was executed, Mel Frank's owner, Dennis Frank, talked with Di-Chem representatives who were touring the premises. Frank asked them what Di-Chem was going to be selling and was told chemicals. The agent brought the lease to Frank for his signature.

The lease appears to be an Iowa State Bar Association form. *See* Iowa State Bar Association Official Form No. 164. The lease was to start June 1, 1994 and end May 31, 1997. The lease limited Di-Chem's use of the premises to "storage and distribution."

Some of the chemicals Di-Chem distributes are considered "hazardous material." There was no testimony that Dennis Frank was aware of this at the time the lease was executed. A Di-Chem representative, who was present during the earlier-mentioned conversation with Dennis Frank, testified that hazardous materials did not come up in the conversation.

The lease contained several provisions that bear on the issues in this appeal. One requires Di-Chem to "make no unlawful use of the premises and . . . to comply with all . . . City Ordinances." There is also a destruction-of-premises provision that allows either party to terminate the lease under certain circumstances.

On July 21, 1995, the city's fire chief and several other city authorities inspected the premises. Following the inspection, the city's fire marshal wrote Di-Chem, stating:

> At the time of the inspection the building was occupied as Hazardous Materials Storage. I have given you a copy of 1994 Uniform Fire Code, which the City has adopted, covering Hazardous Material Storage. As you can see the building does not comply with the Code requirements which creates Health and Life Safety Hazards. The Hazardous Materials must be removed within seven (7) days to eliminate the hazard.

* * * Both Frank and Di-Chem representatives testified they understood the letter to mean that if these deficiencies were eliminated, Di-Chem could

continue to store hazardous material. There was testimony that the changes in the code occurred after Di-Chem took occupancy of the premises. * * *

Thereafter Dennis Frank and Di-Chem representatives met with city officials about what it would take to correct the various code deficiencies to allow Di-Chem to continue storing hazardous materials. Di-Chem representatives and Dennis Frank briefly considered bringing the building up to code. There was talk about the possibility of Di-Chem splitting the costs with Mel Frank, but Dennis Frank felt the cost was prohibitive.

On October 23 Di-Chem notified Mel Frank by letter of its intention to vacate the premises by the end of October. The letter in part stated: "The city's position that we cannot legally store all of our inventory at this site prior to extensive alteration of the building makes the structure useless to us as a chemical warehouse." True to its word, Di-Chem vacated the premises.

II. Proceedings.

Later, Mel Frank sued for breach of the lease and for damages to the property. Di-Chem asserted several affirmative defenses: mutual mistake, * * * and impossibility. * * *

The court found for Mel Frank. The court found that Mel Frank had "no reason to believe or [know] that chemicals classified as hazardous would be stored in the warehouse." The court relied on the testimony of Norm Wirtala, an officer of Di-Chem:

> Mr. Wirtala testified he would be in a "superior position of knowledge" concerning the items to be stored in the building and that he had a general understanding of fire code requirements for the storage of hazardous materials due to his experience in the business although [neither] he nor his agents claimed to have examined the Council Bluffs' fire codes as they may have related to hazardous materials and building specifications for storage of hazardous materials.

With this the court concluded that there was:

> clear and conclusive [evidence] that the plaintiff made no representations to the defendant that the warehouse was suitable for any specific purpose, nor were any discussions or representations made concerning the character of the products to be stored by the defendant. Consequently, this Court concludes the lease was breached by the defendants for va-

> cating the premises and failing to pay the balance of the lease term as required by its terms and conditions and the defendants owe the sum of $55,913.77 for rent [and $2,357.00 for damage to the property].
>
> * * *

IV. Impossibility of Performance.

A. The law. The introduction to the Restatement (Second) of Contracts covers impossibility of performance but with a different title: impracticability of performance and frustration of purpose. *See* Restatement (Second) of Contracts ch. 11, at 309 (1981) [hereinafter Restatement]. According to the Restatement,

> Contract liability is strict liability. . . . The obligor is therefore liable in damages for breach of contract even if he is without fault and even if circumstances have made the contract more burdensome or less desirable than he had anticipated. . . . The obligor who does not wish to undertake so extensive an obligation may contract for a lesser one by using one of a variety of common clauses:. . . . he may reserve a right to cancel the contract. . . . The extent of his obligation then depends on the application of the rules of interpretation. . . .

Id.

Even though the obligor has not restricted his or her obligation by agreement, a court may still grant relief: "An extraordinary circumstance may make performance so vitally different from what was reasonably to be expected as to alter the essential nature of that performance." *Id.* In these circumstances, "the court must determine whether justice requires a departure from the general rule that the obligor bear the risk that the contract may become more burdensome or less desirable." Restatement (Second) of Contracts ch. 11, at 310 (1981). Whether extraordinary circumstances exist justifying discharge is a question of law for the court. *Id.*

The Restatement recognizes three distinct grounds for the discharge of the obligor's contractual duty:

> First, the obligor may claim that some circumstance has made his own performance impracticable. . . . Second, the obligor may claim that some circumstance has so destroyed the value to him of the other party's performance as to frustrate his own purpose in making the contract. . . . Third, the obligor may claim that he will not receive the agreed exchange

> for the obligee's duty to render that agreed exchange, on the ground of either impracticability or frustration.

Id.

The rationale behind the doctrines of impracticability and frustration is whether the nonoccurrence of the circumstance was a basic assumption on which the contract was made. Restatement (Second) of Contracts ch. 11, at 310–311 (1981). The parties need not have been conscious of alternatives for them to have had a "basic assumption." Restatement (Second) of Contracts ch. 11, at 311 (1981). The Restatement gives an example: Where an artist contracts to paint a painting and dies, the artist's death is an "event the nonoccurrence of which was a basic assumption on which the contract was made, even though the parties never consciously addressed themselves to that possibility." *Id.* * * *

B. Discharge by supervening frustration. For reasons that follow, we think the facts of this case fall within the parameters of section 265 of the Restatement. Section 265 provides:

> Where, after a contract is made, a party's principal purpose is substantially frustrated without his fault by the occurrence of an event the nonoccurrence of which was a basic assumption on which the contract was made, his remaining duties to render performance are discharged, *unless the language or the circumstances indicate the contrary.*

(Emphasis added.) As mentioned, this is one of the three grounds the Restatement recognizes for discharging the obligor's contractual duty. *See id.* ch. 11, at 310.

The rule deals with the problem that arises when a change in circumstances makes one party's performance virtually worthless to the other, frustrating the purpose in making the contract. *Id.* § 265 cmt. a, at 335. The obligor's contractual obligation is discharged only if three conditions are met:

> First, the purpose that is frustrated must have been a principal purpose of that party in making the contract. It is not enough that he had in mind some specific object without which he would not have made the contract. The object must be so completely the basis of the contract that, as both parties understand, without it the transaction would make little sense. *Second, the frustration must be substantial. It is not enough that*

> *the transaction has become less profitable for the affected party or even that he will sustain a loss. The frustration must be so severe that it is not fairly to be regarded as within the risks that he assumed under the contract.* Third, the non-occurrence of the frustrating event must have been a basic assumption on which the contract was made. . . . The foreseeability of the event is . . . a factor in that determination, but the mere fact that the event was foreseeable does not compel the conclusion that its non-occurrence was not such a basic assumption.

Id. * * *

Based on the foregoing authorities, we reach the following conclusions. A subsequent governmental regulation like a statute or ordinance may prohibit a tenant from legally using the premises for its originally intended purpose. In these circumstances, the tenant's purpose is substantially frustrated thereby relieving the tenant from any further obligation to pay rent. The tenant is not relieved from the obligation to pay rent if there is a serviceable use still available consistent with the use provision in the lease. The fact that the use is less valuable or less profitable or even unprofitable does not mean the tenant's use has been substantially frustrated.

C. The merits. It is clear from the pleadings and testimony that Di-Chem was asserting a defense of frustration of purpose. Di-Chem had the burden of persuasion to prove that defense. * * * The district court's decision in favor of Mel Frank is a determination that Di-Chem did not carry its burden on this defense.

Di-Chem produced no evidence that *all* of its inventory of chemicals consisted of hazardous material. In fact, its own correspondence to Mel Frank indicates otherwise. For example, Di-Chem's October 23 letter to Mel Frank stated: "The city's position that we cannot legally store *all* of our inventory at this site prior to extensive alteration of the building makes the structure useless to us as a chemical warehouse." (Emphasis added.) A reasonable inference from this statement is that not all of Di-Chem's inventory consisted of hazardous material. * * * Another Di-Chem representative testified that Di-Chem's product line included industrial chemicals and *food additives*. Presumably, food additives are not hazardous materials.

Given the posture of this appeal, Di-Chem has to establish as a matter of law that its principal purpose for leasing the facility—storing and distributing chemicals—was substantially frustrated by the city's actions. Di-Chem presented no evidence as to the nature of its inventory and what percentage of the inventory consisted of hazardous chemicals. The company also failed to show what its lost profits, if any, would be without the hazardous chemicals. Thus, there is no evidence from which the district court could have found the city's actions substantially frustrated Di-Chem's principal purpose of storing and distributing chemicals. Put another way, there is insufficient evidence that the city's action deprived Di-Chem of the beneficial enjoyment of the property for other uses, *i.e.*, storing and distributing nonhazardous chemicals.

Simply put, Di-Chem failed to establish its affirmative defense of what it has termed impossibility. We must therefore affirm the district court's decision as to this issue.

* * *

VII. Disposition.

In sum, we conclude Di-Chem has failed to establish—as a matter of law—that it is entitled to relief via its impossibility defense or the terms of the lease. The district court's erroneous finding that the real estate agent represented Di-Chem was harmless. We affirm.

AFFIRMED.

QUESTIONS AND NOTE

1. Questions about the facts of this case

    1.1. The court found that the local ordinance was enacted after the lease was signed. What difference does that make?

    1.2. The court said that: "The lease appears to be an Iowa State Bar Association form." What does that mean?

    1.3. Did the court make a finding that continued storage of Di-Chem's materials would have been a violation of the local ordinances? Did it have to make such a finding? What else, if anything, could Di-Chem use the premises for?

2. Questions about the law

2.1. If Di-Chem was going to use the space only for hazardous chemicals, what should it have done to ensure that it could break the lease without liability if they were told they couldn't store such materials at the leased premises?

2.2. Is this case more like *Taylor*, or more like *Krell*?

2.3. May Markell insert the following clause into a contract with Epstein and never, ever worry about impracticability?

"Markell and Epstein agree that Epstein hereby assumes all risks, known or unknown, which relate to this contract, and agrees to perform no matter what may happen between the time this agreement is signed and the time this agreement requires Epstein to perform."

3. Notes

3.1. *Impracticability vs. Frustration.* In *7200 Scottsdale Road General Partners v. Kuhn Farm Machinery, Inc.*, 184 Ariz. 341, 909 P.2d 408 (Ariz. Ct. App. 1995), Kuhn, a United States subsidiary of a French manufacturer of farm machinery, booked a block of rooms at a Phoenix resort. Unfortunately, after formation and before performance, the Gulf War of 1991 broke out, bringing with it enhanced fears of terrorism against international air travel, especially travel to the United States. After a drop in attendance caused by the fact that representatives from the French parent would likely not travel by air to the conference, Kuhn sought to cancel and avoid damages on the ground of "apprehension of impossibility." The trial court agreed, but the appellate court reversed, analyzing the problem as follows:

The trial court held that the contract was discharged under the doctrines of impracticability of performance and frustration of purpose. These are similar but distinct doctrines. *See* Restatement (Second) of Contracts ("Restatement") § 265 cmt. a (1981) (discussing the differences between impracticability of performance and frustration of purpose). Impracticability of performance is, according to the Restatement, utilized when certain events occurring after a contract is made constitute an impediment to performance by either party. *See* Restatement § 261. Traditionally, the doctrine has been applied to three categories of supervening events: death

> or incapacity of a person necessary for performance, destruction of a specific thing necessary for performance, and prohibition or prevention by law. *Id.* cmt. a.
>
> On the other hand, frustration of purpose deals with "the problem that arises when a change in circumstances makes one party's performance virtually worthless to the other. . . . " Restatement § 265 cmt. a. "Performance remains possible but the expected value of performance to the party seeking to be excused has been destroyed by a fortuitous event, which supervenes to cause an actual but not literal failure of consideration." . . . While the impact on the party adversely affected is the same regardless of which doctrine is applied, frustration of purpose, unlike the doctrine of impracticability, involves no true failure of performance by either party.
>
> Notwithstanding, some cases speak of a contract as "frustrated" when performance has become impossible or impracticable. . . . This usage is inaccurate. "Frustration is not a form of impossibility even under the modern definition of that term, which includes not only cases of physical impossibility but also cases of extreme impracticability of performance." . . .
>
> Turning to the contract between Kuhn and the resort, Kuhn clearly has no claim for impossibility or impracticability. The contract required the resort to reserve and provide guest rooms, meeting rooms, and food and services. In return, Kuhn was required to pay the monies specified in the contract. Kuhn does not allege that it was impossible or impracticable to perform its contractual duty to make payment for the reserved facilities. Rather, it contends that the value of the resort's counter-performance—the furnishing of convention facilities—was rendered worthless because of the Gulf War's effect on convention attendance. This is a claim of frustration of purpose.

184 Ariz. at 345–346.

In applying the standards of frustration of purpose, the court cited *Krell* and previous Arizona frustration cases. After that summary, it noted:

> We begin our analysis on this point with the proposition that substantial frustration means frustration "so severe that it is not fairly to be regarded as within the risks . . . assumed under the contract."

Restatement § 265 cmt. a. Furthermore, "it is not enough that the transaction has become less profitable for the affected party or even that he will sustain a loss." *Id.* The value of the counter-performance to be rendered by the promisee must be "totally or nearly totally destroyed" by the occurrence of the event. . . .

Here, the conduct of Kuhn and its dealers clearly demonstrates that the value of the resort's counter-performance—the furnishing of its facilities for Kuhn's convention—was not totally or nearly totally destroyed by terrorist threats. In late January, after the United States attacked Iraq and when the threat of terrorism was at its highest level, Kuhn implicitly confirmed the convention date by reducing the reserved room block from 190 to 140. Furthermore, although several dealers canceled in early February, the uncontroverted record demonstrates that over one hundred dealers registered for the convention after the commencement of Operation Desert Storm on January 16, 1991. Thus, the frustration was not so severe that it cannot fairly be regarded as one of the risks assumed by Kuhn under the contract.

* * *

We conclude that Kuhn's cancellation of the convention because of the perceived threat of terrorism was not an objectively reasonable response to an extraordinary and specific threat. The slight risk to domestic air travel by vague threats of terrorism does not equate with the actual and substantial danger of running a naval blockade in time of war. Consequently, Kuhn gains nothing by recasting its frustration of purpose argument as one of "apprehension of impossibility."

Finally, we consider whether Kuhn is entitled to relief on the ground that fear of terrorist activities resulted in less than expected attendance, which in turn made the convention uneconomical. Although economic return may be characterized as the "principal purpose" of virtually all commercial contracts, mere economic impracticality is no defense to performance of a contract. *See* Restatement § 265 cmt. a. ("it is not enough that transaction has become less profitable for affected party or even that he will sustain a loss"). . . . Thus, although the Gulf War's effect on the expected level of attendance may have rendered the convention uneconomical, Kuhn was not on this ground relieved of its contractual obligation.

Id. at 349–351.

Would the Arizona court have ruled the same as the English court in *Krell* if presented with the same facts?

Questions on Impracticability Under Section 2-615 of the U.C.C.

The U.C.C. The Uniform Commercial Code has within it notions of impracticability. Section 2-615 states, in relevant part:

> § 2-615. Excuse by Failure of Presupposed Conditions.
>
> Except so far as a seller may have assumed a greater obligation and subject to the preceding section on substituted performance:
>
> (a) Delay in delivery or non-delivery in whole or in part by a seller . . . is not a breach of his duty under a contract for sale if performance as agreed has been made impracticable by the occurrence of a contingency the non-occurrence of which was a basic assumption on which the contract was made or by compliance in good faith with any applicable foreign or domestic governmental regulation or order whether or not it later proves to be invalid. . . .

1. May a buyer under the U.C.C. raise impracticability? May either party raise frustration of purpose? *See* U.C.C. § 1-103.
2. What are the principle differences between the common law of impracticability and the U.C.C.'s version of the doctrine?

SECTION 5: EXCUSE THROUGH ACTIONS OF A PARTY BEFORE PERFORMANCE IS OTHERWISE DUE

Circumstances are not the only things that may change between formation and performance. Sometimes sellers have second thoughts, or buyers may be riddled with buyer's remorse. Other times, the parties may believe that they have *no* obligations—either because they erroneously believe that there is no contract, or they believe that any obligations they might have are subject to a condition that has not yet occurred.

A. Repudiation and Anticipatory Repudiation as Excuse

What happens in an executory contract (that is, one under which formation has occurred, but both sides still have obligations to perform) if one side indicates that it will not perform when the time comes? Do you have to wait until the appointed time, or can you do something early? The next several cases examine various facets of this question, starting with the classic case in this area.

Hochster v. De La Tour

118 Eng. Rep. 922 [Q.B. 1853]

On the trial, before Erle, J., at the London sittings in last Easter Term, it appeared that plaintiff was a courier, who, in April, 1852, was engaged by defendant to accompany him on a tour, to commence on 1st June 1852, on the terms mentioned in the declaration. On the 11th May 1852, defendant wrote to plaintiff that he had changed his mind, and declined his services. He refused to make him any compensation. The action was commenced on 22d May. The plaintiff, between the commencement of the action and the 1st June, obtained an engagement with Lord Ashburton, on equally good terms, but not commencing till 4th July. The defendant's counsel objected that there could be no breach of the contract before the 1st of June. The learned judge was of a contrary opinion, but reserved leave to enter a nonsuit on this objection. The other questions were left to the jury, who found for plaintiff.

Hugh Hill, in the same Term, obtained a rule Nisi to enter a nonsuit, or arrest the judgment. . . .

LORD CAMPBELL, C.J., now delivered the judgment of the Court.

On this motion in arrest of judgment, the question arises, Whether, if there be an agreement between A. and B., whereby B. engages to employ A. on and from a future day for a given period of time, to travel with him into a foreign country as a courier, and to start with him in that capacity on that day, A. being to receive a monthly salary during the continuance of such service, B. may, before the day, refuse to perform the agreement and break and renounce it, so as to entitle A. before the day to commence an action against B. to recover damages for breach of the agreement; A. having been ready and willing to perform it, till it was broken and renounced by B. The defendant's counsel very powerfully contended that, if the plaintiff was not contented to dissolve the contract, and to abandon all remedy upon it, he was bound to remain ready and willing to perform it till the day when the actual employment as courier in the service of the defendant was to begin; and that there could be no breach of the agreement, before that day, to give a right of action. But it cannot be laid down as a universal rule that, where by agreement an act is to be done on a future day, no action can be brought for a breach of the agreement till the day for doing the act has arrived. If a man promises to marry a woman on a future day, and before that day marries another woman, he is instantly liable to an action for breach of promise of marriage; Short v. Stone, (8 Q.B. 358). If a man contracts to execute a lease on and from a future day for a certain term, and, before that day, executes a lease to another for the same term, he may be immediately sued for breaking the contract; Ford v: Tiley, (6 B. & C. 325). So, if a man contracts to sell and deliver specific goods on a future day, and before the day he sells and delivers them to another, he is immediately liable to an action at the suit of the person with whom he first contracted to sell and deliver them; Bowdef v. Parsons, (10 East, 359). One reason alleged in support of such an action is, that the defendant has, before the day, rendered it impossible for him to perform the contract at the day; but this does not necessarily follow; for, prior to the day fixed for doing the act, the first wife may have died, a surrender of the lease executed might be obtained, and the defendant might have repurchased the goods so as to be in a situation to sell and deliver them to the plaintiff. Another reason may be, that, where there is a contract to do an act on a future day, there is a relation constituted between the parties in the meantime by the contract, and that they impliedly promise that in the meantime neither will do anything to the prejudice of the other inconsistent with that relation. As an example, a man and woman engaged to marry are affianced to one another during the period between the time of the engagement and the celebration of the marriage. In this very case, of traveller and courier, from the day of the hiring till the day when the employment was to begin, they were engaged to each other; and it seems to be a breach of an implied contract if either of them renounces the engagement. This reasoning seems in accordance with the unanimous decision of the Exchequer Chamber in Edlerton v. Emmens, [6 Com. B. 160], which we have followed in subsequent cases in this Court. The declaration in the present case, in alleging a breach, states a great deal more than a passing intention on the part of the defendant which he may repent of, and could only be proved by evidence that he had utterly renounced the contract, or done some act which rendered it impossible for him to perform it. If the plaintiff has no remedy for breach of the contract unless he treats the contract as in force, and acts upon it down to the 1st June 1852, it follows that, till then, he must enter into no employment which will interfere with his promise "to start with the defendant on such travels on the day and year," and that he must then be properly equipped in all aspects as a courier for a three months' tour on the continent of Europe. But it is surely much more rational, and more for the benefit of both parties, that, after the renunciation of the agreement by the defendant, the plaintiff should be at liberty to consider himself absolved from any future performance of it, retaining his right to sue for any damage he has suffered from the breach of it. Thus, instead of remaining idle and laying out money in preparations which must be useless, he is at liberty to seek service under another employer; which would go in mitigation of the damages to which he would otherwise be for a breach of the contract. It seems strange that the defendant, after renouncing the contract, and absolutely declaring that he will never act under it, should be permitted to object that faith is given to his assertion, and that an opportunity is not left to him of changing his mind. If the plaintiff is barred of any remedy by entering into an engagement inconsistent with starting as a courier with the defendant on the 1st June, he is prejudiced by putting faith in the defendant's assertion: and it would be more consonant with principle, if the defendant were precluded from saying that he had not broken the contract when he declared that he entirely renounced it. Suppose that the defendant, at the time of his renunciation, had embarked on a voyage for Australia, so as to render it physically impossible for him to employ the plaintiff as a courier on the continent of Europe in the months of June, July, and August 1852: according to decided cases, the action might have been brought before the 1st June; but the renunciation may have been founded on other facts, to be given in evidence, which would equally have rendered the defendant's performance of the contract impossible. The man who wrongfully renounces a contract into which he has deliberately entered cannot justly complain if he is immediately sued for a compensation in damages by the man whom he has injured: and it seems reasonable to allow an option to the injured party, either to sue immediately; or to wait till the time when the act was to be done, still holding it as prospectively binding for the exercise of this option, which may be advantageous to the innocent party, and cannot be prejudicial to the wrongdoer. An argument against the action before the 1st of June, is urged from the difficulty of calculating the damages: but this argument is equally strong against an action before the 1 st of

September, when the three months would expire. In either case, the jury in assessing the damages would be justified in looking to all that had happened, or was likely to happen, to increase or mitigate the loss of the plaintiff down to the day of trial. We do not find any decision contrary to the view we are taking of this case. . . .

If it should be held that, upon a contract to do an act on a future day, a renunciation of the contract by one party dispenses with a condition to be performed in the meantime by the other, there seems no reason for requiring that other to wait till the day arrives before seeking his remedy by action: and the only ground on which the condition can be dispensed with seems to be, that the renunciation may be treated as a breach of the contract.

Upon the whole, we think that the declaration in this case is sufficient. It gives us great satisfaction to reflect that, the question being on the record, our opinion may be reviewed in a Court of Error. In the meantime we must give judgment for the plaintiff.

Judgment for Plaintiff.

QUESTIONS

1. Questions about the facts of this case

   1.1. What was Hochster hired to do? Why couldn't he do it?

   1.2. What were De La Tour's duties under the contract? Had they yet matured when De La Tour indicated that he would not need Hochster's services?

2. Questions about the law

   2.1. What is a "motion to arrest the judgment"? Sheriffs aren't taking involuntary possession of pieces of paper, are they?

   2.2. If De La Tour's obligations under the contract had not yet matured (he didn't yet owe Hochster anything, right?), how can he be held in breach?

   2.3. Suppose that, on the day after Hochster files his lawsuit, De La Tour relents, and tells Hochster that he'll be happy to hire him as promised. One small problem, though. Hasn't Hochster disabled himself from performing with De La Tour because of his contract with Lord Ashburton? So if De La Tour renounces his renunciation or repudiation, isn't Hochster immediately in breach with either De La Tour or Lord Ashburton?

2.4. On April 1, you are hired by Holmes, King & Sidley to work for the summer after your first year of law school, and agree to show up on May 15. Holmes, King & Sidley agree to pay you $3000 per week. On April 15, the law firm calls you and says "Sorry. We hired too many summer associates and you no longer have a job." What is your legal position?

Most modern applications of the doctrine of repudiation are rarely as cut and dried as *Hochster*. Rather, the parties often are equivocal about their prospective performance, or try to evade it by insisting on terms and conditions that may not have been agreed upon. In the next case, a buyer of land wants the land for a purpose other than what it is currently being used for. But this new use requires zoning changes—a change neither party completely controls. Not to worry. Through the adroit use of conditions, the buyer can tie up the land and nail down a price, while at the same time ensuring that her obligation to pay the purchase price does not mature and become due until the permits or zoning changes are obtained. But what if the condition does not occur (the zoning change isn't obtained), and at least one party wants to go forward anyway, albeit on different terms. Is it the same deal, a new deal or something else?

Truman L. Flatt & Sons Co., Inc. v. Schupf

Appellate Court of Illinois
271 Ill. App. 3d 983, 649 N.E.2d 990 (1995)

Presiding Justice Knecht delivered the opinion of the court:

Plaintiff Truman L. Flatt & Sons Co., Inc., filed a complaint seeking specific performance of a real estate contract made with defendants Sara Lee Schupf, Ray H. Neiswander, Jr., and American National Bank and Trust Company of Chicago (American), as trustee under trust No. 23257. Defendants filed a motion for summary judgment, which the trial court granted.

Plaintiff now appeals from the trial court's grant of the motion for summary judgment. We reverse and remand.

In March 1993, plaintiff and defendants entered a contract in which defendants agreed to sell plaintiff a parcel of land located in Springfield, Illinois. The contract stated the purchase price was to be $160,000. The contract also contained the following provisions:

> "1. This transaction shall be closed on or before June 30, 1993, or upon approval of the relief requested from the Zoning Code of the City of Springfield, Illinois, whichever first occurs ('Closing Date'). The closing is subject to contingency set forth in paragraph 14.
>
> * * *
>
> 14. This Contract to Purchase Real Estate is contingent upon the Buyer obtaining, within one hundred twenty (120) days after the date hereof, amendment of, or other sufficient relief of, the Zoning Code of the City of Springfield to permit the construction and operation of an asphalt plant. In the event the City Council of the City of Springfield denies the request for such use of the property, then this contract shall be voidable at Buyer's option and if Buyer elects to void this contract Buyer shall receive a refund of the earnest money paid."

On May 21, plaintiff's attorney sent a letter to defendants' attorney informing him of substantial public opposition plaintiff encountered at a public meeting concerning its request for rezoning. The letter concluded:

> "The day after the meeting all of the same representatives of the buyer assembled and discussed our chances for successfully pursuing the rezoning request. Everyone who was there was in agreement that our chances were zero to none for success. As a result, we decided to withdraw the request for rezoning, rather than face almost certain defeat.
>
> The bottom line is that we are still interested in the property, but the property is not worth as much to us a 35-acre parcel zoned I-1, as it would be if it were zoned I-2. At this juncture, I think it is virtually impossible for anyone to get that property re-zoned I-2, especially to accommodate the operation of an asphalt plant. In an effort to keep this thing moving, my clients have authorized me to offer your clients the sum of $142,500.00 for the property, which they believe fairly represents its value with its present zoning classification. Please check with your clients and advise whether or not that revision in the contract is acceptable. If it

> is, I believe we can accelerate the closing and bring this matter to a speedy conclusion. Your prompt attention will be appreciated. Thanks."

Defendants' attorney responded in a letter dated June 9, the body of which stated, in its entirety:

> "In reply to your May 21 letter, be advised that the owners of the property in question are not interested in selling the property for $142,500 and, accordingly, the offer is not accepted.
>
> I regret that the zoning reclassification was not approved."

Plaintiff's attorney replied back in a letter dated June 14, the body of which stated, in its entirety:

> "My clients received your letter of June 9, 1993[,] with some regret, however upon some consideration they have elected to proceed with the purchase of the property as provided in the contract. At your convenience please give me a call so that we can set up a closing date."

After this correspondence, plaintiff's attorney sent two more brief letters to defendants' attorney, dated June 23 and July 6, each requesting information concerning the status of defendants' preparation for fulfillment of the contract. Defendants' attorney replied in a letter dated July 8. The letter declared it was the defendants' position plaintiff's failure to waive the rezoning requirement and elect to proceed under the contract at the time the rezoning was denied, coupled with the new offer to buy the property at less than the contract price, effectively voided the contract. Plaintiff apparently sent one more letter in an attempt to convince defendants to honor the contract, but defendants declined. Defendants then arranged to have plaintiff's earnest money returned.

Plaintiff filed a complaint for specific performance and other relief against defendants and American, asking the court to direct defendants to comply with the terms of the contract. Defendants responded by filing a "motion to strike, motion to dismiss or, in the alternative, motion for summary judgment." The motion for summary judgment sought summary judgment on the basis plaintiff repudiated the contract.

Prior to the hearing on the motions, plaintiff filed interrogatories requesting, among other things, information concerning the current status of the property. Defendants' answers to the interrogatories stated defendants had no knowledge of any third party's involvement in a potential sale of the property, defendants had not made any offer to sell the property to anyone, no one had made an offer to purchase the property or discussed the possibility of purchasing the property, and defendants had not sold the property to, received any offer from, or discussed a sale of the property with, any other trust member.

After a hearing on the motions, the trial court granted the defendants' motion for summary judgment without explaining the basis for its ruling. Plaintiff filed a post-trial motion to vacate the judgment. The trial court denied the post-trial motion, declaring defendants' motion for summary judgment was granted because plaintiff had repudiated the contract. Plaintiff now appeals the trial court's grant of summary judgment, arguing the trial court erred because (1) it did not repudiate the contract, and (2) even if it did repudiate the contract, it timely retracted that repudiation.

* * *

Plaintiff first argues summary judgment was improper because the trial court erred in finding plaintiff had repudiated the contract.

> "The doctrine of anticipatory repudiation requires a clear manifestation of an intent not to perform the contract on the date of performance. *** That intention must be a definite and unequivocal manifestation that he will not render the promised performance when the time fixed for it in the contract arrives. [Citation.] Doubtful and indefinite statements that performance may or may not take place are not enough to constitute anticipatory repudiation." * * *

These requirements exist because "anticipatory breach is not a remedy to be taken lightly."* * * The Restatement (Second) of Contracts adopts the view of the Uniform Commercial Code (UCC) and states "language that under a fair reading 'amounts to a statement of intention not to perform except on conditions which go beyond the contract' constitutes a repudiation. Comment 2 to Uniform Commercial Code § 2-610." (Restatement (Second) of Contracts § 250 Comment, b, at 273 (1981).) Whether an anticipatory repudiation occurred is a question of fact and the judgment of the trial court thereon will not be disturbed unless it is against the manifest weight of evidence. * * *

As can be seen, whether a repudiation occurred is determined on a case-by-case basis, depending on the particular language used. Both plaintiff and defendants, although they cite Illinois cases discussing repudiation, admit the cited Illinois cases are all factually distinguishable from the case at hand because none of those cases involved a request to change a term in the contract. According to the commentators, a suggestion for modification of the contract does not amount to a repudiation. (J. Calamari & J. Perillo, Contracts § 12-4, at 524 n.74 (3d ed. 1987) (hereinafter Calamari) * * * Plaintiff also cites cases in other jurisdictions holding a request for a change in the price term of a contract does not constitute a repudiation. * * * Defendants attempt to distinguish these cases by arguing here, under the totality of the language in the letter and the circumstances surrounding the letter, the request by plaintiff for a decrease in price clearly implied a threat of nonperformance if the price term was not modified. We disagree.

The language in the May 21 letter did not constitute a clearly implied threat of nonperformance. First, although the language in the May 21 letter perhaps could be read as implying plaintiff would refuse to perform under the contract unless the price was modified, given the totality of the language in the letter, such an inference is weak. More important, even if such an inference were possible, Illinois law requires a repudiation be manifested clearly and unequivocally. Plaintiff's May 21 letter at most created an ambiguous implication whether performance would occur. Indeed, during oral argument defense counsel conceded the May 21 letter was "ambiguous" on whether a repudiation had occurred. This is insufficient to constitute a repudiation under well-settled Illinois law. Therefore, the trial court erred in declaring the May 21 letter anticipatorily repudiated the real estate contract as a matter of law.

Moreover, even if plaintiff had repudiated the contract, the trial court erred in granting summary judgment on this basis because plaintiff timely retracted its repudiation.* * * The Restatement (Second) of Contracts states:

> "The effect of a statement as constituting a repudiation under § 250 or the basis for a repudiation under § 251 is nullified by a retraction of the statement if notification of the retraction comes to the attention of the injured party before he materially changes his position in reliance on the repudiation or indicates to the other party that he considers the repudiation to be final." . . . (Restatement (Second) of Contracts § 256(1), at 293 (1981).)

The UCC adopts the same position:

> "Retraction of Anticipatory Repudiation. (1) Until the repudiating party's next performance is due he can retract his repudiation unless the ag-

> grieved party has since the repudiation cancelled or materially changed his position or otherwise indicated that he considers the repudiation final." . . . (810 ILCS 5/2-611(1) (West 1992).)

Professors Calamari and Perillo declare section 2-611 of the UCC:

> "*** is in general accord with the common law rule that an anticipatory repudiation may be retracted until the other party has commenced an action thereon or has otherwise changed his position. The Code is explicit that no other act of reliance is necessary where the aggrieved party indicates 'that he considers the repudiation final.' " . . . (Calamari § 12.7, at 528.)

"The majority of the common law cases appear to be in accord with this position." (Calamari § 12.7, at 528 n.93.) Other commentators are universally in accord. Professor Farnsworth states: "The repudiating party can prevent the injured party from treating the contract as terminated by retracting before the injured party has acted in response to it." . . . (2 E. Farnsworth, Contracts § 8.22, at 482 (1990).) Professor Corbin declares one who has anticipatorily repudiated his contract has the power of retraction until the aggrieved party has materially changed his position in reliance on the repudiation. (4 A. Corbin, Corbin on Contracts § 980, at 930–31 (1951) (hereinafter Corbin).) Corbin goes on to say the assent of the aggrieved party is necessary for retraction only when the repudiation is no longer merely anticipatory, but has become an actual breach at the time performance is due. (4 Corbin § 980, at 935.) Williston states an anticipatory repudiation can be retracted by the repudiating party "unless the other party has, before the withdrawal, manifested an election to rescind the contract, or changed his position in reliance on the repudiation." . . . 11 W. Jaeger, Williston on Contracts § 1335, at 180 (3d ed. 1968) (hereinafter Williston).

Defendants completely avoid discussion of the common-law right to retract a repudiation other than to say Illinois is silent on the issue. Defendants then cite * * * authorities * * * for the proposition that after an anticipatory repudiation, the aggrieved party is entitled to choose to treat the contract as rescinded or terminated, to treat the anticipatory repudiation as a breach by bringing suit or otherwise changing its position, or to await the time for performance. The UCC adopts substantially the same position. (810 ILCS 5/2-610 (West 1992).) Defendants here assert they chose to treat the contract as rescinded, as they had a right to do under well-settled principles of law.

Plaintiff admits the law stated by defendants is well settled, and admits if the May 21 letter was an anticipatory breach, then defendants had the right to treat the contract as being terminated or rescinded. However, plaintiff points out defendants' assertions ignore the great weight of authority, discussed earlier, which provides a right of the repudiating party to retract the repudiation before the aggrieved party has chosen one of its options allowed under the common law and listed in Stonecipher, Builder's Concrete, and Leazzo. Plaintiff argues defendants' letter of June 9 failed to treat the contract as rescinded, and absent notice or other manifestation defendants were pursuing one of their options, plaintiff was free to retract its repudiation. Plaintiff is correct.

Defendants' precise theory that plaintiff should not be allowed to retract any repudiation in this instance is ambiguous and may be given two interpretations. The first is Illinois should not follow the common-law rule allowing retraction of an anticipatory repudiation before the aggrieved party elects a response to the repudiation. This theory warrants little discussion, because the rule is well settled. Further, defendants have offered no public policy reason to disallow retraction of repudiation other than the public interest in upholding the "sanctity of the contract."

The second possible interpretation of defendants' precise theory is an aggrieved party may treat the contract as terminated or rescinded without notice or other indication being given to the repudiating party, and once such a decision is made by the aggrieved party, the repudiating party no longer has the right of retraction. It is true no notice is required to be given to the repudiating party if the aggrieved party materially changes its position as a result of the repudiation.* * * Here, however, the defendants admitted in their answers to plaintiff's interrogatories they had not entered another agreement to sell the property, nor even discussed or considered the matter with another party. Defendants had not changed their position at all, nor do defendants make any attempt to so argue. As can be seen from the language of the Restatement, the UCC, and the commentators, shown earlier, they are in accord that where the aggrieved party has not otherwise undergone a material change in position, the aggrieved party must indicate to the other party it is electing to treat the contract as rescinded. This can be accomplished either by bringing suit, by notifying the repudiating party, or by in some other way manifesting an election to treat the contract as rescinded. Prior to such indication, the repudiating party is free to retract its repudiation. The Restatement (Second) of Contracts provides the following illustrations:

"2. On February 1, A contracts to supply B with natural gas for one year beginning on May 1, payment to be made each month. On March 1, A repudiates. On April 1, before B has taken any action in response to the repudiation, A notifies B that he retracts his repudiation. B's duties under the contract are not discharged, and B has no claim against A.

***

4. The facts being otherwise as stated in Illustration 2, on March 15, B notifies A that he cancels the contract. B's duties under the contract are discharged and B has a claim against A for damages for total breach ***." . . . Restatement (Second) of Contracts § 256, Comments a, c (1981).

This rule makes sense as well. If an aggrieved party could treat the contract as rescinded or terminated without notice or other indication to the repudiating party, the rule allowing retraction of an anticipatory repudiation would be eviscerated. No repudiating party ever would be able to retract a repudiation, because after receiving a retraction, the aggrieved party could, if it wished, simply declare it had already decided to treat the repudiation as a rescission or termination of the contract. Defendants' theory would effectively rewrite the common-law rule regarding retraction of anticipatory repudiation so that the repudiating party may retract an anticipatory repudiation only upon assent from the aggrieved party. This is not the common-law rule, and we decline to adopt defendants' proposed revision of it.

Applying the actual common-law rule to the facts here, plaintiff sent defendants a letter dated June 14, which clearly and unambiguously indicated plaintiff intended to perform under the contract. However, defendants did not notify plaintiff, either expressly or impliedly, of an intent to treat the contract as rescinded until July 8. Nor is there anything in the record demonstrating any indication to plaintiff, prior to July 8, of an intent by defendants to treat the contract as rescinded or terminated. Thus, assuming plaintiff's May 21 request for a lower purchase price constituted an anticipatory repudiation of the contract, plaintiff successfully retracted that repudiation in the letter dated June 14 because defendants had not yet materially changed their position or indicated to plaintiff an intent to treat the contract as rescinded. Therefore, because plaintiff had timely retracted any alleged repudiation of the contract, the trial court erred in granting summary judgment for defendants on the basis plaintiff repudiated the contract. Defendants were not entitled to judgment as a matter of law.

The trial court's grant of summary judgment for defendants is reversed, and the cause is remanded.

Reversed and remanded.

Cook and McCullough, JJ., concur.

QUESTIONS AND NOTE

1. Questions about the facts of this case

   1.1. So, did Flatt repudiate the contract? How?

   1.2. If Flatt did repudiate the contract, did it effectively retract that repudiation? How?

2. Questions about the law

   2.1. Can a party to a contract repudiate his or her obligations by asking for an amendment? How?

   2.2. Was it clear that Flatt could waive the condition regarding the rezoning? Does *Wyler, supra,* at 727, help here? What if Schupf was the one who wanted to go forward, notwithstanding the inability to change the zoning?

   2.3. Ponoroff agrees to paint Epstein's house. Ponoroff shows up at the appointed time and place and begins to set up. Epstein, in a hissy fit over the fact that Ponoroff's arrival has caused him to mistime his three-minute egg, tells Ponoroff to pack up and leave; he never wants to see him again. Ponoroff leaves, and when he returns to work to see what to do next, Epstein calls and tells him to come back. Does Ponoroff have to go if he does not wish to be in breach?

3. Note

How unequivocal does the repudiation have to be? In *Wholesale Sand & Gravel, Inc. v. Decker*, 630 A.2d 710 (Maine S. Ct. 1993), Decker, a Maine resident, contracted with Wholesale to replace Decker's dirt driveway with a gravel one. The contract was signed on June 12, about the end of winter in Maine. Payment was to be made within 90 days of the date the contract was signed.

Wholesale began work on the driveway on the weekend after the contract was executed and immediately experienced difficulty because of the wetness of the ground. In fact, Wholesale's bulldozer became stuck in the mud and had to be removed with a backhoe. Wholesale returned to the site the following weekend, when it attempted to stabilize the driveway site by hauling out mud and hauling in gravel. Because the ground was too wet to allow Wholesale to perform the work without substantially exceeding the contract price. Goodenow [Wholesale's president] decided to wait for the ground to dry out before proceeding further.

On July 12, 1989, Decker contacted Goodenow concerning the lack of activity at the site and his urgent need to have the driveway completed. Goodenow responded that he would "get right on it." On July 19, Decker telephoned Goodenow to inquire again about the lack of activity and gave him one week in which to finish the driveway. Again, Goodenow said that he would "get right on it." On July 28, Decker called Goodenow for the purpose of terminating the contract. When Goodenow stated that he would be at the site the next day, Decker decided to give him one more chance. Goodenow, however, did not appear at the site and Decker subsequently terminated the contract.

630 A.2d at 711.

When Decker sues Wholesale for breach, who wins—Decker, because of Wholesale's repudiation through inaction, or Wholesale, because of Decker's termination?

B. Failure to Give Adequate Assurance of Future Performance as Excuse

Given the strong requirements in repudiation doctrine for a definite and unambiguous statement, what is a party to a contract to do if the other side is "just making noises" about not performing? Is there anything that can be done?

The next case tries to answer this in a common law setting. In doing so, it borrows from the U.C.C. How does the court accomplish its result? How does the U.C.C.?

Norcon Power Partners, L.P. v. Niagara Mohawk Power Corp.
Court of Appeals of New York
92 N.Y.2d 458, 705 N.E.2d 656, 682 N.Y.S.2d 664 (1998)

Bellacosa, J.

The doctrine, known as demand for adequate assurance of future performance, is at the heart of a Federal lawsuit that stems from a 1989 contract between Norcon Power Partners, L.P., an independent power producer, and Niagara Mohawk Power Corporation, a public utility provider. Niagara Mohawk undertook to purchase electricity generated at Norcon's Pennsylvania facility. The contract was for 25 years, but the differences emerged during the early years of the arrangement.

The case arrives on this Court's docket by certification of the substantive law question from the United States Court of Appeals for the Second Circuit. Our Court is presented with an open issue that should be settled within the framework of New York's common-law development. We accepted the responsibility to address this question involving New York contract law:

> "Does a party have the right to demand adequate assurance of future performance when reasonable grounds arise to believe that the other party will commit a breach by non-performance of a contract governed by New York law, where the other party is solvent and the contract is not governed by the U.C.C.?" (*Norcon Power Partners v. Niagara Mohawk Power Corp.*, 110 F.3d 6, 9.)

As framed by the particular dispute, we answer the law question in the affirmative with an appreciation of this Court's traditional common-law developmental method, and as proportioned to the precedential sweep of our rulings.

I.

The Second Circuit Court of Appeals describes the three pricing periods, structure and details as follows:

> "In the first period, Niagara Mohawk pays Norcon six cents per kilowatt-hour for electricity. In the second and third periods, the price paid by Niagara Mohawk is based on its 'avoided cost.' The avoided cost reflects the cost that Niagara Mohawk would incur to generate electricity itself or purchase it from other sources. In the second period, if the avoided cost falls below a certain floor price (calculated according to a formula), Niagara Mohawk is obligated to pay the floor price. By the same token, if the avoided cost rises above a certain amount (calculated according to a formula), Niagara Mohawk's payments are capped by a ceiling price. An 'adjustment account' tracks the difference between payments actually made by Niagara Mohawk in the second period and what those payments would have been if based solely on Niagara Mohawk's avoided cost.
>
> "In the third period, the price paid by Niagara Mohawk is based on its avoided cost without any ceiling or floor price. Payments made by Niagara Mohawk in the third period are adjusted to account for any balance existing in the adjustment account that operated in the second period. If the adjustment account contains a balance in favor of Niagara Mohawk—that is, the payments actually made by Niagara Mohawk in the second period exceeded what those payments would have been if based solely on Niagara Mohawk's avoided cost—then the rate paid by Niagara Mohawk will be reduced to reflect the credit. If the adjustment account contains a balance in favor of Norcon, Niagara Mohawk must make increased payments to Norcon. If a balance exists in the adjustment account at the end of the third period, the party owing the balance must pay the balance in full within thirty days of the termination of the third period" (*Norcon Power Partners v. Niagara Mohawk Power Corp.*, 110 F.3d 6, 7, supra).

In February 1994, Niagara Mohawk presented Norcon with a letter stating its belief, based on revised avoided cost estimates, that substantial credits in Niagara Mohawk's favor would accrue in the adjustment account during the second pricing period. "[A]nalysis shows that the Cumulative Avoided Cost Account . . . will reach over $ 610 million by the end of the second period." Anticipating that Norcon would not be able to satisfy the daily escalating credits in the third period, Niagara Mohawk demanded that "Norcon provide adequate assurance to Niagara Mohawk that Norcon will duly perform all of its future repayment obligations."

Norcon promptly sued Niagara Mohawk in the United States District Court, Southern District of New York. It sought a declaration that Niagara Mohawk had no contractual right under New York State law to demand adequate assurance, beyond security provisions negotiated and expressed in the agreement. Norcon also sought a permanent injunction to stop Niagara Mohawk from anticipatorily terminating the contract based on the reasons described in the demand letter. Niagara Mohawk counterclaimed. It sought a counter declaration that it properly invoked a right to demand adequate assurance of Norcon's future payment performance of the contract.

The District Court granted Norcon's motion for summary judgment. It reasoned that New York common law recognizes the exceptional doctrine of demand for adequate assurance only when a promisor becomes insolvent, and also when the statutory sale of goods provision under UCC 2-609, is involved. Thus, the District Court ruled in Norcon's favor because neither exception applied, in fact or by analogy to the particular dispute (decided sub nom. *Encogen Four Partners v. Niagara Mohawk Power Corp.*, 914 F. Supp. 57).

The Second Circuit Court of Appeals preliminarily agrees (110 F.3d 6, supra) with the District Court that, except in the case of insolvency, no common-law or statutory right to demand adequate assurance exists under New York law which would affect non-UCC contracts, like the instant one. Because of the uncertainty concerning this substantive law question the Second Circuit certified the question to our Court as an aid to its correct application of New York law, and with an eye toward settlement of the important precedential impact on existing and future non-UCC commercial law matters and disputes.

II.

Our analysis should reference a brief review of the evolution of the doctrine of demands for adequate assurance. Its roots spring from the doctrine of anticipatory repudiation (*see*, Garvin, *Adequate Assurance of Performance: Of Risk, Duress, and Cognition*, 69 U. Colo. L .Rev. 71, 77 [1998]). Under that familiar precept, when a party repudiates contractual duties "prior to the time designated for performance and before" all of the consideration has been fulfilled, the "repudiation entitles the nonrepudiating party to claim damages for total breach" * * * A repudiation can be either "a statement by the obligor to the obligee indicating that the obligor will commit a breach that would of itself give the obligee a claim for damages for total breach" or "a voluntary affirmative act which renders the obligor unable or apparently unable to perform without such a breach"* * * .

That switch in performance expectation and burden is readily available, applied and justified when a breaching party's words or deeds are unequivocal. Such a discernible line in the sand clears the way for the nonbreaching party to broach some responsive action. When, however, the apparently breaching party's actions are equivocal or less certain, then the nonbreaching party who senses an approaching storm cloud, affecting the contractual performance, is presented with a dilemma, and must weigh hard choices and serious consequences. One commentator has described the forecast options in this way:

> "If the promisee regards the apparent repudiation as an anticipatory repudiation, terminates his or her own performance and sues for breach, the promisee is placed in jeopardy of being found to have breached if the court determines that the apparent repudiation was not sufficiently clear and unequivocal to constitute an anticipatory repudiation justifying nonperformance. If, on the other hand, the promisee continues to perform after perceiving an apparent repudiation, and it is subsequently determined that an anticipatory repudiation took place, the promisee may be denied recovery for post-repudiation expenditures because of his or her failure to avoid those expenses as part of a reasonable effort to mitigate damages after the repudiation" * * *.

III.

The Uniform Commercial Code settled on a mechanism for relieving some of this uncertainty. It allows a party to a contract for the sale of goods to demand assurance of future performance from the other party when reasonable grounds for insecurity exist (*see*, UCC 2-609; II Farnsworth, Contracts § 8.23). When adequate assurance is not forthcoming, repudiation is deemed confirmed, and the nonbreaching party is allowed to take reasonable actions as though a repudiation had occurred (see, 4 Anderson, Uniform Commercial Code § 2-609:3 [3rd ed. 1997 rev.]).

UCC 2-609 provides, in relevant part:

> "(1) A contract for sale imposes an obligation on each party that the other's expectation of receiving due performance will not be impaired.

> When reasonable grounds for insecurity arise with respect to the performance of either party the other may in writing demand adequate assurance of due performance and until he receives such assurance may if commercially reasonable suspend any performance for which he has not already received the agreed return. . . .
>
> "(4) After receipt of a justified demand failure to provide within a reasonable time not exceeding thirty days such assurance of due performance as is adequate under the circumstances of the particular case is a repudiation of the contract."

In theory, this UCC relief valve recognizes that "the essential purpose of a contract between commercial [parties] is actual performance . . . and that a continuing sense of reliance and security that the promised performance will be forthcoming when due, is an important feature of the bargain" (UCC 2-609, Comment 1). In application, section 2-609 successfully implements the laudatory objectives of quieting the doubt a party fearing repudiation may have, mitigating the dilemma flowing from that doubt, and offering the non-breaching party the opportunity to interpose timely action to deal with the unusual development. * * *

Indeed, UCC 2-609 has been considered so effective in bridging the doctrinal, exceptional and operational gap related to the doctrine of anticipatory breach that some States have imported the complementary regimen of demand for adequate assurance to common-law categories of contract law, using UCC 2-609 as the synapse (*see, e.g., Lo Re v. Tel-Air Communications*, 200 N.J. Super. 59, 490 A.2d 344 [finding support in U.C.C. 2-609 and *Restatement (Second) of Contracts* § 251 for applying doctrine of adequate assurance to contract to purchase radio station]; *Conference Ctr. v. TRC—The Research Corp. of New England*, 189 Conn. 212, 455 A.2d 857 [analogizing to U.C.C. 2-609, as supported by *Restatement (Second) of Contracts* § 251, in context of constructive eviction]).

Commentators have helped nudge this development along. They have noted that the problems redressed by UCC 2-609 are not unique to contracts for sale of goods, regulated under a purely statutory regime. Thus, they have cogently identified the need for the doctrine to be available in exceptional and qualifying common-law contractual settings and disputes because of similar practical, theoretical and salutary objectives (e.g., predictability, definiteness, and stability in commercial dealings and expectations) * * *.

The American Law Institute through its Restatement (Second) of Contracts has also recognized and collected the authorities supporting this modern development. Its process and work settled upon this black letter language:

> "(1) Where reasonable grounds arise to believe that the obligor will commit a breach by non-performance that would of itself give the obligee a claim for damages for total breach under § 243, the obligee may demand adequate assurance of due performance and may, if reasonable, suspend any performance for which he has not already received the agreed exchange until he receives such assurance.
>
> "(2) The obligee may treat as a repudiation the obligor's failure to provide within a reasonable time such assurance of due performance as is adequate in the circumstances of the particular case"

(Restatement [Second] of Contracts § 251).

Modeled on UCC 2-609, Restatement § 251 tracks "the principle that the parties to a contract look to actual performance 'and that a continuing sense of reliance and security that the promised performance will be forthcoming when due, is an important feature of the bargain' " (Restatement [Second] of Contracts § 251, comment a, quoting UCC 2-609, Comment 1). The duty of good faith and fair dealing in the performance of the contract is also reflected in section 251 (*see*, Restatement [Second] of Contracts § 251, comment a).

Some States have adopted Restatement § 251 as their common law of contracts, in varying degrees and classifications. * * *

IV.

New York, up to now, has refrained from expanding the right to demand adequate assurance of performance beyond the Uniform Commercial Code. * * *Hence, the need for this certified question emerged so this Court could provide guidance towards a correct resolution of the Federal lawsuit by settling New York law with a modern pronouncement governing this kind of contract and dispute.

Niagara Mohawk, before our Court through the certified question from the Federal court, urges a comprehensive adaptation of the exceptional demand tool. This wholesale approach has also been advocated by the commentators (*see generally, Dowling, op. cit.; Campbell, op. cit.*). Indeed, it is even reflected in the breadth of the wording of the certified question.

This Court's jurisprudence, however, usually evolves by deciding cases and settling the law more modestly* * *. The twin purposes and functions of this Court's work require significant professional discipline and judicious circumspection.

We conclude, therefore, that it is unnecessary, while fulfilling the important and useful certification role, to promulgate so sweeping a change and proposition in contract law, as has been sought, in one dramatic promulgation. That approach might clash with our customary incremental common-law developmental process, rooted in particular fact patterns and keener wisdom acquired through observations of empirical application of a proportioned, less than absolute, rule in future cases.

It is well to note the axiom that deciding a specific case, even with the precedential comet's tail its rationale illuminates, is very different from enacting a statute of general and universal application. * * *

Experience and patience thus offer a more secure and realistic path to a better and fairer rule, in theory and in practical application. Therefore, this Court chooses to take the traditionally subtler approach, consistent with the proven benefits of the maturation process of the common law, including in the very area of anticipatory repudiation which spawns this relatively newer demand for assurance corollary. * * *

This Court is now persuaded that the policies underlying the UCC 2-609 counterpart should apply with similar cogency for the resolution of this kind of controversy. A useful analogy can be drawn between the contract at issue and a contract for the sale of goods. If the contract here was in all respects the same, except that it was for the sale of oil or some other tangible commodity instead of the sale of electricity, the parties would unquestionably be governed by the demand for adequate assurance of performance factors in UCC 2-609. We are convinced to take this prudent step because it puts commercial parties in these kinds of disputes at relatively arm's length equilibrium in terms of reliability and uniformity of governing legal rubrics. The availability of the doctrine may even provide an incentive and tool for parties to resolve their own differences, perhaps without the necessity of judicial intervention. Open, serious renegotiation of dramatic developments and changes in unusual contractual expectations and qualifying circumstances would occur because of and with an eye to the doctrine's application.

The various authorities, factors and concerns, in sum, prompt the prudence and awareness of the usefulness of recognizing the extension of the doctrine of demand for adequate assurance, as a common-law analogue. It should apply to the type of long-term commercial contract between corporate entities entered into by Norcon and Niagara Mohawk here, which is complex and not reasonably susceptible of all security features being anticipated, bargained for and incorporated in the original contract. Norcon's performance, in terms of reimbursing Niagara Mohawk for credits, is still years away. In the meantime, potential quantifiable damages are accumulating and Niagara Mohawk must weigh the hard choices and serious consequences that the doctrine of demand for adequate assurance is designed to mitigate. This Court needs to go no further in its promulgation of the legal standard as this suffices to declare a dispositive and proportioned answer to the certified question.

Accordingly, the certified question should be answered in the affirmative.

Chief Judge Kaye and Judges Smith, Levine, Ciparick and Wesley concur.

Following certification of a question by the United States Court of Appeals for the Second Circuit and acceptance of the question by this Court pursuant to section 500.17 of the Rules of the Court of Appeals (22 NYCRR 500.17), and after hearing argument by counsel for the parties and consideration of the briefs and the record submitted, certified question answered in the affirmative.

QUESTIONS AND NOTES

1. Questions about the facts of this case

   1.1. What was Niagra Mohawk's concern? Why couldn't it have been addressed at the contract formation stage?

   1.2. Where in the written contract is the provision requiring Norcon to even respond to Niagra Mohawk's demand for adequate assurance of future performance?

   1.3. Was Norcon in breach at any time relevant for this opinion? If not, then why is Niagra Mohawk going to prevail?

2. Questions about the law

   2.1. Does the U.C.C. apply in this case? If not, why does the court cite Section 2-609?

   2.2. It seems as if Niagra Mohawk can turn a case of no breach into a case of breach. Why is that? If the day after the contract was signed, and before there was any balance in the Cumulative Avoided Cost Account, Niagra Mohawk had sent the same letter, would the court order the same result?

   2. 3. If you represented Norcon, and your client indicated that it wished to respond to the letter sent, how would you respond? What types of information do you think would satisfy Niagra Mohawk? Just a letter saying "We intend to perform"?

3. Notes:

   3.1. Article 72 of the *Convention for the International Sale of Goods*, which has been adopted by the United States, states as follows:

   (1) If prior to the date for performance of the contract it is clear that one of the parites will commit a fundamental breach of contract, the other party may declare the contract avoided.

   (2) If time allows, the party intending to declare the contract avoided must give reasonable notice to the other party in order to permit him to provide adequate assurance of his performance.

   Is this superior or inferior to the U.C.C. § 2-609? In thinking about this, consider Article 7.3.4 of the *UNIDROIT* principles which states:

   A party who reasonably believes that there will be a fundamental nonperformance by the other party may demand adequate assurance of due performance and may meanwhile withhold its own performance. Where this assurance is not provided within a reasonable time the party demanding it may terminate the contract.

   3.2. In referring this case to the New York Court of Appeals, the Second Circuit had this to say about the possible effects of U.C.C. § 2-609:

   [S]ome authorities argue that the right to demand adequate assurance may not mitigate many of the problems faced by a party who

> has substantial concerns about the ability of the other party to perform the contract. A party, and eventually a court, may have to determine what constitutes "reasonable grounds for insecurity" or "adequate" assurance. "Partly as a result of the uncertain application of the concepts involved, section 2-609 sometimes does little more than extend the minuet between the weaseling party and the contractual counterpart and add a couple of new moves." 1 James J. White & Robert S. Summers, Uniform Commercial Code § 6-2 (4th ed. 1995); cf. Mollohan v. Black Rock Contracting, Inc., 160 W. Va. 446, 235 S.E.2d 813, 816 n.1 (W. Va. 1977) (declining to adopt Restatement position "except to the extent that a demand for assurances and failure to give them may be evidence of repudiation to present to a jury with other evidence to prove . . . positive repudiation and anticipatory breach"). But see 4 Ronald A. Anderson, Anderson on the Uniform Commercial Code § 2-609:6 (3d ed. 1983) ("courts . . . will undoubtedly expand the application of U.C.C. § 2-609 to transactions that do not come within the . . . Code").
>
> *Norcon Power Partners, L.P. v. Niagara Mohawk Power Corp.*, 110 F.3d 6, 8–9 (2d Cir. 1997).

SECTION 6: EXCUSE PROVIDED BY A MATERIAL BREACH BY THE OTHER PARTY

The last category of excuse may seem strange. It is the excuse provided by the other party's breach of its obligations. Many think that such a result—you don't have to perform if the other party doesn't—is so self evident as to not require much thought.

But the consequences of non-performance—of breach—are many and varied. Before looking at cases developing the nuances, let's take an overview of the subject.

A. The Possible Responses to Breach, and the Categories of Breach

Let us say that Markell, badly in need of tutoring in contracts, enters into a contract with Ponoroff for tutoring services. They agree that Ponoroff will tutor Markell every Monday and Wednesday at Markell's house, and will be paid $1000 per month for his services, payment to be made in advance on the first of the month. The contract will last for six months.

All well and good, so far. We have a contract supported by consideration. The contract is executory on both sides—Ponoroff is obligated to teach, and Markell is obligated to pay. There are probably implied obligations of good faith in the performance on both sides.

But what if Ponoroff doesn't show up for the first tutoring session? What can Markell do? First, let's assume that Ponoroff has no excuse; he was drinking heavily after reading *Clark v. West, supra*, at 722, hoping for a muse to allow him to write. Next, let's recall that as indicated at the start of this Chapter and in Section 235 of the *Restatement*, any nonperformance of a contractual duty is a breach.

So Ponoroff is a contract breacher. Shall he burn in hell for his transgression? Not likely, but let's list the possible ways in which Markell might react, or want to react:

- He might just forgive Ponoroff, since he is such a good teacher. In short, he might *waive* his right to pursue Ponoroff for breach.
- He might contact Ponoroff and just tack on another lesson on the back of the deal, or get a credit on next month's fee for the missed class. In short, he might seek to *amend* or *modify* the existing contractual relationship.
- He might seek to keep the whole contract in place, but receive compensation for Ponoroff's breach, in the form of reimbursement of his lost expenses, or the cost of hiring a substitute tutor. In short, he might seek compensation for the *partial breach*, while keeping in place the whole contract
- He might get ticked off at Ponoroff, and without calling off the whole deal, inform Ponoroff that he will not make any more payments, or make arrangements for Wednesday's session, unless Ponoroff gives

Markell adequate assurance of his future performance, along the lines indicated in *Norcon, supra*, at 767. In short, Markell might *suspend* his performance, keeping the contract in limbo, until Ponoroff gives more definite indications of his true intent.

- Finally, Markell might try to cancel or terminate the whole contract; that is, treat it as breached completely and irrevocably, and then either seek to rescind or seek whatever damages or other remedies that he might obtain. In this regard, Markell would take the position that Ponoroff's *total breach* has *discharged* him from further performance.

While these might be the possible responses, are they equally available? The simple answer is no, and the next section explores when a breach by one party can excuse the other party from its performance.

B. Of Material Breach and Substantial Performance

The rule with respect to a party's ability to suspend performance or terminate the contract when the other party breaches is relatively easy to state. You can suspend performance or terminate only when the breach is a "material breach." That much is backed up by the following section of the *Restatement*:

> *§ 237 Effect on Other Party's Duties of a Failure to Render Performance*
>
> *[I]t is a condition of each party's remaining duties to render performances to be exchanged under an exchange of promises that there be no uncured material failure by the other party to render any such performance due at an earlier time.*

Note the legal device used to implement this rule: conditions. The duty to tender performance is conditioned upon the other party's not being in "material breach." This makes the inquiry into what constitutes a "material failure"or a "material breach"critical. The following cases address that issue.

Gibson v. City of Cranston

U.S. Court of Appeals, First Circuit
37 F.3d 731 (1994)

Selya, Circuit Judge.

This appeal arises out of Dr. Diane Gibson's short and stormy stay as superintendent of schools in Cranston, Rhode Island. It stands as a vivid illustration that some of life's most instructive lessons are learned in the classroom of adversity. After educating ourselves about the facts of the case, the applicable law, and the proceedings below, we conclude that the district court correctly refused to give the plaintiff's case a passing grade.

I. BACKGROUND

Because the trial court took this case from the jury and terminated it by means of an instructed verdict, we summarize the facts adduced below in the light most congenial to appellant's claims.

In early 1989, while serving as Assistant Superintendent of Schools in Waterloo, Iowa, plaintiff-appellant Diane Gibson applied for a job as school superintendent in Cranston. The school committee (the Committee) interviewed her twice (once publicly and once privately) and eventually offered her the post. On August 21, 1989, she met in Rhode Island with members of the Committee concerning her employment contract (the Contract). The parties signed it the next day.

The Contract contained 11 sections, counting the preamble, spread over eight pages. It specified a term that ran from October 1, 1989 to June 30, 1992. The Contract contained various clauses related to professional growth, compensation, contract renewal, salary adjustments, termination for cause, and resignation. It also provided for such miscellaneous items as certification, annual medical examinations, and disability protection. Article III described the superintendent's duties, stating that she

> shall be the chief administrator and agent of the Cranston schools and have charge of the administration of the schools under the direction of the Committee. In this capacity she shall implement, among other things, all policies approved by the Committee, provide for efficient administration of the system and provide for the performance evaluation of all administrators, teachers, and quality of the education provided.

The same article stated that the parties' "respective rights and responsibilities . . . shall be as specified in Chapter 2 of Title 16 of the [Rhode Island General Laws]."

Article VI of the Contract has particular pertinence in this litigation. By its terms, the article obligated the Committee to assess in writing the Superintendent's overall performance at least annually. The format and procedure for the evaluation were to be decided upon by the parties no later than 60 days after the Contract's effective date. Once an evaluation emerged, the Committee and the Superintendent were to meet for discussion of it; specifically, the Contract indicated that a meeting dedicated to this purpose would be held between February 15 and March 15 of each contract year. The evaluation was to be used in determining "if the Superintendents's Contract is renewed/not renewed." To this end, Article VI also contained a non-exclusive list of factors to be considered in the evaluation process and required that the end product describe in reasonable detail "specific instances of strengths and commendations as well as specific instances of any unsatisfactory performance."

At the end of the first 60 days of her reign, Dr. Gibson had not heard from the Committee regarding the evaluation process. She brought the matter to the attention of Stephen Dambruch, the Committee's chairman. Dambruch suggested that appellant develop and disseminate a proposed evaluation form. On December 4, 1989, appellant complied. On March 1, 1990, Dambruch notified the Committee that an evaluation was due between February 15 and March 15 of each year. Five of the nine Committee members responded on the form appellant had prepared. Two other members wrote letters commenting upon appellant's performance. Two Committee members kept their own counsel. In any event, the Committee never composed a unified performance evaluation.

This lollygagging took place during a period of considerable turmoil. In January 1990 the Committee voted to restructure the public schools, only to reverse itself two months later. Spurred in part by this dramatic about-face, appellant requested that the Committee provide her with a written statement of its goals. Although a meeting was held to discuss this request, the Committee never complied with it.

In March 1990 appellant became aware that the school system had improperly paid health benefits on behalf of former employees. She brought this matter to the Committee's attention. Dambruch and his colleagues commissioned an ad hoc committee (the AHC) to mull the problem. The

AHC sought to exclude appellant from its deliberations. To compound this contretemps, an assistant city solicitor wrote to Dambruch on June 8, 1990 suggesting that the AHC might be illegally infringing on the Superintendent's administrative prerogatives and might lack the legal authority necessary to arrange for an audit of the school system's records. Eventually, the Committee retained a certified public accountant. Although the accountant completed a study of the situation, the Committee never provided appellant either with the accountant's report or with any feedback regarding the accountant's recommendations.

Cranston held a municipal election in November of 1990. The electoral results significantly affected the Committee's composition. A member suggested that appellant's evaluation be completed before the newly elected members took office. The Committee scheduled a special meeting for this purpose, but appellant resigned before the meeting could be held. In her letter of resignation, dated December 28, 1990, appellant accused the Committee of violating the Contract by not providing a proper evaluation and statement of goals, and by infringing on the scope of her autonomy as superintendent.

All was serene for well over a year. On June 10, 1992, however, appellant, then a citizen and resident of North Carolina, sued for breach of contract in a Rhode Island state court. She claimed that the City of Cranston, acting through the Committee, disregarded duties owed under the contract, and she sought damages including the balance of her salary and benefits for the period from January 1, 1991 through June 30, 1992.[2] [Cranston removed the case to federal district court]

In due course, Chief Judge Lagueux empaneled a jury and trial commenced. At the close of the appellant's case, Cranston moved for a judgment as a matter of law. The district judge assumed arguendo that Cranston had not fulfilled its contractual commitments, but ruled that, even so, the evidence did not permit a rational jury to find a breach of sufficient materiality as to allow appellant to cease performance and recover damages for the balance of the unexpired term. This appeal followed. * * *

---

[2]Although Dr. Gibson originally sued a bevy of defendants, only Cranston and its treasurer remain in the case. Because Rhode Island law treats a suit against the treasurer of a municipality, in his or her official capacity, as a suit against the city, see R.I. Gen. Laws § 45-15-5 (1991), these two defendants are in effect the same entity. We refer to them collectively as "Cranston."

III. ANALYSIS

The substantive law of Rhode Island governs in this diversity case. Under Rhode Island law, a contracting party may cease performance and seek damages if the other contracting party commits a breach that is "material," * * * or that "goes to the essence of the contract" * * *. Some courts and commentators have cast the standard in terms of a "total" breach as opposed to a "partial" breach, with only the former justifying termination of a contract. * * *Because we believe these terms constitute various ways of saying the same thing, we will use them interchangeably.[5]

Appellant invites us to rule that materiality is always a question of fact, thereby eliminating the possibility of a directed verdict where, as here, the issue is disputed. We decline the invitation. While the state supreme court has indicated that, in this context, materiality "is essentially a factual question," and that its resolution ordinarily "requires consideration of all the pertinent evidence and the conduct and relationship of the parties," * * *, the first part of this statement is a generalization, and, like most generalizations, it admits of exceptions. Though questions of materiality are usually to be determined by the trier of fact, in this case the jury, the rule is not universal. As is true of virtually any factual question, if the materiality question in a given case admits of only one reasonable answer (because the evidence on the point is either undisputed or sufficiently lopsided), then the court must intervene and address what is ordinarily a factual question as a question of law.

The task of delineating which particular breaches may justify an injured party ceasing performance and bringing an action for damages is demanding, but the case law affords some insights. In Aiello [Constr., Inc. v. Nationwide Tractor Trailer Training & Placement Corp., 122 R.I. 861, 413 A.2d 85, 87 (R.I. 1980)], for example, the plaintiff, a contractor, sued a property owner for nonpayment of installments due under a construction contract. The Rhode Island Supreme Court upheld a finding that the defendant's failure to pay installments as they came due went to the essence of the contract and, therefore, excused further performance by the plaintiff. See Aiello,

[5]The rigid material/non-material dichotomy may oversimplify the universe of breaches. Although this case, in its present posture, does not require us to make a finer distinction, we do not deprecate the possibility that there may be an intermediate level of breach, i.e., breaches which are not serious enough to warrant repudiation of the contract and a suit for damages by the injured party, but which nonetheless might constitute a defense to an action for damages brought by the party committing the initial breach. Thus, our holding that the Committee's alleged breaches were not material, see infra, does not necessarily betoken that Dr. Gibson would have been liable had the Committee sued her for breach.

413 A.2d at 87. In Dunne [Leases Cars & Trucks, Inc. v. Kenworth Truck Co., 466 A.2d 1153, 1160 (R.I. 1983)], the court upheld a finding that a dealer committed a material breach of its franchise agreement with a truck manufacturer by failing to honor its promise to separate its leasing activities from its dealership operation. See Dunne, 466 A.2d at 1159. In its opinion, the court emphasized the presence of evidence that the leasing activities adversely impacted the truck dealership in the areas of parking, cleanliness, parts sales, and service. See id. at 1158. On this basis, the court concluded that the dealer's breach might be deemed material even though the dealer regularly achieved its sales quota under the franchise agreement. See id. at 1159.

Despite the insights that can be gleaned from these cases, the Rhode Island courts thus far have not precisely defined what constitutes a material breach. Nonetheless, we believe that the proper analysis is informed by certain commentaries and decisions from outside Rhode Island. * * *The Restatement is an especially helpful source of guidance because Rhode Island courts frequently turn to the Restatement to fill gaps in state law. * * *The Restatement lists five factors that may be considered in determining whether a breach is material.[7] Other commentators have espoused slightly different sets of relevant factors for use in determining materiality, such as the extent to which the contract has been performed at the time of the breach, the willfulness *vel non* of the breach, and the degree of seriousness attributable to the breach, expressed in quantitative terms. * * * * We believe that when the occasion arises, the Rhode Island Supreme Court will adopt some variant of these tests to determine the materiality of a breach of con-

[7]These factors are:

(a) the extent to which the injured party will be deprived of the benefit which he reasonably expected;

(b) the extent to which the injured party can be adequately compensated for the part of that benefit of which he will be deprived;

(c) the extent to which the party failing to perform or offer to perform will suffer forfeiture;

(d) the likelihood that the party failing to perform or to offer to perform will cure his failure, taking account of all the circumstances including any reasonable assurances;

(e) the extent to which the behavior of the party failing to perform or to offer to perform comports with standards of good faith and fair dealing.

Restatement (Second) of Contracts § 241 (1979).

tract.[8] In our view, the test will concentrate on factors such as those listed in the Restatement, with special emphasis, in the employment context, on the extent to which the alleged breach interferes with the duties and benefits flowing from the contract in its entirety. We need not dice matters too finely, however, for appellant's proof can meet neither the Restatement standard nor any reasonable variant of it. We explain briefly.

While a material breach of an employment contract need not completely frustrate the entire purpose of the contract, it must be so important that it makes continued performance by the plaintiff virtually pointless. * * * Thus, if Cranston refused to pay appellant, or, conversely, if appellant completely withheld her services for no valid reason, the ensuing breach would reach the essence of the Contract.

But that is not what transpired here. We think it is readily apparent that, under the stringent standard that obtains, the Committee's alleged breaches of the Contract are, as a matter of law, not material. The superintendent's job encompasses a complex and varied set of responsibilities. Under a provision of the Rhode Island General Laws, which is incorporated into the Contract by explicit reference, the post includes a vast array of administrative, supervisory, managerial, and policymaking functions. See R. I. Gen. Laws § 16-2-11 (1988). . . . This elaborate compendium of responsibilities, complemented by the multifarious provisions of the Contract itself, put appellant's grievances into proper perspective. And so viewed, we are unable to see how a reasonable jury could find that the Committee's conduct involved matters of sufficient significance to constitute a material breach.

Appellant's flagship claim pirouettes around the Committee's failure to provide her with a unified evaluation. Given the admitted feedback that appellant received from a majority of the individual Committee members, we cannot discern how the failure to reduce the feedback to a unified evaluation or the other shortcomings in the evaluation process could be deemed a material breach. Without the evaluation, appellant was still able to carry out virtually all of her responsibilities. She still received the overwhelming majority of the benefits to which the Contract entitled her. Her mere testimony that without the evaluation provision she would not have signed the employment agreement cannot make this otherwise unremarkable provision into one that "goes to the essence of the contract." * * * The determination

---

[8]Appellant suggests that "a breach is material if it denies a party a bargained-for exchange." We find this formulation unacceptable, for it does not reflect how significant a contract provision must be before its breach will be deemed material.

of materiality, like other aspects of contract interpretation, must be based largely on a standard of objective reasonableness rather than purely subjective belief. * * * In other words, a party cannot transmogrify a provision that, from an objective standpoint, has only marginal significance into one of central salience by the simple expedient of saying in retrospect that she believed it to be very important.

Here, notwithstanding plaintiff's post hoc rationalization, the Committee's failure to provide a unified evaluation seems much more a matter of form than of substance. It did not in any way shrink plaintiff's major duties or deprive her of the principal benefits of her contractual bargain. Nothing about the failure betokens bad faith or an unfair course of conduct. And the sockdolager is that, at the time Dr. Gibson resigned, there was a high likelihood that the Committee would soon cure its breach by providing an evaluation; a special meeting for this purpose was scheduled to occur less than one week after she precipitously resigned.

Appellant's fallback position is that the Committee never furnished her with a written statement of goals. But appellant had ample contact with the Committee and its members to get a sense of the school system's objectives. Thus, as with the first alleged breach, this failure did not interfere significantly with either her duties or her benefits under the Contract. Consequently, it could not be deemed a material breach.

Finally, appellant alleges that the Committee infringed upon her administrative responsibilities. She offers two incidents to illustrate her contention: a Committee member's action in sending a questionnaire directly to the faculty, . . . and the AHC's attempt to exclude her from its deliberations. Given the minor nature of these supposed infractions and their subsequent resolution, no reasonable jury could find that they constitute a material breach.

IV. CONCLUSION

We need go no further. Considering all the evidence in the light most hospitable to plaintiff, no reasonable jury could find that the Committee's alleged breaches of the Contract gutted it. Consequently, the court below did not err in granting judgment as a matter of law.

Affirmed.

QUESTIONS AND NOTE

1. Questions about the facts of this case

   1.1. What were the breaches by the City of Cranston?

   1.2. Why were they not material?

   1.3. Will Gibson get any compensation for the acknowledged breaches?

2. Questions about the law

   2.1. What types of breaches would this court have found to be material?

   2.2. Had Gibson been well advised, and if she in good faith believed the evaluation clause to be essential, what could or should she have done at formation that would have changed the result in this case?

   2.3. May a party to the contract specify that some, or even all, of the provisions of the contract are material, thus eliminating (at least for that contract) the distinction between material and other breaches? Read the note that follows.

3. Note

In *RW Power Partners, L.P. v. Virginia Electric and Power Co.*, 899 F. Supp. 1490 (E.D. Va. 1995), two power companies had entered into a contract for the provision of power over a long term period. The relationship soured, with Virginia Electric and Power Co. wishing to get out of the contract any legal way it could. It tried to do so when RW Power failed to keep in place a letter of credit (a financial device akin to a bank guaranty) for a seven to ten day period. The contract, however, required continuous coverage by the letter of credit; the gap was, therefore, an incurable breach.

But was the breach material, allowing Virginia Electric to consider its obligations discharged and permitting it to terminate the agreement? Applying the factors set forth in Section 241 of the *Restatement (Second) of Contracts*, quoted in footnote 7 above, the court held that:

> Application of these basic principles in this action leads to the inevitable conclusion that the failure to have in place a letter of credit for a period of

> at most 10 days, during which time no injury befell Virginia Power, was not a material breach of contract. Consequently, Virginia Power was not entitled to terminate the Agreement. It would be entitled to damages for partial breach, but it has shown none.

899 F. Supp. at 1498.

Virginia Electric, however, was not without backup arguments. Pointing to a clause that stated that "If Operator [RW Power] fails to perform any of its obligations pursuant to this Agreement, then Virginia Power may cancel this Agreement," Virginia Electric then argued that the contract of the parties had superceded the common law of material breach, and thus clauses which allow termination for "partial" or "immaterial" breaches are enforceable. The court, while agreeing that parties to a contract may agree to cancellation for any reason, even immaterial breach, did not agree that the contract before it permitted such a cancellation. In trying to give effect to the above language the parties had agreed up for cancellation, the court noted that:

> Where the breach is not material and the contract does not explicitly state that an immaterial breach will excuse further performance, termination of the contract is improper, and the injured party is limited to damages for the breach.

Id. at 1502.

Without the explicit notation that an immaterial breach would be grounds for termination, the court declined to permit Virginia Power to terminate the agreement.

Which leads one to wonder how you should draft clauses in which the parties actually agree that immaterial breaches can permit termination. Do you have to put "AND WE REALLY MEAN IT" after every clause in the contract in order to enforce it as written?

If the breach is not material, can the breaching party still assert rights under the contract? That is, can someone who renders imperfect performance still sue under the contract? The answer turns, in part, on the type of contract. Let us start with another contracts classic from the area of construction contracts.

Jacob & Youngs, Incorporated v. Kent
Court of Appeals of New York
230 N.Y. 239, 129 N.E. 889 (1921)

Cardozo, J:

The plaintiff built a country residence for the defendant at a cost of upwards of $77,000, and now sues to recover a balance of $3,483.46, remaining unpaid. The work of construction ceased in June, 1914, and the defendant then began to occupy the dwelling. There was no complaint of defective performance until March, 1915. One of the specifications for the plumbing work provides that "all wrought iron pipe must be well galvanized, lap welded pipe of the grade known as 'standard pipe' of Reading manufacture." The defendant learned in March, 1915, that some of the pipe, instead of being made in Reading, was the product of other factories. The plaintiff was accordingly directed by the architect to do the work anew. The plumbing was then encased within the walls except in a few places where it had to be exposed. Obedience to the order meant more than the substitution of other pipe. It meant the demolition at great expense of substantial parts of the completed structure. The plaintiff left the work untouched, and asked for a certificate that the final payment was due. Refusal of the certificate was followed by this suit.

The evidence sustains a finding that the omission of the prescribed brand of pipe was neither fraudulent nor willful. It was the result of the oversight and inattention of the plaintiff's subcontractor. Reading pipe is distinguished from Cohoes pipe and other brands only by the name of the manufacturer stamped upon it at intervals of between six and seven feet. Even the defendant's architect, though he inspected the pipe upon arrival, failed to notice the discrepancy. The plaintiff tried to show that the brands installed, though made by other manufacturers, were the same in quality, in appearance, in market value and in cost as the brand stated in the contract—that they were, indeed, the same thing, though manufactured in another place. The evidence was excluded, and a verdict directed for the defendant. The Appellate Division reversed, and granted a new trial.

We think the evidence, if admitted, would have supplied some basis for the inference that the defect was insignificant in its relation to the project. The courts never say that one who makes a contract fills the measure of his duty by less than full performance. They do say, however, that an omission, both trivial and innocent, will sometimes be atoned for by allowance of the resulting damage, and will not always be the breach of a condition to be followed by a forfeiture * * * The distinction is akin to that between dependent and independent promises, or between promises and conditions * * *. Some promises are so plainly independent that they can never by fair construction be conditions of one another. * * *. Others are so plainly dependent that they must always be conditions. Others, though dependent and thus conditions when there is departure in point of substance, will be viewed as independent and collateral when the departure is insignificant * * *. Considerations partly of justice and partly of presumable intention are to tell us whether this or that promise shall be placed in one class or in another. The simple and the uniform will call for different remedies from the multifarious and the intricate. The margin of departure within the range of normal expectation upon a sale of common chattels will vary from the margin to be expected upon a contract for the construction of a mansion or a "skyscraper." There will be harshness sometimes and oppression in the implication of a condition when the thing upon which labor has been expended is incapable of surrender because united to the land, and equity and reason in the implication of a like condition when the subject-matter, if defective, is in shape to be returned. From the conclusion that promises may not be treated as dependent to the extent of their uttermost minutiae without a sacrifice of justice, the progress is a short one to the conclusion that they may not be so treated without a perversion of intention. Intention not otherwise revealed may be presumed to hold in contemplation the reasonable and probable. If something else is in view, it must not be left to implication. There will be no assumption of a purpose to visit venial faults with oppressive retribution.

Those who think more of symmetry and logic in the development of legal rules than of practical adaptation to the attainment of a just result will be troubled by a classification where the lines of division are so wavering and blurred. Something, doubtless, may be said on the score of consistency and certainty in favor of a stricter standard. The courts have balanced such considerations against those of equity and fairness, and found the latter to be the weightier. The decisions in this state commit us to the liberal view, which is making its way, nowadays, in jurisdictions slow to welcome it * * *. Where the line is to be drawn between the important and the trivial cannot be settled by a formula. "In the nature of the case precise boundaries are impossible"* * *. The same omission may take on one aspect or another according to its setting. Substitution of equivalents may not have the same significance in fields of art on the one side and in those of mere utility on the other. Nowhere will change be tolerated, however, if it is so dominant or pervasive as in any real or substantial measure to frustrate the purpose of the contract* * *. There is no general license to install whatever, in the builder's judgment, may be regarded as "just as good"* * *. The question is one of degree, to be answered, if there is doubt, by the triers of the facts* * *, and, if the inferences are certain, by the judges of the law* * *. We must weigh the purpose to be served, the desire to be gratified, the excuse for deviation from the letter, the cruelty of enforced adherence. Then only can we tell whether literal fulfilment is to be implied by law as a condition. This is not to say that the parties are not free by apt and certain words to effectuate a purpose that performance of every term shall be a condition of recovery. That question is not here. This is merely to say that the law will be slow to impute the purpose, in the silence of the parties, where the significance of the default is grievously out of proportion to the oppression of the forfeiture. The willful transgressor must accept the penalty of his transgression* * *. For him there is no occasion to mitigate the rigor of implied conditions. The transgressor whose default is unintentional and trivial may hope for mercy if he will offer atonement for his wrong * * *.

In the circumstances of this case, we think the measure of the allowance is not the cost of replacement, which would be great, but the difference in value, which would be either nominal or nothing. Some of the exposed sections might perhaps have been replaced at moderate expense. The defendant did not limit his demand to them, but treated the plumbing as a unit to be corrected from cellar to roof. In point of fact, the plaintiff never reached the stage at which evidence of the extent of the allowance became necessary. The trial court had excluded evidence that the defect was unsubstantial, and in view of that ruling there was no occasion for the plaintiff to go farther with an offer of proof. We think, however, that the offer, if it had been made, would not of necessity have been defective because directed to difference in value. It is true that in most cases the cost of replacement is the measure* * *. The owner is entitled to the money which will permit him to complete, unless the cost of completion is grossly and unfairly out of proportion to the good to be attained. When that is true, the measure is the difference in value. Specifications call, let us say, for a foundation built of granite quarried in Vermont. On the completion of the building, the owner learns that through the blunder of a subcontractor part of the foundation has been built of granite of the same quality quarried in New Hampshire. The measure of allowance is not the cost of reconstruction. "There may be missions of that which could not afterwards be supplied exactly as called for by the contract without taking down the building to its foundations, and at the same time the omission may not affect the value of the building for use or otherwise, except so slightly as to be hardly appreciable"* * *. The rule that gives a remedy in cases of substantial performance with compensation for defects of trivial or inappreciable importance, has been developed by the courts as an instrument of justice. The measure of the allowance must be shaped to the same end.

The order should be affirmed, and judgment absolute directed in favor of the plaintiff upon the stipulation, with costs in all courts.

McLaughlin, J. (dissenting). I dissent. The plaintiff did not perform its contract. Its failure to do so was either intentional or due to gross neglect which, under the uncontradicted facts, amounted to the same thing, nor did it make any proof of the cost of compliance, where compliance was possible.

Under its contract it obligated itself to use in the plumbing only pipe (between 2,000 and 2,500 feet) made by the Reading Manufacturing Company. The first pipe delivered was about 1,000 feet and the plaintiff's superintendent then called the attention of the foreman of the subcontractor, who was doing the plumbing, to the fact that the specifications annexed to the contract required all pipe used in the plumbing to be of the Reading Manufacturing Company. They then examined it for the purpose of ascertaining whether this delivery was of that manufacture and found it was. Thereafter, as pipe was required in the progress of the work, the foreman of the subcontractor would leave word at its shop that he wanted a specified number of feet of pipe, without in any way indicating of what manufacture. Pipe would thereafter be delivered and installed in the building, without any examination whatever. Indeed, no examination, so far as appears, was made by the plaintiff, the subcontractor, defendant's architect, or any one else, of any of the pipe except the first delivery, until after the building had been completed. Plaintiff's architect then refused to give the certificate of completion, upon which the final payment depended, because all of the pipe used in the plumbing was not of the kind called for by the contract. After such refusal, the subcontractor removed the covering or insulation from about 900 feet of pipe which was exposed in the basement, cellar and attic, and all but 70 feet was found to have been manufactured, not by the Reading Company, but by other manufacturers, some by the Cohoes Rolling Mill Company, some by the National Steel Works, some by the South Chester Tubing Company, and some which bore no manufacturer's mark at all. The balance of the pipe had been so installed in the building that an inspection of it could not be had without demolishing, in part at least, the building itself.

I am of the opinion the trial court was right in directing a verdict for the defendant. The plaintiff agreed that all the pipe used should be of the Reading Manufacturing Company. Only about two-fifths of it, so far as appears, was of that kind. If more were used, then the burden of proving that fact was upon the plaintiff, which it could easily have done, since it knew where the pipe was obtained. The question of substantial performance of a contract of the character of the one under consideration depends in no small degree upon the good faith of the contractor. If the plaintiff had intended to, and had complied with the terms of the contract except as to minor omissions, due to inadvertence, then he might be allowed to recover the contract price, less the amount necessary to fully compensate the defendant for damages caused by such omissions.* * * But that is not this case. It installed between 2,000 and 2,500 feet of pipe, of which only 1,000 feet at most complied with the contract. No explanation was given why pipe called for by the contract was not used, nor was any effort made to show what it would cost to remove the pipe of other manufacturers and install that of the Reading Manufacturing Company. The defendant had a right to contract for what he wanted. He had a right before making payment to get what the contract called for. It is no answer to this suggestion to say that the pipe put in was just as good as that made by the Reading Manufacturing Company, or that the difference in value between such pipe and the pipe made by the Reading Manufacturing Company would be either "nominal or nothing." Defendant contracted for pipe made by the Reading Manufacturing Company. What his reason was for requiring this kind of pipe is of no importance. He wanted that and was entitled to it. It may have been a mere whim on his part, but even so, he had a right to this kind of pipe, regardless of whether some other kind, according to the opinion of the contractor or experts, would have been "just as good, better, or done just as well." He agreed to pay only upon condition that the pipe installed were made by that company and he ought not to be compelled to pay unless that condition be performed. * * *The rule, therefore, of substantial performance, with damages for unsubstantial omissions, has no application. * * *

What was said by this court in *Smith* v. *Brady* * * * is quite applicable here: "I suppose it will be conceded that everyone has a right to build his house, his cottage or his store after such a model and in such style as shall best accord with his notions of utility or be most agreeable to his fancy. The specifications of the contract become the law between the parties until voluntarily changed. If the owner prefers a plain and simple Doric column, and has so provided in the agreement, the contractor has no right to put in its place the more costly and elegant Corinthian. If the owner, having regard to strength and durability, has contracted for walls of specified materials to be laid in a particular manner, or for a given number of joists and beams, the builder has no right to substitute his own judgment or that of others. Having departed from the agreement, if performance has not been waived by the other party, the law will not allow him to allege that he has made as good a building as the one he engaged to erect. He can demand payment only upon and according to the terms of his contract, and if the conditions on which payment is due have not been performed, then the right to demand it does not exist. To hold a different doctrine would be simply to make another contract, and would be giving to parties an encouragement to violate their engagements, which the just policy of the law does not permit." (p. 186.)

I am of the opinion the trial court did not err in ruling on the admission of evidence or in directing a verdict for the defendant.

For the foregoing reasons I think the judgment of the Appellate Division should be reversed and the judgment of the Trial Term affirmed.

QUESTIONS AND NOTES

1. Questions about the facts of this case

    1.1. As far as you can tell from the opinion, what is the difference between Reading pipe and Cohoes pipe? Is this difference what is driving the lawsuit? If not, what do you think is?

    1.2. Was Jacob & Youngs in breach? If so, why should they recover anything?

    1.3. Does it matter that the breach was unintentional? Why?

2. Questions about the law

    2.1. What is the relationship between substantial performance and material breach?

    2.2. Would the result be different if Reading pipe was slightly superior to Cohoes pipe?

    2.3. Would the result be different if Kent had not paid anything with respect to the contract?

2.4. If Jacobs & Youngs had walked off the job when it was half-done, could they have sued Kent on the contract under this case? Why or why not?

2.5. Does this opinion mean that you can never contract for a specific good that may sound goofy to the rest of the world, but is just hunky-dory to you? If not, how can you protect yourself?

2.6. Does the *Peacock* case, *supra*, at 629, have any bearing on this case? Are they consistent? Are there any other cases in this chapter which are relevant to the issues raised by this case?

3. Notes

3.1. The requirement of Reading pipe was found in General Condition 225 of the contract. General Condition 22 of the same contract stated:

> (22) Where any particular brand of manufactured article is specified, it is to be considered as a standard. Contractors desiring to use another shall first make application in writing to the Architect, stating the difference in cost, and obtain their written approval of the change.

Does examination of this clause make the result reached more or less palatable? *See* RICHARD DANZIG, THE CAPABILITY PROBLEM IN CONTRACT LAW: FURTHER READINGS ON WELL-KNOWN CASES 111–12 (1978).

3.2. Almost 75 years after *Jacob & Youngs*, the New York Court of Appeals had the occasion to review part of that opinion. In *Oppenheimer & Co., Inc. v. Oppenheim, Appel, Dixon & Co.*, 86 N.Y.2d 685, 660 N.E.2d 415, 636 N.Y.S.2d 734 (1995), two parties signed a sub-lease of New York office space, but made the effectiveness of the lease expressly conditional on obtaining the landlord's consent to making certain tenant improvements necessary for the sub-leasee's business. In particular, the relevant language required the sub-tenant to obtain:

> 'the Prime Landlord's written notice of confirmation, substantially to the effect that [defendant] is a subtenant of the Premises reasonably acceptable to Prime Landlord.' If such written notice of confir-

> mation were not obtained 'on or before December 30, 1986, then this letter agreement and the Sublease * * * shall be deemed null and void and of no further force and effect and neither party shall have any rights against nor obligations to the other.'

86 N.Y.2d at 688.

The deadline was mutually extended to February 25, 1987, but still the sub-tenant could not comply. As noted by the court:

> However, plaintiff never delivered the prime landlord's written consent to the proposed tenant work on or before the modified final deadline of February 25, 1987. Rather, plaintiff's attorney telephoned defendant's attorney on February 25 and informed defendant that the prime landlord's consent had been secured. On February 26, defendant, through its attorney, informed plaintiff's attorney that the letter agreement and sublease were invalid for failure to timely deliver the prime landlord's written consent and that it would not agree to an extension of the deadline. The document embodying the prime landlord's written consent was eventually received by plaintiff on March 20, 1987, 23 days after expiration of paragraph 4(c)'s modified final deadline.

Id. at 688–689.

Okay, so they had only oral consent, not written consent, by the deadline. That's substantial performance within *Jacob & Youngs*, isn't it?

No. As phrased by the New York Court of Appeals:

> Plaintiff's reliance on the well-known case of *Jacob & Youngs v. Kent*, 230 N.Y. 239, 129 N.E. 889, is misplaced. There, a contractor built a summer residence and the buyer refused to pay the remaining balance of the contract price on the ground that the contractor used a different type of pipe than was specified in the contract. The buyer sought to enforce the contract as written. This would have involved the demolition of large parts of the structure at great expense and loss to the seller. This Court, in an opinion by then-Judge Cardozo, ruled for the contractor on the ground that "an omission, both trivial and innocent, will sometimes be atoned for by allowance of the resulting damage, and will not always be the breach of a condition to be followed by a forfeiture" (230 N.Y., at

241, 129 N.E. 889). But Judge Cardozo was careful to note that the situation would be different in the case of an express condition:

> 'This is not to say that the parties are not free by apt and certain words to effectuate a purpose that performance of every term shall be a condition of recovery. That question is not here. This is merely to say that the law will be slow to impute the purpose, in the silence of the parties, where the significance of the default is grievously out of proportion to the oppression of the forfeiture' (*id*., at 243–244, 129 N.E. 889).

Id. at 694.

So there is no lease; just read the "apt and certain" words of the contract. As the New York appeals court concluded: "Freedom of contract prevails in an arm's length transaction between sophisticated parties such as these, and in the absence of countervailing public policy concerns there is no reason to relieve them of the consequences of their bargain. If they are dissatisfied with the consequences of their agreement, 'the time to say so [was] at the bargaining table.'" *Id.* at 695.

Just in case you thought that courts always accept less than perfect performance, read the next case. Is it consistent with *Jacob & Youngs*? Should it be?

O. W. Grun Roofing & Construction Co. v. Cope

Court of Civil Appeals of Texas
529 S.W.2d 258 (1975)

Cadena, J:

Plaintiff, Mrs. Fred M. Cope, sued defendant, O. W. Grun Roofing & Construction Co., to set aside a mechanic's lien filed by defendant and for damages in the sum of $1,500.00 suffered by plaintiff as a result of the alleged failure of defendant to perform a contract calling for the installation of a new roof on plaintiff's home. Defendant, in addition to a general denial, filed a cross-claim for $648.00, the amount which plaintiff agreed to pay defendant for installing the roof, and for foreclosure of the mechanic's lien on plaintiff's home.

Following trial to a jury, the court below entered judgment awarding plaintiff $122.60 as damages for defendant's failure to perform the contract; setting aside the mechanic's lien; and denying defendant recovery on its cross-claim. It is from this judgment that defendant appeals.

The jury found . . . defendant did not substantially perform the contract [and that] . . . the reasonable cost of performing the contract in a good and workmanlike manner would be $777.60. Although the verdict shows the cost of proper performance to be $777.60, the judgment describes this finding as being in the amount of $770.60, and the award of $122.60 to plaintiff is based on the difference between $770.60 and the contract price of $648.00.

* * *

The written contract required defendant to install a new roof on plaintiff's home for $648.00. The contract describes the color of the shingles to be used as "russet glow," which defendant defined as a "brown varied color." Defendant acknowledges that it was his obligation to install a roof of uniform color.

After defendant had installed the new roof, plaintiff noticed that it had streaks which she described as yellow, due to a difference in color or shade of some of the shingles. Defendant agreed to remedy the situation and he removed the nonconforming shingles. However, the replacement shingles do not match the remainder, and photographs introduced in evidence clearly show that the roof is not of a uniform color. Plaintiff testified that her roof has the appearance of having been patched, rather than having been completely replaced. According to plaintiff's testimony, the yellow streaks appeared on the northern, eastern and southern sides of the roof, and defendant only replaced the non-matching shingles on the northern and eastern sides, leaving the southern side with the yellow streaks still apparent. The result is that only the western portion of the roof is of uniform color.

When defendant originally installed the complete new roof, it used 24 "squares" of shingles. In an effort to achieve a roof of uniform color, five squares were ripped off and replaced. There is no testimony as to the number of squares which would have to be replaced on the southern, or rear, side of the house in order to eliminate the original yellow streaks. Although there is expert testimony to the effect that the disparity in color would not be noticeable after the shingles have been on the roof for about a year, there is testimony to the effect that, although some nine or ten months have elapsed since defendant attempted to achieve a uniform coloration, the roof is still "streaky" on three sides. One of defendant's experts testified that if the shingles are properly applied the result will be a "blended" roof rather than a streaked roof.

In view of the fact that the disparity in color has not disappeared in nine or ten months, and in view of the fact that there is testimony to the effect that it would be impossible to secure matching shingles to replace the nonconforming ones, it can reasonably be inferred that a roof of uniform coloration can be achieved only by installing a completely new roof.

The evidence is undisputed that the roof is a substantial roof and will give plaintiff protection against the elements.

The principle which allows recovery for part performance in cases involving dependent promises may be expressed by saying that a material breach or a breach which goes to the root of the matter or essence of the contract defeats the promisor's claim despite his part performance, or it may be expressed by saying that a promisor who has substantially performed is entitled to recover, although he has failed in some particular to comply with his agreement. The latter mode of expressing the rule is generally referred to as the doctrine of substantial performance and is especially common in cases involving building contracts, although its application is not restricted to such contracts.

It is difficult to formulate definitive rule [*sic*] for determining whether the contractor's performance, less than complete, amounts to "substantial performance," since the question is one of fact and of degree, and the answer depends on the particular facts of each case. But, although the decisions furnish no rule of thumb, they are helpful in suggesting guidelines. One of the most obvious factors to be considered is the extent of the nonperformance. The deficiency will not be tolerated if it is so pervasive as to frustrate the purpose of the contract in any real or substantial sense. The doctrine does not bestow on a contractor a license to install whatever is, in his judgment, "just as good." The answer is arrived at by weighing the purpose to be served, the desire to be gratified, the excuse for deviating from the letter of the contract and the cruelty of enforcing strict adherence or of compelling the promisee to receive something less than for which he bargained. Also influential in many cases is the ratio of money value of the tendered performance and of the promised performance. In most cases the contract itself at least is an indication of the value of the promised performance, and courts should have little difficulty in determining the cost of curing the deficiency. But the rule cannot be expressed in terms of a fraction, since complete reliance on a mathematical formula would result in ignoring other important factors, such as the purpose which the promised performance was intended to serve and the extent to which the nonperformance would defeat such purpose, or would defeat it if not corrected. *See, generally*, 3A Corbin, Contracts Secs. 700–07 (1960).

Although definitions of "substantial performance" are not always couched in the same terminology and, because of the facts involved in a particular case, sometimes vary in the recital of the factors to be considered, the following definition by the Commission of Appeals in *Atkinson v. Jackson Bros.*, 270 S.W. 848, 849 (Tex. Com. App. 1925), is a typical recital of the constituent elements of the doctrine:

> To constitute substantial compliance the contractor must have in good faith intended to comply with the contract, and shall have substantially done so in the sense that the defects are not pervasive, do not constitute a deviation from the general plan contemplated for the work, and are not so essential that the object of the parties in making the contract and its purpose cannot, without difficulty, be accomplished by remedying them. Such performance permits only such omissions or deviations from the contract as are inadvertent and unintentional, are not due to bad faith, do not impair the structure as a whole, and are remediable without doing material damage to other parts of the building in tearing down and reconstructing.

* * *

What was the general plan contemplated for the work in this case? What was the object and purpose of the parties? It is clear that, despite the frequency with which the courts speak of defects that are not "pervasive," which do not constitute a "deviation from the general plan," and which are "not so essential that the object of the parties in making the contract and its purpose cannot, without difficulty, be accomplished by remedying them," when an attempt is made to apply the general principles to a particular case difficulties are encountered at the outset. Was the general plan to install a substantial roof which would serve the purpose which roofs are designed to serve? Or, rather, was the general plan to install a substantial roof of uniform color? Was the object and purpose of the contract merely to furnish such a roof, or was it to furnish such a roof which would be of a uniform color? It should not come as a shock to anyone to adopt a rule to the effect that a person has, particularly with respect to his home, to choose for himself and to contract for something which exactly satisfies that choice, and not to be compelled to accept something else. In the matter of homes and their decoration, as much as, if not more than, in many other fields, mere taste or preference, almost approaching whimsy, may be controlling with the home-owner, so that variations which might, under other circumstances, be considered trifling, may be inconsistent with that "substantial performance" on which liability to pay must be predicated. Of mere incompleteness or deviations which may be easily supplied or remedied after the contractor has finished his work, and the cost of which to the owner is not excessive and readily ascertainable, present less cause for hesitation in concluding that the performance tendered constitutes substantial performance, since in such cases the owner can obtain complete satisfaction by merely spending some money and deducting the amount of such expenditure from the contract price.

In the case before us there is evidence to support the conclusion that plaintiff can secure a roof of uniform coloring only by installing a completely new roof. We cannot say, as a matter of law, that the evidence establishes that in this case that a roof which so lacks uniformity in color as to give the appearance of a patch job serves essentially the same purpose as a roof of uniform color which has the appearance of being a new roof. We are not prepared to hold that a contractor who tenders a performance so deficient that it can be remedied only by completely redoing the work for which the contract called has established, as a matter of law, that he has substantially performed his contractual obligation.

* * *

The judgment of the trial court is affirmed.

QUESTIONS AND NOTE

1. Questions about the facts of this case

    1.1. How much was Grun Roofing paid for its work on the roof?

    1.2. Did the roof leak? Did the roof "serve the purpose for which roofs are designed to serve"?

    1.3. Did the contract provide that the roof was to be a uniform color?

    1.4. Why did Grun Roofing admit that it was its "obligation to install a roof of uniform color"?

2. Questions about the law

   2.1. How did the court define "substantial performance"?

   2.2. What was the basis for the court's determination that the uniformity of the color of the roof was important to the Copes? Would the Texas Court of Civil Appeals have reversed the trial court if the trial court had concluded that Grun Roofing's breach was "trivial and innocent"?

   2.3. Is the court's statement that "It should not come as a shock to anyone to adopt a rule to the effect a person has, particularly with respect to his home, to choose for himself and to contract for something which exactly satisfies his choice, and not to be compelled to accept something else" a shock to anyone who has read *Jacob & Youngs v. Kent*?

3. Note

As *Grun Roofing* illustrates, the rule that a "material breach . . . defeats the promisor's claim" can lead to harsh consequences—Grun Roofing received nothing for its work. There is a tendency on the part of judges, lawyers, law professors and law students to look for ways to avoid or mitigate harsh consequences.

The concept of "divisible" contract is a mitigating doctrine that reduces the harsh consequences in a class of cases. The California Court of Appeals recently explained the concept of divisible contracts in *Filet Menu, Inc. v. C.C.L.& G., Inc.*, 79 Cal. App. 4th 852, 94 Cal. Rptr. 2d 438 (Cal. Ct App. 2000):

> A "divisible" contract is one "under which the whole performance is divided into two sets of partial performances, each part of each set being the agreed exchange for a corresponding part of the set of performances to be rendered by the other promisor. . . . * * * It is one in which two or more separate partial performances on each side are agreed to be exchanged for partial performances on the other side. The failure to perform one part does not bar recovery for performance of another. The "performance of each division of the service will be impliedly a condition precedent to the recovery of a corresponding portion of the price."

> Once a contract is determined to be divisible, various consequences ensue. "If the performances to be exchanged under an exchange of promises can be apportioned into corresponding pairs of part performances so that the parts of each pair are properly regarded as agreed equivalents, *a party's performance of his part of such a pair has the same effect on the other's duties to render performance of the agreed equivalent as it would have if only that pair of performances had been promised*." (Rest.2d Contracts, § 240, italics added.) Comment a to section 240, states: "This Section embodies another mitigating doctrine which reduces the risk of forfeiture in that important class of cases in which it is proper to regard corresponding parts of the performances of each party as agreed equivalents. Its effect is to give a party who has performed one of these parts the right to its agreed equivalent just as if the parties had made a separate contract with regard to that pair of corresponding parts." (Rest.2d Contracts, § 240, com. a.) Thus, if a party has breached one part of a divisible contract, he or she is not precluded from obtaining the consideration that was allocated to that portion of the contract that he or she performed.

79 Cal. App. 4th at 860.

Apply this concept of divisible contract from *Filet Menu* and *Restatement (Second) of Contracts* § 240 to the following problems:

Problems on Divisible Contracts

1. Scavenger, Inc., (S) entered into four separate contracts to develop four different CD-ROM games for GT Interactive Software, Inc. (GT) for $1,000 a game. S only developed one of the games. Should S be able to recover $1,000 from GT under the contract?

2. Same facts as problem 1 except that S and GT sign one contract that provides for payment of $1,000 at the time each of the four games is delivered, instead of four separate contracts. Again, S only develops one of the games. Should S be able to recover $1,000 from GT under the contract?

3. Same facts as problem 1 except that S and GT sign one contract that provides for the payment of $4,000 at the time the four games are

delivered, instead of four separate contracts. Again, S only develops one of the four games. Should S be able to recover from GT under the contract?

4. Ponoroff-Epstein Construction Co. (P) contracts with Markell (M) to build a swimming pool, pool house and fence. The contract provides for the payment of $20,000 on completion of the pool, $30,000 on the completion of the pool house and $4,000 on completion of the fence. P completes the pool house but does not do any work on either the pool or the fence. M can easily find other construction companies who will build the pool for $20,000 and the fence for $4,000. Should P be able to recover from M under the contract?

C. The Option to Continue: Election of Remedies

Among the options an aggrieved party to a contract breach has is to reserve a right to be compensated while continuing to perform under (and presumably, reap the benefits of) the contract. How far can this concept be stretched?

The next case involved a major league dispute between Major League Baseball and the sports cable network, ESPN. Although long, it tries to lay out the myriad of options parties to a long-term deal may have, and some of the perils their actions may produce.

ESPN, Inc. v. Office of the Commissioner of Baseball

U.S. District Court, Southern District of New York
76 F. Supp. 2d 383 (1999)

Opinion and Order

Scheindlin, J.

Introduction

This is a contract dispute between ESPN, Inc. ("ESPN"), an all-sports cable television network, and The Office of Major League Baseball ("Baseball"), which acts on behalf of the Major League Baseball clubs. In 1996, the parties entered into a telecasting agreement (the "1996 Agreement") pursuant to which Baseball granted ESPN the right to telecast regular season major league baseball games on its primary cable service. In exchange, ESPN agreed, among other things, to pay Baseball yearly rights fees and to produce baseball game telecasts on Wednesday and Sunday nights during the regular season.

A. Background

The 1996 Agreement includes two provisions that are the primary focus of this litigation. The first is a representation by ESPN that "it has not made nor will it make any contractual or other commitments that conflict with or will prevent full performance [of the 1996 Agreement]." 1996 Agreement, Ex. Q to 10/15/99 Affidavit of Robert J. Kheel, attorney for Baseball ("Kheel Aff."), at 60. The second provision permits ESPN to preempt up to ten baseball games a season with Baseball's prior written approval, which may not be unreasonably withheld. The preemption provision states:

> With the prior written approval of Baseball, which shall not be unreasonably withheld or delayed, ESPN may . . . preempt any [Baseball game telecast] hereunder, up to a maximum of ten [Baseball game telecasts] per year, for an event of significant viewer interest.

Id. at 48–49. Pursuant to this provision, Baseball may telecast the preempted baseball games on its secondary cable service, ESPN2. Id. at 49 & 1997 Amendment.

On January 13, 1998, ESPN entered into a telecasting contract with the National Football League ("NFL") whereby ESPN obtained the rights to broadcast regular season NFL games on Sunday nights. See JPTO at 23, 38. On January 30, 1998, ESPN requested Baseball's approval to telecast NFL games in place of baseball games on three Sunday nights in September 1998. See id. at 23, 43. Baseball declined to approve ESPN's request. See id. at 23, 44. Despite Baseball's disapproval, however, ESPN substituted NFL games for baseball games on the three Sunday nights in question. See id. at 25, 45. Baseball refused to allow ESPN to broadcast the preempted baseball games on ESPN2. See id. at 25, 41–42.

This exact series of events repeated itself in January 1999, when ESPN again sought Baseball's approval to replace three baseball games scheduled for Sunday nights in September 1999 with football games. See id. at 25, 45. Baseball denied ESPN's preemption request; ESPN preempted the three September 1999 baseball games in favor of football games; and Baseball refused to allow ESPN to broadcast the preempted games on ESPN2. See id. at 26–27; 45.

B. Contentions of the Parties

In April 1999, Baseball terminated the 1996 Agreement contending that ESPN had materially breached the contract. In response, ESPN commenced the instant litigation in which it alleges that Baseball materially breached the contract by (i) unreasonably withholding its approval of ESPN's preemption requests in 1998 and 1999; (ii) precluding ESPN from broadcasting the preempted baseball games on ESPN2; and (iii) improperly terminating the parties' agreement. See id. at 3. ESPN seeks damages and declaratory and injunctive relief. See id.

Baseball has asserted counterclaims against ESPN in which it alleges that ESPN materially breached the 1996 Agreement by (i) entering into a "conflicting" contract with the NFL; (ii) preempting Baseball games in 1998 and 1999 without ESPN's prior written approval; and (iii) utilizing highlight footage of baseball games in excess of the amount authorized by the 1996 Agreement. See id. at 4. Baseball also seeks damages and declaratory and injunctive relief. See id.

* * *

I. Baseball's Motion . . . to Strike the Affirmative Defense of Election of Remedies or in the Alternative for Summary Judgment

In its Amended Answer to Baseball's counterclaim, ESPN asserts the affirmative defense of "election of remedies." By this motion, Baseball seeks to preclude ESPN from asserting such a defense.

A. Election of Remedies

The doctrine of "election of remedies" provides as follows:

> When a party materially breaches a contract, the non-breaching party must choose between two remedies—[it] can elect to terminate the contract and recover liquidated damages or [it] can continue the contract and recover damages solely for the breach. A party can indicate that [it] has chosen to continue the contract by continuing to perform under the contract or by accepting the performance of the breaching party. Once a party elects to continue the contract, [it] can never thereafter elect to terminate the contract based on that breach, although [it] retains the option of terminating the contract based on other, subsequent breaches.

Bigda v. Fischbach Corp., 898 F.Supp. 1004, 1011–12 (S.D.N.Y.1995) (citations omitted). * * *

ESPN contends that because Baseball accepted full performance by ESPN for the 1998 and 1999 seasons, it elected to continue the 1996 Agreement and therefore cannot seek termination of the contract based on any alleged breaches by ESPN during those years. According to ESPN, Baseball can only seek damages for ESPN's alleged breaches of the 1996 Agreement.

B. Ability to Terminate for Alleged 1998 Breaches

To the extent Baseball seeks termination based solely on ESPN's 1998 contract with the NFL or its preemption of three baseball games in 1998—assuming that those acts constitute material breaches of the 1996 Agreement—the election of remedies defense bars such relief. That is, with respect to both of the alleged 1998 breaches, Baseball continued to perform and continued to accept performance under the 1996 Agreement for more than a year, and thus it lost its right to terminate for those breaches. * * *

Baseball concedes that it "continued performance of the 1996 Agreement after ESPN's 1998 breach" but claims that its ability to terminate the agreement based on those breaches is preserved by the contract's broadly worded "no waiver" provision. BB MIL at 5. Essentially, Baseball argues that a contractual "no waiver" provision trumps the common law contract principle of election of remedies. Although Baseball's contention is legally without merit, it raises interesting and seldom addressed issues regarding the relationship between the doctrines of waiver and election and thus merits a more detailed analysis.[3]

1. Waiver Versus Election of Remedies

The doctrines of waiver and election of remedies are complementary rather than competing common law contract principles. Under the doctrine of waiver, "a party may, by words or conduct, waive a provision in a contract or eliminate a condition in a contract which was inserted for [its] benefit." * * * Suppose, for example, that under the 1996 Agreement ESPN is obligated to make bi-weekly payments of $100,000 to Baseball. Suppose further that after several months of making the required bi-weekly payments, ESPN begins to tender monthly payments of $100,000 to Baseball. If Baseball accepts and/or fails to object to ESPN's deficient payments, then Baseball has eliminated or "waived" its contractual right to bi-weekly payments of $100,000 under the 1996 Agreement.[4]

In contrast to a waiver of contractual rights, an election is simply a choice among remedies by the party; it is a decision by that party as to how it should proceed in the wake of the breaching party's nonperformance. In other words, "an election is not a waiver of any rights under the contract but rather a choice between two inconsistent remedies for breach of the contract." * * *

Returning to the hypothetical, suppose that Baseball had, in fact, objected when ESPN began to tender monthly rather than bi-weekly pay-

[3]Baseball also argues that ESPN must demonstrate that it "changed its position to its detriment in reliance on [Baseball's] indication that [it] elected to treat the contract as valid" in order to establish an election of remedies defense. BB MIL at 4. However, the Second Circuit has clearly held that detrimental reliance is not an essential element of an election of remedies defense. * * *

[4]Note that a party's waiver of a contract provision is not absolute. That is, a previously waived provision may be restored " 'by a reasonable notice demanding performance and stating that the contract will be rescinded if the notice is not complied with.'" * * *

ments. Under these facts, Baseball has preserved its contractual right to bi-weekly payments of $100,000, and thus there is no waiver of that provision. However, Baseball must still decide how to proceed in light of ESPN's hypothetical nonperformance. Assuming that ESPN's hypothetical failure to make timely and sufficient payment is a material breach, Baseball has two choices. It can terminate the parties' contract and claim damages for total breach. Or, it can continue the contract and sue for partial breach. The election of remedies simply requires that Baseball choose or "elect" a single course of action. Thus, if Baseball terminates the contract, then it has elected termination, and it cannot continue to perform or expect performance under the contract. If Baseball chooses to continue the contract, then it has elected to continue, and it cannot later decide to terminate based on the same breach. In essence, the election of remedies doctrine is implicated only in the absence of waiver. That is, if a party waives her right to performance under a contract, then she has no remedies to elect because she has waived her ability to enforce the relevant provision. If a party has not waived her right to enforce a provision in the event of breach, then she can elect the appropriate and desired remedy. The key is that once a party has elected a remedy for a particular breach, her choice is binding with respect to that breach.

* * *

The remedy of termination—or, more accurately, the "right" to terminate—is available only where one party has materially breached the contract. A breach is material if it defeats the object of the parties in making the contract and "deprive[s] the injured party of the benefit that it justifiably expected." Farnsworth, Contracts § 8.16 (3d ed.1999). Where a breach is material, the party is justified in refusing to go on, and thus the law provides that party with the right to terminate. And, a party who terminates in response to a material breach presumably does so because it can no longer derive a worthwhile benefit from its contractual relationship.

On the other hand, where a party with the right to terminate chooses instead to continue, the only inference to be drawn is that the party will derive a worthwhile benefit from its contractual relationship. Therefore, the party's election to continue rather than end the contract essentially moots its legal justification for termination. Once a party recognizes contractual benefits in the wake of a material breach, that particular breach can no longer be considered the antithesis of the contract, and it can no longer serve as the basis for termination. Of course, if a party chooses to continue with the contract and the other party subsequently commits another material breach, the party has the right to terminate based on the new breach. This is the scenario to which I now turn.[7]

C. Termination for Alleged 1999 Breach

Baseball elected to continue the 1996 Agreement despite ESPN's alleged material breaches in 1998. As a result, Baseball can no longer terminate the parties' contract based on those breaches. However, to the extent Baseball seeks termination based upon ESPN's preemption of three baseball games in 1999—assuming arguendo that the 1999 preemptions constitute material breaches of the parties' agreement—the election of remedies doctrine does not bar such relief.

In January 1999, ESPN sought permission to preempt baseball games on three Sunday nights in September 1999. On February 11, Baseball declined to approve the requested preemption. On March 1, ESPN advised Baseball that it would preempt the September games notwithstanding Baseball's denial of its request. In response, on April 21, 1999, Baseball terminated the parties' agreement effective at the end of the Baseball season in October. Baseball's notice of termination stated: "As outlined above, ESPN has materially breached the [1996] Agreement. Therefore, Baseball hereby terminates the Agreement pursuant to Paragraph XX.B. thereof effective immediately following the last game of the 1999 regular season." See 5/21/99 letter from Paul Beeston, President and CEO of Baseball, to various officers of ESPN* * *

It is useful to compare Baseball's actions in connection with the alleged 1998 breaches to its actions in connection with the alleged 1998 breaches. In 1998, Baseball clearly elected to continue its contract with ESPN. Although Baseball informed ESPN that it considered the NFL contract and the 1998 preemptions to be material breaches,* * *, and although it "reserved" its right to terminate,* * *, there is no question that Baseball elected to continue and did continue the agreement throughout 1998 and into the 1999 season. In 1999, however, Baseball did not merely mention or reserve its right to terminate, it in fact terminated the agreement.

[7]For all of the reasons discussed in the preceding section, I reject Baseball's similar argument that the doctrine of election is inapplicable because "in its written correspondence with ESPN on this matter, [Baseball] in addition, reserved specifically all its rights." BB MIL at 6. Regardless of how many times Baseball "reserved its rights" in written correspondence regarding the alleged 1998 breaches, Baseball cannot avoid the fact that once it elected to continue the contract, it lost its ability to terminate based on the 1998 breaches. * * *

Despite Baseball's purported election to terminate in April 1999, ESPN maintains that Baseball cannot seek termination based on the 1999 preemptions

> because even while the parties were litigating their claims and counterclaims about the propriety of termination, in which Baseball was insisting that ESPN's actions threatened not just 1998 or 1999 but all five remaining years on the contract, the parties both continued performing under the contract for the full remainder of the 1999 season, with Baseball again receiving from ESPN the full 1999 rights fee of $3.4 million and the national cable telecasting of over 80 of its games.

ESPN Op. at 8. According to ESPN, "Baseball plainly made a choice. It elected to continue the contract in the face of the claimed breaches and anticipatory breaches as to five years of the contract that it now cites as the basis for termination, and elected to obtain substantial benefits under the contract from ESPN by so doing ." Id. In particular, ESPN argues that because Baseball purported to terminate in April 1999 but continued to accept performance under the contract for nearly six more months, it was pursuing two inconsistent courses of action, the very behavior election of remedies disdains.

In response, Baseball asserts that its method of delayed termination was the most reasonable way to sever the parties' contractual relationship. Baseball argues:

> ESPN has cited no cases, nor, we submit, could they, to suggest that Baseball's termination notice was defective because it was not immediately effective at the time the notice was given. Baseball gave ESPN reasonable notice to wind down its relationship with Baseball once Baseball determined that it had no choice but to terminate the 1996 Agreement in view of ESPN's breaches and anticipatory breaches in 1999.

BB Reply at 7. Baseball also states that "the effective date of termination was chosen out of fairness to ESPN and its scheduling arrangements." Id. at 6.

As Baseball notes, there is little guidance regarding whether a party can give present notice of future termination without running afoul of election of remedies. Again, it is helpful to look at the policy underlying that doctrine. To begin, "the doctrine of election permits parties to wait a 'reasonable time' after learning of the alleged breaches before terminating the contract. . . .

[H]ow much time is reasonable depends on the nature of the performance to be rendered under the contract." * * * The critical factor is not the passage of time but "whether the non-breaching party has taken an action (or failed to take an action) that indicated to the breaching party that [it] had made an election." * * *

In the instant case, the issue is not whether Baseball rendered or accepted performance during the time between breach and election but whether Baseball rendered or accepted performance during the time between its election of termination and the effective date of that termination.[8] On the one hand, both Baseball and ESPN tendered and accepted dozens of performances during the six months between April and October 1999. Indeed, ESPN telecast approximately eighty baseball games during the 1999 season. ESPN Op. at 8. However, those individual performances were part of a more global performance. Stated somewhat differently, the 1996 Agreement, in keeping with its subject matter, is seasonal in nature. As a result, it calls for seasonal performance. For example, the baseball games that are ultimately telecast on ESPN are organized and scheduled months in advance. Indeed, under the 1996 Agreement, Baseball must provide ESPN with a regular season schedule of games "no later than August 15th of the calendar year preceding each Baseball season." * * * By the time the baseball season commences each spring, the parties' global performance for that season is already well under way. Games and other programming have been scheduled and those schedules have been published to, and relied upon by, third parties including sponsors, advertisers, the media and the public. Of course, performance continues throughout the summer and fall

---

[8]There is no question that Baseball's April 1999 termination was timely. Pursuant to the doctrine of anticipatory repudiation, Baseball had no duty to "elect its remedies" prior to ESPN's actual breach of the contract in September 1999. Under New York law, where an anticipatory breach has occurred the party may either sue immediately or wait until there has been actual breach:

> When a promisor repudiates a contract, the injured party faces an election of remedies; [it] can treat the repudiation as an anticipatory breach and immediately seek damages for breach of contract, thereby terminating the contractual relation between parties, or [it] can treat the repudiation as an empty threat, wait until the time for performance arrives and exercise [its] remedies for actual breach if a breach does in fact occur at such time.

Silver Air v. Aeronautic Dev. Corp. Ltd., 656 F.Supp. 170, 178 (S.D.N.Y.1987) (internal quotations omitted). Accordingly, Baseball could have waited until ESPN actually preempted the September 1999 baseball games to seek termination of the contract.

as baseball games are telecast and payment is made, but it is clearly all part of the same seasonal undertaking.

This difference is critical because it demonstrates that Baseball did not act inconsistently when it terminated effective at the end of the season. Instead, Baseball's method of termination merely mirrored the nature of the 1996 Agreement. At the time Baseball elected to terminate the contract in April 1999, the 1999 season and performance for that season was well underway. Thus, rather than stop the agreement mid-performance at a high cost to both parties and nonparties, Baseball simply notified ESPN that it would render and accept no "new" performance under the contract; it would not go forward with the 2000 season.[9]

Not only do I find that Baseball's approach did not violate the doctrine of election, I also find that it was eminently reasonable under the circumstances. Had Baseball terminated effective immediately, not only would both parties have suffered enormous hardship, an immeasurable number of third parties including sponsors, advertisers and the public would have been affected. In an industry where so much time and energy is expended in advance preparation, it makes little sense to treat the fruits of those efforts as a wholly separate "performance" for purposes of the election of remedies defense. I suspect that if ESPN were not Baseball's adversary in this litigation, it would appreciate rather than complain of Baseball's considerate approach to termination.

Accordingly, I find as a matter of law that if the 1999 preemptions by themselves or in connection with other alleged breaches constitute a material breach, Baseball has a right to terminate the 1996 Agreement.

* * *

E. Conclusion

As a matter of law, Baseball cannot terminate the 1996 Agreement based on ESPN's 1998 contract with the NFL or its 1998 preemptions of baseball games, regardless of whether those actions constitute material breaches of the 1996 Agreement. However, if the 1999 preemptions constitute a material breach of the parties' agreement then Baseball can terminate the contract.

---

[9]This is markedly different than Baseball's response to the alleged 1998 breaches. In 1998, Baseball not only completed performance of the 1998 season, but it started and continued performance for the new 1999 season.

QUESTIONS

1. Questions about the facts of this case

    1.1. What were the breaches in 1998? How will Baseball be compensated for those breaches?

    1.2. What were the breaches in 1999? How will Baseball be compensated for those breaches?

    1.3. Were there explicit contract provisions on how to terminate the contract? How did the court conclude that the 1999 termination was "eminently reasonable"?

2. Questions about the law

    2.1. Is the court right that Baseball can terminate for reasons other than the ones it states? Recall that Baseball based its termination on the 1998 *and* 1999 breaches by ESPN; the court disallowed termination based on the 1998 breaches.

    2.2. Did ESPN materially breach the contract? What evidence would you point to in formulating your answer, and what additional questions would you ask before giving an answer?

    2.3. Go back to the hypotheticals above regarding Ponoroff's provision of tutoring services, *supra,* at 777–78. If Ponoroff is a no-show for the first tutoring session, advise Markell based upon *ESPN* what to do if Markell wants to be done with Ponoroff and hire Epstein, a cheaper and better tutor. Assume that Markell doesn't really want to pursue any remedies against Ponoroff (being quit of him is sufficient, thank you), but Markell sure doesn't want Ponoroff suing him for breach.

Note on Substantial Performance and Partial Breach

As *ESPN* notes, remedies often turn on whether the breach is "material." To expand upon *ESPN,* there is an essential link between a material breach and how much you can sue for in damages. As stated in section 243(1) of the *Restatement (Second) of Contracts,* "With respect to performances to be exchanged under an exchange of promises, a breach by non-performance gives rise to a claim for damages for total breach only if it discharges the injured party's remaining duties to render such performance . . ."

What is the difference between a total and partial breach? Again, the *Restatement*:

> b. Total and partial breach distinguished. *Although every breach gives rise to a claim for damages, not every claim for damages is one for damages based on all of the injured party's remaining rights to performance under the contract. Such a claim is said to be one for damages for total breach. . . . If the injured party elects to or is required to await the balance of the other party's performance under the contract, his claim is said instead to be one for damages for partial breach. For example, an injured party who claims damages in addition to specific performance claims damages for partial breach. Rules for determining whether a particular breach gives rise to a claim for damages for partial breach, for total breach, or for either partial or total breach at the election of the injured party are stated in §§ 243 [relating to material breach] and 253 [relating to repudiation].*

Restatement (Second) of Contracts § 236, com. b.

Thus, if the breach is material, then the non-breaching party is not only justified in suspending its performance and, if it is sufficiently serious, canceling the contract (thus preventing any executory duties it has from maturing), but it may also then sue for damages measured by the breaching party's failure to perform now, *and* in the future. As indicated above, this is sometimes referred to as suing for "total" breach, and the remedies examined in Chapter Five will often assume that such a total breach exists (that is, the breacher's conduct constitutes a material breach).

But what if the breach is not material, or as in *ESPN*, there is an argument that the other side "accepted" the material breach and continued performance? There still is a breach, and there still is a remedy in damages—but only for the present breach, not for a cessation of all future obligations. This is often referred to a "partial" breach.

An example might be paying one installment of a series of payments 15 days late. In the whole scheme of things, this breach may not be material, and the party receiving payment may not be able to cancel the contract. Moreover, it will have to keep performing. It is entitled to some remedy, however, and if the parties do not agree to one, a court would likely award interest on the payment for the 15-day gap. This would put the non-breaching party in the same place it would have been but for the breach (it's only money, after all), and keeps the parties both in the contract with respect to future obligations.

D. Material Breach and the Perfect Tender Rule Under the U.C.C.

The rules change when dealing in goods, as indicated by this section of the U.C.C., often referred to as the perfect tender rule:

> § 2-601. Buyer's Rights on Improper Delivery
>
> Subject to the provisions of this Article on breach in installment contracts (Section 2-612) and unless otherwise agreed under the sections on contractual limitations of remedy (Sections 2-718 and 2-719), if the goods or the tender of delivery fail *in any respect* to conform to the contract, the buyer may
>
> (a) reject the whole; or
>
> (b) accept the whole; or
>
> (c) accept any commercial unit or units and reject the rest.

The emphasis is added. This section is applied in the next case.

Ramirez v. Autosport
Supreme Court of New Jersey
88 N.J. 277, 440 A.2d 1345 (1982)

Pollock, J:

This case raises several issues under the Uniform Commercial Code ("the Code" and "UCC") concerning whether a buyer may reject a tender of goods with minor defects and whether a seller may cure the defects. We consider also the remedies available to the buyer, including cancellation of the contract. The main issue is whether plaintiffs, Mr. and Mrs. Ramirez, could reject the tender by defendant, Autosport, of a camper van with minor defects and cancel the contract for the purchase of the van.

The trial court ruled that Mr. and Mrs. Ramirez rightfully rejected the van and awarded them the fair market value of their trade-in van. The Appellate Division affirmed in a brief *per curiam* decision which, like the trial court opinion, was unreported. We affirm the judgment of the Appellate Division.

I

Following a mobile home show at the Meadowlands Sports Complex, Mr. and Mrs. Ramirez visited Autosport's showroom in Somerville. On July 20, 1978 the Ramirezes and Donald Graff, a salesman for Autosport, agreed on the sale of a new camper and the trade-in of the van owned by Mr. and Mrs. Ramirez. Autosport and the Ramirezes signed a simple contract reflecting a $14,100 purchase price for the new van with a $4,700 trade-in allowance for the Ramirez van, which Mr. and Mrs. Ramirez left with Autosport. After further allowance for taxes, title and documentary fees, the net price was $9,902. Because Autosport needed two weeks to prepare the new van, the contract provided for delivery on or about August 3, 1978.

On that date, Mr. and Mrs. Ramirez returned with their checks to Autosport to pick up the new van. Graff was not there so Mr. White, another salesman, met them. Inspection disclosed several defects in the van. The paint was scratched, both the electric and sewer hookups were missing, and the hubcaps were not installed. White advised the Ramirezes not to accept the camper because it was not ready.

Mr. and Mrs. Ramirez wanted the van for a summer vacation and called Graff several times. Each time Graff told them it was not ready for delivery. Finally, Graff called to notify them that the camper was ready. On August 14 Mr. and Mrs. Ramirez went to Autosport to accept delivery, but workers were still touching up the outside paint. Also, the camper windows were open, and the dining area cushions were soaking wet. Mr. and Mrs. Ramirez could not use the camper in that condition, but Mr. Leis, Autosport's manager, suggested that they take the van and that Autosport would replace the cushions later. Mrs. Ramirez counteroffered to accept the van if they could withhold $2,000, but Leis agreed to no more than $250, which she refused. Leis then agreed to replace the cushions and to call them when the van was ready.

On August 15, 1978 Autosport transferred title to the van to Mr. and Mrs. Ramirez, a fact unknown to them until the summer of 1979. Between August 15 and September 1, 1978 Mrs. Ramirez called Graff several times urging him to complete the preparation of the van, but Graff constantly advised her that the van was not ready. He finally informed her that they could pick it up on September 1.

When Mr. and Mrs. Ramirez went to the showroom on September 1, Graff asked them to wait. And wait they did—for one and a half hours. No one from Autosport came forward to talk with them, and the Ramirezes left in disgust.

On October 5, 1978 Mr. and Mrs. Ramirez went to Autosport with an attorney friend. Although the parties disagreed on what occurred, the general topic was whether they should proceed with the deal or Autosport should return to the Ramirezes their trade-in van. Mrs. Ramirez claimed they rejected the new van and requested the return of their trade-in. Mr. Lustig, the owner of Autosport, thought, however, that the deal could be salvaged if the parties could agree on the dollar amount of a credit for the Ramirezes. Mr. and Mrs. Ramirez never took possession of the new van and repeated their request for the return of their trade-in. Later in October, however, Autosport sold the trade-in to an innocent third party for $4,995. Autosport claimed that the Ramirez' van had a book value of $3,200 and claimed further that it spent $1,159.62 to repair their van. By subtracting the total of those two figures, $4,159.62, from the $4,995.00 sale price, Autosport claimed a $600–700 profit on the sale.

On November 20, 1978 the Ramirezes sued Autosport seeking, among other things, rescission of the contract. Autosport counterclaimed for breach of contract.

II

Our initial inquiry is whether a consumer may reject defective goods that do not conform to the contract of sale. The basic issue is whether under the UCC, adopted in New Jersey as *N.J.S.A.* 12A:1-101 *et seq.*, a seller has the duty to deliver goods that conform precisely to the contract. We conclude that the seller is under such a duty to make a "perfect tender" and that a buyer has the right to reject goods that do not conform to the contract. That conclusion, however, does not resolve the entire dispute between buyer and seller. A more complete answer requires a brief statement of the history of the mutual obligations of buyers and sellers of commercial goods.

In the nineteenth century, sellers were required to deliver goods that complied exactly with the sales agreement. * * * That rule, known as the "perfect tender" rule, remained part of the law of sales well into the twentieth century. By the 1920's the doctrine was so entrenched in the law that Judge Learned Hand declared "[t]here is no room in commercial contracts for the doctrine of substantial performance." * * *

The harshness of the rule led courts to seek to ameliorate its effect and to bring the law of sales in closer harmony with the law of contracts, which allows rescission only for material breaches. * * * Nevertheless, a variation of the perfect tender rule appeared in the Uniform Sales Act. *N.J.S.A.* 46:30-75 (purchasers permitted to reject goods or rescind contracts for any breach of warranty) * * *. The chief objection to the continuation of the perfect tender rule was that buyers in a declining market would reject goods for minor nonconformities and force the loss on surprised sellers.* * *

To the extent that a buyer can reject goods for any nonconformity, the UCC retains the perfect tender rule. Section 2-106 states that goods conform to a contract "when they are in accordance with the obligations under the contract." *N.J.S.A.* 12A:2-106. Section 2-601 authorizes a buyer to reject goods if they "or the tender of delivery fail in any respect to conform to the contract". *N.J.S.A.* 12A:2-601. The Code, however, mitigates the harshness of the perfect tender rule and balances the interests of buyer and seller. *See Restatement (Second), Contracts*, § 241 comment (b) (1981). The Code achieves that result through its provisions for revocation of acceptance and cure. *N.J.S.A.* 12A:2-608, 2-508.

Initially, the rights of the parties vary depending on whether the rejection occurs before or after acceptance of the goods. Before acceptance, the buyer may reject goods for any nonconformity. *N.J.S.A.* 12A:2-601. Because of the seller's right to cure, however, the buyer's rejection does not necessarily discharge the contract. *N.J.S.A.* 12A:2-508. Within the time set for performance in the contract, the seller's right to cure is unconditional. *Id.*, subsec. (1); *see id.*, Official Comment 1. Some authorities recommend granting a breaching party a right to cure in all contracts, not merely those for the sale of goods. *Restatement (Second), Contracts*, ch. 10, especially §§ 237 and 241. Underlying the right to cure in both kinds of contracts is the recognition that parties should be encouraged to communicate with each other and to resolve their own problems. *Id.*, Introduction p. 193.

The rights of the parties also vary if rejection occurs after the time set for performance. After expiration of that time, the seller has a further reasonable time to cure if he believed reasonably that the goods would be acceptable with or without a money allowance. *N.J.S.A.* 12A:2-508(2). The determination of what constitutes a further reasonable time depends on the surrounding circumstances, which include the change of position by and the amount of inconvenience to the buyer. *N.J.S.A.* 12A:2-508, Official Comment 3. Those circumstances also include the length of time needed by the seller to correct the nonconformity and his ability to salvage the goods by resale to others. *See Restatement (Second), Contracts*, § 241 comment (d). Thus, the Code balances the buyer's right to reject nonconforming goods with a "second chance" for the seller to conform the goods to the contract under certain limited circumstances. *N.J.S.A.* 12A:2-508, New Jersey Study Comment 1.

After acceptance, the Code strikes a different balance: the buyer may revoke acceptance only if the nonconformity substantially impairs the value of the goods to him. *N.J.S.A.* 12A:2-608. * * * This provision protects the seller from revocation for trivial defects. * * *. It also prevents the buyer from taking undue advantage of the seller by allowing goods to depreciate and then returning them because of asserted minor defects. *See* White & Summers, *Uniform Commercial Code*, § 8-3 at 391 (2 ed. 1980). Because this case involves rejection of goods, we need not decide whether a seller has a right to cure substantial defects that justify revocation of acceptance.* * *

Other courts agree that the buyer has a right of rejection for any nonconformity, but that the seller has a countervailing right to cure within a reasonable time. * * *

One New Jersey case, *Gindy Mfg. Corp. v. Cardinale Trucking Corp.*, suggests that, because some defects can be cured, they do not justify rejection. 111 *N.J. Super.* 383, 387 n.1 (Law Div.1970). * * * Nonetheless, we conclude that the perfect tender rule is preserved to the extent of permitting a buyer to reject goods for any defects. Because of the seller's right to cure, rejection does not terminate the contract. Accordingly, we disapprove the suggestion in *Gindy* that curable defects do not justify rejection.

A further problem, however, is identifying the remedy available to a buyer who rejects goods with insubstantial defects that the seller fails to cure within a reasonable time. The Code provides expressly that when "the buyer rightfully rejects, then with respect to the goods involved, the buyer may cancel." *N.J.S.A.* 12A:2-711. "Cancellation" occurs when either party puts an end to the contract for breach by the other. *N.J.S.A.* 12A:2-106(4). Nonetheless, some confusion exists whether the equitable remedy of rescission survives under the Code. * * *

The Code eschews the word "rescission" and substitutes the terms "cancellation," "revocation of acceptance," and "rightful rejection." *N.J.S.A.* 12A:2-106(4); 2-608; and 2-711 & Official Comment 1. Although neither "rejection" nor "revocation of acceptance" is defined in the Code, rejection includes both the buyer's refusal to accept or keep delivered goods and his notification to the seller that he will not keep them. * * * Revocation of acceptance is like rejection, but occurs after the buyer has accepted the goods. Nonetheless, revocation of acceptance is intended to provide the same relief as rescission of a contract of sale of goods. *N.J.S.A.* 12A:2-608 Official Comment 1; N.J. Study Comment 2. In brief, revocation is tantamount to rescission.* * * Similarly, subject to the seller's right to cure, a buyer who rightfully rejects goods, like one who revokes his acceptance, may cancel the contract. *N.J.S.A.* 12A:2-711 & Official Comment 1. We need not resolve the extent to which rescission for reasons other than rejection or revocation of acceptance, *e.g.* fraud and mistake, survives as a remedy outside the Code. *Compare N.J.S.A.* 12A:1-103 *and* White & Summers, *supra*, § 8-1, p. 295, *with N.J.S.A.* 12A:2-721. * * *

Although the complaint requested rescission of the contract plaintiffs actually sought not only the end of their contractual obligations, but also restoration to their pre-contractual position. That request incorporated the equitable doctrine of restitution, the purpose of which is to restore plaintiff to as good a position as he occupied before the contract. Corbin, *supra*, § 1102 at 455. In UCC parlance, plaintiffs' request was for the cancellation of the contract and recovery of the price paid. *N.J.S.A.* 12A:2-106(4), 2-711.

General contract law permits rescission only for material breaches, and the Code restates "materiality" in terms of "substantial impairment". * * * The Code permits a buyer who rightfully rejects goods to cancel a contract of sale. *N.J.S.A.* 12A:2-711. Because a buyer may reject goods with insubstantial defects, he also may cancel the contract if those defects remain uncured. Otherwise, a seller's failure to cure minor defects would compel a buyer to accept imperfect goods and collect for any loss caused by the nonconformity. *N.J.S.A.* 12A:2-714.

Although the Code permits cancellation by rejection for minor defects, it permits revocation of acceptance only for substantial impairments. That distinction is consistent with other Code provisions that depend on whether the buyer has accepted the goods. Acceptance creates liability in the buyer for the price, *N.J.S.A.* 12A:2-709(1), and precludes rejection. *N.J.S.A.* 12A:2-607(2); *N.J.S.A.* 12A:2-606, New Jersey Study Comment 1. Also, once a buyer accepts goods, he has the burden to prove any defect. *N.J.S.A.* 12A:2-607(4); White & Summers, *supra*, § 8-2 at 297. By contrast, where goods are rejected for not conforming to the contract, the burden is on the seller to prove that the nonconformity was corrected.* * *

Underlying the Code provisions is the recognition of the revolutionary change in business practices in this century. The purchase of goods is no longer a simple transaction in which a buyer purchases individually-made goods from a seller in a face-to-face transaction. Our economy depends on a complex system for the manufacture, distribution, and sale of goods, a system in which manufacturers and consumers rarely meet. Faceless manufacturers mass-produce goods for unknown consumers who purchase those goods from merchants exercising little or no control over the quality of their production. In an age of assembly lines, we are accustomed to cars with scratches, television sets without knobs and other products with all kinds of defects. Buyers no longer expect a "perfect tender." If a merchant sells defective goods, the reasonable expectation of the parties is that the buyer will return those goods and that the seller will repair or replace them.

Recognizing this commercial reality, the Code permits a seller to cure imperfect tenders. Should the seller fail to cure the defects, whether substantial or not, the balance shifts again in favor of the buyer, who has the right to cancel or seek damages. *N.J.S.A.* 12A:2-711. In general, economic considerations would induce sellers to cure minor defects.* * * Assuming the seller does not cure, however, the buyer should be permitted to exercise his remedies under *N.J.S.A.* 12A:2-711. The Code remedies for consumers are to be liberally construed, and the buyer should have the option of cancelling if the seller does not provide conforming goods. *See N.J.S.A.* 12A:1-106.

To summarize, the UCC preserves the perfect tender rule to the extent of permitting a buyer to reject goods for any nonconformity. Nonetheless, that rejection does not automatically terminate the contract. A seller may still effect a cure and preclude unfair rejection and cancellation by the buyer. *N.J.S.A.* 12A:2-508, Official Comment 2; *N.J.S.A.* 12A:2-711, Official Comment 1.

III

The trial court found that Mr. and Mrs. Ramirez had rejected the van within a reasonable time under *N.J.S.A.* 12A:2-602. The court found that on August 3, 1978 Autosport's salesman advised the Ramirezes not to accept the van and that on August 14, they rejected delivery and Autosport agreed to replace the cushions. Those findings are supported by substantial credible evidence, and we sustain them. * * * Although the trial court did not find whether Autosport cured the defects within a reasonable time, we find that Autosport did not effect a cure. Clearly the van was not ready for delivery during August, 1978 when Mr. and Mrs. Ramirez rejected it, and Autosport had the burden of proving that it had corrected the defects. Although the Ramirezes gave Autosport ample time to correct the defects, Autosport did not demonstrate that the van conformed to the contract on September 1. In fact, on that date, when Mr. and Mrs. Ramirez returned at Autosport's invitation, all they received was discourtesy.

On the assumption that substantial impairment is necessary only when a purchaser seeks to revoke acceptance under *N.J.S.A.* 12A:2-608, the trial court correctly refrained from deciding whether the defects substantially impaired the van. The court properly concluded that plaintiffs were entitled to "rescind"—*i.e.*, to "cancel"—the contract.

Because Autosport had sold the trade-in to an innocent third party, the trial court determined that the Ramirezes were entitled not to the return of the trade-in, but to its fair market value, which the court set at the contract price of $4,700. A buyer who rightfully rejects goods and cancels the contract may, among other possible remedies, recover so much of the purchase price as has been paid. *N.J.S.A.* 12A:2-711. The Code, however, does not define "pay" and does not require payment to be made in cash.

A common method of partial payment for vans, cars, boats and other items of personal property is by a "trade-in." When concerned with used vans and the like, the trade-in market is an acceptable, and perhaps the most appropriate, market in which to measure damages. It is the market in which the parties dealt; by their voluntary act they have established the value of the traded-in article. * * * In other circumstances, a measure of damages other than the trade-in value might be appropriate. * * *

The ultimate issue is determining the fair market value of the trade-in. This Court has defined fair market value as "the price at which the property would change hands between a willing buyer and a willing seller when the former is not under any compulsion to buy and the latter is not under any compulsion to sell, both parties having reasonable knowledge of relevant facts." * * * Although the value of the trade-in van as set forth in the sales contract was not the only possible standard, it is an appropriate measure of fair market value.

For the preceding reasons, we affirm the judgment of the Appellate Division.

QUESTIONS AND NOTES

1. Questions about the facts of this case

   1.1. Why did the Ramirezes not take delivery of the van? With swapped cushions, wouldn't it have taken them to the same camping destinations?

   1.2. If the book value of the trade-in was really $3,200, and Autosport really spent $1,159.62 to repair the van, then why do the Ramirezes get $4,700 as the value of the car?

2. Questions about the law

   2.1. If the contract between Autosport and the Ramirezes had said "in the event of that the van selected is not available at the designated time of delivery, Autosport reserves the right to substitute another van that in its good faith estimation is equivalent or greater in value", would the result have been different if Autosport had offered a pricier, but bright pink, van in substitution?

   2.2. The court indicated that other values other than the value in the contract might be taken as fair market value. Didn't Autosport offer one such valuation? Why was it rejected?

   2.3. What is the difference under the U.C.C. between cancellation and termination? Which of these terms best describes what happened in this case?

3. Notes

3.1. Is there a divisibility of contract doctrine under the U.C.C.? A hint of an answer comes from the statement of the perfect tender rule itself. Note that section 2-601 starts with the words "Subject to the provisions of this Article on breach in installment contracts (Section 2-612). . . ." Thus, the perfect tender rule does not apply to installment contracts.

What are installment contracts? The U.C.C. is obliging, and offers the following definition:

§ 2-612. "Installment contract"; Breach.

(1) An "installment contract" is one which requires or authorizes the delivery of goods in separate lots to be separately accepted, even though the contract contains a clause "each delivery is a separate contract" or its equivalent.

(2) The buyer may reject any installment which is non-conforming if the non-conformity substantially impairs the value of that installment and cannot be cured or if the non-conformity is a defect in the required documents; but if the non-conformity does not fall within subsection (3) and the seller gives adequate assurance of its cure the buyer must accept that installment.

(3) Whenever non-conformity or default with respect to one or more installments substantially impairs the value of the whole contract there is a breach of the whole. But the aggrieved party reinstates the contract if he accepts a non-conforming installment without seasonably notifying of cancellation or if he brings an action with respect only to past installments or demands performance as to future installments.

3.2. When is the breach of an installment also a breach of the whole contract under the U.C.C.? That issue has been litigated often, but perhaps in no more relevant context (for the law student, at least) as in *Emanuel Law Outlines, Inc. v. Multi-State Legal Studies, Inc.*, 899 F. Supp. 1081 (S.D.N.Y. 1995). There, Emanuel had agreed to provide Multi-State with outlines for nine bar exam subjects for a period of three years. Among the outlines to be provided was a criminal procedure outline supplement for use by Multi-State in its California bar exam courses. The delivery date for the supplement was May 1 (a date critical because Multi-State then had to distribute the outlines to the students taking their bar exam courses which started in mid-May to late June). Because of health problems with the outline's author, the criminal procedure supplements weren't delivered until June 3. Multi-State claimed breach not only of the installment, but of the entire contract, and refused to take delivery of the next year's batch of outlines (which, presumably would include a Contracts outline . . .). In finding that the declaration of total breach was erroneous (that is, in finding that Emanuel did not breach the whole contract), the court said the following:

Even if the Court were to agree that there was an uncured breach of contract by ELO, Multi-State's right to be relieved of its obligations requires a demonstration of substantial impairment of the whole contract. Inasmuch as this contract requires the delivery of goods in separate lots to be separately accepted, it is an installment contract as defined by N.Y.U.C.C. § 2-612(1). Under § 2-612(3), Multi-State's right to cancel the entire agreement required a showing of substantial impairment of the whole contract. Whether a breach constitutes "substantial impairment" is a question of fact. Stinnes Interoil v. Apex Oil Co., 604 F. Supp. 978, 981 (1985). When there is no predicate for finding that the breach substantially impaired the value of the contract, there is no basis for the buyer to repudiate the contract. "[A] late shipment of one installment may be treated as a breach of the entire contract only if the default with respect to one or more installments substantially impairs the value of the whole contract." Trans Works Metals, Inc. v. Southwire Co., 769 F.2d 902, 907 (2d Cir. 1985) (citing N.Y.U.C.C. § 2-612(3)). Here, there is no evidence to support Multi-States [sic] argument that failure to have the supplements ready by May 1, 1993 substantially impaired the entire contract.

Multi-State's only contention with regard to damages is that the company received oral complaints from students enrolled in the course. This claim is tenuous at best, considering that Multi-State offered no proof of any written complaints, nor did it provide any written records of the complaints, and it failed to show that it had to refund any tuition money to students. Moreover, Multi-State's students did in fact receive eight of the nine promised outline [sic] on time and subsequently received the supplement more than a month prior to the bar exam.

> Finally, Multi-State's own actions demonstrate the minor nature of any breach. When ELO shipped the goods in June, Multi-State made no effort to expedite delivery. Because it was responsible for the cost of shipping, it could have utilized any delivery method it desired, including overnight mail. Instead, Multi-State opted for UPS delivery, which is far from the fastest method. Inasmuch as Multi-State's actions do not indicate significant urgency, it would be very difficult for the court to so find.
>
> Nor can it be said that the June delivery of the supplements had any effect on future enrollment in Multi-State's course. After the 1993 course, Multi-State no longer offered the full service California bar review course. It is undisputed that Multi-State's decision was unrelated to the instant action. Since Multi-State no longer offered the full service course, ELO's breach could not have had any damaging effect whatsoever for subsequent years.
>
> The very purpose of the substantial impairment requirement of N.Y.U.C.C. § 2-612(3) is to preclude a party from canceling the contract for trivial defects. Multi-State has failed to demonstrate any substantial or lingering harm incurred from ELO's failure to have the supplement ready by May 1, 1993. Accordingly, Multi-State had no legal justification for not performing on the contract.
>
> 899 F. Supp. at 1087–1088.

Installment Contract Problems Under U.C.C. § 2-612

As you have seen, the U.C.C. treats installment contracts under Section 2-612 very differently from contracts subject to the perfect tender rule of Section 2-601. Test your understanding of the section with these hypotheticals:

1. Markell agrees to sell Ponoroff his prized coin collection for $75,000. They both agree that, given its bulk, Markell will deliver the collection as follows: all his nickels on 1/1, all his dimes on 2/1 and all his quarters on 3/1. Ponoroff agrees to pay $25,000 upon receipt of each delivery.

   On 1/1, Markell shows up with almost all of his nickels; he is missing all of his Denver mint 1950 nickels, which are valuable but not rare. May Ponoroff terminate the entire contract? If he cannot, what can he do? Would your answer be different if Markell showed up without his rare and complete collection of all Buffalo nickels, worth $17,500 standing alone?

2. Now assume that Markell cured his 1/1 default by delivering the nickels. On 2/1, Markell calls Ponoroff and tells him that he can't make it until 2/5. What may Ponoroff do?

3. Markell finally makes good on the dimes. For the 3/3 delivery, Markell shows up, but does not bring one-half of his collection; he wants the purchase price increased before he will do that. Tired of being nickeled and dimed, Ponoroff consults you to see if he can terminate the contract. What do you tell him?

Chapter Five

HOW DOES THE LAW ENFORCE A DEAL?

SECTION 1: THE PROBLEM EXAMINED

We start this chapter making some assumptions: that there is a contract, and that at least one party did not do what she promised to do in it (and there is no excuse for non-performance). The question this chapter investigates is: Now what?

Your studies thus far might cause you to jump to the correct conclusion—a suit seeking a judgment for money damages—but that isn't a necessary jump. Some might say that were society really serious about people keeping their promises, we would simply put contract breachers in jail; that is, we would make an unexcused breach of contract a crime. Alternatively, we could post the breacher's picture in a public place and encourage everyone to avoid future dealings with the cad. Or we could just brand the breacher's forehead with a scarlet "B."

Generally, however, we don't do any of these things. You might take this as an indication of a lack of societal interest in having people honor their contracts, but that would be too hasty a conclusion. While all of these various forms of punishment may discourage or deter future breaches of other contracts, they don't accomplish squat for the party who was expecting performance. For that party (sometimes referred to as the "aggrieved party," and generally assumed to be innocent of any breach), society does provide courts and enforcement mechanisms to allow a chance for redress.

But what form does this redress take? While we don't throw contract breachers in jail, should we make them do what they promised they would do? Put another way, if Markell has a valid contract with Ponoroff to wash

Markell's car for $10 on Monday, and Ponoroff hasn't washed it by lunch, can Markell run to court on his lunch hour and get a court to sign an order directing Ponoroff to wash the car that afternoon?

The next series of cases looks at the issues raised by having courts order people to perform specific tasks that they have promised to perform. This form of redress, or relief, is called "specific performance" and the following case looks at when a court will order that type of relief.

SECTION 2: SPECIFIC PERFORMANCE

You can't always get what you want,
You can't always get what you want,
You can't always get what you want,
But if you try sometimes you just might find
You'll get what you need.

Keith Richards & Mick Jagger of the *Rolling Stones*
You Can't Always Get What You Want,
on LET IT BLEED (ABKCO Records 1969)

Triple-A Baseball Club Associates v. Northeastern Baseball, Inc.

U.S. Court of Appeals, First Circuit
832 F.2d 214 (1987)

Bownes, Circuit Judge.

All parties have appealed in this diversity contract case which was tried without a jury by the district court.

The plaintiffs are: Triple-A Baseball Club, a Maine limited partnership; Jordan Kobritz, general partner of the limited partnership; * * * Plaintiffs will be referred to as "the partnership" and/or "Kobritz," as the reference requires.

Defendants are Northeastern Baseball, Inc. (NBI), a Pennsylvania non-profit corporation; [and] the Multi-Purpose Stadium Authority (MPSA) of Lackawanna County, Pennsylvania, a county and state entity * * *.

The focus of the case is the interpretation of a written contract dated September 3, 1986, between the three plaintiffs and NBI. The district court made extensive and detailed findings of fact and rulings of law. *Triple-A Baseball Club Associates v. Northeastern Baseball, Inc.*, 655 F. Supp. 513 (D. Me. 1987). * * * We * * * hold that the plaintiffs and NBI are bound by the terms of the contract.

HOW THE GAME WAS PLAYED

Before we step onto the playing field for this contract case, a little baseball background is necessary. Baseball is organized into Major Leagues and Minor Leagues. * * * The Minor Leagues are divided into four classifications, Triple-A, Double-A, Single-A, and Rookie Leagues. * * * The game now begins.

John McGee was a man with a self-imposed mission. Indeed, it could be described as an obsession. He wanted to bring Triple-A Baseball to Scranton, Pennsylvania. But there were two problems. One, Scranton did not have a Triple-A franchise, that is, it did not have a right to have a Triple-A team play there. * * * McGee's second problem was that Scranton did not have a stadium suitable for Triple-A baseball. McGee, however, was not deterred. He first convinced the county commissioners of Lackawanna County, in which Scranton is located, that a municipal corporation ought to be formed to build a stadium that would meet Triple-A requirements; MPSA was formed and McGee became its legal advisor. At about the same time, McGee [formed NBI]. * * *

In his quest for a Triple-A franchise, McGee, on June 18, 1986, approached Kobritz who, through the partnership, was the major owner of the Maine Guides, a Triple-A team that played in Old Orchard Beach, Maine. McGee offered to buy the Triple-A franchise and Kobritz indicated an interest in selling. Negotiations continued through the summer. On July 30, McGee sent [a draft contract to] to Kobritz [which] provided that NBI would buy the Triple-A franchise for $2.4 million * * * A check for $100,000 accompanied the drafts. Kobritz did not sign the draft[]; he kept the check but did not deposit it. On August 20, Kobritz sent a proposed draft contract to McGee. Kobritz' proposal was more complicated than McGee's because he had some reluctant partners to deal with. In effect, Kobritz proposed that NBI pay $1.2 million to the limited partnership and $800,000 to the general partners. Kobritz' proposal also made the transfer of the Triple-A franchise to NBI contingent upon [the closing of another deal involving a baseball team.]

On September 3, 1986, the partnership and NBI signed a contract . . . , which was drafted in final form by Kobritz' attorney. It provides as follows. The partnership agrees to sell its Triple-A franchise to NBI for $2.4 million. * * * Paragraph 5 of the contract states: "In the event that the Eastern League of Professional Baseball Clubs shall refuse to approve the [sale of the other baseball team upon which the deal had been made contingent,] then this Agreement shall continue in full force and effect with the following modifications:. . . ." The modifications made the purchase price of the Triple-A franchise $2 million payable by a deposit of $100,000 (which Kobritz already had) and $1.9 million at the closing. Paragraphs 6, 7, and 8 made the agreement subject to the approval on or before September 11, 1986, of the board of directors of NBI, the limited partners of the partnership, and the International League. All three approvals were obtained prior to September 11.* * *

[Later on,] the Eastern League took the position that it had territorial franchise rights to the Scranton area and refused to approve the [other] sale. * * * McGee and his attorney appeared in Portland on the date of the closing prepared to pay Kobritz $1.9 million. He was informed by Kobritz and his attorney that the sale of the Triple-A franchise would not be made. The game then moved to the federal district court.

THE LINEUP

Plaintiffs' Claims

[Triple-A moved for declaratory relief on the grounds that its obligation to transfer the franchise had not yet matured.]

* * *

Defendants' Counterclaims

NBI's counterclaim alleges [that Triple-A's obligations had matured, and] asked that the Triple-A franchise be conveyed in accord with the terms of the contract (Count I); that the plaintiffs breached the contract, specific performance or damages "in excess of $10,000" were sought (Count II).

* * *

THE SEPTEMBER 3 CONTRACT

The Findings and Rulings of the District Court

[After a long analysis, the court concluded that Triple-A's obligation had matured.] The partnership and Kobritz were contractually obligated to transfer the Triple-A franchise to NBI in accord with the terms of the contract.

The next question is the remedy to which NBI is entitled, damages or specific performance. This court can order specific performance even though the district court did not address the issue.* * *As with the other legal issues, the law of Maine on specific performance versus damages is like that of most jurisdictions. The granting of specific performance is a matter of judicial discretion. * * * Specific performance will not be granted unless the terms of the contract are clear enough to enable a court to fashion an appropriate order. * * * Specific performance will not be granted where there exists an adequate remedy at law. * * * The party seeking specific performance has the burden of showing that it is warranted. * * * The party seeking specific performance must show an attempt to tender its own full performance,* * * unless such tender would be futile. * * * Contracts for the sale of realty may be specifically enforced. * * * Maine also allows specific performance on contracts for personalty, in certain circumstances. *Northeast Investment Co., Inc. v. Leisure Living Communities, Inc.*, 351 A.2d 845, 855–56 (Me. 1976) (specific performance was appropriate to enforce an oral contract to purchase stock, where the stock had no readily ascertainable market value, was not easily obtainable elsewhere, and was of special interest to the buyer).

We have been unable to find any Maine case deciding whether specific performance is appropriate with respect to the sale of a franchise. The few courts that have addressed this issue have all decided that specific performance was appropriate. * * *

The Restatement (Second) of Contracts (1981) focuses on the adequacy of a remedy at law. Comment c to § 360(b) states:

> There are many situations, however, in which no suitable substitute is obtainable, and others in which its procurement would be unreasonably difficult or inconvenient or would impose serious financial burdens or risks on the injured party. . . . If goods are unique in kind, quality or personal association, the purchase of an equivalent elsewhere may be im-

> practicable, and the buyer's "inability to cover is strong evidence of" the propriety of granting specific performance. Comment 2 to Uniform Commercial Code § 2-716.

5A Corbin on Contracts § 1142 at 117 (1964 & Supp. 1982) is to the same effect:

> Among the factors to be considered in granting a decree for specific performance, the most important seem to be the following: difficulty and uncertainty in determining the amount of damages to be awarded for the defendant's breach; . . . [and] the insufficiency of money damages to obtain the duplicate or the substantial equivalent of the promised performance, either because the subject matter is unique in character and cannot be duplicated or because the obtaining of a substantial equivalent involves difficulty, delay, and inconvenience. . . .

Although the Uniform Commercial Code, adopted by Maine, is not implicated, we think section 2-716 of the Code is a helpful analogy. It states: "(1) Specific performance may be decreed where the goods are unique or in other proper circumstances." Me. Rev. Stat. Ann. tit. 11, § 2-716(1) (1964). The Maine comment to this section states that it is intended to "broaden[] the rule" as compared to its predecessor section in the Uniform Sales Act. The pertinent Uniform Commercial Code comments to this section state:

> 2. In view of this Article's emphasis on the commercial feasibility of replacement, a new concept of what are "unique" goods is introduced under this section. . . . The test of uniqueness under this section must be made in terms of the total situation which characterizes the contract. . . . However, uniqueness is not the sole basis of the remedy under this section for the relief may also be granted "in other proper circumstances" and the inability to cover is strong evidence of "other proper circumstances".

The emphasis on ability to "cover" as a major criterion in deciding the appropriateness of specific performance is also found in the leading case of *Laclede Gas Co. v. Amoco Oil Co.*, 522 F.2d at 40, where the court ordered specific performance because, in part, "there was uncontradicted expert testimony that Laclede probably could not find another supplier of propane willing to enter into a long-term contract such as the Amoco agreement. . . ."

We think the facts of this case bring it well within the ambit of the rules requiring specific performance. The contract's terms are unambiguous; there is no problem in drafting a clear order. NBI showed its ability and willingness to perform on the closing day and presented convincing evidence of its inability to purchase another Triple-A team. The same factors that impelled specific performance of the sale of corporate stock in *Northeast Invest. Co., Inc. v. Leisure Liv. Com., Inc.*, 351 A.2d at 855–56, are present here: the Triple-A franchise has no readily ascertainable market value, it cannot be easily obtained from other sources, and it is of special interest to NBI.

There can be no doubt that what NBI sought, a Triple-A franchise, was unique. Nor can it be gainsaid that money damages, even if ascertained, could not "obtain the duplicate or the substantial equivalent of the promised performance. . . ." 5A Corbin on Contracts § 1142 at 117. The Restatement, Corbin, the Uniform Commercial Code, and the pertinent case law strongly favor specifically enforcing contracts where the subject of the contract is unique and cannot be duplicated.

Plaintiffs argue: (1) the franchise cases are inapposite because NBI already has a (Double-A) franchise, and (2) damages are quantifiable, hence an adequate remedy at law exists. The first argument is way off base. As this case illustrates, there is a significant difference between a Triple-A and Double-A franchise. Triple-A baseball teams, generally speaking, are superior in quality to Double-A teams and the caliber of the play is consequently higher. Triple-A is the last rung of the baseball ladder leading to the "Majors." The difference between a Triple-A and Double-A franchise is evidenced in this case by the dissent in the partnership over the proposed change from a Triple-A to a Double-A team, by the different stadium requirements of the two Leagues, and especially by the dramatic difference in price for the two teams set in the contract. That NBI has a Double-A franchise is simply not relevant. As to damages, Plaintiffs only offer an amount for the year 1987, based on the difference in profits between a Triple-A team and a Double-A team for that year. This formulation does not take into account the difference in location or facilities. Nor do plaintiffs discuss how to measure future lost profits or how to compensate NBI for any added expenses it will incur in obtaining a Triple-A team in the future—assuming one becomes available for purchase.

We have considered plaintiffs' other arguments on this issue and find them without merit.

* * *

CONCLUSION

We reverse the district court on the September 3 . . . contract. . . .

A specific performance decree shall issue from the district court ordering that, upon payment of two million dollars, Triple-A Baseball Club Associates shall forthwith convey all of its right, title and ownership in its baseball franchise in the International League to Northeastern Baseball, Inc. If there have been any changes in ownership of the Triple-A franchise since the inception of this case, the decree shall be worded so as to reflect such changes.

QUESTIONS AND NOTES

1. Questions about the facts of this case

1.1. If something can be bought and sold, as was the case with the AAA franchise in this case, why aren't damages adequate compensation?

1.2. What was the difference between the August 20 draft of the contract and the contract signed on September 3 with respect to the closing of the deal related to the other baseball team? Why does the court think that it is significant that Kobritz's attorney drafted the final agreement?

2. Questions about the law

2.1. The court indicates that under Maine law (which is reflective of American common law generally) specific performance:

(a) is a matter of discretion;

(b) is unavailable if the terms of the contract are not clear enough; and

(c) is unavailable if there exists a remedy at law.

If the court is correct (and it is) answer the following questions:

(a) Why bother with precedent if ultimately the court is guided by its own discretion?

(b) Is it possible to have a contract with terms that are clear enough to be binding, but not clear enough to be specifically enforced?

(c) When are remedies adequate at law? Does the court's discussion of Kobritz's arguments about the franchise cases help on this point?

2.2. The court also says that real estate contracts may be specifically enforced. Why is there special status given to these contracts?

3. Notes

3.1. The preference for damages over specific performance tends to be limited to Anglo-American systems. The *UNIDROIT Principles of International Commercial Contracts*, for example, states that "[w]here a party who owes an obligation other than one to pay money does not perform, the other party may require performance," subject to certain restrictions such as impossible or unreasonably burdensome performance. Art. 7.2.2.

Similarly, the *Convention on the International Sales of Goods* says, in Article 46(1), that the buyer of goods "may require performance by the seller of his obligations." If the seller delivers goods that do not meet contract specifications, 'the buyer may require delivery of substitute goods" if the goods that were delivered would have represented a fundamental breach of contract (defined in Article 25 of the *CISG*). Finally, if a seller under the *CISG* delivers goods that do not comply with the contract, "the buyer may require the seller to remedy the lack of conformity by repair, unless this is unreasonable having regard to all the circumstances."

3.2. The requirement that there be no adequate remedy at law seems to have its origins in the relatively inflexible nature of the form of the judgment the law courts issued. 1 JOSEPH STORY, COMMENTARIES ON EQUITY JURISPRUDENCE AS ADMINISTERED IN ENGLAND AND AMERICA §§ 27–35 (13th ed., Melville M. Bigelow, ed., 1886); 3 WILLIAM BLACKSTONE, COMMENTARIES ON THE LAWS OF ENGLAND 436–39 (1768). A common law judgment was simply a piece of paper that commanded one party to pay another money. Echos of that heritage is found in Rule 58 of the Federal Rules of Civil Procedure and its "separate document" rule for judgments. Since injunctions commanded the person to do something in a way that might involve some discretion, the form of a law court's judgment was inadequate to the task. Orders which commanded someone to do something (or not do something, as seen in the next case) were thus committed to the courts of equity which could enter judgments directed to the conscience of the party involved. As the result of a long jurisdictional turf war, courts of equity typically deferred to courts of law, but also were not above engaging in fictions in order to establish their jurisdiction. *See e.g.*, BLACKSTONE, *supra*, at 452.

3.3. There is significant debate as to whether the adequacy of remedy rule retains any true vitality. In *The Death of the Irreparable Injury Rule*, 103 HARV. L. REV. 687 (1990), Professor Douglas Laycock argued at length that courts have essentially vitiated the rule that money damages are an adequate substitute for actual performance. His words: "Courts have escaped the rule by defining adequacy in such a way that damages are never an adequate substitute for plaintiff's loss. Thus, our law embodies a preference for specific relief if plaintiff wants it." *Id.* at 691.

Specific performance might work when the subject matter of the contract is a thing or a good to be transferred, but what if the contract is for the special services of a human being? Notwithstanding the 13th Amendment to the Constitution, may a court order a person to specifically perform an employment contract? That is the subject of the next case.

AGH Associates, Inc. v. Fusco

Superior Court of Massachusetts
1998 Mass. Super. LEXIS 40 (1998)

Amended Memorandum and Order on
Plaintiff's Motion for Preliminary Injunction

Lawrence B. Wernick, Justice of the Superior Court:

Plaintiff, AGH Associates, Inc. ("AGH") is an organization which recruits, hires, trains and supervises occupational, physical, speech and language therapists for public schools in Massachusetts and New Hampshire. Defendant Jenny C. Fusco ("Fusco") is a Certified Occupational Therapist Assistant, who entered into a written contract with AGH on or about June 18, 1997, for the school year 1997–98, to provide services in the Springfield area. Under the contract, services were to be provided by Ms. Fusco for up to eight hours per day, up to forty hours per week, for a two-hundred-day contract period. The contract further provided in pertinent part as follows:

NONCOMPETITIVE CLAUSE

> Employee further agrees that she will not perform professional services for any organization or person for which Employee has performed services for AGH unless AGH has employed Employee for the provision of such services to the client. This restriction shall remain in effect for a period of twelve months after the termination of this contract. For the purposes of this section, "client" is defined as any organization, subcontract, municipality, or individual, which during said period of restriction, has engaged AGH directly or indirectly to provide: occupational therapy assistant services.

In accordance with the contract, Ms. Fusco undertook to perform services helping special needs students develop motor skills, including hand-eye coordination, in the Springfield Public School System, beginning in September 1997.

On or about March 13, 1998, Ms. Fusco tendered her resignation to AGH, effective March 31, 1998, in order to accept a position performing similar services for the Westfield Public Schools. Ms. Fusco claims that she did so because her case load for the Springfield School System was approximately eighty children and she was required to work sixty to seventy hours per week, without additional compensation, which far exceeded the hours specified in her contract with AGH. She further claims that, although she initially looked for work after the completion of her contract with AGH, the job offered to her by the Westfield Public Schools was conditioned upon her coming to work on or before April 1, 1998.

By this law suit, AGH seeks specific performance of Fusco's obligations under the contract as well as damages for her breach of contract and damages against the Westfield Public Schools for intentional interference with contractual relations. In addition, AGH seeks injunctive relief in the form of a mandatory injunction ordering Fusco to honor her obligations under her contract with AGH and an injunction enjoining her from working for the Defendant Westfield Public Schools or any other entity until her contract with AGH expires. AGH seeks as well an injunction against Defendant Westfield Public Schools from hiring Ms. Fusco while she is under contract with AGH. Before the Court now is AGH's Motion for Preliminary Injunctive Relief.

A promise to render personal services will not be specifically enforced. *Roce v. D'Arville,* 162 Mass. 559, 560, 39 N.E. 180 (1895); Restatement of Contracts, Second, 367, 42 Am.Jur.2d, 101. The contract in this case is a contract for the rendering of personal services. Accordingly, the mandatory injunction sought by AGH must be denied.

Although an injunction requiring an individual specifically to perform personal services under a contract is not available, there are certain situations in which courts will preclude persons bound by a personal service contract from rendering any such services to another during the term of the contract. These situations arise when the contract itself contains a negative covenant precluding the person providing the services from providing the same services for anyone else, the services are unique or extraordinary, either because of special skill that the provider possesses or because of special knowledge that the provider has acquired of his employer's business, the probable result of injunctive relief will not be to leave the employee without other reasonable means of making a living (in other words, the purpose in granting the injunction is not to force the employee to perform the contract as the only reasonable means of making a living), *and* the party seeking the injunctive relief is not itself in default, or otherwise unable to perform its obligations under the contract. See *Roce v. D'Arville,* 162 Mass. 559, 560, 39 N.E. 180 (1895); Restatement of Contracts, Second, 367; 42 Am.Jur. Second, 101. This case does not present such a situation.

The contract at issue does contain a covenant not to compete, but that covenant is limited to performance of professional services "for any organization or person for which Employee has performed services for AGH unless AGH has employed Employee for the provision of such services to the client." Fusco's employment with the Westfield Public Schools does not violate this covenant. Although AGH did not seek to obtain Fusco's services exclusively for itself, the injunctive relief it requests would accomplish precisely that result. What AGH did not seek to accomplish by contract, it should not now be allowed to accomplish through this injunction, particularly where the effect of the injunction would be to leave Ms. Fusco without any opportunity to make a living, unless she performed services under the contract with AGH. This alone is sufficient to mandate denial of AGH's motion.

Ms. Fusco, furthermore, claims that AGH is itself in breach of the contract by requiring her to work without extra pay, twenty to thirty hours more than the forty-hour maximum specified in the contract. AGH has not submitted any materials to refute this allegation, but does refer to Ms. Fusco's resignation letter which mentions nothing about just cause for her resignation. On this record, the Court is unable to determine which party is more likely to succeed on the issue of just cause for Fusco's termination of the contract.

Finally, with respect to whether Ms. Fusco's services are unique or extraordinary, the Court concludes that AGH is likely to succeed in establishing that the services are of that character. Certified Occupational Therapist Assistants appear to be somewhat difficult to find. More importantly, however, Ms. Fusco has been working with special needs children within the Springfield public school system since the beginning of the school year. Her particularized knowledge of each of these children and their needs renders her services unique or extraordinary. However, where the probable result of a negative injunction would be the Employee's performance of the contract, as the Court concludes it would be in this case, the Court must also consider what effect forcing Ms. Fusco to choose between being idle or performing under the contract might have on the services to be provided under the contract. These services are highly individualized and involve personal relations between Ms. Fusco and each student. If Ms. Fusco is unsatisfied with her working conditions and is, in essence, being forced to work against her will, there is a substantial risk that the services provided to these children might indeed be affected. AGH might argue that services performed begrudgingly and halfheartedly are better than no services at all. The Court is not satisfied that this is the only choice available to AGH and to the Springfield Public Schools, or that rendering services under such circumstances would be in the best interest of the children.

For all of the above reasons, AGH's Motion for Preliminary Injunction is DENIED.

QUESTIONS AND NOTES

1. Questions about the facts of this case

    1.1. What is the difference between ordering someone to perform her personal services contract, on the one hand, and ordering her not to perform similar services for anyone else, on the other?

    1.2. According to this court, what type of activity would have been grounds for a negative injunction of the type AGH sought?

1.3. If you were AGH's attorney, would you redraft the contract after reading this decision? Why? What would you change?

2. Questions about the law

2.1. *AGH* is not a case available through the normal print reporters; it is available only on-line. Does that reduce its precedential value? What sources would you consult to answer that question?

2.2. If Fusco doesn't have to worry about the negative injunction, why did she try to show that AGH was in breach?

2.3. After the matter denying the injunction, does Fusco have any potential liability to AGH?

2.4. If someone's services are indeed unique, how can you fashion a negative injunction that does not "force the employee to perform the contract as the only reasonable means of making a living"? Isn't that self-contradictory?

3. Notes

3.1. *Specific Performance and Personal Property—Current Law.* Transactions in goods are governed by the U.C.C. Currently, Section 2-716(1) governs the ability to get specific performance of a contract to sell goods. Here is what it says:

> (1) Specific performance may be decreed where the goods are unique or in other proper circumstances.

Comment 2 to this section tries to explain what "other proper circumstances" means:

> 2. In view of this Article's emphasis on the commercial feasibility of replacement, a new concept of what are "unique" goods is introduced under this section. Specific performance is no longer limited to goods which are already specific or ascertained at the time of contracting. The test of uniqueness under this section must be made in terms of the total situation which characterizes the contract. Output and requirements contracts involving a particular or peculiarly available source or market present today the typical commercial specific performance situation, as contrasted with contracts for the sale of heirlooms or priceless works of art which were

usually involved in the older cases. However, uniqueness is not the sole basis of the remedy under this section for the relief may also be granted "in other proper circumstances" and inability to cover is strong evidence of "other proper circumstances".

3.2. *Specific Performance and Personal Property—The Future.* Article 2 is going through revisions as this book is being written. Here is the current (Summer 2001) version of the revised form of Section 2-716. What's different?

§ 2-716. Right to Specific Performance or Replevin or the Like.

(1) Specific performance may be decreed where the goods are unique or in other proper circumstances. In a contract other than a consumer contract, specific performance may be decreed if the parties have agreed to that remedy. However, even if the parties agree to specific performance, specific performance may not be decreed if the breaching party's sole remaining contractual obligation is the payment of money.

The proposed comments to this proposed section state:

2. Uniqueness should be determined in light of the total circumstances surrounding the contract and is not limited to goods identified when the contract is formed. The typical specific performance situation today involves an output or requirements contract rather than a contract for the sale of an heirloom or priceless work of art. A buyer's inability to cover is evidence of "other proper circumstances."

3. Subsection (1) provides that a court may decree specific performance if the parties have agreed to that remedy; the parties' agreement to specific performance can be enforced even if legal remedies are entirely adequate. Even in a commercial contract, the third sentence of subsection (1) prevents the aggrieved party from obtaining specific performance if the only obligation of the party in breach is the payment of money. Whether a buyer is obligated to pay the price is determined by Section 2-709, not by this section.

SECTION 3: A SHORT DETOUR: DAMAGES AND THE CONCEPT OF EFFICIENT BREACH

So what's a lawyer to do when a client hands him (as happened to one of your casebook authors on his first day as a lawyer) a contract with a scribbled notation "Get me out of this"? You know from the above text that a court is not likely to enter an injunction compelling your client to do what he promised.

Is it thus "bad" to advise the client to breach and pay damages (assuming you can calculate them)? Many have said no, with one of the earliest being Oliver Wendell Holmes, Jr. In his classic series of lectures, *The Common Law,* Holmes said this in 1881:

> The only universal consequence of a legally binding promise is, that the law makes the promisor pay damages if the promised event does not come to pass. In every case it leaves him free from interference until the time for fulfillment has gone by, and therefore free to break his contract if he chooses.

OLIVER WENDELL HOLMES, JR., THE COMMON LAW 236 (Mark DeWolfe Howe, ed. 1963)

Holmes said it more forcefully some sixteen years later, in his article *The Path of the Law:*

> Nowhere is the confusion between legal and moral ideas more manifest than in the law of contract. Among other things, here again the so-called primary rights and duties are invested with a mystic significance beyond what can be assigned and explained. The duty to keep a contact at common law means a prediction that you must pay damages if you do not keep it—and nothing else. . . . But such a mode of looking at the matter stinks in the nostrils of those who think it advantageous to get as much ethics into the law as they can. . . .

Oliver Wendell Homes, Jr., *The Path of the Law,* 10 HARV. L. REV. 457 (1897).

So, according to Holmes, there is no moral component to the law of contracts. We certainly see part of that in the near-universally held notion that there are no punitive damages awarded for breach of a contract. *Restatement (Second) of Contracts* § 355; U.C.C. § 1-106(1).

But surely no modern intellect of any stature would hold these views seriously, right? Wrong. Many of the "law and economics" school of thought hold dear to the theory of "efficient breach." Just what that is, and how it affects your view of contract breach, is explored in this section.

First, what is "efficient breach"? Here's an excerpt from a recent Delaware Supreme Court case that tries to put the concept in context:

> Traditional contract doctrine is also supported by the more recent theory of efficient breach. The theory holds that properly calculated expectation damages increase economic efficiency by giving "the other party an incentive to break the contract if, but only if, he gains enough from the breach that he can compensate the injured party for his losses and still retain some of the benefits from the breach." *Restatement (Second) of Contracts*, Reporter's Note to Introductory Note to ch. 16, Remedies; see also Barton, *The Economic Basis of Damages for Breach of Contract*, 1 J. Legal Studies 277 (1972). The notion of efficient breach "accords remarkably with the traditional assumptions of the law of contract remedies." Farnsworth, *Contracts* § 12.3 at 155.[19] Punitive damages would increase the amount of damages in excess of the promisee's expectation interest and lead to inefficient results. *Id.* at 155–56.

E.I. Dupont De Nemours and Company v. Pressman, 679 A.2d 436, 445–446 (Del. S. Ct. 1996).

For a start on how efficient breach could affect the doctrine you've learned thus far, let's turn to Judge Richard Posner of the Seventh Circuit Court of Appeals.

---

[19]The theory of efficient breach is certainly not without its critics. *See* Farber, Reassessing the Economic Efficiency of Compensatory Damages for Breach of Contract, 66 Va. L. Rev. 1443 (1980); MacNeil, Efficient Breach of Contract Circles in the Sky, 68 Va. L. Rev. 947 (1982); Friedmann, The Efficient Breach Fallacy, 18 J. Legal Studies 1 (1989).

Paton v. Mid-Continent Systems
U.S. Court of Appeals, Seventh Circuit
841 F.2d 742 (1988)

Posner, J:

[Mid-Continent, a credit card company for truckers, franchised certain areas in Northern Indiana and Illinois. The franchises had certain exclusive dealing provisions, and certain provisions allowing existing franchisees first rights of refusal for any expansion sought by the Mid-Continent. Paton, an owner of a truck stop, complained about infringement of his area; Mid-Continent was licensing another truck stop without his consent, and that infringing truck-stop was taking business away from him. About the same time, Mid-Continent said that it wanted to expand in Paton's area, and gave him the first right to develop the necessary facilities. Paton, understandably, wanted the infringing truckstop cancelled; Mid-Continent said they would if Paton would expand—in effect, putting a condition on their cure of the breach. No resolution could be had. Paton went out of business, ostensibly because of the territory infringement, and sought lost profits as his contract damages. But he also sought something more.]

Indiana allows punitive damages to be awarded in suits for breach of contract if,"mingled" with the breach, are "elements of fraud, malice, gross negligence or oppression." * * * In trying to give concrete meaning to these terms (especially "oppression"), it is important to bear in mind certain fundamentals of contractual liability. First, liability for breach of contract is, prima facie, strict liability. That is, if the promisor fails to perform as agreed, he has broken his contract even though the failure may have been beyond his power to prevent and therefore in no way blameworthy. The reason is that contracts often contain an insurance component. The promisor promises in effect either to perform or to compensate the promisee for the cost of nonperformance; and one who voluntarily assumes a risk will not be relieved of the consequences if the risk materializes.* * *

Even if the breach is deliberate, it is not necessarily blameworthy. The promisor may simply have discovered that his performance is worth more to someone else. If so, efficiency is promoted by allowing him to break his promise, provided he makes good the promisee's actual losses. If he is forced to pay more than that, an efficient breach may be deterred, and the law doesn't want to bring about such a result. * * * Suppose that by franchising Truck-O-Mat in the plaintiffs' territory, Mid-Continent increased its own profits by $150,000 and inflicted damages of $75,000 on the plaintiffs.

That would be an efficient breach. But if Mid-Continent had known that it would have to pay in addition to compensatory damages $100,000 in punitive damages, the breach would not have been worthwhile to it and efficiency would have suffered because the difference between Mid-Continent's profits of $150,000 and the plaintiffs' losses of $75,000 would (certainly after the plaintiffs were compensated) represent a net social gain.

Not all breaches of contract are involuntary or otherwise efficient. Some are opportunistic; the promisor wants the benefit of the bargain without bearing the agreed-upon cost, and exploits the inadequacies of purely compensatory remedies (the major inadequacies being that pre-and post-judgment interest rates are frequently below market levels when the risk of nonpayment is taken into account and that the winning party cannot recover his attorney's fees). This seems the common element in most of the Indiana cases that have allowed punitive damages to be awarded in breach of contract cases; * * * Granted, this is not how the legal test is phrased; in particular the category of "gross negligence" seems unrelated to opportunistic breach. We may have captured the core of the Indiana rule but missed the periphery. But whatever the exact dimensions of the rule, the facts of the present case are pretty clearly outside it.

There is no evidence that the action of Mid-Continent in franchising Truck-O-Mat in the plaintiffs' exclusive territory was opportunistic or even deliberate. So far as can be discerned from the record it was an honest mistake resulting from the ambiguous description of the territory in the franchise agreement with the plaintiffs. However, Mid-Continent's failure to correct the violation year after year after the plaintiffs had called its attention to it—even after it acknowledged the violation—converted an innocent breach into a deliberate one; but no clear and convincing evidence enables the breach to be characterized as malicious, fraudulent, oppressive or even grossly negligent. As we saw in discussing the issue of compensatory damages, the breach did little, perhaps no, damage to either plaintiff, and it is therefore quite possible that it was an efficient breach in the sense that it increased Mid-Continent's profits by more than it caused anyone losses. If so, the refusal to rectify the breach, while deliberate, would not justify an award of punitive damages. * * * Mid-Continent's unfulfilled promises to rectify the breach could be viewed as a form of deceit designed to prevent the plaintiffs from resorting to legal remedies, but this is just the kind of conjecture that seems excluded by the requirement of proving entitlement to punitive damages by clear and convincing evidence.

* * *

The award of punitive damages must be vacated. The finding of breach of contract is affirmed and the case remanded for a new trial limited to compensatory damages.

QUESTIONS

1. Questions about the facts of this case

   1.1. Okay. What is an efficient breach of contract? Was one present here?

2. Questions about the law

   2.1. If the measures of contract damages accurate compensate aggrieved parties, aren't all breaches of contract efficient? Where does the slip come from?

   2.2. Go back to *Jacob & Youngs v. Kent, supra*, at 788, and see how that case could be argued under the efficient breach theory.

Odd rules, such as Indiana's rule that punitive damages may sometimes be awarded in contract actions, can provide a test case for the efficient breach theory—the line between punishment and compensation is a venerable one, and one that frames the issues well. We'll see more about efficient breach and punishment in the next section. But for now, let's look at a logical offshoot of efficient breach theory—the ability to contract not only for a particular performance, but the ability to contract for a particular dollar amount of damages.

To explore that idea, let's go back to the hypothetical that opened this section. Ponoroff agreed, in a valid contract, to wash Markell's car on Monday. It is now Tuesday, and Markell's car is still dirty, and Epstein's Car Wash will do a nice job, complete with Carnuba Wax and hot air drying, for $15, or $5 more than Ponoroff agreed to take for the exact same job. Can Markell get a court order requiring Ponoroff to wash the car? Note now that, due to the passage of time, it is impossible for Markell to get exactly what he bargained for—a car wash on Monday. And given the easy quantification of the value of a car wash, thanks to Epstein, Markell probably have an adequate remedy at law that even Professor Laycock would acknowledge.

But it burns Markell that Ponoroff doesn't have to get wet and messy cleaning his car. And money damages don't seem to count the value of Markell's time in hauling the car down to Epstein's, and the excruciating pain Markell will have to go through listening to Epstein wax on about Contracts while Markell waits for the car to be cleaned.

Markell might be willing to do this, but Ponoroff ought to pay for it. Is there some way? Recall this is contracts, the study of consensual obligations. Can Ponoroff and Markell agree ahead of time what Ponoroff will pay if he flakes off and doesn't do what he promised to do? What if Ponoroff and Markell agree that if the car isn't washed by Monday, and there's no excuse, Ponoroff will pay Markell $500? Can Markell go into court Tuesday, get an order directing Ponoroff to pay him $500 smackers, and then brave the hot air at Epstein's and pocket the extra $485? Whether Markell can do that is the subject of the next section.

SECTION 4: AGREED REMEDIES

You can't always win what you want,
You can't always win what you want,
You can't always win what you want,
But if you try sometimes you just might find
You'll get what you agreed.

David "Rockabilly" Epstein & Bruce "Vegas" Markell
You Can't Always Win What You Want,
on LET THEM READ (Ponoroff Records 2001)

O'Brian v. Langley School
Supreme Court of Virginia
256 Va. 547, 507 S.E.2d 363 (1998)

Kinser, Justice:

This appeal concerns a liquidated damages clause requiring parents to pay tuition for an entire academic year to a school for failure to give timely notice of their decision to withdraw their daughter from the school. Because the circuit court entered summary judgment for the school before permitting the parents to conduct discovery with regard to their defense that the clause is an unenforceable penalty, we will reverse the judgment of the circuit court.

I.

William E. O'Brian, Jr., and Fern P. O'Brian (the O'Brians) enrolled their daughter as a student at Langley School (Langley) for the 1995–96 academic year. On February 29, 1996, the O'Brians executed the "Langley School 1996–97 Membership Agreement" (the Agreement) to enroll their daughter in the second grade for the ensuing academic year. Pursuant to the Agreement, they paid a deposit in the amount of $1,055 to Langley. The O'Brians subsequently decided to withdraw their daughter from Langley, and, in a letter dated June 13, 1996, they notified Langley of their decision.

In response, Langley informed the O'Brians in two separate letters dated June 18 and June 20, 1996, that they were obligated to pay the entire amount of the 1996–97 tuition because they had not timely notified Langley of their decision to withdraw their daughter. Langley based its demand on paragraphs D(1) and (4) of the Agreement. These paragraphs state:

> D. WITHDRAWALS AND REFUNDS:
>
> 1. All withdrawals MUST BE made by June 1, 1996, as follows:
>
> a. The withdrawal must be made in writing stating the name and grade of the child(ren) to be withdrawn.
>
> b. This notice must be received by an authorized administrative employee of the School no later than 4:30 p.m. on June 1, 1996.
>
> * * * * * *
>
> 4. IT IS UNDERSTOOD THAT THERE SHALL BE NO REFUND OF OR RELIEF FROM ANY PORTION OF THE FULL TUITION OR ANY OTHER OBLIGATION ACCEPTED HEREIN FOR ANY REASON IF WRITTEN NOTICE OF WITHDRAWAL OF ANY CHILD IS NOT RECEIVED IN ACCORDANCE WITH THE ABOVE PROCEDURE. SINCE DAMAGE TO THE SCHOOL DUE TO SUCH A WITHDRAWAL WOULD BE DIFFICULT TO DETERMINE, MEMBER AGREES TO PAY AGREED-UPON TUITION AS LIQUIDATED DAMAGES, TOGETHER WITH ANY COURT COSTS AND/OR LEGAL FEES THE SCHOOL MAY BE OBLIGED TO INCUR IN THE COLLECTION OF SUCH LIQUIDATED DAMAGES IN THE EVENT OF WITHDRAWAL AFTER JUNE 1, 1996.

The O'Brians refused to pay the agreed-upon tuition as liquidated damages. Consequently, Langley filed a motion for judgment on September 4, 1996, alleging that the O'Brians had breached the terms of the Agreement. Langley sought judgment against the O'Brians for the tuition that was due under the Agreement, plus late fees and attorney's fees.

During pretrial proceedings, the O'Brians submitted written interrogatories to Langley. In one of the interrogatories, the O'Brians asked Langley whether it had made reasonable efforts to fill the spot made available by the withdrawal of the O'Brians' daughter. In response, Langley stated that it "does not so contend because it has no obligation to do so by virtue of" the Agreement. Langley either partially answered or objected to the remaining interrogatories. The O'Brians then filed a motion to compel discovery, which the circuit court denied. Thereafter, Langley moved for summary judgment. After considering memorandum and oral argument from both parties, the circuit court granted Langley's motion and entered judgment on October 3, 1997, against the O'Brians in the amount of $9,745, plus late payment fees from June 1, 1996, and an attorney's fee in the amount of $8,900. The O'Brians appeal.

II.

The dispositive issue in this case is whether the circuit court erred by awarding summary judgment before permitting the O'Brians to conduct discovery with regard to their defense that paragraph D(4) of the Agreement is not a valid liquidated damages clause. Langley asserts that the circuit court did not err because the O'Brians were asserting a defense that is not legally cognizable. We do not agree.

We have previously enunciated the test for determining the validity of a liquidated damages clause:

> [P]arties to a contract may agree in advance about the amount to be paid as compensation for loss or injury which may result from a breach of the contract "[w]hen the actual damages contemplated at the time of the agreement are uncertain and difficult to determine with exactness and when the amount fixed is not out of all proportion to the probable loss."

301 Dahlgren Ltd. Partnership v. Bd. of Supervisors of King George County, 240 Va. 200, 202–03, 396 S.E.2d 651, 653 (1990) (quoting Taylor v. Sanders, 233 Va. 73, 75, 353 S.E.2d 745, 746–47 (1987)). However, a liquidated

damages clause will be construed as an unenforceable penalty "when the damage resulting from a breach of contract is susceptible of definite measurement, or where the stipulated amount would be grossly in excess of actual damages." Brooks v. Bankson, 248 Va. 197, 208, 445 S.E.2d 473, 479 (1994) (citing Taylor, 233 Va. at 75, 353 S.E.2d at 747); accord 301 Dahlgren, 240 Va. at 203, 396 S.E.2d at 653.

The fact that a party enters into a contract containing a liquidated damages clause does not prevent that party from later litigating the validity of the clause. The party opposing the imposition of liquidated damages is entitled to conduct discovery and present relevant evidence that the damages resulting from breach of the contract are susceptible of definite measurement or that the stipulated damages are grossly in excess of the actual damages suffered by the nonbreaching party. Upon proof of either of these elements, a liquidated damages clause becomes an unenforceable penalty. Brooks, 248 Va. at 208, 445 S.E.2d at 479.

As the party challenging the validity of paragraph D(4) of the Agreement, the O'Brians bear the burden of proof on that issue. [Citations omitted] We believe this allocation of the burden of proof is appropriate since the O'Brians initially assented to the clause when they signed the Agreement. Moreover, the purpose of a liquidated damages provision is to obviate the need for the nonbreaching party to prove actual damages. This purpose would not be served if the nonbreaching party, instead of proving actual damages, had to show that "the damage resulting from a breach of contract is [not] susceptible of definite measurement" and that "the stipulated amount [is not] grossly in excess of actual damages." Brooks, 248 Va. at 208, 445 S.E.2d at 479. However, if the O'Brians are successful in proving that paragraph D(4) is an unenforceable penalty, Langley must then prove its actual damages as in any breach of contract action where the contract does not contain a liquidated damages provision. * * *

In the present case, the circuit court precluded any inquiry into the validity of the liquidated damages clause by denying the O'Brians' motion to compel and subsequently awarding summary judgment before hearing any relevant evidence on the issue. Generally, the granting or denying of discovery is a matter within the discretion of the trial court and will not be reversed on appeal unless "the action taken was improvident and affected substantial rights." Rakes v. Fulcher, 210 Va. 542, 546, 172 S.E.2d 751, 755 (1970). However, the court's actions here substantially affected the O'Brians' ability and right to litigate the validity of the liquidated damages clause.

For these reasons, we will reverse the judgment of the circuit court and remand this case for further proceedings consistent with this opinion.

Reversed and remanded.

QUESTIONS AND NOTE

1. Questions about the facts of this case

   1.1. June 1, 1996, the day the notice was due, was a Saturday. It is likely that no one was in the office then. Which way does that cut with respect to the validity of the clause, and why?

   1.2. Is there any question that the O'Brians did not actually know about the liquidated damages clause? Note: Mr. O'Brian, a Washington, D.C.-based attorney, was his own counsel in this case. His wife, also an attorney, joined him on the briefs.

   1.3. If you represent the Langley School after this case, how much detail would you tell them to insert in their future contracts so that they can avoid being sued by angry parents?

2. Questions about the law

   2.1. What is the test for liquidated damages in *O'Brian*? How many elements does it have?

   2.2. Does it not seem strange that we do not let the parties attack the reasonableness or adequacy of exchange for purposes of finding consideration, but do let them separately litigate the issue of the reasonableness of liquidated damage clauses?

   2.3. Do you see any inconsistency between the court's quotation of *301 Dahlgren* and the court's own statements in the very next paragraph? Focus on the proper role or relevance of actual damages suffered.

3. Note

Section 356 of the *Restatement (Second) of Contracts* states the general test for liquidated damages as follows:

§ 356 Liquidated Damages and Penalties.

(1) Damages for breach by either party may be liquidated in the agreement but only at an amount that is reasonable in light of the anticipated or actual loss caused by the breach and the difficulties of proof of loss. A term fixing unreasonably large liquidated damages is unenforceable on grounds of public policy as a penalty.

The next case is governed by the U.C.C. When reading it, ask yourself if the U.C.C. adopts the same rule for liquidated damages as the common law.

Kvassay v. Murray

Court of Appeals of Kansas

15 Kan.App.2d 426, 808 P.2d 896 (1991)

Walker, District Judge, Assigned:

Plaintiff Michael Kvassay, d/b/a Kvassay Exotic Food, appeals the trial court's finding that a liquidated damages clause was unenforceable and from the court's finding that damages for lost profits were not recoverable. Kvassay contends these damages occurred when Great American Foods, Inc., (Great American) breached a contract for the purchase of baklava. . . .

On February 22, 1984, Kvassay, who had been an independent insurance adjuster, contracted to sell 24,000 cases of baklava to Great American at $19.00 per case. Under the contract, the sales were to occur over a one-year period and Great American was to be Kvassay's only customer. The contract included a clause which provided: "If Buyer refuses to accept or repudiates delivery of the goods sold to him, under this Agreement, Seller shall be entitled to damages, at the rate of $5.00 per case, for each case remaining to be delivered under this Contract."

Problems arose early in this contractual relationship with checks issued by Great American being dishonored for insufficient funds. Frequently one of the Murrays issued a personal check for the amount due. After producing approximately 3,000 cases, Kvassay stopped producing the baklava because the Murrays refused to purchase any more of the product. . . .

In April 1985, Kvassay filed suit for damages arising from the collapse of his baklava baking business. Great American counterclaimed and, in May 1988, the trial court sustained a defense motion to bifurcate the case. The court conducted bench hearings on the validity of the liquidated damages clause. . . . The trial court ruled that liquidated damages could not be recovered. . . . The court also held "as a matter of law" that Kvassay would not be able to recover damages for lost profits in the action because they were too "speculative and conjectural."

* * *

Kvassay first attacks the trial court's ruling that the amount of liquidated damages sought by him was unreasonable and therefore the liquidated damages clause was unenforceable.

Kvassay claimed $105,000 in losses under the liquidated damages clause of the contract, representing $5 per case for the approximately 21,000 cases of baklava which he was not able to deliver. The trial court determined that Kvassay's use of expected profits to formulate liquidated damages was improper because the business enterprise lacked duration, permanency, and recognition. The court then compared Kvassay's previous yearly income (about $20,000) with the claim for liquidated damages ($105,000) and found "the disparity becomes so great as to make the clause unenforceable."

Since the contract involved the sale of goods between merchants,* the Uniform Commercial Code governs. See K.S.A. 84-2-102 [U.C.C. 2-102]. "The Code does not change the pre-Code rule that the question of the propriety of liquidated damages is a question of law for the court." 4 Anderson, Uniform Commercial Code § 2-718:6, p. 572 (3d ed. 1983). Thus, this court's scope of review of the trial court's ruling is unlimited.

Liquidated damages clauses in sales contracts are governed by K.S.A. 84-2-718, which reads in part:

> (1) Damages for breach by either party may be liquidated in the agreement but only at an amount which is reasonable in the light of the anticipated or actual harm caused by the breach, the difficulties of proof of

---

*Okay. We can't let this wait until the *Questions and Notes*. Does a transaction have to be "between merchants" to be within the U.C.C.? *OF COURSE NOT!* If you don't believe us, reread § 2-102. Your purchase of this casebook was governed by the U.C.C., as was your purchase of the highlighter you're using to note this sentence. Those trained in the classics will have heard the phrase, "Even Homer nods," but here we're not even sure the judge qualifies as a Homer of the prairie. Despite this goof, don't discount the rest of the case. Perhaps the judge took the test from the trial court, who *really* made a hash of §2-718. And hash and baklava don't mix; trust us. Eds.

> loss, and the inconvenience or nonfeasibility of otherwise obtaining an adequate remedy. A term fixing unreasonably large liquidated damages is void as a penalty.

To date, the appellate courts have not interpreted this section of the UCC in light of facts similar to those presented in this case. In ruling on this issue, the trial court relied on rules governing liquidated damages as expressed in *U.S.D. No. 315 v. DeWerff*, 6 Kan. App.2d 77, 626 P.2d 1206 (1981). *DeWerff*, however, involved a teacher's breach of an employment contract and was not governed by the UCC. Thus, the rules expressed in that case should be given no effect if they differ from the rules expressed in 84-2-718.

In *DeWerff*, this court held a "stipulation for damages upon a future breach of contract is valid as a liquidated damages clause if the set amount is determined to be reasonable and the amount of damages is difficult to ascertain." 6 Kan.App.2d at 78, 626 P.2d 1206. This is clearly a two-step test: Damages must be reasonable and they must be difficult to ascertain. Under the UCC, however, reasonableness is the only test. K.S.A. 84-2-718. K.S.A. 84-2-718 provides three criteria by which to measure reasonableness of liquidated damages clauses: (1) anticipated or actual harm caused by breach; (2) difficulty of proving loss; and (3) difficulty of obtaining an adequate remedy.

In its ruling, the trial court found the liquidated damages clause was unreasonable in light of Kvassay's income before he entered into the manufacturing contract with Great American. There is no basis in 84-2-718 for contrasting income under a previous unrelated employment arrangement with liquidated damages sought under a manufacturing contract. Indeed, the traditional goal of the law in cases where a buyer breaches a manufacturing contract is to place the seller "in the same position he would have occupied if the vendee had performed his contract." *Outcault Adv. Co. v. Citizens' Nat'l Bank*, 118 Kan. 328, 330–31, 234 P. 988 (1925). Thus, liquidated damages under the contract in this case must be measured against the anticipated or actual loss under the baklava contract as required by 84-2-718. The trial court erred in using Kvassay's previous income as a yardstick.

Was the trial court correct when it invalidated the liquidated damages clause, notwithstanding the use of an incorrect test? If so, we must uphold the decision even though the trial court relied on a wrong ground or assigned an erroneous reason for its decision. To answer this question, we must look closer at the first criteria for reasonableness under 84-2-718, anticipated or actual harm done by the breach.

Kvassay produced evidence of anticipated damages at the bench trial showing that, before the contract was signed between Kvassay and Great American, Kvassay's accountant had calculated the baklava production costs. The resulting figure showed that, if each case sold for $19, Kvassay would earn a net profit of $3.55 per case after paying himself for time and labor. If he did not pay himself, the projected profit was $4.29 per case. Nevertheless, the parties set the liquidated damages figure at $5 per case. In comparing the anticipated damages of $3.55 per case in lost net profit with the liquidated damages of $5 per case, it is evident that Kvassay would collect $1.45 per case or about 41 percent over projected profits if Great American breached the contract. If the $4.29 profit figure is used, a $5 liquidated damages award would allow Kvassay to collect 71 cents per case or about 16½% percent over projected profits if Great American breached the contract.

An examination of these pre-contract comparisons alone might well lead to the conclusion that the $5 liquidated damages clause is unreasonable because enforcing it would result in a windfall for Kvassay and serve as a penalty for Great American. A term fixing unreasonably large liquidated damages is void as a penalty under 84-2-718.

A better measure of the validity of the liquidated damages clause in this case would be obtained if the actual lost profits caused by the breach were compared to the $5 per case amount set by the clause. However, no attempt was made by Kvassay during the bench trial to prove actual profits or actual costs of production. Thus, the trial court could not compare the $5 liquidated damages clause in the contract with the actual profits lost by the breach. It was not until the jury trial that Kvassay attempted to prove his actual profits lost as part of his damages. Given the trial court's ruling that lost profits were not recoverable and could not be presented to the jury, it is questionable whether the court would have permitted evidence concerning lost profits at the bench trial.

The trial court utilized an impermissible factor to issue its ruling on the liquidated damages clause and the correct statutory factors were not directly addressed. We reverse the trial court on this issue and remand for further consideration of the reasonableness of the liquidated damages clause in light of the three criteria set out in 84-2-718 and our ruling on recoverability of lost profits which follows.

* * *

The trial court's decisions with respect to liquidated damages and lost profits are reversed and the case is remanded for a new trial on those issues. . . .

QUESTIONS AND NOTE

1. Questions about the facts of this case

    1.1. What is baklava?

    1.2. Why did Kvassay not introduce evidence of actual lost profits? What should be the difference between the amount of those lost profits and the projections? In other words, what types of additional evidence do you think Kvassay's attorney would have to investigate?

2. Questions about the law

    2.1. What are the differences between the common law standard set forth in the *Restatement* and in *O'Brian*, and the standard set forth in U.C.C. § 2-718?

    2.2. Who measures reasonableness? The court or the jury? Do you think the $5 was unreasonable?

3. Note

    3.1. In May of 2001, U.C.C. Revised Article 2 was presented to the American Law Institute for approval. At that time, the drafters had revised Section 2-718(1) to read as follows:

    § 2-718. Liquidation or Limitation of Damages; Deposits.

    (1) Damages for breach by either party may be liquidated in the agreement but only at an amount which is reasonable in the light of the anticipated or actual harm caused by the breach~~, the difficulties of proof of loss, and the inconvenience or nonfeasibility of otherwise obtaining an adequate remedy. A term fixing unreasonably large liquidated damages is void as a penalty.~~ and, in a consumer contract, in addition the difficulties of proof of loss and the inconvenience or nonfeasibility of otherwise obtaining an adequate remedy. Section

2-719 determines the enforceability of a term that limits but does not liquidate damages.

The deletions to the pre-2001 Article 2 are noted by strikethrough text, and the additions are noted by underlined text.

Upon motion of Professor Jean Braucher, however, the ALI amended the text on the floor of the annual meeting by a close 69–68 vote to read as follows:

Section 2-718. Liquidation or Limitation of Damages; Deposits.

(1) Damages for breach by either party may be liquidated in the agreement but only at an amount which is reasonable in the light of the anticipated or actual harm caused by the breach, the difficulties of proof of loss, and the inconvenience or nonfeasibility of otherwise obtaining an adequate remedy. A term fixing unreasonably large liquidated damages is void as a penalty. Section 2-719 determines the enforceability of a term that limits but does not liquidate damages.

What's going on here?

Sometimes liquidated damages clauses can cause unanticipated results, as you'll see in the next case. When that happens, do you change the law of liquidated damages, or find some other law to offset the odd result? Read on.

Vines v. Orchard Hills, Inc.
Supreme Court of Connecticut
181 Conn. 501, 435 A.2d 1022 (1980)

Peters, J:

This case concerns the right of purchasers of real property, after their own default, to recover moneys paid at the time of execution of a valid contract of sale. The plaintiffs, Euel D. Vines and his wife Etta Vines, contracted, on July 11, 1973, to buy Unit No. 10, Orchard Hills Condominium, New Canaan, from the defendant Orchard Hills, Inc. for $78,800. On or before that date, they had paid the defendant $7880 as a down payment toward the purchase. Alleging that the sale of the property was never consummated, the plaintiffs sought to recover their down payment. The trial court, I. Levine, J., overruled the defendant's demurrer to the plaintiffs' amended complaint;

subsequently, after a hearing, the trial court, Novack, J., rendered judgment for the plaintiffs for $7880 plus interest. The defendant's appeal maintains that its demurrer should have been sustained, that its liquidated damages clause should have been enforced, and that evidence of the value of the property at the time of the trial should have been excluded.

The facts underlying this litigation are straightforward and undisputed. When the purchasers contracted to buy their condominium in July, 1973, they paid $7880, a sum which the contract of sale designated as liquidated damages.[1] The purchasers decided not to take title to the condominium because Euel D. Vines was transferred by his employer to New Jersey; the Vines so informed the seller by a letter dated January 4, 1974. There has never been any claim that the seller has failed, in any respect, to conform to his obligations under the contract, nor does the complaint allege that the purchasers are legally excused from their performance under the contract. In short, it is the purchasers and not the seller whose breach precipitated the present cause of action.

In the proceedings below, the purchasers established that the value of the condominium that they had agreed to buy for $78,800 in 1973 had, by the time of the trial in 1979, a fair market value of $160,000. The trial court relied on this figure to conclude that, because the seller had gained what it characterized as a windfall of approximately $80,000, the purchasers were entitled to recover their down payment of $7880. Neither the purchasers nor the seller proffered any evidence at the trial to show the market value of the condominium at the time of the purchasers' breach of their contract or the damages sustained by the seller as a result of that breach.

The seller's principal argument on this appeal is that the trial court improperly disregarded the parties' valid liquidated damages clause. * * *Whether a party may recover payments made despite its own default and despite its agreement to a liquidated damages clause is a question that presents issues of fact which transcend the legal sufficiency of the complaint, as the trial itself demonstrated. * * * The trial court was, however, in error in its conclusion that the evidence before it was sufficient to sustain a judgment in favor of the purchasers.

---

[1]Paragraph 9 of the contract of sale provided: "DEFAULT: In the event Purchaser fails to perform any of the obligations herein imposed on the Purchaser, the Seller performing all obligations herein imposed on the Seller, the Seller shall retain all sums of money paid under this Contract, as liquidated damages, and all rights and liabilities of the parties hereto shall be at an end."

The ultimate issue on this appeal is the enforceability of a liquidated damages clause as a defense to a claim of restitution by purchasers in default on a land sale contract. Although the parties, both in the trial court and here, have focused on the liquidated damages clause per se, we must first consider when, if ever, purchasers who are themselves in breach of a valid contract of sale may affirmatively invoke the assistance of judicial process to recover back moneys paid to, and withheld by, their seller.

I

The right of a contracting party, despite his default, to seek restitution for benefits conferred and allegedly unjustly retained has been much disputed in the legal literature and in the case law. * * * Although earlier cases often refused to permit a party to bring an action that could be said to be based on his own breach; * * * many of the more recent cases support restitution in order to prevent unjust enrichment and to avoid forfeiture. * * *

A variety of considerations, some practical and some theoretical, underlie this shift in attitude toward the plaintiff in breach. As Professor Corbin pointed out in his seminal article, "The Right of a Defaulting Vendee to the Restitution of Instalments Paid," 40 Yale L.J. 1013 (1931), the anomalous result of denying any remedy to the plaintiff in breach is to punish more severely the person who has partially performed, often in good faith, than the person who has entirely disregarded his contractual obligations from the outset. Only partial performance triggers a claim for restitution, and partial performance will not, in the ordinary course of events, have been more injurious to the innocent party than total nonperformance. Recognition of a claim in restitution is, furthermore, consistent with the economic functions that the law of contracts is designed to serve. See Kessler & Gilmore, Contracts, pp. 4–6 (1970). The principal purpose of remedies for the breach of contract is to provide compensation for loss; * * *; and therefore a party injured by breach of contract is entitled to retain nothing in excess of that sum which compensates him for the loss of his bargain. Indeed, there are those who argue that repudiation of contractual obligations is socially desirable, and should be encouraged, whenever gain to the party in breach exceeds loss to the party injured by breach.* * *To assign such primacy to inferences drawn from economic models requires great confidence that the person injured by breach will encounter no substantial difficulties in establishing the losses for which he is entitled to be compensated. It is not necessary to push the principle of compensatory damages that far, or to disregard entirely the desirability of maintaining some incentives for the performance of promises. A claim in restitution, although legal in form, is equitable in nature, and permits a trial court to balance the equities, to take into account a variety of competing principles to determine whether the defendant has been unjustly enriched. "Even though we adhere to the rule that only compensatory damages are to be awarded, there are other important questions of policy to be considered. One is whether aid is to be given to one who breaches his contract, particularly when the breach is deliberate and without moral justification. Another is whether restitution can be administered without leaving the innocent party with uncompensated damages." 1 Palmer, Restitution § 5.1, p. 574 (1978).

Recognition that there are circumstances under which a defaulting purchaser may be entitled to restitution for benefits conferred upon the innocent seller of land is consistent with parallel developments elsewhere in the law of contracts. Judicial resistance to enforcement of forfeitures has of course long been a commonplace, particularly with regard to contract clauses purporting to liquidate damages. * * * Despite the deference afforded by nineteenth-century courts to freedom of contract in other areas;* * * clauses that might impose forfeitures were invariably carefully scrutinized and frequently denounced as penal. Contract clauses permitting retention of partial payments pursuant to contracts of conditional sale temporarily escaped this obloquy, on the theory that a seller's retention of a property interest in his goods entitled him, upon any default by the buyer, both to retake his goods and to retain any moneys paid. See 1 Gilmore, Security Interests in Personal Property § 3.2 (1965); * * *. The law of conditional sales contracts came, however, in this century, to recognize that avoidance of forfeiture was more important than retention of title, so that conditional sales, like chattel mortgages, were enforced in such a way as to preserve the debtor's equity. See 1 Gilmore, supra, 68; * * * In a similar vein, in real property transactions courts have long protected a debtor's equity from forfeiture by allowing the debtor to show by parol evidence that a deed although absolute on its face was actually intended to be a mortgage. * * * We therefore conclude that a purchaser whose breach is not willful has a restitutionary claim to recover moneys paid that unjustly enrich his seller. In this case, no one has alleged that the purchasers' breach, arising out of a transfer to a more distant place of employment, should be deemed to have been willful. The trial court was therefore not in error in initially overruling the seller's demurrer and entertaining the purchasers' cause of action.

II

The purchaser's right to recover in restitution requires the purchaser to establish that the seller has been unjustly enriched. The purchaser must show more than that the contract has come to an end and that the seller retains moneys paid pursuant to the contract. To prove unjust enrichment, in the ordinary case, the purchaser, because he is the party in breach, must prove that the damages suffered by his seller are less than the moneys received from the purchaser. * * * It may not be easy for the purchaser to prove the extent of the seller's damages, it may even be strategically advantageous for the seller to come forward with relevant evidence of the losses he has incurred and may expect to incur on account of the buyer's breach. Nonetheless, only if the breaching party satisfies his burden of proof that the innocent party has sustained a net gain may a claim for unjust enrichment be sustained. * * *

In the case before us, the parties themselves stipulated in the contract of sale that the purchasers' down payment of 10 percent of the purchase price represents the damages that would be likely to flow from the purchasers' breach. The question then becomes whether the purchasers have demonstrated the seller's unjust enrichment in the face of the liquidated damages clause to which they agreed.

This is not a suitable occasion for detailed review of the checkered history of liquidated damages clauses. Despite the judicial resistance that such clauses have encountered in the past; * * * this court has recognized the principle that there are circumstances that justify private agreements to supplant judicially determined remedies for breach of contract. * * * This court has however refused to enforce an otherwise valid liquidated damages clause upon a finding that no damages whatsoever ensued from the particular breach of contract that actually occurred. * * *

Most of the litigation concerning liquidated damages clauses arises in the context of an affirmative action by the party injured by breach to enforce the clause in order to recover the amount therein stipulated. In such cases, the burden of persuasion about the enforceability of the clause naturally rests with its proponent. * * * In the case before us, by contrast, where the plaintiffs are themselves in default, the plaintiffs bear the burden of showing that the clause is invalid and unenforceable. * * * It is not unreasonable in these circumstances to presume that a liquidated damages clause that is appropriately limited in amount bears a reasonable relationship to the damages that the seller has actually suffered. See Restatement (Second), Contracts § 388, esp. subsection (2) (Tent. Draft No. 14, 1979).[2] The seller's damages, as Professor Palmer points out, include not only his expectation damages suffered through loss of his bargain, and his incidental damages such as broker's commissions, but also less quantifiable costs arising out of retention of real property beyond the time of the originally contemplated sale. 1 Palmer, Restitution §§ 5.4, 5.8 (1978).* * * A liquidated damages clause allowing the seller to retain 10 percent of the contract price as earnest money is presumptively a reasonable allocation of the risks associated with default. * * *[3]

The presumption of validity that attaches to a clause liquidating the seller's damages at 10 percent of the contract price in the event of the purchaser's unexcused nonperformance is, like most other presumptions, rebuttable. The purchaser, despite his default, is free to prove that the contract, or any part thereof, was the product of fraud or mistake or unconscionability.* * * In the alternative, the purchaser is free to offer evidence that his breach in fact caused the seller no damages or damages substantially less than the amount stipulated as liquidated damages. See Norwalk Door Closer Co. v. Eagle Lock & Screw Co., supra, 689.

The trial court concluded that the plaintiff purchasers had successfully invoked the principle of Norwalk Door Closer Co. v. Eagle Lock & Screw Co. by presenting evidence of increase in the value of the real property between the date of the contract of sale and the date of the trial. That conclusion was in error. The relevant time at which to measure the seller's damages is the time of breach. * * * Benefits to the seller that are attributable to a rising

[2]Section 388 of the Restatement (Second) of Contracts (Tent. Draft No. 14, 1979) provides:

"RESTITUTION IN FAVOR OF PARTY IN BREACH.

(1) Subject to the rule stated in Subsection (2), if a party justifiably refuses to perform on the ground that his remaining duties of performance have been discharged by the other party's breach, the party in breach is entitled to restitution for any benefit that he has conferred on the injured party by way of part performance or reliance.

(2) To the extent that, under the manifested assent of the parties, a party's performance is to be retained in the case of breach, that party is not entitled to restitution if the value of the performance as liquidated damages is reasonable in the light of the anticipated or actual loss caused by the breach and the difficulties of proof of loss."

[In the final version of the *Restatement*, the quoted text appears as Section 374. Eds.]

[3]We have, in another context, viewed 10 percent as a reasonable cutoff point to determine presumptively what inferences are to be drawn from ambiguous commercial undertakings. See Granite Equipment Leasing Corporation v. Acme Pump Co., 165 Conn. 364, 368, 335 A.2d 294 (1973).

market subsequent to breach rightfully accrue to the seller. * * * There was no evidence before the court to demonstrate that the seller was not injured at the time of the purchasers' breach by their failure then to consummate the contract. Neither the seller's status as a developer of a condominium project nor the absence of willfulness on the part of the purchasers furnishes a justification for disregarding the liquidated damages clause, although these factors may play some role in the ultimate determination of whether the seller was in fact unjustly enriched by the down payment he retained.

Because the availability of, and the limits on, restitutionary claims by a plaintiff in default have not previously been clearly spelled out in our cases, it is appropriate to afford to the purchasers herein another opportunity to proffer evidence to substantiate their claim. What showing the purchasers must make cannot be spelled out with specificity in view of the sparsity of the present record. The purchasers may be able to demonstrate that the condominium could, at the time of their breach, have been resold at a price sufficiently higher than their contract price to obviate any loss of profits and to compensate the seller for any incidental and consequential damages. Alternatively, the purchasers may be able to present evidence of unconscionability or of excuse, to avoid the applicability of the liquidated damages clause altogether. The plaintiffs' burden of proof is not an easy one to sustain, but they are entitled to their day in court.

There is error, the judgment is set aside, and the case is remanded for further proceedings in conformity with this opinion.

In this opinion the other judges concurred.

QUESTIONS AND NOTE

1. Questions about the facts of this case

   1.1. Was Vines in breach? Why?

   1.2. Did Orchard Hills suffer any loss? Why?

   1.3. Is Orchard Hills just being a pig here?

2. Questions about the law

   2.1. Why should the law ever help those who breach their contracts?

2.2. Does it seem cumbersome to you to blend the law of breach, liquidated damages and restitution just to get a fair result? Why doesn't the court just say that deposits are always refundable if the seller suffers no loss?

3. Note

Justice Peters had this to say about *Vines* in retrospect:

> I had sent Grant [Gilmore, a Yale law professor who Justice Peters knew when she was on the Yale law faculty before being appointed to the Connecticut Supreme Court,] a copy of an opinion I had written for the court in a case involving a reluctant buyer of real property, who, having breached his contract of purchase, sought to recover his down payment. What made the buyer's argument appealing, and persuasive to the trial court, was the fact that, after the buyer's breach, the value of the real estate had soared. The seller, having retained the property, was thus arguably benefitted by the buyer's breach and unjustly enriched by keeping the down payment in addition. We rejected this appealing argument, reasoning that the buyer was imposing the wrong time frame on the measurement of benefit: since the seller's injury arose at the time of the buyer's breach, so his benefit had to be measured at that same time. Grant wrote back, after noting how fascinating a problem the case had presented: "I appreciate the logic of your position. And yet I wonder whether the trial judge may not have blundered into a sort of truth (judicial ignorance is the greatest of law reformers). No doubt the economists would have an answer ready-made."

Ellen Peters, *In Memory of Grant Gilmore: Grant Gilmore and the Illusion of Certainty*, 92 YALE L.J. 8, 11 (1982).

Problems on Liquidated Damages

1. *Liquidated Damages and Specific Performance*

Despite all advice to the contrary, Epstein, Markell and Ponoroff form a law partnership. Being crafty devils, they place in their partnership agreement a non-compete clause, and set liquidated damages for breach of that non-compete clause at $50,000, a sum everyone agrees is on the high side of reasonable given the nature of the proposed practice.

Unfortunately, a year later, to everyone's surprise, Epstein wins a huge case. His name and picture (with a big, toothy grin) is plastered all over the papers. When Markell and Ponoroff refuse to amend the formula used to allocate partnership profits to give Epstein more of a share, Epstein is silent for a second, checks the partnership agreement and then says "G'bye, y'all."

Epstein then sets up shop next door to Markell and Ponoroff and begins competing in direct violation of the non-compete clause. Markell and Ponoroff sue to enjoin Epstein. What result?

If an injunction is not granted, may Markell and Ponoroff show that their real damages from Epstein's blatant violation of the non-compete clause are closer to $200,000, given that Epstein is now sucking all of the legal work in town to his new boutique? Why or why not?

Final variant: Does it make a difference what standard (*Restatement*, *O'Brian*, or U.C.C.) you use with respect to what result you get?

2. *Scare Tactics*

Many retails stores have signs above the counter that say "$25 charge on returned checks." Putting aside for now the question as to whether this sign becomes part of the contract, do you think such a term is enforceable? Would you advise a client to rely on such a sign in light of *O'Brian*? Does the *Restatement* formulation yield a different result?

3. *Scare Tactics (Redux)*

Many contracts for cellular telephone service require you to commit to a year or more of subscription, or they say that they will assess a "termination fee", which sometimes exceeds $200 (when the monthly service charge is only $35). Knowing what you know now, is there any way to attack this fee?

4. *Final Problem*

Most construction contracts call for a per day "penalty" or "fee" to be paid if a job is not completed within the agreed time. Assume that Markell Construction Co. agrees with Epstein to build an addition to Epstein's house for $20,000. The contract says that Markell will pay $100 a day for each day he is late in finishing past the agreed due date of July 1, 2001.

True to form, Markell (as his mother would say) is "slower than molasses running uphill in the month of January." He finishes on July 31, 2001. Can he contest the $3,000 in liquidated damages as a penalty? What more would you want to know before venturing a firm answer?

What if Markell doesn't finish until July 1, 2002? Are Epstein's damages then $36,500?

What if he never finishes?

A. Penalties, Liquidated Damages and Efficient Breach

In *Vines*, Justice Peters, a former academic, refers to significant academic commentary that disapproves of liquidated damages. Some judges makes this disapproval more overt. In *Lake River Corp. v. Carborundum Co.*, 769 F.2d 1284 (7th Cir. 1985), Circuit Judge Richard Posner had the following to say about the liquidated damages/penalty distinction:

> Deep as the hostility to penalty clauses runs in the common law, see Loyd, Penalties and Forfeitures, 29 Harv. L. Rev. 117 (1915), we still might be inclined to question, if we thought ourselves free to do so, whether a modern court should refuse to enforce a penalty clause where the signator is a substantial corporation, well able to avoid improvident commitments. Penalty clauses provide an earnest of performance. The clause here enhanced Carborundum's credibility in promising to ship the minimum amount guaranteed by showing that it was willing to pay the full contract price even if it failed to ship anything. On the other side it can be pointed out that by raising the cost of a breach of contract to the contract breaker, a penalty clause increases the risk to his other creditors; increases (what is the same thing and more, because bankruptcy imposes "deadweight" social costs) the risk of bankruptcy; and could

amplify the business cycle by increasing the number of bankruptcies in bad times, which is when contracts are most likely to be broken. But since little effort is made to prevent businessmen from assuming risks, these reasons are no better than makeweights.

A better argument is that a penalty clause may discourage efficient as well as inefficient breaches of contract. Suppose a breach would cost the promisee $12,000 in actual damages but would yield the promisor $20,000 in additional profits. Then there would be a net social gain from breach. After being fully compensated for his loss the promisee would be no worse off than if the contract had been performed, while the promisor would be better off by $8,000. But now suppose the contract contains a penalty clause under which the promisor if he breaks his promise must pay the promisee $25,000. The promisor will be discouraged from breaking the contract, since $25,000, the penalty, is greater than $20,000, the profits of the breach; and a transaction that would have increased value will be forgone.

On this view, since compensatory damages should be sufficient to deter inefficient breaches (that is, breaches that cost the victim more than the gain to the contract breaker), penal damages could have no effect other than to deter some efficient breaches. But this overlooks the earlier point that the willingness to agree to a penalty clause is a way of making the promisor and his promise credible and may therefore be essential to inducing some value-maximizing contracts to be made. It also overlooks the more important point that the parties (always assuming they are fully competent) will, in deciding whether to include a penalty clause in their contract, weigh the gains against the costs—costs that include the possibility of discouraging an efficient breach somewhere down the road—and will include the clause only if the benefits exceed those costs as well as all other costs.

On this view the refusal to enforce penalty clauses is (at best) paternalistic—and it seems odd that courts should display parental solicitude for large corporations. But however this may be, we must be on guard to avoid importing our own ideas of sound public policy into an area where our proper judicial role is more than usually deferential. The responsibility for making innovations in the common law of Illinois rests with the courts of Illinois, and not with the federal courts in Illinois. And like every other state, Illinois, untroubled by academic skepticism of the wisdom of re-

> fusing to enforce penalty clauses against sophisticated promisors, see, e.g., Goetz & Scott, Liquidated Damages, Penalties and the Just Compensation Principle, 77 Colum. L. Rev. 554 (1977), continues steadfastly to insist on the distinction between penalties and liquidated damages. * * * To be valid under Illinois law a liquidation of damages must be a reasonable estimate at the time of contracting of the likely damages from breach, and the need for estimation at that time must be shown by reference to the likely difficulty of measuring the actual damages from a breach of contract after the breach occurs. If damages would be easy to determine then, or if the estimate greatly exceeds a reasonable upper estimate of what the damages are likely to be, it is a penalty. * * *

Id. at 1288–90.

Ok. That was 1985. Has Judge Posner mellowed any? No. Compare this except from *Lawyers Title Ins. Corp. v. Dearborn Title Corp.*, 118 F.3d 1157 (7th Cir. 1997):

> Parties to a contract can agree on the amount of damages if there is a breach, but for such a "liquidated damages" clause to be enforceable it must be a reasonable estimate of what the promisee's losses are likely to be in the event of a breach. * * * This rule has come in for a lot of academic criticism, running along the following lines. A penalty clause has no effect on anyone except the parties, so why should a court refuse to enforce it, unless there is evidence of fraud or other overreaching not here argued? Penalty clauses can serve a valuable signaling device: by agreeing to a penalty Dearborn manifested a credible determination to break itself of what had become a bad habit of paying its debts to United with checks that bounced. A penalty clause makes particularly good economic sense if there is some probability that a breach will go undetected—for example, if the seller could plausibly blame the buyer for the failure of the seller's product to perform as intended. In such a case, without a penalty clause the seller's expected damages liability will be less than the buyer's actual damages and there will be too many breaches from the standpoint of economic efficiency. It can even be argued that a penalty clause is unlikely to overcompensate the promisee if an ex ante (before the fact) perspective is employed, because the promisor would not agree to such a clause unless it was necessary to compensate the promisee for an expected loss. And as for any concern that penalty clauses might discourage efficient breaches—breaches in which

> the profit from the breach exceeds the cost to the promisee—the promisee can always waive the penalty and will do so if compensated by the promisor. The compensation doesn't have to equal the penalty, since if the promisee refuses to waive its rights under the contract and as a result the promisor adheres to the contract, the promisee will not receive the penalty because there will be no breach.
>
> Against all this it can be argued that penalty clauses, precisely by encouraging the formation of contracts likely to be broken—which presumably is why a promisee would demand such a clause—would, if enforceable, throw more contract cases into the courts. Such a clause might also make the promisee, who may profit greatly from the promisor's breach since it will activate the promisee's entitlement to a penalty, stubborn about agreeing to contract modifications when the promisor gets into trouble. A related point is that penalty clauses turn minor breaches of contract into litigation casus belli by increasing the expected judgment in a breach of contract suit if the judgment includes a penalty. The parties to lawsuits do not pay the full costs that litigation imposes on the judicial system, and so courts are justly concerned with proposed changes in law that would foster additional litigation.

Id. at 1160–61.

Questions on Judge Posner's Views

1. How can the opportunity to breach be worth more than the cost of breach? Again, what is providing the extra value?
2. Also, just what exactly does Judge Posner seem to mean by "efficient"?

B. A Dissenting View from the Bench on Efficient Breach

Not all judges hop on the efficient breach bandwagon (or all academics; see footnote 19 to the Delaware Supreme Court's opinion in *DuPont*, *supra*, at 845, and see Alan Schwartz, *The Case for Specific Performance,* 89 YALE L.J. 271 (1979)). Some judges are worried about the imperfect translation between money and an act. For example, in some contracts, you may want what you bargained for desperately more than a damages substitute. Insurance coverage might be a good example, as the following excerpt from a dissent from the California Supreme Court shows.

Cates Const., Inc. v. Talbot Partners
Supreme Court of California
21 Cal. 4th 28, 980 P.2d 407, 86 Cal. Rptr. 2d 855 (1999)

Baxter, J.;

This case presents issues relating to the contract and tort liability of a commercial surety to a real estate developer under a bond guaranteeing the contract performance of a general contractor on a multimillion dollar condominium construction project. For the reasons set forth below, we conclude that the bond at issue contractually obligates the surety to pay damages attributable to the general contractor's failure to promptly and faithfully perform its contract obligations by the agreed date. We further conclude that, as a matter of law, the developer may not recover in tort for the surety's breach of the covenant of good faith and fair dealing implied in the performance bond. In light of these conclusions, we reverse the judgment of the Court of Appeal insofar as it affirmed the underlying award of tort damages for breach of the implied covenant and permitted an award of punitive damages.

* * *

Mosk, J, dissenting:

* * *

Certainty of performance being the essential value of performance bonds, their worth is deeply undermined if sureties can regularly choose to ignore their obligations, having nothing to fear but contract damages that will approximate what they would pay in performance. As the Court of Appeal reasoned: "The quasi-public nature of the insurance industry arises from the purpose and nature of the contracts and the duties which the insurer assumes. That is, the quasi-public nature arises from the contingent nature of the contract and the public's interest in promoting the conduct of business and personal affairs with confidence that in the event of calamity, there is protection. These factors apply equally to performance bond surety insurance, which is vital to real estate development."

Under most circumstances a breach of contract violates no social policy; the law limits the nonbreaching party's remedies so as to allow for "efficient breach" of the contract. But when a contract exists primarily to provide one party certainty and security in a risky enterprise, the other party's bad faith breach cannot be efficient, because it negates the very purpose of the contract. A tort remedy is justified in this context in order to deter such breaches of the covenant. "Recognizing a cause of action in tort for a commercial surety's breach of its duty to act in good faith compels commercial sureties to handle claims responsibly. When the commercial surety withholds payment of an obligee's claim in bad faith, contract damages do not compensate the obligee for the commercial surety's misconduct and have no deterrent effect to prevent such misconduct in the future. As the Arizona Supreme Court explained in Dodge, contract damages 'offer no motivation whatsoever for the insurer not to breach. If the only damages an insurer will have to pay upon a judgment of breach are the amounts that it would have owed under the policy plus interest, it has every interest in retaining the money, earning the higher rates of interest on the outside market, and hoping eventually to force the insured into a settlement for less than the policy amount.' * * *

QUESTIONS

1. How would Judge Posner respond to Justice Mosk's comments on certainty? How do you?

2. Does this discussion make you want to rethink the current state of the doctrine regarding specific performance? Liquidated damages? How do efficient breach and specific performance interrelate? How do efficient breach and liquidated damages interrelate?

3. If you could reverse the rule regarding the non-availability of attorneys' fees as incidental damages, would that help or hurt the efficient breach hypothesis?

4. Say a person rejects goods in bad faith but consistent with the perfect tender rule of Section 2-601 of the U.C.C.? Is that person in breach? To those who would change the result by pointing to the inherent good faith requirement of Section 1-203, would the proponents of efficient breach have a counter-argument?

SECTION 5. MONEY DAMAGES

You can't always win what you want,
You can't always win what you want,
You can't always win what you want,
But if you try sometimes you just might find
You'll get wads of green.

David "Rockabilly" Epstein & Bruce "Vegas" Markell
You Can't Always Win What You Want,
on LET THEM READ (Ponoroff Records 2001)

A. The General Measure of Money Damages: Receipt of the Benefit of the Bargain (of the Expectancy Interest)

The material in the prior section should have lead you to think that, in drafting a liquidated damages clause, you should avoid drafting a penalty. But how do you do that? It seems that both *O'Brian* and *Vines* tell you to look to what the parties knew at formation. That's all well and good, but the concept of penalty involves some sort of comparison with a benchmark: if the liquidated damages clause comes close to the benchmark, it is okay; if not, it is a penalty.

What is the benchmark? Again, *O' Brian*, *Kvassay* and *Vines* are consistent in the view that the benchmark consists of the standard measure of money damages.

Moreover, we saw in the first case in this chapter, *Triple-A*, *supra*, at 830, that specific performance could be granted only if legal remedies were inadequate. Inadequacy, in turn, translated into the inability to compensate with money damages.

But how are money damages calculated? As we have seen throughout all the cases that have brought you to this point, courts tend to compute damages as the amount necessary to put the aggrieved party in the same position that he would have been in had there been performance. In short, money substitutes for performance. In the normal case of commercial contracts, it may be that this equation—money for performance—works well enough. If Ponoroff breaches his contract to supply widgets to Markell, and Markell has to get widgets elsewhere, it seems reasonable that Markell can be compensated with money.

In the next case, however, the contract arises in a non-commercial setting. Do money damages compensate the plaintiff in the next case for the breach of contract that is found?

Hawkins v. McGee
Supreme Court of New Hampshire
84 N.H. 114, 146 A. 641 (1929)

Assumpsit against a surgeon for breach of an alleged warranty of the success of an operation. Trial by jury. [A $3,000] Verdict for the plaintiff. The writ also contained a count in negligence upon which a nonsuit was ordered, without exception.

Defendant's motions for a nonsuit and for a directed verdict on the count in assumpsit were denied, and the defendant excepted. During the argument of plaintiff's counsel to the jury, the defendant claimed certain exceptions, and also excepted to the denial of his requests for instructions and to the charge of the court upon the question of damages, as more fully appears in the opinion. The defendant seasonably moved to set aside the verdict upon the grounds that it was (1) contrary to the evidence; (2) against the weight of the evidence; (3) against the weight of the law and evidence; and (4) because the damages awarded by the jury were excessive. The court denied the motion upon the first three grounds, but found that the damages were excessive, and made an order that the verdict be set aside, unless the plaintiff elected to remit all in excess of $500. The plaintiff having refused to remit, the verdict was set aside "as excessive and against the weight of the evidence," and the plaintiff excepted.

Branch, J.

The operation in question consisted in the removal of a considerable quantity of scar tissue from the palm of the plaintiff's right hand and the grafting of skin taken from the plaintiff's chest in place thereof. The scar tissue was the result of a severe burn caused by contact with an electric wire, which the plaintiff received about nine years before the time of the transactions here involved. There was evidence to the effect that before the operation was performed the plaintiff and his father went to the defendant's office, and that the defendant, in answer to the question, "How long will the boy be in the hospital?" replied, "Three or four days, not over four; then the boy can go home and it will be just a few days when he will go back to work with a good hand." Clearly this and other testimony to the same effect would not justify a finding that the doctor contracted to complete the hospital treatment in three or four days or that the plaintiff would be able to go back to work within a few days thereafter. The above statements could only be construed as expressions of opinion or predictions as to the probable duration of the treatment and plaintiff's resulting disability, and the fact that these estimates were exceeded would impose no contractual liability upon the defendant. The only substantial basis for the plaintiff's claim is the testimony that the defendant also said before the operation was decided upon, "I will guarantee to make the hand a hundred per cent perfect hand or a hundred per cent good hand." The plaintiff was present when these words were alleged to have been spoken, and, if they are to be taken at their face value, it seems obvious that proof of their utterance would establish the giving of a warranty in accordance with his contention.

The defendant argues, however, that, even if these words were uttered by him, no reasonable man would understand that they were used with the intention of entering "into any contractual relation whatever," and that they could reasonably be understood only "as his expression in strong language that he believed and expected that as a result of the operation he would give the plaintiff a very good hand." It may be conceded, as the defendant contends, that, before the question of the making of a contract should be submitted to a jury, there is a preliminary question of law for the trial court to pass upon, i.e. "whether the words could possibly have the meaning imputed to them by the party who founds his case upon a certain interpretation," but it cannot be held that the trial court decided this question erroneously in the present case. It is unnecessary to determine at this time whether the argument of the defendant, based upon "common knowledge of the uncertainty which attends all surgical operations," and the improbability that a surgeon would ever contract to make a damaged part of the human body "one hundred per cent perfect" would, in the absence of countervailing considerations, be regarded as conclusive, for there were other factors in the present case which tended to support the contention of the plaintiff. There was evidence that the defendant repeatedly solicited from the plaintiff's father the opportunity to perform this operation, and the theory was advanced by plaintiff's counsel in cross examination of defendant that he sought an opportunity to "experiment on skin grafting," in which he had little previous experience. If the jury accepted this part of plaintiff's contention, there would be a reasonable basis for the further conclusion that, if defendant spoke the words attributed to him, he did so with the intention that they should be accepted at their face value, as an inducement for the granting of consent to the operation by the plaintiff and his father, and there was ample evidence that they were so accepted by them. The question of the making of the alleged contract was properly submitted to the jury.

The substance of the charge to the jury on the question of damages appears in the following quotation: "If you find the plaintiff entitled to anything, he is entitled to recover for what pain and suffering he has been made to endure and for what injury he has sustained over and above what injury he had before." To this instruction the defendant seasonably excepted. By it, the jury was permitted to consider two elements of damage: (1) Pain and suffering due to the operation; and (2) positive ill effects of the operation upon the plaintiff's hand. Authority for any specific rule of damages in cases of this kind seems to be lacking, but, when tested by general principle and by analogy, it appears that the foregoing instruction was erroneous.

"By 'damages,' as that term is used in the law of contracts, is intended compensation for a breach, measured in the terms of the contract." Davis v. New England Cotton Yarn Co., 77 N.H. 403, 92 A. 732. The purpose of the law is "to put the plaintiff in as good a position as he would have been in had the defendant kept his contract." 3 Williston Cont. § 1338; Hardie-Tynes Mfg. Co. v. Eastern Cotton Oil Co., 150 N.C. 150, 63 S.E. 676. The measure of recovery "is based upon what the defendant should have given the plaintiff, not what the plaintiff has given the defendant or otherwise expended." 3 Williston Cont. § 1341 . . .

The present case is closely analogous to one in which a machine is built for a certain purpose and warranted to do certain work. In such cases, the usual rule of damages for breach of warranty in the sale of chattels is applied, and it is held that the measure of damages is the difference between the value of the machine, if it had corresponded with the warranty and its actual value, together with such incidental losses as the parties knew, or ought to have known, would probably result from a failure to comply with its terms. . . .

The rule thus applied is well settled in this state. "As a general rule, the measure of the vendee's damages is the difference between the value of the goods as they would have been if the warranty as to quality had been true, and the actual value at the time of the sale, including gains prevented and losses sustained, and such other damages as could be reasonably anticipated by the parties as likely to be caused by the vendor's failure to keep his agreement, and could not by reasonable care on the part of the vendee have been avoided." Union Bank v. Blanchard, 65 N.H. 21, 18 A. 90; . . . P.L. ch. 166, § 69, subd. 7. We therefore conclude that the true measure of the plaintiff's damage in the present case is the difference between the value to him of a perfect hand or a good hand, such as the jury found the defendant promised him, and the value of his hand in its present condition, including any incidental consequences fairly within the contemplation of the parties when they made their contract. 1 Sutherland, Damages (4th Ed.) § 92. Damages not thus limited, although naturally resulting, are not to be given.

The extent of the plaintiff's suffering does not measure this difference in value. The pain necessarily incident to a serious surgical operation was a part of the contribution which the plaintiff was willing to make to his joint undertaking with the defendant to produce a good hand. It was a legal detriment suffered by him which constituted a part of the consideration given by him for the contract. It represented a part of the price which he was willing to pay for a good hand, but it furnished no test of the value of a good hand or the difference between the value of the hand which the defendant promised and the one which resulted from the operation.

It was also erroneous and misleading to submit to the jury as a separate element of damage any change for the worse in the condition of the plaintiff's hand resulting from the operation, although this error was probably more prejudicial to the plaintiff than to the defendant. Any such ill effect of the operation would be included under the true rule of damages set forth above, but damages might properly be assessed for the defendant's failure to improve the condition of the hand, even if there were no evidence that its condition was made worse as a result of the operation.

It must be assumed that the trial court, in setting aside the verdict, undertook to apply the same rule of damages which he had previously given to the jury, and, since this rule was erroneous, it is unnecessary for us to consider whether there was any evidence to justify his finding that all damages awarded by the jury above $500 were excessive.

* * *

New trial.

QUESTIONS AND NOTES

1. Questions about the facts of this case

   1.1. Why wasn't Dr. McGee liable to Hawkins under tort law?

   1.2. Why was Dr. McGee liable to Hawkins under contract law? What exactly was the promise made by Dr. McGee to Hawkins?

   1.3. How does the court characterize Dr. McGee's words with respect to the period of recuperation?

2. Questions about the law

   2.1. What is a warranty? How does it differ, if at all, from a normal promise?

   2.2. What does the court mean when it says "The pain necessarily incident to a serious surgical operation was a part of the contribution which the plaintiff was willing to make to his joint undertaking with the defendant to produce a good hand. It was a legal detriment suffered by him which constituted a part of the consideration given by him for the contract."?

   2.3. Why wasn't Dr. McGee liable for punitive damages?

   2.4. What is the exact measure of damages adopted by this court?

   2.5. Remand.

      a. On remand, would the agreed cost of the original surgery be relevant? Why?

b. What about evidence that Hawkins had been apprenticing as a watchmaker, but he lost that position because he no longer had the necessary manual dexterity?

c. What if Hawkins had a job as a receptionist at a local law firm, and they fired him because they thought he was driving away clients due to the unsightly nature of his hairy hand?

d. What about evidence that Hawkins' pain and suffering lasted far longer than the usual recovery period for such surgeries?

2.6. Does this court seriously believe that a hand is like a "chattel"? By the way, what is a chattel?

3. Notes

3.1. Subsequent research into the facts of this case indicated that before the new trial Dr. McGee settled the lawsuit for $1,400. We know this because Dr. McGee then sued his insurance carrier to recover that sum and an additional $2,850 in expenses, mostly attorneys' fees. Dr. McGee lost, because the insurance policy only covered liability "in consequence of any malpractice, error, or mistake." *McGee v. United States Fidelity & Guaranty Co.*, 53 F.2d 953 (1st Cir. 1931).

3.2. The same appellate case tells us what the main case does not: the condition of Hawkins' hand. In the words of the appellate court, after three months of hospitalization, "the new tissue grafted upon said hand became matted, unsightly, and so healed and attached to said hand as to practically fill the hand with an unsightly growth, restricting the motion of the plaintiff's hand so that said hand has become useless to the plaintiff. . . ."

3.3. Cases such as this inspire doggerel:

A terrible need for a fee
Brought great grief to Doctor McGee.
And his promises airy
Led a patient unwary
To a hand that no mortal should see.

Douglass Boshkoff, *Selected Poems on The Law of Contracts: Raintree County Memorial Library Occasional Paper No. 1*, 66 N.Y.U. L. REV. 1533, 1542 (1991).

If one follows the lead of *Hawkins* and the cases we have read thus far, it would seem that parties have all sorts of pecuniary interests to protect by contract. The best categorization of these interests was the subject of one of the basic articles of contract law of the 20th Century: Lon L. Fuller & William R. Perdue, Jr., *The Reliance Interest in Contract Damages,* 46 YALE L.J. 52 (1936). In that article, Professor Fuller and his student, William Perdue, tried to isolate theories regarding the award of damages. As they summarize:

> It is convenient to distinguish three principal purposes which may be pursued in awarding contract damages. These purposes, and the situations in which they become appropriate, may be stated briefly as follows:
>
> First, the plaintiff has in reliance on the promise of the defendant conferred some value on the defendant. The defendant fails to perform his promise. The court may force the defendant to disgorge the value he received from the plaintiff. The object here may be termed the prevention of gain by the defaulting promisor at the expense of the promisee; more briefly, the prevention of unjust enrichment. The interest protected may be called the restitution interest. For our present purposes it is quite immaterial how the suit in such a case be classified, whether as contractual or quasi-contractual, whether as a suit to enforce the contract or as a suit based upon a rescission of the contract. These questions relate to the superstructure of the law, not to the basic policies with which we are concerned.
>
> Secondly, the plaintiff has in reliance on the promise of the defendant changed his position. For example, the buyer under a contract for the sale of land has incurred expense in the investigation of the seller's title, or has neglected the opportunity to enter other contracts. We may award damages to the plaintiff for the purpose of undoing the harm which his reliance on the defendant's promise has caused him. Our object is to put him in as good a position as he was in before the promise was made. The interest protected in this case may be called the reliance interest.
>
> Thirdly, without insisting on reliance by the promisee or enrichment of the promisor, we may seek to give the promisee the value of the expectancy which the promise created. We may in a suit for specific performance actually compel the defendant to render the promised performance to the plaintiff, or, in a suit for damages, we may make the defendant pay the money value of this performance. Here our object is to put the plain-

> tiff in as good a position as he would have occupied had the defendant performed his promise The interest protected in this case we may call the expectation interest.

Id. at 53–55.

The *Restatement (Second) of Contracts* paid this article the ultimate compliment by adopting this categorization of damages. *Restatement (Second) of Contracts* § 344 (1981). For our present purposes, however, we need to know which of these interests is paramount, and why. As with most law, the rule is easy to find; its proper application, however, is more difficult. Of these three interests, section 345 of the *Restatement (Second) of Contracts* bluntly chooses the third: "the injured party has a right to damages based on his expectation interest. . . ."

But how do you measure someone's expectation interest? It is all well and good to say that a party should get the difference between the value of a normal hand and a deformed and hairy hand, but how is that difference calculated? The *Restatement* has an answer to that too. It states that the expectation interest is measured as:

> (a) *the loss in value to [the injured party] of the other party's performance caused by its failure or deficiency, plus*
> (b) *any other loss, including incidental or consequential loss, caused by the breach, less*
> (c) *any cost or other loss that [the injured party] has avoided by not having to perform.*

Restatement (Second) of Contracts § 347 (1981).

Test this formulation by going to the original contract for car washing between Markell and Ponoroff, *supra*, at 849. Ponoroff was to wash Markell's car on Monday for $10. Recall that Markell could get the same car wash from Epstein for $15. We have seen that Markell cannot compel Ponoroff to wash the car through a decree of specific performance. Assume also that Markell wasn't smart enough to put in a liquidated damages clause.

What's left? Money damages. That is, Markell will seek an order from a court (called a judgment) that Ponoroff owes Markell some money. If Ponoroff does not pay the amount ordered by the court (and does not appeal) Markell will then be able to take that judgment to the local sheriff and start to seize and sell Ponoroff's property until Markell is paid the amount listed in the judgment.

But what amount will the court insert in its judgment? In short, what amount will compensate Markell? Should we award Markell $15, the amount he will have to pay to Epstein? No. Ponoroff will argue successfully that Markell was already going to spend $10 for his service, thus, giving Markell $15 would be the same as giving Markell a free car wash, which is not what the deal was. It also overcompensates Markell, something contract law is loathe to do.

What would Markell get under section 347 of the *Restatement*? It starts with an amount of money equal to "(a) the loss in value to [the injured party] of the other party's performance caused by its failure or deficiency." Here, that would be $5, the difference between what Ponoroff agreed to do the job for, and Epstein's increased price. Markell would also get "(b) any other loss, including incidental or consequential loss, caused by the breach." So if Markell has to drive further to get to Epstein's car wash, he should get some compensation for that. But from all this Markell would have to subtract "(c) any cost or other loss that [the injured party] has avoided by not having to perform." That would be zero here, since the cost of Markell's preparation is no less for Epstein than for Ponoroff. So total damages, assuming no inconvenience to Markell to take the car to Epstein's, would be $5.

Here are some other problems on the basic notion of damages to test yourself.

Basic Problems on Damages

1. Markell agrees to buy Epstein's 1973 Cadillac for $1,000. Epstein breaches. What are Markell's damages if:

    a. Markell has to pay $3,000 to buy a comparable Cadillac; or

    b. Markell can buy another similar Cadillac from Ponoroff for $1,200 but has already paid Epstein $1,000; or

    c. Markell can buy a comparable Cadillac for $800; or

    d. Markell has paid $5,000 to enlarge his garage so that the Cadillac would fit, and he can get a comparable Cadillac for $1,100?

2. Markell agrees to rent Ponoroff's concert hall for a Tom Waits concert for $10,000. The day of the concert, Ponoroff breaches. How much can Markell recover if:

   a. Markell has spent $90,000 on promotions and Waits' nonrefundable fee; and

   b. Markell has received $300,000 from the sale of tickets for this sold-out Waits concert, all of which he will have to refund?

3. *Sneaky Review Question*: Would your answer to question 2 change if instead of breaching on the day of the planned concert, Ponoroff instead stood beside you in the early morning haze, crying, while he watched the concert hall burn to the ground?

The following case tries to apply this test in the case where the numbers are relatively small and there seems to be no dispute as to the basic math. In most cases, however, you won't have that luxury. You must then try to apply the rule the cases state above, after first formulating it accurately.

B. Benefit of the Bargain Measured by Expectations Under the Contract

Leingang v. Mandan Weed Board
Supreme Court of North Dakota
468 N.W.2d 397 (1991)

Evine, Justice.

Robert Leingang appeals from an award of damages for breach of contract. The issue is whether the trial court used the appropriate measure of damages. We hold it did not, and reverse and remand.

The City of Mandan Weed Board awarded Leingang a contract to cut weeds on lots with an area greater than 10,000 square feet. Another contractor received the contract for smaller lots. During 1987, Leingang discovered that the Weed Board's agent was improperly assigning large lots to the small-lot contractor. Leingang complained and the weed board assigned some substitute lots to him.

Leingang brought a breach of contract action in small claims court and the City removed the action to county court. The City admitted that it had prevented Leingang's performance under the contract and that the contract price for the lost work was $1,933.78. A bench trial was held to assess the damages suffered by Leingang.

At trial, Leingang argued that the applicable measure of damages was the contract price less the costs of performance he avoided due to the breach. Leingang testified that the total gas, oil, repair and replacement blade expenses saved when he was prevented from cutting the erroneously assigned lots was $211.18.

The City argued that to identify Leingang's damages for net profits, some of Leingang's overhead expenses should be attributed to the weed cutting contract and deducted from the contract price. The City offered testimony about the profitability of businesses in Mandan and testimony from Leingang's competitor about the profitability of a weed cutting business in Mandan. The City also offered Leingang's 1986 and 1987 federal tax returns. Based on the Schedule C—"Profit or Loss From Business"—in those returns, the City argued that Leingang attributed considerably more expenses to the business of cutting weeds than he had testified he had avoided.

The trial court adopted what it called a "modified net profit" approach as the measure of damages. It derived a profit margin of 20% by subtracting four categories of expenses reported on Leingang's Schedule C, and attributed to the weed-cutting business, from the weed-cutting income reported to the IRS. The trial court selected insurance, repairs, supplies, and car and truck expenses as costs attributed to the weed-cutting business. Applying the profit margin of 20% to the contract price, the trial court deducted 80% from the contract price as expenses and awarded Leingang $368.59 plus interest. Leingang appeals.

Leingang contends that the method used by the trial court to derive net profits was improper because it did not restrict the expenses that are deductible from the contract price to those which would have been incurred but for the breach of the contract, i.e., those expenses Leingang did not have to pay because the City kept him from doing the work. We agree.

For a breach of contract, the injured party is entitled to compensation for the loss suffered, but can recover no more than would have been gained by full performance. NDCC §§ 32-03-09, 32-03-36. Our law thus incorporates the notion that contract damages should give the nonbreaching party the benefit of the bargain by awarding a sum of money that will put that person in as good a position as if the contract had been performed. * * * Where the contract is for service and the breach prevents the performance of that service, the value of the contract consists of two items: (1) the party's reasonable expenditures toward performance, including costs paid, material wasted, and time and services spent on the contract, and (2) the anticipated profits. Welch Mfg. Co. v. Herbst Dept. Store, 53 N.D. 42, 204 N.W. 849, 854 (1925). Thus, a party is entitled to recover for the detriment caused by the defendant's breach, including lost profits if they are reasonable and not speculative. Id. * * *.

Where a plaintiff offers evidence estimating anticipated profits with reasonable certainty, they may be awarded. See King Features Synd. v. Courrier, 241 Iowa 870, 43 N.W.2d 718 (1950). In King Features, the plaintiff proved the value of its anticipated profits by reducing the contract price by the amount it would have spent to perform. The court held that this proof was reasonably certain. In quantifying the costs of performance, the plaintiff did not deduct "overhead" expenses because the evidence established that those expenses were constant whether or not the contract was performed. 43 N.W.2d at 725–26.

The King Features approach fulfills the Welch Mfg. requirement that a plaintiff be compensated for all the detriment caused by the breach. Under King Features, constant overhead expenses are not deducted from the contract price because they are expenses the plaintiff had to pay whether or not the contract was breached. The King Features approach compensates plaintiff for constant overhead expenses by allowing an award of the contract price, reduced only by expenses actually saved because the contract did not have to be performed. The remaining contract proceeds are available to pay constant expenses. See also Buono Sales, Inc. v. Chrysler Motors Corp., 449 F.2d 715, 720 (3d Cir.1971) [because fixed expenses must be paid from the sum remaining after costs of performance are deducted, further reducing contract price by fixed expenses would not fully, or fairly, compensate plaintiff].

Neither side argues that lost profits are not calculable here. Instead, each urges a different method for computing lost profits. In measuring Leingang's anticipated profits, the trial court erroneously calculated a "net profit" margin by deducting general costs of doing business including insurance, repairs, supplies, and car and truck expenses, without determining whether these costs remained constant regardless of the City's breach and whether they were, therefore, not to be deducted from the contract price. King Features, 43 N.W.2d at 726. The reduction from the contract price of a portion of the "fixed," or constant expenses, effectively required Leingang to pay that portion twice. See Buono Sales, Inc., 449 F.2d at 720.

We reverse the judgment and remand for a new trial on the issue of damages.

Erickstad, C.J., and Vande Walle, Gierke and Meschke, JJ., concur.

QUESTIONS AND NOTE

1. Questions about the facts of this case

   1.1. So what should Leingang receive as damages on remand?

   1.2. What doesn't make sense here? If Leingang's general profit margin really is 20%, then why isn't the trial court's ruling correct? If you were the city attorney, and knew what you know now, what types of questions would you ask Leingang at trial?

2. Questions about the law

   2.1. Both *Hawkins* and *Leingang* purport to apply the same general remedy: an award of damages to compensate the non-breaching party for the loss of that party's benefit of the bargain. Are the approaches used in both cases consistent?

   2.2. The court indicates that lost profits must be proved with certainty. We'll look at the issue in more detail below at 929.

3. Note

The web site www.cityofmandan.com/demographics/demographics.html indicates that Mandan is a small town of less that 15,000 inhabitants north of Bismark. The site also indicates that there are only four months during the year when the average snow fall is less than one inch, and (at least during the summer of 2001) had pictures of weed-covered lots. The mowing season must be short.

But what if there is no "market" in the item or service that was the subject of the contract? How do you measure the benefit of the bargain then? Keep in mind that there is no magic, one-size-fits-all formula. As a lawyer, you need to be creative and informed by your client as to how he or she can be best compensated within the law. The next case is one that cries out for creative thought, given the lack of a market to assess the value of the contract.

C. Benefit of the Bargain Measured by Cost of Substitute Performance, Cost of Repair and Other Benchmarks

Rasnick v. Tubbs

Court of Appeals of Ohio, Third Appellate District
126 Ohio App.3d 431, 710 N.E.2d 750 (1998)

Evans, Judge.

This appeal is brought by Dennis Tubbs, d.b.a. Denny's Street Shop ("appellant"), from a judgment of the Marion County Court of Common Pleas finding appellant liable to Charles and Tonyua Rasnick, d.b.a. Bennett & Sieg Auto Wrecking and d.b.a. The Rasnick Family Racing Team ("Rasnicks"), for $15,903.68 in damages for breach of a contract.

The parties in this case entered into a contract for the construction of a race car. In December 1994, appellant orally agreed to construct a 1952 Chevy Pro Modified Race Car from a 1952 Sports Coupe already owned by the Rasnicks. In addition to paying appellant $52,820 for the job, the Rasnicks were to supply the engine, transmission, and clutch assembly for the race car. Any other parts purchased by the Rasnicks would be counted toward the agreed purchase price of $52,820. The construction of the car was to be completed over twenty weeks' time. The Rasnicks agreed to make installments of $1,000 each week for appellant's labor, although the contract did not allocate a part of the purchase price for labor.

By May 12, 1995, the car was not completed and the parties saw the need to enter into a written contract. The written contract embodied substantially the same terms as the oral agreement; however, it provided that appellant would complete construction of the race car within six weeks of receiving the wheels and tires. When the completed race car was finished, as defined in the contract, the Rasnicks would pay the balance due under the contract in a lump sum.

The evidence produced at trial reveals that the wheels and tires were delivered to appellant's shop on or about May 26, 1995. Six weeks after this date the car was still not completed. Nevertheless, the Rasnicks continued to make $1,000 payments to appellant, and appellant continued to work intermittently on the car. By February 29, 1996, the Rasnicks had paid approximately $49,619.25 toward the contract price, and the car was still not finished. A meeting was called by the parties. According to the Rasnicks and one other witness, appellant informed the Rasnicks that he would not finish construction of the race car unless he was paid an additional $20,000. Furthermore, appellant stated that he could not guarantee that the costs to complete the car would not exceed this amount. Refusing to pay more than the contracted price, the Rasnicks removed the partially constructed race car from appellant's shop, with appellant's consent, and subsequently took it to another mechanic for completion. At trial, appellant denied these statements and claimed that he could have finished the car for $5,609.70.

On April 4, 1996, the Rasnicks filed a complaint in the Court of Common Pleas of Marion County, claiming that appellant was in breach of contract and seeking damages in the amount of $25,000, which represented their cost to have the car completed at another shop. A three-day bench trial commenced on February 27, 1997. On June 5, 1997, the trial court issued its judgment entry, granting the Rasnicks $15,903.68 in damages.

Appellant now appeals this decision, asserting two assignments of error.

"Assignment of Error No. One

"The judgment below is contrary to the manifest weight of the evidence and should be reversed because there was no competent credible evidence to establish that the parties had a meeting of the minds and therefore a specific contract that defendant breached that would entitle plaintiff[s] to damages."

Appellant's first assignment of error alleges that the trial court erred in finding a binding contract existed in this case. To the contrary, we find that the trial court had ample evidence before it to determine the existence of a contract.

"A contract is a promise or a set of promises for the breach of which the law gives a remedy, or the performance of which the law in some way recognizes a duty." * * * In order for a party to be bound to a contract, the party must consent to its terms, the contract must be certain and definite, and there must be a meeting of the minds of both parties. * * * Manifestation of mutual assent to an exchange requires that each party either make a promise or begin or render a performance. * * * Normally, mutual assent is effected by offer and acceptance. * * *.

The record in this case is replete with evidence that the parties were of one mind concerning the agreement for the construction of the race car. What began as an oral agreement wherein one party agreed to build a race car and the other party agreed to pay a sum of money in exchange was subsequently put down in a written document entitled a "contract." The terms of the contract were certain and definite. It was stated that the total expenditure by the Rasnicks was to be $52,820, for which they would receive a race car. This price included the cost of parts necessary to complete the car with the exception of the motor, transmission, and clutch assembly. Other parts supplied by the Rasnicks would be deducted from the total purchase price. The Rasnicks agreed to make weekly payments of $1,000 for appellant's labor costs, and appellant was to complete the car within six weeks of receiving the wheels and tires. While the deadline for completion of the car was continually extended, this modification was by agreement of the parties. The parties had a meeting of the minds as to these terms. We find that the record supports the trial court's determination that the parties entered into a binding contract for the construction of a race car. Consequently, appellant's first assignment of error is overruled.

"Assignment of Error No. Two

"The court below erred as a matter of law by failing to deduct the costs of the parts provided by defendant Tubbs in determining the amount of damages awarded."

It is axiomatic that a claimant seeking to recover for a breach of contract must show injuries as a result of the breach in order to recover damages from the breaching party. * * * Damages are not awarded for a mere breach alone. In this case, appellant's failure to fulfill his obligations under the contract resulted in damage to the Rasnicks. The Rasnicks were forced to find another mechanic to finish their car and were faced with thousands of dollars of additional expense. They sought to recover these compensatory costs from appellant. However, when the trial court determined the amount of damages the Rasnicks were entitled to as compensation for appellant's breach of contract, it failed to consider the cost it would take for the Rasnicks to complete their race car. Instead, it appears that the trial court attempted to restore to the Rasnicks the excess monies (benefit) that they had conferred on appellant, thereby granting them restitution damages.

The trial court calculated damages by first determining that the total cost of parts necessary to build the race car was $23,731.57. Deducting this amount from the contract price to be paid by the Rasnicks ($52,820), the court figured that appellant was to receive $29,088.43 for his labor on the project. The trial court then concluded that since the race car was seventy-five-percent complete, appellant should have received only seventy-five percent of $29,088.43, or $21,816.32. Given that the Rasnicks paid him $37,720 for his labor, the trial court found that appellant was overpaid $15,903.68 and awarded the Rasnicks this amount in damages.

The conclusions of law contained in the trial court's judgment entry stated:

> "2. Since defendant has been overpaid $15,903.68, it is logical to assume that figure will compensate the plaintiff[s] and allow the plaintiff[s] to complete the vehicle based on the original agreement of the parties."

We find the trial court's determination of damages to be in error for the following reasons. First, even assuming, *arguendo*, that restitution damages were the correct remedy in this case, the trial court's formula fails to consider costs other than labor incurred by appellant and otherwise fails to employ figures and percentages that can be supported by the record. The evidence at trial was that appellant purchased some of the parts that ultimately comprised the Rasnicks' car; however, the court's award of damages fails to account for these expenditures. To that extent, we sustain appellant's second assignment of error.

Moreover, we can find no evidence in the record justifying the trial court's conclusion that appellant had completed seventy-five percent of the race car construction. Nor does the court explain how it determined that the total cost of parts necessary to complete the car would be $23,731.57. Our review of the record could produce no evidence to support this figure. We recognize that judgments supported by some competent, credible evidence will not be reversed as being against the manifest weight of the evidence.* * * However, as stated above, we find no evidence to support the trial court's determination of damages. Therefore, we must vacate the trial court's award of damages.

Second, we fail to see the logic in the trial court's assumption that the Rasnicks could have their car completed "based on the original agreement of the parties" by another mechanic at the same price they agreed to pay appellant. This statement ignores the fact that not every auto body shop charges the same for labor or has the same markup on parts, as was demonstrated by the testimony and evidence at trial. Furthermore, there was some evidence that appellant may have taken on the race car construction at a lowered price because he thought he would get some advertising benefit from the deal.

This leads us to the final problem with the trial court's award, which is that it fails to give the Rasnicks the compensatory or expectation damages they sought in their complaint. Generally, a party injured by a breach of contract is entitled to his expectation interest or "his interest in having the benefit of his bargain by being put in as good a position as he would have been in had the contract been performed." Restatement of the Law 2d, Contracts (1981) 102–103, Section 344. The fact is that had the contract in this case been performed the Rasnicks would have paid $52,820 for a completed race car. While the trial court's judgment entry cited the often-used principle in contract law that "money damages awarded in a breach of contract action are designed to place the aggrieved party in the same position it would have been in had the contract been performed," the trial court's decision fails to ensure that the Rasnicks reap the benefit of their bargain.

The measure of damages suggested by the Restatement for compensating an expectation interest is calculated as follows:

> "(a) the loss in the value to him of the other party's performance caused by its failure or deficiency, plus
>
> "(b) any other loss, including incidental or consequential loss, caused by the breach, less
>
> "(c) any cost or other loss that he has avoided by not having to perform."

Restatement, *supra*, at Section 347, Comment *e*, Illustration 12; *see Livi Steel, Inc. v. Bank One, Youngstown, N.A.* (1989), 65 Ohio App.3d 581, 589, 584 N.E.2d 1267, 1272.

In this case, the loss in value is the difference between the value of performance rendered without a breach and the value of performance as it was actually rendered. This loss in value is difficult to determine with any certainty, since little if any evidence was presented at trial about the value of appellant's partial performance. Moreover, evidence regarding the percentage of appellant's partial performance was conflicting and did not support the court's finding of seventy-five percent in any event. Because damages for injury to an expectation interest are limited to actual loss, the evidence must establish that loss with reasonable certainty. * * *

Because the loss has not been demonstrated with sufficient certainty, the Rasnicks may recover damages based on "the reasonable cost of completing performance or of remedying the defects if that cost is not clearly disproportionate to the probable loss in value." Restatement, *supra*, at Section 348(2)(b) and Comment *c*, Illustration 2. We find that the record in this case provides evidence regarding such costs. However, it is up to the trial court to determine exactly what value to assign as completion costs, since there was evidence that some expenses incurred by the Rasnicks when finishing the race car may have been avoided. Once the trial court determines the reasonable cost of completing performance, this amount must be decreased by the value of the cost avoided by the Rasnicks. This requires that the trial court determine how much of the original contract price the Rasnicks have paid. The remaining amount that was unpaid under the contract are the costs avoided and must be subtracted from the damages awarded the Rasnicks for completing construction of the race car.

Having found error prejudicial to the appellant herein, in the particulars assigned and argued, we vacate the judgment of the trial court as to the award of damages and remand the cause to the trial court for further proceedings not inconsistent with this opinion. In all other respects, the judgment of the trial court is affirmed.

Judgment affirmed in part, vacated in part and cause remanded.

Shaw, P.J., and Thomas F. Bryant, J., concur.

QUESTIONS

1. Questions about the facts of this case

   1.1. Did Tubbs breach the contract? How? When?

   1.2. Do you think this transaction was handled by parties used to dealing in sizeable business matters? Should that matter?

   1.3. Why did the Rasnicks continue to pay $1000 per week to Tubbs?

   1.4. Do we know what the fair market value of the car was at the time the Resnicks took it back from Tubbs? Is that even relevant?

2. Questions about the law

   2.1. The court skips over the straight application of section 345 of the *Restatement* in favor of a cost of completion formula. Why? What piece of evidence (or put another way, what value) would you need to apply section 345's formula?

   2.2. In applying a cost of completion formula, whose cost of completion is to be accepted? That of Tubbs, or the costs actually paid by the Rasnicks?

   2.3. The Rasnicks now have to go back to trial. What evidence do you think their lawyer should focus on? Who should testify as to these points?

In *Rasnick*, the court did not have evidence as to the diminution in value resulting from defendant's breach and so focused on the cost of completion. What does a court do if it has credible evidence about both the diminution in value and the costs of completion and the two amounts differ significantly?

Groves v. John Wunder Co.
Supreme Court of Minnesota
205 Minn. 163, 286 N.W. 235 (1939)

Stone, Justice:

Action for breach of contract. Plaintiff got judgment for a little over $15,000. Sorely disappointed by that sum, he appeals.

In August, 1927, S. J. Groves & Sons Company, a corporation (hereinafter mentioned simply as Groves), owned a tract of 24 acres of Minneapolis suburban real estate. It was served or easily could be reached by railroad trackage. It is zoned as heavy industrial property. But for lack of development of the neighborhood its principal value thus far may have been in the deposit of sand and gravel which it carried. The Groves company had a plant on the premises for excavating and screening the gravel. Near by defendant owned and was operating a similar plant.

In August, 1927, Groves and defendant made the involved contract. For the most part it was a lease from Groves, as lessor, to defendant, as lessee;

its term seven years. Defendant agreed to remove the sand and gravel and to leave the property "at a uniform grade, substantially the same as the grade now existing at the roadway *** on said premises, and that in stripping the overburden *** it will use said overburden for the purpose of maintaining and establishing said grade."

Under the contract defendant got the Groves screening plant. The transfer thereof and the right to remove the sand and gravel made the consideration moving from Groves to defendant, except that defendant incidentally got rid of Groves as a competitor. On defendant's part it paid Groves $105,000. So that from the outset, on Groves' part the contract was executed except for defendant's right to continue using the property for the stated term. (Defendant had a right to renewal which it did not exercise.)

Defendant breached the contract deliberately. It removed from the premises only "the richest and best of the gravel" and wholly failed, according to the findings, "to perform and comply with the terms, conditions, and provisions of said lease *** with respect to the condition in which the surface of the demised premises was required to be left." Defendant surrendered the premises, not substantially at the grade required by the contract "nor at any uniform grade." Instead, the ground was "broken, rugged, and uneven." Plaintiff sues as assignee and successor in right of Groves.

As the contract was construed below, the finding is that to complete its performance 288,495 cubic yards of overburden would need to be excavated, taken from the premises, and deposited elsewhere. The reasonable cost of doing that was found to be upwards of $60,000. But, if defendant had left the premises at the uniform grade required by the lease, the reasonable value of the property on the determinative date would have been only $12,160. The judgment was for that sum, including interest, thereby nullifying plaintiff's claim that cost of completing the contract rather than difference in value of the land was the measure of damages. The gauge of damage adopted by the decision was the difference between the market value of plaintiff's land in the condition it was when the contract was made and what it would have been if defendant had performed. The one question for us arises upon plaintiff's assertion that he was entitled, not to that difference in value, but to the reasonable cost to him of doing the work called for by the contract which defendant left undone.

1. Defendant's breach of contract was wilful. There was nothing of good faith about it. Hence, that the decision below handsomely rewards bad faith and deliberate breach of contract is obvious. That is not allowable. Here the

rule is well settled, and has been since Elliott v. Caldwell, 43 Minn. 357, 45 N.W. 845, 9 L.R.A. 52, that where the contractor wilfully and fraudulently varies from the terms of a construction contract he cannot sue thereon and have the benefit of the equitable doctrine of substantial performance. That is the rule generally. See Annotation, "Wilful or intentional variation by contractor from terms of contract in regard to material or work as affecting measure of damages." 6 A.L.R. 137.

Jacob & Youngs, Inc. v. Kent, 230 N.Y. 239, 243, 244, 129 N.E. 889, 891, 23 A.L.R. 1429, is typical. It was a case of substantial performance of a building contract. (This case is distinctly the opposite.) Mr. Justice Cardozo, in the course of his opinion, stressed the distinguishing features. "Nowhere," he said, "will change be tolerated, however, if it is so dominant or pervasive as in any real or substantial measure to frustrate the purpose of the contract." Again, "the willful transgressor must accept the penalty of his transgression."

2. In reckoning damages for breach of a building or construction contract, the law aims to give the disappointed promisee, so far as money will do it, what he was promised. (9 Am. Jur., Building and Construction Contracts, § 152.) It is so ruled by a long line of decisions in this state, beginning with Carli v. Seymour, Sabin & Co. 26 Minn. 276, 3 N.W. 348, where the contract was for building a road. There was a breach. Plaintiff was held entitled to recover what it would cost to complete the grading as contemplated by the contract. For our other similar cases, see 2 Dunnell, Minn. Dig. (2 ed. & Supps.) §§ 2561, 2565.

Never before, so far as our decisions show, has it even been suggested that lack of value in the land furnished to the contractor who had bound himself to improve it any escape from the ordinary consequences of a breach of the contract. * * *

Even in case of substantial performance in good faith, the resulting defects being remediable, it is error to instruct that the measure of damage is "the difference in value between the house as it was and as it would have been if constructed according to contract." The "correct doctrine" is that the cost of remedying the defect is the "proper" measure of damages. Snider v. Peters Home Bldg. Co. 139 Minn. 413, 414, 416, 167 N.W. 108.

Value of the land (as distinguished from the value of the intended product of the contract, which ordinarily will be equivalent to its reasonable cost) is no proper part of any measure of damages for wilful breach of a building contract. The reason is plain.

The summit from which to reckon damages from trespass to real estate is its actual value at the moment. The owner's only right is to be compensated for the deterioration in value caused by the tort. That is all he has lost. But not so if a contract to improve the same land has been breached by the contractor who refuses to do the work, especially where, as here, he has been paid in advance. The summit from which to reckon damages for that wrong is the hypothetical peak of accomplishment (not value) which would have been reached had the work been done as demanded by the contract.

* * *

Suppose a contractor were suing the owner for breach of a grading contract such as this. Would any element of value, or lack of it, in the land have any relevance in reckoning damages? Of course not. The contractor would be compensated for what he had lost, i.e., his profit. Conversely, in such a case as this, the owner is entitled to compensation for what he has lost, that is, the work or structure which he has been promised, for which he has paid, and of which he has been deprived by the contractor's breach.

To diminish damages recoverable against him in proportion as there is presently small value in the land would favor the faithless contractor. It would also ignore and so defeat plaintiff's right to contract and build for the future. To justify such a course would require more of the prophetic vision than judges possess. This factor is important when the subject matter is trackage property in the margin of such an area of population and industry as that of the Twin Cities.

* * *

The objective of this contract of present importance was the improvement of real estate. That makes irrelevant the rules peculiar to damages to chattels, arising from tort or breach of contract. Crowley v. Burns Boiler & Mfg. Co. 100 Minn. 178, 187, 110 N.W. 969, 973, dealt with a breach of contract for the sale of a steam boiler. The court observed:

> "If the application of a particular rule for measuring damages to given facts results in more than compensation, it is at once apparent that the wrong rule has been adopted."

That is unquestioned law, but for its correct application there must be ascertainment of the loss for which compensation is to be reckoned. In tort, the thing lost is money value, nothing more. But under a construction contract, the thing lost by a breach such as we have here is a physical structure or accomplishment, a promised and paid for alteration in land. That is the "injury" for which the law gives him compensation. Its only appropriate measure is the cost of performance.

It is suggested that because of little or no value in his land the owner may be unconscionably enriched by such a reckoning. The answer is that there can be no unconscionable enrichment, no advantage upon which the law will frown, when the result is but to give one party to a contract only what the other has promised; particularly where, as here, the delinquent has had full payment for the promised performance.

3. It is said by the Restatement, Contracts, § 346, Comment b:

> "Sometimes defects in a completed structure cannot be physically remedied without tearing down and rebuilding, at a cost that would be imprudent and unreasonable. The law does not require damages to be measured by a method requiring such economic waste. If no such waste is involved, the cost of remedying the defect is the amount awarded as compensation for failure to render the promised performance."

The "economic waste" declaimed against by the decisions applying that rule has nothing to do with the value in money of the real estate, or even with the product of the contract. The waste avoided is only that which would come from wrecking a physical structure completed, or nearly so, under the contract. The cases applying that rule go no further. Illustrative are Buchholz v. Rosenberg, 163 Wis. 312, 156 N.W. 946; Burmeister v. Wolfgram, 175 Wis. 506, 185 N.W. 517. Absent such waste, as it is in this case, the rule of the Restatement, Contracts, § 346, is that "the cost of remedying the defect is the amount awarded as compensation for failure to render the promised performance." That means that defendants here are liable to plaintiff for the reasonable cost of doing what defendants promised to do and have wilfully declined to do.

It follows that there must be a new trial. The initial question will be as to the proper construction of the contract. Thus far the case has been considered from the standpoint of the construction adopted by plaintiff and acquiesced in, very likely for strategic reasons, by defendants. The question has not been argued here, so we intimate no opinion concerning it, but we put the question whether the contract required removal from the premises of any overburden. The requirement in that respect was that the overburden should be used for the purpose of "establishing and maintaining" the grade. A uniform slope and grade were doubtless required. But whether, if it could not be accomplished without removal and deposit elsewhere of large amounts of overburden, the contract required as a condition that the grade everywhere should be as low as the one recited as "now existing at the roadway" is a question for initial consideration below.

The judgment must be reversed with a new trial to follow.

So ordered.

QUESTIONS

1. Questions about the facts of this case

   1.1. The plaintiff in this case sued as "assignee and successor in right of Groves." Does that mean that Groves was paid money to sell his lawsuit? If so, why do we care about whether the land is restored to grade?

   1.2. Why didn't the defendant just volunteer to buy the land for, say, $13,000?

2. Questions about the law

   2.1. The court started off by noting that the breach was wilful. So? Are damages increased just because of the mental state of the contract breacher? If not, then why are the intentions of the breacher relevant?

   2.2. Do you think the court would reach a different result if the cost of repair were $1,000,000 (such as is often the case with environmental cleanups of dumping sites), but the value after repair was still only $12,000? Why or why not?

   2.3. Why does the court mention *Jacob & Youngs*, *supra*, at 788? How are the cases similar? How are they different? Is the breaching party in this case the plaintiff or the defendant? Was the breaching party in *Jacob & Youngs* the plaintiff or the defendant? Does that matter?

   2.4. Recall that the court noted that this contract involves the "improvement of real estate." Why does the court then say that rules for damages for breach of contracts relating to chattels are "irrelevant"?

2.5. Recall the court's discussion of "economic waste." Does the court understand the concept of economic waste? What is the defendant's economic waste argument in this case?

2.6. Can the theory of efficient breach, discussed with *Paton*, *supra*, at 846, be used to explain the result in this case?

Peevyhouse v. Garland Coal & Mining Co.
Supreme Court of Oklahoma
382 P.2d 109 (1962)

Jackson, Justice.

In the trial court, plaintiffs Willie and Lucille Peevyhouse sued the defendant, Garland Coal and Mining Company, for damages for breach of contract. Judgment was for plaintiffs in an amount considerably less than was sued for. Plaintiffs appeal and defendant cross-appeals.

In the briefs on appeal, the parties present their argument and contentions under several propositions; however, they all stem from the basic question of whether the trial court properly instructed the jury on the measure of damages.

Briefly stated, the facts are as follows: plaintiffs owned a farm containing coal deposits, and in November, 1954, leased the premises to defendant for a period of five years for coal mining purposes. A 'strip-mining' operation was contemplated in which the coal would be taken from pits on the surface of the ground, instead of from underground mine shafts. In addition to the usual covenants found in a coal mining lease, defendant specifically agreed to perform certain restorative and remedial work at the end of the lease period. It is unnecessary to set out the details of the work to be done, other than to say that it would involve the moving of many thousands of cubic yards of dirt, at a cost estimated by expert witnesses at about $29,000.00. However, plaintiffs sued for only $25,000.00.

During the trial, it was stipulated that all covenants and agreements in the lease contract had been fully carried out by both parties, except the remedial work mentioned above; defendant conceded that this work had not been done.

Plaintiffs introduced expert testimony as to the amount and nature of the work to be done, and its estimated cost. Over plaintiffs' objections, defendant thereafter introduced expert testimony as to the 'diminution in value' of plaintiffs' farm resulting from the failure of defendant to render performance as agreed in the contract—that is, the difference between the present value of the farm, and what its value would have been if defendant had done what it agreed to do.

At the conclusion of the trial, the court instructed the jury that it must return a verdict for plaintiffs, and left the amount of damages for jury determination. On the measure of damages, the court instructed the jury that it might consider the cost of performance of the work defendant agreed to do, 'together with all of the evidence offered on behalf of either party'.

It thus appears that the jury was at liberty to consider the 'diminution in value' of plaintiffs' farm as well as the cost of 'repair work' in determining the amount of damages.

It returned a verdict for plaintiffs for $5000.00—only a fraction of the 'cost of performance', but more than the total value of the farm even after the remedial work is done.

On appeal, the issue is sharply drawn. Plaintiffs contend that the true measure of damages in this case is what it will cost plaintiffs to obtain performance of the work that was not done because of defendant's default. Defendant argues that the measure of damages is the cost of performance 'limited, however, to the total difference in the market value before and after the work was performed'.

It appears that this precise question has not heretofore been presented to this court. In Ardizonne v. Archer, 72 Okl. 70, 178 P. 263, this court held that the measure of damages for breach of a contract to drill an oil well was the reasonable cost of drilling the well, but here a slightly different factual situation exists. The drilling of an oil well will yield valuable geological information, even if no oil or gas is found, and of course if the well is a producer, the value of the premises increases. In the case before us, it is argued by defendant with some force that the performance of the remedial work defendant agreed to do will add at the most only a few hundred dollars to the value of plaintiffs' farm, and that the damages should be limited to that amount because that is all plaintiffs have lost.

Plaintiffs rely on Groves v. John Wunder Co., 205 Minn. 163, 286 N.W. 235, 123 A.L.R. 502. In that case, the Minnesota court, in a substantially similar situation, adopted the 'cost of performance' rule as-opposed to the 'value' rule. The result was to authorize a jury to give plaintiff damages in the amount of $60,000, where the real estate concerned would have been worth only $12,160, even if the work contracted for had been done.

It may be observed that Groves v. John Wunder Co., supra, is the only case which has come to our attention in which the cost of performance rule has been followed under circumstances where the cost of performance greatly exceeded the diminution in value resulting from the breach of contract. Incidentally, it appears that this case was decided by a plurality rather than a majority of the members of the court.

Defendant relies principally upon Sandy Valley & E. R. Co., v. Hughes, 175 Ky. 320, 194 S.W. 344; Bigham v. Wabash-Pittsburg Terminal Ry. Co., 223 Pa. 106, 72 A. 318; and Sweeney v. Lewis Const. Co., 66 Wash. 490, 119 P. 1108. These were all cases in which, under similar circumstances, the appellate courts followed the 'value' rule instead of the 'cost of performance' rule. Plaintiff points out that in the earliest of these cases (Bigham) the court cites as authority on the measure of damages an earlier Pennsylvania tort case, and that the other two cases follow the first, with no explanation as to why a measure of damages ordinarily followed in cases sounding in tort should be used in contract cases. Nevertheless, it is of some significance that three out of four appellate courts have followed the diminution in value rule under circumstances where, as here, the cost of performance greatly exceeds the diminution in value.

The explanation may be found in the fact that the situations presented are artificial ones. It is highly unlikely that the ordinary property owner would agree to pay $29,000 (or its equivalent) for the construction of 'improvements' upon his property that would increase its value only about ($300) three hundred dollars. The result is that we are called upon to apply principles of law theoretically based upon reason and reality to a situation which is basically unreasonable and unrealistic.

In Groves v. John Wunder Co., supra, in arriving at its conclusions, the Minnesota court apparently considered the contract involved to be analogous to a building and construction contract, and cited authority for the proposition that the cost of performance or completion of the building as contracted is ordinarily the measure of damages in actions for damages for the breach of such a contract. * * *

Even in the case of contracts that are unquestionably building and construction contracts, the authorities are not in agreement as to the factors to be considered in determining whether the cost of performance rule or the value rule should be applied. The American Law Institute's Restatement of the Law, Contracts, Volume 1, Sections 346(1)(a)(i) and (ii) submits the proposition that the cost of performance is the proper measure of damages 'if this is possible and does not involve unreasonable economic waste'; and that the diminution in value caused by the breach is the proper measure 'if construction and completion in accordance with the contract would involve *unreasonable economic waste*'. (Emphasis supplied.) In an explanatory comment immediately following the text, the Restatement makes it clear that the 'economic waste' referred to consists of the destruction of a substantially completed building or other structure. Of course no such destruction is involved in the case now before us.

On the other hand, in McCormick, Damages, Section 168, it is said with regard to building and construction contracts that '*** in cases where the defect is one that can be repaired or cured without undue expense' the cost of performance is the proper measure of damages, but where '*** the defect in material or construction is one that cannot be remedied without *an expenditure for reconstruction disproportionate to the end to be attained*' (emphasis supplied) the value rule should be followed. The same idea was expressed in Jacob & Youngs, Inc. v. Kent, 230 N.Y. 239, 129 N.E. 889, 23 A.L.R. 1429, as follows:

> 'The owner is entitled to the money which will permit him to complete, unless the cost of completion is grossly and unfairly out of proportion to the good to be attained. When that is true, the measure is the difference in value.'

It thus appears that the prime consideration in the Restatement was 'economic waste'; and that the prime consideration in McCormick, Damages, and in Jacob & Youngs, Inc. v. Kent, supra, was the relationship between the expense involved and the 'end to be attained'—in other words, the 'relative economic benefit'.

In view of the unrealistic fact situation in the instant case, and certain Oklahoma statutes to be hereinafter noted, we are of the opinion that the 'relative economic benefit' is a proper consideration here. This is in accord with the recent case of Mann v. Clowser, 190 Va. 887, 59 S.E.2d 78, where, in applying the cost rule, the Virginia court specifically noted that '*** the defects are remediable from a practical standpoint and the costs *are not grossly disproportionate to the results to be obtained*' (Emphasis supplied).

* * *

We therefore hold that where, in a coal mining lease, lessee agrees to perform certain remedial work on the premises concerned at the end of the lease period, and thereafter the contract is fully performed by both parties except that the remedial work is not done, the measure of damages in an action by lessor against lessee for damages for breach of contract is ordinarily the reasonable cost of performance of the work; however, where the contract provision breached was merely incidental to the main purpose in view, and where the economic benefit which would result to lessor by full performance of the work is grossly disproportionate to the cost of performance, the damages which lessor may recover are limited to the diminution in value resulting to the premises because of the non-performance.

We believe the above holding is in conformity with the intention of the Legislature as expressed in the statutes mentioned, and in harmony with the better-reasoned cases from the other jurisdictions where analogous fact situations have been considered. It should be noted that the rule as stated does not interfere with the property owner's right to 'do what he will with his own' Chamberlain v. Parker, 45 N.Y. 569), or his right, if he chooses, to contract for 'improvements' which will actually have the effect of reducing his property's value. Where such result is in fact contemplated by the parties, and is a main or principal purpose of those contracting, it would seem that the measure of damages for breach would ordinarily be the cost of performance.

The above holding disposes of all of the arguments raised by the parties on appeal.

Under the most liberal view of the evidence herein, the diminution in value resulting to the premises because of non-performance of the remedial work was $300.00. After a careful search of the record, we have found no evidence of a higher figure, and plaintiffs do not argue in their briefs that a greater diminution in value was sustained. It thus appears that the judgment was clearly excessive, and that the amount for which judgment should have been rendered is definitely and satisfactorily shown by the record.

We are asked by each party to modify the judgment in accordance with the respective theories advanced, and it is conceded that we have authority to do so. * * *

We are of the opinion that the judgment of the trial court for plaintiffs should be, and it is hereby, modified and reduced to the sum of $300.00, and as so modified it is affirmed.

Welch, Davison, Halley, and Johnson, JJ., concur.

Williams, C. J., Blackbird, V. C. J., and Irwin and Berry, JJ., dissent.

IRWIN, Justice (dissenting). By the specific provisions in the coal mining lease under consideration, the defendant agreed as follows:

> '*** '7b Lessee agrees to make fills in the pits dug on said premises on the property line in such manner that fences can be placed thereon and access had to opposite sides of the pits.
>
> '7c Lessee agrees to smooth off the top of the spoil banks on the above premises.
>
> '7d Lessee agrees to leave the creek crossing the above premises in such a condition that it will not interfere with the crossings to be made in pits as set out in 7b.
>
> '7f Lessee further agrees to leave no shale or dirt on the high wall of said pits. * * *'

Following the expiration of the lease, plaintiffs made demand upon defendant that it carry out the provisions of the contract and to perform those covenants contained therein.

Defendant admits that it failed to perform its obligations that it agreed and contracted to perform under the lease contract and there is nothing in the record which indicates that defendant could not perform its obligations. Therefore, in my opinion defendant's breach of the contract was wilful and not in good faith.

Although the contract speaks for itself, there were several negotiations between the plaintiffs and defendant before the contract was executed. Defendant admitted in the trial of the action, that plaintiffs insisted that the above provisions be included in the contract and that they would not agree to the coal mining lease unless the above provisions were included.

In consideration for the lease contract, plaintiffs were to receive a certain amount as royalty for the coal produced and marketed and in addition thereto their land was to be restored as provided in the contract.

Defendant received as consideration for the contract, its proportionate share of the coal produced and marketed and in addition thereto, the right to use plaintiffs' land in the furtherance of its mining operations.

The cost for performing the contract in question could have been reasonably approximated when the contract was negotiated and executed and there are no conditions now existing which could not have been reasonably anticipated by the parties. Therefore, defendant had knowledge, when it prevailed upon the plaintiffs to execute the lease, that the cost of performance might be disproportionate to the value or benefits received by plaintiff for the performance.

Defendant has received its benefits under the contract and now urges, in substance, that plaintiffs' measure of damages for its failure to perform should be the economic value of performance to the plaintiffs and not the cost of performance.

If a peculiar set of facts should exist where the above rule should be applied as the proper measure of damages, (and in my judgment those facts do not exist in the instant case) before such rule should be applied, consideration should be given to the benefits received or contracted for by the party who asserts the application of the rule.

Defendant did not have the right to mine plaintiffs' coal or to use plaintiffs' property for its mining operations without the consent of plaintiffs. Defendant had knowledge of the benefits that it would receive under the contract and the approximate cost of performing the contract. With this knowledge, it must be presumed that defendant thought that it would be to its economic advantage to enter into the contract with plaintiffs and that it would reap benefits from the contract, or it would have not entered into the contract.

Therefore, if the value of the performance of a contract should be considered in determining the measure of damages for breach of a contract, the value of the benefits received under the contract by a party who breaches a contract should also be considered. However, in my judgment, to give consideration to either in the instant action, completely rescinds and holds for naught the solemnity of the contract before us and makes an entirely new contract for the parties.

* * *

In my judgment, we should follow the case of Groves v. John Wunder Company, 205 Minn. 163, 286 N.W. 235, 123 A.L.R. 502, which defendant agrees 'that the fact situation is apparently similar to the one in the case at bar', and where the Supreme Court of Minnesota held:

> 'The owner's or employer's damages for such a breach (i. e. breach hypothesized in 2d syllabus) are to be measured, not in respect to the value of the land to be improved, but by the reasonable cost of doing that which the contractor promised to do and which he left undone.'

The hypothesized breach referred to states that where the contractor's breach of a contract is wilful, that is, in bad faith, he is not entitled to any benefit of the equitable doctrine of substantial performance.

In the instant action defendant has made no attempt to even substantially perform. The contract in question is not immoral, is not tainted with fraud, and was not entered into through mistake or accident and is not contrary to public policy. It is clear and unambiguous and the parties understood the terms thereof, and the approximate cost of fulfilling the obligations could have been approximately ascertained. There are no conditions existing now which could not have been reasonably anticipated when the contract was negotiated and executed. The defendant could have performed the contract if it desired. It has accepted and reaped the benefits of its contract and now urges that plaintiffs' benefits under the contract be denied. If plaintiffs' benefits are denied, such benefits would inure to the direct benefit of the defendant.

Therefore, in my opinion, the plaintiffs were entitled to specific performance of the contract and since defendant has failed to perform, the proper measure of damages should be the cost of performance. Any other measure of damage would be holding for naught the express provisions of the contract; would be taking from the plaintiffs the benefits of the contract and placing those benefits in defendant which has failed to perform its obligations; would be granting benefits to defendant without a resulting obligation; and would be completely rescinding the solemn obligation of the contract for the benefit of the defendant to the detriment of the plaintiffs by making an entirely new contract for the parties.

I therefore respectfully dissent to the opinion promulgated by a majority of my associates.

QUESTIONS AND NOTE

1. Questions about the facts of this case

   1.1. In what ways is this case factually similar to *Groves*?

   1.2. Is there an allegation of intentional breach here? Does it matter?

2. Questions about the law

   2.1. What would be the waste in forcing Garland to do what it said it would do?

   2.2. Both *Peevyhouse* and *Groves* cite Judge Cardozo's opinion in *Jacob & Youngs v. Kent, supra*, at 788. Who has the better citation?

   2.3. Could this ruling be overcome with "apt and certain" drafting; *e.g.*, could the lease have said "Regardless of the economic waste that might be involved, Garland hereby promises to restore the land to its original state upon completion of the strip mining."? What if the Peevyhouses had inserted a liquidated damages clause of $50,000 upon non-performance of the restoration obligation? $500,000?

   2.4. Which decision—*Groves* or *Peevyhouse*—is more consistent with the protection of expectation approach to contracts damages? Which decision is more consistent with Section 348 of the *Restatement (Second) of Contracts*?

3. Note

Great cases, great doggerel:

We picked a fine time to strip mine, Lucille.
It sure looks to me like we got a raw deal.
That smooth city-slicker said we'd all get rich quicker
I should have known it warn't real.
We picked a fine time to strip mine, Lucille.

* * *

We picked a fine time to strip mine, Lucille.
Make no mistake, hon, we got a raw deal,
I never went to law school,

I didn't know the value rule,
I thought sure we'd win our appeal,
The Supreme Court done gyped us, Lucille.

Sung to the tune of "You Picked a Fine Time to Leave Me Lucille," as sung by Kenny Rodgers. *See* Judith Maute, Peevyhouse v. Garland Coal & Mining Co. *Revisited: The Ballad of Willie and Lucille*, 89 NW. U. L. REV. 1341, 1345 (1995), for the full text of the tune, and for a fascinating examination of the case.

D. Damages Supplementary to Precise Benefit of Bargain: Transaction Costs and Incidental Damages

In a perfect world, the expectation interest would fully compensate. But this is not a perfect world. All sorts of costs are incurred when scrambling to react to another party's breach. Phone calls, return costs and other hassles ensure that the expectation interest, while theoretically sufficient, be practically insufficient.

It would thus seem that many costs associated with breach are not technically part of the calculation of expectation interests. Can they be recovered as part of the general measure of damages? Section 347 of the *Restatement* includes in the calculation of damages "any other loss, including incidental . . . loss, caused by the breach." The example the *Restatement* gives is *Mr. Eddie, Inc., v. Ginsberg*, 430 S.W.2d 5 (Tex. Ct. App. 1968), where a 65-year old man was dismissed improperly from his job as a commercial buyer of women's clothes. In addition to damages related to loss of wages, Ginsberg incurred additional costs as follows:

> In connection with the effort made by appellee to secure employment the evidence shows that he went to a merchandise mart meeting where ninety five percent of the manufacturers showed their lines but he could find no one interested in his services; that he ran an advertisement for eight days in the Womens' Wear Daily, answered every advertisement that appeared in the Womens' Wear Daily, the Wall Street Journal, the Dallas Times Herald, the Dallas News and paid extra to have the Womens' Wear Daily specially delivered to him; that he had a resumé prepared and sent to prospective employers in response to advertise-

> ments, notified all prospective employers that he would relocate anywhere in the world and made job applications for employment in Germany, Israel and Greece; that he listed his availability with employment agencies, made trips to New York and Houston seeking employment and incurred $1,340.36 expense [sic] seeking other employment

Id. at 8.

The court allowed these additional expenses as costs incurred incidental to breach.

The U.C.C. tries to define such damages in section 2-715(1). That section states:

> (1) Incidental damages resulting from the seller's breach include expenses reasonably incurred in inspection, receipt, transportation and care and custody of goods rightfully rejected, any commercially reasonable charges, expenses or commissions in connection with effecting cover and any other reasonable expense incident to the delay or other breach.

This is a fairly broad grant of power to award damages related to the breach, and is reflective of the common law.

One key cost that many aggrieved parties have to pay to get relief is attorneys' fees. Can they be categorized as incidental damages? In America, no. The so-called "American Rule" requires each party to bear his or her own attorneys' fees, unless otherwise provided for in the contract itself (or by statute, as in civil rights cases). *See Bunnett v. Smallwood*, 793 P.2d 157 (Colo. S. Ct. 1990) (*en banc*) (general rule in contracts); *Indiana Glass Co. v. Indiana Michigan Power Co.*, 692 N.E.2d 886 (Ind. Ct. App. 1998) (under U.C.C. § 2-715). Some states, such as California, make the provision of attorneys' fees reciprocal; that is, if one side is entitled to receive them by contract, so is the other side, even if the agreement does not specifically provide. Cal. Civ. Code § 1717.

Try your creativity in connecting costs to breaches with the following problems:.

Problems on Incidental Damages

1. *Interest Costs*

   Epstein goes to Local Car Co. to buy a car. Not only will Local Car Co. sell him a car, but it directs Epstein to a bank to enable him to finance it. The car, unfortunately is a lemon. While Epstein sues Local, however, he still is paying on the loan taken out to acquire the car. General measures of damages will help Epstein pay off the principal balance of this loan, but can Epstein recover the interest and loan fees as incidental damages?

2. *Reliance Costs*

   Ponoroff contracts with Markell to sell Markell swamp land in Florida. Markell incurs title search costs and attorneys' fees in checking out Ponoroff's title (which he said was just fine). This investigation turns up the fact that the property has several mortgages about which Ponoroff just "forgot." Moreover, their existence breaches Ponoroff's agreement with Markell to convey clean title.

   (a) May Markell, in addition to other damages, recover his title search costs and attorneys' fees? Does it matter if the title company used an attorney, and its costs are just the title company's bill with its own attorney?

   (b) Would the result change if Ponoroff had not agreed to convey clean title, but the contract instead made Markell's obligation to pay for the land conditioned on there being clean title?

SECTION 6: LIMITATION ON MONEY DAMAGES

As set forth above, the general measure of damages is measured by the expectation interest. Markell gets as damages that which would have put him in the same position as he would have been had the other party not breached. In most cases, Markell will be satisfied by receiving either costs of repair or the difference between the contract rate and the market rate for whatever was being exchanged.

But what if the breach relates to the acquisition of a good or service that Markell was going to use to make money elsewhere? A generic example would be if Markell ordered a Grade A widgets for $5 each, intending to incorporate them into a machine that transforms widgets into foobars, which he can sell for $10 a piece. For this process Markell needs Grade A widgets; Grade B or C widgets don't cut it. If the vendor of widgets sends Markell a Grade C widget, he has breached. The vendor's first response might be to offer Markell the difference in price between Grade A and Grade C widgets—assume that difference to be $2.

But Markell wants more. He lost the ability to sell the transformed widget (as a foobar) for $10; in short, after deducting the cost of a Grade A widget, Markell lost $5 as a consequence of the vendor's breach. Not surprisingly, such damages are often referred to as "consequential" and sometimes as "special" damages.

An example comes from Judge Richard Posner, of the Seventh Circuit. In *Evra Corp. v. Swiss Bank Co.*, 673 F.2d 951 (7th Cir. 1982) (Evra Corp. was formerly known as Hyman-Michaels Co.), Hyman-Michaels had a deal to ship goods by boat. The price for the contract was $27,000, to be paid in advance. Hyman-Michaels arranged for the funds to go from its bank, Continental, to Swiss Bank, and then from Swiss Bank to Bank Paribas, the bank used by the vessel's owner. Swiss Bank failed to execute its part of the transaction, and had no excuse for its default. When the funds were not received, the vessel's owner canceled the deal. Hyman-Michaels tried to arbitrate the cancellation, and lost. It then sued Swiss Bank for the cost of the arbitration, and the loss of the profit on the deal involving the boat. As Judge Posner explains:

> When a bank fails to make a requested transfer of funds, this can cause two kinds of loss. First, the funds themselves or interest on them may be lost, and of course the fee paid for the transfer, having bought nothing, becomes a loss item. These are "direct" (sometimes called "general") damages. Hyman-Michaels is not seeking any direct damages in this case and apparently sustained none. It did not lose any part of the $27,000; although its account with Continental Bank [from which the $27,000 was to come] was debited by this amount prematurely, it was not an interest-bearing account so Hyman-Michaels lost no interest; and Hyman-Michaels paid no fee either to Continental or to Swiss Bank for the aborted transfer. A second type of loss, which either the payor or the payee may suffer, is a dislocation in one's business triggered by the failure to pay. Swiss Bank's failure to transfer funds to the Banque de Paris when requested to do so by Continental Bank set off a chain reaction

which resulted in an arbitration proceeding that was costly to Hyman-Michaels and in the cancellation of a highly profitable contract. It is those costs and lost profits—"consequential" or, as they are sometimes called "special" damages—that Hyman-Michaels seeks in this lawsuit.

The damages for failure to wire the $27,000 was *$2,100,000*, which is the profit Hyman-Michaels figured it lost when it could not ship the goods because of the cancellation of the shipping contract.

If this all seems a tad metaphysical, perhaps a more concrete example would help. Federal Express charges different rates depending on when you want your package to arrive. For purposes of an example, say that they charge $25 for 9:00 am delivery tomorrow, and $10 for second day delivery. You need to send your resume to a firm so that you can get that hot job next summer paying $8000 per month (which your professor assures you is yours if you timely get in your resumé for consideration). Thus, you need to get the resume to the firm positively, absolutely tomorrow.

You take your resume to FedEx, pay the $25 and go home to await the call that will put you on easy street. But the call doesn't come, since FedEx delivered the letter on the second day after you posted it. When you complain to FedEx, they offer to refund you $15—after all, that is the difference between the performance you requested and the performance they rendered.

But $15 isn't enough, is it? As a consequence of FedEx's breach, you lost out on a lucrative job. Shouldn't FedEx pay you for your lost job opportunity? The next case, a contracts classic, begins the answer to that question. As you read it, think of the "contract of carriage" as a 19th Century version of FedEx.

A. Foreseeability

Hadley v. Baxendale

9 Ex. 341, 156 Eng.Rep. 145 (Court of the Exchequer 1854)

At the trial before Crompton, J., at the last Gloucester Assizes, it appeared that the plaintiffs carried on an extensive business as millers at Gloucester; and that, on the 11th of May, their mill was stopped by a breakage of the crank shaft by which the mill was worked. The steam-engine was manufactured by Messrs. Joyce & Co., the engineers, at Greenwich, and it became necessary to send the shaft as a pattern for a new one to Greenwich. The fracture was discovered on the 12th, and on the 13th the plaintiffs sent one of their servants to the office of the defendants, who are the well known carriers trading under the name of Pickford & Co., for the purpose of having the shaft carried to Greenwich. The plaintiffs' servant told the clerk that the mill was stopped, and that the shaft must be sent immediately; and in answer to the inquiry when the shaft would be taken, the answer was, that if it was sent up by twelve o'clock any day, it would be delivered at Greenwich on the following day. On the following day the shaft was taken by the defendants, before noon, for the purpose of being conveyed to Greenwich, and the sum of 2£. 4s. was paid for its carriage for the whole distance; at the same time the defendants' clerk was told that a special entry, if required, should be made to hasten its delivery. The delivery of the shaft at Greenwich was delayed by some neglect; and the consequence was, that the plaintiffs did not receive the new shaft for several days after they would otherwise have done, and the working of their mill was thereby delayed, and they thereby lost the profits they would otherwise have received.

On the part of the defendants, it was objected that these damages were too remote, and that the defendants were not liable with respect to them. The learned Judge left the case generally to the jury, who found a verdict with 25£. damages beyond the amount paid into Court.

Whateley, in last Michaelmas Term, obtained a rule nisi for a new trial, on the ground of misdirection.

Keating and Dowdeswell showed cause.

Alderson, B. We think that there ought to be a new trial in this case; but, in so doing, we deem it to be expedient and necessary to state explicitly the rule which the Judge, at the next trial, ought, in our opinion, to direct the jury to be governed by when they estimate the damages.

It is, indeed, of the last importance that we should do this; for if the jury are left without any definite rule to guide them, it will, in such cases as these, manifestly lead to the greatest injustice. The Courts have done this on several occasions; and, in Blake v. Midland Railway Company (18 Q.B. 93), the Court granted a new trial on this very ground, and the rule had not been definitely laid down to the jury by the learned Judge at Nisi Prius.

"There are certain established rules," this Court says, in Alder v. Keighley, 15 M. & W. 117, "according to which the jury ought to find." And the Court, in that case, adds: "and here there is a clear rule, that the amount which would have been received if the contract had been kept, is the measure of damages if the contract is broken."

Now we think the proper rule in such a case as the present is this:— Where two parties have made a contract which one of them has broken, the damages which the other party ought to receive in respect of such breach of contract should be such as may fairly and reasonably be considered either arising naturally, i.e., according to the usual course of things, from such breach of contract itself, or such as may reasonably be supposed to have been in the contemplation of both parties, at the time they made the contract, as the probable result of the breach of it. Now, if the special circumstances under which the contract was actually made were communicated by the plaintiffs to the defendants, and thus known to both parties, the damages resulting from the breach of such a contract, which they would reasonably contemplate, would be the amount of injury which would ordinarily follow from a breach of contract under these special circumstances so known and communicated. But, on the other hand, if these special circumstances were wholly unknown to the party breaking the contract, he, at the most, could only be supposed to have had in his contemplation the amount of injury which would arise generally, and in the great multitude of cases not affected by any special circumstances, from such a breach of contract. For, had the special circumstances been known, the parties might have specially provided for the breach of contract by special terms as to the damages in that case; and of this advantage it would be very unjust to deprive them. Now the above principles are those by which we think the jury ought to be guided in estimating the damages arising out of any breach of contract. It is said, that other cases, such as breaches of contract in the nonpayment of money, or in the not making a good title to land, are to be treated as exceptions from this, and as governed by a conventional rule. But as, in such cases, both parties must be supposed to be cognisant of that well-known rule, these cases may, we think, be more properly classed under the rule above enunciated as to cases under known special circumstances, because there both parties may reasonably be presumed to contemplate the estimation of the amount of damages according to the conventional rule. Now, in the present case, if we are to apply the principles above laid down, we find that the only circumstances here communicated by the plaintiffs to the defendants at the time the contract was made, were, that the article to be carried was the broken shaft of a mill, and that the plaintiffs were the millers of that mill. But how do these circumstances show reasonably that the profits of the mill must be stopped by an unreasonable delay in the delivery of the broken shaft by the carrier to the third person? Suppose the plaintiffs had another shaft in their possession put up or putting up at the time, and that they only wished to send back the broken shaft to the engineer who made it; it is clear that this would be quite consistent with the above circumstances, and yet the unreasonable delay in the delivery would have no effect upon the intermediate profits of the mill. Or, again, suppose, that, at the time of the delivery to the carrier, the machinery of the mill had been in other respects defective, then, also, the same results would follow. Here it is true that the shaft was actually sent back to serve as a model for a new one, and that the want of a new one was the only cause of the stoppage of the mill, and that the loss of profits really arose from not sending down the new shaft in proper time, and that this arose from the delay in delivering the broken one to serve as a model. But it is obvious that, in the great multitude of cases of millers sending off broken shafts to third persons by a carrier under ordinary circumstances, such consequences would not, in all probability, have occurred; and these special circumstances were here never communicated by the plaintiffs to the defendants. It follows, therefore, that the loss of profits here cannot reasonably be considered such a consequence of the breach of contract as could have been fairly and reasonably contemplated by both the parties when they made this contract. For such loss would neither have flowed naturally from the breach of this contract in the great multitude of such cases occurring under ordinary circumstances, nor were the special circumstances, which, perhaps, would have made it a reasonable and natural consequence of such breach of contract, communicated to or known by the defendants. The Judge ought, therefore to have told the jury that, upon the facts then before them, they ought not to take the loss of profits into consideration at all in estimating the damages. There must therefore be a new trial in this case.

Rule absolute.

QUESTIONS AND NOTES

1. Questions about the facts of this case

   1.1. Who are the players here, and what are their roles? Who, for example, is "Alderson, B."? Who are Whateley, Keating and Dowdeswell? Where does the opinion begin? For that matter, who is Hadley? Where is Baxendale? Answers to this quiz later.

1.2. Trick question: Did Pickford & Co. receive notice of the urgency of the shipment?

2. Questions about the law

2.1. *Hadley* has been practically unanimously adopted in the United States and is studied by virtually every sentient first year law student; indeed, Grant Gilmore stated that "Hadley v. Baxendale is still, and presumably always will be, a fixed star in the jurisprudential firmament." THE DEATH OF CONTRACT 83 (1974). Can you surmise why?

2.2. What type of notice or knowledge does *Hadley* require in order to be able to collect consequential damages?

2.3. Would it made any difference if the defendant had delivered the crankshaft on time, but so negligently handled the crankshaft in transporting it that the repairs on it cost the mill five days of delay to fix it? Are tort damages different from contract damages in this case? Should they be?

3. Notes

3.1. *Victoria Laundry (Windsor) Ltd. v. Newman Industries, Ltd.* [1949] 2 K.B. 528, 537, 1 All E.R. 997 expressed the opinion that the headnote to *Hadley* is "definitely misleading in so far as it says that the defendants' clerk, who attended at the office, was told that the mill was stopped and that the shaft must be delivered immediately." In *Victoria Laundry*, the defendants had agreed to sell to the plaintiff launderers a large steam boiler which, as the defendants knew, was desired for immediate use. Delivery was made some five months after the date fixed in the contract. The late delivery was a breach. Victoria Laundry commenced an action for loss of bargain, asking: (1) loss of profits of £16 a week for the very large number of new customers they could have serviced with the new boiler, and (2) £ 262 a week which they could have earned under dyeing contracts with the Ministry of Supply. The court of appeal held Newman Industries liable for "business profits" during the five month period, but not liable for the profits plaintiffs would have realized on the "particularly lucrative" dyeing contracts because Newman Industries had not been told of the contract when agreeing to sell the boiler.

3.2. Do you need actual agreement that one party will be liable for consequential damages of a particular sort, or do you just need notice of that fact? Evaluate the following clauses:

a. Seller acknowledges that Buyer needs the widgets being sold hereunder to meet its obligations under a contract with Bamco.

b. Seller agrees and understands that Buyer will use the widgets hereunder to meet its obligations hereunder in Buyer's contract with Bamco. Time is of the essence under the Bamco contract so any failure by seller to make timely delivery of widgets under this contract will result in default under the Bamco contract.

c. Time is of the essence for all performance due under this contract.

d. Seller agrees that should it default, Buyer's damages will include any and all lost profits under Buyer's contract with Bamco, and Seller agrees to assume that risk and responsibility.

Which clause is more likely to result in an award of consequential damages? Which clause is more likely to be agreed to by the parties during their negotiations? If you represented the Seller, and the Buyer presented the language found in item (d), what would advise your client to do? If you represented the Buyer and delivered the language in item (d), would you be surprised if the Seller countered with a price increase request?

3.3. The "Terms and Conditions" for Federal Express' contract with its customers state the following:

[Federal Express] will not be liable for any damage, whether direct, incidental, special or consequential in excess of the declared value of a shipment, whether or not Federal Express had knowledge that such damage might be incurred including but not limited to loss of income or profits.

Do you think FedEx's lawyers have read *Hadley*?

3.4. *Hadley*'s history is unearthed in Richard Danzig, *Hadley v Baxendale A Study in the Industrialization of the Law*, 4 J. LEGAL STUD. 249

(1975). Professor Danzig's article was then substantially incorporated in his excellent book THE CAPABILITY PROBLEM IN CONTRACT LAW 68–107 (1978).

3.5. The concept of small acts leading to large consequences is common and venerable. See the following from Benjamin Franklin:

For want of a nail the shoe was lost;
For want of a shoe the horse was lost;
And for want of a horse the rider was lost;
For the want of a rider the battle was lost;
For the want of the battle the kingdom was lost;
And all for the want of a horseshoe-nail.

Benjamin Franklin, *Preface: Note to Courteous Readers*, POOR RICHARD'S ALMANACK (1758). The poem, in some form, is attributed to George Herbert (1651), *quoted in* JOHN BARTLETT, FAMILIAR QUOTATIONS 270 (15th ed. 1980).

3.6. Answer to quiz from note 1:

"Alderson, B." is Baron Alderson, a law lord of the Court of the Exchequer. He was one of only fifteen judges with general jurisdiction in all of England at the time of the decision. He is hearing an appeal from a county court, where the case was heard in Assize session.

Whateley, Keating and Dowdeswell are counsel for the respective parties; the style of English reports from this time period was to include a summary of the arguments of counsel in the opinion; you can see this in early editions of the reports of the United States Supreme Court as well.

Joseph and Jonah Hadley were the proprietors of City Steam Mills, the flour mill that engaged Pickford & Co. to transport the mill shaft.

Joseph Baxendale was one of the managing directors of Pickford & Co.; under the rules of agency and company law then-existing in England, managing directors were personally liable for the unpaid debts of their unincorporated businesses. It was not until 1855 that England extended limited liability to companies not chartered by Parliament.

3.7. Again, more doggerel:

> There once was a young man named Hadley
> Whose contract of transport went badly.
> "My mill shaft is gone,
> All my goods are in pawn,
> And my business is closed," he said sadly.

Douglass Boshkoff, *Selected Poems on The Law of Contracts: Raintree County Memorial Library Occasional Paper No. 1*, 66 N.Y.U. L. REV. 1533, 1542 (1991).

How does Hadley play out in normal transactions? The following will give you some clue.

Manouchehri v. Heim
Court of Appeals of New Mexico
123 N.M. 439, 941 P.2d 978 (1997)

Hartz, Chief Judge.

Jeff Heim sold Dr. A. H. Manouchehri a used x-ray machine. Manouchehri sued for breach of warranty and was awarded $4400 in damages after a bench trial. Heim appeals, claiming the following errors:* * (2) direct damages based on the cost of repair should not have been awarded because there was no evidence of such cost; and (3) consequential damages should not have been awarded because (a) Manouchehri could have avoided them by obtaining a replacement machine; (b) they were not foreseeable, and (c) they were not proved with the required certainty. We affirm.

I. BACKGROUND

Manouchehri was the sole witness at trial. Heim presented no evidence other than through cross-examination of Manouchehri. We summarize Manouchehri's testimony.

Manouchehri is a physician in Cedar Crest, New Mexico. Heim, a sales representative of a medical supply company, had previously sold various items to Manouchehri. In December 1991 Heim learned that Manouchehri wanted to buy a used 100/100 x-ray machine. The two numbers refer to the rating of the machine in kilovolts and milliamps, respectively. The rating of the machine affects the quality of the image obtained. A weak machine often will not be able to produce adequate images.

On December 9 Manouchehri purchased a machine from Heim. He paid with a check for $1900 on which he wrote at the top "guaranteed to work (install Continental 100-100 x-ray) without limitation" and wrote on the memo line "purchase and installation of Continental 100-100 x-ray." Heim signed his name on the front of the check after Manouchehri read the notations to him.

During the following weeks Manouchehri realized that the machine was performing as a 100/60 machine. The power was sufficient only for x-rays of small children and thin people. Manouchehri notified Heim and asked him to repair it, offering to pay half the repair costs. Although Heim sent someone to inspect the machine, no repairs were made. Manouchehri continued to talk regularly with Heim about the problem until the lawsuit was filed in September 1994. Heim at first denied knowing that the x-ray machine was a 100/60 machine but later admitted that he knew. At that time he indicated that it was the sort of machine one can buy for only $1900.

Manouchehri initially obtained a default judgment, but it was later set aside. After trial on April 4, 1996 Manouchehri obtained judgment in the amount of $4400. Of the total, $1900 was for direct contract damages and $2500 was for consequential damages. The district court denied Heim's motion for reconsideration and Heim appealed.

* * *

III. DAMAGES

Heim does not dispute the district court's finding that he breached a warranty to provide Manouchehri with a 100/100 x-ray machine. His appeal focuses on the propriety of the award of damages. The decretal language of the court's judgment was as follows:

> IT IS, THEREFORE, ORDERED, ADJUDGED AND DECREED that [Manouchehri] is entitled to judgment against [Heim] in the amount of $1,900.00, for the cost of repair of the X-ray machine and the amount of $2,500.00 for incidental damages for a total of $4,400.00.

A contract for the sale of merchandise is governed by Article 2 of the Uniform Commercial Code. See NMSA 1978, § § 55-2-102 and -105(1)

(Repl. Pamp. 1993). For breach of warranty the buyer may recover direct, incidental, and consequential damages. The statutory provisions applicable to this appeal are NMSA 1978, § § 55-2-714 and -715 (Repl. Pamp. 1993). The pertinent portions of Section 55-2-714 state:

> (2) The measure of damages for breach of warranty is the difference at the time and place of acceptance between the value of the goods accepted and the value they would have had if they had been as warranted, unless special circumstances show proximate damages of a different amount.
>
> (3) In a proper case any incidental and consequential damages under the next section may also be recovered.

Section 55-2-715 states:

> (1) Incidental damages resulting from the seller's breach include expenses reasonably incurred in inspection, receipt, transportation and care and custody of goods rightfully rejected, any commercially reasonable charges, expenses or commissions in connection with effecting cover and any other reasonable expense incident to the delay or other breach.
>
> (2) Consequential damages resulting from the seller's breach include:
>
> (a) any loss resulting from general or particular requirements and needs of which the seller at the time of contracting had reason to know and which could not reasonably be prevented by cover or otherwise; and
>
> (b) injury to person or property proximately resulting from any breach of warranty.

Of the $4400 awarded by the district court, $1900 is for direct damages under Section 55-2-714 and $2500 is for damages under Section 55-2-715. Heim challenges both figures. We first discuss direct damages.

A. Direct Damages

The judgment awarded Manouchehri $1900 for the cost to repair the x-ray machine. The cost of repair can be an appropriate measure of direct damages. Although Section 55-2-714(2) sets the measure of direct damages for breach of warranty as the difference between the value of the goods as warranted and the value of the goods as accepted, often that difference can be approximated by the cost to repair the goods so that they conform to the warranty. For example, if it costs $200 to fix the x-ray machine so that it performed as a 100/100 machine, then one could assume that the unrepaired machine (the "goods accepted") was worth $200 less than the repaired machine (the goods "as warranted"). Thus, the cost of repair is commonly awarded as the direct damages. See 1 James J. White & Robert S. Summers, Uniform Commercial Code § 10-2, at 554 (4th ed. 1995); * * *

As pointed out by Heim, however, there was no evidence at trial of the cost to repair the x-ray machine. On the contrary, the evidence at trial was that the machine could not be transformed into a 100/100 machine. Consequently, Manouchehri could not be awarded direct damages based on a cost of repair. As stated in a leading treatise:

> There are many cases in which the goods will be irreparable or not replaceable and therefore the costs of repair or replacement cannot serve as a yardstick of the buyer's damages. In those cases, the court will have to find some other way to measure the difference between the value of the goods as warranted and the value of the goods as accepted.

1 White & Summers, supra, § 10-2, at 557.

Nevertheless, we affirm the award of $1900 as direct damages. When to do so would not be unfair to the appellant, we can affirm a ruling by the trial court on a ground other than what was expressed by that court. * * * Such a course is particularly appropriate in this case because our review of the record indicates that the district court in fact computed the direct damages on a proper ground even though the judgment does not state that ground.

At the hearing on Heim's motion for reconsideration, Heim's attorney properly stated the law, arguing that Manouchehri's direct damages should be limited to the difference between the value of the x-ray machine as warranted and the value of the machine as it was delivered to Manouchehri. He sought to set aside the award of $1900 on the basis that there was insufficient evidence to support it. Acknowledging that the sales price constituted sufficient evidence of the value of the machine as warranted, see 1 White & Summers, supra, § 10-2, at 557 ("The purchase price of the damaged goods may be the best evidence of the value of the goods as warranted."), he focused his argument on the alleged absence of evidence to support a finding regarding the value of the machine delivered to Manouchehri.

The district court did not dispute the contentions of Heim's attorney as to the proper measure of damages, but it rejected the claim that there was insufficient evidence regarding the value of the machine delivered to Manouchehri. Indeed, Finding No. 5 in the district court's decision states: "Any value to [Manouchehri] of the X-Ray machine 'as is' is offset by the cost to [Manouchehri] of having the machine removed from his premises." On appeal Heim has not challenged this finding. As we understand Finding No. 5, the court determined that Manouchehri could not recover any money for the machine; at the conclusion of trial the court had said, "I presume that someone will be willing to remove the machine for its residual value." * * * Hence, we do not find it unfair to affirm the district court's award of $1900 in direct damages as the difference between the value of the x-ray machine as warranted and the value of the machine actually delivered to Manouchehri.

B. Consequential Damages

The district court's judgment awarded "$2500 for incidental damages." Again, the judgment was not prepared with sufficient care. The damage award was clearly for consequential damages, not incidental damages. See § 55-2-715 (defining "incidental" and "consequential" damages). Finding No. 6 of the district court's decision states: "[Manouchehri] has suffered consequential damages in the form of loss of business of at least $2,500.00 during the time [Manouchehri] reasonably waited for [Heim] to repair the X-Ray machine or otherwise perform under the guarantee."

Manouchehri's testimony with respect to consequential damages was straightforward. He said that taking an x-ray would cost him from three to six dollars and he would charge "about $85 to $88" for taking and reading an x-ray. He also claimed that the inadequacy of the machine prevented him from taking at least 30 x-rays a month, although he had no documentation to support his estimate. Using the lowest possible profit per x-ray, Manouchehri contended in closing argument that the monthly loss would be $2370—computed by multiplying $79 net income per x-ray times 30 x-rays a month.

Heim contends that the award is improper for three reasons. First, he contends that Manouchehri failed to present evidence that he could not avoid the damages by renting or buying a substitute machine. Second, he contends that any lost profits were not reasonably foreseeable. Third, he contends that the proof of damages was too indefinite. Each of Heim's arguments has some force. But they must be examined in light of the district court's award of only $2500. It appears that the district court cons dered the three matters raised by Heim and adjusted the award accordingly. We now examine each of Heim's arguments.

1. Failure to Obtain Replacement Machine

Consequential damages are not recoverable if they could "reasonably be prevented by cover or otherwise." Section 55-2-715(2)(a). Heim argues that Manouchehri needed to present evidence that he could not avoid the damages by renting or buying a substitute machine. On the record before us, we reject the argument.

Manouchehri testified that he asked Heim to have someone repair the machine and that Heim responded that he would have someone come to the office for that purpose. Manouchehri further testified that he talked to Heim on a monthly basis regarding the problem and that until about a month before he filed the lawsuit he believed that Heim would fix the problem.

The UCC requirement to take reasonable steps to prevent consequential damages derives from standard contract law. In particular, guidance in interpreting Section 55-2-715(2)(a) can be found in the Restatement (Second) of Contracts § 350 (1981). See 1 White & Summers, supra, § 10-4, at 577 ("Restatement [§ 350] may be regarded as an articulation of the rules embodied in the adverb 'reasonably' in 2-715."). Restatement, supra, Section 350 reads:

> Avoidability as a Limitation on Damages
>
> (1) Except as stated in Subsection (2), damages are not recoverable for loss that the injured party could have avoided without undue risk, burden or humiliation.
>
> (2) The injured party is not precluded from recovery by the rule stated in Subsection (1) to the extent that he has made reasonable but unsuccessful efforts to avoid loss.

The comment to this section states that it may be reasonable to rely on a breaching party's assurances that the breach will be remedied. See id. cmt. g and illus. 19* * * .

We cannot say that it was unreasonable as a matter of law for Manouchehri to delay seeking a replacement machine for a few months. The district court found that Manouchehri "suffered consequential damages in the form of loss of business of at least $2,500.00 during the time [he] reasonably waited for [Heim] to repair the X-Ray machine or otherwise perform under the guarantee." The district court did not state how long it was reasonable for Manouchehri to wait, nor did it state how much business Manouchehri lost in any particular month. Nevertheless, we see no need for mathematical precision in the circumstances of this case. The question is only whether it was rational for the district court to find, on the basis of the evidence presented, that by the time Manouchehri should have stopped relying on Heim's promises, he had lost at least $2500 in profits. Our answer is yes.

2. Foreseeability

Heim next argues that the lost profits cannot be awarded because Manouchehri failed to present any evidence on the issue of foreseeability. He relies on the language in Section 55-2-715(2)(a) that restricts recovery for consequential damages to losses "resulting from general or particular requirements . . . of which the seller at the time of contracting had reason to know. . . ." We are not persuaded.

This was not a sale of a mass-produced item to an anonymous buyer. Heim knew his customer and knew how the x-ray machine was to be used. Any reasonable person in his position would assume that a doctor using such a machine would charge more for its use than the cost of operation and would earn income from it. Moreover, Manouchehri testified to conversations with Heim that at least touched on the economics of the machine. For example, Manouchehri related one occasion when parts from an old failed x-ray machine were in front of his office:

> [Heim] asked that I had that x-ray and what to do with them and how come it was still sitting there. And I told him that this was a failed x-ray and I am stuck with the loss of this much money. And at that time he promised me, quoting from him, that "I know a doctor that has just [the] x-ray that you want. X-ray 100/100 is what you want, and I can get it for you and install in your office for this much money.

On the evidence at trial the district court could properly find that lost income would be a foreseeable consequence of an underpowered x-ray machine. * * * Although Manouchehri did not tell Heim how much income he would earn from use of the machine, he did not need to do so in order to recover consequential damages so long as the consequence of lost income was reasonably foreseeable. The law does not require those who enter into contracts to disclose to other parties the profits they expect to make from the contracts. See Richard A. Posner, Economic Analysis of Law 115 (3d ed. 1986) ("Any other rule would make it difficult for a good bargainer to collect damages unless before the contract was signed he had made disclosures that would reduce the advantage of being a good bargainer—disclosures that would prevent the buyer from appropriating the gains from his efforts to identify a resource that was undervalued in its present use.");* * * Perhaps some limit could be placed on recovery for particularly large lost profits, cf. Restatement, supra, § 351(3) (court may limit damages for foreseeable loss "in order to avoid disproportionate compensation"), but the award of $2500 in this case was within proper bounds.

3. Certainty of Proof of Damages

Finally, Heim argues that the evidence of lost profits was not certain enough. We disagree. We recognize that "when it is possible to present accurate evidence on the amount of damages, the party upon whom the burden rests to prove damages must present such evidence." * * * This requirement must be understood, however, in the context of the amount at stake. What it is "possible" to present in a suit for a million dollars may be an excessive burden for a small claim. Although Manouchehri's evidence was minimal, it was adequate in the circumstances. The absence of detail and documentary corroboration detracted from the weight of the testimony, but the district court could still find it sufficiently credible to support the $2500 award.

IV. CONCLUSION

We affirm the judgment below.

QUESTIONS

1. Questions about the facts of this case

    1.1. What value did the court place on the X-ray machine as delivered?

    1.2. Why do you suppose that Heim put on no evidence? Were you Heim's counsel, what types of evidence would you have introduced?

2. Questions about the law

 2.1. The cost of the X-ray machine was $1900. Why did the court award more than the purchase price?

 2.2. Did this court really say that the Doctor's proof would have been inadequate if the amounts at issue had at three more zeros after them? Why? Isn't this discriminatory justice?

 2.3. What if the item at issue was not an X-ray machine sold by a salesman the doctor knew, but a $2500 mail-order computer? Would consequential damages, in this court's opinion, be proper in that case?

 2.4. Correspondence with counsel confirms that there was no written contract in this case. Review question: How did the plaintiff get by the statute of frauds?

B. Certainty

As indicated in *Manouchehri*, there are two other limitations on damages besides foreseeabilty: damages must be proved with certainty, and the aggrieved party needs to minimize, or mitigate, her damages. Let's take certainty first. How much certainty? Well, remember *ESPN v. Major League Baseball, supra*, at 804? Read on.

ESPN, Inc. v. Office of the Commissioner of Baseball

U.S. District Court, Southern District of New York
76 F. Supp. 2d 416 (1999)

Shira A. Scheindlin, U.S.D.J.:

On October 15, 1999, ESPN, Inc. ("ESPN") and the Office of the Commissioner of Baseball ("Baseball") moved in limine to preclude the admission of certain evidence and argument at their forthcoming trial. Ten separate motions—five by ESPN and five by Baseball—were fully submitted on October 29, 1999. Six of the motions were resolved by opinion dated November 22, 1999 [which is reprinted above, at 804]. Three of the motions were resolved from the bench during a hearing on November 23, 1999. The final motion, ESPN's motion in limine to preclude damages evidence, is the subject of this Opinion and Order.

I. ESPN's Motion in Limine to Preclude Damages Evidence

In my November 22 opinion, I ruled that ESPN breached its 1996 telecasting agreement ("1996 Agreement") with Baseball when it preempted six baseball games scheduled for Sunday nights in September 1998 and September 1999 without the prior written approval of Baseball. See ESPN, Inc. v. Office of the Commissioner of Baseball, 76 F. Supp. 2d 383 (S.D.N.Y. 1999). ESPN broadcast NFL football games rather than the previously scheduled baseball games on those six nights.

Baseball claims that it has been damaged in an amount "believed to exceed millions of dollars" as a result of ESPN's breach of the 1996 Agreement. * * * Baseball attributes its damages to an alleged loss of:

(1) national television exposure;

(2) promotional opportunities and ratings;

(3) value of the "Sunday Night Baseball" television package;

(4) prestige;

(5) potential sponsorships; and

(6) the future value of all of Baseball's national telecast packages

* * * Because Baseball received full payment from ESPN under the contract, it may only seek extra-contractual damages stemming from the six preemptions.

By its motion, ESPN seeks to preclude Baseball from introducing testimony or other evidence of its alleged monetary damages. ESPN contends that "there is no factual basis to support any claim for monetary damages arising from these perceived injuries, and that such claims are the product of speculation and guesswork." * * * Baseball argues that it has made the "requisite showing of damage" and therefore it is "entitled to have the opportunity to prove its damages at trial." * * *

II. Legal Standard

It is well-settled under New York law that

> [a] plaintiff seeking compensatory damages has the burden of proof and should present to the court a proper basis for ascertaining the damages [it] seeks to recover. They must be susceptible of ascertainment in some manner other than by mere conjecture or guesswork.

Dunkel v. McDonald, 272 A.D. 267, 70 N.Y.S.2d 653, 656 (1st Dep't 1947), aff'd, 298 N.Y. 586, 81 N.E.2d 323 (1948). * * * Although it is true that "when the existence of damage is certain, and the only uncertainty is as to its amount, the plaintiff will not be denied recovery of substantial damages," but even then the plaintiff must show "a stable foundation for a reasonable estimate" of damages. * * *

With respect to damages for loss of goodwill, business reputation or future profits, the proof requirements are much more stringent.* * * Not only must the claimant prove the fact of loss with certainty, but the "loss must be 'reasonably certain in amount.' " * * * "In other words, the damages may not be merely possible speculative or imaginary but must be reasonably certain and directly traceable to the breach, not remote or the result of other intervening causes." * * *

III. Baseball's Proffered Damages Evidence

During discovery, ESPN served Baseball with interrogatories regarding its claims for monetary damages. Among other things, ESPN asked Baseball to "state the amount of monetary damages you seek in this action and explain the basis for the computation of your claim." ESPN Interrogatory No. 6, Ex. A to Lobenfeld Aff. at 7. Baseball responded as follows:

> Baseball has not quantified the amount of damages it has sustained by reason of ESPN's willful refusal to carry [baseball] games as required by the 1996 Agreement. A quantification of those damages, however real, is extremely complex and for that reason Baseball insisted, and ESPN agreed, in the 1996 Agreement that ESPN would produce and distribute the telecasts and that its failure to do so could be specifically enforced, without regard to the need for Baseball to prove irreparable harm. At its essence the damages, believed to exceed millions of dollars, are attributable to [loss of national television exposure; promotional opportunities and ratings; value of the "Sunday Night Baseball" television package; prestige; potential sponsorships; and the future value of all of Baseball's national telecast packages].

Id. at 7–8.[2] Nowhere in its response does Baseball set forth any specific dollar amount of monetary damages other than its estimate that damages are "believed to exceed millions of dollars." Nor does Baseball set forth any method of calculating its alleged damages.

As the following excerpts demonstrate, Baseball's [designated] witness on the topic of damages, Baseball's President Paul Beeston, was equally speculative and vague regarding the alleged harm caused by ESPN's breach.

> Q: Has Baseball quantified any of the damages it alleges in this case?
>
> A: No, we have not quantified it to the extent of a specific dollar, no.
>
> Q: Has Baseball made any calculations as to any specific element of its alleged damages?
>
> A: We have not.
>
> Q: Is there a reason why Baseball has not done any calculation of its damages in this case?
>
> A: No. We just believe it's significant. We believe that the case speaks for itself at the present time, and we have not worked out what the dollars are of the damages.

9/27/99 Deposition of Paul Beeston ("Beeston Dep.") at 6–7.

> * * *
>
> Q: What's the basis for your belief that Baseball's alleged damages exceed millions of dollars?

[2]Baseball's interrogatory response is quite revealing. Baseball concedes that it had agreed that in the event of a breach it would seek "specific[] enforcement" without the need to prove "irreparable harm." Baseball's failure to seek that specific enforcement is puzzling and leads one to question whether it really wanted the games aired, or whether it really wanted an excuse to renegotiate a contract which it no longer found sufficiently lucrative. On the other hand, ESPN's behavior is also suspect. In the November 22 opinion, I held that ESPN should not have engaged in self-help but should have sought judicial intervention as to whether Baseball's failure to grant permission to broadcast football in place of baseball games was unreasonable. ESPN's failure leads one to question whether the fear of an adverse ruling, and the accompanying loss of millions of dollars in revenues, caused ESPN to choose the option of intentionally breaching its contract.

> A: Based on what we have right here and what we've said what we've got here going forward. I don't have anything specific, as I said.
>
> Q: If somebody suggested to you that they believed you're right, Baseball was damaged but it's only a hundred thousand dollars, would you be able to point me to anything to say it's not a hundred thousand dollars, it's a million dollars?
>
> A: Specifically I won't be able to say this is what it is, try this calculation and that's the way it works out, no.

Id. at 28.

> * * *
>
> Q: Can you point to anything specific as evidence that ESPN's [breach] has made Baseball less valuable in any way?
>
> A: "Specifically, no if you're asking for one example that I could give you. . . ."
>
> Q: You say you think it probably hurt you. Are you able to point to us specifically—
>
> A: No, I said I cannot.

Id. at 10–11. Not once during his deposition did Beeston offer a concrete example of harm or monetary loss stemming from Baseball's breach. Baseball's expert witness, Robert J. Wussler, was similarly unable to cite specific examples of loss. During his deposition, Wussler testified as follows:

> Q: Are you aware of any money that Baseball lost as a result of those three games?
>
> A: No I'm not.
>
> Q: And the same thing is true in '99, same question with respect to '99?
>
> A: They've lost in perception. It's very hard to evaluate dollars and perception.
>
> Q: I'm not going to ask you about perception. You are not aware of any dollars lost, correct?
>
> A: I'm not.

10/15/99 Deposition of Robert J. Wussler at 92–93.

* * *

Q: Again, just so I'm clear, are you aware of 5 cents of advertising revenue that Baseball lost as a result of the three games being [not shown on ESPN]—

A: No I'm not.

Id. at 107.

* * *

Q: I take it you are not aware of any lost sponsors or lost advertisers; is that correct?

A: That is correct.

Id. at 108.

Finally, on November 23, this Court held oral argument on ESPN's motion to preclude damages evidence. During that argument, this Court specifically asked counsel for Baseball whether Baseball had any "concrete proof of monetary harm." * * *. In response, counsel for Baseball merely reiterated the entirely subjective and speculative assertion that Baseball "feel[s] this was very dilatory [sic] to our position and denigrated our product and cost us in the marketplace and otherwise." * * * Counsel for Baseball was unable to show "any loss of sponsorship, any loss of advertising, [or] any loss of ancillary sales or ticket sales." * * * As counsel for Baseball conceded: "We have not shown specific losses your Honor, we agree with you there. What we have said is we believe it did affect us."[3]

IV. Discussion

As the above-quoted testimony and answers to ESPN's interrogatories demonstrate, there can be no question that Baseball has failed to ade-

---

[3]At the end of oral argument, counsel for Baseball set forth, for the very first time, an alternate theory of damages. Baseball proposed that damages be calculated according to the amount it would have sought had ESPN asked Baseball to "sell the right to dump [Baseball] onto [another channel]." 11/23/99 Tr. at 30. In other words, Baseball seeks to calculate damages based on a hypothetical negotiation or sale of the six preempted games.

Regardless of the merits of Baseball's alternate theory, I reject it as a basis for the calculation of damages. Baseball's failure to mention this alternate theory of damages until six days before trial—months after the close of discovery and weeks after the submission of pre-trial motions—bars it from presenting such a theory at trial.

quately demonstrate either the fact of damages or the amount of damages. Put simply, Baseball's subjective belief that the amount of damages is "significant"—no matter how fervent—does not meet any of the required proofs set forth under New York law. Baseball has not cited a single lost promotional opportunity, sponsor or advertising dollar stemming from ESPN's breach. Nor has Baseball set forth any evidence of a decrease in ratings or box office ticket sales. Although damage to Baseball's prestige and future value are difficult to prove, such difficulty does not allow Baseball to proceed with speculative claims of damages. To the contrary, under New York law, a claim of damages for loss of reputation and future profits must be "reasonably certain." * * *

Baseball's damages claim is based on nothing more than its own vague assertions that it was "hurt." Baseball cites no specific examples of monetary damage, nor does it proffer a method for calculating such damages. The proffered unsupported allegations are simply inadequate to sustain a claim for damages under New York law, and therefore ESPN's motion to preclude damages evidence is granted.

V. Nominal Damages and Materiality

Although Baseball is not entitled to an award of money damages, it may still receive nominal damages. "It is a well-settled tenet of contract law that even if the breach of contract caused no loss or if the amount of the loss cannot be proven with sufficient certainty, the injured party is entitled to recover as nominal damages a small sum fixed without regard to the amount of the loss, if any."* * *.[4] Accordingly, I will instruct the jury that if Baseball proves its breach of damages claim, it is entitled to an award of nominal damages.[5]

Baseball's ability to recover only nominal damages does not impede its ability to present testimony and evidence regarding the materiality of ESPN's breach. Materiality goes to the essence of the contract. That is, a breach is material if it defeats the object of the parties in making the contract and

---

[4]Although unable to prove monetary damage, there is no question that Baseball was harmed by virtue of ESPN's breach. Baseball was entitled to the broadcast of six baseball games during September 1998 and September 1999. When ESPN failed to broadcast those games, ESPN was harmed regardless of whether it can prove any monetary damage.

[5]Although ESPN breached the 1996 Agreement when it preempted baseball games without Baseball's approval, in order for Baseball to prove its breach of contract claim, it must first demonstrate that it substantially performed under the contract.

"deprive[s] the injured party of the benefit that it justifiably expected." Farnsworth, Contracts § 8.16 (3d ed. 1999). Materiality does not depend upon the amount of provable money damages, it depends upon whether the nonbreaching party lost the benefit of its bargain. Thus, although Baseball is only entitled to nominal damages, it may still present evidence and argument to the effect that ESPN's breach was material. * * *

VII. Conclusion

For the reasons set forth above, Baseball is precluded from presenting damages evidence at trial and is only entitled to seek an award of nominal damages.

QUESTIONS

1. Questions about the facts of this case

   1.1. Why are the assertions of Baseball that the breach cost them "millions of dollars" to be believed?

   1.2. Does this opinion state that Baseball was not harmed at all?

   1.3. What amount do you think "nominal" damages should be set at? Why do nominal damages even exist? Why not just dismiss the case for failure of proof of an essential element; that is, damages?

2. Questions about the law

   2.1. Why did Baseball not seek specific performance? Wasn't that fatal to its case?

   2.2. What would be "certain" damages in this case?

   2.3. Does this case look like a good candidate for liquidated damages? If so, how would you set them, and how would you draft that clause in the contract?

   2.4. If you were counsel for Baseball, wouldn't you be embarrassed if your bill exceeded the "nominal" damages awarded? Doesn't Baseball have the resources to hire counsel who should have seen this result coming? What do you think happened?

What happens if the fact of damages is clear, but the amount is uncertain? Do you still try and award expectation damages? Or is there some other measure that is more appropriate. The next case, involving an aging celebrity, provides the standard answer.

Hollywood Fantasy Corporation v. Gabor
U.S. Court of Appeals, Fifth Circuit
151 F.3d 203 (1998)

Before King and Wiener, Circuit Judges, and Rosenthal,* District Judge

Rosenthal, District Judge:

Appellee Hollywood Fantasy Corporation was briefly in the business of providing "fantasy vacation" packages that would allow participants to "make a movie" with a Hollywood personality and imagine themselves movie stars, for one week, for a fee. In May 1991, Hollywood Fantasy planned to offer its second fantasy vacation package, in San Antonio, Texas. Hollywood Fantasy arranged to have Zsa Zsa Gabor as one of two celebrities at the event. Two weeks before the fantasy vacation event, Ms. Gabor canceled her appearance. A short time later, Hollywood Fantasy canceled the vacation event, to which it had sold only two tickets. A short time after that, Hollywood Fantasy went out of business.

Hollywood Fantasy sued Ms. Gabor for breach of contract and fraud. After the trial judge found that Ms. Gabor and Hollywood Fantasy had reached a contract, the jury found that Ms. Gabor had breached that contract. The jury awarded Hollywood Fantasy $100,000 for the breach, as well as $100,000 for fraud. The district court set aside the jury's fraud verdict for lack of evidence and entered judgment in favor of Hollywood Fantasy for $100,000 on the breach of contract claim, plus attorneys' fees and post-judgment interest. Ms. Gabor appealed. We affirm the district court's judgment as to liability; reverse the district court's damages award; and render judgment for a lesser amount of damages.

I. The Facts as to Hollywood Fantasy

Leonard Saffir created Hollywood Fantasy and served as its chief executive officer. The company Mr. Saffir created charged each vacation "client"

*District Judge of the Southern District of Texas, sitting by designation.

$7,500 for a week of "pampering," instruction on making movies, rehearsals, and a "starring" role in a short videotaped film with a "nationally known" television or movie star. Mr. Saffir hoped that "bloopers" and "outtakes" from the videotapes would ultimately become the basis for a television series. A new venture, Hollywood Fantasy had conducted only one vacation event before the package scheduled to take place in San Antonio in May 1991. The first event, held in Palm Springs, California, had received some media coverage, but had lost money.

This case began with a letter Hollywood Fantasy sent Zsa Zsa Gabor dated March 4, 1991. The letter opened with the following language:

> This will confirm our agreement whereby Hollywood Fantasy Corporation (HFC) will employ you under the following terms and conditions: . . .

The letter set out the terms and conditions of Ms. Gabor's appearance in fourteen numbered paragraphs. The terms and conditions specified the dates of employment; the hours of work; the duties required; the payment; and certain perquisites to be provided. The letter stated that Ms. Gabor was to be employed from May 2–4, 1991, in San Antonio, Texas; was to be "on call" from after breakfast until before dinner each day; was to act in videotaped "movie" scenes with the clients, using scripts and direction provided by Hollywood Fantasy, and was to join the clients for lunch and dinner; was to allow Hollywood Fantasy to use her name and photograph for publicity; and was to provide media interviews "as appropriate" during her stay in San Antonio. Hollywood Fantasy was to pay Ms. Gabor a $10,000 appearance fee and $1,000 for miscellaneous expenses. Hollywood Fantasy would also provide Ms. Gabor two first-class round-trip plane fares from Los Angeles; transportation to the Los Angeles airport and in San Antonio; hair and makeup services; meals; hotel expenses, excluding long distance telephone calls; and a hotel suite with "two bath rooms if available."

Ms. Gabor made three handwritten changes to this letter before signing and returning it to Mr. Saffir. * * * The last paragraph of the terms and conditions provided an "out clause":

> [Hollywood Fantasy] agrees that if a significant acting opportunity in a film comes up [Gabor] will have the right to cancel [her] appearance in San Antonio by advising [Hollywood Fantasy] in writing by April 15, 1991.

* * * The parties agree that Ms. Gabor sent Mr. Saffir a telegram dated April 15, 1991, stating:

> In accordance with the contract that exists between us the purpose of this telegram is to inform you that I must terminate it because I am due to be involved in preproduction and a promotion film for a motion picture I am contracted to do. The name of the film is Queen of Justice produced by Metro Films of Los Angeles. . . . I am very sorry to cause you any discomfort but will be happy to try to help in supplying you with a replacement and hopefully we'll be able to do something together in the very near future.

Hollywood Fantasy unsuccessfully attempted to replace Ms. Gabor for the San Antonio event. The San Antonio event was canceled; the two ticket purchasers received their money back; Hollywood Fantasy went out of business; and this litigation began.

* * *After a second trial, the jury awarded Hollywood Fantasy $100,000 on its breach of contract claim and $100,000 on its fraud claim. * * * The district court * * * upheld the jury's finding that Ms. Gabor's cancellation was not based on "a significant acting opportunity in a film," as the contract permitted. The district court entered judgment in favor of Hollywood Fantasy for $100,000, plus attorneys' fees and post-judgment interest. Ms. Gabor timely appealed.

* * *

III. The Cancellation Provision

[The court upheld the finding that Ms. Gabor had no commitments on the relevant dates, finding that the opportunity to act in "Queen of Justice" was not conflicting, and that her 14 second cameo role in Naked Gun 2-1/2 was not significant.]

IV. The Evidence on Damages

At trial, Ms. Gabor moved for judgment as a matter of law that there was insufficient evidence to support the jury's award of $100,000 for breach of contract. The district court denied Ms. Gabor's motion. Ms. Gabor renews her objection here.

* * *

"It is a general rule that the victim of a breach of contract should be restored to the position he would have been in had the contract been performed." * * * "However, an injured party may, if he so chooses, ignore the element of profits and recover as damages his expenditures in reliance." * * *

The $100,000 damages award cannot be supported as the recovery of lost profits. Mr. Saffir testified that Hollywood Fantasy lost $250,000 in profits from future fantasy vacation events and at least $1,000,000 in future profits from the creation of a television series based on "bloopers" and "outtakes" from the videotapes of clients "acting" with Hollywood personalities. Although "[r]ecovery of lost profits does not require that the loss be susceptible to exact calculation," * * *, lost profits must be proved with "reasonable certainty."* * * "[A] party claiming injury from lost profits need not produce in court the documents that support his opinions or estimates." * * * A witness may testify "from personal knowledge as to what profits would have been."* * * However, "[a]t a minimum, opinions or estimates of lost profits must be based on objective facts, figures or data from which the amount of lost profits may be ascertained." * * * "Mere speculation" of the amount of lost profits is insufficient. * * *

Leonard Saffir's testimony that Hollywood Fantasy lost $250,000 in future profits was based on his estimate that Hollywood Fantasy would make a $25,000 profit from each of ten future events. Hollywood Fantasy was a new venture. It had put on one event, in which nine people participated, and in which it had lost money. Two weeks before the San Antonio event, only two people had bought tickets for the event. Hollywood Fantasy had no commitments to, or arrangements for, specific future events. "Profits which are largely speculative, as from an activity dependent on uncertain or changing market conditions, or on chancy business opportunities, . . . or on the success of a new and unproven enterprise, cannot be recovered."* * * "The mere hope for success of an untried enterprise, even when that hope is realistic, is not enough for recovery of lost profits." * * * In Texas Instruments, the Texas Supreme Court made it clear that the relevant "enterprise" in the lost profits inquiry is "not the business entity, but the activity which is alleged to have been damaged." * * * There was no evidence at trial that the "movie fantasy vacation" enterprise promoted by Hollywood Fantasy had been a successful enterprise in any context. There was no evidence that the Hollywood Fantasy management had ever been involved in any prior fantasy vacation enterprise, let alone a successful one. * * *

In Texas Instruments, the Texas Supreme Court stated that even a new enterprise may attempt to recover lost profits when there are "firmer reasons" to "expect [the] business to yield a profit." * * *There was no evidence at trial that Hollywood Fantasy had "firm" reasons to expect a profit. Nine participants attended the [earlier] Palm Springs event; not all of those participants paid the full $7,500 price of admission and only "some" of the Hollywood Fantasy employees were paid for their work. As of April 15, 1991, two weeks before the San Antonio event, only two tickets had been sold. Mr. Saffir's testimony that he still expected twenty participants was based on the optimistic but unsupported assertion that people generally "don't send in their money right away."

Hollywood Fantasy's claim for loss of television revenue is even more speculative. Mr. Saffir admitted that he had not sold a television pilot, let alone a series, based on the fantasy vacation videotapes. Mr. Saffir testified that the actors appearing in the videotapes could have unilaterally declined to permit Hollywood Fantasy to use the tapes in a television pilot. Mr. Saffir testified that unidentified producers and others were enthusiastic about the "concept" of such a television series, but he had difficulty even estimating what the profits from a series might be. No "objective facts, figures, or data" substantiated the estimate of lost profits.

Hollywood Fantasy's claims for lost profits also fail because there was no evidence of how Hollywood Fantasy estimated the profits or what data it used to do so. * * *

Mr. Saffir also testified that Hollywood Fantasy lost $200,000 in "goodwill." Under Texas law, the loss of goodwill or business reputation is not recoverable in a breach of contract action. * * *

Hollywood Fantasy also seeks to support the damages awarded as based on evidence of lost investment in the corporation. Mr. Saffir testified that Hollywood Fantasy lost $200,000 that had been invested in the corporation. Under Texas law, "actual damages may be recovered when loss is the natural, probable, and foreseeable consequence of the defendant's conduct." * * * The record must contain evidence that permits the jury "to assess with reasonable certainty the . . . degree of causation of the damage by the breach or interference relative to other factors." * * * It is pure speculation that but for Ms. Gabor's breach, Hollywood Fantasy would not have gone out of business. Hollywood Fantasy had lost money on the Palm Springs event despite the fact that it had not charged the full fee to several participants and had not paid all of its employees. Hollywood Fantasy had sold only two tickets to the San Antonio event. Hollywood Fantasy is not entitled to an award of damages representing a return of $200,000 invested in the corporation.

Although Hollywood Fantasy did not present evidence to base an award of compensatory damages on either lost profits or lost investment, it did present sufficient evidence as to certain out-of-pocket expenses to justify their recovery. Mr. Saffir testified that Hollywood Fantasy incurred the following out-of-pocket expenses for the San Antonio event: (1) $8,500 in printing costs for color brochures and press releases; (2) $12,000 in marketing costs for mailings and advertising; (3) $22,000 in personnel and miscellaneous expenses, including air fares, staff accommodations, script-writing costs, telephone calls, and logo t-shirts; (4) $9,000 in travel expenses for Mr. Saffir and members of the Hollywood Fantasy "staff," including Margo Mayor, Hollywood Fantasy's president; and (5) $6,000 in expenses relating to preparations to film the San Antonio event for a possible television pilot. These expenses total $57,500.[4]

Ms. Gabor objects that this evidence cannot form the basis of a damages award because Mr. Saffir testified that there were documents relating to a few of these expenses, but did not produce any documents at trial. However, the Texas cases Ms. Gabor cites to support her argument do not hold that documentary evidence is required for the recovery of out-of-pocket expenses. In Black Lake Pipe Line Co. v. Union Constr. Co., 538 S.W.2d 80 (Tex.1976), the plaintiff attempted to prove damages by introducing summaries of records. The court held that the summaries were inadmissible hearsay because the plaintiff had failed to make the underlying records available to the defense. Id. at 92–94. The court's holding was based on the plaintiff's failure to comply with the rules governing the admissibility of summaries of voluminous underlying information. Id. at 93–94. The court did not hold that the summaries were inadmissible because they were not the "best evidence" of damages. Nor did the court hold that oral testimony regarding damages, if based on sources other than the flawed summaries themselves, would have been inadmissible. Id. at 94.

* * *

---

[4]The general rule is that the nonbreaching party may only recover out-of-pocket expenses incurred after the contract was formed. See, e.g., Autotrol Corp. v. Continental Water Sys. Corp., 918 F.2d 689, 695 (7th Cir.1990) (applying Texas law); Hough v. Jay-Dee Realty & Inv., Inc., 401 S.W.2d 545, 551 (Mo.Ct.App.1966); see also 3 FARNSWORTH, FARNSWORTH ON CONTRACTS § 12.16, at 262-63 n. 2; Gregory S. Crespi, Recovering Pre- Contractual Expenditures as an Element of Reliance Damages, 49 SMU L. REV. 43, 44 (1995). Mr. Saffir's testimony does not make it clear whether each of these expenses were incurred after Ms. Gabor returned the March 4, 1991 letter. However, Ms. Gabor does not challenge the jury's award on this ground.

Ms. Gabor presented no evidence controverting Mr. Saffir's testimony as to Hollywood Fantasy's lost out-of-pocket expenses for the San Antonio event. Mr. Saffir's testimony as to Hollywood Fantasy's out-of-pocket expenses is sufficient to support an award of $57,500 for breach of contract, but not to support an award of $100,000.[5] The award of $100,000 is reversed in part on the basis that the evidence disclosed in the record does not support compensatory damages beyond $57,500.

* * *

VI. Conclusion

We affirm the district court's judgment with respect to Ms. Gabor's liability for breach of contract. We reverse the district court's award of $100,000 for breach of contract and render judgment in the amount of $57,500, with post-judgment interest from the date of the district court's judgment to the date it is paid, at the rate previously set by the district court, and the attorneys' fees awarded by the district court.

Affirmed in Part and Reversed and Rendered in Part.

QUESTIONS AND NOTES

1. Questions about the facts of this case

   1.1. What evidence did Saffir have of his losses?

   1.2. If Saffir could testify without backup documentation on his "reliance" expenses, then why could he not testify without documentation or history about his lost profits? Isn't he in the best position to assess those losses?

2. Questions about the law

   2.1. In requiring certainty for admitted losses, aren't we knowingly setting up a system that will systematically undercompensate aggrieved par-

[5] Hollywood Fantasy cannot recover the $15,000 it refunded to the two individuals who had bought tickets to the San Antonio event before it was cancelled. The ticket price refund was not an out-of-pocket expense. Hollywood Fantasy presented no testimony as to what portion, if any, of this amount it would have kept as profit had the event gone forward with Ms. Gabor's participation.

ties? Are "reliance" damages a way of giving at least something but which we know is less than full compensation? Do we adjust other parts of the damages formula to reflect this undercompensation?

2.2. If Zsa Zsa could prove that there was no way on Earth that Saffir could have made money on his venture, should the court award any damages, even for costs incurred in reliance on the contract? Does it matter if the venture would have lost only $10,000? $60,000?

3. Notes

3.1. Although receiving a judgment for $57,000, the plaintiff likely did not collect. During this litigation, Zsa Zsa Gabor filed bankruptcy proceedings in Los Angeles. Before filing, however, Ms. Gabor failed to show up for the first-scheduled trial, and wound up with a $3,000,000 default judgment being entered against her. That default was set aside to allow the trial referred to in the opinion to take place.

3.2. In a part of the opinion omitted, the court held that the common law of Texas no longer observed the strict mirror image rule of offer and acceptance, and found that so long as the handwritten changes by Ms. Gabor were not material, her signature acted as an acceptance. This discussion was notable for its inquiry as to whether Ms. Gabor's request for a Neiman-Marcus wardrobe, a term added by handwriting, was a material change or not.

3.3. This case could be viewed as screwy money-making scheme in which a "can't win" idea's only hope is that a solvent participant will breach. Could Zsa Zsa's attorneys have attacked the scheme as hopeless from the beginning, and paid nothing? But then, Mr. Saffir was once described as:

> In his nearly 68 years, the Brooklyn-born Saffir has been a Marine in the Korean War, a foreign press correspondent, a friend of Ferdinand Marcos in his pre-dictator days, a four-time newspaper publisher, a husband three times, a father three times, a Republican U.S. senator's chief of staff, a smuggler of Hebrew Bibles into Communist Russia, a top New York City public relations executive, an author, a television producer, a past president of a foreign press club, a president of a New Jersey-based Internet company, a suc-

cessful player in The Palm Beach Post's stock market game, and, let the record show, an adversary of Zsa Zsa Gabor.

Palm Beach Post, March 16, 1998, Page 1A.

3.4. Here's what the popular press had to say about this case. Read this article, and see if you can decide if it is accurate:

Court: Failed Fantasy Worth Only $57,500

Janet McConnaughey

NEW ORLEANS—Would you pay $7,500 to spend a week pretending to be a Hollywood star, being videotaped with and dining with Zsa Zsa Gabor in San Antonio, Texas?

Two people sent in their money before Gabor pulled out, two weeks before the "fantasy vacation" was to start.

Leonard Saffir, who set it all up, said her cancellation forced his Hollywood Fantasy Corp. out of business and cost him millions of dollars.

Most of that was pure speculation, a federal appeals court ruled Wednesday. However, it did order Gabor to pay $57,500—Hollywood Fantasy's actual expenses—for breaking her 1991 contract.

Among the questions before the 5th U.S. Circuit Court of Appeals was whether a 14-second cameo during credits of "Naked Gun 2 ½" was a significant acting opportunity for Gabor.

She said that that was one reason she canceled. A federal District Court jury in Midland, Texas, said it wasn't a good enough excuse, and the Appeals Court agreed.

The 5th Circuit is the third court to rule in the case.

Gabor was a no-show at her first trial, and a federal District Court jury in San Antonio ordered her to pay the full $3 million Saffir wanted. Another judge threw out the verdict and heard the case after attorney Melvin Belli said that Gabor had never been told of the trial date in San Antonio.

The second jury ruled that Gabor owed Saffir $200,000, half for breach of contract and half for fraud. The judge threw out the fraud verdict, but accepted the breach of contract claim.

After the 5th Circuit heard arguments in the case, Gabor, under court order to pay Elke Sommers $3.3 million for calling her a haggard Hollywood has-been, asked a bankruptcy court for protection from her creditors.

That stopped Saffir's case until the California bankruptcy court agreed in March 1997 that it could go forward.

The $3 million he claimed in damages included $250,000 in profits from 10 future fantasy vacations and at least $1 million from a planned television series of "bloopers" from the videotapes.

However, the 5th Circuit noted, Hollywood Fantasy had lost money on its only previous fantasy vacation, which attracted nine paying customers; it had sold only two tickets to Gabor's week; and it had no arrangements for any future events.

Nor had Saffir sold a television pilot, and he acknowledged that the actors could have refused to let Hollywood Fantasy use the tapes, the appeals court said.

However it said he did provide enough evidence about his out-of-pocket expenses, including $6,000 to prepare to film the San Antonio event for a possible TV pilot, to add up to the $57,500 award.

THE BATON ROUGE ADVOCATE, Aug. 14, 1998, Page 7B.

C. Mitigation

The final limitation on damages has nothing to do with the breacher's conduct, but the conduct of the party *not* in breach. It responds to the simple question: Must the non-breaching party act so as not to run up damages? Take the following situation: Ponoroff contracts with Epstein to build a shrine to all esteemed Deans of the Tulane Law School. The shrine is to be constructed of bright green material, with a wave motif throughout. In short, it will be so "special" that no one else in their right mind would want it. The agreed price is $50,000. Epstein thinks that the cost of materials will be $35,000. Before purchasing anything or starting any preparation, Ponoroff calls and tells Epstein that he has changed his mind, and that the project is off. Epstein, unfazed, completes the work anyway, and sues for the full contract price, or $50,000.

Does he get it? No. At most, he will get $15,000. Why? When Epstein continued work after being told unequivocally that Ponoroff was breaching, his additional losses after that point can no longer be said to stem from the breach. In short, after hearing of the repudiation, any work he voluntarily takes on after that point is on his dime. He could have avoided the incurrence of the $35,000 of costs by simply not incurring them.

This notion is normally referred to as "mitigation;" that is, a non-breaching party cannot simply continue to perform after being told that the other side will breach, and then charge the breaching party the full contract price. The causal link between breach and damage is broken when the non-breaching party learns that the other side will not pay.

That makes sense when you can avoid additional costs and losses by simply doing nothing. But are there times when you must take affirmative action in mitigation of damages. Read the next two cases.

Fair v. Red Lion Inn

Supreme Court of Colorado
943 P.2d 431 (1997)

Justice SCOTT delivered the Opinion of the Court.

In Fair v. Red Lion Inn, 920 P.2d 820 (Colo. App. 1995), we granted certiorari to address a single question: whether as a matter of law, the refusal of an employee to accept her former employer's unconditional offer of reinstatement, after a breach of contract by the employer, constitutes a failure to mitigate damages on the part of the employee. Because we conclude that a discharged employee has a duty to mitigate damages by accepting an unconditional offer of reinstatement in the absence of special circumstances, we affirm the judgment of the court of appeals.

I.

A.

In June 1987, the respondent, Red Lion Inn (Red Lion), a hotel operator, hired petitioner, Patricia Fair (Fair), as a server in its Colorado Springs restaurant, Maxi's Dining Room. When hired, Fair signed the "Red Lion Inns Employment Agreement Condition of Employment" (Employment Agreement). Among other matters, the Employment Agreement provided that Fair's employment with Red Lion was at will, and that she could be discharged with or without cause. At the same time, Red Lion gave Fair a copy of its employee manual.

The employee manual included a section entitled "Employee Relations Philosophy." In that section, the following language appears:

> The policies, practices and procedures set forth in this Employees' Manual are guidelines for supervision. They are not intended to confer contractual rights of any kind upon any employee or to create contractual obligations of any kind for the Company. The Company may revise, delete or supplement any policy, practice or procedure in this Employees' Manual at any time in its sole discretion.

Also important here, the employee manual set forth certain policies regarding medical leaves of absence: employees were not eligible for a medical leave of absence until after successfully completing a probationary period and working more than three months with Red Lion and, once eligible, an employee was permitted to request a medical leave of absence for a period not to exceed three months. The manual included the following provision:

> During a medical leave of absence, every effort will be made to keep a position available for the employee's return. If it is not possible to keep the position open because of business necessity, preference will be given for a similar position of equal to or lesser pay. Preference will be based upon job openings and qualifications.
>
> . . .
>
> Failure to advise the company of availability to return to work, failure to return to work upon doctor's release or continued absence from work beyond the time approved by the company will be deemed a voluntary termination of employment with Red Lion Inns.

On April 14, 1990, Fair was injured in a non-work related traffic accident. As a result of injuries from the accident, Fair applied for and was granted a medical leave. The term of her approved leave of absence was from May 25, 1990, to June 20, 1990. At the time of her leave of absence, Fair's position of employment with Red Lion was that of coffee break attendant in the room service department. Her duties included lifting, moving, and setting up a heavy banquet table, as well as walking back and forth from the table to the bar several times a day while carrying trays and coffee urns to refill the urns with coffee kept behind the bar. The injury she sustained in the accident made it difficult for Fair to perform her duties. In addition, on or about May 31, Fair learned that she was pregnant.

On June 20, 1990, the date her medical leave was to expire, Fair asked Neal Gustafson (Gustafson), the director of Human Resources, if she could bring in her doctor's release on June 22. Gustafson told her that was "not a problem." Fair submitted a partial release dated June 22, 1990, which permitted her to return to work, but only under certain conditions. The partial release limited Fair's work activities to those that did not involve heavy lifting (more than fifty pounds), prolonged standing or sitting, or abnormal postures (bending, kneeling, etc.). When told that the conditions of the partial release were not acceptable, Fair asked to be allowed to submit a full release by June 29, 1990, and she was again told that to do so would not be a problem. Shortly thereafter, Fair submitted a full release. The second release, dated June 27, 1990, stated that Fair was "capable of returning to work with no restrictions applied as of July 2, 1990."

In early July 1990, however, Fair learned that her employment with Red Lion had been terminated. The termination notice dated June 20, 1990, set forth the following explanation for her termination:

> Patricia's Medical Leave of Absence expired June 20, 1990. Her doctor did not give her a full release until July 2, 1990. The Red Lion is unfortunately unable to hold her position available past the expiration date of June 20, 1990.

On or about July 10, 1990, Fair asked Gustafson whether she was fired or released and he replied that Red Lion could no longer hold the position open.

Believing she was wrongfully discharged, Fair asked her legal counsel, retained due to the accident, to investigate the circumstances of her termination. After requesting and receiving information concerning the termination, Fair's attorney sent Red Lion a letter dated September 17, 1990, stating Fair's position that she had "complied with the Red Lion's policies regarding medical leaves of absence, but that the Red Lion failed to so comply." Citing Fair's "extreme emotional and financial losses as a result of the hotel's actions," her attorney further stated that the purpose of the letter was to "reiterate the facts, as supported by the written documentation, and to see if there is any possibility of reaching some amicable resolution, short of suit." In a September 20 response, Red Lion, through Gustafson, offered Fair "the opportunity to return to her position in Room Service at the Red Lion Hotel, Colorado Springs." The offer (Reinstatement Offer), by its terms, would be held open until October 3, 1990, and if not accepted, would be considered rejected.

Responding to the Reinstatement Offer, by letter dated October 1, Fair's attorney wrote back:

> If all of the monetary damages incurred by Ms. Fair as a result of her wrongful termination could be reimbursed to her, she would be willing to accept a position with the hotel. However, due to the apprehension she feels regarding her security in such a position, she would need to have certain special conditions met:
>
> 1. She would return to a position at the front desk for the Monday through Friday, 8:00 a.m. to 3:00 p.m. shift.
>
> 2. All her employee benefits must be restored without penalty for their interruption.
>
> 3. Certain restrictions must be placed on the Red Lion's termination of employment rights.
>
> 4. She must be able to transfer to another Red Lion Hotel with the same contract of employment.

On October 9, 1990, Gustafson sent a letter to Fair's attorney clarifying the terms of the Reinstatement Offer. The letter stated in part:

> Please be aware that our offer of reinstatement includes restoration of the appropriate benefits with coverage bridged as Ms. Fair would maintain her original hire date.
>
> We have offered to return Ms. Fair to her former position in Room Service as that is the position she is qualified to fill. Your first request to return in a position for which she is not trained and, in essence does not exist due to the hours and days stipulation you have made, cannot be considered.
>
> As an active Red Lion employee, Ms. Fair would have the rights [sic] to transfer based on company policy just as any other employee would. For scheduling purposes, please have Ms. Fair contact me no later than

October 15, 1990 or we will consider she has declined our offer of reinstatement and voluntarily resigned her position.

Neither Fair nor her attorney contacted Gustafson before October 15, nor did they otherwise affirmatively respond to the Reinstatement Offer to further clarify, to accept, or to reject the offer.

At trial, Fair testified that she did not accept the Reinstatement Offer because: (1) she believed that she would be terminated again as a form of retaliation; (2) she was concerned about her physical condition due to her pregnancy; and (3) she was uncertain of the meaning of the term "appropriate benefits" in the Reinstatement Offer. Fair did not, however, convey any of her concerns or otherwise discuss the terms of the Reinstatement Offer with her immediate supervisor, or any other person at Red Lion. Instead, by not responding by October 15, Red Lion assumed that Fair "declined" the Reinstatement Offer. Fair did, however, call the insurance company that provided medical benefits for Red Lion employees to ask whether Red Lion had the ability to bridge benefits. An employee of the insurance company told Fair that the determination to bridge benefits did not belong to Red Lion; rather, the insurance company itself made decisions regarding who was covered.

For reasons not reflected in the record, Fair did not share this information with Red Lion. In addition, Fair did not communicate with Red Lion to express any concerns, about her physical condition or otherwise, regarding the Reinstatement Offer.

B.

On November 13, 1991, Fair commenced this action in the El Paso County District Court by filing her complaint naming Red Lion as the defendant. In the complaint, Fair alleged that Red Lion breached an implied employment contract, among other claims. Through her complaint, Fair essentially asserted that the employment manual and the medical leave of absence form created a valid implied contract of employment that Red Lion failed to honor. The case eventually proceeded to trial.

At trial, Red Lion argued that Fair failed to mitigate her damages by rejecting its offer of reinstatement and, by motion, asked the trial court to direct a verdict and to limit damages. The trial court denied that motion and after the close of evidence, submitted both the questions of liability and damages to the jury. Finding Red Lion liable for breach of contract, the jury awarded Fair $140,000 in actual damages, including damages for loss of salary after Red Lion's offer of reinstatement. The trial court entered final judgment in the amount of $183,414.06, representing the amount of actual damages plus statutory interest of $43,414.06.

Red Lion appealed to the court of appeals. The court of appeals upheld the jury's finding of liability but, concluding that Fair was limited to recovery of damages incurred before Red Lion's unconditional offer of reinstatement, reversed the jury award of damages, and remanded the case for a new trial on damages. See Fair, 920 P.2d at 822–23. Fair filed a petition for certiorari, arguing that the decision of the court of appeals was in error and that Red Lion was not entitled to a directed verdict limiting the amount Fair is entitled to recover under Red Lion's defense that she failed to mitigate her damages. Due to the importance of the questions raised by Fair's petition, we granted certiorari.

II.

* * *

It is well established by our precedent that an injured party claiming breach of contract "has the duty to take such steps as are reasonable under the circumstances in order to mitigate or minimize the damages sustained." * * * "This means that the plaintiff may not recover damages for injuries which he or she reasonably might have avoided." * * * Mitigation or failure to mitigate is an affirmative defense that may be raised by the defendant and the defendant bears the burden of proving the defense.* * *

The defense of failure to mitigate damages is satisfied when the injured party fails to take reasonable steps to minimize the resulting damages. * * * A plaintiff's failure to mitigate damages is excused, however, if mitigation would require inordinate or unreasonable measures or if there were reasonable grounds for the failure to mitigate. * * *

Generally, the question of what constitutes reasonable effort in mitigation of damages is a question of fact to be determined by the trier of fact. * * * However, the defense of failure to mitigate damages will not be presented to the jury unless the trial court determines there is sufficient evidence to support it. * * * A trial court's determination will not be disturbed on appeal unless it is clearly erroneous.* * *

III.

With our settled law as context, we now address the specific issue and question of first impression before us: whether, as a matter of law, Fair presented sufficient evidence to show that she did mitigate her damages and therefore she should not be prohibited from recovering damages for lost compensation after the date of the Reinstatement Offer.

A.

The court of appeals reasoned that:

> Depending upon the substance of the offer and the circumstances under which it is made, an employee may be required to accept an offer of reemployment from the original employer as part of his or her duty to mitigate damages. A claimant may forfeit all or part of claimed rights to back pay if he or she refuses a job offered by the previous employer that is substantially equivalent to the one from which he or she was wrongfully terminated so long as acceptance of the reemployment offer would not effect an abandonment of the employee's rights under the original contract.

Fair, 920 P.2d at 827 (citations omitted). The court of appeals went on to conclude that if the injured party receives an unconditional offer of reinstatement to the same or a similar position and rejects such unconditional offer in the absence of special circumstances, the ongoing accrual of damages must terminate. See id.

* * *

B.

As discussed above, we have previously recognized the general duty of an injured party to mitigate damages flowing from a breach of contract. Today, we unequivocally hold that the same doctrine shall be applied in circumstances involving employment agreements. Hence, we must now determine whether the evidence in this case regarding the circumstances surrounding Fair's rejection of the Reinstatement Offer was sufficient to create an issue for the jury regarding the reasonableness of Fair's failure to mitigate her damages.

Fair argues that the judgment of the court of appeals should be reversed because it is not supported by the record. Fair contends that the issue of whether her refusal of the Reinstatement Offer was a reasonable failure to mitigate is a question of fact solely for the jury and that the trial court judgment should be upheld on appeal. Because we find that the reasons offered by Fair do not, as a matter of law, constitute "special circumstances" evincing a reasonable basis for rejecting Red Lion's offer of reinstatement, we disagree.

* * *

Here, Fair testified that she rejected the Reinstatement Offer because: (1) she believed that she would be terminated again as a form of retaliation; (2) she was concerned about her physical condition due to her pregnancy; and (3) she was uncertain of the meaning of the terms "appropriate benefits" in the Reinstatement Offer. However, at trial Fair did not produce evidence sufficient to articulate a basis for her belief and concerns based upon the specific terms and conditions of the offer or identifiable conduct of Red Lion or its employees or agents. Thus, without more, the reasons proffered by Fair are insufficient as a matter of law to create a triable issue for the jury's consideration.

Fair's first reason—a fear of retaliatory termination after rehire—is not a valid reason for rejecting Red Lion's Reinstatement Offer. Fair testified that she did not accept the Reinstatement Offer because she did not believe that Red Lion had any intention of upholding it. However, Fair did not indicate any basis for such belief, nor did she suggest any conduct by Red Lion or those in its employ which fairly indicates such a predisposition. Moreover, Fair's employment by Red Lion was clearly at will. Red Lion was only required to offer Fair reinstatement to a position of equivalent terms and conditions. Red Lion was not required to offer Fair a position with better terms than she had previously. * * * Consequently, since Red Lion's offer was consistent with Fair's previous employment position, her rejection of the offer due to its lack of assurance against future termination was not reasonable.

In addition, the record fails to suggest and Fair did not specify what, if anything, in the offer or Red Lion's conduct caused her to believe that the offer was anything but a bona fide unconditional offer of reinstatement.* * * The evidence indicates that Fair was both competent and efficient in the performance of her duties and that her supervisors valued her service to the company. In fact, during trial, Fair was very complimentary of her supervisors and spoke positively about her relationship with her supervisors and their influence upon her. Thus, her fear that the offer was not bona fide is not supported by the record and therefore does not constitute a reasonable basis for rejection of the Reinstatement Offer.

Fair's second reason for rejecting the Reinstatement Offer was that she was concerned about performing the duties of a coffee break attendant during her pregnancy. However, on cross-examination, Fair testified that she had no physical restrictions at the time she refused the Reinstatement Offer. Moreover, Fair failed to communicate any concern regarding physical limitations in her letter requesting special conditions. Certainly, the fact of particular limitations due to her pregnancy would have been relevant information to relay to Red Lion. Fair also neglected to discuss any physical restrictions with anyone at Red Lion. Thus, while we do not exclude physical limitations per se as a reasonable basis to reject a reinstatement offer,[13] in this case we are not persuaded that it was sufficiently presented to evince a reasonable basis to reject the Reinstatement Offer.

Fair's third reason for rejecting the Reinstatement Offer—that she was concerned about what benefits were in fact included within the term "appropriate benefits"—is also an unreasonable basis for rejecting the offer. First, it is undisputed that Fair never contacted anyone at Red Lion to discuss her concerns or to inquire about the meaning of "appropriate benefits." Instead, Fair, without further inquiry of Red Lion or communication of her concerns, rejected the offer out of hand. Even if Red Lion's medical insurance carrier had declined to continue insurance coverage for Fair, which it did not do, that alone would not be a sufficient basis for rejecting Red Lion's unconditional offer. As the court of appeals noted, the Reinstatement Offer was not contingent. If the carrier did not provide coverage, Fair would be covered because Red Lion would still be bound, even if forced to incur additional expenses for her coverage. At trial, Fair admitted that despite contrary information from Red Lion's insurance carrier, she assumed that Red Lion had the right to bridge benefits and could do so by paying the insurance company directly. Thus, it is clear that Fair's concern about benefits could not stand as a reasonable basis to reject Red Lion's Reinstatement Offer.

Furthermore, the letter containing the Reinstatement Offer represented a written commitment by Red Lion to provide benefits for Fair. Since the letter

[13]The parties have not argued that Red Lion failed to offer reasonable accommodations for Fair in light of her pregnancy. Therefore, we do not reach the question of whether and to what extent the employer has a duty to accommodate a pregnant employee.

was offering reinstatement to her former position in Room Service, it would be reasonable to assume that "appropriate benefits" would mean as are normally provided for a person in that position, i.e., the same as what she formerly received. However, even if Fair did not read "appropriate benefits" as the same benefits as she had previously, she could have called her supervisor or Gustafson to determine the meaning of that term and to clear up any confusion on her part.

In July, Fair had a full release to return to work stating that she was "capable of returning to work with no [physical] restrictions" whatsoever. Having been so informed by an employee and the employee's physician, it would be unreasonable to require an employer to include within an unconditional offer of reinstatement an accommodation for physical limitations or a change in responsibilities or position of employment solely because the employer is aware the employee is pregnant. Such a result cannot be supported by reason.

The court of appeals concluded that the grounds for refusal presented by Fair do not, as a matter of law, constitute sufficient special circumstances that would permit presentation of the mitigation issue to the jury. See Fair, 920 P.2d at 828. In her testimony at trial, Fair did not articulate a basis for rejecting Red Lion's offer grounded in the terms and conditions of reinstatement different from her position with Red Lion when discharged, nor one based on Red Lion's conduct or specific incidents or events related to her continuing relationship with Red Lion if she accepted the offer. Because at trial Fair did not present sufficient evidence for the issue of reasonableness of Fair's failure to mitigate to go to the jury, the court of appeals correctly decided that the issue of damages should not have been submitted to the jury without a limiting instruction.

IV.

By our holding today, we do not question the reasonableness of Fair's apprehensions. It goes without saying that an employee who has suffered a wrongful discharge will, as a natural consequence, have the trust and confidence once reposed in an employer diminished by the experience. However, this is true of any party to a contract in which the other party has broken its promise and breached their agreement. The injured party will have apprehensions about future dealings under the contract and, of course, the contract relationship will be affected. Nonetheless, sound principles of contract law in the commercial and employment setting and our precedent, confirmed by our decision in Ballow v. PHICO Insurance Co., 878 P.2d 672 (Colo.1994), ordain the principles we acknowledge today: The injured party claiming breach of an employment agreement has a duty to mitigate or minimize damages. In the employment agreement context, such duty includes the acceptance of an unconditional offer of reinstatement where no special circumstances exist to justify rejection.

In sum, we conclude that in the absence of "special circumstances," an employee's rejection of a former employer's unconditional offer of reinstatement constitutes a failure to mitigate damages. The result of such failure to mitigate damages is a loss of any claim to damages based upon the accrual of back pay from the date of the reinstatement offer. Here, we hold that Fair's reasons for rejecting Red Lion's reinstatement offer do not rise to the level of "special circumstances" justifying rejection of the offer. As such, we agree with the court of appeals' conclusion that there was not sufficient evidence on the issue of the reasonableness of Fair's rejection of Red Lion's Reinstatement Offer and that the trial court erred in refusing to limit the damages award.

V.

Accordingly, we affirm the court of appeals' judgment reversing the award of damages and remanding the case for a new trial on damages only.

MULLARKEY, J., dissents, and HOBBS and BENDER, JJ., join in the dissent [which is omitted].

QUESTIONS

1. Questions about the facts of this case

   1.1. What was Red Lion's breach of contract?

   1.2. Can Fair offer on remand any evidence of special circumstances?

   1.3. If she could, what counts as special circumstances under this case?

   1.4. The court said that it does not "question the reasonableness of Fair's apprehensions." Is that statement consistent with the court's holding?

2. Questions about the law

   2.1. Why is there a remand for determination of damages? Does this opinion basically mean that Fair gets nothing?

   2.2. If you were a Colorado lawyer after this case, how would you protect your employee clients who believe that they have special circumstances justifying a rejection of a reinstatement?

Parker v. Twentieth Century-Fox Film Corp.
Supreme Court of California
3 Cal.3d 176, 74 P.2d 689, 89 Cal.Rptr. 737 (1970)

Burke, J:

Defendant Twentieth Century-Fox Film Corporation appeals from a summary judgment granting to plaintiff the recovery of agreed compensation under a written contract for her services as an actress in a motion picture. As will appear, we have concluded that the trial court correctly ruled in plaintiff's favor and that the judgment should be affirmed.

Plaintiff is well known as an actress,* and in the contract between plaintiff and defendant is sometimes referred to as the "Artist." Under the contract, dated August 6, 1965, plaintiff was to play the female lead in defendant's contemplated production of a motion picture entitled "Bloomer Girl." The contract provided that defendant would pay plaintiff a minimum "guaranteed compensation" of $53,571.42 per week for 14 weeks commencing May 23, 1966, for a total of $750,000. Prior to May 1966 defendant decided not to produce the picture and by a letter dated April 4, 1966, it notified plaintiff of that decision and that it would not "comply with our obligations to you under" the written contract.

By the same letter and with the professed purpose "to avoid any damage to you," defendant instead offered to employ plaintiff as the leading actress in another film tentatively entitled "Big Country, Big Man" (hereinafter,

*The plaintiff is more commonly known as Shirley MacLaine. Eds.

"Big Country"). The compensation offered was identical, as were 31 of the 34 numbered provisions or articles of the original contract.[1] Unlike "Bloomer Girl," however, which was to have been a musical production, "Big Country" was a dramatic "western type" movie. "Bloomer Girl" was to have been filmed in California; "Big Country" was to be produced in Australia. Also, certain terms in the proffered contract varied from those of the original.[2] Plaintiff was given one week within which to accept; she did not and the offer lapsed. Plaintiff then commenced this action seeking recovery of the agreed guaranteed compensation.

The complaint sets forth two causes of action. The first is for money due under the contract; the second, based upon the same allegations as the first, is for damages resulting from defendant's breach of contract. Defendant in its answer admits the existence and validity of the contract, that

[1]Among the identical provisions was the following found in the last paragraph of Article 2 of the original contract: "We [defendant] shall not be obligated to utilize your [plaintiff's] services in or in connection with the Photoplay hereunder, our sole obligation, subject to the terms and conditions of this Agreement, being to pay you the guaranteed compensation herein provided for."

[2]Article 29 of the original contract specified that plaintiff approved the director already chosen for "Bloomer Girl" and that in case he failed to act as director plaintiff was to have approval rights of any substitute director. Article 31 provided that plaintiff was to have the right of approval of the "Bloomer Girl" dance director, and Article 32 gave her the right of approval of the screenplay.

Defendant's letter of April 4 to plaintiff, which contained both defendant's notice of breach of the "Bloomer Girl" contract and offer of the lead in "Big Country," eliminated or impaired each of those rights. It read in part as follows: "The terms and conditions of our offer of employment are identical to those set forth in the 'BLOOMER GIRL' Agreement, Articles 1 through 34 and Exhibit A to the Agreement, except as follows:

> "1. Article 31 of said Agreement will not be included in any contract of employment regarding 'BIG COUNTRY, BIG MAN' as it is not a musical and it thus will not need a dance director.
>
> "2. In the 'BLOOMER GIRL' agreement, in Articles 29 and 32, you were given certain director and screenplay approvals and you had preapproved certain matters. Since there simply is insufficient time to negotiate with you regarding your choice of director and regarding the screenplay and since you already expressed an interest in performing the role in 'BIG COUNTRY, BIG MAN,' we must exclude from our offer of employment in 'BIG COUNTRY, BIG MAN' any approval rights as are contained in said Articles 29 and 32; however, we shall consult with you respecting the director to be selected to direct the photoplay and will further consult with you with respect to the screenplay and any revisions or changes therein, provided, however, that if we fail to agree . . . the decision of . . . [defendant] with respect to the selection of a director and to revisions and changes in the said screenplay shall be binding upon the parties to said agreement."

plaintiff complied with all the conditions, covenants and promises and stood ready to complete the performance, and that defendant breached and "anticipatorily repudiated" the contract. It denies, however, that any money is due to plaintiff either under the contract or as a result of its breach, and pleads as an affirmative defense to both causes of action plaintiff's allegedly deliberate failure to mitigate damages, asserting that she unreasonably refused to accept its offer of the leading role in "Big Country."

Plaintiff moved for summary judgment under Code of Civil Procedure section 437c, the motion was granted, and summary judgment for $750,000 plus interest was entered in plaintiff's favor. This appeal by defendant followed.

The familiar rules are that the matter to be determined by the trial court on a motion for summary judgment is whether facts have been presented which give rise to a triable factual issue. The court may not pass upon the issue itself. Summary judgment is proper only if the affidavits or declarations in support of the moving party would be sufficient to sustain a judgment in his favor and his opponent does not by affidavit show facts sufficient to present a triable issue of fact. The affidavits of the moving party are strictly construed, and doubts as to the propriety of summary judgment should be resolved against granting the motion. Such summary procedure is drastic and should be used with caution so that it does not become a substitute for the open trial method of determining facts. . . .

As stated, defendant's sole defense to this action which resulted from its deliberate breach of contract is that in rejecting defendant's substitute offer of employment plaintiff unreasonably refused to mitigate damages.

The general rule is that the measure of recovery by a wrongfully discharged employee is the amount of salary agreed upon for the period of service, less the amount which the employer affirmatively proves the employee has earned or with reasonable effort might have earned from other employment. * * *[4] However, before projected earnings from other employment opportunities not sought or accepted by the discharged employee can be applied in mitigation, the employer must show that the other employment was comparable, or substantially similar, to that of which the employee has been deprived; the employee's rejection of or failure to seek

[4]Although it would appear that plaintiff was not discharged by defendant in the customary sense of the term, as she was not permitted by defendant to enter upon performance of the "Bloomer Girl" contract, nevertheless the motion for summary judgment was submitted for decision upon a stipulation by the parties that "plaintiff Parker was discharged."

other available employment of a different or inferior kind may not be resorted to in order to mitigate damages. * * *

In the present case defendant has raised no issue of reasonableness of efforts by plaintiffs to obtain other employment; the sole issue is whether plaintiff's refusal of defendant's substitute offer of "Big Country" may be used in mitigation. Nor, if the "Big Country" offer was of employment different or inferior when compared with the original "Bloomer Girl" employment, is there an issue as to whether or not plaintiff acted reasonably in refusing the substitute offer. Despite defendant's arguments to the contrary, no case cited or which our research has discovered holds or suggests that reasonableness is an element of a wrongfully discharged employee's option to reject, or fail to seek, different or inferior employment lest the possible earnings therefrom be charged against him in mitigation of damages.

Applying the foregoing rules to the record in the present case, with all intendments in favor of the party opposing the summary judgment motion—here, defendant—it is clear that the trial court correctly ruled that plaintiff's failure to accept defendant's tendered substitute employment could not be applied in mitigation of damages because the offer of the "Big Country" lead was of employment both different and inferior, and that no factual dispute was presented on that issue. The mere circumstance that "Bloomer Girl" was to be a musical review calling upon plaintiff's talents as a dancer as well as an actress, and was to be produced in the City of Los Angeles, whereas "Big Country" was a straight dramatic role in a "Western Type" story taking place in an opal mine in Australia, demonstrates the difference in kind between the two employments; the female lead as a dramatic actress in a western style motion picture can by no stretch of imagination be considered the equivalent of or substantially similar to the lead in a song-and-dance production.

Additionally, the substitute "Big Country" offer proposed to eliminate or impair the director and screenplay approvals accorded to plaintiff under the original "Bloomer Girl" contract (see fn. 2, *ante*), and thus constituted an offer of inferior employment. No expertise or judicial notice is required in order to hold that the deprivation or infringement of an employee's rights held under an original employment contract converts the available "other employment" relied upon by the employer to mitigate damages, into inferior employment which the employee need not seek or accept. (See *Gonzales v. Internal. Assn. of Machinists*, *supra.*, 213 Cal.App.2d 817, 823–824. . . .)

Statements found in affidavits submitted by defendant in opposition to plaintiff's summary judgment motion, to the effect that the "Big County" offer was not of employment different from or inferior to that under the "Bloomer Girl" contract, merely repeat the allegations of defendant's answer to the complaint in this action, constitute only conclusionary assertions with respect to undisputed facts, and do not give rise to a triable factual issue so as to defeat the motion for summary judgment.* * *

In view of the determination that defendant failed to present any facts showing the existence of a factual issue with respect to its sole defense—plaintiff's rejection of its substitute employment offer in mitigation of damages—we need not consider plaintiff's further contention that for various reasons, including the provisions of the original contract set forth in footnote 1, *ante*, plaintiff was excused from attempting to mitigate damages.

The judgment is affirmed.

McComb, J., Peters, J., Tobriner, J., Kaus, J., and Roth, J., concurred.

Dissent: Sullivan, Acting C. J.

The basic question in this case is whether or not plaintiff acted reasonably in rejecting defendant's offer of alternate employment. The answer depends upon whether that offer (starring in "Big Country, Big Man") was an offer of work that was substantially similar to her former employment (starring in "Bloomer Girl") or of work that was of a different or inferior kind. To my mind this is a factual issue, which the trial court should not have determined on a motion for summary judgment. The majority have not only repeated this error but have compounded it by applying the rules governing mitigation of damages in the employer-employee context in a misleading fashion. Accordingly, I respectfully dissent.

The familiar rule requiring a plaintiff in a tort or contract action to mitigate damages embodies notions of fairness and socially responsible behavior which are fundamental to our jurisprudence. Most broadly stated, it precludes the recovery of damages which, through the exercise of due diligence, could have been avoided. Thus, in essence, it is a rule requiring reasonable conduct in commercial affairs. This general principle governs the obligations of an employee after his employer has wrongfully repudiated or terminated the employment contract. Rather than permitting the employee simply to remain idle during the balance of the contract period, the law requires him to make a reasonable effort to secure other employment.[1] He is not obliged, however, to seek or accept any and all types of work which may be available. Only work which is in the same field and which is of the same quality need be accepted.[2]

Over the years the courts have employed various phrases to define the type of employment which the employee, upon his wrongful discharge, is under an obligation to accept. Thus in California alone it has been held that he must accept employment which is "substantially similar" * * *; employment "in the same general line of the first employment" * * *.

For reasons which are unexplained, the majority cite several of these cases yet select from among the various judicial formulations which they contain one particular phrase, "Not of a different or inferior kind," with which to analyze this case. I have discovered no historical or theoretical reason to adopt this phrase, which is simply a negative restatement of the affirmative standards set out in the above cases, as the exclusive standard. Indeed, its emergence is an example of the dubious phenomenon of the law responding not to rational judicial choice or changing social conditions, but to unrecognized changes in the language of opinions or legal treatises. However, the phrase is a serviceable one and my concern is not with its use as the standard but rather with what I consider its distortion.

The relevant language excuses acceptance only of employment which is of a different kind.* * * It has never been the law that the mere existence of differences between two jobs in the same field is sufficient, as a matter of law, to excuse an employee wrongfully discharged from one from accepting the other in order to mitigate damages. Such an approach would effectively eliminate any obligation of an employee to attempt to minimize damage

---

[1]The issue is generally discussed in terms of a duty on the part of the employee to minimize loss. The practice is long-established and there is little reason to change despite Judge Cardozo's observation of its subtle inaccuracy. "The servant is free to accept employment or reject it according to his uncensored pleasure. What is meant by the supposed duty is merely this, that if he unreasonably reject, he will not be heard to say that the loss of wages from then on shall be deemed the jural consequence of the earlier discharge. He has broken the chain of causation, and loss resulting to him thereafter is suffered through his own act." (*McClelland v. Climax Hosiery Mills* (1930) 252 N.Y. 347, 359 [169 N.E. 605, 609], concurring opinion.).

[2]This qualification of the rule seems to reflect the simple and humane attitude that it is too severe to demand of a person that he attempt to find and perform work for which he has no training or experience. Many of the older cases hold that one need not accept work in an inferior rank or position nor work which is more menial or arduous. This suggests that the rule may have had its origin in the bourgeois fear of resubmergence in lower economic classes.

arising from a wrongful discharge. The only alternative job offer an employee would be required to accept would be an offer of his former job by his former employer.

Although the majority appear to hold that there was a difference "in kind" between the employment offered plaintiff in "Bloomer Girl" and that offered in "Big Country" . . ., an examination of the opinion makes crystal clear that the majority merely point out differences between the two films (an obvious circumstance) and then apodically [sic] assert that these constitute a difference in the kind of employment. The entire rationale of the majority boils down to this; that the "mere circumstances" that "Bloomer Girl" was to be a musical review while "Big Country" was a straight drama "demonstrates the difference in kind" since a female lead in a western is not "the equivalent of or substantially similar to" a lead in a musical. This is merely attempting to prove the proposition by repeating it. It shows that the vehicles for the display of the star's talents are different but it does not prove that her employment as a star in such vehicles is of necessity different in kind and either inferior or superior.

I believe that the approach taken by the majority (a superficial listing of differences with no attempt to assess their significance) may subvert a valuable legal doctrine.[5] The inquiry in cases such as this should not be whether differences between the two jobs exist (there will always be differences) but whether the differences which are present are substantial enough to constitute differences in the kind of employment or, alternatively, whether they render the substitute work employment of an inferior kind.

It seems to me that this inquiry involves, in the instant case at least, factual determinations which are improper on a motion for summary judgment. Resolving whether or not one job is substantially similar to another or whether, on the other hand, it is of a different or inferior kind, will often (as here) require a critical appraisal of the similarities and differences between them in light of the importance of these differences to the employee. This necessitates a weighing of the evidence, and it is precisely this undertaking which is forbidden on summary judgment. * * *

[5]The values of the doctrine of mitigation of damages in this context are that it minimizes the unnecessary personal and social (e.g., nonproductive use of labor, litigation) costs of contractual failure. If a wrongfully discharged employee can, through his own action and without suffering financial or psychological loss in the process, reduce the damages accruing from the breach of contract, the most sensible policy is to require him to do so. I fear the majority opinion will encourage precisely opposite conduct.

This is not to say that summary judgment would never be available in an action by an employee in which the employer raises the defense of failure to mitigate damages. No case has come to my attention, however, in which summary judgment has been granted on the issue of whether an employee was obliged to accept available alternate employment. Nevertheless, there may well be cases in which the substitute employment is so manifestly of a dissimilar or inferior sort, the declarations of the plaintiff so complete and those of the defendant so conclusionary and inadequate that no factual issues exist for which a trial is required. This, however, is not such a case.

It is not intuitively obvious, to me at least, that the leading female role in a dramatic motion picture is a radically different endeavor from the leading female role in a musical comedy film. Nor is it plain to me that the rather qualified rights of director and screenplay approval contained in the first contract are highly significant matters either in the entertainment industry in general or to this plaintiff in particular. Certainly, none of the declarations introduced by plaintiff in support of her motion shed any light on these issues.[6]

The plaintiff's declarations were of no assistance to the trial court in its effort to justify reaching this conclusion on summary judgment. Instead, it

[6]Plaintiff's declaration states simply that she has not received any payment from defendant under the "Bloomer Girl" contract and that the only persons authorized to collect money for her are her attorney and her agent. The declaration of Herman Citron, plaintiff's theatrical agent, alleges that prior to the formation of the "Bloomer Girl" contract he discussed with Richard Zanuck, defendant's vice president, the conditions under which plaintiff might be interested in doing "Big Country"; that it was Zanuck who informed him of Fox's decision to cancel production of "Bloomer Girl" and queried him as to plaintiff's continued interest in "Big Country"; that he informed Zanuck that plaintiff was shocked by the decision, had turned down other offers because of her commitment to defendant for "Bloomer Girl" and was not interested in "Big Country." It further alleges that "Bloomer Girl" was to have been a musical review which would have given plaintiff an opportunity to exhibit her talent as a dancer as well as an actress and that "Big Country" was a straight dramatic role; the former to have been produced in California, the latter in Australia. Citron's declaration concludes by stating that he has not received any payment from defendant for plaintiff under the "Bloomer Girl" contract.

Benjamin Neuman's declaration states that he is plaintiff's attorney; that after receiving notice of defendant's breach he requested Citron to make every effort to obtain other suitable employment for plaintiff; that he (Neuman) rejected defendant's offer to settle for $400,000 and that he has not received any payment from defendant for plaintiff under the "Bloomer Girl" contract. It also sets forth correspondence between Neuman and Fox which culminated in Fox's final rejection of plaintiff's demand for full payment. Nor do they attempt to explain why she declined the offer of starring in "Big Country, Big Man." Nevertheless, the trial court granted the motion, declaring that these approval rights were "critical" and that their elimination altered "the essential nature of the employment."

was forced to rely on judicial notice of the definitions of "motion picture," "screenplay" and "director" (Evid. Code, § 451, subd. (e)) and then on judicial notice of practices in the film industry which were purportedly of "common knowledge." (Evid. Code, § 451, subd. (f) or § 452, subd. (g).) This use of judicial notice was error. Evidence Code section 451, subdivision (e) was never intended to authorize resort to the dictionary to solve essentially factual questions which do not turn upon conventional linguistic usage. . . .

The majority do not confront the trial court's misuse of judicial notice. They avoid this issue through the expedient of declaring that neither judicial notice nor expert opinion (such as that contained in the declarations in opposition to the motion)[8] is necessary to reach the trial court's conclusion. Something, however, clearly is needed to support this conclusion. Nevertheless, the majority make no effort to justify the judgment through an examination of the plaintiff's declarations. Ignoring the obvious insufficiency of these declarations, the majority announce that "the deprivation or infringement of an employee's rights held under an original employment contract" changes the alternate employment offered or available into employment of an inferior kind.

[8]Fox filed two declarations in opposition to the motion; the first is that of Frank Ferguson, Fox's chief resident counsel. It alleges, in substance, that he has handled the negotiations surrounding the "Bloomer Girl" contract and its breach; that the offer to employ plaintiff in "Big Country" was made in good faith and that Fox would have produced the film if plaintiff had accepted; that by accepting the second offer plaintiff was not required to surrender any rights under the first (breached) contract nor would such acceptance have resulted in a modification of the first contract; that the compensation under the second contract was identical; that the terms and conditions of the employment were substantially the same and not inferior to the first; that the employment was in the same general line of work and comparable to that under the first contract; that plaintiff often makes pictures on location in various parts of the world; that article 2 of the original contract which provides that Fox is not required to use the artist's services is a standard provision in artists' contracts designed to negate any implied covenant that the film producer promises to play the artist in or produce the film; that it is not intended to be an advance waiver by the producer of the doctrine of mitigation of damages.

The second declaration is that of Richard Zanuck. It avers that he is Fox's vice president in charge of production; that he has final responsibility for casting decisions, that he is familiar with plaintiff's ability and previous artistic history; that the offer of employment for "Big Country" was in the same general line and comparable to that of "Bloomer Girl"; that plaintiff would not have suffered any detriment to her image or reputation by appearing in it; that elimination of director and script approval rights would not injure plaintiff; that plaintiff has appeared in dramatic and western roles previously and has not limited herself to musicals; and that Fox would have complied with the terms of its offer if plaintiff had accepted it.

I cannot accept the proposition that an offer which eliminates any contract right, regardless of its significance, is, as a matter of law, an offer of employment of an inferior kind. Such an absolute rule seems no more sensible than the majority's earlier suggestion that the mere existence of differences between two jobs is sufficient to render them employment of different kinds. Application of such per se rules will severely undermine the principle of mitigation of damages in the employer-employee context.

I remain convinced that the relevant question in such cases is whether or not a particular contract provision is so significant that its omission creates employment of an inferior kind. This question is, of course, intimately bound up in what I consider the ultimate issue: whether or not the employee acted reasonably. This will generally involve a factual inquiry to ascertain the importance of the particular contract term and a process of weighing the absence of that term against the countervailing advantages of the alternate employment. In the typical case, this will mean that summary judgment must be withheld.

In the instant case, there was nothing properly before the trial court by which the importance of the approval rights could be ascertained, much less evaluated. Thus, in order to grant the motion for summary judgment, the trial court misused judicial notice. In upholding the summary judgment, the majority here rely upon per se rules which distort the process of determining whether or not an employee is obliged to accept particular employment in mitigation of damages.

I believe that the judgment should be reversed so that the issue of whether or not the offer of the lead role in "Big Country, Big Man" was of employment comparable to that of the lead role in "Bloomer Girl" may be determined at trial.

Appellant's petition for a rehearing was denied October 28, 1970. Mosk, J., did not participate therein. Sullivan, J., was of the opinion that the petition should be granted.

QUESTIONS AND NOTES

1. Questions about the facts of this case

   1.1. What was Twentieth Century-Fox's breach? What did they offer as evidence that Ms. Parker did not suffer damages?

1.2. What does it mean to take "judicial notice" of studio practices as complained about in the dissent? Doesn't everyone know what a film director is and what she does?

2. Questions about the law

2.1. Again, let's be clear. Shirley MacLaine gets $750,000 for doing nothing more than signing a contract. Were you counsel for Twentieth Century-Fox, what would you have done differently?

2.2. Note the procedural context in this case: the matter comes up after denial of summary judgment. In short, the court is deciding whether there are any factual issues requiring a jury trial. It seems that all but one of the members of the California Supreme Court believe that, as a matter of law, they can determine whether one movie presents the type of different employment required by the mitigation doctrine. On the other hand, if the matter went to trial, would each side try to call Gene Shalit or Roger Ebert? What would that accomplish?

2.3. What did Chief Justice Sullivan mean in footnote one of his dissent that there is no duty to mitigate damages? If there is no duty, then what is the logical or analytical device courts use to reduce damages when the aggrieved party does not attempt to mitigate damages, such as by taking comparable work?

2.4. Is this case consistent with *Fair*?

3. Notes

3.1. Subsequent commentary on this case has brought out other facts. "Bloomer Girl" was based on the life of Amelia Jenks Bloomer, a champion for womens' rights in the 19th Century. Its literary antecedent, a Broadway musical comedy, had strong strains of what we would identify today as feminism and the promotion of racial justice. Shirley MacLaine had publicly identified with both of these themes at or before the time of the contract. Should these facts have mattered? If so, why? *See* Mary Jo Frug, *Re-Reading Contracts: A Feminist Analysis of a Contracts Casebook*, 34 AM. U. L. REV. 1065, 1113–1123 (1985).

3.2. More doggerel:

There once was a lawsuit by Shirley
Who thought the defendant quite surly.
Re the movie she missed,
The defense was dismissed
And the judgment for Shirley came early.

Douglass Boshkoff, *Selected Poems on The Law of Contracts: Raintree County Memorial Library Occasional Paper No. 1*, 66 N.Y.U. L. REV. 1533, 1542 (1991).

Problems on Mitigation of Damages

Imagine that Epstein is lucky enough to get a summer job with Dewey, Cheatam & Howe, a 500-lawyer firm with a gold-plated, international practice. The pay offered is $2000 per week. One month before he shows up, Epstein gets a call from Markell, the managing partner, who tells him that it has just come to his attention that Epstein once contributed money to the American Association for the Prevention of Cruelty to Animals. "We don't hire soft-bellied pinkos here, bub. You can hit the bricks."

a. What are Epstein's damages if he cannot get a job for the 12-week summer season?

b. Do they change if Dewey, Cheatam & Howe can show that they offered Epstein a job in the mail room for the $2000 a month, and Epstein turned them down? Do you have to go to a jury trial?

c. What if Markell finishes the conversation by saying: "But just to show no hard feelings, we've arranged for you to work at Browbeat, Phlogem & Harrassem, a similar-sized firm that likes weak-kneed bleeding hearts, for the same salary." Again, do you have to go to a jury trial?

d. Same facts as problem c, but Browbeat, Phlogem & Harrassem is a plaintiffs' personal injury firm of low repute.

SECTION 7: OTHER REMEDIAL MEASURES—RESTITUTION

We've now examined money damages and specific performance. Are there other ways that contract law spells "relief"? In short, yes. We've seen some of them already, and we'll see a more complete treatment of such relief in Chapter 7, *infra*, but focusing on at least one of them here may serve to highlight the panoply of options aggrieved parties may have.

United States v. Algernon Blair, Incorporated

U.S. Court of Appeals, Fourth Circuit
479 F.2d 638 (1973)

Before Haynsworth, Chief Judge, Bryan, Senior Circuit Judge, and Craven, Circuit Judge.

Craven, Circuit Judge:

May a subcontractor, who justifiably ceases work under a contract because of the prime contractor's breach, recover in quantum meruit the value of labor and equipment already furnished pursuant to the contract irrespective of whether he would have been entitled to recover in a suit on the contract? We think so, and, for reasons to be stated, the decision of the district court will be reversed.

The subcontractor, Coastal Steel Erectors, Inc., brought this action under the provisions of the Miller Act, 40 U.S.C.A. § 270a et seq., in the name of the United States against Algernon Blair, Inc., and its surety, United States Fidelity and Guaranty Company. Blair had entered a contract with the United States for the construction of a naval hospital in Charleston County, South Carolina. Blair had then contracted with Coastal to perform certain steel erection and supply certain equipment in conjunction with Blair's contract with the United States. Coastal commenced performance of its obligations, supplying its own cranes for handling and placing steel. Blair refused to pay for crane rental, maintaining that it was not obligated to do so under the subcontract. Because of Blair's failure to make payments for crane rental, and after completion of approximately 28 percent of the subcontract, Coastal terminated its performance. Blair then proceeded to complete the job with a new subcontractor. Coastal brought this action to recover for labor and equipment furnished.

The district court found that the subcontract required Blair to pay for crane use and that Blair's refusal to do so was such a material breach as to justify Coastal's terminating performance. This finding is not questioned on appeal. The court then found that under the contract the amount due Coastal, less what had already been paid, totaled approximately $37,000. Additionally, the court found Coastal would have lost more than $37,000 if it had completed performance. Holding that any amount due Coastal must be reduced by any loss it would have incurred by complete performance of the contract, the court denied recovery to Coastal. While the district court correctly stated the " 'normal' rule of contract damages,"[1] we think Coastal is entitled to recover in quantum meruit.

In United States for Use of Susi Contracting Co. v. Zara Contracting Co., 146 F.2d 606 (2d Cir. 1944), a Miller Act action, the court was faced with a situation similar to that involved here—the prime contractor had unjustifiably breached a subcontract after partial performance by the subcontractor. The court stated:

> For it is an accepted principle of contract law, often applied in the case of construction contracts, that the promisee upon breach has the option to forego any suit on the contract and claim only the reasonable value of his performance.

146 F.2d at 610. The Tenth Circuit has also stated that the right to seek recovery under quantum meruit in a Miller Act case is clear. Quantum meruit recovery is not limited to an action against the prime contractor but may also be brought against the Miller Act surety, as in this case. Further, that the complaint is not clear in regard to the theory of a plaintiff's recovery does not preclude recovery under quantum meruit. Narragansett Improvement Co. v. United States, 290 F.2d 577 (1st Cir. 1961). A plaintiff may join a claim for quantum meruit with a claim for damages from breach of contract.

In the present case, Coastal has, at its own expense, provided Blair with labor and the use of equipment. Blair, who breached the subcontract, has retained these benefits without having fully paid for them. On these facts, Coastal is entitled to restitution in quantum merit.

> The "restitution interest," involving a combination of unjust impoverishment with unjust gain, presents the strongest case for relief. If, following

[1] Fuller & Perdue, The Reliance Interest in Contract Damages, 46 Yale L.J. 52 (1936); Restatement of Contracts § 333 (1932).

> Aristotle, we regard the purpose of justice as the maintenance of an equilibrium of goods among members of society, the restitution interest presents twice as strong a claim to judicial intervention as the reliance interest, since if A not only causes B to lose one unit but appropriates that unit to himself, the resulting discrepancy between A and B is not one unit but two.

Fuller & Perdue, The Reliance Interest in Contract Damages, 46 Yale L.J. 52, 56 (1936).[6]

The impact of quantum meruit is to allow a promisee to recover the value of services he gave to the defendant irrespective of whether he would have lost money on the contract and been unable to recover in a suit on the contract. Scaduto v. Orlando, 381 F.2d 587, 595 (2d Cir. 1967). The measure of recovery for quantum meruit is the reasonable value of the performance, Restatement of Contracts § 347 (1932); and recovery is undiminished by any loss which would have been incurred by complete performance. 12 Williston on Contracts § 1485, at 312 (3d ed. 1970). While the contract price may be evidence of reasonable value of the services, it does not measure the value of the performance or limit recovery.

It should be noted, however, that in suits for restitution there are many cases permitting the plaintiff to recover the value of benefits conferred on the defendant, even though this value exceeds that of the return performance promised by the defendant. In these cases it is no doubt felt that the defendant's breach should work a forfeiture of his right to retain the benefits of an advantageous bargain. Fuller & Perdue, supra at 77. Rather, the standard for measuring the reasonable value of the services rendered is the amount for which such services could have been purchased from one in the plaintiff's position at the time and place the services were rendered.

Since the district court has not yet accurately determined the reasonable value of the labor and equipment use furnished by Coastal to Blair, the case must be remanded for those findings. When the amount has been determined, judgment will be entered in favor of Coastal, less payments already made under the contract. Accordingly, for the reasons stated above, the decision of the district court is

Reversed and remanded with instructions.

---

[6]This case also comes within the requirements of the Restatements for recovery in quantum meruit. Restatement of Restitution § 107 (1937); Restatement of Contracts §§ 347-357 (1932).

QUESTIONS

1. Questions about the facts of this case

    1.1. So Coastal gets damages even though it would lose money on the contract? What is to stop the Coastals of this world, every time they enter into a losing contract, from goading the other side into breach so that it can get out of the contract with its costs?

    1.2. What amount is the court on remand supposed to calculate? What will it do then?

2. Questions about the law

    2.1. If the contract to Coastal would not return a profit, why should it be awarded anything? Doesn't that undermine the expectancy basis of contract damages?

    2.2. What if Coastal were in breach instead of Blair? The fact that a person is in breach does not affect the value of the services that he has rendered, does it?

SECTION 8: THE INNOVATIONS OF THE UNIFORM COMMERCIAL CODE

The Uniform Commercial Code (U.C.C.) changes some of the common law rules regarding damages. Recall that the U.C.C. deals with transactions in goods—defined as anything that is moveable. U.C.C. § 2-105(1). Goods present all sorts of specific questions about damages; for one thing, there are many markets for new and used goods—new and used car lots, for example—and price discounts are often a way to compensate for difference in quality among the same goods. Just look at the "day old" price for bread and bakery products compared to the prices for the same goods when fresh.

To take into account the differences occasioned by goods, the U.C.C. has an entire article on damages. In section 2-703, sellers' remedies are catalogued; section 2-711 does the same for buyers' remedies. Full examination of these changes awaits you in a Sales course, but for now we'll examine some of the more relevant problems.

A. Changes to the Notion of the Relevant Market—Of Cover and Resale

Article 2 of the U.C.C. attempts to address a practical problem lurking in the market-value based definition of contract damages: proof of a market, and the price in that market at the time you care about. Typically, the plaintiff is not allowed to testify that a market exists and what the prices were in that market at the relevant times. Indeed, some courts won't even let you introduce published accounts of market prices—say the price of stocks from the *Wall Street Journal*—because such testimony would be hearsay.

The U.C.C. attempts to finesse this problem by allowing the plaintiff to enter into a substitute transaction, and to allow the price in that transaction to substitute for the market price. For sellers, the relevant section is Section 2-706. It provides that if a buyer fails to take delivery of goods, the seller may resell the goods himself, and then seek damages equal to the contracted price less the price actually realized (as opposed to the contracted price less some hypothetical "market" price). There are, however, at least two restrictions on the seller's ability to use the price actually obtained: the seller must act in good faith, and in a commercially reasonable manner. Among other things, this means that the seller can't sell at a bargain-basement discount price to her brother-in-law. While still raising factual issues—such as what is "good faith" and "commercial reasonableness"—these issues will be raised only if contested. Were market price still the requirement, it would always have to be proved by outside evidence.

For buyers, Section 2-712 provides the alternative rule. If the seller doesn't deliver the goods, "the buyer may 'cover' by making in good faith and without unreasonable delay any reasonable purchase of or contract to purchase goods in substitution for those due from the seller." If the buyer complies with this section, the damages are the difference between the price she had to pay to get the goods, and the contract price contained in the deal with the breaching seller.

Before looking at a case applying these principles, first try some introductory problems:

Introductory Problems on Damages Under the U.C.C.

What are the damages in each of these cases? (Assume good faith, reasonable purchases in each case).

1. Sales contract for $1000. Seller breaches. Buyer pays $800 for a replacement.
2. Same facts as problem 1 except Buyer pays $1400 for replacement.
3. Same facts as problem 1 except now Buyer does not replace the goods; he goes without. What result if the market price for replacement is $1400? (Question: How can the buyer who does not replace prove market price?).
4. Same facts as problem 1 except Buyer replaces at $800 through her "connections," but alleges (truthfully) that market price for replacement is $1400.

Now see how a court handles these questions.

KGM Harvesting Co. v. Fresh Network

Court of Appeal of California, Sixth Appellate District
36 Cal. App. 4th 376, 42 Cal. Rptr. 2d 286 (1995)

Cottle, P. J.

California lettuce grower and distributor KGM Harvesting Company (hereafter seller) had a contract to deliver 14 loads of lettuce each week to Ohio lettuce broker Fresh Network (hereafter buyer). When the price of lettuce rose dramatically in May and June 1991, seller refused to deliver the required quantity of lettuce to buyer. Buyer then purchased lettuce on the open market in order to fulfill its contractual obligations to third parties. After a trial, the jury awarded buyer damages in an amount equal to the difference between the contract price and the price buyer was forced to pay for substitute lettuce on the open market. On appeal, seller argues that the damage award is excessive. We disagree and shall affirm the judgment. In a cross-appeal, buyer argues it was entitled to prejudgment interest from August 1, 1991, as its damages were readily ascertainable from that date. We agree and reverse the trial court's order awarding prejudgment interest from 30 days prior to trial.

FACTS

In July 1989 buyer and seller entered into an agreement for the sale and purchase of lettuce. Over the years, the terms of the agreement were modified. By May 1991 the terms were that seller would sell to buyer 14 loads of lettuce each week and that buyer would pay seller 9 cents a pound for the lettuce. (A load of lettuce consists of 40 bins, each of which weighs 1,000 to 1,200 pounds. Assuming an average bin weight of 1,100 pounds, 1 load would equal 44,000 pounds, and the 14 loads called for in the contract would weigh 616,000 pounds. At 9 cents per pound, the cost would approximate $55,440 per week.)

Buyer sold all of the lettuce it received from seller to a lettuce broker named Castellini Company who in turn sold it to Club Chef, a company that chops and shreds lettuce for the fast food industry (specifically, Burger King, Taco Bell, and Pizza Hut). Castellini Company bought lettuce from buyer on a "cost plus" basis, meaning it would pay buyer its actual cost plus a small commission. Club Chef, in turn, bought lettuce from Castellini Company on a cost plus basis.

Seller had numerous lettuce customers other than buyer, including seller's subsidiaries Coronet East and West. Coronet East supplied all the lettuce for the McDonald's fast food chain.

In May and June 1991, when the price of lettuce went up dramatically, seller refused to supply buyer with lettuce at the contract price of 9 cents per pound. Instead, it sold the lettuce to others at a profit of between $800,000 and $1.1 million. Buyer, angry at seller's breach, refused to pay seller for lettuce it had already received. Buyer then went out on the open market and purchased lettuce to satisfy its obligations to Castellini Company. Castellini covered all of buyer's extra expense except for $70,000. Castellini in turn passed on its extra costs to Club Chef which passed on at least part of its additional costs to its fast food customers.

* * *

Subsequently, seller filed suit for the balance due on its invoices, and buyer cross-complained for the additional cost it incurred to obtain substitute lettuce after seller's breach. At trial, the parties stipulated that seller was entitled to a directed verdict on its complaint for $233,000, the amount owing on the invoices. Accordingly, only the cross-complaint went to the jury, whose task was to determine whether buyer was entitled to damages from seller for the cost of obtaining substitute lettuce and, if so, in what amount.

The jury determined that seller breached the contract, that its performance was not excused, and that buyer was entitled to $655,960.22, which represented the difference between the contract price of nine cents a pound and what it cost buyer to cover by purchasing lettuce in substitution in May and June 1991. It also determined that such an award would not result in a windfall to buyer and that buyer was obligated to the Castellini Company for the additional costs. The court subtracted from buyer's award of $655,960.22 the $233,000 buyer owed to seller on its invoices, leaving a net award in favor of buyer in the amount of $422,960.22. . . .

DISCUSSION

A. Seller's Appeal

Section 2711 of the California Uniform Commercial Code provides a buyer with several alternative remedies for a seller's breach of contract. The buyer can "'cover' by making in good faith and without unreasonable delay any reasonable purchase of . . . goods in substitution for those due from the seller." (§ 2712, subd. (1).) In that case, the buyer "may recover from the seller as damages the difference between the cost of cover and the contract price. . . ." (§ 2712, subd. (2).) If the buyer is unable to cover or chooses not to cover, the measure of damages is the difference between the market price and the contract price. (§ 2713.) Under either alternative, the buyer may also recover incidental and consequential damages. (§ 2711, 2715.) In addition, in certain cases the buyer may secure specific performance or replevin "where the goods are unique" (§ 2716) or may recover goods identified to a contract (§ 2502).

In the instant case, buyer "covered" as defined in section 2712 in order to fulfill its own contractual obligations to the Castellini Company. Accordingly, it was awarded the damages called for in cover cases—the difference between the contract price and the cover price. (§ 2712.)

In appeals from judgments rendered pursuant to section 2712, the dispute typically centers on whether the buyer acted in "good faith," whether the "goods in substitution" differed substantially from the contracted for goods, whether the buyer unreasonably delayed in purchasing substitute goods in the mistaken belief that the price would go down, or whether the buyer paid too much for the substitute goods.* * *

In this case, however, none of these typical issues is in dispute. Seller does not contend that buyer paid too much for the substitute lettuce or that buyer was guilty of "unreasonable delay" or a lack of "good faith' in its attempt to obtain substitute lettuce. Nor does seller contend that the lettuce purchased was of a higher quality or grade and therefore not a reasonable substitute.

Instead, seller takes issue with section 2712 itself, contending that despite the unequivocal language of section 2712, a buyer who covers should not necessarily recover the difference between the cover price and the contract price. Seller points out that because of buyer's "cost plus" contract with Castellini Company, buyer was eventually able to pass on the extra expenses (except for $70,000) occasioned by seller's breach and buyer's consequent purchase of substitute lettuce on the open market. It urges this court under these circumstances not to allow buyer to obtain a "windfall."[2]

The basic premise of contract law is to effectuate the expectations of the parties to the agreement, to give them the "benefit of the bargain" they struck when they entered into the agreement. In its basic premise, contract law therefore differs significantly from tort law. As the California Supreme Court explained in *Foley v. Interactive Data Corp.* (1988) 47 Cal. 3d 654 [254 Cal. Rptr. 211, 765 P.2d 373], ". . . contract actions are created to enforce the intentions of the parties to the agreement [while] tort law is primarily designed to vindicate 'social policy.'" * * *

"'The basic object of damages is compensation, and in the law of contracts the theory is that the party injured by breach should receive as nearly as possible the equivalent of the benefits of performance.' "* * * A compensation system that gives the aggrieved party the benefit of the bargain, and no more, furthers the goal of "predictability about the cost of contractual relationships . . . in our commercial system." * * *

With these rules in mind, we examine the contract at issue in this case to ascertain the reasonable expectations of the parties. The contract recited that its purpose was "to supply [buyer] with a consistent quality raw product at a fair price to [seller], which also allows [buyer] profitability for his finished product.' Seller promised to supply the designated quantity even if the price of lettuce went up ("We agree to supply said product and amount at stated price regardless of the market price or conditions") and buyer promised to purchase the designated quantity even if the price went down ("[Buyer]

---

[2]In answering special interrogatories, the jury found (1) that if buyer were awarded the difference between the contract price and the cost of cover, it would not result in a windfall to buyer, and (2) that buyer had an obligation to pay Castellini Company for the amount Castellini Company paid buyer to acquire the substitute lettuce. . . .

agrees to purchase said product and amounts at stated price regardless of the market price or conditions, provided quality requirements are met"). The possibility that the price of lettuce would fluctuate was consequently foreseeable to both parties.

Although the contract does not recite this fact, seller was aware of buyer's contract with the Castellini Company and with the Castellini Company's contract with Club Chef. This knowledge was admitted at trial and can be inferred from the fact that seller shipped the contracted for 14 loads of lettuce directly to Club Chef each week. Thus, seller was well aware that if it failed to provide buyer with the required 14 loads of lettuce, buyer would have to obtain replacement lettuce elsewhere or would itself be in breach of contract. This was within the contemplation of the parties when they entered into their agreement.

As noted earlier, the object of contract damages is to give the aggrieved party "'as nearly as possible the equivalent of the benefits of performance.'" * * * * In the instant case, buyer contracted for 14 loads of lettuce each week at 9 cents per pound. When seller breached its contract to provide that lettuce, buyer went out on the open market and purchased substitute lettuce to fulfill its contractual obligations to third parties. However, purchasing replacement lettuce to continue its business did not place buyer "in as good a position as if the other party had fully performed." This was because buyer paid more than 9 cents per pound for the replacement lettuce. Only by reimbursing buyer for the additional costs above 9 cents a pound could buyer truly receive the benefit of the bargain. This is the measure of damages set forth in section 2712.

As White and Summers point out, "Since 2-712 measures buyer's damages by the difference between his actual cover purchase and the contract price, the formula will often put buyer in the identical economic position that performance would have." (White & Summers, *supra*, Buyer's Remedies, Cover, § 6-3, p. 285.) Therefore, "[i]n the typical case a timely 'cover' purchase by an aggrieved buyer will preclude any 2-715 [incidental and consequential] damages.' (*Ibid.*) "Not only does the damage formula in 2-712 come close to putting the aggrieved buyer in the same economic position as actual performance would have," White and Summers conclude, "but it also enables him to achieve his prime objective, namely thatof acquiring his needed goods." (*Id.* at p. 292.)

In this case, the damage formula of section 2712 put buyer in the identical position performance would have: it gave buyer the contracted for 14 loads of lettuce with which to carry on its business at the contracted for price of 9 cents per pound.

Despite the obvious applicability and appropriateness of section 2712, seller argues in this appeal that the contract-cover differential of section 2712 is inappropriate in cases, as here, where the aggrieved buyer is ultimately able to pass on its additional costs to other parties. Seller contends that section 1106's remedial injunction to put the aggrieved party "in as good a position as if the other party had fully performed' demands that all subsequent events impacting on buyer's ultimate profit or loss be taken into consideration (specifically, that buyer passed on all but $70,000 of its loss to Castellini Company, which passed on all of its loss to Club Chef, which passed on most of its loss to its fast food customers). . . .

* * *

As noted earlier, section 2712 "will often put buyer in the identical economic position that performance would have." (White & Summers, *supra*, Buyer's Remedies, Cover, § 6-3, p. 285.) In contrast, the contract-market differential of section 2713 "bears no necessary relation to the change in the buyer's economic status that the breach causes. It is possible that this differential might yield the buyer a handsome sum even though the breach actually saved him money in the long run (as for example when a middleman buyer's resale markets dry up after the breach). It is also quite possible that the buyer's lost profit from resale or consumption would be greater than the contract-market difference." (*Id.*, § 6-4, at p. 294.)

White and Summers argue that the drafters of section 2713 could not have intended to put the buyer in the same position as performance since "[p]erformance would have given the buyer certain goods for consumption or resale" (White & Summers, *supra*, Buyer's Remedies, Cover, § 6-4, at p. 294) which would have resulted in "either a net economic gain for the buyer or a net economic loss." (*Ibid.*) The best explanation of section 2713, they suggest, is that it is a "statutory liquidated damage clause, a breach inhibitor the payout of which need bear no close relation to the plaintiff's actual loss." * * * In discussing the "problem of a buyer who has covered but who seeks to ignore 2-712 and sue for a larger contract-market differential under 2-713," the authors suggest: "If the Code's goal is to put the buyer in the same position as though there had been no breach, and if 2-712 will accomplish that goal but 2-713 will do so only by coincidence, why not force the covering buyer to use 2-712?" (White & Summers, *supra*, at p. 304.) Professor Robert Childres has actually called for the repeal of section 2713 and the requirement of compulsory cover. (Childres, *Buyer's Remedies: The Danger of Section 2-713* (1978) 72 Nw. U. L.Rev. 837.)

With these prefatory comments in mind, we look to the *Allied Canners* case. In *Allied Canners*, [Victor Packing, a] raisin supplier breached another contract to sell raisins in 1976. The buyer, Allied Canners, had contracts to resell the raisins it bought from Victor to two Japanese companies for its cost plus 4 percent. Such a resale would have resulted in a profit of $4,462.50 to Allied. When Victor breached the contract, Allied sued for the difference between the market price and the contract price as authorized by section 2713. As the market price of raisins had soared due to the disastrous 1976 rains, the market-contract price formula would have yielded damages of approximately $150,000. Allied did not purchase substitute raisins and did not make any deliveries under its resale contracts to the Japanese buyers. One of the Japanese buyers simply released Allied from its contract because of the general unavailability of raisins. The other buyer did not release Allied, but it did not sue Allied either. By the time Allied's case against Victor went to trial, the statute of limitations on the Japanese buyer's claim had run.

Under these circumstances, the court held that the policy of section 1106 (that the aggrieved party be put in as good a position as if the other party had performed) required that the award of damages to Allied be limited to its actual loss. It noted that for this limitation to apply, three conditions must be met: (1) "the seller knew that the buyer had a resale contract'; (2) "the buyer has not been able to show that it will be liable in damages to the buyer on its forward contract"; and (3) "there has been no finding of bad faith on the part of the seller. . . ." (*Allied Canners & Packers, Inc. v. Victor Packing Co., supra*, 162 Cal. App. 3d at p. 915.)

The result in *Allied Canners* seems to have derived in large part from the court's finding that Victor had not acted in bad faith in breaching the contract. The court noted, "It does appear clear, however, that, as the trial court found, the rains caused a severe problem, and Victor made substantial efforts [to procure the raisins for Allied]. We do not deem this record one to support an inference that windfall damages must be awarded the buyer to prevent unjust enrichment to a deliberately breaching seller. (Compare *Sun-Maid Raisin Growers v. Victor Packing Co., supra*, 146 Cal. App. 3d 787 [where, in a case coincidentally involving Victor, Victor was expressly found by the trial court to have engaged in bad faith by gambling on the market price of raisins in deciding whether to perform its contracts to sell raisins to Sun Maid].)" (162 Cal. App. 3d at p. 916.)[7]

We believe that this focus on the good or bad faith of the breaching party is inappropriate in a commercial sales case. As our California Supreme Court recently explained, courts should not differentiate between good and bad motives for breaching a contract in assessing the measure of the non-breaching party's damages. (*Applied Equipment Corp. v. Litton Saudi Arabia Ltd.* (1994) 7 Cal. 4th 503, 513–515 [28 Cal.Rptr.2d 475, 869 P.2d 454].) Such a focus is inconsistent with the policy "to encourage contractual relations and commercial activity by enabling parties to estimate in advance the financial risks of their enterprise." (*Id.* at p. 515.) "'Courts traditionally have awarded damages for breach of contract to compensate the aggrieved party rather than to punish the breaching party.' [Citations.]" (*Foley v. Interactive Data Corp.*, *supra*, 47 Cal. 3d at p. 683.) * * *

As the foregoing discussion makes clear, we have serious reservations about whether the result in *Allied Canners*, with its emphasis on the good faith of the breaching party, is appropriate in an action seeking damages under section 2713. We have no reservations, however, in not extending the *Allied Canners* rationale to a section 2712 case. As noted earlier, no section 2712 case, including *Sun-Maid Growers v. Victor Packing Co.*, *supra*, 146 Cal. App. 3d 787, has ever held that cover damages must be limited by section 1106. The obvious reason is that the cover-contract differential puts a buyer who covers in the exact same position as performance would have done. This is the precisely what is called for in section 1106. In this respect, the cover/contract differential of section 2712 is very different than the market/contract differential of section 2713, which "need bear no close relation

[7]In view of Allied Canners' three-part test, we assume the results would have been different here if the court had found Victor was "a deliberately breaching seller.' Perhaps in that case, the court would not have focused on what the aggrieved buyer ultimately would have received on resale but might have focused on what benefits the seller reaped from breaching. In Allied Canners, the price of raisins went up from 30 cents a pound to 87 cents a pound. If seller had not breached, it would have had to go out on the market and buy raisins for Allied at considerably more than it was contracted to sell them for to Allied. By breaching, it avoided a loss that might have been more in the $150,000 range (market-contract differential) than the $4,000 range (Allied's lost profits). Thus, the court prevented a windfall to Allied at the cost of providing a windfall to Victor. Such a result is curious if the intent of contract damages is to effectuate the expectations of the parties to the contract. Here, the parties clearly contemplated when they entered into their fixed price agreement that the price of raisins would fluctuate and that sometimes buyer would receive a price better than the market price and that other times it would have to pay more than the market price.

to the plaintiff's actual loss." (White & Summers, *supra*, Buyer's Remedies, Cover, at p. 295.)

In summary, we hold that where a buyer "'cover[s]" by making in good faith and without unreasonable delay any reasonable purchase of . . . goods in substitution for those due from the seller, . . . [that buyer] may recover from the seller as damages the difference between the cost of cover and the contract price. . . ." (§ 2712.) This gives the buyer the benefit of its bargain. What the buyer chooses to do with that bargain is not relevant to the determination of damages under section 2712.

* * *

DISPOSITION

. . . [The] judgment is affirmed. Costs on appeal to buyer.

Premo, J., and Elia, J., concurred.

QUESTIONS

1. Questions about the facts of this case

    1.1. What is the "good" involved here that invokes the U.C.C.?

    1.2. Why did the seller allege that recovery in this case would result in a windfall?

2. Questions about the law

    2.1. What does this court think is the appropriate result that should follow from a finding that a particular breach of contract was intentional? Why does it even have to discuss that point?

    2.2. The court said that "We believe that this focus on the good or bad faith of the breaching party is inappropriate in a commercial sales case." Does this mean that motive is a proper focus in a consumer case? That Cardozo was wrong in *Jacob & Youngs v. Kent, supra*, at 788, when he said "The willful transgressor must accept the penalty of his transgression* * *. For him there is no occasion to mitigate the rigor of implied conditions." Or is that "different"?

2.3. What in blazes is the relevance of § 1-106? That isn't even in Article 2 of the U.C.C., is it?

The U.C.C. does not make resales or cover purchases mandatory. An aggrieved seller can always prove market based damages, even if the resale was not, for example, not commercially reasonable. U.C.C. § 2-706. As indicated in *KGM,* a buyer may use market-based damages even if she does not cover. U.C.C. §§ 2-713, 2-714.

B. Loss of a Sale to a Volume Seller

What happens if, as is often the case with retail sellers, all the breach does is force the seller to resell the goods to someone else—in short, all that happens is that the seller is just "out of a sale." The next case explores this in the context of whether a liquidated damages clause provides a reasonable estimate of damages, a question we left open after *O'Brian, supra,* at 850.

Rodriguez v. Learjet, Inc.

Court of Appeals of Kansas
24 Kan.App.2d 461, 946 P.2d 1010 (1997)

Before Marquardt, P.J., Pierron, J., and Nancy E. Parrish, District Judge, Assigned.

Marquardt, Presiding Judge:

Miguel A. Diaz Rodriguez (Diaz) appeals from the district court's decision that a liquidated damages clause in his contract with Learjet, Inc., (Learjet) was reasonable and enforceable.

On August 21, 1992, Diaz executed a contract with Learjet to purchase a model 60 jet aircraft. The contract called for a $250,000 deposit to be made upon execution of the contract; a $750,000 payment to be made on September 18, 1992; a $1,000,000 payment to be made 180 days before the delivery date of July 30, 1993; and the balance of the purchase price to be paid upon delivery.

Diaz paid Learjet $250,000 on the day that he executed the contract, but made no other payment.

At the time of the purchase, Diaz worked for Televisa. Diaz was purchasing the aircraft at the request of Alejandro Burillo, his supervisor at Televisa. Near the end of September 1992, Burillo told Diaz that he no longer wanted the aircraft. Diaz testified that he called Alberto Castaneda at Learjet and told him that he was not going to buy the aircraft and that he wanted Learjet to return his $250,000 deposit.

On September 30, 1992, Castaneda sent Diaz a fax, requesting payment. On October 6, 1992, Castaneda wrote Diaz a letter, which stated, in part: "Unless we receive payment from you or your company by October 9, 1992, [Learjet, Inc.,] will consider this agreement terminated and will retain all payments as liquidation damages in accordance with Paragraph C . . . of Section VII . . . of said agreement." By letter dated October 20, 1992, Learjet informed Diaz that it considered their contract terminated and that the $250,000 deposit was being retained as liquidated damages.

The contract provides, in part:

> "Learjet may terminate this Agreement as a result of the Buyer's . . . failure to make any progress payment when due. . . . If this Agreement is terminated by Learjet for any reason stipulated in the previous sentence Learjet shall retain all payments theretofore made by the Buyer as liquidated damages and not as a penalty and the parties shall thenceforth be released from all further obligations hereunder. Such damages include, but are not limited to, loss of profit on this sale, direct and indirect costs incurred as a result of disruption in production, training expense advance and selling expenses in effecting resale of the Airplane."

After Diaz had breached the parties' contract, Circus Circus Enterprises, Inc., (Circus) contracted with Learjet to buy the aircraft. Circus requested that changes be made to the aircraft, which cost $1,326. Learjet realized a $1,887,464 profit on the sale of the aircraft to Circus, which was a larger profit than Learjet had originally budgeted.

Diaz filed suit against Learjet, seeking to recover the $250,000 deposit. Diaz' petition alleged, in part, that the actual amount of Learjet's liquidated damages was not $250,000 and that Learjet's retention of the $250,000 deposit was unreasonable and an unenforceable penalty.

The district court initially granted Learjet's motion for summary judgment, holding that the liquidated damages provision of the contract was reasonable. Diaz appealed that decision. On appeal, this court held that the district court had erred in using the wrong standard to evaluate the liquidated damages clause and in not examining all of the necessary factors and remanded the case to the district court for further consideration of the reasonableness of the liquidated damages clause. *Rodriguez v. Learjet, Inc.*, No. 71,352, 890 P.2d 752, unpublished opinion filed March 10, 1995.

On remand, a bench trial was held. Following the presentation of evidence, the district court found that Learjet was a lost volume seller and that its actual damages included lost profits. The district court held that $250,000 in liquidated damages was reasonable and upheld the liquidated damages clause.

Diaz argues that the district court erred in holding that the liquidated damages clause was reasonable and enforceable. Diaz reasons that the liquidated damages clause was unreasonably large and, therefore, void as a penalty.

A determination concerning the reasonableness and enforceability of a liquidated damages clause is a question of law subject to unlimited review by this court. *Kvassay v. Murray*, 15 Kan.App.2d 426, 429, 808 P.2d 896, *rev. denied* 248 Kan. 996 (1991).

K.S.A. 84-2-718 [UCC § 2-718] governs liquidated damages in contracts for the sale of goods and provides, in part:

> "(1) Damages for breach by either party may be liquidated in the agreement but only at an amount which is reasonable in the light of the anticipated or actual harm caused by the breach, the difficulties of proof of loss, and the inconvenience or nonfeasibility of otherwise obtaining an adequate remedy. A term fixing unreasonably large liquidated damages is void as a penalty."

In Kvassay, 15 Kan.App.2d at 430, 808 P.2d 896, this court noted that "reasonableness is the only test" for liquidated damages under the Uniform Commercial Code. This court paraphrased the three criteria for measuring the reasonableness of a liquidated damages clause provided in K.S.A. 84-2-718: "(1) anticipated or actual harm caused by breach; (2) difficulty of proving loss; and (3) difficulty of obtaining an adequate remedy." 15 Kan.App.2d at 430, 808 P.2d 896.

A liquidated damages clause that "'fixes damages in an amount grossly disproportionate to the harm actually sustained or likely to be sustained'" is considered a penalty and will not be enforced by the courts.* * * If a liquidated damages clause is invalidated as a penalty, then the nonbreaching party may recover actual damages instead. * * * The burden of proving that a liquidated damages clause is unenforceable rests with the party challenging its enforcement. * * *

Diaz' challenge to the reasonableness of the liquidated damages clause focuses on the first factor of K.S.A. 84-2-718—the anticipated or actual harm caused by the breach. The question of whether a seller qualifies as a lost volume seller is relevant when evaluating whether a liquidated damages clause is reasonable in light of the anticipated or actual harm caused by the breach.

Diaz argues that the district court erred in concluding that Learjet qualifies as a lost volume seller. As a lost volume seller, Learjet's actual damages would include lost profits, notwithstanding that Circus purchased the aircraft which Diaz had contracted to buy and that Learjet made a profit on the Circus sale. The two contracts contained identical base prices, and both contracts had escalation clauses. The evidence indicates that the lost profit from the Diaz contract would have been approximately $1.8 million.

Whether a seller is a lost volume seller is a question of fact. * * * An appellate court reviews factual findings to determine if they are supported by substantial competent evidence. * * *

Courts have "unanimously" held that a lost volume seller can recover lost profits under § 2-708(2) of the Uniform Commercial Code.* * *The Kansas Legislature has enacted this statute as K.S.A. 84-2-708(2).

In Jetz, 19 Kan.App.2d at 148, 865 P.2d 1051, this court explained:

> "The 'lost volume seller' measure of damages 'refers to the lost volume of business the non-breaching seller incurs on buyer's breach. When the seller resells the entity he expected to sell to the original buyer, he usually deprives himself of something of value—the sale to a new buyer of another similar entity.' [*Snyder v. Herbert Greenbaum & Assoc.*, 38 Md.App. 144, 154 n. 3, 380 A.2d 618 (1977)]."

Similarly, Restatement (Second) of Contracts § 350, Comment d (1979) notes that if a seller would have entered into both transactions but for the breach, then the seller has lost volume as a result of the breach. Thus, lost profits are awarded to a lost volume seller, notwithstanding that the seller resells the item that a buyer contracted to buy, based on the principle that the seller was deprived of an additional sale and the corresponding profit by the buyer's breach. * * *

Awarding lost profits to a lost volume seller serves the general principle that the purpose of awarding damages is to make a party whole by restoring the nonbreaching party to the position that that party occupied prior to the breach—to place a seller in as good a position as if a buyer had performed. K.S.A. 84-1-106 * * *.

The issue in *Jetz* was whether the plaintiff qualified as a lost volume lessor, and this court did not expressly state the specific requirements for qualifying as a lost volume seller. The Jetz court held that lost volume status is available to businesses providing services and identified the following evidence as sufficient to affirm the trial court's finding that the plaintiff was a lost volume lessor:

> "[J]etz Service is in the business of supplying coin-operated laundry equipment; it has several warehouses in which it has available for lease about 1,500 used washers and dryers; it continually looks for new locations in which to install laundry equipment; it would have been able to fulfill the Kansas City lease without using the machines from Salina Properties; and it is uncontroverted Jetz Service would have been able to enter into both transactions irrespective of the breach by Salina Properties." 19 Kan.App.2d at 152, 865 P.2d 1051.

In *Diasonics*, 826 F.2d at 685, the court held that in order to qualify as a lost volume seller and recover for lost profits, a seller must establish three factors: (1) that it possessed the capacity to make an additional sale, (2) that it would have been profitable for it to make an additional sale, and (3) that it probably would have made an additional sale absent the buyer's breach. See also *R.E. Davis Chemical Corp. v. Diasonics*, 924 F.2d 709, 711 (7th Cir.1991) (restating rule formulated in prior appeal of case); Kansas Comment 2 to 84-2-708 (citing first Diasonics case).

Here, in finding that Learjet qualified as a lost volume seller, the district court referred to *Jetz*, 19 Kan.App.2d 144, Syl. & 2, 865 P.2d 1051.

Applying the more specific criteria established in *Diasonics*, 826 F.2d at 684–85, there is adequate evidence to support the district court's finding. The master scheduler for Learjet testified that Learjet was operating at 60 percent capacity during the relevant time period and that Learjet was able to accelerate its production schedule to produce more of the model 60 planes in any given year. Learjet also presented testimony about its accounting system which indicated that an additional sale would have been profitable to Learjet. Learjet's profit from the Circus transaction and the similarity between the Diaz contract price and the Circus contract price also indicate that the additional sale would have been profitable.

We agree with the district court that Learjet qualifies as a lost volume seller and that the $250,000 in liquidated damages was reasonable in light of the anticipated or actual harm caused by the breach. See K.S.A. 84-2-718(2).

Even if we were to conclude that Learjet was not a lost volume seller, there is authority to support the holding that the liquidated damages clause was reasonable. In *Aero Consulting Corp. v. Cessna Aircraft Co.*, 867 F.Supp. 1480, 1493–94 (D.Kan.1994), the court held that a liquidated damages clause in an aircraft purchase agreement was reasonable under Kansas law. The *Aero* court did not consider the lost volume theory. The base price of the aircraft was $3,995,000. The liquidated damages, which were in the form of a deposit that was retained by Cessna after Aero breached, equaled $425,000. The court found that the liquidated damages clause "was reasonable in light of the damages that Cessna could reasonably anticipate would flow from such a cancellation of the contract." 867 F.Supp. at 1494. The court also noted that "in light of the nature of the production of aircraft and the costs associated with maintaining production, it would not be feasible for Cessna to otherwise obtain an adequate remedy for breach." 867 F.Supp. at 1494. Under both analyses, the liquidated damages claimed by Learjet were reasonable.

Affirmed.

QUESTIONS

1. Questions about the facts of this case

    1.1. So, the Rodriguez deal fizzles, Learjet gets to resell the plane for a larger than anticipated profit *and* it gets to keep $250,000 of Rodriguez' money. Isn't Learjet making out like a bandit on this deal? Is *Vines, supra*, at 860, relevant here?

    1.2. Alternatively, Learjet's profit on the sale to Circus Circus was more than four times the amount of the liquidated damages clause. Shouldn't Learjet amend its form to request more in future cases?

2. Questions about the law

   2.1. Would the case come out differently if the testimony was that Learjet was working at capacity, and could not have made another plane without disappointing another customer? Why, or why not?

   2.2. What if, right after the breach, the federal government ordered Learjet to suspend production for three months so that the FAA could inspect Learjet's plant?

   2.3. Review: Does this court get *Kvassay* right? See *Kvassay*, *supra*, at 855.

C. Alternatives and Limitations on Damage Remedies

As we have seen with agreed damages, parties often try to anticipate the effect of breach and specify its consequences. With the sale of goods, especially those produced on a mass scale, the parties (or at least the seller) knows that a breach to at least some buyers is inevitable. One method of anticipating this is to provide that damages are not available as a remedy—that the seller's efforts to repair or replace the defective goods will be the sole remedy available to an aggrieved buyer.

In the next case, a seller tried to both eliminate some forms of damage, and to require the buyer to accept its efforts to repair or replace defective goods. As we will see, the U.C.C. has sections which specifically deal with these common situations. When reading this case, ask yourself what type of evidence you would have to muster and proffer if your toaster or rice cooker went on the fritz, and the contract under which you bought it had the same provisions on limitations and remedies.

Roneker v. Kenworth Truck Co.
U.S. District Court, Western District of New York
944 F.Supp. 179 (1996)

Decision and Order

Heckman, United States Magistrate Judge.

The parties have consented to have the undersigned conduct all further proceedings in this matter, including entry of judgment, in accordance with 28 U.S.C. § 636(c). Defendants Kenworth Truck Company ("Kenworth") and Detroit Diesel Corp. ("DDC") have moved for summary judgment pursuant to Rule 56 of the Federal Rules of Civil Procedure. For the following reasons, defendants' motions are granted in part and denied in part.

BACKGROUND

Plaintiff is a self-employed truck driver. On December 31, 1992, he purchased a 1993 Kenworth T600B truck, which contained an engine manufactured by DDC. Kenworth's warranty agreement covering the sale provided:

> [E]xcept for engine, engine brake, automatic transmission, tires, wheels and/or rims, and fifth wheel, which are warranted directly to you by their respective manufacturers, . . . [the vehicle] will be free from defects in materials and workmanship during the time and mileage periods set forth in the Warranty Schedule and appearing under normal use and service.
>
> * * *
>
> Your sole and exclusive remedy against Kenworth . . ., arising from your purchase and use of this vehicle, is limited to the repair or replacement of defective materials or workmanship at Authorized Kenworth Class 8 Dealers. . . .
>
> WARRANTY DISCLAIMER AND LIMITATIONS OF LIABILITY
>
> EXCEPT FOR THE ABOVE WARRANTY, KENWORTH . . . MAKE[S] NO OTHER WARRANTIES, EXPRESS OR IMPLIED, AND MAKE[S] NO WARRANTY OF MERCHANTABILITY OR FITNESS FOR A PARTICULAR PURPOSE.

> IT IS AGREED THAT KENWORTH . . . SHALL NOT BE LIABLE FOR INCIDENTAL OR CONSEQUENTIAL DAMAGES including, but not limited to: loss of income; damage to vehicle, attachments, trailers and cargo; towing expenses, attorney's fees and the liability you may have in respect to any other person.

(Item 24, Ex.F(B)).

The DDC warranty covering the engine provided:

> Defects
>
> This warranty covers Engine REPAIRS to correct any malfunction occurring during the WARRANTY PERIOD resulting from defects in material or workmanship.
>
> Repairs
>
> To obtain warranty repairs, you must request the needed repairs within the WARRANTY PERIOD from an authorized DDC service outlet. Only new genuine parts or remanufactured parts or components supplied or approved by DDC will be used. DDC may, at its discretion, replace rather than repair components. . . .
>
> * * *
>
> Incidental or Consequential Damages
>
> DDC is not responsible for incidental or consequential costs or expenses which the owner may incur as a result of a malfunction or failure covered by this warranty, such as communication expenses, meals, lodging, overtime, towing, loss of use of the Engine or vehicle ("downtime"), loss of time, inconvenience, cargo loss or damage, and other similar costs and expenses.
>
> Other Limitations
>
> The performance of REPAIRS is the exclusive Owner's remedy under this warranty. DDC does not authorize any person to assume or create for it any other obligation or liability in connection with the Engine or the Accessories.
>
> THIS WARRANTY AND THE EMISSIONS CONTROL WARRANTY ARE THE ONLY WARRANTIES APPLICABLE TO THE ENGINE AND ACCESSORIES AS USED IN ON-HIGHWAY VEHICLE APPLICATIONS. [DDC] MAKES NO OTHER WARRANTIES EXPRESS OR IMPLIED, INCLUDING

> ANY IMPLIED WARRANTY OF MERCHANTABILITY OR FITNESS FOR A PARTICULAR PURPOSE. [DDC] SHALL NOT BE LIABLE FOR ANY INCIDENTAL OR CONSEQUENTIAL DAMAGES AS DESCRIBED ABOVE.

(Item 21, Ex.A).

Plaintiff claims that he began having problems with the truck almost immediately after he bought it. On October 19, 1993, plaintiff's attorney Susan M. Hassinger, Esq., wrote to Mr. Daniel Perryman, Service Manager for Kenworth of Indianapolis, Inc. (The Kenworth dealership from whom plaintiff bought the truck), detailing the following problems:

1. Despite three front-end alignments and at least 15 service visits, the steering wheel shimmied and plaintiff had to purchase new steering tires twice before reaching 100,000 miles.
2. The engine was consuming five times the normal amount of oil, and plaintiff had to have an oil pan leak repaired. His attorney stated in the letter that plaintiff "does not want the motor to be overhauled. [Plaintiff] purchased a brand new vehicle, not one with an overhauled, refurbished motor."
3. The transmission did not properly shift from 7th to 8th gear, it "hammered" when going into gear, it "howled" at various speeds, and the gearshift lever vibrated and rattled.
4. The hood was repaired for misalignment, but a piece of the hood was still missing.
5. The electronic tachometer "wandered."

The letter stated that, in light of these problems, plaintiff was "seeking replacement with a new vehicle . . . because it appears that with so many things wrong within the first year of operation, it is quite clearly a lemon and does not meet Kenworth's high standards or its warranties" (Item 20, Ex.F).

The repair invoices produced by plaintiff during discovery in this case (attached as Ex. F. to Item 24) indicate the following:

DATE	MILEAGE	PROBLEM	EXHIBIT
1/4/93	2,431	doors, air leak, fuel gauge	J (attached to Item 24, Ex. F)
1/19/93	8,157	oil leak, timer	D
1/26/93	11,154	axle gasket leak	J
2/1/93	13,377	oil leak	D
2/4/93	14,236	oil leak	G
3/1/93	24,650	front and rear alignment	I
3/8/93	28,143	front alignment	J
4/12/93	39,905	vibration, air compressor	J
4/23/93	45,073	window regulator, hood	L
8/20/93	87,984	fuel filter base	N
9/8/93	90,881	air restriction gauge	D
2/3/94	149,052	forward differential	K
5/3/94	170,377	oil leak	F
5/9/94	"	air conditioning	M

In addition, purchase invoices indicate that plaintiff purchased 55-gallon barrels of oil on March 1, June 24 and November 1, 1993, and January 13 and March 20, 1994 (Item 24, Ex. E). Plaintiff purchased new tires on March 8, July 23 and December 19, 1993, and May 3, 1994 (*id.*, Ex. H).

On November 11, 1994, plaintiff's attorney Charles J. Marchese, Esq., wrote to Kenworth's attorney stating that plaintiff was continuing to have front end and engine problems with the truck. Plaintiff's attorney stated that DDC "has refused to meet with [plaintiff] and instead offers a rebuilt engine as a solution, one my client is adamantly opposed to as the engine is obviously defective and a new engine should have been provided" (Item 20, Ex. D). Mr. Marchese also detailed an additional problem with the truck's rear end that necessitated repair work involving a rebuilt unit, which "voided the original 500,000 mile warranty" (*id.*). Mr. Marchese demanded replacement of the truck with a new Kenworth vehicle, and reimbursement for "one-half of [plaintiff's] out-of-pocket loss over the past two years (*id.*)."

On December 19, 1994, plaintiff traded in the 1993 truck for a 1995 Kenworth T600 (Item 20, Ex. H). He received a $60,000.00 trade-in allowance (*id.*).

Plaintiff filed this action on February 21, 1995, presumably on the basis of diversity jurisdiction (although there are no jurisdictional or venue allegations in the complaint) (Item 1). He alleges that he "suffered damages such as loss of income, increased oil expense, increased tire expense [and] other related expenses due to the vehicle's lack of fitness for purpose of its intended use and the cost of replacing the vehicle with one fit for the intended use" (Item 1, & 14). He also claims that defendants breached their written warranties "that the vehicle will be free from defects in materials and workmanship and that the vehicle and engine were merchantable and fit for their particular purpose" (*id.*, & 18). He further alleges that Kenworth breached its contract with respect to several specifications of the 1995 vehicle (*id.*, & 23). He seeks "actual, consequential and replacement damages" in the amount of $650,000.00.

Both Kenworth and DDC move for summary judgment on the ground that the breach of warranty claims and consequential damages alleged in the complaint are barred as a matter of law by the provisions of the respective warranties covering the sale.

DISCUSSION

A. Summary Judgment.

Summary judgment is appropriate if the pleadings, discovery materials, and affidavits on file "show that there is no genuine issue as to any material fact and that the moving party is entitled to a judgment as a matter of law." Fed.R.Civ.P. 56(c). * * *

B. Breach of Warranty.

In this case, plaintiff alleges that both Kenworth and DDC failed to remedy the numerous problems he had with the 1993 vehicle and engine, causing significant "down time" resulting in loss of income and other consequential damages. Defendants argue that the language in their respective warranties precludes plaintiff's claims for consequential damages and for breach of implied warranty of merchantability or fitness for a particular purpose.

Section 2-719 of the New York Uniform Commercial Code provides:

Contractual Modification or Limitation of Remedy

(1) Subject to the provisions of subsections (2) and (3) of this section and of the preceding section on liquidation and limitation of damages,

> (a) the agreement may provide for remedies in addition to or in substitution for those provided in this Article and may limit or alter the measure of damages recoverable under this Article, as by limiting the buyer's remedies to return of the goods and repayment of the price or to repair and replacement of non-conforming goods or parts; and
>
> (b) resort to a remedy as provided is optional unless the remedy is expressly agreed to be exclusive, in which case it is the sole remedy.
>
> (2) Where circumstances cause an exclusive or limited remedy to fail of its essential purpose, remedy may be had as provided in this Act.
>
> (3) Consequential damages may be limited or excluded unless the limitation or exclusion is unconscionable. Limitation of consequential damages for injury to the person in the case of consumer goods is prima facie unconscionable but limitation of damages where the loss is commercial is not.

N.Y.U.C.C. § 2-719.

Here, the warranties both exclude consequential damages and limit plaintiff's remedy to repair and replacement. Plaintiff argues that the remedy of repair and replacement failed of its essential purpose of this case, and that therefore the exclusion of consequential damages can be disregarded under N.Y.U.C.C. § 2-719(2). This precise question was addressed in *Cayuga Harvester, Inc. v. Allis-Chalmers Corp.*, 95 A.D.2d 5, 465 N.Y.S.2d 606 (4th Dept.1983). In that case, the Fourth Department held that an exclusion of consequential damages under § 2-719(3) should be given effect even where the plaintiff has shown under § 2-719(2) that the limited remedy of repair and replacement has failed of its essential purpose. According to the Fourth Department:

> "The limited remedy of repair and a consequential damages exclusion are two discrete ways of attempting to limit recovery for breach of warranty. The Code . . . tests each by a different standard. The former survives unless it fails of its essential purpose, while the latter is valid unless it is unconscionable. We therefore see no reason to hold, as a general proposition, that the failure of the limited remedy provided in the contract, without more, invalidates a wholly distinct term in the agreement excluding consequential damages."

* * * As explained in the *Cayuga Harvester* case:

> The purposes of the two clauses are totally discrete: that of the first is to restrict defendant's obligations under the transaction to repairing or replacing defective parts, while that of the second is to rule out a specific type of damage. Each clause stands on its own and may be given effect without regard to the other.

Cayuga Harvester, *supra*, 95 A.D.2d at 14, 465 N.Y.S.2d at 613. Thus, even if the plaintiff succeeds in establishing that the limited remedy of repair has failed of its essential purpose, an exclusion of consequential damages that is not unconscionable will be given effect "where the failure of the repair and replacement warranty is not due to bad faith or willfully dilatory conduct. . . ." *Id.*, 95 A.D.2d at 15, 465 N.Y.S.2d at 614.[3]

Under New York law, therefore, a sales contract limiting the buyer's remedy to repair or replacement and excluding the recovery of consequential damages is subject to a two-part analysis to determine (1) whether the limited remedy failed in its essential purpose, and (2) whether the exclusion of consequential damages was unconscionable. *Siemens*, *supra* at 694–96; *Cayuga Harvester*, *supra*. The court now turns to this two-part analysis.

1. Failure of Essential Purpose.

Whether a limited remedy in a contract fails in its essential purpose is a question of fact. * * * A remedy fails in its essential purpose when, while it may have appeared fair and reasonable at the inception of the contract, as a result of later circumstances it operates to deprive a party of a substantial benefit of the bargain. * * * As explained in *Cayuga Harvester*:

> The damage to the buyer is the same whether the seller diligently but unsuccessfully attempts to honor his promise or acts negligently or in bad faith. Moreover, a "delay in supplying the remedy can just as effectively deny the purchaser the product he expected as can the total inability to repair. In both instances the buyer loses the substantial benefit of his purchase."

Cayuga Harvester, *supra* (quoting *Chatlos Systems*, *supra*, 635 F.2d at 1085); * * *

---

[3]The complaint in this case does not allege, and the record before the court does not suggest, bad faith or dilatory conduct on the part of either Kenworth or DDC.

In this case, plaintiff has made a sufficient prima facie showing for this court to find that material factual issues exist as to whether the limited remedy of repair or replacement failed of its essential purpose. Plaintiff alleges that he repeatedly took the truck in for repairs, and that the dealer was unable to repair the various problems. As outlined above, plaintiff has produced copies of repair bills, work orders and purchase invoices for work performed on the 1993 vehicle during the two-year warranty period (*see* Table at p. 5, *infra*, and Item 24, Ex. F(D-O)). Apparently, plaintiff has not produced a detailed repair log or list of warranty claims. *See Cayuga Harvester*, *supra*, 95 A.D.2d at 12, 465 N.Y.S.2d at 612. However, the documents in the record at least raise a material issue of fact as to whether the remedy of repair failed of its essential purpose.

Defendants claim that they are entitled to summary judgment on the limitation of remedy issue because plaintiff refused to accept the remedy of repair offered by defendants and instead unilaterally demanded replacement of the 1993 truck with an entirely new one. However, whether plaintiff's demands were reasonable under the circumstances likewise presents an issue of fact for the jury. * * * In addition, neither Kenworth's nor DDC's warranty expressly limits the remedy to repair or replacement using only remanufactured parts.

Based on the record before the court, I find that the question of whether the limited remedy of repair or replacement warranted by defendants failed of its essential purpose should be left for the jury to determine "upon proof of the circumstances occurring after the contract [was] formed." * * * Should plaintiff prevail on this question, he would be free to pursue his remedies under other provisions of the U.C.C. as if the limited remedy did not exist. * * *

2. Exclusion of Consequential Damages.

As discussed above, even if plaintiff succeeds in establishing that the repair and replacement warranty failed of its essential purpose, the exclusion of consequential damages will remain in effect unless the exclusion is unconscionable. Consequential damages are defined in the U.C.C. as follows:

> Consequential damages resulting from the seller's breach include
>
> (a) any loss resulting from general or particular requirements and needs of which the seller at the time of contracting had reason to know and which could not reasonably be prevented by cover or otherwise; and

(b) injury to person or property proximately resulting from any breach of warranty.

N.Y.U.C.C. § 2-715(2). "The determination of unconscionability is a matter of law for the court to decide." * * *

Unconscionability requires "an absence of meaningful choice on the part of one of the parties together with contract terms which are unreasonably favorable to the other party." *Williams v. Walker-Thomas Furniture Co.*, 350 F.2d 445, 449 (D.C.Cir.1965) * * *. "The basic test is whether, in light of the general commercial background and the commercial needs of the particular trade or case, the clauses involved are so one-sided as to be unconscionable under the circumstances existing at the time of the making of the contract." N.Y.U.C.C. § 2-302, Official Comment 1. Factors that courts have considered in determining unconscionability include disparity in bargaining power, an atmosphere of haste and pressure, and lack of understanding by one of the parties. * * *

In cases involving transactions of a commercial nature, courts have rarely found unconscionability. * * * Indeed, "there is a presumption of conscionability when the contract is between businessmen in a commercial setting." * * *

In this case, the transaction was indisputably commercial in nature. The record shows that plaintiff is a self-employed truck driver who has been in the business for over thirty years (Item 20, Ex. F). He had purchased several Kenworth vehicles prior to purchasing the 1993 vehicle (*id.*, Ex. D) and an additional one after the 1993 vehicle. Plaintiff signed the Kenworth warranty agreement, acknowledging that he had read the agreement and understood and accepted its terms (Item 24, Ex. F(B)). Although plaintiff may not have the bargaining power to persuade defendants to change their warranty language, I refuse to find that the warranty claim was unconscionable.

Accordingly, plaintiff is barred from recovering consequential damages. The record is unclear as to whether plaintiff is claiming damages that are not consequential in nature. To the extent that he is, plaintiff can proceed to trial on the first issue—whether the remedy of repair failed of its essential purpose.

In this court's view, "the precise demarcation between direct and consequential damages is a question of fact . . . [which] must be left for resolution at trial." *American Elec. Power Co. v. Westinghouse Elec. Corp.*, 418 F. Supp. 435, 459–60 (S.D.N.Y. 1976). In making its determination, the jury should consider the commercial context in which the contract was made as well as the express language of the exclusion clauses themselves. *Id.* at 459. "Suffice it to say that the scope of direct damages recoverable by plaintiff [ ], should [he] prevail at trial, must provide a 'fair quantum of remedy for the breach of the obligations or duties outlined in the contract.' " *Id.* at 460 (quoting N.Y.U.C.C. § 2-719, Official Comment 1).

CONCLUSION

For the foregoing reasons, defendant Kenworth's motion for summary judgment (Item 23) and defendant DDC's motion for summary judgment (Item 18) are granted in part and denied in part.

SO ORDERED.

QUESTIONS

1. Questions about the facts of this case

   1.1. At trial, what facts would you point to to show, on behalf of Roneker, that the repair or replace remedy had failed of its essential purpose?

   1.2. What facts would you adduce if you represented Kenworth?

   1.3. Do you think this judge might change his view of what unconscionability is after reading the California Supreme Court's decision in *Donovan v. RRL Corp., supra,* at 254.

2. Questions about the law

   2.1. Following the standard measure of damages, shouldn't the court award the difference between a good Kenworth truck and the lemon Roneker bought? Indeed, if at trial Roneker can show failure of an essential purpose, then Section 2-714 of the Uniform Commercial Code provides that the measure of damages is the difference at the time and place of acceptance of the goods between the value of the goods at that time and the value of the goods had they had been as promised. Will that satisfy Roneker? How would he prove both values?

2.2. Why couldn't Roneker get specific performance of the "repair or replace" clause?

2.3. Does it seem inconsistent to let Roneker out of the "repair or replace" clause, but not the limitation on consequential damages?

Chapter 6

WHEN DO YOU HAVE RIGHTS AND/OR DUTIES UNDER A CONTRACT THAT YOU DID NOT MAKE?

We have now covered the story of a contract from beginning to end. We have considered the questions

- is there a contract, *i.e.*, an agreement that is legally enforceable?
- if so, what are its terms?
- have the two contracting parties performed pursuant to those terms?
- if not, is the nonperformance excused?
- and, if not, what are the legal remedies?

While we have covered the entire story, it has been a two character or a two party story. We now need to consider when third parties have rights or duties under a contract that they did not enter into themselves. More specifically, we need to consider third party beneficiaries, assignees of contract rights and delegatees of contract duties.

SECTION 1: THIRD PARTY BENEFICIARIES

Issues of third party beneficiary law arise in situations in which a person who is not a party to a contract and who did not provide the consideration for that contract claims that she can enforce the contract because the parties intended for her to benefit from performance of the contract.

The most obvious example of a third party beneficiary contract is a life insurance contract. For example, Epstein enters into a life insurance contract with the Allstate Insurance Company in which Epstein agrees to make annual premium payments of $1,000 and Allstate agrees to pay $25,000 in policy benefits to Sharon Stone on Epstein's death. When Epstein dies, Allstate refuses to pay Sharon Stone, contending that it never contracted with her and never received consideration from her. Even though Sharon Stone was not a party to the Epstein-Allstate contract and provided no consideration to Allstate, she can enforce that life insurance contract. She is a third party beneficiary.

It is important to understand that example and to understand that it is an example based on general contract law rather than special life insurance law. The legal basis for Sharon Stone's rights against Allstate is the general contract law concept of third party beneficiary rather than some special life insurance law rule.

Consider a third party beneficiary example unrelated to life insurance. Ponoroff owed Markell $300. Ponoroff later entered into a contract whereby Ponoroff loaned Epstein $300 and Epstein promised to repay that $300 to Markell, thus satisfying Ponoroff's debt to Markell.

Under these facts, Markell is not a party to the contract between Ponoroff and Epstein. Under these facts, Markell did not provide the consideration to Epstein in exchange for Epstein's promise to pay him as $300. Nonetheless, Markell as a "third party beneficiary" can enforce the promise of the "promisor," Epstein.

This Ponoroff-Markell hypothetical is similar to *Lawrence v. Fox*, which is generally regarded as the seminal case recognizing rights of certain third party beneficiaries.

Lawrence v. Fox

Court of Appeals of New York
20 NY 268 (1859)

APPEAL from the Superior Court of the city of Buffalo. On the trial before Mr. Justice MASTEN, it appeared by the evidence of a bystander, that one Holly, in November, 1857, at the request of the defendant, loaned and advanced to him $300, stating at the time that he owed that sum to the plaintiff for money borrowed of him, and had agreed to pay it to him the then next day; that the defendant in consideration thereof, at the time of receiving the money, promised to pay it to the plaintiff the then next day. Upon this state of facts the defendant moved for a nonsuit, upon three several grounds, viz.: That there was no proof tending to show that Holly was indebted to the plaintiff; that the agreement by the defendant with Holly to pay the plaintiff was void for want of consideration, and that there was no privity between the plaintiff and defendant. The court overruled the motion, and the counsel for the defendant excepted. The cause was then submitted to the jury, and they found a verdict for the plaintiff for the amount of the loan and interest, $344.66, upon which judgment was entered; from which the defendant appealed to the Superior Court, at general term, where the judgment was affirmed, and the defendant appealed to this court.

H. GRAY, J.

The first objection raised on the trial amounts to this: That the evidence of the person present, who heard the declarations of Holly giving directions as to the payment of the money he was then advancing to the defendant, was mere hearsay and therefore not competent. Had the plaintiff sued Holly for this sum of money no objection to the competency of this evidence would have been thought of; and if the defendant had performed his promise by paying the sum loaned to him to the plaintiff, and Holly had afterwards sued him for its recovery, and this evidence had been offered by the defendant, it would doubtless have been received without an objection from any source. All the defendant had the right to demand in this case was evidence which, as between Holly and the plaintiff, was competent to establish the relation between them of debtor and creditor. For that purpose the evidence was clearly competent; it covered the whole ground and warranted the verdict of the jury.

But it is claimed that notwithstanding this promise was established by competent evidence, it was void for the want of consideration. It is now more than a quarter of a century since it was settled by the Supreme Court of this State—in an able and pains-taking opinion by the late Chief Justice SAVAGE, in which the authorities were fully examined and carefully analysed—that a promise in all material respects like the one under consideration was valid; and the judgment of that court was unanimously affirmed by the Court for the Correction of Errors. (Farley v. Cleaveland, 4 Cow., 432; same case in error, 9 id., 639.) In that case one Moon owed Farley and sold to Cleaveland a quantity of hay, in consideration of which Cleaveland promised to pay Moon's debt to Farley; and the decision in favor of Farley's right to recover was placed upon the ground that the hay received by Cleaveland from Moon was a valid consideration for Cleaveland's promise to pay Farley, and that the subsisting liability of Moon to pay Farley was no objection to the recovery. The fact that the money advanced by Holly to the defendant was a loan to him for a day, and that it thereby became the property of the defendant, seemed to impress the defendant's counsel with the idea that because the defendant's promise was not a trust fund placed by the plaintiff in the defendant's hands, out of which he was to realize money as from the sale of a chattel or the collection of a debt, the promise although made for the benefit of the plaintiff could not enure to his benefit. The hay which Cleaveland delivered to Moon was not to be paid to Farley, but the debt incurred by Cleaveland for the purchase of the hay, like the debt incurred by the defendant for money borrowed, was what was to be paid.

That case has been often referred to by the courts of this State, and has never been doubted as sound authority for the principle upheld by it. It puts to rest the objection that the defendant's promise was void for want of consideration. The report of that case shows that the promise was not only made to Moon but to the plaintiff Farley. In this case the promise was made to Holly and not expressly to the plaintiff; and this difference between the two cases presents the question, raised by the defendant's objection, as to the want of privity between the plaintiff and defendant.

But it is urged that because the defendant was not in any sense a trustee of the property of Holly for the benefit of the plaintiff, the law will not imply a promise. I agree that many of the cases where a promise was implied were cases of trusts, created for the benefit of the promiser. The duty of the trustee to pay the cestuis que trust, according to the terms of the trust, implies his promise to the latter to do so. In this case the defendant, upon ample consideration received from Holly, promised Holly to pay his debt to the plaintiff; the consideration received and the promise to Holly made it as plainly his duty to pay the plaintiff as if the money had been remitted to him for that purpose, and as well implied a promise to do so as if he had been made a trustee of property to be converted into cash with which to pay. The fact that a breach of the duty imposed in the one case may be visited, and justly, with more serious consequences than in the other, by no means disproves the payment to be a duty in both. The principle illustrated by the example so frequently quoted (which concisely states the case in hand) "that a promise made to one for the benefit of another, he for whose benefit it is made may bring an action for its breach," has been applied to trust cases, not because it was exclusively applicable to those cases, but because it was a principle of law, and as such applicable to those cases.

It was also insisted that Holly could have discharged the defendant from his promise, though it was intended by both parties for the benefit of the plaintiff, and therefore the plaintiff was not entitled to maintain this suit for the recovery of a demand over which he had no control. It is enough that the plaintiff did not release the defendant from his promise, and whether he could or not is a question not now necessarily involved; but if it was, I think it would be found difficult to maintain the right of Holly to discharge a judgment recovered by the plaintiff upon confession or otherwise, for the breach of the defendant's promise; and if he could not, how could he discharge the suit before judgment, or the promise before suit, made as it was for the plaintiff's benefit and in accordance with legal presumption accepted by him until his dissent was shown. Suppose the defendant had given his note in which, for value received of Holly, he had promised to pay the plaintiff and the plaintiff had accepted the promise, retaining Holly's liability. Very clearly Holly could not have discharged that promise, be the right to release the defendant as it may.

No one can doubt that he owes the sum of money demanded of him, or that in accordance with his promise it was his duty to have paid it to the plaintiff; nor can it be doubted that whatever may be the diversity of opinion elsewhere, the adjudications in this State, from a very early period, approved by experience, have established the defendant's liability; if, therefore, it could be shown that a more strict and technically accurate application of the rules applied, would lead to a different result (which I by no means concede), the effort should not be made in the face of manifest justice.

The judgment should be affirmed.

COMSTOCK, J. (Dissenting.)

The plaintiff had nothing to do with the promise on which he brought this action. It was not made to him, nor did the consideration proceed from him. If he can maintain the suit, it is because an anomaly has found its way into the law on this subject. In general, there must be privity of contract. The party who sues upon a promise must be the promisee, or he must have some legal interest in the undertaking. In this case, it is plain that Holly, who loaned the money to the defendant, and to whom the promise in question was made, could at any time have claimed that it should be performed to himself personally. He had lent the money to the defendant, and at the same time directed the latter to pay the sum to the plaintiff. This direction he could countermand, and if he had done so, manifestly the defendant's promise to pay according to the direction would have ceased to exist. The plaintiff would receive a benefit by a complete execution of the arrangement, but the arrangement itself was between other parties, and was under their exclusive control. If the defendant had paid the money to Holly, his debt would have been discharged thereby. So Holly might have released the demand or assigned it to another person, or the parties might have annulled the promise now in question, and designated some other creditor of Holly as the party to whom the money should be paid. It has never been claimed, that in a case thus situated, the right of a third person to sue upon the promise rested on any sound principle of law. We are to inquire whether the rule has been so established by positive authority.

The cases in which some trust was involved are also frequently referred to as authority for the doctrine now in question, but they do not sustain it. If A delivers money or property to B, which the latter accepts upon a trust for the benefit of C, the latter can enforce the trust by an appropriate action for that purpose.

A fund received under such an agreement does not belong to the person who receives it. He must account for it specifically; and perhaps there is no gross violation of principle in permitting the equitable owner of it to sue upon an express promise to pay it over. Having a specific interest in the thing, the undertaking to account for it may be regarded as in some sense made with him through the author of the trust. But further than this we cannot go without violating plain rules of law. In the case before us there was nothing in the nature of a trust or agency. The defendant borrowed the money of Holly and received it as his own. The plaintiff had no right in the fund, legal or equitable. The promise to repay the money created an obligation in favor of the lender to whom it was made and not in favor of any one else.

The judgment of the court below should therefore be reversed, and a new trial granted.

QUESTIONS AND NOTE

1. Questions about the facts of this case

    1.1. To whom did the plaintiff loan money?

    1.2. From whom is the plaintiff trying to collect that debt?

    1.3. Why is the plaintiff trying to collect his debt from the defendant instead of his borrower? Does the court answer that question? Should it?

2. Questions about the law

   2.1. Who was the third party beneficiary?

   2.2. Who was the promisor? Who was the promisee?

   2.3. Why is the court considering consideration?

   2.4. Is there any question as to whether the defendant received consideration for its promise to pay the plaintiff $300?

   2.5. Did the defendant receive consideration from the plaintiff?

   2.6. What is the purpose of requiring consideration?

   2.7. What is privity? Are the plaintiff and the defendant in privity? Didn't the defendant promise to pay the plaintiff? Why is the court discussing implied promises?

   2.8. Who could have sued whom? Could the plaintiff have sued Holly for $300? Could the plaintiff have collected the $300 from Holly and still sued the defendant?

   2.9. If the plaintiff sued Holly because the defendant refused to pay the plaintiff, could Holly have then sued the defendant for breach of contract?

3. Note

For a more complete understanding of why Lawrence sued Fox instead of Lawrence suing Holly or Holly suing Fox, *see* Anthony Jon Waters, *The Property in the Promise: A Study of the Third Party Beneficiary Rule*, 98 HARV. L. REV. 1109 (1985).

Professor Waters' article provides not only an understanding of what happened in *Lawrence v. Fox* but also what happened after *Lawrence v. Fox*:

> The second Part of this Article deals impressionistically with the question of how this new rule, quite at odds with received wisdom, became all but universally accepted in American jurisdictions, state and federal. This inquiry centers on the work of Arthur Corbin, Professor of Law at Yale Law School, author of six articles on the subject of third party contract rights, and highly influential in the formulation of both Restatements of Contracts. Between the years 1918 and 1930, Corbin managed nothing less than a campaign on behalf of the third party beneficiary rule, singling out

for a special brand of jurisprudential hounding those jurisdictions that denied or tightly limited third party recovery and basing much of his work on flagrant misrepresentation of the law of those states. It is an extraordinary story of how one well-placed academic influenced the development of the common law.

* * *

During the sixty years or so between the New York Court of Appeals decision in *Lawrence v. Fox* and the beginning of Arthur Corbin's activity in this area, the third party beneficiary rule enjoyed a fitful existence. In 1918, Corbin launched what became a campaign on behalf of the third party beneficiary rule, a campaign that would last about fifty years and would culminate in the "Corbinized," "intended beneficiary" rule of the Second Restatement.

Arthur Linton Corbin was born in 1874, fifteen years after the New York Court of Appeals decided *Lawrence v. Fox*. He died in 1967, the same year that the American Law Institute unveiled the 'intended beneficiary' formulation. During his life he became the most influential academic figure in American contract law, achieving a preeminence that no one since has matched. * * *

When Arthur Corbin first published on the subject of third party beneficiary doctrine, the courts had been struggling with the doctrinal repercussions of this judicial innovation for more than half a century. The rule of *Lawrence v. Fox* had quickly generated difficult questions that could not be answered by the logical application of doctrine, for there was, as yet, no doctrine to apply. By 1918, when Corbin published the first of his six articles on the subject, there was enough case law, enough controversy, and enough chaos to have warranted several attempts, by various people, to set things straight. Williston, for example, began his 1902 article "Contracts for the Benefit of a Third Person," with this quote:

"In no department of the law has a more obstinate and persistent battle between practice and theory been waged than in regard to the answer to the question: Whether a right of action accrues to a third person from a contract made by others for his benefit? Nor is the strife ended; for if it be granted that the scale inclines in favor of practice, yet the advocates of this result are continually endeavoring to extend the territory which they have conquered and to apply the doctrines thereby established to cases which should be governed by other principles."

From the outset of his lengthy crusade on behalf of the third party beneficiary, Corbin was resolute in his belief that the rule was supported by many practical considerations and opposed only by empty formalism. Here, as elsewhere, Williston and Corbin disagreed. Williston took the position that a beneficiary's recovery on the contract, while theoretically anomalous, was sometimes justified by the equities of the case. By contrast, Corbin pushed for the recognition of third party enforcement as the general rule rather than the exception.

98 HARV. L. REV. at 1148–51.

The debate Corbin and Williston conducted in contracts law treatises and law review articles and Restatements was not, in the main, a debate over whether traditional contracts concepts such as consideration or privity precluded a third party from ever enforcing a contract. Rather the focus of the debate was on when third parties could enforce contracts. This debate continues today not only in contract law treatises and law review articles and but also in cases such as the following two cases: *Ex parte Stamey* and *Midwest Grain Products of Illinois, Inc. v. Productization, Inc. and CMI Corp.*

A. When a Third Party is a "Third Party Beneficiary"

Ex Parte Stamey

Supreme Court of Alabama
776 So.2d 85 (2000)

HOUSTON, Justice.

Gary Stamey and Deborah Stamey, third-party plaintiffs in an action currently pending in the Mobile Circuit Court, petition for a writ of mandamus directing the trial court to vacate its order compelling arbitration of the Stameys' claims against Green Tree Financial Corporation, Hallmont Homes, Inc., and Hallmont employees Jarod Hall and Gaylon Hall. We deny the writ.

In December 1996, the Stameys contracted with Hallmont Homes, Inc., to purchase land and a mobile home. The contract also included assurances that Hallmont would prepare a foundation for the mobile home and would install a septic system and a light pole. The Stameys claim that the septic system and the light pole were never installed. The Stameys had borrowed money from Green Tree to pay for these purchases and installations. Included in the financing agreement between Green Tree and the Stameys was this arbitration provision:

> "ARBITRATION: ALL DISPUTES, CLAIMS OR CONTROVERSIES ARISING FROM OR RELATING TO THIS CONTRACT OR THE PARTIES THERETO SHALL BE RESOLVED BY BINDING ARBITRATION BY ONE ARBITRATOR SELECTED BY YOU WITH MY CONSENT. THIS AGREEMENT IS MADE PURSUANT TO A TRANSACTION IN INTERSTATE COMMERCE AND SHALL BE GOVERNED BY THE FEDERAL ARBITRATION ACT AT 9 U.S.C. SECTION 1. JUDGMENT UPON THE AWARD RENDERED MAY BE ENTERED IN ANY COURT HAVING JURISDICTION. THE PARTIES AGREE AND UNDERSTAND THAT THEY CHOOSE ARBITRATION INSTEAD OF LITIGATION TO RESOLVE DISPUTES. THE PARTIES UNDERSTAND THAT THEY HAVE A RIGHT OR OPPORTUNITY TO LITIGATE DISPUTES IN COURT, BUT THAT THEY PREFER TO RESOLVE THEIR DISPUTES THROUGH ARBITRATION, EXCEPT AS PROVIDED HEREIN. THE PARTIES VOLUNTARILY AND KNOWINGLY WAIVE ANY RIGHT THEY HAVE TO A JURY TRIAL, EITHER PURSUANT TO ARBITRATION UNDER THIS CLAUSE OR PURSUANT TO A COURT ACTION BY YOU (AS PROVIDED HEREIN). THE PARTIES AGREE AND UNDERSTAND THAT ALL DISPUTES ARISING UNDER CASE LAW, STATUTORY LAW AND ALL OTHER LAWS INCLUDING, BUT NOT LIMITED TO, ALL CONTRACT, TORT AND PROPERTY DISPUTES WILL BE SUBJECT TO BINDING ARBITRATION IN ACCORD WITH THIS CONTRACT.

Dr. Bernard Eichold II, in his capacity as health officer of Mobile County, sued for injunctive relief against the Stameys, alleging that their property was in violation of state health laws—specifically, his complaint alleged a violation concerning the septic system on the Stameys' property. The Stameys filed an answer, along with a third-party complaint against Hallmont and Green Tree, alleging conversion, fraud, and breach of contract. The Stameys contend that Hallmont and/or Green Tree caused the problem with the septic system for which the Stameys were sued. Hallmont and Green Tree both moved the trial court to compel arbitration of the claims asserted against them. Hallmont was not a signatory to the arbitration agreement. The trial court granted the motions to compel. * * *

While the Stameys' contract with Green Tree contains an arbitration agreement, neither the sale contract between the Stameys and Hallmont nor any other document to which Hallmont was a signatory contained an arbitration agreement. Hallmont's motion to compel arbitration was based on the arbitration provision in the contract between Green Tree and the Stameys.

Normally, in order to have a valid arbitration provision, there must be an agreement to arbitrate, and if no agreement exists, then a party cannot be forced to submit a dispute to arbitration. The question whether one has assented to an arbitration provision is governed by ordinary principles of a state's common law and statutory law governing the formation of contracts. Assent to arbitrate is usually to be manifested through a party's signature on the contract containing the arbitration provision. However, both Federal courts and Alabama courts have enforced exceptions to this rule, so as to allow a nonsignatory, and even one who is not a party, as to a particular contract, to enforce an arbitration provision within that same contract. * * * If Hallmont is a third-party beneficiary, then it should be able to enforce the arbitration provision included in the contract between the Stameys and Green Tree. Thus, we must determine whether Hallmont is a third-party beneficiary of that contract.

A party claiming to be a third-party beneficiary, "must establish that the contracting parties intended, upon execution of the contract, to bestow a direct, as opposed to an incidental, benefit upon the third party." Weathers Auto Glass, Inc. v. Alfa Mut. Ins. Co., 619 So.2d 1328, 1329 (Ala.1993). In other words, Hallmont must show that the Stameys and Green Tree intended for Hallmont to receive a direct benefit from the financing contract. This issue will be determined with the intent of the parties as indicated by the language used. [W]e look to the language of the entire financing contract between the Stameys and Green Tree. We conclude that they did intend for Hallmont to receive a direct benefit.

The financing contract is a standard contract that provides for a secured transaction in which Green Tree received a security interest in the manufactured home and in which Green Tree would pay Hallmont for the manufactured home on behalf of the Stameys. In other words, this contract allows Green Tree to pay the obligation of the Stameys to Hallmont. The section of the contract entitled "ITEMIZATION OF THE AMOUNT FINANCED" sets out the amounts that were to be "paid on [the Stameys'] behalf." Included in this chart are the amounts that were paid on behalf of the Stameys to Hallmont for the cost of the manufactured home, the cost of the land, and the cost of the installations.

Furthermore, the language of the contract clearly shows that the parties contemplated Hallmont as a third-party beneficiary. The last section of the contract states:

> "WAIVER OF JURY TRIAL: I HEREBY WAIVE ANY RIGHT TO A TRIAL BY JURY THAT I HAVE IN ANY SUBSEQUENT LITIGATION BETWEEN ME AND THE SELLER, OR ME AND ANY ASSIGNEE OF THE SELLER, WHERE SUCH LITIGATION ARISES OUT OF, IS RELATED TO, OR IS IN CONNECTION WITH ANY PROVISION OF THIS AGREEMENT, WHETHER THE AGREEMENT IS ASSERTED AS RELATED TO, OR IS IN CONNECTION WITH ANY PROVISION OF THIS AGREEMENT, WHETHER THE AGREEMENT IS ASSERTED AS THE BASIS FOR A CLAIM, COUNTERCLAIM OR CROSS CLAIM, OR A DEFENSE TO A CLAIM, COUNTERCLAIM OR CROSS CLAIM."

(Emphasis added.) By this section, the Stameys clearly waived the right to a jury trial, not against Green Tree, but against Hallmont—"the seller."

The language of the two sections mentioned in the two preceding paragraphs clearly indicates an intent on behalf of the Stameys and Green Tree to benefit Hallmont through the financing contract. Therefore, we conclude that Hallmont is a third-party beneficiary of the financing contract and that it has all the rights that exist under that contract. As a result, Hallmont can enforce the arbitration agreement set out in that contract. * * *

QUESTIONS

1. Questions about the facts of this case

    1.1. Did the contract between the Stameys and Hallmont have an arbitration clause?

    1.2. Who is alleging that it is a third party beneficiary?

    Who is the promisor?

    1.3. Why would the Stameys and Green Tree intend for Hallmont to receive a benefit from the financing contract?

2. Questions about the law

   2.1. Did Hallmont provide any consideration for the Stameys' promise to arbitrate?

   2.2. Would this case have been decided differently if the last section of the contract, the "waiver of jury trial" set out in the end of the opinion, had been omitted?

   2.3. How would this case have been decided by a judge applying *Restatement (Second) of Contracts* § 304 (and § 302)? By the judge in the next case?

Midwest Grain Products of Illinois, Inc. v. Productization, Inc. and CMI Corp.
U.S. Court of Appeals, Seventh Circuit
228 F.3d 784 (2000)

DIANE P. WOOD, Circuit Judge.

This case presents a classic contract dispute: A orders a product from B, and B turns to C to manufacture it. When A receives the product, it is not satisfied, and it wants to hold C responsible for the alleged flaws. We must decide whether there is enough evidence of some kind of warranty, either express or as a matter of law, to allow Midwest Grain Products (Company A) to move beyond summary judgment in its action against CMI Corporation (Company C). (Midwest settled its claims against Productization, Inc. (PI) (Company B), and so that actor has not been part of this case for some time.) The district court concluded that Midwest's evidence was lacking and that CMI was entitled to judgment as a matter of law. It also ruled that CMI was not entitled to its attorneys' fees. Each company has appealed from the part of the judgment adverse to it, but, finding no error in the district court's disposition of the action, we affirm.

I.

On January 12, 1993, Midwest Vice President Anthony Petricola sent a letter to PI President Andrew Livingston requesting a quote on grain dryers to be used in Midwest's expansion of its facility in Pekin, Illinois. Livingston responded on January 26 with an offer on PI's behalf to provide two dryers for a total price of $1,515,800. Midwest accepted PI's offer on February 25, through a purchase order sent to Livingston.

With the deal in hand, PI then turned to CMI to manufacture the dryers. On April 29, 1993, it sent CMI a set of specifications for the dryers Midwest wanted. CMI replied with a fax giving price terms and stating that "[a]cceptance of the order will be subject to receipt by CMI of a letter from Midwest Grain agreeing to make payment, with checks made payable jointly to CMI and Productization." * * *

On May 10, Midwest's Petricola sent the requested letter directly to CMI. The letter commits Midwest to "make payment for equipment purchased by Productization, Inc. from CMI Corporation for its [*i.e.*, Midwest's] project in Pekin, Illinois, with check(s) payable jointly to Productization, Inc. and CMI Corporation." It also mentions the shipment, price, and storage terms of the PI/CMI agreement and states that CMI will issue waivers of liens to Midwest upon CMI's receipt of payment.

This was Midwest's only direct appearance into the dealings between PI and CMI. The latter two companies continued to work out the details of their contract. * * *

* * * Paragraph 8 addressed warranties, and said in pertinent part:

> CMI warrants such equipment, accessories, parts and other goods covered by this order and as are manufactured by CMI against defective material or workmanship for a period of six (6) months after date of first delivery or for one thousand (1,000) hours of use, whichever comes first;. . . . THIS WARRANTY IS EXPRESSLY IN LIEU OF AND EXCLUDES ALL OTHER WARRANTIES, EXPRESSED OR IMPLIED (INCLUDING ANY WARRANTY OF MERCHANTABILITY AND FITNESS OF ANY PRODUCT OR GOODS FOR A PARTICULAR PURPOSE), AND ALL OTHER OBLIGATIONS OR LIABILITIES ON CMI'S PART, AND CMI NEITHER ASSUMES NOR AUTHORIZES ANY OTHER PERSON TO ASSUME FOR CMI ANY OTHER LIABILITY IN CONNECTION WITH THE SALE OF CMI'S PRODUCTS. THERE ARE NOT ANY WARRANTIES WHICH EXTEND BEYOND THE DESCRIPTION ON THE FACE OF THIS ORDER.

* * *

The first dryer reached Midwest in February 1994, but it was not put into service until 1995. The other dryer was delivered in April 1994 and was put into service two months later. Midwest experienced a variety of problems with both units. Initially, CMI and PI serviced them. Later, still unhappy with PI and CMI, it filed this action.

* * *

We begin with the question whether, under Oklahoma law, Midwest has any claim to third-party beneficiary status to the agreement between CMI and PI.

* * *

Under Oklahoma law, a party may be a third-party beneficiary to an agreement only if the contracting parties intended the benefits of the contract to run to the third party. * * * "[I]t is not necessary that third-party beneficiaries be specifically identified at the time of contracting, but it must appear that the contract was expressly made for the benefit of a class of persons to which the party seeking enforcement belongs."

There are only two pieces of evidence in this record that link the CMI/PI contract to Midwest: first, the fact that CMI knew that PI wanted the dryers so that it could then sell them to Midwest, and second, the fact that CMI insisted that it be paid by checks that Midwest made payable jointly to PI and to itself. Nothing in Oklahoma law the parties have cited, and nothing in Oklahoma law that we have been able to find ourselves, comes close to holding that an ultimate buyer is a third-party beneficiary of every contract its seller enters into with suppliers in order to fulfill the contract. Nor are we referred to, or can we find, any Oklahoma decision indicating that the kind of financial arrangement CMI secured here is enough to give the ultimate buyer third-party beneficiary status. That step was enough to make Midwest a surety for PI, and in that sense it allowed CMI to look not only to PI for payment (a right it had under the basic contract) but also to Midwest. But it did not indicate that the contract was expressly for Midwest's benefit. From CMI's point of view, it was a contract for the sale of goods, and it was not CMI's problem in the final analysis what PI wanted to do with the dryers once it received them.

Indeed, in the section of Midwest's brief entitled "Plaintiff's third-party beneficiary status was ignored or improperly addressed," it cites not a single decision of an Oklahoma court. It refers instead to one Illinois case, *Olson v. Etheridge*, 177 Ill.2d 396, 226 Ill.Dec. 780, 686 N.E.2d 563 (Ill.1997), and one decision from this court in a diversity case governed by Illinois law. States vary in their approach to rules like those governing the recognition and rights of third-party beneficiaries, and we would at least need some reason to conclude that Oklahoma and Illinois take the same approach before these authorities would be persuasive.

If Midwest was not a third-party beneficiary of the CMI/PI contract, which is our best predication of what an Oklahoma court would find, then it has no case. * * *

In the final analysis, the party that Midwest needed to pursue was its seller, PI. Indeed, it did include PI in this action at the outset. The terms of its settlement with PI are not pertinent to its case against CMI and are not in any event a matter of record. We hold only that, under the facts as presented and the governing law, the district court correctly granted summary judgment in the case Midwest wanted to bring against CMI.

QUESTIONS

1. Questions about the facts of this case

    1.1. Who bought what from whom?

    1.2. Why is the buyer Midwest suing CMI instead of PI?

    1.3. What facts support Midwest's contention that it is a third party beneficiary of the CMI/PI contract?

2. Questions about the law

    2.1. Why is Midwest arguing that it is a third party beneficiary of the contract between PI and CMI?

    2.2. In omitted dictum, Judge Wood stated: "Indeed, as a general matter, the Oklahoma courts do not seem to be inclined to adopt rules from the Contracts restatement, perhaps because Title 15 of the Oklahoma Code is a comprehensive legislative statement of the law of contracts in that state." 238 F.3d at 790. Is Judge Wood's "prediction" of Oklahoma law in this case consistent with *Restatement (Second) of Contracts* § 304? Is this case consistent with the Alabama Supreme Court's decision in *Ex parte Stamey, supra*?

    2.3. There is no omitted dicta regarding U.C.C. section 2-318. The opinion does not mention U.C.C. section 2-318. Is the contract in this case within the scope of Article 2? Should Judge Wood have discussed 2-318? Is U.C.C. section 2-318 relevant to understanding this case? Is U.C.C. section 2-318 relevant to a more general understanding of third party beneficiary law?

B. Cancellation and Modification of the Rights of the Third Party Beneficiary and Defenses Against the Third Party Beneficiary

The previous three cases focused on the question of whether a third party has any right to enforce a contract entered into by others. That is the primary focus of most of the reported third party beneficiary cases.

The next case deals with (i) the related question of when the rights of a third party beneficiary can be cancelled or modified—a question raised but not considered in *Lawrence v. Fox*—and (ii) the question of what defenses can be asserted against a third party beneficiary.

Olson v. Etheridge
Supreme Court of Illinois
686 N.E.2d 563 (1997)

[Plaintiffs (the third party beneficiaries) sold their John Deere dealership to Etheridge (the promisee) pursuant to Agreement I with annual payments to be made by Etheridge to Plaintiffs pursuant to Note I. Subsequently, in 1983, Etheridge sold one-half of the business to Engelhaupt (the promisor) pursuant to Agreement II with annual payments to be made pursuant to Note II. Agreement II and Note II provided that Engelhaupt's payments were to be made to Plaintiffs to reduce Etheridge's obligation to Plaintiffs under Note 1. In 1986, Etheridge and Engelhaupt and Princeton Bank entered into Agreement III which provided for Engelhaupt to pay the remaining balance of Note II to Princeton Bank to satisfy one of Etheridge's other debts. Engelhaupt made such a payment. Etheridge defaulted on its obligations under Agreement I and Note I. Plaintiffs sued both Etheridge and Engelhaupt for the unpaid balance of Note I.]

Justice BILANDIC delivered the opinion of the court:

Bay v. Williams, 112 Ill. 91, 1 N.E. 340 (1884), established the rule in Illinois that the rights of a third-party beneficiary in a contract are subject to immediate vesting and, once vested, cannot be altered or extinguished through a later agreement of the contracting parties without the assent of the beneficiary. We are here called upon to determine the continued validity of the *Bay* rule.

The four plaintiffs in this case are third-party beneficiaries of a promise contained in a contract entered into by the appellant and another party. The circuit court of Bureau County awarded summary judgment to the plaintiffs based on *Bay*. The appellate court affirmed. We now reverse this award of summary judgment and remand for further proceedings, for the reasons set forth below.

* * *

Engelhaupt's appeal focuses on the appellate court's rejection of his claim that he is not subject to liability to the plaintiffs because all his obligations under Agreement II and Note II were discharged by the actions taken between him, Etheridge, and Princeton Bank on February 10, 1986. The actions pointed to by Engelhaupt are his $83,385 payment to Princeton Bank on Note II, and Princeton Bank's agreement that this constituted full payment; and his $100 payment to Princeton Bank for Agreement II, and Princeton Bank's and Etheridge's assignments of all their interests in Agreement II over to Engelhaupt. Engelhaupt concedes that the vesting rule in Bay commands a contrary conclusion, but argues that the *Bay* rule should be replaced with the vesting rule set forth in section 311 of the Restatement (Second) of Contracts (1981). According to Engelhaupt, if section 311 is applied, the summary judgment entered in favor of the plaintiffs was improper because questions of material fact remain to be determined.

* * *

Before addressing the parties' arguments, we briefly summarize third-party beneficiary law. The well-established rule in Illinois is that if a contract is entered into for the direct benefit of a third person, the third person may sue for a breach of the contract in his or her own name, even though the third person is a stranger to the contract and the consideration. This principle of law is widely accepted throughout the United States, because allowing a third-party beneficiary to sue the promisor directly is said to be manifestly just and practical. In cases such as this one, it increases judicial efficiency by removing the privity requirement, under which the beneficiary must sue the promisee, who then in turn must sue the promisor.

An important corollary to this principle is that the promisor may assert against the beneficiary any defense that the promisor could assert against the promisee if the promisee were suing on the contract. This is because the third-party beneficiary's rights stem from a contract to which the beneficiary is not a party. Accordingly, the promisor in this case, Engelhaupt, may assert against the plaintiffs-beneficiaries any defense that he could assert against the promisee, Etheridge, if Etheridge were suing him on Agreement II. Engelhaupt here asserts the defense that all his obligations under Agreement II and Note II were discharged when he made full payment to Princeton Bank on Note II and obtained assignments of both Princeton Bank's and Etheridge's interests in Agreement II.

The plaintiffs maintain, however, that Engelhaupt is not entitled to assert this defense against them because their rights as third-party beneficiaries had "vested." The vesting doctrine is an exception to the above rule that the promisor may assert against the beneficiary any defense that the promisor could assert against the promisee. Under this doctrine, once a third-party beneficiary's rights vest, the original contracting parties cannot modify or discharge those rights without the beneficiary's assent. The "question of vesting arises only where the promisor and the promisee purport to vary or discharge the rights of the beneficiary"; otherwise, "the topic of vesting is irrelevant." Before proceeding, then, we must determine in this case what rights the plaintiffs are asserting under Agreement II, and whether Engelhaupt and Etheridge attempted to vary or discharge those rights.

The plaintiffs here are asserting third-party beneficiary rights in Agreement II. In particular, they claim that they are the beneficiaries of Engelhaupt's promise in Agreement II "to assume" one-half of Etheridge's obligation to pay the plaintiffs under Agreement I and Note I. This assumption by Engelhaupt of one-half of Etheridge's obligation to pay is a classic example of a delegation. Unlike an assignment, which involves only a transfer of rights, a delegation involves the appointment of another to perform one's duties. ("Rights are assigned; duties are delegated"); J. Calamari & J. Perillo, Contracts § 18-1, at 722 (3d ed.1987). When a duty is delegated, the delegating party continues to remain liable for performance. The effects of this delegation are as follows: Etheridge remains liable to the plaintiffs under Agreement I and Note I, while Engelhaupt is liable to the plaintiffs under the third-party beneficiary theory. The plaintiffs therefore have a claim against both Etheridge and Engelhaupt, but are entitled to only one satisfaction. Thus, in count V, the plaintiffs are asserting their rights as third-party beneficiaries to payment from Engelhaupt, as provided for in Agreement II.

* * *

We now turn to the primary issue in this case: how vesting should be defined in this context. The plaintiffs urge application of the vesting rule declared in *Bay*. Engelhaupt, on the other hand, asks us to apply the vesting rule set forth in section 311 of the Second Restatement of Contracts.

In *Bay*, 112 Ill. 91, 1 N.E. 340, Williams sold land to Newman and Sissons in exchange for a down payment and promissory notes payable in installments. Newman and Sissons then sold the land to Bay. The deed tendered to Bay contained an express promise by Bay to pay the balance due on the promissory notes executed by Williams and Newman and Sissons. Bay later obtained a release of his obligation to pay Williams from Sissons. Newman went bankrupt without giving Bay a release. Williams exercised her power of foreclosure and sold the land, but was left being owed $3,559 on the notes. She sued Bay for that amount as third-party beneficiary of the deed between Newman and Sissons and Bay.

Bay argued that he was absolved from his promise to pay the promissory notes by Sissons' release. He proposed three different theories: (1) that third-party beneficiary rights do not vest until suit is brought; (2) that third-party beneficiary rights do not vest until the beneficiary relies upon or accepts the promisor's promise; and (3) that the promisor's promise to pay is a mere indemnity, which cannot be reached until the promisee is insolvent or on some other equitable ground. This court in *Bay* rejected these views, holding:

> "[The promisor's] promise invests the person for whose use it is made with an immediate interest and right, as though the promise had been made to him. This being true, the person who procures the promise has no legal right to release or discharge the person who made the promise, from his liability to the beneficiary. Having the right, it is under the sole control of the person for whose benefit it is made,—as much so as if made directly to him."

Consequently, *Bay* established the rule in Illinois that third-party beneficiary rights vest immediately and cannot be altered or extinguished through a later agreement of the original parties to the contract, unless the beneficiary assents.

Engelhaupt urges us to replace the *Bay* rule with the "modern view" as set forth in section 311 of the Second Restatement. Section 311, entitled "Variation of a Duty to a Beneficiary," stands in direct contrast to *Bay*. It provides that, in the absence of language in a contract making the rights of a third-party beneficiary irrevocable, the parties to the contract "retain power to discharge or modify the duty by subsequent agreement," without the third-party beneficiary's assent, at any time until the third-party beneficiary, without notice of the discharge or modification, materially changes position in justifiable reliance on the promise, brings suit on the promise or manifests assent to the promise at the request of the promisor or promisee. Restatement (Second) of Contracts § 311 (1981).

Section 311 now represents the majority view on the subject of vesting. In contrast, the immediate vesting rule as set forth in *Bay* represents the minority view, followed by only a handful of states.

Engelhaupt maintains that we should adopt section 311. He asserts that section 311 represents the majority rule on vesting because it better conforms to modern commercial practices and general principles of contract law. According to Engelhaupt, parties should remain free to modify or discharge their contracts as they see fit, without the assent of a third-party beneficiary, subject only to the three exceptions provided for in section 311. Section 311 makes sense, Engelhaupt contends, because third-party beneficiaries should not be able to enforce contracts for which they do not give any consideration, unless they demonstrate some detriment or act of faith in reliance on the contract.

Engelhaupt asserts that the superiority of the Restatement approach over the *Bay* rule is demonstrated by the facts present in this case. As he explains, the plaintiffs here freely chose to extend credit to Etheridge, who was then bound to pay them under Agreement I and Note I. Etheridge and Engelhaupt then freely contracted with each other that Engelhaupt would make one-half of Etheridge's payments to the plaintiffs, in Agreement II and Note II. The plaintiffs, however, were not bound to accept Engelhaupt's promise to pay in Agreement II and Note II in replacement of Etheridge's promise to pay in Agreement I and Note I, and did not do so. Consequently, the plaintiffs' contractual remedies against Etheridge in the event of Etheridge's nonpayment under Agreement I remained intact. Engelhaupt asserts that, in this situation, he and Etheridge should not be forever barred from modifying or discharging their agreement without the plaintiffs' assent, which is precisely what *Bay* mandates. Rather, Engelhaupt asserts, the third-party beneficiary plaintiffs should be found to have obtained vested rights in his and Etheridge's contract only if they meet one of the circumstances set forth in section 311.

Finding Engelhaupt's arguments persuasive, we hereby adopt the vesting rule set forth in section 311 of the Second Restatement. The rationale underlying section 311's vesting rule is that "parties to a contract should remain free to amend or rescind their agreement so long as there is no detriment to a third party who has provided no consideration for the benefit received." This rationale is compelling. Moreover, we find this rationale to be consistent with the general principles running throughout contract law. Contract law generally favors the freedom to contract. Contract law also allows for equitable remedies where the facts compel such a result.

In contrast, the immediate vesting rule of *Bay* curtails the freedom to contract. It provides, in essence, that every promise which benefits a third-party beneficiary carries with it another term, implied at law, that the parties to the contract are prohibited from modifying or discharging the promise that benefits the beneficiary, without the beneficiary's assent. We do not believe that the modern law of contracts should always imply such a term. To do so can work a great injustice upon the parties involved in a particular case. Although, as the plaintiffs contend, the *Bay* rule is clear and easy to apply, this does not persuade us to retain it. Our concern is that the rule of law we expound best serves the pursuit of justice, not that it is the easiest rule of law for courts to apply.

We note, moreover, that the plaintiffs' argument against adoption of the Restatement rule is not persuasive. They maintain that the Restatement position has fluctuated so much over the past century that it is not stable. We do not agree with this characterization. In fact, the Restatement position regarding creditor beneficiaries, such as the plaintiffs, is essentially the same as it has always been. Under the original Restatement, the rights of creditor beneficiaries vested once the beneficiary brought suit or otherwise materially changed position in reliance on the promise. Restatement of Contracts §§ 142, 143 (1932). Today, creditor beneficiaries are called intended beneficiaries, and their rights vest once the beneficiary brings suit on the promise, materially changes position in justifiable reliance on the promise or manifests assent to the promise at the request of the promisor or promisee. Restatement (Second) of Contracts §§ 302, 311 (1981). As to donee beneficiaries, the original Restatement provided that their rights vested immediately. Restatement of Contracts §§ 142, 143 (1932). This was changed after substantial criticism. Now donee beneficiaries are also classified as intended beneficiaries, and their rights vest as in the same manner stated above. Restatement (Second) of Contracts §§ 302, 311 (1981). Even were we to agree with the plaintiffs' characterization of the Restatement view as unstable, however, this would not impact our decision. We find the current Restatement position on vesting to be consistent with general principles underlying contract law. This court is free to reject any later revisions of the Restatement.

In conclusion, we adopt the vesting rule set forth in section 311 of the Second Restatement. *Bay* is hereby overruled. The circuit court awarded summary judgment to the plaintiffs based on the *Bay* rule. The circuit court did not consider the plaintiffs' motion for summary judgment in the context of the vesting rule of section 311. We therefore reverse this award of summary judgment for the plaintiffs and remand to the circuit court for further proceedings, consistent with section 311's vesting rule. * * *

QUESTIONS

1. Questions about the facts of this case

   1.1. Who is the third party beneficiary of Agreement II?

   1.2. Who is the promisor in Agreement II?

   1.3. Has the promisor paid all amounts that he promised to pay in Agreement II?

2. Questions about the law

   2.1. At trial, Engelhaupt argued that the plaintiffs were not intended third party beneficiaries of Agreement II. The trial court held that the plaintiffs were intended third party beneficiaries and Engelhaupt did not challenge that holding on appeal. Do you agree with that decision? Would Judge Wood agree? Recall that this case, *Olson v. Etheridge*, was the one case referred to in the *Midwest Grain Products* case.

   2.2. Would this case have been decided differently if Etheridge was in default under Agreement I after 1985 but plaintiffs had not foreclosed because of the promised payments from Engelhaupt under Agreement II?

   2.3. What is the practical significance, if any, of the court's statement in this case that "the promisor may assert against the beneficiary any defense that the promisor could assert against the promisee if the promisee were suing on the contract"? What if in *Lawrence v. Fox*, the $300 that Holly "loaned and advanced" to the defendant was counterfeit funds?

2.4. On January 15, 2002, Batman contracts to provide protection to Gotham for the remainder of 2002 in exchange for Gotham's promise to pay Robin $20,000 on December 31, 2002. Notwithstanding this contract, Batman fails to provide any protection to Gotham. Does Gotham still have to pay Robin $20,000 on December 31, 2002?

2.5. Do you agree with the statement in *Olson* that "the vesting doctrine is an exception to the . . . rule that the promisor may assert against the beneficiary any defense that the promisor could assert against the promisee"?

2.6. Do you understand the statement in *Olson* that "the assumption by Engelhaupt of one half of Etheridge's obligation to pay is a classic example of a delegation"? Was *Lawrence v. Fox* also a "classic example of a delegation"? What is the difference between a delegation and a third party beneficiary transaction? Between a delegation and an assignment?

SECTION 2: ASSIGNMENT AND DELEGATION

A. Introduction to Assignment and Delegation: What Are They?

A contract creates both rights and duties. If for example, Markell contracts to buy Epstein's car for $400, Markell has a right to obtain Epstein's car and a duty to pay $400. Epstein has a right to be paid $400 and a duty to deliver his car.

Similarly, if Epstein contracts with BAR/BRI to do contracts bar review lectures in New York for $10 a lecture, Epstein has a right to be paid $10 and a duty to deliver contracts lectures. BAR/BRI has a right to Epstein's lectures and a duty to pay $10.

A contracting party's later transfer of his contract rights to a third party is generally referred to an assignment. If, for example, Markell transfers his right to obtain Epstein's car to Ponoroff, that is an "assignment" and, (as you have long suspected), Markell is an assignor and Ponoroff is an assignee. The *Olson* case above provides another example of an assignment. Recall that in *Olson* Etheridge assigned the right to payment from Engelhaupt under Agreement II to Princeton Bank.

A contracting party's later transfer of his contract duties to a third party is generally referred to as a delegation. If, for example, Epstein gets Ponoroff to do the BAR/BRI contracts bar review lectures in New York, that is a delegation and Epstein is a delegator and Ponoroff is a delegatee. Again, the *Olson* case provides another example of a delegation. Recall that in Agreement II in *Olson*, Etheridge got Engelhaupt to agree to pay one-half of what Etheridge owed to Plaintiffs, *i.e.*, Etheridge delegated that duty to Engelhaupt.

A contracting party can both assign his contract rights and delegate his contract duties. Epstein and Ponoroff agree that Ponoroff will get the right to collect the $10 and will do the New York BAR/BRI lectures provided for in Epstein's earlier contract with BAR/BRI.

There are three questions about contract assignments and delegations that lawyers and first year law students need to be able to answer:

1. How is an assignment of rights under a contract factually different from a contract intended to benefit a third party? (In other words, when do you look to the law regarding third party beneficiaries and when do you look to the law regarding assignments?)
2. What are the legal consequences of an assignment and/or a delegation?
3. What are the limitations on the making of an assignment and/or a delegation?

You should be able to answer the first question from the material in this part of the chapter, and you should be able to answer the next two questions from the materials in the next two parts of the chapter.

B. Consequences of an Assignment and Delegation: Who Can Sue Whom?

1. Assignee Can Sue Obligor

Illustration 1 to *Restatement (Second) Contracts* § 317 illustrates that the assignee can sue the obligor:

1. *A has a right to $100 against B. A assigns his right to C. A's right is thereby extinguished, and C acquires a right against B to receive $100.*

QUESTIONS

1. Markell enters into a contract with Epstein to purchase Epstein's 1973 Cadillac for $400. The contract provides that Markell will pay Epstein for the car within ten days after delivery. Epstein delivers the car to Markell. Epstein then assigns his right to the $400 payment under the Markell contract to Ponoroff. Markell refuses to pay Ponoroff. Can Ponoroff sue Markell for breach of contract even though Ponoroff was not a party to that contract?

2. Under the facts in question 1 above, can Epstein sue Markell for breach of contract?

3. In questions 1 and 2, should it matter whether Ponoroff paid Epstein or Epstein simply made a gift to Ponoroff?

4. Epstein's klezmer band, The Alter Kochers, signs a contract with Bad Boy Records to record "Bubba's Bar Mitzvah." The contract provides for the payment of royalties to Epstein based on sales. Subsequently, Epstein's assigns his right to "Bubba's Bar Mitzvah" royalty payments to Markell. To whom should Bad Boy make the royalty payments? What if Bad Boy makes a royalty payment to Epstein after the assignment but before it had been notified of the assignment?

2. Obligee Can Sue Delegator

The *Restatement* does restate the law with respect to who can sue whom after a delegation of duties to perform under a contract. Please read section 318 of the *Restatement (Second) of Contracts* set out below and apply it in the questions below.

§ 318 Delegation of Performance of Duty

(1) An obligor can properly delegate the performance of his duty to another unless the delegation is contrary to public policy or the terms of his promise.

(2) Unless otherwise agreed, a promise requires performance by a particular person only to the extent that the obligee has a substantial interest in having that person perform or control the acts promised.

(3) Unless the obligee agrees otherwise, neither delegation of performance nor a contract to assume the duty made with the obligor by the person delegated discharges any duty or liability of the delegating obligor.

Comments & Illustrations:

Illustrations:

1. A owes B $100, and asks C to pay B. Payment or tender to B by C has the effect of payment or tender by A.

2. A contracts to deliver to B coal of specified kind and quality. A delegates the performance of this duty to C, who tenders to B coal of the specified kind and quality. The tender has the effect of a tender by A.

3. A contracts to build a building for B in accordance with specifications, and delegates the plumbing work to C. Performance by C has the effect of performance by A.

. . .

d. Delegation and novation. *An obligor is discharged by the substitution of a new obligor only if the contract so provides or if the obligee makes a binding manifestation of assent, forming a novation. See §§ 280, 328 and 329. Otherwise, the obligee retains his original right against the obligor, even though the obligor manifests an intention to substitute another obligor in his place and the other purports to assume the duty. The obligee may, however, have rights against the other as an intended beneficiary of the promise to assume the duty.*

Illustrations:

9. A borrows $50,000 from B and contracts to repay it. The contract provides that, if a corporation C is organized and assumes the debt under described conditions, A will be under no further obligation. C is or-

ganized and in good faith assumes the debt as provided. A is discharged.

10. A contracts with B to cut the grass on B's meadow. A delegates performance to C, who contracts with A to assume A's duty and perform the work. C begins performance with B's assent, but later breaks the contract. C is liable to B, but A is not discharged.

QUESTIONS

1. Epstein contracts with BAR/BRI to do bar review lectures in New York for $10. Being the wonderful friend that he is, Ponoroff agrees to do the lectures for Epstein without charge. And, being the wonderful friend that he is, notwithstanding this agreement, Ponoroff does not do the lectures. Can BAR/BRI sue Epstein for breach of contract?

2. Same facts as question 1. Can BAR/BRI sue Ponoroff for breach of contract?

3. Would your answers to questions 1 and/or 2 change if Epstein paid Ponoroff $30 to do the lectures?

4. Would your answers change if BAR/BRI had agreed that Ponoroff could do the lectures instead of Epstein? (Hint: you do not have to be a Catholic to know what a "novation" is.)

5. H enters into a contract with M under which M loans H $50,000 and H grants M a mortgage on H's house. Subsequently, H sells the house to T who assumes the mortgage. If T misses a mortgage payment, can M still sue H? Can M sue T? What, if any, needed facts are missing?

6. Is the following statement doctrine as well as doggerel: "A delegation for consideration results in a third party beneficiary obligation"?

C. Limitations on Assignment and Delegation

It should be obvious that there are limitations on a contracting party's ability to assign her contract rights and/or delegate her contract duties. If not, consider the following easy questions:

1. Sharon Stone enters into a contract with Ponoroff in which she promises to pay him $1,000 and he promises to paint a full body nude portrait of her. Can Sharon Stone assign her rights under this contract to Markell so that Ponoroff paints Markell in the nude instead of Stone?
2. Chipper Jones enters into a contract to play third base for the Atlanta Braves. Epstein, who played third base in Little League* and who has been a Braves fan for fifty years, has always wanted to play third base for the Braves. Can Chipper Jones delegate his contract duties to Epstein so that he (Chipper) can spend even more time at Hooters? Can Chipper Jones delegate his duties to Derek Jeter?

As the first question illustrates, there is a common law prohibition on assignments that "materially change the duty of the obligor." *See Restatement (Second) of Contracts* § 317(2)(a). And, as should be obvious from the second illustration, delegation is not permitted if "the obligee has a substantial interest in having that person perform or control the acts promised." *See Restatement (Second)* § 318(2).

The final three cases illustrate less obvious limitations on assignment and delegation.

The Macke Co. v. Pizza of Gaithersburg, Inc.

Court of Appeals of Maryland
270 A.2d 645 (1970)

SINGLEY, Judge.

The appellees and defendants below, Pizza of Gaithersburg, Inc.; Pizzeria, Inc.; The Pizza Pie Corp., Inc. and Pizza Oven, Inc. . . . operated at six locations in Montgomery and Prince George's Counties. The appellees had

*Okay, I learned my lessons from George O'Leary. I was not a starter at third base. More often, I played right field. In the last three innings. DGE.

arranged to have installed in each of their locations cold drink vending machines owned by Virginia Coffee Service, Inc., and on 30 December 1966, this arrangement was formalized at five of the locations, by contracts for terms of one year, automatically renewable for a like term in the absence of 30 days' written notice. A similar contract for the sixth location was entered into on 25 July 1967.

On 30 December 1967, Virginia's assets were purchased by The Macke Company (Macke) and the six contracts were assigned to Macke by Virginia. In January, 1968, the Pizza Shops attempted to terminate the five contracts having the December anniversary date, and in February, the contract which had the July anniversary date.

Macke brought suit in the Circuit Court for Montgomery County against each of the Pizza Shops for damages for breach of contract. From judgments for the defendants, Macke has appealed.

The lower court based the result which it reached on two grounds: first, that the Pizza Shops, when they contracted with Virginia, relied on its skill, judgment and reputation, which made impossible a delegation of Virginia's duties to Macke; and second, that the damages claimed could not be shown with reasonable certainty. These conclusions are challenged by Macke.

In the absence of a contrary provision—and there was none here—rights and duties under an executory bilateral contract may be assigned and delegated, subject to the exception that duties under a contract to provide personal services may never be delegated, nor rights be assigned under a contract where delectus personae was an ingredient of the bargain.[1] * * *

The six machines were placed on the appellees' premises under a printed 'Agreement-Contract' which identified the 'customer,' gave its place of business, described the vending machine, and then provided:

"TERMS

"1. The Company will install on the Customer's premises the above listed equipment and will maintain the equipment in good operating order and stocked with merchandise.

[1] Like all generalizations, this one is subject to an important exception. Uniform Commercial Code § 9-318 makes ineffective a term in any contract prohibiting the assignment of a contract right: *i.e.*, a right to payment. Compare Restatement, *Contracts* § 151(c) (1932).

"2. The location of this equipment will be such as to permit accessibility to persons desiring use of same. This equipment shall remain the property of the Company and shall not be moved from the location at which installed, except by the Company.

"3. For equipment requiring electrity and water, the Customer is responsible for electrical receptacle and water outlet within ten (10) feet of the equipment location. The Customer is also responsible to supply the Electrical Power and Water needed.

"4. The Customer will exercise every effort to protect this equipment from abuse or damage.

"5. The Company will be responsible for all licenses and taxes on the equipment and sale of products.

"6. This Agreement-Contract is for a term of one (1) year from the date indicated herein and will be automatically renewed for a like period, unless thirty (30) day written notice is given by either party to terminate service.

"7. Commission on monthly sales will be paid by the Company to the Customer at the following rate: * * *."

The rate provided in each of the agreements was '30% of Gross Receipts to $300.00 monthly[,] 35% over [$]300.00,' except for the agreement with Pizza of Gaithersburg, Inc., which called for '40% of Gross Receipts.'

We cannot regard the agreements as contracts for personal services. They were either a license or concession granted Virginia by the appellees, or a lease of a portion of the appellees' premises, with Virginia agreeing to pay a percentage of gross sales as a license or concession fee or as rent . . . and were assignable by Virginia unless they imposed on Virginia duties of a personal or unique character which could not be delegated. . . .

The appellees earnestly argue that they had dealt with Macke before and had chosen Virginia because they preferred the way it conducted its business. Specifically, they say that service was more personalized, since the president of Virginia kept the machines in working order, that commissions were paid in cash, and that Virginia permitted them to keep keys to the machines so that minor adjustments could be made when needed. Even if we assume all this to be true, the agreements with Virginia were silent as to the details of the working arrangements and contained only a provision requiring Virginia to 'install * * * the above listed equipment and * * * maintain the equipment in good operating order and stocked with merchandise.' We think the Supreme Court of California put the problem of personal service in proper focus a century ago when it upheld the assignment of a contract to grade a San Francisco street:

> 'All painters do not paint portraits like Sir Joshua Reynolds, nor landscapes like Claude Lorraine, nor do all writers write dramas like Shakespeare or fiction like Dickens. Rare genius and extraordinary skill are not transferable, and contracts for their employment are therefore personal, and cannot be assigned. But rare genius and extraordinary skill are not indispensable to the workmanlike digging down of a sand hill or the filling up of a depression to a given level, or the construction of brick sewers with manholes and covers, and contracts for such work are not personal, and may be assigned.' *Taylor v. Palmer*, 31 Cal. 240 at 247–248 (1866).

. . . Moreover, the difference between the service the Pizza Shops happened to be getting from Virginia and what they expected to get from Macke did not mount up to such a material change in the performance of obligations under the agreements as would justify the appellees' refusal to recognize the assignment.

* * *

Restatement, *Contracts* § 160(3) (1932) reads, in part:

> 'Performance or offer of performance by a person delegated has the same legal effect as performance or offer of performance by the person named in the contract, unless,
>
> (a) performance by the person delegated varies or would vary materially from performance by the person named in the contract as the one to perform, and there has been no * * * assent to the delegation * * *.'

In cases involving the sale of goods, the Restatement rule respecting delegation of duties has been amplified by Uniform Commercial Code § 2-210(5), which permits a promisee to demand assurances from the party to whom duties have been delegated.

As we see it, the delegation of duty by Virginia to Macke was entirely permissible under the terms of the agreements. * * *

QUESTIONS

1. Questions about the facts of the case

   1.1. Who was the assignor? The assignee? The delegator? The delegatee? The third party beneficiary?

   1.2. What, if any, contract language was important to the court in making its decision?

2. Questions about the law

   2.1. The court stated, "We cannot regard the agreements as contracts for personal services." Why not? Did the court nonetheless regard the agreements as contracts for personal services? If not, why did the court mention the "delectus personae rule," *i.e.*, "duties under a personal services contract may never be delegated . . . where delectus personae was an ingredient of the bargain"? Why did the court discuss Joshua Reynolds and Claude Lorraine and the *Restatement* § 160(3)?

   2.2. Why does the court discuss section 2-210(5) of the Uniform Commercial Code? Is *Macke* a case involving a contract for the sale of goods? Is the *Nexxus* case, *infra*, which also discusses section 2-210, a case involving a contract for the sale of goods?

   2.3. What result if the contract had provided "the President of Virginia Coffee Service, Inc. shall personally keep the machines in working order"? Professor James Nehf suggests:

   > The general rule is that contracts are assignable unless the assignment will materially alter the rights or obligations of the nonassigning party. In deciding whether the assignment will change the contract materially, contract language can be critical.
   >
   > The typical scenario involves the nonassigning party complaining that the assignment will substitute an inferior actor for the original contracting party, now the assignor. In one often-cited case, an owner of several pizza shops contracted with a vending machine company to stock and service its vending machines. This particular vending company was chosen because its president personally tended to the maintenance, paid commissions in cash, and allowed

> the shops to keep a key to the machines, making minor adjustments fast and easy. When the vending company sold its assets and assigned all its contracts, the pizza shops terminated the agreement. The court held that the contract was assignable. There would not be a material change in service even though the new company did not pay cash commissions or allow the shops to keep a key on hand. A deciding factor was that the contract did not mention these benefits which the non-assigning party now claimed were so important. The lesson for contract drafters is that all important expectations should be spelled out in the contract; otherwise, it may be difficult to contend later that they were material parts of the bargain that would be altered through an assignment.

James P. Nehf, *Writing Contracts in the Client's Interest*, 51 S.C. L. Rev. 153, 179 (1999)

2.4. What result if the contract had provided "This contract may not be assigned"? The next case involves a contract provision prohibiting assignment.

Rumbin v. Utica Mutual Insurance Co.
Supreme Court of Connecticut
757 A.2d 526 (2000)

VERTEFEUILLE, J.

The defendant Safeco Life Insurance Company (Safeco), appeals from the judgment of the trial court approving the transfer by the plaintiff, Marco Rumbin, of payments due to him under an annuity issued pursuant to a structured settlement agreement between the plaintiff and the named defendant, Utica Mutual Insurance Company (Utica Mutual).[1] The plaintiff proposes to sell the remaining payments to the intervening plaintiff, J.G. Wentworth.[2] The principal issues in this appeal are: (1) whether General Statutes § 52-225f invalidates antiassignment provisions that are included in structured settlement agreements and annuities issued pursuant to such agreements; and (2) whether the antiassignment clause contained in the

---

[1]The only party objecting to the sale of the annuity contract is Safeco, the issuer of the annuity contract. Utica Mutual is not a party to this appeal

annuity issued by Safeco for the plaintiff beneficiary invalidates his assignment to Wentworth. We conclude that § 52-225f does not invalidate such antiassignment provisions. We further conclude that, under Connecticut common law, the antiassignment provision in the annuity contract does not invalidate the plaintiff's assignment of his right to payments under the annuity to Wentworth. In accordance with case law and § 322 of the Restatement (Second) of Contracts, an antiassignment provision that does not limit the power to assign or expressly invalidate the assignment does not render the assignment of the annuity ineffective. Safeco, however, has the right to recover damages for the plaintiff's breach of the antiassignment provision. We therefore affirm the judgment of the trial court.

The record reveals the following facts. In April, 1998, the plaintiff and Utica Mutual entered into a structured settlement agreement to resolve a personal injury claim. Pursuant to that settlement agreement, the plaintiff was to receive from Utica Mutual a lump sum payment, followed by a series of periodic payments over the next fifteen years.[5] The structured portion of the settlement was funded by the annuity contract issued by Safeco. The annuity contract provided under its "Assignment" provision that "[n]o payment under this annuity contract may be . . . assigned . . . in any manner by the [plaintiff]. . . ."[6]

Approximately six months after the execution of the settlement agreement and the issuance of the annuity, the plaintiff had become unemployed and faced a mortgage foreclosure action against his home, where he lived with his family. In order to resolve his financial troubles, the plaintiff decided to sell his right to the annuity payments. In November, 1998, he filed a declaratory judgment action seeking court approval to transfer his right to the remaining annuity payments to Wentworth in exchange for a lump sum payment and other consideration. * * *

---

[5]Under the terms of the settlement agreement, the plaintiff was entitled to receive $52,000 within thirty days of its execution, thirty semiannual payments of $1323.09 beginning on March 6, 1999, and a final lump sum payment of $44,000 on March 6, 2014.

[6]The plaintiff has not claimed that the annuity contract is a contract of adhesion. Typically, "life insurance contracts are [considered] contracts of adhesion because [t]he contract is drawn up by the insurer and the insured, who merely adheres to it, has little choice as to its terms. . . . Standardized contracts of insurance continue to be prime examples of contracts of adhesion, whose most salient feature is that they are not subject to the normal bargaining processes of ordinary contracts." *Aetna Casualty & Surety Co. v. Murphy*, 206 Conn. 409, 416, 538 A.2d 219 (1988). A review of the annuity contract in the present case reveals that it is a preprinted, standardized insurance contract in which the plaintiff was the named annuitant. It was not a contract arrived at by actual negotiation between the parties. * * *

The primary issue raised by this case is whether, under Connecticut common law, an antiassignment provision in an annuity contract invalidates the plaintiff payee's transfer of his right to future payments under the annuity to a third party. We conclude, in accordance with case law and § 322 of the Restatement (Second) of Contracts, that the antiassignment provision at issue here does not render the assignment of the annuity ineffective, but, instead, gives the annuity issuer, Safeco, the right to recover damages for breach of the antiassignment provision.

Although we previously have addressed the issue of the validity of contractual provisions prohibiting the assignment of contractual rights; *see Lewin & Sons, Inc. v. Herman*, 143 Conn. 146, 149, 120 A.2d 423 (1956) (upholding validity of contractual provision that prohibited assignment without consent); the law of contracts has changed considerably since our earlier decision. Accordingly, we now reexamine the basic legal principles regarding contractual antiassignment provisions.

* * * Common-law restrictions on assignment were abandoned when courts recognized the necessity of permitting the transfer of contract rights. * * *

The parties to a contract can include express language to limit assignment and courts generally uphold these contractual antiassignment clauses. Given the importance of free assignability, however, antiassignment clauses are construed narrowly whenever possible.

In interpreting antiassignment clauses, the majority of jurisdictions now distinguish between the assignor's "right" to assign and the "power" to assign (modern approach). For example, in *Bel-Ray Co. v. Chemrite (Pty.) Ltd.*, 181 F.3d 435, 442 (3d Cir.1999), the United States Court of Appeals for the Third Circuit recognized that numerous jurisdictions followed the general rule "that contractual provisions limiting or prohibiting assignments operate only to limit [the] parties' *right* to assign the contract, but not their *power* to do so, unless the parties manifest an intent to the contrary with specificity." (Emphasis added.) The court concluded, however, that the "assignment clauses [did] not contain the requisite clear language to limit [the] 'power' to assign" and, therefore, held the assignment valid and enforceable. The court acknowledged that contracting parties could limit the *power* to assign by including an "assignment provision [that] generally states that nonconforming assignments (i) shall be 'void' or 'invalid,' or (ii) that the assignee shall acquire no rights or the nonassigning party shall not recognize any such assignment." Without such express contractual language, however, "the provision limiting or prohibiting assignments will be interpreted merely as a covenant not to assign. . . . Breach of such a covenant may render the assigning party liable in damages to the non-assigning party. The assignment, however, remains valid and enforceable against both the assignor and the assignee."

* * *

The modern approach offers the advantage of free assignability together with full protection for any obligor who actually suffers damages as a result of an assignment. An assignor who breaches a contractual provision limiting his or her right to assign will be liable for any damages that result from that assignment. * * *

This approach is also adopted in the Restatement (Second) of Contracts. Section 322(2)(b) of the Restatement (Second), supra, provides that the general rule is "[a] contract term prohibiting assignment of rights under the contract, unless a different intention is manifested . . . (b) gives the obligor a right to damages for breach of the terms forbidding assignment but does not render the assignment ineffective. . . ."

In the present case, the annuity contract provided that "[n]o payment under this annuity contract may be . . . assigned" by the plaintiff. This antiassignment provision limited the plaintiff's *right* to assign, but not his *power* to do so. The provision did not contain any express language to limit the power to assign or to void the assignment itself. Therefore, in accordance with the modern approach, we conclude that the plaintiff's assignment to Wentworth is valid and enforceable despite the plaintiff's breach of the contract's antiassignment provision. We further conclude, however, that Safeco is free to sue for any damages that it might sustain as a result of the assignment by bringing an action for breach of contract against the plaintiff as assignor. Alternatively, Safeco may pursue damages from Wentworth, who, as the assignee, " 'stands in the shoes of the assignor.' " . . . Safeco, therefore, is fully protected against any actual damages that it might sustain as a result of the plaintiff's breach of the antiassignment provision.[11] The modern

[11] At the trial court hearing, Safeco did not show any actual damages resulting from the assignment. It argues, however, that upholding the assignment increases the risk of losing certain purported favorable federal tax treatment afforded to both the insurance company and the annuitant. More specifically, an insurer can fund its liability under a structured settlement agreement by purchasing an annuity that grows tax free while the annuitant receives tax free payments from that annuity. Safeco argues that allowing a party to assign his rights to payments frustrates the public policy of ensuring a steady source of income to that party and creates a risk that the favorable tax treatment will be lost. We agree with the trial court's

approach thus serves the dual objectives of free assignability of contracts together with full compensation for any actual damages that might result from an assignment made in breach of an antiassignment provision.

The judgment is affirmed.

QUESTIONS AND NOTE

1. Questions about the facts of this case

   1.1. Who was the assignor? The assignee? The obligor?

   1.2. Was there an "antiassignment" provision in the contract between the plaintiff and Utica Mutual? Why?

2. Questions about the law

   2.1. Is this decision consistent with the language of the contract? With the intention of the parties to the contract?

   2.2. Would this court have reached a different decision if the contract had added the words "and any assignments will be void"?

   2.3. Would the court have reached a different decision if Safeco produced evidence that it was damaged by the assignment? If you were representing Safeco, what evidence could you offer to show damage from the assignment?

3. Note

   "Consider the argument that these provisions should be upheld because they were freely bargained for by both parties. If the only reason for bargaining for these provisions was because of potential adverse tax consequences that in fact do not exist, then there is little justification for upholding these provisions in light of basic contract law principles that invalidate provisions against assigning contract rights, especially when the

---

findings that "[Safeco] . . . has not offered evidence of danger of suffering adverse tax effects as a result of the transfer nor is there other evidence of any detriment to it by virtue of the transfer." Although Safeco has raised the specter of a risk of losing its favorable tax treatment, it has not provided any evidence that there will be an actual adverse effect if this court were to uphold the assignment.

right is simply to receive money." Note, *Structured Settlements: The Assignability Problem*, 9 S. CAL. INTERDISC. L.J. 465, 492 (2000).

Do you agree?

Sally Beauty Co., Inc. v. Nexxus Products Co., Inc.
U.S. Court of Appeals, Seventh Circuit
801 F.2d 1001 (1986)

CUDAHY, Circuit Judge.

Nexxus Products Company ("Nexxus") entered into a contract with Best Barber & Beauty Supply Company, Inc. ("Best"), under which Best would be the exclusive distributor of Nexxus hair care products to barbers and hair stylists throughout most of Texas. When Best was acquired by and merged into Sally Beauty Company, Inc. ("Sally Beauty"), Nexxus cancelled the agreement. Sally Beauty is a wholly-owned subsidiary of Alberto-Culver Company ("Alberto-Culver"), a major manufacturer of hair care products and a competitor of Nexxus'. Sally Beauty claims that Nexxus breached the contract by cancelling; Nexxus asserts by way of defense that the contract was not assignable or, in the alternative, not assignable to Sally Beauty. The district court granted Nexxus' motion for summary judgment, ruling that the contract was one for personal services and therefore not assignable. We affirm on a different theory—that this contract could not be assigned to the wholly-owned subsidiary of a direct competitor under section 2-210 of the Uniform Commercial Code.

I.

Only the basic facts are undisputed and they are as follows. Prior to its merger with Sally Beauty, Best was a Texas corporation in the business of distributing beauty and hair care products to retail stores, barber shops and beauty salons throughout Texas. Between March and July 1979, Mark Reichek, Best's president, negotiated with Stephen Redding, Nexxus' vice-president, over a possible distribution agreement between Best and Nexxus. Nexxus, founded in 1979, is a California corporation that formulates and markets hair care products. Nexxus does not market its products to retail stores, preferring to sell them to independent distributors for resale to barbers and beauticians. On August 2, 1979, Nexxus executed a distributorship agreement with Best, in the form of a July 24, 1979 letter from Reichek, for Best, to Redding, for Nexxus:

Dear Steve:

It was a pleasure meeting with you and discussing the distribution of Nexus Products. The line is very exciting and we feel we can do a substantial job with it—especially as the exclusive distributor in Texas (except El Paso).

If I understand the pricing structure correctly, we would pay $1.50 for an item that retails for $5.00 (less 50%, less 40% off retail), and Nexus will pay the freight charges regardless of order size. This approach to pricing will enable us to price the items in the line in such a way that they will be attractive and profitable to the salons.

* * *

While we feel confident that we can do an outstanding job with the Nexus line and that the volume we generate will adequately compensate you for your continued support, it is usually best to have an understanding should we no longer be distributing Nexus Products—either by our desire or your request. Based on our discussions, cancellation or termination of Best Barber & Beauty Supply Co., Inc. as a distributor can only take place on the anniversary date of our original appointment as a distributor—and then only with 120 days prior notice. If Nexus terminates us, Nexus will buy back all of our inventory at cost and will pay the freight charges on the returned merchandise.

Steve, we feel that the Nexus line is exciting and very promotable. With the program outlined in this letter, we feel it can be mutually profitable and look forward to a long and successful business relationship. If you agree that this letter contains the details of our understanding regarding the distribution of Nexus Products, please sign the acknowledgment below and return one copy of this letter to me.

Very truly yours,

/s/ Mark E. Reichek

President

Acknowledged /s/ Stephen Redding Date 8/2/79. Appellant's Appendix at 2–3.

In July 1981, Sally Beauty acquired Best in a stock purchase transaction and Best was merged into Sally Beauty, which succeeded to Best's rights and interests in all of Best's contracts. Sally Beauty, a Delaware corporation with its principal place of business in Texas, is a wholly-owned subsidiary of Alberto-Culver. Sally Beauty, like Best, is a distributor of hair care and beauty products to retail stores and hair styling salons. Alberto-Culver is a major manufacturer of hair care products and, thus, is a direct competitor of Nexxus in the hair care market.

Shortly after the merger, Redding met with Michael Renzulli, president of Sally Beauty, to discuss the Nexxus distribution agreement. After the meeting, Redding wrote Renzulli a letter stating that Nexxus would not allow Sally Beauty, a wholly-owned subsidiary of a direct competitor, to distribute Nexxus products:

> "As we discussed in New Orleans, we have great reservations about allowing our NEXXUS Products to be distributed by a company which is, in essence, a direct competitor. We appreciate your argument of autonomy for your business, but the fact remains that you are totally owned by Alberto-Culver.
>
> Since we see no way of justifying this conflict, we cannot allow our products to be distributed by Sally Beauty Company."

In August 1983, Sally Beauty commenced this action by filing a complaint in the Northern District of Illinois, claiming that Nexxus had breached the distribution agreement. * * * Nexxus filed a motion for summary judgment on the breach of contract claim the next day.

The district court granted Nexxus' motion for summary judgment. * * *

In ruling on this motion, the district court framed the issue before it as "whether the contract at issue here between Best and Nexxus was of a personal nature such that it was not assignable without Nexxus' consent." It ruled:

> The court is convinced, based upon the nature of the contract and the circumstances surrounding its formation, that the contract at issue here was of such a nature that it was not assignable without Nexxus's consent. First, the very nature of the contract itself suggests its personal character. A distribution agreement is a contract whereby a manufacturer gives another party the right to distribute its products. It is clearly a contract for the performance of a service. In the court's view, the mere selection by a manufacturer of a party to distribute its goods presupposes a reliance and confidence by the manufacturer on the integrity and abilities of the other party. . . . In addition, in this case the circumstances

surrounding the contract's formation support the conclusion that the agreement was not simply an ordinary commercial contract but was one which was based upon a relationship of personal trust and confidence between the parties. Specifically, Stephen Redding, Nexxus's vice-president, travelled to Texas and met with Best's president personally for several days before making the decision to award the Texas distributorship to Best. Best itself had been in the hair care business for 40 years and its president Mark Reichek had extensive experience in the industry. It is reasonable to conclude that Stephen Redding and Nexxus would want its distributor to be experienced and knowledgeable in the hair care field and that the selection of Best was based upon personal factors such as these.

* * *

We cannot affirm this summary judgment on the grounds relied on by the district court. * * * Although it might be "reasonable to conclude" that Best and Nexxus had based their agreement on "a relationship of personal trust and confidence," and that Reichek's participation was considered essential to Best's performance, this is a finding of fact. Since the parties submitted conflicting affidavits on this question,[3] the district court erred in relying on Nexxus' view as representing undisputed fact in ruling on this summary judgment motion.

We may affirm this summary judgment, however, on a different ground if it finds support in the record. Sally Beauty contends that the distribution agreement is freely assignable because it is governed by the provisions of

---

[3]Reichek stated the following in an affidavit submitted in support of Sally Beauty's Memorandum in Opposition to Nexxus' Motion for Summary Judgment:

> At no time prior to the execution of the Distribution Agreement did Steve Redding tell me that he was relying upon my personal peculiar tastes and ability in making his decision to award a Nexxus distributorship to Best. Moreover, I never understood that Steve Redding was relying upon my skill and ability in particular in choosing Best as a distributor. I never considered the Distribution Agreement to be a personal service contract between me and Nexxus or Stephen Redding. I always considered the Distribution Agreement to be between Best and Nexxus as expressly provided in the Distribution Agreement which was written by my brother and me. At all times I conducted business with Nexxus on behalf of Best and not on my own behalf. In that connection, when I sent correspondence to Nexxus, I invariably signed it as president of Best. Neither Stephen Redding nor any other Nexxus employee ever told me that Nexxus was relying on my personal financial integrity on executing the Distribution Agreement or in shipping Nexxus products to Best . . .

the Uniform Commercial Code (the "UCC" or the "Code"), as adopted in Texas. Appellants' Brief at 46–47. We agree with Sally that the provisions of the UCC govern this contract and for that reason hold that the assignment of the contract by Best to Sally Beauty was barred by the UCC rules on delegation of performance, UCC § 2-210(1).

* * * Texas applies the "dominant factor" test to determine whether the UCC applies to a given contract or transaction: was the essence of or dominant factor in the formation of the contract the provision of goods or services? No Texas case addresses whether a distribution agreement is a contract for the sale of goods, but the rule in the majority of jurisdictions is that distributorships (both exclusive and non-exclusive) are to be treated as sale of goods contracts under the UCC.

Several of these courts note that "a distributorship agreement is more involved than a typical sales contract." This is true of the contract at issue here (as embodied in the July 24, 1979 letter from Reichek to Redding). Most of the agreed-to terms deal with Nexxus' sale of its hair care products to Best. We are confident that a Texas court would find the sales aspect of this contract dominant and apply the majority rule that such a distributorship is a contract for "goods" under the UCC.

The fact that this contract is considered a contract for the sale of goods and not for the provision of a service does not, as Sally Beauty suggests, mean that it is freely assignable in all circumstances. The delegation of performance under a sales contract (whether in conjunction with an assignment of rights, as here, or not) is governed by UCC section 2- 210(1). The UCC recognizes that in many cases an obligor will find it convenient or even necessary to relieve himself of the duty of performance under a contract, *see* Official Comment 1, UCC § 2-210 ("[T]his section recognizes both delegation of performance and assignability as normal and permissible incidents of a contract for the sale of goods."). The Code therefore sanctions delegation except where the delegated performance would be unsatisfactory to the obligee: "A party may perform his duty through a delegate unless otherwise agreed to or unless the other party has a substantial interest in having his original promisor perform or control the acts required by the contract." UCC § 2-210(1). Consideration is given to balancing the policies of free alienability of commercial contracts and protecting the obligee from having to accept a bargain he did not contract for.

We are concerned here with the delegation of Best's duty of performance under the distribution agreement, as Nexxus terminated the agreement because it did not wish to accept Sally Beauty's substituted performance.[6] Only one Texas case has construed section 2-210 in the context of a party's delegation of performance under an executory contract. In *McKinnie v. Milford*, 597 S.W.2d 953 (Tex.Civ.App.1980, writ ref'd, n.r.e.), the court held that nothing in the Texas Business and Commercial Code prevented the seller of a horse from delegating to the buyer a pre-existing contractual duty to make the horse available to a third party for breeding. "[I]t is clear that Milford [the third party] had no particular interest in not allowing Stewart [the seller] to delegate the duties required by the contract. Milford was only interested in getting his two breedings per year, and such performance could only be obtained from McKinnie [the buyer] after he bought the horse from Stewart." *Id.* at 957. In McKinnie, the Texas court recognized and applied the UCC rule that bars delegation of duties if there is some reason why the non-assigning party would find performance by a delegate a substantially different thing than what he had bargained for.

In the exclusive distribution agreement before us, Nexxus had contracted for Best's "best efforts" in promoting the sale of Nexxus products in Texas. UCC § 2-306(2), states that "[a] lawful agreement by either buyer or seller for exclusive dealing in the kind of goods concerned imposes unless otherwise agreed an obligation by the seller to use best efforts to supply the goods and by the buyer to use best efforts to promote their sale." This implied promise on Best's part was the consideration for Nexxus' promise to refrain from supplying any other distributors within Best's exclusive area. *See* Official Comment 5, UCC S 2-306. It was this contractual undertaking which Nexxus refused to see performed by Sally.

In ruling on Nexxus' motion for summary judgment, the district court noted: "Unlike Best, Sally Beauty is a subsidiary of one of Nexxus' direct competitors. This is a significant distinction and in the court's view, it raises serious questions regarding Sally Beauty's ability to perform the distribution agreement in the same manner as Best." We agree with these assessments and hold that Sally Beauty's position as a wholly-owned subsidiary of Al-

[6]If this contract is assignable, Sally Beauty would also, of course, succeed to Best's rights under the distribution agreement. But the fact situation before us must be distinguished from the assignment of contract rights that are no longer executory (*e.g.*, the right to damages for breach or the right to payment of an account), which is considered in UCC section 2-210(2), Tex.Bus. & Com.Code Ann. S 2-210(b) (Vernon 1968), and in several of the authorities relied on by appellants. The policies underlying these two situations are different and, generally, the UCC favors assignment more strongly in the latter. *See* UCC § 2-210(2) (non-executory rights assignable even if agreement states otherwise).

berto-Culver is sufficient to bar the delegation of Best's duties under the agreement.

We do not believe that our holding will work the mischief with our national economy that the appellants predict. We hold merely that the duty of performance under an exclusive distributorship may not be delegated to a competitor in the market place—or the wholly-owned subsidiary of a competitor—without the obligee's consent. We believe that such a rule is consonant with the policies behind section 2-210, which is concerned with preserving the bargain the obligee has struck. Nexxus should not be required to accept the "best efforts" of Sally Beauty when those efforts are subject to the control of Alberto-Culver. It is entirely reasonable that Nexxus should conclude that this performance would be a different thing than what it had bargained for. At oral argument, Sally Beauty argued that the case should go to trial to allow it to demonstrate that it could and would perform the contract as impartially as Best. It stressed that Sally Beauty is a "multi-line" distributor, which means that it distributes many brands and is not just a conduit for Alberto-Culver products. But we do not think that this creates a material question of fact in this case. When performance of personal services is delegated, the trier merely determines that it is a personal services contract. If so, the duty is *per se* nondelegable. There is no inquiry into whether the delegate is as skilled or worthy of trust and confidence as the original obligor: the delegate was not bargained for and the obligee need not consent to the substitution. And so here: it is undisputed that Sally Beauty is wholly owned by Alberto-Culver, which means that Sally Beauty's "impartial" sales policy is at least acquiesced in by Alberto-Culver—but could change whenever Alberto-Culver's needs changed. Sally Beauty may be totally sincere in its belief that it can operate "impartially" as a distributor, but who can guarantee the outcome when there is a clear choice between the demands of the parent-manufacturer, Alberto-Culver, and the competing needs of Nexxus? The risk of an unfavorable outcome is not one which the law can force Nexxus to take. Nexxus has a substantial interest in not seeing this contract performed by Sally Beauty, which is sufficient to bar the delegation under section 2-210. Because Nexxus should not be forced to accept performance of the distributorship agreement by Sally, we hold that the contract was not assignable without Nexxus' consent.

The judgment of the district court is AFFIRMED.

POSNER, Circuit Judge, dissenting.

My brethren have decided, with no better foundation than judicial intuition about what businessmen consider reasonable, that the Uniform Commercial Code gives a supplier an absolute right to cancel an exclusive-dealing contract if the dealer is acquired, directly or indirectly, by a competitor of the supplier. I interpret the Code differently.

Nexxus makes products for the hair and sells them through distributors to hair salons and barbershops. It gave a contract to Best, cancellable on any anniversary of the contract with 120 days' notice, to be its exclusive distributor in Texas. Two years later Best was acquired by and merged into Sally Beauty, a distributor of beauty supplies and wholly owned subsidiary of Alberto-Culver. Alberto-Culver makes "hair care" products, too, though they mostly are cheaper than Nexxus's, and are sold to the public primarily through grocery stores and drugstores. * * *

* * * So far as appears, the same people who distributed Nexxus's products for Best (except for Best's president) continued to do so for Sally Beauty. Best was acquired, and continues, as a going concern; the corporation was dissolved, but the business wasn't. Whether there was a delegation of performance in any sense may be doubted. The general rule is that a change of corporate form—including a merger—does not in and of itself affect contractual rights and obligations.

The fact that Best's president has quit cannot be decisive on the issue whether the merger resulted in a delegation of performance. The contract between Nexxus and Best was not a personal-services contract conditioned on a particular individual's remaining with Best. If Best had not been acquired, but its president had left anyway, as of course he might have done, Nexxus could not have repudiated the contract.

* * *

Steel companies both make fabricated steel and sell raw steel to competing fabricators. General Motors sells cars manufactured by a competitor, Isuzu.

* * *

Suppose there had been no merger, but the only child of Best's president had gone to work for Alberto-Culver as a chemist. Could Nexxus have canceled the contract, fearing that Best (perhaps unconsciously) would favor Alberto-Culver products over Nexxus products? That would be an absurd ground for cancellation, and so is Nexxus's actual ground. At most, so far as the record shows, Nexxus may have had grounds for "insecurity" regarding the performance by Sally Beauty of its obligation to use its best efforts to promote Nexxus products, but if so its remedy was not to cancel the contract but to demand assurances of due performance. *See* UCC § 2-609; Official Comment 5 to § 2-306. No such demand was made. An anticipatory repudiation by conduct requires conduct that makes the repudiating party unable to perform. The merger did not do this. At least there is no evidence it did. The judgment should be reversed and the case remanded for a trial on whether the merger so altered the conditions of performance that Nexxus is entitled to declare the contract broken.

QUESTIONS AND NOTES

1. Questions about the facts of this case

    1.1. What fact did the court treat as the most important fact in the case? Do you agree?

    1.2. What facts do you think should be important?

        (a) Was there language in the contract between Nexxus and Best regarding assignment and delegation of the contract? Is that important?

        (b) Is it important that the contract made Best the exclusive distributor for Nexxus' products for most of the State of Texas?

        (c) Is it important that Texas is sometimes referred to as the "Big Hair State"?

2. Questions about the law

    2.1. Why did the court apply Article 2? Which contract was a contract for the sale of goods—the distributorship contract between Nexxus and Best or the contract between Best and Sally transferring the distributorship contract? If Article 2 applies in this case, should the court in *Macke* also have applied Article 2?

    2.2. Why did the court look to section 2-210(1) instead of section 2-210(2)? Under section 2-210(1), which of the parties in this case is the "party"? The "original promisor"? The "other party"? In this case, what is the "substantial interest in having his original promisor perform"?

2.3. What is the court's holding? Is it that the contract could not be delegated, or that the contract could not be delegated to a competitor of the obligee? Would the Seventh Circuit have decided this case differently if Sally Beauty had been owned by Alberto Markell, Bruce Markell's South American cousin, instead of Alberto-Culver, a competitor of Nexxus? Should a court applying section 2-210(1) decide the two cases differently?

2.4. If the contract between Nexxus and Best had stated "This contract is not assignable", would Sally have filed this law suit? *Cf.* section 2-210(3). Would Sally have still given the same amount of consideration to the prior owners of Best in order to acquire Best?

3. Notes

3.1. The *Nexxus* case involves not only the transfer of contracts rights but also a stock purchase transaction and a merger—stuff covered in second and third year courses on business associations. (And stuff covered by a casebook that Epstein has co-authored on business structures (a/k/a "bs").)

3.2. Increasingly, the transfer of contract rights are governed by statutes. Articles 3 and 4 of the Uniform Commercial Code deal with the transfer of rights under contracts that are negotiable instruments; Article 9 of the Uniform Commercial Code deals with transferring rights under accounts receivable and other contracts as security for loans courses on the U.C.C. (And stuff covered by a casebook that Ponoroff has co-authored.) The Bankruptcy Code provides special rules for transfers of contract rights by or to a person who is debtor in a bankruptcy case—stuff covered in second and third year courses in bankruptcy. (And stuff covered by a casebook that Epstein and Markell have co-authored.) We, of course, hope that you take these courses and use our books.

Chapter 7

WHAT ARE THE ALTERNATIVES TO CONTRACTS AND CONTRACT LAW? (QUASI-CONTRACT AND RESTITUTION)

SECTION 1: NATURE AND ORIGINS OF QUASI-CONTRACT

As we discussed way back in Chapter 1, contract liability is distinguished from other forms of liability in that it is *consensual.* That is to say, a contractual obligation exists because it is voluntarily undertaken by the promisor rather than, as in the case of tort or criminal liability, imposed as a matter of societal judgment about what forms of behavior will be deemed culpable. Our legal regime has, however, devised another form of liability which is neither purely fault-based nor truly promise-based, although, for historical reasons discussed more fully below, the terminology used to describe this type of liability sounds eerily like the terminology used to describe conventional contract liability. In fact, this form of liability has come to bear the appellation of *Quasi-Contract.*

A quasi-contractual claim, which exists somewhere in-between classic contract and classic tort liability, is based neither on an express agreement nor an agreement implied-in-fact. Instead, it is a legal fiction, or an *implied-in-law* agreement, that rests on the proposition or general theory of obligation that one party should not be permitted to be enriched unjustly at the expense of a second party unless the first party makes compensation to the second party for the value of the benefit conferred. In effect, then, the cause of action for quasi-contract is based on the doctrine of *unjust enrichment.* It is a separate theory of liability (distinct from ordinary contract liability) that provides a remedy, namely, *restitution*, in circumstances where no true contract exists.

Restitution is its own area of law, with its own history, its own jurisprudence, and even its own *Restatement*. You will recall that when we considered how the law enforces a deal in Chapter 5, we looked at "restitutionary" recovery as an alternative to recovery under the contract based on either the expectation or reliance interests. Indeed, the law of restitution pertains to situations wholly unrelated to contract, such as cases involving fraud and conversion, as well as cases that arise in the more typical contractual or quasi-contractual contexts. Thus, the term restitution really has two meanings: it refers to both the substantive legal rules that embody the right of an innocent party to recover for unjust enrichment and the remedy, at law or equity, that is available to redress an unjust enrichment. For present purposes, however, what is critical is that you understand two things: (1) the formal distinction between a genuine contract (whether express or implied-in-fact) and a quasi or implied-in-law contract; and (2) the fundamentally different purposes served by these separate areas of law. To this end, consider the following explanation offered more than a hundred years ago by Professor Maine.

HENRY SUMNER MAINE, **ANCIENT LAW**
3rd American Ed. 332–33 (1888)

The part of Roman law which has had most extensive influence on foreign subjects of inquiry has been the law of Obligation, or, what comes nearly to the same thing, of Contract and Delict. The Romans themselves were not unaware of the offices which the copious and malleable terminology belonging to this part of their system might be made to discharge, and this is proved by their employment of the peculiar adjunct *quasi* in such expressions as Quasi-Contract and Quasi-Delict. 'Quasi,' so used, is exclusively a term of classification. It has been usual with English critics to identify the quasi-contracts with implied contracts; but this is an error, for implied contracts are true contracts, which quasi-contracts are not. In implied contracts, acts and circumstances are the symbols of the same ingredients which are symbolized, in express contracts, by words; and whether a man employs one set of symbols or the other must be a matter of indifference so far as concerns the theory of agreement. But a quasi-contract is not a contract at all. The commonest sample of the class is the relation subsisting between two persons, one of whom has paid money to the other through mistake. The law, consulting the interests of morality, imposes an obligation on the receiver to refund; but the very nature of the transaction indicates that it is not a contract, inasmuch as the convention, the most essential ingredient of contract, is wanting. This word 'quasi,' prefixed to a term of Roman law, implies that the conception to which it serves as an index is connected with the conception with which the comparison is instituted by a strong superficial analogy or resemblance. It does not denote that the two conceptions are the same, or that they belong to the same genus. On the contrary, it negatives the notion of an identity between them; but it points out that they are sufficiently similar for one to be classed as the sequel to the other, and that the phraseology taken from one department of law may be transferred to the other, and employed without violent straining, in the statement of rules which would otherwise be imperfectly expressed.

In order to understand how claims for unjust enrichment came to be based on a fictional contract, it must be emphasized that early common law lawyers in seeking redress for a particular kind of action thought not in terms of *rights*, as modern lawyers tend to do, but in terms of *remedies*. This was because, in medieval England, a plaintiff seeking relief against a particular defendant was required to fit his claim into a recognized form of action or *writ*. For example, the modern law of contracts was developed through extension of the form of trespass on the case known as *special assumpsit* (literally that the defendant undertook or promised to perform a particular act).* Early on, however, assumpsit, which was really a tort-based remedy, was not available if the action of *Debt*—to recover a sum certain—more neatly fit the facts. But the older action of Debt was still subject to the ancient procedure known as "wager of law," pursuant to which a defendant could avoid liability by producing a number of professional "oath-sayers" who would swear that the defendant was telling the truth. This made the action of Debt easy for the defendant to manipulate in order to avoid a just debt. Therefore, ingenious common law judges,** desirous of providing a remedy in deserving cases,

*For more on the history of the development of the writ of assumpsit, *see* A.W.B. SIMPSON, A HISTORY OF THE COMMON LAW OF CONTRACT: THE RISE OF THE ACTION OF ASSUMPSIT (1975); KEVIN M. TEEVEN, A HISTORY OF THE ANGLO-AMERICAN COMMON LAW OF CONTRACT, 27–50 (1990); James Barr Ames, *The History of Assumpsit,* 2 HARV. L. REV. 1 (1888).

**Lord Mansfield is generally credited with bringing quasi-contract into the mainstream of English common law. *See* Moses v. Macferlan, 2 Burr. 1005, 97 Eng. Rep. 676 (K.B. 1760) ("In one word, the gist of this kind of action is, that the defendant, upon the circumstances

gradually began to permit actions for payment of a sum certain to be brought in assumpsit. However, to circumvent the cumbersome action of Debt, this action was known as *general assumpsit* and, unlike special assumpsit, it did not depend on the existence of a real promise or an actual contract. Instead, it rested on a promise implied in law where one party had already performed but received nothing in return from the party benefited by that performance. For this reason, in addition to an alternative to either an action of Debt or special assumpsit, this action proved useful when the defendant had received a clear benefit from the plaintiff, but no express promise could be proved or established. In effect, general assumpsit would lie where one party had been unjustly enriched at the expense of another party because the court would indulge the fiction that the benefit was conferred by the plaintiff *at the request* of the defendant and with the attendant obligation to compensate the plaintiff for the value of the benefit conferred. In the parlance of the common law at the time, such claims were said to arise *quasi ex contractu,* and the enduring link between contract law and unjust enrichment was forged.

SECTION 2: ELEMENTS OF A QUASI-CONTRACTUAL CLAIM

A. In General

John W. Wade, *Restitution for Benefits Conferred Without Request*
19 Vand. L. Rev. 1183, 1183–84, 1211–12 (1966)

I. Introduction

The principle is now fully recognized in this country that a "person who has been unjustly enriched at the expense of another is required to make restitution to the other." This is the language of the first section of the *Restatement of Restitution.* When one person confers a benefit upon another without the latter's solicitation, the benefit received constitutes an enrichment—a windfall, so to speak. This benefit may take one of several forms. It

---

of the case, is obliged by the ties of natural justice and equity to refund the money" [paid by mistake]).

may involve (1) transferring property to the defendant, (2) saving, preserving or improving his property, (3) rendering personal services for him, or (4) performing for him a duty imposed directly by law by his own contractual arrangements. In any of these situations there is an enrichment, and the principle quoted above comes into play if the enrichment is "unjust." When is it unjust? Obviously, it would not be so characterized if it were intended as a gift; just as obviously, the opposite is true if the plaintiff acted under legal compulsion and against his will. In making the determination, considerable weight is given to the circumstances that the benefit was not requested by the defendant.

The common law has long had a pronounced policy that benefits may not be forced upon a party against his will, so as to require him to pay for them. This idea has been forcefully expressed on a number of occasions. Said the court in the leading English case, "Liabilities are not to be forced upon people behind their backs any more than you can confer a benefit upon a man against his will." Most of the time this idea has been indicated by applying an epithet to the plaintiff. The term most frequently used is that of "volunteer." Applied to the plaintiff, particularly if it carries the adjective "mere," it has played the "kiss of death" and the sure indication that he will not be allowed to recover. Other derogatory terms used include meddler, intermeddler, interloper, mere stranger, mere impertinence. The Restatement uses the adjective "officious," which carries a somewhat more restricted connotation.[1] All of these terms embody the policy that one should not be required to pay for benefits which he did not solicit and does not desire.

* * *

IV. Conclusion

The restrictions on recovery which have been spelled out at considerable length have all been presented from a negative standpoint.

It may now be possible to summarize them and present a general principle stated in a positive fashion.

Perhaps the following two sentences will prove helpful in this regard:

---

[1]"A person who officiously confers a benefit upon another is not entitled to restitution therefor." *Restatement, Restitution* § 2 (1937). "Officiousness means interference in the affairs of others not justified by the circumstances under which the interference takes place." Id., comment a.

> One who without intent to act gratuitously, confers a measurable benefit upon another, is entitled to restitution, if he affords the other an opportunity to decline the benefit or else has a reasonable excuse for failing to do so. If the other refuses to receive the benefit, he is not required to make restitution unless the actor justifiably performs for the other a duty imposed upon him by law.

QUESTIONS

Dean Wade's definition suggests that a mere volunteer, one who confers a benefit gratuitously, is not entitled to restitution under this doctrine. Why not? Can you think of some examples where this limitation would preclude a quasi-contractual recovery? Suppose, without being asked, Markell rushes out and washes Epstein's filthy car. Does Markell have a claim against Epstein for payment? Does it matter if Markell can show that the rear window was so dirty that it was becoming a safety hazard?

Patterson v. Patterson

Court of Appeals of New York
59 N.Y. 574 (1875)

[This case was filed by the executrix of the estate of William Patterson to foreclose a mortgage executed by the defendant and given to the testator to secure the payment of $1,200 due upon William Patterson's death. By way of counterclaim, the defendant raised his right to set off against this claim, among other amounts, the sum of $180.30, representing the amount paid by the defendant to the undertakers to defray the cost of the testator's funeral expenses. The trial court held in favor of the plaintiff on the basis that, under applicable statutes, the defendant could not setoff a debt arising after the death of the testator against a debt due from the defendant arising during the life of the testator. The defendant appealed].

FOLGER, Justice.

* * *

I have no doubt but that the reasonable and necessary expenses of the interment of the dead body of one deceased, are a charge against his estate, though not strictly a debt due from him. The ground of this is the general right of every one to have decent burial after death; which implies the right to have his body carried, decently covered, from the place where it lies to a cemetery or other proper inclosure, and there put under ground. (*Regina v. Stewart*, 12 Ad. & Ell., 773, citing *Gilbert v. Buzzard*, 2 Hagg. Consist. R., 333; see, also, *Chapple v. Coope*, 13 M. & W., 252.) In the last case, in which an infant, a widow, was held liable on her contract for the funeral expenses of the burial of her deceased husband, it was said, that "there are many authorities which lay it down that decent Christian burial is a part of a man's own rights; and we think it not great extension of the rule to say, that it may be classed as a personal advantage and reasonably necessary to him." This right existing, the law casts upon some one the duty of seeing that it is accorded. So it would seem, at common law, that if a poor person of no estate dies, it is the duty of him under whose roof his body lies, to carry it, decently covered, to the place of burial. The husband surviving is bound to bury the corpse of his wife; and in his absence, another, a relative, with whom she has lived up to her death, having directed the funeral and paid the expense, may recover it of the husband. * * * And where the owner of some estate dies, the duty of the burial is upon the executor. * * * And our Revised Statutes (2 R. S., 71 § 16) recognize this duty, in that the executor is prohibited from any interference with the estate until after probate, except that he may discharge the funeral expenses. From this duty springs a legal obligation, and from the obligation the law implies a promise to him who, in the absence or neglect of the executor, not officiously, but in the necessity of the case, directs a burial and incurs and pays such expense thereof as is reasonable. * * * It is analogous to the duty and obligation of a father to furnish necessaries to a child, and of a husband to a wife, from which the law implies a promise to pay him who does what the father or the husband, in that respect, omits. * * *

No statutory provisions are now in mind which interpose an obstacle. Though our statute of payment of debts and legacies (2 R.S., p. 87 § 27) gives the order in which the executor shall make payment of debts against the estate, and though there is no provision there for a priority of payment of funeral expenses, it is not to be held therefrom that the common-law rule is abrogate. Those expenses are not to be treated as a debt against the estate, but as a charge upon the estate, the same as the necessary expenses of administration. * * * The expenses of probate of will precede the formal authority to the executor, but are allowed to him on an accounting. So should funeral expenses be. The decent burial of the dead is a matter in which the public have concern. It is against the public health if it do not take place at all, and against a proper public sentiment, that it should not take place with decency. * * *

Can the defendant set off these expenses in this action? His cause of action is against the plaintiff on a promise implied by law from her. He had no cause of action therefor, against the testator. As the cause of action against the defendant, arose after the death of the testator, and to the plaintiff, it appears that the two demands are mutual debts respectively due to and from defendant, and to and from the plaintiff in the same capacity. This demand may therefore be set off.

The judgment appealed from, must be modified so as to allow to the defendant, in diminution of the amount of the claim established against him, the sum of $180.30. He is also entitled to the interest thereon.

The judgment so modified, should be affirmed, without costs to either party in this court.

QUESTIONS

1. Questions about the facts of this case

   1.1. What was the relationship between William Patterson and the defendant?

   1.2. The court concludes that William Patterson's estate is liable for the costs incurred by defendant in arranging for the burial of the testator. Did William Patterson, during his life, agree to reimburse the defendant for the costs of paying Mr. Patterson's funeral expenses? Did the executrix agree to reimburse those expenses? If the answer to both questions is "no," then what were the key facts from which this obligation could be said to arise?

2. Questions about the law

   2.1. The court also concludes that the set-off sought by the defendant for funeral expenses was proper because "the two demands are mutual debts respectively due to and from the defendant, and to and from the plaintiff in the same capacity." What does this mean? If mutuality of obligation is a requirement to the right of set-off, did the court properly apply it in this case? Wasn't the defendant's debt owed to William Patterson and his claim against the estate?

2.2. Under the trial court's reasoning, would the defendant have been able to recover for the $180.30 paid to defray funeral expenses?

B. At the Request of the Defendant

Schott v. Westinghouse Electric Corporation

Supreme Court of Pennsylvania
436 Pa. 279, 259 A.2d 443 (1969)

Pomeroy, J.

During the period 1962 to 1965 (the relevant times for the purpose of this case), there was in effect at Westinghouse Electric Corporation (hereinafter "Company") a formalized suggestion program under which its employees were invited to submit to the Company any suggestions they might have for increasing production and reducing costs. The question in this case is whether the Company may have become contractually obligated to one of its employees, appellant herein, by virtue of the actions of both parties pursuant to the program. This appeal is from the sustaining of preliminary objections by the Company in the nature of a demurrer. Consequently, the facts before us are confined to the appellant's complaint, as amended, and the demurrer admits for present purposes every well pleaded material fact set forth in the pleading to which it is addressed, as well as the inferences reasonably deducible therefrom. * * *

The terms of the suggestion program are set forth in the documentary exhibits attached to the complaint. In pertinent part, the basic form of the suggestion system provides as follows:

> "With a view toward increasing production and reducing costs, thereby promoting employment, the Westinghouse Electric Corporation encourages practical suggestions from employes.

> "Cash awards ranging from a minimum of $5.00 to a maximum of $15,000 will be paid for each suggestion adopted . . .
>
> "Suggestions must be submitted on this form . . . All suggestions will be passed upon as soon as possible, and suggesters will be notified as to the action taken . . ."

Space was provided for the statement of the employee's suggestion. Beneath that space and immediately above the signature line where the employee-suggester was to sign was the following stipulation:

> "In submitting this suggestion, I agree that the decision of the local Suggestion Committee on all matters pertaining to this suggestion, my eligibility for an award, and the amount of award, if any, will be final. I further understand that if this suggestion is rejected, I have the right to reopen it within 12 months from the date of rejection, or to re-submit it as a new suggestion at any time thereafter.
>
> "Note: If adopted; Minimum Award—$5.00
>
> Maximum Award—$15,000"

In May, 1962, the appellant, an employee of the Company, submitted a suggestion that certain panels used on circuit breakers manufactured by the Company be made from fabricated heavy gauge steel rather than the material then used, cast aluminum. Appellant submitted the suggestion, as required, on the standard form with its stipulation that the decision of the Suggestion Committee should be determinative as to all matters. Thereafter, the Suggestion Committee informed the appellant in writing that his suggestion had been rejected (Exhibit C to the complaint). This communication stated that a change of the panels would necessitate large expenditures for design work, the building of models, and laboratory tests, and that these costs would more than offset any savings which might be realized from the proposed change. Appellant was informed that "If breaker re-design is started for other reasons in the future, this idea will be considered." He was also advised, in the same communication, that his suggestion could be reopened within a year or resubmitted after a year.

In September, 1963, appellant resubmitted his suggestion, again using the Company's prescribed form for his submission; in January, 1964, he was informed that the suggestion had again been rejected. In explaining its action, the Suggestion Committee cited its original reasons, adverted to further problems in the design of the panels resulting from the need to use nonmagnetic materials in the panel, and mentioned that redesign of the panels to include partial nonmagnetic materials was being undertaken as part of an independent cost reduction study.

At this point in the narrative, resort must be had to the complaint itself, as distinguished from the documentary exhibits. The complaint averred, in paragraph 8, that thereafter, probably in 1964, the Company "did adopt and utilize" the recommendations advanced by the suggestion, and the plaintiff (appellant) thereupon requested reconsideration of his suggestion. The Company apparently made such a review and communicated the results thereof to appellant in a letter of May, 1965 (Exhibit F to the complaint). This letter adverts to the Company's "application of the same basic idea [as that contained in appellant's suggestion] in a redesign" and confirms the Company's view that the reason given for the initial rejection of the suggestion in 1962 had been valid at that time. It further states the opinion of the writer (General Manager of the Switchgear Division) that "the action taken [by the Company] in 1964 changing the back plate was the result of independent action taken without knowledge of your [appellant's] suggestion," and reaffirmed the Company's refusal to make an award to appellant.

In November, 1966, appellant filed a complaint which averred that the Company had adopted the appellant's suggestion and prayed for an accounting as to the Company's savings therefrom, and damages equal to 20% thereof. The Company filed preliminary objections, on the ground that the complaint did not set forth a valid claim against the Company on which relief could be granted. In support of this conclusion the objections cited the stipulation that "the decision of the Local Suggestion Committee on all matters pertaining to this suggestion . . . will be final." The lower court in sustaining the Company's objections, found that the suggestion program of the Company was an invitation to its employees to make an offer; that the offer of the appellant was by its terms subject to acceptance or rejection by the Company through its Committees; and that the offer had been duly and consistently rejected by the Company. The court further held: "Plaintiff is bound by the statement to which he agreed that the decision of the Suggestion Committee will be final on all matters pertaining to his suggestion and his eligibility for an award unless there is fraud or deceit practiced by or an unjust enrichment inuring to the defendant and no such allegations are made in this case." Finding that no enforceable contract had been pleaded by appellant, the court sustained defendant's preliminary objections and granted plaintiff leave to amend his complaint.

Thereafter, appellant filed an amended complaint seeking damages both under a theory of contract and under a theory sounding in unjust enrichment, properly set forth in a separate count. The amended complaint alleged no new facts but charged appropriation of plaintiff's valuable idea.

The Company again filed preliminary objections, renewing its position that appellant had failed to state a cause of action sounding in contract and further asserting that no cause of action based on unjust enrichment had been set forth. The lower court (McKenna, Jr., J.) found that the amended complaint added no substantial allegation to the original complaint. Holding that appellant was bound by the adverse determinations of the Suggestion Committee, the court below sustained the objections and dismissed the amended complaint. * * *

The present appeal is from the order of the lower court dismissing appellant's amended complaint. Appellant argues that he was entitled to recover the value of his suggestion, either under a theory of performance of a unilateral contract or under a theory of unjust enrichment.

We agree with the lower court that the appellant cannot recover under a contract theory, but under the facts averred we believe the appellant has stated a cause of action in unjust enrichment. Accordingly, we are obliged to reverse and remand.

I

As we view the first cause of action, we need not decide whether the purported contract was unilateral or bilateral in nature. Whichever interpretation is adopted, it is clear that appellant agreed to abide by the decision of the Suggestion Committee on "all matters" (including the acceptableness of the suggestion itself). The Committee rejected the suggestion, and that rejection bars the appellant's recovery under his first cause of action, not because appellant was thereby made ineligible for an award under a valid contract with the Company, but rather because, in view of the Committee's action, no contract existed between the parties.

* * *

II

Appellant's alternative position is that, relying on the Company's promise in the suggestion invitation, he submitted a valuable idea to the Company in hope of securing a monetary award therefor; that the Company "adopted" or appropriated the idea to its own use and benefit; that the Company has refused to make payment to appellant therefor in accordance with the terms of the suggestion system; that in consequence appellant is entitled to the full value of the saving realized by the Company from its use of his idea. The Company responds that these are but conclusory averments and that no cause of action is set forth. * * *

Returning to the applicable law, we note that this Court has found the quasi-contractual doctrine of unjust enrichment inapplicable when the relationship between parties is founded on a written agreement or express contract. * * * But in the present case, having found that no legal contract bound the parties, it would be manifestly unjust to fail to consider appellant's claim on the ground that there might have been a contract or that the parties had attempted to enter into a contract.

Quasi-contracts, or contracts implied in law, are to be distinguished from express contracts or contracts implied in fact. "[U]nlike true contracts, quasi-contracts are not based on the apparent intention of the parties to undertake the performances in question, nor are they promises. They are obligations created by law for reasons of justice." Restatement (Second) of Contracts, § 5, comment b at 24 (Tent. Draft No. 1, 1964). See also Corbin, Contracts, § 19 (1950); * * *. Quasi-contracts may be found in the absence of any expression of assent by the party to be charged and may indeed be found in spite of the party's contrary intention. * * * Consequently, the failure of the Company's Suggestion Committee to accept the appellant's suggestion is not determinative of appellant's quasi-contractual cause of action.

* * *

Mr. Justice Roberts (concurring):

I agree that appellee's preliminary objections should be dismissed and this case should be permitted to go to trial, but I do so because, in my view, appellant's complaint alleges facts which if established would prove that appellee's actions have created a contract.

* * *

I cannot accept, however, the majority's conclusion that appellant can withstand appellee's preliminary objections on an "unjust enrichment" theory. When appellant submitted his suggestion on appellee's form, in accordance with appellee's procedure, in my view he gave up any claim he might have had to unjust enrichment damages. If appellant is to recover at all, it must be within the limitations of appellee's procedure for offering suggestions. I do not believe that it is wise to become entangled in metaphysical notions of whether appellee extended an offer or an invitation to deal, and whether appellant thus tendered an acceptance or an offer. In my view it is enough to say that appellant cannot, under these circumstances, recover outside of appellee's established procedure, a procedure appellant accepted when tendering his suggestion, and thus unjust enrichment in my judgment is not appropriate.

* * *

Mr. Chief Justice Bell (dissenting):

The Majority admits there was no fraud or deceit by defendant. I am strongly opposed to the doctrine of unjust enrichment. Furthermore, even if the doctrine be judicially adopted by this Court, it cannot be applied in this case in view of the written contract which so clearly prescribes and defines, and thus limits, the rights of the parties.

QUESTIONS AND NOTE

1. Questions about the facts of this case

   1.1. Did the court believe that the company's redesign of the panels was "independent action" taken without knowledge of Schott's earlier suggestion? Does it matter?

   1.2. If the reasons for the company's rejection of Schott's suggestion were valid when made, is it unjust for the company to later use that suggestion, after circumstances change, without compensating Schott?

   1.3. What is the significance of the fact that, at the time of the resubmittal of Schott's suggestion, the company acknowledged that it was undertaking an effort to redesign the panels to include partial nonmagnetic materials?

   1.4. What do you suppose Chief Justice Bell has against the doctrine of unjust enrichment?

2. Questions about the law

   2.1. Why was the dismissal of the plaintiff's breach of contract claim affirmed on appeal?

   2.2. Do you agree with Chief Justice Bell that the parties can, by their contract, preclude the possibility of a claim for restitution?

   2.3. Justice Roberts seems to believe that the existence of a valid contract would preclude a claim for restitution. Do you agree? If Justice Roberts' view had prevailed, what would Schott's argument be on remand to establish the existence of a contract?

   2.4. Note that Schott's complaint prayed for damages equal to 20 percent of the savings realized by the company for use of his suggestion, as determined by an accounting. Was that proper in view of the fact that the suggestion program promised cash awards ranging from $5 to $15,000?

3. Note

The aim of restitution is to make the defendant account for the value of the benefit conferred on the defendant. Suppose, however, that during the course of contractual negotiations, one party performs work at the request of the other, but those negotiations never ripen into an enforceable contract. If those services do not *benefit* the requesting party can the person providing the services nevertheless bring a claim for unjust enrichment? *See Earhart v. William Low Co.*, 25 Cal. 3d 503 (1979).

C. Not at the Request of the Defendant

Cablevision of Breckenridge, Inc. v. Tannhauser Condominium Association

Supreme Court of Colorado
649 P.2d 1093 (1982)

LOHR, J.

We granted certiorari to review the decision of the Colorado Court of Appeals in *Cablevision of Breckenridge, Inc. v. Tannhauser Condominium Association*, * * * which reversed the judgment of the Summit County District Court awarding the plaintiff, Cablevision of Breckenridge, Inc. (Cablevision), damages for the wrongful conversion of its subscription cable service. We reverse the decision of the court of appeals and remand for reinstatement of the district court judgment.

I.

This case was tried to the district court under a stipulated set of facts which included those that follow. Cablevision is a corporation engaged in providing cable television and FM radio to its subscribers in areas where the television signals are weak or nonexistent. This is a frequently encountered problem in the vicinity of Breckenridge, Colorado, because the topography of the community and its distance from the originating broadcast stations generally result in an inability to receive a useful broadcast signal when using only the traditional antennas normally employed by individual households.

In order to provide its service, Cablevision constructed several antennas on a mountain peak near Breckenridge, by which it receives six television stations as well as FM radio. At the point of reception, the television signals are strong enough to reproduce a black and white picture, but are too weak to allow color reproduction. Consequently, the signals are fed into a "pre-amp," which magnifies their strength. The signals are then transmitted to a "head-end" building, located near the receiving antennas, where they are passed through a channel processor and mixer for the purpose of improving the clarity of the picture produced by the transmission. From this building, the signals are sent by coaxial cable to the "hub" facility in Breckenridge, and thence through distribution lines to the individual subscribers. Additional amplification of the signals is necessary as they are transmitted through the system, so amplifiers are installed along the distribution lines. Cablevision's capital investment in the transmission system is approximately $450,000.

The stipulated facts further establish that in October 1972 Cablevision entered into an oral agreement for the provision of subscription cable services with Judy Keller, who was acting on behalf of the owners of the condominium units comprising the Tannhauser I development in Breckenridge. The Tannhauser I building consisted of 33 condominium units, and each was to receive the Cablevision service. Pursuant to this agreement Cablevision installed the equipment necessary to provide its service to each of the units. This was accomplished by running a connecting line from the distribution system to an amplifier located inside Tannhauser I. The signals were then transmitted from this amplifier to individual wall plates serving each of the units. From January 1, 1972, through March 1974, Tannhauser I paid for the service to these 33 units at a specified rate per unit.

Effective May 1974, Cablevision ceased billing for service to 33 units and began billing for service to only three units. This was done at the request of Jerry White, whose status is not described in the stipulation but who apparently acted as a representative for the Tannhauser I owners. The stipulation reflects disagreement over the exact events leading to this change in service, but it is undisputed that the Cablevision amplifier inside Tannhauser I was removed; that White then substituted his own amplifier and connected it to the Cablevision line; and that, following May 1, television and FM radio service was still provided to all 33 units of Tannhauser I despite the payment to Cablevision for service to only three of those units. This state of affairs continued from May 1, 1974, to approximately December 1, 1976.

In the fall of 1974 a second building, known as Tannhauser II and comprised of 25 condominium units, was constructed near Tannhauser I. Cablevision was never requested to supply service to Tannhauser II. However, the new building was wired internally for cable television and FM radio, and in November 1974 White supervised and assisted in the installation of a cable between Tannhauser I and Tannhauser II enabling extension of the Cablevision service to each of the 25 units in Tannhauser II. Tannhauser II began receiving the Cablevision transmission approximately November 30, 1974. Cablevision subsequently discovered the unauthorized use of its transmission by Tannhauser I and II and terminated all service to the condominiums about December 1, 1976.

Thereafter, Cablevision brought the present action, naming the condominium associations for Tannhausers I and II and the owners of the individual condominium units as defendants. Cablevision's amended complaint contained eight claims for relief, including breach of contract, concealment, conversion, various claims of unjust enrichment, and a request for injunctive relief.

However, as part of the pre-trial stipulation of facts summarized above, the parties submitted for judicial resolution the following single stipulated issue:

> Have the Defendants, or any of them, breached any contract with Plaintiff, written or oral, in fact or implied, for which Plaintiff is entitled for damages, actual or punitive?

After a hearing, the trial court entered an oral ruling incorporating the parties' stipulated facts, and holding that the defendants were liable for conversion of Cablevision's service. The parties had originally provided in their stipulation that, in the event of recovery, the damages would be $12,195, plus appropriate interest. However, the defendants advised the court subsequent to entry of the stipulation that they objected to this figure, so a further hearing was held on the question of damages. The court then entered its written judgment. The court again adopted the stipulation of the parties as its findings of fact and concluded:

> The plaintiff's property and services in the furnishing of cable television is a legally protected interest for which it is entitled to charge an appropriate and lawful rate to its subscribers. The defendants, through the actions stated in the Stipulation, have converted those protected interests without fully paying for them.

Based upon the damages hearing, the court entered judgment for actual damages of $11,597.50 plus statutory interest and court costs, and denied the prayer for punitive damages. The defendants then appealed.

The court of appeals reversed. It held that the trial court erred in ruling that the defendants were liable on the basis that they converted Cablevision's property interests because, pursuant to the parties' stipulation, "the only issue before the trial court was whether any defendant breached any contract with [Cablevision]." It further held that, because the stipulation did not establish the essential elements of a contract, Cablevision had not proved its breach of contract claim. Therefore, it directed the trial court to enter judgment for the defendants.

We accepted certiorari to review the court of appeals' decision. * * * [W]e do not address these arguments because we conclude that the judgment of the trial court is supported by an alternative basis of liability raised by the stipulated issue submitted by the parties.

II.

As stipulated by the parties, the issue for decision was whether "the Defendants, or any of them, *breached any contract* with Plaintiff, written or oral, in fact or implied." (Emphasis added.) We read the mention of "implied" contracts as a reference to the doctrine of quasi-contract or unjust enrichment, under which courts imply a contract as a matter of law where necessary to avoid unjust enrichment. This interpretation is based in part upon the apparent intent of parties in distinguishing "implied contracts" and contracts "in fact," and draws further support from the inclusion of unjust enrichment claims in the complaint.

In addressing only the issue of whether the stipulated evidence established a contract in fact, the court of appeals did not consider this alternative basis of liability. We conclude that the facts of this case present an appropriate basis for application of the doctrine of unjust enrichment, and reverse the decision of the court of appeals for that reason.

To recover under a theory of quasi-contract or unjust enrichment, a plaintiff must show (1) that a benefit was conferred on the defendant by the plaintiff, (2) that the benefit was appreciated by the defendant, and (3) that the benefit was accepted by the defendant under such circumstances that it would be inequitable for it to be retained without payment of its value. * * * Application of the doctrine does not depend upon the existence of a contract, express or implied in fact, but on the need to avoid unjust enrichment of the defendant notwithstanding the absence of an actual agreement to pay for the benefit conferred. * * * The scope of this remedy is broad, cutting across both contract and tort law, with its application guided by the underlying principle of avoiding the unjust enrichment of one party at the expense of another. 1 G. Palmer, *The Law of Restitution* § 1.1 (1978); 66 *Am. Jur. 2d Restitution and Implied Contracts*, *supra*, § 11.

In the present case, we conclude that a benefit was conferred upon the defendants by Cablevision and that the defendants appreciated this benefit. The defendants' initial payment for this service in connection with the 33 Tannhauser I condominium units and their continued payment for service to three of those units amply demonstrate both the beneficial service provided by Cablevision and the appreciation of that service by the defendants. Instructive in this regard is the broad definition of benefit contained in the *Restatement of Restitution* § 1, comment b (1937):

> A person confers a benefit upon another if he gives to the other possession of or some other interest in money, land, chattels, or choses in action, performs services beneficial to or at the request of the other, satisfies a debt or a duty of the other, or in any way adds to the other's security or advantage. He confers a benefit not only where he adds to the property of another, but also where he saves the other from expense or loss. The word "benefit," therefore, denotes any form of advantage.

We also conclude that the defendants have retained this service under such circumstances that it would be inequitable to allow its use without payment for its value. The stipulated facts demonstrate that Cablevision never intended to provide its service to all of Tannhausers I and II in exchange for payment in connection with only three units. Indeed, upon discovery of the unauthorized use of its signals, Cablevision terminated all service to the defendants. Further, the defendants were not innocent or unwilling recipients of this benefit, but actively facilitated its provision.

* * *

The defendants have accepted a service from Cablevision that is customarily paid for and, in fact, was initially paid for by these defendants. The defendants were active participants in obtaining this benefit from Cablevision, and, based on the initial agreement to serve Tannhauser I, their representatives must have acted with the knowledge that Cablevision expected compensation for each Tannhauser unit receiving the Cablevision transmission. Under these facts, restitution is appropriate to avoid unjust enrichment to the defendants. * * *

The damages awarded were based upon the rate prescribed in Cablevision's franchise from Breckenridge, which correspond to the rate paid for the three Tannhauser I units during the period of unauthorized use of the Cablevision signals. This was an appropriate measure of the benefit conferred upon the defendants and the amount of restitution due.

* * *

We reverse the decision of the court of appeals and return the case to that court for remand to the trial court with directions to enter judgment in accordance with the views expressed in this opinion.

QUESTIONS

1. Questions about the facts of this case

 1.1. Why did Cablevision's lawyer agree in the pre-trial stipulation that the only issue to be resolved at trial was the issue of breach of contract? Was that a mistake? Was it malpractice?

 1.2. Did the residents of the Tannhauser units know they were getting for free a service that other people pay for? Was that fact important to the court? Should it matter? If an ATM malfunctions and gives you twice as much cash as you requested, without charging your account, is it a good defense to the bank's unjust enrichment claim if you can show that you were unaware of the error?

 1.3. How important was the fact that the Tannhauser I units had received and paid for cable service for over two years?

2. Questions about the law

 2.1. What was the key difference in the interpretation given to the parties' pre-trial stipulation by the Colorado Court of Appeals and the Colorado Supreme Court? Did the supreme court conclude that there had been a breach contract in the traditional sense?

 2.2. The court awarded damages based on the rate prescribed in Cablevision's franchise from the City of Breckenridge* during the period of the unauthorized use. Was that appropriate? If you represented the defendants, what kind of evidence would you have sought to introduce to justify a lesser recovery?

---

*Actually, Breckenridge is a "kingdom," not a city, and, as far as we know, the only such governmental entity in the country. But that's another story.

Watts v. Watts

Supreme Court of Wisconsin

137 Wis. 2d 506, 405 N.W.2d 303 (1987)

Abrahamson, J.

This is an appeal from a judgment of the circuit court for Dane County, William D. Byrne, Judge, dismissing Sue Ann Watts' amended complaint, pursuant to sec. 802.06(2)(f), Stats. 1985–86, for failure to state a claim upon which relief may be granted. * * *

The case involves a dispute between Sue Ann Evans Watts, the plaintiff, and James Watts, the defendant, over their respective interests in property accumulated during their nonmarital cohabitation relationship which spanned 12 years and produced two children. The case presents an issue of first impression and comes to this court at the pleading stage of the case, before trial and before the facts have been determined.

* * *

We test the sufficiency of the plaintiff's amended complaint by first setting forth the facts asserted in the complaint and then analyzing each of the five legal theories upon which the plaintiff rests her claim for relief.

I.

The plaintiff commenced this action in 1982. The plaintiff's amended complaint alleges the following facts, which for purposes of this appeal must be accepted as true. The plaintiff and the defendant met in 1967, when she was 19 years old, was living with her parents and was working full time as a nurse's aide in preparation for a nursing career. Shortly after the parties met, the defendant persuaded the plaintiff to move into an apartment paid for by him and to quit her job. According to the amended complaint, the defendant "indicated" to the plaintiff that he would provide for her.

Early in 1969, the parties began living together in a "marriage-like" relationship, holding themselves out to the public as husband and wife. The plaintiff assumed the defendant's surname as her own. Subsequently, she gave birth to two children who were also given the defendant's surname. The parties filed joint income tax returns and maintained joint bank accounts asserting that they were husband and wife. The defendant insured the plaintiff as his wife on his medical insurance policy. He also took out a life insurance policy on her as his wife, naming himself as the beneficiary. The parties purchased real and personal property as husband and wife. The plaintiff executed documents and obligated herself on promissory notes to lending institutions as the defendant's wife.

During their relationship, the plaintiff contributed childcare and homemaking services, including cleaning, cooking, laundering, shopping, running errands, and maintaining the grounds surrounding the parties' home. Additionally, the plaintiff contributed personal property to the relationship which she owned at the beginning of the relationship or acquired through gifts or purchases during the relationship. She served as hostess for the defendant for social and business-related events. The amended complaint further asserts that periodically, between 1969 and 1975, the plaintiff cooked and cleaned for the defendant and his employees while his business, a landscaping service, was building and landscaping a golf course.

From 1973 to 1976, the plaintiff worked 20–25 hours per week at the defendant's office, performing duties as a receptionist, typist, and assistant book-keeper. From 1976 to 1981, the plaintiff worked 40–60 hours per week at a business she started with the defendant's sister-in-law, then continued and managed herself after the dissolution of that partnership. The plaintiff further alleges that in 1981 the defendant made their relationship so intolerable that she was forced to move from their home and their relationship was irretrievably broken. Subsequently, the defendant barred the plaintiff from returning to her business.

The plaintiff alleges that during the parties' relationship, and because of her domestic and business contributions, the business and personal wealth of the couple increased. Furthermore, the plaintiff alleges that she never received any compensation for these contributions to the relationship and that the defendant indicated to the plaintiff both orally and through his conduct that he considered her to be his wife and that she would share equally in the increased wealth.

The plaintiff asserts that since the breakdown of the relationship the defendant has refused to share equally with her the wealth accumulated through their joint efforts or to compensate her in any way for her contributions to the relationship.

* * *

The plaintiff's fourth theory of recovery involves unjust enrichment. Essentially, she alleges that the defendant accepted and retained the benefit of services she provided knowing that she expected to share equally in the wealth accumulated during their relationship. She argues that it is unfair for the defendant to retain all the assets they accumulated under these circumstances and that a constructive trust should be imposed on the property as a result of the defendant's unjust enrichment. In his brief, the defendant does not attack specifically either the legal theory or the factual allegations made by the plaintiff.

Unlike claims for breach of an express or implied in fact contract, a claim of unjust enrichment does not arise out of an agreement entered into by the parties. Rather, an action for recovery based upon unjust enrichment is grounded on the moral principle that one who has received a benefit has a duty to make restitution where retaining such a benefit would be unjust. * * *

Because no express or implied in fact agreement exists between the parties, recovery based upon unjust enrichment is sometimes referred to as "quasi contract," or contract "implied in law" rather than "implied in fact." Quasi contracts are obligations created by law to prevent injustice. * * *

In Wisconsin, an action for unjust enrichment, or quasi contract, is based upon proof of three elements: (1) a benefit conferred on the defendant by the plaintiff, (2) appreciation or knowledge by the defendant of the benefit, and (3) acceptance or retention of the benefit by the defendant under circumstances making it inequitable for the defendant to retain the benefit. * * *

The plaintiff has cited no cases directly supporting actions in unjust enrichment by unmarried cohabitants, and the defendant provides no authority against it. * * *

As part of his general argument, the defendant claims that the court should leave the parties to an illicit relationship such as the one in this case essentially as they are found, providing no relief at all to either party. * * *

As we have discussed previously, allowing no relief at all to one party in a so-called "illicit" relationship effectively provides total relief to the other, by leaving that party owner of all the assets acquired through the efforts of both. Yet it cannot seriously be argued that the party retaining all the assets is less "guilty" than the other. Such a result is contrary to the principles of equity. Many courts have held, and we now so hold, that unmarried cohabitants may raise claims based upon unjust enrichment following the termination of their relationships where one of the parties attempts to retain an unreasonable amount of the property acquired through the efforts of both.

In this case, the plaintiff alleges that she contributed both property and services to the parties' relationship. She claims that because of these contributions the parties' assets increased, but that she was never compensated for her contributions. She further alleges that the defendant, knowing that the plaintiff expected to share in the property accumulated, "accepted the services rendered to him by the plaintiff" and that it would be unfair under the circumstances to allow him to retain everything while she receives nothing. We conclude that the facts alleged are sufficient to state a claim for recovery based upon unjust enrichment.

As part of the plaintiff's unjust enrichment claim, she has asked that a constructive trust be imposed on the assets that the defendant acquired during their relationship. A constructive trust is an equitable device created by law to prevent unjust enrichment. * * * To state a claim on the theory of constructive trust the complaint must state facts sufficient to show (1) unjust enrichment and (2) abuse of a confidential relationship or some other form of unconscionable conduct. The latter element can be inferred from allegations in the complaint which show, for example, a family relationship, a close personal relationship, or the parties' mutual trust. These facts are alleged in this complaint or may be inferred. * * * Therefore, we hold that if the plaintiff can prove the elements of unjust enrichment to the satisfaction of the circuit court, she will be entitled to demonstrate further that a constructive trust should be imposed as a remedy.

* * *

Problem: The Good Samaritan and the Greedy Doctor

One day, Epstein, an elderly man, was crossing the street when he was hit by a car. Markell, an attorney who had dropped out of medical school several years earlier, witnessed the accident and rushed to Epstein's aid. Able to draw on his prior medical training, Markell saved Epstein's life. Thereafter, he submitted a bill to Epstein for the reasonable value of his services. Epstein balked at paying, so Markell now brought his legal training to bear and filed suit. Should Markell recover? Would it make a difference if Epstein had not survived the accident? How about if Markell were a real doctor? How about if the basis for Epstein's refusal to pay is his strong religious convictions against seeking medical intervention under any circumstances? *See In re Crispin's Estate*, 107 N.W.2d 907 (1961).

D. At the Request of a Third Party

Flooring Systems, Inc. v. Radisson Group, Inc.
Supreme Court of Arizona
160 Ariz. 224, 772 P.2d 578 (1989)

Corcoran, Justice.

Plaintiff Flooring Systems, Inc. appeals from summary judgment entered in favor of defendants Radisson Group, Inc. and CSA, Inc. We granted review to consider whether summary judgment was properly granted on Flooring's unjust enrichment claim. * * *

Facts

In July 1985, CSA, as Radisson's agent, invited Flooring to bid on carpeting work for the Scottsdale Radisson Resort. Flooring submitted a bid, which CSA accepted in August 1985.

In October 1985, Radisson chose Five Star Services, Inc. as the general contractor for the renovations and an agreement was executed. Five Star then entered into a subcontract agreement with Flooring for the same carpeting work included in Flooring's bid that CSA accepted. Neither Radisson nor CSA was a party to this subcontract agreement. During renovation, Flooring submitted all payment requests to Five Star, not Radisson.

Although Flooring completed its work, Five Star failed to pay Flooring the full amount due under the subcontract. Because of Five Star's default, Radisson withheld approximately $25,000 due under its general contract with Five Star. Section 6.2 of Radisson's general contract with Five Star permitted Radisson to withhold final payment until Five Star satisfied "all known indebtedness" connected with the work.

Flooring sued Radisson, CSA and Five Star to recover the amount due. Five Star later filed for bankruptcy and was dismissed as a party.

Procedure and Issue

In its complaint, Flooring alleged breach of contract and unjust enrichment. Radisson and CSA moved for summary judgment, arguing that, * * * the existence of a subcontract agreement between Five Star and Flooring precluded any recovery from Radisson and CSA under an unjust enrichment theory. The trial court granted summary judgment against Flooring. The court of appeals affirmed * * * .

Discussion

Flooring contends that it is entitled to recover on its unjust enrichment claim because it has sold and installed $59,000 worth of carpet, and Radisson has paid no one for at least $25,000 of it. In response, Radisson and CSA rely on *Stratton v. Inspiration Consol. Copper Co.,* 140 Ariz. 528, 683 P.2d 327 (App.1984), and *Advance Leasing & Crane Co. v. Del E. Webb Corp.*, 117 Ariz. 451, 573 P.2d 525 (App.1977).

In *Stratton*, the defendant hired a general contractor to do remodeling. The general contractor subcontracted the painting work to the plaintiff. Defendant approved the general contractor's hiring of plaintiff and inspected the work from time to time, but no contract existed between defendant and plaintiff. Defendant fully paid the general contractor pursuant to the contract and later change orders, but the general contractor did not pay plaintiff. Attempting to recover from defendant, plaintiff filed a mechanic's lien and sued to foreclose on defendant's property. The complaint also alleged unjust enrichment.

The trial court granted summary judgment in defendant's favor. The court of appeals affirmed, stating that "the doctrine of unjust enrichment has no application to the owner where an explicit contract exists between the subcontractor and the prime contractor." 140 Ariz. at 531, 683 P.2d at 330.

The *Stratton* court relied on *Advance Leasing*, in which the court of appeals also held that a contract between a general contractor and a subcontractor precluded recovery by the subcontractor against the owner. 117 Ariz. at 452, 573 P.2d at 526. In so holding, the court indicated its agreement with *Restatement of Restitution* § 110 (1937), which states:

> § 110 Restitution from Beneficiary of a Contract with Third Person Who Has Failed to Perform.
>
> A person who has conferred a benefit upon another as the performance of a contract with a third person is not entitled to restitution from the other merely because of the failure of performance by the third person.

The facts in *Advance Leasing* were similar to those in *Stratton*: no contract existed between the owner and the subcontractor and, although the owner fully paid the general contractor, the general contractor failed to pay the subcontractor.

In support of its position, Flooring relies on *Commercial Cornice & Millwork, Inc. v. Camel Constr. Serv. Corp.*, 154 Ariz. 34, 739 P.2d 1351 (App.1987), and *Costanzo v. Stewart*, 9 Ariz. App. 430, 453 P.2d 526 (1969). The plaintiff in *Commercial Cornice*, a subcontractor, alleged that the owner had agreed to pay the full amount due under the contract between plaintiff and the general contractor. In fact, the owner had paid a portion of the amount due, but neither the owner nor the general contractor paid the remainder. The trial court granted the owner's motion to dismiss for failure to state a claim because of plaintiff's contract with the general contractor.

The court of appeals held that dismissal was inappropriate, despite the existence of the contract between the subcontractor and the general contractor. The court distinguished *Stratton* and *Advance Leasing* by noting that in both cases the owner had fully paid the general contractor, and thus was not unjustly enriched.

The owner in *Costanzo* had assured the subcontractor that "the money for the job was in escrow and that he would write a check to him and [the general contractor] when the job was finished. . . ." 9 Ariz. App. at 431, 453 P.2d at 527. The subcontractor completed the job, but the bank did not honor the general contractor's check to him. In permitting the subcontractor to recover from the owner on an unjust enrichment claim, the court of appeals commented, "Costanzo [the owner] has paid no one anything for the work done." 9 Ariz. App. at 431, 453 P.2d at 527, citing *Restatement of Restitution* § 40, comment d (1937),[1] the court stated:

> The trial court found, and the testimony shows, that defendant [the owner] knew plaintiff [the subcontractor] was concerned about his payment and he assured him escrow arrangements had been made. These facts establish a good case for restitution. 9 Ariz. App. at 432–33, 453 P.2d at 528–29.

---

[1]Restatement of Restitution § 40, comment d (1937) provides:

> [W]here a person accepts services from another, having reason to know that the other is under a belief that the recipient or a third person has promised compensation or is otherwise under a duty to pay for them . . . the recipient is liable for the reasonable value of the services irrespective of their value to him.

Neither party cites our decision in *Murdock-Bryant Constr., Inc. v. Pearson*, 146 Ariz. 48, 703 P.2d 1197 (1985). In that case, we held that a general contractor's joint venturers were liable for benefits received from a subcontractor, even though they became joint venturers after the general contractor had contracted with the subcontractor. We stated that "a party may be liable to make restitution for benefits received, even though he has committed no tort and is not contractually obligated to the plaintiff." 146 Ariz. at 53, 703 P.2d at 1202. We set forth the following analysis to be used in deciding unjust enrichment claims:

> In determining whether it would be unjust to allow the retention of benefits without compensation, a court need not find that the defendant intended to compensate the plaintiff for the services rendered or that the plaintiff intended that the defendant be the party to make compensation. This is because the duty to compensate for unjust enrichment is an obligation implied by law without reference to the intention of the parties. 1 S. Williston, Contracts § 3A at 13 (3rd ed. 1957). What is important is that it be shown that it was not intended or expected that the services be rendered or the benefit conferred gratuitously, and that the benefit was not "conferred officiously."

146 Ariz. at 54, 703 P.2d at 1203, *quoting Pyeatte v. Pyeatte,* 135 Ariz. 346, 353, 661 P.2d 196, 203 (App.1982). We explained that the subcontractor's contract with the general contractor

> has importance in considering [the] claim for unjust enrichment because it both evidences [plaintiff's] expectation of compensation and the circumstances which make it unjust to allow [defendant] to retain the benefits.

Id.

Using the above analysis, we find that Radisson and CSA were not entitled as a matter of law to prevail on Flooring's unjust enrichment claim. Flooring clearly did not intend to provide carpeting work gratuitously or officiously; its contract with Five Star evinces its intent to be paid for its services. Although Flooring has completed its work, it has not been paid fully for its services. CSA invited Flooring to bid on the job and accepted Flooring's bid. Radisson obviously knew that Flooring had not been paid and on that basis Radisson withheld final payment from Five Star. Under these circumstances, to permit Radisson and CSA to retain the full benefit of Flooring's work at Flooring's expense may be unjust. We therefore hold that summary judgment in favor of Radisson and CSA on this issue was improper.

Radisson argues that it is merely protecting itself from having to pay an amount in excess of that contracted for, should other subcontractors on the remodeling job also seek payment, and that it will pay the approximately $25,000 retained to Five Star and/or its creditors after the court enters a final, non-appealable judgment in its favor. Radisson may have a remedy through interpleader, requiring all parties with potential claims to the retained funds to bring their claims before a single court for resolution. However, Radisson may not merely retain the money, making promises of disbursement at some future time.

CONCLUSION

We hold that summary judgment was improperly granted on Flooring's unjust enrichment claim and therefore reverse the trial court's judgment on that issue, as well as the trial court's award of attorneys' fees to Radisson and CSA. * * * We vacate that portion of the opinion that is inconsistent with this opinion, including the award of attorneys' fees to Radisson and CSA, and remand the case to the trial court for proceedings consistent with this opinion.

* * *

QUESTIONS AND NOTE

1. Questions about the facts of this case

   1.1. How important in this case was the fact that CSA had solicited Flooring Systems' original bid for the carpeting work?

   1.2. How important was it to the decision in *Flooring Systems* that Radisson had withheld a portion of the contract price due to the general contractor, Five Star Services?

2. Questions about the law

   2.1. Is the court saying that it is always unjust for an owner to retain the benefits of a subcontractor's work without paying?

   2.2. On remand, should Flooring Systems' recovery be limited to the amount withheld ($25,000), even though its claim was for a greater amount ($59,000)? If so, what about other unpaid subcontractors who come along later; are they just out of luck? If not, what should Radisson do? Will the interpleader technique suggested by the court be a viable approach?

3. Note

In most states, subcontractors, suppliers, and laborers who work on a construction project are protected by statutory mechanic's liens. These statutes differ considerably from state to state in terms of scope and procedure. Generally speaking, however, they allow unpaid suppliers of goods and services on the project to file a *lien* against the owner's property for the amount they are owed by the general contractor. A lien is a charge against the property rather than an *in personam* claim against the owner. Ultimately, the lien must be satisfied through a judicial foreclosure proceeding in which the property is auctioned to the highest bidder and the lienholder is paid with the proceeds. In the typical situation, the owner will already have paid the general contractor the full contract price. However, if the general contractor is dishonest or insolvent, it will not always make payment under its subcontracts with laborers and suppliers, thus giving rise to their lien claims. To avoid the loss of her property, obviously the owner will have to pay the lien. This means the owner will end up having paid twice for the same work and will be left only with what often amounts to a worthless claim against the general contractor. Knowing how these mechanic's liens work, why didn't Flooring Systems seek to enforce a lien against Radisson rather than suing for breach of contract and unjust enrichment? If you are contracting for a major renovation on your house, what steps might you take to ensure that the property does not later become subject to such liens?

Problem on Third Party Benefits

Ponoroff retained Epstein, attorney-at-law, to pursue a claim against the Great South Health Network, Ponoroff's health insurer, for failing to pay expenses incurred by Ponoroff at the Tulane Medical Center ("TMC"). As a result of Epstein's adroit lawyering skills, Great South finally capitulated and agreed to pay the disputed charges. Thereupon, Epstein sued TMC claiming that the latter benefited from his services by virtue of receiving a payment for services from Ponoroff's insurer that Ponoroff never would have paid out of his own pocket. What result? *See generally Lynch v. Deaconess Medical Center*, 113 Wash.2d 162, 776 P.2d 681 (1989).

E. Breach of Fiduciary Duty

George E. Palmer, Law of Restitution
§ 1 at 2 (1978)

Restitution based upon unjust enrichment cuts across many branches of the law, including contract, tort, and fiduciary relationship, but it also occupies much territory that is its sole preserve.

Wiener v. Lazard Freres & Co.
Supreme Court of New York, Appellate Division
241 A.D.2d 114, 672 N.Y.S.2d 8 (1998)

Milonas, J. P.

At issue in this action is the nature of the relationship between plaintiffs and the Lazard defendants (hereinafter collectively referred to as Lazard) in the context of plaintiffs' efforts to repurchase from the mortgagee bank a building on whose mortgage plaintiffs had defaulted. Plaintiffs are partners of 1500 Realty, which owned an office building at 1500 Broadway. In the spring of 1994, the partnership defaulted on the building's mortgage held by Crossland Federal Savings Bank and filed for bankruptcy pursuant to chapter 11 of the Bankruptcy Code (11 USC). In April 1995, plaintiffs and Crossland entered into an agreement by which Crossland would release plaintiffs from the limited personal guaranty executed in connection with the mortgage in exchange for certain payments as well as plaintiffs' cooperation in transferring the property to the bank. Two months later, a reorganization plan was approved in the bankruptcy proceeding, whereby the property was to be transferred to Crossland or its designee.

However, both prior to and after defaulting on the mortgage, plaintiffs were engaged in an effort to raise sufficient funds to enable them to settle with Crossland and retain ownership of the building. Their intent was to secure Crossland's consent to a transfer of the building to a new entity under plaintiffs' ownership and control, free and clear of the original $75 million mortgage, for a price in the $40 million to $60 million range. To this end, plaintiffs made preliminary arrangements with Credit Lyonnais for a first mortgage in the amount of up to $30 million; they then initiated contact with Lazard to secure a second mortgage for the balance of the purchase price. By letter dated December 22, 1993, Lazard proposed extending an interim first mortgage loan in the amount of $50 million to $55 million, to be replaced within a year by financing from an outside lender in the $35 million to $50 million range, with Lazard retaining a subordinated mortgage of $15 million to $17 million.

Plaintiffs decided to proceed with Lazard's proposal and to work with Lazard in dealing with Crossland. Plaintiffs and Lazard executed a commitment letter dated September 16, 1994, pursuant to which Lazard, as lender, agreed to provide $45 million as interim financing for the purchase or refinancing of the Crossland mortgage, in return for a $300,000 application fee. Lazard was given the exclusive right to provide the financing during an "exclusive period," as defined in the letter, unless it elected earlier not to proceed with the loan.

In connection with Lazard's due diligence under this commitment letter, plaintiffs were to provide Lazard with information regarding the financial history, physical condition and all other relevant data in their possession as owners of the property. Plaintiffs considered this information highly confidential and refused to disclose it until after a formal agreement was executed. It was, and remains, plaintiffs' contention that, as owner of the property, their detailed knowledge of every aspect of the building's operation—from the specifics of its construction and safety-related conditions to negotiations with tenants and labor unions—placed them in a uniquely advantageous position in terms of making the best (i.e., the highest) offer to Crossland. Once the commitment letter was executed, plaintiffs provided this information to Lazard, which reviewed it and arranged for the necessary financial and environmental audits of the property.

By letter dated November 16, 1994, Lazard indicated that it was prepared to go ahead with the interim financing described and asked plaintiffs to sign an "agreement to proceed" under which they would pay a $400,000 deposit by December 1, 1994. This agreement was never signed, however, because Crossland would not agree to a transaction at the price specified in the commitment letter; Crossland also insisted that any agreement be made within the context of the then-pending bankruptcy proceeding, whereby Crossland would become the owner. At this point, according to plaintiffs, the parties agreed that Anthony Meyer, a Lazard executive, would take over the negotiations with Crossland on behalf of plaintiffs, while the latter would attempt to finalize a reorganization plan and resolve their obligations under the personal guaranty executed in conjunction with the Crossland mortgage.

Thus, according to plaintiffs, as of December 1994 through August 1995, they believed that Lazard was actively negotiating with Crossland on their behalf to effect the purchase of the property, with the financing to be provided by a Lazard affiliate and/or Credit Lyonnais. Pursuant to their understanding to this effect, plaintiffs went ahead and reached an agreement with Crossland on the reorganization plan, by which 1500 Realty would transfer the property to Crossland or its designee in exchange for the settlement of plaintiffs' personal guaranty.

Apparently, however, unbeknownst to plaintiffs and contrary to the agreements just described, Lazard decided not to proceed with the plan contemplated in the commitment letter and instead entered into a relationship with defendant Zapco that culminated in Zapco's acquisition of the property from Crossland on terms similar to those Lazard was ostensibly negotiating on behalf of plaintiffs. Zapco's August 1995 contract to purchase the property for $55 million under the reorganization plan was based on financing provided by Lazard and Credit Lyonnais on terms similar to those proposed for plaintiffs.

According to plaintiffs, Lazard not only worked with Zapco to this end while Lazard was supposedly working on plaintiffs' behalf, but also shared with Zapco the confidential information plaintiffs had provided regarding the property's operation, thus enabling Zapco to make an offer that would be acceptable to Crossland—and one that was comparable to plaintiffs' intended offer. Plaintiffs claim that Lazard's dealings with Zapco constituted a gross violation of ethical standards applicable to investment bankers and advisors as well as a clear breach of fiduciary duty.

Plaintiffs' original complaint alleged causes of action for unjust enrichment and breach of fiduciary duty. Defendants moved to dismiss on the grounds that a defense was based on documentary evidence that plaintiffs had failed to state a cause of action and that the complaint failed to set forth in sufficient detail the alleged breach of fiduciary duty. Plaintiffs thereafter served an amended complaint, amplifying the factual allegations underlying their claims and adding the claim of unfair competition based on the misappropriation of plaintiffs' trade secrets, the building's operating data. Construing the dismissal motions as against the amended complaint at defendants' request, the court concluded that plaintiffs had failed to state a cause of action against the Lazard defendants or Zapco and dismissed the complaint. We disagree. Accepting the allegations as true and according them every favorable inference, we find that plaintiffs have sufficiently stated causes of action against the Lazard defendants for breach of fiduciary duty and for unjust enrichment as to the $300,000 application fee.

The Unjust Enrichment Claims

A cause of action for unjust enrichment is stated where "plaintiffs have properly asserted that a benefit was bestowed ... by plaintiffs and that defendants will obtain such benefit without adequately compensating plaintiffs therefor" (*Tarrytown House Condominiums v. Hainje,* 161 AD2d 310, 313). Where defendants have reaped such benefit, equity and good conscience require that they make restitution. In dismissing the unjust enrichment claims, the court found that plaintiffs had failed to show how defendants had been enriched or that any enrichment had been at plaintiffs' expense. According to the court, plaintiffs did no more than allege that Lazard received a benefit from them (the application fee) as well as benefits from Zapco (fees, equity interest and future profits). The court further found that the Zapco deal was not made "at plaintiffs' expense" because Crossland would never have concluded a deal with plaintiffs under any circumstances; thus, plaintiffs were never in a position to have made such a deal for themselves.

As plaintiffs correctly argue in the first instance, the court, in reaching these conclusions on motions to dismiss, made improper findings of fact. It is well established that, on such a motion, the pleadings must be liberally construed and the facts alleged accepted as true; the court must determine "only whether the facts as alleged fit within any cognizable legal theory" * * *.

Here, while the court determined that Crossland would never have sold the property to plaintiffs, the pleadings only refer to Crossland's unwillingness to sell to plaintiffs at the $45 million price specified in the commitment letter. According to plaintiffs' allegations, once it became clear that this price was not acceptable, Crossland continued to negotiate with plaintiffs, with Meyer now conducting the negotiations on plaintiffs' behalf. Thus, the court erred in dismissing the unjust enrichment claims on this ground.

With respect to the benefit bestowed on defendants, the receipt of a benefit alone, pursuant to the standard set forth above, is insufficient to establish a cause of action for unjust enrichment * * * Here, having been paid $300,000, defendants did not fulfill the terms of their agreement to work to secure a deal for plaintiffs but instead secured a deal for Zapco, using plaintiffs' confidential information. Defendants argue that, as to the $300,000 fee, plaintiffs are precluded from asserting that their payment of this fee constituted unjust enrichment when, in the commitment letter, plaintiffs specifically agreed that the fee "shall be deemed fully earned by us [Lazard]." According to Lazard, plaintiffs thereby acknowledged that the fee had been earned—that Lazard had an absolute right to it—and therefore cannot now claim to the contrary. In making this argument, defendants insist on too literal a reading of the phrase. Indeed, the language establishes to the contrary that the fee has not actually been earned at all; it is "deemed" earned, i.e., it is a nonrefundable sum paid pursuant to the parties' understanding as to what Lazard will do on plaintiffs' behalf. Thus, plaintiffs may claim that a benefit ($300,000) was bestowed upon Lazard, for which Lazard has not adequately compensated plaintiffs (in that it abandoned its efforts on plaintiffs' behalf and secured a deal for Zapco instead). As to this benefit, the cause of action for unjust enrichment should not have been dismissed.

The remaining benefits alleged by plaintiffs, consisting of whatever flowed from the Crossland-Zapco deal to Lazard—fees paid and any equity interest or profits to be paid in the future—cannot be said to be benefits bestowed on defendants for which plaintiffs should have been compensated or to which plaintiffs were entitled. Thus, to the extent the unjust enrichment claims were based on these benefits, they were properly dismissed.

The Breach of Fiduciary Duty Claim

[The court also reinstated the plaintiffs' breach of fiduciary duty claim against the Lazard defendants.]

* * *

SECTION 3: PROMISSORY RESTITUTION

Webb v. McGowin

In *Webb*, *supra*, at 414, the Alabama Court of Appeals recognized, and the Alabama Supreme Court affirmed that an exception to the general rule that past consideration is not good consideration exists when the promise is made in recognition of an antecedent benefit conferred on the defendant by the plaintiff. As we saw, the so-called "material benefit rule" is now codified in § 86 of the *Restatement (Second) of Contracts.* Take a moment to review § 86 again. It sets forth the elements that must be established in order for a party to recover on a promise even though the benefit which induced the promise occurred before it was made. Do these elements sound familiar? In fact, do they even sound a little bit like the elements for recovery under quasi-contract? The similarity is no accident. There is unquestionably a relationship between the material benefit rule and the doctrine of unjust enrichment. Consider whether, if McGowin had not made the promise to pay Webb $15 every two weeks, Webb could have succeeded in an action for unjust enrichment? Clearly, the benefit conferred was material; McGowin's life, and the exigency of the situation would excuse Webb's failure to give McGowin the opportunity to deny the benefit. So far so good. But was there really an expectation of compensation on Webb's part? Probably not; the act was gratuitous. However, when you add to the mix McGowin's subsequent decision to agree to pay a reasonable amount in recognition of the benefit conferred, the case for enforcement becomes sufficiently compelling, or so the argument goes, to justify the case for enforcement. Professor (later, Judge) Robert Braucher, the first Reporter for the *Restatement (Second) of Contracts*, in commenting on an earlier draft of § 86, stated that the section fairly "bristles with nonspecific concepts." Do you agree? At the same time, however, he also noted that the provision "seeks to draw a distinction between the cases involving moral obligation based on gratitude and sentiment and those cases which are on the borderline of quasi-contract. . . ." Braucher, *Freedom of Contract and the Second Restatement*, 78 YALE L.J. 598, 605 (1969).

Recall in Chapter 2 we examined two other cases (*Harrington v. Taylor, supra*, at 403, and *Mills v. Wyman, supra*, at 404) in both of which the court rejected the argument that past consideration creates a moral obligation sufficient to support enforcement of a subsequent promise of payment. Instead of asserting the enforceability of the actual promises made by the defendants in *Harrington* and *Mills,* what if the plaintiffs in those cases had brought a claim for restitution based on unjust enrichment? Would either or both of them have prevailed? Why did the court in *Mills* stress the age of the defendant's son? If the son had been a minor or a dependent how would that have helped the case for recovery for breach of contract? For unjust enrichment?

Look again at the elements of § 86, specifically subsection (2), which provides that the promise is *not* binding if (a) the promisee conferred the benefit as a *gift*, or (b) the promisor has not been unjustly enriched. Can an act be gratuitous and still not intended as a gift? We think so. Was Webb making a gift when he decided to fall with the 75-pound pine block? The other limitation in § 86(2) is that the promise will not be enforced to the extent that its value is disproportionate to the benefit. Is there a link to the doctrine of unjust enrichment here, too? In answering that question for yourself, consider the material in the next section dealing with how to measure damages in a quasi-contract action.

SECTION 4: MEASURING THE VALUE OF THE RESTITUTIONARY INTEREST

The idea behind quasi-contract is to prevent the inequitable enrichment of one party at the expense of the other. Thus, the benefit conferred must be restored if equity is to be done. That is to say, the defendant must make *restitution.* But sometimes that can be easier said then done, particularly when the benefit is not an object or commodity that is capable of being physically returned to the plaintiff. Also, when the basis of the plaintiff's claim is an action for unjust enrichment, then, unlike in a conventional breach of contract action where the object is to enforce a broken promise, it is not necessarily appropriate to award the plaintiff her "expectation" (*i.e.*, what she would have received had an actual promise been made by the defendant). Instead, in many cases, the court will have to determine the *reasonable value* of the benefit conferred in order to fashion an appropriate remedy. But often value, like beauty, is in the eye of the beholder.

Pull v. Barnes

Supreme Court of Colorado
142 Colo. 272, 350 P.2d 828 (1960)

Per Curiam:

The parties appear here in the same order they appeared in the trial court, namely Burnard T. and Margaret H. Pull as plaintiffs, and Margaret Barnes and Mary E. Moffat as defendants. * * *

The action was brought by the plaintiffs in September of 1956 in the district court of Jefferson County to determine the boundary line between properties owned by the plaintiffs and the defendants, for damages and other relief.

In June of 1953 the plaintiffs located a parcel of land about one acre in size in Jefferson County, upon which they desired to build a mountain home and began to search out the owners of it. Just west of the piece of land selected was a line of an old fence which had upon it "No Trespassing" signs. Plaintiffs proceeded to negotiate with and buy from the parties who, in good faith, asserted the title to the land now in question. It later was determined by a survey that the defendants Barnes and Moffat, who owned the land west of the fence line, actually owned most of the land east of the fence line which the plaintiffs believed they had purchased, and upon which they had constructed their cabin.

Prior to constructing their cabin the plaintiffs hired a licensed surveyor to stake out the corners of the cabin site, but did not ask him to survey the land itself to determine the boundary lines between their property and that of the defendants'. Construction of the cabin upon the site, with a concrete slab floor and foundation, was begun in August 1953 and substantially completed by the fall of 1953.

During the construction the defendants several times were on the scene and acted as neighbors-about-to-be. The evidence clearly discloses that neither party knew or even suspected at the time of the construction of the cabin that it was being built upon land belonging to defendants.

After the cabin was completed the defendant Barnes negotiated with plaintiffs for a right-of-way through the land upon which the plaintiffs had built their cabin, and upon being refused hired a surveyor, and for the first time learned that the cabin which the plaintiffs had erected was solely upon her and the defendant Moffatt's land. Thereupon defendants erected a fence excluding the plaintiffs from the cabin and the land until a preliminary injunction was entered in this case some two years later.

Defendants now assert dominion over the cabin, contending that the plaintiffs had no rights therein, it having been built on defendants' land and as a result became a part of the land by operation of law.

Plaintiffs contend that the principles laid down by *Golden Press v. Rylands,* 124 Colo. 122, 235 P. (2d) 592, which permitted relief to a party who had encroached to a small extent on his neighbor's land, should apply. Plaintiffs further contend that the defendants are estopped by reason of their conduct from asserting title to the house.

On the other hand defendants urged that the facts in the present case do not bring it within the rule of *Golden Press, supra,* and further in the light of *Jacobs v. Perry,* 135 Colo. 550, 313 P. (2d) 1008, the doctrine of estoppel cannot apply here.

The trial court held that the boundary line of the property was the line surveyed east of the old fence line, thereby placing the cabin entirely within the land owned by the defendants, and held that the doctrine announced in *Golden Press, supra,* did not apply and that *Jacobs, supra,* forbade the application of the doctrine of estoppel. Judgment was entered for the defendants. In the course of its findings the court said:

"We would be inclined to grant some relief with reference to this building if it were within our power to do so. However, the only suggestion that has been made to us would be relief under the principle as laid down in the case of *Golden Press v. Rylands,* 124 Colo. 122, and we believe that the principle of encroachment set forth in that case is not applicable."

The trial court was correct in determining that *Golden Press, supra,* presented a different fact situation than is presented here; however, it is clear from the trial court's finding that it was searching for an equitable remedy which it could apply and which would prevent the harshness of the ruling.

As an abstract principle of law it is true that the moment a house is built upon land, it belongs to the owner of the land by mere operation of law and he may possess and enjoy it as his own. But this is merely stating the technical rule of law by which the owner seeks to hold what, in a just sense, he never had the slightest title to; that is, the house if it were not attached to the realty. It is not answering the objection by merely and dryly stating that the law so holds; for admitting this to be so, in law, such a situation furnishes a strong ground why equity should and does interpose and grant relief in proper cases.

Here the powers of the trial court were invoked to settle a boundary dispute and the problems arising from the situation in which the plaintiffs and the defendants found themselves without bad faith on the part of any of the parties. The matter having been presented to the court, it was the court's duty to grant the relief in equity which the situation demanded.

We think the applicable rule is stated in *Johnson v. Dunkel (1955)*, 132 Colo. 383, 288 P. (2d) 343, and is peculiarly applicable to the situation before us. In that case the adjoining owner who had in good faith erected improvements on adjoining land, believing it to be his own, was granted the right to remove same if feasible and if not, then was given an equitable lien on the property for the value thereof.

The judgment is accordingly reversed with directions to the trial court to hold a further hearing to determine whether it would be practical and feasible for Pull to remove the improvements from the land in question, and if so to specify the conditions under which it shall be done. If removal of the cabin is not feasible, then the value thereof should be determined and the land subjected to a lien in favor of plaintiffs in an amount equal to the value so determined.

QUESTIONS AND NOTES

1. Questions about the facts of this case

   1.1. What facts are most helpful to the plaintiffs' case?

   1.2. What facts are most helpful to support the defendants' contentions?

2. Questions about the law

   2.1. What do you understand the court to be saying in this case about the relationship between law and equity?

   2.2. On remand, if the trial court in *Pull* determines that removal is not feasible and, therefore, decides to impose an equitable lien on the defendants' property for the value of the cabin constructed on the defendants' land, how should "value" be determined under these circumstances? *See Restatement (Second) of Contracts* § 371. What if the defendants didn't really like the design of the cabin and planned to tear it down because they considered it an eyesore?

   2.3. If removal of the cabin were practicable, can plaintiffs recover the costs associated with doing so?

3. Notes

   3.1. In *Watts v. Watts, supra*, the plaintiff requested that a *constructive trust* be imposed on the defendant's assets acquired during the course of the relationship. In *Pull v. Barnes*, the Colorado Supreme Court directed that if removing the cabin was not feasible, the defendants' land should be subjected to an *equitable lien* in favor of the plaintiffs for the value of the improvements made on the land. As we noted earlier, a lien creates a charge against the property for the amount owed to the lienholder such that good title to the land cannot be conveyed until the lien is discharged by payment to the lienholder. Most liens, like most trusts, are created by agreement between the parties. In *Pull*, however, the court imposed the lien as a matter of law, rather than as a matter of contract, hence the term *equitable lien.* Similarly, a constructive trust is not a real trust in the conventional sense of the term, but instead is a remedy whereby the party with legal title to certain assets is deemed to hold title for the benefit of the party with a superior claim to such assets. Both constructive trusts and equitable liens are restitutionary remedies that may be employed by the court to prevent unjust enrichment. How would you describe the difference between the two? Why would the constructive trust not have been an appropriate remedy in *Pull*?

3.2. Sometimes a court will simply award damages based on the monetary value of what the defendant has unjustly received from the plaintiff. Indeed, this is the traditional remedy at common law for recovery in a quasi-contract action. Historically, an action in quasi-contract was sometimes referred to as a count (cause of action) of *quantum meruit* (literally, "as much as it deserves"), and that terminology still shows up in cases today. How does such a recovery differ from a recovery under the contract? In addition, when the benefit conferred consists of something other than money, for example property or services, how would you attempt to prove the value of the benefit conferred? Consider that question as you read the next case and the "Note on Measuring the Value of the Restitutionary Interest" that follows.

Britton v. Turner

Supreme Court of New Hampshire
6 N.H. 481 (1834)

Syllabus:

Assumpsit for work and labour, performed by the plaintiff, in the service of the defendant, from March 9th, 1831, to December 27, 1831.

The declaration contained the common counts, and among them a count in quantum meruit, for the labor, averring it to be worth one hundred dollars.

At the trial in the C. C. Pleas, the plaintiff proved the performance of the labor as set forth in the declaration.

The defence was that it was performed under a special contract—that the plaintiff agreed to work one year, from some time in March, 1831, to

March 1832, and that the defendant was to pay him for said year's labor the sum of one hundred and twenty dollars; and the defendant offered evidence tending to show that such was the contract under which the work was done.

Evidence was also offered to show that the plaintiff left the defendant's service without his consent, and it was contended by the defendant that the plaintiff had no good cause for not continuing in his employment.

There was no evidence offered of any damage arising from the plaintiffs departure, farther than was to be inferred from his non fulfillment of the entire contract.

The court instructed the jury, that if they were satisfied from the evidence that the labor was performed, under a contract to labor a year, for the sum of one hundred and twenty dollars, and if they were satisfied that the plaintiff labored only the time specified in the declaration, and then left the defendant's service, against his consent, and without any good cause, yet the plaintiff was entitled to recover, under his quantum meruit count, as much as the labor he performed was reasonably worth, and under this direction the jury gave a verdict for the plaintiff for the sum of $95.

The defendant excepted to the instructions thus given to the jury.

Parker, J.

It may be assumed, that the labor performed by the plaintiff, and for which he seeks to recover a compensation in this action, was commenced under a special contract to labor for the defendant the term of one year, for the sum of one hundred and twenty dollars, and that the plaintiff has labored but a portion of that time, and has voluntarily failed to complete the entire contract.

It is clear, then, that he is not entitled to recover upon the contract itself, because the service, which was to entitle him to the sum agreed upon, has never been performed.

But the question arises, can the plaintiff, under these circumstances, recover a reasonable sum for the service he has actually performed, under the count in quantum meruit.

* * *

That such rule in its operation may be very unequal, not to say unjust, is apparent. * * *

The case before us presents an illustration. Had the plaintiff in this case never entered upon the performance of his contract, the damage could not probably have been greater than some small expense and trouble incurred in procuring another to do the labor which he had contracted to perform. But having entered upon the performance, and labored nine and a half months, the value of which labor to the defendant as found by the jury is $95, if the defendant can succeed in this defence, he in fact receives nearly five sixths of the value of a whole year's labor, by reason of the breach of contract by the plaintiff a sum not only utterly disproportionate to any probable, not to say possible damage which could have resulted from the neglect of the plaintiff to continue the remaining two and an half months, but altogether beyond any damage which could have been recovered by the defendant, had the plaintiff done nothing towards the fulfillment of his contract.

* * *

We hold then, that where a party undertakes to pay upon a special contract for the performance of labor, or the furnishing of materials, he is not to be charged upon such special agreement until the money is earned according to the terms of it, and where the parties have made an express contract the law will not imply and raise a contract different from that which the parties have entered into, except upon some farther transaction between the parties.

In case of a failure to perform such special contract, by the default of the party contracting to do the service, if the money is not due by the terms of the special agreement he is not entitled to recover for his labor, or for the materials furnished, unless the other party receives what has been done, or furnished, and upon the whole case derives a benefit from it. * * *

But if, where a contract is made of such a character, a party actually receives labor, or materials, and thereby derives a benefit and advantage, over and above the damage which has resulted from the breach of the contract by the other party, the labor actually done, and the value received, furnish a new consideration, and the law thereupon raises a promise to pay to the extent of the reasonable worth of such excess. This may be considered as making a new case, one not within the original agreement, and the party is entitled to "recover on his new case, for the work done, not as agreed, but yet accepted by the defendant." 1 Dane's Abr. 224.

If on such failure to perform the whole, the nature of the contract be such that the employer can reject what has been done, and refuse to receive any benefit from the part performance, he is entitled so to do, and in such case is not liable to be charged, unless he has before assented to and accepted of what has been done, however much the other party may have done towards the performance. He has in such case received nothing, and having contracted to receive nothing but the entire matter contracted for, he is not bound to pay, because his express promise was only to pay on receiving the whole, and having actually received nothing the law cannot and ought not to raise an implied promise to pay. But where the party receives value—takes and uses the materials, or has advantage from the labor, he is liable to pay the reasonable worth of what he has received. * * * And the rule is the same whether it was received and accepted by the assent of the party prior to the breach, under a contract by which, from its nature, he was to receive labor, from time to time until the completion of the whole contract; or whether it was received and accepted by an assent subsequent to the performance of all which was in fact done. If he received it under such circumstances as precluded him from rejecting it afterwards, that does not alter the case—it has still been received by his assent.

* * *

It is easy, if parties so choose, to provide by an express agreement that nothing shall be earned, if the laborer leaves his employer without having performed the whole service contemplated, and then there can be no pretence for a recovery if he voluntarily deserts the service before the expiration of the time.

The amount, however, for which the employer ought to be charged, where the laborer abandons his contract, is only the reasonable worth, or the amount of advantage he receives upon the whole transaction, and, in estimating the value of the labor, the contract price for the service cannot be exceeded. * * *

If a person makes a contract fairly he is entitled to have it fully performed, and if this is not done he is entitled to damages. He may maintain a suit to recover the amount of damage sustained by the non performance.

The benefit and advantage which the party takes by the labor, therefore, is the amount of value which he receives, if any, after deducting the amount of damage; and if he elects to put this in defence he is entitled so to do, and the implied promise which the law will raise, in such case, is to pay such amount of the stipulated price for the whole labor, as remains after deducting what it would cost to procure a completion of the residue of the service, and also any damage which has been sustained by reason of the non fulfillment of the contract.

If in such case it be found that the damages are equal to, or greater than the amount of the labor performed, so that the employer, having a right to the full performance of the contract, has not upon the whole case received a beneficial service, the plaintiff cannot recover.

This rule, by binding the employer to pay the value of the service he actually receives, and the laborer to answer in damages where he does not complete the entire contract, will leave no temptation to the former to drive the laborer from his service, near the close of his term, by ill treatment in order to escape from payment; not to the latter to desert his service before the stipulated time, without a sufficient reason; and it will in most instances settle the whole controversy in one action and prevent a multiplicity of suits and cross actions.

* * *

The defendant sets up a mere breach of contract in defense of the action, but this cannot avail him. He does not appear to have offered evidence to show that he was damnified by such breach, or to have asked that a deduction should be made on that account. The direction to the jury was therefore correct, that the plaintiff was entitled to recover as much as the labor performed was reasonably worth, and the jury appear to have allowed a pro rata compensation, for the time which the plaintiff labored in the defendant's service.

As the defendant has not claimed or had any adjustment of damages, for the breach of the contract, in this action, if he has actually sustained damage he is still entitled to a suit to recover the amount.

* * *

Judgment on the verdict.

QUESTIONS AND NOTE

1. Questions about the facts of this case

 1.1. Why do you think Turner failed to offer any evidence of damages arising from Britton's breach of his employment contract?

 1.2. Was the court concerned with the reasons why Britton left Turner's employ before the end of the one-year? Is that fact relevant to the legal issue in the case?

2. Questions about the law

 2.1. Look at the trial court's instruction to the jury. Did the court permit Britton to recover under the contract?

 2.2. Could you argue that Britton "substantially performed"? How would the analysis and/or the outcome have been different if the court had concluded that there had been substantial performance?

 2.3. What, if anything, would Turner have had to pay to Britton if Turner had been able to show that it cost him $50 to hire someone else to perform Britton's duties for the balance of the contract term? Suppose the cost was only $15?

 2.4. In estimating reasonable value of the employee's services for which the employer might be charged, why should the contract price operate as a ceiling?

 2.5. Suppose Turner had been able to show that the contract price was above market rates for similar services, or that Britton performed his job in a sloppy manner. Would either of these facts affect the amount Britton should be able to recover in a quantum meruit claim?

 2.6. What are the policy issues the court was concerned with? Does the rule devised by the court in this case advance those policies?

3. Note

Today, in virtually all jurisdictions, employers are required by statute to pay their employees periodically (*i.e.*, bi-weekly or monthly) without regard to either the quality of the employee's work or whether the employee has substantially performed the contract. In effect, employment contracts are made divisible by statute. However, the "net benefit rule" established in *Britton v. Turner* still has enormous viability in other contexts, including construction services and independent contractor arrangements.

Note on Measuring the Value of the Restitutionary Interest

Restatement (Second) of Contracts § 371 provides that when a sum of money is awarded to protect a party's restitution interest, it may be measured *either* by the cost to obtain the same benefit from a third party in the claimant's position *or* the extent to which the other party's property has been increased in value or his other interests advanced. Thus, one approach looks to the reasonable value of market substitutes while the other focuses on net enrichment. Which approach did the court follow in *Britton v. Turner*? The answer is that it is difficult to tell without knowing whether the original employment contract was at, above, or below market rates for comparable services. The *Britton* court did state, however, that even if it had been a below-market contract, such that the value of the services rendered by the plaintiff were *greater* than the stipulated contract price, the plaintiff's recovery could not exceed the contract rate. What policy is served by that rule? *See Restatement (Second) of Contracts* § 373(2).

To understand the difference between the "cost saved" and the "net enrichment" approaches, suppose the cabin erected by the plaintiffs in *Pull v. Barnes, supra*, increased the value of the defendants' property by $5,000; that is to say, if the property were put on the market with and without a cabin of the kind plaintiffs' erected, the difference in what could be obtained in an arms-length sale would be $5,000. It is often the case, however, that the costs of constructing improvements or making repairs upon property do not translate into a dollar-for-dollar increase in the market value of the underlying property. In other words, had the defendants contracted to have such a cabin built, a reasonable bid to do the work may have been $7,500. Which measure should the court use? If the purpose for the doctrine of unjust enrichment is not to compensate or make the benefit-provider whole, but rather to make the benefit-receiver restore the benefit, then a good case for the less generous net enrichment approach can be made. Under what circumstances, then, might a court nevertheless be inclined to adopt the "costs saved" approach?

In Chapter 5, we saw that restitution is sometimes available as an alternative remedy for breach of contract. In *Britton v. Turner*, of course, it was the party *in breach* who sought to recover the reasonable value of his services, net of the damages flowing from his breach. This rule has found its way into the *Restatement*. *See Restatement (Second) of Contracts* § 374. In measuring the value of the restitutionary interest, should it make a difference to the court whether the party seeking restitution is the breaching or the non-breaching party? If so, how?

Final Note from the Authors

We hope you enjoyed your study of *Making and Doing Deals.* We hope you learned something in the process, too. We also hope you enjoyed using our book. In fact, we hope you enjoyed it so much that you decide to keep it rather than to sell it back to the bookstore! Either way, we wish you the best of luck throughout the remainder of your law school career.

DGE
BAM
LP

Appendix

INTRODUCTION TO LAW, LAW SCHOOL AND CONTRACT LAW

SECTION 1: THE RULE OF LAW

This is a book about "contract law." But contract law represents only a narrow slice of our overall legal system. Any mature legal system is grounded firmly in the "rule of law"—the notion that the resolution of any particular problem and the exercise of any authority is ultimately to be guided and, when necessary, constrained by a single set of known or knowable principles that apply even-handedly to all members of society. In a law review article, Markell had this to say about the rule of law: "The concept of the rule of law contains within it the central notion that governmental actions and decisions should proceed in accordance with known or knowable rules and norms. Put another way, legal texts or norms constrain those in power. This restraint can be positive or negative; a decision has legitimacy—and commands respect and obedience—only if justified by resort to some text or some norm. The text could be a statute, a decree, or something promulgated in a way that gives it legitimacy. Conversely, a decision is illegitimate—and thus need not be followed—if it cannot be tied to an authorizing text or norm." Bruce A. Markell, *A View From the Field: Some Observations on the Effect of Interpretational Commercial Law Reform Efforts on the Rule of Law*, 6 IND. J. GLOBAL LEGAL STUD. 497, 498–99 (1999).

When we speak of "law" and the "rule of law" it's important to recognize that we're speaking of more than rules of law as written in codes, statutes, decrees, and regulations. The written law is important of course. Historical documents, like the Declaration of Independence and the federal Constitution, impose limits on the exercise of power by those in authority and this is a critical aspect of the rule of law. Published statutes and regulations provide guidelines and limitations for private transactions as well, ensuring a measure of certainty and consistency for the parties involved. Being able to predict the legal consequences of a particular course of action is important to commercial actors since it allows them to order their affairs with the comfort of knowing that their previous arrangements, if within the letter of the law, will be recognized and enforced. Textual rules of law not only codify received and settled rules that may not be written down, they are often supplemented by norms and customs that guide action and official discretion in ways that are just as binding as a written text. In Anglo/American jurisdictions, the common law typically embodies these unwritten rules of law that restrain the exercise of power. In international relations, customary international law contains the unwritten rules of interstate behavior, just as written treaties provide the written rules governing behavior among nations. Together, this body of text and unwritten norms are the "law," in the sense that they prescribe what can and cannot be done by those in power.

Texts and norms, however, are not always applied as written or understood. In fact, in some instances they are honored more in the breach than in the observance. This practice represents another component of the rule of law; namely the rule of law *as applied.* Bureaucratic tendencies toward administrative convenience, or political pressures toward expediency, will sometimes create practices at odds with the spirit, if not the text, of the law. This divergence between law and practice reflects the existence of both a formal legal code and an "operational code."

Unavoidably, a certain measure of retained discretion for government officials resides within the texts and norms that operate behind the rule of law. This retained discretion is not necessarily harmful to the legitimacy of a legal system. Lawmakers and judges understand intuitively that the law as written cannot anticipate all contingencies that may arise after the fact. Therefore, the legal system must allow those who administer the law some leeway to accommodate the "unprovided for" case. To be sure, however, too much discretion in application can be destructive if the opportunity to vary rules for exigent or emergency situations also gives rise to latitude in the determination of what constitutes exigent or emergency situations. On the other hand, often just the pretext of compliance with the written law can be used to undermine the salutary effects of the rule of law. Delay can be a potent weapon, frequently working to the advantage of one side over another. Thus, unless there is a separate norm that reserves some discretion in the law-applier, even the best drafted rules will fail to achieve their aims. The key, however, is that such discretion should be used to further the public good, rather than private profit.

There is one further component of a regime governed by a rule of law, and not a rule of men, that goes beyond the constraints of power and political discretion imposed by the positive law both as written and applied. A system that adheres to the rule of law has within it certain shared cultural underpinnings and understandings. For instance, the limits on the discretion that may exist to override the written rule to achieve justice in the particular case is something that is often learned rather than prescribed. In many cases, the use of power for the general common good, as opposed to personal gain, is not something that can be prescribed and history has repeatedly demonstrated that such instincts do not often arise naturally or in abundance. It is in this respect, then, that cultural norms and habits create the difference between a system that resembles Western democratic societies' notion of the rule of law and a system that pays lip service to those values, but ultimately uses the law to further personal goals or consolidate personal power in ways that contravene those values and expectations. Thus, the *role* of law in a deeper cultural sense dramatically influences how the *rule* of law operates in a society.

SECTION 2: WHAT IS "CONTRACTS"?

In common parlance, the term *contract* is often used to refer to the written document which embodies the agreement of the parties. For instance, one can visualize the newspaper photo of the star college athlete waving a piece of paper after signing his first professional contract. But that's not a contract in the true legal sense of the term at all; at most, it's a memorialization of a contract. In the technical, but not always commonly understood, sense a contract, be it oral *or* written, is a promise or set of promises that the law recognizes by way of enforcement. There are two key terms in that definition that bear closer scrutiny: *promise* and *enforcement.*

All contracts have in common the notion of a *promise* which, by definition, relates to the happening or non-happening of a future event. For example, in a contemporaneous sale of goods for cash (*e.g.*, you purchase a hot dog for a dollar) there is no contract because there is no promise; the transaction occurs wholly in the present. However, were you to take the hot dog today with the understanding that you would not have to pay for it until next week the relationship becomes contractual in nature.

The term *promise* also connotes that the liability that a party to a contract incurs upon breach is suffered only because that party has knowingly and voluntarily agreed to that liability by making the promise in the first place. Other forms of liability, such as tort liability, arise out of external social judgments about the reasonableness of particular forms of behavior. Thus, if A runs a red light and smashes into B's car, and B sues A to recover for damages done to his vehicle, it is no defense for A to say that he never promised to observe the traffic signal. Instead, a court would say A was culpable—at fault—in running the light and, hence, must be held accountable for the financial consequences of his action. Similarly, if A steals B's car and is prosecuted by the state for theft, it would be no defense in the criminal case for A to assert that he never promised not to filch B's car. By contrast, were B to sue A for not paying B $10,000 to purchase her car, it would be very relevant if A could convince the court that he never promised to buy B's car for $10,000.

The term *enforcement* indicates that the law of contracts is concerned only with those promises the breach of which will give rise to liability; that is to say, for which the aggrieved party can seek recourse in a court of law. Not all promises are legally enforceable. While the making of any promise may carry a moral obligation to see to its fruition, the point is that not all promises are legally effective. Rather, each society must choose which promises will be enforced and which will not. For example, most societies will not enforce a promise to commit an illegal act. In that instance, the public policy favoring enforcement of promises bends to the stronger public policy of discouraging the commission of illegal acts.

Because there can be no promise unless there is also someone to whom the promise is made, any contract inevitably involves a legal relationship between at least two parties. Moreover, more often than not each of the parties will be bound by reciprocal promises to one another. This is because the only reason A may have made a promise to B—was willing to give up $10,000—was that B promised in return to sell her car to A. Therefore, most contracts involve *exchange* relationships where A's promise was motivated by the return promise from B, which, in turn, was induced by A's promise. We will, in this course, be concerned primarily with *exchange transactions.* This is because under the English common law system, from which our own law of contracts evolved, courts are (except in special circumstances) unwilling to enforce a promise unless something is given or promised in return. More technically put, an enforceable promise must be supported by *consideration.*

The promise, "I'll sell you my car for $1,000," if accepted, is enforceable. The promise, "I'll give you my car next Tuesday," is not, because nothing was given or promised in return and the *nudum pactum* (naked promise) is not enforceable under traditional principles of contract law. As should be obvious to you, contract law, and the doctrine of consideration, derive from and, in turn, serve the needs of trade and commerce. A market-driven economy relies heavily on direct, bilateral exchanges between private parties to allocate economic resources and it is these transactions that our law of contracts developed to facilitate. It is not as if contract law is irrelevant or indifferent to promises made in the social or familial situation, but it is true that contract law is less concerned with those promises and, as we will see, contract law operates less elegantly when applied in those non-commercial settings.

At bottom, contract law exists to satisfy the basic impulse—to which most people subscribe—that the reasonable expectations excited by a promise, if and when disappointed without legal excuse, are entitled to recompense in a court of law. Nevertheless, because not all promises can be enforced, there is considerably less agreement today on when, and, in particular, the reasons *why,* the coercive power of the state should be brought to bear to enforce certain broken promises.* Is it to ensure fairness and promote justice; because of the moral obligation attendant to the making of any promise; or simply to promote commerce and aggregate social wealth? No one can answer this question for you, but how *you* answer the question has enormous implications for deciding which promises ought to be enforced and which not. Consider these thoughts from Professor Farnsworth about wanting to make a commitment and regretting being committed.

**See generally* Randy Barnett, *A Consent Theory of Contract,* 86 COLUM. L. REV. 269 (1986) (reviewing competing theories of contractual liability).

E. ALLAN FARNSWORTH, CHANGING YOUR MIND: THE LAW OF REGRETTED DECISIONS
13–14, 16–18, 24, 26–27 (1998)

[T]he function of promising is usually very different from the function of resolving. While you make a resolution with a view to self-control, you most often make a promise with a view toward self-interest. You make it in order to get what you want from someone else whose self-interest is in having your commitment in return. You make it as part of an exchange in which you swap your commitment for something that you want.* * *

Complete freedom to renege on your promises would make it difficult for you to deal with others by lowering your worth in their eyes. Keeping your resolutions may be of little concern to others, but keeping your promises is an altogether different matter. Who would swap for your promises if you were free to renege on them?

To be sure, even if the law imposed no restraints you might honor your promises because of extralegal restraints. Some of these restraints are external: You might fear diminished standing among peers, harm to reputation, impairment of relationships, or loss of future opportunities. * * * Other restraints are internal: you might be moved by a sense of integrity, acquired by upbringing, education, or introspection. Why else do we use the word "honor" in this connection? * * *

For the law the question is not *why* do you honor your promises but *when* should you be restrained from reneging on your promises. Since extralegal restraints cause some promisors to honor their promises quite without regard to what the law requires, the law has an impact in restraining promisors only to the extent they would otherwise renege.

Even though you wanted to be committed at the time you made your promise, you may in hindsight wish you were not. Rare is the promisor who has never felt regret—the sensation that comes from such hindsight. * * *

Promises are made in the face of an uncertain future. Even if your promise reflected your existing preferences, so that you had no cause for regret, you might nevertheless have cause for regret after the passage of time. For this there are two possible reasons.

First, because you were poor at predicting external circumstances, you may find that they have changed and you made an improvident decision. Because contracts are devices for dealing with uncertainty by allocating risks of future changes, courts have tended to be markedly less paternalistic [i.e., intervene to allow you out from your promise] when faced with excuses based on improvident decisions than when confronted with excuses based on uninformed decisions. * * *

Second, because you were poor at predicting your preferences, you may find they have changed even though external circumstances have not, and that you have made an obsolete decision. * * *

Country-music star Willie Nelson, when asked about his four marriages, replied, "I've changed. I'm not the same guy that was married to this person or that person. . . . [E]ach of my wives was married to a different person."[37] But contract law is not so forgiving. Even a financial disaster that not only alters one's preferences but leaves one unable to perform is dismissed as mere "subjective impossibility, that is, impossibility that is personal to the promisor and does not inhere in the nature of the act performed" and so is no excuse.[38]

* * *

To sum up, only rarely will a court allow you to change your mind and renege on a binding promise, though there is a trend toward tolerance of reneging and in this sense toward paternalism.

Professor Farnsworth's comments underscore the reasons why, once each party has voluntarily made a promise to the other, the law holds the parties to their promises, regardless of what might happen in the future that makes one of those promises more burdensome or less advantageous than originally contemplated. This idea is what we mean when we use the phrase "freedom of contract"—expressing the policy that parties are free to bargain about the terms of their deal, but once the deal is struck there is no turning back. But how far does this principle of freedom of contract extend? Consider that question often as you read the cases in this book.

---

[37] 60 Minutes, April 20, 1997 (CBS).

[38] B's Co. v. B.P. Barber & Assocs., 391 F.2d 130, 137 (4th Cir. 1968).

SECTION 3: WHY DO LAWYERS AND LAW STUDENTS NEED TO KNOW ABOUT CONTRACTS AND CONTRACT LAW?

In a democratic society, contracts and contractual relationships permeate almost every aspect of day-to-day life. Perhaps nobody has put it quite so well as Sir Henry Maine who, at the end of the nineteenth century, observed that, "The movement of the progressive societies has hitherto been a movement from status to contract."* We each make numerous contracts of every stripe every year; for example, when we lease an apartment, open a checking account, buy a car, subscribe for cellular phone service, or sign our student loans. Not surprisingly, therefore, contract law, the law of promissory liability and enforcement, touches virtually every field of legal practice, from intellectual property to labor law to real estate. For this reason, every lawyer must be conversant with, and every law student must have exposure to, the basic rules and principles of contract law.

Ultimately, however, contract law is economic in focus and orientation. Business and commercial dealings and relationships in this country and, for that matter, throughout the free world are fundamentally contractual in nature. A market-based economy, or free enterprise system, relies heavily on voluntary, private exchange transactions to allocate goods and services in society. "Contracts" is the area of law that facilitates trade and commerce by setting forth the rules governing economic exchanges and enforcement of commercial obligations. It is important to recognize that businesspeople and companies relate to the rest of the world through their contracts, including contracts with employees, customers, suppliers, lenders, and many others. Indeed, most forms of business transaction, whether a big corporate merger or the routine purchase of office supplies, involve at their core a *contract* between two or more parties; that is to say, each of these parties has undertaken a legally binding performance obligation to the other in order to secure some desired reciprocal performance in return.

As should be apparent to you already, the law of "contracts" applies to an exceedingly wide array of transactions in an equally wide variety of settings. Having said this, however, it is also important to point out that certain types of contracts involve special rules because of the unique nature of the relationship involved. For example, if you plan to study labor law, there is a complex

*HENRY SUMNER MAINE, ANCIENT LAW 141 (New Universal Library ed. 1905).

statutory framework governing labor/management agreements that you will have to master. Likewise, insurance contracts, government contracts, and consumer credit contracts are the subject of detailed regulatory schema that address the special concerns and issues that arise in each of those areas. However, even the special rules governing these particular kinds of contracts are built upon the basic principles of common law contracts and, in many instances, rely on those principles to fill the gaps where the applicable legislation is silent. Thus, it is the study of those basic rules and principles that this course and book are devoted to because no lawyer worth her salt, whatever her area of expertise, can function effectively in ignorance of them.

SECTION 4: THE CASE METHOD: PROS AND CONS

This book is filled with cases, mostly appellate decisions. Virtually all of the cases in the book have been *edited* by us, your authors. That is to say, we have omitted certain portions of the courts' discussion from the actual decisions that we considered extraneous or simply not relevant for our purposes. Indeed, sometimes we edited a case simply to make it more readable for you. In any event, whenever you see three asterisks ("* * *"), that is our signal to you that we have deleted some material from the opinion as actually reported.

Since the latter part of the nineteenth century, it has been traditional to teach first-year (and often upper-level) courses through the case method, and we are, at least in this respect, traditionalists. There is much to be said for the case method of instruction. In a common law system such as our own, the rule of judicial precedent, *stare decisis* (not to unsettle things that are established), is critically important to understanding the evolution and application of the law. All U.S. jurisdictions follow in the English common law tradition, with the partial exception of Louisiana, which, because of its unique history and heritage, still operates under a *civil law* system.

Although the line between the two has blurred considerably over the course of the last century, the essential difference between a civil and a common law system is that the law in the former is *codified,* whereas common law is largely judge-made law advanced through the doctrine of precedent. This difference has its most profound effect in the style of judging that occurs under the two systems. This is because a decided case in a common law system not only resolves the dispute between the litigants, but it also serves as *precedent* should the same or a similar dispute arise between other litigants in a subsequent case. Therefore, in deciding individual cases, judges in a common law system must be, and are, much more conscious of their "law-making" function than their civil law counterparts. In addition, because the role of the civil law judge is more administrative than policy-making in nature, the judiciary in a civil law system tends to be composed of members of a class of professional judges who have chosen that occupation as a career and have been trained accordingly. In contrast, common law judges come almost exclusively from the ranks of the practicing bar, whether they are either popularly elected or appointed.

Now, how do these differences in legal culture relate to the case method of instruction? Because in a common law system the decision of a judge in one case will be binding on a judge hearing a similar claim in a subsequent case, the case method teaches you how to reason by analogy from one set of facts to another and how to abstract general principles from specific cases, which is at the essence of what lawyers and judges in a common law system do. In addition, the case method teaches different modes of argument about the meaning of words and specific rules of law that may be used or useful in advancing legal positions. In short, the case method not only exposes you to the rules of law, but also allows you to develop the skill of solving legal problems by providing the environment in which you can see how the very same rule, when applied to a subtlely different factual mosaic by a different decision-maker and at a different time, may yield a very different outcome.

We think it is a mistake to "learn the law" as an abstraction, wholly disassociated from the cooperative human society that it is supposed to serve. Put a different way, legal rules are not some collection of fixed, static principles of eternal truth simply waiting to reveal themselves to anyone prepared to pay the price of admission, or, in your case, more precisely, the price of tuition. By definition, law is dynamic; it is influenced by prevailing social, cultural, and economic factors and, in turn, those forces are influenced by the law.

This is why we think it is valuable to learn the law—in our case, contract law—by reading and analyzing cases. Let us speak for a moment, however, on how we, and we suspect your professor, approach these cases in class. Here, of course, we are speaking of the so-called "Socratic method" of instruction, which is a grandiloquent way of saying that you may be called upon to recite the facts of a case, frame the issue, state the holding, or render an opinion about that holding or its applicability on slightly different facts. The Socratic method is consistent with learning a process and a skill. If the object of this course is not only to learn a set of rules, but also to learn to reason analytically, to discern the nuance in the facts from one case to the next and articulate why the rule should perhaps be applied differently from one case to the next—or even changed in light of evolving societal attitudes and mores—then you must actively participate in the exercise.

You might be able to memorize a bunch of rules simply by being a passive receptor, but you cannot come to grips with the functioning of a complex, dynamic system without becoming actively involved in the endeavor. In fact, if you think back to your college years, you will probably agree that the most important thing you learned was not specific information but rather the ability to acquire new knowledge and integrate that knowledge into your daily life. So, too, we believe that by reading cases and having a dialog about those cases in class, you will acquire the skill of, and develop an effective process for approaching, reasoning, and ultimately solving legal problems.

The case method is not, however, without its limitations. To begin with, lawyers don't decide cases, judges do. Therefore, by just reading appellate opinions you do not learn a great deal about the lawyering process. Furthermore, the appellate decision is just the tip of the iceberg in what was a real dispute between real parties that eventually ended up in litigation, *i.e.*, having to be resolved by a judge or jury. However, the reality is that in the vast majority of settings in which lawyers act they serve as problem *solvers,* not progenitors. The point is that being a good lawyer entails more than being a ferocious advocate or an encyclopedia of legal rules. A good lawyer must be able to evaluate and apply those rules in specific situations; to advise clients when it's in their interest to invoke the judicial process and when they should attempt to proceed by conciliation and private settlement. This can be a complex calculation involving a variety of both legal and nonlegal considerations. In the final analysis, however, the true measure of a good lawyer is the ability to plan in advance and in a manner that avoids or at least minimizes the likelihood of problems arising in the future. And in the area of "contracts," perhaps more so than any other area of law, the parties and their lawyers have the greatest opportunity, through careful and creative planning, to resolve future disputes without the need for litigation. Therefore, throughout this book we also consider the role of the lawyer and ask you not only how you might have handled the case, but also what you might have done differently to avoid the problem in the first place.

The other major problem with the case method is that it tends to inculcate in students new to the area the false impression that most rules of contract law are ambiguous and that most contract disputes are resolved by trial. In fact, the vast majority of contractual obligations are simply performed without incident. This is in part because many of the rules of contract law and liability are in fact clear and unambiguous. Moreover, when disputes do occur, the vast majority of those are settled amicably by the parties either without the necessity for litigation or prior to trial if suit is actually filed. Finally, increasingly many forms of contract dispute are resolved by resort to private arbitration, mediation, and other forms of alternative dispute resolution. While the pivotal role that a lawyer plays in the formal adjudicatory process is well-known and understood, the advice and assistance of counsel is often equally critical in the negotiation of private settlements or resolution through informal dispute resolution mechanisms.

Finally, we hasten to add that we understand that for first year law students, new to the case method of instruction with its emphasis on analytic reasoning skills and oral recitation, preparing for class can be confounding. The cases must not only be read carefully, they must be read with a view toward appreciating all sides of the issue. After all, when a rule clearly applies, there is little need for lawyers and not much to litigate about. Therefore, we suggest that at least early on in the course you get into the habit of asking yourself, and answering, a series of questions as you read each case.

- *Who is suing whom?* This means not only knowing the names of the parties, but their position in relation to one another as well. *E.g.,* A is an employee suing his boss, B.

- *What is the basis for the plaintiff's claim? E.g.,* X claims Y breached a written contract for the sale of land.

- *What does the plaintiff want?* This means what is the plaintiff asking the court for: money damages, an injunction, a declaration of rights, etc.?

- *What happened?* Know the facts; how this case arose. See, too, if you can identify those factual findings which are critical to the court's determination

- *What is the specific question presented?* Try to hone in on the specific legal issue(s) on which the outcome of the case hinges.
- *What are the arguments of each side on this question?* Make your own independent evaluation of these arguments.
- *Who wins and why?* Be aware that the "why" can often be just as, if not more, important than the "who."
- *Are you satisfied with the result?* Here, consider whether you feel the court's decision was doctrinally sound and whether it was fair or "right."
- *Are there any limits to the court's holding?* This means you should consider the precedential effect of the decision; how broadly or narrowly should the holding be construed?
- *Are there any concurring or dissenting opinions?* If so, make sure you can articulate exactly where the opinions of the judges diverge from one another.
- *How does the court's decision relate to the material previously discussed?* This may be at the same time the most important and the most frequently overlooked step, because, to do well in this course, eventually you will be called on to synthesize all of the material that was studied in a coherent fashion. Therefore, as you go along, it is not sufficient only to breakdown (analyze) each case you read. You must also begin to see how the cases interrelate with one another to form a systemic whole.

Here is what Professor Clark Byse, the inspiration for Professor Kingsfield in the movie *The Paper Chase,* told his contracts students at Harvard (and later Boston University) in their very first class meeting:

> On the first day of the class on Contracts, there is a temptation to lecture because, as Adlai Stevenson said when he was the speaker at a college commencement, "This is a wonderful opportunity, for there is so much that I, a man in his fifties, have learned in my lifetime that would be of great value to you in your early twenties." At this point, Mr. Stevenson paused, shook his head slightly, and said in a mournful tone, "But it would do no good for me to tell you those things, for what is important and lasting in life must be learned—by action, by participation, rather than by passive absorption." So never forget that the emphasis in this

> class is on what and how you think, not on what some judge or treatise writer or your instructor thinks. My function is to assist you to develop your lawyerly skills and understanding of the institution of Contract and of the legal process and the role of law in our society. Developing those skills and understanding can and will be an exciting experience for some. For others, the experience at times may be frustrating, even unpleasant. Some will enjoy being called on and speaking in class. For others, speaking in front of 100 hearers may be embarrassing, even painful—something to be avoided at all costs. To those who dread being called on, I say, Relax. We are all in this together, to learn, to improve ourselves. Of course, mistakes will be made. This is why there are erasers on pencils. There is nothing wrong about making a mistake. What would be wrong is not learning from one's mistakes.

Clark Byse, *Introductory Comments to the First-Year Class in Contracts*, 78 B.U. L. REV. 59 (1998).

SECTION 5: WHERE DOES CONTRACT LAW COME FROM?

A. English Common Law Origins and the Evolution of *Assumpsit*

E. Allan Farnsworth, *The Past of Promise: An Historical Introduction to Contract*
69 Colum. L. Rev. 576, 592–98 (1969)

The view that promises are not generally enforceable, which started from the premise of Roman law that a mere agreement did not beget an action, was held by the common law. Its choice was scarcely surprising. It accorded well with the procedural niceties of common law courts, where recovery was not to be had unless the claim could be fitted within one of the established forms of action; and it suited the status-oriented society of the Middle Ages, which was anything but conducive to the flowering of promise. Furthermore, there was no great pressure for enforceability as contracts were not a significant part of the business of the common law courts. * * *

The challenge that faced [the courts in developing a general basis for the enforcement of promises] was to work within the framework of the forms of action, first to develop exceptions as the Romans had done, and then to so fashion these exceptions as ultimately to achieve what the Romans had never achieved—a general theory of contract. This challenge was met by the common law courts in the course of the fifteenth and sixteenth centuries. * * * The achievement was all the more remarkable in view of the fact that when this development began, the English law of contracts was little more advanced than that of many primitive societies. How was it brought about?

The common law courts found the answer in the law of torts. They had already recognized that liability in tort arose when a person undertook (*assumpsit*) to perform a duty and then performed it in such a way as to cause harm. Suit could be brought on the special variety of trespass on the case that came to be known as assumpsit. At the beginning of the fifteenth century it was available only where there had been misfeasance in performance of the undertaking. This example was given in 1436: "If a carpenter makes a covenant with me to make me a house good and strong and of a certain form, and he makes me a house which is weak and bad and of another form, I shall have an action of trespass on my case."[74] In such cases of misfeasance it was not hard to justify liability in tort. But might not the same remedy lie when there had merely been nonfeasance, a failure to perform the undertaking? At first the answer was no. In 1410 it was said: "Certainly it would lie [if the carpenter had built the house badly], because he would then answer for the wrong which he had done, but when a man makes a covenant and does nothing under that covenant, how can you have an action against him without a deed?"[75]

Nevertheless, by the second half of the fifteenth century there was a growing tendency among the common law judges to make the first major extension in the action of assumpsit by enforcing such promises even where there had been only nonfeasance. * * * But some limits had to be placed on what promises would be enforced, for the judges were not about to allow "that one shall have trespass for any breach of covenant in the world."[76] The courts were therefore forced to find a test to distinguish instances where nonfeasance was actionable from those where it was not. Since the

---

[74]Y.B. 14 Hy. VI, at 18. 3 W. Holdsworth [A History of English Law] 430 [(4th ed. 1936)].

[75]Y.B. Mich. 11 Hy. IV, pl 60, 3 W. HOLDSWORTH, *supra* note [74], at 433–34.

[76]Y.B. Hil. 3 Hy. VI, pl. 33, 3 W. HOLDSWORTH, *supra* note [74], at 435.

misfeasance cases that had originally given rise to the action in assumpsit were characterized by a detriment incurred by the promisee in reliance on the promise, it was natural to formulate an analogous test and to allow enforcement where the promisee had changed his position on the faith of the promise, and had been consequently damaged by its nonperformance.

* * *

As the sixteenth century drew to a close, however, the common law courts, conscious of the expanding jurisdiction of Chancery and anxious to preserve their own powers, made a second major extension of the action of assumpsit. Thus it was held that a party who had given only a promise in exchange for the other's promise had, nonetheless, suffered a detriment by having his freedom of action fettered, since he was in turn bound by his own promise. * * *

On this ground the extension of the action of assumpsit to include the mere exchange of promises can be justified.

The action was to experience yet one more important extension. The procedure in actions of assumpsit, in which the plaintiff was entitled to a jury trial, was more favored by creditors than that in actions of debt, in which the defendant could resort to wager of law.[*] The next step in the common law's development of the law of contract was to permit assumpsit to supplant debt. By the middle of the sixteenth century, it had been recognized that an action in assumpsit could be brought against a defendant who, being already indebted (*indebitatus*), expressly undertook (*assumpsit*) to pay a particular sum. This action was called one in "*indebitatus assumpsit*", to distinguish it from the older "special assumpsit." Toward the end of the century, it began to be held that a debt alone, without a subsequent express promise, would support such an action. The final triumph of this view came at the beginning of the seventeenth century in Slade's case in which, on a jury finding that "there was no other promise or assumption, but only the said bargain,"[83] all the judges of England resolved "that every contract executor

*The debt form of action permitted the defendant to invoke the archaic "wager of law" as the method of trial, instead of trial by jury. Under this system, the party accused of owing a debt could avoid liability by reciting a scripted oath, in effect swearing he did not owe such debt, and supporting his own oath with those of certain hired "oath sayers" who, for a price, would swear that the defendant's testimony was unperjured. The plaintiff was not permitted to cross-examine the oath sayers, meaning that if the defendant was prepared to lie under oath he could in fact get away with it. Eds.

83Slade's Case, 4 Co. Rep. 92 b, 76 Eng. Rep. 1074 (Q.B. 1602).

imports in itself an assumpsit."[84] The creditor was at last assured of the benefits of jury trial in place of wager of law and was freed of the technicalities of pleading in debt.

Over the course of the fifteenth and sixteenth centuries the common law courts had succeeded in evolving a general basis for the enforceability of promises through the action of assumpsit. During the sixteenth century the word "consideration," which had earlier been used without technical significance, came to be used as a word of art to express the sum of the conditions necessary for an action in assumpsit to lie. It was therefore a tautology that a promise, if not under seal, was enforceable only where there was "consideration," for this was to say no more than that it was enforceable only under those circumstances in which the action of assumpsit was allowed. In this fashion, however, the word "consideration" came to be applied to the test of enforceability of a simple promise and to be used to distinguish those promises that in the eyes of the common law were of sufficient significance to society to justify the legal sanctions of assumpsit for their enforcement.

B. Classical Era of American Contract Law

LAWRENCE M. FRIEDMAN, CONTRACT LAW IN AMERICA
17–18, 20–22 (1965)

Quite clearly, Anglo-American law now pays more attention to contract than medieval English law ever did. The rise of contract to legal prominence is fairly recent. Blackstone's classic exposition of the common law was written shortly before the American Revolution; in it, only a few short sections include contract, while the special doctrines of real-property law fill almost the whole of one of the four books of the *Commentaries* and color much of the rest. * * * The nineteenth century was very different. Even in the lawyer's narrow sense, the law of contract swelled into one of the main branches of legal learning. There were no important treatises on the law of contracts published until the nineteenth century; the appearance then of such works was a sure sign that the lawyers saw bread-and-butter importance to the field. When Christopher Columbus Langdell [Dean of the Har-

[84] Id. at 1077.

vard Law School] in the 1870s undertook to reform legal education and to establish the case method of instruction, he began the career of the law school case-book with a volume on contracts. In the mid-twentieth century the subject remains an immutable pillar of the first-year curriculum of every law school.

* * *

The law of contract is, therefore, roughly coextensive with the free market. Liberal nineteenth-century economics fits neatly with the law of contracts so viewed. It, too, had the abstracting habit [of removing from the realm of concern all particularities concerning persons and subject-matter]. In both theoretical models—that of the law of contracts and that of liberal economics—parties could be treated as individual economic units which, in theory, enjoyed complete mobility and freedom of decision. * * * The correspondence between law and economic theory was never exact. Contract law was not a book written by Adam Smith. Nobody purposely sat down to turn contract law into an applied branch of liberal economics. But a free market developed, and grew; the law of contract was the legal reflection of that market and naturally took on its characteristics. Contract was abstract; the free market was abstract; and the two institutions directed behavior along similar channels.

C. Demise of Classical Principles of Contract Law

"Classical contract law," of which Professor Friedman speaks, flourished more or less from 1850 through 1940, holding at its core the first principle of *freedom of contract* and the corollary of that principle, *pacta sund servanda* (promises are to be kept). But what do we mean by "freedom of contract"? The phrase encompasses the notion that private bargains, freely and voluntarily entered into, should be enforced without reservation and certainly blind to the identities of the parties or the relative equities of their positions under the contract. This judicial "hands-off" approach reflected the bias, consistent with the pervading economic theory of the day, that the good of the economy, and ergo society as a whole, would best be served by allowing tough, rugged individualists to bargain it out in the marketplace free from interference or regulation by the state except in extreme cases of fraud, duress, or illegality.

Under the classical principles of contract law, it was not perceived as the role of the courts to review, rewrite, or evaluate the underlying fairness of the deal; the role of the courts was simply to ensure that a bargain had been struck and, if so, to enforce it, nothing less and certainly nothing more. This ensured the stability, predictability, and certainty on which business relied and efficient commercial relations depended. Of course, these principles only existed in idealized form; the reality of contract law and enforcement was always a more complex and nuanced phenomenon. Nevertheless, as you will see, the principles that govern contractual relations today bear only the faintest resemblance to the principles that exemplified classical contract law just over a hundred years ago.

In the main, the second half of the twentieth century witnessed a number of changes in contracts doctrine, but none more important than the removal by both legislative and judicial intervention of various issues that had previously been left to the realm of private bargain of the parties. In effect, as to these matters, freedom of contract has been, if not eliminated, at least curtailed. For example, today, parties are free to negotiate over and reach agreement on the rate of interest that one party will have to pay the other in a loan transaction, but only to a point because their agreement is subject to applicable state law governing usury. Therefore, even though knowingly and voluntarily agreed to, a promise to pay a usurious rate of interest will simply not be enforced. Unlike many of the rules of contract law which can be "contracted around" if the parties so choose,* these types of rules cannot be altered by the parties. This is because they represent a form of external regulation of the exchange relationship, typically imposed because of social judgments about either the need to protect parties to contract relationships or the need to protect society as a whole from certain types of conduct.

Professor Grant Gilmore, in his famous work titled THE DEATH OF CONTRACT 95–96 (1974), neatly summed up the reasons for this evolution in contract law theory and doctrine as follows:

---

*Because it is impossible for the parties to address every aspect of their relationship in detail, an important function of contract law is to supply the rule that will apply in the absence of specific agreement of the parties. These rules are sometimes called "default" rules to contrast them from other kinds of rules which are mandatory or "immutable." *See generally* Richard Carswell, *Contract Law, Default Rules, and the Philosophy of Promising,* 88 MICH. L. REV. 489 (1989).

> As we look back on the nineteenth century theories, we are struck most of all, I think, by the narrow scope of social duty which they implicitly assumed. No man is his brother's keeper; the race is to the swift; let the devil take the hindmost. For good or ill we have changed all that. We are now all cogs in a machine, each dependent on the other. The decline and fall of the general theory of contract and, in most quarters, of laissez-faire economics may be taken as remote reflections of the transition from nineteenth century individualism to the welfare state and beyond.

There are any number of social, cultural, and economic factors and attitudes that can be identified as contributing to the demise of classical contract law and the erosion of unbridled freedom of contract. Among the most significant, however, has been the increasing complexity and interdependency of our economic system. The growth of large, powerful corporations and other commercial enterprises, coupled with the perfection of the "standard printed form," has meant that the relative equality in bargaining strength and position that was the unstated assumption on which the principle of freedom of contract was predicated no longer reflects the reality of many exchange relationships in contemporary society. This has led courts to take a much more activist role in monitoring the fairness of contractual relationships, particularly where there is a significant disparity in bargaining power between the parties. The hard and fast rules of contract doctrine that tended to confine the discretion of the court in earlier times has in general given way to more open-ended and flexible standards that leave significant room for the court to do particularized justice in individual cases.*

A drawback, arguably, of this trend in the law has been some loss in the certainty, predictability, and stability of contractual relationships. Unlike the era when the policy of freedom of contract reigned supreme, parties can no longer be sure that their bargains, freely and voluntarily entered into, will be enforced. Business and commerce rely on clear rules, as much if not more than they do on the content of those rules. Consider the court's statement in *Shreve v. Cheesman,* 69 F. 785, 791 (8th Cir. 1895): "It is universally conceded that it is often more important that rules [affecting property rights] should be certain and changeless than that they should be right. Men engaged in active business buy and sell in reliance on them." Do you agree with this

**See generally* P.S. ATIYAH, THE RISE AND FALL OF FREEDOM OF CONTRACT (1979).

statement? How much certainty should be sacrificed in the interests of justice? Need one always come at the expense of the other?

One of the ways in which this evolution in judicial attitudes toward contract enforcement has manifested itself is in a greater willingness on the part of courts to view contract enforcement as something more than an all-or-nothing proposition. Historically, if the court found that there had been a breach of contract, the aggrieved party was entitled to its remedy under the contract. Today, in certain situations—for example, employee noncompetition covenants—a court might only enforce the portion of the contract that it considers to be fair and reasonable but not the part it thinks is unfair or unreasonable.

Regulation of bargain relationships, and the waning deference to private autonomy, goes far beyond post hoc judicial review of the fairness of existing contracts. Congress and the state legislatures have also gotten into the act, wholly removing certain types of contracts from the realm of general principles of contract law. As we noted earlier, today, labor contracts, insurance contracts, consumer credit agreements, and others are the subject of comprehensive statutory enactments that regulate in detail the form and terms of the contract, as well the permissible scope of what the parties may or may not bargain over by private agreement. Sometimes these statutes create rights in one party to the agreement that the party did not himself bargain for. For example, recognizing that people caught unaware in their homes by a slick, experienced salesman might end-up agreeing to buy something (encyclopedias or a vacuum cleaner) that they really didn't want, the Federal Trade Commission, acting under authority of a federal law, adopted a regulation (an administrative rule) giving consumers in door-to-door sales transactions a three-day "cooling off period" during which they retain the right to cancel the deal even though they signed a "binding contract." 16 C.F.R. § 429 (effective June 7, 1974).

We are not much concerned with these specialized kinds of contracts in this book, even though the common law continues to operate interstitially even with respect to these types of agreements. Rather, our focus is confined largely to the general body of principles comprising "contract law" that has been developed over several hundred years by courts employing the common law style of reasoning and analysis. This is not to say, however, that contract law is wholly caselaw. As we see in the next section, some aspects of contract law have always been statutory and the trend toward *codification* of the law has intensified, particularly over the last half-century. Even with respect to statutory law, however, it is important not to lose sight of the pivotal role still played by the courts. Unlike the application of legislative codes in civil law jurisdictions, where judicial decisions tend to have little impact or effect except upon the litigants to the particular the case under decision, in a common law system when courts decide specific cases by interpreting a governing statutory provision they may also be placing their own *gloss* on that rule. Often, that gloss becomes part of the law and, thus, may affect the interests of litigants in future cases.

D. Sources of Modern Contract Law

For most of our history the basic rules and principles of contract law evolved in the common law style. That is to say, the general principles of contract law were derived from a wide variety of cases decided by the English common law—and to an extent the chancery—courts with some but relatively few statutory modifications. Of course, the common law courts did not act wholly without structure. They were, in the first instance, guided by the principle of *precedent* and influenced to a considerable degree by other bodies of law such as Roman law, Canon Law and, particularly, The Law Merchant, which was a separate system of rules that developed (reaching its heyday during the sixteenth century) in England to govern commercial transactions, largely administered by local mercantile authorities. The law of contracts that was imported into the American legal system was essentially this common law of contracts as it existed at the end of the eighteenth century.

Beginning early in the twentieth century, however, a trend developed, which continues to the present day, to *codify* our laws, including the law of contracts. The first major codification effort was the Uniform Sales Act, patterned on its English predecessor of 1893, which was approved by the National Conference of Commissioners on Uniform State Laws (the NCCUSL) in 1906. Professor Samuel Williston, also the author of a major treatise on contract law, was the principal draftsperson of the Uniform Sales Act, which was eventually adopted by over thirty states.

The Uniform Sales Act was eventually replaced by the Uniform Commercial Code (the U.C.C.), a much more comprehensive statute governing a wide range of commercial transactions. Contracts involving the sale of goods are the subject of Article 2 of the U.C.C. The U.C.C., the first official text of which was approved in 1952, was the product of a joint effort by the NCCUSL and the American Law Institute (the ALI). The U.C.C. has enjoyed near-universal acceptance in the states (Louisiana has now adopted most of the U.C.C. except for Article 2), and, since its inception, has been the subject of continuing revision and modernization. In 1987, for example, a whole new Article dealing with personal property leases, Article 2A, was approved and has received widespread adoption. Also, as of this writing, a wholesale revision to Article 2 is being considered by the NCCUSL and the ALI.

The Code's Permanent Editorial Board, established by the joint sponsors of the U.C.C. in 1961 to promote uniform state enactment and interpretation of the Code, is responsible for evaluating the operation of the Code in the various states and determining when revisions to the various Articles may be appropriate. With each such revision, a new official text of the uniform version of the Code is promulgated. The most current official text, and the one we refer to when citing to Code provisions in this book, is the 2000 Official Text.

The primary architect of the U.C.C., and the principal draftsperson of Article 2, was Karl Llewellyn. The statute very much reflects his normative view of law, and those of a generation of legal scholars roughly classified together as *Legal Realists.* The realists were decidedly pragmatic. They rejected the idea of law as a "science." Instead they believed that the law was a tool to serve societal and economic interests and, therefore, legal rules should be crafted to conform with people's expectations of how the law *ought* to work. The realist attitude about the role of the commercial law is evident in section 1-102(2) of Article 1 of the Code, which broadly sets forth the purposes of the U.C.C. as intending "to simplify, clarify, and modernize the law governing commercial transactions; to permit the continued expansion of commercial practices through custom, usage and agreement of the parties; to make uniform the law among the various jurisdictions."

The U.C.C. has been very influential even in transactions that do not fall within its broad scope. For example, Article 2 supplies the governing law only if the subject matter of the contract involves a transaction in goods. Nevertheless, Article 2 has had a profound effect upon the development of contract law in non-sale of goods cases, such as contracts involving real estate or services of one kind or another. This is because courts will frequently look to the provisions of Article 2, and even apply those provisions by analogy, in deciding these non-sale of goods cases.

The second major development in contract law in the last century was the *Restatements of Contracts* developed under the aegis of, and published by, the American Law Institute. The American Law Institute was founded in 1923 "to promote clarification and simplification of the law and its better adaptation to social needs, to secure the better administration of justice, and to carry on scholarly and scientific legal work." Its membership is composed of distinguished judges, lawyers, and law teachers. Work on the first *Restatement of Contracts* began in 1923, and it was finally approved in 1932. Professor Williston was the Reporter for the project. Among his advisors was Professor Arthur Corbin, the author of another major treatise on contract law. Professors Williston and Corbin's views about and approach to contract law are frequently contrasted. Williston was much inclined to see the law as fixed and immutable. Sometimes described as a *positivist* view of law, Williston tended to regard law as a science; a closed system of rules which could be consistently applied to resolve any fact situation. Professor Corbin's approach to contract law was much less mechanical and formalistic. A principal figure in the legal realist movement, Corbin was willing to accept a much greater degree of indeterminacy in the law than Williston in order to assure a just or fair result. Corbin felt that the hard and fast rules of contract law needed to be applied much more flexibly, tempered by the prevailing norms, mores, and attitudes of the social and economic milieu in which the rules operated. Thus, Corbin was much more open to incorporating into the law broad, open-ended considerations of ethics and justice.

The enormous pace of new developments in contract law in the quarter century following adoption of the first *Restatement* led to the decision in the early 1960s to begin work on the *Restatement (Second) of Contracts*, with Professor Robert Braucher serving as Reporter. Professor Alan Farnsworth replaced Professor Braucher in 1971, after Braucher was appointed to the Supreme Judicial Court of Massachusetts. Work on the *Restatement (Second)* was finally completed in 1981. Heavily influenced by Corbin's perspective on the law, as well as by the U.C.C., the *Restatement (Second)* took a decidedly normative turn from its predecessor, placing a much greater emphasis on protecting parties' detrimental *reliance* on promises and forsaking bright-line rules for more flexible, open-ended standards.

It is important to realize that the *Restatements*, unlike the U.C.C., do not have the force of law. No state legislature has enacted a *Restatement*. Instead, they reflect a systemic distillation of the prevailing rules and principles of the common law of contracts, albeit sometimes with a deliberative normative twist, into a single code-like document. Thus, while very influential in judicial decisionmaking because of the prestige of the American Law Institute and the individuals selected to work on these projects, a court is not bound to apply the *Restatement* if it believes the applicable rule is wrong or, more likely, not in accord with the common law in that jurisdiction.

While contract law is predominantly state law, there are federal laws relating to specific matters of federal concern, such as interstate commerce or the procurement of goods and services by federal governmental units and agencies. Moreover, the trend toward codification of the law of contracts has not been limited to domestic law. In 1990, the United Nations Commission on International Trade submitted a draft of the *Convention on Contracts for the International Sale of Goods* (*CISG*), which governs in the case of contracts between citizens of ratifying nations. The United States formally ratified *CISG* in 1986. Finally, in 1994, the International Institute for the Unification of Private Law (UNIDROIT) announced its *Principles of International Commercial Contracts*, reflecting rules derived from both civil and common law legal systems that might desirably apply to international contracts. Not a formal treaty, which would require adoption by member-nations, the *UNIDROIT Principles* are more like a *Restatement*, although they may be made applicable to a transaction by agreement of the parties. They can also be referred to by an international tribunal as an authoritative source of rules for resolving a dispute between parties from different countries.

SECTION 6: WHAT IS THE LAWYER'S ROLE IN CONTRACT LAW?

Two parties considering entering into a contractual relationship are initially under no obligation to, and have no rights against, one another. Instead, unlike in most areas of law, they have the opportunity, subject only to very minimal restriction, to define by agreement what their rights and obligations will be. That is to say, the essence of contractual liability is that it is a consensual form of liability. This notion is reflected in the core contract law principle of *freedom of contract.* Freedom of contract means that the parties are free to establish their corresponding rights and duties by private bargain. By the same token, the principle of freedom of contract implies its corollary, namely, the principle of freedom *from* contract, which means that neither party is obligated to conclude a deal with the other. Thus, either party may elect to break off negotiations at any point prior to the formation of a binding contract. How does the lawyer fit into this dynamic?

The permutations are innumerable. In the case of large, sophisticated business parties, the lawyer's role tends to be more purely legal; giving advice relating to legal issues and considerations, and drafting the definitive documentation of the transaction. With smaller business clients and individuals, the lawyer will perform these functions and often will also be consulted on the business points of the deal. In both instances, the role of the lawyer is predominantly a *planner* and not an *adversary.* Moreover, while the lawyer is always looking out first and foremost for the interests of her client in the transaction, in many contractual settings there is a substantial identity of interests between the parties and a common or shared desire to achieve a mutually satisfactory accommodation of those interests. This is particularly so in situations where the parties anticipate a long-term mutually advantageous relationship, such as, for example, a partnership arrangement. In some of these cases, with the consent of the parties, the lawyer may actually represent both parties. This will, however, preclude the lawyer's representation of either party individually should there be a falling out in the future because such representation would constitute a conflict of interest and a violation of the lawyer's ethical obligations. However, even when the parties approach one another at arms-length and have their own separate counsel, the lawyers' objectives are often to reach reasonable accommodation on the key points of negotiation rather than solely to maximize their client's interests at the expense of the other party. In short, the role is much more collaborative in nature than is ordinarily true of the lawyer's role in representing a party once a dispute has broken out under a contract.

It is also important to recognize that lawyers encounter contracts in virtually all aspects of practice. "Contracts" does not itself represent a discrete area of legal practice in the same way, for example, we might speak of a criminal or a personal injury law practice. Rather, contract law and contractual relationships transcend many different areas of practice, but, in particular, form the foundation of the commercial law. At the same time, whether the transaction being handled by the lawyer at the moment involves a real estate conveyance, a corporate combination, a financing arrangement, or an employment or agency relation, more often than not the key to the deal is an acceptable contractual arrangement. Thus, the "hired gun" image typically associated with the lawyer in the traditional litigation model is simply inaccurate in the contract negotiation and formation stages of the deal. How well suited are most lawyers to playing these roles? Consider these comments from Professor Macneil concerning the lawyer's role in planning contractual transactions.

Ian R. Macneil, *A Primer of Contract Planning*

48 S. CAL. L. REV. 627, 639 (1975)

Finally, all planning is complicated by what Professor [Lon] Fuller describes as "tacit assumptions."[27] These lie "somewhere between the superficial layer of consciousness and the dark inner recesses of the human psyche probed by the psychoanalysts."[28] His example of the absent-minded professor reading a book as he steps out of the office demonstrates well what he means by tacit assumptions: the professor assumes that the hall floor is still there, although consciously he never gives any thought to the matter.

Tacit assumptions are as important in contract planning as they are in any other human behavior. Just as people constantly make tacit assumptions while they are eating, driving, playing football, operating a computer, or making love, so too they make tacit assumptions when they are planning contractual relationships.

In light of the foregoing complexities any description of the planned portion of a contract must necessarily be a description of an ideal that actual contract planning may approach but certainly never achieve. The ideal is the complete and exact mapping of all "territories to be," totally understood in precisely the same way by all parties with all details in sharp conscious focus at the same time, with all being entirely unaffected by anything external

---

[27]His highly original note on this subject now appears in L. Fuller & M. Eisenberg, Basic Contract Law 804–808 (1972).

[28]Id. at 806.

to that mapping, including tacit assumptions of the parties. Such an ideal is as unobtainable as the Holy Grail.

Perhaps the most critical lawyer responsibility is the responsibility for *drafting* the actual written terms of the transaction. Even when contracts are "custom drafted," the lawyer will inevitably begin by retrieving an agreement from a prior deal to use a form. This is because most contracts will contain what has come to be referred to *boilerplate*. The term boilerplate is used to refer to contractual provisions and language that are routinely included as part of any agreement. There is nothing wrong with boilerplate if it fits, but the draftsperson who includes boilerplate from a form without consciously considering its applicability and appropriateness in the current transaction runs the risk of doing the client a grave disservice.

On other occasions, the lawyer will be faced with a contract where there is no opportunity to participate in the drafting of the proposed agreement. This is because the client will have been presented with a "take it or leave it" deal. In the area of consumer transactions, for example, since World War II businesses have increasingly come to rely upon the standard printed form, representing the only basis on which the merchant will do business with a prospective customer. If you'd like to test this assertion, go down to a new car dealership. Decide on the make and model you'd like and negotiate a price. Then tell the salesperson that you'll draft the contract up that evening and be back in the morning. Now, watch his or her reaction. But what's wrong with you drafting the contract rather than using the dealership's form? In truth, nothing's "wrong" with it, it just "ain't gonna happen."

If you're forced to do business on the dealer's form, how valid is the principle of freedom of contract in these circumstances? Should the courts take a different attitude toward enforcement in consumer cases? As a practical matter, how many of these kinds of contracts do you suppose are actually reviewed by lawyers before they're signed? We haven't actually counted, but we think bloody few.

Even in the non-consumer or commercial setting, often times the parties will not approach one another from a position of equal bargaining strength. In these situations, the party in the superior position may insist the deal be done on its terms or not at all. For instance, how much opportunity do you suppose that the average worker has to negotiate the terms of his or her employment arrangements? In these cases, a lawyer counseling a client plays a somewhat different role. Because there will be very little opportunity to control the terms of the contract, the lawyer's job is to help the client understand the risk so that the client can intelligently decide whether to take the job or look for one that offers greater security.

All of the cases in this book consist of deals that went bad. That's why there was lawsuit. We think it might be useful for you to ask yourself from time-to-time what you, as the lawyer for one of the parties to the deal, might have done differently to have, if not avoided the problem, at least, better protected your client's interest. Remember, freedom of contract means not only considerable freedom for the party to the contract to affect the terms and conditions of the deal, but considerable freedom for the party's lawyer to help structure the transaction in a manner that best serves the client's interest.

Table of Cases

[Principal cases in italics. All other cases appear in roman type. References are to pages.]

C

G

H

M

T

U

V

Index

[References are to pages.]

A

[References are to pages.]

[References are to pages.]

[References are to pages.]

D

E

[References are to pages.]

F

[References are to pages.]

[References are to pages.]

[References are to pages.]

[References are to pages.]

[References are to pages.]

[References are to pages.]

[References are to pages.]

U

V

W